Luigi Albertini

THE ORIGINS OF

THE WAR OF

1914

Translated and edited by
ISABELLA M. MASSEY
M.A. (Cantab.), Dr. phil. (Marburg).

VOLUME III

THE EPILOGUE OF THE CRISIS OF JULY 1914
THE DECLARATIONS OF WAR AND OF NEUTRALITY

ENIGMA BOOKS

Enigma Books
580 Eighth Avenue, New York, NY 10018
www.enigmabooks.com

This edition reprinted by Enigma Books by
arrangement with
Oxford University Press.
First published by Oxford University Press in 1952.
Copyright © The Estate of Luigi Albertini, 1952.
Copyright © 2005 Enigma Books

ISBN 1-929631-33-2 [Volume III]
Printed in the United States of America

Library of Congress Cataloging-in-Publication Data

Albertini, Luigi, 1871-1941.
  [Origini della guerra del 1914. English]
  The origins of the war of 1914 / Luigi Albertini ; translated and
edited by Isabella M. Massey.

  3 v. : maps ; cm.
  Includes bibliographical references and index.
  Contents: v. 1. European relations from the Congress of Berlin
to the eve of the Sarajevo murder -- v. 2. The crisis of July 1914.
From the Sarajevo outrage to the Austro-Hungarian general
mobilization -- v. 3. The epilogue of the crisis of July 1914 -- The
declarations of war and of neutrality.
  ISBN: 1-929631-26-X (set)
  ISBN: 1-929631-31-6 (v.1)
  ISBN: 1-929631-32-4 (v.2)
  ISBN: 1-929631-33-2 (v.3)

  1. World War, 1914-1918--Causes. 2. Europe--Politics and
government--1871-1918. 3. World War, 1914-1918--Diplomatic
history. I. Massey, Isabella Mellis. II. Title. III. Title: Origini
della guerra del 1914.

D511 .A5713 2005
940.3/11

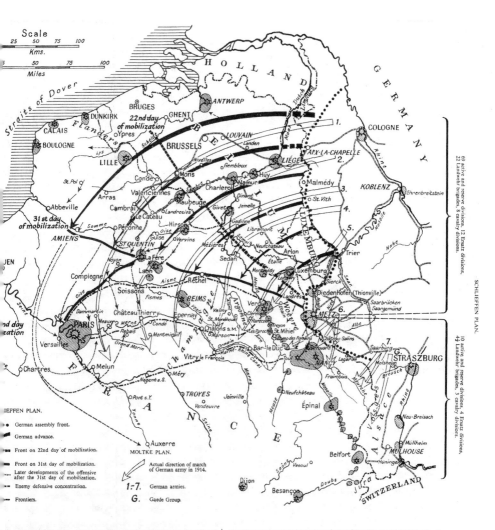

Count Schlieffen's plan of operations, after a sketch by Joh. Victor Bredt, member of the Committee nominated by the Reichstag to investigate the war guilt question. | The hollow arrows, representing the lines of march followed in the 1914 Schlieffen plan as modified by Moltke, are taken from a sketch by the German General Friedrich von Bernhardi.

TABLE OF CONTENTS

VI. ITALY'S ATTITUDE AFTER THE FIUGGI CONVERSATION. NEGOTIATIONS ON COMPENSATION. 254

VII. THE ITALIAN DECLARATION OF NEUTRALITY (29 JULY-2 AUGUST). 296

VIII. LAST ENGLISH EFFORTS FOR NEUTRALITY AND FIRST STEP TOWARDS INTERVENTION. 364

IX. BELGIAN NEUTRALITY AND THE GERMAN ULTIMATUM.

412

X. BRITAIN AT WAR.   476

XI. AUSTRIA AT WAR WITH THE TRIPLE *ENTENTE*.   526

XVI. MONTENEGRO MAKES COMMON CAUSE WITH SERBIA.

XVII. THE ATTITUDE OF THE OTHER STATES.

ABBREVIATIONS

Abbreviations are confined to works quoted more than three times. For the collections of diplomatic documents, the number of the volume and the number of the document are given. The French diplomatic documents are divided into three series. For them and for the Russian documents (INT. BEZ.) the series number is given in the first place. Authorised English translations are quoted, but not abridgements or selections.

A.F-R.: Ministère des Affaires Etrangères.—*L'alliance franco-russe. Origines de l'alliance 1890-1893. Convention militaire 1892-1899, et convention navale 1912* (Paris, 1918).

ASQUITH: Asquith, Herbert Henry.—*The Genesis of the War* (London, 1923).

BACH: Bach, A.—Deutsche Gesandtschaftsberichte zum Kriegsausbruch 1914.—*Berichte und Telegramme der badischen, süchsischen und württembergischen Gesandtschaften in Berlin aus dem Juli und August 1914. Im Auftrag des Auswärtigen Amtes herausgegeben* von August Bach (Berlin, 1937).

BARNES: Barnes, Harry Elmer.—*The Genesis of the World War. An Introduction to the Problem of War Guilt* (New York and London, 1929).

BD.: *British Documents on the Origins of the War 1898-1914.* Ed. by G. P. Gooch and Harold Temperley. Vols. I-XI (London, 1926-38).

BENCKENDORFF : Benckendorff, Alexander Graf von.—*Diplomatischer Schriftwechsel hrsg. von Benno von Siebert* (Berlin and Leipzig, 1928).

BETHMANN: Bethmann Hollweg, Theobald von.—*Betrachtungen zum Weltkriege.* 2 vols. (Berlin, 1919-22).

BRANDENBURG: Brandenburg, Erich.—*From Bismarck, to the World War* (London, 1933); *Von Bismarck yum Weltkrkg* (Leipzig, 1939).

BREDT: Bredt, Joh. Victor.— *Die belgische Neutralist und der Schlieffensche Feldzugsplan* (Berlin, 1929).

BULG: *Die bulgarischen Dokumente zum Kriegsausbruch 1914*, in KSF., March 1928 (Berlin).

BÜLOW: Bülow, Prince Bernard von.—*Memoirs (1905-9).* 4 vols. (London and New York, 1931-2).

CDD.: *Collected Diplomatic Documents relating to the Outbreak of the European War* (London, 1915).

CHURCHILL: Churchill, Winston Leonard Spencer.—*The World Crisis.* 6 vols. (London, 1923-31).

CONRAD: Conrad von Hotzendorf, Franz Graf.—*Aus meiner Dienstyeit 1906-1918.* 5 vols. (Vienna, 1921-5).

CROKAERT: Crokaert, J.—*L'ultimatum allemand du 2 août,* in *Le Flambeau* of Brussels, 31 March 1922.

CZERNIN : Czernin, Ottokar Count.—*In the World War* (London, New York, 1919).

DA.: Republik Österreich, Staatsamt für Äusseres.—*Diplomatische Aktenstücke zur Vorgeschichte des Krieges 1914.—Erganyungen und Nachtrage zum Österreichisch-Ungarischen Rotbuch (28. Juni bis 27. August, 1914).* 3 vols (Vienna, 1919; *Deutsche Verlagsgesellschaft für Politik und Geschichte in*

Berlin. Translated as: *Austrian Red Book. Official Files pertaining to Pre-War History.* 3 parts (London, 1920).

DD.: *Die Deutschen Dokumente zum Kriegsausbruch.—Vollständige Sammlung der von Karl Kaufsky zusammengestellten amtlicben Aktenstücke mit einigen Ergänzungen. Neue durchgesebene und vermebrte Ausgabe.* 4 vols. (Berlin, 1927). *Outbreak of the World War.* Carnegie Endowment for International Peace. 1 vol. (O.U.P. 1924).

DIRR: Dirr, Pius.—*Bayerische Dokumente zum Kriegsausbruch mdvyim Versailler Schuldspruch* (Munich and Berlin, 1928).

DF.: Ministère des Affaires Étrangères. Commission de publication des documents relatifs aux origines de la guerre de 1914.—*Documents diplomatiques Français (1871-1914).* III Serie: *1911-14* (Paris, 1929-36).

DOBROROLSKI: Dobrorolski, Sergei Kostantinovich.—*La mobilisation de l'armee russe en 1914,* in *Revue d'Histoire de la Guerre Mondiale* (Paris, April-July, 1923).

FISCHER: Fischer, Eugen.—*Die kritischen 39 Tage von Sarajevo bis zum Weltbrand* (Berlin, 1928).

FOERSTER: Foerster, Wolfgang.—*Graf Scblieffen und der Weltkrieg* (Berlin, 1925).

FRANGULIS: Frangulis, A. F.—*La Grèce. Son statut international, son histoire diplomatique* (Paris, 1934).

FRONT WIDER BÜLOW: Thimme, Friedrich.—*Front wider Bülow. Staatsmanner, Diplomaten und Forscher zu seinen Denkwiirdigkeiten* (Munich, 1931).

GALET: Galet, Émile Joseph.—*Albert King of the Belgians in the Great War* (London, 1931).

GERIN: *Les responsabilités de la guerre. Quatorze questions par Rene Gerin; quatorze réponses par Raymond Poincaré* (Paris, 1930).

GIOLITTI: Giolitti, Giovanni.—*Memoirs of My Life* (London and Sydney, 1923).

GP.: *Die grosse Politik der europäischen Kabinette (1871-1914). Sammlung der diplomatischen Akten des Auswdrtigen Amies.* 39 vols. and Index vol. (Berlin, 1922-7).

GR.: Ministére des Affaires Étrangères de Grece.—*Documents diplomatiques 1913-17* (Athens, 1917).

GREY: Grey, Sir Edward (Lord Grey of Fallodon).—*Twenty-five Years 1892-1916.* 2 vols. (London, 1925).

HAUSER: *Histoire diplomatique de l'Europe (1871-1914)* publieé sous la direction de Henri Hauser par J. Ancel, L. Cahen, R. Guyot, A. Lajusan, P. Renouvin et H. Salomon. 2 vols. (Paris, 1929).

HERRE: Herre, Paul.—*Die kleinen Staaten und die Entstebung des Weltkriegs,* in *Berliner Monatsheffe* (KSF.) of May and July 1933 and February and April 1934.

HUGUET: Huguet, Général V. J. M.—*L' intervention militaire bntannique en 1914* (Paris, 1928); *Britain and the War. A French indictment* (London, 1928).

INT. BEZ.: *Die internazionalen Beziehungen im Zeitalter des Imperialisms. Dokumente aus den Archiven der Zarischen und der Provisorischen Regiernng.* Ed. O. Hoetsch. (Berlin 1931-40).

IZVOLSKY: *Der diplomatische Schriftwechsel Iswolskis, 1911-14.* Ed. Friedrich Stieve. 4vols. (Berlin, 1926).

JOFFRE: *Memoirs of Marshal Joffre.* 2 vols. (London, 1932).

KAUTSKY: Kautsky, Karl.—*The Guilt of William Hohenyolkrn* (London, 1920).

KSF: *Die Kriegschuldfrage. Zeitscbrift zur Vorgescbicbte und Geschicbte des Weltkrieges* (Berlin, 1923-8). Under the title *Berliner Monatsbefte,* edited by A. von Wegerer (Berlin, 1929-37).

LAS.: *Correspondence diplomatique du Gouvernment Serbe., 16/29 juin–3/16 août 1914* (Paris 1914; in CDD).

LGB.: Royaume de Belgique: Ministére des Affaires Étrangères. I^{ier} *Livre gris beige. Correspondance diplomatique relative à la guerre de 1914 (24 juillet-29 août 1914)* (Paris, 1914); in CDD. 2me *Livre gris beige. Correspondance diplomatique relative a la guerre de 1914* (Paris, 1915).

LICHNOWSKY: Prince Lichnowsky.—*Heading for the Abyss* (London, 1928).

LJF.: Ministére des Affaires Étrangères. *Livre Jaune Français: Documents diplomatiques 1914. La guerre européenne. Pièces relatives aux négotiations qui ont precede les declarations de guerre de V Allemagne a la Russie (1 août 1914) et a la France (3 août 1914). Declaration du 4 septembre 1914* (Paris, 1914); in CDD.

LLOYD GEORGE: Lloyd George, David.—*War Memoirs.* 6 vols. (London, 1933-6).

LN.: *Un Livre Noir.—Diplomatie d'avant-guerre d'apres les documents des archives russes. 1910-1917.* 3 vols. in 6 parts (Paris, 1922-34).

LUTZ : Lutz, Hermann.—*Die europäische Politik in der Julikrise 1914. Gutachten* (Berlin, 1930).

MAGRINI: Magrini, Luciano.—*Il dramma di Sarajevo. Origini e responsabilità della guerra europea* (Milan, 1929).

MARGUTTI: Margutti, Albert von.—*Ui tragedie des Habsbourg* (Paris and Vienna, 1919).

MOLTKE: Moltke, Helmuth von.—*Erinnerungen, Briefe, Dokumente 1877-1916.* Ed. Eliza von Moltke (Stuttgart, 1922).

MONTGELAS: Montgelas, Max, Count.—*The Case for the Central Powers* (London, 1925).

MORLEY: Morley, John, Viscount, of Blackburn.—*Memorandum on Resignation, August 1914* (London, 1928).

NICOLSON: Nicolson, Harold George.—*Sir Arthur Nicolson, Bart., First Lord Carnock.—A Study in the Old Diplomacy* (London, 1930).

OE-U.: *Österreich-Ungarns Aussenpolitik von der bosnischen Krise 1908 bis zum Kriegsausbruch 1914.* 8 vols. and Index vol. (Vienna, 1930).

PALEOLOGUE: Paléologue, Maurice.—*An Ambassador's Memoirs.* 3 vols. (London, 1923).

POINCARE: Poincaré, Raymond.—*Au service de la France. Neuf atmees de souvenirs.* 10 vols. (Paris, 1926-33).

POURTALÈS: Pourtalès, Friedrich, Graf.—*Meine let^fen Verhandlungen in Skt. Petersburg. Ende Juli 1914* (Berlin, 1927).

PRIBRAM: Pribram, A. F.—*The Secret Treaties of Austria-Hungary.* Vol. I *Texts of the Treaties and Agreements.*Vol. II. *Negotiations leading to the Treaties of the Triple Alliance* (Harvard University Press, 1920, 1921).

RECOULY: Recouly, Raymond. *Les heures tragiques d'avant-guerre* (Paris, 1922).

RENOUVIN: Renouvin, Pierre.—*The Immediate Origins of the War* (Yale U.P., 1928); *Les origines immédiates de la guerre (28 juin-4 août 1914)* (Paris, 1927).

SALANDRA: Salandra, Antonio.—*La Neutralità italiana (1914)* (Milan, 1928).

SAZONOV: Sazonov, Serge.—*Fateful Years, 1909-1916* (London, 1928).

SCHÄFER: Schäfer, Theobald von.—*Generaloberst von Moltke in den Tagen vor der Mobilmachung und seine Einwirkung auf Österreich* (KSF., Berlin, August 1926).

SCHILLING: *How the War began in 1914. Being the Diary of the Russian F.O. from the 3rd to the 20th July 1914.* With a foreword by S. D. Sazonov and an introduction by Baron Schilling (London, 1925).

SCHMITT: Schmitt, Bernadotte E.—*The Coming of the War.* 2 vols. (New York, 1930).

SCHOEN: Schoen, Wilhelm Eduard, Freiherr von.—*Memoirs of an Ambassador* (London, 1922).

SELLIERS DE MORANVILLE: Selliers de Moranville, Lieutenant Général.—*Contribution à l'histoire de la guerre mondiale 1914-1918* (Paris, 1933).

SETON-WATSON, *Romanians*: Seton-Watson, R. W.—*A History of the Romanians* (Cambridge, 1934).

SHEBEKO : Schebeko, N.—*Souvenirs. Essai historique sur les origines de la guerre de 1914* (Paris, 1936).

SIEBERT: Siebert, Beuno von.—*Ententè Diplomacy and the World* (London, 1921).

SPENDER: Spender, John Alfred.—*Life of Herbert Henry Asquith, Lord Oxford and Asquith.* 2 vols. (London, 1932).

STEED: Steed, Henry Wickham.—*Through Thirty Years 1892-1922.* 2 vols. (London, 1924).

STIEVE: Stieve, Friedrich.—*Izvolsky and the World War* (London, 1926).

TAUBE: Taube, M.—*Der grossen Katastrophe entgegen* (Leipzig. 1937).

TIRPITZ, *Memoirs*: Tirpitz, Alfred von.—*My Memoirs.* 2 vols. (London, 1919); *Erinnerungen.* 1 vol. (Berlin and Leipzig, 1927).

TIRPITZ, *Dokumente:* Tirpitz, Alfred von.—*Politische Dokumente. 2 vols.* Vol. I. *Der Aufbau der deutschen Wehrmacht* (Berlin, 1924). Vol. II. *Deutsche Ohnmachtspolitik im Weltkriege* (Berlin, 1926).

TITTONI, *Nuovi Scritti*: Tittoni, Tornmaso.—*Nuovi Scritti dipolitica interna ed estera* (Milan, 1930).

U.S.A.: Department of State; *Diplomatic Correspondence with Belligerent Governments relating to Neutral Rights and Duties. Nos. 2, 3* (Washington, 1915, 1916).

WEGERER, *Weltkreig*: Wegerer, Alfred von.—*Der Ausbruch des Weltkrieges.* 2 vols. (Berlin, 1939).

WEGERER, *Refutation*: Wegerer, Alfred von.—*A Refutation of the Versailles War Guilt Thesis* (New York and London, 1930).

WULLUS-RUDIGER: Wullus-Rudiger, J.—*La Belgique et l'equilibre européen* (Paris, 1935).

ZWEHL: Zwehl, Hans von.—*Erich von Falkenhayn, General der Infanterie. Eine biographische Studie* (Berlin, 1926).

ACKNOWLEDGEMENT

The editor desires to express sincere thanks to Professor Bernadotte E. Schmitt for his kindness in reading the present volume.

CHAPTER I

THE PROCLAMATION OF THE
KRIEGSGEFAHRZUSTAND IN GERMANY;
THE GERMAN ULTIMATUM TO RUSSIA

(1) *The Chancellor and the Kaiser's marginalia: his 'That means I have got to mobilize as well!' (p.* 1). (2) *Moltke's sudden change-over to readiness for war (p.* 6). (3) *Bethmann confesses to his Cabinet colleagues that he has lost control of events; his promise to the Generals (p.* 14). (4) *Sazonov's formula for mediation received in Berlin; the Kaiser's perplexities on the afternoon of 30 July (p.* 18). (5) *Haeften's revelations and what they amount to (p.* 24). (6) *How King George V's telegram to the Kaiser was communicated to Vienna (p.* 27). (7) *News of the Russian general mobilization becomes known in Berlin (p.* 31). (8) *The Kaiser's wrathful outbursts; his ignorance of the real situation, and his groundless optimism at the last moment (p.* 34). (9) *Proclamation of the* Kriegsgefahrzustand *and the German ultimatums to Russia and to France (p.* 38). (10) *The Kaiser's telegram to Francis Joseph; Moltke's startling proposals to Conrad (p.* 45). (11) *Bethmann's renewed approach to London; Grey's last urgent appeal to Berlin (p.* 50). (12) *A telegram from the Tsar to Wilhelm; Sazonov's successive states of mind (p.* 55). (13) *Pourtalès hands Sazonov the German ultimatum with a twelve-hour time limit (p.* 61).

1. *The Chancellor and the Kaiser's marginalia; his 'That means I have got to mobilize as well!'*

On the night of 29-30 July the Chancellor had reached the point of telegraphing to Tschirschky:

We are, of course, prepared to fulfill our duty as allies, but must decline to let ourselves be dragged by Vienna, irresponsibly and without regard to our advice, into a world conflagration.[1]

Shortly afterwards he had learnt that, despite his urgent plea, Berchtold had told Tschirschky he could not give an immediate answer to the *Halt in Belgrade* proposal, approved by London and on the acceptance of which all Berlin's hopes were fixed.[2] This delay boded ill for such hopes especially in view of the fact that Russia had ordered partial mobilization and that Sazonov had told Pourtalès it could not be revoked.[3] It might have been expected, therefore, that on the morning of the 30th Bethmann would have redoubled his efforts at Vienna,

---

[1] DD. II, 396. See Vol. II, p. 525.   [2] DD. II, 388. See Vol. II, pp. 525-6.
[3] DD. II, 401. See Vol. II, p. 562.

even telephoning to Tschirschky, as the Wilhelmstrasse was wont to do when occasion demanded. Instead of so doing, Bethmann had no communication at all with Tschirschky on the morning of the 30th and his attitude showed a weakening which was not attributable to any change in the situation, since the news of the Russian partial mobilization had reached him already on the evening of the 29th and he had then telegraphed to Tschirschky:

> In order to prevent general catastrophe, or at any rate put Russia in the wrong, we must urgently desire that Vienna should initiate and pursue conversations as indicated.[1]

This weakening on Bethmann's part was to have disastrous consequences. If in the course of 30 July Germany had put further resolute pressure on her ally before she herself on the 31st ordered general mobilization, the crisis might well have had a different issue. But action would have had to be taken with the utmost speed and determination. It would have meant Bethmann's telephoning, rather than telegraphing, to say that, cost what it may, Berchtold must agree to the *Halt in Belgrade*. The documents do not show why after making his effort on the previous evening Bethmann let it drop on the 30th, and on the afternoon of that day began his surrender to Moltke, a surrender which by evening was complete. Certain facts do, however, allow of a conjecture.

First of all we must see what the Kaiser was doing. On waking up on the morning of the 30th, Wilhelm found bad news awaiting him. In the night, as already mentioned, there had arrived the Tsar's telegram telling that 'the military measures which have now come into force were decided five days ago'.[2] What these measures were the Kaiser learnt at 6 a. m. by a message from Bethmann belatedly informing him of that telegram from Pourtalès, received the previous day at 2.52 p. m., announcing the mobilization of the four Russian military districts facing the Austrian frontier.[3] Thereupon Wilhelm wrongly jumped to the conclusion that the mobilization had begun five days earlier and minuted the Tsar's telegram as follows:

> So that is almost a week ahead of us. And these measures are supposed to be of defense against Austria, who is not attacking him!!! I cannot commit myself to mediation any more, since the Tsar, who appealed for it, has at the same time been secretly mobilizing behind my back. It is only a maneuver to keep us dangling and increase the lead he has already gained over us. My task is at an end.[4]

The Chancellor's message accompanying the Pourtalès telegram received sundry marginal annotations, among which are the following:

---

[1] DD. II, 385. See Vol. II, p. 504.   [2] DD. II, 390. See Vol. II, p. 560.
[3] DD. II, 343, 399.   [4] DD. II, 390.

'According to this the Tsar with his appeal for my help has simply been acting a part and leading us up the garden path!'—'That means I have got to mobilize as well!'—the mobilization 'which began already on the 24th'. There followed a footnote saying that the Russian mobilization,

according to the Tsar's telegram of the 29th, had been ordered five days earlier, therefore on the 24th, immediately after the delivery of the ultimatum to Serbia. Therefore long before the Tsar telegraphed asking me for mediation. His first telegram expressly said he would probably be compelled to take measures which would lead to a European war. He thereby takes the blame on his own shoulders. In reality the measures were already in full swing and he has simply been lying to me. The sending of Tatistchev and the wish that I should not let myself be deterred from my role as mediator by his mobilization measures are childish and meant only to set a trap for us (*uns auf den Gänsedreck führen*)! I regard my mediatory action as mistaken, since, without straightforwardly awaiting its effects, the Tsar has already and without a hint to me been mobilizing behind my back.[1]

Only a superficial perusal of the Tsar's telegram could leave room for this suspicion and invective on Wilhelm's part. However clumsy and inexpedient it was for Nicholas to say: 'the military measures which have now come into force were decided five days ago', the words gave no grounds for the assumption that Russian mobilization had begun five days earlier, nor for regarding this as a reason for breaking off all mediatory action, nor for ordering German mobilization. The Kaiser's conclusions all the more reveal his lack of judgment when it is remembered that this same partial mobilization to which the Tsar alluded had been declared by Jagow not to be a ground for German counter-measures.

The injudiciousness of the Kaiser's marginal notes in this connection is admitted even by Montgelas, though he maintains that they

could not have had the slightest influence on the decision the responsible director of Germany's policy had long since taken.[2]

That no such 'decision' had been taken by 'the responsible director of German policy' is evident from the fact that a veiled threat from Grey was sufficient on the evening of the 29th to direct the Chancellor's efforts into quite different channels from those of the previous days. To the present writer it does not seem possible to rule out the assumption that the Kaiser's annotations to the two documents in question affected the Chancellor's actions on the morning of the 30th, while it is practically certain that they influenced those of the German Chief of Staff with decisive results.

[1] DD. II, 399.
[2] Montgelas, *The Case for the Central Powers* (London, 1925), p. 149.

Already on the morning of the 30th Bethmann had received back the Tsar's telegram from Wilhelm with his marginal comments. This is proved by the fact that at 11.15 a. m. that same morning a letter went off from Bethmann to Wilhelm with thanks and suggestions for an answer to the Tsar's telegram.[1] The Kaiser himself notes that at 7 a. m. that morning he also read the Pourtalès telegram; hence it is evident that the latter, complete with his marginal notes, went back to Bethmann at the same time as the Tsar's telegram. Marginalia and footnotes all show the Kaiser expressing his intention of throwing up the role of mediator and mobilizing, in the belief that he is already six days behind Russia. What was the impression produced on the Chancellor by this expression of his Imperial master's intentions?

The relations between the two men were not those of full mutual confidence. The Kaiser had no great opinion of the Chancellor, who in his turn sought to let his Sovereign know as little as possible about what he was doing and saying. He could not do otherwise than acquaint Wilhelm of the more important of the Ambassadors' telegrams, but he did so with deliberate belatedness, with textual alterations, and above all with the omission of information on the action taken by himself. Strangely enough the Kaiser, autocrat though he was, did not demand to see copies of all diplomatic correspondence, as did the King of Italy, at least when the Liberals were in power. Thus Wilhelm did not see the text of the telegrams sent by Bethmann to Tschirschky on the night of the 29th. All he was allowed to know was contained in a few colorless sentences of the short letter sent at 1 1 . 15 a. m. on the 30th accompanying the Lichnowsky telegram which reported Grey's threat of the evening of the 29th.[2] Such concealment made it impossible for the Kaiser to exercise effective control over the Government's doings, know what was going on, or intervene in time. This, however, does not imply that the Government could leave the Kaiser's views out of account. It had been his will that Austria was to be given unconditional support and urged to take strong action, and that Tschirschky should abstain from exercising any restraining influence. Then with his usual fickleness Wilhelm on the 28th had manifested a desire to avoid a war and proposed the *Halt in Belgrade,* Bethmann being obliged to follow suit, first against his will, and then, after the threat from Grey, with eagerness and conviction. But now Wilhelm was apparently changing his mind once more and talking of mobilizing.

It is permissible to assume that the Kaiser's new mood and new proposals threw the Chancellor off his bearings and made him doubt the feasibility of getting Vienna to accept a compromise on pain of losing German support. What Bethmann ought to have done was

[1] DD. II, 408.   [2] DD. II, 407.

to go straight to Potsdam and clear the matter up, especially in view of that disquieting telegram from Lichnowsky. Did his Sovereign really want peace, or was his mind made up for war? If Wilhelm did want peace, as in truth he did in spite of his outbursts, and if war offered itself in the most unfavorable conditions, then Berchtold must at once be spoken to in no uncertain terms, even to the point of refusing recognition of the *casus foederis.* But Bethmann was not the man for such bold and clear-cut measures. He may, after the effort of the previous night, have not found the strength in himself to renew his pressure. It would have meant admitting to Berchtold, and forcing Berchtold also to admit, that the pair of them had taken the wrong turning and that they must back out of danger even at the price of humiliation. Instead of deciding one way or another, what he in fact did was to place the fate of Germany on the knees of the gods. Had he not been pressing Vienna to accept the *Halt in Belgrade?* Then surely, before thinking of mobilizing—since this was tantamount to going to war—ought he not at least to wait and see what Austria would reply? In the letter of 11.15 a. m. by which he thanked Wilhelm for returning the Tsar's telegram and suggested a draft for a reply, he ended up with the words:

As this telegram, too, will become a particularly important document for history, I would humbly recommend that in it Your Majesty should not—as long as there is no decision from Vienna—make the statement that Your Majesty's mediatorial role is already at an end.[1]

Thus Bethmann was back again at his old devices for putting Russia in the wrong and saving appearances. In these ways he wasted the last precious hours when it would still have been possible to persuade Vienna to accept the solution offered in accord with London. He did, at 11.30 a. m., telegraph Lichnowsky to ask that Grey should insist on the dropping of military preparations by France and Russia on grounds that

Austria will hardly be able to refrain from answering Russian mobilization with corresponding measures. Our position becomes extremely critical on this account.[2]

But he gave no sign of life to Vienna, though this was what was most urgently needful, because if Vienna had agreed to the proposal, inspired by Wilhelm and regarded as satisfactory by Grey, the situation might still have been saved. His silence showed that he was giving up the attempt. Indeed, everything that Bethmann was to do and say on that last decisive day, 30 July, betrays faint-heartedness, irresolution, bewilderment and lack of confidence. The Kaiser, on the other hand,

[1] DD. II, 408.   [2] DD. II, 409. See Vol. II, p. 635.

lightly tossing aside his first impressions and anything but eager to
run the risk of war, at once fell in with his Chancellor's proposals.
Slightly modifying Bethmann's English draft and adding a final sentence, he telegraphed at 3.30 p. m. on the 30th to the Tsar as follows:

> Best thanks for telegram. It is quite out of the question that my ambassadors [*sic*]
> language could have been in contradiction with the tenor of my telegram. Count
> Pourtalès was instructed to draw the attention of your Government to the danger and
> grave consequences involved by a mobilization; I said the same in my telegram to
> you. Austria has only mobilized against *Serbia* and only a *part* of her army. If, as is
> now the case, according to the communication by you and your Government,
> Russia mobilizes against Austria, my role as mediator you kindly entrusted me with,
> and which I accepted at you[r] express prayer, will be endangered if not ruined. The
> whole weight of the decision lies solely on you[r] shoulders now, who have to bear
> the responsibility for Peace or War.[1]

2. *Moltke's sudden change-over to readiness for war.*

The views, or rather the outbursts, of the Kaiser had a still more
visible effect on Moltke than they had on Bethmann. On learning from
Falkenhayn that Bethmann 'had asked Falkenhayn and Tirpitz to see
him at 1 p. m. on the 30th, Moltke appeared at the meeting uninvited'.[2]
Why this meeting was called and what was said and decided at it
are not known. At 11.50 a. m. the Wilhelmstrasse had received an
urgent telegram from Pourtalès, sent off at 11 a. m., announcing:

> Mobilization comprises military districts of Kiev, Odessa, Moscow, Kazan,
> Cossack armies of the Don, Kuban, Terek, Astrakan, Orenburg, Ural. Apart from
> the mobilization of the fleet, no call up has been ordered in the military districts of
> Warsaw, Vilna and St. Petersburg.[3]

Russian partial mobilization was a known fact, but here the exact
details were given, and it is not unlikely that the Chancellor felt the
need of discussing them with the War Minister and the army chiefs.
After the meeting Wenninger, the Bavarian Military Attaché, telegraphed to Munich that the Kaiser was

definitely on the side of Moltke and the War Minister,

who wanted to have the *Kriegsgefahrzustand* proclaimed.[4] But this
statement was incorrect. Although no document proves (and lack of
time furthermore rules out the possibility) that Moltke and Bethmann
discussed the matter with Wilhelm, it is an ascertained fact that
Wilhelm, despite all the marginalia and footnotes which we have
considered, was by no means in favor of mobilization, and at once

---

[1] DD. II, 420.   [2] DD. IV, No. 5, p. 157.
[3] DD. II, 410.   [4] DD. IV, p. 157; Dirr., p. 226.

agreed to telegraph the Tsar along the lines proposed by Bethmann. In the afternoon of the 30th and morning of the 31st he was far from being as bellicose as he was to show himself later. But what becomes clear beyond doubt is that during the talk which Moltke had with the Chancellor at about 1 p. m. on the 30th, he took a firm stand in favor of war. This was a new development. Though in his memorandum of 28 July Moltke had written that only a miracle could

prevent at the eleventh hour a war which will annihilate the civilization of almost the whole of Europe for decades to come,[1]

and though he was reported by Lerchenfeld to have said months earlier that

the moment is militarily favorable to a degree which cannot occur again in a foreseeable future,[2]

he behaved calmly and cautiously at the Potsdam meeting on the 29th, lending no support to Falkenhayn's proposal to proclaim the *Kriegsgefahrzustand,* the prelude to general mobilization and war, and only asking for military protection of key-points on the railway system.[3] When on the evening of the 29th there came news that Russia was proceeding to partial mobilization, Bethmann negatived the suggestion that this rendered German mobilization inevitable

against slight, very, very slight opposition from Moltke.[4]

Nay more. On the following morning (the 30th) Moltke scandalized Conrad by telling Captain Fleischmann, the Austrian liaison officer with the German General Staff, in full accord with Bethmann's point of view:

Russian [partial] mobilization still no reason for [German] mobilization; not until commencement of state of war between Monarchy and Russia.[5]

It was an hour after making this last statement that Moltke suddenly changed his mind, to the great astonishment of Falkenhayn, who

was struck by this change of mood.[6]

Lieutenant-Colonel Schäfer also records that

the opinion of Colonel-General von Moltke on the decisive question whether the great war could still be avoided or not, underwent a change in the course of 30 July,

and that the change must have taken place about noon.[7] In Schäfer's

---

[1] DD. II, 349. See Vol. II, p. 489.   [2] DD. IV, 151. See Vol. II, p. 487.
[3] See Vol. II, p. 491.   [4] Zwehl, p. 57. See Vol. II, p. 502.
[5] Conrad, IV pp. 151-2. See Vol. II, p. 671.
[6] Zwehl, p. 8.   [7] Schäfer, p. 527.

opinion the deciding factor must have been the Russian partial mobilization. But this cannot be so, since Russia already the previous day had announced her intention to carry this out, and Moltke that very morning (the 30th) had told Fleischmann: 'Russian mobilization still no reason for mobilization.' Schäfer goes on to say that Moltke's change of attitude may have been caused partly by the fact that, contrary to expectation,

Russia's conduct in this matter seemed not to encounter disapproval from the other Powers. The disposition of England, Italy and Romania grew increasingly doubtful, and this in itself constituted an extraordinary intensification of the danger of war.[1]

But this argument is not convincing because, if anything, it should have preserved Moltke from all temptation to plunge into a venture which would begin under unfavorable auspices. Why, therefore, the change?

As we have previously noted, the docility and circumspection manifested by Moltke during 29 July and Falkenhayn's air of resignation were in all probability entirely due to the Kaiser's pacific state of mind at Potsdam on that date.[2] As long as the Sovereign was openly in favor of peace, his Chief of Staff did not venture to ask for war. Then came Wilhelm's marginalia and footnotes to the two telegrams from St. Petersburg, which gave the impression that he no longer meant to use his influence to compose the conflict and intended on the contrary to mobilize. This was just what Moltke wanted. Doubtless regretting what he had said to Fleischmann, fully understanding the difficult position of Austria, knowing how the Schlieffen mobilization plan was designed to work, he did not wait for the statesmen to straighten out their ideas but suddenly dropped his cautious attitude and launched out into vigorous action in favor of war.

But how did he find out so soon about the Imperial marginalia? There is much likelihood that somebody very high up at the Wilhelmstrasse, who, like him, thought that war was necessary, kept him abreast of all that went on there.[3] When Pourtalès's telegram arrived at 11.30 a. m. on the 30th[4] with details of the districts in which Russian partial mobilization was being operated, Moltke learnt immediately of its contents. He in his turn at once informed Fleischmann, who at 1.15 p. m. telegraphed the news to Vienna, adding:

Chief of General Staff requests communication of decision taken by you.[5]

[1] Schäfer, p. 527.   [2] See Vol. II, pp. 496-7.
[3] Leuckart, the Saxon military plenipotentiary at Berlin, sent word to the Saxon War Minister, Carlowitz, on 28 July: 'At the War Ministry and the General Staff feverish activity is noticeable. . . . Between General Staff and Foreign Ministry there is a constant coming and going—I saw Staff officers driving up to the Foreign Ministry in cars of the motorized battalion' (Bach, p. 84).
[4] DD. II, 410.   [5] Schäfer, p. 524. See Vol. II, p. 672.

It may be objected that this proves nothing, since the news from Pourtalès was of a nature to be communicated at once to the Chief of Staff. But we shall see farther on that a very important telegram sent to Vienna by Bethmann on the evening of the 30th to persuade Berchtold to agree to the *Halt in Belgrade* and mediation also became at once known to Moltke, who thus had time to enter protest against it and get the instructions contained in it cancelled. This could only happen if someone in a very high position was in league with him. Therefore nothing was more natural than that as soon as Moltke's informant read the Kaiser's comments and thus learnt what he had in mind, this personage at once let the General know that he could go ahead without fear of being at cross-purposes with his Imperial master. Only in this way can it be explained that at 10 a. m. Moltke was speaking to Fleischmann in terms which made Conrad feel doubtful of German support, while about noon he was suddenly saying the very opposite.[1] It is also the explanation of Wenninger's telegram saying that the Kaiser was 'definitely on the side of Moltke and the War Minister' who wanted the *Kriegsgefahrzustand to* be proclaimed.[2]

We can only conclude that Wenninger, too, got wind of the Kaiser's marginal notes and learnt that Moltke was pressing the Chancellor for mobilization. That would be a reason for his telegraphing as he did.

Many other factors confirm that the Kaiser's words throwing up the role of mediator and contemplating mobilization leaked out.

The Berlin correspondent of the *Neues Wiener Tagblatt,* on information from one of the Kaiser's Aides-de-Camp, telegraphed to his paper at 10 a. m. announcing German general mobilization.[3] The same news was given at 1 p. m. in an extra edition of the *Berliner Lokal-Anzeiger,* a semi-official publication regularly read by the Kaiser and much in favor in high circles. This extra edition, of which we have already spoken,[4] contained the announcement:

We learn that the Kaiser has just ordered the immediate mobilization of the German army and navy.

Now Eugen Fischer who, as secretary of the Reichstag Commission for the Investigation of War Origins, had opportunities for forming

---

[1] Eugen Fischer also takes this view and writes of 'Moltke, in appropriate subordination to the Kaiser's will, itself subordinated to that of the Chancellor'. For the 30th he notes that Moltke was 'obviously immediately informed' of the Kaiser's marginal notes and at once sent for the Austrian Military Attaché to tell him that Austria must mobilize against Russia and that Germany would recognize the *casus foederis.* But Fischer places the first Moltke-Fleischmann interview on the evening of the 29th, instead of the morning of the 30th, which latter date makes it much more significant (Fischer, pp. 218-9).

[2] See p. 6; DD. IV, 157.

[3] R. Puaux, Le *mensonge du 3 août* 1914 (Paris, 1917), p. 72.

[4] See Vol. II, p. 57;.

a well-founded opinion, is convinced that the *Lokal-Anzeiger* derived its information from the War Ministry. The military now thought the moment had come for an attack on 'lanky Theobald' *(der lange Theobald)*, as they disrespectfully called the Chancellor. 'He himself would never have enough courage.'

The nation *(Volk)* was to burst into enthusiasm. Then it could be said to the Kaiser: Your Majesty, You will need this enthusiasm, it cannot be kept in cold-storage. Take advantage of it. Mobilize. Then wouldn't lanky Theobald open his eyes wide! And no sooner was the telegram off than it would be at Vienna, Paris, St. Petersburg and London too. It would give the Viennese a prod. It would perhaps make Paris take immediate counter-measures.[1]

Wegerer casts doubt on Fischer's interpretation, basing his own on evidence given by an assistant editor and two members of the newspaper staff of the *Lokal-Anzeiger:*

On 30 July about noon the editor's office learnt from several sources news that sounded reliable to the effect that the proclamation of mobilization was to be expected in a couple of hours or so. In view of the extreme importance of the news the editorial staff, as often in such cases, discussed the question how most speedily to inform the public of the mobilization, if the news received official confirmation.

In the end the order was issued for the preparation of an extra edition, the copy being held in readiness until the news was confirmed. The technical staff printed an edition of 2,000 copies and, by a mistake, 150 were sold at a street corner in about two minutes before sales were stopped.[2] To those with newspaper experience Wegerer's story will hardly carry much conviction. They will incline more to believe that there was a leakage of the Kaiser's marginal note, perhaps brought about intentionally by the General Staff. The motives for such a maneuver are obvious. Bethmann was still awaiting a reply from Vienna about the *Halt in Belgrade* and had not yet given up all hope of peace. Above all, he was anxious not to appear in the guise of the aggressor, and thus bring England in against Germany, so that at the interview of 1 p. m. he did not, there and then, yield to Moltke's demand for the immediate proclamation of the *Kriegsgefahrzustand* followed in due course by mobilization. Schäfer thinks Moltke used the argument that, since between the two measures there would be a twenty-four to forty-eight hour interval, the first possible day of mobilization would be 1 August. This would mean that Germany would be a full week behindhand in relation to Russia.[3]

---

[1] Fischer, pp. 220–1.
[2] A. von Wegerer, *Das Extrablatt des Lokal-Anzeigers,* in KSF., Nov. 1929, pp. 1040 ff.
[3] Schäfer, p. 531.

Failing to gain Bethmann's consent, Moltke went back to his room in a state of annoyance but determined to foil the Chancellor and induce Austria to mobilize and reject the *Halt in Belgrade*. To this end he sent for the Austrian Military Attaché, Lieutenant-Colonel Bienerth, who writes:

It may have been about 2 p. m. His Excellency, as far as my memory serves, came from the Foreign Ministry and was extremely agitated, as I had never before seen him. . . . Moltke said he would think the situation critical unless the Austro-Hungarian Monarchy at once mobilizes against Russia. . . . This would give the *casus foederis* for Germany. Bring about honorable arrangement with Italy by assurances of compensation. . . . Reject renewed English *démarche* for maintenance of peace. Last means of preserving Austria-Hungary is to fight out *(durchhalten)* a European war. Germany with you unconditionally.[1]

Later that same evening Moltke himself telegraphed direct to Conrad in the same sense, using the words: 'Germany will mobilize'.

Schäfer quotes Waldersee as explaining:

We in Berlin were anxious about how things were going in Vienna, even in the purely military field. We knew . . . the slow pace of Austro-Hungarian mobilization, we feared that Vienna's secretiveness towards Italy would give Rome an excuse to desert us and we had grounds for feeling apprehensive that at this critical moment Austria-Hungary would disperse her resources not only by fixing her teeth into Serbia but by leaving corps stationed on the Italian frontier.[2]

This is all very well, but the fact remains that Moltke's action constituted a usurpation of the powers of the Chancellor. The thesis has been put forward that Moltke was not Bethmann's subordinate, that the two were of equal status in relation to the Kaiser, who decided between them in case of difference.

Nor was Moltke an undisciplined person accustomed to going his own way. What seems probable therefore is that Moltke sent his message to Conrad in the knowledge that the Emperor agreed with him.[3]

Eugen Fischer, in reply to an enquiry from the present writer, wrote that in his opinion Moltke's change of front in the course of 30 July was due to the change in the attitude of the Kaiser. His letter runs:

No document dealing with this question exists even in the form of a note in the Kaiser's hand, or as an instruction from him to the Chief of Staff or to the Chancellor or Foreign Minister. . . .

The Tsar's telegram, which reached the telegraph office in the Neues

[1] Conrad, IV, p. 152. See Vol. II. p. 673.   [2] Schäfer, p. 532.
[3] Bernadotte Schmitt, *The Coming of the War*, 1914, II, p. 198.

Palais at 1.45 a. m., may be regarded as the cause of the change in the attitude of the Chief of Staff. This telegram must have been handed to the Kaiser when he rose in the morning, if not already during the night. 'I cannot', commented Wilhelm 'commit myself to mediation any more, since the Tsar, who appealed for it, has at the same time secretly been mobilizing behind my back. It is only a maneuver to keep us dangling and increase the lead he has already gained over us. My task is at an end.'

If Moltke came to know of this it is certainly understandable that he regarded a new situation as having arisen. The most natural thing is to suppose that the Aide-de-Camp, General von Plessen, who was ordered by the Kaiser, for example on 27 July, to hand on information to Moltke, remained all the time in continual close contact with him and may have passed on to him, perhaps even at the Kaiser's bidding, the text of the Tsar's telegram.

Still more eloquent is the Kaiser's marginal note to the Chancellor's report giving news of the Russian mobilization against Austria, telegraphed by Pourtalès and confirmed by the Russian Ambassador at Berlin: 'That means I have got to mobilize as well. . . .'

Bethmann's report went off at 6 a. m. and was shown at once to the Kaiser, who dated it and added '7 a. m.'. He had already read the Tsar's telegram when he wrote the marginal notes to Bethmann's report. Moltke may have been informed of the Kaiser's views at the same time through the two documents 390 and 399. As regards both of them there also exists the possibility that the information reached him through the Wilhelmstrasse, for the Chancellor in a letter to the Kaiser, dispatched at 11.15 a. m., already alludes to the Kaiser's annotations to his report,[1] expressing thanks for having been shown the Tsar's letter to the Kaiser. Hence Bethmann's report came back to the Foreign Ministry in the course of the morning, in fact in time for the Chancellor to be able at 11.15 to send a reply to Potsdam with a draft for another telegram to the Tsar composed by Jagow.

In connection with the behavior of Moltke during the 30th, the present writer sent a letter of inquiry to the ex-Kaiser Wilhelm, and he, after 'deep reflection' on the questions contained in it, commanded his Aide-de-Camp, Sell, to reply on 11 March 1936

that as early as 30 July General Moltke saw war as inevitable is perfectly true. The German General Staff was obliged to come to that conviction because hour by hour news reached it of the beginnings of Russian partial mobilization against Austria-Hungary. Hence it was his duty as Chief of the General Staff to warn his Viennese colleagues of the absolute necessity for the most speedy Austro-Hungarian counter-measures. It is thus entirely understandable that late on the evening of the 30th General Moltke asked the Chancellor to postpone, in particular, instruction No. 200 by which Bethmann Hollweg sought to urge Vienna to concessions. It would be absolutely mistaken to see in the action of General Moltke the expression of a bellicose state of mind. He was prompted solely by a justifiable concern about the perilous position of our ally. This estimate of the situation on the

---

[1] DD. II, 408.

part of Moltke resulted from the fact that a Russian partial mobilization would give rise to corresponding counter-measures on the part of Austria; and after there had occurred a clash between Russia and Austria, it would no longer have been possible to avoid intervention by Germany on the basis of our obligations under the alliance. To these conclusions he was all the more entitled as Russian military measures on the German frontier, arising both from the coming into force of the 'period of preparation' for war, and the behavior of the Russian rulers, gave the quite correct impression that Russia would take military measures against Germany as well. Naturally His Majesty was kept most fully informed of the progress of Russian mobilization.[1]

In all this the real question, worded to elicit whether during 30 July Moltke had acted with the Kaiser's knowledge, remains unanswered.

Leaving aside the possibility of a harmony of views between the Kaiser and Moltke, the latter had no right to encroach on the Chancellor's functions with the mistaken idea of saving his country. His pressure for mobilization assumed forms which robbed the political leadership of its freedom of action. On the afternoon of the 30th Jagow and Zimmerman complained to the Spanish Ambassador and Jules Cambon of the pressure from the military:

One of the Ambassadors with whom I have very close relations saw Herr von Zimmermann at 2 o'clock. According to the Under-Secretary of State the military authorities are very anxious that mobilization should be ordered, because all delay makes Germany lose some of her advantages. Nevertheless, up to the present, there is said to have been successful resistance to the haste of the General Staff, which in mobilization sees war.[2]

And of his own talk with Jagow, Cambon writes:

I remarked to the Secretary of State that he himself had told me Germany would not consider herself obliged to mobilize unless Russia mobilized on her frontiers, which was not the case. He replied that this was true but that the army chiefs were insisting, because all delay was a loss of strength for the German army and that the words of which I reminded him did not constitute a binding engagement on his part.[3]

But it was not true that enough resistance was being offered to stop the military from prejudicing the decisions which the situation demanded, foremost among which was resolute perseverance in endeavors for peace. The Chancellor was losing heart and beginning to surrender to the will of the Chief of Staff.

[1] Letter in possession of the present writer.
[2] DF. 3. XI, 339; it appears with some alterations as No. 105 of the *French Yellow Book* (CDD., p. 214).
[3] DF. 3. XI, 380, appearing with alterations as No. 109 of the *French Yellow Book* (CDD., p. 217).

3. Bethmann confesses to his Cabinet colleagues that he has lost control of events; his promise to the Generals.

A few hours after his talk with Moltke, Bethmann presided at a meeting of the Prussian Cabinet held, not at noon, as is stated by most historians, but at 5 p. m. according to the written evidence produced for the Investigating Commission on 26 January 1924 by the Under-secretary of State, Heinrichs, who had drawn up the minutes of the meeting.[1] It is of great importance in many cases to know the exact hour at which certain events took place, because this knowledge throws light on words and actions which would otherwise be hard to explain. In the present case Bethmann's attitude and the statements he made to his colleagues would be difficult to understand if they were not seen as resulting from pressure, and probably also from promises given by him to Moltke.

The Chancellor opened by saying:

He had summoned the Ministers of State to today's meeting to give them a survey of the present political situation, as far as this was possible. The situation varied from hour to hour and was still doubtful in view of the uncertain factors in developments. His Majesty had tried to get an under-standing between the Vienna and St. Petersburg Governments. The Vienna Government, after the Serbian rejection of its terms, had made a declaration at St. Petersburg that it had no territorial aims and did not wish to infringe the integrity of the Serbian State [a statement which had never been made by Berchtold.[2]] The German Government had suggested to that of Vienna that a statement be made at St. Petersburg to the effect that Serbia had only partially agreed to fulfill the wishes of Vienna, moreover it was in a high degree doubtful whether she would keep her promises. Therefore the Vienna Government proposed by a temporary occupation to take a gage for its demands and for the good behavior of the Serbian Government. This *démarche*, made yesterday, had as yet received no answer. [Was the Chancellor ashamed to say

---

[1] Max Montgelas, 'Le 31 Juillet a Berlin et a Petersbourg', in *Évolution* (Paris, 15 Nov., 1926, p. 7).

[2] This observation has already been made in Vol. II, p. 576. The Austrian collection of documents furnishes no evidence of any statement by Berchtold on which Bethmann could base this assertion of his. On the 27th, by a telegram in cipher of 10.20 p. m., Berchtold authorized the Austrian Ambassador at St. Petersburg, 'without entering into a binding engagement, to converse with M. Sazonov and your Italian colleague in the sense that as long as the war between Austria-Hungary and Serbia remains localized, the Monarchy does not plan any territorial acquisitions' (Oe-U. VIII, 10834. See Vol. II, p. 684). On the 30th (but this telegram was enciphered at 1 p. m. and cannot have been laid before the Prussian Cabinet meeting) Berchtold telegraphed to Szögyény: 'It would seem to me necessary that Count Pourtalès should be instructed to indicate to M. Sazonov that Count Szápáry is furnished with detailed instructions for an explanation with the Russian Minister to the effect that in our action against Serbia we plan no territorial gain and have absolutely no intention to destroy the independent existence of the Kingdom' (Oe-U. VIII, 11020). But even in this telegram, which contains the fullest formulation arrived at by Berchtold, there is no word of 'having no wish to infringe the integrity of the Serbian State' and the way was thus still left open for diminishing Serbia for the benefit of adjoining states.

that the *démarche* had been made as early as the evening of the 28th?] The deciding factors in Germany's attitude in the present conflict were the following: The greatest importance must be attached to presenting Russia as the guilty party and that would be achieved by this Austro-Hungarian statement, which would reduce the assertions of the Russian Government to absurdity; next it must be borne in mind that, except on small points, the Serbian reply had in fact responded to the Austro-Hungarian desiderata. [Only forty-eight hours earlier, in his circular to the Prussian envoys to the other German Federal Governments, Bethmann had been writing that 'the answer of the Serbian Government . . . shows that authoritative quarters in Serbia do not intend to renounce their previous policy and subversive activity![1]]

Parallel with these negotiations with Vienna an exchange of telegrams had been carried on between His Majesty and the Tsar. . . . The telegrams had crossed, and a further exchange had been rendered difficult by the intervening of Russian mobilization. . . . Germany and England had taken all steps to avoid a European war. . . . His Majesty approved that, before further decisions, the above-mentioned *démarche* at Vienna should be brought to a conclusion. As regards military measures: proclamation of imminent danger of war meant mobilization, and this in our circumstances—mobilization on both fronts—meant war. One could not fittingly carry on political and military actions at the same time. Probably today in Vienna the decision would be taken in the matter of the German and English proposals.

As for the attitude of the other nations, there was practically no hope of England. England would be sure to side with the [Franco-Russian] Dual Alliance. Italy's attitude was not clear. The Austro-Serbian conflict was unpopular in Italy, because it was regarded as endangering Italian interests in the Balkans. He had urged Austria to come to an understanding with Italy, but this had so far not been done, Austria being in fact very difficult to deal with in the conduct of her policy. Romanian aid could not be counted on, nor that of Bulgaria, because its present Government would probably be overthrown and replaced by one friendly to Russia.

The picture was a terrifying one and its hues were rendered more somber still by Bethmann's closing remarks:

In concluding, the Minister-President emphasized that all the Governments—including that of Russia—and the great majority of the nations are in themselves pacific, but the situation had got out of hand (*es sei die Direktion verloren*) and the stone had started rolling. As a politician, however, he did not yet, as long as his *démarche* had not been rejected by Vienna, give up hopes and endeavors for the preservation of peace. The decision might come in a short time, then another marching route would be taken. The general atmosphere in Germany was good (approval from all sides). Even from Social Democracy and the Social Democrat party leadership nothing of any consequence was to be feared; this he felt

---

[1] DD. II, 307.

entitled to say after negotiations with the Reichstag deputy, Südekum. Of a general or partial strike or sabotage there would be no question.[1]

Here is Bethmann frankly stating that the Serbian reply 'except on small points had in fact responded to the Austro-Hungarian desiderata' and that 'Germany and England had taken all steps to avoid a European war', and again, with the same frankness, that English intervention was practically certain, that Italy would probably default, that Romania and Bulgaria could not be relied on, and he goes on no less frankly to admit that neither the governments nor the peoples wanted war and yet that it was likely to break out because 'the situation has got out of hand and the stone has started rolling'. In other words, the political leaders were no longer in control; the war machine was getting under way and threatening to overwhelm everything. Janushkevich and Joffre on the one side, Conrad and Moltke on the other, had thrust themselves into the foreground and were taking the situation more and more under their control. The German Chancellor laments the disaster and ranks himself among its victims. He gives the impression that in his dismay and anguish he felt the need of making a full confession and sharing the burden of responsibility with his colleagues. It is almost as if he hoped in making these gloomy and unvarnished statements that some Minister would guess his own and his Sovereign's desperation and come forward with the question: Why, if matters were so, if Serbia had practically given Austria satisfaction, if English proposals for peace were identical with those of Germany, if nobody wanted war, and if, should it break out, it would be in conditions disastrous for the two Empires, why was it not being avoided at all cost and the civil government again put in the position of control which it ought never to have let slip? But not one of the men in power in Germany, whether civilian or soldier, rose that day in Berlin to save Prussia and the Empire, just as on the morrow in Vienna no one rose to save the Monarchy. Bethmann more and more lost all control. To be sure, he had said that 'as a politician he did not, as long as his *démarche* had not been rejected by Vienna, give up hopes and endeavors for the preservation of peace'. But what he meant by the limitation 'as a politician' remains unclear. In any case, five hours later the politician was completely overwhelmed by the military, to whom he had already begun to yield ground.

His speech, if closely scrutinized, already proves this. 'The decision might come in a short time, then another marching route would be taken.' The decision was that about to be taken by Vienna on the *Halt in Belgrade* proposal, and he felt in advance that it would be a refusal. When this refusal would come, instead of using further strong pressure on Austria to obtain at all cost her consent to the peace formula,

[1] DD. II, 456.

'another marching route would be taken', the route chosen by Moltke.

This logical interpretation of Bethmann's words, which have given rise to much discussion, finds confirmation in the message telegraphed to Munich at 5.30 p. m. by Wenninger, the Barvarian Military Attaché at Berlin, and in a report telephoned later by the Bavarian Minister. Lerchenfeld. Wenninger's telegram runs:

If Vienna rejects today's German attempt at mediation, there will today follow imminent danger of war and then mobilization.[1]

Lerchenfeld at last managed to see Bethmann on the evening of the 30th and conveyed his ideas to Munich:

For the moment there is no reply from Vienna but tonight the Chancellor has roundly told the Vienna Cabinet that Germany cannot let herself be taken in tow by the Balkan policy of Austria. In the event of an affirmative reply from Austria, the Chancellor does not give up hope of preserving peace. This is, however, not sure, because the mobilization already begun by Russia greatly increases the difficulty of a Russian retreat. Germany's course is rendered difficult by the fact that it is not known how much is bluff and how much seriousness in the measures taken by Russia and France.

Until the Austrian reply comes in, Germany will not proceed to the proclamation of the 'state of imminent war danger', which, as things stand in Germany, has to be followed by mobilization, in fact, under our military dispositions, by the mobilization of the whole army. Germany cannot wait very long before deciding, for we should otherwise fall behindhand in respect of Russia and France.

There follow prognostications on the attitudes of England, Italy, Romania and Bulgaria more or less corresponding to what Bethmann had said at the Cabinet meeting except for the statement: 'Italy will stand by the Triple Alliance and has only announced a certain alteration in military aid'. In conclusion Bethmann had said to Lerchenfeld:

It is sad to have to say that a war that nobody wanted was possibly being unleashed, as it were, by elemental forces and by the long-standing state of exacerbation of one Cabinet against another.[2]

The strong pressure alluded to in the first lines of the above quotation must be that contained in the much-talked-of telegram No. 200, to which we shall soon come. The other statements show that Bethmann expected a reply from Vienna in the negative, the arrival of which would hand the victory to Moltke, who was refusing to wait any longer and to whom Bethmann must have made some promise. Falkenhayn and Moltke, writes the former's biographer, Zwehl, under the date of 30 July,

[1] Dirr, p. 223.   [2] DD. IV, 144-5.

secured an assurance that by noon next day at the latest a decision would be taken about declaring 'imminent danger of war'.[1]

Zwehl does not say whether the promise was made to the two Generals at the interview of 1 p. m. or at a later one which, according to Schäfer, they had with the Chancellor about 9 or 10 o'clock in the evening.[2] But what Bethmann said at the Cabinet meeting at 5 p. m. and the messages sent by Wenninger and Lerchenfeld make it probable that the promise was made at the 1 p. m. meeting. To the Cabinet he had said: 'proclamation of imminent danger of war meant mobilization and mobilization meant war. . . . One could not fittingly carry on political and military action at the same time. . . . Probably today in Vienna the decision would be taken in the matter of the German and English proposals'. Thus the German decision would be taken at the latest by noon on the morrow, 31 July.

Now to give the generals such a promise was a serious thing, for it meant that Germany was leaving the decision on peace or war to Austria. On the previous evening Bethmann had instructed Tschirschky to tell Berchtold forcefully:

> We are, of course, prepared to fulfill our duty as allies, but must decline to let ourselves be dragged by Vienna wantonly and without regard to our advice into a world conflagration.[8]

This meant that either Vienna must be reasonable and agree to yield, or Germany would leave her to her fate. On the 30th, on the contrary, the Chancellor no longer insisted on the acceptance of his peace formula. He might still beg her to accept it, but if she did not, never mind, the die would be cast and war accepted.

4. *Sazonov's formula for mediation received in Berlin; the Kaiser's perplexities on the afternoon of 30 July.*

Bethmann was placed in a quandary by the telegram from Pourtalès which he received at 3.32 p. m., and which contained the following formula for conciliation, wrested by Pourtalès from Sazonov:

> If Austria states that, recognizing that her conflict with Serbia has assumed the character of a question of European interest, she declares herself ready to eliminate from her ultimatum the points which infringe the sovereign rights of Serbia, Russia engages to cease all military preparations.[4]

Either Sazonov was not acting in good faith when he drafted the formula for Pourtalès or else he immediately forgot having done so, for soon afterwards he went to ask the Tsar to proclaim general mobilization.

[1] Zwehl, pp. 57-8.   [2] Schäfer, p. 532.
[3] DD. II, 396. See Vol. II, p. 525.   [4] DD. II, 421. See Vol. II, p. 563.

But Berlin could not know this, and what the Wilhelmstrasse ought to have done was to make up its mind at once whether or not to clutch at this life-belt, and send the answer, whether affirmative or negative, by Pourtalès, since it was he who had asked and received the formula from Sazonov. One day earlier the Chancellor would not have hesitated to reject the formula offhand, since it contained two demands which till now Bethmann had flatly declined to entertain: recognition of the European character of the Austro-Serbian conflict, and revision and softening of the ultimatum. But after Grey's words to Lichnowsky on the afternoon of the 29th things were different, and Bethmann, though he never answered the Pourtalès telegram, minuted it as follows:

What points of the Austrian ultimatum has Serbia rejected? As far as I know, only the participation of Austrian officials in law-court trials. Austria could dispense with this participation on condition that she occupies parts of Serbia with her troops until the end of the negotiations.

Brief but significant! It reveals that the man in charge of the policy of an Empire now being dragged into a mortal struggle, had not acquainted himself with the content of a document of vital importance in the dispute, namely, the Serbian reply to the ultimatum. It also reveals that, having till then demanded that any solution by conciliation should be based on a resounding diplomatic victory for Austria, and by repercussion for Germany, taking the form of full acceptance by Serbia of the Austrian ultimatum with the supine acquiescence of Russia, and having brought Europe to the brink of war by refusing to consent to a softening of the ultimatum terms, Bethmann was now at the eleventh hour expecting Austria to abandon her stiffest demand. He had traveled a long way in the twenty-four hours since the arrival of the English warning! True, at 10.30 p. m. on the 30th the Russian Ambassador, Sverbeev, called on Jagow to ask what impression he had of Sazonov's formula for conciliation, transmitted to the Wilhelmstrasse by Pourtalès but not yet received by Sverbeev from his Government, and Jagow's reply had been that it was too 'humiliating for Austria to be able to accept it'.[1] But by 10.30 p. m., when Jagow was saying this to Sverbeev, all resistance on the part of the Chancellor had collapsed or was about to do so.

Until about that hour he had not given everything up for lost but was sitting on thorns because of the non-arrival of Vienna's reply. In the afternoon Stumm telephoned to Tschirschky, but the reply was not reassuring, as may be inferred from a telegram of Tschirschky's:

This afternoon before and after the telephone conversation with Herr von Stumm I again took occasion to have a very serious discussion in our sense

[1] *Int. Bez.* i. V, 305.

with Counts Forgach and Hoyos. Both assured me that feeling in the army and among the public made them regard it as impossible to limit military operations. Tomorrow morning Count Tisza is expected in Vienna, and his opinion in so weighty a decision will have to be heard.[1]

But then if the decision was not yet taken, there still remained time once again to press Berchtold to accept the Anglo-German proposal, a move which would not have been displeasing to Wilhelm, since he himself that afternoon was again showing signs of wanting peace. He had 'gratefully' received King George V's message and at 2.15 p. m. had given his approval to the sensible telegram of reply sent by Prince Henry of Prussia.[2] A little earlier, at 1 p. m., he had read Lichnowsky's telegram of the previous evening reporting Grey's threatening words and had written on it the irate footnote already quoted,[3] and no less violent marginal notes such as:

The biggest, most unheard-of piece of English pharisaism I have ever seen! Never will I make a naval agreement with such scoundrels! . . . Oho! the mean cheat!!

But of mobilization there was not a single word from the ebullient Sovereign's pen, in fact he showed plain signs of panic. The document was returned to the Wilhelmstrasse probably in the afternoon, when the Kaiser, equally worried by Vienna's silence, asked for a draft of a telegram to be sent by him to Francis Joseph (another sign of an anything but bellicose mood). We have already taken cognizance of its text, drafted by Jagow, and dispatched from the Neues Palais at 7.15 p. m. Beginning with a word about his role as mediator to prevent a world conflagration, he goes on to the proposal, to be conveyed by Tschirschky, that 'after occupying Belgrade or other places, Austria should make known her terms', and ends: 'I should be most sincerely obliged to you if you would let me know your decision as soon as possible'.[4]

It cannot fail to strike one that he does not urge his brother Sovereign to accept the proposal, but only to come to a decision on it. Was this a voluntary or involuntary omission on the part of, say, Jagow, who drafted the text? Much still remains obscure in connection with the events of 30 July at Berlin. For example, when, by the Stumm-Tschirschky telephone conversation, Berlin learnt that Vienna would not reply before noon on the following day, after Tisza would have arrived, Bethmann wrote a two-line telegram with the news for the Kaiser and then jotted down, probably for Jagow, on an enclosed sheet of paper:

[1] DD. II, 465. See Vol. II, p. 666.   [2] DD. II, 417. See Vol. II, p. 637.
[3] DD. II, 368. See Vol. II, p. 517.   [4] DD. II, 437. See Vol. II, p. 674.

I suppose it is necessary to send appended telegram to H.M., don't you agree? If no objections, please have it sent off.[1]

Why the doubt? Was he afraid of Wilhelm's reactions to the news?

But the Kaiser's mood was patently such as to render it possible if not, indeed, imperative to make a further *démarche* at Vienna for which there were other reasons as well. At 5.56 p. m. Lichnowsky's telegram reached Berlin summarizing the first of his two conversations with Grey on the afternoon of the 30th, which have already been discussed, while two other telegrams relating to the second conversation did not arrive until 8.45 p. m.[2] Lichnowsky was reporting that he had been assured by Grey 'that the French were using their whole influence at St. Petersburg in the cause of peace. . . . Real war preparations . . . had not taken place.' Grey was going to have a talk with Cambon and Benckendorff and hoped that Bethmann would mediate at Vienna as he himself was mediating at St. Petersburg to bring about an understanding. The telegram ended:

To an intimate he [Grey] said this morning that if Anglo-German co-operation were this time successful in saving the peace, he was convinced that our relations would be safeguarded for all times and that by corresponding influence on his associates he would be successful in preventing the repetition of similar crises.[3]

It was probably under the stimulus of the latest Imperial marginal notes, together with Lichnowsky's telegram, that Bethmann, moved by the warmth of the English proposal and annoyed at the Austrian delays and ambiguities, nerved himself to make a fresh attempt at Vienna. He had just received the three telegrams from Tschirschky, which avoided going to the root of the matter and simply beat about the bush.[4] The only one containing real information, as has already been noted, was not dispatched until 1.35 a. m. on the 31st, reaching Berlin at 4.33 a. m.[5]

Believing, therefore, that there was still time for a last effort, the Chancellor himself wrote out the following telegram to Tschirschky, which bears the number 200 in the archives of the Ministry and is known to historians under that designation:

If, as is to be presumed from Your Excellency's telephone conversation with Herr von Stumm, all compromise, in particular Grey's proposal, is rejected, it will scarcely be possible to cast the blame on Russia for the European conflagration now about to break out. At the Tsar's request His Majesty has undertaken

[1] DD. II, 440.   [2] DD. II, 435, 438, 439.
[3] DD. II, 435 See Vol. II, p. 635.
[4] DD. II, 432, 433, 434, See Vol. II, pp. 660, 665.
[5] DD. II, 465. See Vol. II, pp. 665-6.

mediation at Vienna, because he could not decline without arousing the irrefutable suspicion that we wanted the war. The success of this intervention is, it is true, hampered by the fact that Russia has mobilized against Austria. This we have communicated today to England with the addition that we had already in a friendly way suggested at St. Petersburg and Paris a suspension of Russian and French military measures, and therefore felt that we could only make a fresh *démarche* in that direction by an ultimatum which would mean war. We have therefore made strong representations that he on his side should act in this sense at Paris and St. Petersburg and have just received a corresponding assurance through Lichnowsky. If England succeeds in these efforts while Vienna rejects everything, then Vienna brings documentary proof that it really wants war into which we shall be drawn, while Russia remains free from blame. That will put us in an untenable position in the eyes of our own people. We can therefore only recommend most urgently that Austria should accept Grey's proposal, which in every respect preserves her status. Your Excellency should at once hold most emphatic language in this sense with Count Berchtold, and, if necessary, with Count Tisza.[1]

There is a very distinct softening of tone between this document and those of the previous night, particularly the one, already mentioned, which stated that 'we decline to let ourselves be dragged by Vienna wantonly and without regard to our advice into a world conflagration'.[2] But now, if any impression was to be made, it would be necessary to speak still more strongly. It would not be enough to 'hold most emphatic language' and to 'recommend most urgently' to Berchtold and Tisza. They would have to be told plainly that the *casus foederis* would not be recognized. Unless the Chancellor was prepared to go to that length, all talking was useless. And it was a pointless and ineffectual maneuver on the part of Jagow to tell Szögyény on the evening of the 30th that he could not, as Berchtold had requested the previous evening, threaten St. Petersburg with a joint German and Austrian mobilization, having 'already spoken in this sense at St. Petersburg and Paris. We, therefore, would ask Austria to make the *démarche* alone.'[3]

In any case, whether ineffectual or not, this fresh German pressure for peace was never put into operation. The telegram ordering it left Berlin at 9 p. m., reaching Vienna in the night of 30-31 July. But at 11.20 p. m. it was followed by another urgent one *en clair* written in Zimmerman's hand:

Please do not for the time being carry out Instruction No. 200.[4]

To explain this suspension Zimmermann himself drafted yet another telegram for Tschirschky, also for Bethmann's signature:

[1] DD. II, 441.   [2] DD. II, 396.
[3] Oe-U. VIII, 10937; DD. II, 442. See Vol. II, pp. 655, 659, 674.
[4] DD. II, 450.

I have suspended the execution of Instruction No. 200 because General Staff just tells me that military preparations of our neighbors, especially on the east, compel speedy decision if we do not wish to expose ourselves to surprises. General Staff urgently desires to be informed definitely and with the least possible delay of decisions taken in Vienna, especially those of a military nature. Please act quickly so that we receive answer tomorrow.[1]

This meant the end of all pressure on Vienna to accept Grey's proposal and of all interest in what Vienna's decision might be in the matter. All that now mattered was to be told what the military steps were to be. In other words, all attempt to save the peace was abandoned; what was now being prepared for was war. What had happened to justify such a change within a couple of hours? The Chief of Staff was no longer allowing the political leadership to waste time in attempts to save the peace and compose the conflict. Learning from his informants at the Wilhelmstrasse that the Chancellor had sent Instruction No. 200 to Tschirschky, Moltke had intervened and represented the necessity of revoking it on the ground that it might have fatal effects from the military point of view.

Eugen Fischer gives the explanation:

The General Staff heard of the Chancellor's telegram. Had not their Chief a few hours earlier enjoined on the Austrian Military Attaché that Vienna was to mobilize at once and not entertain the English proposal? How much longer was the Chancellor going on with his efforts to preserve appearances? The General Staff rose in protest. If the Chancellor's telegram were to have the effect of making Vienna postpone still longer its mobilization against Russia, then German mobilization would not be able to get under way. The Russians would be enabled to complete theirs against Germany undisturbed. It just would not do. Nobody could put up with that! Had the Chancellor still not recovered from his 'English malady' [play of words on this popular German name for 'rickets']? Herr Zimmermann got to hear of it and made himself the spokesman of the General Staff with the Chancellor. Tschirschky received a message countermanding the instruction. He was not to carry out the order and on the contrary was to press Vienna for a military decision. The Chief of General Staff, or his representative, could drive back satisfied to the Red House.[2]

It is not impossible, from what Fischer says, that Moltke's informant and adherent at the Wilhelmstrasse was Zimmermann himself. R. Grelling writes:

The mouthpiece of the General Staff at the Foreign Ministry was the Under-Secretary of State, Zimmermann, whose task it was to undo the next day the cloth that the Chancellor, like another Penelope, had woven during the night—particularly in the night of 29-30 July—and by skilful counter-measures, orders, counter-orders, disorders, render harmless (from the point

---

[1] DD. II, 451.   [2] Fischer, pp. 224-225.

of view of the General Staff) Bethmann's feeble mediatory *démarche* with Berchtold.[1]

The part played by Zimmermann on the evening of the 30th seems to confirm what Grelling says. But in any case the reader who has followed in the preceding pages the Chancellor's gradual collapse in the course of 30 July will not be surprised at his capitulation in suspending Instruction No. 200. He had doubtless never actually given Moltke and Falkenhayn his word not to make further representations to Vienna, but he had prejudiced his freedom of action by promising to let them have his decision the following day. Moltke must have carried away the impression that he could now go to considerable lengths, seeing that on coming away from his talk with the Chancellor he exhorted Conrad to obtain the rejection of all proposals for peace.[2] He would have found himself in an awkward position if Instruction No. 200 had been carried out. Doubtless he painted the military situation in very gloomy colors to persuade the Chancellor to revoke the instruction. The General Staff in the course of the 30th had received more or less alarming, but vague and untrustworthy, news of Russian war preparations. All that was certain was that Russia was mobilizing against Austria, not against Germany. Or did Moltke late in the evening get wind of the Russian general mobilization proclaimed at 5 in the afternoon?

5. Haeften's revelations and what they amount to.

In connection with this point the *Norddeutsche Allgemeine Zeitung* of 31 September 1917 published revelations by Major-General von Haeften, a member of the German General Staff. According to this story, in the night of 30 to 31 July 1914, between midnight and 1 a. m., Moltke, on returning from his interview with Bethmann, sent for Haeften and, after expressing views on the situation identical with those embodied in his memorandum of 28 July,[3] went on further to say:

---

[1] R. Grelling, *La campagne innocentiste en Allemagne* (Paris, 1925), pp. 45-6. On the subject of the action taken by Berlin on 30 July, Grelling aptly writes: 'In the night of 29-30 July —by telegrams 395 and 396—Bethmann had again endeavored (on his own behalf and by inadequate measures) to foil the military party's set determination to have a war, as revealed at the Potsdam Crown Council on the afternoon of 29 July, gain a favorable reception at Vienna for Grey's formula, or at the very least awaken a desire on the part of Vienna to enter into definite negotiations with St. Petersburg. By these means he sought to restrain Moltke, Falkenhayn and their fellows, who were heading at full speed for war. Bethmann's efforts in the night hours for peace, inadequate in themselves and not backed by a categoric threat to break the alliance, ended at daybreak (on 30 July), like ghosts vanishing at the first rays of the sun. In the course of that decisive day the General Staff gained the upper hand of the feeble leader of the Foreign Ministry and every sentence of Bethmann's speech to the Cabinet betrayed that the Chancellor felt himself defeated in his efforts for peace. One is aghast at the impotence and spinelessness of this 'statesman' in whose hands rested the fate of a nation of seventy million souls!' (pp. 55-6).

[2] Conrad IV, p. 152. See Vol. II, p. 673.

[3] DD. II, 349. See Vol. II, pp. 488-9.

Meanwhile the situation has grown clearer. We have two reliable and independent reports that Russia has already ordered the mobilization of her entire forces. Barring a miracle, i.e., unless Russian mobilization is revoked, war would seem to be inevitable. Germany can purchase the preservation of peace now only at the price of severe national humiliation, for any treating under pressure of Russian mobilization is tantamount to national humiliation. Yet if we mobilize, it means war. Should Germany now delay this measure on the plea of gaining time for parleys the result will be that if, as is to be anticipated, these parleys fail, Germany will enter the war in the most unfavorable conditions. We should thereby be allowing our enemies to carry war into German territory. If we linger over mobilization, our military position will become every day more unfavorable and may have the most disastrous consequences for us, should our probable adversaries go on making their preparations unmolested. . . . This war will develop into a world war in which England also will take a hand. Few can have any idea of the dimensions, the duration and the end of this war. How it will all end, nobody today knows. . . . Tomorrow at noon the decision will be taken about peace or war. The Chancellor, the War Minister and I are together to have an audience of His Majesty. But before I can advise His Majesty to proclaim mobilization I intend to wait for yet a third confirmation of the announcement of Russian mobilization. I expect it tomorrow morning at the same time as the intimation from Vienna whether the Austro-Hungarian forces have been mobilized or not. The truth is there is barely a glimmer of hope still for the preservation of peace.[1]

Haeften's revelation that on the evening of the 30th Moltke had received 'two reliable and independent reports that Russia has already ordered the mobilization of her entire forces' is not strictly true. In the first place, it must be ruled out that the reason for Bethmann's suspending Instruction 200 was his having learnt from Moltke that 'two reliable and independent reports' had shown that Russia had ordered general mobilization. We have already seen that the explanation drafted by Zimmermann for dispatch to Tschirschky states: 'General Staff has just told me that military preparations of our neighbors, especially to the east, compel speedy decision, if we do not wish to expose ourselves to surprises.' 'Military preparations', therefore, not mobilization, which would have caused the General Staff to speak another language and the Chancellor to have taken a different course of action. More-over, it is self-evident that if Moltke had had reliable information of Russian general mobilization, he would not have contented himself with confiding this to Major Haeften, as he was then, in order that Haeften might use it three years later to prove German innocence. He would have at once passed on the news to the Kaiser, the Chancellor, and the Minister for War, using it to support his thesis of the necessity for immediate mobilization. Moreover, if this had been Moltke's course of

[1] Schulthess, *Geschichtskalender,* 1917, II, pp. 996-7.

action the fact would have been recorded, not in a Staff Major's reminiscences but in the diplomatic documents themselves, that Berlin learnt of Russian general mobilization, not at noon on the 31st, but on the evening of the 30th. Bethmann would have telegraphed to Pourtalès asking for confirmation of the grave news. Pourtalès would have replied and Moltke and Falkenhayn would have recorded the event. The fact is that no trace of any such story exists either in diplomatic documents, or in Moltke's memoirs, or in Falkenhayn's comments. In vain would one seek a trace of the two communications of the evening of 30 July in the pages of Colonel Nicolai who, as Director of Military Intelligence of the German General Staff, would have been the first to learn of it. All he says is:

> Only when on the morning of 31 July an intelligence officer from the Russian frontier reported that Russia was fully mobilized against Germany, too, did war seem inevitable. But even then I still found that General von Moltke harbored doubts born of his feelings of responsibility. The positive assurance of this intelligence officer that he would be personally responsible for the truth of his report was necessary before his information was finally credited. General von Moltke then telegraphed it to the Kaiser at Potsdam. . . . Only with the help of unusual strength of will did General von Moltke order that on 31 July at midday the state of 'imminent danger of war' was to be decreed.[1]

The accounts given by Haeften and Colonel Nicolai make it almost seem that Moltke had waited for Russia to proclaim general mobilization before putting forward the demand that Germany must do the same. However, there is proof, on the contrary, that Russian mobilization had not yet been proclaimed when, at 2 p. m. on the 30th, Moltke sent for the Austrian Military Attaché, Bienerth, and asked for Austro-Hungarian general mobilization which would create the *casus foederis* for Germany and bring about the European war offering Austria her last hope of salvation. Moltke's memorandum of 28 July had laid down that (1) Austria ought to mobilize in advance of Russia in order to have her rear secure while she dealt with Serbia; (ii) Austrian mobilization would bring about an Austro-Russian war; (iii) this would give the *casus foederis* for Germany.[2] On the 29th Moltke had lain low because he perceived that the Kaiser strongly inclined to a peaceful solution. But on the 30th, thinking Wilhelm had changed his mind, Moltke felt he could win the day, and, after talking to Bienerth, telegraphed personally to Conrad: 'Mobilize at once against Russia. Germany will mobilize'.[3]

Does this mean that Haeften invented his story from beginning to end? The present writer does not think so. No doubt, in order to prove

---

[1] W. Nicolai, *The German Secret Service*, London, 1924, pp. 66-8.
[2] DD. II, 349. See Vol. II, p. 489.   [3] Conrad, IV, p. 152. See Vol. II, 673.

that Germany only decided on mobilizing after learning that Russia had already done so, he exaggerates and amplifies the actual substance of the information reaching the General Staff on the evening of the 30th which can now be reconstructed on the basis of known documents. The order for general mobilization issued at St. Petersburg about 5 p. m. was not long in reaching the frontier posts, where there began the burning down of customs buildings, the closing of public offices, and the removal of their strong-boxes to the interior.[1] These operations could not long remain hidden from the Germans on the other side of the frontier whose vigilance during those days must have been intensified, aided by the customary daily contacts between the staffs on the two sides of the frontier. News was at once sent back to German Headquarters, probably by telephone, and Moltke drew the legitimate conclusion that the Russian measures were the prelude or the signal of general mobilization, intimating this to Haeften.

6. How King George V's telegram to the Kaiser was communicated to Vienna.

Hardly had Bethmann surrendered when at 11.8 p. m. on the 30th there arrived in Berlin the telegram from King George replying to that of Prince Henry. As we have seen, it said:

My Government is doing its utmost suggesting to Russia and France to suspend further military preparations if Austria will consent to be satisfied "with occupation of Belgrade and neighboring Serbian territory as a hostage for satisfactory settlement of her demands, other countries meanwhile suspending their war preparations. Trust William will use his great influence to induce Austria to accept this proposal, thus proving that Germany and England are working together to prevent what would be an international catastrophe. Pray assure William I am doing and shall continue to do all that lies in my power to preserve peace of Europe.[2]

Did these warm, sincere words cause the Chancellor a pang of remorse at having surrendered when a further powerful effort at Vienna might have landed him in the safe harbor of peace? Certainly they placed him in a quandary. What use could he make of them? The order suspending the execution of Instruction No. 200 had not yet been dispatched. He withdrew it and replaced it by the following, also drafted by Zimmermann but the final sentence of which is in Bethmann's hand:

I have suspended the execution of Instruction No. 200 in consideration of the following telegram from the King of England to Prince Henry: 'Thanks for your telegram . . . peace of Europe'. Your Excellency should communicate the telegram immediately to Count Berchtold and hand him a copy, if he

---

[1] BD.XI,337.
[2] DD. II, 452, See Vol. II, p. 638.

so desires, for possible submission to Emperor Francis Joseph. A definite decision from Vienna in the course of today is urgently requested.[1]

One rubs one's eyes on reading this document, thinking one cannot have read it aright. Instead of causing the suspension of Instruction No. 200 it should have had the logical effect of renewing it. To say that its execution was suspended in consideration of King George's telegram is nonsense, such nonsense that Schäfer is driven to saying that, because of King George's telegram, Instruction No. 200 remained in force and that Tschirschky ought to have used it to press home the demand for acceptance of mediation.[2] But his theory does not hold water in view of Bethmann's own words: 'I have suspended the execution of Instruction No. 200 in consideration of', etc.[3] In the opinion of the present writer the only explanation of Bethmann's telegram is that it was not sent in good faith. He may have thought it necessary, perhaps in anticipation of a command from the Kaiser, to acquaint Vienna of King George's reply. But, not venturing to advise that no notice be taken of it after what he himself had telegraphed the night before in support of the *Halt in Belgrade* proposal, he adopted this misleading phraseology. Had he been honest, he would have had to write: 'I have suspended Instruction No. 200 in spite of the following telegram from King George, because', etc. But by expressing himself as he did Bethmann was in a position to say to the Kaiser, if necessary, that he had acquainted Berchtold of King George's appeal, while making sure that, not being supported by Berlin, it would have no effect. He was no longer expecting Vienna to listen to peace proposals, but only to send him in the course of the day an answer that would give him a free hand.

A free hand for what? Besides having promised Moltke and Falkenhayn to give a decision about noon on their demand for the proclamation of the *Kriegsgefahrzustand,* besides having ceased to press Vienna any further to accept the *Halt in Belgrade,* Bethmann on the 30th had taken a still more serious decision, namely, that on the morrow he would send an ultimatum to Russia demanding the suspension of her military preparations independently of the reply Vienna might give to the Anglo-German proposal, even though it were to be an acceptance.

[1] DD. II, 464.
[2] Schäfer, p. 533.
[3] It must be added that the Austro-Hungarian and German documents reveal no sign of Tschirschky's having shown King George's telegram to Berchtold. Moreover, if Berchtold had known of it, he would not have failed to mention it at the morning meeting with Conrad (Conrad, IV, p. 148) or at the meeting of the Council of Ministers also held that forenoon of the 30th. One cannot, however, rule out the possibility that the telegram was followed by a telephone call instructing Tschirschky not to bring the King's message to Berchtold's knowledge.

This is a point it is of immense importance to make clear because of the conclusions which can be drawn from it. In Berchtold's report to Francis Joseph of 31 July it is stated:

> This morning on the authority of a telephone call from Berlin, Herr von Tschirschky informed me that the Chancellor intends to send an ultimatum to Russia immediately about suspending mobilization.[1]

Conrad in his memoirs writes:

> On the morning of the 31st the Foreign Ministry told me that Germany was going to send an ultimatum to Russia about her armaments.[2]

Realizing the significance of this piece of evidence, Wegerer seeks to discredit it on the authority of Stumm. Wegerer says that it was not possible to find out at Vienna when Berchtold wrote that report nor when Tschirschky gave Berchtold that news. Berchtold himself was unable to throw light on the matter. But Stumm, at that time head of the Political Section of the German Foreign Ministry, gave Wegerer the following information:

> After we had forwarded the English mediation proposal of 29 July 1914 to Vienna with an urgent plea for acceptance, I, on the Chancellor's instructions, repeatedly telephoned our Embassy at Vienna to find out about the attitude of the Austro-Hungarian Government. Early on 31 July I again called up the Ambassador asking him to let me know that the answer of the Vienna Cabinet might be expected not to be in the negative. Herr von Tschirschky at the same time told me that—as counter-measure to the Russian mobilization of the military districts of Kiev, Odessa, and Kazan—general mobilization had been ordered. In the course of the forenoon I was summoned to the Reichskanzlerpalais to a conference pre-sided over by the Imperial Chancellor, von Bethmann Hollweg, and attended by the Chief of General Staff and the War Minister, at which a discussion took place on the increasingly threatening bulletins about Russian military measures also on the German frontier. The discussion was proceeding when the telegram from Count Pourtalès was brought in announcing the general mobilization of the Russian army and navy. A decision was then taken to address the well-known ultimatum to Russia, summoning her to suspend her military measures. After that the meeting broke up and I went off to the Foreign Ministry. Hardly had I got there than I was called up on the telephone by our Embassy at Vienna. Legation Secretary von Bethmann Hollweg, a nephew of the Chancellor, was on the telephone. He in-formed me of the attitude of the Vienna Government to the English mediation proposal. I replied that this question had become outdated on account of the mobilization of the whole Russian army, news of which had just come in and which had made it necessary for us to re-quest by an ultimatum the revocation by Russia of her mobilization. The news of the general mobilization of the Russian army most

---

[1] Oe-U. VIII, 11201. [2] Conrad, IV, p. 152.

likely reached the Imperial Chancellor shortly after twelve noon; my telephone conversation with Vienna will have taken place round about 12.30 p. m.[1]

It is understandable that Stumm felt it necessary to affirm that the ultimatum to St. Petersburg was decided on after the arrival of Pourtalès's telegram announcing Russian general mobilization. But against his statement there remains the fact that Berchtold's report gives the time at which he received the news from Tschirschky as the morning and not the afternoon of the 31st, and that the accuracy of his account is confirmed by Conrad's entry in his diary, recording that he heard the news from Berchtold on the morning of the 31st. Since neither Berchtold nor Conrad in writing had any idea what conclusions would be deduced many years later from their words, there is no need to doubt their truthfulness in the matter. Even were there any doubt, their evidence finds authoritative confirmation in another unchallengeable document, which Wegerer passes over in silence. At 11.15 a. m. on the 31st, before knowing of Pourtalès's telegram with the news of the Russian general mobilization, Lerchenfeld, the Bavarian envoy at Berlin, whose sources of information were official and first hand, telephoned to Munich:

Reply from Vienna not yet received, as Tisza's arrival in Vienna is still awaited, but it is expected this afternoon. Should Vienna agree to the German and English proposal for mediation, it will be telegraphed to the Tsar, by-passing Sazonov, and at the same time an ultimatum will be presented about suspension of armaments. England works with us and it is not impossible that even at the eleventh hour she will stop the whole action; situation remains critical, because Russian attitude to mediation proposal doubtful; General Staff here presses for a decision.[2]

If Lerchenfeld was able to telephone this to Munich before noon, Stumm was able to telephone it to Tschirschky first thing in the morning. And it was certainly in the earlier of his two telephone calls, rather than in the later, that he told Tschirschky of Berlin's decision to send an ultimatum to Russia. But why an ultimatum? A few hours earlier Bethmann had been wanting Vienna to agree to the *Halt in Belgrade,* rightly thinking that this would save the peace. Now he was no longer concerned to save the peace. Nay more, even had Vienna, contrary to expectation, agreed to it, he was going to send this news to the Tsar and accompany it with an ultimatum to St. Petersburg demanding suspension of mobilization. Did he not realize that such an intimation, which would have torn open afresh and deepened the wound of March 1909, could never have been accepted by Russia and that war

---

[1] A. von Wegerer, *Die russische allgemeine Mobilmachung und das deutsche Ultimatum an Russland,* KSF., November 1928, pp. 1061-3.

[2] DD. IV, 147; Dirr, p. 170.

would become a certainty? He could not but know this. But, having lacked the courage to resist the pressure from the all-powerful army chiefs, he perhaps thought that, before consenting to mobilization, which meant war, he might as well try playing this card once more. He certainly had Bülow's success of 1909 in his mind. It has already been said that Bülow advised him not to repeat the dangerous experiment. *'Nec bis in idem'*. But Bethmann had replied 'in a ruffled voice that even he might one day score a success on the same terrain over which I had moved with such agility'.[1] Now, five years later, the occasion offered itself. If Russia yielded, it would be a triumph for him. If she did not, the big guns would do the talking. And this latter hypothesis being the more probable, Jagow telegraphed that night to the German Ambassador at Paris (the telegram went off at 1.30 a. m. on the 31st):

Departure of Germans advisable.[2]

From this documentation the conclusion may be drawn that, with or without Russian general mobilization, with or without Austrian acceptance of the Anglo-German proposals, the treatment of Russia on 31 July would have been the same and the European war would have broken out all the same. This conclusion does not seek to lift all blame from the shoulders of the Russian Government, for, if the latter had not proclaimed partial mobilization, the General Staffs at St. Petersburg, Paris, Berlin and Vienna would never have been able to thrust themselves into the foreground and some peaceful solution of the conflict would have been found. What it does seek to make clear is that it was the Russian partial mobilization, not the general mobilization, which brought Europe to war. The partial mobilization took place, it is true, after the Austrian mobilization against Serbia. But the Austrian mobilization of eight army corps against Serbia was not a threat to the safety of Russia. It was Russia, beyond doubt, who was the first to set the war machine in motion against a Great Power, thus bringing the military chiefs of the other Powers upon the scene and ousting the political leadership. But if on the 30th Bethmann had not let himself be overruled by Moltke, had insisted with Berchtold, on pain of non-recognition of the *casus foederis,* that Austria should content herself with the Anglo-German proposals, and had then waited for Sazonov to follow suit, the peace of the world might have been saved.

7. News of the Russian general mobilization becomes known in Berlin.

We have now reached the decisive 31 July, on the morning of which the Chancellor had a talk with the English Ambassador, Goschen.

---

[1] Bülow, III, p. 12. See Vol. II, p. 163.   [2] DD. II, 461.

Goschen summarized it in two telegrams to Grey[1] and then on the same day wrote to Nicolson:

This morning before 10 o'clock, I went to see the Chancellor to give him the answer of Sir E. Grey to his 'neutrality' proposal.[2] On my going into his room he said that I came *à point* as he was just going to ask me by telephone to come and see him. He then told me that he had just received news from the Russian frontier, which, if confirmed, would create a very grave and dangerous situation and might oblige Germany to make a serious communication to the Russian Government. The news in question was that the Russian Government had destroyed their customs houses on the German frontier, had sealed their public offices in the neighborhood of the frontier, and had carried off their money chests into the interior. I said that these proceedings, if true, seemed to me to be not so much a menace to Germany, as measures of precaution, in a palpably grave situation, to meet all emergencies. He maintained on the contrary that, taken with other reports which had reached him both from Russia and Sweden, the above news threatened general mobilization; he hoped not, and he, and the Emperor also, at the urgent request of the Czar, were still doing their best to mediate at Vienna, but he feared the worst. At the close of our conversation on this subject I read to him Sir E. Grey's answer to the neutrality proposal. He paid but little attention to it and certainly made no comment; but I left him with a full paraphrase of Sir E. Grey's telegram. Subsequently I saw Jagow, who confirmed the Chancellor's views as to the gravity of the situation.[3]

It is obvious that if Moltke had received news of Russian general mobilization from the two 'reliable' reports of which Haeften speaks, the Chancellor would have been in a position to tell Goschen about them the following morning. Most likely the reports which Moltke mentioned to Haeften were the two of which the Chancellor spoke in his conversation with Goschen, and which suggested the possibility of Russian general mobilization without making it seem certain. They served the Chancellor as a prelude to prepare London for the news of his decision to send an ultimatum to St. Petersburg, a decision the taking of which caused him great agitation. He was feeling so depressed that he could not pay proper attention while Goschen read out Grey's important message in reply to the German request for English neutrality. He could not pay attention because he had now embarked on another course, and one which was practically certain to lead to war. He told Goschen that

he was going to see the Emperor and he wished me to tell you that it was quite possible that in a very short time, perhaps even today, they would have to take some very serious step.[4]

---

[1] BD. XI, 336, 337.   [2] BD. XI, 303. See Vol. II, p. 633.
[3] BD. XI, 677.   [4] BD. XI, 337.

Moltke was in much the same state of mind as the Chancellor. He suspected, not without reason, that Russia was mobilizing also on the German frontier. But he needed proof of it before getting permission for the proclamation of the *Kriegsgefahrzustand* which would immediately be followed by mobilization. Bethmann had promised him a decision by noon. This decision could not be other than in the affirmative if he could make certain that the Russian mobilization was general, not partial. If it were only partial, Heaven knows how endless would be the hesitations of the irresolute Chancellor. He would send the ultimatum to Russia all the same. But supposing Russia were to yield for the time being? What Moltke was after was not a diplomatic success for Bethmann, but war. Let us recall what Lerchenfeld wrote to the Bavarian Prime Minister that very day (31st):

Military circles here are most optimistic. Months ago the Chief of the General Staff, Herr von Moltke, expressed the view that the situation is from the military point of view favorable to a degree which cannot occur again in a foreseeable future.[1]

At 7 a. m., therefore, General Moltke rang up General Hell, Chief of the General Staff of the XX Army Corps at Allenstein, to inquire:

'Have you at the frontier the impression that Russia is mobilizing?' Hell: 'Yes, I have thought so for several days'. M.: 'What makes you think so?' H.: 'The frontier is hermetically sealed. Nobody crosses in either direction. Since yesterday they have been burning the frontier guard-houses, and red mobilization notices are said to be posted up in Mlava'. M.: 'Why have you not got hold of one of the notices?' H.: 'Everything is being done to get one but the closure of the frontier has so far prevented it'. M.: 'You must get me one of those red notices; I must make certain whether they are mobilizing against us. Till then I cannot obtain the promulgation of a mobilization order.'[2]

A few hours after this conversation a Russian red mobilization order was in the hands of the Allenstein Command, and almost at the same time First Lieutenant Köstring from Moscow who had just managed to get across the frontier at the last moment, brought definite news that mobilization was actually in full swing on the German frontier.[3]

But even before confirmation arrived by these channels, the telegram from Pourtalès reached the Wilhelmstrasse at 11.40 a. m., having been dispatched from St. Petersburg at 11.20 a. m.:

General mobilization army and navy ordered. First day of mobilization 31 July.[4]

---

[1] DD. IV, 151. See Vol. II, p. 487.
[2] Schulthess, *Europäischer Geschichtskalender* (Berlin, 1917), II, p. 1000.
[3] Schäfer, p. 535.
[4] DD. II, 473.

We have it on Stumm's testimony that the telegram arrived when Bethmann was in conference with Falkenhayn and Moltke. The decision was at once taken to proclaim the *Kriegsgefahrzustand* forthwith and to warn Russia to suspend her armament. But the decision needed the Kaiser's approval. He, on learning over the telephone of Pourtalès's telegram, returned hot haste to Berlin. Here, before proceeding further, it is necessary to say something about him.

8. *The Kaiser's wrathful outbursts, his ignorance of the real situation, and his groundless optimism at the last moment.*

We have seen that after the outburst of the morning of the 30th, when the Kaiser hinted at the idea of mobilizing and throwing up the role of mediator between St. Petersburg and Vienna, he calmed down and, on learning of the warning words Grey had used to Lichnowsky on the evening of the 29th, gave vent to anger with England inspired by fear of a war presenting itself under bad auspices. Later, at 7 p. m. on the 30th, he was shown the telegram from Pourtalès which had reached Berlin at 7.10 in the morning, the one summarizing the midnight conversation at which Sazonov had said that partial mobilization (against Austria) could not be revoked. This caused Wilhelm to vent his feelings in a lengthy footnote, a good part of which it is worth while reproducing for its dramatic quality and historical interest:

Irresponsibility and weakness are to plunge the world into the most terrible war, aimed in the last resort at ruining Germany. For no doubt remains in my mind: England, Russia and France—basing themselves on our *casus foederis* in relation to Austria—are in league to wage a war of annihilation against us, taking the Austro-Serbian conflict as a pretext. That explains Grey's cynical remark to Lichnowsky 'as long as the war remains localized between Russia and Austria England would sit still, only if we mixed ourselves and France with it would he be forced to take action against us'. In other words, we are either basely to betray our ally and leave him a prey to Russia—thereby breaking up the Triple Alliance—or, for our loyalty to the alliance, be fallen upon by the combined Triple *Entente* and punished. . . . That is the real naked situation in a nut-shell, slowly and surely prepared by Edward VII, carried forward and systematically developed in disavowed conversations held by England with Paris and St. Petersburg; finally brought to a conclusion and put into operation by George V. The stupidity and clumsiness of our ally has been turned into a noose for our necks. So the famous 'encirclement of Germany' has at last become a complete actuality. . . . Edward VII in the grave is still stronger than I who am alive! And to think there have been people who believed England could be won over or pacified by this or that petty measure!!! Ceaselessly, relentlessly, she has pursued her aim by notes, proposals of [naval] holidays, scares, Haldane, etc. And we have fallen into the snare and have even introduced the keel-for-keel rate of naval construction in the pathetic hope of pacifying England thereby!!!... Now we have the

English so-called thanks for it! . . . Now this whole trickery must be ruthlessly exposed and the mask of Christian pacifism roughly and publicly torn from the face [of England] and the Pharisaical peace sham put in the pillory!! And our consuls in Turkey and India, agents, etc., must fire the whole Mahometan world to fierce revolt against this hateful, lying, unprincipled nation of shopkeepers; for if we are to bleed to death, England shall at least lose India.[1]

This outburst reveals the whole man. The bankruptcy of his policy made him fall into towering rages from which all sense of the truth was banned. It was he who had threatened the existence of England by building a navy of such proportions as to leave no doubt that it was intended one day to try its strength against that of Britain and give Germany the hegemony of the world. It was he who had rejected the offers of alliance from London and the repeated appeals for agreement on the pace and rate of naval construction. In short, he, more than any "other man, had brought about the situation over which he was now wringing his hands and which, nevertheless, would not have ended in a European war if he and his Chancellor had not given Austria permission to solve the Serbian problem by resort to war, thus for a second time offering provocation to Russian feelings. He ought to have foreseen that Russia would not a second time climb down as in 1909, that she would never look on quietly while the little Slav state was crushed, that the loyalty of Germany to the Dual Monarchy would be matched by that of France to Russia, and that England would not stand aside from the conflict and doom the Triple *Entente* to destruction. Now for the first time, when the spectre of defeat loomed up before him, the Kaiser was beginning to perceive all this. What he should immediately have done was to call the Chancellor and discuss what steps could be taken. Would it not perhaps have been a case for threatening Vienna to leave her to her fate unless she yielded?

Wilhelm's isolation on that fateful 30 July is incomprehensible. It was this isolation of his, enabling Moltke to gain the upper hand with Bethmann, and leaving Bethmann free to drop his efforts to influence Vienna and take the decision to send an ultimatum to Vienna, which may perhaps be regarded as the factor that finally turned the scales. For the Kaiser, far more clearly than his subordinates, had grasped that a war might well end in defeat for Germany and as late as 31 July desired a peaceful solution and was confident of achieving it. This is proved by his actions on that morning. While Moltke was eagerly waiting for the news of Russian general mobilization which would give the signal for Germany to mobilize, while Bethmann was preparing the way for the ultimatum he had decided to send to Russia, Wilhelm

[1] DD. II, 401.

with the usual time lag was reading Tschirschky's telegram of the afternoon of the 30th which held forth hope of a resumption of direct
conversations between St. Petersburg and Vienna. Berchtold was
promising that 'after the conclusion of peace' Austria 'planned a purely
temporary occupation of Serbian territory in order to enforce on the
Serbian Government the integral fulfillment of her demands and the
furnishing of guarantees for future good behavior'. The Kaiser, who
did not perceive the trickery in this phrasing, commented: 'Practically
my proposal accepted' and gave the whole telegram the final mark:
'Good'.[1] He saw things through rose-colored spectacles that morning.
His Military Plenipotentiary at the Russian Court, General Chelius,
telegraphed on the evening of the 30th that he had heard from several
officers of high rank that Russian [partial] mobilization could not be
stopped. But

in Russia between the commencement of mobilization and the beginning of war
there was a long step which could still be used for peaceful negotiations. I have the
impression that they have mobilized here for fear of coming events without
aggressive intention and are now scared at what they have done.

'Right. That is how it is', wrote Wilhelm in the margin against this
last sentence.[2]

Still more in evidence was his optimism in a letter which he himself
composed on the morning of the 31st for the information of Tirpitz
and the Naval General Staff. After touching on the contrast between
King George's pacific message and Grey's threatening words to
Lichnowsky, summarizing the reply sent at his request by Prince Henry
of Prussia to King George, and enclosing the latter's answering telegram, the letter proceeded:

His proposals coincide with mine that I have suggested to the Vienna Cabinet,
which has left us for six days without an answer. . . . Between Vienna and Peterhof
diplomatic conversations have at last been begun. . . . At St. Petersburg, by today's
report from the Ambassador, there is absolutely no enthusiasm for war, on the
contrary a depressed mood . . . anxiety at what they have done with their premature
mobilization.[3]

All was going well—thought Wilhelm—and his bright idea of the
Halt in Belgrade was going to save the peace of the world. No monarch

---

[1] DD, II, 433. See Vol. II, p. 660.   [2] DD. II, 445.

[3] DD. II, 474. The present writer checked up on the original of the Kaiser's letter and found there
the erroneous statement that 'for six days' he had been waiting for the Austrian reply. This mistake
would seem to be an oversight on the Kaiser's part. This is also the opinion of Wegerer, to whom the
present writer sent a written inquiry. His reply states: 'The proposal which the Kaiser had in mind
could only be that of the *Halt in Belgrade,* formulated by him on the morning of the 28th in his letter to
the Secretary of State, Jagow (DD. II, 293), and sent to Tschirschky at 10.15 p. m. that same day
(DD. II, 323)'.

believing himself to hold the threads of the situation could possibly have been more ill informed, more devoid of any grasp of the situation, and this was so because Wilhelm did not maintain contact with his subordinates and had no knowledge of what they were doing. The above letter of his bears the date 31 July, 12 noon. This was the very hour at which the news arrived that Russia, far from repenting of her mobilization against Austria, was mobilizing also against Germany.

The Kaiser, changeable as he ever was, took cognizance of this news without reacting to it. Just before leaving Potsdam he arranged to send two telegrams, one to King George V and one to the Tsar. The one to King George seems to have been dispatched at 12.58 p. m., while the one to the Tsar went off at 2.48 p. m., both from the Neues Palais, Potsdam. But the one to the Tsar seems to have been written before the one to King George, since it makes no mention of Russian general mobilization, while this is mentioned in the telegram to King George. Probably Wilhelm wrote to the Tsar knowing only of the frontier reports mentioned by Bethmann to Goschen. Had he known of the general mobilization, either he would not have telegraphed at all, or he would have expressed himself in different terms from the ones he used:

On your appeal to my friendship and your call for assistance [I] began to mediate between your and the Austro-Hungarian Government. While this action was proceeding your troops were mobilized against Austro-Hungary, my ally. Thereby, as I have already pointed out to you, my mediation has been made almost illusory.

I have nevertheless continued my action. I now receive authentic news of serious preparations for war on my eastern frontier. Responsibility for the safety of my empire forces preventive measures of defense upon me. In my endeavors to maintain the peace of the world I have gone to the utmost limit possible. The responsibility for the disaster which is now threatening the whole civilized world will not be laid at my door. In this moment it still lies in your power to avert it. Nobody is threatening the honor or power of Russia, who can well afford to await the result of my mediation. My friend-ship for you and your empire transmitted to me by my grandfather on his deathbed has always been sacred to me and I have honestly often backed up Russia when she was in serious trouble, especially in her last war.

The peace of Europe may still be maintained by you, if Russia will agree to stop the military measures which must threaten Germany and Austro-Hungary.[1]

This, as can be seen, is a strong appeal for peace. Wilhelm is still asking Russia to await the results of his mediation, not knowing that his Chancellor and his Chief of Staff were working in the opposite direction. More distant, but no less calm, is the telegram to King George, written after he learnt of Russian general mobilization:

[1] DD. III, 480.

Many thanks for your kind telegram. Your proposals coincide with my ideas and with the statements I got this night from Vienna which I had forwarded to London. I just received news from chancellor that official notification has just reached him that this night Nicky has ordered the mobilization of his whole army and fleet. He has not even awaited the results of the mediation I am working at and left me without any news, I am off to Berlin to take measures for ensuring safety of my eastern frontiers where strong Russian troops are already posted.[1]

Thus Wilhelm was off to Berlin to take security measures against Russia, not to bring about war. But on arriving there he was immediately swept off his feet by the state of things he found there. Military and civil authorities were now bent on resorting to extreme measures. Divided in opinion twenty-four hours earlier, they had drawn much closer together between the afternoon and evening of the 30th. Now the news of Russian general mobilization played into Moltke's hands and overcame the Chancellor's last hesitations. Already they had settled the procedure to be followed: proclamation of the *Kriegsgefahrzustand;* ultimatum to Russia, which was practically certain to be rejected; mobilization, i.e., war. Faced with this agreement between civil and military powers, the Kaiser either allowed himself to be convinced or lacked the strength and courage to impose his own will to peace by instilling into his lieutenants his fears as to the outcome of a European war. And so the starting signal was given.

9. Proclamation of the Kriegsgefahrzustand *and the German ultimatums to Russia and to France.*

The proclamation of the *Kriegsgefahrzustand* involved: (*a*) guarding of the railways; (*b*) prohibition of publication by the press of military news; (*c*) proclamation of martial law within the Reich; (*d*) recall of effectives on leave; (*e*) return of troops to garrison; (*f*) suspension of private traffic in the frontier areas and supervision of postal traffic with countries abroad; (*g*) protection of frontiers by covering troops; (*h*) protection of North Sea islands.[2] At the Prussian Cabinet meeting on the 30th, Tirpitz and Falkenhayn intimated that the measure also included the call-up of reservists.[3] Was mobilization a necessary consequence of the first precautionary measure? At that Cabinet meeting Bethmann stated that

proclamation of imminent danger of war meant mobilization and this in our circumstances—mobilization on both fronts—meant war.[4]

But, as Montgelas observes, the Chancellor himself on the previous day had telegraphed the very opposite to Schoen.[5] And on 31 July, in

---

[1] DD. II, 477.   [2] Montgelas, art. at. in *Evolution,* November 1926, p. 15.
[3] DD. II, 456.   [4] DD. II, 456.   [5] DD. II, 341. See Vol. II, p. 599.

telegraphing to London, St. Petersburg, Paris, and Rome the announcement of the measure, he added that mobilization would follow only if Russia did not drop all war preparations against Germany and Austria within twelve hours.[1] In short, it was still possible to turn back if Russia gave way. But in the present case it was regarded as practically certain that Russia would not give way and that therefore the 'state of imminent danger of war' would be followed by mobilization and war. Accordingly Bethmann at 1.45 p. m. on 31 July telegraphed to Tschirschky:

> After the Russian total mobilization we have proclaimed imminent danger of war, which will probably be followed within forty-eight hours by mobilization. This inevitably means war. We expect from Austria immediate active participation in the war against Russia.[2]

Not long after, between 3.10 and 3.30 p. m. (the time necessary to draft and encipher them), the four telegrams just mentioned left Berlin for London, St. Petersburg, Paris and Rome respectively, constituting the first steps in the diplomatic action preluding the opening of hostilities. Bernadotte Schmitt thinks that their dispatch was held up until the arrival at 2.45 p. m. of the reply from Vienna in the shape of a telegram from Francis Joseph to Wilhelm saying that the threatening attitude of Russia would not stop Austria from acting against Serbia.[3] To the present writer, however, it seems evident that a telegram reaching the Berlin Schloss at 2.45 p. m. would be too late to influence a series of telegrams sent off between 3.10 and 3.30 p. m. It must be remembered, moreover, that at 4.35 on the morning of the 31st the Wilhelmstrasse had received Tschirschky's telegram of 1.35 a. m. saying that Vienna was practically certain to reject mediation, but that the final decision must await Tisza's arrival on the morning of the 31st.[4] Thus, if Tisza was against the rejection of the Anglo-German proposal, the plan (which Lerchenfeld outlined to Munich that morning) could be put into operation of telegraphing the Austrian acceptance of the *Halt in Belgrade* to the Tsar, accompanied by the ultimatum calling for the suspension of Russian mobilization. But probably the official news of Russian general mobilization made the Chancellor decide (no doubt under pressure from Moltke, who did not want Austria to give way and the crisis to end peacefully) not to wait for a possible, but extremely improbable Austrian acceptance of the mediation proposals. It is not impossible, nay it is even highly probable, that Tschirschky telephoned the decision taken by the Ballplatz after the arrival of Tisza on the

---

[1] DD. III, 488, 490, 491, 492; Montgelas, art. cit. in *Évolution,* p. 14.
[2] DD. II, 479.
[3] Schmitt, II, p. 267; DD. III, 482. See Vol. II, p. 675.
[4] DD. II, 465. See Vol. II, pp. 665-6.

morning of the 31st.[1] That the telephone between the German Embassy at Vienna and the Wilhelmstrasse was worked hard during the 31st seems likely from the circumstance that the official documents only produce three telegrams from Tschirschky for that date, the overnight one mentioned above [2] and two others dealing with matters unconnected with the Austro-German main question.[3]

At all events the telegram was sent off to Lichnowsky telling him:

In spite of still pending and apparently not unavailing mediation, and although we ourselves had taken no mobilization measures, Russia has today decreed the mobilization of her entire army and navy, hence also against us. We have had to proclaim imminent danger of war, which must be followed by mobilization if Russia within twelve hours does not stop all war measures against us and Austria. I do not think it impossible that Russian mobilization is attributable to the fact that rumors current here yesterday, utterly false and officially at once contradicted, were reported as facts to St. Petersburg.[4]

The telegram to Pourtalès, like those to Schoen and Flotow, went off at 3.30 p. m. It was written in the Chancellor's hand—the others were written by Jagow and somewhat altered by Bethmann—and runs:

In spite of the still pending negotiations for mediation and although we had up to the present taken no measures for mobilization, Russia has mobilized entire army and navy, that is also against us. By these Russian measures we have been compelled for the security of the Empire, to proclaim imminent danger of war, which does not yet mean mobilization. But mobilization must follow unless within twelve hours Russia suspends all war measures against ourselves and Austria-Hungary and gives us a definite assurance to that effect. Please notify M. Sazonov of this at once, and wire hour of notification. I know that Sverbeev yesterday telegraphed to St. Petersburg that we had mobilized, which to the present hour is still not the case.[5]

The telegram to Schoen runs:

In spite of our still pending mediatory action and although we ourselves had taken no mobilization measures, Russia has decreed mobilization of her entire army and navy, thus also against us. We have, thereupon, proclaimed imminent state of war, which must be followed by mobilization unless within twelve hours Russia suspends all war measures against ourselves and Austria. Mobilization inevitably means war. Pray ask French Government whether it will remain neutral in a Russo-German war. Answer must be given within eighteen (18) hours. Wire at once hour when demand presented. Utmost speed necessary.

Secret: If, as is not to be presumed, French Government declares willingness to remain neutral, will Your Excellency declare to French

---

[1] See Vol. II, pp. 675-6.   [2] DD. II, 465.   [3] DD. III, 493, 510.
[4] DD. III, 488. See Vol. II, p. 650.   [5] DD. III, 490.

Government that as guarantee for neutrality we must demand the fortresses of Toul and Verdun which we would occupy and restore after end of war with Russia. Answer to latter question would have to be here by tomorrow afternoon 4 o'clock.[1]

Thus the ultimatum to Russia was accompanied by an ultimatum to France. The certainty of French solidarity with Russia raised the problem of Italy. Hence a telegram was sent to Flotow identical in its first part with the one to Schoen and also saying: 'Mobilization means war.' It then continues:

We have put the question to France whether she will remain neutral in a Russo-German war. Time limit eighteen (18) hours. If the French answer is in the negative, as is to be anticipated, war between France and ourselves will have to be declared immediately.

We definitely count on Italy's fulfillment of the engagements into which she has entered.[2]

As can be seen, all these four documents take practically the same things for granted. But the two first lack an intimation of capital importance which figures in the two latter. The telegram to Lichnowsky in Jagow's handwriting ran:

We have had to proclaim imminent danger of war which must be followed by mobilization. War with Russia seems hardly avoidable if Russia within twelve hours does not stop all war measures against us and Austria.

But the Chancellor, not wanting to alarm Grey, struck out the words 'War with Russia seems hardly avoidable'. On the other hand, when the draft for Schoen's telegram in Jagow's hand, speaking of mobilization but not of war, was submitted to him, Bethmann added the sentence: 'Mobilization inevitably means war', and Jagow himself inserted them into his draft of the telegram for Flotow. Bethmann judged the wording right for Paris as it stood, but removed the word 'inevitably' from the telegram for Rome. No great harm so far. But when with his own hand he wrote out the ultimatum to Russia he entirely omitted to explain that for Germany to mobilize meant to begin war. Of all of them, Sazonov was the one who should have received the warning that, if Russia did not revoke her mobilization, Germany not only would mobilize but would go to war immediately. The whole ultimatum should have hinged on this. By not making the point plain, Bethmann ran the risk that Sazonov would argue with the Tsar: 'But Germany is mobilizing too; we can go on negotiating and discussing just the same'. And, indeed, as we shall see, that is exactly how he did argue.

Was this most serious omission involuntary on Bethmann's part?

The answer is: No, because he himself was at pains to fill in the omission in the telegram prepared by Jagow for Paris. Nay more! On the following day (1 August), in telling the *Bundesrat* that he had sent Russia an ultimatum demanding the suspension of her mobilization within twelve hours with a warning that, in the event of her refusal, Germany herself would mobilize, he added:

There exists, I imagine, no misapprehension as to what mobilization means with us.[1]

Then on 4 August, explaining to the *Reichstag* how the war broke out, he went still further, saying that Germany had

as late as on 31 July called upon Russia to demobilize as the only measure which could still save the peace of Europe,

and that the German Ambassador to St. Petersburg had been instructed to warn Russia

that in the event of a refusal of our request we should be obliged to regard the state of war as having come into being.[2]

When we come to examine this speech it will be explained why Bethmann gave the *Reichstag* a different version of his communication to Sazonov from that presented to the *Bundesrat.* Both versions are equally far from the truth. All that he had telegraphed to Pourtalès was:

Mobilization must follow unless within twelve hours Russia stops all war measures against ourselves and Austria-Hungary and gives us a definite assurance in this respect.

The silence, therefore, on the import of German mobilization was intentional on his part.

It may be objected that its import was known to St. Petersburg. Even Sazonov in *Fateful Years,* writes:

In Germany mobilization immediately led to war as the German Ambassador had warned me.[3]

But Sazonov's memory has deceived him. This is proved by evidence which is above suspicion as coming from Pourtalès himself. Of a talk with Sazonov on 26 July he writes :

Sazonov put the question: 'Surely mobilization is not equivalent to war with you, either, is it?' I replied: 'Perhaps not in theory. But . . . once the button is pressed and the machinery of mobilization set in motion, there is no stopping it'.[4]

[1] DD. III, 553.
[2] Schulthess, *Geschichtskalender* (1914), I, pp. 383-4; CDD., pp. 136-9.
[3] Sazonov, p. 210.
[4] Pourtalès, p. 25. See Vol. II, p. 481.

This seemed to imply that mobilization was not yet war. It is true that the following day Pourtalès gave Sazonov the message telegraphed by Bethmann:

Preparatory military measures on the part of Russia directed in any way against us would oblige us to take counter-measures which would have to consist in the mobilization of the army. Mobilization, however, means war.[1]

But the import of these words obviously escaped Sazonov, since Pourtalès describes him as saying of this and another telegram communicated to him, that they 'produced a very good impression on him'.[2]

On 29 July Pourtalès had to convey to Sazonov the imperious instructions from Bethmann:

You should impress on M. Sazonov very seriously that further progress of Russian mobilization measures would compel us to mobilize and that then European war would scarcely be to be prevented.[3]

'Scarcely', but not 'not at all'. The final and most convincing argument is that Sazonov himself brought up the matter again when Pourtalès handed him the ultimatum, and even then, as we shall see, carried away the distinct impression that German mobilization was not equivalent to war and that there was still room for discussion and negotiation.

Kautsky writes:

In the text intended for Russia, this decisive sentence, which makes the communication an ultimatum, is wanting. Why was this? The omission can be explained in two very different ways: first from the desire of the General Staff not to arouse Russia prematurely, to keep her still in the belief that in spite of the mobilization, negotiations could be continued and thus prevent her hastening mobilization unduly. The omission might, however, have arisen from the desire of the Chancellor not to break down all bridges, in spite of mobilization.[4]

This latter explanation does not hold water, since mobilization would break down all bridges, and in fact did so. The first explanation, however, makes sense. But it shows that what was now regarded as important was, not to save the peace, but to win the war, and that to win the war precautions were neglected which might in fact have saved the peace.

Without even waiting for a reply from St. Petersburg, an ultimatum was sent to Paris the final section of which horrified even the German Ambassador charged with delivering it. Writing after the war he

---

[1] DD. I, 219.
[3] DD. II, 342. See Vol. II, p. 491.
[2] Pourtalès, p. 29.
[4] Kautsky, p. 205.

describes the idea of demanding from France that she should hand over
the fortresses of Toul and Verdun as 'not a happy one'. The demand

showed a lack of correct appreciation of French national sentiment. If the French had
even for only a passing moment thought of agreeing to the proposal of neutrality,
the demand for the surrender of their most important fortresses would have nipped
any understanding in the bud. . . . The demand for a guarantee in such a form
must have been urged on those responsible for our foreign policy by parties with no
political training and the reason for not refusing it was only the certainty that
France's attitude would make it useless to raise the question.[1]

This was indeed the case. The truth was, however, that Germany did
not possess two plans for mobilization and war, one preparing for
defense in the west and attack in the east against Russia. There was only
one single German plan: to throw her whole might, through Belgium,
against France, knock her out, and then settle accounts with Russia,
who meanwhile was to be held by Austrian forces. It would be a
catastrophe if France upset this plan by declaring herself neutral. To
prevent this the only thing to do was to make conditions for neutrality
such as she could not accept. Bethmann is, therefore, not being perfectly
straightforward when he seeks to justify himself by the plea:

Had France actually made a declaration of neutrality, we should have had to
reckon with the French army's completing its preparations down to the last detail
under cover of ostensible neutrality, in order at the given moment to fall on us when
we were deeply involved in the east. Against this we needed strong guarantees;
according to military opinion these would have been provided by the occupation of
Toul and Verdun for the duration of the war. This military consideration had to be
taken into account in issuing instructions to the Ambassador.[2]

The handing over of the fortresses of Toul and Verdun would not
in itself have sufficed to secure Germany's rear while she was turning
all her strength against Russia. In fact, it is doubtful whether the
military authorities would have asked for or agreed to such a thing,
since it would not in any way make up for the lack of a plan of mobilization drawn up for a war against Russia alone. The demand was made
solely because it was known that France would be sure to recognize
the *casus foederis* and reject so humiliating a suggestion, which Schoen,
as we shall see, never had occasion to present. Indeed, the telegram to
him had hardly been sent off when the Wilhelmstrasse, still on the
31st, drafted a declaration of war on France which was revised on
1 August and never dispatched.[3] Moreover, in the telegram addressed
by the Kaiser that evening to the King of Italy there occur the words:

---

[1] Schoen, pp. 195-6.   [2] Bethmann, I, p. 165, note.
          [3] DD. III, 608.

I have just had the question put to Paris whether in a Russo-German war France would be willing to remain neutral. The answer, unfortunately, cannot be in doubt.[1]

The demand for the handing over of Toul and Verdun is the indication of a will to war which, with the General Staff in full mastery, brushed aside all political considerations in order to attain its end with the utmost speed, no matter by what means. Politically it would have been more skilful to await the answer about Russian intentions before approaching France, and to refrain from laying down terms for French neutrality until France had expressed willingness to consider the possibility of neutrality. But Moltke was in a hurry and determined to bring things to a head, and the Chancellor's surrender was now followed by that of the Kaiser.

10. The Kaiser's telegram to Francis Joseph and Moltke's startling proposals to Conrad.

Stumm had drafted, and Zimmermann and the Chancellor had initialed, the text of a telegram for Francis Joseph from the Kaiser announcing the ultimatum about to be sent to Russia, and saying that, if Russia failed to yield, German mobilization would follow, but not mentioning that the order for mobilization signified the beginning of war. The text continues:

I hope to God that He may yet at the eleventh hour lighten the understanding of the Tsar and avert the terrible misfortune which the procedure of Russia threatens to bring upon the world. But if it is not to be so, I trust that shoulder to shoulder in the war forced upon us, we shall win the victory.[2]

For reasons we do not know, this text was never used and at 4.5 p. m. it was replaced by another which struck a different note:

The preliminary mobilization of my whole army and navy, ordered by me today, will be followed with the briefest delay by the definitive mobilization. I reckon with 2 August as first day of mobilization and am prepared in fulfillment of my obligations under the alliance to begin war immediately against Russia and France. In this hard struggle it is of the greatest importance that Austria should employ her main strength against Russia and not disperse it by a simultaneous offensive against Serbia. This is all the more important as a large part of my army will be tied down by France. In the gigantic struggle upon which we enter shoulder to shoulder Serbia plays a quite subordinate part, requiring only the most essential defensive measures. Success in the war, and with it the survival of our monarchies, can only be expected if we two meet the new, powerful opponent with our full forces. I further beg you to do everything to induce Italy to take part by the greatest

---

[1] DD. III, 530.
[2] DD. III, 502.

possible deference to her wishes; everything else must be put into the back-ground in order that the Triple Alliance may unitedly enter the war.[1]

The difference between the two texts is striking. In the first there still breathes a faint whisper of peace. In the second all possibility of peace is ruled out and war is regarded as certain. This is even more the case here than in the telegram sent by Bethmann to Tschirschky which said that 'imminent danger of war' would 'as far as can be foreseen' be followed by mobilization.[2] One might think that it was in the interval between them that all hope of a peaceful solution faded. But this is not the case, for all hope had practically been abandoned the night before. Probably the first text was phrased in order not to alarm the aged Emperor too much by saying that war was certain, while the second was prompted by the idea of rousing him to drop the Serbian war and give Germany full backing against Russia. The German General Staff thought a sharp eye must be kept on Austria, while Austria on her side had been afraid that Germany would back out at the last minute. The German mistrust was due not only to a general feeling of scant esteem for the energy and efficiency of the Austrian ally, but also to the telegrams from Vienna manifesting an intention of pushing forward with the war against Serbia when, with the entry of Russia into the fray, it was important not to waste strength on the minor opponent but to concentrate on the chief enemy. On the 30th Conrad had addressed a telegram to Moltke (which was only dispatched on the morning of the 31st) saying:

On the basis of His Majesty's decision the resolve is: to go forward with the war against Serbia. Mobilize remainder of army, assemble in Galicia.[3]

A later telegram also from Conrad to Moltke, dispatched from Vienna at 12.50 and received in Berlin at 11 p. m., runs:

General mobilization is expected today. 4 August first day of mobilization. Deployment and operation against Serbia still remain on their previous scale.[4]

At 2.45 p. m. this Austrian program was confirmed by Francis Joseph's reply to Wilhelm:

The action of my army now in progress against Serbia cannot suffer interruption on account of the menacing and challenging attitude of Russia.[5]

Here was a matter to cause concern to Moltke! It was probably he who prompted the Kaiser's telegram to Francis Joseph. And it was very likely on his advice that the Kaiser sent for the Austrian Military

---

[1] DD III, 503.   [2] DD. II, 479.
[3] Oe-U. VIII, 11119. See Vol. II, pp. 672-3.
[4] Schäfer, p. 539.   [5] DD. III, 482.

Attaché, Bienerth, and, at 5 p. m. on the 31st, made him a long speech. Wilhelm began by telling of his exchange of telegrams with the Tsar and King George V, and went on to recount all he had done to keep Romania faithful to the Triple Alliance, obtain the co-operation of Turkey, discourage Greece from siding with Russia, and keep Italy true to her pledges. He recalled all this with the idea of strengthening the determination of Austria to strike at Russia, since Germany had to turn her main forces at first against France and, only after the latter's defeat, would be free to take the offensive against Russia.[1] But in spite of this effort by the Kaiser, Moltke's alarm must have increased shortly afterwards when at 4.15 p. m. there came the following telephone call from Conrad:

> Austro-Hungarian mobilization against Russia is due only to Russian mobilization. It is only for the purpose of taking precautions against attack from Russia, without any intention of declaring or beginning war.[2]

When Moltke read the written record of this call he must have been struck dumb. So Vienna was taking not the slightest notice of what he had told Bienerth at about 2 p. m. on the 30th, of his own telegram to Conrad [3] and of Bethmann's to Tschirschky which ended:

> We expect from Austria immediate active participation in the war against Russia.[4]

Did this mean that Austria did not intend to hurl herself against Russia and was determined to push on with the offensive against Serbia? If so, vigorous action was necessary. Accordingly, between 6 and 7.15 p. m. he had the following message telephoned to Conrad:

> Chief of General Staff has received telephone communication from His Excellency Conrad that Austria does not intend to wage war against Russia. Germany will proclaim mobilization of entire military forces probably 2 August and open hostilities against Russia and France. Will Austria leave her in the lurch? (*'Willes Österreich im Stich lassen').*[5]

This telephone message deeply shocked Conrad—remarks Schäfer —but did not clear matters up. On the contrary, it caused Conrad to put through another call at 9.30 p. m. (reaching Berlin at 10.30 p. m.):

> By ordering concentration of forces in Galicia, Austria-Hungary has already proved will to war. Concluding statement of my last communication re postponement of declaration of war and opening of hostilities was only in response to German desire to avoid appearance of aggressive act on part of Austria

---

[1] Oe-U. VIII, 11133, 11134. [2] Schäfer, p. 539.
[3] See Vol. II, p. 673. [4] DD. II, 479.
[5] Schäfer, p. 541.

against Russia and to await declaration of war and opening of hostilities on part of Russia. Moreover, at time of dispatch of my last communication no news had come in about Germany's intentions of mobilization. Thus I could count on finishing off (*durchzuführen*) war against Serbia before move against Russia necessary. Information arriving only today makes known Germany's intention to begin war against France and Russia. Request statement by return whether this the correct interpretation of German intention, in order to regulate our own action accordingly.[1]

Twenty minutes later Conrad put through a second call, which seems to be the continuation of its predecessor and reached Berlin at 10.30 p. m.:

I beg His Excellency von Moltke for a definite statement whether it is now necessary to reckon with waging a major war against Russia immediately and unconditionally, that, in other words, there is no likelihood of our desisting from the war against Serbia without coming to grips with Russia. This definite statement is indispensable and urgent for our own decision.

At 11.20 p. m. Moltke replied:

Long-distance call 10.30 p. m. received. Germany has sent ultimatum to Russia and France, which has to be answered by 4 p. m. on 1 August. If reply unsatisfactory, mobilization will be ordered tomorrow.

At 2.20 a. m. on 1 August, probably in answer to Conrad's second call, Moltke, on returning from the Foreign Ministry, dictated the following long-distance telephone message:

Germany has demanded of Russia immediate withdrawal of all military measures taken against Germany and Austria. If Russia rejects this demand, German declaration of war follows immediately. Russian reply demanded with twelve-hour time limit. Thus decision must be taken tomorrow. I regard acceptance of German demand by Russia as impossible.[2]

By now Conrad certainly understood that Germany meant to mobilize and go to war. But meanwhile the decision was still subject to the reply from Russia. Moreover, the tartness of Conrad's language

---

[1] Schäfer, p. 541. The recorded text of this call as published by Schäfer, who found the document in the Reich Archives, differs from the text given by Contad (IV, pp. 155-6), which runs: 'By general mobilization and the order for concentration in Galicia, Austria-Hungary has proved will to war. The last paragraph [of telegram] was written in deference to the wish of Germany not to direct an attack against Russia but to await Russian declaration of war. Moreover, telegram was dispatched at a moment when there was no news of Germany's intentions to mobilize, and on the contrary the negotiations with England led rather to the conclusion that Germany intended to compose the conflict by peaceful means. We were forced into war against Serbia, Russia has mobilized; we have still no certainty whether Russia is only threatening, therefore we cannot allow ourselves to be turned aside from our action against Serbia. A quite different situation arises if Germany declares that she means at once to carry through (*durchführen*) the war. Request enlightenment on this point'.

[2] Schäfer, pp. 541-2.

probably betrays lingering irritation at what Moltke had said to Fleischmann the previous day, and an intention to make it seem as if he were conferring a favor in acceding to the German request. Hence Moltke was kept on tenterhooks until, at 2.10 a. m. on 1 August, he received the following reassuring message from Kageneck, the German Military Attaché at Vienna:

Just now conversation with Chief of General Staff [Conrad] about His Majesty's telegram in the matter of active participation war against Russia. Chief of General Staff says if only Germany had made up mind twenty-four hours earlier. Now she has placed us in very difficult position. Tell Berlin we shall do all in our power. I told Chief of General Staff that earlier decision impossible on diplomatic grounds.[1]

Thus in the night of 31 July to 1 August the misunderstanding between the two General Staffs was for the time being cleared up, though, as we shall see, it reappeared later. But on 1 August Conrad wrote Moltke a letter to make plain that the blame for what had happened rested with the German Chief of Staff:

We hoped to be able to wage this war as a localized one without further complications. . . . It is natural that for this war we prepared forces which, already by their numbers, vouched for success. But when, by mobilizing her southern districts, Russia took a hostile stand against the Monarchy, we turned to Germany with the request that she should declare this move against us to be unacceptable to Germany also. Simultaneously the mobilization of the remainder of the army was ordered, and its concentration in Galicia was taken in hand. At this stage, as was also urgently requested by Germany, we found it necessary to declare that our hostile measures were devised only against Serbia and that further mobilization was only a defense measure against the Russian threat. . . . Meanwhile our transports in a southward direction began to operate. The diplomatic negotiations then in progress gave us the impression that, if we were attacked by Russia, Germany would, without doubt, honor her obligations under the alliance, but would prefer to avoid a major war. We were obliged, therefore, to pursue our intention of proceeding with the action against Serbia, entrusting the defense against Russia, against whom we alone could not start an offensive war, to our forces which were to be concentrated in Galicia, to the threat from Germany and to the intervention of the other Powers. Only on 31 July came suddenly the definite declaration on the part of Germany that she herself now intended to carry through the major war against France and Russia. This created an entirely new situation. As a result thereof we made plans to employ the main weight of our strength in the north, and I beg to assure Your Excellency that this will be carried through, in spite of the great complications created by the already completed transport of troops to the south. But I hope that even the difficulties which arise from the present situation will be overcome.

[1] Schäfer, p. 543.

I will send Your Excellency concrete data as soon as the position can be reviewed in detail and request similar information from you about your position and plans.[1]

This extremely fair summing up of the situation elicited from Moltke the following letter, which reached Vienna at 4.45 p. m. on 2 August:

I fully appreciate Your Excellency's difficulties in these last days. But in spite of all endeavors I was not able to speed up the tasks of the diplomatists and give Your Excellency enlightenment earlier about our mobilization. Now things have got under way. We march against France and Russia, and operations begin at once. I know that Your Excellency's purposeful energy will at this moment once again meet with success in overcoming all difficulties. The one goal, the overthrow of Austria-Hungary's mortal enemy Russia, will be kept in view in all measures taken. The hour demands that all available forces shall be used for this objective. Serbia can be kept in check with limited forces.[2]

This reply clearly displays Moltke's embarrassment. He extricates himself by alleging his inability to speed up the task of the diplomatists. We, however, know that until noon on the 30th he had remained passive, had then come forward and gained the upper hand with the Chancellor, demanding and obtaining the abandonment of negotiation and the decision to resort to war. It was worth our while to turn our attention to this Moltke-Conrad correspondence because it so well illustrates Moltke's abrupt transition from passivity to a usurpation of powers outside his field, and above all the abrupt change of direction in German policy.

11. Bethmann's renewed approach to London; Grey's last urgent appeal to Berlin.

Undeterred by Grey's warnings and Lichnowsky's forebodings, by Grey's scornful rejection of the German appeal of the 29th for British neutrality, by the fact that Russia had been presented with an ultimatum which was about to be followed by the declaration of war, Bethmann still persevered on the 31st in his endeavors to persuade England to take a favorable view of German conduct, vaguely hoping that she would remain neutral. At 3.10 p. m. he had sent Lichnowsky the telegram we have already noticed acquainting London with the proclamation of the *Kriegsgefahrzustand* and adding that it would be followed by German mobilization unless Russia demobilized. He said nothing to London about the sending of the ultimatum to Russia, still less about the fact that mobilization meant war, for fear of alarming London.[3] It was a paltry subterfuge since Grey was bound soon to learn the truth from St. Petersburg. Not till evening did Bethmann make up his mind

[1] Conrad, IV, pp. 164-5.   [2] Conrad, IV, pp. 318-9.
[3] DD. III, 488. See p. 40.

to give Grey his version of the facts in a telegram of 8.30 p. m. to Lichnowsky.

On 29 July the Tsar asked His Majesty the Kaiser by telegraph to mediate between Austria-Hungary and Russia. The Kaiser at once declared his readiness to do so; he so informed the Tsar by telegram, and immediately took the necessary steps at Vienna. Without waiting for the result, Russia then mobilized against Austria-Hungary, whereupon the Kaiser at once informed the Tsar that such action rendered his mediation illusory; the Kaiser further requested the Tsar to stop the military preparations against Austria. This was, however, not done. The German Government nevertheless persevered with its mediation at Vienna. In putting forward the urgent proposals that it did, the German Government went to the utmost limit possible with a sovereign State which is its ally. The suggestions made by the German Government at Vienna were entirely on the lines of those put forward by England, and the German Government recommended them for serious consideration at Vienna. They were considered this morning at Vienna. While the deliberations were taking place, and before they were even terminated, Count Pourtalès announced from St. Petersburg the mobilization of the whole Russian army and navy. This action on the part of Russia rendered any answer by Austria to the German proposal for mediation impossible. It also affected Germany, whose mediation had been solicited by the Tsar personally. We were compelled, unless we wished to neglect the safety of the Fatherland, to answer this action, which could only be regarded as hostile, by serious counter-measures. We could not idly watch Russia mobilizing on our frontier. We therefore told Russia that if she did not stop her warlike measures against Germany and Austria-Hungary within twelve hours we should mobilize, and that would mean war. We asked France whether in a Russo-German war she would remain neutral. Please use all means to induce the English press to give due consideration to this sequence of events.[1]

Bethmann evidently thought that 'due consideration' would render English public opinion hostile to intervention.

We need hardly dwell on the speciousness of this reasoning, especially in view of the fact that Russian partial mobilization had to a certain extent received the approval of Berlin and that Vienna never had any intention of accepting the Anglo-German proposal for the *Halt in Belgrade.* We will, however, note that this second telegram gave London the alarm and led in the night of 31 July–1 August to King George's sending a telegram to the Tsar of which more will be said further on.[2] This telegram reached St. Petersburg at 5 p. m. on 1 August and was read by the Tsar after Germany had declared war on Russia. It is evident that it would have been dispatched much earlier if Bethmann, in his first telegram to Lichnowsky of 3.10 p. m., had said what he at last made up his mind to say in his second. This point is passed over in silence by those German historians who

---

[1] DD. III, 513; BD. XI, 372. [2] See p. 125.

accuse Buchanan of having failed to give his royal master's message in good time to the Tsar, with the result that Nicholas did not learn of King George's wish for the suspension of Russian mobilization until the declaration of war rendered the situation irreparable. It is undoubtedly true that the Tsar would have found it very difficult to give an order suspending mobilization, especially as he thought that mobilization did not preclude the continuance of negotiations. But it is not in the light of subsequent knowledge that the actions of that time have to be judged. Were it so, it would have been essential for Bethmann to have approached London without wasting a moment, even before 3 p. m., as soon as the *Kriegsgefahrzustand* was proclaimed. If he did not do so and dealt out his information at intervals in two portions, this was because he was now endeavoring to prevent, not war, but English intervention, and thought he could do so by presenting the facts in that manner. How-ever, he was still not sure of having achieved his purpose, for a few hours later he reverted to the subject in yet another telegram to Lichnowsky:

> It will be Your Serene Highness's duty to promote understanding of the fact that our geographical and military situation left us no choice but to answer Russian mobilization with the proclamation of imminent state of war. . . . If Russia completes her mobilization without our mobilizing, East and West Prussia, perhaps Posen and Silesia too, will be given up defenseless to the Russians. In the Tsar's last telegram to His Majesty he promised he would refrain from all 'provocative action'. That will not fail to produce its effect in England when it is known. . . . A mobilized Russian army on our frontier without our having mobilized is a mortal danger to us even without 'provocative action'. . . . No German would understand it if we failed to answer it with sharp measures.[1]

This document, too, is neither frank nor sincere. The Chancellor claims in it the right to resort to 'sharp measures', a right which was not disputed by the Tsar when on 1 August he telegraphed to Wilhelm:

> Understand you are obliged to mobilize but wish to have the same guarantee from you as I gave you that these measures do not mean war and that we shall continue negotiating, etc.[2]

But the right which Bethmann proposed to exercise was something quite different, namely, to reply to Russian mobilization by breaking off negotiations and going to war, even though on that 31 July he saw that England was coming further to meet Germany than she had ever done in the preceding days. This is a point which deserves to be made clear.

---

[1] DD. III, 529; BD. XI, 397.   [2] DD. III, 546. See p. 64.

The telegrams containing the ultimatums to St. Petersburg and Paris were about to be dispatched at 3.30 p. m. on the 31st when at 3.25 Lichnowsky's telegram reached the Wilhelmstrasse reporting his talk with Grey of that morning. It was a talk of such capital importance that the Wilhelmstrasse ought to have thought afresh whether it were not advisable to reverse the decisions taken and refrain from extreme measures, i.e., cancel mobilization. Lichnowsky had been instructed to acquaint Grey with Tschirschky's telegram of 30 July announcing Berchtold's specious consent to the resumption of direct conversations between St. Petersburg and Vienna.[1] Grey

said at first that Russia had become somewhat sensitive in the matter of war measures. . . . He will, however, endeavor to use his influence in this sense. In regard to Austro-Russian talks, he thought everything depended on Austria's making such a concession that Russia would be in the wrong if she rejected it, then he would be in a position to put pressure on Paris and St. Petersburg. . . . He would have to be in a position, at need, to motivate an attitude of reserve on the part of England by some tangible evidence of Russia's being in the wrong. . . . He let it clearly be understood that he could sponsor the idea of not immediately taking the part of France only if he were in a position to point to some evidence of a conciliatory spirit [on the part of Germany]. He repeatedly stressed that England was bound by no treaties. I surmise that he has in mind his original suggestion for the suspension of military operations in Serbia. . . . From my knowledge of Vienna I feel sure that only extremely strong pressure from Berlin will induce Vienna to make such a concession as would decisively influence the attitude of England in case war were to break out after all.[2]

This was a life-line thrown to Bethmann which he could have grasped if he had at heart really wanted to avoid war. By not doing so he was plunging his country into a struggle under unfavorable auspices. Had he insisted on Vienna's acceptance of the *Halt in Belgrade,* he not only would have enabled Austria to penetrate into Serbia with the consent of the Powers and deal the Pan-Serb movement a perhaps mortal blow, but he would have divided England from France and Russia, especially as Grey's promise had been actually more sweeping than was apparent in Lichnowsky's telegram. Grey's own account of it to Goschen runs:

I said to German Ambassador this morning that if Germany could get any reasonable proposal put forward which made it clear that Germany and Austria were striving to preserve European peace and that Russia and France would be unreasonable if they rejected it, I would support it at St. Petersburg and Paris and go to the length of saying that, if Russia and France would not accept it, His Majesty's Government would have nothing to do with the

[1] DD. II, 433, 434. See Vol. II, pp. 660-5.
[2] DD. III, 489. See Vol. II, p. 641.

consequences; but, otherwise, I told German Ambassador that if France became involved we should be drawn in.[1]

As a result of Grey's instructions, Goschen went to see Jagow late on the night of 31 July. His report, dispatched at 2 a. m. on 1 August, runs:

I spent an hour with Secretary of State for Foreign Affairs urging him most earnestly to accept your proposal and make another effort to prevent terrible catastrophe of a European war. He . . . said it was impossible for the Imperial Government to consider any proposal until they received an answer from Russia to their communication of today; this communication, which he admitted had the form of an ultimatum, being that, unless Russia could inform the Imperial Government within twelve hours that she would immediately countermand her mobilization against Germany and Austria, Germany would be obliged on her side to mobilize at once. I asked His Excellency why they had made their demand even more difficult for Russia to accept by asking them to demobilize in south as well.[2] He replied that it was in order to prevent Russia from saying all her mobilization was only directed against Austria. His Excellency said that if the answer from Russia was satisfactory he thought personally that your proposal merited favorable consideration.[3]

Goschen's question to Jagow why Germany was demanding that Russia should demobilize in the south as well was an embarrassing one. Jagow knew that Russia could not agree to it and that the whole proposal would therefore end in the waste-paper basket. But he took neither heed nor alarm when Goschen put a question to him which was a clear pointer to the way England was likely to act. At 5 p. m. on the 31st Grey had telegraphed to Goschen and Bertie:

I still trust that situation is not irretrievable, but in view of prospect of mobilization in Germany it becomes essential to His Majesty's Government, in view of existing treaties, to ask whether French Government is prepared to engage to respect neutrality of Belgium so long as no other Power violates it. A similar request is being sent to the German Government.[4]

Faced with this demand, reports Goschen, Jagow said

he could not possibly give me an answer before consulting the Emperor and the Chancellor. I said that I hoped that the answer would not be too long delayed. He then gave me to understand he rather doubted whether they could answer at all, as any reply they might give could not fail, in the event of war, to have the undesirable effect of disclosing to a certain extent, part of their plan of campaign. . . . He told me in confidence that Belgium had already committed certain acts which he could only qualify as hostile. On my asking him for details, he gave me as an instance that the Belgian Govern

---

[1] BD. XI, 340. See Vol. II, p. 642.   [2] BD. XI, 185. See Vol. II, pp. 481-2.
[3] BD. XI, 385.   [4] BD. XI, 348.

ment had already embargoed a consignment of grain destined for Germany. . . . In any case it would be necessary for them to know what France replied to your inquiry. I shall speak to him again on the subject tomorrow, but I am not very hopeful of obtaining a definite answer.[1]

12. A. telegram from the Tsar to Wilhelm; Sazonov's successive states of mind.

The intransigent attitude on the part of the German leaders seems all the more insensate when one considers that while London was making these warm and tempting appeals for peace, coupled with threats of intervention if they were not heeded, the ultimatum had not created an irretrievable situation at St. Petersburg. Before receiving the order to present the ultimatum to Sazonov, Pourtalès had once more made endeavors to avert the catastrophe. He writes that on the morning of 31 July he was just preparing to go to the Russian Foreign Ministry to communicate the two telegrams which had arrived in the night (the more important being the one containing Tschirschky's bogus news of the 30th that Berchtold had authorized the resumption of conversations with St. Petersburg[2]) when the Military Attaché, Major Eggeling, came in with the news that notices of the general mobilization of the army and navy had just been posted up at the street-corners. Knowing that Sazonov was at Peterhof, Pourtalès called on his assistant, Neratov, and told him

that the prospects of an understanding opened up by the telegram from Vienna had unfortunately been definitely brought to naught by the mobilization directed against us. The proclamation of the Russian mobilization would in my opinion act like a thunderbolt. . . . It could only be regarded by us as showing that Russia was bent on war.[3]

Neratov, taken aback by this language, said he would bring the matter to Sazonov's knowledge. Pourtalès, on his part, rang up Sazonov at Peterhof.

The relevant entry in Schilling's diary, however, gives Pourtalès as having seen Sazonov personally, and having been told by him

that the decision [to mobilize] taken by the Imperial Government merely constituted a precautionary measure necessitated by the unconciliatoriness manifested in Berlin and Vienna, and that Russia for her part would do nothing that was irrevocable, but that, despite her mobilization, peace could be maintained if Germany would consent before it was too late to exercise a moderating influence upon her ally.[4]

Not satisfied with what Sazonov had told him, Pourtalès made up his mind to ask for an audience of the Tsar, which was immediately granted for the afternoon of the same day (31st).

---

[1] BD. XI, 383.
[3] Pourtalès, pp. 64-5.
[2] DD. II, 433. See Vol. II, p. 660.
[4] Schilling, p. 69.

I particularly emphasized that the mobilization was a threat and a challenge to Germany and, as it occurred at the moment when our Kaiser was endeavoring to mediate between Russia and Austria, must be regarded as an insult to His Majesty. The Tsar . . . at first only answered: 'Vous croyez vraiment?' My impression was that His Majesty . . . had not yet fully grasped the seriousness of the situation. When I remarked that the only thing which in my opinion might yet prevent war was a withdrawal of the mobilization order, the Tsar replied that I, as a former officer, must realize that on technical grounds a recall of the order issued was no longer possible. . . . The Tsar . . . dwelt on the necessity for us to exercise strong pressure on Austria-Hungary. . . . I answered that our moderating influence on Austria-Hungary had been repeatedly in evidence during the Balkan war. . . . We could no longer be asked to exercise powerful pressure on Austria-Hungary. . . . I then attempted to call the Tsar's attention to the dangers that this war represents for the monarchic principle. His Majesty agreed and said he hoped things would turn out right after all. Upon my remarking that I did not think this possible if Russian mobilization did not stop, the Tsar pointed heavenwards with the words: 'Then there is only One who still can help'.[1]

This reliance on divine help did not, however, prevent Nicholas II, even if he could not stop the machinery of mobilization which had been set in motion by his order, from doing all he knew how to save the peace by negotiation which he still regarded as possible. He did not know that for Germany mobilization was equivalent to war and showed Pourtalès a telegram he was on the point of sending to Wilhelm in answer to the latter's reply to his of the 30th.[2] This telegram, dispatched from Peterhof at 2.55 p. m., crossed with the one from the Kaiser already noticed[3] and showed how the Russian Sovereign hoped and believed he could avert the opening of hostilities.[4] It runs:

I thank you heartily for your mediation which begins to give one hope that all may yet end peacefully. It is technically impossible to stop our military preparations which were obligatory owing to Austria's mobilization. We are far from wishing for war. As long as the negotiations with Austria on Serbia's account are taking place my troops shall not make any *provocative* action. I give you my solemn word for this. I put my trust in God's mercy and hope in your successful mediation in Vienna for the welfare of our countries and for the peace of Europe.[5]

[1] Pourtalès, pp. 66–9.   [2] DD. II, 420. See p. 6.   [3] DD. III, 480. See p. 37.

[4] The Tsar also showed Pourtalès a letter he was writing to Wilhelm. This is probably the one which appears on pp. 283–4 of the *Correspondance entre Guillaume II et Nicolas II, 1894–1914* and is of no great importance. It blames Austria for assuming that the Serbian Government was implicated in the Sarajevo murder and sending an ultimatum with a time limit of only forty-eight hours. 'Repressive expeditions can be undertaken only in one's own land or one's colonies. That is why this war has aroused such indignation in my country; it will be very difficult to calm down the warlike mood manifested here. . . . I appeal to you, Austria's ally, to be a mediator with the aim of maintaining peace'.

[5] DD. III, 487.

This simple and warmhearted appeal reached the Berlin Schloss (owing to the difference of hour) at 2.52 p. m. on the 31st at the very moment when the decision was being taken to send the ultimatum to Russia. At the same time Sazonov, like his Sovereign, was making efforts to save the peace. A telegram from Sverbeev of the 30th told him that Jagow had declared his formula, drafted in the early hours of that day for Pourtalès,[1] to be unacceptable, but had added that

Szápáry was instructed to continue conversations with Your Excellency, and in addition there were fresh proposals from Grey which no doubt had already arrived in St. Petersburg.[2]

Jagow was alluding to Grey's telegram to Buchanan, shown by Grey to Lichnowsky and summarized by the latter in a telegram to Berlin[3] and then forwarded in the original text.[4] Grey had made some modifications to Sazonov's formulation:

I think Russian Minister for Foreign Affairs' formula might be changed to read that the Powers would examine how Serbia could fully satisfy Austria without impairing Serbian sovereign rights or independence. If Austria, having occupied Belgrade and neighboring Serbian territory, declares herself ready, in the interest of European peace, to cease her advance and to discuss how a complete settlement can be arrived at, I hope that Russia would also consent to discussion and suspension of further military preparations provided that other Powers did the same.[5]

On the basis of these suggestions Sazonov on 31 July drew up an amended formula, but Buchanan's telegram giving this news to London on 1 August was never received in London.[6] The Russian documents show that after his talk with Buchanan Sazonov telegraphed to the five Russian Ambassadors accredited to the other Great Powers:

The English Ambassador has conveyed to me his Government's desire to introduce certain changes into the formula which I had yesterday proposed to the German Ambassador. I replied that I agreed to the English proposal and the formula, amended accordingly, will be transmitted to you as No. 2.[7]

A succeeding telegram contained the new wording:

If Austria agrees to stop the march of her troops into Serbian territory and if, in recognition of the fact that the Austro-Serbian conflict has assumed the character of a question of European interest, she agrees that the Great Powers shall enquire into the satisfaction which Serbia might give to the Austro-Hungarian Government without infringement of her rights as a sovereign state and her independence, Russia engages to maintain her waiting attitude.[8]

---

[1] DD. II 421. See Vol. II, p. 563.
[2] *Int. Bez.* i. V, 305.
[3] DD. II, 439.
[4] DD. II, 460.
[5] BD. XI, 309. See Vol. II, p. 635.
[6] BD. XI, 393 and note.
[7] *Int. Bez.* i. V, 342.
[8] *Int. Bez.* i. V, 343.

On the face of it the new Russian formula did not sound entirely conciliatory. It did not agree to the cancellation of mobilization any more than did the Tsar's telegram to Wilhelm. It also gave no explicit consent to the occupation of Belgrade and neighboring territory not yet occupied by the Austrians. But both Sazonov and the Tsar—of whose letter to the Kaiser Sazonov informed Buchanan and Paléologue —were under the impression that mobilization could be completed without harming negotiation and that therefore there was no reason for stopping it. He omitted mention of Belgrade probably in order not to lay stress on a painful concession, but he regarded Austrian troops as having already entered Serbian territory and made no demand that they should evacuate it. He may have thought that, having suffered bombardment, Belgrade was already occupied or about to be so. In any case he declared himself in agreement with Grey's proposal and so much believed the method of negotiation still to be feasible that he suggested to Buchanan the holding of conversations in London

as atmosphere there was far more favorable to pacific solution. . . .

In conclusion, His Excellency begged me to convey to you his warm thanks for what His Majesty's Government have done in the cause of peace. If Germany had made this last pacific 'geste' and if war was actually averted, it would be in great measure due to the firm attitude adopted by Great Britain. This was a service which neither Emperor, Government, nor Russian people would ever forget.[1]

Buchanan's telegram makes no mention of the Sazonov-Szápáry conversation of the 31st, which makes it probable that this took place after Sazonov had talked with Buchanan and Paléologue. This conversation has already been fully discussed and the versions given by Szápáry and Sazonov compared. After it Sazonov telegraphed with a sense of great relief to the Russian Ambassadors:

The Austrian Ambassador called on me and conveyed to me the consent of his Government to enter into a discussion on the content of the ultimatum presented to Serbia. I expressed my satisfaction over this and indicated to the Ambassador that it would be preferable that the negotiations should be carried on in London with the participation of the Great Powers. We hope that the English Government will undertake to preside over these discussions whereby it would earn the gratitude of all Europe.

For a successful prosecution of such negotiations it would be very important that Austria should suspend her military operations on Serbian territory.[2]

---

[1] BD. XI, 393. For Paléologue's account see DF. XI, 453, and Poincaré, IV, pp. 462-3. In the *Yellow Book* Paléologue's telegram is published as No. 113 (CDD., p. 220), prefaced with an invented preamble which has no counterpart in the document reproduced in the authoritative French collection.

[2] *Int. Bez.* i. V, 348. See Vol. II, pp. 681-3.

These concluding words are enough to show that Sazonov believed the Austrian army to have already entered Serbia and that he was conceding a great deal in regarding it as 'very important' but not indispensable that the invasion should not go farther. But he was, as we know, mistaken in stating that Berchtold had agreed to discussions on the ultimatum to Serbia, though the fault was not entirely his, since Szápáry, as has already been said, used very ambiguous language in speaking to him about this matter.

Sazonov's diplomatic activity in the course of 31 July leaves the impression that, although he had willed the mobilization, he was making sincere efforts to save the peace and was not without hopes of succeeding, even to the point of speaking with premature satisfaction. Bernadotte Schmitt thinks that Sazonov was

perhaps grasping at a straw. But it is more likely that he wished to gain time by negotiations while the mobilization was being executed . . . and that he was maneuvering for position, just as were Count Berchtold and Herr von Bethmann. This is borne out by what the Serbian Premier Pašić wrote to his Chief of Staff, Putnik, on 31 July:

'The reports from our Minister in St. Petersburg declare that Russia is now talking and drawing out the negotiations in order to gain time for the mobilization and concentration of her army. When that is complete she will declare war on Austria.'

Schmitt lists certain precautions taken by Russia at Paris and London, and certain instructions to Russian representatives in Serbia, Bulgaria, and Romania, which seem to indicate that she regarded war as now certain.[1] Now, undoubtedly, Sazonov thought that war was highly probable and acted in accordance with this belief. We have just seen how he expressed the gratitude which Russia would feel to England 'if war was actually averted.' Thus the above precautions and telegrams prove nothing. As for Pašić's letter to Putnik, one only need read it to see that it contains general statements of doubtful value and anterior to the 31st. It shows no knowledge of German mobilization, and goes on to say:

There is still a belief that it will be possible to avoid a general war which would involve all Europe. . . . [Russia's] wish is to settle the dispute or conflict in a peaceful way and without bloodshed, while, however, safe-guarding Serbia's dignity.[2]

Thus it is much more logical to think, as Schmitt himself throws out by way of a suggestion, that Sazonov was still sincere in clutching at these last straws, even if he had not much confidence in them.

[1] Schmitt, II, pp. 314-15.
[2] *Pashitch on the Situation on July 31, 1914*, in KSF., November 1926, pp. 836-8.

The man was by nature weak, vacillating, muddleheaded, and impulsive. It would be a mistake to credit him with continuity of thought and to qualify his contradictorinesses as cunning and machiavellism. At times we find him excited and unyielding, at others depressed and conciliatory. On 24 July he was convinced of the inevitability of war, deciding to mobilize against Austria and advising the Serbs to resist. On the 25th, on the contrary, he advised them to ask for English mediation. On the 26th, 27th and, up to a certain hour, on the 28th, he seemed dominated by groundless optimism and thought the conflict could be averted. But when on the afternoon of the 28th he learnt that Austria had declared war on Serbia, he was again violently seized with warlike impulses. Anxious not to draw Germany into the dispute, he first decided to mobilize only against Austria until, under pressure from the generals, he persuaded the Tsar on the 29th to authorize general mobilization. When the Tsar revoked this, Sazonov in the early hours of 30 July improvised a peace formula which he gave to Pourtalès, and then, without awaiting Berlin's reply, went and begged the Tsar to order general mobilization. On 31 July he thought the sky was clearing a little, drew a deep breath and reverted to optimism. One must always bear in mind the fact of his determination to surmount the crisis without submitting to the will of the Central Powers as Izvolsky had done in 1909. But he did not want war; on the contrary, he dreaded it. And so he accepted Grey's proposal, toning it down somewhat and thanking England, as we have seen. He gave a friendly reception to Szápáry and attached too much weight to the latter's specious words. He expressed his satisfaction not only to Sverbeev and Shebeko, as he would have done had he wanted to throw dust in the eyes of Germany and Austria, but to all the Russian Ambassadors. He sent a copy of the relevant telegram to the Tsar, whom he had no interest in deceiving, and who annotated the document:

The one thing [i.e., discussions to be held in London] does not rule out the other [i.e., direct discussions with Vienna]. Continue the conversations with the Austrian Ambassador. Peterhof, 1 August 1914.[1]

It must always be borne in mind when one tries to understand the state of mind and line of conduct of those in charge of Russian (not to speak of Austrian) policy, and of Grey as well, that they did not regard mobilization as necessarily followed by war. The fact that war did follow on the heels of mobilization has led many historians astray, because they look back with a knowledge of what came after. But there exists a series of documents which prove that, although mobilization was regarded as a serious step, it was not in 1914 regarded as an

----

[1] *Int. Bez.* i. V, 348. See Vol. II, p. 683.

irrevocable one by the Government of any Great Power with the sole exception of Germany. It was the case that mobilization required a certain number of days during which it was still regarded as possible to save the peace. Accordingly, St. Petersburg was not alarmed beyond measure at receiving Izvolsky's telegram of 31 July reporting that Jules Cambon had sent word from Berlin that

Jagow had sent for him and said that in view of Russian general mobilization Germany to her regret was obliged to take military measures corresponding to the 'war danger' situation. . . . Germany requests Russia to demobilize; otherwise she herself will mobilize.[1]

The same news came also from Sverbeev. He had seen Jagow that morning and there had been some sharp words. Jagow had expressed alarm at the Russian measures against Germany and had threatened retaliatory measures.[2] But Berlin did not yet know that Russian general mobilization had been ordered. When Jagow learnt of it he sent for Sverbeev and told him 'with extreme agitation'

that he was obliged to reply with immediate general mobilization and this very day with the declaration that Germany is in a state of 'imminent danger'.[3]

But this advance announcement did not unduly alarm Sazonov, just as even the ultimatum, when it came, did not alarm him to more than a certain degree.

13. *Pourtalès hands Sazonov the German ultimatum with a twelve-hour time limit.*

In his diary Pourtalès records more fully than in his telegram of 1 a. m. on 1 August[1] what was said at his interview with Sazonov, which took place about midnight on the 31st. He had only at 11.10 p. m. received Bethmann's telegram summoning the Russian Government to stop mobilization. Sazonov in reply repeated what the Tsar had said to Pourtalès earlier in the day, namely, that technical reasons rendered it impossible to revoke mobilization but that it

did not at all imply the intention of going to war, and negotiations could be continued in spite of mobilization.

The Tsar's solemn word that Russian troops would not begin hostilities while negotiations were being continued ought to be sufficient reassurance. Pourtalès replied

that this assurance could not satisfy us. The Tsar was not engaging to keep the peace if negotiations should fail as a result of Russia's rigid adherence to her demands. I asked the Minister whether he were in a position to give me any guarantees in this respect. When M. Sazonov said he could not, I replied that one could not

[1] *Int. Bez.* i. V, 354.   [2] *Int. Bez.* i V, 358.
[3] *Int. Bez.* i. V, 359.   [4] DD. III, 536.

take it amiss if our Supreme Command refused to wait until Russia had assembled her mighty army masses on our frontier. The Minister then reverted to the point that mobilization still need not mean making war and repeated the question whether we, too, could not mobilize without its necessarily meaning that there would be war. On this point I could only refer to my previous statements and declared definitely that if Russia did not stop her mobilization and therefore obliged us to mobilize, we should find ourselves on the brink of war.[1]

These notes recorded by Pourtalès reveal the extreme importance attached by Sazonov to the question, already raised by him in this connection at a previous interview, whether German mobilization meant the immediate outbreak of war, the Ambassador's reply being such as to give the impression that once mobilization was ordered, war would be not inevitable but very probable. One can, accordingly, only conclude that if the telegram conveying the ultimatum had contained the plain statement made in those addressed to Schoen and Flotow, that mobilization inevitably meant war, Sazonov would have attached far greater importance to the announcement than he actually did and would have reacted in a very different manner. His reaction, in actual fact, was slight, quite incommensurate with the importance of the document read out to him, and showed that he had not grasped its importance. Pourtalès had not entirely grasped it himself and, in his brief report to the Wilhelmstrasse, said that Sazonov had again referred to technical difficulties which made the stopping of mobilization impossible. He

again sought to persuade me that we overrate the importance of Russian mobilization, which is not to be compared with ours. He urgently begged me to represent to Your Excellency that, in today's telegram from H.M. Tsar Nicholas to H.M. the Kaiser and King, the Tsar's assurance on his word of honor ought to reassure us about Russia's intentions.[2]

Here we have the unperturbed reply of one who feels no great concern and who is not alive to the seriousness of returning a refusal, even if only implicitly. Still more revealing is the telegram Sazonov himself sent on the morning of 1 August to all the Russian Ambassadors, which runs:

At midnight the German Ambassador on instructions from his Government told me that, unless within twelve hours—that is by Saturday noon—we began demobilization not only against Germany but also against Austria, the German Government would be compelled to give the order to mobilize. Upon my asking whether that was equivalent to war the Ambassador answered that such was not the case, but that we should be extraordinarily near to war.[3]

---

[1] Pourtalès, pp. 74-5.   [2] DD. III, 536.   [3] *Int. Bez* i. V, 385.

Appended to the text of this telegram in the archives is a note from Sazonov to Schilling:

I think one ought to send the Tsar a report of my nocturnal conversation with Pourtalès. This should be done at once and it ought to be added that at 2 p. m. a Council of Ministers will be held which I must in all circumstances attend.

It is obvious that, if Sazonov had realized he was dealing with a definite war ultimatum, and that, unless he yielded to the Chancellor's demand, hostilities would be opened, he would never have confined himself to giving these casual instructions to Schilling. He would have had the Tsar wakened and given him the news over the telephone, or he would have gone to Peterhof first thing in the morning in order to be able to give Pourtalès his answer by noon, since he alone could not take a decision on the issue of peace or war, i.e., on the fate of Russia. On the contrary, not only did he fail to understand the bearing of Pourtalès's communication, but he even went to the length of ruling out the possibility of its having the worst meaning when, in answer to his question whether if Germany were to mobilize it would be the equivalent of war, Pourtalès answered 'that such was not the case but that we should be extraordinarily near to war'. This to his mind afforded still a short breathing space. The above interpretation of the documents differs from the picture retrospectively given by Sazonov in *Fateful Years.* There he claims:

I had been for several days prepared for this step on the part of the Berlin Cabinet; I clearly realized that the cause of peace upon which we had spent endless efforts was lost irretrievably, and that in a few hours the ultimatum would be followed by the last and final step.[1]

This is not at all true. His very words and those of Pourtalès belie it. How can he have been expecting German mobilization for several days when Russian general mobilization had been proclaimed only the previous day and when her partial mobilization had received the implicit assent of Jagow? From time to time Sazonov is tendentious in his reconstruction of events in his book. What he is anxious to prove is that it was not Russian partial or general mobilization which let loose the European war, but the German determination to have war. The truth, as we have seen, is much more complex. Moreover, his memory often betrays him, as, for instance, when he writes:

When the time limit for our capitulation before the Central Powers was drawing to its close, the Austrian Government suddenly expressed its consent to resume negotiations with Russia—a consent it obstinately with-held so long as the negotiations were likely to be of some use.[2]

[1] Sazonov, p. 211.   [2] Sazonov, p. 211.

As we have seen, his interview with Szápáry, at which this request was brought forward, took place before, and not after the ultimatum, to which Sazonov did not capitulate, but which was not understood as implying immediate war either by him or by the Tsar or even by Pourtalès.

A further proof of this is furnished by the events which took place on the morning of 1 August. At 7 a. m. Pourtalès took the step of addressing a letter to Count Fredericks, the influential Minister at the Court of the Tsar, who the previous, day had asked him to call in on him after the audience with the Tsar, offering to do all he could to avoid a war, which he regarded as disastrous, and expressing willingness to convey to his Sovereign any communication which Pourtalès desired to make. In the letter Pourtalès said:

> The situation has become extremely grave and I seek everywhere means to avert a misfortune. For a war would be an immense danger for all the monarchies. I received the order last night to tell M. Sazonov immediately that we are not yet mobilizing, but that if by noon today Russia does not positively state to us that she is stopping her war preparations against our-selves and Austria the order for mobilization will be given today. You no doubt know that what means with us. We cannot hide from ourselves that in that case we are only a finger's breadth from war, a war which neither you nor we desire.[1]

'A finger's breadth' from war, but not actually at war. Had Bethmann written to him, as he did to Schoen and Flotow, that 'mobilization inevitably means war', Pourtalès would have spoken and written differently and his words would have met with a hearing. But as things were, he was not understood any better by Fredericks than by Sazonov and the Tsar. About 2 p. m. Fredericks rang up Pourtalès from Peterhof to read out to him a letter which the Tsar was sending in answer to the one from Wilhelm of 31 July mentioned above.[2] It left St. Petersburg at 2.6 p. m. and, owing to the difference of hour, reached Berlin at 2.5 p. m.

> I received your telegram. Understand you are obliged to mobilize but wish to have some guarantee from you that these measures do not mean war and that we shall continue negotiating for the benefit of our countries and universal peace dear to all our hearts. Our long proved friendship must succeed, with God's help, in avoiding bloodshed. Anxiously, full of confidence await your answer.[3]

As Fredericks received Pourtalès's letter at 10.30 a. m. it is evident that the Tsar, even if not immediately informed by Sazonov of the German intimation to cease mobilization, learnt of it from this letter.

---

[1] DD. III, 539.   [a] DD. III, 480. See p. 37.   [3] DD. III, 546.

His telegram shows that he was aware of the German intention to mobilize, though there had been no mention of it in Wilhelm's telegram. Aware, but not alarmed, and taking the mobilization as a matter of course, under the illusion that negotiation could still continue. Evidence of this comes also from Buchanan, who had an audience of the Tsar at 11 p. m. on 1 August, i.e., after war was declared.

In the course of conversation His Majesty observed that mobilization did not necessarily entail war, and that there had been frequent cases in history where it had been followed by demobilization.[1]

Is it necessary to add more to prove the extent of misunderstanding arising from the fact that the Russian leaders did not know and were not warned that in Germany mobilization and war were the same thing? It was this misunderstanding which caused the German ultimatum not to receive all the attention it deserved, either on the part of the Russians or of Pourtalès himself. In fact, after the expiry of the time limit set for the reply he did not call on Sazonov to receive it and he sent nothing more to Berlin after the short telegram of 1 a. m. on 1 August summarizing his midnight talk with Sazonov.[2] Anxious to work for peace, he probably thought that the Russian reply was made sufficiently plain in his message, and did not want to make Sazonov pronounce a definite 'no', which would have made the situation irretrievable. Indeed, his attitude and that of Sazonov might have borne different fruits if Berlin had been in a different state of mind, i.e., if Moltke's will to war had not been in the ascendant, ruining all the prospects of peace which were on the skyline right up to the last. The very fact that Russia was not taking the ultimatum dead seriously, had it only been understood in Berlin from Pourtalès's telegram, would have enabled the Wilhelmstrasse to give further consideration to Grey's proposal, Goschen's words, and the revealing and alarming English inquiry with reference to Belgium. This might have led Berlin to negotiate further before mobilizing, i.e., going to war. But German diplomatic activity had come to an end. The military were in command and, oblivious to the consequences of their deeds, they swept their country on to defeat.

[1] BD. XI, 490.   [2] DD. III, 536. See p.61.

CHAPTER II

GENERAL MOBILIZATION IN FRANCE

(1) *French anxiety; Poincaré's letter to King George V; Joffre presses for frontier* couverture (*p.* 66). (2) *The first news of Russian general mobilization and the German proclamation of the* Kriegsgefahrzustand (*p.* 70). (3) *Schoen's* démarche *to ascertain French intentions; Viviani's evasive reply* (*p.* 73). (4) *Viviani's telegram to Paléologue of 31 July and the circumstances which gave rise to it* (*p.* 76). (5) *The reasons for French acquiescence in the Russian general mobilization* (*p.* 80). (6) *The assassination of Jaurès on 31 July and the atmosphere in which it took place* (*p.* 85). (7) *Bertie's inquiry as to the French attitude on Belgium; Paléologue's telegram confirming Russian general mobilization* (*p.* 88). (8) *Joffre on the evening of 31 July asks for French mobilization* (*p.* 91). (9) *The Szécsen incident and the Quai d'Orsay's manoeuvres* (*p.* 92). (10) *The French Cabinet decides to order general mobilization* (*p.* 99). (11) *Viviani's manifesto and the thesis that mobilization is not war* (*p.* 105). (12) *The last conversation between Schoen and Viviani on 1 August; Viviani's tactics, and two revealing telegrams from Izvolsky* (*p.* 108).

1. French anxiety; Poincaré's letter to King George V; Joffre presses for frontier couverture.

We have already noted the anxiety which filled the minds of the French leaders during the whole of 31 July when war seemed inevitable while at the same time there was reason to fear that England meant to keep out of it.[1] At 11.25 p. m. on the 30th Paris had received Paléologue's telegram, which had been sent off at 9.15 p. m. and said nothing of the fact that general mobilization had been ordered at St. Petersburg at 5 p. m., merely stating that the Russian Government 'has decided to proceed secretly to the first measures of general mobilization'.[2] This, however, was not the news which caused such great alarm at the Quai d'Orsay, where it was thought that the moves announced by Paléologue were of a different order from a regular general mobilization. Those Frenchmen who accuse Poincaré and Viviani start from the assumption that Paléologue's telegram was the announcement of Russian general mobilization and see in the fact that it produced no strong reaction in the two statesmen a proof of their complicity and will to war. In the opinion of the present writer this accusation is unwarrantable. How could Paris imagine that, if regular general mobilization was ordered in Russia, Paléologue would maintain silence about it and twist the news as he actually did? Hence Poincaré is not wrong in writing:

[1] See Vol. II, pp. 646 9.   [2] See Vol. II, pp, 620-1.

In the information given . . . by M. Paléologue . . . it was only a question of preparatory measures, not in any way of a final and official decision.[1]

In other words, the measures in question were those which Margerie had suggested to Izvolsky, and Messimy to Ignatiev, as being moves which could be made secretly and appeared advisable without having the serious implications of a general mobilization.

The real cause of the French Government's anxiety on 31 July was the telegrams coming in from Berlin and the military preparations in Germany. Joffre overrated their extent both in his own mind and to the Ministers and pressed for authorization to take counter-measures. These in reality were not called for by the needs of the situation and were politically dangerous, but would have been necessary, had there been a real foundation for the alarming news which he took to be true. Joffre was perturbed because on the 30th he had received permission to operate the covering movement by moving troops towards the lines only on foot, not by railway transport, and without calling up reservists.[2] He thought that Germany had gone much farther in the matter of *couverture* and above all had called up reservists by individual notifycation. In the telegram which Viviani sent to Paul Cambon at 12.30 p. m. on the 31st he laid stress on the 'tens of thousands' of German reservists thus called to the colors.[3] The rumor was devoid of foundation. The German parliamentary inquiry, held after the war, made public the German War Minister's dossier containing exact information on the measures taken in July 1914. The recall of men on leave and the return to garrison of the troops on maneuver were ordered only in the night 29-30 July, after these measures had been taken by France and Russia. On the morning of the 30th the Kaiser proposed that the frontier troops should be reinforced by the recall of men on leave, but nothing came of his proposal or of the request from the Metz High Command on the evening of the 30th that *couverture* troops should be dispatched in response to similar measures taken by the French. In any case, secret mobilization by individual call-up was impracticable, and it seems extraordinary that the French General Staff should have given credence to the rumor. The truth is that, just as Berlin exaggerated the extent and the dangers of the measures taken by France, so Paris ascribed to Germany preparations she was not making. Montgelas writes:

Official mobilization, the only mobilization possible in Germany, was decreed at 5 p. m. on 1 August and was not preceded by any secret mobilization. Far from being prepared on 1 August for a large-scale maneuver, the German

[1] Poincaré, IV, p. 445. See Vol. II, pp. 604-6, 621.
[2] See Vol. II, p. 628.
[3] Poincaré, IV, p. 435. See Vol. II, p. 647.

armies did not complete their strategic muster on the western front until 17 August, the 16th day of mobilization. The earlier attack on Liége was carried out by troops on a peace footing, when the companies did not count more than 150–160 rifles.[1]

However, all this was only learnt later. Today, when the truth is more or less known, there is a tendency to underestimate the natural effect on the decisions of the military chiefs produced by the alarmist and often unfounded reports reaching them regarding the enemy's preparations, reports which they were not in a position to verify. This is in reality a point of considerable importance. In France nervousness was intensified by the fear that England was not going to take her stand with France. It was in the panic caused by British 'insular serenity' in the face of what was developing on the Continent that Poincaré obtained Viviani's authorization to address the letter to King George which has been mentioned already[2] and which we must now regard more closely.

The letter laid great stress on the increasing pace of German military preparations while France on the contrary was confining herself to the most essential precautionary measures:

It is, I believe, on the language and attitude of the English Government that the last possibilities of a peaceful solution now depend. We, ourselves, from the beginning of the crisis have recommended to our Allies a moderation from which they have not departed. In accord with the English Government and conformably to Sir Ed. Grey's suggestions, we shall continue to act in the same sense. But if all efforts for conciliation are applied on the same side, and if Germany and Austria can calculate on English abstention, the Austrian demands will remain inflexible, and an accord between her and Russia will become impossible. I am deeply convinced that the more England, France, and Russia at the present moment give a strong impression of unity in their diplomatic action, the more it will still be legitimate to count on peace being preserved.[3]

That France had enjoined moderation on Russia right from the beginning was unfortunately not true, as we have seen already. 'Sazonov must be firm, and we must back him up' had been Poincaré's injunction to Paléologue,[4] and Paléologue had obeyed it with a zeal which had the most disastrous influence on the weak Sazonov. Poincaré himself, while losing no time in appealing directly to King George, took no steps to telegraph to the Tsar urging him not to precipitate matters. The truth is that he was now convinced that a conflict was inevitable. A letter of Bertie's to Grey of 30 July runs:

[1] Montgelas, 'Le 30 Juillet à Berlin et à Petersbourg' (*Évolution,* November 1926).
[2] See Vol. II, p. 648.   [3] Poincaré, IV, pp. 438–40.
[4] Paléologue, I, p. 19.

The Spanish Ambassador [Urrutia] has been here just as the messenger is about to leave for London. He says that the President of the Republic told a friend this morning that he considers war inevitable.[1]

This makes it difficult to escape the impression that the appeal was made to King George not so much because Poincaré believed that a word from Britain could yet save the peace as because he hoped that, in speaking such a word, Britain would involve herself in an undertaking eventually to take the field. Paris seemed to be seconding Grey's efforts for peace. When on the morning of the 31st Viviani received communication from Bertie of the peace formula telegraphed the previous evening by Grey to Buchanan,[2] he, in his turn, with Poincaré's approval, telegraphed to Paléologue:

> Please inform M. Sazonov urgently that the suggestion of Sir E. Grey appears to me to furnish a useful basis for conversations between the Powers, who are equally desirous of working for an honorable arrangement of the Austro-Serbian conflict.[3]

But what value had this recommendation, chiefly intended to please England and only sent off at 5 p. m. on the 31st, when the first flames of the conflagration were already leaping up?

This was certainly the impression gained by Joffre, who writes that when about 2 p. m. on the 31st he learnt of the German ultimatum to Russia of the afternoon of 29 July, he felt it his duty

> to place the Government squarely in face of its responsibilities.[4]

In reality the German message of the 29th was not actually an ultimatum, even if Sazonov regarded it almost as such.[5] The real ultimatum was presented at midnight on the 31st. How and why it was only on the 31st that Joffre received inaccurate news of the German *démarche* of the 29th it is difficult to understand. The fact remains that it caused him to draft a note which he handed to Messimy at 3.30 p. m. on the 31st as Messimy was leaving for the afternoon meeting of the Cabinet. (Another Cabinet meeting had been, held from 9 a. m. till 12 noon but had only dealt with financial measures.) Joffre's note stated:

> If the Germans, under cover of diplomatic conversations, continue to take the . various steps comprised in their plan for mobilization—though without pronouncing that word—it is absolutely necessary for the Government to understand that, starting with this evening, any delay of twenty-four hours in

[1] BD. XI, 320 b.
[2] BD. XI, 309, 342. See Vol. II, p. 635.
[3] DF. 3, XI, 405; LJF 112; CDD., p. 220; Poincaré, IV, p. 461.
[4] Joffre, *Memoirs*, I, p. 125.
[5] DD. II, 342. See Vol. II, pp. 491, 553.

calling up our reservists and issuing orders prescribing covering operations, will have as a result the withdrawal of our concentration points by from ten to twelve miles for each day of delay; in other words, the initial abandonment of just that much of our territory. The Commander-in-Chief must decline to accept this responsibility.[1]

2. *The first news of Russian general mobilization and the German proclamation of the* Kriegsgefahrzustand.

Joffre's note was read to the Cabinet, which gave its approval and at 5.15 p. m. authorized Joffre to send a telegram ordering the necessary movements for providing *couverture,* but not for the time being to call up reserves. According to Poincaré this authorization was given when it became known that Germany had proclaimed the *Kriegsgefahrzustand*[2] Faced with this proclamation

no French Cabinet, I am sure, would have behaved otherwise.[3]

But it is not at all sure that things were quite like that. At 3.30 p. m. the Quai d'Orsay had received an urgent telegram dispatched by Jules Cambon at 2.17 p. m.:

According to a report reaching me, the German Ambassador at St. Petersburg seems to have telegraphed that Russia had just decided on total mobilization in reply to Austrian total mobilization. In these conditions the almost immediate publication is to be expected of the German order for general mobilization.[4]

Then at 4.25 p. m. came another telegram of 3.30 p. m. from J. Cambon:

The Secretary of State [Jagow] has just sent for me; he said that he much regretted to inform me that in face of the total mobilization of the Russian army, Germany, in the interest of the security of the Reich, found herself obliged to take serious precautionary measures. A decision has been taken called 'imminent danger of war' enabling the authorities, if they deem it expedient, to proclaim martial law, to suspend certain public services, and close the frontier. At the same time St. Petersburg is being asked to demobilize, failing which Germany would be obliged to mobilize on her side. Herr von Jagow told me that Herr von Schoen was instructed to inform the French Government of the Berlin Cabinet's decisions and to ask what attitude it thought necessary to adopt. Herr von Jagow has few illusions; he appeared to me deeply moved; he strongly deplored the precipitancy of Russia which renders useless the German Kaiser's mediation, that, according to him, had been asked for by the Russian Tsar and that Austria

[1] Joffre, I, p. 125.
[2] Poincaré, IV, p. 458.
[3] Gerin, p. 118.
[4] DF. 3. XI, 402; Poincaré, IV, pp. 445-6. This telegram does not appear in the *Yellow Book.*

was preparing to accept. On my part, I deplored the attitude taken up by Austria since the beginning of the crisis.[1]

This was the first document from which Paris learnt of the proclamation of the *Kriegsgefahrzustand*. But as it arrived at 4.25 p. m. and had first to be decoded, it hardly seems possible for it to have been read at the Élysée in time to influence the decision taken at the Cabinet meeting to authorize measures *couverture*. This decision was taken, as we have seen, at 5.15 p. m., after the reading of Joffre's note and a certain amount of discussion.[2] The first telegram, itself sufficiently disquieting, may perfectly well have been before the Ministers during the Cabinet meeting. But one can only say that, if they had it before them, they would have derived the impression from it that war was imminent and would therefore have agreed to Joffre's other demand, i.e., that there should be a call-up of reservists. They would also have asked Paléologue for the explanation in regard to Russian general mobilization which they only demanded later, after Schoen had made his *démarche*. The impression left by a perusal of *L'Union Sacrée* is that Poincaré often recasts the story of events to fit his own theses. For instance, in reproducing those two telegrams of Jules Cambon's, Poincaré adds a third in which Cambon says:

> The Russian Ambassador, to whom Herr von Jagow made the same communication as to me, told me that he had no information from St. Petersburg leading him to believe in the total mobilization of Russia.[3]

Poincaré comments:

> In the face of so many obscurities and contradictions, M. Viviani and I felt surprised at having still received nothing from St. Petersburg on the

---

[1] DF. 3. XI, 403; Poincaré, IV, pp. 446-7. In LJF. 116 (CDD., p. 222) the latter part of the telegram, beginning with 'Herr von Jagow has few illusions', is omitted.

[2] Izvolsky also telegraphed St. Petersburg that the Council of Ministers met after Jules Cambon's second telegram had been received *{Int. Bez.* i. V, 354) and Messimy told Recouly: 'The Council of Ministers, given much more freedom by the publication of the *Kriegsgefahrzustand,* accords full satisfaction to General Joffre' (Recouly, p. 79). As regards Izvolsky it is easy to prove that his information was incorrect. The Cabinet meeting, as Messimy told Recouly, lasted from 4 to 6.30 p. m. (Recouly, p. 80), and this is corroborated by Joffre, who writes that he gave his note to Messimy at 3.30 p. m. 'just as he was leaving for the Cabinet meeting' (Joffre, I, p. 125). It is true that further on Joffre contradicts himself, giving the hour of the Cabinet meeting as 5 p. m. But he then adds that the note received Cabinet approval at 5.15 p. m. (Joffre, I, p. 126), which would have given no time for the Ministers to read and discuss it. In any case, even if the Cabinet had met only at 5 p. m., it could not have been because of a telegram of considerable length arriving in cipher at 4.25 p. m. Messimy's memory was no longer quite clear about these events when he told the story to Recouly. What he actually did say was: 'In the afternoon of the 31st Schoen came to acquaint M. Viviani that the Kaiser had ordered the *Kriegsgefahrzustand*. Almost at the same hour General Joffre handed me a note', etc. (Recouly, p. 78), the truth being that the note was handed him at 3.30 p. m. and the conversation between Schoen and Viviani took place at 7 p. m. after the Cabinet meeting had ended.

[3] DF. 3. XI, 434.

subject of the *Ukaze* which was said to have been issued that morning, and we asked one another which was telling the truth, the German Ambassador in Russia, or the Russian Ambassador in Germany.[1]

While it is evident that Poincaré finds it useful to maintain that he did not at once give credence to the news of Russian general mobilization, it must be noted not only that Sverbeev did not deny the mobilization, merely expressing doubt on the ground that he had not been informed of it, but also that Jules Cambon's third telegram arrived at 8.45 p. m. after Schoen had made his *démarche,* which was too serious to be based on unconfirmed news, and, above all, that at 8.30 p. m. there had come the telegram from Paléologue announcing at last that Russia had ordered general mobilization, news of which also reached Paris through *Havas* telegrams and those of other newspapers. Poincaré and Viviani cannot, therefore, have exchanged the remarks recorded by Poincaré.

The probabilities are that the first two Cambon telegrams, the second of which intimates that Russian general mobilization was responsible for the breaking off of negotiations and the imminent approach of war, were never laid before the Cabinet meeting, where they might have given rise to undesirable reactions and discussions. For instance, since J. Cambon foreshadowed Schoen's impending *démarche,* the Cabinet would most likely have laid down the lines on which Viviani was to act. This was not done. In actual fact the decisions were taken entirely by Poincaré and Viviani. They probably received the two telegrams during or at the end of the Cabinet meeting, since, as we shall soon see, they discussed them together before Viviani's return to the Quai d'Orsay.[2]

Were they in any doubt whether the news of Russian general mobilization was true? Had not even the War Ministry received a telegram from the Military Attaché, General Laguiche, telling the truth about what had happened? He, at least, cannot have been ignorant of the fact that Russia was mobilizing on the 30th. Must one, therefore, assume that he, too, was in league with Paléologue to give his Government tendentious information and hide from it news of the utmost gravity? One is led to incline to this hypothesis. That the Quai d'Orsay on the afternoon of the 31st did not know of St. Petersburg's having ordered general mobilization (a different matter from the first secret measures of general mobilization mentioned by Paléologue the previous evening[3]) can be deduced from a telegram in which Izvolsky tells Sazonov of the message from Jules Cambon announcing the proclamation in Germany of the *Kriegsgefahrzustand* in consequence of Russian general mobilization, and then goes on to say:

---

[1] Poincaré, IV, p. 447.   [2] See pp. 77-8.   [3] See Vol. II, p. 620.

To the above communication Margerie added that France will immediately respond to a mobilization of the German army by mobilizing her armed forces. It is worthy of note that a Havas Agency telegram coming in from Berlin speaks also of a 'general mobilization' of the Russian army, which gives rise to the thought that Germany for some purpose or other intends prematurely to provoke a corresponding measure on the part of France.[1]

This produces the impression that Margerie would never have spoken thus to Izvolsky (who, in turn, would have written differently to St. Petersburg) if Paris had known of the proclamation of general mobilization in Russia. The only singular thing is that, on learning of Jules Cambon's two telegrams, the Quai d'Orsay did not at once demand immediate explanations from Paléologue before Schoen made his appearance to ask, as foreshadowed by Jules Cambon, what were France's intentions in the event of a conflict. To this point we shall shortly return.[2] For the moment we must turn our attention to Schoen's *démarche.*

3. *Schoen's* démarche *to ascertain French intentions; Viviani's evasive reply.*

Before Schoen received the telegram of instructions to inform the French Government of the ultimatum sent to Russia and tell them that for Germany 'mobilization inevitably means war', asking for a reply within eighteen hours 'whether, in a war between Germany and Russia, France would remain neutral',[3] he had displayed a certain amount of optimism and had telegraphed to Berlin at 12.5 p. m. on the 31st:

Public opinion today less excited thanks to efforts of Government. Hope revived of success of negotiations in progress. Suspicions that we are out for war are subsiding. In the event of peace not being maintained a mood of resigned determination.[4]

On receiving the Chancellor's telegram with the ultimatum, Schoen called at the Quai d'Orsay about 7 p. m., and after executing his instructions, reported to Berlin by a telegram which was dispatched in cipher from Paris at 8.17 p. m. It was markedly laconic:

Prime Minister says he has no news of Russian general mobilization but only of precautionary measures. He will therefore still not entirely give up hope of avoiding the worst. He promised answer to question about neutrality by tomorrow 1 o'clock at the latest.[5]

On Schoen's *démarche* the *French Diplomatic Documents* give only the following short note penciled by Berthelot on 31 July, with three additions in ink written afterwards and here printed in italics:

---

[1] *Int. Bez* i. V, 354.
[3] DD. III, 491. See pp. 40-1.
[2] See p. 77
[4] DD. III, 483.
[5] DD. III, 528.

Christian Jordan sent by German Ambassador to ask the audience in which Baron Schoen announced the decree of 'Kriegszustand' (state of war) promulgated about 3 p. m. at Berlin in answer to Russian mobilization. German Ambassador came at 6 p. m. to announce that the German Government had given the Russian Government 12 hours to demobilize *on the two frontiers, Austrian and German* (but he did not know at what hour the time limit started) (*from midnight to noon on 1 August*).

To the inquiry what the Government of the Republic would do *in a Russo-German conflict* M. Viviani gave no answer. Baron Schoen having asked when he could give him an answer, the Prime Minister replied: 'Tomorrow at 1 o'clock.' (He proposes at that moment to reply that the Government of the Republic will have regard to its own interests.[1])

A more detailed version of the conversation is given by Poincaré based, perhaps, on things that Viviani told him. Viviani, according to this account, had no information of Russian general mobilization either from Paléologue or from Izvolsky and thought that the proclamation of the *Kriegsgefahrzustand* did not necessarily mean the end of the negotiations then in progress, J. Cambon's telegram gave Jagow as saying only:

If Russia does not demobilize, we ourselves shall mobilize.

He did not say:

If Russia does not demobilize we shall declare war on her.[2]

Baron von Schoen, moreover, no more than Herr von Jagow, announced Germany's intention to declare war on Russia, should she fail to demobilize. He simply put forward such a war as an ultimate possibility and asked M. Viviani what France would do in such a case. Would she maintain neutrality? M. Viviani had anticipated the question. He had discussed it with me. We both thought that, if it were put, prudence would require that there should not be the immediate reply that France would fulfill her duty as an ally. Every minute in which international differences were not emphasized could be a minute gained for peace. Therefore M. Viviani evaded the question and simply told Herr von Schoen: 'Let me still hope that extreme decisions will be avoided and permit me to take time to reflect.' Herr von Schoen said he would come for the answer on the morrow at the beginning of the afternoon. It was a polite and barely veiled ultimatum.[3]

Here we have Poincaré putting forward an assertion which, as will be shown later, is of far-reaching significance.

If the facts were as he relates, it would have to be recognized that Schoen did not fully carry out his instructions to warn France that a Russian refusal to demobilize would mean war. It would imply that, in order not to aggravate the situation, Schoen left the French Government under a misapprehension as to the nature and significance of the

---

[1] DF. 3. XI, 417.   [2] Poincaré, IV, p. 447.
[2] Poincaré, IV, pp. 448–9.

communication he was making, and thus gave it no inducement to take the bold action at St. Petersburg which would have been necessary to avert the conflict, and which, given a knowledge of the true facts, it might well have decided to take. But can one believe that, having received a direct order to present an ultimatum to France, with a demand for the handing over of two French forts in the event of an affirmative reply and with a time, limit of eighteen hours for that reply, Schoen can have willfully evaded so momentous a task by suppressing the most important and decisive part of the communication which he had to make?

Poincaré goes on to the length of saying:

> In fact, Baron Schoen had not told M. Viviani all. He thought the mission which he had received from Berlin so brutal that he did not entirely carry it out, and he did not utter to the Prime Minister the fundamental sentence of the instructions issued to him: 'mobilization inevitably means war'.[1]
> M. Viviani could not guess what the Ambassador had not dared to tell him.[2]

Schoen, however, vigorously denied this accusation. Questioned by the *Berliner Monatshefte* he rebutted Poincaré's statement as follows:

> In order to induce the French Government to declare its attitude it was imperative to acquaint it unreservedly and in full detail with the extremely tense situation which had forced this unusual step upon us. Such was my task, and I am convinced that I fulfilled it in the most conscientious manner. It is not surprising if today, after over eighteen years, I am, in spite of my good memory, not able to recall every word spoken at the interview, but I am certain that I did not underemphasize or slur over any point of importance. I had the less reason to avoid uttering a serious warning about the inevitability of war in that I regarded our *démarche* less as a warlike threat to France—Poincaré speaks of 'intimidation'—than as a last urgent appeal to co-operate in saving the peace that was in dire peril.[3]

This statement is so cogent and convincing that it leaves no room for doubt. However, there is a point here which must not escape attention. Schoen had been ordered to warn Paris that German 'mobilization inevitably means war', and this order he carried out. But there is a shade of meaning which needs to be made clear. The Chancellor's phrase did not fully explain the true German position. It might be taken to mean that at the moment of ordering mobilization the German Government would declare war by an act of its own will because it judged this to be the right thing to do. In reality this was not so. The true fact was that, independently of the will of the German Government and as a consequence of the Schlieffen plan, the order for mobilization

---

[1] Poincaré, IV, p. 450.   [2] Poincaré, IV, p. 452.
[3] Georges Demartial, *Un point d'interrogation,* KSF. 1932, pp. 1139-40.

implied the immediate commencement of military operations, in short, the opening of hostilities. This automatic sequence left no room for second thoughts and was thus infinitely more serious. And as such it would have appeared to the French Government, had it known the facts. But Schoen was unable to enlighten it because he, like Pourtalès and Tirpitz, was ignorant of this himself. He only said what he knew, namely, that if Germany mobilized she went to war. The warning was less effective than it would have been had it been known that the German mobilization plan made war inevitable. However, it was sufficiently serious to rule out all hesitation. Viviani cannot but have heeded it and reported it to Poincaré. In fact, Poincaré has himself disproved his own story by relating that at the end of the interview:

> The Ambassador . . . said to M. Viviani: 'If I am obliged to leave Paris, I count on your being good enough to facilitate my departure. . . . Will you kindly present my respects to the President of the Republic and hand me my passports.'

Viviani courteously protested:

> M. de Pourtalès is still at his post in St. Petersburg, the Austrian Ambassador is here. Why give the signal of departure, and without orders shoulder such a responsibility? . . . Margerie, who was present at the interview, added: 'You have given proof of moderation all through your career, you cannot end it in bloodshed.' M. de Schoen bowed and, in leaving, repeated that he would return next day, 1 August, for the answer to his question.[1]

Schoen's request for his passports before ever receiving an answer, his cold and unbending attitude, could only mean that, but for a miracle, all was at an end. Berlin demanded to know France's intentions within eighteen hours because Germany would go to war with Russia if Russia did not demobilize, as she was hardly likely to do.

4. Viviani's telegram to Paléologue of 31 July and the circumstances which gave rise to it.

It may be objected that if Schoen had spoken clearly, Viviani, in the telegram he sent to Paléologue after the interview, would have reproduced what Poincaré rightly calls the 'fundamental sentence' of the Ambassador's message, that German 'mobilization inevitably means war'. But in fact there is no word of this, nor of the intimation that war would break out if Russia did not consent to demobilize. But the objection falls to the ground if it can be proved that Viviani's silence was intentional, that the telegram was worded in view of tactical considerations which we shall examine later after having read the text itself.

[1] Poincaré, IV pp. 449-50.

Drafted by Margerie and signed by Viviani, it runs (the phrases in brackets are omitted from the *Yellow Book*):

The German Government (on the ground that the Russian Government has ordered the *total* mobilization of its land and sea forces) decided at midday to take all military measures implied by the state called 'state of danger of war'. In communicating this decision to me at 7 o'clock this evening, Baron von Schoen added that the Government required at the same time that Russia should demobilize. If the Russian Government has not given a satisfactory reply within twelve hours Germany will mobilize in her turn.

I replied to the German Ambassador that I had no information at all about an alleged total mobilization of the Russian army and navy which the German Government invoked as the reason for the new military measures which they are taking today.

Baron von Schoen finally asked me, in the name of his Government, what the attitude of France would be in case of war between Germany and Russia. (I did not give him a reply.) He told me that he would come for my reply tomorrow, Saturday, at one o'clock.

I have no intention of making any statement to him on this subject, and I shall confine myself to telling him that France will have regard to her interests. The Government of the Republic need not, indeed, give any account of her intentions except to her ally.

I ask you to inform M. Sazonov of this immediately (and to report to me, as a matter of urgency, as to the reality of the alleged general mobilization in Russia). As I have already told you, I do not doubt that the Imperial Government, in the overruling interests of peace, will on its side avoid anything which might open up the crisis.[1]

First of all, one remark. Having learnt from Jules Cambon's telegram of 3.30 p. m., as well as through the *Havas* agency, to say nothing of telegrams from newspaper correspondents, that St. Petersburg had ordered general mobilization, no notice of which had been sent by Paléologue, Viviani might have been expected to have telegraphed him at once as a matter of urgency, demanding information and explanations, particularly if he felt doubts about the matter. It is something that the high officials at the Quai d'Orsay could have done even without awaiting Viviani's return from the afternoon meeting of the Cabinet. They did no such thing, and the fact is suspicious.

Another remark. To the sentence in Viviani's telegram: 'I shall confine myself to telling him that France will have regard to her interests', Poincaré appends the annotation: 'It was the formula agreed between Viviani and myself.'[2] And before that he had written: 'Viviani

---

[1] DF. 3. XI, 438; LJF. 117; CDD., pp. 222-3; Poincaré, IV, pp. 452 3. The last phrase in the *Yellow Book* runs: 'that might render inevitable or precipitate the crisis'
[2] Poincaré, IV, p. 453.

had anticipated the question and had spoken with me about it.'[1] As has been said, the inference is that, after J. Cambon's warning of the impending *démarche* by Schoen, Viviani took counsel with Poincaré on what was to be done.[2] Obviously he would not have sent Paléologue the telegram he actually did send immediately after Schoen had left him without submitting it to Poincaré unless there had been previous agreement between the two, since Viviani never acted otherwise than with Poincaré's approval. It will be remembered that in the night of 30 July, when Izvolsky brought him news of a telegram from Sazonov of much less importance than the telegram from Bethmann which Schoen had now communicated to him, Viviani went and wakened Poincaré to get his opinion and submit the draft reply for his approval.[3]

What the nature was of the agreement reached between Poincaré and Viviani under the imminence of the German *démarche* cannot, of course, exactly be known. One can only attempt to reconstruct it by inference from their actions. These show:

(1) That no request for explanations was addressed to St. Petersburg before Schoen called to carry out his instructions, therefore not before about 8 p. m., though the Russian mobilization had been known since 3.30 p. m.

(2) That the German Ambassador's message was received with expressions of extreme surprise and he was told that nothing was known of the 'alleged' Russian total mobilization, whereas information of it had come in from several sources and it was regarded as a next step after Paléologue's intimation of the previous evening that the Russian Government had decided 'to proceed secretly to the first measures of general mobilization'.[4]

[1] Poincaré, IV, p. 449.

[2] The possibility cannot be ruled out that Messimy, who was definitely in favor of war, was also present at this consultation. The conjecture is made by Fabre-Luce in the review *Europe* (15 August 1926): 'In 1914, the crowning decision in regard to approval of Russian general mobilization was taken outside the Cabinet at a late night meeting attended only by Viviani and Messimy in addition to him (Poincaré).' Poincaré quotes this to deny it (IV, p. 454). If not a case of actual approval, it was a case of acquiescence. But the decision to acquiesce must have been taken not at a late night meeting after the third Cabinet meeting of the day, held at 9 p. m., but after the afternoon meeting, i.e., before Viviani had the talk with Schoen and sent Paléologue the telegram mentioned above (DF. 3. XI, 438). Messimy's attitude is revealed in an incident related by him to Recouly after the war: 'A disagreement arose in the Cabinet over the exodus of Austrians and Germans who were hastily leaving the country by the trainload. I proposed to detain them on some pretext or other. . . . I estimate that between 100,000 and 150,000 enemy subjects, at least half or a third of them of military age, got away. . . . Unfortunately I and Abel Ferry were alone in taking this line. All the other Ministers, including the Head of the State, ranged themselves against us. They protested against the measure as being brutal, unworthy, barbarous' (Recouly, pp. 80-1; see also, Messimy, *Mes Souvenirs* (Paris, 1937), p. 143).

[3] See Vol. II, pp. 601-3,

[4] See Vol. II, p. 620.

(3) That the Idea of Schoen's asking for his passports gave rise to protests, as if it were not obvious and as if he had not in fact said that the anticipated refusal of Russia to mobilize would lead to war.

(4) That an inquiry for information was then addressed to Paléologue by telegram manifesting ignorance of the decisions taken by St. Petersburg and telling him nothing of the warning uttered by Schoen that for Germany to mobilize was to go to war.

(5) Finally, that this telegram, expressing confidence that 'in the overruling interest of peace' Russia, on her part, 'would avoid anything which might open up the crisis', i.e., general mobilization, was making a feint of not believing in the reality of the Russian mobilization. In view of the facts known to us and the nature of Schoen's communication to Viviani, this whole method of procedure gives the impression of lacking in straightforwardness, and it is not difficult to discern the motives underlying it.[1]

By not omitting that Schoen had carried out the most essential part of his instructions, i.e., had said: *'If we mobilize there will inevitably be war'*; or in no less exact terms: *'If we mobilize, we shall attack immediately'*[2]; by putting on an appearance of being ignorant and incredulous of the fact that Russia had mobilized, not only against Austria but also against Germany; by professing to be sure that St. Petersburg would avoid anything which might open up the crisis, i.e., general mobilization, it became possible to refrain from reacting in any way to this rash and dangerous step on the part of the Russian Government and to be aware of it without saying so, feigning to regard the situation not as catastrophic, but as allowing negotiations to continue even

---

[1] August Bach writes: 'When the German Ambassador called at the Quai d'Orsay at 7 p. m. on 31 July, Viviani was already informed of the order for Russian general mobilization by (1) Paléologue's telegram of the evening of 30 July (LJF. 102; CDD. p. 211); J. Cambon's telegram from Berlin of the afternoon of 31 July (LJF. 116; CDD. p. 222); a Havas Agency report from Berlin of the afternoon of 31 July. . . . The circumstance that after the German Ambassador's call Viviani urgently requested Paléologue to apprize him of the truth of the alleged Russian mobilization does not do away with the fact that his behavior to Schoen was anything but straightforward (LJF. 117). Strangely enough, the compilers of the *Yellow Book* have omitted this inquiry of Viviani's from his telegram to Paléologue. This is all the more incomprehensible in that its publication would have furnished an explanation of Viviani's alleged ignorance.' (A. Bach, *Die französische Regierung und die russische Mobilmachung 1914*, KSF., August 1923, pp. 32–3). The actual facts are that no such telegram was sent by Viviani to Paléologue; the request for information 'as a matter of urgency as to the reality of the alleged general mobilization in Russia' was contained in the telegram (quoted on p. 77 above) and the sentence in question was omitted from No. 117 of the *Yellow Book*. Taken in conjunction with the omission, in the first sentence of this dispatch, of the words 'on the ground that the Russian Government has ordered the *total* mobilization of its land and sea forces', this further omission shows the embarrassment felt by the compilers of the *Yellow Book* about repeating the statement that on the evening of the 31st the French Government still did not believe the news of Russian general mobilization which converged on Paris from too many different sources not to be treated as authentic.

[2] Gerin, p. 134.

though Germany should mobilize. As Poincaré himself writes:

> He [Jagow] would have exercised an unquestionable right in replying to a general mobilization by a general mobilization and, as Nicholas II asked of Wilhelm II, negotiations could have continued. Unfortunately this is not what Berlin wanted.[1]

It is quite true that Berlin refused to negotiate unless Russia demobilized; but Poincaré and Viviani knew this, because Schoen had told them so and because it was obvious from the whole situation.

5. The reasons for French acquiescence in the Russian general mobilization.

Why did Paris accept the *fait accompli* of Russian general mobilization which was a step towards war, had been deprecated the previous day, and was a breach of the terms of the Dual Alliance? Let it be noted that Viviani's telegram to Paléologue of the 31st was still less firm in tone than the already none too forceful telegram dispatched on the morning of the 30th. On the 30th he had sent Sazonov the message that

> it would be opportune that in the precautionary and defensive measures to which Russia believes herself obliged to resort, she should not immediately proceed to any measure which might offer Germany a pretext for a total or partial mobilization of her forces.[2]

In the later telegram not even as much as that! Only a vague and fatuous phrase which meant nothing at all. Why this lowered key at the very moment when it was urgent not to give Germany a pretext? Had there been a genuine determination to stop such a plunge and save the peace, no difficulty would have been encountered in finding the right words. That very day Poincaré had sought and obtained authorization from the Cabinet to send a letter to King George asking for English support. He might equally well have obtained similar authorization to telegraph to the Tsar saying that the general mobilization of the Russian armed forces, directed, as it would be, not only against Austria, but also against Germany, was an infringement of the alliance and might have the most disastrous consequences in making the Russian Empire appear as the aggressor and thus giving England every right to remain neutral, while bringing about Italian intervention on the side of the Central Powers, and that, therefore, if unfortunately the order for mobilization had already been issued, it must be revoked in the supreme interests of their two countries. Nothing of this kind entered the head of the President of the Republic, who held the virtual

---

[1] Poincaré, IV, pp. 447-8.   [2] See Vol. II, pp. 603-4.

control of French foreign policy. Was he, in his heart of hearts, bent on war? In a speech in the French Chamber on 6 July 1922 Poincaré drew attention to an article published a few months previously by Steeg, who had been Minister of the Interior in Poincaré's Ministry in 1912. The article quoted the following words uttered by Poincaré at a Cabinet meeting in 1912:

> Even though I were sure in advance that a war would bring us victory, I would never take the responsibility of letting it be declared.[1]

It is, however, one thing to declare war and quite another to accept war in favorable conditions. The man who recoiled from declaring war did not quite conceal his real thoughts when, in reply to one of Gerin's questions, he confessed in 1930:

> We [the men of Poincaré's generation] said to ourselves: 'Who knows? A day will come perhaps when Europe in time of peace will undertake a general settlement of the questions which divide her and where we may hope to recover what was taken from us in war. Perhaps also, unfortunately, there will come a day when the German Empire, more and more infected by megalomania, will take it into its head to attack us. Let us remain strong. Let us, if possible, have allies. If ever war is declared on us, let us fight it out ('soutenons-la') to victory and let us restore French unity.'[2]

The first of these eventualities was completely out of the question, but the second was now offering itself to Poincaré in a way he could never have dreamt of. Here was a crisis brought about by the Central Powers. If war broke out, it was manifestly a war provoked by them. This fact would in itself cause England to range herself on the side of France and Russia, and would oblige Italy to declare her neutrality, a set of circumstances which gave hope of a decisive victory. This prospect of victory did not escape the notice of certain currents of French public opinion. On the morning of 1 August 1914, the *Matin* appeared with an article containing the following passage:

---

[1] Gerin, p. 71.

[2] Gerin, p. 176. In that same speech in the Chamber of 6 July 1922 Poincaré recalled having also said at a banquet in 1912: 'That from so much honest effort to preserve peace a war could result— and what a war! the most terrible which could ever descend upon the world—would be something in defiance of all common sense, all civilization, all humanity.' And he went on to reaffirm: 'The words I used in 1912, which have been reproduced by M. Steeg, exactly expressed my deepest conviction: never, never would I have been willing to take the responsibility of a war even if, I repeat, I had been sure of victory. But if I was determined to do everything to avoid this war, I was no less determined to do everything in order that, if it broke out in spite of all our endeavors for peace, it should end in victory and the liberation of Alsace-Lorraine. It is this double thought—whatever people may say, there is nothing self-contradictory about it—which for thirty-five years has inspired my whole political life.' In theory these two ideas were, it is true, not incompatible, but to be guided by them was like walking on a tight-rope above an abyss, a superhuman effort would be needful to maintain the balance between them, and the slightest false movement would lead to catastrophe.

We well know that never has war offered itself under aspects more favorable to us. When Austria has thrown her best troops against the Near East, when Russia has just built up her army anew, when the three-years term of service has just come into full force in France, when Germany will have to bear almost alone the brunt of the attack from the *Entente* armies and navies, in truth if we were inclined to war, if we were not deeply attached to the cause of civilization and peace, would we not feel the strong temptation of war? Nevertheless it is not for this war that we shall be held responsible by posterity. If it comes, we shall meet it with high hopes. We are convinced that it will bring us the reparations which are our due (*les réparations du Droit*).[1]

This was all perfectly true. But now occurred a hitch. The Russian general mobilization was threatening to reverse the situation to the detriment of the Dual Alliance in the eyes of England and of world opinion. By mobilizing not only against Austria but also against Germany, Russia was making herself appear to be in the wrong. In a note to a report of 10 August 1892, General Boisdeffre, then Chief of General Staff, had written:

To carry out a general mobilization against Austria and Italy alone (*contre l'Autriche et l'Italie seules*) is to assume the role of an aggressor in Europe and to create a difficult situation for us in regard to the neutrals. On the other hand, by waiting, while at the same time taking precautions, for it to be Germany who mobilizes, it is she who will play the aggressor role with all its drawbacks, while Russia and France will, right to the end, have shown their desire to preserve peace and affirmed their purely defensive intentions.

Also in the event of Italy's attacking France, the latter, to avoid the role of an aggressor, would confine herself to mobilizing the single regions strictly necessary to contain her.

It would seem that it would be advantageous likewise for Russia to act in the same way in regard to Austria, all the more so since her mobilization is relatively slow and since this waiting attitude would enable her to get forward with it.[2]

Now if this held good when it was a question of resisting attack by Austria, it was still more pertinent when the attack was being made, not by Austria on Russia, but by Russia on Austria. And if this was the way France reasoned in 1892, still more should it have been the way she reasoned in 1914 when Russia, taking the role of an aggressor, was rendering it much more difficult for the English Government to persuade Parliament and public opinion of the necessity for the country to take its stand with Russia and France in the resultant war.

---

[1] *Évolution*, October 1933, p. 494. Poincaré's enemies record a similar thought expressed by him to Senator Trystram on landing at Dunkirk on 29 July in reply to a question whether he thought that war could be avoided. 'It would be a great pity', answered M. Poincaré. 'We should never again find conditions better.' (A. Charpentier, *Les responsabilités de M. Poincaré, Évolution*, 15 April 1926, p. 57.)

[2] A.F.-R., p. 68.

What could be done to remedy matters? Ask Russia to admit her mistake and revoke the mobilization order? But how could France's ally be expected to withdraw her rash move at the cost of a humiliation still more galling than that of 1909 when, moreover, in refusing to yield, she had been acting on the advice of Poincaré himself, and after his departure on that of his representative, Paléologue? What had the latter been saying and doing during the preceding days? The statement attributed to him in Sazonov's telegram of 29 July showed that Paléologue had irreparably committed himself to promising unconditional support from France.[1] There was no way out. Anything rather than isolation and the ruin of France. In replying at question time on 16 July 1922 to the accusation leveled at him by Léon Blum of not having warned Russia in 1912 that, if she provoked a European war over Serbia, France could not recognize the *casus foederis,* Poincaré said:

I was not prepared to say I would desert Russia because I know what would have happened: the alliance would have definitely broken up. One day or other Germany, after attacking Russia, would have attacked France and at the beginning we should have stood alone.[2]

Poincaré must be blamed for his previous mistakes but not for this line of reasoning. Its correctness is not disputed even by one of the stoutest champions of German innocence, Montgelas. In an article devoted to a scrutiny of Poincaré's defense, in *L'Union Sacrée,* of his own and the French Government's handling of the crisis of July 1914, Montgelas writes:

As a result of its unpardonable silence on Russian war preparations, of its unpardonable silence on the Russian mobilization against Austria, and of Messimy's unpardonable advice [to Ignatiev] on the evening of 30 July, the French Government had put itself in a disastrous position. The Russian decision [for general mobilization] forced it to choose between peace and war. A decision for peace would have necessitated a condemnation of the Russian measures and would thus probably have led to the collapse of the Franco-Russian alliance on which French policy had been based for twenty-four years. A decision for war involved deceiving the French people, the Allies and, as far as possible, the neutral nations, in regard to the true facts.[3]

[1] *Int. Bez.* i. V, 221. See Vol. II. pp. 556, 601-2.
[2] Gerin, pp. 15-7.
[3] Max Montgelas, *Das Plaidoyer Poincaré,* KSF., February 1928, p. 159. If Montgelas is fair-minded in admitting that this was France's position, Jagow is otherwise in writing: 'Could not the President of the French Republic—if he was as pacific as he says he was and the treaty only bound him in respect of an (of course spontaneous) act of aggression— declare himself for neutrality? The war brought on by Russia would have been localized and for France peace would have been preserved.' From the German point of view this is a convenient argument. From the European point of view it is easy to reply that the best way to avoid the crisis was for Austria not to declare war on Serbia and to bring her case before the tribunal of the Powers, Jagow, however, ignores this and goes on to say: 'How little we desired to be drawn into a war with France is shown by our offer in London on

The French Government's choice of the latter decision will be discussed fully farther on. Here it is necessary to add at once what Montgelas passes over in silence, namely, that the German ultimatum to St. Petersburg and Paris, which was the forerunner of the German declaration of war on the Dual Alliance Powers, put good cards into the hands of France and Russia and to a certain extent mitigated the evil effects of Russia's false step. Now it would be the German Government which would play the part of the aggressor if, having urged Austria to send Serbia an ultimatum, declare war on her and reject all mediation, it then went to war with France and Russia simply because they both mobilized. As Poincaré says, Germany was acting within her rights in mobilizing, but not in going to war. (And in the eyes of the world—not, be it noted, through any guile on the part of France—the Central Powers, and especially Germany, at once stood branded as the aggressors.) Hence the French Government need only let things take their course for Germany to appear as the wrong-doer. Simply by being cautious it could avoid all risk of being blamed if the war went badly, could appear innocent in the eyes of the nation, avoid alienating England and causing embarrassment to Italy. It would be anything but cautious if in an official document which might someday come to light the French Government acknowledged that, in contravention of the treaty of alliance, Russia had taken the step of mobilizing without the previous consent of France and if the Government had not at the same time in the same document forcefully demanded the withdrawal of the measure as leading to catastrophe. If it was no longer possible or desirable to make such a demand, the rejection of which would have entailed a refusal by France to recognize the *casus foederis,* the only course left open to the French Government was to feign ignorance, draft as colorless a document as possible, suitable to be shown at the moment to the English and also to future generations, and of such a nature as to have no influence on the course of events; in short, tacitly to accept the fact of Russian mobilization without saying so.

The thought that any other course of action would have no better success in persuading Russia to draw back, while it would undoubtedly lead to the collapse of the alliance, was certainly the factor which led Viviani, influenced as he was by Poincaré, to take the line he did of not sending an *aut-aut* to St. Petersburg, of acquiescing in the *fait accompli* of the mobilization and signing the telegram submitted to him by

1 August that, if France would remain neutral, we would abstain from all attack on her and employ our troops elsewhere' (Gottlieb von Jagow, *Herr Poincaré,* KSF., July 1930, pp. 601-11). But before this last-minute offer Germany had, on 31 July, requested France to clarify her intentions by agreeing that, should she pledge herself to remain neutral, she would hand over the fortresses of Toul and Verdun as a guarantee. This was equivalent to rendering it impossible for France to declare herself neutral. Moreover, even the offer of 1 August was made by Wilhelm in complete bad faith, as will be shown farther on.

Margerie. Between 30 and 31 July, under the pressure of the pro-war movement which had gained the upper hand in Paris and overridden any will to resist on the part of the pacifist elements, Viviani and his colleagues resigned themselves more or less willingly to the idea of war and *révanche,* and gave up all attempt to prevent it. What had taken place on 30 July in Berlin when the Chancellor had yielded to the will of the military authorities, now in other circumstances took place in Paris, where the President of the Republic, inspired by the ideas and feelings already described, held the reins of authority. And just as in Berlin, all efforts were concentrated on casting the blame for the war on Russia in order that England might be kept neutral, so in Paris the dominating idea was, not to restrain Russia, but to act in such a manner that Germany would open hostilities, so that England would range herself with France and Russia, the victims of attack. This is confirmed by a telegram of the evening of 31 July sent by Izvolsky to Sazonov. After reporting Schoen's call on Viviani, Izvolsky goes on to say:

> Margerie, who has just given me the above particulars, said that Viviani will probably not give the Ambassador an answer tomorrow either. He regards the German action as a trick to put the blame for the declaration of war on France.[1]

At 1 a. m. on 1 August Izvolsky again telegraphed to St. Petersburg:

> The War Minister, who assures me in solemn, heart-felt tones of the Government's firm resolve to fight, begged me to confirm the hope of the French General Staff that all our efforts will be directed against Germany and that Austria will be regarded as a negligible quantity.[2]

In just the same way, Germany on 31 July begged Austria to regard Serbia as a negligible quantity and throw the weight of her attack against Russia.[3]

6. The assassination of Jaurès on 31 July and the atmosphere in which it took place.

Jean Jaurès, a stormy petrel in French political life in the decades preceding the war, was an idealist who was one of the most courageous champions of Dreyfus, a Socialist who sought to reconcile Marxism with the French Socialist tradition based on moral aspirations and not tied to the mechanical certitude of a proletarian revolution, which is the core of Marxism. He regarded the French policy of the pre-war decades as fraught with danger for European peace. On 20 October 1912 he wrote in his organ *Humanité:*

> Morocco will lead on to Tripolitania. Tripolitania will lead on to war in the Balkans. War in the Balkans will give rise to the danger of world war.

---

[1] *Int. Bez.* i. V, 355.   [2] *Int. Bez.* i. V, 356.   [3] DD. III, 503.

He was not blind to the menace of German policy and armaments, but the fear uppermost in his mind was that it was through her Russian alliance that France would be drawn into war with Germany, and in the Chamber he fought against the bill for the three-year term of military service. On 7 July 1914 he spoke against the credit of 400,000 francs required for Poincaré's state visit to St. Petersburg on grounds that the visit was particularly inopportune at a moment when complications in the Near East might drag the country into serious trouble in virtue of treaties of which it was in ignorance.[1] In the last stages of the crisis, however, at a meeting in Brussels on 29–30 July of the International Socialist Bureau, of which *Humanité* of 30 July published an account, Jaurès said:

Look at the diplomatists of Austria-Hungary; they have just achieved a masterpiece; they have obscured all responsibilities other than their own. . . . And Germany? If she knew the Austro-Hungarian note she is beyond excuse for having permitted such a *démarche*. And if official Germany did not know the Austrian note . . . what is the significance of the Triple Alliance? . . . We French socialists have a plain duty; we have not to impose a policy of peace upon our Government. Its policy is one of peace. I personally, who have never hesitated to call down the hatred of our Chauvinists upon my head by my obstinate, unfaltering will for a Franco-German rapprochement, have the right to say that at the present moment the French Government has the will to peace and is working for peace.[2]

Jaurès's views had long since made him anathema to the French Right, whose press conducted an incessant campaign of abuse against him, echoed even by organs of more moderate opinion. Paul Boncour relates that from 1913 onwards hardly a day passed without some fresh press attack.[3] Tardieu, in the *Temps* of 2 March 1913, wrote that Jaurès acted 'against the national interest as an advocate for the foreigner' and was 'a sinister agent of negation and disruption'. Léon Daudet, in the *Action Française,* 21 April 1913, said that Jaurès 'would be deserving of condign punishment in any organized state'. Maurice de Waleffe, in *Paris-Midi,* 2 April 1913, asserted: 'He has vowed to give Paris to the Prussians', and on 28 November 1913 harped on: 'I continue to accuse him of high treason towards the country.' On 17 July 1914 an overt incitement to assassination came from the same pen:

If on the eve of war a general were to detail half a dozen men and a corporal to put Citizen Jaurès up against a wall and pump the lead he needs into his brain at point-blank range—do you think the general would be doing anything but his elementary duty? Aye, and I would help him in it.

[1] KSF. 1929, p. 880.
[2] Jaurès, *Oeuvres, Pour la Paix,* V (Paris, 1939), pp. 393-5.
[3] Paul Boncour, *Trois Plaidoiries* (Paris and Neufchâtel, 1934), p. 38.

The *Action Française* also waged a merciless war against Jaurès. In its issue of 23 July 1914, Charles Maurras reiterated the incitement to murder:

We have no wish to incite anyone to political assassination, but M. Jean Jaurès may well shake in his shoes! His article . . . may perhaps give some fanatic the desire to settle by the experimental method the question whether anything would be changed in the invincible order of things if M. Jean Jaurès were to suffer the fate of M. Calmette.

The 'fanatic' was soon found. After Jaurès's return from Brussels, he was dining at a Paris café on 31 July when at 9.40 p. m. he was shot dead by two bullets from the revolver of a total stranger, Raoul Villain. The trial, which ended with the acquittal of the assassin, threw no light on the influences which led this colorless and insignificant young man to commit the crime. After the war an attempt was made to cast suspicion on the Russian Ambassador, Izvolsky, whom Jaurès had ceaselessly attacked as the evil genius of French foreign policy. In *Humanité* of 6 January 1913 Jaurès had written:

In M. Izvolsky, who in times to come will have the immortal fame of having been both the accomplice and dupe of M. Aehrenthal, the Balkan movement produces the illusion of a *revanche*. . . . Has France no other ambition and design than to serve the rancours of M. Izvolsky?

And on 27 July 1914, seeing Izvolsky in the ante-chamber of Bienvenu-Martin, the acting Prime Minister during Viviani's visit to Russia, Jaurès was heard to say: 'There goes that scoundrel Izvolsky. It is here, that war he was wanting' *(Il la tient, sa guerre),* words which, though Izvolsky pretended not to hear them, made his monocle drop from his eye. But even the German historian August Bach, in a special study of the question, concludes that the evidence is too flimsy to support an accusation against Izvolsky.[1]

The murder of Jaurès deeply shocked public opinion. Poincaré at once wrote to his widow expressing 'his great admiration for the character and ability' of her husband. And the *Temps,* in whose columns Tardieu had so often insulted Jaurès, deplored the disappearance of 'a great force', declaring that 'public opinion paid homage to his undeniable ability, the uprightness of his character, and the fine dignity of his life'. Fearing riots the Government retained in Paris two cavalry regiments bound for the frontiers, but all remained quiet, and cries of *'Vive la France, Vive l'armée'* greeted the departing troops. But the embittered strife between the Left and Right was a factor with which the Government had to reckon while the issue of peace or war was being decided.

[1] August Bach, *Jaurès Ermordung,* KSF., September 1929, pp. 880-98.

In the years after the war much discussion went on in France as to how Jaurès would have acted once war had broken out and after the German Socialists had voted for the war. Would he have stood aside like Karl Liebknecht in Germany and later Turati in Italy? Or would he have joined those Socialists (and even the anarchist Kropotkin) who supported the war? Poincaré is quite sure that this latter is what he would have done.

There is no doubt but that his patriotism and generosity of soul would have made him, like Guesde and Sembat, the valuable collaborator of a Cabinet of national defense in the event of war.[1]

But, even if accepting the necessity for war, he would certainly have opposed the *jusqu'auboutistes* with might and main. By his death the French Socialists were left leaderless and it is not possible from their actual behavior to deduce what it might have been, had their leader been with them.

7. Bertie's inquiry as to the French attitude on Belgium; Paléologue's telegram confirming the Russian general mobilization.

The French Cabinet meeting had not long heard of the assassination of Jaurès at 9.50 p. m. when at 10.30 p. m. Viviani was called away for a moment to speak to the English Ambassador, who had asked to see him on an urgent matter. At 8.30 p. m. Bertie had received a telegram from Grey, dispatched at 5.30 p. m., asking

whether the French Government is prepared to engage to respect neutrality of Belgium so long as no other Power violates it. A similar request is being addressed to German Government. It is important to have an early answer.[2]

Bertie at 1.10 a. m. on 1 August replied that Viviani

took note of the enquiry as to the respecting by France of the neutrality of Belgium. . . . He told me that a communication had been made to you by the German Ambassador in London of the intention of Germany to order a general mobilization of her army if Russia does not demobilize at once. . . . Minister for Foreign Affairs also told me that the German Embassy is packing up.[3]

(This is another indication of Viviani's knowledge, denied by Poincaré, that if Germany mobilized she would inevitably go to war.)

At the Cabinet meeting Bertie's inquiry must have been regarded as an auspicious omen. Another good omen was a telegram from Barrère in Rome saying that San Giuliano had confided to him under 'the most complete secrecy'

---

[1] Poincaré, IV, p. 474.   [2] BD. XI, 348. See Vol. II, p. 649.
[3] BD. XI, 380.

that the Italian Government was inclined to regard the Austrian attack on Serbia as an act of aggression of a nature to absolve it from action in favor of Austria. He further thought that the articles of the Triple Alliance, which, moreover, were consonant with the 1902 agreement, were such as to enable Italy, without failing in the loyalty she owes to her allies, to abstain from participation in any conflict. He added that this action on the part of Italy must be conditional on the restraint shown by France and Russia.[1]

This was saying that France and Russia must not appear as the aggressors, since, if they did so, Italy would be obliged to recognize the *casus foederis* laid down in the Triplice treaty.

Let us now see how the French Government behaved when at 8.30 p. m. Paris at last received Paléologue's telegram, dispatched at 10.43 a. m.:

An order has been issued for the general mobilization of the Russian army.[2]

This laconic telegram must certainly have been decoded in a few minutes. It left no more room for doubt as to the reality of Russian general mobilization. A note of Viviani's, written for the Quai d'Orsay on 3 January 1923,[3] states that Viviani left the Ministry building at about 8 p. m. to go home for dinner, before attending the 9 p. m. meeting of the Cabinet. However, either Margerie or Berthelot or both of them were certainly at the Quai d'Orsay that tragic evening. They cannot but have perceived that this confirmation of Russian mobilization rendered Viviani's telegram No. 117 to Paléologue nugatory. It had not yet even been dispatched in its entirety. The first part of it went off at 9 p. m. and the second at 9.30 p. m. Even assuming the first part already to have gone off, the second certainly had not done so. But no attempt was made to hold it up. No telephone message was sent to Viviani asking for further instructions. No later telegram followed up No. 117 taking account of Russian mobilization and giving the French Government's views. Yet the Cabinet meeting lasted from 9 p. m. until midnight. And at it or immediately after it the order was given that Margerie should at once call on Bertie with the message:

French Government are resolved to respect the neutrality of Belgium. . . . This assurance has been given several times. President of the Republic spoke of it to the King of the Belgians, and the French Minister at Brussels has spontaneously renewed the assurance to the Belgian Minister for Foreign Affairs today.

The message further stated:

---

[1] DF. 3. XI, 411; Poincaré, IV, p. 473. This telegram was not included in the French *Yellow Book.*
[2] DF. 3. XI, 432. See Vol. II, p. 622.
[3] Poincaré, IV, p. 457.

It would only be in the event of some other Power violating that neutrality that France might find herself under the necessity, in order to assure defense of her own security, to act otherwise.[1]

Now, if such quick action could be taken when it was a question of making sure of English approval, similar quick action could have been taken at St. Petersburg to save the peace. But nothing was done. The question obtrudes itself: what discussions and decisions took place at the Cabinet meeting when *Schoen's démarche* and Paléologue's telegram were made known? It looks as if there were none, since Viviani afterwards said he did not even remember whether the telegram was sent him at the Élysée or whether he read it later.[2] Poincaré maintains:

In fact, the telegram was actually brought to us, if I am not mistaken, while the Cabinet meeting was in progress.

Such a tentative statement about so important a document gives rise to the suspicion that the less said about it and about when it was received the better.

Moreover [continues Poincaré] it no more than confirmed the indirect information we had already received.[3]

Here is the avowal that the French Government was already aware of Russian mobilization and that Viviani's telegram No. 117 was a mere maneuver devoid of sincerity.

The most likely thing is that Viviani's second supposition is the correct one and that the Quai d'Orsay officials showed him Paléologue's telegram, containing nothing that was not already known, either when he returned to the Ministry after the Cabinet meeting, if he did go back, or when he came in on the morning of 1 August. The same thing would seem to have happened to this telegram as to the two sent by Jules Cambon in the afternoon, which in the present writer's opinion were not produced at the Cabinet meeting.[4] Poincaré must have known all this, and his 'if I am not mistaken' sounds ironically disingenuous The same impression is produced by his explanation why telegram No. 117 was not stopped when confirmation came in of Russian general mobilization:

---

[1] BD. XI, 382. Bertie sent this telegram at 1.12 a. m. on 1 August. That same day the message was also telegraphed by Viviani to the French representatives at London, Berlin, and Brussels. The text as published in the *Yellow Book* (No. 122; CDD., p. 227) has a slightly different wording: 'It would only be in the event of some other Power violating that neu trality that France might find herself brought to enter Belgian territory, with the object of fulfilling her obligations as a guaranteeing Power.'

[2] After the Cabinet meeting ended at midnight, Viviani had gone and sat for a long time beside the bier of the murdered Jaurès, only getting home at 2 a. m. (Poincaré, IV, p. 457).

[3] Poincaré, IV, p. 457.

[4] See pp. 70-2.

Useless as [Viviani's] instructions had now become they proved once again not only that France had remained extraneous to the general mobilization of Russia, but that she continued to deplore that measure and to judge it precipitate.[1]

In other words, they served to place the French Government in a favorable light but not to avert the catastrophe which was now being accepted as inevitable. That this was so is shown by Messimy's words to Izvolsky after the Cabinet meeting,[2] and by the fact that on the evening of 31 July the Cabinet was in favor of ordering general mobilization.

8. Joffre on the evening of 31 July asks for French mobilization.

Joffre narrates that on learning of Schoen's inquiry on 31 July what would be the attitude of France in the case of a conflict between Germany and Russia, he immediately urged Messimy

to give orders for our general mobilization without an instant's delay, for I considered it imperative. Messimy promised me to insist on this step when the Cabinet assembled in the evening.[3]

By then, however,

it was too late for the first day to be fixed sooner than 2 August at midnight. The Cabinet, therefore, decided to wait a few hours more, though at the same time giving me the assurance that, if no improvement took place in the situation, the order would be issued before 4 p. m., the last possible limit which would allow of its reaching the most distant villages and ensure its execution the following morning. But I obtained permission from the Minister to send to all army corps a preparatory warning, stating that 'most likely orders for mobilization will be issued today, 1 August, during the evening. Proceed at once to make all preparations which would facilitate mobilization'.[4]

Poincaré glides away over the details given by Joffre, saying merely that the Cabinet meeting 'yesterday postponed the consideration of the question [of mobilization] until this morning'.[5] But nothing better illustrates the spirit animating the French Government once it had learnt of the Russian mobilization and German intentions. Poincaré therefore, in the present writer's opinion, is not on strong ground when he resents the statement made in the *Comments by the German Delegation on the Conditions of Peace*[6] that the French

---

[1] Poincaré, IV, 454.   [2] See p. 85.
[3] Joffre, I, 126.   [4] Joffre, I, p. 127.
[5] Poincaré, IV, p. 479. Be it noted that when in 1926–7 Poincaré gave *L'Union Sacrée* to the printers there had already appealed Volume I of the 1922 edition *of Les Armées Françaises dans la Grande Guerre* in which the above-quoted preparatory notice was reproduced (1922 edn., p. 80, 1936 edn., p. 108).
[6] (American Association for International Conciliation, New York. 1919), p. 558.

Government, knowing the gravity of the measure taken at St. Petersburg, kept the Russian mobilization secret as long as possible.[1] This is exactly what it did do, or rather, Poincaré feigned unbelief to save having to take up a position in the matter, an understandable attitude, to be sure, as has already been said. Bernadotte Schmitt observes:

> As matters stood on the evening of 31 July, a discussion of the meaning, wisdom or necessity of the Russian mobilization would have been quite academic. France, having decided for reasons of high policy to support Russia on the Serbian question, was constrained to accept the consequences of the action by which the Russian Government sought to secure respect for its views, even if M. Viviani would have preferred that mobilization should not have been ordered. Theoretically the French Premier might have taken the position that, since Russia had not respected his wishes, and had given Germany a 'pretext for mobilization', the terms of the alliance did not apply. Practically and politically such a course was out of the question.[2]

Schmitt's estimate accords with what has been said above in explanation of telegram No. 117 and of Poincaré's attitude. However, one cannot but agree with Jules Isaac's comment on this summing up:

> It is the language of common sense with which one can associate oneself with the following reservation: Certainly, from the moment war broke out there could be no question for France of abandoning her ally, but up to that moment her duty was to guard against dangerous moves, impulsive gestures on the part of the Russian Government. Now, can it be said that French diplomacy fulfilled this duty of caution? Or may it not have sacrificed this to what (perhaps) seemed to be a more imperative duty, that of taking in the rear the supposed, the suspected, the predetermined enemy—Germany?[3]

Inevitable or not, the course followed by France differs substantially from the one she claims to have taken from the beginning and pursued to the end, and shows her Government to be answerable on counts which it had not the courage to acknowledge, nay, which it was at pains immediately to disclaim by resorting to devices which we shall soon consider. But first we must narrate the facts in the order in which they took place.

9. *The Szécsen incident and the Quai d'Orsay's maneuvers.*

While the Cabinet meeting was still in progress the Austrian Ambassador, Szécsen, was received in Viviani's absence by Berthelot, to whom he communicated the telegram from Berchtold to which reference has been made already. It instructed Szécsen to point out to

---

[1] Poincaré, IV, p. 454.   [2] Schmitt, II, pp. 302-3.
[3] Isaac, p. 214

Viviani that Austria had officially declared at St. Petersburg that she did not intend to annex Serbian territory or infringe Serbian sovereignty. He was also to calm the apprehensions, which he had reported to exist in Paris, that Austria had intentions of reoccupying the Sanjak and give an official denial of this to the French Government.[1] As has already been said,[2] this telegram from Berchtold had been sent at the suggestion of Szécsen himself, he being in ignorance of the true state of things and imagining he held a trump card which he could play in support of peace. He lost no time in taking up the matter, and as his actions caused a hubbub among the accusers of the French Government, it is well to devote a few pages to them.

Szécsen habitually dined at the Union club, where he regularly met the Romanian Minister, Lahovary, to whom, as the latter relates in the *Matin* of 4 January 1921, he always maintained that the Serbian question was the sole concern of Austria, who would not tolerate the interference of other Powers in it. But on the evening of 31 July Szécsen took a different line and gave Lahovary to understand that his Government would no longer refuse to make a statement about the additional demands[3] which it would present to the Serbian Government if the latter appealed to it directly or by the intermediary of a friendly Power. Lahovary also received information of negotiations in Vienna between Berchtold and Shebeko and gained the impression that there was a desire on the part of Austria to arrive at a peaceful settlement. His first thought was to tell Vesnić, the Serbian Minister in Paris, of this new turn in the Viennese attitude. But first he sought out the Swiss Minister, Lardy, whom he regarded as one of the ablest of European diplomats and legal authorities, to ask whether Lardy would go with him to call on Vesnić. Lardy said that he must first receive permission from his Government (which in fact gave him leave to associate himself with any peace move that might be made). Meanwhile he urged Lahovary to go and see Vesnić at once, which Lahovary forthwith did. Vesnić agreed to accompany him at 10 p. m. to the Quai d'Orsay, where Margerie received them. Lahovary gave him an account of what had happened. Margerie thanked him for his call, 'which might perhaps lead to further mediation', and said that he would at once telegraph Dumaine in Vienna for exact particulars.

But no such telegram was ever sent. If it had been, it would have come to the knowledge of Berthelot, who was called upon to throw light on the incident in the following circumstances. On 18 November 1920 Mathias Morhardt, acting on behalf of the *Société d'études critiques*

---

[1] Oe-U. VIII, 11121. See Vol. II, p. 685.   [2] See Vol. II, p. 685.

[3] Lahovary cannot have understood aright. It will later be made clear from Szécsen's own words that he spoke not of additional demands on the part of Austria, but of unreserved acceptance by Serbia of the ultimatum terms.

sur la guerre, wrote the president of the *Ligue des droits de l'homme* an account of the Szécsen episode of which the *Société d'études* took a grave view, in that the French Government had apparently let drop a serious and reasonable proposal for peace made by the Austrian Ambassador. Victor Basch, on behalf of the *Ligue des droits de l'homme,* on 9 December 1920 asked Poincaré for an explanation, and Poincaré in turn passed on the inquiry to the official involved, Philippe Berthelot, who in 1914 had been Assistant Director of the Political Section at the Quai d'Orsay. Having obtained the permission of his Minister, Leygues, Berthelot forwarded to Poincaré, who claimed to know nothing of the affair, a copy of the notes on the Szécsen incident taken by himself on the evening of 31 July at the Quai d'Orsay, accompanying them with an explanatory letter.[1]

But in this instance, as in so many others, the French account does not tally with that given by the non-French parties concerned. Lahovary can hardly have invented the detail that Vesnić went to the Quai d'Orsay, not alone, but accompanied by Lahovary himself, at about 10 p. m., being received by Margerie, who gave the promise mentioned above. In his reply to Poincaré of 12 December 1920, Berthelot reproduces his penciled notes of a talk with Vesnić at 11 p. m., notes which do not rule out the possibility that Lahovary and Vesnić were received also by Margerie. Berthelot's letter, states however that Vesnić (he makes no mention of Lahovary) had a talk with him (and therefore not with Margerie) without making any proposal, or asking that the matter should be followed up, since 'Szécsen's suggestion, like the German proposal, only tended to oblige Russia and the Powers to look on helplessly while Serbia was crushed by Austria'. But then, if Szécsen's suggestion was devoid of sincerity, why did Berthelot treat it as worthy of consideration in a document which we must now examine?

As has been said, Szécsen called on Berthelot (here there is no doubt) at 10.15 p. m., and, according to notes made by Berthelot himself that same evening, began by reading out Berchtold's telegram without comment. Then, 'speaking in a personal capacity', he added

that it ought to be possible still to settle the question, mobilization not being war and leaving a few days still for conversations. It was for Serbia to ask Austria for terms.

Berthelot

replied, speaking quite privately, that it seemed extremely late and that they had been overtaken by events.[2]

The version telegraphed by Szécsen to Vienna is on the same lines. Berthelot

[1] Poincaré, IV, pp. 464-8.   [2] DF. 3. XI, 443.

expressed the personal opinion that in view of the German *démarche* of today the Serbian question fell entirely into the background.[1]

Twelve years later Szécsen published his recollections of the incident. He writes that late on the evening of 31 July he hastened to the Quai d'Orsay with the telegram giving the assurance that Austria would not infringe the sovereignty and territorial integrity of Serbia:

To my intense amazement [Berthelot] assured me that he knew nothing of this, adding that it was now too late for negotiations. . . . I dissented from this opinion and said that in my personal view the conflict might still be composed if Serbia would make up her mind to fulfill to the letter the demands formulated by my Government in its note with a time limit of 23 July. The objection continually raised by the French that direct diplomatic contact between Belgrade and Vienna was broken off constituted no obstacle in this case, for Serbia could always ask for the mediation of a genuinely neutral Government not interested in the question in order to get a statement to this effect conveyed to Vienna and to negotiate. This was the suggestion made by me on my own authority, which M. Viviani in a circular telegram of 1 August (No. 120 of the *French Yellow Book)* described as 'vague'. Had Serbia then been prepared to take this step, the possibility of further negotiation would have opened up.

From the whole attitude of my interlocutor I could not but derive the impression that the Quai d'Orsay did not regard a peaceful settlement of the conflict with Serbia as attainable or even desirable. M. Berthelot showed no inclination to discuss in any way the possibility of a direct, peaceful settlement, he even omitted to give a communiqué to the press about my *démarche,* which would certainly have had a quieting effect.[2]

We shall judge later how much basis there was for this thesis of Szécsen's. At present let us recall that in his letter to Poincaré of 12 December 1920 Berthelot vindicated himself from Szécsen's accusation by claiming that soon after the conversation, at 6 a. m. on 1 August, he sent off to the French Embassies at St. Petersburg, Vienna and Rome a full text of Berchtold's telegram with the comment:

The few words added by the Austrian Ambassador as a private opinion give the impression that he not did yet regard all conciliation as impossible; the Austrian Ambassador's *démarche* with M. Sazonov, of which M. Izvolsky has just informed me,[3] deepens that impression. Since on the other hand the Russian Government accepts the English proposal (which implies the cessation of military preparations by all concerned) it therefore seems, that even at this late hour the peace may be preserved (Russia linking the cessation of her preparations to the cessation of those of Austria and the other Powers) if at Berlin the desire for peace is sincere.[4]

---

[1] Oe-U. VIII, 11164.

[2] Graf Szécsen, *Ein vergeblicher Versuch für die Erhaltung des Friedens im Sommer* 1914, KSF., February 1926, pp. 66-9.

[3] *Int. Bez.* i. V, 348. See Vol. II, p. 683.   [4] Poincaré, IV, 465-6.

In the *Documents Diplomatiques Français* this telegram, dispatched not at 6 a. m. but at 11.20 a. m. on 1 August, appears over Viviani's signature and bears the footnote that the minute was drafted by Berthelot.[1] It remains incomprehensible—and Berthelot's letter to Poincaré gives no enlightenment—why and how, after having rather curtly dismissed Szécsen's communication, Berthelot came to treat it with such consideration in the telegram to the French Ambassadors. If this was the result of a change of mind on his part, how comes it that a few hours later, when on the morning of 1 August the Swiss Minister, Lardy, called at the Quai d'Orsay to support Szécsen's suggestion, he was told that it was 'too late'? Indeed, according to the article of Lahovary's published in the *Matin* of 4 January 1921, Lardy received the reply 'that all hope was gone because on the previous day Germany had suddenly declared war on Russia'. Lahovary also received this reply when on the morning of 1 August he went to inquire what had resulted from the moves of the preceding evening. Now in actual fact the declaration of war was handed to Sazonov only at 7 p. m. on 1 August.

Nor is this all. It must further be noted that in his letter to Poincaré of 12 December 1920 Berthelot himself relates that half an hour after leaving the Quai d'Orsay at midnight on 31 July, Szécsen wrote to the Political Director, Margerie, to say that on returning home he had found a telegram from Berchtold announcing that:

in view of the Russian mobilization on our frontiers, we are obliged to take similar measures in Galicia. These measures are of a *purely defensive* nature, we regret being obliged to take them, having no hostile intentions towards Russia and desiring the continuance of good relations. The *pourparlers* between Vienna and St. Petersburg, which we hope will help to bring about a pacification, continue on friendly terms. I thought that this might interest you.[2]

The telegram to which Szécsen alluded is one already referred to.[3] How, then, is it to be explained that in Viviani's telegram of 11.20 a. m. he made no allusion to this significant message which lent added weight to Szécsen's previous move? Finally, why after sending his telegram did Viviani on 1 August repeat the same statements to the Ambassadors without any reference to the telegram of 11.20 a. m.?

The hour of dispatch of this telegram is of some importance, coming as it did after a long telegram (sent off in two parts at 10.55 and 11 a. m.) to the Embassies at London and Berlin, and beginning:

Two *démarches* were made yesterday evening by the Austrian Ambassadors —the one at Paris, which was rather vague, the other at St. Petersburg, precise and conciliatory.

[1] DF. 3. XI, 484.   [2] DF, 3. XI, 472; Poincaré, IV, p. 467-8.
[3] Oe-U. VIII, 11120. See Vol. II, p. 679.

There follows a detailed account of what had been said by Szécsen and Szápáry.

The deduction from these facts is that Austria would at least seem to show herself ready to come to an agreement, just as the Russian Government is ready to enter into negotiations on the basis of the English proposal. Unfortunately these arrangements, which allowed one to hope for a peaceful solution, appear in fact to have been rendered useless by the attitude of Germany.[1]

In short, this is an amplified duplicate of the telegram of 11.20 to the Embassies at St. Petersburg, Vienna, and Rome, with a concluding passage which we must now glance at. It must be noted that the passage in question is at complete variance with the thesis maintained by the Quai d'Orsay a few hours later in regard to Austria and the role played by her. But that aspect of the question is of such importance in another connection that it will be studied in detail in the next chapter.

It is not necessary to dwell further on the Szécsen episode after assessing its importance, which is minimal and in no way justifies the sensation it caused in France and the reverberations of this sensation among the upholders of German innocence. The Szécsen suggestion was nothing further than an encore to that of San Giuliano and had no more solid a foundation. Just as the Serbian Chargé d'Affaires at Rome had no authority to give the impression that Serbia was willing to accept the ultimatum, so Szécsen had no authority to say in Paris that, if Serbia made known to Vienna, or to some intermediary, her acceptance of the Austrian ultimatum, the dispute might be settled peacefully. A settlement on that basis was an impossibility. It would not have found acceptance either at Belgrade or at St. Petersburg, where the demand was that the terms should be reviewed and softened. Nor would it have been accepted by Vienna, which was not even willing to engage to confine military operations to the occupation of Belgrade. Hence Berthelot was not wrong in saying on 31 July to Szécsen that his suggestion came too late and was overtaken by events. After the general mobilization in Russia, the Austro-Serbian conflict fell into the background. What came now to the forefront was the Russo-German conflict, and that, after the German ultimatum to St. Petersburg and Paris, could only be composed by a Russian pledge to demobilize.[2]

Here we reach the very heart of the question. And this is the reason why Viviani's two telegrams of 1 August make no sense except in as far as they form part of a series of maneuvers undertaken by the Quai

---

[1] DF. 3. XI, 481; LJF. 120; CDD., p. 225.

[2] These obvious considerations are entirely disregarded by Bach in his article in KSF., February 1928, entitled *Die letzten Versuche zur Erhaltung des Friedens in Paris am 31. Juli und 1. August 1914*, pp. 204–15. In support of the thesis of German innocence he attributes an importance to the Szécsen episode which it entirely lacks.

d'Orsay from 31 July onwards to avoid confessing the truth that
after the Russian general mobilization, which Paris either was
not able or was not willing to ask St. Petersburg to revoke, war
had become unavoidable. These maneuvers were to make it
possible to cast the blame on Germany for what was bound to
follow.

The maneuver is patent in Nos. 120 and 121 of the *Yellow
Book*. No. 120 is one of the few telegrams in the *Yellow Book*
published without alterations. Here is its concluding passage:

> The ultimatum [from Germany to Russia] is not justified, for Russia has
> accepted the British proposal which implies a cessation of military
> preparations by all the Powers. The attitude of Germany proves that she
> wishes for war. And she wishes for it against France. Yesterday when Herr
> von Schoen came to the Quai d'Orsay to ask what attitude France proposed
> to take in case of a Russo-German conflict, the German Ambassador,
> although there has been no direct dispute between France and Germany, and
> although from the beginning of the crisis we have used all our efforts for a
> peaceful solution and are still continuing to do so, added that he asked me
> to present his respects and thanks to the President of the Republic, and
> asked that we would be so good as to make arrangements for his own person
> *(des dispositions pour sa propre personne);* we know also that he has already
> put the archives of the Embassy in safety. This attitude of breaking off
> diplomatic relations without any direct dispute and although he has not
> received any definitely negative answer, is characteristic of the determination
> of Germany to make war against France. The want of sincerity in her
> peaceful protestations is shown by the rupture which she is forcing upon
> Europe at a time when Austria had at last agreed with Russia to begin
> negotiations.

This last idea was inserted also into J. Cambon's telegram
from Berlin on 1 August, to whose original text the compilers of
the *Yellow Book* have added the following:

> Germany's ultimatum, coming at the very moment when an agreement
> seemed about to be reached between Vienna and St. Petersburg, is
> characteristic of her warlike policy. In truth the conflict was between Russia
> and Austria only, and Germany could intervene only as an ally of Austria:
> in these circumstances, since the two Powers which were interested as
> principals were prepared for conversations, it is impossible to understand why
> Germany should send an ultimatum to Russia instead of continuing, like all
> the other Powers, to work for a peaceful solution, unless she desired war on
> her own account.[1]

It is obvious that these documents talk of everything but the
real cause of the two ultimatums, the Russian mobilization, and
this silence is covered over by two falsehoods, namely, that
Russia had agreed to demobilize if the other Powers did the
same, and that an Austro-Russian agreement was almost

---

[1] DF. 3. XI, 521; LJF. 121; CDD., pp. 226-7

achieved. It is true that Berchtold's artfulness had created the impression that an agreement was possible; but it was a long road from that to a genuine agreement, seeing that Berchtold had no intention of yielding a single inch. Moreover, it was a complete invention to say that Russia had agreed to Grey's formula and had declared her readiness to demobilize on those terms. The actual facts were that on 31 July Sazonov had telegraphed to the Russian Ambassadors that he 'was in agreement with the English proposal'. But he had added that he was sending them a modified formula, pledging Russia only 'to maintain her waiting attitude', not to suspend the general mobilization.[1] Of this Viviani was perfectly well aware through a telegram from Paléologue of 31 July, which reached Paris at 4 a. m. on 1 August.[3] Thus the Quai d'Orsay was simply putting up a smoke-screen to hide the Russian mobilization which was leading to war. There had been signs of this already on the previous evening. The smoke-screen was in full operation on the morning of 1 August with the dispatch of telegram No. 120 before Schoen paid a forenoon call on Viviani, and also during this call, which took place while the first Cabinet meeting of the day was in progress.

10. The French Cabinet decides to order general mobilization.

Already at 8 a. m. on 1 August Joffre had renewed his importunities with another note to Messimy, saying:

Information received up to the present shows that five classes of German reservists have been recalled for 2 August at the latest: requisitions and purchases of horses began on 30 July, possibly before. It can, therefore, be said that on 4 August, even without the order for mobilization having been issued, the German army will be entirely mobilized; in this way a start of over forty-eight hours, perhaps of three days, will have been secured.

Joffre's account continues:

In handing M. Messimy this note I once more urged the imperative necessity of ordering our mobilization. For in France this measure cannot be effected little by little and with the concealments which are possible in Germany; it has to be accomplished once for all. As I took my leave I reminded the Minister that the last possible time limit for publishing the order would expire at 4 p. m.[3]

[1] *Int. Bez.* i. V, 342, 343. See p. 57.

[2] DF. 3. XI, 453; LJF. 113; CDD., pp. 220-1; Poincaré, IV, pp. 462-3. The *Yellow Book* under 113 reproduces the first sentence of DF. 3. XI, 340 ('The news of the bombardment of Belgrade during the night and morning of yesterday has provoked very deep feeling in Russia') ; then come the following words invented by the compilers: 'One cannot understand the attitude of Austria, whose provocations since the beginning of the crisis have regularly followed Russia's attempts at conciliation and the satisfactory conversations exchanged between St. Petersburg and Vienna.' Then follows the text of DF. 3. XI, 453.

[3] Joffre, I, p. 128; Recouly, p. 83.

And Messimy later told Recouly that Joffre had added:

If the Government delays the issue of the order for general mobilization, I cannot possibly continue to bear the crushing responsibility of the high office which it has entrusted to me.

The Cabinet met at 9 a. m. and Messimy asked Joffre to attend it:

He [Joffre] repeated to all my colleagues the explanations he had given me. There was no protest, no comment.[1]

Joffre does not mention this appearance of his at the Cabinet meeting. What he tells us is that

while it was going on, news came that the Italian Government had decided to maintain neutrality in case of a conflict. . . . I immediately sent additional instructions . . . prescribing that in case of mobilization the covering troops designated for the south-eastern frontier should remain in their mobilization centers, ready to entrain for the northeast.[2]

Poincaré confirms the fact that Joffre attended the Cabinet meeting:

Joffre appeared with the placid face of a calm, resolute man whose only fear is lest France, outstripped by German mobilization, the most rapid of all of them, might speedily find herself in an irreparable state of inferiority.[3]

The decision for general mobilization had not yet been taken when about 11 a. m. Viviani was summoned to the Quai d'Orsay, where Schoen had appeared before the hour fixed for his appointment to receive the answer to his question of the previous day about the intentions of France. This answer had been drawn up at the Cabinet meeting of the previous evening: 'France will have regard to her own interests.' According to Viviani's account, Schoen, after a moment's reflection, asked:

'I confess that my question is rather ingenuous. But, after all, have you not got a treaty of alliance?' 'Exactly', replied Viviani.[4]

Schoen's version, in a brief telegram to Berlin of 1.05 p. m. on 1 August, runs:

In reply to a definite and repeated question whether France would remain neutral in a Russo-German war, Prime Minister replied *hesitatingly:* France would do what her interests dictated. He motivated the vagueness of this statement by the fact that he regards situation as changed since yesterday. An official communication has been received here that *Sir Ed. Grey's proposal for a cessation of military preparations on the part of all concerned* has been accepted by Russia in principle and that Austria-Hungary has announced that she will not infringe Serbian integrity and sovereignty.[5]

[1] Recouly, p. 84.   [2] Joffre, I, p. 128.   [3] Poincaré, IV, 479.
[4] Viviani, *Réponse au Kaiser,* pp. 204-5.   [5] DD. III, 571.

On Viviani's telegram to the Ambassadors informing them of this second call of Schoen's he wrote:

I put him in possession of the facts as to the *pourparlers* which have been carried on since yesterday:

(1) An English compromise, proposing, besides other suggestions, suspension of military preparations on the part of Russia, on condition that the other Powers should act in the same way; adherence of Russia to this proposal.

(2) Communications from the Austrian Government declaring that they did not desire any aggrandizement in Serbia, nor even to advance into the Sanjak, and stating that they were ready to discuss even the basis of the Austro-Serbian question at London with the other Powers.

I drew attention to the attitude of Germany, who, abandoning all *pourparlers,* presented an ultimatum to Russia at the very moment when this Power had just accepted the British formula (which implies the cessation of military preparations by all the countries which have mobilized) and regarded a diplomatic, rupture with France as imminent.[1]

Schoen's version differs from that of Viviani only in lacking the statement that Austria was 'ready to discuss even the basis of the Austro-Serbian question at London with the other Powers'. The statement was, of course, devoid of foundation and Schoen was nonplussed by it and answered

that he did not know the developments which had taken place in this matter in the last twenty-four hours, that there was in them perhaps a 'glimmer of hope' for some arrangement . . . and that he was going to get information.

Accordingly

Baron von Schoen did not allude to his immediate departure and did not make any fresh request for an answer to his question concerning the attitude of France in case of an Austro-Russian conflict. He confined himself to saying of his own accord that the attitude of France was not doubtful.

Viviani adds the comment:

It would not do to exaggerate the possibilities which may result from my conversation with the German Ambassador for, on its side, the Imperial Government continues the most dangerous preparations on our frontier. However, we must not neglect the possibilities, and we should not cease to work towards an agreement. On her side France is taking all military measures required for protection against too great an advance in German military preparations. She considers that her attempts at solution will only have a chance of success so far as it is felt that she will be ready and resolute if the conflict is forced on her.[2]

[1] DF. 3. XI, 505; LJF. 125; CDD., pp. 228-9.
[2] DF. 3. XI, 505; LJF. 125; CDD., pp. .229.

Viviani's falsehoods can only be explained by (1) his embarrassment at having to admit that Russia had mobilized and was not demobilizing, and that France had not requested her to do so or thought she ought to do so and was, on the contrary, on the point of ordering mobilization herself; (2) the intent to make it appear that not only had Russia and France the most pacific intentions but that even Austria had the same, so that it was Germany alone who desired to bring about a war. Poincaré must have noticed that Viviani had played tricks with the truth. His version of the Viviani-Schoen interview runs:

> M. Viviani himself explains the indefinite character of his statement by the fact that since yesterday he thinks the situation improved. Austria-Hungary has declared that she does not intend to infringe the territorial integrity of Serbia. Sir E. Grey is renewing his *démarche* for the opening of Four-Power negotiations and the suspension of military preparations.

No! What Viviani had really said to Schoen, and thus misled him, was that Austria was 'ready to discuss even the basis of the Austro-Serbian question at London with the other Powers'. And it is inconceivable that after the interview he can, as Poincaré writes, have returned to the Élysée *'le front moins soucieux'* and told the Cabinet that Schoen 'has said nothing more about his departure and everything is on the point of being settled'.[1] Here the misstatement is Poincaré's, not Viviani's. Poincaré ascribes to Viviani a state of mind which cannot have been his. Even if Schoen may have been nonplussed and not asked for his passports, this was only because he had been told that Russia was agreeing to suspend mobilization, and this Viviani knew to be untrue. So much did Viviani know it that on his return to the Élysée, where he was awaited by the Cabinet and by Poincaré, far from proposing to refrain from general mobilization—which would have had no justification, had the situation been as he described it to Schoen, and which it was dangerous to order when Germany had not yet ordered hers—he obtained the Cabinet's approval for it without a dissentient voice and with a precaution which Joffre describes as follows:

> When the Prime Minister returned to his seat he informed his colleagues that in spite of the vague assurances given by Baron von Schoen, he was now fully convinced that I was right, and in face of the dangerous preparations already made by the Germans, he was ready to sign the order for general mobilization. However, in order to hold open until the very last minute the possibility of an arrangement, he asked the Minister of War to keep this order in his personal possession up to the last minute which would make it possible to begin the mobilization on 2 August at midnight. This order was signed by MM. Poincaré, Viviani, Augagneur [Minister of Marine] and Messimy,   and   entrusted   to   the   last   named;   at   3.30   p.   m.,

[1] Poincaré, IV, pp. 478-9.

the moment of execution having arrived, I sent General Ebener to get it. At 3.45 the telegrams, already prepared, were delivered at the central telegraph office. . . . The whole of France was thus immediately informed that 'the first day of mobilization would be Sunday, 2 August'.[1]

Messimy, however, relates that shortly before 4 p. m. Viviani came to his office just as the telegram was going off and asked for a brief postponement of its dispatch:

A talk which he had just had with Herr von Schoen gave a gleam of hope of an arrangement. After consulting General Ebener by telephone I answered that the order had already gone and that the first measures were being carried out. It was too late, the mechanism had been set in motion. We shook hands with emotion. We had the feeling of having done everything in our power to avert the catastrophe.[2]

Either Messimy's memory has deceived him, or Viviani was not frank with him in motivating his request by hopes raised in a fresh conversation with Schoen. He had not seen Schoen again after their interview at 11 a. m.[3] On the contrary, at 12.50 p. m. on 1 August the Quai d'Orsay had received a telegram from Paléologue dispatched at 4.25 a. m.:

The German Ambassador has just declared to the Russian Government that the general mobilization of the German army will be ordered tomorrow morning, 1 August.[4]

Here a parenthesis is necessary. In quoting this telegram Poincaré adds:

This decision, therefore, was taken at Berlin as early as yesterday, whereas we ourselves on the contrary had delayed ours.

He coolly continues:

But M. Paléologue's telegram is incomplete, . . . In reality Count Pourtalès went at midnight to tell M. Sazonov, on orders from his Government, that if within twelve hours, i.e., by Saturday 1 August at noon, Russia does not begin her demobilization . . . the Berlin Government will see itself obliged also to decree mobilization.[5]

---

[1] Joffre, I, p. 128.   [2] Recouly, pp. 85-6.

[3] B. Schmitt explains this by the conjecture that Viviani called on Messimy after Schoen's second visit, which took place at 5.30 p. m. (Schmitt II, p. 336 note). But it is difficult to believe this, as Viviani knew the mobilization order would be published at 4 p. m. Actually it was about 4 p. m. that he called on Messimy. Moreover, in any case, Schoen's second visit gave no cause for optimism.

[4] DF. 3. XI, 490; Poincaré IV, p. 480.

[5] As further evidence that the German decision to mobilize antedates that of France, Poincaré recalls that on 31 July at 4.40 p. m. Wilhelm telegraphed to Francis Joseph that the *Kriegsgefahrzustand* would be followed as soon as possible by general mobilization (Poincaré, IV, pp. 481-82). Quite true; but it is equally true that, had Russia agreed to demobilize, Germany would have refrained from mobilizing.

A neat way of glossing over a real falsification of the facts of which the French Ambassador was guilty. Sazonov had at once told Paléologue that Pourtalès was threatening German mobilization unless Russia revoked hers, but Paléologue intentionally withheld the news from his Government and made it believe that Germany had informed Russia that German mobilization would with certainty be ordered on the morning of 1 August.[1] The obvious purpose of this was that Paris should be led to believe that Germany was going to mobilize in any case, lest the Quai d'Orsay should be tempted to urge St. Petersburg to agree to demobilize. What it should do was on the contrary to order French mobilization without losing time. It will be remembered that Paléologue had played the same trick on his government on 30 July in telegraphing:

> According to information received by the Russian General Staff the general mobilization of the German army will be ordered tomorrow, 30 July.[2]

Viviani was evidently not taken in by this maneuver of Paléologue's. He was able to learn the truth both from Schoen's *démarche* and from that of Pourtalès at St. Petersburg, which Sazonov immediately communicated to Izvolsky by telegram.[3] If Viviani had believed what Paléologue wrote he would never have called on Messimy with the request to wait before issuing the order for French mobilization. His action must have been prompted by doubts and fears which made him repent of having too easily yielded to Joffre's demand. It may have seemed to him that the soldiers were regarding the matter purely from their own one-sided point of view, completely forgetting the political aspect of the measures for which they asked and which might be disastrous militarily as well. Supposing, for example, premature mobilizations, such as those in Russia and France, were to have an unfavorable effect on the attitude of England and Italy! In actual fact, not only was Russian mobilization premature, but French mobilization was decided before noon and promulgated at 3.55 p. m. on 1 August, while German mobilization was decided at 5 p. m. (4 p. m. French time) that same day and promulgated shortly afterwards. Apart from the few minutes' precedence in beginning French mobilization, there is the

---

[1] In connection with this date of 1 August one remark must be made. If Paléologue telegraphed thus at 4.25 a. m. on 1 August, the 'tomorrow' to which he referred would be the 2nd and not the 1st. It may be replied that he perhaps drafted the telegram before midnight on the 31st. However, Pourtalès states that he made his *démarche* at midnight; moreover, he could not have done so earlier, since Bethmann's instructions only reached him at 11.10 p. m. Hence 1 August may be presumed to be the true date. It is clear that to be able to send such immediate notice of Pourtalès's *démarche*, Paléologue must have been present in one of the rooms at the Foreign Ministry. Indeed, from what one can see, he seems to have spent most of his time there.

[2] See Vol. II, p. 614; DF. 3. XI, 302.

[3] See above p. 62, *Int. Bez.* i. V, 385.

fact that the decision to mobilize was taken before Paris actually knew that Germany herself was on the point of mobilizing. The consequences of this might have been very serious if, after the English *démarche* about Belgium, Berlin had decided not to proceed with mobilization. Although the species of ultimatum presented by Schoen could in a certain sense serve as a justification for French mobilization, the decision to resort to such a measure would have placed the Republic in an awkward position morally, especially as it was Russia who had set the bad example of ordering general mobilization.

That this was the feeling in Paris is shown in Izvolsky's telegram of shortly before noon on 1 August:

> On the other hand, for political reasons relating both to Italy and still more to England, it is very important for France that her mobilization shall not precede that of Germany but be the answer to it. The question is at this very moment under discussion at the Cabinet meeting at the Élysée and it is highly probable that the Cabinet will decide on general mobilization.[1]

And, in fact, this is what it did.

11. Viviani's manifesto and the thesis that mobilization is not war.

Viviani realized the dangers of the decision. His uneasiness is apparent in the manifesto which he drafted during that morning's Cabinet meeting to explain the reasons for mobilizing to the nation and to which he obtained the signatures of Poincaré and the whole Cabinet:

> For some days the state of Europe has been considerably deteriorating, and despite the efforts of diplomacy the horizon has grown dark. At the present moment most of the countries have mobilized their forces. Countries whose constitutional and military legislation do not resemble our own have, without a previous decree of mobilization, begun and continued preparations equivalent in reality to actual mobilization and in fact effecting it in advance. France . . . has now taken the first essential measures for safeguarding her territory. . . . Mobilization is not war. In the present circumstances it appears, on the contrary, the best means of assuring peace with honor. Strong in the ardent desire to achieve a peaceful solution of the crisis, the Government, under shelter of these necessary precautions, will pursue its diplomatic endeavors and still hopes to be successful. . . . At this hour there are no longer parties. There is only eternal France, pacific and resolute France. There is only the homeland of law and justice completely united in calmness, vigilance and dignity.[2]

With all its eloquence this manifesto, by the very artifices it employed to cultivate the illusion that peace could yet be saved, was the confession of an uneasy conscience. How could peace yet be saved

---

[1] *Int. Bez.* i.. V, 405.   [2] Poincaré, IV, pp. 483-6.

unless Russia demobilized? And would Russia demobilize without being asked to do so by her ally, when yielding to the German demand would be a fresh diplomatic defeat infinitely more humiliating than that of 1909? But the most serious accusation which has been leveled at Viviani is that of having stated that 'mobilization is not war' while knowing that mobilization was war. Various historians have gone to work to prove that he knew this by producing copious quotations from the negotiations between General Boisdeffre and the Russian General Obruchev in which it was laid down that the order for mobilization would be inseparable from the order to open hostilities. This question has been dealt with in the preceding volumes[1] and need not be discussed here. Suffice it to say that the principle laid down in those negotiations was revoked and could not apply in particular to a country like France where, as Poincaré remarks,

mobilization and martial law cannot be confounded with the declaration of war inasmuch as the former depend on the Government alone, whereas the latter demands the intervention of Parliament and the passing of a law.[2]

And earlier, in *L'Union Sacrée,* Poincaré had written:

Between civilized nations the equation (mobilization = war) has no justification either in law or in fact. Mobilization is an internal measure to which the nation which orders it remains free not to give a bloodstained sequel. Only the declaration creates the state of war.[3]

There may, indeed, be war without a declaration, but this does not mean that mobilization is war. That which happened in Germany, and happened necessarily as a result of the Schlieffen plan, has led many historians to maintain that mobilization is war, but they are wrong. Russia, Austria, Italy, and France could mobilize without crossing their frontiers. Austria ordered mobilization against Serbia on the evening of 25 July and declared war on 28 July. She informed Germany, to the latter's annoyance, that she would not open hostilities until 12 August. It is, thus, undeniable that if Germany's plan for mobilization and war had not been what it was, nothing need have prevented the conflict from being brought to a settlement in two or three days. This is recognized by Walter Schücking, who writes:

But would it not have been possible to continue diplomatic negotiations even after Russian and German mobilization had taken place? Theoretically it undoubtedly could. For mobilization is a government measure which does not necessarily always lead to war. Often enough in the course of history mobilized armies have faced one another across frontiers and yet war has been successfully averted by diplomatic action. It had been thus on the Galician frontier between

[1] See Vol. I, p. 77; Vol. II, pp. 579-80.   [2] Gerin, pp. 46-7.
[3] Poincaré, IV, 530.

Russia and Austria during the crisis of the Balkan war; and again after war had begun between Germany and Russia [in August 1914], as a result of a word from Grey there was a brief moment in which Berlin hoped that France would remain neutral and that German and French troops could stand to arms on their respective sides of the frontier without attacking.[1]

But these considerations are not incompatible with the admission that in writing in the manifesto that 'mobilization is not war', after being told by Schoen that for Germany 'mobilization inevitably means war', Viviani was not being entirely frank. This is especially apparent in his next words: 'In the present circumstances it appears, on the contrary, the best means of assuring peace with honor.' It was a grievous overstatement to claim that mobilization was a means of assuring peace. And Viviani must all the more have seen it to be so on receiving at 3.47 p. m. the following telegram which Paléologue had sent off at 10.50 a. m. on 1 August:

General mobilization continues with precision and activity. Even among the working class war with Germany evokes keen enthusiasm.[2]

Recouly thus describes the scenes in Paris and outside a newspaper office where the little blue mobilization order had been posted up.

The crowd gathered in front of one of the windows of the office where a small blue paper was affixed. . . . Those who had read it made way for others. . . . Demonstrations, processions on the boulevard, on the Place de la Concorde where an innumerable crowd surged to and fro. 'Mobilization is not war' said M. Poincaré in his message to the people. To tell the truth no one believed him. If it was not war, it was certainly something terribly near to it.[3]

Nor can Viviani have believed it either. When he wrote the words, what was uppermost in his mind was the effect that the news of French general mobilization would produce in London, and he lost no time in sending a long telegram to Paul Cambon in which he gives his own version of the events leading up to the mobilization, making statements which will later be shown to be untrue and repeating on the lines laid down in the manifesto:

Our decree of mobilization is an essential measure of protection . . . Mobilization is not war . . . it is the best means for France of safeguarding peace; the Government of the Republic will redouble its efforts to bring the negotiations to a conclusion. Will you be good enough to bring all these points urgently to the notice of Sir Edward Grey, and point out to him that

---

[1] Walter Schücking, *Die völkerrechtliche Lehre des Weltkrieges* (Leipzig, 1918), p. 196. Professor Schücking and Montgelas were in charge of the publication of the German documents collected by Kautsky.

[2] DF. 3. XI, 506.   [3] Recouly, p. 116.

we have throughout been governed by the determination not to commit any act of provocation. I am persuaded that in case war were to break out, English opinion would see clearly from which side aggression comes, and that it would understand the strong reasons which you have given to Sir Edward Grey for asking for armed intervention on the part of England in the interest of the future of the European balance of power.[1]

It was these same considerations which caused Messimy immediately after the Cabinet meeting to repeat the order to the troops not to enter the 10-Kilometre zone:

> Late in the evening the President of the Republic summoned me to the Élysée. He told me that according to telephone messages received by his department certain cavalry elements had penetrated into the neutral zone. I renewed for the fourth time the strict order not to enter this zone.[2]

The order was dispatched at 10.30 p. m. signed by Poincaré and Messimy and stating that those who disobeyed it would be court-martialed. But when at 5.30 p. m. Schoen returned to the Quai d'Orsay to ask again what France intended to do, Viviani again acted as if he thought the situation not at all hopeless and said he hoped things would turn out all right.

12. *The last conversation between Schoen and Viviani on 1 August; Viviani's tactics, and two revealing telegrams from Izvolsky.*

Schoen, who in the forenoon had been considerably perplexed by the news given him by Viviani, especially by the statement that Russia had agreed to suspend mobilization provided the other Powers did the same, had meanwhile received a peremptory telegram from Bethmann sent off at 1.5 p. m.:

> Your Excellency is empowered if necessary to give the French Government a time limit of two hours, until 3 p. m., French time, to reply to our proposal regarding eventuality.[3]

Probably the word 'eventuality' was an allusion to the second part of his telegram of the 31st:

> If, as is not to be presumed, French Government declares willingness to remain neutral, will Your Excellency declare to French Government that as guarantee for neutrality we must demand the fortresses of Toul and Verdun.[4]

There was no possibility that France would declare herself neutral or need time to make up her mind about declining to hand over the two fortresses, a matter which Schoen had no occasion to mention.

---

[1] DF. 3,. XI, 523; published with some alterations as No. 127 of the *Yellow Book;* CDD., p. 231.

[2] Recouly, p. 86.   [3] DD. III, 543.   [4] DD. III, 491. See p. 41.

But this further telegram made it plain that the ultimatum was still in force, and Schoen, who did not receive it until after 3 p. m., hastened to the Quai d'Orsay to ask for an immediate answer.

At 7.5 p. m., after having seen Viviani, he telegraphed to Berlin as follows:

> At a further interview with Prime Minister at 5.30 p. m., he, in spite of all I could urge, declined to depart from the formula of this forenoon in the matter of France's attitude in a Russo-German war ['France will have regard to her own interests']. Prime Minister assured me the mobilization, just ordered here (1st day, Sunday) betokens no aggressive intentions, as is also stated in the proclamation. He says there is still room for the continuation of negotiations on the basis of Sir E. Grey's proposal to which France has agreed and 'which she warmly supports. To prevent frontier clashes, he says, the precaution has been taken of marking off a 10 km. zone on the French side. He refuses to give up hope of peace.[1]

We do not possess the French version of this conversation. Its place must be taken by Viviani's long telegram to Paul Cambon, which figures as No. 127 of the *Yellow Book* and expatiates on the pacific attitude of France and Russia and its contrast to that of Germany. It has in part been discussed above.[2] But not one word does dispatch No. 127 let fall about Schoen's second visit, whose import could not be misunderstood and of which all the French Ambassadors should have been informed. If this was not done, as seems probable, it is because Viviani was still keeping up the pretence of not having grasped the seriousness of the German demand, now repeated for the third time, and of thinking negotiation still possible. These tactics show through clearly in Izvolsky's telegram to Sazonov giving an account of the evening conversation between Viviani and Schoen. On the morning of 1 August Izvolsky had already reported Szécsen's two calls on Viviani the previous evening, Schoen's appearance on 1 August before the hour of his appointment with Viviani, and the Cabinet meeting which was in progress as he wrote and was discussing whether France should mobilize and was anxious that French mobilization should not precede that of Germany.[3] Another telegram followed with the news that the decision for general mobilization had been taken

> in consequence of the arrival of a telegram from Paléologue that the German Ambassador has acquainted you of the German decision to proclaim general mobilization. . . . The German Ambassador has just paid a second call on Viviani but made no fresh communication, alleging that it had not yet been possible to decode the telegrams which had arrived. Viviani informed him that in answer to German mobilization, the mobilization decree had been issued, and expressed surprise that Germany had resorted to a measure of that kind just at a moment

---

[1] DD. III, 598.   [2] See pp. 107-8.   [3] *Int. Bez.* i. V, 405.

when the friendly exchange of views between Russia, Austria and the Powers was in progress; he added that mobilization does not yet mean war and that just as the Russian Ambassador at Vienna and the Austrian Ambassador at St. Petersburg were still at their posts, there were no grounds for the departure of Baron Schoen, who in fact did not renew his threat.[1]

This telegram is full of untrue statements which Izvolsky certainly did not invent but which were fed to him by the Quai d'Orsay. In the first place, it was not true that the decision to mobilize was taken in consequence of Paléologue's telegram announcing German general mobilization for the morning of 1 August, since the telegram arrived at 12.50 p. m. when the French mobilization decree was already signed. This is corroborated by Poincaré himself when he writes:

> Hardly had the Cabinet meeting [at which the decision was taken] come to an end when a telegram from M. Maurice Paléologue, etc.[2]

Neither was it true that Viviani had said to Schoen that French mobilization was a reply to that of Germany, which had only been ordered an hour and a half earlier and of which Paris was still in ignorance. Moreover, had Viviani said anything of the kind to Schoen on a basis of Paléologue's telegram, Schoen would undoubtedly have intimated this to his Government. It is obvious that the Quai d'Orsay was anxious to appear, even in the eyes of allied Russia, guiltless of having mobilized before Germany did so and assumed the same pacific mien with Izvolsky as Viviani had assumed with Schoen.

After the war Poincaré continued the same tactics. In reproducing Schoen's telegram, both in *L'Union Sacrée* and in his reply to the second question put by Gerin, he comments:

> The German Ambassador at Paris, Baron von Schoen, quite admitted that mobilization was not war when on 1 August at 7 p. m. he telegraphed to Berlin.[3]

This is not so. Schoen made no such admission; he simply reported on Viviani's pacific tone and words without expressing belief or disbelief. Was Viviani being sincere? Poincaré maintains:

> No one who knew Viviani could ever for an instant doubt the sincerity of his declarations. Like all of us, up to the last hour he refused to believe in a definitive rupture.[4]

It must be admitted that Viviani was anxious to avoid a definitive rupture, but it is impossible to believe that he still remained hopeful after learning that Russia was not demobilizing and knowing that she

---

[1] *Int. Bez.* i. V, 406.   [2] Poincaré, p. 480. See p. 103.
[3] Gerin, pp. 45-6.   [4] Poincaré, IV, 482.

had never been asked by France to do so. Nor were any hopes felt by Poincaré. He simply uses Viviani's words to Schoen to acquit the French Government of failing to influence St. Petersburg and pretends that the Government still did not regard negotiations as at an end when in fact it was only a question of answering yes or no to the German ultimatum. In other words, Viviani was not being straightforward in holding such pacific, conciliatory language with Schoen. He, like Poincaré, and the Quai d'Orsay officials, was maneuvering. All of them were conscious that, in consequence of the Russian general mobilization, war was now certain.

This certainty is revealed by two telegrams sent by Izvolsky, the first of which follows on after the one quoted above and reports:

Margerie tells me that according to information from a very reliable source Italy, manifestly having regard to the way the present crisis has come about, has decided for the time being to remain neutral and to make a definite decision one way or another according as events turn out.[1]

The second telegram is from the Russian Military Attaché, reporting:

The War Minister expressed a wish (1) for influence to be used with Serbia to induce her to take the offensive more speedily, (2) for daily reports on the German army corps deployed against us, (3) for an announcement of the date of the opening of our offensive against Germany. The preferred direction of our offensive still is Warsaw-Posen.[2]

It was now a question, not of negotiating, but of winning a war, and midnight had hardly struck on 1 August when Paris knew for certain that negotiation had come to an end since Germany, a few hours earlier, had declared war on Russia.

This declaration played into the hands of France. Austria by the ultimatum to Serbia and the declaration of war on her, Germany by the ultimatum to St. Petersburg, the demand for French neutrality, the declaration of war on Russia and the invasion of Belgium, now appeared as aggressors in the eyes of the whole world. In the competition between the German and French Governments each to appear innocent and lay the blame on the other, the French Government had scored a clear advantage. It was only a question of waiting a few hours more and the success would be complete in spite of the mistake made by Russia in proceeding to general mobilization, a mistake which both St. Petersburg and Paris would try to retrieve.

[1] *Int. Bez.* i. V, 407.   [2] *Int. Bez.* i, V, 408.

CHAPTER III

THE LEGEND THAT THE AUSTRIAN GENERAL MOBILIZATION PRECEDED THAT OF RUSSIA

(1) *Whether it was possible for Paris on 31 July to receive the impression that the Austrian mobilization preceded that of Russia* (p. 112). (2) *The first assertion of the priority of Austrian mobilization made by Poincaré to Bertie on the morning of 1 August* (p. 116). (3) *The manipulations in the* Yellow Book: *documents falsified and invented. The priority of Austrian mobilization in the British* Blue Book *and the Russian* Orange Book (p. 120). (4) *Austria accused of having been the first to mobilize in the Tsar's reply to the supreme appeal from King George V* (p. 125). (5) *The hour of the arrival of King George's telegram; two meetings of Sazonov, Buchanan and Paléologue* (p. 128). (6) *Buchanan's belated telegram to London about the Russian general mobilization* (p. 135). (7) *How the Tsar was induced to assert the priority of the Austrian general mobilization* (p. 138). (8) *First doubts in France and first reactions, the truth revealed in documents brought to light after the war* (p. 141). (9) *Paléologue's diary, Poincaré's lectures in 1921, the debate in the French Chamber on 5 July 1922* (p. 145). (10) *The exchange of letters between the President of the* Ligue des Droits de l'Homme *and Poincaré on the falsifications in the* YellowBook (p. 151). (11) L'Union Sacrée *and the admission of the truth. How Poincaré explains the falsifications in the* Yellow Book (p. 157). (12) *The publication of the* Documents diplomatiques français (p. 161).

1. *Whether it was possible for Paris on 31 July to receive the impression that the Austrian mobilization preceded that of Russia.*

In the previous chapter some account has been given of the manoeuvre whereby Viviani and the Quai d'Orsay officials sought to evade the real issue raised by the Russian general mobilization which had led to the German ultimatum to St. Petersburg. The maneuver consisted in declaring that Russia had agreed to suspend mobilization if the other Powers suspended theirs, that Russia and Austria were on the point of reaching an agreement, and that, therefore, if war broke out, it was because Germany willed it at any price. To this maneuver was added on 1 August a new one, which soon displaced it. Developed at length in the *Yellow Book*, it was maintained with persistence after the war and its effects are still to be traced in many recent French works. Whereas the first maneuver absolved Austria and concentrated the blame on Germany, the second sought to establish that Russian mobilization, which was regarded by many as the cause of the war, had been proclaimed later than the Austrian general mobilization, and was thus provoked by it. As we have seen, the truth was that Austria proclaimed her mobilization some twenty hours after the Russian mobilization. But, particularly in France, the contrary came to be believed, and the fact was of considerable importance when the question of the war guilt of the Imperial Powers came up for discussion. Since much ink has flowed on this point, the present chapter is designed to throw light into dark corners which are not without interest both in themselves and because of the personalities involved.

First of all let one point be made clear. Even had it been true that the Austrian general mobilization preceded the Russian, the one in the wrong would be not Austria but Russia, who—as has always been agreed without question—first ordered mobilization against Austria, described as partial only because it did not include the forces which would have operated against Germany, but total in respect of Austria, and hence of a nature, as Renouvin admits,[1] to compel Austria to reply with a similar measure. Thus it was confusing the issues to claim that, because Austria had ordered general mobilization, Russia was right to do the same, it being evident that the widening of Russian mobilization from partial to general mobilization constituted a threat not only to Austria but also to Germany. In spite of all this the French Government regarded the thesis as a good defense for the rash act of its ally and used it without scruple before war broke out, while war lasted, and even after the peace.

Did the idea arise from a genuine misunderstanding? Before the publication of *L'Union Sacrée* the view prevailed, or at least was put forward, that the Quai d'Orsay was unwittingly misled by the order in which the two mobilizations were communicated to it. At 7.30 p. m. on 31 July Paris received a telegram dispatched from Vienna at 5 p. m. saying:

> The order for general mobilization has just been issued to the Austro-Hungarian armies,[2]

while, on the other hand, Paléologue's telegram announcing the Russian general mobilization arrived at 8.30 p. m. But could this circumstance in any way suffice to create the impression, nay conviction, that the Austrian general mobilization was anterior to the Russian and the cause of it? The answer is: No, certainly not! Paléologue's telegram left St. Petersburg at 10.43 a. m., that of the Military Attaché left Vienna at 5 p. m. But while Paléologue said that mobilization had been ordered in Russia without stating when—it might have been during the night or the previous evening—the telegram from Vienna stated that at 5 p. m. the Austrian mobilization order *vient d'être donné*. However, in 1927 Poincaré revealed the telegram from Jules Cambon which we

---

[1] Renouvin, p. 217.   [2] DF. 3. XI, 419.

already know and which had left Berlin at 2.17 p. m., arriving at Paris at 3.30 p. m.:

According to a report reaching me, the German Ambassador at St. Petersburg seems to have telegraphed that Russia had just decided on total mobilization in reply to Austrian total mobilization.[1]

Poincaré declares that it was this telegram which led the French Government to believe that the Austrian mobilization was earlier than the Russian.

In reply to Austrian total mobilization, said Jules Cambon, and he thought this to be the version also of the German Ambassador at St. Petersburg; and we at Paris, on receiving this disjointed news, inevitably had the same impression. It was not altogether correct, and in reality, as will be seen in a moment, the two decisions had been about contemporaneous.[2]

In actual fact they were hardly contemporaneous, there being nearly a day's interval between them, and at that juncture a day was a very great deal. Did this telegram furnish legitimate grounds for the assumption that the Austrian general mobilization had preceded that of Russia? In the first place Jules Cambon had used the conditional tense, '*aurait télégraphié*', implying that he had not seen the telegram himself but was simply reporting a rumor which the Quai d'Orsay would not believe without confirmation. Not only was there no confirmation but, shortly after, J. Cambon was sent for by Jagow, who spoke of the Russian general mobilization and deeply deplored it. It may be imagined that J. Cambon would not have failed to ask whether this mobilization had been preceded by that of Austria, and that, if Jagow had admitted this, Cambon would have reported the fact to Paris. But actually in his next telegram, which arrived at 4.25 p. m., he reported the conversation with Jagow without a mention of Austrian mobilization.[3]

Nay more. If Viviani had given credence to J. Cambon's first telegram and had, as Poincaré asserts, been persuaded by it that Russian mobilization was a reply to that of Austria, he would undoubtedly have raised the point with Schoen when the latter called at 7 p. m. on 31 July to make the fact of Russian mobilization the basis of a German threat to mobilize and go to war and of a demand that France should make plain her intentions within eighteen hours. The fact, however, is that Viviani not only made no allusion to the priority of Austrian mobilization in talking with Schoen but said that he

had no information at all of an alleged total mobilization of the Russian army and navy which the German Government invoked as the reason for the new military measures which they are taking today,

---

[1] DF. 3 XI, 402.   [2] Poincaré, IV, pp. 445-6. See p. 70
[3] DF. 3. XI, 403. See pp. 70-1.

and he telegraphed Paléologue

to report to me, as a matter of urgency, as to the reality of the alleged general mobilization in Russia.[1]

It is self-evident that if he had believed that Russia had mobilized because Austria had done so he would neither have cast doubt on and disclaimed all knowledge of Russian mobilization nor would he have failed to point out that it was a consequence of Austrian mobilization. And if Paléologue had thought that Vienna had first given the bad example he would have sent a very different telegram from the one he actually sent on the evening of 31 July. There is a still further point. If the Quai d'Orsay had thought thus on 31 July, Berthelot would have brought up the matter in his talk with Szécsen at 11.15 p. m. He would have told Szécsen that his pacific words ill accorded with the actions of his Government, which by mobilizing was setting the match to the powder-cask. Far from this, Viviani gave what was said by Szécsen as a basis for telegraphing to the French ambassadors at 11.20 a. m. on 1 August that

it seems . . . that even at this late hour peace may be preserved . . . if the desire for peace at Berlin is sincere.[2]

How, moreover, can it be imagined that the Quai d'Orsay got no inkling of the truth when, on the evening of the 30th, Paléologue telegraphed that Russia had decided

to proceed secretly to the first measures of general mobilization?[3]

The news of 31 July made it appear very probable that those 'first measures' had a much wider scope and that Russian general mobiliza- tion had been in progress since the evening of 30 July. Actually this was openly stated in press telegrams to the *Matin* from St Petersburg. On 1 August the *Matin* published:

St. Petersburg, 31 July. General mobilization has been ordered. It was late last night when the Government decided it.

Immediately under this telegram was printed another saying:

Vienna, 31 July, 4.30 p. m. Mobilization in Austria-Hungary has become general by Imperial order. The notices relative to the mobilization are being posted up at this moment.

This was true. General mobilization had been proclaimed at St. Petersburg on the 30th, however much Paléologue maintained silence about it, and at Vienna on the 31st. And it has been shown above that Paris never believed otherwise. Had it done so, documents of the 31st

[1] See p. 77.   [2] DF. 3. XI, 484.   [3] See Vol. II, p. 620.

would have shown traces thereof. But there are none. The lie came to birth on 1 August. How and through whom is what we must now proceed to examine.

Writing in 1930, Poincaré states:

In Paris the Minister for Foreign Affairs and his colleagues in 1914 sincerely believed that the Austrian mobilization preceded the Russian. Viviani said this to me on several occasions and I myself repeated it to Sir F. Bertie.[1]

Since, as we shall soon see, it was on the morning of 1 August that Poincaré repeated to Bertie what Viviani had said to him 'on several occasions', one can only conclude that Viviani had made the statements on the evening of 31 July or the morning of 1 August. But it has been shown above that neither the documents written by Viviani nor the actions of his officials on the evening of 31 July and morning of 1 August show traces of any belief on the evening of the 31st that the Austrian mobilization had preceded and caused the Russian. In fact, there is proof of the contrary. At 9 a. m. on 1 August the Cabinet met. But it was certainly not then that Viviani began misleading Poincaré, for at 11 a. m. he left the Élysée Palace for his interview with Schoen. And to Schoen he never hinted that Russia had been driven to mobilize because of Austria's having previously done so, an accusation he would undoubtedly have made and which would have been most useful to him if it had as much as entered his head.

2. The first assertion of the priority of Austrian mobilization made by Poincaré to Bertie on the morning of 1 August.

So either Poincaré's memory betrayed him or he was consciously not telling the truth. It is a fact that the earliest known document in which the priority of Austrian over Russian mobilization is alleged is Bertie's report of his conversation with Poincaré on the morning of 1 August.

But first of all the time of the talk, as given by Poincaré, does not tally with that given in Bertie's telegram. Poincaré writes:

Sur la fin de l'après-dîner Sir Francis Bertie asked an audience of me.[2] Bertie's

telegram states, on the other hand:

I have seen President of the Republic and have communicated to him your urgent telegram this morning,[3]

and, in fact, his telegram left Paris at 12.30 p. m., reaching London at 2.30. Thus the audience took place before 12 noon, probably during the pause in the Cabinet meeting while Viviani absented himself for his conversation with Schoen at the Quai d'Orsay at 11 a. m. How comes

[1] Gerin, p. 153.   [2] Poincaré, IV, p. 489.   [3] BD. XI, 403.

it that Poincaré, so exact in certain particulars and no doubt using notes taken at the time, makes a mistake about the hour of so important a *démarche* ? The present writer cannot believe the mistake to be involuntary, especially as, when Poincaré was: writing, Bertie's telegram had already been published in Vol. XI of the *British Documents,* brought out in 1926. We shall return to the point later. Meanwhile we continue the narrative.

At 3.30 a. m. on that same day, 1 August, Grey had telegraphed to Bertie communicating to him a telegram of King George to the Tsar, which has been already briefly mentioned and will be discussed again later.[1] Here it is enough to say that King George was forwarding to the Tsar a telegram, sent by Bethmann to Lichnowsky and by Lichnowsky passed on to the Foreign Office, explaining and deploring the disastrous consequences of the Russian general mobilization.[2] King George added:

I cannot help thinking that some misunderstanding has produced this deadlock. . . . I therefore make a personal appeal to you to remove the misapprehension, which I feel must have occurred, and to leave still open grounds for negotiation and possible peace.[3]

Grey, in forwarding these documents, instructed Bertie:

You should apply to the President at once for an audience and communicate to him the following message sent by the King to the Emperor of Russia.

And this is what Bertie did.

In his report of the audience Bertie wrote to London:

[Poincaré] says the German Government were endeavoring to put on Russia responsibility for critical state of affairs, *that Emperor of Russia did not order a general mobilization until after a decree of general mobilization had been issued in Austria;* that measures already taken by German Government, though not designated a general mobilization, are so in effect; that France is already forty-eight hours behindhand as regards German military preparations and that a French general mobilization will become necessary for self-defense; that whereas German troops are actually on the French frontier, and have made incursions on it in places, orders to French troops are not to go nearer to the German frontier than a distance of 10 km. from it, so as to avoid any ground for accusations of provocation to Germany; that Emperor of Russia has expressed his readiness, notwithstanding mobilizations, to continue his conversations with German Ambassador with object of preservation of peace, which is sincere desire of France, whose wishes are markedly pacific; and that French Government do not quite despair of war being avoided.[4]

[1] BD. XI, 384. See pp. 51, 125.   [2] DD. III, 513; BD. XI, 372.
[3] BD. XI, 384.   [4] BD. XI, 403.

Poincaré in *L'Union Sacrée* vouchsafes no account of what passed between himself and Bertie at this audience. He only adds:

I communicated this note [i.e., King George's telegram to the Tsar] to M. Viviani and he agreed with me in approving this new initiative and associating himself with it as with all the others.[1]

But Bertie's telegram does not speak of Poincaré's support, nor is there any trace in the *Yellow Book*, the *Documents Diplomatiques Français*, or Poincaré's own memoirs of any document by which the French Government associated itself with King George's initiative, so that it is hard to believe that one ever existed. On the other hand, Bertie's dispatch makes it plain that Poincaré was so warm in his defense of the Russian action that he was practically refusing to put pressure on Russia. The same line of conduct, in short, as that of the previous evening, only justified by a new and apparently decisive argument, namely, that Austria had been the first to decree general mobilization and therefore (though he did not actually say so) to cause Russia to mobilize.

Who first suggested this argument? We shall see the answer to this later on.[2] For the moment it is enough to establish that the first to use it was Poincaré, and the question obtrudes itself whether he relegated the audience with Bertie to *la fin de l'après-dîner*—an unusual, vague expression—either to create the impression that King George's initiative was not supported for lack of time (Paris learnt at 11.30 p. m. on 1 August that Germany had declared war on Russia) or, above all to make it seem that Margerie and Viviani were the first to say that Austria mobilized before Russia, hence that he himself was only repeating it.

But it was not true that Margerie and Viviani were the first to say so. In the afternoon of 1 August Bertie saw Margerie, and his telegram, dispatched at 7.10 p. m., reports:

Political Director tells me that German Ambassador called at Ministry for Foreign Affairs this morning. He was informed that French Government do not comprehend for what reason his communication yesterday evening was made. It seemed to them strange that, at a moment when Russia and Austria were ready to converse, German Government presents an ultimatum at St. Petersburg requiring immediate demobilization by Russia, *general mobilization in that country not having been ordered until after decree of Austrian general mobilization,* and Russian Government having expressed its readiness to demobilize if all Powers did likewise.[3]

But Viviani had not said any such thing to Schoen. Or rather he had made the untrue statement that

---

[1] Poincaré, IV, p. 491.   [2] See p. 139.   [3] BD. XI, 428. Italics ours.

Sir Ed. Grey's proposal for a cessation of military preparations on the part of all concerned has been accepted by Russia in principle,

but had not in any way claimed that Austria had mobilized before Russia. Had he done so Schoen would have telegraphed this to Berlin. Not only does it not figure in Schoen's own telegram, but Viviani makes no mention of such a thing in the circular telegram he sent to the French ambassadors giving an account of what he had said to Schoen.[1] On the contrary, far from accusing Austria, Viviani was ascribing ultra-pacific intentions to her. Nor did he breathe a word of the accusation to Schoen when the latter called on him for a second time at 5.30 p. m. to receive an answer about the intentions of France. Therefore, Margerie's statement to Bertie was without foundation, and Margerie himself cannot have believed it. Margerie presumably saw Bertie at about 5 p. m., to judge by the hour at which the latter's telegram was dispatched, and his next caller was Szécsen, whose dispatch, sent off at 10.50 p. m., runs:

France has today ordered general mobilization. . . . French mobilization, says M. Margerie, is purely defensive and merely an answer to German measures. . . . Mobilization is, moreover, a long way from being a declaration of war, especially here, where consent of Parliament necessary. . . . Between Germany and France, he maintains, no controversial questions exist, and the German attitude and the Ambassador's language can only be interpreted here as based on the desire of Germany to bring about war. I dissented from this opinion. My interlocutor mentioned with satisfaction our discussions with St. Petersburg and emphatically stressed French desire to bring about *détente.*[2]

However, there exists one document, bearing Viviani's signature and dated 1 August, in which the trick, excogitated at the Élysée that morning and adopted by Margerie in the afternoon, of putting the blame for the Russian mobilization on Austria, is fully developed. It is the notorious No. 127 of the *Yellow Book,* which has been mentioned already [3] and has been the cause of much discussion and criticism of Viviani:

We are warned through several channels that the German and the Austrian Governments are trying at this moment to influence England by making her believe that the responsibility for war, if it breaks out, will fall on Russia. Efforts are being made to obtain the neutrality of England by disguising the truth. France has not ceased, in co-operation with England, to advise moderation at St. Petersburg; this advice has been listened to. From the beginning M. Sazonov has exercised pressure on Serbia to make her accept all those clauses of the ultimatum which were not incompatible with her sovereignty. He then engaged in a direct

---

[1] DD. III, 571; DF. 3. XI, 505; LJF. 125; CDD., pp. 228-9. See p. 101.
[2] DA. III, 93.   [3] See pp. 107-8.

conversation with Austria; this was fresh evidence of his conciliatory spirit. .... M. Sazonov consented to modify the first formula which he had put forward, and he has drawn up a second which is shown not to differ materially from the declaration which Count Szécsen made yesterday to M. de Margerie. . . . It would then seem that an agreement between Sir Edward Grey's suggestion, M. Sazonov's formula and the Austrian declarations could easily be achieved. . . . But while these negotiations were going on, and while Russia in the negotiations showed a good will which cannot be disputed, *Austria was the first to proceed to a general mobilization. Russia has found herself obliged to imitate Austria,* so as not to be left in an unfavorable position, but all the time she has continued ready to negotiate. It is not necessary for me to repeat that, so far as we are concerned, we will, in co-operation with England, continue to work for the success of these *pourparlers.* But the attitude of Germany has made it absolutely compulsory for us to make out the order for mobilization today. Last Wednesday, well in advance of Russian mobilization. . . . Herr von Schoen announced to me the impending publication of the *Kriegsgefahrzustand.* This measure has been taken by Germany, and under the protection of this screen she immediately began a mobilization in the proper sense of the word. Today M. Paléologue telegraphed that Count Pourtalès had notified the Russian Government of German mobilization. Information which has been received by the Ministry of War confirms the fact that this mobilization is really in full execution. Our decree of mobilization is then an *essential measure* of protection.[1]

Let us first note the change of attitude which this document betrays. No longer is it asserted that Russia agreed to demobilize if the other Powers did the same, nor that Austria was willing to seek an agreement with Russia. These untrue statements were dropped, and instead the new allegation of the priority of Austrian mobilization went a step further than Poincaré and Margerie had done in saying that 'Russia has found herself obliged to imitate Austria'.

3. *The manipulations in the* Yellow Book: *documents falsified and invented. The priority of Austrian mobilization in the British* Blue Book *and the Russian* Orange Book.

In the *Yellow Book* we can watch the development of the maneuver to make Russia appear innocent and Austria guilty. To attain this end documents are manipulated and falsified to an extent which caused great scandal when the matter came to public knowledge.

On the evening of 30 July Paléologue had sent a telegram explaining the reasons for the Russian general mobilization which had shortly before been decreed and which he announced in the equivocal form:

In consequence the Russian Government has decided to proceed secretly to the first measures of general mobilization.

[1] LJF. 127; CDD. pp. 230-1.

The telegram, as has been already shown, was inserted into the second part of No. 102 of the *Yellow Book,* but the vital sentence, just quoted, which was the proof that Russia as early as the evening of 30 July, i.e., before Austria did so, was at least beginning to proceed to general mobilization, was left out.[1] Furthermore, in reproducing the telegrams of 31 July from Paléologue and Dumaine announcing respectively the Russian and the Austrian mobilizations, that of Dumaine, which was dispatched at 6 p. m., was, as No. 115, put before that of Paléologue (No. 118), which was dispatched at 10.43 a. m. This would hardly have mattered if the *Yellow Book* had printed the hours of dispatch and receipt of each document. But since it (like all the other collections of documents then made public by the belligerent Powers) omitted to do so, the documents would have had to be arranged in order of dispatch if misrepresentations were to be avoided. But in the present case the misrepresentation was so intentional that Dumaine's dispatch was given in the following form:

General mobilization for all men from 19 to 42 years of age was declared by the Austro-Hungarian Government this morning at 1 o'clock. My Russian colleague still thinks that this step is not entirely in contradiction to the declaration made yesterday by Count Berchtold.[2]

The telegram as actually sent by Dumaine, at 6 p. m., went on further to say:

He supposes that by this stationing of troops on her frontiers, Austria seeks to obtain a forced localization of the conflict.

But still more important is the fact that the telegram does not contain the words 'this morning at 1 o'clock'.[3] And since it had been preceded by one from the Military Attaché at Vienna, dispatched at 5 p. m. and received at 7.30 p. m. on 31 July, saying:

The order of general mobilization has just been given to the Austro-Hungarian armies,[4]

i.e., just before 5 p. m., the addition of the words 'this morning at 1 o'clock' in the *Yellow Book* appears as an intentional tampering with the truth. And the same holds good of No. 118, which runs as follows:

---

[1] See Vol. II, p. 620.   [2] LJF. 115; CDD., p. 222.
[3] DF. 3. XI, 431; Poincaré, IV, p. 459. The original telegram bears an annotation by Berthelot: 'Austrian general mobilization 31st (5 a. m.). Russian mobilization follows (10 a. m.). German *Kriegszustand* (3 o'clock). Convocation of French covering troops (6 o'clock).' The editors of the *Documents Diplomatiques Français* comment that another jotting on the corner of the page: '31 July, 1914, 118', must have been made at the time when the *Yellow Book* was being prepared, but they add that it is not possible to determine whether the annotation itself was made at that moment or at the time when the telegram was originally received (DF. 3. XI, 431 note).
[4] DF. 3. XI, 419.

As a result of the general mobilization of Austria and of the measures for mobilization taken secretly, but continuously, by Germany for the last six days, the order for the general mobilization of the Russian army has been given, Russia not being able, without most serious danger, to allow herself to be further outdistanced; really she is only taking military measures corresponding to those taken by Germany. For imperative reasons of strategy the Russian Government, knowing that Germany was arming, could no longer delay the conversion of her partial mobilization into a general mobilization.[1]

It will be remembered that Paléologue had confined himself to telegraphing at 10.43 a. m. on the 31st:

An order has been issued for the general mobilization of the Russian army.[2]

This laconic line was the source which inspired the compilers of the *Yellow Book* to the whole flight of fancy of No. 118, which was phrased to corroborate the falsification perpetrated on Dumaine's telegram. No. 115 lays down that Austrian mobilization started (on the 31st) 'this morning at 1 o'clock'. No. 118 develops the logical consequence that 'As a result of the general mobilization of Austria', etc. No. 127 amplifies the idea still further: 'Austria was the first to proceed to a general mobilization. Russia has found herself obliged to imitate Austria.'

The thesis was a bold one. But when the *Yellow Book* appeared on 1 December 1914 there had already been published the British *Blue Book* on 5 August, the Russian *Orange Book* on 7 August, and a second edition of the British *Blue Book* on 24 September, in all of which the thesis was either indirectly supported or explicitly confirmed. The Quai d'Orsay may well have thought that if the Germans and Austrians attacked it they would be met by a united Franco-Anglo-Russian front to which world opinion would give more credence, as was indeed the case for a considerable time. But the question then arises: was it the British and Russian Governments which first falsified the facts? The answer is: No. It was Paris which first alleged the priority of Austrian mobilization, notwithstanding the circumstance that the *Blue Book* and the *Orange Book* were issued before the *Yellow Book*. At this point it is necessary to make a long diversion to explain how the lie made its way into the *Blue Book* and especially into the *Orange Book*.

In the *Blue Book*, Buchanan's telegram announcing the Russian general mobilization appears as No. 113, dated 31 July. But it lacked the footnote which was inserted in the *British Documents* of 1926:

The date of dispatch seems to be wrong. . . . The telegram was probably sent at 6.40 p. m. on 30 July and delayed in transmission and a mistake made by the clerk who deciphered the original telegram.[3]

---

[1] CDD., p. 223.   [2] DF. 3. XI, 432. See Vol. II, p. 622.
[3] BD. XI, 347 and note.

Thus the impression was created that the Russian general mobilization had been ordered after the Austrian, as was asserted by Poincaré and Margerie in their talks on 1 August with Bertie, whose telegrams appear in paraphrase as Nos. 125 and 136 of the. *Blue Book.*[1] Is it to be inferred that the compilers of the British *Blue Book* intentionally altered the date of Buchanan's telegram, because to give the real date would have destroyed the French thesis of the priority of Austrian mobilization? In France this has been maintained, among others, by G. Demartial.[2] But it cannot be accepted. There are omissions and paraphrases in the *Blue Book* but nothing in the nature of falsification of documents—and such a change of date would be a falsification—all the more so since it is highly probable, if not entirely certain, that, as will be shown farther on, the telegram in question is in reality of 31 July.[3]

The assertion that Austria ordered general mobilization before Russia did so occurs, however, in a letter of 1 September 1914 from Bunsen, the English Ambassador at Vienna, to Grey:

> It is deplorable that no effort should have been made [by Austria] to secure by means of diplomatic negotiations the acquiescence of Russia and Europe as a whole in some peaceful compromise of the Serbian question by which Austrian fears of Serbian aggression and intrigue might have been removed for the future. Instead of adopting this course the Austro-Hungarian Government resolved upon war. The inevitable consequence ensued. Russia replied to a partial Austrian mobilization and declaration of war against Serbia by a partial Russian mobilization against Austria. Austria met this move by completing her own mobilization, and Russia again responded, with results that have passed into history.[4]

Bunsen wrote thus in perfect good faith. From where he was he did not and could not know the sequence of events and his mistake was a natural one. In actual fact, Austria on 30-31 July had decided to resort to general mobilization in response to Russia's having ordered partial mobilization directed against her on 29th, not as a result of learning that on 30 July Russia had changed the partial into a total mobilization. This latter was a step affecting Germany, not further threatening Austria. It was not surprising, therefore, that at Vienna it could be thought that the Austrian general mobilization had preceded the Russian.

This order of events is still more explicitly set forth in the Russian *Orange Book.* Before the German declaration of war Sazonov made no

---

[1]   (*Blue Book*) *Great Britain and the European Crisis. Correspondence and Statements in Parlia ment together with an introductory narrative of events* (London, 1914).
[2]   G. Demartial, 'Les responsabilités de la guerre. Histoire d'un mensonge', *Évolution,* May 1931, p. 37.
[3]   See p. 135-6.   [4] *Blue Book,* 161; BD. XI, 676.

claim that the Russian general mobilization was a result of the Austrian. As a justification for the partial mobilization, he said on the 29th to Pourtalès that

Austria had mobilized eight army corps and this measure must be regarded as partly directed against Russia.[1]

On the evening of that same day he telegraphed to Izvolsky:

We, in fact, made these preparations only on account of the mobilization already undertaken of eight army corps by Austria,[2]

as if these eight army corps were threatening Russia.

Now Sazonov's statement was not made in good faith, because he knew well enough that the eight army corps were destined for operations against Serbia and that their mobilization was not a threat to Russia. And he dropped this pretext later on. Very probably, however, in persuading the Tsar to consent to the military measures he desired to carry out, Sazonov used the argument that Austria was arming also against Russia. The *Journal of the Russian General Staff Committee* of 25 July, summarizing the decisions taken at the audience at Krasnoe Selo that afternoon, records:

From messages coming in Austria-Hungary and Italy would seem already to be taking certain preliminary steps towards mobilization. Therefore H.M. the Tsar was pleased to confirm the decree of the Council of Ministers that the pre-mobilization period shall begin in the night of 25–26 July.[3]

In the next few days after the 25th the Tsar's advisers must have persuaded him that Austria was mobilizing in Galicia, so that on the 29th they obtained his signature to the decrees for partial and for general mobilization. This can be seen in the telegram sent by the Tsar to Wilhelm in the night of 29/30 July:

The military measures which have now come into force [i.e., partial mobilization] were decided five days ago for reasons of defense on account of Austria's preparations.[4]

But on the 30th Wilhelm replied:

Austria has only mobilized against Serbia and only a part of her army.[5]

This did not convince the Tsar, who replied at 2.55 p. m. on the 31st:

It is technically impossible to stop our military preparations, which were obligatory owing to Austria's mobilization.[6]

[1] DD. II, 343. See Vol. II, p. 549.
[2] *Int. Bez.* i. V, 221. See Vol. II, p. 556,
[3] *Int. Bez.* i. V, 79.
[4] DD. II, 390. See Vol. II, p. 560.
[5] DD. II, 420. See p. 6.
[6] DD. III, 487. See p. 56.

This was evidently a deep-seated conviction with the Tsar; and Sazonov, to say the least of it, took no steps to undeceive him, appearing, in fact, to share the same conviction in the friendly conversation he had with Szápáry in the afternoon of 31 July. Szápáry's dispatch narrates that as an excuse for the Russian mobilization Sazonov alleged:

> Moreover we [the Austrians] had mobilized first, an assertion which I distinctly denied, so that the Minister said: 'Let us leave chronology aside.'[1]

Were the words of the Tsar and of Sazonov allusions to the Austrian mobilization against Serbia or to the Austrian mobilization which Berchtold on the afternoon of the 30th had notified in advance to Shebeko as being a reply to the Russian mobilization against Austria?[2] It is possible, as will be shown later, that the allusion was to the latter. Be that as it may, one thing is certain, namely that the priority of the Austrian general mobilization over the Russian was first definitely asserted in the Tsar's telegram of 2 August, replying to the already mentioned telegram from King George,[3] to which it is now necessary to turn our attention.

4. Austria accused of having been the first to mobilize in the Tsar's reply to the supreme appeal from King George V.

It has already been narrated above that on the evening of 31 July Bethmann Hollweg had belatedly telegraphed to Lichnowsky:

> We have told Russia that unless the warlike measures were suspended within twelve hours we would mobilize and that would mean war. We have asked France whether she will remain neutral in a Russo-German war.[4]

Lichnowsky communicated the telegram to Tyrrell, and it so alarmed Asquith that he had King George wakened and got him to send the German statement on to the Tsar immediately, accompanied by the following message:

> I cannot help thinking that some misunderstanding has produced this deadlock. I am most anxious not to miss any opportunity of avoiding the terrible calamity which at present threatens the whole world. I therefore make a personal appeal to you to remove the misapprehension which I feel must have occurred, and to leave still open grounds for negotiation and possibly peace. If you think I can in any way contribute to that all-important purpose, I will do everything in my power to assist in reopening the interrupted conversations between the Powers concerned. I feel confident that you are as anxious as I am that all that is possible should be done to secure the peace of the world.[5]

---

[1] DA. III, 97; see Vol. II, p. 682.
[2] *Int. Bez.* i. V, 307. See Vol. II, p. 662.
[3] See p. 117.
[4] DD. III, 513. See p. 51.
[5] BD. XI, 384; CDD., p. 536.

The instruction to Buchanan by which this is prefaced runs:

You should at once apply for an audience with His Majesty the Emperor and convey to him the following personal message from the King.

It went off at 3.30 a. m. on 1 August and the Tsar replied at 3.10 p. m. the next day:

I would gladly have accepted your proposals had not German Ambassador this afternoon presented a note to my Government declaring war. Ever since presentation of the ultimatum to Belgrade, Russia has devoted all her efforts to finding some pacific solution of the question raised by Austria's action. Object of that action was to crush Serbia and make her a vassal of Austria. Effect of this would have been to upset balance of power in Balkans, which is of such a vital interest to my Empire as well as to those Powers who desire maintenance of balance of power in Europe. Every proposal, including that of your Government, was rejected by Germany and Austria, and it was only when favorable moment for bringing pressure to bear on Austria had passed that Germany showed any disposition to mediate. Even then she did not put forward any precise proposal. Austria's declaration of war on Serbia forced me to order a partial mobilization, though, in view of threatening situation, my military advisers strongly advised a general mobilization owing to quickness with which Germany can mobilize in comparison with Russia. I was eventually compelled to take this course in consequence of complete Austrian mobilization, of the bombardment of Belgrade, of concentration of Austrian troops in Galicia, and of secret military preparations being made by Germany. That I was justified in doing so is proved by Germany's sudden declaration of war, which was quite unexpected by me, as I had given most categorical assurances to the Emperor William that my troops would not move so long as mediation negotiations continued.

In this solemn hour I wish to assure you once more that I have done all in my power to avert war. Now that it has been forced on me, I trust your country will not fail to support France and Russia in fighting to maintain balance of power in Europe. God bless and protect you.[1]

In this, as in all the Tsar's messages, there is a note of sincerity which must be borne in mind in any appraisement of the man and his actions. His estimate of the situation is substantially correct, except for the statement: 'I was eventually compelled to take this course in consequence of complete Austrian mobilization.' Let it be here repeated once more that there was no sense in this statement since Austria was already covered by the Russian partial mobilization, and that her general mobilization was a measure directed against Germany. It was, moreover, quite natural that Austria should reply to Russian partial mobilization by her own general mobilization. This was well understood at St. Petersburg. But for this very reason when the *Orange Book* was being compiled the falsification was carried much further. As

---

[1] BD. XI, 490; *Int. Bez.* i. V, 451.

the Russian partial mobilization had been ordered on the evening of 29 July, the Austrian general mobilization was made to appear as having been ordered still earlier. What Shebeko had telegraphed from Vienna on 28 July was:

In all, eight army corps have been mobilized up to the present, i.e., half the entire Austro-Hungarian army.[1]

But the *Orange Book* invents a telegram of 28 July from Shebeko: The order for general mobilization has been signed.[2]

The forgery is admitted in the official collection of Russian documents. As a footnote to Shebeko's real telegram the forged telegram appears with the comment:

This telegram is not in the Archives of the former Foreign Ministry.

The same falsehood was repeated in more general terms in two later documents. In Sazonov's telegram to Izvolsky of 29 July, mentioned above,[3] which said: 'We . . . made these preparations only on account of the mobilization already undertaken *of eight army corps* by Austria', the words in italics were omitted, making the sentence read: 'on account of the mobilization already undertaken by Austria'.[4] Again on 2 August, after war had been declared, Sazonov sent a telegram to Benckendorff declaring:

Germany endeavors in the eyes of the world to cast the responsibility for the rupture on Russia. The general mobilization in Russia has been, provoked solely in view of the immense responsibility which the Russian Government would have taken upon its shoulders if it had not taken all the precautionary measures which had become absolutely necessary to its security at the moment when Austria was confining herself to negotiations of a dilatory nature and was bombarding Belgrade.[5]

This was the truth. But in the *Orange Book,* where the telegram figures as a message to all Russian Representatives Abroad, the relevant passage runs:

if we had not taken all possible precautionary measures at a time when Austria, while confining herself to discussions of a dilatory nature, was bombarding Belgrade and *was undertaking general mobilization.*[6]

It is singular that the original telegram lacks this falsehood which the Tsar had been made to utter or allowed to utter on the previous evening. Did Sazonov fight shy of repeating it? This would seem to be the case, since he did not venture to allege the priority of the Austrian

---

[1] *Int. Bez.* i. V, 190.
[3] *Int. Bez.* i. V, 79; see p. 124.
[5] *Int. Bez.* i. V, 452; BD. XI, 532.

[2] *Orange Book,* 47; CDD., p. 283.
[4] *Orange Book,* 58.
[6] *Orange Book,* 78; CDD., p. 297.

general mobilization even in the speech he made in the Duma on 8 August:

Time was passing. Negotiations were making no progress. Austria was fiercely bombarding Belgrade. . . . In these circumstances we could not do otherwise than take obvious measures, all the more as Austria had already mobilized half her army. When the mobilization was ordered in Russia, our Tsar gave the Kaiser of Germany his imperial word that Russia would not make use of arms so long as there still remained a hope of a peaceful solution on the moderate terms already mentioned. This voice was not listened to. Germany declared war first on us and then on our allies.[1]

This was the truth. Does it, therefore, follow that the Tsar alleged the priority of Austrian general mobilization of his own initiative and that Sazonov had no hand in drawing up the reply to King George? We must examine the circumstances in which the drafting of it took place. It is a point which has given rise to much discussion in Germany and it is not fully cleared up.

5. The hour of arrival of King George's telegram; two meetings of Sazonov, Buchanan and Paléologue.

King George's appeal to Nicholas II could not fail to have a profound effect on the men in charge of Russian policy, since any failure to pay heed to it might have incalculable consequences. Asquith and Tyrrell attached so much importance to the King's intervention that, as has been said, they did not hesitate to have him wakened in the night in order to submit the draft to him, and it went off at 3.30 a. m. on 1 August. Already at 2.5 a. m. preliminary warning of it had been sent by Crowe to Bertie:

An important and urgent telegram of some length is going to you in cipher. Please arrange to have it deciphered without delay.[2]

The warning was not sent to Buchanan, and this may be explained by a desire that the King's telegram should reach Paris before it reached St. Petersburg in order that the Quai d'Orsay should support it by pressure at St. Petersburg, pressure which, as we have seen, was never exercised. We learn from a letter of Buchanan's to Nicolson of 3 August:

The King's telegram to the Emperor reached me at 5 o'clock on Saturday afternoon,

i.e., too late to influence the situation.[3]

The German historian Bach has cast doubts on this hour of arrival on grounds that, in view of its urgent nature, it ought to have been

[1] Schulthess, 1914. Vol. II, pp. 841–2.
[2] BD. XI, 381.
[3] BD. XI, 665.

delivered much earlier and that Buchanan's telegram ordinarily took only six or seven hours to reach London.[1] King George telegraphed to Wilhelm in the afternoon of 1 August:

Last night I sent an urgent telegram to Nicky. . . ,[2]

From this Bach concludes

that King George's telegram was dispatched in good time so that it could with certainty have been in the Tsar's hands before 12 noon on 1 August and that therefore it was possible for the telegram to have exercised an influence on the Tsar before the expiry of the German ultimatum to Russia which fell due at that hour.[3]

It may be objected that, when Buchanan writes that he received the telegram at 5 p. m., he means that it was then he received it decoded; he may even have been absent from the Embassy when the telegram arrived and found it awaiting him on his return. But in any case, even allowing that an urgent telegram should not have taken all those hours to arrive, it could not have arrived in time for Buchanan to read it decoded, to request and obtain an audience, make the journey to Peterhof and be received by the Tsar before 11 a. m. For that, King George's telegram would have had to go off several hours earlier, and this, as has been shown already, might have happened, had Bethmann's telegram to Lichnowsky, which gave rise to King George's appeal, been dispatched at noon on the 31st instead of at 8.30 p. m.[4]

Still better would it have been if King George had telegraphed directly to the Tsar *en clair,* as the Tsar and Wilhelm always did to each other, by-passing Buchanan, who—and here Bach is certainly right— did not treat this important document with the urgency it deserved. On this occasion his behavior gives rise to doubts, as being so greatly in contrast with that of the preceding days when he had endeavored to restrain Sazonov from military measures which would be certain to set the dangerous mechanism of mobilization in motion. By the time Buchanan received the appeal, as he says, at 5 p. m., seventeen hours had already elapsed since the German ultimatum had been presented to Sazonov. Buchanan should not have lost a moment in making every effort to see the Tsar immediately, as Grey desired. He would have been too late all the same, but this was something he could not know at the time, and every hour gained might have been invaluable. What Buchanan did was to call on Sazonov, not only to ask for an audience, but also to discuss with Sazonov and Paléologue the King's message and how the Tsar should answer it. Had he instructions to do this? He

---

[1] August Bach, *König Georgs Telegramm an den Zaren,* KSF., 1932, pp. 1221-9; see also Gustav Roloff, *Englands Anteil an der Kriegsschuld,* KSF., 1928, pp. 917-50 and *König Georg von England und der Ausbruch des Weltkrieges,* KSF., 1931, pp. 927-38.
[2] DD. III, 574.   [3] Bach, KSF., 1932, p. 1222.   [4] DD. III, 513.

is silent on this point in his letter to Nicolson, and his silence is significant. But the *Documents Diplomatiques Français* reproduce the following telegram from Paléologue, dispatched from St. Petersburg at 8.30 p. m. on 1 August:

> King George V has just telegraphed to Tsar Nicholas addressing a supreme appeal to his pacific sentiments. My English colleague, who undertakes to deliver the telegram, at once asked for an audience of the Tsar; he will probably be received at Peterhof tonight. M. Sazonov, Sir G. Buchanan and I have just been discussing the reply which His Britannic Majesty's appeal calls for. I pressed that Tsar Nicholas should reiterate and if necessary underline the statements he made yesterday in his personal telegram to Kaiser Wilhelm,[1] begging King George to confirm, nay even to guarantee, to the German Emperor the sincerity of these assurances. I particularly pointed out that the Tsar's reply must leave no doubt as to his will to save the peace still, for this reply will perhaps decide whether England will or will not take sides against Germany.[2]

Certainly the King, Asquith, and Grey never dreamt of Paléologue's having a finger in what the Tsar was to say and to do. On the evening of the 29th a telegram from Wilhelm had sufficed to make Nicholas II telegraph to Janushkevich ordering the suspension of the general mobilization which he had authorized a few hours earlier.[3] The King of England was appealing to him, not to his Ministers, still less to the French Ambassador.

Nor is this all. Let us see what happened after this discussion. Paléologue's telegram indicates that it took place before Pourtalès delivered the declaration of war at 7 p. m., let us say between 5 and 7 p. m. This tallies with the hour at which Paléologue's telegram was dispatched, i.e., 10.30 p. m. However, Bach maintains—and regards it as a proof that King George's telegram arrived before 5 p. m.—that the three diplomats met earlier than 5 p. m. because Schilling's Diary says that Sazonov was at a Council of Ministers in Elagin Island between 5 and 7 p. m. But what Schilling's Diary really says is:

> Between 4 and 5 p. m. Count Pourtalès called up Baron Schilling on the telephone and said that it was indispensable that he should see the Minister at once. Baron Schilling replied that at the present time S. D. Sazonov was in Elagin Island attending a Council of Ministers, and promised to inform the Ambassador directly the Minister returned. This was done soon after
> 6 p. m.[4]

This makes it possible that Sazonov got back to his Ministry soon after six and, before Pourtalès's arrival, had a word with Buchanan, who was probably waiting in the antechamber with Paléologue.

[1] DD. III, 546. See p. 64.   [2] DF. 3. XI, 536; Poincaré, IV, p. 497.
[3] See Vol. II, pp. 559-60.   [4] Schilling, p. 76.

The two *Entente* Ambassadors could not have been long gone when Pourtalès presented himself with the declaration of war, news of which Sazonov telephoned to Buchanan at 7.15 p. m., adding that the Tsar was expecting him at 10 p. m.[1] The declaration of war rendered King George's intervention nugatory and also made it very difficult for the Tsar to frame a reply, since Russia must now justify herself for causing so great a catastrophe. Sazonov entrusted the task to one of the senior officials at the Ministry, laying down the general lines of the reply. Then at 8 p. m. he went to dine at the British Embassy, where he again found Paléologue. Buchanan's letter to Nicolson tells:

He [Sazonov] happened to be dining with me that evening,[2]

but is silent on the presence of Paléologue, as about the earlier meeting of the three.[3] The letter to Nicolson gives the following account of what followed:

Just before I started in my motor for Peterhof, a messenger brought a draft of the reply which he had drawn up for the Emperor's approval. I arrived at a little villa on the shores of the Gulf, where the Imperial Family always live, at 10.45 p. m. and was at once received by His Majesty. In reply to a question which he addressed to me, I told him frankly that the draft reply in French was, in my opinion, couched in too official language and that I should personally greatly prefer it if His Majesty would answer the King in his own words. The Emperor expressed his entire concurrence, and we then proceeded to discuss the whole situation. Finally His Majesty sat down at his writing table and asked me to help him in drawing up the reply. This was by no means an easy task as, though he talks English fluently, he evidently found some difficulty in putting what he wanted into words; and I virtually had to dictate the telegram to him on the lines of the draft which Sazonov had given me and on what His Majesty had told me. I was with him for an hour and a half and only got back at 2 o'clock [a. m. 2 August].

One would have thought that immediately on his return Buchanan would have had the Tsar's reply enciphered by a clerk, held in readiness to do so, and that it would have been sent off without delay. But in fact it only went off at 3.10 p. m. on 2 August. The delay is so extreme as to rouse suspicion as to whether it was intentional, i.e., whether Buchanan kept the telegram back, either in order first to have it read and approved by Sazonov, or lest it should adversely influence the decisions of his own country, of which he felt none too sure. How uncertain he felt is shown by the comment with which he accompanied the Tsar's reply:

---

[1] Sir George Buchanan, *My Mission to Russia* (London, New York, 1923), I, p. 205.
[2] BD. XI, 665.
[3] Buchanan, *op. cit.* I, p. 205. Paléologue's presence is attested by Buchanan's daughter, Meriel Buchanan, *The Dissolution of an Empire* (London, 1932), p. 90.

German statement [i.e., the one forwarded to the Tsar by King George] entirely misrepresents case, and its evident object is to persuade His Majesty's Government that responsibility for war rests with Russia in the hope of inducing them to remain neutral. I would venture to submit with all respect that if we do not respond to Emperor's appeal for our support, we shall at end of the war, whatever be its issue, find ourselves without a friend in Europe, while our Indian Empire will no longer be secure of attack by Russia.[1]

Let us recapitulate the facts noted in this account: scant eagerness on Buchanan's part to deliver his King's appeal, since he showed it to Sazonov and Paléologue before giving it to the Tsar; the telegram discussed by the three but no mention of the discussion in Buchanan's letter to Nicolson; active interference of Paléologue in laying down the lines of the reply to be made by the Tsar before the latter had even seen the King's message;[2] outright refusal to consider King George's expressed desire that Russia should demobilize; second meeting of the three diplomats at the dinner, this also not mentioned in Buchanan's letter; draft for a reply taken with him by Buchanan; abnormal delay on Buchanan's part in telegraphing to London the text entrusted to him by the Tsar; addition by him to the Tsar's message of a comment stressing Russian innocence and advocating support for her. These features seem to point to some sort of intrigue to avert the danger of England's remaining neutral in consequence of the Russian mobilization which seemed to have brought about the catastrophe. Indeed, the query obtrudes itself whether the idea of denying that Russia was the first to order general mobilization and accusing Austria of so doing did not perhaps occur to one of the three diplomatists at that dinner.

At the dinner itself, and not at the previous discussion, because otherwise some trace of the idea would have been visible in the draft of a reply for which Sazonov gave instructions before going to the dinner and which was brought him at the end of it. This draft is preserved among the Russian documents and makes no suggestion of Austrian mobilization having preceded that of Russia. It runs as follows:

Austria began to mobilize on a scale disquieting for us and there immediately followed the to me unexpected news of the declaration of war on

---

[1] BD. XI, 490.

[2] In his two articles, mentioned above, G. Roloff maintains that the Tsar must have been informed by Sazonov of the contents of King George's telegram when Sazonov telephoned to ask for an audience for Buchanan. This would mean that the postponement of the audience 'by some five hours, until after expiry of the ultimatum' had the Tsar's approval (KSF., 1928, p. 939). To this the reply is: that the ultimatum expired at noon; that Roloff brings no proof of his assertions; that it was not in the Tsar's character to resort to such subterfuges. He who had shown the utmost promptness in replying to Wilhelm's telegram and in receiving Pourtalès, would not have delayed five hours in granting Buchanan an audience if he had been cognizant of the important nature of the document to be presented. It is more logical to suppose that it was Sazonov who concealed this from him and suggested the late hour for the audience itself.

Serbia and the bombardment of Belgrade. In view of these facts and having become convinced of the uselessness of negotiations, which only wasted time, I found myself compelled to mobilize on my part.[1]

It was not true that before the Russian general mobilization Austria had begun mobilizing on a scale disquieting to Russia. But this exaggeration was trifling in comparison with the assertion which figured in the Tsar's final version, namely, that the Russian partial mobilization had been changed into general mobilization 'in consequence of Austrian general mobilization'. Unless this version emanated from the Tsar, it must have originated in the mind of one of the three diplomats and been agreed upon when they met again at dinner at the British Embassy, by which time Sazonov had just received the German declaration of war. This must have been the main theme of their conversation and they must have been anxious to make the best of the situation.

That something had to be done was beyond doubt. On that same day, 1 August, Benckendorff had telegraphed to Sazonov from London:

I am having it stated in the press that responsibility for extremely dangerous crisis falls on German demand that there must be demobilization within twelve hours, that this demand is tantamount to putting match to the powder barrel at the very moment when favorable negotiations have been resumed by England. Pacifist party, supported by pro-Germans, tries to throw the responsibility on Russia, whose mobilization order preceded the proclamation of *Kriegsgefahr* in Germany.[2]

It is doubtful whether this telegram arrived in St. Petersburg and was read by Sazonov before he went to the British Embassy, but in any case Buchanan may well have known how matters stood and explained the position to his guests, with the result that they persuaded him to put forward the thesis of the priority of the Austrian general mobilization. It was, in fact, during Buchanan's audience with the Tsar that this statement was inserted into the Tsar's answer to King George, and it was Buchanan, no doubt by previous agreement with his two dinner guests, who asked and received the Tsar's consent to the publication of his reply to King George along with other papers.[3]

---

[1] *Int. Bez.* i. V, 451.   [2] *Int. Bez.* i. V, 398.

[3] BD. XI, 490. In the article in KSF. mentioned above Roloff comments: 'The trio [Buchanan, Sazonov, Paléologue] simply shouldered aside the King of England's express wish and did not take the telegram seriously, regarding it, as Paléologue's account shows, merely as an opportunity to justify the policy of the *Entente* and exercise influence on England. For that purpose publicity was necessary. And this point at once occupied their attention, for Buchanan telegraphed home the Russian answer, adding: "Emperor said that he had no objection to above being published with other papers" (BD. XI, 490). That this thought occurred to the Tsar spontaneously will hardly be believed; it is obvious that Buchanan must have asked for the permission. And use was made of it at once: immediately after the English declaration of war the two telegrams were published in the press, thus serving as the first propaganda measures' (KSF. 1928, p. 942).

If this were pure imagination, the only explanation left would be that it was the Tsar himself who introduced into the draft an account of events which was at variance with the truth. And he would have had to do so in good faith, because Nicholas II, of mediocre intelligence and unimaginative though he was, would never have been capable of such an invention, and he was, moreover, too sincere and honest to lie to his brother sovereign, with whom he was on terms of friendship and who in any case would have soon found out the lie. There were, however, two telegrams from Shebeko in Vienna which may have misled him and made him believe that Austria had replied to the Russian partial mobilization by her own general mobilization, before Russia on the afternoon of 30 July transformed her partial into general mobilization. The first of these telegrams was of 29 July and runs:

Tomorrow the order for the general mobilization is expected.[1]

On the 30th the order never came. But late in the evening of the 30th or in the early morning of the 31st St. Petersburg received another telegram from Shebeko reporting the friendly and promising conversation which he had had with Berchtold in the afternoon of the 30th and of which we have already spoken[2]:

Count Berchtold asked me to call on him today and said in the friendliest manner that in view of our mobilization Austria saw herself compelled on her side to mobilize her troops on our frontier. He requested me to inform you that this measure contained no threat against Russia, with whom Austria had no quarrel and with whom she wished to remain further on good terms. The measure has been taken purely in view of our military preparations.[3]

Thus on 30 July Berchtold was telling Shebeko that Austria found herself obliged to mobilize in Galicia. But mobilization in Galicia following on mobilization against Serbia amounted to general mobilization. It was this general mobilization which the Tsar, if not also Sazonov, may have understood as having been already ordered when Berchtold gave official notification of it. This would explain not only the Tsar's telegram to Wilhelm of 31 July saying:

It is technically impossible to stop our military preparations, which were obligatory owing to Austria's mobilization,[4]

but also Sazonov's brush with Szápáry, when he flung out the remark that it was the Austrians who had 'mobilized first'.[5] It would further explain the telegram mentioned not far back[6] by which Buchanan notified London of the Russian general mobilization. It is necessary to dwell a little on this telegram to clear up not only the line taken by

---

[1] *Int. Bez.* i. V, 242.
[3] *Int. Bez.* i. V, 307.
[5] DA. III, 97. See Vol. II, p. 682.

[2] See Vol. II, pp. 661-2.
[4] DD. III, 487. See p. 56.
[6] See p. 122.

Buchanan, but also an obscure point in regard to the date of dispatch of this telegram. If it was sent off on the 30th Buchanan deserves credit for his promptitude in sending the news to his Government, but if it did not go off until the 31st, an unfavorable light is thrown upon his behavior at this critical juncture.

6. Buchanan's belated telegram to London about the Russian general mobilization.

The text of the telegram is given in the *British Documents* as follows:

St. Petersburg, July 31 1914. D. 6.40 p. m. R. 5.20 p. m.
It has been decided to issue orders for general mobilization. This decision was taken in consequence of report received from Russian Ambassador in Vienna to the effect that Austria is determined not to yield to intervention of Powers, and that she is moving against Russia as well as against Serbia. Russia has also reason to believe that Germany is making active military preparations and she cannot afford to let her get a start.[1]

Is the allusion to Shebeko's telegram of 30 July? Bernadotte Schmitt thinks so,[2] but does not perceive the implications of this assumption. The conversation with Berchtold summarized in this telegram took place in the afternoon or evening of the 30th and Sazonov cannot have known of it earlier than the night of 30/31 July or the morning of the 31st. In that case, Buchanan's telegram No. 347 must be assigned to 6.40 p. m. on the 31st, as given in the *British Documents,* and not to 6.40 p. m. on the 30th, as is generally believed. This would mean that Buchanan waited twenty-four hours before notifying London of the Russian general mobilization, thus beating Paléologue's record of seventeen hours and showing that he, too, was involved in a conspiracy of silence between the representatives of the Triple *Entente* at St. Petersburg in regard to Russian general mobilization.

The historians who edited the *British Documents* found it impossible to believe that Buchanan was so remiss. No doubt they thought, after the outcry in France over the belatedness of Paléologue's telegram, that such remissness would be regarded as having been intentional. But they were not able to clear up doubts by consulting the original cipher telegram sent in from the Post Office because these were not preserved by the Foreign Office. They therefore reproduced the times as given in the decoded copy, i.e., D. 6.40 p. m. on 31st, R. 5.20 p. m. on 31st. Thus the telegram took only forty minutes in transit, Russian time being two hours ahead of Greenwich time. The Editors remark that: 'The hour of receipt is correct', because 'at 4.45 p. m. on 31 July Prince Lichnowsky telegraphed to Berlin:

---

[1] BD. XI, 347; *Blue Book,* 113, dated 31 July; CDD., p. 87.
[2] Schmitt, II, p. 246, note.

Sir William Tyrrell informs me that the Government here has no news of any kind about the mobilization of the whole Russian army and navy'.[1]

It was thus somewhere about 4 p. m. on the 31st that London learnt from Lichnowsky about the mobilization. Therefore, in Volume XI of the *British Documents* the telegram appears with the day and hours as given in the decoded copy, and reproduced in the *Blue Book*. But the Editors add the comment:

It is most improbable that Sir George Buchanan should have dispatched a telegram on the evening of the 31st announcing that it had been decided to issue orders for general mobilization; on that day he must have said that the orders for general mobilization had been issued. The telegram was probably sent at 6.40 p. m. on 30 July and delayed in transmission and a mistake made by the clerk who deciphered the original telegram. . . . From this time onwards there was much delay in the telegraphic service with Russia, and it became necessary to arrange that telegrams should be sent by a circuitous route via Aden.[2]

This has been the view generally accepted by historians, but there are reasons for calling it in question. In the first place, acceptance of it rules out the possibility that Buchanan was alluding to Shebeko's telegram of 30 July, whereas the allusion is patent. In the second place, it seems excessive that telegram No. 347 should have taken over twenty-four hours in transmission. It is not true that from 30 July onwards Buchanan's telegrams, except for those sent via Aden (of which there were only two), suffered great delay. Apart from the two-line telegram No. 405, dispatched July 30 at 1.30 p. m., received 1 August at 3 p. m., and thus taking over two days to arrive, all his other telegrams were transmitted very quickly. The long telegram No. 410 of 1 August took only one hour and fifty minutes. The very lengthy No. 490 of 2 August, containing the Tsar's reply, took barely four hours. This gives rise to the thought that there may have been a special reason for the holding back of No. 405 since it contained military news from the Warsaw region. In the third place, there is a very serious and convincing piece of evidence. All Buchanan's telegrams appear in the *British Documents* accompanied by the numbering given them at the Embassy in St. Petersburg, with the exception of two, i.e., No. 153 and No. 347. In the case of No. 153 there is no difficulty since the telegram was—as it indicates—a private one to Sir Edward Grey and was not entered in

---

[1] DD. III, 518.

[2] Another error in dating occurs in Buchanan's telegram No. 445: 'German Ambassador handed to Minister for Foreign Affairs formal declaration of war this evening at 7 o'clock.' This telegram of 1 August is printed in the *British Documents* as having been dispatched at 1.20 p. m. and received at 11.15 p. m. But Buchanan clearly could not at 1.20 p. m. give news of something that happened at 7 p. m., that he learnt of a few minutes later and was able to communicate in cipher at about 8 p. m.

the Embassy register. But it is extremely surprising that No. 347 bears no registry number[1] and that the editors give no reason for the omission. We can, however, arrive at the reason by inference. Buchanan's telegrams of 30 July which appear in the *British Documents* bear the registry numbers 185, 187, 188. No. 186 is lacking. But it cannot be No. 347 of the *British Documents* because No. 186 necessarily preceded No. 187. Now 187 went off at 1.30 p. m., while No. 347 only left at 6.40 p. m. and could not have done so earlier. The telegrams of 31 July are all in order. They bear the Embassy registry numbers 189, 192, 193, 194, respectively, Nos. 190 and 191 are lacking. But a note to 193 (No. 393 of the *British Documents*) tells that 191 was never received in London. Thus No. 347 cannot be the missing 191, but might very well be 190. Since No. 189 went off at 9.23 a. m. and No. 192 at 8.27 p. m., No. 190 (i.e., No. 347) might very well have gone off at 6.40 p. m. on the 31st. So far the train of reasoning fits the facts without a flaw. But this is not yet all. Let us read No. 194 (No. 410 of the *British Documents*):

St. Petersburg, 31 July 1914. D. 1 August 3.10 p. m. R. 1 August 3 p. m. Following from Military Attaché for War Office:

Mobilization ordered in Kiev, Odessa, Moscow and Kazan military districts on 30 July. Naval reservists in Petersburg called out on same date.

Notices posted up at 4 a. m. on 31 July ordering general mobilization, etc.

Thus it was only at 3.10 p. m. on 1 August that the Military Attaché's telegram was dispatched notifying London of the order for Russian partial mobilization issued on the evening of 29 July, and adding that the calling-up notices of general mobilization had been posted up at 4 a. m. on the 31st. The first of these two news items was over sixty hours old and the second thirty-five hours old. Now if the Military Attaché waited so long before sending news which was public property in St. Petersburg and was posted up in all its streets, may not the Ambassador have been doing the same thing, keeping just slightly ahead of the Military Attaché? And to keep just ahead, may he not even perhaps have held back the Military Attaché's telegram for a certain number of hours? That the telegram was held back is beyond doubt. There is no other way of explaining how and why, though dated 31 July, it was only dispatched at 3.10 p. m. on 1 August, at least fifteen hours later. All this leads to the conclusion that there must be a revision of the generally accepted view that Buchanan notified the Foreign Office of the Russian general mobilization on the evening of 30 July. If, as seems probable, his telegram is really of the 31st, he would have been still more tardy than Paléologue in informing his Government, though his

---

[1] The Librarian of the Foreign Office kindly confirms that telegram No. 347 bears no registry number [Ed.].

motives would have been different. His delay, in other words, must be linked with his behavior after the proclamation of this serious measure which he, unlike Paléologue, had endeavored to prevent. What he was perhaps trying to do was to avert its consequences, which he thought would be disastrous.

7. *How the Tsar was induced to assert the priority of the Austrian general mobilization.*

Let us turn back a moment to Shebeko's telegram of 30 July, which may in the beginning have led not only the Tsar and Sazonov but even Buchanan to regard the Austrian mobilization in Galicia as justification for the Russian general mobilization. The truth of the matter is that— unless it referred to the Austrian mobilization against Serbia, in which case it was sheer sophistry—there was no substance in this justification, because in any case it was Russia who by her partial mobilization had first mobilized against Austria, not the other way round, while what was here being done was to link not the partial, but the general Russian mobilization with the Austrian general mobilization, although as regards Austria they amounted to the same thing.

But even admitting all this, it still remains to be explained how a mistaken opinion, which might have been held up to a certain hour on 31 July, was reiterated on the evening of 1 August, after the arrival on the evening of 31 July of the following further message from Shebeko:

Today there was proclaimed the general mobilization for which Count Berchtold had prepared me yesterday.[1]

Whatever St. Petersburg may have thought before, it was no longer possible after this telegram to think that the Austrian general mobilization had been ordered on the 30th. And, in fact, during 1 August Sazonov never stated either in conversation or in telegrams that the Austrian mobilization had preceded and provoked the Russian, nor did he do so in his speech of 8 August. Is it possible that he kept Shebeko's telegram of the 31st from the Tsar's knowledge in order not to disturb the comforting conviction that the Austrian general mobilization had the priority?

The puzzle must remain unsolved. One can only say that the behavior of the three who dined together that night at the British Embassy bears out the hypothesis of their having come to an agreement that this excuse should be used by the Tsar. Though Sazonov never himself uttered the falsehood in speech or writing, he did not prevent its being uttered by the Tsar, whose answer to King George's message he had before him on the morning of 2 August. Moreover, it was by Sazonov's will or with his consent that the *Orange Book* repeated the

[1] *Int. Bez.* i. V, 361.

falsehood in three documents, one of which, the invented telegram of 28 July from Shebeko, is very damning.[1] Buchanan, who helped in the drafting of the Tsar's reply, and who, after being in such close contact with Sazonov, must have known the truth, also raised no objection to Nicholas II giving King George a falsified version of the facts. Paléologue, too, played a part to which we must now turn our attention.

It must be borne in mind that on one and the same day, at a few hours' interval, France and Russia had the same idea of accusing Austria of being the first to order general mobilization. Such a coincidence would seem a miracle if fortuitous. But in the present writer's opinion it was not fortuitous. Nor need the fact that the accusation was formulated categorically in Paris earlier than in St. Petersburg lead to the conclusion that it originated in Paris. It was already implied in the Tsar's telegram to Wilhelm and in Sazonov's remark to Szápáry. As will also be remembered, Paris on the evening of 31 July and first thing on 1 August made no mention of any Austrian priority in mobilization, describing Austria, on the contrary, as conciliatory, desirous of peace, and ready to come to an understanding with Russia.[2] It was just before noon on 1 August that a sudden change of attitude became manifest when Poincaré told Bertie

that Emperor of Russia did not order a general mobilization until after a decree of general mobilization had been issued in Austria.[3]

Was it because of some telegram that Poincaré gave this explanation of Russian general mobilization different from the one advanced by Berthelot and Viviani? Yes, it was. At 5.15 a. m. on 1 August Paris received a telegram from Paléologue sent off at 7.31 p. m. on 31 July:

Kaiser Wilhelm telegraphed this morning to Tsar Nicholas guaranteeing the conciliatory attitude of Austria if Russia ceases her military preparations. It is to confirm this telegram that the German Ambassador asked an audience of the Tsar. After having received Count Pourtalès, Tsar Nicholas telegraphed to Kaiser Wilhelm thanking him for his mediation 'which begins to give one hope that all may yet end peacefully'.[4] He added that it was technically impossible to stop the mobilization of the Russian army and that this mobilization was solely motivated by the previous mobilization of the Austro-Hungarian army and does not imply any aggressive intention on the part of Russia; he ended by giving his word that the Russian army will not attack Austria as long as the negotiations between St. Petersburg and Vienna are not broken off.[5]

To telegraph this Paléologue must have read the text of the Tsar's telegram[6]. It is noteworthy that in regard to the point which here

[1] See p. 127.   [2] See pp. 98-9.   [3] BD. XI, 403. See p. 117.
[4] DD. III, 487.   [5] Poincaré, IV, p. 462.   [6] See p. 56.

concerns us, Paléologue goes a step farther than the Tsar. The Tsar had written that the Russian 'military preparations' were 'obligatory owing to Austria's mobilization'. Paléologue telegraphed that Russian mobilization was 'solely motivated by the previous mobilization of the Austro-Hungarian army'. It was this statement of Paléologue's which probably put it into Poincaré's head to say to Bertie, as the Tsar had said to Wilhelm, that the Russian mobilization had been ordered after that of Austria, and to pass the idea on to Margerie. This is, no doubt, why Paris and St. Petersburg were in unison on 1 August in falsifying the facts and why this unison lasted on in their respective diplomatic documents.

It may be objected that in all this Paléologue played a perfectly innocent part. With his quick mind he may immediately have perceived the value of the argument used by the Tsar and passed it on in still more clear-cut form to the Quai d'Orsay, but without realizing the uses to which it could be put. This may be so. Pursuing the matter still further, however, one cannot but observe that when in the *Revue des Deux Mondes* of 15 January 1921 Paléologue published the first install-ment of his *Diary,* he reproduced the Russian *Orange Book*'s bogus telegram: 'Vienna, 28 July. The order for general mobilization has been signed,'[1] well knowing it to be bogus. Demartial thinks he did so to make his account tally with the French *Yellow Book.*[2] It is a question of which was first, the hen or the egg. If anything, his concern was to bring his account into line with the *Orange* not the *Yellow Book* since the latter said nothing about Austria's having mobilized as early as 28 July. But why should he have wanted to bring his account into line with the *Orange Book* if he had had no hand in what was done at St. Petersburg? This does not mean that it was Paléologue's own idea to accuse Austria of being the first to order general mobilization, thus forcing Russia to follow suit. Bernadotte Schmitt, overlooking the telegram revealed by Poincaré, thinks that Paris was influenced by another telegram of Paléologue's, not known to us, and writes that 'Sazonov may have offered such an explanation to Paléologue', i.e., that the priority rested with Austria.[3] But this is inconceivable, given the close relations between the two men and the full knowledge possessed by Paléologue of everything that went on. Never during the whole crisis was Sazonov lacking in frankness or sincerity with Paléologue who was installed at the Foreign Ministry almost as if he were at home there. It is more in keeping with the facts to assume the two, or rather the three, diplomatists on the evening of 1 August, like

[1] *Orange Book,* 47.
[2] Demartial, 'Les responsabilités de la guerre', *Évolution,* May 1931, p. 19.
[3] Schmitt, II, note to p. 299.

drowning men clutching at a floating spar, seized upon the hint espied in Shebeko's telegram[1] the previous day; indeed, it is not inconceivable that the possibilities thereby opened up were intimated to Paris in some other telegram of Paléologue's which we shall never know.

Here ends the long digression caused by the necessity of clearing up the genesis of the interrelated falsehoods in the *Orange* and *Yellow Books,* fabricated to support the thesis that Russia was forced to order general mobilization because Austria had done so. Now we must turn our attention to the way in which this thesis struck root in French public opinion. It is a point which may seem to fall outside the purview of the present work, but this is not so. An account of how the truth came to be known and the obstacles, which were put in its way throws a revealing, if indirect light upon the problem of war guilt, which after so many years is still unsettled.

8. First doubts in France and first reactions; the truth revealed in documents brought to light after the war.

When the war broke out the French were unanimous in the belief that France had been attacked and that the Central Powers, with Germany as the leader, were solely responsible for the war, as Viviani put it in the chamber on 4 August 1914. Had Jaurès lived the Socialists might perhaps have taken another line, but, he being dead, only a small group of trade unionists, whose organ was the monthly review *'La Vie Ouvrière,* opposed the war, spurred on by the appeal to the world entitled *Au-dessus de la Mêlée* published in the *Journal de Genève* of 22-3 September by Romain Rolland, who had been caught by the war in Switzerland. When in December 1914 the Committee of the French Federation of Trade Unions decided not to answer an invitation from the Socialists of the neutral countries, one of its members, Monatti, resigned from the Committee and, in defiance of the censorship, published a pamphlet saying:

This war . . . passes as a war for the liberation of Europe . . . to destroy militarism all over the world! What an illusion! This war, for which the Sarajevo murder has been merely a pretext, has its real causes in Anglo-German economic competition and the rivalry between Teuton and Slav. The alliance with Russia, already a disgrace to the French Republic, has plunged our country into this abyss.

About the same time, the end of 1914, doubts of the veracity of the published official documents throwing the whole blame upon the Central Powers assailed Georges Demartial not as a result of any political or pacifist ideology. As Director at the Colonial Ministry,

[1] *Int. Bez.* i. V, 361.

Demartial had been chairman of Poincaré's election committee at the last elections and had supported the unpopular law imposing the three-year term of military service. The *Yellow Book* had not yet appeared, but the English *Blue Book* and the Russian *Orange Book,* as well as the German *White Book,* seemed to Demartial to show that Germany was not solely responsible for the war. In November 1914 he raised the question with a group of scholars, the *Union pour la Vérité,* but only aroused general indignation. He did, however, enlist the support of the eminent economist, Charles Gide, of the University of Paris.[1]

Thus towards the end of 1914 two movements against the official thesis came into being, one political, using the war guilt question as a weapon in the anti-war struggle, the other serving the interests of historical scholarship. The former lies outside our inquiry.[2] The latter, though of lesser dimensions and general influence, concerns us closely. It would have found a far better hearing with French public opinion if its exponents had not early fallen into the error of overstating their case, forgetting that, if France and Russia were not exempt from all blame, the conflagration had arisen in consequence of the Austrian ultimatum to Serbia and of the German demand that the Austro-Serbian conflict should remain 'localized' and not be submitted to mediation.[3] The professional historians, furthermore, maintained silence about the activities of those who accused the French Government and forthwith accepted the French Government's version of the cause of the war without demur, especially after the appearance on 1 December 1914 of the *Yellow Book* with its documents. The *Yellow Book* was only just out when there appeared a pamphlet *Who Wanted war?* by Durkheim and Denis, professors of sociology and history respectively at the Sorbonne. The pamphlet was one of a series of *Studies and Documents on the War* published by a team of well-known professors under the general editorship of the historian Lavisse and widely circulated in millions of copies. In this pamphlet appears the following statement in italics:

[1] Much of what now follows is derived from Demartial's writings, in particular from his long article 'Les responsabilités de la guerre' in *Évolution,* May 1931, pp. 1–45.

[2] On the political movement in France, see A. Rosenberg's article 'La question des responsabilités en France pendant la guerre', *Évolution,* July 1929, pp. 5–22.

[3] Writing in *Évolution,* which was the organ of the French Revisionists and which had Demartial as one of its chief contributors, one of these exponents, Gouttenoire de Toury, admits that the Revisionist minority in the *Ligue des Droits de l'Homme* never managed to become a majority because of its own extremism. 'In their justifiable desire to demolish the untenable thesis of the unilateral responsibility of the vanquished for unleashing the war they had gone to such extremes that for them the responsibility for the war fell exclusively on the *Entente* Governments, while the Governments of the Central Powers were made to appear as white as snow' ('Le congrès de la Ligue des Droits de l'Homme et la révision du Traité de Versailles', *Évolution,* November 1932, p. 680). It may be added that as a result of the French revisionist campaign Demartial was suspended for five years from his rank as officer of the *Légion d'Honneur.*

This important fact that the general mobilization of Austria was anterior to the general mobilization of Russia is nowhere mentioned in the German *White Book*. Yet that it was anterior is certain.

And it led them to the conclusion:

Germany has wished to make the Russian Government responsible for the war on account of its general mobilization on the 31st. She willfully forgot that such a measure had been imposed on Russia by a similar measure that had already been taken by Austria. Russia could not content herself with opposing the few army corps she was mobilizing against the millions of men that Austria was preparing for battle.[1]

Montgelas tells us that the true facts were that while

the entire field army [of Austria] comprised only fifty divisions in all, twenty-three of which were marching on Serbia far away from Russia's frontiers, the so-called Russian partial mobilization, which should more correctly be described as the Russian mobilization against Austria, comprised fifty-five infantry divisions, five more than the whole army of the Danubian Monarchy.[2]

In any case, not only Russia's partial but also her general mobilization preceded the Austrian general mobilization, and while Durkheim and Denis's pamphlet was still in the press, this fact was proclaimed in a reply to the *Yellow Book* published by the *Deutsche Allgemeine Zeitung* of 21 December 1914.

The German article stated that the Austrian mobilization was ordered in the course of the day of 31 July, while that of Russia was ordered in the night of 30/31 July (the truth being that it was ordered in the afternoon of 30 July). But in an added note the two French professors raised specious objections to the German statement. Because in the *White Book* the German Government, in ignorance of the truth, had declared the Russian mobilization to have been ordered 'am Vormittag', i.e., in the forenoon of the 31st, Durkheim and Denis affirmed that it must clearly have been ordered in the latter part of the forenoon, i.e., about 11 a. m. on 31 July, after that of Austria,[3] and they were thus able to assert that

Russia's act loses the aggressive character imputed to it and becomes a simple measure of self-defense.[4]

Remaining still unconvinced by the documentation of the *Yellow Book*, Demartial submitted his doubts to the *Ligue des Droits de L'Homme*. This society had come into being in connection with the Dreyfus case, its membership was drawn mainly from the university

[1] Durkheim and Denis, *Who Wanted War?* (Paris, 1915), pp. 40, note 2; 54-5.
[2] Max Montgelas, *Das Plaidoyer Poincarés*, KSF. February 1928, p. 161.
[3] Durkheim and Denis, op. cit., pp. 61–2.
[4] Durkheim and Denis, op. cit., p. 38.

world, and its aims were to vindicate truth and justice against the encroachments of the *raison d'état.* The secretary of this society, Mathias Morhardt, one of its founders and on the staff of the *Temps,* soon became prominent as a strong opponent of the Government version of the origin of the war and brought the question before the committee of the society. It was discussed at a meeting at Easter 1915, but the committee did not adopt his standpoint, and the vice-president of the League, the Sorbonne professor, Victor Basch, shortly after-wards published *La Guerre de 1914 et le Droit* in which the Austrian mobilization was given as anterior to the Russian. A similar line was taken by the *Ligue d'Éducation Morale,* and so Morhardt, Demartial, and Charles Gide founded the *Société d'études critiques et documentaires sur la guerre* which attracted some distinguished people as members and had Morhardt as its president. Demartial raised his question with the committee and had no difficulty in convincing the membership at meetings which were held frequently without police interference, except during the summer of 1917, but which had no influence on public opinion because the censorship prevented the publication of any reports of them. Meanwhile, the official historians continued to main-tain the priority of the Austrian mobilization despite the fact that in England Philips Price in the *Diplomatic History of the War* (London, 1914), had subjected the dates of the various mobilizations to an analysis and had established the true facts, and that in Russia the trial of the former War Minister, General Sukhomlinov, had revealed, and the Kerensky Government soon confirmed, that the Russian general mobilization, ordered on the 29th and invoked on the same evening by the Tsar, had been definitely proclaimed on the 30th.

Nor did the French historians revise their opinions when the war was over and light began to be shed from various quarters. At the beginning of 1919, when the Peace Conference was opening. Professor Pokrowski published a series of articles on 'The Men responsible for the War' in the Moscow Communist daily *Pravda.* They reproduced documents from the archives of the Russian Foreign Ministry which showed that No. 78 of the *Orange Book* had been tampered with. About that same time the English Professor Oman, who had been granted access to the British documents, published his *Outbreak of the War* which, while accepting the *Yellow Book*'s false statement that the Austrian mobilization was ordered in the early hours of 31 July, gave the Russian as having been decided on the afternoon of the 30th and ordered on the morning of the 31st At the Peace Conference the Commission appointed to investigate the war guilt question declared Germany guilty of the aggression but did not accuse Austria of having been the first to mobilize, maintaining silence on the Russian general mobilization. When later in 1919 the Austrian Government brought out the *Red Book* containing the most important documents of the July-August crisis 1914 and the German Government published the four volumes of documents selected by Kautsky, the truth ought to have made its way in France, but the French official world persisted in not recognizing it.

In April 1920 Caillaux was brought to trial on a charge of intelligence with the enemy and conspiracy against the security of the State. In Caillaux's possession had been found an unpublished manuscript entitled *Les Responsables* putting forward the thesis that the French Government could have averted the war by preventing, above all, the Russian mobilization. Viviani, called as a witness, deposed to the contrary, giving, among others, the reason that the Russian mobilization, ordered at 11 a. m. on the 31st, was in reply to the Austrian, ordered at 1 a. m. on the same day. Demartial, in *Humanité*, showed the falsity of this deposition, but the French press passed over his refutation in silence. And Berthelot in his letter of 12 December 1920, mentioned above,[1] went to the length of writing to Poincaré:

> It was on 31 July at noon that the German Government, under the false pretext that the Russian Government had ordered the mobilization of its land and sea forces, decreed the *Kriegsgefahrzustand,* i.e., mobilization under a hypocritical name.[2]

How could Berthelot describe as a false pretext the fact that Russia had already mobilized when Germany proclaimed the *Kriegsgefahrzustand,* which was not identical with mobilization, as Paris well knew?

9. Paléologue's diary; Poincaré's lectures in 1921; the debate in the French Chamber on 5 July, 1922.

Only a few days were to pass, and Viviani and Berthelot were to be confuted indirectly by none other than Paléologue himself, when on 15 January 1921 the first installment of his diary appeared in the *Revue des Deux Mondes.* Under the date of 29 July it repeated the false statement in the *Orange Book,* No. 47, that Vienna issued the general mobilization order on the 28th, and then goes on to record the events of 29 and 30 July, as we have already seen,[3] thus revealing that Russian general mobilization had received the Tsar's authorization at 4 p. m. on the 30th and therefore earlier than the Austrian mobilization, which Viviani had placed at 1 a. m. on 31 July but which belonged to the afternoon of that day. To this evidence provided by Paléologue Poincaré turned a blind eye in his series of lectures on the origins of the war delivered in Paris in the first months of 1921. He possessed copies of all the genuine documents, and in his lectures made public one hitherto

[1] See p. 94. [2] Poincaré, IV, p. 466.
[3] See Vol. II, pp. 583, 619-21.

unpublished document, but he refrained from any attempt to use them to throw light on this or any other point that remained obscure. He kept strictly along the track of the *Yellow Book,* and in his last lecture, delivered at the beginning of March, repeated word for word the two notorious forged telegrams Nos. 115 and 118 of the *Yellow Book,* vouching thus for their authenticity, saying that 115 arrived after 118 and giving it to be understood that the Austrian mobilization preceded the Russian. Equally lacking in straightforwardness was the Sorbonne professor, Émile Bourgeois, who, also in 1921, published with Pagès *Les Origines et les Responsabilités de la Grande Guerre,* an investigation undertaken at the request of the Senate Sub-committee of Inquiry. Though admitting (on p. vi) that he had had access to 'all the documents preserved at the Quai d'Orsay', this historian reproduces Nos. 115 and 118 as if he had found them in the archives and then remarks: 'Which of the two mobilizations preceded the other? Or were they simultaneous? It is a point difficult to decide in the absence of all documentary indication (*toute indication de pièces*).[1]

Nor was Viviani more scrupulous when on 5 July 1922 he made a speech in the Chamber when the war guilt question was being debated, Poincaré being then again Prime Minister. The Communist deputy, Vaillant-Couturier, was making a speech reviewing in the spirit of Jaurès the course of French policy leading up to the war, criticizing the subservience of French policy to that of Russia and the influence exercised on it by Poincaré during his term as President of the Republic. He was just pointing out that from Paléologue's diary it was now known that the Russian general mobilization had been decreed at 4 p. m. on 30 July, and asking where in the *Yellow Book* was Paléologue's dispatch conveying that information, adding:

Dispatch 118 of the *Yellow Book,* by which M. Paléologue announces the Russian mobilization as a consequence of the Austrian mobilization, this by the way is an inexactitude. . . .

when Viviani asked to be allowed to interrupt. Viviani from his seat then plunged into a long story of events during his Premiership from 16 June onwards, his account showing that he not only did not remember, but had perhaps never properly understood the real sequence of developments leading to the outbreak of war. He began by paying homage to Poincaré, who was listening from the Government front bench, as

the man who, enclosed in a constricting constitution, not able to take action, yet by the incomparable lucidity of his mind, the fluency and clarity of his words in summing up debates, persuasively brought into prominence the

[1] Bourgeois et Pagès, op. cit., p. 42.

view which seemed to him the practical one, the man of hard work and courage.

Warming to his theme, Viviani proceeded:

We come now to speak of the mobilization. There is . . . a crucial fact which unhappily disappears under the pens of the majority of historians, and which is the story of the first ultimatum addressed by Germany to Russia. It was on 29 July that Austria partially mobilized 11 army corps on the Galician frontier. What could Russia do? She was obliged to mobilize army corps—on the Galician, not on the German frontier. . . . The ultimatum from Germany. What was its reason? The German frontier was not threatened by a single Russian soldier. . . . War was on the point of being declared. The decision was taken on the evening of 29 July. But at that same moment England intimated that she would keep a free hand if France became involved in the conflict. Therefore, a change of front! M. Sazonov turned to me. I remember that tragic night, and so do you, too, M. Poincaré, when I came to see you. M. Sazonov asked me: 'Can I count on the alliance engagements.' I replied over my own signature: 'France will remain faithful to the obligations of the alliance. But in the preparations perhaps required of you by national security, do not do anything which could give Germany a pretext.' My dispatch, by the way, was in vain. Why? Change of front again: the attitude of England did not allow [Germany] to unleash war against Russia on the 29th on grounds of a partial mobilization, rendered necessary by the Austrian mobilization. The ultimatum was withdrawn. Something else will then be prepared which will appear more plausible. . . . Then comes a second Austrian mobilization. We are nearing the drama. . . . Austria mobilizes 'generally'. I affirm that Austria mobilized generally on 30 July at 1 a. m. This has been admitted by M. Bethmann Hollweg. On what date, I ask you, did Russia mobilize 'generally', and especially at what hour? It is this point which is, in fact, under discussion. The night of 30/31 July was when Austria mobilized. And I personally declare to you that according to German documents which can be at once available to you if anyone wishes to consult them, the Russian mobilization was made operative at 11 a. m. on 31 July. . . . Thus it is posterior to the Austrian mobilization.

Every sentence of this incoherent retrospect contains an egregious misstatement. Austria had not mobilized in Galicia before 31 July, nor had Germany presented an ultimatum to Russia on 29 July, she had simply given warning after Sazonov's announcement of partial mobilization

that further progress of Russian mobilization measures would compel us to mobilize and that then European war would be scarcely to be avoided.[1]

Nor had Sazonov ever had occasion to inquire of France whether he could count on the alliance engagements. In Paléologue's telegram of 30 July Sazonov, on the contrary,

---

[1] DD. II, 487. See Vol. II, pp. 491, 553.

expressed thanks for Paléologue's official declaration that 'France is determined to meet all the obligations of the alliance'.[1] Another fabrication was the statement that Germany revoked her mobilization decree because England would not allow her to attack Russia. Lastly, there was no truth in his assertion of the priority of Austrian mobilization, giving as his authority the outdated pamphlet of Durkheim and Denis of 1914. But in the French Chamber there was no one in a position to rectify his statements, nor would the Chamber have tolerated this being attempted. Viviani's version satisfied the feelings of the immense majority of the members, who accompanied it with continuous applause, ending with an ovation and a vote that the speech should be posted up on all municipal notice boards, after which Poincaré and Viviani embraced.

Similar enthusiasm welcomed Poincaré on the following day when he spoke after the Communist deputy Cachin, denying the imputations made by the latter against him. He protested that his policy had always been inspired by peaceful intentions but without entering into particulars or touching on the subject of the respective times of mobilization, a much safer line than that taken by Viviani. After Poincaré, the chief speakers were another Communist, Ernest Lafont, and the leader of the Socialists, Léon Blum. Shouting and angry interruptions accompanied their speeches, although—the fact is worthy of note—they both prefaced them by statements that they regarded the Central Powers as the real authors of the war. Blum expressed himself as follows:

> We do not regard a debate like this as one which could in any way exercise a retroactive influence on the reparations question. . . . What I say is intended to express the truth as we see it, not in any way to lighten, mask, or diminish the responsibility of the Germans. . . . Between those who, consciously or unconsciously, voluntarily or involuntarily, piled up the inflammable material and the one who set light to it, we do and always shall make an infinite distinction. . . . This decision for war, this will to war, this decisive act by which and after which war came into being, we have never doubted that it lies at the door of Germany.

Then before passing on to his arraignment of Poincaré's policy, Blum said that to the question of priority in mobilization he attached little importance:

> I confess I regard the question as practically devoid of importance. It would be altogether too simple if one could escape appearing as the aggressor in the eyes of posterity just by not letting mobilization in one's country become official until a day or a few hours after the others.

The two facts which convinced Blum of the guilt of the Central Powers were: the ultimatum to Serbia and the instruction that Schoen

---

[1] See Vol. II, p. 618.

should ask Paris to hand over the fortresses of Toul and Verdun, compliance with which would have been 'a veritable moral suicide'.

The following quotations from Blum's very long speech indicate the main lines of his indictment of Poincaré:

> I am going to say . . . why . . . we nevertheless have the right to say . . . *Poincaré-la-Guerre.*[1] It is not necessary to have willed war, to have declared war, to have premeditated war, it is enough not to have gone to the very end of human endeavor in order to prevent war, it is enough to have accepted the idea of war. . . . I noticed something new in French policy [when Poincaré came to power in January 1912]. No longer is the motto: anything rather than war. It is now: rather war than any infringement, I do not say of the independence or even the honor, but of the dignity of France. . . . Rather war than a lowering of the prestige of France in Europe, rather war than a modification of the European balance of power, rather war than a change in the distribution of strength in Europe to the detriment of France; rather war than a success for Germany. . . . You have taken the attitude of a man who does not desire war for his country, who will never declare war, who will never premeditate war, but who, within certain limits and at a favorable moment might accept the idea of war if it were to offer the necessary compensations. . . . I believe that is what is at the bottom of your policy. That is the meaning of the article from which another speaker has just now read out passages—whether it is written by M. Colrat or not seems to me of slight importance—and which substantially expresses the ideas I have just been outlining.'

Colrat, a friend and former secretary of Poincaré, was the proprietor of the periodical *Opinion* and directed its policy, though he does not seem to have been the author of the article several times quoted in the course of the debate. A salient passage in this article runs:

> If Metz and Strasbourg have been recovered, this is not due only to the magnificent achievement of our soldiers, living and dead, of the dead more than of the living, it is the consummation of a whole policy. M. Poincaré pursued it with a skill and perseverance which sacrificed, when necessary, the accessories to the essentials, the means to the end, the individual to the task.

'You', said Blum to Poincaré, 'have had the glory of this policy, now shoulder the responsibility for it'.

Tardieu for the Right and Herriot for the Left rose to defend Poincaré from these charges. Poincaré might have silenced his accusers at home and abroad by accepting the proposal made in a calmly reasoned speech by the Socialist Bracke that a parliamentary sub-committee of thirty-five members should be appointed to collect, examine and publish the diplomatic documents relating to the origins of the war and

---

[1] Title of an article published by Blum.

the peace offers made during the war. This motion was defeated by 487 to 65 votes and in its stead the Chamber, by 532 votes to 65, adopted a motion brought forward by extreme Right wing deputies, including Siegfried, Castelnau, Barrès, and beginning:

> The Chamber, repudiating and condemning with the full force of its contempt the campaign of calumny organized and carried on to the benefit of Germany in order to impute the responsibility for the war to France, etc.

No one in the course of the debate had gone so far as to impute the responsibility for the war to France. But no one had demonstrated that France bore no share of it, least of all Viviani, who, as Prime Minister in July 1914, was the one to do so. When in later years it became plain that his two chief statements were not in accordance with the truth, Poincaré as we shall see, came forward in defense of Viviani's good faith, and in this Poincaré may have been right. Viviani was superficial and irresponsible. He had never gone thoroughly into the question or read the documents as they became accessible. And so his speech was made at random, without real knowledge and following the lines of the *Yellow Book*. His shallowness and vacuity were displayed to the full in his *Réponse au Kaiser* which he published the following year. A poor performance, it bristles with errors, arbitrary statements and bombast, leaving a very unflattering impression of the author's personality. Though published when an abundance of material was available, it gives a survey of the mobilizations which is enough to make one's hair stand on end. According to Viviani, Austria ordered partial mobilization on 28 July, Russia replied with partial mobilization on the 29th; on the 29th Germany sent Russia an ultimatum, and Russia in the night of 29th to 30th agreed to demobilize; on 30th July Austria began a general mobilization by order of Germany, who on 31st decreed the *Kriegsgefahrzustand,* 'the equivalent of mobilization'; consequently French mobilization, ordered at 4 p. m. on 1 August, was over a day later than what 'is for everybody the real German mobilization'. Not a single one of all these statements is true.[1] Mark that Viviani claimed to have read the statements made by Dobrorolski, saying that

---

[1] Viviani, *Réponse au Kaiser,* pp. 142-210. It is true that Asquith's account is not much less inaccurate: On 31 July Russia and Austria mobilized against each other. Conflicting statements were issued as to which Power took the first step in substituting general for partial mobilization. Austria, according to her intimation was 'compelled to respond to Russia's action'. On the other hand, the Russian order was described at St. Petersburg 'as a result of the general mobilization of Austria and of the measures for mobilization taken secretly but continuously by Germany for the last six days'. *The Genesis of the War* (London, 1923), p. 198. These words are no doubt a reminiscence of those used by the Tsar in his telegram to King George V (see p. 126), but before writing on the genesis of the war Asquith would have done well to make use of the documents and works which had already appeared on the question.

they corroborated his own! Mark, also, that his speech of 5 July 1922 had given rise to a protest of responsible opinion in France which had brought to light a serious blemish in the *Yellow Book.*

10. *The exchange of letters between the President of the* Ligue des Droits de l'Homme *and Poincaré on the falsifications in the* Yellow Book.

Eleven days after Viviani's speech, the *Ligue des Droits de l'Homme,* on the initiative of Morhardt and other members, decided to take the matter up. At the time of the Dreyfus affair the *Ligue* had brought to light the false statements issued by the Ministry of War. It had now set up a committee to investigate the origins of the Great War. In June 1922 it had held a general congress at Nantes at which a strong group had supported Gouttenoire de Toury's motion in favor of a revision of the Treaty of Versailles. This motion would probably have been passed if the Central Committee for the *Ligue* had not opposed its being put to the vote. But the pressure from the minority was too strong to be ignored. The result was that on 16 July 1922 the President of the *Ligue,* Ferdinand Buisson, addressed a letter to Poincaré containing two definite questions. Paléologue in the *Revue des Deux Mondes* of 15 January 1921 and Dobrorolski *in Die Mobilmachungm der russischen Armee* had both stated that the decree for Russian general mobilization had been signed by the Tsar on 29 July. Dobrorolski had related how, just as it was about to be issued towards 9 p. m., it was replaced by the order for partial mobilization. Paléologue therefore had only informed Paris of the latter. On the following day at 4 p. m. the Tsar had definitely ordered general mobilization. But on the 31st, Viviani, in a dispatch to Paléologue (No. 117 of the *Yellow Book),* three times repeated that he knew nothing 'of an alleged total mobilization of the Russian land and sea forces'.

Yet M. Paléologue must evidently have telegraphed the news to Paris, it figures as No. 118 in the *Yellow Book.* But his dispatch, dated 31 July and classified as the last but one of that date, must therefore have arrived quite late in the evening. To crown it all M. Paléologue gives no indication of the exact time at which the Russian mobilization was ordered. The Committee of Investigation would like precise information on two points: At what hour was M. Paléologue's telegram (No. 118) dispatched from St. Petersburg, and at what hour did it reach Paris?[1]

On 9 August 1922 Poincaré replied that

the first measures of general mobilization' had been decided by the Russian Government on the evening of the 29th and that they were countermanded by Tsar Nicholas II in the night of 29/30 July. They were ordered anew on

[1] Mathias Morhardt, Les *Preuves,* pp. 165-7.

the 30th at the end of the afternoon. But the general mobilization was only ordered in the night of 30/31 July. M. Paléologue notified the French Government of it by telegram dispatched from St. Petersburg at 10.45 a. m. This telegram, for reasons which I cannot explain, no doubt because of congestion on the lines, was not received in Paris until 8.30 p. m. Thus M. Viviani could not know of it at 4p. m. when he sent off the telegram which figures as No. 117 in the *Yellow Book*.[1]

Poincaré's reply took over a copyist's error contained in Buisson's letter giving the time of dispatch of No. 117 as 4 p. m., when in reality it went off at 9.21 p. m. after Schoen's call on Viviani. Poincaré also made his answer tally with Paléologue's uninformative and misleading telegrams.

The truth, as we know, was very different. What was ordered in the evening of 29 July and again at 6 p. m. on the 30th was not 'first measures' but general mobilization, which Poincaré gave as having been ordered only in the night of 30/31 July. Poincaré cannot have been ignorant of this, since both Paléologue's diary and Dobrorolski's booklet had been published and were known to him.

His reply did not satisfy the Revisionists of the *Ligue,* who were encouraged to continue their campaign by further material that came to light. In 1919 Kaiser Wilhelm had written for his own use the *Vergleichende Geschichtstabellen,* 'Comparative Historical Tables from 1887 to the Outbreak of War, 1914'. These tables were printed 'as manuscript' in 1920 in a limited number of copies which were given away to certain people. One copy came into the hands of the Dutch newspaper *Het Volk,* which published it in 1921. In December 1921 the German edition was issued at Leipzig, and in the latter half of 1922 a French translation appeared in Paris preceded by an *Introduction aux Tableaux d'Histoire de Guillaume II* by the French historians Charles Appuhn and Pierre Renouvin and a preface by Poincaré. The *Introduction* refuted the errors and pointed out the omissions in Wilhelm's work, and Poincaré's preface commented:

Wilhelm ignores everything that does not suit him, and, when he finds nothing to support his one-sided statements, he invents. This is what he calls comparative history.[2]

Certainly the Kaiser's compilation cannot count as comparative history, but neither can what had been said till then by Poincaré or at his bidding.

When, for the purpose of disproving a statement of Pokrowski's which had been reproduced by Wilhelm, Appuhn and Renouvin were

[1] Mathias Morhardt, *Les Preuves,* p. 167.

[2] *Introduction aux tableaux d'histoire de Guillaume II. Avant-propos de Raymond Poincaré* (Paris, 1923) p. II.

granted access to the Quai d'Orsay archives, they could not do otherwise than reveal Paléologue's telegram of 30 July, dispatched at 9.15 p. m. and received in Paris at 11.25 p. m. which figures as the second part of No. 102 of the *Yellow Book* but is minus the sentence:

> In consequence the Russian Government has decided to proceed secretly to the first measures of general mobilization.[1]

This was treasure trove for the French Government's accusers, who regarded these words as proof that Paris learnt of the Russian general mobilization on the evening of the 30th. The result was that on 10 November 1922 the *Ligue des Droits de l'Homme,* under pressure from Morhardt, sent Poincaré another long letter signed by Buisson, asking Poincaré to rectify the copyist's error contained in their previous letters and putting two further questions:

> The Committee is glad to learn the hour of arrival in Paris [of No. 118] but . . . still thinks this indication is not enough. What it would like to know is the hour at which the decoded message was laid before the Prime Minister. It will not have escaped you that the vital point is to know whether in sending off telegram No. 117 after Baron Schoen's call, the Prime Minister did or did not know of the Russian mobilization announced in No. 118. The Committee thinks M. Viviani cannot have known No. 118 before dispatching No. 117, But its opinion will only be generally accepted as valid proof in France and elsewhere after an exact determination and comparison of the hour by which No. 118 was decoded and the hour when No. 117 was dispatched.
>
> Finally the Committee notes that since your letter of 9 August, another telegram from M. Paléologue has been published by MM. Appuhn and Renouvin in the *Introduction aux Tableaux d'Histoire.* This is the dispatch of 30 July . . . reporting that 'the Russian Government has decided to proceed secretly to the first measures of general mobilization'. . . . Leaving aside the phrase which we have just quoted, the importance of which is obvious and which the *Yellow Book* has omitted to reproduce, the *Yellow Book* differs considerably from the text published by MM. Appuhn and Renouvin [and in fact, the first part of No. 102 was not in the telegram published by Appuhn and Renouvin]. Of these two versions the Committee asks us which is authentic, i.e., conforms strictly to the original. In case neither reproduces the original text, the Committee would be grateful if you, *Monsieur le President,* would at last give public opinion the satisfaction of a definitive, complete, and faithful version of this telegram. For it is impossible to continue working on inaccurate documents.
>
> No doubt the diplomats who during the war compiled the *Yellow Book* believed they were serving the country by altering the nature of the texts it was their task to publish. The *Ligue* as a body protests against such a conception of propaganda.

[1] See Vol. II, p. 620.

But whatever may have been their motive, we know today that the authors of the *Yellow Book* have given us neither a complete collection nor a faithful text. The rectified texts are made public by chance as a result of controversy or of other publications. We are anxious to have them as a collection. We expect this of the Government in the interests of the truth and in the interests of France, who has nothing to fear from the truth.

We, therefore, ask you once more to order the publication of all the documents in the archives of the Ministry for Foreign Affairs bearing on the origins of the war, to surround this publication with all the safeguards necessitated by the methods of critical editorship, and to entrust the task to a Commission of independent men qualified by their professional training to gather, date, classify and publish historical documents.

As there was no reply from Poincaré the *Ligue* repeated its request on 8 December 1922, and on 9 January 1923 it received an answer:

The questions you asked me have received the closest attention and have necessitated a considerable amount of research. Moreover, I have been obliged to consult M. Viviani, who has been particularly busy and detained away from Paris.[1]

Poincaré gave the facts as we have already noted them about the hours of dispatch of Viviani's telegram No. 117 and receipt of Paleologue's telegram No. 118: Viviani's telegram had gone off in two portions at 9 p. m. and 9.30 p. m. and was being encoded when Paléologue's telegram came in, so that Viviani could not have read this before receiving Schoen and before drafting (in reality before signing, since the drafting was done by Margerie) No. 117, seeing that at 8 p. m. he left the Ministry building. Viviani could not remember whether he received No. 118 during the Cabinet meeting or after it.[2]

As regards Paléologue's telegram of the 30th, published by Appuhn and Renouvin and of which a mutilated text had appeared in the *Yellow Book,* Poincaré revealed that No. 102 was a fusion of two telegrams from Paléologue, Nos. 311 and 315. No. 311, dispatched from St. Petersburg at 4.31 p. m. on the 30th, had remained entirely unknown hitherto and Poincaré gave its text.[3] No. 315 was the one made known by Appuhn and Renouvin.

It is not necessary to repeat here what has already been said about these documents and the light they throw on Paléologue's disingenuous maneuvers.[4] But Paléologue was not to blame if the French Government, to justify its own conduct, fabricated No. 102 of the *Yellow Book* by fusing two of his telegrams and suppressing the most important news in the second one: i.e., that the Russian Government had 'decided to proceed secretly to the first measures of general

---

[1] Mathias Morhardt, *Les Preuves* (Paris, 1925), pp. 177-182.
[2] See p. 90.   [3] DF. 3. XI, 342.   [4] See Vol. II, pp. 615-21.

mobilization'. So the Russian mobilization had become known in Paris on the evening of the 30th! Then how had it been regarded by the Quai d'Orsay? Thus the Buisson-Poincaré correspondence had not silenced Poincaré's accusers. They returned to the charge soon after in connection with Viviani's telegram to Paléologue of the morning of 30 July deprecating the Russian general mobilization.[1] In a lecture given on 23 February 1923 Renouvin gave a text of it which differed from that of No. 101 of the *Yellow Book*. Which was the genuine one? was the question put to Poincaré by Buisson on 18 June 1923. On 5 July Poincaré replied that the genuine text was that of Renouvin, but that

the collation of the two versions shows that there is no substantial difference. . . . If the text of the passage in the *Yellow Book* which is the subject of your question does not entirely conform to the original, it is because its form has been slightly modified to safeguard as far as possible the secret of the cipher code.[2]

Even were it so that there is no substantial difference between the versions, it is not true that the changes were due to the necessity of not betraying the cipher code. This could be discovered from the documents or portions of documents which the *Yellow Book* published unaltered. The real reason why this telegram was manipulated was for the purpose of suppressing the reference contained in it to Viviani's telegram of 27 July,[3] which for some mysterious reason was left out of the *Yellow Book*.

This, of course, was only known later. But at the time Poincaré's admissions gave rise to demands that the truth should be made known also about the suspect No. 115 of the *Yellow Book*. Here, however, they encountered stronger resistance, because it was harder to own up to this falsification. A vain appeal was made in 1924 by Bernard Lazare, the author of *À l'Origine du Mensonge,* and the President of the *Ligue des Droits de l'Homme* put the question to Herriot. On behalf of the Quai d'Orsay, Herriot replied on 16 February 1925 that No. 115 had been dispatched by Dumaine at 6 a. m. on 31 July, the truth being that it went off at 6 p. m. By this device the words *ce matin à la première heure,* which had been inserted in the *Yellow Book* but the insertion of which was not acknowledged in Herriot's letter, was made to harmonize with the alleged hour of dispatch of the telegram. Thus the forgery was perpetuated, not to the credit of the French Foreign Ministry, which ought by then to have seen that it was not possible to prevent the truth being known, and that it was injudicious at a time when the

---

[1] See Vol. II, pp. 603-4.
[2] Mathias Morhardt, *Les Preuves,* pp. 276-8
[3] See vol. II, pp. 536,593.

thesis of Germany's sole responsibility for the war was being vigorously attacked in France to cling to the deplorable expedients used by the compilers of the *Yellow Book* in 1914. Alfred Fabre-Luce's *La Victoire,* published in 1924, had sought to establish the formula:

> Germany and Austria made the gestures which rendered war possible; the Triple *Entente* made those which made it certain.[1]

This was an overstatement. Germany and Austria, having rendered war possible, made a powerful contribution towards rendering it inevitable. There was also Victor Margueritte, who in *Les Criminels* of 1925 was still more severe with the leaders of his country. Neither of them, however, went to the lengths of Georges Demartial in his *L'Évangile du Quai d'Orsay* of 1926. Like others of the same persuasion, Demartial seeks in this work to absolve the Central Powers of all war guilt, throwing the whole blame for the European war on Russia and France. This thesis had less foundation than that of putting the whole blame on Germany. But in the summer of 1925 Victor Margueritte managed to collect 102 signatures to his *Appel aux Consciences,* which was a violent protest against Art. 231 of the Treaty of Versailles. His protest, however, did not concern itself with the merits of the case, but only with the pressure by which the signature of the German representatives to this article was obtained.

It was in the first half of 1925 that Pierre Renouvin at last published *Les Origines Immédiates de la Guerre.* As head of the *Bibliothèque-Musée de la Guerre,* Renouvin had access to the documents relating to the outbreak of the Great War. He and Appuhn had been entrusted with the task of refuting the already mentioned *Vergleichende Geschichtstabellen* of Kaiser Wilhelm, and the semi-official *Société de l'Histoire de la Guerre* had also procured his appointment to a chair of the history of the European War. Thus he was, and still is, the chief French authority on this subject, and on its appearance his book became a standard work in his country. To his honor be it said that he increasingly dissociated himself from the version of the official historians and set forth the true facts on many points. Demartial, whose judgment in this matter is above suspicion, writes of Renouvin and his book:

> As he could not bring himself to endorse false documents, false dates and false statements, he was led, so far as material facts are concerned, to depart from the official version at almost every point, especially on the important question of the mobilizations—a departure over which, as was natural for a man in his position, he endeavored to cast a pious veil, but which a simple comparison with the official documents makes absolutely clear. This example of professional conscience is all the

[1] *Op. cit.,* p. 232.

more honorable because French professors generally have shown much less of it, both during and after the war.[1]

It looks as if Renouvin were trying to adopt a gradual procedure in clearing away the falsifications contained in the *Yellow Book*. With Appuhn he had begun by revealing the authentic text of the first part of No. 102. Then he published that of No. 101. In his book he went further and stated that at 10.43 a. m. on 31 July Paléologue had confined himself to telegraphing:

An order has been issued for the general mobilization of the Russian army.[2]

But did this not imply that the lengthy No. 118 of the *Yellow Book* had been fabricated four months afterwards at the Quai d'Orsay? That was, however, further than Renouvin was willing to go. He confined himself to writing in a footnote:

Yellow Book, 118 gives a longer message, Telegram No. 318 which is inaccurate.[3]

Worse than inaccurate, it was an invention from start to finish! So much so that Poincaré in his two replies to Buisson had hedged on this point, giving the hours of dispatch and receipt of Paléologue's telegram, but not telling the whole truth any more than did Renouvin. Although having access to the archives of the Foreign Ministry, Renouvin, after publishing the authentic text of No. 118, had not the courage to publish that of No. 115 in which the hour of the Austrian mobilization had been falsified to make it precede that of Russia. This he passed over in silence, though making it clear that the Russian mobilization was anterior to that of Austria.

11. *L'Union Sacrée, and the admission of the truth. How Poincaré explains the falsifications in the* Yellow Book.

Poincaré himself found the courage to give the true No. 115 when in 1927 he published *L'Union Sacrée,* the fourth volume of his memoirs. Dispatched from Vienna at 6 p. m., this telegram from Dumaine followed and confirmed another of 5 p. m. which said:

The order for general mobilization has just been given to the Austro-Hungarian armies.

It therefore did not contain the words: 'this morning at 1 o'clock', added in the *Yellow Book*.[4] It should have been Poincaré's duty to follow up the publication of this and other genuine texts by some mention of

---

[1] Demartial's article appeared in *Current History* of 1 March 1926, pp. 787-93, in KSF. of the same date, p, 134, and in *Évolution* of 15 March 1926 under the title: *L'état de la question des responsabilités en France,* p. 39.
[2] See Vol. II, p. 622.   [3] Renouvin, p 199, note 14.   [4] See p. 121.

those that had been altered in the *Yellow Book,* even if not going so far as to proffer an explanation of how the falsifications came to be made. Nothing of this does Poincaré attempt. He glides over the ticklish point as if it did not exist, as if the *Yellow Book* had made no changes. He never even stops to produce an excuse for having in his lectures of 1921 read out as authentic both No. 115 and No. 118, while having the original documents among his papers. The only thing he did was to produce a document which had escaped the attention not only of the compilers of the *Yellow Book* but also of Bourgeois and Renouvin, although it to some extent furnished the explanation of how Paris gained the impression of the priority of the Austrian mobilization. This is Jules Cambon's telegram, received at 3.30 p. m. on 31 July:

> According to a report reaching me the German Ambassador at St. Peters-burg seems to have (*aurait*) telegraphed that Russia had just decided on total mobilization in reply to Austrian mobilization.[1]

Apart from the observations already made about this document[2] it is curious to note that, after having disclosed it in *L'Union Sacrée,* Poincaré makes no further use of it, even when at the end of 1929, in reply to No. XI of the questions put to him by R. Gerin, he dealt more fully with the point.[3]

He began his reply by stating that he was not in any way connected with the publication of the *Yellow Book*:

> You will be good enough to recognize that as President of the Republic I have been entirely extraneous to the compilation of the *Yellow Book.* . . . The *Yellow Book* was prepared by the Quai d'Orsay services under the authority of a Minister who had at that moment more imperious and more urgent duties. . . . But when in connection with the *Yellow Book* you speak of *falsification* or of words *fraudulently* added, I venture to remind you that in 1914, before and after the declaration, and particularly at the moment when the *Yellow Book* was published, the French Government genuinely believed that the Austrian general mobilization had preceded the Russian general mobilization. . . . [The telegram] by which M. Paléologue announced the general mobilization of the Russian army . . . did not arrive in Paris until 8.30 p. m. . . . The official news of the Austrian general mobilization had reached the Quai d'Orsay at 7.30 p. m.

The absurdity of this reasoning has already been pointed out. A glance at the times of dispatch of the two telegrams, the second of which, though addressed to the Ministry of War, reached the Quai d'Orsay at 7.30 p. m. and was communicated to the Ministry of War at 11 p. m., is proof of the contrary.[4] Then why did Poincaré not rather

---

[1] See p. 70.   [2] See pp. 113-16.
[3] Gerin, pp. 148-156.   [4] DF. 3. XI, note to 419. See p. 113.

adduce J. Cambon's telegram quoted above? True, even this proof would have convinced no one, but it was slightly more valid than the other. Poincaré then went on to say that it was Viviani and his colleagues at the Foreign Ministry who had led him to believe in the priority of the Austrian mobilization, an assertion which has been shown above to be untrue.[1] Mentioning as proof of Viviani's belief the latter's statements in the Chamber on 5 July 1922, Poincaré admitted that the Russian mobilization had been decided about 4 p. m. on 30 July and the Austrian at 11.30 a. m. on the 31st, but he did so against the grain and glossing it over with the comment:

If the Austrian mobilization did not precede the Russian mobilization, neither was it influenced by the latter or ordered in reply to it. But for a matter of a few hours they in reality coincided.

This was completely disingenuous in view of the fact that they were separated by an interval of practically twenty hours. Moreover, if the Austrian general mobilization was not ordered in reply to that of Russia, it was undoubtedly provoked by the Russian partial mobilization, which in respect of Austria was a general mobilization. Hence, even if one can agree with Poincaré that

none of those who have known M. Viviani would ever allow that he sought either in 1922 or in 1914 to deceive the Chamber and public opinion. He only expressed an idea which had been suggested to him by defective information which, at the time, had been that of his services,

one cannot equally agree as to the good faith of those who in the *Yellow Book* misled him with such information. Poincaré's reply ends:

When the *Yellow Book* was compiled in the first weeks of the war it is probable that in order to state exactly the chronology of events in a sense that was believed to be accurate, the editors thought they might add to telegram No. 118 the words in which you perceive a falsification. I had no cognizance of this addition, but it corresponded to the Minister's deep conviction and therefore does not deserve the severity with which you judge it.

Although the documents published in the *Yellow Books* are consistently more or less modified because of the cipher, I myself had such faith in the basic accuracy of the documents published in 1914 that, as you say, I quoted them as they stood in my lectures of 1921. But in consequence of the questions put to me on 10 November and 8 December 1922 by M. Ferdinand Buisson, then President of the *Ligue des Droits de l'Homme,* I had fresh inquiries made at the Quai d'Orsay and in addition asked M. Viviani to sort out his recollections. On 9 January, 1923 I sent M. F. Buisson the information I had collected, which M. Herriot in his turn has confirmed and supplemented by a letter of 16 February 1925 addressed to the *Ligue.* In so

[1] See p. 116.

doing I myself checked the texts and times of the telegrams 117 and 118, and, as the *Union Sacrée* was published after this checking, I, of course, regarded it as a duty to give in it the text that I had in my hands.[1]

Let it be noted that (1) 'in order to state exactly the chronology of events in a sense that was believed to be accurate' No. 118 is ten times the length of Paléologue's actual brief telegram: 'An order has been issued for the general mobilization of the Russian army.'[2] In the *Yellow Book* this becomes:

> As a result of the general mobilization of Austria . . . the order for the general mobilization of the Russian army has been given. . . . Really she [Russia] is only taking military measures corresponding to those taken by Germany,[3]

whereas J. Cambon's telegram had made it perfectly clear that

> what is called *Kriegsgefahrzustand* . . . allows the authorities, if they deem it expedient, to proclaim martial law, to suspend some of the public services, and to close the frontier,

and was therefore not at all the equivalent of general mobilization.[4] Moreover, in No. 115, on which Poincaré did not dwell, the addition of the words 'this morning at one o'clock', far from 'stating exactly the chronology of events', falsified it, as has been shown above.[5]

(2) Poincaré asserts that: 'the documents in the *Yellow Book* are consistently more or less modified because of the cipher'. This plea does not hold water. No end would have been served by tampering with the documents. The German *White Book* and the Austrian *Red Book* were incomplete, but they did not contain manipulated documents. The British *Blue Book* had lacunae but no falsifications. The Russian *Orange Book* is full of authentic documents which were dangerous from the point of view of the cipher, as were also the authentic documents and passages of the *Yellow Book*. The safeguarding of the cipher is, therefore, not the reason for which all the documents in the *Yellow Book* were more or less modified. Of all the diplomatic books published after the outbreak of war, it is without doubt the one which least mirrors the truth.

(3) Can it be imagined that Poincaré set about preparing his lectures on the origins of the war without going through the relevant papers? Especially as in the last lecture of the series, the one at which he read out No. 115 and No. 118, he disclosed an unpublished telegram from

---

[1] Gerin, pp. 155-6.   [2] DF. 3. XI, 432.   [3] LJF. 118.
[4] Poincaré, IV, p. 446; LJF. 116; DF. 3. XI, 403. See p. 70. The text of Cambon's telegram as published in the *Yellow Book* lacks its final paragraph: 'Herr v. Jagow has few illusions, he appeared to me deeply moved; he complained strongly of the precipitancy of Russia which rendered useless the German Kaiser's mediation, asked for, according to him, by the Tsar.. . . "   [5] See p. 121.

Paul Cambon which served his purpose.[1] Furthermore, there was in France a spate of accusations against himself and the French documents which certainly did not escape the notice of Poincaré, who kept abreast of all that was written, readily taking up the cudgels in his own defense. How could he deal exhaustively with the origins of the war without going to the sources? And why, having, as he himself relates, gone to the sources in 1923 and the beginning of 1925, did he not seize the occasion to make the truth known when in October 1925 he published his article 'The Responsibility for the War' in *Foreign Affairs.*

On the contrary, it is only by determined endeavors that the truth was extracted from those in possession of the secrets. Proofs had to pile up on all sides, accusations to become more and more widely and insistently voiced, the *Ligue des Droits de l'Homme* had to take the field and call Poincaré on to the scene, official history with Renouvin as its mouthpiece had to repudiate the thesis of the *Yellow Book,* the *British Documents* had to make their appearance at the end of 1926, preceded by the Austrian and German and followed by the Russian documents, before Poincaré in *L'Union Sacrée* at last decided to discard the *Yellow Book* and publish some essential documents, though with superhuman efforts to adapt facts to the need of defending himself and the Government of that day. Even today the truth has not gained admittance to many important works published in France.[3] Moreover, even after the publication of *L'Union Sacrée* and the great collection of French diplomatic documents, there still remains a doubt whether the whole truth has been made known to us.

12. *The publication of the* Documents Diplomatiques Français.

The obstructionism practiced by the high officials of the Quai d'Orsay in regard to the publication of the French diplomatic documents is not an edifying spectacle. Zealous for the traditions and prestige of their

---

[1] Poincaré, *Les origines de la guerre,* p. 262.

[2] In a school text-book of 1922 Jules Isaac had accepted the incorrect version of the order in which the two mobilizations were decreed, but he rectified the statement in the next edition. His example, however, found no imitators. In *Un débat historique, 1914,* he comments that, although for a good many years the point had been settled beyond doubt, eminent French writers were still stating that Russia ordered general mobilization because Austria had done so. This is true of J. Bainville in *Histoire de France* (Paris, 1930); M, Muret in *Guillaume II d'après les plus récents témoignages*; Marshall Foch in his *Memoirs*; V. Giraud in *Hisioire de la Grande Guerre,* and several others. The historian Émile Bourgeois, in the *Manuel historique de politique étrangère,* wrote in 1926 that the Tsar yielded to the requests of his General Staff in consequence of the announcement of the German general mobilization made in the special issue of the *Berliner Lokal-Anzeiger* (IV, p. 627), which was not true. Moreover, French works in general assert that the proclamation of the *Kilegsgefahrzustand* in Germany was the equivalent of the proclamation of general mobilization, "when the contrary is plain from the message telegraphed to Paris by Jules Cambon on 31 July (see p. 70) and from the German plan of mobilization which the French General Staff had got hold of in May 1914 (Les *armées françaises dans la Grande Guerre* (Paris, 1922), I, p. 39; (1936), I, pp. 62-4).

department, they induced successive Foreign Ministers to speak in opposition to the publication in full of all the documents which had been asked for by the *Ligue des Droits de l'Homme* as early as 10 November 1922, recommending that the bona fides of a critical edition should be guaranteed by entrusting the task to a commission of independent experts.[1] Receiving no satisfaction of this legitimate demand, the *Ligue* renewed it in 1925, and on 5 November of that year the then Foreign Minister stated that a preliminary classification of French diplomatic documents was being undertaken and that a commission would 'shortly' be appointed to undertake the task of editing them. But as nothing was done the *Ligue* again raised the matter on 18 February 1927. On 20 April 1927 the Foreign Minister replied that the corresponding German and English publications referred to by the *Ligue* were mainly concerned 'not with the war period but with the pre-war period'. This caused the *Ligue* on 25 June 1927 to express surprise at the Foreign Minister's ignorance of the four volumes of *Deutsche Dokumente zum Kriegsausbruch* issued by the German Government in 1919 and to express a wish to see at long last 'a complete *Yellow Book* consisting entirely of authentic documents'.

The wish was granted at the end of 1927. The budget estimates for 1928 included a credit of 200,000 francs for the publication of the French diplomatic documents relating to the origins of the war. A decree of 29 January 1928 appointed the special commission charged with the carrying out of the publication. Its chairman was Charlety, and it was composed of three categories of members. The first were historians and specialists and included Auerbach, Aulard, Camille Bloch, Émile Bourgeois, Eisenmann, General Gilard, René Pinon, Pierre Renouvin, Seignobos. The second were diplomatists, Jules Cambon, Berthelot, Barrère, Paléologue, Bompard, Bonin, Dumaine, Jusserand, Pichon. The third category were members of the *Institut.* Thus the list did not include a single member of the *Ligue des Droits de l'Homme,* which had done so much to bring about the publication of the documents, nor of the *Société des Études Documentaires et Critiques* nor of anyone of those who had been critical of the line taken by France, while, on the other hand, among those appointed were the diplomatists who were themselves the authors of documents to be published, beginning with Paléologue.

The commission divided the documents into three series and in the first half of 1929 began publication with one volume in each series. The first begins with 1871, the second with 1901, the third with 4 November 1911. The two first series were not completed when the second European war broke out in 1939. The third series was com

[1] See p. 154.

pleted by Vol. XI (24 July-4 August 1914), which appeared at the end of 1936. The *British Documents,* on the other hand, began with Vol. XI dealing with the outbreak of war, and the German and Austrian documents also followed this order. It is needless to dwell on the fact that the lateness in setting up the commission, its composition, and the delay in issuing the documents relating to July 1914 betray the great difficulty with which official France overcame its unwillingness to publish the documents. On 26 December 1932 the *Ligue des Droits de l'Homme* held a general meeting attended by more than 1,500 delegates representing the 180,000 members which it then numbered. It again brought up the question of the revision of the Treaty of Versailles and the motion was carried *nem. con.*

It may be that the French Government found it painful and difficult to admit the full truth after all that had been done to hide it. But for France it is always possible, nay fitting, to entrust the defense of her cause to worthier arguments than the falsehoods to which she then resorted. These falsehoods may have been understandable at the time they were uttered, because France and Russia did not want to seem to be in the wrong in the eyes of England. It was a danger that appeared serious. Not only did Benckendorff bring it to Sazonov's notice on 1 August,[1] but when Grey learnt of the Russian mobilization on the evening of 31 July, he said to Cambon:

> This, it seemed to me, would precipitate a crisis, and would make it appear that German mobilization was being forced by Russia.[2]

Cambon did not report this outburst to Paris. It is recorded in a letter written by Grey to Bertie on 31 July. Bertie only received it after his talk with Poincaré at about 11 a. m. on 1 August and in any case had no reason to bring it to the knowledge of Paris. But even without knowing that Grey had expressed himself thus the Quai d'Orsay might well fear that the decision taken at St. Petersburg would have an adverse influence on the enigmatic attitude of England. One cannot be greatly surprised if Poincaré and Margerie sought to obviate this by taking up the suggestion indirectly made in Paléologue's telegram.

But why persist in the falsehood to the extent of inventing and falsifying the documents in the *Yellow Book* a good four months after the outbreak of the war? Because, says Demartial, it was also necessary to explain why Russia ordered her mobilization, which caused the war, and to make the Central Powers bear the responsibility for her having done so.[3] To this it may be replied that on 4 August neither Poincaré

[1] *Int. Bez.* i. V, 398. See p. 133.
[2] BD. XI, 367. See Vol. II, p. 646. In the *Blue Book* the sentence containing these words is omitted. This is symptomatic.
[3] Demartial, *Evolution,* 15 March, 1926, p. 40.

nor Viviani alleged the Austrian general mobilization as the justification for the Russian. Poincaré confined himself to general terms, and Viviani, with his habitual irresponsibility, accused Germany of having sent St. Petersburg an ultimatum 'on pretext that Russia had mobilized', thus even denying that Russian general mobilization was ordered before the German ultimatum. Another big falsehood, it is true. But to assign the blame to where it belonged there was no need to resort to misrepresentations, and this is where Demartial and his associates put themselves in the wrong. They do not see, as even the Socialist and Communist leaders in France saw, that the French Government might legitimately have presented the facts in the following way: Austria sent Serbia an unacceptable ultimatum which infringed her sovereign rights; Germany demanded that the Monarchy should be given a free hand to settle accounts with Serbia as she pleased; the other Powers especially Russia, could not permit this violation, hurtful to their feelings and to their own interests; moreover while Serbia had accepted the greater part of the Austrian demands, the Powers had in vain proposed that the issue should be submitted to a conference of Ambassadors as in 1912-13, and had put forward other mediatory formulas which were rejected; in consequence of these repulses, and especially of the Austrian declaration of war on Serbia, Russia had mobilized against Austria, and this had been regarded by Germany as permissible; as, however, Russia did not have a plan for partial mobilization, she had been obliged to order general mobilization, pledging herself, at the same time, not to undertake hostilities as long as the negotiations, which had taken a promising turn, were continued. Germany had then demanded that Russia should demobilize and had followed this up by a declaration of war; France also received an ultimatum demanding that she remain neutral; she could not engage to abandon her ally, and in consequence Germany declared war on her. This summary of events would have been substantially true to the facts and would have afforded good grounds for defending the line taken by France. Certainly, France had encouraged Russia to be firm, had promised unconditional support, and had not objected to the Russian partial mobilization which had been regarded as natural by England and as tolerable by Germany herself. France had, on the other hand, advised against general mobilization. She could not, however, ask Russia to revoke it for fear of endangering the alliance. Yet, even in spite of the Russian general mobilization the conflict might have been settled without war if the German Government had not decided to precipitate matters. Or rather, it was not the German Government (which after 29 July had shown a disposition to be conciliatory), it was the German General Staff which decided on war. This has been admirably shown by Poincaré in the article which he wrote for the

American periodical *Foreign Affairs* in 1925, summarizing events on the lines just indicated without resorting to falsehoods or artifices to make out that the French Government acted otherwise than it actually did.[1]

This mode of presentation would, it is true, have been at the same time a criticism of the line taken by France, which was anything but prudent and was probably motivated by the *arrière-pensée* that if war came it would after all come in conditions favorable to the Triple *Entente*. But it would have avoided the lamentable falsehoods which seemed to be a confession of guilt. When lies are used to defend a case which can be justified on good grounds that case is weakened instead of being strengthened and runs the risk of being lost in spite of its good grounds.

And thus it is that the French Government has been put in the dock for falsifying the facts and has been blamed not only for what it did do but also for the sins committed by the Central Powers. This lengthy analysis of its mistakes is intended to make its errors quite plain but also to clear it of accusations which it does not deserve and which were not made in those tragic last days of July 1914 when, without need of documents, European and, in particular Italian, public opinion clearly saw the threat to peace of the Austrian action and instinctively felt that unless the Vienna and Berlin Governments would accept a compromise the outcome would be war.

[1] R. Poincaré, 'The Responsibility for the War', *Foreign Affairs,* October 1925, pp. 1-19.

CHAPTER IV

THE GERMAN DECLARATIONS OF WAR

ON RUSSIA AND FRANCE (1–3 AUGUST)

(1) *The Chancellor's speech to the Bundesrat; the mobilization order signed at the Berlin Schloss (p. 166). (2) A telegram from London raises German hopes of French neutrality (p. 171). (3) The order to abstain from occupying Luxemburg; confusion reigns at Berlin (p. 175). (4) Pourtalès delivers the declaration of war to Sazonov; Izvolsky asks France for her support (p. 181). (5) Tirpitz and Bethmann; stormy scenes between the German political and military chiefs (p. 186). (6) Draft of a declaration of war on France; breakdown of the political leadership of the Reich (p. 193). (7) Moltke's illusions; Luxemburg occupied; an ultimatum sent to Belgium (p. 197). (8) The incidents on the Franco-German frontier on 2 and 3 August (p. 204). (9) The false report of the bombing of Nuremberg; the German declaration of war sent to France (p. 209). (10) The Chancellor's speech in the Reichstag on 4 August (p. 219). (11) Poincaré's message and Viviani's speech to the French parliament (p. 225).*

1. *The Chancellor's speech to the Bundesrat; the mobilization order signed at the Berlin Schloss.*

We now reach the epilogue of the tragedy. Berlin had sent the ultimatum to St. Petersburg, had requested Paris to define the French line of conduct and was now awaiting the two replies. The Russian answer had to be given by noon on 1 August, the French by 2 p. m. Some time during the small hours of 1 August Pourtalès's telegram must have arrived telling of his having served the ultimatum on Sazonov at midnight on the 31st and adding:

M. Sazonov again alluded to the technical impossibility of stopping the military measures.[1]

But this immediate objection did not amount to the formal rejection which Germany needed before proceeding to the extreme step. And Russia had been given a twelve-hour time limit in which to reply. In the meantime the Chancellor explained the situation to the Bundesrat, asking for the approval of the other States of the Confederation to the line of action he proposed to follow.

Taking the assassination of the Archduke as its starting-point, his review of events was an apologia for the free hand given to Austria culminating in the pledge:

[1] DD. III, 536. See p. 61.

It goes without saying that if the *casus foederis* arises we shall stand loyally beside you.

Serbia, he said, had accepted some of the Austrian demands but had rejected or made reservations about certain others. Germany had asked the other Powers to let the conflict remain localized, and all had agreed except Russia, who began secretly to arm. The Tsar asked for the mediation of the Kaiser, who was willing to act. Austria was advised to make one more solemn declaration of her territorial *désintéressement* to St. Petersburg and to reaffirm that

the aim of her military intervention was simply to lay hold of a bargaining counter for the fulfillment of her demands by occupying parts of Serbian territory.

This was on similar lines to the English mediation proposal which Berlin had sent on to Vienna. Then all of a sudden the news arrived on the 30th of Russian partial and, on the 31st, of her general mobilization.

Yesterday [the 31st] was to be the day on which Vienna made the decision to address Russia either on the lines of our proposal or that of England. In either case Austria-Hungary at our request had resumed the direct negotiations with Russia which had been broken off. Yesterday, therefore, Vienna was in negotiation for an understanding . . . . At that moment Russia mobilized her total land and sea forces.

We need not dwell on the inaccuracy and mendacity of this summary. The facts are already sufficiently known to the reader. Bethmann went on to say:

Russia tries to make out that her mobilization is not to be regarded as an act of hostility towards us. If we were to accept this view, we should commit a crime against the safety of our fatherland. . . . We should be in danger of losing the advantage of our greater speed of mobilization. . . . Therefore we have felt ourselves obliged to send an ultimatum to Russia in reply to the mobilization. . . . Her answer is due at 12 noon today. I do not yet know what form it will take. . . . The French reply is due at 1 p. m. . . . If the Russian reply is unsatisfactory and there is no absolutely unambiguous declaration of neutrality from France. . . the Kaiser will have the Russian Government informed that he must regard himself as in a state of war with Russia brought on by Russia herself, and to France he will have the statement made that we are at war with Russia and that, as France does not guarantee her neutrality, we must assume that we are also in a state of war with France. . . . We have not willed the war, it has been forced upon us. . . . But we trust . . . in God's help.

The representatives of the other States of the German Confederation voted unanimously that in the event of satisfactory declarations not being made by Russia and France, H.M. the Kaiser should cause both of these states to be informed that they had brought about a state of war with the German Empire.

Whereupon Bethmann said in conclusion:

Thus my survey has met with the general approval of the High Confederated States. When now the iron dice are cast, may God be our help.[1]

The Russian reply did not arrive at 12 noon, hence, of course, Bethmann could not know what it was because, as has been stated above,[2] Pourtalès did not present himself after 12 noon to receive the Russian answer, nor did he send any further telegram after the one of 1 a. m. summarizing his midnight conversation with Sazonov of 31 July/1 August.[3] But the Wilhelmstrasse, feeling it had no time to lose, had at 12.52 p. m. on 1 August telegraphed to Pourtalès the text of the declaration of war which was to be served on the Russian Government if it did not return a 'satisfactory reply'. The declaration was worded in such a way as to be used either if Russia rejected the German intimation to demobilize or if she returned no reply. The telegram runs:

In the case of the Russian Government's not returning a 'satisfactory reply' to our demand, Your Excellency will kindly hand it the following declaration this afternoon at 5 p. m. Central European time:

'The Imperial Government has endeavored since the beginning of the crisis to bring it to a peaceful solution. Acceding to a wish which had been expressed to him by H.M. the Tsar of Russia, H.M. the Emperor of Germany, in agreement with England, had sought to fulfill a mediatory role between the Cabinets of Vienna and St. Petersburg, when Russia, without awaiting its outcome, proceeded to the mobilization of the totality of her land and sea forces.

'In consequence of this threatening measure, not motivated by any military preparations on the part of Germany, the German Empire found itself faced with grave and imminent danger. I the Imperial Government had failed to take measures against this danger it would have jeopardized the security and the very existence of Germany. In consequence the German Government finds itself obliged to address itself to the Government of H.M. the Tsar of all the Russians insisting on the cessation of the said military acts. Russia having refused to accede _____ to this demand and having shown not having thought it necessary to reply

by this refusal that her action was directed against Germany, I have the attitude

honor, on the order of my Government, to inform Your Excellency as follows:

---

[1] DD. III, 553.   [2] See p. 65.   [3] DD. III, 536.

'H.M. the Emperor, my august Sovereign, in the name of the Empire, accepts the challenge and considers himself in a state of war with Russia.'[1]

A similar document, prepared for a declaration of war on France but not sent, will be discussed farther on.[2] Now we must turn our attention to what was going on in Berlin while this telegram to Pourtalès was on its way. There was anxious waiting and the generals were impatient about Pourtalès's silence. In the evening Falkenhayn again spoke to the Chancellor of the dangers of being behindhand with mobilization. Falkenhayn's diary entry for 1 August runs:

As up to 4 p. m. there has been no reply from Russia although the ultimatum expired at midday, I drove to the Chancellor's to get him to go with me to see the Kaiser and ask for the promulgation of the mobilization order. After considerable resistance he consented and we rang up Moltke and Tirpitz. Meanwhile His Majesty himself rang and asked us to bring along the mobilization order. At 5 o'clock in the afternoon the signing of the order by His Majesty on the table made from timbers of Nelson's 'Victory.' As he signed I said: 'God bless Your Majesty and your arms, God protect the beloved Fatherland.' The Kaiser gave me a long hand shake and we both had tears in our eyes. Those present were the Imperial Chancellor, Moltke, Tirpitz, Lyncker, Plessen.[3]

It was, indeed, a solemn moment about which various more or less apocryphal rumors got about. According to Admiral Mark Kerr, Princess Bülow was told by her husband that, after signing the mobilization decree, the Kaiser

stood up and faced the officers standing round him and, throwing down the pen, said: 'Gentlemen, you will live to rue the day when you made me do this.' Kerr also quotes the late Henry White, former American Ambassador to Italy and France, as saying that in the last days of July 1914 Bülow told him [White]: 'That the peace party at the Palace is ruining us. We cannot get him to sign the mobilization,' and that Falkenhayn told him: 'We cannot get the Emperor to sign the mobilization, he still has hopes of peace. We are forty-eight hours behind, and all the trains are getting jammed up.' As a matter of fact, White was not in Berlin in the last days of July 1914; he reached there immediately after hostilities had begun. He dined with Falkenhayn at

---

[1] DD. III, 542. The *Deutschen Dokumente zum Kriegsausbruch* reproduces three drafts of this declaration of war, the results of repeated efforts of Mirbach, Stumm, Rosenberg, and Bethmann himself, its text having to be worded in French. The wording of the final sentence caused particular difficulty: what was to be the reason for declaring war? The first draft said that the Kaiser *'déclare accepter la guerre qui lui est octroyée'*. Obviously the man who drafted it did not know that in French *'octroyer'* means 'to bestow', 'to grant as a favor'. Next the word *'octroyée'* was replaced by *'imposée'*, but this evidently was not regarded as quite suitable, since in the second and third drafts the *'guerre . . . octroyée'* becomes simply *'le défi'* which the Kaiser *'re/ère'* and which justifies his having to 'consider himself in a state of war' with Russia.

[2] DD. III, 608. See p. 194.   [3] Zwehl, p. 58.

the War Office and made a memorandum of their conversation. In this memorandum, published in Allan Nevin's *Life of Henry White*, White quotes Falkenhayn as saying: 'Those Peace People at the Palace had held back the mobilization of the German Army for nearly forty-eight hours after he him-self had thought it necessary because of Russian mobilization.'[1]

No word of any remark made by the Kaiser. In fact, if the Kaiser had said such things Falkenhayn would certainly have recorded them in his diary and reported them to Tirpitz, who conceals nothing and records fully all that he knew and heard in the days preceding the outbreak of war. This does not make it impossible that Wilhelm signed the decree with reluctance due to fear of English intervention. Falkenhayn confided to White that

of course they never expected for one moment that England would enter the war. . . . the coming in of England had made all the difference in the world, both to the probable duration of the war [which he thought 'was likely to last at least three or four years'], and possibly even to its outcome.[2]

The signing of the ultimatum was certainly premature, not only, as will be shown at length further on, because efforts to negotiate could and should have been continued before resorting to the declaration of war,[3] but also because for Germany the mobilization order implied the opening of hostilities and this involved the immediate occupation of Luxemburg before it was known whether Germany was at war with Russia or not. The instructions to Pourtalès containing the declaration of war had begun:

In the case of the Russian Government's not returning a 'satisfactory reply' to our demand. Your Excellency will . . .[4]

So if because of a change of mind on the part of the Tsar, or because of King George's appeal, or for any other reason, Sazonov at 7 p. m. on 1 August had returned a 'satisfactory reply' to Pourtalès's demand, thrice repeated, that Russia should demobilize, the result would have been that with unexampled levity Germany would have set fire to the powder magazine before completing the necessary procedure in regard to the ultimatum. One may go still further and say that supposing Sazonov, on the expiry of the time limit set by the ultimatum, i.e., noon on 1 August, had accepted its terms, Berlin would most probably have heard of his acceptance after German mobilization had been proclaimed, i.e., after she had gone to war. This is a point which has escaped the notice of historians, who tend to confine themselves to what actually happened without considering what might logically have happened. But responsibility for acts that have been committed

---

[1] Schmitt, II, p. 324 note.
[3] See pp. 232-6.

[2] Schmitt, II, p. 324 note.
[4] See p. 168.

is not to be measured only on a basis of the consequences that actually followed from them. Account must also be taken of the consequences they might potentially have had. Clearly if mobilization signified going to war, Berlin before mobilizing should have awaited the reply to the ultimatum. As this was not done, the consequence was that in the night of 1/2 August Germany did not know whether she was at war with Russia or not, whether or not to send an ultimatum to Belgium and declare war on France. This lack of knowledge and this indecision led to a serious and significant incident immediately after the signing of the mobilization order.

2. A telegram from London raises German hopes of French neutrality.

Those summoned to the Schloss to be present at the signing of the mobilization order were still there discussing the declaration of war on Russia[1] when Jagow appeared with the news that

a very important dispatch had come in from England which would soon be decoded and brought along.

Tirpitz, for motives of which we shall speak later, suggested that Moltke and Falkenhayn should not leave before reading it. This was a very reasonable suggestion. What if the message were such as to render immediate mobilization unnecessary? Nothing shows up more vividly the levity of the German decisions and the untrammeled power of the military than the fact that the two generals 'went straight off with the signed orders . . . without waiting for the English dispatch'.[3] They had their own reasons for so doing. Having shared and, indeed, inspired the mood of 'supreme confidence' which, as the English Military Attaché noted, 'reigns in military circles in Berlin',[3] they on the one hand were in a hurry to send out the mobilization order, and on the other were afraid lest the telegram from Lichnowsky might cause the Kaiser to change his mind and revoke the order. Better lose no time and issue it. Ten minutes after the departure of the two army chiefs the telegram was brought and read out to those who remained. Dispatched at 11.14 a. m. and received at 4.23 p. m., this astounding telegram runs:

Sir E. Grey has just sent word by Sir W. Tyrrell that he hopes this after-noon to make a communication to me about the results of a Cabinet meeting now in progress, which may be of a nature to avert the great catastrophe. From Sir William's indications it seems to mean that if we were not to attack France, England would remain neutral and guarantee the passivity of France. I shall learn

[1] See p. 193.
[2] Tirpitz, *Dokumente* II, pp. 16-7.
[3] BD. XI, 404. Lerchenfeld also reported to Munich on 2 August: 'The mood in military circles here is one of absolute confidence' (DD. IV, p. 145).

particulars this afternoon. Sir E. Grey has just called me to the telephone and asked whether I feel able to give an assurance that in the event of France's remaining neutral in a Russo-German war, we would not attack France. I assured him I could make myself responsible for that and he will use this statement at today's Cabinet meeting.

P.S. Sir W. Tyrrell urged me to use my influence so that our troops should not violate the French frontier. He said everything depended on this.[1]

We shall not dwell here on this fantastic English move or the motives behind it. They will be fully discussed later.[2] Here it is only needful to say that this was not an actual proposal but only the pre-announcement of a proposal, and one that on the face of it appeared unworthy of credence. The sensible thing to do would have been to wait till afternoon and see what would come of it. But the telegram opened up such unhoped-for prospects, seemed so much the fulfillment of the highest German hopes, that it was taken as an outright promise from England to observe neutrality if Germany attacked Russia but did not attack France. Falkenhayn and Moltke were speedily called back, and Moltke, in a memoir he wrote at Homburg in November 1914, tells that he found those who had stayed behind 'in a joyful state of mind'.[3] Well might they be! To be given leave to attack Russia with the forces of the two Empires without interference from France and England was such a heaven-sent blessing that, as Tirpitz writes,

Kaiser, Chancellor, Jagow welcomed this dispatch with great joy,[4] and Moltke writes:

The Kaiser said to me: 'Then we simply deploy in the east with the whole army.'[5]

Such remarks, while revealing Wilhelm's jubilation, show his abysmal ignorance of military matters. Though aware that Germany did not possess a mobilization plan for a war against Russia alone and that German troops were poised to cross the western front as laid down in the only existing plan for a war on two fronts, he thought it quite easy to send them against Russia. Moltke was aghast.

I assured His Majesty that this was not possible. The deployment of an army of a million men was not a matter of improvisation. It was the product of a whole heavy year's work and, once worked out, could not be changed. If His Majesty insisted on leading the whole army eastwards, he would not have an army ready to strike, he would have a confused mass of disorderly armed men without commissariat. The Kaiser insisted on his demand and grew very angry, saying to me, amongst other things: 'Your uncle would have given me a different answer!' which hurt me very much. I have never claimed to be the equal of the Field-Marshal. Nobody seemed to

---

[1] DD. III, 562.   [2] See pp. 380-6.   [3] Moltke, p. 19.
[4] Tirpitz, *Dokumente*, p. 17.   [5] Moltke, p. 19.

reflect that it would bring disaster upon us if we were to invade Russia with our entire army, leaving a mobilized France in our rear. How, even with the best will, could England have prevented France from attacking us in the rear! In vain did I object that France was already mobilizing and that a mobilized Germany and a mobilized France could not possibly come to an agreement to leave each other alone. The atmosphere grew more and more excited and I stood in a minority of one. I finally managed to persuade His Majesty that our concentration of strong forces against France and light defensive forces against Russia must be carried out as planned unless the most unholy muddle was to be created. I told the Kaiser that, once the concentration had been carried out, it would be possible to transfer forces at will to the eastern front, but that the concentration itself must proceed unchanged, or else I could not be responsible for things.[1]

Tirpitz's account is substantially the same:

When the two army chiefs returned there was a sharp clash between the Chief of Staff and the Chancellor. The Chief of Staff (supported rather half-heartedly by the War Minister) declared that he could not take the responsibility if changes were made in the concentration as laid down under mobilization. This declaration was a reply to the Imperial Chancellor's proposal to stop the concentration against France. Chief of Staff said if this happened the Kaiser would have a mass of men, but not an army. Threat the Imperial Chancellor declared that then he on his part could not take the political responsibility. After the first violence of the encounter had somewhat abated, I supported the Chancellor and the Kaiser in the view that, whether bluff or no, we could not reject Grey's proposal out of hand because, when Grey's dispatch was published, we should be put flagrantly in the wrong. The Kaiser strongly agreed. The War Minister asked the Kaiser's permission to go aside with Moltke and discuss the matter.[2]

What was said between the two men can be gathered from Falkenhayn's diary:

He [Moltke] said he was absolutely cut up because the Kaiser's decision showed that he still hopes for peace. I comforted Moltke. I shared his opinion of His Majesty's idea but could not see anything to hurt Moltke's feelings in the temporary postponement of some of his arrangements, and the Kaiser's humane thoughts only do him credit. Of course I do not for one moment believe that the telegram will change anything in the tremendous drama which started at 5 o'clock.[3]

The upshot was that Moltke made up his mind to agree to acceptance of the English proposal on the condition, already mentioned, that the mobilization plan should take its course also on the French frontier, leaving it open for the army to be sent east against Russia later. Moltke's consent was given with a heavy heart.

[1] Moltke, pp. 19-21.   [2] Tirpitz, *Dokumente* II, p. 17.
[3] Zwehl, p. 59.

In the course of this scene I nearly fell into despair. I regarded these diplomatic moves, which threatened to interfere with the carrying out of our mobilization, as the greatest disaster for the impending war. . . . Years earlier the Foreign Ministry had told me that France might possibly remain neutral in a war between Germany and Russia. I had so little faith in this possibility that I said even then that, if Russia declared war on us, we should have to declare war on France at once were there the least doubt about her attitude.[1]

Such being his views, he would only have been willing to accept the English proposal if France had for the time being ceded the fortresses of Toul and Verdun as bargaining-counters. But this was ruled out as showing mistrust of England. Falkenhayn asserts that it was he who drafted the reply to Lichnowsky[2] which the *Deutschen Dokumente* state to be in Jagow's handwriting. Tirpitz, however, whose information is always full and accurate, writes:

The telegram was then drafted on these lines in an adjoining room by the Imperial Chancellor, Jagow, and the two military chiefs[3]:

'Germany is prepared to accede to the English proposal if England guarantees with her entire armed strength the unconditional neutrality of France in the Russo-German conflict, a neutrality which must last until the final settlement of this conflict. It must rest with Germany to decide when this settlement is attained.'

'German mobilization took place today on grounds of the Russian challenge and before Telegram No. 205 [No. 562 of the German Diplomatic Documents] was received. Consequently it is too late to change our concentration on the French frontier. But we engage until Monday, 3 August, 7 p. m., not to cross the French frontier if by that time acceptance by England has been received.'[4]

While this telegram was being drafted by those mentioned above, Tirpitz suggested to Wilhelm that he should send a personal telegram of the same content to the King of England. The telegram was accordingly drafted by Tirpitz and Admiral von Müller 'in a still more friendly tone'.

When the others had read out their telegram and the four men agreed on its wording the personal telegram to the King of England was also read aloud and most gratefully accepted by the Imperial Chancellor.[5]

It runs as follows:

I just received the communication from your Government offering French neutrality under guarantee of Great Britain. Added to this offer was the inquiry whether under these conditions Germany would refrain from attacking France. On technical grounds my mobilization which had already

---

[1] Moltke, p. 21.   [2] Zwehl, p. 59.   [3] Tirpitz, *Dokumente* II, p. 18.
        [4] DD. III, 578.   [5] Tirpitz, *Dokumente,* II, p. 18.

been proclaimed this afternoon must proceed against two fronts east and west as prepared. This cannot be countermanded because I am sorry your telegram[1] came so late. But if France offers me neutrality which must be guaranteed by the British fleet and army I shall of course refrain from attacking France and employ my troops elsewhere. I hope that France will not become nervous. The troops on my frontier are in the act of being stopped by telegraph and telephon [*sic*] from crossing into France.[2]

Wilhelm's message went off at 7.2 p. m. and Bethmann's at 7.15 p. m. on 1 August but they did not end the diplomatic activity necessitated by the great event that lay ahead. At 7.20 p. m. Jagow telegraphed to Lichnowsky:

Please give Sir Edward Grey best thanks for proposal, which unfortunately only reached here after promulgation of mobilization, but may, it is to be hoped, still be successful. Detailed reply goes off in cipher at the same time as this and requires to be dealt with immediately.[3]

Next, at 8.45 p. m., Jagow telegraphed to Schoen—in answer to Schoen's dispatch, received at 6.10 p. m. and reporting the morning conversation with Viviani[4]—confidentially informing him of what Lichnowsky's telegram foreshadowed, and adding:

Please keep the French quiet for the time being.[5]

3. The order to abstain from occupying Luxemburg; confusion reigns at Berlin.

'Unfortunately' the English proposal only reached Berlin after the promulgation of mobilization, wrote Jagow, echoing similar words of the Kaiser's. And Moltke writes:

I am convinced that the Kaiser would never have signed the mobilization order if Prince Lichnowsky's dispatch had arrived half an hour earlier.[6]

But how could he have not signed it, having declared war on Russia, who was not prepared to demobilize and whom France and England were going to allow him to attack, thus assuring him of an easy triumph? One cannot help thinking that the expressions of regret were prompted rather by the hazards of carrying through a mobilization plan designed for an attack on France and operating on the French frontier. One of the difficulties which might have sobered German hopes, even if a settlement on the lines of Lichnowsky's telegram had been possible, was raised at the Schloss gathering. The plan provided for the immediate occupation of Luxemburg by the 16th Division to ensure that the Luxemburg railways, needed for the German

---

[1] This must mean Lichnowsky's telegram.
[3] DD. III, 579.
[5] DD. III, 587.
[2] DD. III, 575.
[4] DD. III, 571. See p100.
[6] Moltke, p. 23.

concentration, would not be seized by the French. What brought the matter up was the Chancellor's remark that

the occupation of Luxemburg must not on any account be carried out, as it was a direct threat to France.[1]

No doubt the Kaiser at once saw that the invasion of Luxemburg would not only be a threat to France but would violate the neutrality of a State which Germany was pledged to respect. Moltke's account continues:

As I stood there the Kaiser, without asking me, turned to the aide-de-camp on duty and commanded him to telegraph immediate instructions to the 16th Division at Trier not to march into Luxemburg. I thought my heart would break. The danger arose afresh that our concentration would be thrown into confusion. What that means can probably only fully be realized by one familiar with the complicated business of mobilization, which has to be worked out down to the smallest details. Where every move is laid down in advance to the minute, any change cannot but have disastrous effects. I tried in vain to convince His Majesty that we needed and must secure the Luxemburg railways. I was snubbed with the remark that I should use other railways instead. The order must stand.

Therewith I was dismissed. It is impossible to describe the state of mind in which I returned home. I was absolutely broken and shed tears of despair. When the telegram to the 16th division was submitted to me, repeating the order sent by telephone, I slammed down the pen on the desk and said I would not sign. I could not put my signature, the first since the issue of the mobilization order, to an order revoking what was carefully planned, it would at once be regarded by the troops as a sign of indecision. 'Do as you like with the telegram,' I said to Lieutenant-Colonel Tappen. 'I am not going to sign it.' So I sat on inert in my room in a state of despondency, until at about 11 o'clock at night I was again summoned to the Schloss by His Majesty.[2]

What was the reason of this fresh summons? Had something new happened? That evening, after the stormy meeting, the Kaiser had retired to rest full of optimism. About 10 p. m. he had given an audience to Szögyény, who brought him Francis Joseph's reply to his telegram of the previous day[3] and who had found him surrounded by his family in a little garden of the Schloss. The Kaiser was in excellent humor. He talked to Szögyény of the Tsar's telegram full of contradictions which he could not describe otherwise than as 'lies', suggested perhaps by the War Minister, if not by Rasputin. He said that no reply had come in from St. Petersburg and Paris to the intimations sent to them but that, on the other hand, Grey, with King George's assent,

---

[1] Moltke, pp. 21-2.   [2] Moltke, pp. 22-3.
[3] DD. III, 503, 601; Oe-U. VIII, 11118.

had offered by telegram to guarantee the neutrality of France in case of a war between Germany and Russia, that, of course, he [the Kaiser] would demand a gage of France, that he had the impression that the mobilization of Germany had frightened France to an extreme degree, that in these conditions it was a matter of persevering calmly but with great firmness in the path pursued up to the present; that above all he was determined to settle accounts with France in which he hoped to be completely successful.

Finally:

The Kaiser again expressed himself in eulogistic terms on the manly behavior of the Imperial Chancellor, praising the exactitude which he displayed in the execution of his plans.[1]

Incredible euphoria on the part of the unstable and impulsive monarch, who veered from abject depression to irrational optimism. Lichnowsky's telegram had evidently gone to his head, and in a swaggering mood he deluded himself that with the consent of England he was going to make short work first of Russia and then of France, of which latter he would demand a 'gage' of her neutrality, perhaps the handing over of Toul and Verdun, as desired by Moltke but without Bethmann's approval. With these rosy expectations he took leave of Szögyény and repaired to rest. He can hardly have gone to sleep when there came King George's reply to his telegram of 7.2 p. m. shattering his beautiful dream:

In answer to your telegram just received I think there must be some mis-understanding as to a suggestion that passed in friendly conversation between Prince Lichnowsky and Sir Edward Grey this afternoon when they were discussing how actual fighting between German and French armies might be avoided while there is still a chance of some agreement between Austria and Russia. Sir Edward Grey will arrange to see Prince Lichnowsky, early tomorrow to ascertain whether there is a misunderstanding on his part.[2]

This was not what Lichnowsky had telegraphed or Berlin understood. By now war on Russia must have been declared and the hope that Lichnowsky had raised in Berlin was that this war could perhaps be fought without England and France coming in. A foolish hope, but one justified by the wording of the telegram. Now it was at an end, and the only thing to do was to send for Moltke again and give him a free hand. Moltke's story continues:

The Kaiser received me in his bedroom, he had already been in bed but had got up again and thrown on a coat. He handed me a telegram from the King of England . . . The Kaiser was extremely agitated, and said to me: 'Now you can do as you will.' I drove home at once and telegraphed to the 16th Division that the invasion of Luxemburg   was   to   proceed.   To   give   some   reason   for   this

[1] DA. III, 105.   [2] DD. III, 612.

renewal of the order, I added: 'as it has just been learnt that France has ordered mobilization.'[1]

There was no need for the order because in spite of the Kaiser's standstill order the smooth-working mobilization machinery, set in motion before the order was received, had already carried the 16th Division into Luxemburg. But in spite of his free hand Moltke's nerves did not recover from the shock. He writes:

I never got over the effects of this experience, it destroyed something in me that could not be built up again, confidence and trust were shattered.[2]

This confession elicits from Falkenhayn's biographer, Zwehl, the comment:

In the vicissitudes of those critical days, [Moltke's] frame of mind, as his memoirs show was no longer one of equanimity such as is needed by a commander in chief who must daily and hourly take the rough with the smooth and be ready with expedients when difficulties arise, not allowing them to drive him to outbursts of despair. To what degree this was the case, with Moltke as early as 1 August, perhaps under the after-effects of a double Karlsbad cure, emerges from his *Memoirs*.[3]

Such was probably the impression prevailing in Berlin, for Falkenhayn's diary for 10 August records:

Lyncker thinks he has grounds for asking me whether in the event of Moltke's losing his nerve I would take over his duties. Of course I cannot say otherwise than: Yes.[4]

It will be necessary to return to this singular episode later on in speaking of the line taken by Grey, who in fact did get Tyrrell to make to Lichnowsky the statements reported in the latter's dispatch.[5] The details here given cast a significant light on the personalities of the men who set in motion this measureless tragedy and bring out the contrast between the fecklessness with which they made their decisions and the appalling consequences of these decisions. The lives, the belongings, the future of millions of human beings, perhaps of the whole human race, were in their hands. Did they show any awareness of this? In any case, what a disproportion between their intellectual and moral endowments and the gravity of the problems which faced them, between their acts and the results thereof! How could Berlin ever imagine that France would leave Russia exposed to the attack of the Central Powers only to see them impose their will and their unchallenged domination first in the Balkans and then on the rest of Europe, or that England would hold the ring for so disastrous an encounter which could not but harm and disgrace herself! True, that is what Lichnowsky's telegram

---

[1] Moltke, p. 23.   [2] Moltke, p. 23.   [3] Zwehl, p. 60.
[4] Zwehl, p. 61.   [5] See pp. 380-6.

said, but it was obvious that either Lichnowsky had not understood aright or Grey had lost his head and would back out or be made to do so. But not one of those present at the Schloss voiced a doubt about the credibility of the proposal or its tentative form. It was acted upon as if it were a certainty and Wilhelm recounted to Szögyény how he was going to settle accounts first with Russia, then with France, and would demand the surrender of Toul and Verdun, as Moltke desired. The Kaiser's conversation with the Austrian Ambassador is characteristic of the German mentality and, as an expression of the true mind of the German leaders, throws a side light on the whole war-guilt question. It was the same state of mind which, three days earlier, had led Bethmann to inquire of Grey on the evening of 29 July whether England in return for certain guarantees would remain neutral in a Franco-German conflict. It is the state of mind of men who have no repugnance for war in itself, but only for losing a war, and would with alacrity fight a war in the east and the west and on the high seas if they were certain of winning it.

Moltke brushed aside what scruples there were by his certainty of being victorious even if England were to side with France and Russia, and the action he took created a situation from which there was no turning back, even though Wilhelm and his Chancellor still vacillated. Did they repent of having challenged the forces of the Triple *Entente* when Italy and Romania seemed unlikely to recognize the *casus foederis?* Were not the joy and credulity with which they welcomed Lichnowsky's telegram symptoms of a change of mind? And was this what Moltke meant when he said that the Kaiser would not have signed the mobilization order if the telegram had arrived an hour earlier? This may be so. In the present writer's opinion the doubts felt by the Chancellor and his Sovereign as to their wisdom in setting fire to the powder cask can be perceived in the extraordinary telegram sent to the Tsar by the Kaiser on that same evening of 1 August in reply to the Tsar's message, received at the Schloss at 2.5 p. m., saying:

[I] understand you are obliged to mobilize but wish to have the same guarantee from you as I gave you, that these measures *do not* mean war and that we shall continue negotiating. . . [1]

Certainly the idea of subduing Russia in the conditions outlined by Lichnowsky was attractive. But supposing it turned out otherwise and the worst happened, i.e., France and England went to the help of Russia? In any case, London would be most favorably impressed by the Tsar's pacific message, which ended:

Anxiously, full of confidence await your answer.

[1] DD. III, 546. See p. 64.

The Kaiser's answer, therefore, must at least give an impression of not wishing to bar the road to peace. But how could it do this when in all probability war had already been declared? The only way out was to ignore the declaration of war, act as if it had been neither sent nor delivered, and word the telegram to make it appear that the Tsar still had time to bow to the German demand for demobilization. At any rate, at 9.45 p. m. the Chancellor sent the Kaiser a draft reply composed by Wedel to which Wilhelm made some alterations and additions and which in that form went off at 10.30 p. m.:

> Thanks for your telegram. I yesterday pointed out to your Government the way by which alone war may be avoided. Although I requested an answer for noon today, no telegram from my Ambassador conveying an answer from your Government has reached me as yet. I therefore have been obliged to mobilize my army.
>
> Immediate, affirmative, clear and unmistakable answer from your Government is the only way to avoid endless misery. Until I have received this answer, alas, I am unable to discuss the subject of your telegram. As a matter of fact I must request you to immediately order your troops on no account to commit the slightest act of trespassing over our frontiers.[1]

The cavalier style of this message reminds one of the way Bethmann finally told Tschirschky to suspend the notorious Instruction No. 200.[2] Already five and a half hours had gone by since the issue of the mobilization order, which meant the beginning of war operations, and four and a half since the 5 p. m. hour when Pourtalès was to present Sazonov with the declaration of war, and yet here was the Kaiser telling the Tsar that disaster could be avoided if Russia demobilized and asking him to prevent his troops from crossing the frontier.[3] Interestingly enough, Wedel's original draft did not contain the second request, but, in forwarding it to the Kaiser, Bethmann wrote:

> In sending this the idea occurs to me whether Your Majesty could not perhaps put in a word about the Tsar's giving an immediate definite order that his troops should not commit any frontier violation.[4]

It will never be known what passed through the Chancellor's mind when he made this suggestion to the Kaiser, but the fact that Wilhelm adopted it and added a final sentence shows that the move was concerted

---

[1] DD. III, 600.

[2] DD. II, 464. See p. 27.

[3] Writing on 1 August to Nicolson Goschen reported: 'The last thing I hear is that Russia . . . has demanded three hours more to consider the German demand' (BD. XI, 510), But first of all, there is not, nor from the way in which Sazonov received the ultimatum, could there be, in any diplomatic document, proof of any such demand from Russia. In the second place it would offer no explanation for Wilhelm's telegraphing thus to the Tsar after mobilization had been ordered and war declared.

[4] DD. III, 599.

between them. Was it designed to hoodwink London, or to give the Tsar a chance to think better of it? The latter hypothesis might appear to be supported by Wilhelm's marginal note to Pourtalès's telegram of 2 August, which reported the astonishment of the Tsar and Sazonov at the Kaiser's sending such a message after declaring war on Russia and asked that any further explanations might be transmitted through the Italian Ambassador as Pourtalès himself was leaving in three hours. The marginal note runs:

> As Russians have already burned down Prussian villages and blown up railways my answer is not necessary. Russia, after all, has never answered us.[1]

So if the Russians had not committed acts of hostility, negotiation could still have continued! Wegerer goes so far as to assert:

> Nor can it be said that after the declaration of the state of war every possibility of re-establishing peace had vanished. As a matter of fact, the personal negotiations between the Tsar and the Kaiser continued after the declaration of the state of war.[2]

But as we have seen it was not the Tsar who continued negotiating but only Wilhelm, and if he had meant it seriously he would have had to suspend the declaration of war.

4. Pourtalès delivers the declaration of war to Sazonov; Izvolsky asks France for her support.

If the purpose of this singular telegram was to continue negotiations, Berlin soon learnt that it had not attained its object. We must now turn our attention to events in St. Petersburg after the delivery of the declaration of war.

Sazonov's state of mind before receiving it may well be imagined. After Pourtalès handed him the German ultimatum about midnight on the 31st he must have received Izvolsky's telegram of the 31st reporting that at 6.30 p. m. (French time) Schoen had called on Viviani and notified him that Russia had been requested to demobilize, and that, if within twelve hours she did not comply, Germany would mobilize. Schoen had also said that he was instructed to ask what line France would take if there were war between Germany and Russia and that he would call again on the morrow, meanwhile asking that the necessary steps should be taken in connection with his departure. As Izvolsky was sending this telegram the French Cabinet was holding an emergency meeting presided over by Poincaré.[3] Schoen's action threw light on that of Pourtalès and indicated that Germany no longer intended to negotiate but was moving towards war. This did not make it any the

---

[1] DD. III, 666.   [2] Wegerer, *Refutation,* p. 315.
[3] *Int. Bez.* i. V, 355.

more possible to draw back and demobilize when there was no
guarantee that the Central Powers were prepared to make adequate
concessions, On the other hand there was satisfactory news not only
from Paris but also from London. On the evening of 31 July (the
telegram went off at 1 a. m. on 1 August) Izvolsky forwarded a
message from the Russian military attaché in Paris:

The War Minister, who in noble and heartfelt accents expressed the
Government's firm determination for war, asked me to confirm the hope of
the French General Staff that all our efforts will be directed against Germany
and that Austria will be regarded as a negligible quantity.[1]

As regards England it is improbable that by the afternoon of 1
August St. Petersburg had received Benckendorff's telegram of that
same day reporting Grey's inquiry whether Germany and France
would respect Belgian neutrality and adding:

France has answered in the affirmative. Grey told Cambon that the German
Government has stated it cannot categorically reply to that question.[2]

This foreshadowed English intervention.

Meanwhile the twelve-hour time limit laid down in the German
ultimatum had expired, and Pourtalès had not appeared to receive his
answer. Sazonov no doubt "knew of his having written a letter to
Fredericks and sent a Counsellor of Embassy to plead the cause of
peace with the Minister of Agriculture, Kvrivoshein.[3] But his non-
appearance made it seem that he had received fresh instructions from
Berlin, a bad sign. Schilling's account runs as follows:

Between 4 and 5 p. m. Count Pourtalès called up Baron Schilling on the
telephone and said that it was indispensable that he should see the Minister at
once. Baron Schilling replied that at the present time S. D. Sazonov was in
Elagin Island attending a council of Ministers and promised to inform the
Ambassador directly the Minister returned. This was done soon after 6 p. m.
and Count Pourtalès promptly came to the Ministry. When S. D. Sazonov was
informed of this, he gave up all hope and said to Baron Schilling: 'He will
probably bring me the declaration of war.'[4]

The hour given by Schilling differs from that given by Pourtalès,
who writes that the text of the declaration of war reached St.
Petersburg only at 5.45 p. m. Deciphering took one hour; thus he went
to the Ministry about 7 p. m. Sazonov's account corroborates that of
Schilling:

Count Pourtalès came to see me at 7 o'clock in the evening and after the
very first words asked me whether the Russian Government was ready to give
a favorable answer to the ultimatum presented the day before. I answered

---

[1] *Int. Bez.* i V, 356.   [2] *Int. Bez* i V, 402.
[3] Pourtalès, pp. 77-9. See p. 64.
[4] Schilling, p. 76; *Int. Bez.* i. V, 396. See p. 130.

in the negative, observing that although general mobilization could not be cancelled, Russia was disposed, as before, to continue negotiations with a view to a peaceful settlement. Count Pourtalès was much agitated. He repeated his question, dwelling upon the serious consequences which our refusal to comply with the German request would involve. I gave the same answer. Pulling out of his pocket a folded sheet of paper, the Ambassador repeated his question for a third time in a voice that trembled. I said that I could give no other answer. Deeply moved, the Ambassador said to me, speaking with difficulty: 'In that case my Government charges me to give you the following note.' And with a shaking hand Pourtalès handed me the Declaration of War. It contained two versions which, through an oversight of the German Embassy, were included in the same text.[1] I did not notice this at the time, for the meaning of the note was perfectly obvious and I did not have time at the moment to go over it word for word.

After handing the note to me, the Ambassador, who had evidently found it a great strain to carry out his orders, lost all self-control and leaning against the window burst into tears. With a gesture of despair he repeated: 'Who could have thought that I should be leaving St. Petersburg under such circumstances!'

In spite of my own emotion, which I managed to overcome, I felt sincerely sorry for him. We embraced each other and with tottering steps he walked out of the room.[2]

In Pourtalès's account it was Sazonov who threw his arms round his neck, exclaiming: 'Believe me, we shall see you again.' Sazonov then accused Tschirschky of being the one who had really brought on the war, Pourtalès replying that the men responsible were those who had induced the Tsar to order mobilization. The two men were both right, but the shaft struck home at Sazonov, who, at variance with the truth, replied:

What could I as Foreign Minister do when the War Minister told the Tsar that the mobilization was necessary?

Pourtalès replied:

In my opinion he, in his position, knowing from the previous negotiations what would necessarily be the consequences of the mobilization, was the one competent to restrain the Tsar from this fatal step.

We, however, know that he was the one who entreated the Tsar to order it. Pourtalès asked for his passports and took his leave, and later wrote:

[1] The two variants are those given above: Russia 'having refused to accede to this demand' and 'not having thought it necessary to reply to, etc.' Pourtalès, however, writes that he expressly drew attention to the two variants and signed the aide-mémoire at Sazonov's wish (Pourtalès, pp. 84-5). In any case neither he nor Sazonov thought of settling which of these variants was to be regarded as applicable and as canceling the other.
[2] Sazonov, pp. 212-3.

Sazonov at this last interview gave me an impression of utter helplessness, which confirmed my view that in the final phase of the crisis he just allowed himself to drift with the current, letting himself be the passive tool of the warmongers.[1]

Arrangements were made for Pourtalès to leave on the morrow, 2 August, at 8 a. m., and he was taking his rest when at 4 a. m. on the 2nd Sazonov called him up:

Herr Sazonov has just asked me over the telephone how to explain the following: H.M. the Tsar of Russia a few hours ago received a telegram from our gracious Master dated 10.45 p. m. expressing in its concluding sentence the request that Tsar Nicholas will order his troops not in any conditions to cross the frontier. Herr Sazonov asks how I can explain such a request after my presenting the note of yesterday evening. I answered I knew of no other explanation than that my Kaiser's telegram must have been dispatched the day before yesterday at 10.45 p. m. If there is anything further to add or to explain, I beg you to do so directly or through the Italian Ambassador, as I leave in three hours via Stockholm.[2]

This explanation was, indeed, the only one that would have made sense of the Kaiser's message and brings out its inconsistency.

After receiving the declaration of war Sazonov went to dine at the British Embassy, as has been already narrated in the previous chapter.[3] Did he feel sure of French support? There can be no doubt that he did after what Paléologue had said to him and seeing that Paris made no kind of reservations. It is noteworthy that the one who felt least calm or, rather, most distressed was Izvolsky. When about 11 p. m. he received news of the German declaration of war on his country[4] he went straight to the Élysée and asked to see Poincaré on a matter of urgency. It was from him that the French Government learnt of what

---

[1] Pourtalès, pp. 86-8. The impression produced at the St. Petersburg Court by the German declaration of war is described by Anna Virubova, an intimate friend of the Imperial family: 'When at 8 p. m. on 1 August the Court learnt the news that Germany had declared war, the Tsar, the Tsarina and the Grandduchesses burst into tears. I was living in a little villa near the Alexander Palace. I had spent that afternoon with the Tsarina pouring forth our anguish in prayer. Then with the Tsarina, the Tsar and the four Grand-duchesses—the Tsarevich was ill—I had attended service at the Court chapel, and we all stood up in fervent prayer. After supper the Tsarina sent for me, when she saw me, she told me that Germany had declared war on Russia and burst into tears. . . . The Tsar looked utterly depressed' (Luciano Magrini. La caduta e l'assassinio dello Zar Nicola II, Milan, 1928, pp. 224-5). Pierre Gillard, the Tsarevich's tutor, narrates that after the German declaration of war he found the Tsar wearing an 'expression of great weariness, his complexion earthy, the pockets under his eyes which he had when he was tired, had become huge'. The following day as the Tsar was about to go to the Council at the Winter Palace, he looked still worse. His eyes shone as if he had the fever (Magrini, Dramma di Sarajevo, p. 293).

[2] DD. III, 666.   [3] See p. 131.

[4] This document is referred to in a note to Int. Bez. i. V, 393 of 1 August mentioning that on that same day a circular telegram about the German declaration of war was sent to all representatives of Russia abroad.

had happened, since Paléologue's dispatch, as usual, came egregiously late. Not until 1.19 a. m. on 2 August did he send Paris the following telegram, which was received at 2 p. m. on the same day:

> The German Ambassador has just handed M. Sazonov a declaration of war.[1]

Paléologue had known this fact since about 8 p. m. the previous evening.

Poincaré relates that Izvolsky entered with a somber air and haggard features. After giving news of the declaration of war he asked in a voice trembling with emotion:

> In this tragic hour I thought it my duty, *Monsieur le President,* to address myself to the head of the State which is our ally in order to put the question: 'What is France going to do?' And he stood there in front of me in no way resembling, I affirm, the legendary portrait so often drawn of him since his death. Far from congratulating himself or rejoicing over what has been called 'his war,' he was aghast at it.[2]

Poincaré's reply is best given in the more detailed account sent to St. Petersburg by Izvolsky:

> Poincaré declared to me categorically that both he and the entire Cabinet were firmly determined to fulfill in every respect the engagements arising for France from the treaty of alliance. But there arises a series of highly complicated questions of both political and strategic nature. Under the Constitution the Government, for a declaration of war, needs a vote of Parliament the summoning of which will take at least two days. Although Poincaré has no doubts about this vote, he would prefer to avoid public debates on the application of the treaty of alliance; for this reason and for considerations mainly touching England it would be better if the declaration of war were to come not from France but from Germany. One must also not lose sight of the fact that today is the first French mobilization day and that it would be more advantageous for both allies if France did not begin military operations until mobilization had gone further. Poincaré also indicated that Germany will not wait for France to declare war on her and will attack France without warning without leaving her time to complete her mobilization. Immediately after the end of the discussion of these questions by the Cabinet Poincaré will send for me to let me know the result.[3]

The Cabinet held its meeting and Izvolsky stayed on at the Élysée to hear the results. Poincaré says that Viviani was entrusted with the following message by the meeting while Izvolsky says that it was brought him by Poincaré himself:

> The Cabinet meeting again confirmed its resolution to fulfill to the utmost the engagements imposed on France by the treaty of alliance. The Cabinet agreed that the interests of the two allies require that France should complete

---

[1] DF. 3. XI, 582.   [2] Poincaré, IV, p. 495.   [3] *Int. Bez.* i. V, 409.

her mobilization before the opening of military operations, and this will take ten days. At that moment the Houses will be summoned. Poincaré still fears that Germany will immediately attack France in order to hinder the completion of mobilization. What I have said is a matter of the greatest secrecy.[1]

Poincaré writes:

M. Izvolsky would have preferred an immediate and public pronouncement. But he ended by contenting himself with our reply and departed with a lugubrious air.[2]

It seems strange that Izvolsky would have preferred an immediate and public statement from France. Obviously it was more expedient with regard to not only French and British but also Italian public opinion that the declaration of war should come from Germany or that Germany should begin the war. Such being the case, France must not give a public assurance of support in advance, since that would have justified German action. Viviani had skillfully avoided making any such statement each of the three times that Schoen had called on him. It was certainly not the moment to do so at this critical juncture when the German army was preparing to open hostilities and to attack France before moving against Russia.

But how was Germany to open hostilities without declaring war? Here was the Gordian knot now confronting her. That she should mobilize would be taken amiss by no one, seeing that Russia and France had done so. But, as we already know, German mobilization involved the immediate invasion of Luxemburg by German troops and the sending of an ultimatum to Belgium as a prelude to the invasion of France, while for the time being Russia was merely contained. Hence if a declaration of war was not patently necessary as regards Russia, it was essential in respect of France. But war on France could only be justified if Germany were at war with France's ally, Russia. Therefore the procedure must be first to declare war on Russia and then on France. But by so doing Germany would in the eyes of the world appear the aggressor, and this would have far-reaching political, moral, and military repercussions. For one thing it would give Italy and Romania the right not to recognize the *casus foederis,* while giving Britain good reasons for going to the aid of her friends who were now attacked.

5. *Tirpitz and Bethmann; stormy scenes between the German political and military chiefs.*

Had this problem been weighed by the leaders of Germany before they embarked on the mobilization which for them meant war? Yes, it had, but they had come to the conclusion that they could not find

[1] *Int. Bez.* i. V, 412.   [2] Poincaré, IV, p. 496.

another solution than the one they chose. In other words, the Chancellor, who all the time had endeavored to manage matters in such a way that, if it came to an armed conflict, the aggressor would appear to be Russia, now cast aside such considerations and declared war first on Russia and then on France, though fully realizing that this action would render, or appear to render, Germany responsible for the European conflagration. He himself writes:

By so doing we appeared as the aggressors, even if we thought we could allege aggressive acts of French troops in extenuation. I do not think that we could have avoided this dilemma. The rapidity of the military decisions to which we were unavoidably forced by the Russian mobilization left us no scope for marking time nor even time for diplomatic arrangements which might have improved our political position. As is always the case with the offensive, Russia in being the attacker dictated the course we had to take.[1]

This course of action had the sanction of Wilhelm and received the approval of the Bundesrat when Bethmann laid it before the delegates in his speech of 1 August. But there were certain people in Berlin who foresaw its disastrous consequences and sought to get it modified. Foremost among these was the Navy Minister, Grand Admiral Tirpitz, the creator of the German navy and perhaps the most outstanding figure in the Reich after the fall of Bülow. It is necessary at this point to dwell a little on this personage and gather an idea of his views, which are illuminating.

It was certainly the work of Tirpitz if Germany had alienated England by the creation of a navy which threatened her sovereignty of the seas and her very existence, and if, consequently, in 1914 what Germany feared above everything was English intervention in support of France and Russia. Conscious of this responsibility of his, Tirpitz in his *Memoirs* exculpates himself by the line of argument that in 1914

the danger of war became more improbable every year in proportion as respect for the German fleet grew. . . . The fundamental feeling that we ought to be repressed had not altered. . . . But the moment for striking us down was felt in wide circles in England to be past.[2] . . . Meanwhile the strengthening of Russian power had on the whole brought the danger of a world war steadily nearer. . . . The preparations for war of both Russia and France had intensified to the utmost limits. The fact that England favored these preparations . . . renders England's historical guilt irrefutably clear, particularly as she . . . to a certain extent checked by her cooler temperament the increased explosive force of the *Entente* within the unstable European situation. . . . We had almost passed the unavoidable 'danger zone' of our fleet-building, and our object, the peaceful equalizing of our rights with those of England, was within   sight   of   fulfillment.   .   .   .   There   was   another   guarantee

---

[1] Bethmann, I, pp. 165-6.   [2] Tirpitz, I, pp. 209, 237.

in the proportion of five German to eight English squadrons with which we had declared our ultimate aim satisfied . . . and in the simple and fundamental fact . . . that we had gained in and by peace more than was ever imaginable in the most glorious war. . . . A real balance of power was appearing on the political horizon. British statesmen naturally did not stress the fact . . . that it was mainly the presence of our nearly completed fleet in the North Sea that had produced their respectful tone. . . . The American Ambassador Gerard said to me after the outbreak of war that he could not understand our allowing the war to happen for we should have outstripped the English by peaceful means within a few years. . . . The ill-will of the *Entente* Powers ought never for a moment to have been underestimated. But in spite of this, the situation was not lost for German diplomacy when the Serbian challenge was sent to Austria in the summer of 1914. . . . An immediate request from our Kaiser to the Tsar, asking the latter to assist in obtaining satisfaction, might have been successful and would at least have influenced our political situation favorably. So far as Germany was concerned, there was never a menace at any moment in the will to war, but solely in the fatal mediocrity of the politicians in office. . . . The Chancellor was right when he considered that sufficient satisfaction must be given by Serbia to Austria. For it was only by this means that Austria could once more be made a useful member of the Triple Alliance and her internal decay perhaps stopped. The mistake made in Berlin and Vienna only began with the treatment of the whole affair. . . . Bethmann and Berchtold were unable to imagine that sufficient satisfaction could be obtained in other ways than by threatening an invasion by Austrian troops. . . . [Bethmann] drew from the assumption that the *Entente* did not want a war the short-sighted conclusion that Austria could probably force an entry into Serbia regardless of the *Entente,* without endangering the peace of the world. . . . On 31 July the Chancellor had been informed on the essential points of the intended ultimatum on which I received a communication from my deputy while in Tarasp. . . . My first impression was that this ultimatum was unacceptable to the Serbians and might easily lead to a world war. . . . I never believed in the possibility of 'localizing' the Austro-Serbian passage of arms, just as little as I had any faith in England's neutrality in a continental war. I wrote to my deputy in this sense and recommended an agreement with the Tsar. 'The Chancellor is . . . bewitched by his idea of courting the favor of perfidious Albion. . . . *Coûte que coûte* we must come to an agreement with Russia and set the Whale against the Bear.' . . . The question of interrupting my cure was then settled by the Chancellor asking me not to return to Berlin, so as to avoid sensation. As late as 24 July the Chancellery telephoned to the [German] Admiralty that my return would render the situation more acute. . . . Particularly the news of the return of our fleet to home waters finally caused me to return home on 27 July without consulting the Chancellor. . . . From the moment the Serbian answer became known German policy presents the most puzzling psychological problem. . . .

Bethmann Hollweg and Count Berchtold underrated the extent of the diplomatic success which had been achieved. . . . Trust in the peaceful intentions of the *Entente,* of England particularly, gave rise to a hope . . . of localizing the Serbian conflict, and led to a stiffening of Vienna's tone towards Serbia. In order to put a complete stop to the undermining of Austria by the Serbs, they plunged into a far greater danger and as has been said, jumped out of the frying-pan into the fire. . . . Bethmann could have at, once accepted Grey's proposal of an ambassadorial conference on condition that Austria-Hungary should be allowed to secure a gage in Serbia. . . . When Grey's warning words were known after the delivery of the ultimatum: 'The situation would be very dangerous, and a war between the four Great Powers might easily result,' the pundits of the Wilhelmstrasse extracted from this sentence the assurance . . . that no danger of war existed with the fifth Great Power, England. . . . I must raise against the British Cabinet the grave charge that . . . it brought upon itself a large share of the responsibility for the outbreak of the war by uncertainty as to England's attitude during the crisis. . . . Grey could have preserved peace if he had in time made clear to Bethmann England's attitude in the event of the Austro-Serbian conflict extending to the rest of Europe. That he omitted to do this is the more surprising since in July 1911 Lloyd George did not hesitate to threaten us openly on orders from the Cabinet. . . . Whether history will succeed in bringing to light the real extent and the reasons for this British ambiguity, I must leave to the future. . . . Some time in July a moment did occur in England, of which Grey had said to Sazonov in September 1912: 'that if the circumstances in question were to occur, England would do all she could to inflict the most serious possible blow to the power of Germany.' . . . When in the course of July England realized the cul-de-sac into which Bethmann had got himself, she turned away from the business-like peace policy . . . and to the no less business-like policy of war in order, in her character of 'perfidious Albion,' to make Russians and Germans kill one-another. . . . We ought to have taken all the more care not to give them the opportunity of carrying it out. As I said in 1904, every opening which we offered the enemy as a pretext for war was scrupulously to be avoided. . . . [In conversation with Wangenheim] according to the latter's version of 23 April 1914, Bethmann also spoke about 'policy without war.' . . . Thus thought the Chancellor, who three months later handled the Serbian affair alone with the Foreign Ministry in the absence of the chief military representative. . . . It is a lie on the part of our enemies to say that Bethmann intended by this means to break the peace of the world. . . . I can produce yet another valid proof that our Government did not want the war. It was convinced from the very beginning that we should not win. . . . The mistake of our Government lay in the belief that an Austro-Serbian passage of arms could be localized. . . . Not only the German nation, which is on the whole one of the most peace-loving in the world, but Bethmann Hollweg's Government also, is perfectly innocent of the world war so far as its own will is concerned. . . . How is the whole question of guilt then to be answered? The *causa remota* of the world war lies . . . in the English policy of encirclement.[1]

---

[1] Tirpitz, I, pp, 238-69; some slips corrected with the German original. [Ed.].

When writing thus in April 1919 Tirpitz did not know the documents which subsequently came to light and which proved beyond question that (i) the English Government acted most unskillfully but made every endeavor to save the peace thinking—whether rightly or wrongly— of all else rather than of seizing the chance of inflicting a death-blow on German trade and the German navy; (ii) on learning on 29 July of a possible British intervention, Bethmann definitely—but not with sufficient forcefulness—pressed Vienna to accept a formula of conciliation; but the following day, before general mobilization was ordered at St. Petersburg or known in Berlin, surrendered to Moltke's wish for war. Thus Tirpitz's diagnosis of the origins of the war is vitiated by material errors of fact, which, with his Anglophobia, he would perhaps never have admitted, just as he could never see that the so-called 'policy of encirclement' was the inevitable consequence of his program of naval construction. But despite all this, by the admissions he makes and authority with which he speaks, he furnishes an important contribution to the clearing up of the problem of his country's responsibility for the war, and one which has to be taken into account. Like Bülow, he recognizes that it was the German leaders who approved, or better, urged that Austria should plunge into an adventure which, if all proposals for conciliation were rejected, would end in a European conflagration.

Let us now see what efforts Tirpitz made at the height of the crisis to get his ideas adopted.

On 31 July shortly before noon the Foreign Ministry received confirmation of the Russian general mobilization. A few moments later the Admiralty Staff informed me: 'that according to news just received from the Foreign Ministry, war is imminent. The Foreign Ministry inquires whether surprise attack on English fleet is possible, Admiral Pohl says that he will reply in the negative'.[1]

If the idea was to forestall the consequences of the dreaded intervention of England, it would have justified Lord Fisher's suggestion to King Edward VII in 1908 that he should 'copenhagen' the German navy *à la Nelson* by a surprise attack on Kiel in time of peace. But probably what was being proposed was a surprise attack as soon as war was declared. This was expected to happen at any moment now that news had come of the Russian general mobilization of which Tirpitz heard about 12.30 p. m. on the 31st from Bethmann, who told him of the impending proclamation of the *Kriegsgefahrzustand.* But in the afternoon he was shown the Kaiser's optimistic estimate, mentioned above,[2] written at noon for Tirpitz and the Naval General Staff and

---

[1] Tirpitz, *Dokumente,* II, p.5.　　　　[2] See p. 36.

reaching him at 2.50 p. m.[1] What was the explanation of the discrepancy between the Kaiser's assurance that 'a complete material agreement had been arrived at between us and London' and the Imperial order for the *Kriegsgefahrzustand?* This was the question Tirpitz put to Bethmann at a discussion they had not at 12.30, but at 4.30 p. m. on the 31st.

The Chancellor said he thought the Kaiser was mixing up several things.[2] The Russian mobilization would be such an unheard-of procedure against us that we could not put up with it; if Russia went on with it, we should have to mobilize too and an ultimatum ought to have been dispatched to the Tsar so as not to let our mobilization fall too much in arrears. That was my view too. . . . In reality the Russians had been mobilizing since the 25th, and this start made things difficult for us when the war machines began to move. However, I gave the Chancellor to understand that I thought it right once more to point out in the ultimatum the fact that substantial agreement existed, and that a favorable mediation was in progress. The Chancellor replied testily that this had been said all along and Russia had just answered it by mobilizing. . . . I can only state here that as late as the 31st, following my instinct more than my reason, I advised the Chancellor to insert a peaceable paragraph into the ultimatum. In so doing I scarcely hoped to stay the wheel of fate which the Russian mobilization had set in motion, but in any event to lay the responsibility of what was coming still more exclusively upon the enemy.[3]

Had Tirpitz known that the *Halt in Belgrade* solution, on which London and Berlin were agreed, had been rejected not by St. Petersburg but by Vienna and that Russia had mobilized because of the Austrian refusal to accept mediation, he might have been convinced that reason, more than instinct, demanded a very different line of action on the part of Bethmann. There was a clash between the two men on the following day:

On 1 August I learnt at the Federal Council that we had followed up the ultimatum with a declaration of war on Russia. I thought that very disadvantageous for Germany. In my opinion we ought to have turned the advantage that we were militarily on the defensive with regard to Russia diplomatically to account by leaving the declaration of war to the Russians. We must not inspire the moujik with the conviction that the Kaiser intended to attack the White Tsar. The devaluation of our alliance treaty with

---

[1] DD. II, 474. Tirpitz's memory is not very exact. In his *Memoirs* he writes: 'In the early hours of 31 July, I learnt from the Naval Staff . . . that Jagow had asked whether we were ready to attack the English fleet' (I, p. 275). In the *Dokumente* he says he learnt of the inquiry a few moments after the arrival of the news of the Russian general mobilization (II, p. 5). Similarly he writes in his *Memoirs* (I, p. 275) that he received the Kaiser's letter at mid-day on the 31st, whereas it was written by Wilhelm at mid-day and received in the early hours of the afternoon. This shows that the discussion between Moltke and the Chancellor took place not at 'between 12 and 1 o'clock' as is stated in the *Memoirs* (I, p. 275), but at 4.30 p.m. as is stated in the *Dokumente* (II, p. 10).

[2] Tirpitz, *Dokumente,* p. 10.   [3] Tirpitz, I, pp. 275-6.

Romania was also to be weighed. This treaty, like that with Italy, had been designed by Prince Bismarck for defense; both States were only pledged to help us if we were attacked by Russia or France. By our declaration of war on Russia we formally gave the Romanians the right to leave us alone in the war, just as we did to the Italians later by our declaration of war on France. Did Bethmann really never consider the enormous disadvantages accruing to us by our not leaving the act of declaration of war to the enemy?

I had the impression that our action even in this direction was completely unconsidered, and took place without any system and my feelings revolted at our having to assume, through the fault of the jurists of the Foreign Ministry, the odium of the attackers in the face of the world, although we could not possibly intend to march into Russia, and although we were in reality the attacked party. I therefore asked the Chancellor, as the meeting broke up, why the declaration of war had to coincide with our mobilization. The Chancellor replied that this was necessary because the army wanted immediately to send troops over the frontier. The reply shocked me, because at the most it could only be a question of patrols. But through all those days Bethmann was so agitated and irritable that it was impossible to speak to him. . . . When I asked Moltke afterwards the actual relation between the crossing of the frontier and our declaration of war, he denied any intention of sending troops over the frontier forthwith. He also told me that from his own point of view he attached no value to the declaration of war.[1]

Bethmann on the other hand writes:

Falkenhayn considered the declaration of war against Russia a blunder not because, after the Russian mobilization, he in any way regarded war as avoidable, but because he feared damaging political consequences. Moltke, on the contrary, was in favor of the declaration of war because our mobilization plan, designed for a two-front war, was framed on the assumption that military operations would begin immediately, and because our chances in the struggle depended entirely on the extreme speed of our action.[2]

There is no reason for disbelieving the Chancellor's statement. His answer to Tirpitz related not to the offensive against Russia, but to that against France, while Moltke ruled out the notion of sending troops into Russia but not of taking immediate action against France. It is true that Falkenhayn's diary entry for 1 August begins:

I persuade Moltke to come with me to see Jagow, to prevent the foolish and premature declaration of war on Russia. The answer is: 'too late.'[3]

But Wegerer has shown that Falkenhayn and Moltke called on Jagow not on the 1st but on the 2nd August and that it was by a slip that Falkenhayn dated it the 1st.[4]

[1] Tirpitz, I, pp. 276-7.   [2] Bethmann, I, p. 156.   [3] Zwehl, p. 58.
[4] Alfred von Wegerer, *Gerards Ansichten über den preussischen Militarismus,* KSF. July 1926, p. 465, *Zu den Memoiren des Generals von Falkenhayn,* KSF., August 1927, pp. 784-5.

So one must conclude that at the beginning Moltke was in favor of declaring war and only later yielded to the objections raised by Tirpitz and Falkenhayn.

Tirpitz reiterated his objections at the gathering of 1 August at the Schloss for the signing of the mobilization order. In the hearing of all present he asked Moltke whether he meant to invade Russian territory immediately, and Moltke replied that this could not be done for a few days. Why then, declare war on Russia immediately? Tirpitz's question was interrupted by the announcement of the telegram from Lichnowsky of which we have already taken cognizance. But the subject came up again during the night when at 2.30 a. m. Bethmann summoned Jagow, Zimmerman, the chief officials from the Foreign Ministry (Stumm, Hammann, Kriege), the generals and Tirpitz to

an agitated discussion about the declaration of war on Russia—whether we are to be regarded as in a state of war—and the declaration of war on France, which will, they say, have to be issued today because we intend to march through Belgium.[1]

6. Draft of a declaration of war on France; breakdown of the political leadership of the Reich.

As we have already seen, Pourtalès on the previous afternoon had delivered the declaration of war on Russia to Sazonov. But his telegram reporting this, which was dispatched at 8 p. m. on 1 August, never reached the Wilhelmstrasse.[2] The Ambassador's silence must have led Berlin to believe that he had carried out his orders and that the telegram failed to arrive because war was now declared. But in the afternoon and evening of 1 August and in the night of 1/2 August confusion reigned in the German capital, and, in doubt whether Germany was at war with Russia or not, Bethmann sought the advice of the generals. Did he tell them that the declaration of war not only had gone off to St. Petersburg but must have been delivered several hours ago? From Tirpitz's account we shall see that he did not conceal from them that it had been sent off, but, as will soon be evident, he did not tell them that it was to have been delivered at 5 p. m. on the previous day.[3] The reason for this obviously is that he realized the opposition his action would arouse in them and thought it better to keep their attention focused on the problems connected with the declaration of war on France.

This had been drafted on the 31st mainly by Rosenberg and was signed on 1 August by Jagow, who completed it after the arrival at 6.10 p. m. of Schoen's telegram of 1.5 p. m. reporting his morning conversation with Viviani.[4] The Chancellor and Hammann had made

---

[1] Tirpitz, *Dokumente,* II, p. 20.   [2] DD. III, 588.
[3] See p. 191.   [4] DD. III, 571. See p. 100.

certain alterations and additions which gave the document its final form:

In the event of the French Government returning no satisfactory reply to our inquiry, will Your Excellency hand it the following declaration this afternoon at 6 o'clock, Central European time:

The German Government has from the beginning of the crisis made endeavors to find a peaceful compromise. But while, at the wish of H.M. the Tsar of Russia and in contact with England, it was still mediating between Vienna and St. Petersburg, Russia has mobilized her entire army and navy. By this measure, which was preceded by no extraordinary military preparations in Germany, the German Empire is threatened in its security. Not to take measures against such a danger would hazard the existence of the Reich. The German Government has therefore requested of the Russian Government the immediate cessation of the mobilization against Germany and her ally, Austria-Hungary. Simultaneously the German Government notified the Government of the French Republic thereof and, in view of the known relations of the Republic with Russia, requested of it a declaration whether in a Russo-German war France will remain neutral. To this the French Government returned the ambiguous and evasive answer that France will have regard to her own interests. By this answer France leaves herself free to range herself on the side of our adversaries and is in a position to fall on our rear at any moment with her army, mobilized in the meantime. Germany cannot but see a threat in this behavior, all the more as a request to Russia to desist from the mobilization of her forces has still received no answer a long time after the expiry of the time limit, and a Russo-German war has therefore broken out. Germany cannot leave to France the choice of the moment at which the threat to her western frontier becomes a reality, and, threatened on two sides, must at once set her defense in motion.

Accordingly I am charged with informing Your Excellency:

H.M. the German Kaiser declares in the name of the Reich that Germany regards herself as being in a state of war with France.[1]

This declaration would have probably been sent to its destination if Lichnowsky's telegram with its mirage of French neutrality had not given rise to a new situation and a new state of mind. Moreover—as Wegerer observes:

It is worth noting the assurance that the French frontier will not be crossed before 7 p. m. on 3 August.[2]

After the misunderstanding was cleared up by King George's telegram at about 11 p. m. on 1 August it would have been logical for the declaration to be dispatched, but this was held up by the doubts, uncertainties and qualms of which we have spoken.[3] These led to a discussion in the middle of the night between the Chancellor and the service chiefs, a minute of which was drafted at once by Tirpitz. It is

---

[1] DD. III, 608.   [2] Wegerer, *Refutation,* p. 287   [3] See p. 179.

valuable as allowing us to be spectators at a scene of the utmost historical interest:

I said I had not quite understood why the declaration of war on Russia had been published before mobilization; I could also see no use in launching the declaration of war on France before we actually marched into France. March through Belgium, according to Ambassador's [Lichnowsky] reports, would immediately have war with England as a consequence. I was not in a position to judge whether army could make any modification on this point, i.e., postpone the march through Belgium. War Minister arrived, was rather brusque with the Chancellor, saying that the war was there after all and the question of a declaration of war on France was of no account. Moltke arrived and also said it did not matter, the war was there, and that was that. The Chancellor replied that after all we must under international law have some confirmation. Rather violent scene between Chancellor and Moltke, followed by mutual apologies for loss of temper. Moltke said it was known that shots had been fired, first by Russians; thereupon the Chancellor: 'Then, of course, the case is clear, that means the Russians have been the first to start and I shall have the declaration of war handed over the frontier by the nearest General.' In the question of the march through Belgium Moltke's view was that there was no other way open, we must go through with it. This obviously the only possibility worked out in General Staff's plan; no possibility of interfering with transport mechanism. I said in that case we must at once reckon on war with England. Every day for mobilization so much gained, therefore declaration to Belgium as late as possible. It was agreed that this should be kept back until second day of mobilization. General impression: political leadership has completely lost its head. The reins have slipped entirely out of the Imperial Chancellor's hands. Obviously he had no previous knowledge about march through Belgium, tried to prevent it. Kriege sharply snubbed by Moltke when he tried to make legal objections. General Staff obviously not clear about military, political, and economic significance of a war with England, at all events ruthlessly brushing this whole aspect aside and thinking of nothing but the army and of carrying on a land war. It came to light that Austria had never even been asked whether she would take the field with us against Russia. It was agreed that this must speedily be remedied; instructions given to Tschirschky. Italy likewise has been given no information about our declaration of war on Russia. Political leadership patently in considerable confusion *(dérouté)*. As we left, Moltke, the War Minister, and I were horror-stricken at this confusion. Moltke said he thought he would now have to take the political conduct of affairs in hand.[1]

It is obvious that Moltke would not have urged that war should not be declared on France or on Russia, had he known that in all probability the declaration of war had already been served on St. Petersburg a matter of twelve hours previously. He and Falkenhayn were so much under the impression that the blunder could be prevented that in the small hours

---

[1] Tirpitz, *Dokumente,* II, pp. 20-1.

of the morning Falkenhayn persuaded Moltke to go with him and see Jagow 'to prevent the foolish and premature declaration of war on Russia',[1] Jagow replying that it was 'too late'. The meaning of this 'too late' is not quite clear. Does it mean that he owned up to the two generals that the declaration of war was to have been delivered the previous evening? Falkenhayn does not explain. Perhaps Jagow only meant it to mean that by then Germany was at war with Russia. He himself at 6 a. m. on 2 August telegraphed to Tirpitz:

In consequence of the crossing of our frontier by Russian troops we are in a state of war with Russia.[2]

But in any case, even if it were too late to avoid war with Russia, it was not too late to refrain from making the same blunder with regard to France. On this point, although Tirpitz does not say so, the defeated Chancellor surrendered to the pressure from Moltke, who must have told him, either at their meeting or immediately after it:

According to an announcement from the General Staff (today 4 a. m.) attempted destruction of railway and advance of two squadrons of Cossacks on Johannisburg,

because the Kaiser received this notice from the Chancellor sometime early in the morning of the 2nd with the addition:

This constitutes an actual state of war. The above forwarded at once to Vienna and Rome with request for statement *re* fulfillment of alliance engagements, to Rome with addition that we anticipate French attack. . . . According to agreement with War Ministry and General Staff, declaration of war on France not today necessary on military grounds. Therefore not yet sent in hope that French attack us.

Communiqué to the public about state of war with Russia this morning at 4.30 by Wolff telegram. No news from St. Petersburg.[3]

So completely had the Chancellor lost his head that he failed to warn his subordinates of the decision not to send a declaration of war to France. The result was that Kriege, who was head of the legal section at the Foreign Ministry and had had that clash with Moltke, immediately on returning to his office drafted a telegram, which Jagow signed, instructing Schoen:

In delivering the declaration of war please hand a written statement to the Government in Paris that we shall detain merchant vessels flying their flag in our ports, releasing them if within forty-eight hours we receive an assurance of reciprocity.[4]

[1] Zwehl, p. 58. See p. 192.   [2] DD. III, 623.
[3] DD. III, 629. For telegrams to Vienna and Rome cf. DD. III, 627, 628.
[4] DD, III, 625.

On reading this telegram Bethmann feared Schoen might take it as authorizing him to declare war on France, so at 9.10 a. m. on the 2nd he sent Schoen an 'urgent' telegram:

Telegram No. 187 does not mean that Your Excellency is to deliver the declaration of war right now.[1]

But still Bethmann did not feel quite reassured and it was probably at his desire that at 10 a. m. on the 2nd at the Schloss, in the presence of the Kaiser, the discussion was resumed between Moltke, Plessen and Tirpitz. The latter records the following account of what was said:

Moltke and the Chancellor in somewhat excited debate on the question of the declaration of war on France. Moltke gave evidence of a whole series of hostile acts on the part of the French. War, he said, was an actual fact and there was no stopping the whole business. To the declaration of war he attached no importance. I said the army must lose no time in marching into Belgium. I could not see why a declaration of war need be made at all, as it always had an aggressive flavor. The Imperial Chancellor took the view that without a declaration of war on France he could not present the demand on Belgium. (I cannot understand this reasoning.) So the Imperial Chancellor was empowered to notify England that we should make the march through Belgium only under the compulsion of circumstances and of French actions, and that in other respects we should respect Belgian sovereignty and pay for everything. Even after a victorious war we had the most definite intention in no way to infringe the integrity of Belgium. The Imperial Chancellor left the Schloss. Moltke asked the Kaiser to make the political leadership understand that we were already at war with France, which they still did not realize. He said he had sent a message to the Imperial Chancellor setting forth clearly our present attitude towards every State (a political recipe for the Foreign Ministry, in other words). The fact was, he said, the Foreign Ministry was in a deplorable state and no preparations had been made for this situation. They refused to believe that a tremendous avalanche like the one now starting was impossible to stop; they still went on thinking that notes were still of use. I told the Kaiser I felt the same way about it. My view was that the Foreign Ministry had been working badly for years, but it had not been my business to tell him so (the seriousness of the hour now compelled me to do so). I advised the Kaiser to replace Jagow by Hintze. The Kaiser said we could not make changes at this moment. I said: 'Very well, Your Majesty, but Your Majesty might recall Hintze.'[2]

7. Moltke's illusions; Luxemburg occupied; an ultimatum sent to Belgium.

There can be no doubt that the Chancellor had lost his head and was incapable of carrying on his duties. But it cannot be said that the generals, whose pressure had reduced him to that state, were any more capable of reasoning than he in spite of their self-complacency not only in military but also in diplomatic

[1] DD. III, 632.   [2] Tirpitz, *Dokumente,* II, pp. 21-2.

questions. To get an idea of Moltke's abilities as a diplomatist it is sufficient to read the memorandum sent by him in the afternoon of the 2nd to the Wilhelmstrasse giving his advice on the situation:

Turkey is to declare war on Russia as soon as possible. Attempts must be made to rouse a revolt in India if England comes in as an opponent. Ditto in Egypt and in the Dominion of South Africa. Should England make her neutrality conditional on a German assurance 'to observe moderation in a victory over France', this assurance can definitely be given. . . . Sweden must be induced to mobilize all her forces and send her 6th Division as soon as possible to the Finnish frontier. . . . If Sweden declares her readiness to join Germany in military action, Copenhagen is at once to be informed, with the request to do the same as Sweden. . . . Japan is to be invited to seize the opportunity to satisfy all her aspirations in the Far East. . . . Persia is to be invited to use the favorable opportunity to cast off the Russian yoke.

England was to be asked to regard German action in regard to Belgium 'only as an act of self-defense against French threats to German territory'. The attitude of Greece and Romania was to be-clearly ascertained.

It is essential to obtain a statement whether Italy is willing to take an active part in the forthcoming war in accordance with her engagements under the Triple Alliance. I do not mind whether Italy sends the full number of promised reinforcements to Germany. . . . Even if it is only a single cavalry division, that will satisfy me. . . . Declaration of war on Russia or by Russia on us has lost all importance as a result of the Russian invasion of our eastern frontier. If Russian declaration of war has not yet been delivered or only after the Russian operations began, Russia has violated the Hague Convention.

The paragraph on France runs:

Our eventual declaration of war is entirely independent of the *démarche* made in Belgium. The one does not entail the other. I do not regard it as needful to serve the declaration of war on France yet, on the contrary I calculate that, if we for the moment refrain, France will be forced by popular opinion to order military operations against Germany without war being formally declared. Probably France will march into Belgium in the role of protector of Belgian neutrality as soon as the German *démarche* against Belgium is known in Paris. On our side orders have been issued that crossing of the French frontier shall be avoided until French operations provoke it.[1]

One can hardly imagine a greater jumble of wishful thinking, practically all of it unattainable, ingenuous in its arrogance and based on utterly mistaken premises. Without dwelling on all of the paragraphs, let us consider the one dealing with France. Tirpitz had the

[1] DD. III, 662.

good sense to disapprove of the whole affair, the war, the declaration of war and the invasion of Belgium. If Germany had to mobilize, let her at least remain on the defensive, not crossing the frontier either in the east or in the west, leaving it to the enemy to open hostilities and thus throwing the responsibility for the conflagration on Russia and France. But this could not be, because the German mobilization plan required the immediate opening of military operations. Falkenhayn and Moltke knew this, and Tirpitz was finally won over when he realized that the only existing plan of mobilization involved a march through Belgium. But their idea that they could avoid appearing to be the aggressors simply by refraining from declaring war while invading Belgium and Luxemburg was childish in the extreme. It was this idea that made Moltke say that the 'declaration of war is entirely independent of the *démarche* made in Belgium' and that 'the one does not entail the other', when the opposite was clearly the case.

The inference from all this is that by comparison with the service chiefs Bethmann was a paragon of wisdom. Article I of the Hague Convention on the Outbreak of Hostilities of 18 October 1907 laid down:

The Contracting Parties recognize that hostilities among them should not begin without a previous unequivocal notification, which must have either the form of a declaration of war provided with reasons or that of an ultimatum with a conditional declaration of war.

But here was Germany opening hostilities by occupying or preparing to occupy Luxemburg and Belgium in violation of their neutrality. It was no use to hide the fact by statements at variance with the truth, as Tirpitz seeks to do:

We could carry out the *démarche* just as well without the declaration of war on France giving as our motive that, in view of the military agreements known to us relating to Belgium, our armies were compelled to take up position facing France to prevent the possibility of the war being carried into our Rhenish province.[1]

Everybody knew that Germany was occupying Belgium, not to defend herself, but for reasons of offence, i.e., the more easily to invade France. Nor was there any agreement enabling France and England to enter Belgium unless Germany invaded her. The pretext might have acquired some appearance of plausibility if there had been war between Germany and France, but there would have been no war had Germany not declared war first on Russia and then on France. Wegerer remarks:

If the Germans had invaded Belgium without a declaration of war on Russia and France, the result would have been that England would have had

---

[1] Tirpitz, *Dokumente,* II, p. 13.

her desired pretext for war and that Russia and France would have followed her into the war. It cannot be said that such a course would have had any advantages for Germany either during or after the war.[1]

Therefore it is hard to understand why Montgelas should write:

According to the German plan of campaign, Germany had no military interest in hastening the commencement of operations in the east. It seems that the step was taken more for formal legal reasons, and it is the more to be regretted, because, according to the facts now known, if Germany had waited a little longer, France would probably have forestalled her declaration of war, just as she forestalled her mobilization.[2]

Evidently Montgelas thinks that as France mobilized some minutes earlier than Germany without knowing of the German mobilization, she would probably have declared war before Germany did so because of her engagements with Russia. He forgets that French mobilization was consequent on the German ultimatum to Paris, which was the prelude to the declaration of war (in fact, Falkenhayn and Moltke did not want either an ultimatum or a declaration of war) and that for France mobilization was a very different matter from going to war. In truth, what motive would she have had for going to war if Germany had not declared war on Russia? Would it have rendered any service to her ally's offensive? But Russian mobilization was a lengthy business, nor would the Tsar have ever sanctioned an attack before diplomatic negotiations had come to a standstill. Moreover, France would never have let such a thing happen either, her prime consideration being not to appear the aggressor in the eyes of England. And even assuming that, when negotiations failed, the Russian army would have been the first to go into action, it would have operated against Austria, not against Germany, without need of aid from France and without the right to ask for it. Germany, on the contrary, was bound by her treaty with Austria to fling her army immediately against a Russia which attacked Austria. Only in that case would France have intervened and then without formal obligation to do so. None of the Powers except France grasped that this would be the necessary sequence of events.

The *10 km. withdrawal* proves that France fully grasped the risks she would run in regard to both England and Italy by behaving otherwise.[3] Moreover, she could afford to wait, whereas once France had begun

---

[1] Wegerer, *Refutation,* pp. 314-15.

[2] Max Montgelas. *The Case for the Central Powers* (London, 1925), p. 188.

[3] Even after the war French historians and political writers who lay the whole blame for the war on Germany cite the *10 Km. withdrawal* as proof positive of France's will to peace. In reply to an inquiry from the present writer, Gabriel Hanotaux, a former French Foreign Minister, wrote on 17 Nov. 1937: 'These matters are, as you think, full of imponderables. France withdrew her troops 10 Kms. from her frontiers—a definite fact and one which leaves no doubt as to her sentiments.'

mobilization Germany could not delay hers without jeopardizing the success of her strategic plan based on the immediate invasion of Belgium.

If such self-evident truths were overlooked by Bülow, it was that his personal animosity towards Bethmann blinded him to the extent of making him write:

If it is to a certain extent understandable that we wanted to make the thrust against France as soon as possible after being at war with Russia, it is senseless and incomprehensible that we took the step of declaring war on Russia. This, wrongly, but in a manner difficult to refute, made us appear in the eyes of the world to be the incendiaries. General Moltke repeatedly assured me that he not only did not desire the premature declaration of war on Russia, but would have preferred us to have delayed the breach with Russia as long as possible.[1]

The politically unversed Moltke might think it quite in order for Belgium to be notified that she must allow herself to be invaded before war had even been declared on Russia or France. But Bülow must have known better, and Jagow is quite justified in his reproach:

The precondition justifying our action in the west was, as Bülow rightly says, that we should 'be at war with Russia'. If Bülow rightly saw the political dangers involved in our plan of campaign (i.e., of appearing as aggressors and committing a breach of law against Belgium), would he not have done better to insist when he was Chancellor on a change in the plan of campaign, instead of making irrelevant criticisms *ex post*?[2]

Both Bülow and Tirpitz, who was also an opponent of Bethmann, cite Ballin as their authority for attributing the declaration of war on Russia to considerations of domestic policy. Bülow writes:

Why was there this precipitate haste to declare war on Russia on 1 August? The reason for our blunder in diplomacy . . . must be sought in our domestic situation, or rather the anxieties it caused the Chancellor. Albert Ballin gave me a vivid description of a scene he witnessed on the day of the declaration of war on Russia in the Chancellor's Palace. . . . He saw the Chancellor . . . pacing to and fro . . . with great strides. Geheimrat Kriege sat at a table covered with folios. . . . From time to time Bethmann would ask him the impatient question: 'Is the declaration of war on Russia not ready yet? I must have my declaration of war on Russia at once.' . . . Ballin ventured the question: 'Why such enormous haste to declare war on Russia, Your Excellency?' . . . Bethmann answered: 'If I don't, I shan't have the Socialists with me.'[3]

---

[1] Bülow, III, pp. 162-3. This passage is translated afresh from pp. 166-7 of the German original text. [Ed.]

[2] *Front wider Bülow*, pp. 217-8.

[3] Bülow, III, p. 163; German text, pp. 167-8; Tirpitz, *Dokumente*, p. 14.

Apart from the unlikelihood of the scene, it is difficult to see how the approval of the Socialists was to be won by making the German Government appear as an aggressor against Russia and the cause of a European war. Moreover, all the documents show that Bethmann was obsessed by the idea of putting Russia in the wrong and would never have committed the blunder of declaring war on her had his hand not been forced by the exigencies of the Schlieffen plan and by Moltke himself, who was now disavowing them and whom the Chancellor for the moment had allowed to have things his own way.

In actual fact, after the 10 a. m. discussion at the Schloss on 2 August, the already prepared declaration of war on France was not dispatched, although at 2.5 p. m. a telegram was sent to Below-Saleske, the German Minister at Brussels, telling him to open at once the note which had been sent him on 29 July[1] and to carry out that same evening at 8 p. m. (German time) the instructions contained in it, i.e., to present the ultimatum to the Belgian Government.[2] Further, at 5.30 p. m. on 2 August a telegram went off to Lichnowsky explaining the ultimatum on the lines suggested by the generals:

We have reliable information that the French, despite their declaration, have concentrated considerable forces on Belgian frontier and are making preparations for invasion of Belgium. To prevent surprise we shall probably be compelled to take counter-measures. . . . It is desirable that England should regard this step simply as an act of self-defense against French threat. Even in event of military conflict with Belgium, Germany means to respect integrity of Belgium on the conclusion of peace.[3]

It is incomprehensible how the German leaders could imagine they could take in the rest of the world with such deceits. They resorted to the same pretexts to justify the occupation of Luxemburg, the Prime Minister, Eyschen, having on 31 July sent inquiries to both France and Germany whether they would give an assurance to respect the neutrality of Luxemburg.[4] France gave the assurance,[5] Germany did not reply. The occupation was carried out on the evening of 1 August. On 2 August Eyschen and the Grandduchess of Luxemburg telegraphed their protest to Berlin.[6] Shortly before their protests reached Berlin and perhaps in order to forestall them, Moltke had proposed the sending to Brussels of a note dictated by himself:

To its great regret the German Government has been so suddenly put under the necessity of sending light advance troops on to Luxemburg territory

---

[1] DD. II, 375, 376. See Vol. II, p. 503   [2] DD. III, 648 See p. 455.
[3] DD. III, 667.   [4] Poincaré, IV, pp. 472-3; DD. III, 486.
[5] DF. 3. XI, 591. In the *Yellow Book* this telegram, No. 129, bears the date 1 August. The authentic text is dated 2 August at 4 20 p. m.
[6] DD. III, 637, 638.

for the protection of the German railways in Luxemburg that there was no time to come to an understanding with the Luxemburg Government. This measure was rendered unavoidable by the news from France that French forces are advancing towards the Luxemburg frontier.[1]

Bethmann decided to adopt a less pharisaical text drafted by Stumm and sent at 11.30 a. m.:

Our military measures in Luxemburg are not meant as an act of hostility against Luxemburg, but simply as a measure to secure the railways under our management against French attack.[2]

But at 2.10 p. m. Jagow followed it up by telegraphing to Eyschen:

These military measures have to our great regret been rendered necessary by the fact that according to reliable information French forces are advancing on Luxemburg.[3]

On the morning of 3 August Tulff von Tscheepe, the General commanding the 8th Army Corps, which had occupied Luxemburg, distributed the following proclamation:

Since France, disregarding Luxemburg neutrality, as has been established beyond doubt, has opened hostilities against Germany from Luxemburg soil, His Majesty has given orders to German troops to enter Luxemburg.[4]

In bringing this proclamation to the notice of the Chancellor, the Luxemburg Prime Minister added:

This is erroneous. On Luxemburg soil there is not a single French soldier, nor any indication whatever of a threat to neutrality from France. On the contrary, on Saturday evening 1 August on French soil the rails were torn up near Mont St. Martin Longwy.

To explain to the French Government on 2 August why Luxemburg was violated when there was as yet no state of war between Germany and France, Bethmann telegraphed to Schoen at 12.15 p. m.:

Our military measures in Luxemburg do not constitute a hostile act but are merely a protective measure for the railway there which is by state treaty under our management.[5]

To Lichnowsky the text ran:

We were compelled to take military measures in Luxemburg for the protection of the railway there, by state treaty under our administration and management, against a threatened attack from the French.[6]

---

[1] DD. III, 639.   [2] DD. III, 640.   [3] DD. III, 649.
[4] DD. III, 730.   [5] DD. III, 642.   [6] DD. III, 643.

To the German Minister at the Hague at 6 p. m. Jagow telegraphed:

Our military measures in Luxemburg became unavoidable as a protection for our army and our railway there, because, according to our information, French forces were advancing towards Luxemburg.[1]

A light is thrown on the friendliness of German intentions in Luxemburg by an inquiry at 7.10 p. m. from the German Minister there:

General Fuchs [commanding the 16th Infantry Division] on reading text of Telegram No. 12 [i.e., DD. III, 640] asks me to convey that he feels very serious scruples whether to carry out the order he has received in reference to the arrest of various high Luxemburg officials and asks for a reply by return.[2]

The same general at 8 p. m. telegraphed to the Wilhelmstrasse:

How is the Divisional Command to treat the French Minister here in the matter of his sending news to his Government?[3]

Receiving no reply, he again telegraphed at 4.15 p. m. on 4 August:

Reply to yesterday's inquiry not received. After consultation with Luxemburg Government I have today requested French Minister to leave Luxemburg.[4]

And the request was regretfully echoed under duress by Eyschen.[5]

While this was happening in Luxemburg, Below-Saleske at 7 p. m. (Brussels time) on 2 August handed the German ultimatum to the Belgian Foreign Minister. We shall speak later of what happened in Brussels and the repercussions of this ultimatum on London. Here all that we need say is that the violation of Luxemburg neutrality and the impending violation of that of Belgium furnished such unmistakable evidence of the quarter from which the aggression emanated that it quickly revealed the unsubstantiality both of Moltke's objections and of his forecasts, and brought again to the fore the necessity for a declaration of war on France, who, it was clear, was not going to take on the role of aggressor. For about forty-eight hours after the issue of the respective mobilization orders the two armies stood face to face, each waiting and hoping that the other would be the first to open hostilities, while the two Governments and the two General Staffs vied with each other in recording frontier violations and incidents caused by the opposite side, signalizing them to London to persuade Grey from which quarter the aggression emanated.

8. *The incidents on the Franco-German frontier on 2 and 3 August.*

A detailed analysis of the mutual accusations and rebuttals would not only be tedious but would be of no importance. The main events of

---

[1] DD. III, 671.   [2] DD. III, 684.   [3] DD. III, 787.
[4] DD. III, 842.   [5] DF. 3. XI, 769; LJF., 156.

those two days before hostilities opened suffice to indicate the atmo-sphere that prevailed. Joffre writes:

It now became my duty to decide upon the mission of the troops once they were detrained. The prohibited belt of ten kilometres behind our frontier complicated the situation, for we had to abandon positions which we undoubtedly would be obliged to recover later on at the price of costly fighting. The situation now appeared to me sufficiently clear to make it possible for us to move into this prohibited territory. I explained my point of view to the Minister of War but . . . M. Messimy considered that it was more than ever necessary to avoid any clash on the frontier. All he thought it possible to do was to reduce the zone to a width of two kilometres, and he promised to submit this modification to the Cabinet.

During the early part of the afternoon, however, news arrived in Paris that the French frontier had been violated in several places, notably at Longwy and near Cirey, Sainte-Marie-aux-Mines and various other points; it was learnt that thirty-five motor-cars loaded with German officers and soldiers had penetrated into Luxemburg. These events were undoubtedly sufficient to convince the French Government, for about 2 o'clock the Minister of War telephoned . . . that 'the Government gives the Commander-in-Chief full liberty of action for the execution of his plans, even if these should lead to crossing the German frontier'. During the evening of 2 August I . . . prescribed, in spite of the latitude just given me, that, in order to leave the Germans entire responsibility for hostilities, 'our covering troops should confine themselves to driving any attacking forces back across the frontier, refraining from pursuing them farther or entering upon the adversary's territory'.[1]

Viviani, on his part, lodged a protest with Schoen and wrote to Jules Cambon in Berlin about a series of German violations of the French frontier, in one of which a French customs post was fired upon by German soldiers and in another of which, north of Delle, two German patrols advanced to the villages of Joncherey and Baron, more than ten kilometres from the frontier, killing a French soldier.[2] To this Berlin replied at 10 a. m. on 3 August:

According to positive statements from military authorities, German troops have so far not crossed French frontier at any point; on the other hand, on account of continual violations of the frontier by French troops, the rupture of diplomatic relations is imminent.[3]

Jagow also telegraphed to the Ambassadors in London and Rome at 9.15 a. m.:

All French information *re* crossings of French frontier by German troops complete fabrication.[4]

[1] Joffre, I, pp. 132-3; *Les Armées françaises dans la Grande Guerre,* I, pp. 82-3 (1922); pp. 114-15 (1936).
[2] DD. III, 705, 722; DF. 3. XI, 609, 616; LJF. 139; CDD. pp. 236-7.
[3] DD. III, 716 and 722 note.   [4] DD. III, 713, 725.

And when at 9.37 a. m. on 3 August Lichnowsky telegraphed:

Entry into France without war has produced disastrous impression here. . . . Morning papers condemn our action,[1]

Jagow replied at 2.20 p. m.:

So far no German soldier has crossed French frontier.[2]

Jagow wrote this because the decision had now been taken to declare war on France on grounds of French acts of hostility and there was no truth in his denial. Grey telegraphed it on to Bertie,[3] who replied on 4 August:

French War Office states that bodies of two Germans, one an officer and the other either an officer or under-officer, are on French soil and the French authorities are in possession of their clothes and identification papers.[4]

This was admitted that same day by Moltke in a note to the Wilhelmstrasse:

Of the complaints of the French Government about German frontier violations one only is to be admitted. Against express order a patrol of the XIV Army Corps on 2 August, apparently led by an officer, crossed the frontier. It seems to have been shot up. Only one man returned.[5]

That this happened 'against express order' may well be believed. The incidents that happened on both sides were no doubt all local affairs, not only contrary to orders but deplored by both General Staffs.

On 3 August fresh violations took place in Lorraine at Remereville, Arracourt and other localities and a German airplane dropped bombs on Lunéville. In all, the French collected details of twenty-nine frontier violations by German patrols, sixteen of them on 2 August and ten on the 3rd up to the declaration of war, and of nine frontier violations by airships, and one bombing by airplane.[6]

Many of these incidents undoubtedly took place and were of some seriousness. But certain other accusations made against the Germans were quite unfounded. For example, on 2 August the French Embassy In London telephoned to the Foreign Office

to say that they have received a telegram from the Havas Agency from Liége stating that 20,000 German troops have invaded France near Nancy.[7]

Crowe gave Lichnowsky to understand that this news

[1] DD. III, 731.
[2] DD. IV, 742, 744.
[3] BD. XI, 529.
[4] BD. XI, 613.
[5] DD. IV, 869.
[6] For full documentation see René Puaux, *Le mensonge du 3 Août* 1914 (Paris, 1917), pp. 243-365.
[7] BD. XI, 486.

would make a bad impression on the Cabinet . . . and perhaps not be without influence on the final decision.[1]

But the report was entirely without foundation.

The Germans replied by counter-accusations. Montgelas lists twenty cases of frontier violations by French patrols, and there were reports of thirty-six others, but he himself offers the very plausible explanation that those which occurred after the issue of the mobilization order at 3.55 p. m. on 1 August were most likely due to an assumption on the part of commanding officers that this order superseded that of the '10 kilometre withdrawal'.[2] On 2 August Jagow telegraphed to Rome:

According to an announcement by the general in command of the 3rd Bavarian Army Corps, French fliers are bombing the environs of Nuremberg. Moreover, French patrols have crossed the frontier.

But the object of this message is revealed in the next sentences:

These hostile acts before declaration of war signify attack on us by France. Thus the *casus foederis* arises. Russia, too, yesterday opened hostilities before declaration of war.[3]

On the same day the Chancellor sent a similar message to London and Lichnowsky notified the Foreign Office:

According to absolutely reliable news, France has committed the following acts against Germany:

1. A patrol of French cavalry has passed this morning the frontier near Alt-Muensterol in Alsatia.

2. A French aviator has been shot while flying over German territory.

3. Two Frenchmen have been shot whilst attempting to blow up the tunnel near Cochem on the Moselle railway.

4. French infantry have passed the Alsatian frontier and have opened fire.[4]

Bethmann's telegram to Lichnowsky containing these statements ends with the injunction:

Please notify the Government in London of these facts and seriously represent to Sir Edward Grey the perilous position in which Germany is being placed by these unscrupulous provocations and the serious decisions being forced on her. Your Excellency will, I trust, succeed in convincing England that, having stood for peace to the utmost bounds of possibility, Germany, by the provocations of her opponents, is compelled to take up arms to preserve her existence.[5]

---

[1] DD.III, 689.

[2] Montgelas. *Grenzverletzungen vor Kriegsausbruch* 1914. KSF. 1927, pp. 977-82; also *Deutsche Allgemeine Zeitung,* 25 June, 1919.

[3] DD. III, 664.   [4] BD. XI, 539 (I).   [5] DD. III, 693.

These words showed too plainly the purpose pursued by the allegations, and Grey simply forwarded them to Bertie, whose reply of
4 August runs:

Military Attaché reports French War Office informs him that: Firstly it
has no information of any French patrol having crossed the frontier even a
few yards. . . . Secondly, it is correct that a military aviator lost his way on
3 August in Alsace. He landed by mistake in the suburbs of Mülhaus, and
left again, arriving at Belfort without harm. Thirdly, no person . . . has
received instructions to blow up the tunnel of Cochem or any other tunnel. .
. . Fourthly, it has not received any information reporting the crossing of the
Alsatian frontier by French infantry.[1]

Apart from the one flying incident, France, having issued
strict orders, which were generally obeyed, against any crossing
into German territory, steadily denied all the German allegations,
some of which sounded preposterous. For instance, on 2 August
Jagow telegraphed to London, The Hague, and Brussels:

This morning eighty French officers in Prussian officers' uniform in twelve
cars tried to cross German frontier near Walbeck, west of Geldern. This
constitutes the gravest conceivable infringement of neutrality on the part
of France.[2]

The allegation was without foundation and received a vigorous
denial from Paris via London.[3] Equally baseless was the allegation
telegraphed by Jagow to Rome and London on 2 and 3 August
respectively:

A French doctor with the help of two disguised officers attempted to
infect the wells of the Metz suburb of Montsigny with cholera bacilli. He
was court-martialed and shot.[4]

The German General Staff itself protested against the
publication of such fantastic statements. An editorial footnote to
the above telegram runs:

Cf. Stumm's note of 3 August: General Staff . . . urgently requests not
to publish or use such information until checked by General Staff.

On the afternoon of 3 August Bethmann sent Goschen a
written communication containing a list of hostile acts attributed
to the French identical with the one which we shall see figuring in
the declaration of war dispatched to France at the same time. In
sending it on to London, Goschen added:

The official who brought me this communication informed me verbally at
the request of the Chancellor that in some cases, as necessary measures of
precaution, German patrols had crossed German frontier.[5]

[1] BD. XI, 609.   [2] DD. III, 677.
[3] BD. XI, 541, 542; DF. 3. XI, 651; LJF, 146; DD. IV, 782.
[4] DD. III, 690, 721.   [5] BD. XI, 553.

This statement is confirmed by Moltke himself in a note to Jagow of 4 August:

Of the complaints made by the French Government about German frontier violations only one is to be admitted. Against express orders a patrol of the XIV Army Corps, apparently under an officer, crossed the frontier. It seems to have been shot up. Only one man returned. . . . But long before this one little frontier violation took place French fliers dropped bombs on our railways in the heart of Bavaria near Nuremberg, French troops attacked our frontier defense troops in the Schlucht pass. It was the French who fired the first shot. . . . Only when French frontier violations multiplied was permission given on 3 August to push forward across the frontier on reconnaissance.[1]

This tells how at least some of the frontier incidents complained of by the French on 3 August actually took place.

A balance sheet of the various incidents would seem to show that neither General Staff wanted them to happen; that the order to refrain from all acts of hostility was more strictly observed by the French than by the German troops; that nevertheless the German High Command on 3 August authorized reconnaissance forays beyond the German frontier; that the German General Staff and Government sought to make frontier incidents the pretext for declaring themselves attacked by France, and that consequently their accusations were still more exaggerated and unfounded than those of the French, especially as regards bombing. Bombing seemed a specially suitable grievance to serve as pretext for the declaration of war. To the alleged incidents near Nuremberg, Wesel, Karlsruhe, mentioned above, must be added others near Mainz, Cologne, Saarburg, Neustadt-an-der-Hardt and Koblenz.[2] The greatest notoriety was achieved by the protest issued on 2 August against the alleged bombing of the outskirts of Nuremberg.[3]

9. The false report of the bombing of Nuremberg; the German declaration of war sent to France.

On 2 August the Bavarian II Army Corps reported:

Fliers dropping bombs in vicinity of Nuremberg.

The report was forwarded to the General Staff with the comment: 'reliable information not procurable'. It soon turned out that the news was false and this was telephoned on to the General Staff, which had taken no steps to get the news confirmed and ignored the correction. Montgelas goes so far as to admit:

[1] DD. IV, 869.   [2] DD. III, 725; IV, 759.
                [3] DD. III, 664; IV, 869; BD. XI, 553.

This is a case of deplorable levity on the part of the telephone officer concerned.[1]

It may have been so, but one hesitates to believe it. The speed with which the report was published by the Wolff Agency and the German press, and the alacrity with which it was made known to Goschen and telegraphed to Rome—to Rome with the comment: 'Thus the *casus foederis* arises'[2]—shows how welcome was the news. Its accuracy ought to have been and could easily have been checked by telephone. This was not done because nobody wanted to do so. But the Wilhelmstrasse learnt that the report was false even though making no inquiries and though Moltke would have liked to keep the fact dark.

On 2 August, Treutler, the Prussian Envoy in Munich, telegraphed to Bethmann:

> The military announcement, published here by the *Süddeutsche Korrespondenzbureau*, that French fliers today dropped bombs in the vicinity of Nuremberg has not yet been confirmed. Only unknown planes were seen, which were apparently not military aircraft. The dropping of bombs is not confirmed, still less, of course, that the fliers were French.[3]

This document does not bear a record of its hours of dispatch and receipt. What is preserved in the archives is only a copy which is known to have come into the archives of the Foreign Ministry on the afternoon of the 3rd. This does not mean that the Chancellor received it on the 3rd. Many of the documents addressed to him are registered as being received in the archives a day or two after their arrival at the Ministry. On the other hand, there is no question of Treutler's having sent such a document by post. He must have either telephoned or telegraphed it; and this means it arrived on the 2nd, not on the 3rd. There can be no doubt that, whether by Treutler's correction or by some other channel, the Wilhelmstrasse most probably knew by the afternoon of the 2nd that the bombing of Nuremberg was a fabrication. There is proof of this in the fact that Jagow, who had been at pains to talk of it to Goschen between 12 and 1 o'clock, and had telegraphed it to Rome at 4.35 p. m., made no allusion to so serious an incident in the telegram which at 6.55 p. m. he sent to London, The Hague and Brussels with the story about the eighty French officers in Prussian officers' uniform trying to pass the frontier at Walbeck.[4] To Brussels he mentioned 'acts of war, bomb-dropping by airplanes', but without details.[5] Further, at 12.25 a. m. on 3 August Bethmann telegraphed to London a list of allegations against the French, but the bombing of Nuremberg did not figure among them, and Jagow, in making additions to the Chancellor's

[1] Max Montgelas, *Der angebliche Bombenabwurf bei Nürnberg,* KSF. 1927, pp. 672-5.
[2] BD. XI, 477; DD. III, 664.   [3] DD. IV, 758.
[4] DD. III, 677.   [5] DD. III, 682.

original draft, made no attempt to add it.[1] It seems difficult to explain their silence except on the assumption that by the 2nd they knew there had been no such bombing. Even supposing Treutler's contradiction to have arrived only late in the evening of the 2nd or in the night of 2/3 August, this is no excuse for the fact that on the morning of 3 August the bombing of Nuremberg is back in favor again as an item in the list of accusations against France.

At 11 a. m. on the 3rd Jagow actually called on Jules Cambon to complain of the acts of aggression committed by French airmen at Nuremberg and Koblenz.[2] The Nuremberg story was, in addition, introduced into the German declaration of war on France, to which we shall soon come, and figured in the memorandum sent by Bethmann to Goschen on the afternoon of the 3rd, mentioned a little while back. As in the declaration of war, this memorandum averred:

French aviators yesterday threw bombs on railways in the neighborhood of Karlsruhe and Nuremberg.[3]

As late as 4 August Moltke was still repeating the allegation in a report he made to the Wilhelmstrasse [4] which Bethmann used in his Reichstag speech of 4 August. In this speech, it is true, he did not dare to say directly that the bombs were dropped near Nuremberg, he said:

French airplanes have dropped bombs on our railways,

an oblique allusion to the Nuremberg allegation. It is difficult to believe that he was making the statement in good faith. Montgelas asserts:

In the correct test of the declaration the Nuremberg incident plays quite a secondary part.[5]

But it played an essential part in the text of the declaration of war as delivered by Schoen, and for two years the Germans continued to think that the French had really dropped bombs near Nuremberg until a denial was published by the Burgomaster, Dr. Schalbe, on behalf of the municipality of Nuremberg (in the *Deutsche Medizinische Wochenschrift* of 18 May 1916). And in fact the whole declaration of war was devoid of good faith.

It was drafted in the forenoon of 3 August when the decision was taken to file and not use the declaration drafted on 1 August,[6] which

---

[1] DD. III, 693.

[2] Poincaré, IV, pp. 524-5; DF. 3. XI, 775; LJF. 155; CDD., pp. 243-9. The *Yellow Book* has additions which treble the length of the first part of the authentic document.

[3] BD. XI, 553.

[4] DD. IV, 869.

[5] Montgelas, *Case for the Central Powers*, p. 222.

[6] DD. III, 608. See p. 194. To this declaration had been appended the Kaiser's approval, reproduced in DD. III, 540a, and there associated with DD. III, 491. [Ed.].

was much less unworthy than the later one but was put aside under pressure from the generals. This is also the view of Wegerer, who writes:

In this text of the German declaration of war on France, prepared and later not transmitted, the deeper causes are expressed very clearly. Today we can only regret that this declaration was not sent. . . .[1]

The Chief of the General Staff was present part of the time while this [new text] was being drafted. At his suggestion the report was also incorporated that enemy fliers had bombed the railway near Nuremberg. This report was later proved untrue.[2]

Moltke, as we have seen, was against war being declared by Germany and counted on hostilities being opened by France.[3] Had he perhaps become convinced by the forenoon of 3 August that things were not going to happen that way and that the invasion of Belgium, ordered in the afternoon of 3 August, would have to be explained on the ground of the war with France? Wegerer thinks that two telegrams from Lichnowsky played a part in convincing the Wilhelmstrasse of the need for declaring war on France. One of 2 August, already mentioned, reports Crowe as having given Lichnowsky to understand that the news of a German invasion of France before a declaration of war

would make a bad impression on the Cabinet . . . and perhaps not be without influence on the final decision.[4]

The other, of 3 August, is in the same sense.[5]

The second one can have had no influence, since it came too late, but the first may well have overcome hesitations and led to the use of almost wholly fictitious and in any case trivial border incidents as pretexts for presenting Germany as the aggrieved party. What incredible blindness!

The text of the telegram drafted by Jagow, sent to Schoen over the Chancellor's signature, and dispatched at 1.5 p. m. on 3 August, runs:

German troops have had till now orders strictly to respect French frontier and have everywhere obeyed it. On the other hand, in spite of the assurance of the 10 km. zone, French troops yesterday evening crossed German frontier near Altmünsterol and the mountain road in the Vosges and are still on German territory. French airman, who must have flown over Belgian territory, was yesterday shot down while attempting to destroy railroad near Wesel. Several other French airplanes were yesterday definitely identified over Eifel region. These, too, must have flown over Belgian territory. Yesterday French fliers dropped bombs over railways in vicinity of Karlsruhe and Nuremberg.

---

[1] Wegerer, *Refutation*, p. 292.   [2] Wegerer, *Refutation, p.* 294.
[3] DD. III, 662. See pp. 195, 198.   [4] DD. III, 689. See p. 207.
[5] DD. III, 731.

By these acts France has placed us in a state of war. Will Your Excellency please communicate the above to French Government today at 6 p. m., ask for passports, and take your leave, handing affairs to American Embassy.[1]

The last paragraph in Jagow's original draft ran somewhat differently:

We are therefore obliged to recognize a breach of the peace by France, the creation of a state of war, and the violation by France of Belgian neutrality, and we enter protest against the same.

Bethmann may have thought it was going too far to accuse France of having violated Belgian neutrality, as he had no doubt been requested to do by the General Staff, and Zimmermann had been asked to redraft the last sentence. But no amount of redrafting could do anything to bolster up the weakness of the German case. Even if there had been any truth in the wretched pretexts alleged, they furnished no justification for a declaration of war. The bad impression they produced on world opinion was further intensified by the fact that the telegram reached Schoen in so garbled a form as to be at many points unintelligible. Schoen therefore drafted another text, in which the only accusations leveled against France were the fictitious bombings. Schoen in his *Memoirs* gives the following story of what happened:

On the afternoon of 3 August, just when the tension was at its height, a telegram in cipher arrived with the Imperial Chancellor's signature, a sign that it concerned a matter of special importance. There was no doubt in my mind that its contents would be decisive. Unfortunately the telegram was so mutilated that, in spite of every effort, only fragments of it could be deciphered. It was clear, however, that air attacks had been made by the French on Nuremberg, Karlsruhe and Wesel, that I was to ask for my pass-ports at 6 o'clock, hand over the Germans to the protection of the American Ambassador, and leave. There was no time to make any inquiry as to the illegible part. As I knew from other sources that we felt bound to declare war in consequence of a French air attack on Nuremberg, I had to make up my mind to fall back on the little that could be clearly understood from the telegram to justify the declaration of war.[2]

Was the garbling of the telegram carried out by the French telegraph service? This was the accusation leveled at France by the German Government via a Wolff Agency telegram of 7 August 1914 reproducing the authentic text of the declaration of war.[3] The accusation was of course denied by the French. Wegerer makes the comment:

In the garbling of the text it is striking that the statements on frontier violations unfavorable to the French could not be deciphered, except for the erroneous announcement of the attacks on Karlsruhe and Nuremberg, while the rest of the telegram concerning the declaration of war and the departure of the

---

[1] DD. III, 734.   [2] Schoen, p. 200.   [3] DD. III, 734, C.

Ambassador can be clearly made out. It seems likely, there-fore, that the mutilation was intentional for the purpose of keeping the French people in the dark concerning the real reasons for the declaration of war. The only point clear in the telegram was that the state of war began at 6 p. m.[1]

Here it must be noted that on the 3rd Schoen had received another undecipherable telegram, which he twice asked Berlin to repeat. Its text as drafted by Jagow runs:

According to positive statements from military authorities, German troops have so far not crossed French frontier at any point; on the other hand, on account of continual violations of the frontier by French troops, the rupture of diplomatic relations is imminent.[2]

Schoen writes:

A strange coincidence: in both telegrams the very same portions of the text, namely, those that concerned the frontier violation by the French troops, were made unreadable by the transposition of the code-ciphers and in fact by unmistakable systematic falsification. Moreover, it is striking that the two German telegrams were over five hours on the way, but a telegram of the French Ambassador in Berlin, sent almost at the same time as the second one, was only three hours on the way. And this telegram was not garbled.[3]

If the German thesis were correct it would mean that the French had been wily enough to suppress the passage in the declaration of war relating to the crimes imputed to them, i.e., the frontier violations, leaving only the accusation of the air raids, which was without basis, so that war would have been declared on France on the basis of a falsehood. For this to be possible the further assumption would have to be made that the French possessed the German cipher code. But Poincaré says:

Since the end of 1911 the services at the Quai d'Orsay no longer possessed the German cipher and only discovered it much later in the war.[4]

The whole question has been carefully gone into by Professor Aulard, who examined the jumbled cipher text received by Schoen and given by him to the Wilhelmstrasse on his return to Berlin on 6 August.[5] Aulard reaches the conclusion:

It may be regarded as a product of the imagination of Herr von Schoen himself or one of his subordinates, intended to make Herr

---

[1] Wegerer, *Refutation,* p. 296.
[2] DD. III, 716; IV, 776, 809. See p. 205.
[3] Letter of Schoen to Barnes published in *American Historical Review,* October 1929, p. 78.
[4] Poincaré, IV, p. 525
[5] DD. III, 734, 734a.

von Bethmann Hollweg believe that the telegram was jumbled as an excuse for Herr von Schoen's not having read the first passage to M. Viviani.[1]

Among other things, Aulard found in post-office records that Berlin sent the telegram in duplicate by two different routes and that a second copy reached Schoen unmutilated by 5 p. m. on 3 August. Why then did Schoen, in executing his mission to Viviani at about 6.30 p. m., fail to read out the opening passage of the ultimatum?

Renouvin comes to the conclusion that it was because

the ambassador had just received a protest concerning the Joncherey incident [in which a German reconnoitring party had killed a French corporal on French territory], and now he "was to be compelled, without making the slightest explanation, and under instructions from his Government, to declare that not a single German detachment had crossed the frontier! . . . He had thus a personal interest in omitting the passage concerning the violation of the territorial frontier.[2]

Schoen must have felt repugnance for the task he had to perform. As Poincaré remarks:

Herr von Schoen's probity was sorely strained by the wretched pretexts excogitated by his Government.[3]

And, indeed, Schoen writes in his *Memoirs:*

However desirable it may have seemed for military reasons to turn the moment to account and accuse the French of having started hostilities, the step was too momentous to be taken without careful inquiry into the justification for it. Even if the alleged hostile acts had actually taken place, it would have been just as rash to attach the importance of a military offensive to them as it would have been unjustifiable in respect of the indiscretions of a few Hotspurs on our side. The French, as a rule so impulsive, were wise enough not to look on these isolated occurrences as a reason for declaring war, and to leave the odium of taking the offensive to us.[4]

Another fact noted by Aulard is that, in contrast to his action in connection with the earlier undecipherable telegram, Schoen did not telegraph to Berlin asking for the message to be repeated, although what was in question was nothing less than a declaration of war from which it was essential that nothing should be omitted of the grounds of justification on which it was based in the original text. Schoen in his *Memoirs* replies:

There was no time to make an inquiry as to the illegible part. As I knew from other sources [i.e., from Szécsen] that we felt bound to

---

[1] A. Aulard, 'Ma controverse avec le professeur Delbrück', R*evue de Paris,* 1 May 1922, pp. 28-43.

[2] Renouvin, p. 269.   [3] Poincaré, IV, 527.

[4] Schoen, pp. 210-11.

declare war in consequence of a French air attack on Nuremberg, I had to make up my mind to fall back on the little that could be clearly understood from the telegram to justify the declaration of war.[1]

To this statement it has been objected that Schoen should at least have telegraphed to his Government stating how it came about that the ultimatum as delivered by him differed from the original text of his instruction. All he did, however, was to telegraph to the Wilhelm-strasse at 8.30 p. m. on 3 August that he had received and executed his instructions. This telegram does not appear in Kautsky's collection of German documents. Aulard says it is doubtful whether it was ever sent off by the Paris Central Telegraph Office, since it was dispatched two hours after the beginning of the state of war. But the French deciphered most of it and Aulard publishes the cipher original.[2] The telegram makes no mention of the garbling of the message, nor does Schoen in his *Memoirs* claim to have telegraphed to his Government in that sense. What he does claim is that he at once brought the matter to the notice of Viviani.

The Premier, Viviani, to whom I first conveyed the declaration of war by word of mouth, to be followed immediately by a written announcement, received it without any sign of emotion, somewhat as a matter of course. But he most emphatically declined to accept the reason given for it. He said at once that it was out of the question that any of the air attacks spoken of could actually have taken place. I had not omitted to mention that, in consequence of the telegram having been so mutilated, a considerable part of the instructions which had reached me were undecipherable and presumably concerned French hostilities elsewhere.[3]

This statement was rebutted by Viviani in a letter to Aulard of 2 April 1922:

Herr v. Schoen never made any allusion to telegraphic alterations such as might have limited his communication.[4]

But Schoen stuck to his story and amplified it by declaring not only that he told Viviani in Margerie's presence that part of the telegram was undecipherable and related to still other French hostile acts, but that Margerie also remarked that jumbled telegrams had also been received by the Quai d'Orsay in the preceding days.[5]

There is no reason to disbelieve Schoen. What interest had he in suppressing any part of the document he received? Not because it denied that German troops had crossed the French frontier while Viviani declared they had done so. Schoen was not more bound to believe Viviani's word than that of his own Government, which, in instructing him to deliver the ultimatum, formally stated that French

---

[1] Schoen, pp. 200-1.
[3] Schoen, pp. 201-2.
[5] Schoen, *Die Nation,* July 1922, p. 547.

[2] Aulard, *Revue de Paris,* 1 May, 1922, p. 42.
[4] Aulard, *Revue de Pans,* 1 May, 1922, p. 37.

troops had crossed the German frontier at Altmünsterol and on the Vosges mountain road, both of which were on German territory. He had no reason to omit these definite accusations, which would have strengthened the ultimatum. And how could he have exculpated himself for doing violence to a document of such importance if it had arrived decipherable and been correctly deciphered by the Embassy staff? He would have needed to obtain the connivance of the staff, an unthinkable supposition given the character of Schoen, to whose 'probity' even Poincaré pays tribute.

If the French had possessed the cipher they might have had a certain interest in rendering the text of the declaration of war unintelligible, since Schoen would then have had to ask Berlin to repeat it as he had done for the earlier telegram. Not that he would have received a reply, because the Germans, in opening hostilities at 7 p. m.,[1] would have cut the telegraph wires. In that case Germany would have gone to war without declaring war and have therefore appeared still more clearly as the aggressor. But on the other hand, supposing the French had possessed the cipher and had skillfully altered the parts of the text which did not suit them, as the Germans assert, they would have had to make the whole telegram unintelligible in order to prevent what in fact happened, namely, Schoen's using the intelligible part of it to deliver the declaration of war. Probably the truth will never be known, and it may well be that the jumbling was an accident or the result of carelessness. The one certainty is that Schoen was able to draw up a version of the document and convey it without delay to Viviani.

He was just starting out for the Quai d'Orsay about 6.15 p. m. when a man jumped on the running-board of his car in front of the Embassy and forced his way into it, gesticulating wildly and using threatening language. He was immediately followed by a second. Schoen called the police to rid him of the intruders, and two officers got into the car, a third seating himself beside the chauffeur. The American Ambassador had undertaken to look after German interests and had warned the Quai d'Orsay to expect Schoen's call. He was received by Viviani, who on hearing of the episode in the car tendered apologies, which Schoen acknowledged by a bow. He drew from his pocket the declaration of war framed as a letter to Viviani, read it aloud to the Prime Minister and to Margerie, who was also in attendance, and left the document with them. It runs as follows:

The German administrative and military authorities have established a certain number of flagrantly hostile acts committed on German territory by French military airmen. Several of these latter have openly violated the neutrality of Belgium by flying over the territory of that country. One of them has attempted

[1] DF. 3. XI, 678, 725.

to destroy buildings near Wesel, others have been seen over the Eifel region, another dropped bombs on the railway near Karlsruhe and Nuremberg.

I am instructed and have the honor to inform Your Excellency that in the presence of these acts of aggression the German Empire considers itself in a state of war with France in consequence of the acts of this latter Power.

I have at the same time the honor to bring to Your Excellency's knowledge that the German authorities will detain the French merchant vessels lying in German ports, but that they will release them within forty-eight hours if complete reciprocity is assured.

My diplomatic mission having thus come to an end, it only remains for me to request Your Excellency to be good enough to furnish me with my passports, and to take the steps you consider suitable to assure my return to Germany, with the staff of the Embassy, as well as with the staff of the Bavarian Legation and of the German Consulate General in Paris.

Be good enough, M. le President, to receive the assurances of my deepest respect.[1]

Poincaré narrates:

M. Viviani listened in silence while this was being read and took the sheet of paper which the Ambassador handed him. He then protested against the injustice and insanity of the Imperial thesis. He recalled that, far from having permitted incursions into German territory, France had kept her troops ten kilometres away from her frontiers and that, on the contrary, it was German patrols which had come on to our soil and to that distance to kill our soldiers. M. de Schoen said he knew nothing. He had nothing more to say, nor had M. Viviani. The Prime Minister accompanied the Ambassador as far as the courtyard of the Ministry and waited while M. de Schoen entered his carriage. The Ambassador bowed deeply and drove away. On the following day he was to return peacefully to Germany, treated with all possible consideration by the French authorities, while M. Jules Cambon, obliged by the declaration of war to leave Berlin, was refused permission to travel by the route chosen by him, had to make payments in gold, because cheques were not accepted for the traveling expenses of the Embassy staff, and travel in locked carriages like a sort of prisoner.[2]

Poincaré's indignation at the treatment meted out to the French Ambassador has every justification. One cannot read the account given by Jules Cambon himself without sharing the indignation at such gross discourtesy. Cambon's wish had been to travel via Holland or Belgium.

---

[1] DD. IV, 734b; CDD., pp. 240-1. Wegerer writes: 'In the transmission of the declaration of war there was no indication as to whether 6 p. m. Paris time or 6 p. m. Central European time was meant. The Embassy assumed that Paris time was meant, while the Wilhelmstrasse had had Central European time in mind. Consequently, since the Wilhelmstrasse notified the General Staff in accordance with Central European time the German forces crossed the frontier one hour earlier than the notification given to Paris would have warranted' (*Refutation*, p. 363, note 145.)

[2] Poincaré, IV, pp. 521-3.

This was refused (while his English colleague was later accompanied to the Dutch frontier) and he was told he could go via Denmark or Switzerland. He chose Switzerland, but then this was forbidden and he was asked to travel via Vienna. Before agreeing Cambon asked for an assurance that he would not be detained at Vienna. This was given, and he was preparing to make the journey via Vienna when he was told he would be sent to Denmark. His protests were disregarded. The journey to the Danish frontier took him and his staff more than twenty-four hours. As the train neared the Kiel canal the military invaded their coaches.

They ordered windows and curtains of the carriages to be closed. Each of us had to remain alone in his compartment, forbidden to rise from his seat or touch his luggage. In the corridors of the coaches in front of the door of each of our compartments, which were kept open, stood a soldier holding a revolver with his ringer on the trigger. . . . During the twenty-four hours no meals were served for either myself or my staff. . . . Major von Rheinbaben, rather confused, came and told me that the train would not proceed to the Danish frontier unless I paid the price of the train. . . . I offered to pay by cheque on one of the big Berlin banks; this was refused. With the help of my companions I managed there and then to raise the sum demanded of me, which amounted to 3,611 marks 75 pfennigs.[1]

The German Government eventually had the good grace to refund this sum through the Spanish Embassy.

10. *The Chancellor's speech in the Reichstag on 4 August.*

It now remains to consider the speeches by which on 4 August Bethmann in Berlin and Viviani in Paris announced the outbreak of war to their respective parliaments.
Bethmann's began as follows:

A stupendous fate is breaking over Europe. For forty-four years . . . we have lived in peace and have protected the peace of Europe. . . . The feeling that animated everyone from the Kaiser down to the youngest soldier was this: Only in defense of a just cause shall our sword fly from its scabbard. The day has now come when we must draw it against our wish and in spite of our sincere endeavors. Russia has set fire to the building. We are at war with Russia and France—a war that has been forced upon us.

Gentlemen, a number of documents, composed during the pressure of these last eventful days, are before you. Allow me to emphasize the facts that determine our attitude.

From the first moment of the Austro-Serbian conflict we declared that this question must be limited to Austria-Hungary and Serbia, and we worked with this end in view. All Governments, especially that of Great Britain,

[1] DF. 3. XI 775.

took the same attitude. Russia alone asserted that she had to be heard in the settlement of this matter. Thus the danger of a European crisis raised its threatening head.

As soon as the first definite information regarding the military preparations in Russia reached us, we declared at St. Petersburg in a friendly but emphatic manner that military measures against Austria would find us on the side of our ally, and that military preparations against ourselves would oblige us to take counter-measures, but that mobilization would come very near to actual war.

Russia assured us in the most solemn manner of her desire for peace, and declared that she was making no military preparations against us.

Anyone listening to this part of the speech with an open mind would note that Germany was putting forward as a pretext for her action a claim which even a slight knowledge of the international situation would reveal to be untenable, namely, that Russia should leave Serbia at the mercy of Austria and that an Austro-Serbian conflict could remain localized. Equally obvious would be the fact that all the Cabinets, and particularly the English Cabinet, could not possibly—and indeed did not—agree to any such 'localization'. And, in fact, in the *White Book,* which had been laid before the Reichstag on 3 August and to which Bethmann referred in his speech, he refrained from producing any telegram from Lichnowsky in proof of his assertion. On the contrary, Grey had said to Lichnowsky:

So long as it is a question of a localized conflict between Austria and Serbia, it did not concern him, but it would be another matter if public opinion in Russia compelled the Government to take action against Austria. . . . Were Austria to invade Serbia the danger of a European war would loom very close.[1]

Yet in spite of this warning, Berlin urged Vienna to invade Serbia as soon as possible.[2]

Nor was the Chancellor's statement more correct about the attitude taken by Germany towards the Russian military measures. He claimed to have warned St. Petersburg 'that military measures against Austria would find us on the side of our ally and that military measures against ourselves would oblige us to take counter-measures; but that mobilization would come very near to actual war'. In the preamble with which the *White Book* opens, Bethmann goes further and claims to have instructed Pourtalès on 26 July to warn Sazonov:

Preparatory military measures by Russia will force us to counter-measures which must consist in mobilizing the army. But mobilization means war.[3]

---

[1] DD.I, 157.
[2] Oe-U. VIII, 10656. See Vol. II, p. 426.
[3] CDD., p. 408.

Here the omission of certain words borders on falsification. The actual telegram sent on the 26th to Pourtalès runs:

Preparatory military measures on the part of Russia directed in any way *against ourselves* would force us, etc.[1]

The two texts do not mean at all the same thing, and the author of the preamble to the *White Book,* perceiving this, therefore falsified the dispatch. It was one thing to ask Russia not to mobilize against Germany, and another to ask her not to mobilize at all, i.e., against Austria. In actual fact, the mobilization against Austria was not deprecated by the German Government. Jagow raised no objection to it.[2] It was only subsequently that Moltke protested against it, when the thing was done. In the beginning Berlin saw no harm in it. Neither did Grey, who on 25 July said to Lichnowsky that he 'thought it certain that Russian mobilization would follow that of Austria' (against Serbia).[3]

Bethmann went on to speak of the Tsar's appeal to the Kaiser for his mediation, adding:

But scarcely had active steps on these lines begun when Russia mobilized all her forces directed against Austria, while Austria-Hungary had mobilized only those of her corps which were directed against Serbia.

He omitted, of course, to say that the reason for Russia's action was the Austrian declaration of war on Serbia.

In spite of this we continued our task of mediation at Vienna and carried it to the utmost point which was compatible with our position as an ally. Meanwhile Russia of her own accord renewed her assurances that she was making no military preparations against us.

We come now to 31 July. The decision was to be taken at Vienna. Through our representations we had already obtained the resumption of direct conversations between Vienna and St. Petersburg after they had been for some time interrupted. But before the final decision was taken at Vienna the news arrived that Russia had mobilized her entire forces, and that her mobilization was therefore directed against us also.

This, too, was not in accordance with the truth. Berlin had sought to exercise pressure on Vienna (though it was, in fact, frustrated by Tschirschky's behavior) for the last time on the night of 29/30 July. On the evening of the 30th, not yet aware of the Russian general mobilization, and seeing that Austria was not yielding, Bethmann would have liked to renew his pressure. But he was dissuaded from so doing by the generals and decided to send an ultimatum to St. Petersburg. Moreover, his mediation, such as it was, had not the slightest

[1] DD. I, 219. See Vol. II, p. 428.   [2] See Vol. II, p. 482.
[3] DD. I, 180; DB. XI, 116. See Vol. II, p. 338.

success. Vienna would have nothing to do with his formula of the *Halt in Belgrade,* and the resumption of direct conversations was pure sham.[1]

Bethmann's speech continued:

> While we were mediating at Vienna in compliance with Russia's request, Russian forces were appearing all along our extended and almost entirely open frontier, and France, though indeed not actually mobilizing, was admittedly making military preparations. . . . Were we now to wait further in patience until the nations on either side of us chose the moment for their attack? (*Loud cries of No, No! Acclamation.*) It would have been a crime to expose Germany to such peril. Therefore on 31 July we called upon Russia to demobilize as the only measure which could still preserve the peace of Europe. The Imperial Ambassador at St. Petersburg was also instructed to inform the Russian Government that in case our demand met with a refusal, we should have to consider that a state of war existed.
>
> The Imperial Ambassador has executed these instructions. We have not yet learnt what Russia answered to our demand for demobilization. Tele-graphic reports on this question have not reached us, even though the wires still transmitted much less important information.
>
> Therefore, the time-limit having long since expired, the Kaiser was obliged to mobilize our forces on 1 August at 5 p. m.

The question will be discussed further on whether Germany could have waited twenty-four or forty-eight hours before mobilizing or not.[2] Here, be it noted, the Chancellor's speech made it appear as if Pourtalès had been instructed, after delivering the ultimatum, to warn the Russian Government in suitable time that unless it agreed to demo-bilize, Germany would regard the 'state of war' as having arisen. Bethmann understandably phrased his statement in such a way as to create the impression that Russia had been well warned of the conse-quences of a refusal to demobilize, i.e., that she had been made to understand that a refusal would automatically give rise to a state of war, but this statement does not correspond to the facts, as has been fully shown above.[3] True, before declaring war, Pourtalès had thrice asked Sazonov to agree to demobilizing. But while it was one thing to explain the matter to Sazonov and the Tsar at the moment of presenting the ultimatum or before its time-limit had expired, it was another to do so after the expiry of the time-limit. Moreover, even had Sazonov been willing to yield when at 7 p. m. Pourtalès carried out his instruc-tions to declare that, Russia not having demobilized, Germany con-sidered that a state of war existed, his yielding would have come too late. By then German mobilization had already been ordered and war begun. It was not true that, as Bethmann said in his speech, German

---

[1] See Vol. II, Ch. XI, *passim.*   [2] See pp. 232-6.
[3] See pp. 40-1, 61-4.

mobilization was ordered, 'the time-limit having long since expired'. It was a bare six hours since the time-limit had expired, a time so short that, as has been shown above, if Sazonov had bowed to the ultimatum not at 7 p. m. but as early as noon on 1 August, when the time-limit was due to expire, his acceptance would not have become known in Berlin in time to stop the German mobilization.

In the afternoon of 1 August the German military leaders became obsessed with the fear of falling behindhand and urged the Berlin Government to speed up the tempo, with the result that it was placed in acute embarrassment both by the arrival of Lichnowsky's telegram raising hopes of French neutrality and by the silence of Pourtalès, who had not reported whether Russia had rejected the ultimatum or whether war had been declared. By a stroke of good luck, in the night of 1–2 August news came in of Russian crossings of the frontier, which clarified the situation and enabled the compiler of the preamble to the *White Book* to twist the facts and write that, before the confirmation of the declaration of war

as early as the afternoon of 1 August, i.e., the same afternoon on which the Tsar's telegram, cited above [promising not to let his troops cross the frontier], was sent, Russian troops crossed our frontier and marched into German territory. Thus Russia began the war against us.[1]

Kautsky justly comments:

Just think! The German Government commissions their Ambassador in St. Petersburg to declare war on Russia at 5 p. m. On the 'afternoon of the same day, 1 August' Russian troops cross the German frontier; therefore, concludes the Government, Russia has begun the war for—this happened at a time when there was as yet no report in Berlin of the declaration of war in St. Petersburg![2]

In the second part of his speech the Chancellor turned to the question of France:

To our direct question whether she would remain neutral in the event of a Russo-German war, France replied that she would do what her interests demanded. . . . In spite of this, the Kaiser ordered that the French frontier was to be unconditionally respected. This order with one single exception, was strictly obeyed. France, who mobilized at the same time as we did, assured us that she would respect a zone of 10 kilometres on the frontier. What really happened? Airmen dropped bombs, and cavalry patrols and French infantry detachments appeared on Reich territory! Though war had not been declared, France thus broke the peace and actually attacked us. . . .

Gentlemen, we are now in a state of self-defense (*Notwehr*) and necessity (*Not*) knows no law. (*Great applause.*) Our troops have occupied Luxemburg and perhaps have already entered Belgian territory.

---

[1] CDD. 413.   [2] Kautsky. *Tie Guilt of William Hohenzollern*, p. 213.

Gentlemen, that is a breach of international law. It is true that the French Government declared at Brussels that France would respect Belgian neutrality as long as her adversary respected it. We knew, however, that France stood ready for an invasion. France could wait, we could not. . . . Thus we were forced to ignore the rightful protests of the Governments of Luxemburg and Belgium. The wrong—I speak openly—the wrong we thereby commit we will try to make good as soon as our military aims have been attained. He who is menaced as we are and is fighting for his highest possessions, can only consider how he is to hack his way through (*sich durchhauen*). (*Great and repeated applause, intense excitement.*)

In this part of the speech occur notorious phrases which constitute a damning indictment of Germany. Nothing of what the Chancellor said was true and not much acumen was needed to perceive this. It was untrue that war had been declared on France on such trivial grounds, untrue that France was preparing to invade Belgium, and that Germany feared some deadly attack on the Lower Rhine. The invasion of Belgium took place not with a defensive but with an offensive aim. It made clear that the aggression came from Germany. The Chancellor deluded himself that he was winning favor for the German case by confessing his guilt, but his words were on the contrary regarded as cynical and brutal, outraging the conscience of the world and ranging it against Germany with fatal results.

Incredible to say, Bethmann even then, on 4 August, still had lingering hopes of English neutrality!

As for England's attitude, the statements made by Sir Edward Grey in the House of Commons yesterday show the standpoint assumed by the English Government We have informed the English Government that, as long as England remains neutral, our fleet will not attack the northern coast of France, and that we will not violate the territorial integrity and independence of Belgium. These assurances I now repeat before the world, and I may add that, as long as England remains neutral, we would also be willing, upon reciprocity being assured, to take no warlike measures against French commercial shipping.

Amid frantic applause and the highest enthusiasm also in the galleries Bethmann concluded his speech:

Now the great hour of trial has struck for our people. But with clear confidence we go forward to meet it. Our army is in the field, our navy is ready for battle—behind them stands the entire German nation—the entire German nation united to the last man.[1]

It was not even true that Bethmann and his Kaiser were going forward to meet the trial with clear confidence. Tirpitz writes of Bethmann:

[1] CDD., pp. 436-9.

Since the Russian mobilization the Chancellor gave one the impression of a drowning man,

and of the Kaiser:

An old intimate friend of his, who saw much of him during the first days of August, declared that he had never seen such a tragic and disturbed face as that of the Kaiser at the time.[1]

One can well believe it! The venture was beginning under bad auspices. It had come about after a series of diplomatic defeats. Failure had befallen the calculation that the conflict could be 'localized'; failure had ended the hopes of French and Russian inaction; failure had overtaken the plan of making Russia appear the aggressor; failure was about to engulf the main assumption on which the whole venture had been undertaken, namely, that England would remain neutral, while, on the other hand, from Italy and Romania no support was forthcoming.

11. *Poincaré's message and Viviani's speech to the French parliament.*

Greater confidence probably reigned in Paris, where the effect of the German aggression was to bring about a more lasting consciousness of unity than was the case in Germany. War appeared as having been thrust upon the country and there was no other choice, than to meet the challenge, relying on the sympathy that would be universally felt for the victims of aggression. On the morning of 4 August there took place the funeral of Jaurès. The Speakers of the two Chambers and the Prime Minister stood surrounded by all the representative men of the country. Maurice Barrès represented the *Ligue des Patriotes.* Jouhaux, the Secretary of the *Confédération Générale du Travail,* spoke:

In the name of the trade unions, in the name of all the working men who have already rejoined their regiments and of those, of whom I am one, who leave tomorrow, I declare that we take the field with the determination to drive back the aggressor.[2]

At 3 p. m. the two Chambers met and listened to the reading of a message from the President of the Republic. It began:

Gentlemen, France has just been the object of a brutal and premeditated aggression which is an insolent defiance of the law of nations. . . . Ever since the Austrian ultimatum opened a crisis which threatened the whole of Europe, France has persevered in following and in recommending on all sides a policy of prudence, wisdom and moderation. To her can be imputed no act, no gesture, no word which was other than pacific and conciliatory. . . . Up to the last moment she has made supreme efforts to avert the war now

---

[1] Tirpitz, I, pp. 279, 280.   [2] Poincaré, IV, pp. 541-2.

about to break out, the crushing responsibility for which the German Empire will bear in the eyes of posterity. On the very morrow of the day when we and our allies were publicly expressing the hope of seeing negotiations, which had been begun under the auspices of the London Cabinet, carried to a peaceful conclusion, Germany suddenly declared war upon Russia, has invaded the territory of Luxemburg and has outrageously insulted the noble Belgian nation, our neighbor and our friend, and attempted treacherously to fall upon us in the midst of diplomatic conversation. But France was on the watch. No less alert than pacific, she was prepared; and our enemies will encounter on their path our valiant covering troops, who are at their fighting stations. . . . France is loyally seconded by Russia, her ally; she is supported by the sincere friendship of England. And already from all corners of the civilized world come sympathy and good wishes. For today once more she stands in the eyes of the universe for freedom, justice, reason. In the war which is beginning France will have on her side law (*le droit*), whose eternal moral power neither nations nor individuals can with impunity disregard.[1]

This brief and skilful summary of events contained one highly exaggerated statement, namely, that France up to the last moment had 'made supreme efforts to avert the war'. It is completely silent on the fact that the catastrophe had come about in consequence of the Russian general mobilization, which had caused Germany first to send an ultimatum to Russia and then declare war on her. Thus it did not reveal the true factors of the situation, but from the French point of view it admirably fulfilled the needs of the moment.

The reading of the Presidential message was followed by a longer and more detailed statement by Viviani on behalf of the Government. It look as its starting-point the Austrian ultimatum to Serbia, to which Serbia submitted 'almost without reservation'.

This submission, which constituted a success for Austria-Hungary . . . was not unconnected with the advice tendered to Belgrade from the first moment by France, Russia, and England.

But the Austrian Minister at Belgrade declared that the Serbian reply was unacceptable and broke off diplomatic relations.

On Friday, 24th, the German Ambassador came and read to the French Minister for Foreign Affairs a *note verbale* asserting that the Austro-Serbian dispute must remain localized, without intervention by the Great Powers. . . We immediately, in agreement with our allies and our friends, took a conciliatory course and invited Ger-many to join in it. . . . Our intentions and our efforts met with no response from Berlin. . . . On Tuesday, 28 July, Austria-Hungary declared war on Serbia. . . . On Wednesday the 29th, the Russian Government, . . . faced by the Austrian mobilization and declaration of war, decided as a precautionary measure to mobilize . . the formations echeloned along the Austro-Hungarian frontier exclusively. In

---

[1] Poincaré, IV, pp. 544-6.

taking this step, the Russian Government was careful to inform the German Government that its measures, restricted as they were and without any offensive character towards Austria, were not in any degree directed against Germany. . . . The German Secretary of State for Foreign Affairs acknowledged this without demur. On the other hand, all the efforts made by England, with the adherence of Russia and the support of France, to bring Austria and Serbia into touch under the moral patronage of Europe were encountered at Berlin with a predetermined negative. . . . This . . . made it probable that there existed at Berlin intentions which had not been disclosed. . . . In fact, on 31 July, Germany, by proclaiming 'a state of danger of war', cut the communications between herself and the rest of Europe. . . . Already for some days, and in circumstances difficult to explain, Germany had prepared for the transition of her army from a peace footing to a war footing. . . . On the evening of 31 July the German Government . . . addressed an ultimatum to the Russian Government under the pretext that Russia had ordered a general mobilization of her armies, and demanded that this mobilization should be stopped within twelve hours. This demand . . . was put forward at a moment when, at the request of England and with the knowledge of Germany, the Russian Government was accepting a formula of such a nature as to lay the foundation for a friendly settlement of the Austro-Serbian dispute and of the Austro-Russian difficulties by the simultaneous arrest of military operations and of military preparations. . . . The same evening [of 1 August] at 7.30, Germany, without waiting for the acceptance by the Cabinet of St. Petersburg of the English proposal, . . . declared war on Russia. The next day, Sunday, 2 August, . . . German troops crossed our frontier at three points. At the same time . . . they invaded the territory of the Grand Duchy [of Luxemburg] and so gave cause for a protest by the Luxemburg Government. Finally the neutrality of Belgium was also threatened. The German Minister, on the evening of 2 August, presented an ultimatum to the Belgian Government requesting facilities in Belgium for military operations against France. . . . The Belgian Government refused, and declared that it was resolved to defend its neutrality with vigor. . . . The German Ambassador . . . came yesterday evening to ask me for his passport, and to notify me of the existence of a state of war.

Viviani then read out the text of the declaration of war, pointing out the absurdity of the pretexts on which it was based.

The first part of this statement was tolerably accurate, but in the latter part he, like Poincaré, entirely ignored the Russian general mobilization and declared, in defiance of the truth, that Russia had accepted the English proposal on the lines of the German *Halt in Belgrade,* implying the suspension of mobilization. Thus the French Government's declaration, no less than that of the German Government, altered the facts to present its case in the best light. Not yet in a position to promise Parliament the support of England, Viviani read out the letters exchanged on 22–23 November between Grey and Paul

Cambon and made public the pledge given by England, in circumstances of which we shall speak later, that the British fleet would
intervene to protect the French coasts and the French navy in the event
of attack by the German navy.

Viviani ended his speech with a survey of the moral position of the
Republic, which,

> by the restoration of her national forces and the conclusion of diplomatic
> agreements unswervingly adhered to, has succeeded in liberating herself
> from the yoke which even in a period of profound peace Bismarck was able
> to impose on Europe. . . . It seems to me that this work of peaceful
> reparation, of liberation, and honor, finally ratified in 1904 and 1907 with
> the general co-operation of King Edward VII of England and the
> Government of the Crown, this is what the German Empire wishes to destroy
> today by one daring stroke.

In vain in 1904 and 1911 had France been willing to discuss
with Germany over Morocco and other questions. In vain had
Russia yielded to Austria in 1909 and shown the same
moderation in the Balkan wars.

> Useless sacrifices, barren negotiations, vain efforts, since today in the very
> act of conciliation we, our allies and ourselves, are attacked by surprise.
> No one can honestly believe that we are the aggressors. Vain is the desire to
> overthrow the sacred principles of right and liberty to which nations, as
> well as individuals, are subject. Italy, with that clarity of insight possessed
> by the Latin intellect, has notified us that she proposes to preserve neutrality.
> (*Prolonged applause, all the deputies rising to their feet.*) . . . The object of
> attack is the liberties of Europe, which France, her allies, and our friends are
> proud to defend. . . .
>
> A free and valiant people that sustains an eternal ideal, and is wholly
> united to defend its existence; a democracy which knows how to discipline
> its military strength and was not afraid a year ago to increase its burden as
> an answer to the armaments of its neighbor; a nation armed, struggling for its
> own life and for the independence of Europe—here is a sight which we are
> proud to offer to the onlookers in this desperate struggle that has for some
> days been preparing, with the greatest calmness and method. We are without
> reproach. We shall be without fear.
>
> France has often in less favorable circumstances proved that she is a
> most formidable adversary when she fights, as she does today, for liberty
> and for right.
>
> In submitting our actions to you, Gentlemen, who are our judges, we
> have, to help us in bearing the burden of our heavy responsibility, the
> comfort of a clear conscience and the conviction that we have done our duty.[1]

Poincaré related that, after the end of the sitting of the
Chamber, the Ministers hastened to the Élysée palace:

[1] *Journal Officiel,* 5 August 1914; LJF, No. 159; CDD., pp. 255-64.

Never, they told me, had they seen a more impressive sight than the one at which they had just been present. They vied with one another in repeating: 'Why could not you have been there ? In living memory there has never been anything finer in France.'[1]

This affirmation, which forms the conclusion of *L'Union Sacrée,* shows that at least in Government circles in Paris confidence outweighed apprehension. But the confidence was in great measure due to the terms under which the struggle was opening. Today it is possible to express misgivings as to the way the facts of the Franco-Russian case were presented by Poincaré and Viviani. And this has been done. But it cannot be denied that it was the mistakes made by the Central Powers which enabled their adversaries to present their case in so favorable a light. Not only to present it, but sincerely to regard it in that light. By her conduct Germany gave everyone, including her enemies, the clearcut impression of having willed the war and of being determined, with her imposing strength and remarkable organization, to carry it through without scruple to a victory which would have radically altered not only the map but also the political and moral configuration of Europe. The lineaments of the struggle, as depicted by Poincaré and Viviani on 4 August, and as represented by Italy in her declaration of neutrality, remained, indeed grew more pronounced in the course of the struggle and brought about the collapse of the two Empires. The moral factor outweighed all others, inspiring in the camp of Germany's adversaries heroic resistance in the face of dire military defeat and an unexpected degree of cohesion powerful enough to make up for the defection of Russia. Would it not have been possible, notwithstanding the Russian general mobilization, for the German leaders to avoid the conflict when they saw the unfavorable conditions in which it offered itself to their country?

It is a question which has been touched upon but which must now be examined more closely.

[1] Poincaré, IV, p. 548.

CHAPTER V

THE SCHLIEFFEN PLAN AND THE OUTBREAK OF THE EUROPEAN WAR

(1) *The mistakenness of both the Russian and the German mobilization* (*p.* 230). (2) *Germany could have saved the peace by the* Halt in Belgrade *formula* (*p.* 232). (3) *The arguments brought forward by Moltke; the Schlieffen plan* (*p.* 236). (4) *Moltke opposed to the violation of Dutch neutrality; modifications of the Schlieffen plan* (*p.* 238). (5) *The Chancellor under pressure from Moltke* (*p.* 242). (6) *Reasons alleged in defense of the Schlieffen plan; how it limited Germany's choice of action* (*p.* 245). (7) *Lack of co-ordination between the Army and Navy General Staffs* (*p.* 248). (8) *Consequences of the personal rivalries between the German leaders* (*p.* 251).

1. *The mistakenness of both the Russian and the German mobilization.*

Now that we have seen how the great tragedy began which brought affliction to the whole human race and from whose consequences we still suffer and our children's children will go on suffering, we must ask ourselves the question whether there was any justification for the way Germany acted from 30 July onwards. In other words, was it inevitable that the Russian mobilization should let slip the dogs of war in Berlin and cause the abandonment of all attempt to compose the conflict?

There is not the slightest doubt that the Russian partial mobilization, decided in principle as early as 24 July and ordered on the evening of the 29th, was a blunder of the first magnitude, and that in the circumstances and for the reasons we have examined, it led on to her general mobilization which Germany made the reason for carrying out a predetermined procedure of ultimatum, general mobilization, war. This partial mobilization was a very serious mistake, and one without justification, because so long as Austria mobilized only eight army corps for operations against Serbia, Russia had no reason to arm. On the contrary, it would have been from the military point of view of great advantage to her to let Austria send those eight army corps against Serbia, intervening herself, if needful, when the Dual Monarchy had thus diverted part of its forces to a minor field of operations. This had not escaped the attention of Moltke, who in his memorandum of 28 July had written that Austria would not be able to wage war on Serbia

without making Russian intervention certain. That means she will have to mobilize the other half of her army, for she cannot possibly put herself at the mercy of a Russia ready for war.

Thus the mere threat of Russian partial mobilization, or rather the bare possibility of it, would oblige Austria to protect herself by mobilizing her whole army. And then it would not be Russia who gave the bad example and bore the responsibility for mobilizing. She could say, as Moltke foresaw: 'You, Austria, are mobilizing against us; that means you intend to make war on us.'[1] On the other hand, by mobilizing first against Austria, Russia was forcing Austria to take similar measures in self-defense, the fault lying with Russia, and it also meant bringing Germany on to the scene. Sazonov did not perceive the danger. At the beginning he wanted the partial mobilization, not in order to take active measures, but to frighten Austria and obtain diplomatic satisfaction. But such weapons cannot rashly be resorted to with impunity. By transferring the conduct of affairs from the hands of the politicians to those of the generals, they produce the very opposite effect to the one intended, that is they cause the failure of diplomatic action. And, as events showed, once partial mobilization had been decided, unobjectionable as it was held to be even by Jagow, the Russian generals showed that it was impossible of execution and that general mobilization was required. Unfortunately, Sazonov was talked over by their arguments, instead of giving up the idea of even partial mobilization.

Nevertheless, having agreed that Sazonov was mistaken about the consequences which would follow from partial mobilization and that, instead of suspending it, he took the fatal step of ordering general mobilization, for which he bears the entire blame, one is faced with the question whether this measure was such a menace to Germany that she was constrained forthwith to throw up all attempts to achieve the peaceful solution which was already in sight. The pro-German writers avoid touching on this aspect of the situation which presented itself to Berlin at noon on 31 July. They prefer to attack the standpoint of those who maintain that Germany could have confined herself to mobilizing without going to war, on the lines suggested by Sazonov and the Tsar, namely, that the mobilized armies should stand at ease so long as negotiations went on. The thesis of these writers is that 'static' mobilization is a chimera, because all mobilization is necessarily bound up with a plan of offensive operations beyond the frontiers of the State in question. This point has been examined in an earlier chapter.[2] Here it is sufficient to repeat that, in all countries except Germany, mobilization was a proceeding which required a certain amount of time, and the plan of war only came into operation when mobilization was completed. This meant that between mobilization and war there was a considerable interval of time during which, if it were

---

[1] DD. II, 349. See Vol. II, pp. 488-9.   [2] See Vol. II, pp. 479-82.

so desired, there was the possibility of carrying on and concluding a
train of negotiations, without attaching too great importance to such
frontier incidents as might occur. A sufficient proof hereof is the case
of Austria, where Conrad, to the disapproval of Berlin, decided that,
although war was declared on Serbia on 28 July, operations were not
to begin until 12 August. Germany, however, was not in that category.
As has repeatedly been stated, she had given herself a plan of campaign
which laid down that the act of mobilization was immediately followed
by an advance beyond the frontiers. Thus the pro-German writers are
correct in maintaining that Germany could not mobilize and then await
the outcome of negotiations in progress, even if of short duration. The
opposite view is taken by Kautsky, who writes:

> That Germany should mobilize in her turn after the Russian mobilization was
> quite understandable. If Germany had regarded mobilization simply as a
> precautionary measure, as did all other nations—even France—there would be nothing
> to condemn in this step. . . . If Germany had accompanied her mobilization with
> similar assurances [to those given by Russia], negotiations could have really gone on
> and finally ended peacefully. Had not Russia and Austria mobilized in 1913 without
> coming to blows? . . . Mobilization, therefore, did not necessarily mean war.
> Demobilization could still follow it at the last moment without this bloody result, if
> people came to an under-standing meanwhile.[1]

In theory this was true, but in practice the German plan of mobilization ruled out the possibility.

2. *Germany could have saved the peace by the* Halt in Belgrade *formula.*

In spite of this it cannot be proved that after the Russian general
mobilization the German leaders had no other resource than to send
St. Petersburg and Paris the ultimatums which set Europe ablaze. If on
the evening of 30 July the Chancellor had not let the situation get 'out
of hand', if he had not capitulated to Moltke's will to war, a way of
escape could still have been found. Let it not be objected that Moltke
was justified in maintaining that every hour lost endangered the success
of the German plan, based as it was on speed and surprise. Moltke was
doubtless induced to maintain this chiefly by the fear that, if the negotiations lasted on, the conflict might be composed. However, from the
military point of view the fact remains that the German plan did not
provide for an offensive against Russia, but only for one against France
through Belgium. Now, so long as France did not mobilize—and
France would not have mobilized if both she and Russia had not
received an ultimatum on 31 July—the success of the German plan
would not have been directly jeopardized. It would have been so

[1] Kautsky, pp. 202-3.

indirectly in as far as Russia could have taken advantage of any delay on the part of Germany to push forward her own mobilization and put herself into a position to take the initiative in East Prussia. As Bethmann telegraphed to Lichnowsky at 1.50 a. m. on 1 August:

> A mobilized Russian army on our frontier, without our having mobilized, is a mortal danger to us even without 'provocative action'.

And Stumm's original draft had continued:

> For instance, our East Prussian province and perhaps also Posen and Silesia would be abandoned beyond recall to Russian conquest.[1]

But it is not the case that a start of twenty-four or even forty-eight hours would definitely have tipped the scales in favor of Russia, whose mobilization was an exceedingly slow affair. This was admitted even by Falkenhayn when on 29 July he wrote in his diary that there was no need for haste in ordering mobilization,

> for it was to be assumed that our mobilization, even if two or three days later than that of Russia and Austria, would be more rapid than theirs.[2]

What he thought ought to be done first was to proclaim the *Kriegsgefahrzustand*, which would enable preparations to be begun without actual mobilization and the opening of hostilities. Here is the proof that, in view of the immense issue at stake, Germany could well have afforded to wait a moment. If this was not realized by Moltke, who was soon to prove himself altogether unfitted for his task, it was intuitively felt by both Wilhelm and the Chancellor, who had been counting on the neutrality of England and the intervention of Italy and Romania, and now saw these essential preconditions of their venture failing them.

We have seen that on 31 July there still existed a basis of negotiation: the *Halt in Belgrade*. Knowing what the position was and that the *Halt in Belgrade* was a suggestion of Grey's and would therefore have his backing, Berlin could have taken advantage of the silence of Vienna (whence at noon on the 31st no answer had yet been received to the appeal sent on the evening of the 28th) to take a decisive step which Germany, as the country on whom would fall the brunt of the war, had a perfect right to do, namely, to give a promise to St. Petersburg that she would recommend at Vienna the *Halt in Belgrade*, which had also the backing of London, in return for a suspension of mobilization. The *Halt in Belgrade* would not of course be satisfactory to Sazonov if it implied the unconditional acceptance by Serbia of all the demands of the ultimatum. Wilhelm showed appreciation of this when he wrote to Jagow:

[1] DD. III, 529.   [2] See Vol. II, p. 502.

The few reservations made by Serbia on single points can in my opinion well be cleared up by negotiation.[1]

The Chancellor, it is true, in sending on the Kaiser's suggestion to Tschirschky had added that 'the temporary occupation of Belgrade and other definite points on Serbian territory' would serve 'to force the Serbian Government to integral fulfillment of Austrian demands'.[2]

The difference between the two formulas was serious, and that of Bethmann would certainly never have been accepted by Sazonov, who was determined to have guarantees against any infringement of Serbian independence, guarantees which were to be fixed by negotiation. However, by the 30th Bethmann had shown himself prepared to take a long step towards meeting Sazonov's wishes when, to a telegram from Pourtalès communicating Sazonov's last peace formula, he appended the minute:

> What points of the Austrian ultimatum has Serbia rejected? As far as I know only the participation of Austrian officials in law-court trials. Austria could dispense with this participation on condition that she occupies parts of Serbia with her troops until the end of the negotiations.[3]

Only one more step forward, even at the risk of somewhat forcing the hand of Vienna, and conciliation would have been achieved.

Grey would certainly have lent his aid. It must not be forgotten that on the evening of the 30th he had telegraphed to Buchanan proposing a variant of Sazonov's formula:

> If Austrian advance were stopped after occupation of Belgrade, I think Russian Minister for Foreign Affairs' formula might be changed to read that the Powers would examine how Serbia could fully satisfy Austria without impairing Serbian sovereign rights or independence.[4]

And Sazonov himself in that last formula of his had, as Pourtalès commented, asked no more than that Austria should refrain from entering Serbia. On receiving Grey's variant, Sazonov had merged his proposal with Grey's to form the formula which has already been quoted and elucidated above.

> If Austria agrees to stop the march of her troops into Serbian territory and if . . . she agrees that the Great Powers shall inquire into the satisfaction which Serbia might give to the Austro-Hungarian Government without infringement of her rights as a sovereign state and her independence, Russia engages to maintain her waiting attitude.[5]

But this was still not what the situation demanded. What was needed was that Russia should undertake to revoke the mobilization order.

[1] DD II 293. See Vol. II, pp 468-9   [2] DD. II, 323. See Vol. II, pp 476-7.
[3] DD. II, 421. See p. 18.   [4] BD. XI, 309. See Vol. II, p. 635.
[5] Int. Bez. i V, 343. See p, 57,

This would not have been beyond the bounds of possibility, as can be perceived from the optimistic language in which Sazonov thanked the English Government through Buchanan for what it had done in the cause of peace,[1] and in the similar message sent to Benckendorff:

> Be so good as to express to Sir Edward Grey our lively gratitude for his friendly attitude and the firmness and clarity of the views which it has expressed and communicated to the German and Austro-Hungarian Governments. Thanks to the point of view put forward by Sir Edward Grey all hope of a peaceful solution is not ruled out.[2]

The goal was in sight. To reach it, all that would have been necessary was that Grey, as he said to Mensdorff on the 30th, had something to offer St. Petersburg, and that something was the *Halt in Belgrade*.[3] Nay more, to Lichnowsky on the morning of 31 July Grey had gone so far as to say that

> if Germany could get any reasonable proposal put forward which made it clear that Germany and Austria were striving to preserve European peace and that Russia and France would be unreasonable if they rejected it, I would support it at St Petersburg and Paris and go to the length of saying that if Russia and France would not accept it, His Majesty's Government would have nothing more to do with the consequences.[4]

What proposal could be more reasonable than this of Grey? Only, in order to result in peace, it ought to have been presented at St. Petersburg by Berlin in place of the ultimatum in a supreme effort to avert German mobilization and war.

This was not done. And—be it noted—the reason why it was not done was not the proclamation of general mobilization at St. Petersburg. As early as the evening of the 30th, when the mobilization was not yet known, Berlin, as we have seen, decided to give Russia no other choice than to accept the demand that she should cease her military preparations, which then were thought to be directed only against Austria.[5] And this came about because, as the Chancellor himself confessed on the 30th to the Prussian Cabinet, 'the situation had got out of hand and the stone had started rolling',[6] or rather, as Tirpitz puts it, because of the 'stupidity of our political leadership. . . . Since the Russian mobilization the Chancellor gave one the impression of a drowning man'.[7] Had Bethmann not lost his nerve, he would not have ceased putting pressure on Vienna at the very moment when a formula had been found on which Germany and England could agree, and when Grey had promised that he would leave Russia and France to their fate

---

[1] BD. XI, 393. See p. 58.
[2] *Int.* Bez. i. V, 346; BD. XI, 409.
[3] Oe-U VIII, 11064. See Vol. II, pp. 633-4.
[4] BD. XI, 340. See Vol. II, p. 642.
[5] See pp. 22-3.
[6] DD. II, 456. See p. 16.
[7] Tirpitz, *Memoirs,* I, p. 279.

if they did not accept it. Armed with such a series of powerful arguments Bethmann could have firmly resisted the pressure from the generals to drop all further negotiation, instead of which he either made no use of them or used them lamely and belatedly.

3. *The arguments brought forward by Moltke; the Schlieffen plan.*

Before discussing these arguments, let us first take a look at those used by Moltke. He, as has already been said, thought that Germany ought to crush the enemy coalition before it grew stronger.[1] However, he did not go so far as to say so on the afternoon of the 30th. In fact, on the 29th he had raised no strong objection to the Chancellor's view that the Russian partial mobilization did not call for mobilization on the part of Germany, and on the morning of the 30th had spoken in this sense to the Austrian Major Fleischmann, to Conrad's great dismay.[2] This may have been either because his temperament did not incline to undertaking responsibilities to which he did not feel equal—in 1906 he had begged the Kaiser not to appoint him to his post—or because he did not venture to oppose the Kaiser's pacific intentions. But about midday on the 30th an unexpected change took place in his attitude in circumstances explained above.[3] Once bent on war, however, he naturally wanted to speed up the pace of action. Not only was Russia mobilizing against Austria and was Germany taking the measures prescribed for the 'period preparatory to war',[4] but France, too, was arming. This was the worst, because the French preparations boded no good for the success of the Schlieffen plan whereon hung the fate of the war on two fronts about which it is necessary to say a few words.

Schlieffen, the German Chief of General Staff from 1891 to 1905, was undoubtedly a remarkable general who never had the chance to display his notable gifts of intelligence, force of will and daring which were the marvel of his subordinates. His admirers regard him as a mighty figure and deplore that he was removed from the supreme command when he might still have rendered signal service.[5] However, after he vacated his post the spirit of Schlieffen still reigned in the German General Staff through his writings, which were regarded as gospel up to 1913, the year of his death.

Like Bismarck, he thought that 'War with France was unavoidable; sometime or other accounts must be settled between the two nations'.[6]

---

[1] See Vol. II, p. 487.   [2] See Vol. II, p. 671.
[3] See pp. 6-13.   [4] See Vol. II, pp. 304-6.
[5] Among these admirers one of the foremost is Lieutenant-Colonel Wolfgang Foerster, the Director of the Imperial Archives, who is the author of an important work, *Graf Schlieffen und der Weltkrieg* (Berlin, 1925). It is the source of the technical details here given.
[6] Foerster, p. 5.

He had made a close study of the battle of Cannae, which he regarded as the model of a decisive battle, and he meant to inflict a 'Cannae' on France. Hannibal, though weaker than Terentius Varro, had attacked the latter on both flanks and in the rear and destroyed him.

Weapons and military methods—wrote Schlieffen—have entirely changed in two thousand years. The basic conditions of battle remain unchanged. . . . The target of the main attack is not the enemy front. . . . The essential is to crush in the flanks. . . . Annihilation is completed by an attack on the enemy rear.[1]

Placing no reliance on the co-operation of Italy, which he regarded as an 'illusion',[2] Schlieffen saw

Germany and Austria-Hungary exposed alone to the concentric attack of a world of enemies simultaneously on several fronts. 'At the given moment the gates were to be opened, the drawbridge let down, and armies of millions, devastating and annihilating, were to surge across the Meuse, the Konigsau, the Niemen, the Bug, even across the Isonzo and the Tirolese Alps'.[3]

But since the combined forces of the Central Powers were inferior to those of their enemies, they could not wage war at the same time on Russia and France. They must beat them one by one and do so quickly, since time was not on their side.

Which should they attack first? The great Moltke and his successor, Waldersee, had thought the decision should be sought first in Russia, leaving the defense on the French front based on the fortresses of Metz and Strasbourg and the fortified line of the Rhine. In case of need Waldersee was even prepared to sacrifice this line and withdraw eastwards behind the Main.[4] But Schlieffen took a different view. For one thing, the strategic premises from which the older Moltke started had undergone a change. The Russian plan now, if attacked by Austria and Germany, was to deploy in the interior and this would render an early, decisive battle impossible. Moreover, if Germany were to allow the French to reach the Rhine it would mean sacrificing the Saar coal-basin and the rich mineral and industrial region of Lorraine. Finally there was the danger that France might violate the neutrality of Belgium by crossing her territory to invade the Rhineland. The first need therefore was to put France out of action before she could muster her full strength and receive the reinforcement of the English Expeditionary Force.

The whole of Germany must hurl itself against one opponent, the one who is the strongest, most powerful, most dangerous; this cannot but be France-England. Austria need feel no anxiety. The Russian army, destined to serve

---

[1] Foerster, p. 10.   [2] Foerster, p. 17.   [3] Foerster, p. 18.
[4] General H. von Kuhl, *Ost-oder Westaufmarsch* 1914?, KSF., 1923, pp. 73-6.

against Germany, will not march on Galicia before the die has been cast in the west, and the fate of Austria will be decided, not on the Bug, but on the Seine.[1]

While the attack on France was proceeding, East Prussia was to be protected by a weak strategic defense based on the Masurian Lakes, at the worst even by the evacuation of the territory east of the Vistula and a withdrawal behind that river. For, as Schlieffen wrote shortly before his death:

Better sacrifice a province than divide an army with which one is determined and destined to win victory.[2]

To deal France a knock-out blow the assault must be made, not against the powerfully fortified, impregnable Verdun-Belfort line, but against the weak, probably ill-defended, more northerly line of Dunkirk-Lille-Maubeuge, wheeling then southwards and encircling the French forces. This entailed the violation of Belgian neutrality, and it was well understood that such violation would in all probability call England on to the scene. The German General Staff therefore gave serious attention to devising ways and means of avoiding this, but came to the conclusion that without violating Belgian neutrality it would not be possible to destroy the enemy quickly, and that if the Germans did not violate Belgian neutrality the French would probably do so in order to reach the Rhineland.

In 1905, shortly before Schlieffen ceased to be Chief of Staff and when plans were being drawn up for a war against France and England alone, the attack was entrusted to a powerful right wing:

The mass of the western force—seven armies with 69 divisions, counting front line and reserve, 8 cavalry divisions, 22 *Landwehr* brigades—was to concentrate in the Rhine Province, with sections also in Lorraine on the Saar. For the decisive offensive they were to advance first against the Dunkirk-Verdun line in a vast leftward wheel with Metz as its pivot, the 8 *Ersatz* army corps were to follow as soon as they were available. In Lorraine only one army was to be retained with 10 divisions, counting front line and reserve, 3 cavalry divisions, 1 *Landwehr* brigade, apart from the war-time garrisons of Metz and Strasbourg. On the Upper Rhine only 3½ *Landwehr* brigades were to remain. Upper Alsace was to be left undefended. The relative strengths of the right and left wings of the army in front line and reserve divisions was approximately 7:3.[3]

4. *Moltke opposed to the violation of Dutch neutrality; modifications of the Schlieffen plan.*

Holland, also, was not spared by the Schlieffen plan. The Dutch province of Limburg forms a salient jutting forty miles southward, and thus covers part of the Belgian frontier against

---

[1] Foerster, p. 27.   [2] Foerster, p. 24.   [3] Foerster, p. 30.

Germany, constituting an obstacle to the direct westward advance of the German right wing. To avoid it, the German right wing would be obliged to strike south before turning west through the Liége defile.

Operational expediency gave rise to the idea of letting the extreme right wing pass through this Dutch territory. Count Schlieffen accordingly contemplated this possibility—but only on condition that German diplomacy succeeded in persuading Holland at the beginning of the war to attach herself to the Central Powers. He started from the assumption that England was as dangerous an enemy to the Dutch colonial empire as to Germany and that awareness of this would perhaps bring the Dutch Government over to our side.[1]

On becoming Schlieffen's successor, Moltke adopted the strategic concept carrying the sanction of his predecessor's authority and prestige, although he was not entirely convinced of its merits. In his memoirs he writes that he was in agreement with Schlieffen about the necessity of circumventing the French belt of fortifications and that this could only be achieved by using Belgian territory. He differed profoundly, however, over the methods to be pursued.

My predecessor's plan of deployment was so conceived that the German right wing would have to advance via Roermond, thus crossing not only Belgian but also Dutch territory. Count Schlieffen took the view that Holland would confine herself to a protest and would otherwise allow the violation of her territory to take place unhindered. I had the gravest doubts about this opinion. I did not believe that Holland would quietly tolerate violation, and on the other hand I anticipated that a hostile Holland would mean a loss to the German right wing of such considerable forces that it would no longer have the necessary striking power against the west. The advance through Belgium could, in my view, only be carried out under the assumption of a strictly neutral Holland.

Though I did not know what attitude England would take in a war of Germany against Russia and France, I regarded it as more than likely that she would side with our foes as soon as we violated Belgian neutrality. ... It was clear to me that on this ground alone respect of Dutch neutrality was an essential demand, and I allowed for all the difficulties which must necessarily attend our deployment and advance if we meant not to touch Dutch soil. ... I think that circumstances have proved me to be in the right. One need only think how they would have shaped themselves if we had found ourselves faced with a hostile Holland, whose coasts stood open to an English landing, what would have become of the expedition against Antwerp if the Schelde had not been neutral, how many troops would have been needed to cover our rear when we advanced westward. I was and still am convinced that the campaign in the west would have failed if we had not spared Holland. Moreover, I saw that it must at all costs be preserved as an airpipe for our

---

[1] Foerster, p. 30.

economic life. Moreover, if we spared Holland, England, having declared war on us allegedly for the defense of small neutrals, could not possibly violate Dutch neutrality on her own account.[1]

This apologia on the part of Moltke elicits from Schlieffen's champion the footnote:

If Moltke rather boasts of having eliminated the operational possibility of crossing Dutch territory from his plans, it must be pointed out that this rests on a different political basic concept, namely that our diplomacy would not be successful in attracting Holland to our side. The thought of doing violence to Holland by infringing her neutrality was as remote from Count Schlieffen as from Colonel General von Moltke.[2]

But supposing Holland did not join with Germany? In a letter to Lutz, Foerster writes:

Count Schlieffen planned the deployment of the German right wing in such a manner that the advance could take place either by crossing or by avoiding Dutch territory. March routes were provided for both eventualities. The plan taking in Holland was to come into force if German diplomacy were successful in persuading Holland at the outbreak of war to come to an amicable settlement with Germany. Failing that, the advance was to proceed leaving Dutch neutrality intact exactly as actually took place in 1914.

Lutz adds the comment:

This categoric affirmation stands in contrast to the equally categoric written statements of Moltke. . . . Foerster's evidence has not been regarded as convincing in Dutch military circles.[3]

Moltke realized that the violation of Belgian neutrality would have serious consequences and he was disquieted by the idea that the enormous right wing of the German deployment, having crossed Belgium, would plunge into the unknown. The French might put up strong opposition in the north, or they might carry out a counter-offensive and penetrate into Lorraine. This latter possibility perturbed Moltke more than Schlieffen, who felt confident of retaining the initiative and was prepared, if need be, to withdraw his left wing as far as the right bank of the Rhine. Moltke, moreover, had to plan for a war not merely against France, with or without English help, but against France and Russia acting in concert. The case might, it is true, arise that Germany would have to act against Russia alone, if France and England at the beginning remained neutral, leaving open the possibility that they might intervene later. To meet this contingency Moltke prepared the so-called Plan No. 2.

[1] Moltke, pp. 428-32.
[2] Foerster, p. 30, note 1.
[3] Lutz, pp. 531-2.

On 30 January 1910, in a long letter to Conrad discussing what was to be done if, in the event of a war against Russia, Italy and France at the beginning assumed a waiting attitude without the Central Powers having any assurance that their neutrality would be permanently maintained (as in fact happened with Italy in 1914-15), he wrote:

The only radical means of clarifying this critical situation would be an immediate declaration of war on the untrustworthy neutrals. Such a means is, however, not applicable on legal, political, and general human grounds. I have therefore proposed that if war between the allies and Russia comes to be regarded as unavoidable and impending, the German Government should demand an immediate, full, and unambiguous declaration from the French Government as to the attitude it intends to take on the outbreak of war [as was actually done on 31 July 1914]. . . . If France promises to maintain strict neutrality . . . the entire army will be mobilized but the forces not destined for immediate service against Russia will for the time being remain at their stations. In accordance with these considerations the military arrangements made by the General Staff are such that in the event of a satisfactory declaration of neutrality by France the troops destined for the east will be dispatched immediately, while the rest of the army for the time being remains mobilized on home territory and can at need be sent to the east later or used immediately against France if her neutrality proved doubtful. This procedure has, no doubt, the disadvantage for Germany that she may be obliged for a considerable time to send only inferior forces against her most dangerous foe.[1]

However, before the war Moltke came to the conclusion that there was no probability of France's remaining neutral and dropped Plan No. 2. He thus came to the same conclusion as Schlieffen, namely, that France must be put out of action before the attack on Russia was begun.

If Colonel-General von Moltke destined only 9 infantry divisions, 1 cavalry division, 1 *Landwehr* corps and 3 *Landwehr* brigades for the eastern front he was going down to the lowest permissible limit. It clearly shows how convinced he was of the need to concentrate all available forces in the first place on the great decisive battle in the west. . . . At the opening of the war the German forces in the west consisted of 72 front-line and reserve divisions, 10 cavalry divisions, 6½ *Ersatz* divisions and 19½ *Landwehr* brigades. . . . The relative strengths of the two wings, the right for the main offensive via Belgium and Luxemburg, and the left for a subsidiary task in Alsace-Lorraine, shows a profound departure from Schlieffen's plan. In Alsace-Lorraine and Baden were concentrated two armies, the 6th and 7th, with a total of 16 front line and reserve divisions,[2]

thus reducing the relative strength of the right wing from the 7:1 ratio planned by Schlieffen to one of 3:1, a fundamental change.

[1] Conrad, II, pp. 57-60.   [2] Foerster, pp. 35-6.

A modification of the 1905 plan had been worked out by Schlieffen in December 1912, shortly before his death, leaving Holland uninvaded as cover for the Rhineland industrial area and meeting the case where neutral frontiers at both ends of the enemy's territory rendered the enveloping movement on his extreme left impracticable. In this case the attack was to be launched along the entire length of the enemy front, leading to a tactical breakthrough in breadth at a suitable point from which the severed portions of the enemy line could be rolled up and enveloped from the rear. The most suitable area for the breakthrough, in Schlieffen's opinion, was in Belgium, and to the Abbeville-St. Quentin section of the line his plan assigned twenty-one army corps. And the last words he murmured as he lay dying were: 'Be sure and make the right wing strong.' This plan was substantially the one put into operation by Moltke in August-September 1914, but with a lowered ratio of right to left wing, a factor profoundly altering the character of the plan.[1] Moreover, as events were to show, Moltke was prepared in certain circumstances to allow himself to be enveloped, and this proved his undoing.

But the weakening of his right wing made Moltke think it all the more necessary not to waste any time. The week of political negotiations had been precious not only to France and Russia. It had enabled Belgium and England also to take vital military measures. Such negotiations must be brought to an end. Too much precious time had already been lost.[2]

5. The Chancellor under pressure from Moltke.

If this was the line of reasoning of the military, it should have been the right and duty of the civil authorities to counter it with their own arguments, which were strong. Why was it, indeed, that the Great General Staff had prepared only one strategic plan, as if there were no other possibility than that of a war on two great fronts and that France would necessarily make common cause with Russia? Supposing that in France a Government had come or returned to power of other views than those of Poincaré, Delcassé, Millerand, a Government determined not to be dragged into a conflagration caused by the Balkan interests of Russia? Was France to be attacked all the same because that was laid

---

[1] Foerster, pp. 41-3.

[2] Tirpitz writes: 'The subject of the conversation between Bethmann and Goschen was certainly known in Brussels the same day. . . . Thus Belgium gained precious time to organize resistance against us. This resistance had an extraordinarily unfavorable influence on the whole course of the war. England also learnt of our plans earlier than was strictly necessary. This enabled her to take military and naval measures which had bad consequences for us. . . . A delay of even only a few days in the preparation of the English expeditionary force and its transport to France might have been of the greatest importance to us' (Tirpitz, *Dokumente,* II, p. 13.)

down in the Schlieffen plan? One may reply that Russia would never have shown herself so unbending had she not known she could count on France. But this assumption was not something to be depended on, since it might unexpectedly be proved wrong by the facts. It should have been the General Staff's duty to provide for several alternatives, and prepare the relevant plans of mobilization and concentration, so that the political authorities would be free in whatever international crisis to choose the solution most in accordance with the interests of the Reich.

Among the various possible alternatives there was one not provided for in the Schlieffen plan, not even in Plan No. 2, which Moltke threw aside. As has just been mentioned, it was designed to meet the case in which France would declare neutrality, but a neutrality on which too much reliance could not be placed. It might have served Germany—indeed, would have served her in 1914 to prevent English intervention and not give Italy the right to declare herself neutral—to operate the plan of the elder Moltke and Waldersee, maintaining the defensive towards France while taking the offensive against Russia, even though the outcome of the eastern offensive might appear much more doubtful and less decisive than the Schlieffen maneuver. The sound basis of this assumption was demonstrated in 1936 when the Germans militarily reoccupied the Rhineland, which they had pledged themselves to leave demilitarized, and began to fortify it for the purpose of remaining on the defensive towards France and Belgium so as to have a free hand in the south and east. Had some such plan been prepared and the necessary fortifications executed, it would have been possible for Germany to ask for English neutrality in return for a promise to refrain from attack not only on the French coast and navy, as was actually proposed in 1914, but also on the French army, only reserving the right of self-defense in case an attack were made by France. There is likelihood that Grey would have given a different reception to a request for English neutrality on such a basis than he did to the disgraceful suggestion made by Bethmann to Goschen on the evening of 29 July. Nor can it be objected that it was impossible to remain on the defensive towards France. A Metz-Strasbourg line could have been rendered no less impregnable than was actually the Verdun-Belfort line. Moreover, the danger that France might invade the Rhineland by way of Belgium could have been averted by suitable fortification works, and was, in fact, purely imaginary, since it would never have been tolerated by England. The Germans knew this perfectly well. They merely used it as a pretext to cover up the invasion they themselves had planned.

Besides compelling Germany, in the event of a conflict with Russia, to throw her full weight against France and to that end violate the neutrality of Belgium even though it were inadvisable to do so, the

Great General Staff, by preparing a plan of war under which hostilities began with the act of mobilization, placed the German Government in the painful position of being unable to order a measure of mobilization corresponding to that of Russia without unleashing a European war. In other words, the Government had only the choice between leaving Germany disarmed or plunging her headlong into the mortal perils of a general war. Historians have failed to dwell sufficiently on this aspect of the tragedy. Taking for granted that the German principle was a universal practice and basing themselves on utterances of French and Russian generals which were never meant to be taken in this rigid sense, they have drawn the conclusion that mobilization was in every case the equivalent of going to war. It has been shown above that nothing is further from the truth, save in the one case of Germany herself.[1] Mobilization was an affair of more than a few days during which frontier incidents might well occur, but there was no need to pay much attention to them unless they were wanted to serve as a pretext for war. If on 1 August the Berlin Government had been able to order general mobilization in reply to that of Russia without implying the occupation of Luxemburg and the sending of an ultimatum to Belgium, the probabilities are that the Kaiser and the Chancellor, fearing English intervention no less than Italian and Romanian neutrality, would have authorized mobilization but not war and the Anglo-German formula of conciliation would have had time to bear fruit.

At the worst the Germans would have avoided appearing as the aggressors, to their own great advantage, material and moral, a fact which was realized at the moment when hostilities opened not only by Tirpitz but also by Falkenhayn and Moltke. Schlieffen's apologist, Foerster, could not but perceive how seriously the great general's plan handicapped the German Government, compelling it to declare war on Russia and France and thus to take on its shoulders the responsibility of causing the European conflagration. On this point he writes:

It is a completely mistaken opinion, though widespread both at home and abroad and much exploited by propaganda, that the Schlieffen plan of marching through Belgium forced Germany to assume the role of aggressor. But the declaration of war on Russia of 1 August was not the result of any strategic necessity. The correctness of Bethmann Hollweg's assertion that General von Moltke advised it on military grounds is highly questionable. In agreement with the War Minister von Falkenhayn, Moltke in the early hours of 2 August attempted, alas in vain, to prevent the declaration of war on Russia. The German Supreme Command would have been satisfied as regards Russia with the mobilization which had been ordered on 1 August. And even the declaration of war on France of 3 August did not stand in any

[1] See Vol. II, pp. 479-82.

causal connection with the planned move in Belgium. As late as 2 August, in a memorandum to the Imperial Chancellor, Moltke explicitly stated: 'Our eventual declaration of war [on France] is entirely independent of the *démarche* made in Belgium. The one does not entail the other. I do not regard it as needful to serve the declaration of war on France yet, on the contrary I calculate that, if we for the moment refrain, France will be forced by popular opinion to order military operations against Germany without war being formally declared'.[1] If, therefore, the political leaders of the Reich acted otherwise during those days and by declaring war brought upon Germany the odium of being the aggressor in the eyes of the outside world, it was not by the Schlieffen plan that they were forced to do so.[2]

This is the opposite of the truth. It was precisely the Schlieffen plan which dictated their action and it is childish to imagine that, simply by omitting the declaration of war, the odium would have been avoided. What caused the odium was the act of aggression, and this would have made an even worse impression than it did, had it taken place without being preceded by a declaration of war.

6. Reasons alleged in defense of the Schlieffen plan; how it limited Germany's choice of action.

Germany could not act otherwise, reply the politicians, military experts, and historians in Germany who have made a study of the question, and they find strong support in those scholars of other countries who are determined to absolve Germany from all guilt.[3] The words of Wegerer will serve as an illustration of their line of argument:

Surveying the military situation which faced Germany early in August 1914 . . . we understand why Germany could not afford to await inactively the outbreak of hostilities. She had to utilize her slight remaining advantage of operation on the inner line and defend herself as best she could. Accordingly, the struggle of the Central Powers against the expected coalition of Russia, Serbia, France, Belgium and England required not only the speediest mobilization and marshalling of the German and Austrian forces but also an immediate attack for the purpose of making the effectual co-operation of the enemies impossible. . .For the purpose of defense. . .the German

---

[1] DD. III, 662. See p. 198.

[2] Foerster, p. 28.

[3] Among these foreign scholars one of the foremost is G. Demartial who writes: 'The Russian Government was the first to know that the mobilization of the Russian army would provoke not only German mobilization, but war, since Germany, for strategic reasons which a baby could understand, could not mobilize without attacking' (G. Demartial, 'L'état de la question des responsabilités de la guerre en France', in *Évolution*, 15 March, 1926, p. 40). Demartial's assumption is baseless. Russia had no knowledge of the fact that for Germany mobilization meant going to war (See Vol. II, pp. 579-81.) Germany might have mobilized without attacking if, beside the Schlieffen plan, there had existed other less dangerous and ambitious plans of war, which without inflicting a Cannae on the French army, might have not led Germany to the total defeat which was in store for her notwithstanding the Schlieffen plan.

General Staff had since the beginning of the century adopted the plan outlined by General von Schlieffen, namely, of defeating by means of an offensive that opponent who was strongest and who could most readily be attacked—France. If neutral territory were not to be invaded, Germany's offensive against France could be executed only along the short line between Switzerland and Luxemburg. But the territory facing this line could not be rapidly invaded on account of the concrete construction of the forts and barriers at the frontier. The accuracy of this assumption was later proved by the struggles at Verdun which alone cost Germany several hundred thousand men. At the beginning of the campaign, therefore, the hopeless struggles for the French Thermupylean passes had to be avoided and the attempt made to invade northern France by strategically circling round the left flank of the enemy. But the protection of the German industrial region made it necessary also to create a *glacis,* which could be obtained by carrying the war into the enemy's country. Thus we see that the Russian general mobilization forced Germany to resort to an offensive against France, and that this offensive had to be conducted in Belgium.[1]

In these terms Wegerer seeks to defend both the Schlieffen plan and the necessity contained in it of beginning operations with the act of mobilization. But he says nothing which disproves the basis of the objections that can be raised against the plan itself and the necessities it takes for granted. He makes assumptions but brings no proofs. Nor can he do so, in view of the fact that Germany's experiences with the plan were, to say the least of it, anything but happy. Let us leave aside the moral aspect of the violation of Belgian neutrality to which the Germans in general attach no importance, arguing with the utmost candor that if, in order to crush France, who had been guilty of the indelicacy of erecting impregnable defenses along her frontier, Germany had no other way open than to pass through Belgium, it was quite natural that she should do so in breach of the pledge she had given.[2] Let us rather ask Wegerer whether in the conjuncture presenting itself in July 1914, when it was a matter of putting Serbia in her place and restoring Austrian prestige, influence, and security in the Balkans,

---

[1]   Wegerer, *Refutation,* pp. 309-10.
[2]   A sample of the cool effrontery with which the question is treated and regarded in Germany is provided by the following words of Tirpitz: 'The General Staff had for decades considered the possibility of an invasion through Belgium all the more seriously since the French policy of *revanche* began to support itself on the Russian armies. There could not exist a doubt in the whole world that the French were at least morally the aggressors in a Franco-German war. In warding off a French war of *revanche,* which threatened us on the Vistula just as much as on the Meuse and the Moselle, our march through neutral Belgium could only be justified in the eyes of the world if the political offensive of France against us was made as clear as day' (Tirpitz, *My Memoirs,* I, p. 281). He goes on to say: 'Those who were specially engaged on this question on the General Staff . . . had been led to the conviction by many symptoms during the few years before the war, that the French and the English would march through Belgium to attack the Rhineland.' This assumption does not attenuate the cynicism of the words just quoted.

it was necessary for Germany to regard the crushing of the French army as the principle underlying her military action.

Wars, it will be replied, are waged by the methods which ensure maximum military success. That may be so. But one sets about them in such a manner as not to add to the number of one's enemies and diminish the number of one's friends; in other words, one does not endanger the final result because of an attachment to a risky plan of operations, however brilliant. Designed to inflict a mortal blow on the Dual Alliance in a war in which Italy and Romania would march with the Central Powers and England would remain neutral, the Schlieffen plan, especially after the modifications introduced by Moltke, was not sufficient to assure victory in a war of aggression, i.e., one in which Italy would take no part while England would range herself in the opposite camp. As events were to show, the larger forces available to France on the Marne as a result of Italian neutrality and the presence there of the British Expeditionary Force brought about the failure of all the high hopes placed on the grand maneuver of the German right wing. Even had these hopes been realized, there is no certainty that they would have led to final victory. Victory on land was not enough. There must also be victory at sea.

In this connection Tirpitz writes :

> On 6 August I was visited by Jagow. . . . I remonstrated with him on the subject of the complete *déroute* of the political leaders, who ought to have given the event of war a certain amount of preliminary consideration. ... In reply to my question what would happen if we beat France and Russia but not England, Jagow shrugged his shoulders. The conflict of opinion came to the surface when I said: 'Couldn't you promise Russia the passage of the Dardanelles and anything they like, to prevent the war?' Jagow replied: 'If you had only brought us a little naval agreement with England, the war would not have been necessary.'[1]

They were both right. Precisely because Tirpitz had opposed the naval agreement offered by London the German Government should have been doubly careful to avoid giving England any pretext or reason for going to war with Germany. To propose not only to invade France and take her colonies but also to invade Belgium, in other words to carry out the Schlieffen plan, was to offer this very pretext or reason. It would never have been necessary to do this if, alongside of that plan, Germany had had another, less ambitious but better suited to the end proposed, which was neither to crush France nor to go to Moscow, but to save the existence of Austria. On all sides it has been agreed that Germany had nothing to gain from war. In peace she was every year increasing in strength and influence, expanding and becoming ever

---

[1] Tirpitz, *My Memoirs,* I, pp. 283-4; *Dokumente,* II, p. 27.

more feared and respected. Far from wanting to attack her, England had actually come to an agreement with her over the Baghdad railway. Thus even if Germany was obliged to take up arms in defense of her ally and of the latter's Balkan interests, she would have done so at smaller cost and with less risk, even though sacrificing the possibility of inflicting a colossal Cannae on the French and Russians. Wars can, moreover, be won without victories like that of Cannae. It is often wiser to be victorious only up to a certain point. Furthermore, the enemy's power of resistance has to be measured not only by military but also by political standards. Theoretically, it might be right to crush the French army first. Practically, it was doubtful, because Russia at the opening of the struggle was politically and morally in such a state that she would have quickly collapsed under the combined attack of the Central Powers. These would then have found themselves in 1915 in a position to negotiate a peace similar to the one they negotiated at Brest Litowsk in 1917.

7. *Lack of co-ordination between the Army and Navy General Staffs.*

But for that to happen the military authority would have had to be subordinated to the political. It would have been for the political authorities to weigh the various possibilities of conflict that might arise and expect the General Staff to supply different plans to suit the different cases. In Germany, however, the military caste, represented by the Chief of Staff, who ranked as equal to the Chancellor, would never have allowed the latter to interfere in such problems. And at the decisive moment the military took over the direction of affairs and imposed their law. Nor was Bethmann the man to change a state of things to which his predecessors had submitted and which he could not have altered without entering into conflict with his Sovereign. Moltke on 30 July outstepped his powers and invaded those of the Chancellor, who might quite well have resisted. But to do so he would have had to be endowed with the requisite powers of mind and of will.

What, above all, Bethmann should have done in the terrible emergency was to measure the handicap which the Schlieffen plan constituted for Germany in preventing her from mobilizing without going to war, making her appear as responsible for the war in the eyes of the world, rendering English intervention inevitable and justifying the neutrality of Italy and Romania. It was too late to change the plan and, create another, but it was not too late to make a supreme effort to save peace. Just because in going to war Germany would have to entrust her fate to the Schlieffen plan it was to her supreme interest to act with the utmost caution and to refrain from mobilization as long as there was any possibility of negotiating and while there still existed a prospect of reaching agreement on a peace formula. Thus it was on 30 July, not on 1 August, that the Chancellor should have considered this problem of the declarations of war and discussed it with the military chiefs, in order that if it proved intractable, in other words, if the declarations could not be foregone but would make the German Government appear as the aggressor, everything should be done to compose a conflict presenting itself in conditions so overwhelmingly unfavorable to Germany.

The fact is that Bethmann, who had made every effort to cast the blame on Russia, failed to see that his endeavors would be defeated by the very demands of the Schlieffen plan. Had he but realized this and resisted the pressure from Moltke and Falkenhayn, he would certainly have had the support of the Kaiser, who was temperamentally disinclined for war, and still more of Tirpitz, who had fully grasped the madness of what was being done not only by the declarations of war but also by the violation of Belgian neutrality and the challenge to England. It was a real disaster that, because of his jealousy of the Grand Admiral, Bethmann never took counsel with him and sought to keep him away from Berlin during the days of crisis on the pretext that his return would make things more difficult. If in 1912 there had been a difference of opinion between the two men about the naval agreement, desired by London, Bethmann being willing to agree to it and Tirpitz unwisely opposing it, Tirpitz was nevertheless more alive to the need for saving the peace than was Bethmann. He would have thrown his weight on the side of conciliation if for no other reason than that he had no high opinion of the political leadership of the Reich any more than of its military leadership. In his memoirs he writes:

I was troubled by the feeling that the General Staff was not correctly estimating the meaning of a war against England and was heedlessly going on with the war against France because this apparently meant only a short war. The decisions of the hour were never guided by previously considered politico-strategical plans of mobilization for the whole war.[1]

Just so! There had been no collaboration between the army and navy General Staffs. Germany had acquired a powerful navy worthy to measure swords with that of England. But the navy chiefs were not asked for their opinion on the problems raised by a possible European war. And yet the invasion of Belgium created a situation which concerned the navy no less than the army. As Tirpitz asked Jagow on 6 August:

What would happen if we beat France and Russia and found ourselves alone in face of England?[2]

[1] Tirpitz, *My Memoirs,* I, p. 280.   [2] Tirpitz, *Dokumente,* II p. 27.

In truth, Tirpitz frames a very serious accusation against the highest authorities of the Reich when he writes:

In his fear of clearness, the Chancellor was so little prepared for the war that collective consultations between the political and military leaders never took place, either on the politico-strategical problems of the conduct of the war or even on the prospects of a world war at all. I was never even informed of the invasion of Belgium, which immediately raised naval questions when it took place. The question might here be raised whether in time of peace I on my side would not have been in a position to urge the preparation of a mobilization of the collective leadership of the Reich. Anyone knowing the conditions existing in our Government at that time would not ask such a question.[1]

This is an accusation directed against Tirpitz himself, who never explains what obstacle prevented co-operation between the political and military authorities. In the very interests of the powerful navy which he had created, he should have insisted on the absolute necessity, of such co-operation. He writes:

If the Chancellor had consulted me, as was his duty—he ought to have explored the military possibilities in every direction before taking such a course—then I should have had to tell him that from the standpoint of the navy the danger of war, in itself undesirable, would be presenting itself at a strategically unfavorable moment. Dreadnought construction, by the introduction of which England automatically doubled the fighting force of our navy, had only been going on for four years. The Kiel Canal was not yet ready. The navy would not reach its maximum until 1920.[2]

Why, when he realized the gravity of the situation, did not Tirpitz write at once on these lines to the Chancellor?

The German navy, it is true, was a recent growth to which no doubt the spiritual heirs of Frederick the Great and of the illustrious Moltke, who had beaten first Austria and then France and on these victories had reared the edifice of the Reich, would have refused to pay deference. But the Grand Admiral had perhaps more influence with the Kaiser than anyone else, as his own narrative shows:

On Monday, 3 August at 8.30 a. m. I received the following missive from the Kaiser:

'In my opinion this position is absolutely untenable under international law; England, while claiming to be neutral and prepared to remain so stands guard over the French coast and ties down my fleet, although I am at war with France and France has already committed acts of hostility against us. England must at once be reminded by Ambassador that this attitude would have to be regarded by us as an act of war against us. ... Ambassador must tell England to make up her

---

[1]Tirpitz, *Erinnerungen*, p. 228; *My Memoirs*, I, pp. 263-4.
[2]Tirpitz, *My Memoirs*, I, pp. 262-3.

mind whether she means to be at war with us or neutral. Any concentration against us to cover France would be regarded as an act of war. My fleet must have freedom of movement.'

Tirpitz perceived the folly of this attitude and wrote to the Kaiser and Bethmann:

Urgently recommend Chancellor to telegraph to Lichnowsky:
No action against French coast intended as long as England remains neutral.

And to the Chancellor's proposed statement to the Reichstag on 4 August Tirpitz obtained the addition of the words:

And I may add that as long as England remains neutral we should be prepared, in the event of reciprocity, to refrain from taking hostile measures against French mercantile shipping.[1]

8. Consequences of the personal rivalries between the German leaders.
The conclusion to be drawn is that it was personal rivalries and jealousies between the various authorities which prevented their taking timely counsel together about the problems raised by the possibility of a European war. Bethmann, Moltke, Tirpitz each went his own way without seeking contact with the others until noon on 30 July when Moltke declared that the fate of Germany would be irreparably jeopardized if his opinion was not heeded.[2]

The Chancellor yielded, but after the die was cast the discussion on the question of French neutrality, hopes of which had been raised by Grey, and on whether or not it was necessary to send declarations of war brought to light a difference of opinion which, if it had been known before the dispatch of the ultimatum to Russia, would have prevented the taking of this fatal step. But coming to light after things had gone too far it brought about that moral and nervous collapse of the Kaiser, the Chancellor and Moltke which is copiously displayed in the Kaiser's marginalia and in the memoirs of Tirpitz, Falkenhayn and Moltke, and had an adverse influence on the course of operations. Moltke was visibly not master of himself when he telegraphed to Conrad: 'Will Austria leave her [Germany] in the lurch?'[3]

Foerster writes of Moltke:

His nature inclined to introspection (*Grübeln*) and was not inaccessible to attacks of pessimism. . . . Severe struggles in the days immediately before and during the outbreak of war had shaken the equilibrium of his sensitive soul. . . . Moltke emerged from these struggles in the end as victor. But their after-effects had not been completely effaced when operations began.[4]

---

[1] Tirpitz, *Dokumente*, II, pp. 25-6.   [2] See pp. 7-13.
[3] See p. 47.   [4] Foerster, pp. 27-8.

These were the men whom the world regarded with awe and reverence, reverence for them personally and for their main instrument, the German army, the perfect expression of the incomparable German genius for organization unbeaten in all fields of human activity. The world did not perceive that the marvelous machine that Germany was, was in the hands of men who were unequal to their task. Sovereign, Chancellor, Chief of Staff were launching the country on a hazardous, all but desperate venture, the two former well knowing, the third not realizing, what the consequences would be if Italy and Romania were to refuse their co-operation, England were to aid the enemy with her navy and her small but dauntless army, and Belgium were to offer resistance. Nor can Tirpitz be absolved of all responsibility however much more clearly than the others he saw the danger. To his action more than to anyone else's was due the 'encirclement' in which Germany found herself caught at the outbreak of the war. Creator of a fine navy, which performed prodigies in the battle of Jutland, Tirpitz never comprehended, never wanted to comprehend, that by refusing all understanding with the Power which could not yield up the command of the seas without imperiling its very existence, he was preparing the most calamitous end for his navy in his country's defeat. He was to live long enough to see this come to pass.[1]

The most unrivalled qualities of discipline and organization are not in themselves sufficient to assure the welfare of a great and powerful nation. It is undeniable that in 1914 neither the Kaiser nor his Chancellor wanted a European war, any more than it was wanted by Berchtold, Sazonov and Grey. All of them would willingly have continued to

---

[1] Tirpitz's efforts at self-defense and his Anglophobia involve him in much self contra-diction. Perceiving that his vast plans of naval construction and his opposition to any agreement on the pace of construction had driven England towards France and Russia, he exculpates himself, as we have seen (see pp. 187-9), by maintaining that England had let the right moment slip for defeating the German navy which had passed the 'danger zone'. England, in fact, showed every consideration for Germany and made colonial concessions which by the irony of fate were sent by Lichnowsky to Berlin for signature on the very day war was declared. Two more years of peace and Germany would have had nothing more to fear. These two years she might have had—since, as Tirpitz writes, it was untrue 'that in view of the enemy's malevolence the world war could not have been arrested', were it not that 'the fatal mediocrity of the men in office' gave the Triple *Entente* a reason for making war on Germany. 'So the old pirate State, England, has again succeeded in letting Europe tear herself to pieces' (Tirpitz, *My Memoirs*, I, p 287). More illogical than this it would be difficult to be. England had her faults, as has been shown. But if she had let the right moment slip for defeating the German navy, if 'the inclination for an understanding, which was rising in England in spite of everything, reposed . . on a sober estimate of the decreasing profitableness of a war' (Tirpitz, *My Memoirs,* I, p. 255), if war was avoidable provided the German statesmen refrained from provoking it or furnishing a pretext for it, it is self evident that it was not 'the old pirate State' which sought the European war. On the contrary it had allowed the German navy to attain proportions which would have rendered it unassailable had the German rulers not declared war on Russia and France and perpetrated the violation of Belgian neutrality which inevitably brought England into the arena.

negotiate for the peaceful solution of the conflict. It is a source of amazement to historians that notwithstanding this, the war did break out. There is no doubt that the mediocrity of all the personages just mentioned played an important part in bringing about the disaster. But if one seeks to specify how and why Germany—since it was she who set fire to the powder-cask—was led to this grievous action, one must draw the conclusion from what has been said above that she was led to it by the requirements of the Schlieffen plan, which no doubt was a masterpiece of military science, but also a monument of that utter lack of political horse-sense which is the main cause of European disorders and upheavals.

CHAPTER VI

ITALY'S ATTITUDE AFTER THE FIUGGI CONVERSATION. NEGOTIATIONS ON COMPENSATION

(1) *Italian inaction after the Fiuggi conversation (p. 254).* (2) *Avarna on 25 July promises a benevolent attitude on the part of Italy; Berchtold's satisfaction (p. 258).* (3) *How Italy supported the prolongation of the ultimatum to Serbia and the holding of an ambassadors' conference (p. 264).* (4) *The Consulta advises unconditional acceptance by Serbia of the Austrian Note (p. 266).* (5) *San Giuliano's proposal and the Serbian Chargé d'Affaires in Rome (p. 269).* (6) *Berchtold desirous of postponing the discussion of compensation to Italy; Merey opposed to all concessions (p. 271).* (7) *The Italian note on compensation (p. 276).* (8) *Italian silence on the demand for the Trentino; Tschirschky's views and activities (p. 279).* (9) *German pressure on Vienna to keep Italy in the Triple Alliance (p. 282).* (10) *The concession of compensation to Italy in the formula of 28 July (p. 286).* (11) *San Giuliano's disappointment; renewed pressure on Vienna from Berlin (p. 289).* (12) *Compensation conceded in the Tschirschky-Berchtold formula of 31 July and accepted by Avarna (p. 292).*

1. Italian inaction after the Fiuggi conversation.

Account has already been given of the Italian Government's first reaction on learning of the Austrian ultimatum to Serbia, and the instructions telegraphed to the Italian Ambassadors at Berlin and Vienna have been reproduced in the text given by Salandra in his book *La Neutralità Italiana* (1914).[1]

At that point the story of San Giuliano's action was broken off except for a mention of his belated proposal of 28 July to Grey for the settlement of the Austro-Serbian conflict.[2] Now it is time to examine with the aid of the Austrian and German official documents the action taken by Rome after 24 July, i.e., after the conversation which Salandra and San Giuliano had with the German Ambassador Flotow at Fiuggi, and to see how the Italian declaration of neutrality came about.

The telegram sent by San Giuliano to Avarna and Bollati pointed out that Austria had not the right to undertake an action such as the *démarche* at Belgrade without previous accord with her allies, that the tone and content of the note showed that she wished to provoke a war, and therefore

---

[1] See Vol. II, pp. 311-22.   [2] See Vol. II, pp. 417-24.

therefore in view of this behavior on the part of Austria and of the defensive and conservative character of the treaty of the Triple Alliance, Italy is under no obligation to go to the help of Austria in case that, as a result of this *démarche* of hers, she finds herself at war with Russia, since any European war in this case is the consequence of an act of provocation and aggression by Austria.[1]

However, although no obligation existed, the possibility was not entirely ruled out that it might be to the interest of Italy to take part in such a war. But in that case the country would need to have 'the certitude of an advantage commensurate to the risks and of a nature to surmount the opposition of public opinion to a war fought in the interest of Austria'. In any case the Italian Government desired to know whether its allies were in accord with its interpretation of Article VIII relative to Italy's right to compensation. Were this not the case,

we shall be compelled to follow a policy contrary to that of Austria in all Balkan questions except Albania on which special agreements exist between Italy and Austria . . . The Austrian communication does not for the time being require a reply and consequently we for the moment have no motive for making a pronouncement.[2]

It has already been noted how inept and misguided this policy was. The Italian Government ought to have made the most vigorous protest against Vienna's flagrant violation of the terms of Articles I and VII of the Triplice treaty. It should have frankly told its allies: 'Take good heed that Italy will never enter this war of aggression on your side. We, therefore, advise you not to provoke it and to accept the proposals which will be made for a friendly settlement of the dispute, failing which, not only shall we be unable to march at your side, but we shall be compelled to claim our clear and evident right to compensation on the basis of Article VII and exert ourselves to prevent the balance of power in the Balkans from being changed to our disadvantage.' Instead of this, what the Italian Government did say was that Italy was not obliged to intervene in a war brought about by Austria's action, but might do so if assured of adequate reward, whereas if she were not assured as to the interpretation of Article VII she would take action which would be in opposition to that of Austria. By saying in conclusion that 'the Austrian communication does not for the time being require a reply', the Italian Government backed out of using any pressure to save the peace of Europe—a pressure which should have taken the form of an immediate statement that in the event of war Italy would remain neutral. Italy thus exposed herself to the accusation of having deceived and betrayed her allies. The only way to avoid

---

[1] See Vol. II, pp. 314-15.   [2] See Vol. II, pp. 315-16.

this accusation would have been to warn Vienna in time, as had been done in July 1913,[1] and such a warning would have had great effect. To forsake the open high road and slink down devious byways in pursuit of the chimera of compensations was to be left in the end with empty hands and a tarnished reputation.

If San Giuliano had been capable of such perception, it would never have happened that between 24 July and 28 July, the day on which Austria declared war on Serbia, the Consulta took no steps to prevent a general war. Only in the evening of the 28th did San Giuliano request Rodd to submit to Grey his proposal for conciliation which has been already mentioned.[2] London did not receive it until the morning of the 29th after the Austrian declaration of war on Serbia when it had been overtaken by events and was therefore dropped. The proposal was never made directly to Italy's allies as should have been the case. San Giuliano refrained from so doing for fear of giving offence and thus prejudicing the success of his demand for compensations in return for any gains that Austria might make in Serbia. Moreover, how could he work for peace when he was promising Vienna diplomatic support if Austria accepted the Italian interpretation of Article VII? Pledged in this event to support the Austrian case, San Giuliano was bound to refrain from making difficulties for Berchtold or asking for a prolongation of the ultimatum to Serbia. He must either keep silence, as he did for four days, or, as he next did, propose to Serbia that she should accept the Austrian terms in full, subject to getting a pronouncement by the Powers on the harshest points. In order to be able to maintain silence he adopted a simple device. His duty should have been to be present at the Consulta during the days preceding the ultimatum, of whose dangerous nature he was fully aware. What he did was to stay at Fiuggi all through those days until the afternoon of the 27th, only going to Rome for a few hours in the afternoon of the 25th. Clearly he did so in order to avoid contact with the representatives of the Central Powers, especially the Austrian Ambassador, to whom he had no wish to 'make a pronouncement'. At Fiuggi there was the German Ambassador, and that sufficed him.

But while he was taking the waters events took a serious turn. Weak and inadequate as were his words to Flotow, they did at least contain something in the nature of a reservation. But the line taken by Bollati in Berlin and Avarna in Vienna departed so far from the terms in which San Giuliano's telegram summarized the Fiuggi conversation as to make it seem that Italy was in connivance with Austria. Bollati called at the Wilhelmstrasse on the 24th. An account of what he said is given in a telegram of 9.15 p. m. sent by Jagow to Tschirschky:

[1] See Vol. I, pp. 458-9.   [2] See Vol. II, p. 423.

Italian Ambassador has just informed me of his Government's standpoint: with reservation regarding maintenance of her freedom of action and her interests under Article VII of the Triplice treaty, Italy is prepared to adopt a very benevolent and friendly attitude towards Austria and create no difficulties for her. Italy is willing to pursue a harmonious policy with her allies over all Balkan questions; this would, however, only be possible if she received assurances about the interpretation of Article VII. Failing this, Italian policy would be obliged to aim at preventing any territorial aggrandizement of Austria-Hungary. Signor Bollati tells me that Austrian Ambassador in Rome says Austria-Hungary does not aim at territorial aggrandizement, but cannot bind herself on the point.

Solely for Your Excellency's personal information: Signor Bollati told me in strict confidence that in the event of Austrian acquisition of territory Italy would demand Trento in compensation and, if Austria took part of Albania, then Valona. The latter is not desired by Italy.

Article VII speaks of *région des Balkans;* Austrian interpretation that only Turkish territory is in question does not, therefore, seem to us to be applicable. Moreover, theoretical polemics over interpretation of treaty seem to me now out of place. Decisions are necessary which are consonant with the political situation. Will Your Excellency please express yourself in this sense.[1]

Be it noted in the first place that Bollati said nothing of the first statement in San Giuliano's telegram to him, which was of considerable moral and practical importance, namely, that Austria could not act as she was doing without coming to some agreement with Italy, and that the tone and content of her note showed that she wished to provoke a war. A telegram of the 25th from Szögyény to Berchtold reports that Bollati expressed surprise that the text of the ultimatum had not previously been communicated to the Italian Government. But this remark has neither the import nor the vigor of the phraseology in San Giuliano's telegram and Jagow met it with the barefaced lie that Germany had also been not informed in advance by Austria and that he

regarded this as the correct procedure since the present conflict is to be viewed as an affair between Austria-Hungary and Serbia.[2]

Now had Bollati followed the line taken by San Giuliano at Fiuggi, as indicated in the first statement of the telegram, he would have had to declare: (i) that if a general war were to result, the *casus foederis* would not arise, (ii) that this did not rule out the possibility of Italy's taking the field with her allies in return for adequate compensation. Nothing of this did Bollati say. He only talked of Italy's 'freedom of action' without explaining how this would be exercised, i.e., that, given satisfactory compensation, Italy would march at the side of the Central Powers. All

[1] DD. I, 150.   [2] Oe-U. VIII, 10655.

he said was: (i) that Italy was 'prepared to adopt a very benevolent and friendly attitude towards Austria and create no difficulties for her ... if she received assurances about the interpretation of Article VII. Failing this, Italian policy would be obliged to aim at preventing any territorial aggrandizement of Austria-Hungary'; (ii) any such territorial aggrandizement would have to be compensated with the Trentino, or, in certain conditions, Valona. Did San Giuliano mean compensated with the Trentino even if Italy took no part in the war? We do not know, and probably San Giuliano himself did not know either. But for Bollati to have raised the question with Jagow he must have received instructions the nature of which is not known.

2. Avarna on 25 July promises a benevolent attitude on the part of Italy; Berchtold's satisfaction.

Berlin, at all events, received an exact account of the Fiuggi conversation in Flotow's report.[1] Not so Vienna, because San Giuliano kept out of the way of Merey, who in any case was ill. Contact took place through Avarna, who held a language so pleasing to the ears of the Ballplatz officials that Berchtold lost no time in taking advantage of it for his own ends. Making his call, not on the 24th, as Bollati had done, but on the 25th, Avarna did not see Berchtold, who was on the way to Ischl, but spoke with Macchio. With the help of Dipauli and Musulin, who may have been present at the conversation, Macchio drew up the following report of it:

> The Italian Ambassador appeared here today and, in connection with the conflict between the Monarchy and Serbia, said that in the event of the conflict taking a warlike turn and leading to even only a provisional occupation of Serbian territory, the Royal Italian Government reserves to itself to claim the compensation due to it under Article VII of the Triplice treaty. On a basis of the article of the treaty just mentioned the Royal Italian Government is of the opinion that we must come to an agreement with it in the event of any occupation of Serbian territory. For the rest, in the event of an armed conflict between Austria-Hungary and Serbia the Royal Italian Government intends to adopt a friendly attitude consonant with the obligations of the alliance.[2]

The discrepancy between Avarna's words and those of Salandra and San Giuliano to Flotow is enormous. Not a word here of the first principle laid down at Fiuggi that any war resulting in such circumstances would not constitute the *casus foederis* for Italy. Italian diplomatic support for Austria was promised unconditionally without any proviso that Austria must recognize the Italian interpretation of Article VII. How is Avarna's radical departure from his Government's

---

[1] DD. I, 168. See Vol. II, pp. 316-17.   [2] Oe-U. VIII, 10680.

views to be accounted for? In the course of the following narration it will be shown that at this juncture Avarna's attitude was determined, not by the instructions he received, but by his personal conviction that Italy must stand shoulder to shoulder with her allies or at least raise no obstacle to their actions. Did he of his own initiative reverse the instructions given him? Or was the telegram published by Salandra followed by instructions from San Giuliano which caused the two Ambassadors to speak as they did? Proofs of this are lacking but it seems difficult to rule out the possibility, especially since the telegram as reproduced by Salandra only reported what had been said at Fiuggi and gave no instructions, whereas the situation demanded that exact instructions should be issued. One thing certain is that, after his angry outburst at Fiuggi on 24 July, San Giuliano, under the pressure of events, took a step backwards instead of the step forward of refusing in still more forcible terms to recognize the *casus foederis*. As long as he did not regard war as imminent he made little or no mention of the *casus foederis*, either to rule it out or to recognize it, and consequently he no longer made recognition of it conditional on an assurance of substantial compensation. It will be remembered that in his letter of 24 July to the King he wrote that it

is most difficult, perhaps impossible, and certainly extremely dangerous to drag Italy into taking part in an eventual war provoked by Austria and waged in the interest of Austria.

Not that he entirely ruled it out, but he spoke of it as

our eventual, but not probable participation in the war, a participation to be decided pro or contra freely when the time comes.[1]

To hold out to the Central Powers the prospect of obtaining Italian co-operation in exchange for solid advantages meant to run the risk that the acknowledgement of Italian claims to compensation would be made subject to Italian recognition of the *casus foederis*, which San Giuliano described as 'perhaps impossible'. Indeed, as will be shown, this is precisely what happened. Understandably if San Giuliano foresaw it he would be anxious to divert attention from the point, keep up the ambiguity, and leave his allies under the illusion that if they offered satisfaction under Article VII Italy would go the whole way with them. To this end Bollati and Avarna had to receive instructions as to their respective lines of approach. Bollati was to press strongly for compensations, specifying the Trentino in the event of an Austrian annexation of Serbian territory. Avarna was to be more guarded, make vague promises, give no offence, create a friendly atmosphere, and gather the fruits of the pressure from Berlin. This seems the only

[1] See Vol. II, p. 320.

possible explanation of the line taken on the one hand by Bollati and on the other by Avarna. San Giuliano himself, on learning what Avarna had said, took not the slightest steps to get the Ambassador's statements rectified or rendered more complete. And yet the effect produced by them was sensational.

On returning from Ischl and learning of what Avarna had said, Berchtold on 25 July at once telegraphed it to Merey, adding:

I have not yet found an opportunity of explaining our standpoint towards his declaration. As it is today still uncertain whether and to what extent we may find it necessary to carry out a temporary occupation of Serbian territory, any discussion of this topic would seem to me premature, and I shall endeavor to postpone it for the time being. Meanwhile will Your Excellency kindly take occasion to convey to Marquis San Giuliano that his announcement of a friendly attitude on the part of Italy corresponding to the obligations of the alliance has made a most agreeable impression on me.[1]

Berchtold instructed Szögyény to give Berlin the glad news and he circulated it to the other Austrian Ambassadors in Europe and to the Austrian Ministers in Greece, Bulgaria, Romania and Sweden.[2]

Already informed by Tschirschky, Jagow in his turn on 27 July passed on the unexpected Italian declaration to Lichnowsky for communication to the Foreign Office.[3] The impression was to be given everywhere that Italy consented to the conquest of Serbia.

San Giuliano, however, did not learn of Berchtold's satisfaction by official channels. Merey was ill and sent Ambrozy on the 27th to the Consulta to carry out the instruction,

and in order not to end with thanks which are in my opinion as yet un-deserved in view of the rather questionable attitude of the Italian Government on the subject of compensation, I instructed Ambrozy to add that Your Excellency reserved a discussion of the above question for a danger-free moment.[4]

If not through Merey, the Consulta and all Italy learnt of the jubilation in Vienna from a communiqué which Berchtold, with Avarna's permission, had published on 27 July by the semi-official agency, the *Korrespondenz-Büro:*

The Italian Government has made a declaration to the Austro-Hungarian Government that in the event of an armed conflict between Austria-Hungary and Serbia it will maintain a friendly attitude in conformity with the terms of the alliance. The *Wiener Zeitung* comments: This spontaneous declaration is a counterpart to the brilliant demonstration of the allied loyalty of the German Empire which has been enthusiastically welcomed by the entire

---

[1] Oe-U. VIII, 10746.
[2] Oe U. VIII, 10746, 10753.
[3] DD. I, 212, 272. See p. 281.
[4] Oe-U. VIII, 10911.

Monarchy and has been received in Vienna with an expression of satisfaction and gratitude as a response to the loyalty felt by Austria-Hungary. It cannot but awaken the liveliest echo in our whole population, strengthening and deepening the warm feelings for the allied Kingdom.[1]

In telegraphing this communiqué from Vienna the correspondent of the *Corriere della Sera* added:

Yesterday evening the burgomaster gave expression to these sentiments during a demonstration held in front of the town hall. Addressing the demonstrators the burgomaster, after a salute to the aged Emperor, extolled the Triple Alliance and revealed to the crowd the *démarche* made at Vienna by the Duke d'Avarna in affirmation of Italian fidelity to the alliance. The crowd broke out into enthusiastic cheers and cries of 'Long live Italy', 'Long live Victor Emmanuel!' Then with bared heads some demonstrators sang the Royal March and the Garibaldi hymn. Enthusiastic demonstrations also took place at Brünn in Moravia, where several thousand persons yesterday assembled in front of the Italian consulate shouting 'Long live Italy'.

Tschirschky sent the same news to Berlin, adding:

Count Stürgkh tells me in confidence that these demonstrations in favor of Italy have been organized by him. In this connection I inquired of him whether he was considering the idea of doing Italy a favor in the field of domestic politics. Count Stürgkh said he was studying ways and means of making the Italian university a reality as soon as possible.[2]

What deduction can be drawn from this episode? Certainly it raises the question why, if Avarna was not instructed to say what he did, San Giuliano, on learning how his ideas were misunderstood in Vienna and how Italy was seeming to be the accomplice of Austria in the impending aggression on Serbia, did not at once telegraph Avarna for explanations and insist on a rectification in regard to the position of the Italian Government. In *La Neutralità Italiana* Salandra asserts that Italy told Vienna:

Until Berchtold accepts our and the German interpretation of Article VII no *de facto* Triple Alliance will exist on Balkan questions, because we shall have to pursue a policy conforming to that of all the Powers who, like ourselves, have an interest in preventing any territorial aggrandizement of Austria.[3]

The words given as a quotation are placed in quotation marks in Salandra's text, which means that they reproduce a document not known to us. We shall see that something of this kind was said to Flotow by San Giuliano on 26 July,[4] but it was not said to Merey

---

[1] Schulthess, *Geschichtskalender* 1914, Part II, p. 718.
[3] Salandra, pp. 99-100.
[2] DD. II, 302.
[4] DD. I, 211. See p. 283.

nor at Vienna by Avarna. Not only did the latter do nothing to rectify his statement of 25 July but on the 27th he gave consent by implication to the military action of the Monarchy even before the Austrian declaration of war on Serbia, by asking the English Ambassador, Bunsen, if he thought the following might be usefully proposed:

Austria to repeat to Powers in form of positive engagement promise already made to Russia to the effect that she desires neither to annex any territory nor to crush Serbia nor to deprive her of her independence, but merely to obtain guarantees for future.[1]

And to Berchtold on 28 July he said

that the Royal Italian Government in the event of a passage of arms between Austria-Hungary and Serbia would adopt a friendly attitude in accordance with the obligations of the alliance.[2]

Nor is this all. There is a further significant fact which must be noted. Those days offered San Giuliano another opportunity to restate his original standpoint and he failed to take it. On 25 July Bethmann Hollweg received a letter from Waldburg, the German Chargé d'Affaires in Romania, written on the 20th reporting an animated conversation between himself and the Italian Minister at Bucharest, Fasciotti.

He expressed the view that it would be no good for anyone to have a war which might degenerate into a world war. It was understandable that in the event Austria should demand satisfaction from Belgrade but it must be of such a nature that Serbia could accept it. If warlike complications broke out between Austria and Serbia, Russia would not be able to look on passively. ... Italy for the time being was not financially in a position to go to war.[3]

Fasciotti saw things clearly and spoke to the point, even if he did not mention that Italian intervention was impossible for political even more than for financial reasons. But he must have made this opinion known to Romanian political circles, for on the evening of the 26th Jagow telegraphed to Flotow in Rome:

As Your Excellency knows, Romania is willing to honor her engagements. As the Romanian Minister tells me in confidence, M. Bratianu alone is again and again made to waver somewhat by the language of the Italian Minister, who says that Italy cannot join in the conflict and cannot at present wage war at all. It would be desirable that Marquis San Giuliano should instruct the Minister [Fasciotti] how to behave.[4]

What San Giuliano ought to have said to Flotow when he raised the question was that Fasciotti, in speaking thus, was giving a personal opinion, but that he, San Giuliano, had made it

---

[1] BD. XI, 175.   [2] Oe-U. VIII, 10909, See p. 287.
[3] DD. I, 177.   [4] DD. I, 227.

quite clear that, if war broke out, Italy did not feel bound to intervene. Instead of this Flotow telegraphed back from Rome on 27 July:

> Marquis San Giuliano has instructed Minister, Bucharest: (i) to request Romanian Government to recommend compliance in Belgrade, (ii) to state to Romanian Government that it was to the interest both of Italy and of Romania that Serbia should not be completely crushed. If Minister [Fasciotti] had added: 'Italy cannot join in the conflict, etc' he had exceeded his instructions and he [San Giuliano] would call him to order.[1]

By thus disavowing Fasciotti, San Giuliano was creating a grave misunderstanding. What value had the reservations made at Fiuggi and reiterated in the telegram reproduced by Salandra if they were thus to be thrown overboard?

For these reasons one is led to the belief that Avarna acted in accordance with instructions of a very different tenor from those contained in the telegram reporting the statements made to Flotow at Fiuggi on 24 July. This belief receives support from Jagow's telegram to Tschirschky of 27 July:

> Marquis San Giuliano much concerned because Count Berchtold expressed satisfaction at Duke Avarna's declaration of benevolent attitude on part of Italy while saying nothing of Article VII and compensations. Italian Ambassador acquainted me of content of a communication in which Marquis San Giuliano makes discussion of Article VII and compensation (at least in principle) a preliminary condition for the attitude of Italy.[2]

This telegram proves that San Giuliano had placed his hopes on Avarna's declaration and makes one think it was made on his instructions, even though on 27 July Rodd wrote:

> Telegrams from Vienna to press here stating Austria is favorably impressed with declarations of Italian Government had no foundation.[3]

Merey comments from Rome on the 28th:

> It is symptomatic that the news of the Italian assurances of friendship for the alliance has reached the Italian press only from Vienna, whereas they have been withheld from the papers by the Consulta.[4]

San Giuliano thought it necessary to say one thing at Vienna, another at Berlin, and yet another at London and Paris, and he was afraid of

---

[1] DD. I, 261.   [2] DD. I, 269.

[3] BD. XI, 202. On the same day Barrère reported to Paris: 'Marquis San Giuliano returned this evening to Rome and I saw him immediately. He severely criticized the contents of the Austrian note and formally assured me he had no previous knowledge of it. . . . I asked him if he had (as certain newspapers assert) authorized an expression at Vienna of approval of the Austrian action and of assurance that Italy would discharge her obligations as an ally of Austria.' 'In no way', replied the Minister. 'We were not consulted, we were told nothing. We therefore had no reason to make a communication of that nature to Vienna.' (DF. 3. XI, 159.)

[4] Oe-U. VIII, 10912.

uncovering his game to the Italian press, especially to the anti-Austrian section of it. However the case may be, even if Avarna to some extent acted on his own initiative, it is certain that San Giuliano did not object. His attitude was one of passivity, if not of acquiescence towards the Austrian ultimatum which placed the peace of Europe in jeopardy and was a threat to Italian interests. And it was this attitude which prevented him from taking an effective part in the endeavors that were being made to arrive at a peaceful issue.

3. How Italy supported the prolongation of the ultimatum to Serbia and the holding of an ambassadors' conference.

Salandra writes that with San Giuliano he discussed the line to be taken by Italy in the crisis, the first resolution upon which they agreed being 'to associate ourselves in word and deed with all endeavors to avert a general conflagration'. Accordingly: 'We gave our support to the Russian request that the term of the ultimatum might be extended. . . . We at once actively associated ourselves with Grey's unsuccessful efforts to devise a diplomatic settlement of the approaching conflict. Indeed, we suggested modifications of the proposals put forward for a conference and mediation.'[1]

But things were not as Salandra here describes them, as we shall now proceed to see.

It must first be said that on 23 July Strandtmann, the Russian Chargé d'Affaires at Belgrade, had telegraphed Sazonov asking

whether it is not possible to persuade the King of Italy, the Crown Prince's uncle, to intervene.[2]

On the 24th Strandtmann had reported:

The Council of Ministers has resolved the dispatch of a telegram from the Crown Prince to the King of Italy with the request to exercise influence on Vienna for prolongation of ultimatum and softening of its terms.[3]

The text of this note and that of the Italian reply are not known, but a telegram from Flotow at Fiuggi of 26 July says that the Crown Prince 'has received only a polite, evasive reply'.[4] We do, however, know what happened to Sazonov's request for postponement, made on the evening of the 24th and circulated to the Powers for their support. Krupensky, the Russian Ambassador at Rome, received the relevant instructions on the morning of the 25th and wrote to Sazonov in reply:

Three-quarters of the time-limit were over and only a few hours remained before its expiry when I hastened to the Prime Minister (Marquis San Giuliano was not in Rome) with whom I also met the Secretary General of

---

[1] Salandra, pp. 82, 95.   [2] *Int. Bez.* i. V, 75.
[3] *Int. Bez.* i- V, 36.   [4] DD. I, 220.

the Foreign Ministry. Signor Salandra . . . told me he would at once telegraph to Fiuggi to obtain San Giuliano's opinion on the *démarche* at Vienna proposed by you, but feared that he would not be able to give me an answer before 6 p. m., i.e.,, until after the expiry of the time-limit accorded to Serbia (I saw him at 11 a. m.). . . . At 6 p. m. Marquis San Giuliano arrived in Rome. . . . He had already talked with the Prime Minister and told me that he had already at 1 p. m. telegraphed the Italian Ambassador in Vienna instructions to ask Count Berchtold for an extension of the time-limit for the ultimatum if he had the slightest hope of the success of such a step. If not, San Giuliano would regard the step as on the whole harmful, annoying Austria needlessly. . . . Marquis San Giuliano confided to me that a few days ago he received a telegram from Marquis Carlotti in which the latter expressed the opinion that in the event of an Austro-Serbian war Russia could not do otherwise than intervene. 'With the idea of serving the cause of peace and calming the zeal of Austria I immediately sent on this telegram to Berlin and Vienna, where a different opinion prevails.'[1]

The German and Austrian documents reveal no trace of cognizance of Carlotti's telegram, nor of Avarna's having asked for an extension of the time-limit, and, it must be admitted, on the 25th it was already too late to ask for it. Austria had allowed Serbia only forty-eight hours in which to accept her demands precisely in order that the Powers should not have time to intervene. But this does not alter the fact that San Giuliano's answer that Italy would support the Russian request if there were any hope of its success was tantamount to a *fin de non recevoir*. For pressure to have any effect, it would have to be applied by each one of the Powers. Italy especially, if she meant to exercise a decisive influence, must not shrink either from expressing disapproval of such an ultimatum, dispatched without her knowledge, or from causing annoyance to her ally.

Much the same reception was given to the proposal of an ambassadors' conference to be held in London, formulated by Grey on 26 July after Austria had broken off diplomatic relations with Serbia.[2] It arrived on the evening of the 26th when San Giuliano was at Fiuggi, but Rodd was able to telegraph the Italian reply at 10.6 p. m. the same evening, having perhaps received it by telephone. It was to the effect that Italy welcomed the proposal but thought

it would be prudent that Italy in her position as an ally should refer to Berlin and Vienna before undertaking formally to request the latter to suspend all action.[3]

Here, too, the reservation neutralized the effect of the acceptance in principle. How could the conference ever operate if war were to begin? Moreover, in view of the fact that the attack on Serbia was an

---

[1] *Int. Bez.* i. V, 95.   [2] BD. XI, 140. See Vol. II, p. 392.
[3] BD. XI, 154. See Vol. II, p. 395.

open violation of Article VII of the Triplice treaty, which bound Austria-Hungary and Italy not to proceed to any occupation of the Balkans, whether temporary or permanent, without previous agreement, was San Giuliano right in making his consent to a peaceful method of settling the conflict, such as was the conference proposed by Grey, conditional on the approval of an ally who had failed to carry out her treaty obligations? How little San Giuliano was acting in good faith towards Grey is revealed in Flotow's account of his talk with the Italian Foreign Minister on 26 July:

In reference to Sir E. Grey's proposal for mediation if there were danger of a conflict between Russia and Austria, Marquis San Giuliano said to me that one must be careful not to reject brusquely any of Sir Ed. Grey's proposals for mediation. With his character that would dishearten him and drive him into the other camp, whereas his co-operation is now precious.[1]

Thus it is clear that when Salandra maintains that Italy also joined in asking for an extension of the ultimatum and approved of the English proposal for a conference, either his memory served him badly or he had never really known what took place. The same inference is to be drawn from a note in which he states that the American historian Barnes had commended 'the Italian proposal made on 27 July for a conference of the Powers as the most concrete one made in the course of the crisis'.[2] The idea of reviving the Powers' conference in London emanated, not from Italy, but from England.

4. *The Consulta advises unconditional acceptance by Serbia of the Austrian Note*

What San Giuliano did propose and what earned the commendation of Barnes was something quite different and it is strange that Salandra says nothing of it. Is he, peradventure, anxious to cover up the fact that the Italian proposal for saving the peace was that Serbia should submit to the Austrian ultimatum and accept all its terms? The idea may have originated with De Martino, the Secretary General to the Consulta, who first gave a hint of it to Rodd in the forenoon of the 25th:

He [De Martino] is of opinion that Austria-Hungary will only be restrained by unconditional acceptance of note by Serbia, occupation of Serbian territory is contempted.[3]

San Giuliano immediately took up the suggestion. During the few hours spent in Rome in the afternoon of 25 July he saw not only Krupensky but also the Serbian Chargé d'Affaires. Krupensky's telegram of 26 July reports:

Besides me the Foreign Minister received the Serbian Chargé d'Affaires

---

[1] DD I, 225.   2 Salandra, p. 96.
[3] BD. XI, 113. See Vol. II, p. 417.

and asked him to telegraph his friendly advice to Belgrade to yield to the Austrian demands in spite of all their monstrousness. In his opinion Austria would only win a shadow victory thereby; in practice on many points an agreement could be arrived at.[1]

It is obvious that this advice was in keeping with the ideas and temperament of San Giuliano, who was unwilling to displease Vienna. By advising Serbia to yield unconditionally he was giving support to the Austrian demands. On the other hand, if Belgrade had accepted his advice, there would have been no war and wiser counsels might have prevailed. But if this expedient had some sense before Serbia returned her reply to the Austrian note on the evening of the 25th, it was inapplicable to the situation created by that reply, which, by not accepting the note unconditionally, led first to the rupture of diplomatic relations between the two countries and then to the declaration of war. In any case, not a minute should have been lost in making the proposal. But San Giuliano on the 25th failed to do this. He returned to Fiuggi the same evening when the time-limit had expired and the crisis was mounting to an intensity which was reflected in the telegrams from St. Petersburg. About midnight on the 25th Carlotti telegraphed to the Consulta that Paléologue had said to him

that the Council of Ministers this forenoon has taken decisions on the necessary directives and measures to be put into force in the war against Austria and Germany, now regarded as imminent. He added that France was ready to fulfill her duty as an ally to the full. . . . Paléologue ended with the remark that the only gleam of hope left comes from London and Rome, where perhaps an effort is being made to use their great influence in Berlin in order to make an attempt at mediation for the preservation of peace.[2]

Paléologue was not mistaken. As things then were the only sound policy was for London and Rome to try to frustrate the Austrian plan of aggression. And the right moment to do so was when Serbia, by returning a reply which sounded satisfactory not only to London but also to Berlin, provided an opening for the exercise of pressure on Vienna not to start a war which could not remain localized and would therefore involve the allies on both sides, one of whom, not having been consulted in advance, would refuse to recognize the *casus foederis*. Such a *démarche,* made at that juncture, would have reached Berlin on 26 July when Moltke was telling Bethmann he regarded it as

urgently necessary that Italy should be kept firmly with the Triple Alliance,[3]

when on the 27th Bethmann began to have doubts about England, and when on the 28th the Kaiser began to realize that all reason for war was

[1] *Int. Bez.* i. V, 95.
[2] KSF., May 1924, p. 164. See Vol. II, p. 308.
[3] DD. I, 202. See Vol. II, p. 427.

vanishing and proposed the *Halt in Belgrade.* The *démarche* would, therefore, have had a decisive effect. But to make it and thus block the way for Austria, San Giuliano would have had to be fully conscious of the great influence which the Italian attitude would exercise on the decisions of the Central Powers, would have had to be determined to use it and speak his mind boldly without fear of their wrath. This, at bottom, was what Sazonov was urging the Italian Government to do when he telegraphed to Krupensky on the 26th:

We are of the opinion that Italy could play an outstanding part in the preservation of peace if she would exercise suitable influence on Austria and adopt a definitely disapproving attitude towards the conflict, since this cannot remain localized. It would be desirable that you should give it as an opinion of your own that it will be impossible for Russia to refrain from going to the help of Serbia.[1]

Krupensky carried out these instructions in the afternoon of the 27th as soon as San Giuliano at last left Fiuggi and returned to his room at the Consulta, which during those days he ought never to have left. San Giuliano's reply to the message from Sazonov runs:

'Since the beginning of the crisis we have endeavored to bring about a peaceful solution, so far without success. We shall continue to do all in our power to attain our object but I think our zealous effort would be easier if we did not stand alone in our endeavor. England is inclined to associate herself with us and we are exchanging views on the subject. But I am firmly convinced that whatever one may think of the form and substance of the Austrian ultimatum and the Serbian reply, the Vienna Cabinet will not alter a line of its note, and that, if a solution were successfully brought about, it could only be on the basis of integral acceptance by Serbia of the Austrian note. . . . Marquis San Giuliano thinks that if before the delivery of the note Austria had consulted Germany, she would probably have been advised to soften it. But now, even if contrary to expectation the Vienna Cabinet should approach the Berlin Cabinet, the latter would advise against any change in the note because the lowering of Austrian prestige which this would entail would be contrary to the views of Germany.' Upon my [Krupensky] remarking that Russia could not do otherwise than come to the help of Serbia, Marquis San Giuliano, who shared my opinion, said . . . that you [Sazonov] had said that Russia would take up arms on behalf of Serbia if Austria had intentions of making conquests, which, according to the positive assurance of the Vienna Cabinet, she has not. . . .

P.S. Upon my remarking . . . that several of the Austrian demands were impossible of fulfillment even if Serbia were willing, and could therefore not be accepted, Marquis San Giuliano answered: *'Mais qu'est-ce que cela fait qu'ils acceptent, quitte à ne pas remplir ce qu'ils on accepté.'*[2]

---

[1] *Int. Bez,* i, V, 84.   [2] *Int.* Bez. i, V, 131.   I

Did San Giuliano really believe that Austria had sent such an ultimatum without Berlin's consent? And who could ever have told him that Russia would go to war only if Austria took away territory from Serbia, since that would have meant waiting till the Austro-Serbian war was over? And how could he say so when, as has just been narrated, he himself two days earlier had told Krupensky that Carlotti had telegraphed that Russia would not fail to intervene in an Austro-Serbian war! There is no evidence that Carlotti ever conveyed such an illusion to the Consulta. On the contrary, San Giuliano on the 29th deplored with Barrère that Berlin, according to a message from Bollati, was counting on Russia's not moving.[1] Most likely San Giuliano spoke to Krupensky as he did in order to evade taking any action, seeking cover behind his convenient formula of the 25th: *qu'est-ce que cela fait qu'ils acceptent, quitte à ne pas remplir ce qu'ils ont accepté.*

5. San Giuliano's proposal and the Serbian Chargé d'Affaires in Rome.

This formula owed something to the Serbian Chargé d'Affaires in Rome, Mihailović.

The following message telephoned from Rome in the night of 26 July appeared in the *Corriere della Sera* of 27 July:

> We are in a position to communicate the following last-minute news for the accuracy of which we can vouch:
> Count Ambrozy, First Counsellor of the Austro-Hungarian Embassy, states that the present situation is to be regarded not as a state of war but as the beginning of preparations for war.
> M. Mihailović, the Serbian Chargé d'Affaires, declares that the present situation must be regarded as a simple rupture of diplomatic relations. He further states that Serbia would be ready to submit in principle to the Austrian demands, but only at a conference of all the Powers.

There followed the announcement of the English proposal and of Italian support subject 'to acceptance by the German Government'. Obviously the Milan paper had received this hand-out from the Consulta, where optimism reigned. But the correspondent had also questioned the Serbian Chargé d'Affaires, who had said that 'he had no further news than that given by the press'. In other words, he did not know—had probably not been told—what reply his Government had returned to the Austrian note. Then by whom was he authorized to say that Serbia would submit to its demands at a conference of all the Powers? By no one. What he expressed was a purely personal opinion devoid of any basis, as is proved by the documents. But his opinion enabled San Giuliano on the morning of the 27th before returning to Rome to say to Flotow that he still had some hope that the conflict would be avoided.

[1] DF. 3. XI, 280; LJF. 96; CDD., p. 207.

According to his information—he gives no particulars—Serbia would be prepared to accept the Austrian demands if they were presented by Europe. On the other hand, Russia would only intervene if Austria permanently occupied Serbian territory.[1]

Neither statement had any truth in it, but on arriving in Rome in the course of the 27th San Giuliano, besides speaking with Krupensky on the lines we have already noted, told Rodd that

he greatly doubts whether Germany will be willing to invite Austria to suspend military action pending conference, but had hope that military action may be practically deferred by fact of conference meeting at once. He does not, as at present informed, see any possibility of Austria receding from any point laid down in note to Serbia, but believes that if Serbia will even now accept it Austria will be satisfied and, if she had reason to think such will be advice of Powers, Austria may defer action. Serbia may be induced to accept note in its integrity on advice of four Powers invited to conference. This would save her face in allowing her to think she had yielded to Europe and not to Austria alone. This is also view of Serbian agent here, provided some explanation could be given as to how points 5 and 6 of conditions would be applied.[2]

This last sentence implies that Mihailović was expressing a purely personal opinion, and that on his own responsibility he laid down a condition which had not been formulated by San Giuliano and which would tone down the effect of an unconditional acceptance. It remains to be seen whether Mihailović arrived at his opinion entirely by himself or whether he was talked into it by the Consulta. The fact that the formula was roughly sketched out by De Martino on the 25th and sent on the 25th to Belgrade as a piece of advice from San Giuliano, no less than the expressions used by San Giuliano in speaking with Rodd, gives the impression that the idea originated with the Consulta and that Mihailović was asked to approve of it and did so, save for the reservation noted above. It is, however, curious that in spite of Mihailović's approval San Giuliano did not on the 27th propose a settlement of the conflict on the suggested lines but waited until the afternoon of the 28th, when—although he did not know it—Austria had declared war on Serbia, before making his proposal in a negative form and with the negative results which were described in Volume II of the present work.[3] It is symptomatic of San Giuliano's state of mind that on the 28th he made the proposal not to all the Powers but only to England, obviously not venturing to approach Berlin and Vienna with it.

Unacceptable to Serbia and Russia, finding scant favor with Austria, who was now bent on war, belated and put forward only by London, the proposal was dropped and had no influence on the course of events.

---

[1] DD. I, 249.   [2] BD. XI, 202.   [3] See Vol. II, pp. 417-24.

Nor did it deserve a better fate, designed as it was not to offend Vienna or frustrate the Austrian designs. It may even be doubted whether San Giuliano ever seriously expected that it could save the situation and whether he did not take it up simply in order not to appear indifferent to all attempts to preserve the peace. One thing certain is that in the days preceding the outbreak of war San Giuliano was less concerned with preserving peace than with securing compensations, and it was this latter preoccupation combined with the strong dose of veneration and trepidation in his attitude towards the Central Powers, which held him back from frankly opposing the Austrian scheme, dissociating himself from its consequences and thus acting as a powerful deterrent which might well have averted the whole tragedy.

And yet a warning not to lay himself open to misunderstanding was given San Giuliano by one whose long experience in the conduct of Italian foreign policy invested him with signal authority to impart advice. Save for a five-month interval Tittoni had been head of the Consulta from the end of 1903 to the end of 1909 and was now Ambassador in Paris. He was on a cruise in the North Sea when, on learning of the international crisis, he wirelessed to San Giuliano:

> I am of the opinion that in common honesty we ought to lose no time in telling Vienna and Berlin that the ultimatum to Belgrade, prepared without previous diplomatic negotiations and without our knowledge, constitutes a provocation to war on the part of Austria and rules out the agreements under the Triple Alliance even in the event of Russia's joining in the war. This had better be said at once than later under the pressure of Italian public opinion.

In reproducing this wireless message, Salandra comments that Tittoni 'had a true perception right from the first'.[1] Indeed he had! He at once realized that, as has been said, Italian public opinion would irresistibly prevent the Government from involving the country in war on the side of the Central Powers and that in common honesty this ought at once to be made clear to them. Salandra goes on to say: 'The reader knows that this is what we did say to Vienna and Berlin as early as the 24th.' Alas, this is the opposite of the truth, as has already been shown and as will emerge still more clearly in what will now be narrated.

6. Berchtold desirous of postponing the discussion of compensation to Italy; Merey opposed to all concessions.

It has already been said that as early as 15 July Jagow had telegraphed to Tschirschky instructions to draw Vienna's attention to the need of discussions with Italy on the compensations to which she was undoubtedly entitled:

[1] Salandra, p. 143.

In strict confidence, the only compensation regarded as adequate in Italy would be the acquisition of the Trentino.[1]

Without venturing to name the Trentino, Tschirschky had brought up the question on 20 July in conversation with Berchtold, who had rejected out of hand the idea of any right of Italy to compensation and had telegraphed in this sense to Merey and Szögyény. These two Ambassadors were instructed to take the line that, since Austria did not aim at territorial acquisitions in Serbia, a purely temporary occupation of Serbian territory could not furnish grounds for compensation to Italy, especially in view of the fact that Article VII of the Triple Alliance Treaty in speaking of the *status quo* 'in the regions of the Balkans or of the Ottoman coasts and islands in the Adriatic and in the Aegean Sea' referred only to regions in Turkish possession. When it came to the point, however, Merey on instructions from Berchtold refrained from giving San Giuliano on 21 July any pledge of territorial *désintéressement* on the part of Austria in a possible war against Serbia.[2]

After the presentation of the Austrian note, as we have seen, Avarna had told Macchio on the 25th that the Italian Government reserved the right to claim compensation under Article VII of the Triplice Treaty but that

in the event of an armed conflict between Austria-Hungary and Serbia, the Royal Italian Government intends to adopt a friendly attitude consonant with the obligations of the alliance.[3]

On his return from Ischl on 26 July after the rupture of Austro-Serbian relations, Berchtold sent this news to Szögyény with instructions to say to Berlin that he had not yet had the chance of clarifying the Austrian standpoint towards the Italian interpretation of Article VII:

In order to avoid fruitless discussions and undesirable disquisitions on the subject, we do not at present intend to raise this controversy. We will rather impress on the Italian Government that, as an occupation of Serbian territory by us is not contemplated—temporary war operations cannot of course be regarded as occupation, even as provisional occupation—the question of compensation even from the Italian point of view is not relevant for the moment. . . . Any discussion on the subject would seem to be premature and I shall endeavor to postpone it.[4]

In his parallel message to Merey in Rome Berchtold wrote in similar terms, adding, however:

[1] See Vol. II, pp. 229-30.
[2] See Vol. II, pp. 238-9.
[3] Oe-U. VIII, 10680. See p. 258.
[4] Oe-U. VIII, 10746.

Will Your Excellency take occasion to convey to Marquis San Giuliano that his announcement of a friendly attitude on the part of Italy corresponding to the obligations of the alliance has made a most pleasant impression on me.[1]

But as has already been related, Merey on the 27th was ill in bed and sent Ambrozy to carry out the message. In the reply to Berchtold, which went off at 1.30 a. m. on the 28th, Merey wrote:

In order not to end with thanks which are in my opinion as yet undeserved in view of the rather questionable attitude of the Italian Government on the subject of compensation, I instructed Ambrozy to add that Your Excellency reserved a discussion of the above question for a danger-free moment. Minister for Foreign Affairs to whom Ambrozy gave his message was very taken up with business and asked for the communication to be repeated to one of his secretaries, who noted it down. He then sent word to Ambrozy that he would reply tomorrow.[2]

The 'questionable attitude of the Italian Government on the subject of compensation' had become apparent to Merey when on the 25th he received a call, not from San Giuliano, who wanted to keep away from him, but from San Giuliano's secretary, Biancheri, who inquired after Merey's health and proceeded to give him the Italian Government's views about the conflict with Serbia, views which Avarna had not ventured to express to Vienna.

My interlocutor, who was obviously expressing the ideas of his chief, pointed to the tone of our note, unacceptable to any State, the fact that it was not previously communicated to the Cabinets, so that the latter are not bound by any engagements, and that it was subsequently communicated to them after all, giving them the chance to intervene, a fact incompatible with the thesis that it was purely a matter between ourselves and Serbia. Why this communication to the signatory Powers? Italy, who was neither consulted nor informed in advance, cannot be expected to unsheathe the sword for us in the further course of the conflict. If it resulted in a temporary or definitive occupation by us, Italy's claim to compensation would be beyond question.

How came it that a secretary was employed to make a statement of this importance and not the Italian Ambassador? Merey's report concludes:

I vigorously rebutted all these theses but found to my regret if not to my surprise that, as regards criticism of the form of our note and our omission to make preliminary communication of it and of compensation, Signor Biancheri claims identity of views theoretically between Rome and Berlin. I am convinced that Italy will put forward every possible proposal for mediation and compensation to bind us down. My view is that we should

---

[1] Oe-U. VIII, 10746. See p. 260.   [2] Oe-U. VIII, 10911. See p. 260.

reject them all, make no promises and let the Italian Government and press shout. The more resolute and unshakeable we are, the better effect it will have in Italy.[1]

After Ambrozy's call at the Consulta Merey sent a second telegram to Vienna at 1.30 a. m. on 28 July putting Berchtold on his guard against a too optimistic interpretation of Avarna's assurances of the 25th.

It is clear that they are primarily, if not exclusively, intended as a preliminary to claims for compensation, and the friendly, but vague and noncommittal phraseology was doubtless only a *captatio benevolentiae*. The rather enthusiastic reception given to it, coupled with avoidance of all discussion of the difficult subject, seems to me unwise, since the Italians may take it either as tacit acceptance or as an intimation that we do not reckon with a military conflict and hence regard compensation question as not applicable. . . . My *ceterum censeo* is to deny outright all claims to compensation and not to enter into awkward discussions or engagements. Otherwise we shall put Italy into the position of a man who says to his friend who has fallen into the Danube: 'I am not going to pull you out, And if you save yourself by your own exertions, you will have to give me compensation.'[2]

Can anyone imagine a greater contempt for the Triple Alliance or a grosser inability to understand its terms? Merey's Italophobia reveals itself still further in two letters, one official and another private, which he sent on the 29th to his friend, Berchtold. The official letter tells that when on the 21st he saw San Giuliano, who did not yet know of the ultimatum, and began to prepare his mind for what was afoot,

Marquis San Giuliano assumed the cautious, reserved, apprehensive attitude towards possible territorial acquisitions on the part of the Monarchy which I had anticipated.

After the ultimatum had become known:

The vehemence of form and content of our note to the Serbian Government and our determination up to the present to go to extremes, i.e., to provoke war with Serbia and shoulder the risk of a European conflagration, has caused consternation and amazement here. Nothing impresses the Italians more than cool determination and ruthless energy which calmly and imperturbably pursues its purpose regardless of danger. Moreover, the Italians particularly—and perhaps also the Romanians—will doubtless have shivered a little on reading our note. Such a severe procedure against an irredentist movement will make them see a certain analogy, even if on a different scale, and will lead them to examine their own guilty consciences. So if our determination is serious this time and we stick to our guns (*durchhalten*) this will have an extremely good future effect in Italy. Even a certain deterioration in our relations will be outweighed by the respect which we shall have inspired here.

[1] Oe-U. VIII, 10750.   [2] Oe-U. VIII, 10912.

But if, by complete submission on the part of Serbia before the opening of our military operations or even by our consenting to some kind of diplomatic intervention, whether from Russia or from Italy or from several Powers, a peaceful solution of the conflict were to be brought about . . . then the whole episode, as far as Italy is concerned, would end not only with a deterioration of relations but with a fresh decline in our prestige and authority. Already all along the line it is claimed that Italy was not notified in advance and therefore has a free hand. . . . In the event of our occupying foreign territory, temporarily or permanently, the traditional Italian gesture of the outstretched palm is in evidence. Faithful to tradition, Italy must be given something, make a profit which will be pure gain without return service or risk. On this point the Italian Government will be adamant and—as it seems—will regrettably have the support of the Berlin Cabinet. . . . As I regard any undertaking on our part ruling out territorial acquisition or agreeing to compensation as inadvisable and prejudicial, my feeling would be to confine ourselves to a standpoint of rigid negation, letting the Government and press in Italy scream or even threaten and refraining from entering into explanations. In my view no serious danger can result from this. The bad state of the army and finances, the frequent internal disturbances, the weakness of the present Government, the difficulties of Italy's position in Libya, the Dodecanese, and Asia Minor will, I think, limit the range of her action. . . . Italy will not leave the Triple Alliance, because, for one thing, three-quarters of the population would be absolutely against it. The worst that could happen would be an Italian action in Southern Albania. I am not at all of the opinion put forward by Germany that we should quietly allow this to happen. But I think that our position would then not be a bad one, because Italy by so doing would thoroughly put herself in the wrong.[1]

In the private letter, part of which we have looked at already,[2] Merey goes on to say:

As regards Italy, my opinion is that in the event of a European conflagration she will certainly honor her obligations under the alliance. The King and the German Government will make sure of this.[3] . . . With pettifogging legal arguments a case can of course be made out for the Italian standpoint. That is why I am in favor not of discussion but of outright, uncompromising rejection. . . . So let me once more entreat you: '*Landgraf, werde hart*' [Landgrave, get tough].[4]

Such is the estimate of Italy expressed by the obtuse and presumptuous Magyar who was the representative of the Dual

---

[1] Oe-U. VIII, 10989.   [2] See Vol. II, p. 383.
[3] In La *Neutralità Italiana* (p. 101), Salandra writes that Merey advocated at Vienna that 'no undertaking of any sort was to be given to Italy whose neutrality he foresaw in any case (and in this he was right)'. The above document proves that this was not so.
[4] Oe-U. VIII, 10991. The quotation is from a historical ballad '*Der Edelacker*' by W. Gerhard (*Gedichte,* II, p. 24) in which the blacksmith of Ruhla, angered by his Landgrave's mildness, shouts these words to the rhythm of his hammer.

Monarchy at Rome. But it must be confessed that in the feeble and subservient handling of the crisis by the Consulta there was nothing which could have undeceived him.

7. The Italian note on compensation.

When Merey penned the above words on 29 July, he had already received, on the 28th, San Giuliano's note of reply, written in French, to Ambrozy's *démarche.*

The Italian Government, animated by the friendliest feelings towards Austria-Hungary, has made and will continue to make every effort to persuade Serbia to accept the demands contained in the I. and R. Government's note of 24 July 1914 and has on several occasions advised her to pursue a correct policy of good neighborliness towards Austria-Hungary. The Italian Government has retained very good memories of the friendly attitude of Austria-Hungary towards Italy in the concluding period of the Italo-Turkish war. This war had as its object a province situated very far from the sphere of interests of Austria-Hungary, whereas the present conflict between. Austria-Hungary and Serbia is developing in territories in the vicinity of Italy and may have serious consequences for our vital interests. In effect one of the bases and *raisons d'être* of the Triple Alliance for us is Article VII, which applies to the whole Balkan peninsula and is completed by the 1909 agreement on the Sanjak of Novibazar, this agreement having been reaffirmed on the occasion of the renewal of the Triple Alliance. It is on the basis of Article VII and of the agreements on the Sanjak of Novibazar and on Albania that the cordial collaboration of Italian and Austro-Hungarian diplomacy must be founded, and without this basis it is to be feared that it will not be possible: it is on this basis that reciprocal friendship and confidence between the two allied Powers must rest. Germany participates in our interpretation of Article VII. As regards Count Berchtold's intention to discuss the theme of compensations *à un moment donné,* it is evident that agreement on this point is urgent, for so long as it has not been arrived at and doubt can subsist as to the interpretation given by Austria-Hungary to Article VII, Italy cannot pursue a policy such as would now or later facilitate occupations by Austria-Hungary, whether temporary or permanent, and must, on the contrary, favor whatever would lessen the probability of such occupations, while, however, endeavoring as far as possible to reconcile this line of conduct, imposed by the need for safeguarding her vital interests, with her keen desire to render more and more intimate the relations between the two allied Powers, which have made so much progress in recent years and may well make further progress on a basis of the harmony and conciliation of mutual relations for the good of both countries. We therefore hope that the friendly, sincere, and frank conversations which are at present taking place between the three allied Powers at Vienna and Berlin will lead as soon as possible to a result permitting of their collaboration in a common policy.[1]

[1] Oe-U. VIII, 10988.

If for the first time in this document San Giuliano ventures to say to Vienna that Italian diplomatic support depended on the already mentioned condition, nevertheless Italian interests were being sacrificed to so injurious an extent that the note makes painful reading. Here was Italy declaring her readiness in return for acceptance of her interpretation of Article VII 'now or later to facilitate occupations [of Serbian territory] by Austria-Hungary, whether temporary or permanent'. Let us leave aside for the moment the question whether the Trentino, then the goal aimed at, even with the addition of the Isonzo line, asked for later, would have indemnified Italy for the damage done to her by a further advance of Austria eastwards and above all by the gain to Austria in power, prestige, and aggressiveness accruing from the subjugation of Serbia. Let us further disregard the perils to which this 'blackmail', as it was termed, would expose Italy, once the Austro-Serbian issue was settled. Let us confine ourselves here to the matter of most immediate concern, namely, the duty incumbent on the Italian Government to aim above all things at preventing a war for which the country was unprepared and which would raise the disquieting problem of fidelity to the alliance. And what do we find? That by authorizing Austria under certain conditions to occupy Serbian territory temporarily or permanently, nay pledging himself 'to pursue a policy such as to facilitate' such occupation, San Giuliano was working, not for peace, but for war. As we have seen, nothing could prevent war if Austria so much as hinted at an intention to take possession of an inch of Serbian territory. Vienna realized this and promised territorial *désintéressement* to keep Russia quiet. Not so Rome. What Rome said is: 'Promise me compensation and I will help you to dismember Serbia for your own benefit, but if, on the other hand, you do not recognize my right to compensation I shall make all the difficulties for you in my power.' Never should such words and deeds have been possible at a moment like this when both Italy's paramount interest not to promote the Austrian march to Salonika and her own honor were at stake.

San Giuliano's behavior is the more incomprehensible as he cannot be thought to have been unaware of the harm which the crushing of Serbia would cause to Italy. We know from Salandra, that on 20 July he had sent word to Berlin to say:

We could not support the Austrian demands on Serbia if they ran counter to the principles of our liberal code of public law and might create a precedent also affecting ourselves. Further: it was to our interest that Serbia should not be crushed and that Austria-Hungary should not be enlarged.[1]

We have also noted a magnificent page in which Salandra himself declares that the overthrow of Serbia, with or without territorial loss,

---

[1] Salandra, pp. 71-2. See Vol. II, p. 240.

would be an unparalleled defeat for Italy.[1] Well then, if it was so much Italy's interest to prevent the violation of Serbia, why lend a hand to promoting it?

Nor is this all. Vienna was being asked to agree to an interpretation of Article VII without being given any indication of the compensations that were to be demanded. This meant that Italy would be pledging herself to lend support to the pernicious Austrian advance into the Balkans in exchange for a purely generic promise of unspecified indemnification. In his Campidoglio speech of 2 June 1915, Salandra maintains on the contrary:

> On 27 or 28 July we put in plain terms to Berlin and Vienna the question of ceding the Italian provinces of Austria and declared that, if we did not obtain adequate compensation (I repeat the actual wording), *The Triple Alliance would be shattered beyond repair.*

Salandra is misinformed. In a note appended to this speech when it was published in his volume *I discorsi della guerra* he stated that the documents and extracts quoted were given him by the Secretary General of the Foreign Ministry, Giacomo De Martino.[2] But in his later book, *La Neutralità italiana,* Salandra no longer claims that Vienna was threatened with a break-up of the alliance unless Italy received the Italian provinces of Austria. He repeats, however, that his Government on 27 July declared:

> The only possible territorial compensation for us is the cession of a part of the Italian provinces of Austria commensurate with her territorial aggrandizement elsewhere.[3]

Of the document mentioned in the Campidoglio speech there is no word here and its place is taken by this new version. Even it, however, has no foundation in fact and therefore Salandra does well to put on other shoulders the responsibility for such assertions. Neither on the 27th nor on the 28th or earlier were such statements made at Berlin or Vienna. At Berlin, as we have seen, Bollati said to Jagow on the 24th

in strict confidence that in the event of Austrian territorial acquisition Italy would demand Trento in compensation and, if Austria took part of Albania, then Valona.[4]

The proposal made no stir at Berlin, since Jagow himself had anticipated as early as 15 July that Italy would ask for the Trentino.[5] But the demand was not official, nor was it made to Vienna, nor was the

[1] Salandra, pp. 87-8. See Vol. II, pp. 320-1.
[2] Antonio Salandra, *I discorsi della guerra* (Milan, 1922), p. 59.
[3] Salandra, p. 100.
[4] DD. I, 150. See p. 259.
[5] DD. I, 46. See Vol. II, pp. 229-30

statement ever made that if Italy were denied the Trentino 'the Triple Alliance would be shattered beyond repair'. It was only on 3 August, as we shall see, that San Giuliano in a conversation with Merey, discussing the possibility of Italian intervention on the side of the Central Powers, ventured to mention the Trentino, ruling out the consideration of any other compensations. But Merey's answer was such that San Giuliano dared not insist, still less threaten to leave the Triple Alliance, an idea which never entered his head,[1]

8. Italian silence on the demand for the Trentino; Tschirschky's views and activities.

Why this trepidation about saying clearly what Italy wanted? There is but one reason and it has been explained above.[2] It was impossible to ask for the Trentino if Italy remained neutral, while San Giuliano did not want to promise intervention in a war. Indeed, in his telegram of 24 July to Bollati and Avarna he had implicitly, and in his letter to the King explicitly, laid down two categories of compensations, the one in return for intervention, the other 'doubtless very minor compensations, or at least guarantees that our interests shall not be damaged, in return for any diplomatic support given to our allies'.[3] This is further borne out by the fact that when on 3 August he mentioned the Trentino to Merey, he spoke of it as 'the only conceivable compensation' for 'the enormous sacrifices and dangers for Italy' arising from a war.[4] But if this reason explains, it does not excuse San Giuliano's lack of plain speaking. It does not lessen the monstrous fact that he was agreeing to facilitate the violation of Serbia in exchange for a compensation that remained undefined, assuming that any compensation could exist which would indemnify Italy for the indirect harm thus caused her.

No purpose was served by San Giuliano's failure to speak out. We have already seen how, under pressure from Berlin, Vienna received the Italian claims. When on the 24th Bollati explained the Italian attitude towards the Austrian ultimatum to Serbia, Jagow that same evening sent Tschirschky a telegram we have already noted, asking him to express German support for the Italian interpretation of Article VII. 'Decisions are necessary which are consonant with the political situation.'[5] On the 26th Tschirschky accordingly once more raised the question of compensation with Berchtold, who, as has been seen, had that same day telegraphed to Merey and Szögyény that 'any discussion of this topic would seem to me premature and I shall endeavor to postpone it for the time being'.[6]

[1] DA. III, 127.
[2] See pp. 257-8, 259-60,
[3] See Vol. II, pp. 315-16, 319.
[4] DA. III, 127, See p, 334.
[5] DD. I, 150. See pp. 256-7.
[6] Oe-U. VIII, 10746. See p. 260.

On this conversation there exists a lengthy memorandum of the 26th by Berchtold recording that after giving the substance of Bollati's talk with Jagow, Tschirschky had added that in respect of the interpretation of Article VII the German Government's view supported that of the Italian Government. Berchtold objected that when Italian troops occupied a number of Turkish islands in the Aegean during the Libyan War, Austria had raised no claim to compensation.

Furthermore, I expressed the view that at the present moment when we had no intention of occupying Serbian territory either temporarily or permanently—transitory military operations could not be classed as a temporary occupation—the question was not one for immediate discussion.[1]

That same day, in a long telegram to Merey and Szögyény, Berchtold enlarged on the topic of the Aegean islands in anticipation of a possible attempt on the part of Italy

to represent our attitude during the Libyan War as one that hindered Italian action and to exploit our reference at that time to Article VII for her own ends. . . . 'We refused express consent to acts from which we anticipated dangerous repercussions in the Balkans',

while raising no objection to the Italian occupation of the more southerly islands situated, properly speaking, in the Mediterranean.

Our friendly attitude in conformity with the alliance was acknowledged by Duke Avarna in a declaration of 5 July 1912 stating that his Government would seek to strengthen more and more the ties of friendship and alliance with the Monarchy.[2]

Berchtold was obviously speaking as if he had forgotten that an Austrian veto on military operations on the European mainland had prevented Italy from threatening Turkey in a vital spot and thus hastening the end of the Italo-Turkish war, while he was also feigning not to realize that Austria, now in 1914, was seeking radically to alter the whole balance of power in the Balkans to her own advantage, his purpose being to deny the right of the Italian Government to invoke Article VII, which had been purposely formulated in such a manner as to preserve that balance to the benefit of both partners in the alliance. Berchtold was perfectly aware of this and admitted as much at the Council of Joint Ministers of 31 July when he said that only two courses were open to Austria. Either she must insist on her own interpretation of Article VII offering Italy compensation as a *beau geste,* or accept the Italian interpretation, but only in the event of a permanent occupation of Serbian territory.

[1] Oe-U. VIII, 10715. [2] Oe-U. VIII, 10747.

In conclusion he would like to point out that during the Libyan campaign we had given a very rigid interpretation to Article VII.[1]

It was not when Austria was plunging into a life and death struggle that her interest in keeping Italy within the alliance should have been treated in this off-hand manner. But, as Tschirschky wrote to Jagow on 26 July reporting on his conversation with Berchtold,

Austrians always will be Austrians. Arrogance and irresponsibility combined are not to be overcome either easily or quickly! I know them well.[2]

Tschirschky, however, opined that Berlin was unduly anxious about the attitude of Italy. In the same letter to Jagow he repeated the news, already given in his dispatch, of Avarna's assurances that Italy would 'maintain a friendly attitude consonant with her obligations under the alliance'. He went on to say:

Avarna today repeated this to me himself and assured me that Italy had no intention of splitting off from the Triple Alliance. . . I cannot help thinking . . . that San Giuliano is trying . . . to sell his neutrality in the Austro-Serbian conflict at the highest possible figure. What Avarna receives from Rome is much milder in tone than what is said to us and the above quoted latest declaration from the Rome Cabinet is fresh proof thereof. This explains why Berlin is so surprised by Italy's favorable attitude [at Vienna]. All the same that is no reason why, even in our own interest, every effort should not be made to arrive at a practical solution of the question of compensations. Yesterday . . . I worked on Macchio in the first instance, so as through him to influence Berchtold. . . . He [Macchio] too, quite sees that Austria will have to compensate Italy if she enlarges her own territory. 'Only the Italians cannot expect us to carve the compensation out of our own flesh', he added. The Trentino will never, I think, be given up by the aged Emperor—nor by the army. I can only imagine the bare possibility of such a thing after a big, successful war, assuming Austria to have received a completely free hand in the Balkans. If the Italians think they can get the Trentino in barter for some small increase of Austrian territory . . . they are much mistaken, and it seems to me we should destroy any such illusions in Rome.

The letter then went on to give a fuller account of the conversation of the 26th than was contained in the dispatch of that day.[3] Conrad had also been present at it, and Tschirschky narrates:

My very emphatic statement that the [Austrian] interpretation did not have the support of Germany made a great impression especially on Conrad. The bad thing is that the Austrian interpretation of Article VII goes back to the so-called 'great' Aehrenthal . . . and Berchtold is reluctant to renounce this 'legacy' of his celebrated predecessor. Conrad, who does not share these scruples, realized that the Italians must be given something and remarked confidentially that he would have no objections if the Italians were invited to occupy Montenegro. ... I made the suggestion both to Macchio and to Berchtold and Conrad as a personal view of my own that—without referring to Article VII in order not to give up their theoretical standpoint—they ought to say to Italy that Austria would recognize an Italian right to compensation in the event of the Monarchy's enlarging its territory in the Balkans. Avarna also thought this a good solution. More than that Italy cannot ask for, since, as far as I know, nothing is said in the Triple Alliance Treaty about where such compensations are to be situated and how great they are to be. That would have to be settled by negotiation.[1]

This document is of importance both as showing what an error of judgment it was to instruct Avarna to speak as he did at Vienna and as throwing light on Tschirschky's scant obedience to his instructions from Berlin to press Vienna to satisfy Italian wishes. His aim was to fob Italy off with empty words, giving her a mere shadow of satisfaction not based on the rights conferred on her by Article VII. And in this Tschirschky was helped by Avarna, whose confidences were such as to frustrate the action of the Italian Government. The fact that Avarna's instructions were 'much milder' than those sent to Berlin confirms the present writer's surmise, expressed above, that there exist telegrams from Rome very much less decided in tone than the one quoted by Salandra.[2] Nothing more clearly reveals the mood of both San Giuliano and Avarna than the postscript which Tschirschky added on the 28th to his letter of the 26th. On the 26th he had written:

Avarna now has instructions to discuss the compensations question directly with Berchtold.

But this postscript relates:

I received a call from Avarna. Appealing to our personal friendship and with an urgent plea not to betray him, he told me the following: he had been instructed to raise the question of compensations, but today word had come not to do so because Rome feared that only friction would come of it, which they wanted to avoid.

With a Foreign Minister in such terror of Vienna and an Ambassador whom this terror betrayed into such indiscretions, how was any policy possible? But let us resume the thread of our story.

9. *German pressure on Vienna to keep Italy in the Triple Alliance.*

While on 26 July Berchtold in Vienna was seeking to elude the question of compensation, Bethmann in Berlin was telegraphing to Tschirschky that Moltke

---

[1] DD. II, 326.   [2] See pp. 261, 276.

regards it as urgently necessary that Italy be kept firmly with the Triplice. An understanding between Vienna and Rome is therefore necessary. Vienna must not equivocate with questionable interpretations of the treaty and must take resolutions commensurable with the seriousness of the situation.[1]

This telegram reached Tschirschky at 7.10 p. m. after his unfruitful talk with Berchtold mentioned above. He brought up the matter again on the 27th and reported to Jagow that he had had a talk with Berchtold and Forgach lasting an hour and a half

in which I spoke as emphatically as was possible. At the end Count Berchtold explained: 'I see the position quite clearly. I am Shylock crying "I'll have my bond", and getting nothing.' I think that by this conversation I have persuaded them to take the initiative in a discussion with Italy.[2]

But Tschirschky's pressure must have been less forcible than that which he had to apply on the following day, 28th, in pursuance of fresh instructions from Berlin, where the news coming in from Rome was anything but reassuring. At 3.40 p. m. on the 26th Flotow had telegraphed from Fiuggi:

Marquis San Giuliano keeps on telling me that the procedure of Austria is highly questionable in Italian eyes. Austria might employ the same procedure tomorrow against Italy because of the Irredenta. Therefore Italy could not consent to measures such as these. From confidential reports from Bucharest it would seem that the King of Romania is of the same opinion because of the Romanians living in Hungary. I said to the Minister that he ought not to invent cases which did not exist.

The Austrian assurances that no Serbian territory will be claimed still finds no credence with the Minister. He therefore thinks it necessary to prepare Austria soon for Italian claims for compensation. But he does not feel able to treat directly with Vienna in the matter. Neither Baron von Merey here, nor the Duke of Avarna at Vienna, is suited to do so. Moreover, the mistrust prevailing between Vienna and Rome makes any such negotiations difficult. The only practicable road passes via Berlin. I told him I did not know what my Government thought about it. At the present moment it seemed to me premature. The Minister hinted that without compensations Italy would be obliged 'to step in Austria's way'.

Marquis San Giuliano gave me a telegram from Signor Bollati saying that the Secretary of State for Foreign Affairs [Jagow] showed satisfaction at these statements.

In confidential talk the Minister said it seemed to him as if the German Government gave too much encouragement to Austria. I denied this and told him we confined ourselves to fulfilling our engagements under the alliance. The press in general is still relatively favorable. *Corriere della Sera* refused to take the part of Austria.[3]

---

[1] DD. I, 202. See Vol. II, p. 242.   [2] DD. II, 326.   [3] DD. I, 211.

It was not unreasonable on San Giuliano's part to fear that, if Austria were to restore her prestige by a victorious attack on Serbia, she might attempt to carry out similar designs against Italy. It should, however, also have occurred to him that Italy's demand for compensations and the necessity of letting her have them would in the long run only make Austria the more determined to give Italy that good hard lesson for which Conrad had clamored in the preceding years. In the discussions and polemics which raged during the period of Italian neutrality one of the points most frequently made by the advocates of intervention was that compensations would only weaken Italy if in return she gave Austria a free hand against Serbia. It would simply mean that the Monarchy would first settle the Yugoslav problem in its own favor and then, with the new strength thus acquired, would turn and crush the other irredentist movements and punish the 'treacherous blackmailer'. How correct this estimate was is borne out by the testimony of Conrad himself. His diary entry for 11 August 1914 opens as follows:

In two very good reports of 8 and 9 August Lieutenant Field Marshal Count Stürgkh, our delegate at German Chief Headquarters, after touching on the elation reigning there as a result of the initial successes against France, communicates an utterance of General von Moltke to the effect that 'we should do best to secure our rear at the price of the Trentino. Once the war with Russia was over we could challenge Italy to a duel and Germany would be our second'. Kaiser Wilhelm expressed himself to Count Stürgkh in the same sense. He, too, thought that we should buy security from Italy at the price of the Trentino, and later on he would help us to get it back again. Any obligations that might be raised against this were of no account, what must now be pursued was the main objective, which was to attack Russia with full strength.[1]

It is a curious fact that Rome, at that moment, had no consciousness of this serious, if not immediate, threat while fighting shy of coming to a clear understanding with Merey and Berchtold and taking refuge under the wing of the German eagle to the not unmixed satisfaction of the German Government. Indeed, in the early hours of 27 July Jagow, replying to a telegram of the 26th from Fiuggi, telegraphed to Flotow:

About compensations Italy must herself negotiate at Vienna.[2]

What he said to Szögyény is summarized in the latter's dispatch to Berchtold of 5 p. m. on 27 July:

Secretary of State is in full agreement with the reply given by Your Excellency to the Italian Ambassador[3] and thinks it entirely appropriate that you did not for the time being embark upon explanations as to the

---

[1] Conrad, IV, p. 197.   [2] DD. I, 239.   [3] Oe-U. VIII, 10746. See p. 272.

interpretation of Article VII of the Triplice treaty [i.e., Jagow endorses Tschirschky's standpoint]. Nevertheless, Herr von Jagow is of the opinion that without reference to Article VII Your Excellency should now explicitly declare to the Italian Government that if, contrary to our wishes, a more than merely temporary occupation of Serbian territory were to be regarded as an unavoidable measure, Your Excellency would consent to some compensation for Italy, without indicating its extent. Herr von Jagow and Herr Zimmermann think that Italy, who is continually making representations here in this matter, would be calmed down by some such statement.[1]

And when Flotow telegraphed at 5.35 p. m. on the 27th from Fiuggi:

Till now I have not in any way stated or hinted that we support or are preparing claims for compensation on behalf of Italy. May I request instructions, as soon as allowable, as it would be tactically of value here in order to hold Italy securely,[2]

Jagow telegraphed back at 9.30 a. m. on the 28th:

Kindly say that we support Italian wishes for compensation in so far as we have already pointed out to Vienna the need for an understanding and still do so.[3]

Such words were lacking in sufficient force, and the Kaiser saw this when on the morning of the 27th Bethmann laid before him the second of Flotow's two telegrams of the 25th reporting the conversation with Salandra and San Giuliano of the 24th.[4] Wilhelm's comment appears as a footnote to this dispatch, appended by Bethmann on the 27th:

H.M. regards it as absolutely essential that Austria should arrive at an understanding with Italy in time to be of use. This is to be communicated to Herr von Tschirschky for him to hand it on to Count Berchtold at the express orders of H.M.[5]

Jagow dispatched the relevant instruction to Tschirschky at 9 p. m. that same evening.[6] Half an hour later, still under the impression of the Kaiser's order, Jagow in another telegram revoked his approval of Berchtold's evasive treatment of the compensation question, expressed to Szögyény that very afternoon. This second telegram, which reported a communication from Bollati, has been quoted in part above,[7] and runs:

Marquis San Giuliano much concerned because Count Berchtold expressed satisfaction at Duke Avarna's declaration of benevolent attitude on part of Italy but said nothing of Article VII and compensations. Italian Ambassador acquainted me of content of a communication in which Marquis San Giuliano makes discussion of Article VII and compensation (at least in principle) a preliminary condition for the attitude of Italy. This might otherwise turn

---

[1] Oe-U. VIII, 10789. [2] DD. I, 260. [3] DD. II, 287.
[4] DD. I, 244. See Vol. II, pp. 317–18. [5] DD. I, 244, n. 2.
[6] DD. I, 267. [7] See p. 261.

actually anti-Austrian. I therefore regard speedy exchange of views between Count Berchtold and Duke Avarna as urgently necessary.[1]

10. *The concession of compensation to Italy in the formula of 28 July.*

This time Tschirschky was compelled to take action. On the 28th he decided to speak plainly to Berchtold and reported having done so in a dispatch of 9.10 p. m. on 28 July:

I at once acquainted Count Berchtold of His Majesty's message. As a result of my urgent representations made yesterday at a very serious discussion with Count Berchtold and Count Forgach, they have both become convinced that account must be taken of them.

An agreed formula was worked out for dispatch to Szögyény and Merey, the text of which Tschirschky enclosed.[2] How this formula was arrived at was more fully explained in Berchtold's telegrams of the 28th to Merey and Szögyény which Tschirschky alluded to in his dispatch. To Merey Berchtold wrote:

The German Ambassador has yesterday and today made urgent *démarches* on personal instructions from H.M. Kaiser Wilhelm, the Chancellor and the Secretary of State, asking me 'for Heaven's sake' to come to a clear understanding with Italy over the interpretation of Article VII of the Triplice treaty in view of the serious situation and the dangers that threaten. In Italy our procedure against Serbia is regarded as an act of aggression also against Russia, and therefore the standpoint is maintained that because of the defensive nature of the Triplice treaty Italy cannot regard herself as pledged to be on our side in the event of a resultant war with Russia. . . . Herr von Tschirschky, who was instructed to tell me that the German Government interpreted Article VII in the same way as the Italian, made a solemn and emphatic appeal to me to clear up this situation as soon as possible, as the whole military action of our German ally would be jeopardized if Italy were not to recognize the *casus foederis.* Duke Avarna, who also called on me today, made a statement to me on behalf of his Government similar to the one recently—of the 25th—to Baron Macchio, to the effect that Rome would have expected us in a case like the present *(démarche* in Belgrade), as falling under the terms of Article VII of the Triplice treaty (*'dans les Balkans'*), to concert with our two allies beforehand on procedure. He further said

---

[1] DD. I, 269.
[2] DD. II, 328. It may be noted that Tschirschky waited until 9.10 p. m. before sending Berlin this news which could have gone off many hours earlier. The discussion with Berchtold and Forgach took place fairly early in the forenoon since Berchtold's lengthy telegrams to Merey and Szögyény reporting it were enciphered by 1 p. m. Berchtold and Forgach then lunched with Tschirschky and in the afternoon Forgach read out to him the text of the telegram which was being sent to Szögyény. Everything indicates that Tschirschky's delay was intentional. It was a frequent device of his not to send off certain telegrams until late in order that they might be read only on the following morning when their effect would be less immediate and they would be overtaken by events. Italy was to put be off with empty words and the way to do this was to let matters drag on as long as possible.

that in the event of the threatening conflict assuming a military form and leading to an occupation, even though only temporary, of Serbian territory, the Royal Italian Government reserves to itself to claim the compensation due to it under Article VII of the Triplice treaty, about which a preliminary under-standing would have to be achieved. He said in conclusion that in the event of a passage of arms between Austria-Hungary and Serbia the Royal Italian Government intended to adopt a friendly attitude conforming to the obligations of the alliance. I replied to the Italian Ambassador that our dispute with Serbia concerned only ourselves and Serbia, that we moreover did not contemplate territorial acquisitions, that an occupation of Serbian territory was therefore not in question. To Avarna's remark that it would be of great advantage with regard to the Powers if we would give a binding undertaking to this effect, I answered that this was not possible because at the present moment it could not be foreseen whether in the course of the war we might not be forced into occupying Serbian territory against our will. If developments took a normal course this was not to be anticipated as we had absolutely no interest in adding to the number of our Serbian subjects. I beg Your Excellency to communicate the above declaration of Duke Avarna's and my reply to Marquis San Giuliano and, with regard to the claim to compensation based on Article VII of the Triplice treaty, to make the following observations: As has already been stated to the Italian Ambassador, territorial acquisitions are not at all in our intentions. Should we be obliged, however, contrary to our intentions to proceed to an occupation of Serbian territory which must be regarded as purely temporary, we are prepared to enter upon an exchange of views with Italy on compensation in this case. On the other hand, we expect of Italy that the Kingdom will not impede its ally in the action necessary to the attainment of its ends, and will steadily maintain the foreshadowed friendly attitude towards us in accordance with the treaty.

In order that there might be no misunderstandings about the nature of the compensation asked for by Italy, Szögyény was instructed to say at Berlin 'that the question of detaching any portion of the Monarchy could not form the subject of any discussion whatsoever', and Merey also received intimation of this. The dispatch to Merey further contained the 'secret' additional words:

> I have decided to meet the Italian standpoint in this matter because the present game is for high stakes, involves considerable difficulties, and would be absolutely impracticable without the firm cohesion of the Triplice Powers.[1]

This documentary evidence shows: (1) that on the 28th Berchtold was not willing to give a pledge to Avarna ruling out Austrian territorial conquests at the expense of Serbia; (2) that in return for a vague promise of undefined compensation which excluded the Trentino and was only to be granted in the event of

---

[1] Oe-U. VIII, 10909.

permanent occupation—Article VII provided for compensation even in the case of temporary occupation—Italy was to second Austria in the attainment of her far-reaching designs to the point of giving support in the subjection of Serbia and recognizing the *casus foederis*. What also becomes apparent is that San Giuliano was caught in a noose. He had refrained from opposing the Austrian designs, from preannouncing the neutrality of Italy in the event of a European conflagration and by these and other means taking effective action to save the peace, his sole aim being to get the Trentino for Italy, and now he found himself empty-handed. Not only was the Trentino ruled out, but to get any compensation at all Italy would have to join her allies in making war, a step which San Giuliano deemed 'extremely difficult, perhaps impossible, certainly dangerous'. Hence when Merey, having recovered from his indisposition, called on the 29th to convey the message contained in Berchtold's dispatch of the 28th

the Minister, who noted down the substance in key words, said that as it was an important and delicate matter he must reflect and discuss with the Prime Minister before replying. In so replying he again remarked (under the pretext that he was not feeling well after the cure) that the question should be negotiated at Vienna,[1]

very likely because he did not care to discuss it with Merey.

And in this he was fully justified, since Merey's attitude towards the Italian demand for compensation grew increasingly antagonistic, and Flotow wrote to Berlin about this interview:

Unfortunately the Austrian Ambassador is violently opposed to any concessions to Italy and yesterday had a very acrimonious discussion with Marquis San Giuliano.[2]

Tschirschky's own account of the interview, sent off in the small hours of the 29th, contains the words:

The Italian Government only cares about the compensation question, seeks to force the matter . . . even sounds an extortionist note and characteristically seeks to carry on the relevant conversations at Vienna and Berlin. The more courteous, pleased and grateful we show ourselves for the Italian attitude, the more far-reaching and insistent will be the Italian claims."

And on the evening of the 28th, on receiving Berchtold's telegram announcing the slight concession vouchsafed to Italy in response to German pressure[4] which has been quoted above, Merey felt that his opinion had been flouted and fell into a rage which he vented in a postscript to his private letter to Berchtold of the 26th:

[1] Oe-U. VIII, 11085. [2] DD. II, 419.
[3] Oe-U. VIII, 10987. [4] Oe-U. VIII, 10909.

After all, as your Ambassador in Rome, I am, at least in rank, the foremost expert in matters concerning Italy. . . . I really wonder why we afford ourselves the luxury of an Ambassador at Rome . . . and do not rather transfer the representation of our interests in Italy to the German Embassy, which is obviously much more competent. . . . As things are we have gained nothing while making gratis a concession of incalculable significance.[1]

11. San Giuliano's disappointment; renewed pressure on Vienna from Berlin.

In San Giuliano's eyes, however, the concession was of no significance at all. He made no mention of it in his interview with Flotow on the afternoon of the 29th confining himself to a general plan, perhaps because he did not know how to approach the subject. To do so he would have had to reveal that he wanted compensation even in the case of Italy's not entering the war, as was almost certain to be the case. But then he would have lost the support of Berlin. Hence all he found to say was that

Austria's procedure was against Italy's interests so long as Austria did not acknowledge Article VII of the Triplice treaty as still operative and so long as Austria did not grant compensation in the event of territorial occupation in Serbia. Till then Italy could not give Austria full diplomatic support. In the matter of compensation he remained of the opinion that direct negotiations with Vienna would lead to a rupture. Therefore it was necessary that Berlin should at least initiate the negotiations. In any case he declined to discuss them with Baron von Merey. That would be certain rupture. On my insistent representations he had, he continued, till now avoided any outright opposition to the Austrian procedure which obstructed Italian interests, but time was short. The moment was approaching when Italy must decide whether she would take sides diplomatically for or against Austria. To him things looked black as regards the Lovčen. The Austrian military party was determined to have the mountain.[2]

San Giuliano was thus voicing his distrust of Tschirschky's assurance to Berlin on 28 July 'that Austria-Hungary has no intention of occupying the Lovčen unless Montenegro violated neutrality towards Monarchy'.[3] Flotow ended this account of his talk with San Giuliano by observing:

To the best of my endeavor and without Austrian support I have restrained the [Italian] press till now, but I, too, think that frank Austro-Italian discussion is in the long run unavoidable.

Berlin, as we know, thought this too and was much disquieted by Vienna's double game of giving St. Petersburg solemn promises of territorial *désintéressement* and promising Italy

---

[1] Oe-U. VIII, 10991.   [2] DD. II, 363.   [3] DD. II, 312.

compensation if Serbian territory were occupied. We have seen that Bethmann wrote anxiously to Jagow on the 29th:

Is it not necessary to send another telegram to Vienna in which we sharply declare that we regard this way of handling the question of compensation with Rome as absolutely unsatisfactory and hold Vienna entirely responsible for any attitude Italy may take in a possible war? If on the eve of a possible European conflagration Vienna threatens in this way to shatter the Triple Alliance, the whole alliance system will be undermined. Vienna's statement that it will behave itself properly with Italy in the event of a permanent occupation of Serbian territory stands in contradiction with the assurances it gave St. Petersburg of territorial *désintéressement.* The statements made in Rome will certainly become known in St. Petersburg. We, as allies, cannot support a policy with a false bottom.[1]

The result was that at 8 p. m. on 29 July a telegram was sent off to Tschirschky ending with the words:

Please point out to him [Berchtold] that the instructions to Baron Merey can scarcely satisfy Italy.[2]

These words allude to the formula, telegraphed to Berlin by Tschirschky on the 28th, which had been given by Berchtold to Avarna on the 28th and communicated to Merey. By regarding it as unsatisfactory Bethmann was offending Tschirschky, who had thought it settled the matter and on 30 July telegraphed in reply:

I was told at the time that the formulation of the instruction sent on to Rome was based on an exchange of views that had taken place in Berlin.

He also enclosed a copy of Szögyény's telegram to Berchtold of the 27th, mentioned above, which began:

Secretary of State is in full agreement with the reply given by Your Excellency to the Italian Ambassador and thinks it entirely appropriate that you did not for the time being embark upon explanations as to the interpretation of Article VII of the Triplice treaty. Nevertheless Herr von Jagow is of the opinion that without reference to Article VII Your Excellency should now explicitly declare to the Italian Government that if, contrary to our wishes, a more than merely temporary occupation of Serbian territory were to be regarded as an unavoidable measure, Your Excellency would consent to some compensation for Italy, without indicating its extent.[3]

Was not this exactly what had been done? But the fact was that in that tragic night of 29-30 July there had come the first threat of English intervention and the situation was no longer that of the 27th. It was now necessary to make the best of things. The intimation of this was given to Vienna by Szögyény in a

---

[1] DD. II, 340. See Vol. II, p. 492.   [2] DD II, 361.
[3] DD. II, 443; Oe-U. VIII, 10789.

telegram from Berlin of 5.30 p. m. on 30 July which reveals the importance attached by Berlin to the solidarity of Italy and hence how much the Consulta could have accomplished by a sincere and timely effort on behalf of peace:

Whereas until recently in all influential circles here I have found the greatest calmness over the possibility of a European conflict, I must confess I now have the feeling that in these last days they have been seized by an attack of nerves which is not to be accounted for by the greater imminence of the question. The reason of this swing round of public opinion is the fear, which a previous telegram of mine has already reported to you, that in the general conflict Italy will not fulfill her engagements in regard to the Triple Alliance and that her general attitude towards us may even be extremely dubious. But, as the German Government goes on to reason, if the Triple Alliance cannot be regarded as a solid block, our prospects in the event of a major conflict would be very seriously impaired. It is therefore absolutely necessary to retain Italy within the Triple Alliance as an active factor. Hence Your Excellency is most urgently advised from here to be as generous as possible in the interpretation of Article VII of the Triplice treaty, to meet Italy's wishes to the greatest possible extent, and to declare as soon as possible a readiness (in a spirit of the most generous complaisance) to enter upon immediate negotiations relative to the interpretation of Article VII, recognizing an obligation to give compensation. (While at the same time even in the opinion of Berlin there can of course be no question of the Trentino.) This desire on the part of Germany is in my firm opinion due not to any falling off in her loyalty towards her Austro-Hungarian ally but simply and solely to the conviction that Austria-Hungary and Germany absolutely need Italy in order to be able to engage with safety in the general conflict. The concessions to Italy announced in Your Excellency's telegram of the 28th inst. have, according to reports from the German Ambassador in Rome, been declared inadequate by the Italian Cabinet.[1]

Perturbed by this message, Berchtold, who had not yet received Merey's long letter of the 26–8 July, turned to him for advice in the early hours of 30 July, enclosing a copy of Szögyény's telegram.[2] Merey's reply, sent off from Rome the following night, may be imagined:

A threat that has extorted three parts of what it demanded will press, of course, all the more insistently for the remainder. In fact the Foreign Minister remarked to me today that in his reply to this statement from Vienna he called it vague and inadequate. . . . My conviction is that the question whether Italy takes part in the war or remains neutral will not depend on compensation but chiefly on the estimate made of the whole European situation and on military considerations. We risk giving far-reaching undertakings in the question of compensations without attaining our object of Italian military co-operation. In view of the fact that we ourselves are not clear about the nature of the compensation and cannot fix any compen

---

[1] Oe-U. VIII, 11030. [2] Oe-U. VIII, 11084.

sation without knowing what we are to receive in exchange, my opinion is that we can at most only take the further step of declaring that after the end of the—localized or general—war, we are prepared to grant adequate compensation to Italy on a basis of Article VII of the Triplice treaty in the event of our occupying territory in the Balkans, whether permanently or for a length of time exceeding that of the Italian occupation of the Dodecanese, and in the event of Italy's fulfilling exactly her engagements under the alliance.[1]

Merey was quite right in saying that Italy would decide on neutrality or intervention on other grounds than the question of compensation. Public opinion was awakened and the Government had to reckon with it. It was not surprising if Merey claimed that the Italian right to compensation should be contingent on recognition of the *casus foederis*. It only shows up San Giuliano's folly in shirking his duty of laying down a clear line of conduct for Italy. But by the time Merey's advice reached Vienna on 1 August, Berchtold had already been obliged to take measures and the measures he took were the opposite of those suggested by Merey.

12. *Compensation conceded in the Tschirschky-Berchtold formula of 31 July and accepted by Avarna.*

By 30 July the situation had become such as to compel the Monarchy to decide on general mobilization in principle as war seemed practically certain. Something therefore had to be done to meet the wishes of Italy. The problem was discussed at the meeting of Joint Ministers of Austria-Hungary on the morning of the 31st, summoned to sanction general mobilization. Berchtold opened it with a summary of the negotiations that had already taken place. After some discussion Berchtold continued:

He could see only two courses which Vienna could now take. Either to insist on its own interpretation of Article VII but by a 'beau geste' accord Italy compensation, or to accept the Italian interpretation of Article VII with the express proviso that Italy would have claim to compensation only if we were to proceed to a permanent occupation of territory in the Balkan peninsula. In conclusion he would like to point out that during the Libyan campaign we had given a very rigorous interpretation to Article VII.

Baron von Burian and Count Tisza insisted that not only the Italian interpretation of Article VII of the treaty could be disputed but also the Italian Government's view that the *casus foederis* did not arise. Hence con-cessions should only be made on condition that in the event of a major war Italian co-operation should actually materialize. Herr von Bilinski pointed out that the impending great struggle was for the Monarchy a struggle for existence. If effective help from Italy in this struggle were really of such great value, no doubt a sacrifice would have to be made to procure it. Count Stürgkh took the view that Italy could not lay claim to compensation unless upon the outbreak of the major war she fulfilled her obligations as an ally. The Council of Ministers thereupon empowered the chairman in principle to hold out the prospect of compensation to Italy in the event of our proceeding to a permanent occupation of Serbian territory, and if circumstances demanded and Italy actually fulfilled her obligations as an ally, also to discuss the cession of Valona to Italy, in which case Austria-Hungary would secure for herself the preponderant influence in Northern Albania.[1]

Having obtained this authorization Berchtold took up the matter with Avarna and at their first conversation arrived at an agreement the substance of which he reported to Merey in a telegram of 11.30 p. m. on the 31st which was also sent to Szögyény:

Today I had a long conversation with Duke Avarna about the question of compensation at which we arrived at complete agreement. On the basis of our conversation the German and Italian Ambassadors drew up a text entirely satisfactory to Duke Avarna. I trust that the question now seems solved by agreement with all the Triplice Powers. Your excellency will at once inform Marquis San Giuliano of the above, adding that we now definitely reckoned on the fact, which I had never doubted, that Italy would fulfill to the utmost her obligations under the alliance.[2]

In reality the agreement was completed only on the following day, as is apparent from the telegram which Tschirschky, who had acted as go-between, sent to Berlin at 6.5 p. m. on 1 August:

After Duke Avarna yesterday afternoon had for the first time discussed the question of compensation directly with Count Berchtold and approximate success had been attained, I with Duke Avarna yesterday evening drew up the following statement which Count Berchtold was to deliver to the Ambassador this forenoon:

'If, however, by the force of circumstances Austria-Hungary were to be compelled to make territorial acquisitions in the Balkan peninsula, particularly in Serbia and Montenegro, the I. and R. Government is ready to concert with Italy on the subject of compensations to be granted her provided that Italy gives Austria her support in the case that the *casus foederis* contemplated by the treaty presents itself, or that she gives her support without the *casus foederis* presenting itself. This statement contains the elements forming the substance of the interpretation given by Italy to Article VII and which I agree to concede to Italy although I do not join in this actual interpretation.'

According to the written confirmation, given me this morning by Duke Avarna at my request, that the above statement was satisfactory to him I submitted the statement this morning to Count Berchtold, who also accepted it. Thus full agreement has been reached within twenty-four hours.[3]

Berchtold, who, as we have seen, had already announced the agreement to Merey on the 31st, sent confirmation at 12.5 p. m.

---

[1] Oe-U. VIII, 11203.   [2] Oe-U. VIII, 11165.   [3] DD. III, 573.

on August 1 that I have come to an agreement with Duke Avarna and Herr Tschirschky to adopt the Italian interpretation of Article VII of the Triplice treaty on condition that Italy in the present conflict completely fulfills her obligations under the alliance.[1]

But at 1.5 p. m. Berchtold sent Merey the actual text of the agreement, which differed considerably from Tschirschky's draft:

I consider that a difference of views on the interpretation of Article VII constitutes an element of uncertainty in our present and future relations which might be prejudicial to the intimate relationship between the two countries. I accept the interpretation given by Italy and Germany to Article VII on condition that Italy observes a friendly attitude in respect of the war operations now undertaken by Austria-Hungary and Serbia, and fulfills her engagements as an ally in the case in which the present conflict should lead to a general conflagration.[2]

Which of these formulations was the one accepted by Avarna is not known. They differ between themselves in that Tschirschky's formula specified that compensation was due to Italy only if the Monarchy 'were to be compelled to make territorial acquisitions in the Balkan peninsula', hence not in the case of a temporary occupation, while Berchtold's formulation accepted the Italian interpretation of Article VII that compensation was due also in respect of a temporary occupation. In either formula, however, the granting of compensation was made conditional on Italy's maintaining a friendly attitude to Austria in her war with Serbia and recognizing the *casus foederis* in the event of a European war. This was reiterated by Francis Joseph to Wilhelm, who in his telegram of 4 p. m. on the 31st had said:

I beg you to do everything to induce Italy to take part by the greatest possible deference to her wishes; everything else must be put into the background in order that the Triple Alliance may unitedly enter the war.[3]

On 1 August Francis Joseph replied:

In view of the seriousness of the situation my Ambassador in Rome has already received instructions to say to the Italian Government that we are prepared to accept its interpretation of Article VII of the treaty provided that Italy now completely fulfills her obligations under the alliance.[4]

It was much ado about nothing. There was no real difference between what Berchtold agreed to on 28 July and on 1 August. Tschirschky had not persuaded him to give more satisfaction to the Italian Government than he had given in the formula of 28 July. The difference was purely formal. In the first formula compensation was promised without reference to Article VII. In the second

---

[1] DA. III, 86.   [2] DA. III, 87.
[3] DD. III, 503. See pp. 45-6.   [4] DD. III, 601; DA. I, 81b.

compensation was promised as a result of acceptance of the Italian interpretation of Article VII. But practically it amounted to the same thing. The impression remains that there was collusion between Berchtold and Tschirschky, probably on the latter's initiative, to throw dust in Avarna's eyes and fob him off with a promise valueless to the Italian Government, valueless because the Trentino, the object of San Giuliano's ambition, would never come into consideration as compensation and also because, to get any compensation whatever, Italy would have to give Austria a free hand against Serbia and go to war on the side of Austria, were a general war to result.

Avarna, however, without awaiting instructions from Rome expressed in writing his satisfaction at the solution proposed by Berchtold and Tschirschky. Had he received an intimation beforehand to do so in any case? Tschirschky must certainly have shown him Jagow's telegram of the evening of 27 July reporting Bollati as having said that San Giuliano asked for discussions on Article VII and compensation 'at least in principle'.[1] And now 'at least in principle' the question was settled, and settled in a manner which satisfied Avarna, who never contemplated the possibility of Italy's declaring herself neutral and sought to arrange matters in such a way as would force Italy to recognize the *casus foederis*. But the actual responsibility for the approval given to the Tschirschky-Berchtold formula rested with San Giuliano, who was later to reject it. He rejected it, however, only when, partly as a result of his own inaction, the European conflagration did break out and Italy was obliged to make a decision whether to go to war or to declare neutrality. In other words, it was not until the general war had broken out that he was to find courage to declare, and even then in rather uncertain tones, that Italy would keep out of it. San Giuliano, therefore, gave Italy the appearance of being false to her word, when it was in reality she who had most respected the spirit and the letter of the Triple Alliance.

[1] DD. I, 269.

CHAPTER VII

THE ITALIAN DECLARATION OF NEUTRALITY (29 JULY–2 AUGUST)

1. *Italian diplomatic activity after the Austrian declaration of war on Serbia.*

When on the afternoon of 28 July San Giuliano made his proposal to Rodd based on Belgrade's acceptance of all the demands of the ultimatum the Italian Government did not yet know that Austria had declared war on Serbia. As soon as he learnt of it San Giuliano saw that his proposal fell to the ground, and realizing the dangers of the situation created by this precipitate action of Austria, he showed himself anxious and desirous to avert the conflict. In proof of the thesis that 'we pressed for this even after Austria had precipitately opened hostilities' (in reality she did not open hostilities but only declared war on Serbia) Salandra quotes a telegram sent to Bollati on 29 July containing a message to Jagow that he should remember that England would not remain neutral, and continuing:

Finally it is well that Jagow should know that Italian public opinion would not allow or forgive it if the Government neglected any possible means of preventing a European war and the crushing of Serbia. I therefore have told Rodd and will tell Imperiali to maintain close contact between the Italian and British Governments in order that, together or preferably jointly with Germany and France, they may work without delay and without ceasing in complete agreement for the attainment of those two ends, which are, in fact,

inseparable, since Russia would go to war rather than let Serbia or Montenegro be crushed or dismembered and would have the military support of
France and England, while Italy is under no obligation to go to war and
might be dragged by public opinion into regrettable developments if Austria
seized the Lovčen. Now, as Italy, together with England, must necessarily
work for European peace by all means suitable to assuring it, Jagow must
be made to understand the necessity of Germany's co-operating in this
pacificatory action.[1]

The German diplomatic documents show no trace of any
words spoken by Bollati in the sense of this telegram of the
29th, nor do the British documents reveal action by Imperiali in
either this or any other sense. But among the British documents
there exists a telegram from Rodd of 12.5 a. m. on 29 July
summarizing a talk with San Giuliano in the evening following
on the one he had had with him in the afternoon of the 28th and
occasioned, no doubt, by the arrival of the news that Austria had
declared war on Serbia, thus making the situation very much
more dangerous. This telegram is much on the lines of the one
to Bollati published by Salandra:

But Minister for Foreign Affairs understands that it is rather the 'conference' than the principle which creates difficulty. He is telegraphing to
Berlin tonight urging that idea of an exchange of views in London should
be adhered to, and suggests that German Secretary of State for Foreign
Affairs might propose formula which he could accept. Minister for Foreign
Affairs thinks that this exchange of views might be concomitant with direct
communication between St. Petersburg and Vienna and would keep door
open if latter failed to have any result. He is also informing Berlin that public
opinion here will not pardon the Government if every possible step has not
been taken to avoid war and urging that in this Germany must co-operate.
Even if it proved impossible to induce Germany to take part, he would still
advocate that Italy and England should still continue to exchange views,
each as representing one group. He added that there seemed to be a difficulty
in making Germany believe that Russia was in earnest and thought it would
have a great effect if she believed that Great Britain would act with Russia
and France.[2]

Another indication of San Giuliano's activities in this
direction is given in a telegram from Flotow of 30 July:

Marquis San Giuliano is much alarmed at the news that direct negotiations
between Austria and Russia are broken off. It is—he says—no longer to be
questioned that Russia is ready for war and that England will take part in it.
Actual difference between Russia and Austria is quite slight now that Austria
has declared she has no intentions to acquire territory. It is now a matter of
finding out what Austria really wants and then asking St. Petersburg whether
Russia can allow Austria to carry out her intentions. It was absolutely

---

[1] Salandra, pp. 96–7.   [2] BD. XI, 252. See Vol. II, p. 419.

necessary for the German Government to get in touch with Vienna, not in order to persuade Austria to yield, but simply to ascertain Austrian intentions and demands. Then the other Powers, especially England, but also Italy, could negotiate in St. Petersburg on this basis to avert a European war.[1]

And to Merey San Giuliano said much the same thing on 30 July.[2]

But general expressions such as these were not likely to have any influence on the course of events. And he made no protest either at Vienna or at Berlin against the Austrian declaration of war on Serbia, though he plainly saw and said that it was leading Europe to war. But it was to Rodd that he said it on 28 July and not to Flotow on either the 28th or 29th. When he saw Flotow on the 29th all he did was to put in a plea for compensation.[3] It was only in the afternoon of the 30th that he went so far as to say to Flotow that 'it was absolutely necessary for the German Government to get in touch with Vienna, not in order to persuade Austria to yield, but simply to ascertain Austrian intentions and demands'. Was this a way to talk if, as Salandra says, the Italian Government's aim was to save the peace? One is dumbfounded to find San Giuliano advising England to scare Germany by threatening intervention when he himself had not the courage to use the one real weapon at his disposal for preventing war, namely, a straightforward warning to his allies, which would also have taken a great responsibility off his own shoulders, that Italy would not be, with them in a war of aggression.

In this connection it should be noted that one of the points settled at the discussion between San Giuliano and Salandra was, as the latter records: if it proved not possible to avoid war, state that Italy was under no obligation to take part in it.[4] But in the first place why wait to make such a statement till war was knocking at the door? The time for giving warning was right at the beginning, as soon as the crisis began to loom and when the warning would have influenced the plans of the Central Powers and deterred them from dangerous courses, as it did in 1913. In the second place, the phrasing of the warning, as recorded by Salandra, is highly ambiguous. It is one thing to state in good time that, if a general war were to break out, Italy would definitely not take part in it in support of her allies, thus making them think twice before provoking it; it is quite a different matter when the situation is practically beyond remedy to go no further than a denial of the obligation to participate in war while holding out hope of participation under certain conditions. By acting thus San Giuliano let Berlin and Vienna believe that with a little good will on their part over acceptance of the Italian interpretation of Article

[1] DD. II, 446.   [2] Oe-U. VIII, 11166.
[3] DD. II, 363. See p. 289.   [4] Salandra, p. 82.

VII, Italy would recognize the *casus foederis*. So persuaded was Berlin of this that when on the 29th Szögyény received Berchtold's telegram of the 28th reporting Tschirschky's pressure for some concession to the Italian standpoint[1] he sent back the following report of his next call at the Wilhelmstrasse:

I communicated Your Excellency's telegram of yesterday to Under-secretary of State [Zimmermann], Secretary of State not being available. As regards the first part of Herr von Tschirschky's communication that Italy would regard military action by us against Serbia as an aggressive act also against Russia and would, therefore, regard herself as released from her Triplice obligations in the event of a conflict with Russia, the Under-Secretary of State said there seemed to be some misunderstanding. It is true this had once been said by Italy at the beginning of our dispute, but had never been repeated. Moreover, my Italian colleague [Bollati], whom I questioned on the above-mentioned standpoint of the Italian Government as a personal matter reaching me as a rumor, told me that this had certainly been said on one occasion by an Italian representative abroad [Fasciotti], but the latter had received an immediate reprimand from Rome. He could assure me 'quite categorically' that this was not at all the view of the Italian Cabinet.[2]

2. San Giuliano on 29 July allows the possibility of Italian intervention on the side of the Central Powers; the illusions at Berlin and Vienna.

San Giuliano's behavior on 29 July, when it seemed hardly likely that war would be avoided, is mirrored in the dispatch sent to Vienna by Merey in the small hours of 31 July:

The Foreign Minister spontaneously discussed the Italian attitude in the event of a European war. Since the Triple Alliance is of a purely defensive character and we had provoked the European conflagration by our violent action against Serbia and had not previously concerted with the Italian Government, Italy had no obligation to take part in the war. This did not, however, mean that, if the eventuality materialized, Italy will not ask herself the question whether her interests were better served by taking military action on our side or remaining neutral. He, personally, inclined more to the former alternative and regarded it as the more likely one, provided that Italian interests in the Balkans were at the same time safeguarded and that we were not aiming at changes which would give us a preponderant position at the expense of Italy.[3]

Next morning (30 July) San Giuliano said the same thing to Flotow, who telegraphed at 11.45 a. m. to the Wilhelmstrasse:

As Your Excellency knows, Marquis San Giuliano makes no secret that he regards the Austrian procedure against Serbia as a war of aggression and

---

[1] Oe-U. VIII, 10909. See pp. 286-7. [2] Oe-U. VIII, 10943.
[3] Oe-U. VIII, 11090..

that therefore Italy under the Triplice treaty is not obliged to take part in a world war resulting from this war. Moreover, the infringement of Article VII of the Triplice treaty releases Italy from the duty of following suit. Upon my contesting this view he persistently replied: 'I do not say that Italy *will* not take part in the end; I merely register the fact that she is not *bound* to do so.' It grows increasingly apparent that the Italian intention is to get something for Italy out of this affair and it would be well to consider whether the present situation makes it politically advisable to offer her the prospect of some advantage. All Italian arguments about Article VII of the Triplice treaty in my opinion have this end in view. The decision will rest with Austria.[1]

At 9.30 p. m. on the same day Flotow telegraphed again:

Marquis San Giuliano tells me he gives the most definite assurance that the news of an agreement between Italy and England not to attack each other in the event of war is a baseless invention. He is convinced, he says, that England will come into the war. This very fact is sufficient to rule out any secret arrangement with England at the moment.[2]

Here once again we have proof on San Giuliano's own direct admission to Merey and Flotow that the desire to secure compensation was causing him to contemplate the possibility of going to war on the side of his allies and was therefore holding him back from making a genuine effort to save the peace. His telegram of 29 July to Bollati which Salandra has published, says:

It is well that Jagow should know that Italian public opinion would not allow or forgive it if the Government neglected any possible means of pre-venting a European war and the crushing of Serbia.[3]

But Jagow might have retorted that in working for compensation, Rome was working for war, even though it might prefer not to have war and not to have compensation. In this connection it is well to recall what Salandra gives us of the note from San Giuliano to Merey of 28 July asking for an agreement on the interpretation of Article VII:

An agreement on this point is urgent, for until it comes to pass . . . Italy cannot pursue a policy of a nature to facilitate now or later occupation by Austria whether temporary or permanent.

Thus if Italy could make profit out of it she might even let Serbia be crushed, taking the risk that the Austrian action might lead Europe to war. Salandra obviously was blind to this point when he tells how Flotow on the 30th as a deterrent to Russia pressed Italy for a declaration of support for her allies, even if later she were not to go to war, and then quotes San Giuliano as replying that 'it was not possible to

---

[1] DD. II, 419.   [2] DD. II, 458.
[3] Salandra, p. 97. See pp. 296–7.

take such an attitude until we got definite assurances from Austria on the interpretation of Article VII of the treaty'.[1]

So Austria need only give Italy these assurances and Italy would engage to take her part and support her in all her other plans! San Giuliano began supporting Austria when on the 29th he promised Merey to advise Montenegro to remain neutral, i.e., not to make common cause with Serbia,[2] and when on the 28th and 29th he telegraphed Carlotti asking that Sazonov should do the same.[3] He told Carlotti that this was in order that Austria should not have a pretext for occupying the Lovčen. But the best way to prevent this was to avoid war, since no great reliance could be placed on Austrian assurances about the Lovčen, to which San Giuliano seemed to attach so great importance. And what would that mountain matter if Austria were to attain her ambitions in the Balkans about which Merey sought to throw dust in his eyes at their conversation of 30 July?

As Marquis San Giuliano mentioned . . . that we had declared our intention (I interjected: 'but without a formal engagement') of not annexing any Serbian territory and respecting the integrity and independence of Serbia, I affirmed for all eventualities that the communication made by me to him referred solely to the ruling out of territorial acquisitions.[4]

In other words: no formal engagement, still less any pledge to respect the integrity and independence of Serbia. San Giuliano uttered no protest against these statements, doubtless calculating that if Austria made no gains in Serbia she could not give compensation to Italy, while he on the other hand did not want to come out of the crisis empty-handed.

But however wrong his behavior in not restraining Berlin and Vienna by timely plain speaking, that does not hide the fact that the Governments of the Central Powers and their representatives at Rome showed an utter lack of all political sense in imagining that Italy could ever associate herself with them in a war of such a kind. Just as they grossly deceived themselves in counting on Russian acquiescence in the localization of the Austro-Serbian conflict and on English neutrality, so they deceived themselves as to the attitude which Italy would eventually adopt. It is true, as we have seen, that Szögyény's telegram of the 30th speaks of the growing fear in Berlin 'that in the general conflict Italy will not fulfill her engagements in regard to the Triple Alliance and that her general attitude towards us may be extremely dubious'.[5] It is also true that on the morning of the 30th Bethmann instructed Tschirschky to warn Berchtold that:

[1] Salandra, p. 97.
[2] Oe-U. VIII, 11087.
[3] *Int. Bez.* i, V, 183, 237.
[4] Oe-U. VIII, 11166.
[5] Oe-U. VIII, 11030. See p. 291.

we are faced with a conflagration in which England will be against us, Italy and Romania to all appearances will not be with us and we should be two Great Powers against four.[1]

But Vienna was not alone that day in refusing to repent and turn back from the path chosen. Bethmann's chief aim in sending the warning was to put pressure on the Austrian Government to make concessions to Italy. And if he had doubts of Italy's reliability he had not lost all hope of it. Indeed, Lerchenfeld on 30 July reported to the Bavarian Government having been told by Bethmann that

Italy would stand by the Triple Alliance and had only given notification of a certain modification in her mode of support.[2]

This news item was confirmed by Lerchenfeld in a letter of 30 July to the Bavarian Prime Minister:

As I write, things have become clear. England will side with the *Entente*. As regards Italy it is believed that she will remain with the Triple Alliance but will want to make some profit out of the occasion. But not Valona, that she rejects.[3]

Nor was Vienna any less optimistic. By the 31st Berchtold had probably received Merey's private letter of the 29th, which said:

As regards Italy my opinion is that in the event of a European conflagration she will certainly fulfill her obligations under the alliance.[4]

In any case Berchtold telegraphed on the evening of the 31st to Merey and Szögyény:

From a secret but reliable source we learn that the Romanian Government has sounded Rome about whether in the event of a general war Italy would recognize the *casus foederis,* since Romanian public opinion would probably be won over to active co-operation with Austria-Hungary only in the event of an affirmative answer. . . . I should regard it as extremely urgent and important that the Italian Government should not only make its loyal adherence to the Triple Alliance known at Bucharest, but should if possible request the King of Romania to make the existence of the alliance relationship publicly known.[5]

---

[1] DD. II, 395. See Vol. II, pp. 522-3.
[2] DD. IV, *Anhang* IV, 18. p. 145.
[3] Dirr. p. 175.
[4] Oe-U. VIII, 10991. See p. 275.
[5] Oe-U. VIII, 11122. It is not known what went on between Rome and Bucharest during the crisis of July 1914. If the Italian Government had from the first decided on remaining neutral, it would obviously have had to take measures to persuade the Romanian Government to follow suit, not only as a demonstration to the world at large that in a war of this kind the *casus foederis* did not arise, but also to have Romania on the side of Italy in the event of Italy's intervening against Austria. But no diplomatic activity on these lines has come to light. On the contrary Fasciotti received instructions to refrain from statements

Berchtold believed, therefore, that Rome would not only intervene but would use its good offices at Bucharest. And in a report to Francis Joseph of 31 July he wrote

that in view of the menacing situation it was absolutely necessary to ensure the loyal co-operation of Italy, and to this end, although according to our interpretation Article VII of the Triplice treaty does not apply to the armed conflict with Serbia, make some concession to the divergent Italian view. . . . The possibility of ceding the Albanian port of Valona was considered, no serious objections being raised by Admiral Kailer provided that there was an embargo on the development of this port into a naval base. Baron Conrad hopes to persuade Italy to place troops at our disposal for Galicia in addition to fulfilling her engagements under the alliance against France.[1]

This hope may have been inspired by a report of 29 July from the Austrian Military Attaché in Rome, Lieutenant Colonel Szeptycki:

I have gathered in conversation that Italy quite seriously thinks of co-operating in the event of a European conflict. . . . The difficulties, however, are said to be by no means negligible [as a result of the Libyan war]. . . . All this shows how difficult it is for Italy to carry out mobilization. But I have noticed that for the last two days the official and unofficial attitude of Italy towards Austria-Hungary has changed and that there is a willingness to do everything to help us.[2]

How did this misunderstanding arise?

3. The Military Conventions of the Triple Alliance and Cadorna's proposals for co-operation with the Central Powers.

Here a considerable digression is needed, which is not without interest as showing that an attitude favorable to the Triple Alliance was widespread in Italy not only among the diplomats, the upper middle class and in educated circles, but also in the army. In the Italian army the German army was regarded as the finest model of an army, capable of swift victory over that of France, which had been so lamentably beaten in 1870 and was the creation of a republic in which military institutions did not enjoy the prestige and attention bestowed on them in Germany. The leading Triplicist in the Italian army had been none other than General Alberto Pollio, who was its Commander-in-Chief

to the effect that Italy would not march with her allies (DD. I, 177, 227, 261. See pp. 262–3), thus playing into the hands of the Central Powers. Among the Russian documents there is a message from Krupensky in Rome. 'The Minister [San Giuliano] told me today that Romania would obviously take part against us in the war. Romanian public opinion is not in sympathy with this, but the King is said to be determined on it' (*Int. Bez.* i. V, 494). Worse informed than this the Consulta could not be, all for lack of contact and failure to make direct approaches for the purpose of concerting a common policy.

[1] DA. III, 80.
[2] Oe-U. VIII, 10992.

until his death on 28 June 1914. Pollio's extreme ardor for the Triple Alliance determined the tone of the negotiations carried on by him in 1913 and 1914 for Italian military co-operation with Germany and Austria, leading him to actions and utterances of extreme gravity.

His predecessor, General Cosenz, had held the view that in consequence of the construction by France of an extensive system of fortifications along the Italian frontier, Italy, if the *casus foederis* arose, would be compelled to wage long-drawn-out and exhausting static warfare which would absorb a large proportion of her forces and that the decisive theatre of operations would be the Franco-German front. Hence in the Military Convention of 1888 he had engaged to send via Austria to the Rhine the III Army, consisting of five army corps and two cavalry divisions, to co-operate with the German army. This undertaking remained in force until the end of 1912, when Pollio sent Colonel Zupelli to Berlin to tell Moltke that owing to the situation in Libya Italy would act against France in the Alps but could not send the III Army out of the country, and that, therefore, if naval predominance in the Mediterranean could be secured, she would make a landing in Provence and carry out operations in the Rhone valley.[1]

Conrad expressed very sharp anger at this. On 14 December he wrote to Berchtold that he was transmitting the communication which had been made by the Italian Military Attaché, Albricci, and

which permits me to declare with satisfaction that I was not deceived in my appraisal of Italian friendship. I can only regret that we did not come to a reckoning "with this unreliable neighbor' years ago, as I repeatedly pointed out the necessity of doing.[2]

But Conrad went too far and was mistaken about Pollio, who on 21 December 1912 assured Moltke that if the *casus foederis* were to arise Italy would mobilize all her forces and take the offensive against France without delay. At the same time Pollio proposed joint action between the two navies in the Mediterranean for the purpose of guarding the Italian coast-line and gaining command of the sea, which was necessary to carry out the landing in Provence and operations in the Rhone valley. Moltke warmly approved of this plan and about the middle of January 1913 sent his Quartermaster General, Waldersee, to Rome and Vienna for talks with Pollio and Conrad. Waldersee reported that Pollio made an excellent impression. His words had the King's approval and could not possibly conceal any trickery. Pollio was a sincere adherent of the Triple Alliance and 'saw the weal of his country in the holding down of France'. He had said that for the moment, on account of

---

[1] A. Alberti, *Il Generale Falkenhayn, Le relazioni tra i capi di S. M della Triplice* (Rome, 1924), pp. 67-8.
[2] Pribram, II, p. 175, n. 417.

commitments in Libya, he could not part with an army to send it to Germany; but he hoped soon to make troops available. He had then expatiated at some length on the necessity of co-operation between the naval forces of the Triplice for the purpose of gaining control of the Mediterranean, first destroying the English naval units stationed there and then the French navy. France must be prevented from bringing over her forces from North Africa, and then the united Triplice navies would provide protection for the landing in Provence of the Italian army, which was to be used for an offensive there.

In Vienna Waldersee found Conrad skeptical of the duration and extent of Pollio's influence. However, Conrad was in favor of making a naval agreement, parleys for which were begun in Vienna in April 1913 and led to the signing of the convention on 23 June 1913. The following are its main points.

The naval forces of the Triple Alliance which may be in the Mediterranean shall unite for the purpose of gaining naval control of the Mediterranean by defeating the enemy fleets, the plan of operations being prepared in time of peace by the Admiralty Staffs and Naval Section of the Ministries of War of the Triplice Powers. The Supreme Command of the Naval Forces of the Triple Alliance in the Mediterranean may be entrusted to an Austro-Hungarian or to an Italian Flag-Officer whose nomination shall have been decided in time of peace. The nomination to the Supreme Command was conferred, by Section I of a Supplementary Agreement of 23 June 1913, on the Imperial and Royal Austro-Hungarian Admiral Anton Haus.[1]

At the German autumn maneuvers of 1913, in discussions between the three Commanders-in-Chief at which Wilhelm presided, the main subject dealt with was Italian co-operation in case of war. Pollio expressed the opinion that in such a case the Triplice 'should act as a single state'. He expressed his readiness with the consent of his Government to send two cavalry divisions to Germany and to reconsider the dispatch to the Upper Rhine of an army, but below strength. Pollio received the consent of the Italian Government at the beginning of 1914 and the new agreement was drafted. But he would have liked to go still further. On 20 April 1914 he said to Lieutenant-Colonel Kleist, the German Military Attaché at Rome, that he would most willingly put many more corps at Germany's disposal once he was sure that the war would remain 'localized'; but one objection presented itself. 'Think', he said, 'of the possibility that Russia may bring into action greater numbers with greater speed than in the past. Can Austria, in such a case, carry out her task alone if Serbia attacks her in the rear, and must we not send Austria several army corps to aid her

---

[1] Pribram I, pp. 282-305. See Vol. I, pp. 557-9.

against Serbia?" Kleist in his report of this conversation added the comment: 'I nearly fell off my chair when I heard this. The Italian Chief of Staff seriously thinking of the possibility of sending Italian army corps to the help of Austria! How times have changed! Or else is it a speculation on a "thanks" in the shape of Trieste or Trento?'[1]

Pollio's hint of the possibility of sending Italian forces to Austria was caught on the wing by Moltke. On 12 May in a talk with Conrad at Carlsbad he told him that Italy was prepared to send more than the three corps earmarked for Germany and asked Conrad how he would use them. Conrad answered that he was not sure whether he would use them against Serbia or against Russia and that he would need more facts before making a decision. But the draft convention of 1914 definitely laid down that the Italian forces were to be used on the Rhine and not against Russia. Hence on 29 May General Calderari, the Italian Military Attaché at Berlin, reported Moltke's wish to Pollio that in the convention 'the place of assembly of the Italian forces in Germany should not be rigidly laid down'. Sending on Calderari's letters to General Zuccari on 16 June, Pollio commented:

> In regard to the use of the Third Army against Russia, I do not rule it out that the events of the war may justify it, and once war was declared I would even take responsibility for such use. However, if I can agree to its being discussed now, I cannot in the present political and military situation bring it up with the Government and ask for the necessary authorization to insert it in the convention. I can only agree to an exchange of views without official ratification.[2]

The exchange of views was continued. A letter of Conrad's, which we shall soon read, shows that protracted, highly secret negotiations by word of mouth went on between himself and Pollio, where and when we do not know, or whether directly or by intermediaries. The military agreements were on the point of being concluded and signed when on 28 June Pollio died suddenly at Turin. His death was a blow to the Central Powers. Even Francis Joseph was affected by it and, in giving an audience to Tschirschky on 2 July, displayed more grief over Pollio's death than, over that of the Heir Apparent, Francis Ferdinand. Tschirschky records:

> The Emperor then mentioned that General Pollio's sudden death was a bitter loss for Italy and also for ourselves. 'Everybody is dying around me', said His Majesty, 'it is too sad'.[3]

Pollio's successor, General Luigi Cadorna, who took over the command on 27 July 1914, found a spiritual heritage and tradition of

---

[1] See Vol. I, pp. 559-61.
[2] General A. Alberti, *Il Generale Falkenhayn. Le relazioni tra i capi di S. M. della Triplice* (Rome, 1924), p. 87.   [3] DD. I, 11.

studies which from the outset swept him along in the wake of his predecessor. He never doubted that Italy would range herself with her allies and therefore on 29 July ordered 'the emergency military measures necessitated by the international situation'. The first four army corps for concentration on the French frontier were to recall their effectives. Storehouses and shelters in the Alps were to be reprovisioned. The V, VII and XI corps of the Rhine army and the first two cavalry divisions were to be brought up to strength, as were the four First Army corps. Fortress artillery was dispatched to the fortifications barring the Alps. Authorization was sought for the immediate transfer of artillery from the eastern to the western frontier, leaving the Austrian frontier undefended in order to strengthen the French frontier. Moreover, on 31 July Cadorna laid before the King a *Short memorandum on the northwestern concentration and on the transport to Germany of the largest possible force.* After summarizing the previous agreements and referring to the promise lately made to Germany to dispatch three army corps and two cavalry divisions to the Rhine, Cadorna continued:

It is my firm conviction that the proposed solution will not fully meet the needs of the Triple Alliance until it reaches the limits of its capacity. In other words, I think we ought not only to reassign five army corps (in addition to the cavalry divisions) to the army destined for Germany (this, moreover, was one of the wishes and proposals of the late General Pollio); but we must also aim at sending to what will be the chief scene of operations in the war all surplus forces in excess of our needs on the north-west frontier and at home. . . . Our interests cannot but coincide with the general interest of the alliance group to which we belong. The balance of power between the hostile groups of States is tending to tilt against the Triple Alliance; failure on our part to exert our full strength in order to restore stability would be disastrous for the general interest and for ours in particular.[1]

Two days later, on 2 August, General Brusati, the King's first aide-de-camp, replied to Cadorna that 'H.M. the King, to whom I submitted the *Short Memorandum on the northwestern concentration and on the transport to Germany of the largest possible force,* approves of the basic conceptions developed by Your Excellency'.[2] This, however, does not mean that on 1 August the King was persuaded to enter the war on the side of Germany and Austria-Hungary. He in fact always read all diplomatic communications both incoming and outgoing and had on 24 July received the already quoted letter from San Giuliano as well as others that probably followed it, since it was San Giuliano's habit to write his royal master overnight, telling of what he had done and what his thoughts were. Brusati's answer gives the impression that, as the Government

[1] Luigi Cadorna, *Altre pagine sulla grande guerra* (Milan, 1925), pp. 15-23.
[2] Angelo Gatti, *La parte dell'Italia* (Milan, 1924), p. 45.

was hesitating what course to take, the King did not commit himself with the Chief of Staff and merely approved the basic conceptions of the latter's *Memorandum*. But this gives rise to the question: did the Government not arrange to maintain contact with the Chief of Staff, if for no other reason than to prevent him from taking decisions either way? The answer is in the negative. Salandra declares that he only learnt of the existence of Cadorna's *Memorandum* when it was published in 1925 by Cadorna in his *Altre pagine sulla grande guerra* and adds that if Cadorna had spoken to him of it he would have told him 'to spare himself the trouble'.[1] In reality it was the duty of the Prime Minister, who ought not to have been in ignorance of the military agreements annexed to the Triple Alliance, to inform the Chief of Staff of the uncertain position with regard to the *casus foederis* in order to prevent his taking premature action and thus prejudicing the situation.

The fact is that between the political and the military leadership the necessary close understanding was lacking. For instance, it is highly probable, not to say certain, that Salandra was in ignorance of Pollio's intentions and preparations to send Italian troops to Austria. One cannot but think that had he known of them he would have enlightened the Chief of Staff about the impossibility of so doing in view of the relations between Austria and Italy. Hence while the Government was preparing to deny the occurrence of the *casus foederis* Cadorna sent word to Szeptycki by Colonel Montanari that he was making every effort to collaborate with the allies, with the result that Conrad on 1 August wrote him the following letter:

The serious situation which has suddenly arisen compels me to request Your Excellency to proceed with those negotiations, begun verbally, which I personally carried on in strict secrecy with his late Excellency, Pollio. The substance of them was that, over and above the forces which, in pursuance of already existing agreements, Italy is to send in direct support of Germany, further forces are to be rendered available for the Triplice war and placed at its disposal for the direct support of Austria-Hungary.

I beg Your Excellency kindly to furnish information what these forces would be and where they are available and further ask you to allow the requisite agreements to be made between the two General Staffs for the taking over and transport of these forces as was already the case for the forces put at the disposal of Germany.

I beg you to send Your Excellency's delegate to Vienna and provide him with the requisite plenary powers.[2]

This letter shows that Pollio had gone a good long way with Conrad without leaving documentary trace. Cadorna's *Short Memorandum* makes no mention of the idea of sending Italian troops to Austria.

---

[1] Salandra, p. 264.   [2] Conrad, IV, 158.

Luckily Conrad's letter did not arrive until after neutrality had been decided on, so that Cadorna's reply runs:

In answering by return the letter of 1 August with which Your Excellency has favored me, it is my duty to inform Your Excellency that in obedience to the declaration of neutrality of the Royal Italian Government it is impossible for me at the present moment to reply on the matter raised by Your Excellency in the above-mentioned esteemed letter.[1]

Let us now see whether after neutrality was declared Cadorna received instructions from the Government to guide him in his dealings with the Austrian Military Attaché, Colonel Szeptycki. There exists a telegram of 4 August sent by Berchtold to Merey summarizing the gist of Cadorna's reply to Conrad's request for military discussions between the Triplice allies in view of the imminent war:

Discussions useless because Italian Cabinet has decided neutrality. 'Light' mobilization ordered. If Austria-Hungary does not occupy Lovčen and disturb equilibrium in Adriatic, Italy will 'never' act against Austria-Hungary.[2]

In a further telegram, also of 4 August, Berchtold adds that this statement was made by Cadorna to the Austrian Military Attaché in Rome.[3] Conrad in his memoirs wrongly attributes Szeptycki's telegram to Cadorna,[4] who on reading the memoirs wrote a denial in a letter of 16 January 1924:

I should never have taken the liberty of giving an assurance that Italy would never attack Austria-Hungary unless the latter attacked the Lovčen, since, if I had done so, I should have been usurping the role of the Government, having no authority to give any such assurance.[5]

Cadorna had in fact not sent a telegram to such an effect, but his perhaps all too sweeping denial gave it to be understood that he had never at any time made a statement of that nature either in writing or by word of mouth. Now in the second volume of *Österreich-Ungarns letzter Krieg,* which reproduced Conrad's error of attributing the telegram about the Lovčen to Cadorna,[6] there is an appendix giving Szeptycki's written report to Vienna of his conversation with Cadorna of which he had telegraphed the short summary wrongly ascribed in the Austrian *Red Book* and by Conrad to Cadorna himself. The written report runs:

The call-up of classes 90, 89 and the remainder of 91 (i.e., cavalry and artillery) is for the purpose of placing on a normal footing the army, so

---

[1] Alberti, *Il Generale Falkenhayn, Le relazioni tra i capi di S. M. della Triplice* (Rome, 1924), p. 82.

[2] Conrad, IV, p. 176; DA. III, 128.   [3] DA. III, 129. See p. 333.

[4] Conrad, IV, p. 176.

[5] Alberti, *op, cit.,* p. 92.   [6] *Ibid,* II, p. 285.

greatly reduced by the Libyan malady [i.e., the Libyan campaign]. For the time being there is no intention of calling up other classes. Italy does not regard herself as having left the Triple Alliance, but only deems that this war is not a *casus foederis*. Thereat I asked, why therefor armed neutrality and against whom actually this arming is directed. Was it after all directed against us? Thereupon the answer: 'No, certainly not, for we should never use the opportunity to snatch away provinces from Austria-Hungary, when she was busy elsewhere. But should Austria-Hungary occupy the Lovčen or upset the balance of power in the Adriatic in our disfavor, then—and only then—we should ask ourselves why this was being done. But since Austria-Hungary will have enough to do with Russia and Serbia she will not think of the Lovčen and will not disturb the balance of power in the Adriatic' I further asked: 'Can Your Excellency give me the assurance that if we strip the Tirol of troops Italy will not stick the knife into our back?' Answer: 'This will never happen: you can tell the Chief that the Tirol can perfectly well be left without troops; how can it be thought that we could do such a thing and that there could be such doubts of our loyalty?' (The question was put pointedly by me on purpose). . . . [1]

It is unthinkable that Szeptycki can have invented this dialogue. On the other hand, it would be doing an injustice to Cadorna to imagine that among the tremendous problems created by the European war the only one he singled out for attention was the minor Lovčen question which so greatly agitated San Giuliano. It seems likely, therefore, that in raising it with Szeptycki, Cadorna was acting on a suggestion of the Foreign Minister's. And in fact General Alberti—who at the time of writing knew neither of the telegram nor of Szeptycki's report and therefore denies that Cadorna made such a statement to Conrad—maintains that Colonel Montanari's 'day-to-day' notes show that 'the General asked the Minister in what terms and in what tone he was to reply' to the Austrian Military Attaché. Does Minister here mean War Minister? In that case the War Minister would have consulted his colleague of the Foreign Office, who must have advised the Chief of Staff to make a main issue of the Lovčen and give the fullest assurances on all other counts.

4. The Austrian Emperor and the Kaiser appeal to Victor Emmanuel; the Italian declaration of neutrality; San Giuliano's reply to the compensation formula of 31 July

We now return to 31 July, the fateful day on which the Italian Government was to take the decision to declare neutrality. Having received news of the Russian general mobilization and proclaimed the *Kriegsgefahrzustand* in Germany, and having, at 3.30 p. m. on the 31st, sent off his ultimatum to St. Petersburg, the German Chancellor sent Flotow a telegram, which has already received our notice, containing

---

[1] *Österreich-Ungarns letzter Krieg* (Vienna, 1931), II, pp. 793–4.

instructions to inform Rome of these happenings and of the fact that mobilization was equivalent to war, that France had been requested to clarify her intentions within eighteen hours, and that if France did not engage to remain neutral, war would be declared on her immediately. In that case

we definitely count on Italy's fulfillment of the engagements into which she has entered.[1]

Wilhelm telegraphed in the same sense to Victor Emmanuel in the small hours of 1 August, his message ending:

I have just had the question asked at Paris whether in a Russo-German war France would remain neutral. The reply, unfortunately, cannot be in doubt. At this supreme moment, remembering the cordiality of the relations of friendship and alliance which exist between ourselves and our two countries, my thoughts turn to you with complete confidence.[2]

The Emperor Francis Joseph addressed a similar appeal to Victor Emmanuel in the following telegram of 1 August:

Russia arrogates to herself the right to interfere in our conflict with Serbia, has mobilized her army and navy, and threatens the peace of Europe. In agreement with Germany I have decided to defend the rights of the Triple Alliance and have ordered the mobilization of all my military and naval forces. We owe thirty years of peace and prosperity to the treaty uniting us, the identical interpretation of which by our two Governments I note with satisfaction. I am happy at this solemn moment to be able to count on the support of my Allies and their valiant armies, and I cherish the warmest wishes for the success of our arms and a glorious future for our countries.[3]

From Salandra we learn of the effect produced by this appeal and at what moment the decision for neutrality was taken:

On 31 July, the day of Germany's hasty ultimatums to Russia and France, a meeting of the Italian Cabinet was held. San Giuliano gave a detailed survey of the international situation and an account of our actions up to that day. I drew the conclusions therefrom, adding the reasons of internal policy which rendered the decision for neutrality advisable. Rumors have been circulated of disagreement, discussion, debate for and against. On the contrary, there were only brief expressions of agreement, prepared, of course, by private exchanges of views between individual Ministers and myself. The decision was, without difficulty, unanimous. There was no foundation either for the boast, attributed to me by some, of having brought round that firm adherent of the Triple Alliance, San Giuliano. Like myself, San Giuliano had no other concern than the interests of Italy and was moved by no other preconceptions or feelings. Possibly my unfamiliarity with diplomatic caution made me more outspoken in the expression of my ideas. It was only a euphemism if later

---

[1] DD. III, 492. See p. 41.   [2] DD. III, 530.   [3] DA. III, 100 A.

San Giuliano told his friend Flotow in confidence that he stood alone defending Austria against the chorus of his angry colleagues.[1] No official communiqué was issued about this Cabinet meeting save for a denial of current rumors of military measures. Semi-official hints were dropped of the decision for neutrality, which was now irrevocable.

On that same day the German Ambassador formally intimated to the Consulta that Germany had proclaimed the 'danger of war' which would immediately be followed by mobilization and the declaration of war on Russia and France. He ended with the words: 'Germany expects that Italy will fulfill her obligations arising under the alliance.' San Giuliano replied textually as follows: 'With the approval of the Prime Minister and as a result of today's Cabinet meeting, Italy, in accordance with the spirit and letter of the treaty of the Triple Alliance, does not hold herself bound to take part in this war, which is not of a defensive character.' On the morning of 2 August, the King, who had been kept informed of events, arrived in Rome. I saw him at once. He authorized the official declaration of neutrality, the text of which, passed at another Cabinet meeting, was published on the 3rd. Next day England declared war.[2]

This account of events is not quite exact. The Cabinet meeting took place at 10 a. m. on the 31st before news had reached Berlin of the Russian general mobilization and when the German ultimatum had therefore not yet been sent off—in other words, when hopes of a peaceful settlement were still possible.

These hopes only vanished when about 8 p. m. on the 31st Flotow called at the Consulta to communicate the Chancellor's telegram of 3.30 p. m. speaking of German mobilization and war as virtually certain and appealing for Italian support. San Giuliano then sought out Salandra and had a long discussion with him, after which, shortly after midnight, the press was told that in the event of war Italy would remain neutral. In fact, on the morning of 1 August the *Corriere della Sera* appeared with big headlines: 'War now regarded as inevitable. The spirit and letter of the Triple Alliance are such that for Italy a *casus foederis* does not arise. Italy will observe a friendly attitude of a diplomatic character towards the allies and will await the development of events.' The situation created by the German ultimatum was not discussed by the Cabinet until 10 p. m. on 1 August, and afterwards the following communiqué was issued to the press: 'The Cabinet has discussed the situation and expressed approval of the line of action pursued by the Foreign Minister during these last days; in other words, the Cabinet has ratified the decision taken jointly by the Prime Minister and the Foreign Minister yesterday evening and contained in a communiqué published in the press.' Yet it was still not the official and final decision. This was taken at a further Cabinet meeting, which was held at

[1] DD. III, 534.   [2] Salandra, pp. 106-8.

6.30 p. m. on 2 August, after the King's return to Rome, and was published on the morning of the 3rd. It ran:

Since certain European Powers are in a state of war and since Italy is at peace with all the belligerents, the King's Government, the citizens and authorities of the Kingdom are in duty bound to observe the obligations of neutrality under existing legislation and in accordance with the principles of international law. Anyone who infringes these obligations will suffer the consequences of his own acts and incur, if the case arises, the penalties laid down by the law.

This chronicle of events drawn from the press of those days conflicts with the fact that at 11.45 p. m. on the 31st Flotow telegraphed to Berlin:

The Italian Government has already taken its decision about Italy's attitude to the war at the Cabinet meeting held today. . . . She will have to declare herself neutral.[1]

But there exist two other telegrams from Flotow saying that the Cabinet decision was only taken on the evening of 1 August. At 10.55 p. m. on 1 August Flotow telegraphed:

Jointly with Austrian Ambassador I have once again sharply insisted on [Italy's] joining with her allies. Marquis San Giuliano alleged that he was without news from Vienna, made no promises, but was ready to bring the matter up again at the Cabinet meeting this evening [1 August].[2]

On 2 August Flotow further reported:

State of war announced here. Marquis San Giuliano replied that yesterday's Cabinet meeting had come to decision that *casus foederis* did not arise, as it was a question of a war of aggression.[3]

This reconstruction of events shows that the decision for neutrality was not taken at the Cabinet meeting of the morning of 31 July, as Salandra writes. Probably, indeed almost certainly, the meeting discussed the whole question, perhaps not for the first time, as a matter of principle, inclining towards neutrality without taking a definite decision which the situation did not call for when Germany had as yet not issued an ultimatum to Russia. This hypothesis finds confirmation in the following telegram from Merey, which bears the date of 1 August because it was dispatched in the small hours of that day, but narrates events of the 31st:

The Foreign Minister tells me that at a Cabinet meeting held today a tendency has manifested itself that in the event of a European war Italy should remain neutral. . . . After a lively discussion San Giuliano ended

[1] DD. III, 534.   [2] DD. III, 614.   [3] DD. III, 675.

by saying that after all it was not impossible—as a formal decision had not been taken—that Italy might nevertheless take part—perhaps later if the case arose—in the war. Thereat the word compensation was once more uttered.[1]

This, therefore, was the idea of some members of the Cabinet, which as a whole had not definitely made up its mind. Probably while it was meeting, San Giuliano had received news of the Russian general mobilization and this had prompted him first to ascertain the sense of the Cabinet, and then to stretch out a begging hand to Merey in anticipation of what might happen. It is in this connection that it is important to fix the exact sequence of events. San Giuliano realized that since 24 July he had left his allies in doubt as to what line Italy would take in the event of war, and therefore on the 31st, before even hearing of the German ultimatum, he felt he ought to undeceive them. But he had left it till too late when he was no longer in time to give a useful warning and found himself faced with an accomplished fact.

5. How Vienna and Berlin were notified of the Italian declaration of neutrality.

We must now see how the Italian Government intimated to its allies its refusal to follow them into war, the way the Central Powers reacted and their immediate efforts to gain Italian collaboration. Not even when the decision for neutrality had been taken did San Giuliano manage to muster enough courage to speak out boldly and put his allies in the dock, as would have been right and proper, if only to make sure that Italy would not find herself in the dock in their stead. But as things turned out, Italy slunk into neutrality by the back door, tendering apologies, cringing, still making promises which were to be flung back in her face when the day came for her intervention. On the evening of 31 July when Flotow notified the Consulta of the German ultimatums to Russia and France and of the certainty of war, asking for Italian support, San Giuliano told him that the Italian Government regarded the Austrian action against Serbia as an aggression and that the *casus foederis* therefore did not arise.

The Minister further declared that Italy had received no preliminary intimation of the Austrian move against Serbia and can all the less be expected to take part in the war, since Italian interests would be injured by Austrian move. All he could now say was that the Italian Government reserved to itself to examine whether it would later deem it possible to intervene in the war on the side of the allies, provided that in so doing Italian interests were adequately safeguarded. The Minister, who was highly excited, added in explanation that the entire Cabinet except for himself had manifested strong aversion for Austria. He was all the less in a position to combat this

---

[1] DA. III, 88.

since Austria, as I knew, persisted in a conscious injury to Italian interests by violating Article VII of the Triplice treaty and by her refusal to guarantee the integrity and independence of Serbia. He regretted that the German Government had not made greater efforts in this respect, in order to persuade Austria to timely compliance. I have the impression that all hope here for the future need not be given up if the Italians are met on the above-mentioned requirement, i.e., if they are offered compensation.[1]

Thus Berlin did not think the game was definitely lost provided that Italian interests could be adequately safeguarded.

The conversations were resumed on the morning of 1 August, and at 1.30 p. m. Flotow telegraphed:

When I again today pointed out to Marquis San Giuliano the bad effect of the Italian proclamation of neutrality on all classes of our people, the Minister said that in this decision the Prime Minister, Salandra, had been swayed by vital considerations regarding the Monarchy. Participation in a war waged against Italian interests in the Balkans might conceivably sweep away the Monarchy. On the question of compensation I found the Minister more pessimistic than before; he thought it difficult to find compensation. Valona he would not have at any price; all that Italy wanted was that Valona should not be in other hands.

Consideration of England had definitely influenced Italian attitude. But today Minister thought English participation in the war not irrevocably decided; he believed that Italian neutrality would be regarded in England as a factor in favor of English neutrality.[2]

In the afternoon of 1 August the conversation was resumed:

Jointly with Austrian Ambassador I have once again sharply insisted on [Italy's] joining with her allies. Marquis San Giuliano . . . was ready to bring the matter up again at the Cabinet meeting this evening. He continually repeated the outward and inner reasons which here weigh against participation in the war. (Kaiser: Scoundrel. The King has not even answered me yet.) Austrian Ambassador, like myself, has impression that consideration for English attitude the determining factor here. Marquis San Giuliano continually repeats that Italian coastline and harbors could not be exposed to English heavy guns. There is also anxiety here that the troops in Libya might be cut off from supplies. From a confidential agent of M. Barrère I hear that Italian Government has taken steps to approach English Government. Perhaps, in spite of Marquis San Giuliano's denials, some arrangement with England has been arrived at (Kaiser: so even actual betrayal of the allies!).[3]

From Merey there exist two telegrams, one of 1 August, the other of 2 August. The former, written on 31 July, has already been mentioned. It reports San Giuliano as saying that although the Triple Alliance was purely defensive, although no preliminary intimation had been given to Italy, and although she could   not   be   expected   to   make   sacrifices   and

---

[1] DD. III, 534.   [2] DD. III, 566.   [3] DD. III, 614.

run risks for an aim which conflicted with her own interests, 'after all it was not impossible—as a formal decision had not been taken—that Italy might nevertheless take part—perhaps later if the case arose—in the war. Thereat the word compensation was once more uttered.' This elicited from Merey the comment:

> I still have the impression that it is a question of blackmail, already successful on the whole. Italy means to get paid in advance for her attitude, whether it is a case of a localized or of a general war.[1]

In his telegram of 2 August, summarizing the talk of 1 August Merey reported having notified San Giuliano of the agreement arrived at by Berchtold and Avarna at Vienna on the 31st on the subject of compensation.[2] The report continues:

> Our concessions would only be valid in the event of Italy's integral fulfillment of her obligations as an ally. In spite of my insistence Marquis San Giuliano declined to pronounce himself. . . . As I continued to press him he told me that his first impression was not favorable because of the way in which the terms are formulated, that in any case this statement was at most a single factor in the situation as a whole and that the answer to the question whether Italy would take part in the war or remain neutral did not depend only on the satisfactory settlement of this matter.[3]

So much for what San Giuliano did on the evening of 31 July and during 1 August.

On 2 August the Cabinet decided in favor of neutrality, and on 2 August the decision was to be submitted for the royal assent. But the Central Powers did not know this officially when at 6.35 a. m. on 2 August the Chancellor telegraphed to Flotow that German mobilization had been decreed at 5 p. m. on the 1st, and that they were at war with Russia, whose troops had crossed into German territory and attacked.

> War with Russia will also have as a sequel a French attack on us and war with France. We expect from Italy fulfillment of her obligations as an ally. Please communicate the above to Italian Government and wire reply.[4]

Here is a puerile attempt to get it believed that because Russian troops had attacked and French would follow suit, the war resulted from these attacks and therefore it was France and Russia who were attacking Germany and not the contrary. This would make it obligatory for Italy to recognize the *casus foederis*. As has already been mentioned, Moltke had pressed for this in his memorandum to the Foreign Ministry of 2 August:

> It is essential to obtain a statement whether Italy is willing to take an active part in the forthcoming war in accordance with her engagements

---

[1] DA. III, 88. See pp. 313-14.   [2] See pp. 292-4.
[3] DA. III, 107.   [4] DD. III, 628.

under the Triple Alliance. I do not mind whether Italy sends the full number of promised reinforcements to Germany. If on account of the general political situation Italy can send but few troops to Germany, even if it is only a single cavalry division, that will satisfy me. What matters is not that Italy should actively support us with strong forces but that the Triple Alliance as such should enter the war united. That will be achieved with a minimal dispatch of troops. I draw attention to General Pollio's communication No. 2 to the Foreign Ministry: The [Italian] Government directs me to say to Your Excellency, etc.[1]

No wonder a cavalry division would satisfy Moltke, seeing that the Italian army would be a threat to France's southern frontier, compelling her to tie up forces there which would be badly needed on the Marne.

On 2 August Flotow on Bethmann's instructions notified San Giuliano of the state of war between Germany and Russia:

Marquis San Giuliano replied that yesterday's Cabinet meeting had decided that the *casus foederis* did not arise, as it was a war of aggression. Italy had not been previously asked, and was therefore under no obligation. She had not even been given time to make any military preparations. For this reason she would for the time being have to remain neutral, reserving decisions to be taken later in favor of her allies. The minister several times emphasized this possibility.

News of attack of Russian troops on German territory made impression on him. But when he presumed to suggest that it was probably a matter of minor frontier clashes which perhaps did not necessitate such severe measures, I had a sharp altercation with him.

In reply to my reproaches the Minister said he would tell me in strict confidence that according to unanimous and reliable reports the Italian Government would have revolution in the land if it went to war. It must be granted that this danger cannot altogether be denied. For the past year conditions have become very disquieting. I think, however, that not so much this as fear of England accounts for the Italian decision, and that, therefore, practically nothing will be achieved here unless English partici-pation in the war can be prevented.[2]

These documents make painful reading. It is deplorable to see it stated that Italy could not go to war for fear that the Monarchy would fall, that there would be revolution, that Italian coasts and harbors would be exposed to bombardment by the British navy, when it would have been so much worthier, nobler and more intelligent to answer: 'It is you who have violated both spirit and letter of the Triple Alliance, setting Europe ablaze in pursuit of a design which so much runs counter to the terms of our agreements and to Italian interests that you have thought it better to keep us absolutely in the dark about what you were plotting. Can you be surprised if Italy does not lend you her aid, in fact demands compensation under

[1] DD. III, 662. See pp. 197-8.   [2] DD. III, 675.

Article VII for the damage that will be inflicted on her? Remember what was said in July 1913 at Vienna to discourage a previous attempt. Then the Italian warning was issued in conjunction with a similar warning from Germany. If Germany has now changed her mind, Italy has not done so and never can, seeing that her interests, her liberal traditions, her love of peace forbid.' Obviously such plain speaking would have precluded all holding out hopes of 'later intervention, all begging for compensation. And so it came about that Flotow continued to send misleading information to Berlin. On the morning of the 3rd he again reported that the real reason for Italy's neutrality was fear of unrest in the country.

> Both the Austrian Ambassador and I having advocated intervention in the most incisive way and using all arguments, I do not for the present expect greater success with the Cabinet. On the other hand, both I and Baron von Merey have gained the impression from some striking articles in papers in touch with the Government, such as the *Popolo Romano, Giornale d'Italia,* etc., criticizing attitude of Government and neutrality, that Marquis San Giuliano's plan is to make public opinion compel him to intervene later on our side. This chimes in with his first statement [at Fiuggi] that 'he hopes perhaps later to take steps for us', and second statement that 'he will continue to influence the press in a sense favorable to co-operation with us'.[1]

It was not until the discussion had grown thoroughly acrimonious that San Giuliano found courage to speak in terms the situation demanded, though mingling with them deplorable references to unrest at home. The occasion was when Flotow, after having on the 2nd in vain tried to maintain that the war with Russia was provoked by attacks from Russian troops, returned on the 3rd, following instructions sent during the night both to him and to Lichnowsky[2], with reports that the French had opened hostilities on the French frontier. The following is a summary of the conversation dispatched by Flotow at 2 p. m. on the 3rd:

> Marquis San Giuliano takes the view that all these acts of France do not constitute *casus foederis,* as they are only the consequence of the previous aggressive steps by Austria. My argument with him about it reached such a degree of acrimoniousness that its resumption seems to me inadvisable. He reproaches us with having concocted the whole game with Austria in order to face Italy with a *fait accompli.* One cannot, said he, involve a Great Power in a conflict of this nature without previous consultation. We would now have to take the consequences of Italy's refusal to let herself be caught unawares. He had not even been given time to make military preparations. The country could not be laid open to Anglo-French attack in this manner. To this must be added the great dangers of the internal situation. We should

---

[1] DD. IV, 748.   [2] DD. III, 693, 694. See pp. 210-11.

see what, would become of Austria in this conflict. She was a corpse that could never be brought to life again. She would now be entirely destroyed.[1]

Well and good! Here was San Giuliano telling Germany some simple home-truths and foretelling for Austria the fate which was eventually to overtake her. But such outbursts were brief, and the tone of his official utterances, especially those to Vienna, was very different, as is shown by the following incident. We have seen that on 1 August Merey had conveyed to him Berchtold's acceptance of the Italian interpretation of Article VII of the Triplice treaty but only 'on condition that Italy observes a friendly attitude in respect of the war operations now undertaken by Austria-Hungary and Serbia and fulfills her engagements as an ally in the case in which the present conflict might lead to a general conflagration'.[2]

As this was something San Giuliano could not do, he found himself left empty-handed, and on 2 August he wrote Merey a long letter explaining his views and those of Salandra. It runs as follows:

Count Berchtold subordinates acceptance of our interpretation of Article VII to the attitude which Italy would take in the present crisis. One can subordinate the modification of a treaty to this or that condition, but not the interpretation of a treaty, since it is not a question of expressing the present wishes of the contracting parties but of recognizing their intention at the moment they concluded the pact. . . . In the second place the present crisis must be regarded as transitory, whereas the Triple Alliance is designed to last twelve years and may be renewed; and it is desirable, I may even say necessary, that during this long period the policy of Italy and Austria-Hungary in Balkan questions should be identical. . . . To this end it is indispensable that we should be entirely reassured as to the interpretation of Article VII. This necessity is still more manifest in the present crisis even if we do not participate in the war, for it is above all in the most difficult moments when the occasions for applying Article VII seem more probable that, in order by our diplomatic attitude to give the military action of our allies our steady, clear and resolute support, we need to be entirely reassured as to Austria-Hungary's interpretation of Article VII.

However, her acceptance of our interpretation of Article VII, while of great importance for our diplomatic attitude, is not in itself sufficient to eliminate all the very serious reasons which prevent us, at least for the present, from taking part in the war.

In fact, that general formula does not lay down a clear and definite agreement on the nature and value of eventual compensations and their relation to the dangers and enormous sacrifices which exceed those to which our allies expose themselves. This immense difference between the dangers and sacrifices on one side and the advantages on the other is precisely the reason which explains why Austria-Hungary wanted a war which she could easily

---

[1] DD. IV, 745.   [2] DA. III, 87. See p. 294.

have avoided, while we have done all in our power to spare Europe this terrible calamity. We, nevertheless, hope that, even without our taking part in war, openings will present themselves to prove our sincerely friendly feelings for our ally and we therefore count on an agreement of a kind which will reconcile our respective interests.

All these considerations, however serious they may be, would not hinder us from fulfilling our duty if this duty existed, but since the *casus foederis* is not applicable to the present war the Council of Ministers yesterday evening decided on neutrality, reserving the right to take decisions later on more in conformity with the desires of our allies, if such be our duty or shall be consistent with our interests.

The balance of power in Europe, in the Balkan peninsula and on the seas which surround Italy is a vital interest of our country and it will not recoil from any sacrifice, any decision which the safeguarding of its existence may impose.

Since the day on which I took over the direction of the foreign policy of my country, one of the principal aims of my activity has been to tighten the bonds of mutual friendship between Italy and Austria-Hungary. It is to this end that I shall continue to direct all my efforts, for I regard it as essential to the interests of our two countries. To achieve it their interests must be brought into harmony so that the interests of the one may receive satisfaction without injury to those of the other.

I count on Count Berchtold and you, my dear Ambassador, to aid me in fulfilling this task.[1]

Although in the latter part of this epistle a faintly menacing note can be detected, its tone is very different from that of Salandra's Campidoglio speech of 2 June 1915:

> On the 27 and 28 July in plain notes to Berlin and Vienna we posed the question of ceding the Italian provinces of Austria and declared that, if we did not receive adequate compensation (I repeat the actual wording), the Triple Alliance would be shattered beyond repair.[2]

Neither on 27 or 28 July nor even on 2 August was the question raised of the Trentino or of denouncing the Triple Alliance. On the contrary, it was said that 'the present crisis must be regarded as transitory, whereas the Triple Alliance is designed to last twelve years', that San Giuliano had been and would still be its staunch supporter and would prove his friendship for his allies even without joining in the war if he were promised compensation also in the event of Italy's remaining neutral. But he never ventured to specify the nature of such compensation. He even reserved 'the right to take decisions later on more in conformity with the desires of our allies, if such shall be our duty or shall be consistent with our interests'. In all this, not one word worthy of the seriousness of the occasion, no statement that Italy's line of action was a

---

[1] DA. III, 109.   [2] See p. 278

consequence of Austria's breach of the treaty. The begging went on to no purpose.

6. San Giuliano's letter of 3 August to Avarna and Bollati.

On the morning of 1 August Merey had telegraphed to Berchtold that despite the efforts of himself and Flotow the balance was tilting in favor of neutrality.

This tendency, which has been gaining ground only in the last few days, arises—I am fully convinced—primarily from the decisive fact that, contrary to what had been anticipated here (and in Berlin), England will not remain neutral but will intervene. . . . Add to this the utter disorganization of the army after the Libyan campaign . . . and, as I learn from a reliable source, the fear of unrest at home. The final word has not yet been spoken, but for the time being the watchword is: neutrality.[1]

This last sentence deserves notice. Neutrality, it suggests, may be only a temporary solution, since the last word has not been spoken. Berchtold replied to Merey as follows:

It appears from Your Excellency's telegram of the 1st inst. that the Italian Government intends, if the case arises, to intervene later actively in the European war which is to be expected. In view of this circumstance I today asked Duke Avarna to call on me and spoke to him as follows:

'In order to avoid all misunderstanding I think it necessary to make clear that the overtures made on the 1st inst. to Duke Avarna in respect of the interpretation of Article VII of our treaty of alliance have been made on the basis of our firm conviction that Italy will from the first fulfill her duties as an ally in conformity with Article III of the treaty of alliance.' The fact of Russian mobilization, ordered without motive against ourselves and Germany, and the further fact, just announced, that Russian detachments have crossed the Russo-German frontier at several points, seems to give sufficient grounds for the *casus foederis.* I beg Your Excellency to speak in this sense to the Italian Minister for Foreign Affairs. I add for Your Excellency's personal information that Duke Avarna has expressed to me in warm terms his conviction that—even if the strictly literal interpretation of the Triple Alliance treaty allowed the existence of the *casus foederis* to be denied—Italy was under a moral obligation to support her allies. That he had urgently written in this sense to Rome but did not know whether his voice carried sufficient weight to tilt the balance.[2]

Berchtold's words that Austrian acceptance of the Italian interpretation of Article VII was given 'on the basis of our firm conviction that Italy will from the first fulfill her duties as an ally in conformity with Article III of the treaty of alliance' demonstrates the utter ineptitude of the Consulta's handling of

---

[1] DA. III, 90.   [2] DA. III, 106.

the crisis of July 1914. Not only did Austria receive no warning that Italy would not join her in a general war, but Avarna received no briefing about Italy's right to do this and about the serious violation of the Triplice treaty committed by Austria. Hence his regrettable disavowal of his Government. And this disavowal he was to repeat on 3 August when he called at the Ballplatz bearing the official message:

On orders from my Government I have the honor to acquaint Your Excellency that the Italian Government has decided to maintain neutrality in the present conflict.[1]

What passed at this interview has been recorded in a report drawn up by Berchtold:

I answered Duke Avarna that this betokened no very friendly attitude on the part of Italy, an attitude incompatible with the Triplice treaty now that Germany had been attacked by Russia, and France had sided with Russia, whereby the *casus foederis* became operative. Even aside from these circumstances I could only describe it as a very unwise policy for Italy to part company with her allies at such a turning-point of history. . . . If she stood by her allies an opportunity offered itself for her to realize far-reaching aspirations, such as for Tunis, Savoy, etc. . . . It was an idea devoid of all sense to panic over an Austro-Hungarian increase of power in the Balkans. We aimed at no such thing, only at the maintenance of the *status quo*. . . . Nothing was further from our thoughts than the wish to change the existing balance of power with Italy. . . . I could not believe that Marquis San Giuliano meant to deceive me when at Abbazia he repeatedly assured me with great emphasis that Italy wanted and needed a strong Austria-Hungary. How did that harmonize with the fact that he was now preparing to pursue a policy ultimately aimed against the continued existence of the Monarchy in its present form? It made a specially bad impression that the moment chosen for this was one in which a revulsion of feeling in favor of Italy, a wave of warm friendliness towards the allied Kingdom, was making itself felt. It could not have escaped his notice what friendly demonstrations, acclamations of the Royal March, and even of the Garibaldi hymn, had recently taken place. The Government meant to avail itself of this improved atmosphere to the benefit of the Italian element, thus in those very days the Council of Ministers had decided on the creation of an institute for Italian students at Vienna University, which would approximate to the creation of an Italian faculty. And just at this very moment came the rejection by the Italian Government of its obligations under the alliance.[2]

What Avarna may have replied to this travesty of the truth in regard to Austria's intentions in the Balkans and her treatment of the Italian element in her population may be surmised from a telegram sent by Tschirschky to Berlin on 31 July:

[1] DD. IV, 757.
[2] DA. III, 134.

Duke Avarna, who called on me this morning, expressed the opinion that it would be desirable if the German Government on the grounds of Russian aggression, clearly demonstrated by mobilization, should draw attention in Rome to the *casus foederis*.[1]

How Avarna reacted to Berchtold's protests about the Italian declaration of neutrality is outlined in a report of Berchtold's of 4 August:

When, in conclusion, I laid stress on the loyalty which since the first day of the alliance our gracious Sovereign showed towards Italy at all moments of crisis, the Ambassador could no longer hide his dissatisfaction with the course taken by his Government. He confessed having, '*entre nous soit dit*', sent his Minister a report probably stronger than any Minister ever received from his Ambassador, one which would not be easy to swallow. Also that he had begged Marquis San Giuliano to grant him a brief personal conversation, and that, in case of need, he would return for a few days to Rome.

Whereas on all other occasions Duke Avarna always most conscientiously endeavors to support his Cabinet's views by all imaginable arguments, he has in the present case made no effort to shield the Italian Government. He confines himself to remarking that our action against Serbia has been regarded as a provocation to Russia.[2]

How far Avarna went in his dereliction of duty is further told in a dispatch of 7 August from Merey in Rome:

Arrival of Italian Ambassador to Vienna on evening of day before yesterday; conversations with Foreign Minister, Prime Minister; today audience of King. He called on me yesterday, and today explained Your Excellency's well known standpoint, declaring himself determined to resign. Marquis San Giuliano mentioned Ambassador's intention of resigning, adding that he hoped to keep him in Vienna at least till the end of the war. Duke Avarna told me he had spoken his mind plainly to Government and King and insisted on resigning. Minister and King had tried to explain to him impossibility of another course for Italy, not only politically, inasmuch as by our and Germany's behavior the *casus foederis* did not arise, but also on the material side because Italy is neither militarily nor financially prepared for war, hence country could not be exposed to devastation by English and French navies, revolution would break out and the dynasty would be endangered. The Ambassador is to have further talks, seems to insist on resigning, reserving his decision on the moment for his actual departure. My impression is that he will choose the moment when he learns of the first signs of eventual action by Italy against us.[3]

[1] DD. III, 510.
[2] DA. III, 134.
[3] Conrad IV, 187-8. Berchtold telegraphed to Merey that Avarna had said to him under the seal of secrecy 'that in the event of an intention to change the course of Italian policy towards us, he would no longer regard himself as suited to represent Italy at Vienna' (DA. III, 141).

Bollati in Berlin did not go to quite such lengths, though even he showed what his feelings were by not presenting the Italian declaration of neutrality in person but sending it accompanied by a note beginning:

Extremely indisposed, I am absolutely prevented from coming to the Department today.[1]

Was his indisposition physical or moral? The Kaiser thought it was moral, underlining the first four words and adding the marginal note: 'That I well believe. He does not want to deliver such a betrayal.' That the Kaiser should regard it as a betrayal is not surprising, but it is hard to understand why it could be regarded as such by the Italian Ambassadors who knew the treaty, still less how Avarna could behave as he did.

All this only throws into relief San Giuliano's total failure to enlighten them and instill the Government's views and intentions into their minds. Had he talked with them clearly and straightforwardly, citing the text of the alliance and the precedent of 1913, had he stated his views in time without making reservations and half-promises, the Italian Ambassadors could not have acted as they did. Even after neutrality was declared, they were still kept in the dark, as is shown by the following letter, written to each of them by San Giuliano on 2 August and published by Salandra:

I expose to Your Excellency all the reasons for which the Royal Government has had to declare the neutrality of Italy in the present conflict. I expose them with complete frankness confidentially to Y.E. for your sole use; and of course I leave you to judge of the limits and modes in which you can in part make use of them in your conversations.

In a democratic country like Italy it is not possible to make war, still less a major, dangerous war against the wishes and feeling of the nation. Now, save for a small minority, the nation has suddenly shown itself unanimously opposed to a war originating in an act of overbearing on the part of Austria towards a small nation which, contrary to liberal principles and the principle of nationality, she wants to crush for more or less well dissimulated political and territorial ambitions inimical to the interests of Italy. In a country like Italy it may be possible without serious internal and external dangers to drag the nation into a war not in accordance with national feeling provided that the good sense of our people can be shown benefits commensurate with the danger and sacrifices.

But this is not today the case; we should have to burden the budget and the national economy, already none too flourishing and giving rise to widespread and dangerous discontent, "with immense sacrifices which would aggravate the discontent, expose existing institutions to grave risks and retard for half a century the growth of the country's general wealth, which is essential in order to preserve us from more serious political and social upheavals and to maintain our position in the world.

[1] DD.IV,756,757.

We should expose our maritime cities to heavy attack with dangerous repercussions throughout the country, risking the loss of our colonies and the troops stationed in them, and, still worse, "we should see our navy destroyed by the Anglo-French fleet and remain for years deprived of a navy with lasting damage to all our political and economic interests and our whole position in the Mediterranean and the rest of the world. And all this to what end?

Needless to recount what dire consequences would result from the defeat of the Triple Alliance. But even if it won a bare victory it would not be in a position to give us adequate compensation; and if it won a complete victory, reducing France and Russia to impotence for years, there would be neither the interest nor the will to give us compensation proportionate to our sacrifices.

In fact Y.E. remembers that Austria and Germany have always declined to fix compensations, and Merey has always ruled out that they can consist as a whole or in part of the Italian provinces of Austria.

In any case, even after joint war and victory, won by us at high cost, the disappointment in the country would be very great and dangerous for our institutions. Nevertheless, I do not overlook the seriousness of the difficulties and also of the dangers which face us as a result of the decision to maintain neutrality, and it is precisely the existence, nature, and quality of these difficulties and dangers, together with the best ways of forestalling, averting or meeting them, on which I ask Y.E. to enlighten me with your experienced advice and by the frequent sending of information, forecasts and estimates.[1]

The document is noteworthy both for its content and because it is reproduced *in toto*. No fault can be found with the ideas in it as far as they go, but they are totally at variance with San Giuliano's policy, which consisted precisely in seeking to obtain compensation and promising help to Austria in crushing Serbia if she were granted compensation. It is because his policy was in contradiction with the ideas in this letter that San Giuliano only wrote it after war had broken out, when it came far too late to exercise any influence on the two Ambassadors' opinion of his conduct. Furthermore, it was not enough for him to explain what reasons Italy had for not going to war. He ought to have shown that Italy had a right not to go to war. For this it was not enough to stand on the defensive. He ought to have taken the offensive with a vigorous exposition of the treaty violations committed by the other two partners. But, in the words of the final paragraph, San Giuliano was deterred from so doing by 'the seriousness of the difficulties and also of the dangers which face us as a result of the decision to maintain neutrality'.

7. Victor Emmanuel's telegram to Wilhelm, and his statement to Kleist.

The difficulties and dangers of the situation, as will be shown later, were such that San Giuliano advised the King to send the following telegram of reply to Wilhelm. Presented on the 3rd by Bollati, it was

[1] Salandra, pp, 144-6.

totally out of keeping with the needs of the moment, the delicacy of Italy's position and the advisability of making no promises for the future:

> I have just received Your telegram. I deeply regret that Your noble efforts, to which our own have been joined, to avert the serious international consequences of Austria-Hungary's initiative have failed. My Government has from the beginning intimated ['beginning' twice underlined by the Kaiser with the marginal comment 'a lie'] to Your Government and that of Austria-Hungary that, as at present the *casus foederis* laid down by the treaty of the Triple Alliance does not arise, it will apply all its diplomatic activity to supporting the legitimate interests of our allies and ourselves and to working for the cause of peace.
>
> I send You the sincere expression of my most cordial wishes for Your weal and the weal of Germany.
>
> Your Brother and Ally!! (Insolence!)
>
> Victor Emanuel.   (Scoundrel. W.).[1]

It was not a lie to say that Berlin received warning from the beginning that Italy did not regard the *casus foederis* as having arisen. But it was unfortunately true that the Consulta had not at once made it clear, as it ought to have done, that there was no prospect at all of Italian co-operation, nay had held out hopes of co-operation under certain conditions. It was this which caused the deplorable misunderstanding and led the Central Powers to think that, in return for some sort of compensation, Italy would march with them. But, leaving aside Wilhelm's irate comments, we cannot but ask: why was the King allowed to say that Germany had tried to save the peace, when the opposite was the case and when San Giuliano, as we have already seen, on 3 August had uttered this very reproach to Flotow.[2] And why did San Giuliano promise to support 'the legitimate interests of our allies', when his letter to the two Ambassadors showed that he regarded the Austrian action as inimical to Italian interests and that, as we shall now see, there was the possibility, perceived from the beginning by San Giuliano, of Italy's ranging herself with the other side?

Nor was the King less ill-advised in what he said to Lieutenant-Colonel von Kleist, whom the Kaiser dispatched to Rome to plead for Italian solidarity, and whom the King received twice, on the mornings of 3 and 4 August. Kleist's first report to his Imperial master runs:

> Today, Monday, 9 a. m. I presented your message to King of Italy asking for immediate mobilization of army and navy and aid as covenanted under the terms of the alliance.

[1] DD. IV, 755.   [2] DD. IV, 745. See pp. 318-19.

King replied that he personally was wholeheartedly with us and up to a few weeks ago never for a moment doubted that in event of war Italy would actively help her allies. The incredible tactlessness of Austria towards Italian popular feeling had so antagonized public opinion towards Austria in recent weeks that any active co-operation with Austria would now raise a storm. The Cabinet did not wish to risk a revolt. He, the King, unfortunately had no power, only influence. Were he to dismiss the present Cabinet, no other would take on responsibility. All this chiefly because Austria has till now not been prepared to give any definite promise for the future, whereby perhaps a swing round in popular feeling might have been brought about; whether this was still possible was very doubtful.

As nation did not understand the difference, Italy, because of Austria's tactlessness, would not keep her word even to Germany, to the King's great sorrow. He would use his influence once more with the Cabinet and let me know his success.[1]

It was obviously too late to turn back, even had there been the will to do so, seeing that the official announcement of Italian neutrality had been made on 2 August. Hence the King's promise to use his influence with the Cabinet was nothing more than an empty expression of politeness to the Kaiser. The audience of 4 August was reported by Kleist as follows:

H.M. the King received me this morning and said: In spite of his repeated efforts yesterday the Government held firmly to its attitude of neutrality. Active aid to Allies would be regarded by nation *only as help for Austrian plans of expansion in the Balkans,* since Austria had not so far even definitely engaged to refrain therefrom. (Kaiser: Our conflict with France has nothing to do with that. After all, Italy will fight side by side with us, not with Austria.) Nation will always fail to discriminate between Germany and Austria, (Kaiser: Of course, if the Government does nothing about it; senseless all the same), hence if the Government at the present moment gave active help to Germany, it would risk revolt. (Kaiser: A definite lie!) He, the King, could only say once more that he was unfortunately powerless, as Government view was shared by majority of parliament. Even the recently returned Giolitti, the *friend of the Triple Alliance,* took view that *casus foederis* did *not occur.* (Kaiser: unspeakable scoundrel!), that *country needed peace,* must stay neutral, since there was no *obligation* to give armed assistance.

Pollio's death very deplorable, as he was of a *quite different opinion* and *possessed great influence.*

Three years of reservists now mobilized, so that cavalry and artillery as well as navy are on a war footing, companies are 150 strong. Three further classes would be enough approximately to complete the front-line army. Government intends to be armed against 'all eventualities'. Upon my replying that as eventuality did not include assistance, the idea must obviously be an armed threat to Austria, there being no other eventuality, King said, one never knows *what the Government men would do* (Kaiser: In other words, he

[1] DD. IV, 771.

drops out entirely!); for the *moment* he, the King, *calculated* that this would not happen.

My impression from audiences: Italy annoyed with Austria, ascribes expansionist intentions in the Balkans to her which she has *never bindingly* engaged to renounce. If Italian mistrust is *strengthened* by Austrian *evasiveness* or if it *finds confirmation,* Italy will regard this as *injurious* to her interests and is preparing not to tolerate it. (Kaiser: Vienna must, whatever happens, give binding promises and offer big compensation attractive enough to be an enticement, ought to have been done long since.)[1]

The King's words at the first audience so exactly echo the ideas and words of San Giuliano as to be the exact reflection of his influence. It was the nation that was represented as not wanting war, and the Government that yielded for fear of revolt; to make the nation change its mind, Austria would have to make definite promises and this she refused to do. Not the slightest hint of the violation of both letter and spirit of the Triple Alliance committed by the two Central Powers, no allusion to the precedent of 1913 which San Giuliano was prevented from making by the fact of his having kept it concealed from Salandra. Austria had been tactless, unskillful, nothing more.

In short, the great arguments on Italy's side were cast aside in favor of the most despicable ones. So it had been from the beginning, and such was the line the King was now advised to take. However, his words threw into high relief, more than San Giuliano's had ever done, the fact that Austria had never actually pledged herself not to expand her territory at Serbia's expense. Berchtold at once saw how damaging this was when he learnt of the substance of Kleist's telegrams from Tschirschky. He therefore immediately telegraphed to Szögyény on 5 August:

I beg Your Excellency to declare to Herr von Jagow that we consider ourselves bound by the unequivocal and reasoned assurances on this subject Which we have given the Italian Government, and there will be no objection if the German Government in our name makes at Rome the statement of principle that Austria-Hungary does not aspire to any acquisition of territory in the Balkans, that the aim of our war with Serbia is sufficiently known to the Italian Government, that what we want is to put an end to Serbian propaganda aiming at the dissolution of the Monarchy . . . that military operations will oblige us to make Serbia the theatre of war but that we are already determined to evacuate it as soon as the war has achieved its aim; that we have no intention of attacking Montenegro. . . . The above clear and precise statements should suffice to reassure Italy as to our intentions if she is in good faith.[2]

Let us pause a moment to note how far Berchtold himself was from acting in good faith in continuing to avoid giving an

---

[1] DD. IV, 850. The words in italics were underlined by the Kaiser.
[2] DA. III, 148.

unequivocal pledge not to annex any part of Serbian territory and in instructing the Ambassadors to do the same. It will be recalled that on 27 July he had telegraphed them instructions to say 'without entering into a binding engagement that, as long as the war remains localized between Austria-Hungary and Serbia, the Monarchy has no designs of territorial conquest'.[1] True, on the next day, as we have seen, he declared to Avarna that the Monarchy did not contemplate territorial acquisition.[2] And on 31 July he telegraphed Szécsen

to remind M. Viviani at once of the fact that we have already officially stated at St. Petersburg that we have no territorial aims in connection with our action against Serbia and no intention of infringing the sovereignty of Kingdom.[3]

But we have already remarked that even this did not constitute a binding engagement any more than did the above quoted telegram of 5 August intimating to Jagow

that there will be no objection if the German Government in our name gives the 'assurance in principle' [*prinzipielle Zusicherung*] that Austria-Hungary 'does not aim at' [*anstrebe*] any acquisition of territory in the Balkans.[4]

The import of these expressions had been made clear by Berchtold on 28 July in reply to Avarna's remark that it would be a great advantage with regard to the Powers if Austria 'would give a binding undertaking to this effect'. Berchtold's answer was

that this was not possible because at the present moment it could not be foreseen whether in the course of the war we might not be forced into occupying Serbian territory against our will.[5]

That 'against our will' sounds very much like humbug and rendered Berchtold's assurances devoid of significance. He was playing with words in speaking with Avarna, just as he was playing with words and throwing dust in people's eyes when he talked of the Monarchy's territorial *désintéressement,* a very different thing from respect of the territorial integrity of Serbia, which he was careful not to promise, since his intention was to diminish Serbia for the benefit of Bulgaria and Albania. Merey saw through the trick immediately, as is seen in his dispatch of 3 o July:

As Marquis San Giuliano mentioned . . . that we had declared our intention (I interjected: 'But without a formal engagement') of not annexing any Serbian territory, etc.[6]

Still more clearly were the Austrian aims formulated on the 30th by Conrad at an audience with Francis Joseph.

[1] Oe-U. VIII, 10835. See Vol. II, pp. 384-5.   [2] Oe-U. VIII, 10909. See p. 287.
[3] Oe-U. VIII, 11121. See Vol. II, p. 685.   [4] DA. III, 148.
[5] Oe-U. VIII, 10909. See p. 287.   [6] Oe-U. VIII, 11166. See p. 301.

At the audience there was a discussion on what was to be demanded of Serbia in the event of her now coming to heel. She would have to accept the terms of our ultimatum word for word and reimburse all expenditure occasioned by the mobilization. I added that one would have to ask for cessions of territory such as would at least secure our military position: Belgrade and Sabac with adjacent territory for the construction of extensive fortifications the cost of which would have to be borne by Serbia.[1]

If such were Conrad's demands in the event of its being possible to avoid war with Serbia, what would they have been after a victorious war? But Berchtold listened to them without letting fall a word about the promises of territorial *désintéressement* he had given at St. Petersburg and Rome. All he found to say was: 'Count Tisza, too, requests that we demand no cession of territory.' But even Tisza at the Council of Ministers of 19 June had waived his objection to 'frontier rectifications for military reasons', and the Council of Ministers had unanimously passed a resolution

that immediately on the outbreak of war the foreign Powers shall receive a statement that the Monarchy is not waging a war of conquest and does not propose to annex the Kingdom. Strategically necessary frontier rectifications together with the reduction of Serbia for the benefit of other states and such temporary occupation of Serbian territory as may eventually become necessary are, of course, not ruled out by this resolution.[2]

This places it beyond doubt that Berchtold sought to throw dust in the eyes of both the Italian and the German Governments. But it is equally beyond doubt that neither of them showed the slightest desire to bring him to book. On San Giuliano's side the reason was that he aimed at compensation which he could only obtain if Austria made territorial acquisitions at the expense of Serbia, while Jagow, wanting to satisfy San Giuliano, himself suggested to Vienna on 27 July that 'if a more than temporary occupation of Serbian territory were to be regarded as an unavoidable measure' some compensation should be granted to Italy.[3] This enabled Berchtold to maintain the ambiguity even in the instructions he sent out after learning of the observations made by the King of Italy to Kleist.

Besides touching on the point that Austria had refrained from any engagement not to expand in the Balkans, the King also sounded a note which does not occur with equal distinctness in the records of San Giuliano. He intimated to Kleist that Italy was arming. And when Kleist replied that 'the idea must obviously be an armed threat to Austria', Victor Emmanuel's answer was: 'One never knows what the Government men would do.' Only in politeness did he add that 'for

[1] Conrad, IV, p. 150.   [2] Oe-U. VIII, 10393. See Vol. II, p. 256.
[3] Oe-U. VIII, 10789. See pp. 284-5.

the moment he calculated that this would not happen'. Kleist went away with the impression that if Italian mistrust found confirmation Italy was preparing not to tolerate any injury to her interests.[1] None of Merey's reports shows any trace of this possibility and only one of Flotow's of 3 August[2] drops a hint of it, as we shall soon see. Kleist, who as an *ad hoc* diplomatist showed greater perception than either Flotow or Merey, realized that the statement was of especial significance as coming from the King, who, foreseeing what would happen, or more likely knowing of San Giuliano's first approaches to the *Entente,* which we shall soon consider, thought it advisable not to leave things in doubt.

8. *Victor Emmanuel's telegram to Francis Joseph; San Giuliano drops a hint about the Trentino; Merey's and Berchtold's reactions.*

At the first sign of the Austrian *démarche* what would have been needful was an honest, intelligent policy, not diplomatic tactics prompted by second-rate Machiavellism such as might serve at ordinary times but not at a serious moment when the country's honor and future were at stake. This also holds good for the telegram submitted by the Government on 2 August to the King as his reply to Francis Joseph's telegram of 1 August:

I have received Your Majesty's telegram.[3] I need not assure Your Majesty that Italy, who has made all possible efforts to assure the maintenance of peace and who will do all she can to contribute to re-establishing it as soon as possible, will observe a cordially friendly attitude towards her allies conformably to the treaty of the Triple Alliance, her own sincere sentiments and the great interests which it is her duty to safeguard.[4]

Here, too, not a sign of protest or of reservations, no affirmation of Italy's rights, only a promise to 'observe a cordially friendly attitude' which it was impossible to fulfill. In vain does one seek an explanation in Salandra's book, which does not even mention the King's telegrams to the two Emperors and devotes only six lines to the audience given to Kleist, saying that the King was 'courteous but prudent and firm'.[5] More than courteous, he was making promises in order to appease his allies' anger. But, however things might seem on the surface, their resentment remained unabated, as the following will show.
On 2 August Wenninger telegraphed from Berlin to Munich:

About the same time as Italy's uncertain attitude became known, a high-ranking Italian naval officer arrived in Berlin asking on instructions for the German plans of naval concentration. He was not received. This much is certain,

---

[1] See p. 328. [2] DD. IV, 748. [3] See p. 311.
[4] DA. III, 100 B. [5] Salandra, p. 109.

whether Italy now goes with us or against us, the present war will be followed by an Austro-Italian war.[1]

This state of mind is reflected with greater discretion in the diplomatic documents. In an already mentioned telegram to Berchtold of 1 August Merey proposed:

Perhaps we and Germany could contemplate declaring to Italy that if she did not loyally carry out her engagements under the alliance down to the last man and remained neutral, we also should throw up our alliance engagements and regard Italy as having quitted the Triple Alliance.[2]

On 3 August V passed on this advice of Merey's to the Wilhelmstrasse with the comment:

Although in the event of neutrality I would advocate the exclusion of Italy from the Triple Alliance after the war, I query whether the threat at the present moment would not bring the risk of Italy's at once passing over to the enemy camp.

Bergen and Zimmermann both annotated the telegram, Bergen asking whether the answer returned to the Austrian Embassy should run: 'that such a threat at present seems to us *not* [twice underlined] indicated', and Zimmermann adding: 'Yes, undoubtedly.'[3] And in this judgment Berchtold concurred. In sending to Szögyény on 3 August a summary of San Giuliano's letter of the 2nd, mentioned above,[4] he appended to it the following:

I beg Your Excellency to communicate the above to Herr von Jagow and observe that it seemed to me superfluous to add a commentary to this Italian enunciation. In these circumstances the most important thing would seem to be to content ourselves with Italy's neutrality, put a good face on it and avoid everything that could induce Italy to pass into the opposite camp. From this standpoint we must endeavor to awaken the belief in Italy that; in view of the other important reasons determining her neutrality, we are prepared to acquiesce in it. Should Italy pursue the question of compensation further we would politely avoid any conversation on grounds that we have so far not occupied any territory belonging to a Balkan State.

If we can manage to persuade Turkey and Romania to recognize the *casus foederis* and actively intervene, Italy will perhaps feel moved to bow to our interpretation of Article III. But it would seem to me advisable not to use possible intervention by Turkey on our side as a means of exerting pressure in Rome, since we should run the risk of last-minute efforts by Italy to counter our action at Bucharest and Constantinople.[5]

On 5 August Jagow sent a message to Berchtold that he, too, thought it well to 'put a good face on it', but that on the question of compensations he thought it 'would not be light

---

[1] DD. IV, *Anhang* IVa, 12; Dirr., pp. 230-1.   [2] DA. III, 90.
[3] DD. IV, 760. There is some slip in the punctuation of this telegram; no quotation mark shows where Merey's suggestion ends and Szögyény's comment begins.
[4] DA. III, 109. See pp. 19-20.   [5] DA. III, 117.

if, in the event of Italy's raising the matter again, she were to receive an evasive reply. Italy was on the verge not merely of remaining [neutral] but of joining hands with the enemy'.[1]

Jagow was prompted to speak of this danger not only by Kleist's telegram of the previous evening[2] but also by the concluding words of Flotow's telegram of 3 August:

In these circumstances I would think it preferable to avoid an open breach with Italy for the time being and, in the absence of other instructions, will regulate my already quite stiff attitude accordingly. It must also be borne in mind that from hints dropped by Marquis San Giuliano it cannot entirely be ruled out that Italy might turn against Austria.[3]

Before this latter possibility dawned on them the Austrians had been describing the neutrality of Rome as 'blackmail'. In a telegram of 2 August Merey wrote to Berchtold:

As Your Excellency sees, neutrality has been decided and provides the mathematical proof that—as I have always maintained—the indulgence in the question of compensation advised by Germany is only a surrender to blackmail and will not attain the desired results.[4]

Berchtold used the same term in his telegram of 4 August to Merey in passing on Cadorna's reply to the Austrian Military Attaché, Szeptycki:

As Your Excellency can gather from the above utterance of the Italian Chief of Staff, the blackmailing policy is being carried further.[6]

Cadorna's utterance, as we have seen, referred to the Lovčen, and on 4 August Berchtold telegraphed to Merey and Szögyény:

In order to show extreme complaisance to Italy I have induced the Austro-Hungarian Chief of Staff to issue an order eliminating the occupation of the Lovčen from the plan of operations. . . . Even if Montenegro were to attack us, our soldiers will refrain from seizing the Lovčen out of consideration for Italian nervousness.[6]

On 5 August Merey replied:

Foreign Minister seemed pleased and remarked that this concession made things much easier for him. He only regretted that the matter had to be kept secret. . . . Marquis San Giuliano expressed readiness once again to enjoin neutrality on Cetinje.[7]

[1] DA. III, 137.   [2] DD. IV, 850. Seep. 328.   [3] DD. IV, 748.
[4] DA. III, 108.   [5] DA. III, 128. See p. 309.   [6] DA. III, 129.
[7] DA. III, 140.

But it was clear that if these concessions were made to Italy they were accompanied by a repressed rage which could not remain concealed and which burst forth when, on 3 August, San Giuliano for the first time mentioned the Trentino as compensation for the entry of Italy into the war on the side of the Central Powers. Merey's telegram of 4 August runs:

In yesterday's talk the Foreign Minister reverted to reasons making it necessary for Italy to remain neutral. Among other things he dwelt on the thesis that the enormous sacrifices and dangers were out of all proportion to the gains. Not only was Nice French, but it had been ceded by Italy herself. Tunis was a fine colony, but Italy already had too many of them. Albanian territory might be joined to a State of mixed nationalities like the Monarchy, but would be a burden to a nationally unified State. It would be a different matter, he concluded, if the Trentino were in question. That would be the only conceivable compensation. I cut short the conversation at this point with the remark that if in the course of years I had often spoken undiplomatically sharply in our many and often violent discussions, I atoned for that fault at the present moment by not answering his inadmissible suggestions with abuse. That Marquis San Giuliano now dares to speak of the Trentino is characteristic and a bad symptom.[1]

It is hard to say what battle of ideas was going on in San Giuliano's mind in uttering the above words. One can only note by what process of elimination he arrived at his timid request for the Trentino as the only gain that could conceivably be in proportion to the 'enormous sacrifices and dangers' of war. Was he still in doubt of English intervention and hence in fear that Italy might have to join the war with her allies? It is hard to say. At all events Berchtold on 5 August replied:

I fully approve of Your Excellency's reaction to Marquis San Giuliano's remark about the Trentino. If Marquis San Giuliano again speaks of the Trentino, will Your Excellency decline all conversation on the subject and confine yourself to remarking that . . . it is singular that as only conceivable compensation Italy should name a territory which the Monarchy would have to carve out of its own flesh.[2]

A request for the Trentino in a semi-official conversation seemed such a serious sign to Berchtold that he followed up the telegram of 5 August to Szögyény containing instructions to tell Jagow

that there will be no objection if the German Government makes at Rome in our name the statement of principle that Austria does not aspire to any acquisition of territory in the Balkans,[3]

with another of 6 August saying:

[1] DA. III, 127.   [2] DA. III, 142.
[3] DA. III, 148. See p. 329.

I beg Your Excellency . . . to add that the subsequent message from Herr von Merey that in the course of unofficial conversation San Giuliano said he could regard only the cession of the Trentino to Italy as acceptable compensation, taken in conjunction with the noticeably deceitful and hostile behavior of the Rome Cabinet, makes it seem to me extremely inadvisable to give the above assurance. If emphasis is laid on the binding nature of the assurance in question the Italian Government would in all probability reply with a request for compensation in advance in case the engagement could not be fulfilled. This extorted tribute, as we have now learnt from San Giuliano's words, can only be the Trentino. Our inevitable refusal would necessarily bring on the conflict. In these circumstances the giving of the assurance in question seems to me not only pointless but actually dangerous.[1]

There exists yet another proof of the assertion made above that Berchtold's promises of territorial *désintéressement* were made to deceive. On 5 August Merey wrote in a dispatch to Berchtold

Sooner or later Italy will no doubt abandon neutrality. If our group gains a quick decisive success, Italy will probably join it and perhaps be more timid in her claims for compensation. In the opposite case she may be tempted to reinforce the moral extortion by military threats or measures against us.[2]

In his telegram to Francis Joseph of 2 August Wilhelm wrote that the King of Italy 'has shamefully betrayed our trust and has not fulfilled his obligations under the alliance'.[3]

And Moltke ended a letter of 5 August to Conrad with the postscript:

Italy's felony will avenge itself in future history. God give you victory now that you may later settle accounts with those scoundrels.[4]

Although it was not a felony, although the Central Powers were perfectly aware that Italy was not under an obligation to go to their aid, Berchtold continued indirectly to repeat the charge in the reply which on 9 August he instructed Merey to give to San Giuliano's letter of the 2nd. Merey was to begin by saying

that Vienna agreed with Rome in deeming it 'highly desirable that during the long period of twelve years which the present treaty still is to last and in view of the possibility of its renewal on the expiry of that period, the policy of Austria-Hungary and Italy on Balkan questions should be tuned to one and the same keynote. . . . Accordingly, when we decided to adopt the Italian interpretation of Article VII, we did not limit its application to the present conflict with Serbia and Montenegro. . . . We must strongly emphasize that the present great war was forced upon ourselves and Germany by Russia, who tried to prevent our punishing the behavior of a State not dependent on Russia, a behavior which shocked the whole civilized world and threatened our own existence.

[1] DA, III, 150. [2] DA. III, 139. [3] DD. IV, 766.
[4] Conrad, IV, p. 194.

The indisputable fact that we have endeavored for years in most difficult circumstances and at the sacrifice of important interests to avoid a conflict is the surest proof that it was not we who wanted to have war. When a settlement of the dispute with Serbia had become unavoidable we had hoped that the conflict might remain localized. Germany supported us in this endeavor. We are not blind to the undeniable fact that participation in the struggle will impose sacrifices and dangers on Italy, but we cannot accept the view that these sacrifices and dangers are greater than those with which we ourselves have to reckon. Italy may be exposed to extremely threatening attacks from the English and French navies, but even the most disastrous ending of any such encounter would not imperil her integrity or existence. On the other hand, a victorious ending would bring incalculable advantages to Italy, predominance in the western Mediterranean and the primacy among the Latin peoples. We take note with satisfaction of the reservation expressed by the Italian Government of its willingness eventually at a later stage to take decisions in conformity with the wishes of the Allies and are ready in every possible way to contribute to making such a turn possible. In regard to the circumstance of the formulation of Article VII being inadequate and not stipulating clearly the nature and extent of eventual compensation, it must be observed that we ourselves have stated our intention not to make acquisitions in the Balkans. In these circumstances we have till now had no occasion to invite Italy to an exchange of views on concrete compensations'.[1]

In other words, the conflagration had broken out through the fault, not of Austria, but of Russia, hence the *casus foederis* existed for Italy even though her coasts should be exposed to attack and the war would be a costly one for her. Berchtold spoke as if the alliance were still a living force, though how well he knew that it was already dead is seen in a telegram of Tschirschky's of 4 August:

Count Berchtold said every effort must be made to endeavor to hold Italy fast, at least to her neutrality.[2]

[1] Österreichisch-ungarisches Rotbuch. *Diplomatische Aktenstücke betreffend die Beziehungen Österreich-Ungarnszultalien in der Zeit von 20. Juli 1914 bis 23. Mai 1915* (Vienna, 1915), 35.

[2] DD. JV, 862. Concessions were to be made to Italy not only to keep her neutral but also to make her neutrality serve a useful purpose. Moltke wrote on 4 August: 'For the prosecution of the war now in progress it is of the greatest importance, on which enough stress cannot be laid, that food imports via Italy, should remain open for Germany. Now that Italy has not fulfilled her obligations under the alliance, but has promised benevolent neutrality, the least she can do to show her benevolence is to make no difficulties for us in this respect' (DD. IV, 804). Jagow, also on the 4th, telegraphed to Merey: 'Now that Italy leaves us in the lurch in the matter of active assistance, we definitely expect that promised benevolent neutrality includes at least transport of food supplies in the widest sense via Italy' (DD. IV, 806). Flotow replied: 'Italian Government already making difficulties about extensive Austrian grain consignments. Country short of grain' (DD. IV, 859). In the small hours of 5 August Berchtold telegraphed to Szögyény: 'It would be well to persuade Italy to make the observance of strict neutrality towards France and England on land and sea conditional on the abstention of their fleets from passing the latitude of Otranto so long as the Austro-Hungarian maritime forces do not do so. Reason given to Italy: Austria-Hungary conserves its navy which in the altered balance of forces after the war may be of great value for the maintenance of Italian domination in the Mediterranean, if our navy

Some may incline to regard this immediate acquiescence of Berlin and Vienna in the situation created by the Italian declaration of neutrality as a success for San Giuliano's policy. But this view cannot be shared by those who remember the figure that Italy cut in the eyes of the world in those days. Her neutrality could not be other than a first step towards intervention against her former allies and the honorable course to pursue with this end in view was for Italy to dissociate herself from them clearly from the outset.

9. The gravity of the Italian decision and the part played in it by Salandra.
Viewed in retrospect after many years with a knowledge of the documents published later, the texts of secret treaties, and the diplomatic correspondence preceding the European conflagration, and especially in the light of subsequent developments and the way the war ended, it may seem as if Italy chose the obvious solution to the problem with which she was faced by the outbreak of hostilities. But those who lived through the days and years leading up to the war and know what was the state of public opinion in that memorable July 1914 must say in all sincerity that even if Italian interests rendered neutrality imperative, even if no other course seemed or actually was open to the country, it was so momentous a decision as to send a painful throb of emotion pulsating through all hearts. It was not only that for thirty years Italy had been bound to the Central Powers by a treaty which on the face of it seemed to pledge her to range herself at their side, but also the fact that everybody, and especially everybody in Italy, was spellbound by their power, by the superlative quality of their armaments, their overwhelming might, their invincibility. In no less degree than they honored and valued their allies of yesterday, the Italians despised and distrusted themselves and the *Entente.* For France, moreover, they felt an animosity fanned by memories of the humiliation inflicted on them by Poincaré in connection with the *Manouba* and *Carthage* incidents during the Libyan war. Thus a sense of honor, allegiance and doubt as to the outcome of the conflict combined to create a state of acute emotion and anguish, a pause for reflection which in the life of a nation, no less than that of an individual, is the precursor of supreme decisions, even if these are imposed by fate, even if they are inevitable.

These words do not conflict with the judgment expressed above on the line of conduct pursued by San Giuliano. Quite the contrary. On

were destroyed Italy would be unconditionally at the mercy of the Anglo-French preponderance after the war. I request urgent telephonic communication of German standpoint' (DA. III, 135). The reply was not promising. Jagow said 'he must first of all get in touch with the Naval Staff. . . . In Herr von Jagow's personal opinion the suggestion of the R. and I. Navy Department would not meet with success' (DA. III, 152). It was obviously not to the advantage of the German navy that the enemy should be able to move all his forces from the Mediterranean.

those who enacted this tragedy, who were aware of all that led up to it, who knew the treaty binding Italy to the Central Powers and who knew the agreement with France, devolved the duty of having the courage to take the requisite decision however grave. Not only had they had a breathing space of several days in which to fathom the designs of Austria and Germany and decide on the measures to be taken, but they had also the possibility of drawing guidance from what had happened a year earlier almost to the very day when Italy had refused her support to Austrian designs of aggression on Serbia. If in 1913 her attitude had been endorsed by Germany, it did not mean that in 1914 Italian rights and duties under the treaty of alliance were altered by the fact of Germany's choosing to make common cause with Austria. That was Germany's affair. But Italy, who in 1914, unlike 1913, had not even been informed of what Berlin and Vienna were plotting, who was notified of the Austrian ultimatum to Serbia only after it had been delivered at Belgrade, had no reason in 1914 to take a line differing from that of 1913. And to save the peace and escape all accusation of betrayal, action ought to have been taken in good time, as in 1913.

The chief responsibility for not having done so rests on San Giuliano. As head of the Consulta since 30 March 1911, he had conducted Italian foreign policy throughout the Libyan and Balkan wars, had several times seen the spectre of war hover over Europe precisely because of Austro-Serbian discord, and on 12 July 1913 had peremptorily warned Vienna that Italy would not recognize the *casus foederis* in a conflagration brought about by Austrian aggression against Serbia. He knew, therefore, that the line he ought to take was the one laid down by Giolitti in 1913. Salandra, on the other hand, neither had special knowledge of foreign affairs, never having taken any interest in them, nor was in the Government during the crisis of the preceding years, nor had been told by San Giuliano of what had passed between him and Merey in their conversation of 12 July 1913.[1] He was thus to all intents and purposes a novice in the matter and may be believed when he writes in *La Neutralità Italiana:*

> I do not exaggerate in saying that the almost instantaneous decision which I was compelled to take in those few July days cost me more intense effort of reflection and greater strength of determination than the more tragic decision for intervention which matured by slow degrees.[2]

Certainly his task would have been easier if he had been told, by the man who could and should have given him the necessary enlightenment, that a year earlier in a similar situation his predecessor had once before settled the question in the same way as he in his ignorance was to end by doing.

[1] See Vol. I, pp. 458-9; Vol. II, pp. 242-4; 246-7.   [2] Salandra, p. 130,

Deliberately we say that it was Salandra who settled it. He maintains that he cannot claim the credit of converting San Giuliano to neutrality, in other words, denies that San Giuliano intended to support the Central Powers, nor are we in a position to contradict him. But close scrutiny of the documents reveals beyond all doubt that San Giuliano played a double game aimed at keeping open the possibility of bringing Italy in on the side of her allies and gaining compensation, which would, of course, be greater in the case of intervention than in that of neutrality. His silence with Salandra about the precedent of the year before, the absence of any allusion to it in his conversations with Flotow and Merey, and his instructions to Avarna and Bollati are not only corroboration of this thesis but proof of his fear that any such revelation might make Salandra decide instantly on neutrality. Nor was he mistaken therein. A decision for neutrality offered by far the greatest advantages to the head of any Government conscious of his country's political and financial weakness and military unpreparedness. If there were an honorable way of escaping the dangers and sacrifices of war, still more, if it were morally right not to take part in aggression against a small State which barred Austria's road to Salonika and to the command of the Balkans, why not take it? And on the other hand, what difficulties would have to be overcome before the country could be brought into the war on Austria's side against France and England! How would it be possible to overcome the violent opposition of Socialists, Radicals, Republicans and Freemasons? Salandra had only just escaped by a narrow margin from the sandbanks of parliamentary obstructionism. With what alacrity would he not have seized the opportunity of cutting a fine figure by displaying the rectitude and consistency of Italian foreign policy through a refusal of support to the aggressors who were destroying the peace of Europe! San Giuliano was too astute, too expert a navigator in Montecitorio waters not to be aware of all this. That is why he held his peace and depicted the situation to Salandra in quite different colors.

For one thing he could not allow Salandra to learn the exact nature of Italian engagements with France about which it is worth while to quote what Salandra writes:

Merey, the Austrian, was ill and more than ever difficult to deal with. . . . Flotow, the German, saw San Giuliano constantly but was not a man who carried weight with him. . . . Krupensky, the Russian, was a decent fellow but crude and not very bright. Rennell Rodd, the Englishman, [was] hampered up to the last day by the uncertainty of his Government. . . . Only Barrère, the able Ambassador who for many years with unqualified success had represented France at Rome, maintained continuous and diligent contact with San Giuliano and myself. He could not conceal the anxiety which weighed him down at the appalling threat overhanging

his country. As early as the 26th, in San Giuliano's absence, I had told him
what I thought from the purely legal standpoint of Austria's lack of frankness
with us before the ultimatum. But this did not satisfy him. He wrongly
imagined that we were undergoing strong and influential pressure from the
Central Powers. During the Cabinet meeting on the 31st, he sent in an
urgent request to San Giuliano for an immediate brief conversation. San
Giuliano absented himself for a short time from the Council Chamber and
on his return spoke of the Ambassador's intense anxiety. Next day Barrère
came again to see me; and when I, without revealing the definite decision,
which had not yet received the Royal assent, said to him: 'Vous n'avez rien
à craindre de nous', and authorized him to telegraph these words of mine to
Paris, I saw glistening in his eyes the signs of a genuine and unwonted
emotion.[1]

The *Documents Français* show that Barrère saw Salandra not
on the 26th but on the 27th July. Shortly before that he had seen
Ferdinando Martini, the Colonial Minister, who had said to him:

I do not see any possibility of this country marching at the side of Austria.
Everything is opposed to it, public opinion above all.[2]

And of his conversation with Salandra Barrère sent the
following report:

From what he said I have gathered the impression that in the event of a
conflict the Government would like to stay out and maintain an attitude of
watchfulness. In this connection M. Salandra said: 'It would be crazy for an
Italian to want to go to war; and that is just the feeling now uppermost in
public opinion. It would only change if faced with a threat or a danger.
Accordingly we shall make the greatest efforts to prevent peace from being
broken. Our position is somewhat similar to that of England, who does not
seem inclined to launch into adventures (I must comment here that the
attitude attributed to the Foreign Office has produced a great impression
here). Perhaps we could do something in a pacific direction with the
English.' M. Salandra confirmed that the Austrian note had been communicated to Rome at the last moment. He added that in his opinion Austria
ought to have intimated her intentions to her Italian ally and that in not
doing so she had *dégagé la solidarité et l'indépendance de cette dernière.*[3]

In the evening of the 27th Barrère saw San Giuliano
immediately on the latter's return to Rome:

He expressed severe criticism of the content of the Austrian note and formally assured me that he had no previous knowledge of it. . . . I asked him
whether it was true that he had, as certain papers claimed, expressed his
approval of the Austrian action to Vienna and given the assurance that Italy
would fulfill her obligations as an ally towards Austria. 'Not at all',
replied the Minister. . . . Marquis San Giuliano thinks Serbia would have
acted more wisely if she had accepted the note in its entirety, thus placing
Austria

---

[1] Salandra, pp. 110-1.   [2] DF. 3. XI, 144.   [3] DF. 3. XI, 153.

in an embarrassing position. He still thinks it would be the only thing to do.[1]

On the 29th Barrère telegraphed:

The Consulta thinks that in spite of the Austrian declaration of war on Serbia, there are no grounds for desisting from diplomatic efforts in favor of the holding of a conference in London with the aim of mediation.[2]

But he evidently did not feel confidence in San Giuliano for on the 30th he telegraphed:

The Foreign Minister, whatever his inclinations, does not like responsibility. . . . To sum up, the attitude of Italy in the event of a conflagration is uncertain, although public opinion still remains anti-Austrian. Considerable efforts on the part of the Austrians and their friends are being made at this moment with the principal newspapers to counteract this state of mind.[3]

On 31 July Barrère asked San Giuliano what Italy's attitude would be in the event of a war and reminded him of the Franco-Italian agreements of 1902. Under the seal of secrecy San Giuliano replied

'that the Italian Government was inclined to consider the Austrian attack on Serbia as an act of aggression of a nature exempting it from action in favor of Austria.' He further thought that the clauses of the Triple Alliance, which by the way were in harmony with the 1902 agreements, were such as would enable Italy, without failing in the loyalty she owes her allies, to abstain from participation in any conflict, He added that this action on the part of Italy would be contingent on the prudence displayed by France and Russia.[4]

Barrère's uncertainty was dispelled when on 1 August, having called on San Giuliano at 8.30 a. m. to learn exactly what the Italian attitude would be in the event of a general war, he received the news that Italy had declared herself unable to take part in the war.[5]

It is obvious that the above documents do not tally perfectly with Salandra's account. In the conversation of the 27th he had not confined himself to saying what he thought, from a purely legal standpoint, and had dropped a hint of the intention to remain neutral. Nor had he on 2 August been the first to announce the decision to Barrère, who had already learnt of it from San Giuliano on 31 July and 1 August. Indeed as early as 26 July Rodd had telegraphed to London:

I gather that Italian Government will endeavor to argue . . . that inasmuch as Austria did not consult Italy before delivering note, and inasmuch as by her mode of attack on Serbia she would be constructively provoking Russia, the *casus foederis* contemplated by alliance would not arise.[6]

[1] DF. 3. XI, 159.   [2] DF. 3. XI, Z37.   [3] DF. 3. XI, 332.
[4] DF. 3. XI, 411.   [5] DF. 3. XI, 482.   [6] BD. XI, 148.

Tyrrell also said the same thing to Lichnowsky on the 29th[1] and Szögyény reported that fact to Vienna the same day.[2] This is, however, not the important point. What concerns us more is the following statement by Salandra:

The French Ambassador, after the matter was settled, let it be understood that we could not have decided otherwise on account of engagements entered upon in the Prinetti-Barrère agreement of 1902. Not assuredly from forgetfulness but rather from tactful scrupulousness he -was careful not to remind us of these definite obligations in the days preceding the decision. He was well aware how elastic and adaptable are the vague terms aggression and provocation.[3]

Here Salandra reveals his lack of diplomatic experience and shows that San Giuliano had not explained even this aspect of the question to him. He reproduces the written statement given by Prinetti to Barrère:

In the case that France were to be the object of a direct or indirect aggression on the part of one or more Powers, Italy will maintain strict neutrality. The same will happen if France, in consequence of direct provocation, should find herself compelled in defense of her honor and her security to take the initiative in the declaration of war.[4]

This engagement—comments Salandra—'was formally consistent with the text of the Triplice; but to have entered into it was an unmistakable symptom of the slackening of the alliance'. This is perfectly true; in fact, a yet more serious criticism can be made of the Prinetti-Barrère agreement. Apart from all question whether Italy had or had not the right to make this secret agreement with France, it was of enormous advantage to France while tying the hands of Italy without compensating benefit, since if France were attacked by Germany in a European war, she could be no danger to Italy, whereas if Italy ranged herself with Germany she would oblige France to concentrate considerable forces on the Italian frontier. And, as the future was to show, the victory on the Marne was only rendered possible by Italian neutrality. This is not to say that in 1914 neutrality was not the right choice for Italy, but only that there was no point in her giving a guarantee of neutrality without receiving some equivalent in return. She would have been in a very different position towards France in 1914 had there been no Prinetti-Barrère agreement giving France a right to Italian neutrality.

Salandra comments that the vague terms aggression and provocation can be made to bear a very elastic meaning. But this is not so. He evidently did not know that after obtaining Prinetti's signature to that agreement, Barrère—taking advantage of Prinetti's resentment against

---

[1] DD. II, 355.   [2] Oe-U. VIII, 10948.
[3] Salandra, pp. 111-2.   [4] See Vol. I, pp. 127-32.

his allies, especially against Bülow, for their refusal to consent to modifications of the Triplice treaty which would have satisfied his restless ambition—secured precise assurances from Prinetti as to the interpretation to be given lo its terms, assurances through the medium of examples which went much further than might reasonably be claimed.[1] But what was still worse, Salandra's utter lack of diplomatic experience, here makes itself evident. He narrates that as early as the 26th he had told Barrère what he thought 'from the purely legal standpoint of Austria's lack of frankness with us before the ultimatum'. But Barrère was the last person to whom he should have spoken thus. To tell this astute and forceful diplomatist at this particular juncture that from the legal standpoint the *casus foederis* was not established was indirectly to admit that in any conflagration resulting from the ultimatum Italy was under an obligation to refrain from attacking France. Of course this was undoubtedly the case if Italy denied that the *casus foederis* was established. And when, as actually happened, Italy did deny it, she did so on the ground that the European conflict arose from Austrian provocation and aggression. But in so doing Italy herself interpreted Prinetti's statement in a sense favorable to France, so that in July 1914 she did not have all the three courses to choose from which San Giuliano contemplated in the documents published with approval by Salandra.[2] In other words, Italy was bound either to march at once with her allies on grounds that they were directly or indirectly attacked, or to proclaim her neutrality. To go to their aid later on when it suited her and she had received from Austria the promise of the Trentino or something else could not be done without violating first in appearance the Triple Alliance and then in actual fact the agreement with France. This latter further involved the question of Italy's relations with England, to which we must now turn our attention.

10. *Italy, England, and the Triple Alliance.*

The Triple Alliance came into being when, if England did not actually join it, she was gravitating towards it. The Italian Minister, Mancini, who in 1882 concluded it, secured the inclusion in the treaty of a statement that its provisions 'cannot—as has been previously agreed—in any case be regarded as being directed against England'.[3] This was tantamount to a declaration that Italy could not and would not go to war with England, entering into alliance with the Central Powers only in as much as these were on the best possible terms with England. The Mancini declaration was omitted from the first renewal of the alliance by Robilant in 1887 and in the second renewal by

---

[1] DF. 2. II, 329, 340. See Vol. 1, p. 131.   [2] See Vol. II, pp. 247-53.
[3] Pribram, I, pp. 70-1. See Vol. I, p. 45.

Rudini in 1891 in view of the fact that in 1887 a Three Power agreement had been concluded between Austria, Italy and England, and that in 1891 there was a prospect that England would join the Triple Alliance. In these conditions a repetition of the Mancini declaration did not seem necessary. But the mistakenness of omitting it became apparent to Rudini when in 1896, before deciding whether or not to renew the treaty, he asked for the reinstatement of the Mancini declaration on the grounds that it had not proved possible to persuade England to renew the Three Power agreement and that, in view of the deterioration in her relations with Germany, there was no more prospect of her joining the Triple Alliance. The request was curtly refused by Berlin.[1] Prinetti ought to have raised the question again in 1902 when, though unsuccessfully, he asked Bülow for several changes in the treaty, without mentioning this point, the most essential of all. After the danger, caused by the Franco-German friction over Morocco in 1905-6, of a European war (in which England would range herself on the side of France), the Central Powers expected Italy to ask afresh for the restoration of the Mancini declaration when, before 8 July 1907, she had the possibility of not renewing the treaty. And being in absolute need of Italy after the conclusion of the Anglo-French *Entente Cordiale* in 1904, they were prepared to consent. But Tittoni took no action. Still less did San Giuliano raise the matter during the negotiations leading to the last renewal of the alliance in 1912, despite the fact that Anglo-German relations were worse than ever and that, if a general conflagration were to arise, England would in all probability make common cause with France.

Not that either San Giuliano or Tittoni was unaware that it was impossible for Italy with her long coastline and her need for supplies from overseas to be at war with France and England together. General Pollio, to be sure, in his conversations with the German General Staff had calmly envisaged such a situation, believing Italy capable of meeting it, but he was the only one to think so. Traditional Italian policy had always ruled out the possibility of Italy's being in a camp hostile to England, especially when England was associated with France. But for fear of her allies, of Germany in particular, Italy after 1896 had not ventured to ask for what even Rudini had demanded at the time of Adowa and would have been so much more necessary and more easily attained now that England had become reconciled with France and Russia, Berlin being well aware that Italy could not go to war with England and France and that therefore the Central Powers had no other choice than to accept the fact. Hence in 1914 Italy had no right to reopen the question. On the contrary, among the reasons underlying

---

[2] See Vol. I, pp. 86-8.

the decision for neutrality the one most frequently put forward by the Italian Government to justify the decision in the eyes of its allies was the likelihood of English intervention.

Paraphrasing a dictum of Bismarck in *Reflections and Reminiscences,* Salandra writes:

> No Government can feel authorized to lead its country consciously to ruin in obedience to the formal observance of a treaty,[1]

and quotes in justification of his own policy the passage from Bismarck:

> All contracts between great States cease to be unconditionally binding as soon as they are tested by the 'struggle for existence'. No great nation will ever be induced to sacrifice its existence on the altar of fidelity to contract when it is compelled to choose between the two. The maxim . . . holds good in spite of all treaty formulas.[2]

Perfectly true! Yet it is far preferable not to be obliged to resort to such breaches of contract. Italy should have made her position in regard to England perfectly clear to her allies in good time, insisting that her allies gave due acknowledgement of it. And as that had not been done, it would have been better for her not to allege English intervention or other still less creditable reasons for her neutrality when in fact it was her allies who had violated both the spirit and the letter of the treaty, thus giving her the right, or rather making it her duty, to deny the occurrence of the *casus foederis.*

11. The mirage of the Trentino and the key to San Giuliano's policy.

For what reasons was this straight highroad not chosen? Undoubtedly one important factor determining the conduct of the Italian Government was the mirage of the Trentino, a lodestone of all patriotic Italians. In this connection Gaetano Salvemini comments:

> If before sending the ultimatum to Serbia the Governments of Berlin and Vienna had come to terms with that of Rome by promising the Trentino and a fair share in the colonial profits of victory, it is certain that the great majority, not of the Italian people, but of Italian political men, would unhesitatingly have agreed to intervention on the side of the Central Powers and forced it upon the country.[3]

The present writer does not go so far as that. On the contrary, he is convinced that given the freedom of discussion then enjoyed by Italians it would have been impossible to carry the country into a war in support of Austria, repugnant to public opinion and injurious to

---

[1] Salandra, p. 93.
[2] *Reflections and Reminiscences* (London, 1898), II, p. 270.
[3] Gaetano Salvemini, *Dal Patto di Londra alla Pace di Roma* (Turin, 1925), pp. XV- XVI.

Italian interests, and that this was the general feeling among politically-minded Italians. Salandra justly writes:

At all times, and more than ever at that moment, Italian public feeling was opposed to any association with Austria that would have led to the blood of our soldiers being shed in a war started by Austria in her own exclusive interest. Public feeling corresponded to the level-headed estimate of our vital interests.[1]

These vital interests are defined by Salandra in a passage which has been in part quoted already, but which must here be given in full as penetrating to the essence of the problem with which Italy was confronted through the action of Austria:

The conquest of Serbia, with or without loss of territory, her reduction, as was intended, to impotence or vassalage meant the definitive hegemony of Austria and through her the triumphant invasion of the Balkan peninsula by *Deutschtum*, the end of all possibility of Italian expansion, our commercial and military loss of the Adriatic. . . . From the wedge of the Trentino pointing at the heart of the Peninsula, from Garda rapidly becoming Germanized, from Trieste, the German emporium for the Near East, we should have been more and more forcibly surrounded, penetrated, strangled by *Deutschtum*. . . . The kingdom of Italy, even if sharing in their victory, would have been at best the first vassal state of the Reich.[2]

True! Excellently spoken! Only if there were some in Italy who perceived this clearly right from the beginning, with Salandra it was hindsight, acquired about one year later, for the policy of his Government fulfilled none of the above criteria. In other words, Salandra, San Giuliano and Sonnino negotiated with Austria for some measure of compensation in return for giving her a free hand against Serbia, notwithstanding the disastrous consequences that the crushing of Serbia would bring upon Italy. Not that the opposition of public opinion to the crushing of Serbia was based on a 'level-headed estimate' of Italian interests, however much San Giuliano used this argument in conversations with the allied Governments as a ground for his claim to compensation. But it does mean that, if the Italian Government had attempted to force the country into the opposite course, there would have been a revolt of public opinion. As Salandra writes, a current of opinion had developed in Italy 'against which no interpretation of the treaty could have made headway'.[3]

San Giuliano was aware of this but he did not yet-dare to cut loose from the policy of attachment to the Central Powers which he had undeviatingly pursued since 1911. He perhaps did not despair of

---

[1] Salandra, p. 87.   [2] Salandra, pp. 87-8. See Vol. II, p. 321.
[3] Salandra, p. 134.

converting Parliament and public opinion in a certain set of circumstances to the idea of making some sacrifice to close the open wound of the Trentino and perhaps even something more. After all, how was one to know? Perhaps it might be possible to heal the wound even without sacrifices, as Sonnino later tried to do. All depended on how bright were the Central Powers' prospects of victory and how much pressure Italy could bring to bear on them. Supposing England had remained neutral, the chances were that the Central Powers would be victorious and this prospect might overcome many objections. Supposing again the invasion of France through Belgium carried the German army swiftly to Paris and placed the French army in an impossible position. In that case the Italians might feel tempted to join in with her allies to get the Trentino.

Was this the way Salandra, too, looked at the question? From what he writes one would say it was. His profession of opposition to the Triple Alliance in *La Neutralità Italiana* is a late affair. After setting forth the disastrous consequences for Italy of the possible victory of her allies, he claims to have felt strong doubts about the strength of the thirty-year-old alliance now 'not adapted to the changed conditions of international policy' and 'no longer compatible with the dignity and consolidated structure of the Italian state'. Not compatible with its dignity because Italy was regarded by the Central Powers as an appanage, necessary 'but below the rank of an equal, a junior partner of low moral and military value, troublesome and unreliable'.[1] With bitter scorn Bismarck had spoken of Italy's 'jackal policy':

> Insatiable Italy with furtive glance roves restlessly hither and thither, instinctively drawn on by the odor of corruption and calamity—always ready to attack anybody from the rear and make off with a bit of plunder,

and, as Pribram writes, Bismarck had not 'any too exalted an opinion of Italy's military strength'.[2]

Holstein, too, the *éminence grise* of the Wilhelmstrasse, had said of the Triple Alliance in 1887:

> It is a question not of a permanent alliance but of acquiring a paid corps of auxiliaries like the *Lanzknechte* of the Middle Ages.[3]

If there were any still blind to all this the scales must have fallen from their eyes when in 1914 Italy was to be made to shoulder the burdens of the alliance by being confronted with a *fait accompli*. It would have meant submitting to an alliance like the one of which Livy says: *sub umbra foederis aequi servitutem pati possumus*. But after recognizing this Salandra continues:

[1] Salandra, p. 90,   [2] Pribram, II, pp. 3, 6.
[3] Pribram, II, p. 70.

Nevertheless, if the victory of the Central Powers had seemed to us certain, we should have had to stifle our feelings and, seeking as best we could to protect our interests, accept within the limits of our material possibilities the *simpliste* interpretation placed on the treaty by the two Kaisers in their solemn invitations to the King of Italy. But we did not let ourselves be blinded by the prevailing idolatry of Teutonic might. Imposing as was the weight of Russia, whose inner corrosion was known to us, though not to the extent subsequently revealed, we were guided in our forecasts, and hence in our decisions, by the certainty of English intervention.[1]

The present writer remains of the opinion that neither Salandra nor anyone else could have stifled public opinion and forced the country to agree to recognition of the *casus foederis* in such a war. Any politician taking such an attitude would have encountered the opposition of all parties and newspapers of the extreme left, the Freemasons, the greater part of the moderate left, and Liberal organs like the *Corriere della Sera* and others. They would have formed an avalanche which would have swept away any opposing ideas. It is not true, as Salandra writes, that during 'that torturing last week of July the Italian Government found itself *almost alone* in taking responsibility for the decision for neutrality' or that 'public opinion, bewildered by the sudden rush of events, had not yet taken its bearings or, save in a few newspapers, found concrete expression'.[2]

In the first place, the expression of public opinion appearing in certain newspapers was of great importance; and secondly it is indisputable that Socialists and Republicans at once began to threaten, while the partisans of Germany in the governing classes, who came so much to the fore during the period of neutrality, had not the time nor the wish to ask for the observance of the treaty. The Nationalists agitated a little, but they were neither numerous nor influential enough to gain a hearing. Who, in any case, could guarantee the victory of the Central Powers? Even were England to declare her neutrality, how long would it last? And afterwards, if she joined France and Russia, what would be the position of an Italy at war in the opposite coalition?

One thing, however, is certain. San Giuliano and Salandra were bent on not coming away empty-handed from the occasion. Italy was to gain the Trentino and perhaps something more. And as Austria refused to cede the Trentino and, moreover, her victory and that of Germany was far from certain, San Giuliano made haste to establish contact with the opposite camp. This fact only receives brief mention here and no account will be given of its further developments since these lie outside the scope of the present work. On 4 August Sazonov telegraphed to Izvolsky reporting a conversation of the 3rd:

[1] Salandra, pp. 90-1.   [2] Salandra, p. 110.

Highly confidentially I was told today that the Italian Foreign Minister, in acquainting the German Ambassador of Italy's intention to remain neutral, had added that Italy was ready to examine possibilities of aiding her ally if beforehand conditions were definitely laid down appropriate to Italian interests. Among these conditions is apparently the satisfaction of Italian claims to the Trentino and Valona. In this connection we were told that in consequence of the poor prospects of obtaining this satisfaction from Germany and Austria, Italy might enter into an exchange of views with us. Basing ourselves on your telegram No. 224 we answered that not only we but also France would certainly agree to giving Italy the possibility of acquiring Valona. As regards the Trentino we for our part have no objections to raise against its union with Italy; but we expressed no opinion because we first wanted to hear from you what France thinks about this point.

I assume that if the French Government is willing we might open highly confidential discussions with Italy to ascertain what help she could give us in the fight against Austria and Germany as the price of the above-mentioned discussions.[1]

Sazonov's second telegram to Izvolsky of 4 August names the source of his information:

The Italian Ambassador today resumed the discussion with me of the terms on which Italy would decide to join ourselves and France in the struggle against Austria. He indicated that in addition to the acquisition of the Trentino Italy desired to secure the hegemony of the Adriatic and for this end would like to receive Valona. She would have no objections to territorial acquisitions by Greece and Serbia on the Adriatic coast. In view of the fact that Franco-Italian relations were not yet distinguished by sufficient mutual confidence, the Ambassador expressed the wish that negotiations should proceed with us as intermediaries.[2]

Thus the King was assuring Francis Joseph 'that Italy . . . will observe a cordially friendly attitude towards her allies conformable to the treaty of the Triple Alliance', etc., in the very days when the first foundations were being laid of the event which was to come to fruition on 24 May 1915. However, it would be wrong to regard this step as determined solely by the desire for territorial gain. The mirage of the Trentino had a considerable influence on the conduct of the Italian Government, but another emotion was still more powerful, namely, fear of its allies' anger and of the consequences thereof. This is why San Giuliano refrained from challenging them by denouncing their violation of the letter and spirit of the Triplice treaty, why instead he made promises, and why he sought to establish contact with their enemies. Remembering the expressions used by him in his letter of 2 August to Bollati and Avarna: 'I do not overlook the seriousness of the difficulties and also of the dangers which face

---

[1] *Int. Bez.* i. V, 421.   [2] *Int. Bez.* i. V, 529; DDI. V. I, 65.

us as a result of the decision to maintain neutrality',[1] and reflecting on his waverings, his wariness, especially towards Vienna, his assurances of diplomatic support and of possible later intervention given to both Vienna and Berlin, one will find that the key to all his deeds and words is fear, fear not meant in a disparaging sense as something ignoble. In international relations, in decisions affecting the life and future of a nation, it is very necessary to feel fear of enemies or of enemy coalitions more powerful than oneself or the coalition to which one belongs. All sane foreign policy is dictated by fear of this kind and no one was more open to it than Bismarck in his diplomatic dealings. But it must be a well-founded fear based on reason, whereas the fear dominating the rulers of Italy both before and after the outbreak of the European conflagration was more akin to panic.

12. Italy's treachery disproved by the documents.

In formulating these conclusions the present writer has many times asked himself whether there is some gap in his memories of the situation at that moment as generally judged and whether it was not perhaps prudent, wise, nay necessary, to behave towards the Central Powers with the caution displayed by San Giuliano in only theoretically asserting Italy's right to stay out while giving half-promises of cooperation at a later date, asking for compensation so as not to be left empty-handed, but without using threats, then, once war had broken out, declaring neutrality, still with temperate words and gestures and with assurances of a friendly attitude while taking re-insurance measures by immediate overtures to the opposite camp. It was, in truth, not possible to forget the past and the fear felt in Italy at certain moments that she would, as Conrad desired, be attacked by Austria and put once and for all in her place by a punitive expedition. *Straf-expedition!* That was, in fact, the threat overhanging Italy before the war, during her neutrality, and after her entry into the war. And supposing—said many during the neutrality period—the Germans and Austrians, so powerful, so militarily superior to their enemies, decided to make Italy pay dearly for her treason by falling upon her? Or supposing they fell on her once they had rid themselves of France and Russia, perhaps even of England? Thus San Giuliano's caution was but wise, especially as he had also to allow for the possibility that the conflict might be composed and that Italy might find herself having made bold, compromising, dangerous gestures to no purpose.

A paragraph in Salandra's book reveals how much during the July crisis the Italian Government was influenced by the apprehension that if it declared neutrality the Central Powers might inflict immediate chastisement:

[1] DDI. V, I, 2.

It is undoubted that our army chiefs were not without concern about the possibility of an unexpected Austro-German aggression to meet which they did not feel sufficiently prepared.[1]

In proof of this assertion Salandra remarks in a footnote that in La *Guerra sulla Fronte Italiana* Cadorna writes:

It is no exaggeration to say that if as soon as our neutrality was declared Austria had attacked us we should have been virtually defenseless.[2]

But it is one thing to note such a degree of unpreparedness and another to believe it possible that at such a moment Germany and Austria could contemplate creating another enemy for themselves by attacking Italy. In any case, as Salandra himself confesses in another part of his book, he was not at that period in contact with Cadorna, whose opinion was that Italy ought to go to war at the side of her allies. It was not Cadorna who raised that scare, but the Government, who felt it on their own account.

Unreasoning fear is a bad counsellor and can give rise to words and deeds which are both dishonorable and injudicious. There was no occasion to be obsessed with the omnipotence and invincibility of the Central Powers to the extent of crediting them with the desire and the capacity to hurl themselves against Italy when they had their hands full with settling accounts with so many and such formidable enemies. There ought to have been a consciousness that, after the formation of the Triple *Entente,* the Italian alliance had become valuable, especially to Germany, and that as a member of the Triplice Italy could stand up for her own opinions and interests with dignity and firmness. Where San Giuliano went astray was in not having this consciousness, in having failed to study the lesson of the 1887 negotiations conducted by Robilant for the first renewal of the treaty, and in not having learnt from him how to speak to and what to ask of Bismarck's Germany and Kalnoky's Austria when these had need of Italy. Nor is this all. There should have been a realization in 1914—indeed the whole situation hinged on this factor—that what would cause the damage to Italy's relations with the Central Powers would not be her saying truthfully what her attitude would be, but her not joining in their war, consequently that the best way not to join in their war was to prevent them from ever beginning it by telling them unequivocally in good time what the Italian line would be. If there were risks attending this course, still greater were the risks incurred by practicing deception, giving promises that could not be kept, making excuses, haggling over compensation, both because such tricks made no attempt to deter the Central Powers from their plans and because, had their plans succeeded,

---

[1] Salandra, p. 180.　　　　[2] Luigi Cadorna, *op. cit.* (Milan, 1923), p. 180.

Italy would very soon have had to pay dearly for her non-fulfillment, explained away, as it was, by such poor reasons. Of this San Giuliano can have been in no doubt. Indeed, as we have seen, he remarked to Flotow on 26 July

that the procedure of Austria is highly suspect in Italian eyes. Austria might employ the same procedure tomorrow against Italy because of the Irredenta.[1]

This was very different from fearing that Austria would attack immediately and was a well-founded fear. But the policy it called for was the antithesis of the one followed.

The above estimate of Italy's position is at variance with the line taken not only by San Giuliano at that moment but by his successor, Sonnino. It was to form the subject of endless discussion during the neutrality period, which itself could not be other than the prelude to intervention on the opposite side and hence should not have led Italy into the ignoble temptation of seeking rewards without taking part in the struggle, rewards which would have been no less dishonorable than dangerous, and at the end of the war might have been roughly snatched from her by Austria whether victorious or vanquished. To view the situation in this light would be to be guided not by unreasoning fear but by rational apprehension. No such apprehension, unfortunately, was felt by those in and outside the Government who wanted Italy to content herself with the compensation obtainable through negotiations such as those begun by San Giuliano, continued by Sonnino, and regarded by the Central Powers as blackmail. Far from necessitating a policy of deceitful super-diplomacy, such rational apprehension called for a frank and courageous policy of awareness that certain perils can be fended off neither by flight nor by concealment but only by looking the enemy squarely in the face, prepared to fight for one's rights.

The absence of plain speaking, the profusion of excuses and obeisances gave those who did not know the true facts the impression that Italy was in the wrong, and those who knew the truth, namely, the real offenders, though all the time well knowing that Italy had a perfect right not to support them in their war, were led into temptation to represent the Italians as traitors and blackmailers who were to be fobbed off for the time being but with the idea of wreaking vengeance on them at a more opportune moment.

As one studies the documents of the Central Powers one is struck by the absence of any detailed exchange of views on the Italian 'betrayal', because the betrayal had no existence. If in 1914 San Giuliano feigned to forget the interpretation of the Triple Alliance given by him to Merey on 12 July 1913, Berchtold knew of it, enshrined as it

[1] DD. I, 211. See p. 283.

was in the Ballplatz archives, and it had certainly not slipped his memory, especially as in connection with the conversation leading up to it he had had an incident with Merey. Berchtold also knew that he had not protested against that interpretation, not being able to do so seeing that it was shared also by Berlin.

In this connection it may be well to recall certain of the documents. Right at the beginning of the Balkan wars, when it was suspected that Austria was meaning to prevent Serbia from harvesting the fruits of her victories, Wilhelm on 9 November 1912 drew the attention of his Chancellor and Secretary of State for Foreign Affairs to the possibility that Germany might become involved in war with Russia and France simply because Austria did not want Serbia in Albania and at Durazzo. He went on to say:

> So far-reaching an engagement is not in accordance with the spirit of the Triple Alliance, which was designed *a limine* to guarantee the existence of actual possessions. It would far outstep the bounds of a treaty and even of the *casus foederis,* which can in no wise ever be so interpreted as to cause the German army and people to be placed directly at the service and, so to speak, held at the disposal of the whim of another State's foreign policy. The Triplice treaty assures reciprocally only the actual territory in possession of the three States, but does not require unconditional participation in friction over the possessions of others! Of course, if Austria is attacked by Russia, the *casus foederis* arises. But only if Austria has not provoked Russia to the attack. At present such a position might arise with regard to Serbia. And this Vienna must at all costs avoid.[1]

There could be no more clear and convincing demonstration of Italy's good right to act as she did in 1914. And the same interpretation was confirmed a few months later by Bethmann Hollweg, who on 6 July 1913, when Vienna was talking of attacking Serbia, told Szögyény that any such attack would mean a European war, adding:

> This would most seriously affect the vital interests of Germany and I must therefore expect that before Count Berchtold makes any such resolve, he will inform us of it.[2]

Therefore any action against Serbia would cause a conflagration which Austria must not provoke without coming to an agreement with her allies. In 1914 she came to an agreement with Berlin but not with Rome, hence for Rome the *casus foederis* did not arise.

That this was the only admissible interpretation of the Triplice was acknowledged even by the Austrians. At the beginning of 1913 the Heir Apparent, Francis Ferdinand, said to Albert of Wurtemberg:

---

[1] GP. XXXIII, 12349. See Vol. I, pp. 399-400.
[2] GP. XXXV, 13490. See Vol. I, p. 456.

A conquest of Serbia would be senseless; if a general war were to threaten because of it, the *casus foederis* would not exist for the allies.[1]

Merey, too, in 1913 had implicitly maintained that in a conflagration resulting from an Austrian attack on Serbia Italy was not obliged to assist her ally. In his telegram reporting what San Giuliano had said to him on 12 July 1913 he wrote:

When I—*without being personally convinced of the justice of my argument*—objected that Vienna would receive the impression that Italy always took a selfish line in interpreting the Triplice treaty, only invoking it and taking her stand on it where some basic Italian interest was involved, the Minister rebutted my assertion with the utmost vigor.[2]

The words in parenthesis, here italicized, speak volumes, and it must be added that nowhere in his telegrams or letters of 26–31 July does Merey assert that Italy was violating the Triplice treaty by not co-operating with Austria, nor was this ever asserted by either Berchtold or Bethmann Hollweg or Jagow or Tschirschky in communicating with one another. Salandra aptly quotes Erzberger's words:

It is true that even in Foreign Ministry circles in Berlin the view was taken that the conflict between Austria-Hungary and Serbia did not constitute a *casus foederis* for Italy; Foreign Ministry jurists attempted to establish this in a detailed memorandum.[3]

The opposite view was taken by the Kaiser, forgetting what he had said and written on 9 November 1912. This is true also of Moltke, military circles, and the general run of the public in all countries, all, in short, who had no knowledge of the clauses of the treaty but had the crude idea that when one ally went to war all the others were bound to rush to his assistance even if he had acted without consulting them and without regard to the terms of the treaty. A crude conception. No nation can be expected to risk its existence and sacrifice itself to the utmost limits in defense of an ally without first being consulted and giving approval to the enterprise on which that ally proposes to embark.[4]

---

[1] GP. XXXIV[1], 12788.

[2] Oe-U. VI, 7748. See Vol. I, p. 458.

[3] Salandra, p. 108; Erzberger, *Erlebnisse im Weltkriege* (Stuttgart and Berlin, 1929), p. 2.

[4] In this connection it is worth noting that on 9 August, 1914, Ambrozy, then Chargé d'Affaires at Rome, drew Berchtold's attention to a statement in the *Tribuna* to the effect that the *White Book* showed that Germany and Austria had a long time before concerted the action against Serbia in all particulars while Italy was kept in the dark (DA. III, 164). On 10 August Berchtold, realizing the seriousness and the well-foundedness of the accusation, replied saying that he had said enough to Avarna about the projected *démarche* at Belgrade for the purpose of 'procuring for us' the necessary guarantees for the future. He adds: 'It is true that our note to Serbia could only receive its final shape shortly before its presentation, and that is why it was not communicated either to the German or to the Rome Cabinet until the last moment. The fact that we have proceeded to partial mobilization only

Just because, as a result of that crude idea, the accusation of treachery and felony would certainly be raised, as in fact it was, there was need to foresee, forestall, and foil it by timely and appropriate action such as would warn Italy's partners and safeguard her own honor. If Italy had an undoubted right to stand aside from their venture, it was at the same time no less undoubted that the exercise of this right was a fateful step, and one open to misconstruction. The only way to avoid misconstruction and not be treated as the prisoner in the dock was for Italy herself to become the accuser, laying bare her reasons, and above all citing the precedent of 12 July 1913. Never can enough stress be laid on the consequences of San Giuliano's omission in the days before the outbreak of war to inform Salandra and remind the Central Powers of this precedent, and reveal it to the world as the complete vindication of Italy's right to declare her neutrality. The sensation caused in the Chamber by Giolitti's disclosure of it on 5 December 1914 and the use made of it by historians to prove the guilt of the Central Powers make clear how effective it would have been if revealed immediately and accompanied by proofs that the warning had been repeated in time to be effective both before the Austrian ultimatum and after it. Italy would have occupied a dignified and unassailable position, and her later intervention would have appeared as the logical development of the honorable course previously pursued.

Would it in that case have been necessary to denounce the Triple Alliance immediately instead of waiting until 4 May 1915? No. Italy could perfectly well have stated and documented her case without denouncing the alliance, which though in actual fact a dead letter, might formally have continued to exist even though Italy were not bound to take part in the war. Austria and Germany, it is true, had violated the terms of Article I of the treaty, which engaged them 'to an exchange of views on political and economic questions of a general nature that might arise'. Austria had further violated the terms of Article VII, which bound her not to proceed to a temporary or permanent occupation in the Balkans without previous accord with Italy based on the principle of compensation. But just because that Article gave Italy rights and advantages on which discussion was still open it was not expedient for her to dissociate herself from the alliance on grounds of those violations until such time as she had decided to uphold her

after the rejection of our demands by Serbia and that for the preparation of this mobilization no measure had previously been taken sufficiently proves that we had counted on the probability of our demands being accepted' (DA. III, 167). Nothing could be more misleading than this version of the facts, as has been shown in Vol. II, Ch. vii, pp. 254-268 of the present work. The true facts are that Berlin was kept fully informed and not only approved but egged Vienna on. Moreover the demands were so formulated that Serbia could not but reject them and that the result would be war. Italy received no information as to the nature and scope of the step that was about to be taken at Belgrade.

interests by going to war. The denunciation of the treaty could precede intervention only by a few days. This point must be made clear, even while it is agreed that, given San Giuliano's tendencies, he would in any case never have ventured suddenly to sever the links with the Central Powers, however needful it might be to do so.

One can but agree wholeheartedly with Salandra's statement to the Senate on 15 December 1914:

> If we had negotiated our neutrality we should have dishonored it.

There can be no dispute that in such a crisis Italy could not let her policy be a subject of bargaining, and in this connection it is worth while to look at the arguments used by Salandra in *La Neutralità Italiana* in support of his celebrated phrase.

> The reasons are many. In the first place the sense of honor, the only one mentioned by me to the Senate, it not being the moment to expatiate on the others. This certainly was of supreme importance since—apart from all motives of sentiment— in a State with a civilization such as ours, self-respect and the esteem of others, the maintenance of national dignity and prestige constitute a real element of strength at home and abroad. In a Europe accustomed for decades to regard us as united in life and death to Germany and Austria we had above all to vindicate our good right to clear the State and the Sovereign personally of the accusation of defaulting on engagements. Could we allow the further accusation to be made that they did so for mercenary reasons? Posterity, it is true, has condoned, nay even lauded, many another desertion and *volte face,* but only when these were crowned with complete success. To sustain a blackmailing neutrality right from the first we should have had not only to throw over all moral scruples but to have a big army in the Po valley ready to turn east or west. As is now known to all, we had no such army in the summer of 1914 and the heads of foreign armies were aware of this.[1]

The present writer does not think that posterity would have con-doned and even lauded such a *volte face* even if crowned with complete success. Nor could Salandra have thought so either. And if not, what is the meaning of Salandra's words about feeling it his duty to clear the State and the Sovereign personally of the accusation of defaulting on engagements? The sole question which has to be asked in this connection is: did the Italian Government act in July 1914 in the best way to fulfill its duty.

The present writer would fain be mistaken but fears that this is not the case, as he thinks he has shown above. But that does not mean that the errors of procedure committed by the Salandra Ministry were not in great measure redeemed by the credit it earned both by its declaration of neutrality and by its declaration of war.

[1] Salandra, *Neutralità,* pp. 179-80.

13. The Italian ruling classes and the Vatican in the crisis of July 1914.[1]

From 1900 onwards a rapprochement of far-reaching importance had taken place between France and Italy, which culminated in the support given to France at Algeciras by Emilio Visconti Venosta, to whose initiative the rapprochement owed its inception. But after the Poincaré Government came to power at the beginning of 1912 relations between the two countries were seriously disturbed by the *Manouba* and *Carthage* incidents wherein Poincaré displayed an animosity towards Italy which outlasted even the. European war. Poincaré's anti-Italian policy was undoubtedly intensified by the ultra-Triplicistic policy of San Giuliano. There thus came about a decline in Italian friendship with Russia, England, and France and an improvement in Italo-German relations, at least at Government level. This improvement did not extend to relations between Italy and Austria. These, despite San Giuliano's good will, had been growing worse ever since the Libyan war, but had brought about no change in the feeling of attachment felt by the Italian governing classes for the Triplice, particularly for Germany, the pillar on which the Triplice mainly rested. Their feeling was compounded of aversion, not so much for the French people as for the way France had behaved towards Italy, and of admiration and reverence for Germany, her might, her prestige, her science, her economic strength, the excellence of her government institutions, above all her army and navy, prepared for ventures of the greatest magnitude. Loyalty to the Crown and conservatism also operated in favor of friendship with Germany and in this tradition were reared the aristocracy, all those in charge of Italian diplomacy, the heads of the fighting services, the university professors, members of the middle parties in parliament, financiers, industrialists, in short all the leaders of the nation who were strongly represented in the Senate. Their friendly feelings for Germany made them willingly accept the alliance with Austria, who inspired a certain fear and of whom it seemed more prudent to be the ally than the enemy. Moreover, since the road to Vienna passed via Berlin it was not possible to keep company with Berlin without accepting the company of Vienna. For all these reasons germanophilia and triplicism coalesced into a uniform attitude of respect and fear of the two Empires, alliance with which strengthened the confidence of the monarchist and conservative element. Be it not overlooked that the text of the Triplice treaty begins with the preamble:

Their Majesties the Emperor of Austria, King of Bohemia, etc., and Apostolic King of Hungary, the Emperor of Germany, King of Prussia, and the King of Italy, animated by the desire to increase the guarantees of the general peace, to fortify

[1] Abbreviated from L. Albertini, *Venti Anni di Vita Politica* (Milan, 1951), pp. 252-69.

the monarchical principle and thereby to assure the unimpaired maintenance of the
social and political order in Their respective States, have agreed to conclude a Treaty
which, by its essentially conservative and defensive nature, pursues only the aim of
forestalling the dangers which might threaten the security of Their States and the
peace of Europe.[1]

The diplomatic service was triplicist almost to a man. It is true that
Imperiali in London was pro-English in his sympathies, and Carlotti
at St. Petersburg russophil, that being because unfortunately the Italian
ambassadors somewhat, nay, too much, tended to take the color
of the surroundings in which they worked. But the phalanx at the
Consulta was solidly triplicist. The hostility with which Bollati and
Avarna received neutrality was an expression of the general feeling of
their class, a feeling over which Bollati exercised some restraint but
which in Avarna assumed forms of indirect rebellion. In other words,
while Bollati, as was his right and duty, voiced his opinion to the
Government that Italy should make common cause with her allies in
a matter which involved

the dignity, the power, the very life of our country, bound up as it is with that of
the Triple Alliance, which till now has formed the basis of our foreign policy,[2]

Avarna on 31 July called on Tschirschky and told him

it was desirable that the German Government should plainly intimate the *casus
foederis* to Rome pointing to the Russian attack, clearly documented by the
mobilization. My Italian colleague's expressions were not to be understood as
anticipating a disloyal attitude on the part of Italy, but he was under the impression
that frank speaking to Rome by Berlin would be advisable. I venture to request that
Duke Avarna's suggestion be treated as highly confidential, since any leakage would
compromise my Italian colleague who has consistently proved his loyal attachment
to the Triple Alliance.[3]

Thus while the Italian Government was preparing to reiterate to its
allies, this time in a final form, that the *casus foederis* did not obtain,
its representative at Vienna was advising Germany to point out plainly
to Rome that it did.

A telegram which matches this of Tschirschky's about Avarna was
sent to Berlin on 3 August by another German Ambassador, Wangenheim, in Constantinople. It is on the subject of Marquis Garroni, the
well-known Giolittian prefect suddenly promoted by Giolitti to be
Italian Ambassador to the Sultan. The telegram runs:

When I sharply taxed Marquis Garroni today about the attitude of Italy my
colleague at first endeavored as Ambassador to excuse his Government,

---

[1] Pribram, I, pp. 64-5.   2 Salandra, *Neutralità*, p. 147.
                    [3] DD. III, 510.

but then as a private individual said he most strongly disapproved of San Giuliano's behavior and had already telegraphed him in this sense. Italy's defection might well prove to be an indelible stain on Italian national honor. He himself, he continued, had been for months at odds with San Giuliano and had twice already—the last time only a few days ago—tendered his resignation, which was not accepted. He would at once telegraph my opinion to Rome but strongly urged that Berlin should exercise the firmest pressure on San Giuliano, who could do with a smart rap. In his own mind he resolutely believed that in the end Italy would march.[1]

During that last week of July the Italian upper classes, the aristocracy and upper middle class, the scientific, literary, and philosophic intelligentsia, the Senate and Court circles had no chance to demonstrate their germanophil and triplicist sympathies. It was the height of the holiday season; all the better classes were absent from Rome and, as Salandra writes, 'political circles were dispersed and disbanded for the parliamentary summer recess'.[2] However, the voices were raised of the few but noisy Nationalists, pro-German but, above all, anti-French. The executive committee of their organization on 29 July passed a resolution to the effect that in view of the complexity and diversity of the interests of Italy the line she should take could not be laid down in advance and that

the imperative need of the hour is to prevent the conscience and discipline of the nation from being confused by noxious deviations of sentimentalists or compromised by criminal demagogic ventures.

The significance of this resolution became plain in the debate carried on at the meeting of the Rome branch on 29 July, an account of which appeared in the issue of *Idea Nazionale* of 31 July. The speakers were Federzoni, Roberto Forges Davanzati, and Maffeo Pantaleoni, and the report of their speeches filled a whole page of the paper. Federzoni inveighed against the Socialists, who were advocating neutrality, but condemned as

no less antipatriotic the attitude of the Democrats, who still go on defending and advocating the abstract principle of nationality, but only bring it into practical operation when it is a matter of opposing the interests and honor of our own Italian nationality.

Still more revealing was the second speech, that of Forges Davanzati, who opined that the press was wasting its time asking what had gone before, inquiring into how the situation had come about and the procedure by which Austria had served the ultimatum on Serbia.

Such an inquiry is completely useless and not only leads the discussion astray but does an infinite amount of harm by providing sustenance for that

[1] DD. IV, 815.　　　[2] Salandra, *Neutralità*, p. 130.

current of anti-Austrian sentimentality which is the chief hindrance to the dissemination in the country of clear ideas about what Italian interests really are. . . . If a conflict arises in which we are obliged to side with one of the parties we must form an opinion of the respective strengths of the disputants. In the conflict of which we speak, who is the stronger? German public opinion, which backs the German Government in its plans of intervention on behalf of Austria-Hungary if the conflict grows more entangled and extended, is admirably prepared for war and confident of victory. The German has already coolly weighed the conflicting forces as we ought to have done and has chosen his side. We must now do the same, shaking off our ingrained habit of letting ourselves be guided by sentimental considerations and preconceived preferences.

The third speaker, Maffeo Pantaleoni, to whose speech the *Idea Nazionale* gave special prominence by printing it in italics, concurred with the views of Federzoni and Forges Davanzati but added that he was going to speak more plainly than they about things that had been left unexpressed.

Man does not live by bread alone, still less do nations. They live also by honor. Now, we have engagements with other countries and these must at all costs be met. Moreover, our recent acquisition, Libya, is not a matter of concern to Germany or Austria while it is to someone else. Do we want after our long wait on the doorstep to be driven out again ignominiously if victory goes to those who on various occasions in the immediate past have sought easy laurels at our expense? . . . What can we do by ourselves for peace except give advice that no one asks for and that we cannot enforce? We can only make our contribution to peace by ranging ourselves with those to whom we are bound by honor and interest.

Strongly favorable to the cause of Austria was the Vatican and its press organs, whose attitude it is important to define. The diplomatic documents show that the Vatican not only did nothing to avert the Austro-Serbian conflict but gave its approval both to the ultimatum and to the Austrian war against Serbia. The following telegram was sent on 24 July by Herr von Ritter, the Bavarian Chargé d'Affaires at the Vatican, to the Government at Munich:

Pope approves armed measures by Austria against Serbia, and in the event of war with Russia has no high estimate of the Russian and French armies. Cardinal State Secretary likewise hopes that Austria will this time take a firm stand and says he does not know when she would ever be likely to go to war if she is not even resolved to repel with arms a foreign agitation which has led to the murder of the Heir Apparent and, what is more, in the present state of affairs is a threat to the very existence of Austria. Herein is expressed the Curia's intense fear of Pan-Slavism.[1]

---

[1] Dirr, p. 206.

Still more serious is the dispatch that was sent from Rome on 29 July by the Austrian Minister to the Vatican, Count Pállfy, and received on 31 July, reporting to Vienna an important conversation with Cardinal Merry del Val in which the Cardinal explained the reasons for which the Pope unreservedly supported the Austrian action:

When two days ago I called on the Cardinal State Secretary he naturally led the conversation round to the big questions and problems occupying Europe today. Of gentleness or conciliatoriness there was no trace to be felt in His Eminence's observations. While describing the note to Serbia as exceedingly sharp, he unreservedly approved of it and in so doing indirectly gave utterance to the hope that the Monarchy will see the matter through to the end. It was of course a pity, said the Cardinal, that Serbia had not long since been 'cut-up small', since that would then have perhaps been feasible without its involving such incalculable possibilities as it does today. This utterance corresponds with the opinion of the Pope, for in the course of recent years His Holiness has several times expressed regret that Austria-Hungary has failed to 'chastise' her dangerous neighbor on the Danube. One might wonder how it is to be explained that at a moment when the Catholic Church is led by a saint-like Supreme Pontiff imbued with apostolic ideas it manifests such bellicose tendencies? The answer is simple. Pope and Curia see in Serbia the rodent ulcer which is slowly eating its way into the vital tissues of the Monarchy and in time would inevitably destroy it. Now in spite of all explorations in other directions made by the Curia in recent decades Austria-Hungary continues to be the Catholic State κατ' ἐξοχήν, the strongest bulwark of the faith remaining in our times to the Church of Christ. The destruction of this bulwark would mean the loss to the Church of her chief mainstay and the downfall of her stoutest champion in the fight against the Orthodox Church. Just as for Austria-Hungary it is a dictate of self-preservation to remove the rodent ulcer from her organism, if need be with the knife, so for the Catholic Church it is indirectly imperative to take or approve of all action tending to this goal. Viewed in this light it is easy to perceive a bridge connecting apostolic ideas and warlike spirit.[1]

The attitude of *Unità Cattolica* and other clerical organs during the July crisis was in keeping with that attributed by Pállfy to the Holy See. Certain journals of the Catholic trust *(Corriere d'Italia, Avvenire d'Italia,* etc.), which had deplored the Austrian ultimatum to Serbia received on 26 July a rebuke from *Unità Cattolica* on its own count while at the same time it published in heavy black type a Vatican note which stated that 'Austria has waited too long in demanding reparation' and that 'a bad impression had been created in Rome by the indiscretion and irresponsibility with which the above journals of the Catholic trust discuss or attack the Austrian Government's note, necessary as it is, however strong its terms'. On 27 July the Vatican official organ, *Osservatore Romano,* expressed itself in the same sense: 'Before the voice of the cannon, the word of the

---

[1] Oe-U. VIII, 10993.

politicians is heard widely and loudly.' Thus before any declaration of war had been issued the 'voice of the cannon' was taken as a certainty. It was, to be sure, understandable— the articles continued—that Catholic publicists should take up position in the matter, but it must be one, not of battle, but 'of upright and sane judgment which in the Austro-Serbian conflict perceives beyond the carnage of a war between two peoples, a great danger to universal peace'. This 'upright and sane judgment', if it 'does not avail to prevent the conflict between two nations, prompts the Catholic press to formulate the wish in advance that this conflict may not spread to other areas and may be composed in the shortest possible time and with the least possible damage by the good sense and generosity of the respective Governments and their heads'.

Hereby the *Osservatore Romano* was asking for that very 'localization of the conflict' which the Central Powers sought to impose on Europe. Again on 31 July it wrote that the task of those who ruled the nations should be at any cost to avert a European conflagration because 'the sword ought never to be drawn from the scabbard save to give the nations that tranquility, that moral and material well-being which is unlawfully denied them'. In other words, Austria might draw the sword against Serbia, who disturbed her tranquility and well-being, but the others must not do so against Austria.

It would have been difficult to deprecate Italian neutrality in the name of Christian precept, and on 3 August the official Vatican organ the *Osservatore Romano* recommended that Catholics all over the world, 'while fulfilling the duties imposed on them by an upright conscience', should render themselves 'meritorious towards civilization by neither deploring nor aggravating the horrors of the war between the nations'. This train of thought might well have led the Vatican organ to advocate Italian neutrality and support it, after it was declared. On the contrary it manifested its disapproval of the Italian abandonment of Austria by mainly reproducing comments of the anti-neutralist press such as *Popolo d'Italia, Mattino, Resto del Carlino,* and on 4 August *Unità Cattolica,* which was consistently more extreme, reproduced, under the title 'Perils of Neutrality. A forceful judgment of the *Popolo Romano',* the following:

We recognize that in playing her due part in the Triple Alliance Italy at this moment would find herself exposed to damage and dangers perhaps greater than those incurred by our allies; but the moral danger of having failed to honor the engagements of an alliance which for thirty-five years has powerfully contributed to the peace of Europe will inevitably have incalculable consequences. Of course the Triple Alliance from now on must be regarded as lapsed, with all the consequences, which may be enormous. We henceforward are too old and so we commend our children's children to the Lord that they may have the strength to bear these consequences with fortitude.

And throughout the period of Italy's neutrality and after her entry into the war the attitude of the Vatican laid it open to criticism.

Of experienced Italian statesmen not in the Government Giolitti at the time of the crisis was abroad. As he explained to San Giuliano in a letter of 5 August:

> I have been in Vichy, then in Paris and London and must confess I did not believe it possible that a European war could be brought on with such levity. I did not believe it until 31 July, and on 1 August rushed back to Italy from London.

On his way through Paris on 1 August he called at the Italian Embassy to find Tittoni absent on a cruise to the North Cape; but to the Chargé d'Affaires, Ruspoli, he gave it as his opinion that

present circumstances do not constitute the *casus foederis* for us.

Telegraphed at 4.45 p. m. on 2 August, this opinion was received after the Italian Government had taken its decision.[1]

Another statesman who might have been, but was not, consulted and whose experience and authority surpassed that of any other political figure in Italy was Emilio Visconti Venosta, the 'last survivor of the Risorgimento', who had a full knowledge of the terms of the Triplice treaty, and who, as Salandra writes, 'had no equal in his long experience of international politics and high tradition of patriotism'.[2] He was at his villa at Santena during the crisis and spontaneously sent Salandra a telegram expressing entire concurrence in the decision against intervention. The *Corriere della Sera* received news of this telegram from Turin on 3 August and published it the same day. In that way the country received from its most revered elder statesman the reassurance that the decision for neutrality was compatible with the terms of its alliance. This was to remain the only authoritative opinion made widely known at the time. Otherwise public opinion was left at the mercy of a propaganda war between the Nationalists on the one hand and on the other the Socialists, of the strict and of the reformist observance, who, as was their wont, simplified issues on doctrinaire lines.

[1] Giolitti, *Memorie* (Milan, 1945), pp. 513-15.
[2] Salandra, *Neutralità*, p. 133.

CHAPTER VIII

LAST ENGLISH EFFORTS FOR NEUTRALITY AND FIRST STEP TOWARDS INTERVENTION

1. *The dissensions within the English Cabinet and their effect on Grey's policy.*

We now turn our attention to the stages by which England arrived at the decision to intervene. It is a story of considerable interest as showing how a great democracy in the gravest international crisis which it could be called upon to face grew 'slowly wise'. So gradual, arduous, and tardy was the process that the impression it produces is anything but inspiring. If there is a certain grandeur in the spectacle of a nation refusing to engage in mortal combat before its decision has been well weighed, it is saddening to think that if this nation's leaders had only given timely intimation of their intentions to the prospective foe, there might well have been no European war.

The difficulties of giving a lead to public opinion and not being led by it are undoubtedly the greater under the English Cabinet system by the fact that its members exercise more control over major Government decisions than is the case with the Council of Ministers in countries of more recent parliamentary traditions. However, Lloyd George writes that during the eight years before the war when Sir Edward Grey was head of the Foreign Office the Cabinet devoted a ridiculously small percentage of its time to the consideration of foreign affairs. The 1906-14 Governments and Parliaments were engrossed in a series of passionate controversies over home affairs. Certain aspects of foreign policy were familiar to those Ministers who attended the Committee of Imperial Defence, but the Cabinet as a whole was never called into genuine consultation upon the fundamental aspects of the foreign situation.

For instance [continues Lloyd George] nothing was said about our military commitments. There was in the Cabinet an air of 'hush hush' about every allusion to our relations with France, Russia, and Germany. Direct questions were always answered with civility, but were not encouraged. . . . There is no more conspicuous example of this kind of suppression of vital information than the way in which the military arrangements we entered into with France were kept from the Cabinet for six years. They came to my knowledge, first of all, in 1911 during the Agadir crisis, but the Cabinet as a whole were not acquainted with them before the following year. . . . When in 1912 (six years after they had been entered into) Sir Edward Grey communicated these negotiations and arrangements to the Cabinet, the majority of its members were aghast. Hostility barely represents the strength of the sentiment which the revelation aroused: it was more akin to consternation. Sir Edward Grey allayed the apprehensions of his colleagues to some extent by emphatic assurances that these military arrangements left us quite free, in the event of war, to decide whether we should or should not participate in the conflict. . . . These commitments undoubtedly added a good deal to the suspicions which made the task of Sir Edward Grey in securing unanimity in 1914 very much more difficult.[1]

Grey writes:

There was a demand [in 1912] that the fact of the military conversations being non-committal should be put into writing. . . . I agreed, readily and at once, to the proposal that this condition should be put in writing. We proceeded to draft the letter in the Cabinet. . . . The letter, as approved by the Cabinet, was signed and given by me to Cambon [on 22 November 1912], and I received one in similar terms from him in exchange.[2]

Thus Grey had to reckon with the views of his Cabinet colleagues, who were not all of one mind; or rather were of one mind in wanting to save the peace, but not about what was to be done if that proved impossible.

J. A. Spender sums up the situation as follows:

Roughly it may be said that when the trouble began there was on one side a small party which held that, if Germany attacked France, both honor and policy would require us to intervene, and on the other side a small party which was equally clear that in no circumstances ought we to intervene. Between the two, the main body of the Cabinet held that we were under no moral obligation to intervene in a war between the European alliances, that it would impolitic to do so unless we were attacked or until the course of events compelled intervention in our own interests.[3]

[1] Lloyd George, *War Memoirs,* I, pp. 46-51. [2] Grey, I, pp. 96-7.
[3] Spender, *Life of Lord Oxford and Asquith,* II, p. 95.

Churchill and Grey were interventionist. The pacifists were headed by the elderly Lord Morley, the distinguished biographer of Gladstone, who embodied the old liberal tradition and was much respected by his colleagues. It is difficult to say who were the out-and-out pacifists. In the event only Morley and the Labour leader, John Burns, behaved as such. But Simon, Beauchamp, Hobhouse, Harcourt and Lloyd George seemed up to the last moment to lean more that way than towards Grey, while Crewe, McKenna and Samuel remained suspended between the two groups. The great majority was against war, and the Prime Minister, who thought that sooner or later intervention would be inevitable, felt that his first concern was to keep the Cabinet and the party together. He realized, as Lord Crewe put it,

that the break-up of the Cabinet, involving his own resignation, would mean a war conducted by a Conservative Government, the time being in no way ripe for a Coalition. . . . The country would have been divided, perhaps irreparably, with an unknown number of people determined to stop the war at the earliest possible moment. He was, therefore, anxious not to force matters, in the Cabinet and not to move ahead of public opinion in the country.[1]

Asquith incurred much criticism for this 'wait and see' policy; but, as Grey remarks, 'when there is division on such an issue as peace or war, it cannot be bridged by formulas'. He adds:

It [the anti-war party] did not appear in Cabinet discussions, for neither I nor anyone tried to force a decision while there was still any hope of peace. . . . But outside the Cabinet I felt sure that the anti-war group were meeting, were arranging concerted action. . . . I made no attempt to counteract this movement either inside or outside the Government . . . . I felt that, if the country went into such a war, it must do so whole-heartedly, with feeling and conviction so strong as to compel practical unanimity.[2]

However, Morley, Churchill and others make it clear that the division of opinion in the Cabinet did not remain concealed. 'The Cabinets ended in growing tension'.[3] And Grey writes:

It was clear to me that no authority would be obtained from the Cabinet to give the pledge for which France pressed more and more urgently, and that to press the Cabinet for a pledge would be fatal.[4]

There was more than the division of opinion in the Cabinet, there was division in Parliament and in the country. The country in general wanted peace. The notion of being involved in war about a Balkan quarrel was repugnant. Even in the Conservative Party there was no unanimity. Its leader, Bonar Law, who during the last week of July

[1] Spender, *ibid.,* II, p. 95.   [2] Grey, I, pp. 333-4.
[3] Churchill, I, p. 215.   [4] Grey, I, pp. 334-5.

came daily to Grey's room to ask for news of the crisis, expressed doubts whether the party 'would be unanimous or overwhelmingly in favor of war, unless Belgian neutrality were invaded'.

The Cabinet was, in short, up to the time when violation of Belgian neutrality became imminent, unable to give any pledge to anybody, and in that it reflected the state of feeling and opinion in Parliament and the country. By 1 August, after Germany had evaded the request to respect Belgium's neutrality, this period of indecision, as far as the Cabinet was concerned, was coming to an end.[1]

Thus Europe was bursting into flames which were threatening to engulf Britain herself, yet those in charge of her safety, who more than anyone were in a position to put out the blaze, hung back from taking action.

Spender writes:

To urge mediation, to keep on urging it, and to exhaust every possibility, however remote or unpromising, of building bridges between the two European groups was . . . the only line on which either Cabinet or national unity could have been secured.[2]

True, but before deciding one way or another the two European groups needed to know what line the mediator would take if war did break out. Spender maintains that 'a strong declaration on the side of France and Russia' was precluded. But what was wanted was not a declaration in favor of France and Russia but pressure on both groups to make them show the utmost readiness for conciliation, failing which Germany would be faced with English intervention, while France and Russia would have to reckon with English neutrality. So much was this a possible course for England to take despite Cabinet divisions that it was the course which Grey actually took. On 29 July, as we have already seen, Grey spoke to Lichnowsky in such terms that in the night of 29/30 July the Chancellor brought himself to put strong pressure on Vienna, which failed to have effect both because of Tschirschky's unwillingness and above all because it came too late.[3] Had Grey spoken earlier in this sense, Berlin would never have egged Vienna on to measures from which on the 30th it was difficult to retreat. Still better would it have been if Grey had said to Lichnowsky on 24 July what he said on the morning of the 31st:

I said to German Ambassador this morning that if Germany could get any reasonable proposal put forward which made it clear that Germany and Austria were striving to preserve European peace, and that Russia and France would be

---

[1] Grey, I, pp. 334-42.
[2] Spender, *Life of Lord Oxford and Asquith,* II, p. 97.
[3] See Vol. II, pp. 513-4, 520-6.

unreasonable if they rejected it, I would support it at St. Petersburg and Paris and go the length of saying that if Russia and France would not accept it, His Majesty's Government would have nothing more to do with the consequences; but otherwise, I told the German Ambassador that if France became involved we should be drawn in.[1]

Now these words of Grey's, which were exactly what was wanted to restrain both sides, were spoken without the approval of the Cabinet, which on the 31st was still in the main set on neutrality. Nevertheless, Grey spoke them, and this is proof that he could do so. If he did not speak sooner it is because he himself was slow to see how matters stood and, even after he began to understand, was trammeled by doubts and scruples which he with difficulty dared to overcome after the conflagration had broken out.

Paul Cambon's impression of him has been recorded by Recouly:

There was something truly tragic about the case of the Foreign Secretary, Sir Edward Grey. At heart he is a philanthropist, a man of peace, one may even say a pacifist. With his generous, idealistic nature he tends to attribute to others the sentiments which animate himself. All through that terrible week he was not one man but two who could not see eye to eye, indeed who were at war the one with the other; on the one hand the Foreign Secretary, who was receiving the reports of all his Ambassadors and could not but know that events were moving at full speed towards war, and on the other hand the idealist unable to make up his mind to utter a word or take any step that might seem in the nature of a threat or likely, as he thought, to lead to England's being plunged into war. This was the conflict which went on within him. He was deeply unhappy and could not bring himself to make up his mind, to declare himself.[2]

A true impression! To which need only be added that Grey's mind worked slowly, hence he did not at first grasp the significance of the Austrian ultimatum to Serbia and what it would lead to, and therefore failed to act with the necessary vigor and speed. This can be seen not only from what has been already narrated but also from the disclosures made by Morley in his *Memorandum on Assignation.* Though rambling and often inaccurate as to detail, this document sheds considerable light on events.

On or about 24–27 July Grey took a very important line in the Cabinet. He informed us of the contents of Buchanan's telegram of 24 July from Petersburg describing Sazanov's hopes that England would not fail to proclaim her solidarity with France and Russia.[3] . . . Then Grey in his own quiet way, which is none the less impressive for being so simple and so free from the *cassant* and over-emphatic tone that is Asquith's vice on such occasions, made a memorable pronouncement. The time had come, he said,

---

[1] BD. XI, 340. See Vol. II, p. 642.   [2] Recouly, pp. 45-6.
[3] BD. XI, 101. See Vol. II, pp. 295-6.

when the Cabinet was bound to make up its mind plainly whether we were to take an active part with the two other Powers of the *Entente,* or to stand aside in the general European question, and preserve an absolute neutrality. We could no longer defer a decision. Things were moving very rapidly. We could no longer wait on accident, and postpone. If the Cabinet was for neutrality, he did not think he was the man to carry out such a policy. Here he ended in accents of unaffected calm and candor. The Cabinet seemed to heave a sort of sigh, and a moment or two of breathless silence fell upon us. I followed him, expressing my intense satisfaction that he had brought the inexorable position, to which circumstances had now brought us, plainly and definitely before us. It was fairer to France and everybody else, ourselves included. . . . We rambled, as even the best Cabinets are apt to do. . . . I could not, on the instant, gather with any certainty in which direction opinion was inclining. No wonder. Everybody had suddenly awakened to the startling fact that nothing less than the continued existence of the Ministry was this time—the first time—in sharp peril from differences within.[1]

This does not show much understanding of the real state of affairs, and what Churchill writes brings confirmation of the confusion that reigned:

The Cabinet was overwhelmingly pacific. At least three-quarters of its members were determined not to be drawn into a European quarrel, unless Great Britain were herself attacked, which was not likely. Those who were in this mood were inclined to believe first of all that Austria and Serbia would not come to blows; secondly, that if they did, Russia would not intervene; thirdly, if Russia intervened, that Germany would not strike; fourthly, they hoped that if Germany struck at Russia, it ought to be possible for France and Germany mutually to neutralize each other without fighting.[2]

Such almost unbelievable political obtuseness was not conducive to the taking of measures rendered necessary by the situation. It should have been Grey's duty to enlighten his colleagues, but this he did not do, or at least not in sufficient degree. It is not even certain that he administered the shock to his colleagues of telling them straight away at the beginning that he 'was not the man for neutrality'. Spender writes:

Lord Morley's suggestion that Lord Grey said early in the day that 'he was not the man for neutrality' is denied by Lord Grey and does not accord with the memory of his colleagues. Neither he nor Asquith ever threatened their colleagues with resignation or attempted to force their hands in any way.[3]

But Spender overlooks Asquith's entry in his diary under 1 August:

Grey declares that if an out-and-out and uncompromising policy of nonintervention at all costs is adopted he will go.[4]

[1] Morley, pp. 1-3.   [2] Churchill, I, p. 199.
[3] Spender, *Life of Lord Oxford and Asquith,* Vol. II, p. 95.
[4] Asquith, *Memories and Reflections,* Vol. II, p. 7. See p. 378.

Later—continues Morley—we were pressed by the Prime Minister and Grey to examine the neutrality of Belgium and our obligations under the treaty of 1839. But it was thrown back day after day as less urgent than France. . . . A Cabinet usually thinks of one thing at once, and the question of Belgium was up to this date, and in truth up to the morning of 3 August, . . . secondary to the pre-eminent controversy of the Anglo-French *Entente.* One of these days Grey rather suddenly let fall his view, in the pregnant words that German policy was that of a great 'European aggressor, as bad as Napoleon'. 'I have no German partialities', I observed, 'but you do not give us evidence.'

With one as blind as Morley to German designs both on the continent of Europe and on the high seas it would have been easy for Grey to produce proof in plenty, but evidently he did not do so, because Morley adds: 'Perhaps he might have cited the series of Naval Laws.'[1]

Meanwhile—continues Morley—Harcourt had been busy organizing opinion among his Cabinet colleagues in favor of neutrality. . . . Harcourt got me to his room in the House of Commons . . . and I found Beauchamp,. M'Kinnon Wood, Hobhouse, Pease. . . . They calculated to a tune of eight or nine men in the Cabinet likely to agree with us. . . . Lloyd George, not by design, furthered the good cause by a very remarkable piece of intelligence communicated to the Cabinet. . . . He informed us that he had been consulting the Governor and Deputy Governor of the Bank of England, other men of light and leading in the City, also cotton men, and steel and coal men, etc., in the North of England, in Glasgow, etc. . . . and they were all aghast at the bare idea of our plunging into the European conflict; how it would break down the whole system of credit . . . how it would cut up commerce and manufacture . . . how it would hit labor and wages and prices.[2]

Lloyd George, who had brandished the threat of war at the time of Agadir, now preached peace for demagogic reasons of which Morley says:

He knew that his 'stock' had sunk dangerously low; peace might be the popular card against the adventurous energy of Winston.[3]

Morley himself brought up further arguments against intervention:

'Have you ever thought'—I put to them—'what will happen if Russia wins? If Germany is beaten and Austria beaten, it is not England and France who will emerge pre-eminent in Europe. It will be Russia. Will that be good for Western civilization? I at least don't think so. If she says she will go to Constantinople, or boldly annex both northern and neutral zone in Persia, or insist on railways up to the Indian and Afghan frontier, who will prevent her? Germany is unpopular in England, but Russia is more unpopular still. And people will rub their eyes when they realize that Cossacks are their

---

[1] Morley, pp. 3-4.   [2] Morley, pp. 4-5.   [3] Morley, pp. 20-1.

victorious fellow-champions for Freedom, Justice, Equality of man (especially Jew man), and respect for treaties (in Persia for instance).' They listened rather intently, and Lloyd George told me after that he had never thought of all this.[1]

This drawing off attention from the imminent German danger to the more remote and less immediate Russian danger led Burns, after the Cabinet of the 29th, to press Morley's arm and say with vehement emphasis: 'Now, mind, we look to you to stand firm.'

Curiously enough—continues Morley—as it soon fell out, on the 29th I happened to have a party for Lord Kitchener [before his impending departure for Egypt] at the United Services Club. Present, besides him, Jellicoe, Winston, Crewe, Haldane, Biyce, Knollys, Guy. Bryce was shocked at Haldane's war talk. I told him afterwards he must no longer think us a Peace Cabinet. Within ten days Kitchener was installed in my chair in the Cabinet![2]

Events were moving with speed.

2. *What Grey said to Paul Cambon; pressure for and against intervention.*

Spender has published certain letters written after each Cabinet by Asquith, or by Lord Crewe on Asquith's behalf, to King George V to inform him, as was customary, of what went on at the meeting. Unfortunately many letters are lacking, but the few that are known help to throw light on certain phases of the situation. The first refers to the Cabinet of 25 July and is of no great interest. The second, referring to the Cabinet of 28 July, contains the passage:

So far as the country is concerned, the position may be thus described. Germany says to us: 'If you will say to St. Petersburg that in no conditions will you come in and help, Russia will draw back and there will be no war.' On the other hand, Russia says to us: 'If you won't say you are ready to side with us, your friendship is valueless, and we shall act on that assumption in the future.' It was agreed to consider at the next Cabinet our precise obligations in regard to the neutrality of Belgium.[3]

The first thing that should have been done was to decide whether it was not Germany who was in the wrong in claiming that Austria must be allowed to subjugate Serbia with Russian approval, hence whether Germany should be called to order without delay. But no decision was reached. The Cabinet of 29 July discussed both the question of Belgium and the general situation. What was said about Belgium will be considered later.[4] As regards the general situation Asquith reported to the King:

[1] Morley, pp. 6-7.   [2] Morley, pp. 7-9.
[3] Spender, *Life of Lord Oxford and Asquith*, Vol. II, p. 81.
[4] See p. 410.

After much discussion it was agreed that Sir E. Grey should be authorized to inform the German and French Ambassadors that at this stage we were unable to pledge ourselves in advance, either under all conditions to stand aside, or in any conditions to join in.[1]

A decision worthy of Pontius Pilate! But at any rate it enabled Grey that same afternoon of the 29th to warn Lichnowsky, as the latter telegraphed at 6.39 p. m., that if war were to break out between Germany and France 'the British Government might possibly find itself compelled to take rapid decisions'.[2] To Paul Cambon, Grey said that 'if eventually France found herself drawn into the conflict, then it would be a question touching the European balance of power and England would be obliged to consider whether she ought to intervene'.[3] The words spoken to Lichnowsky were perhaps a shade stronger than represented the opinion of the Cabinet though they did not bind it in any way. But the effect they had was immediate, as has already been shown.[4]

Next day, 3 o July, Cambon reminded Grey of the exchange of notes of 22 November 1912 laying down that the two Governments should act together to prevent aggression and to preserve peace, if either Government had grave reason to expect something that threatened the general peace. Cambon pointed out that France was now threatened with aggression from Germany and that from one day to another a general war might be unleashed. It was urgent to agree on a joint line of action. Grey answered that on the morning of 31 July there was to be a Cabinet meeting and that in the afternoon he would give his reply.[5] Asquith's report of this Cabinet meeting to the King has not come to light, nor is there any trace of it in Morley's *Memorandum* for the 31st. There are, however, various reasons for thinking that the dating in the *Memorandum* is not always correct, so that Morley was probably alluding to the Cabinet of the 31st, or, at least, part may really belong to the 31st of what he assigns to the Cabinet of 2 August, about which he writes:

Main question resumed was the language to be held by Grey to Cambon in the afternoon. . . . Grey admitted that we were not bound by the same obligation of honor to France as bound France to Russia. He professed to stand by what he had told Cambon in his letter of 1912, that we were left perfectly free to decide whether we would assist France by armed force.[6]

This corresponds exactly with Grey's instructions of 31 July to Bertie on what the latter was to say to Poincaré:

[1] Spender, *Life of Lord Oxford and Asquith,* Vol. II, p. 81.
[2] DD. II, 368. See Vol. II, pp. 521-3.
[3] DF. 3. XI, 281.   [4] See Vol. II, pp. 521-4.
[5] See Vol. II, p. 636.   [6] Morley, p. 10.

Nobody here feels that in this dispute, so far as it has gone yet, British treaties or obligations are involved. Feeling is quite different from what it was in Morocco question, which was a dispute directly involving France. In this case France is being drawn into a dispute which is not hers. I have told French Ambassador that we cannot undertake a definite pledge to intervene in a war.[1]

And Grey spoke in exactly the same sense to Cambon in the afternoon of 31 July, though on 2 August he was to speak differently.[2]

Morley's account shows that these statements, which threw Cambon into such consternation,[3] were not made at the behest of the Cabinet but uttered by Grey on his own initiative. When he made them on the morning of the 31st he was still in ignorance of the Russian general mobilization and the effect it had had in Germany. But in the afternoon of that day just before 5 p. m. Schubert, the Secretary of the German Embassy, had called to read out the Chancellor's telegram giving news

that Russia had proclaimed a general mobilization of her army and her fleet; that in consequence of this, martial law would be proclaimed for Germany; and that, if within the next twelve hours Russia did not withdraw her general mobilization proclamation, Germany would be obliged to mobilize in her own defense.4

It must be noted that the telegram read out by Schubert was singularly reticent. It did not say that a regular ultimatum had been sent to Russia; above all, it was silent about the fact that for Germany mobilization meant war. As has been pointed out above, the Chancellor had wished that this all-important warning should not be included either in the telegram to London or in the telegram to St. Petersburg.[5] The consequence was that, just as the presentation of the ultimatum did not alarm Sazonov, who did not immediately perceive its significance,[6] so the telegram read out by Schubert only slightly perturbed Grey. It seemed to him natural that, as Russia had mobilized, Germany should do likewise. With reference to Russian mobilization he merely remarked to Cambon:

This, it seemed to me, would precipitate a crisis, and would make it appear that German mobilization was being forced by Russia.'

The reality was, however, that Russian general mobilization led not only to German mobilization but to war.

So far was Grey from realizing this that it did not occur to him to make any change in the statement which on behalf of the Cabinet he was to make to Cambon, however much it had been overtaken by events.

[1] BD. XI, 352. See Vol. II, pp. 630-1, 639.   [2] See pp. 406-8.
[3] See Vol. II, pp. 645—9.
[4] BD. XI, 344; BD. XI, 347 n.; DD. III, 488. See p. 39.
[5] See pp. 40-1.   [6] See pp. 58-60.   [7] BD. XI, 367. See Vol. II, p. 646.

I said that we had come to the conclusion, in the Cabinet today, that we could not give any pledge at the present time. The commercial and financial situation was exceedingly serious; there was danger of a complete collapse that would involve us and everyone else in ruin; and it was possible that our standing aside might be the only means of preventing a complete collapse of European credit, in which we should be involved. I went on to say to M. Cambon that . . . we could not pledge Parliament in advance. . . . Further developments might alter this situation and cause the Government and Parliament to take the view that intervention was justified. The preservation of the neutrality of Belgium might be, I would not say a decisive, but an important factor in determining our attitude. . . . It might be that I should ask both France and Germany whether each was prepared to undertake an engagement that she would not be the first to violate the neutrality of Belgium.[1]

This raises the question whether, in speaking thus to Cambon while asking Paris and Berlin to respect Belgian neutrality, Grey was not perhaps seeking a way of overcoming the opposition in the Cabinet to intervention by basing intervention not on obligations towards France or British self-interest, but on Germany's violation of Belgian neutrality, which seemed probable if not certain and which could not be tolerated by England. The account of what followed will throw some light on this accusation which has been made against Grey by enemies and critics. We will return to the point further on.

First of all it must be noted that Grey's colleagues at the Foreign Office, who were familiar with his mentality and well realized the urgent need of intervention, were on 31 July a prey to the anxiety that their country might be about to shirk the dangers and sacrifices necessitated by its role in world affairs and were even in doubt regarding the intentions of their Chief. How else can one explain certain letters from Nicolson to Grey, certain notes of impassioned appeal from Crowe? On learning of the German decisions consequent upon Russian general mobilization Nicolson wrote to Grey:

It seems to me most essential, whatever our future course may be in regard to intervention, that we should at once give orders for mobilization of the army. It is useless to shut our eyes to the fact that possibly within the next twenty-four hours Germany will be moving across the French frontier—and if public opinion, at present so bewildered and partially informed, is ready in event of German invasion of France to stand by the latter, if we are not mobilized our aid would be too late. Mobilization is a precautionary and not a provocative measure—and to my mind essential.[2]

This was minuted by Grey: 'There is much force in this. We ought to prepare and I think it should be considered early tomorrow.'

---

[1] BD. XI, 367. The telegram requesting France and Germany to respect the neutrality of Belgium was dispatched at 5.30 p. m. on 31 July (BD. XI, 348).
[2] BD. XI, 368.

That same day, 31st, Grey received a memorandum from Sir E. Crowe:

The theory that England cannot engage in a big war means her abdication as an independent State. She can be brought to her knees and made to obey the behests of any Power or group of Powers who *can* go to war, of whom there are several. . . . If the theory were true, the general principle on which our whole foreign policy has hitherto been declared to rest would stand proclaimed as an empty futility. A balance of power cannot be maintained by a State that is incapable of fighting and consequently carries no weight. . . . At the opening of any war in all countries there is a commercial panic. The systematic disturbance of an enemy's financial organization and the creation of panic is part of a well-laid preparation for war. . . . The panic in the City has been largely influenced by the deliberate acts of German financial houses, who are in at least as close touch with the German as with the British Government. . . . It has been the unremitting effort of Germany to induce England to declare herself neutral in case Germany were at war with France and Russia. The object has been so transparent that His Majesty's Government have persistently declined to follow this policy, as incompatible with their duty to France and Russia and also to England herself. The proposal was again pressed upon us in a concrete form yesterday. It was rejected in words which gave the impression that in the eye of His Majesty's Government the German proposal amounted to asking England to do a dishonorable act. If it be now held that we are entirely justified in remaining neutral and standing aside whilst Germany falls upon France, it was wrong yesterday to think that we were asked to enter into a dishonorable bargain, and it is a pity we did not close with it. For at least terms were offered which were of some value for France and Belgium. We are apparently now willing to do what we scornfully declined to do yesterday. The argument that there is no written bond binding us to France is strictly correct. There is no contractual obligation. But the *Entente* has been made, strengthened, put to the test and celebrated in a manner justifying the belief that a moral bond was being forged. The whole policy of the *Entente* can have no meaning if it does not signify that in a just quarrel England would stand by her friends.[1]

Crowe in his memorandum is at particular pains to refute the arguments against intervention used that day by Grey in his

---

[1] BD. XI, 369. In addition to the pressure from Nicolson and Crowe one may note the more deferential but no less explicit advice from Buchanan when transmitting on 2 August the Tsar's reply to King George's telegram: 'I would venture to submit with all respect that if we do not respond to Emperor's appeal for our support, we shall at end of the war, whatever be its issue, find ourselves without a friend in Europe, while our Indian Empire will no longer be secure from attack by Russia. If we defer intervention till France is in danger of being crushed, sacrifices we shall then be called upon to make will be much greater' (BD. XI, 490. See p. 132). Bertie on the other hand, as we have several times noted, showed scant enthusiasm for English participation in the war and on 3 August wrote privately to Grey: 'I am not surprised at H.M. Government declining to send a military force to France. I think that it would be of advantage to us to give naval aid in the war, for it would bring it to an end sooner by starving Germany and it would give us a *locus standi* to determine the conditions of peace' (BD. XI, 566).

talk with Cambon when he had said that the danger of commercial and financial collapse 'might be a paramount consideration in deciding our attitude'.[1] It has already been noted that Lloyd George was the bearer to the Cabinet of alarmist rumors from the City. This is why Crowe writes: 'The panic in the City has been largely influenced by the deliberate acts of German financial houses, who are in at least as close touch with the German as with the British Government, and who are notoriously in daily communication with the German Embassy.' This opinion was also that of Paul Cambon, who on the evening of the 30th had telegraphed:

It is to be noted that in the last few days powerful German influences have been at work in the press and Parliament emanating from the City, which is populated by financiers of Teutonic origin. Several Cabinet members are affected by these influences.[2]

And again, on 2 August, Cambon notes:

Extraordinary efforts are being made by the business world to prevent the Government from intervening against Germany. The City financiers, the Governors of the Bank of England, more or less under the domination of bankers of German origin, are carrying on a very dangerous campaign. Sir Edward Grey tells me that the big North Country industrialists are likewise opposed to intervention.[3]

That German influence had infiltrated even into the Cabinet, is confirmed by L. J. Maxse, then editor of the *National Review* and an active advocate of intervention. He writes:

I was also told at the time. . . that some emissary of the Potsdam Pacifist Party in our Cabinet, either of his own motion or at the instigation of certain Ministers who were then busily intriguing against their colleague at the Foreign Office, took upon himself to inform the German Embassy—probably von Kuhlmann, who was very thick at the time with our pro-German politicians and pro-German journalists—that Sir Edward Grey's declaration need not be taken too seriously as, owing to dissensions in the Cabinet, it would be impossible for him to carry a majority of his colleagues on any war policy.[4]

But there will never be actual proof of this. On the other hand, evidence of intrigues on the part of financiers of German origin or affiliations is given by Henry Wickham Steed, who, in leading articles in *The Times,* was an advocate of intervention:

An attempt . . . was made on 31 July to silence *The Times.* At the urgent request of the head of one of the chief financial houses in the City, the

---

[1] BD. XI, 367.
[2] DF. 3. XI, 363; Poincaré, IV, pp. 433-4.
[3] DF. 3. XI, 612; Poincaré, IV, p. 507.
[4] L. J. Maxse, *Politicians on the Warpath* (London, 1920), p. 46.

financial editor of *The Times,* Mr. Hugh Chisholm, called upon him, and was actually told that the leading articles in *The Times* must cease immediately. These articles, the financial magnate claimed, were hounding the country into war. The City of London, he declared, was on the brink of a catastrophe such as the world had never seen. The only way to avert it would be for England to maintain strict neutrality. He produced a letter he had written to the head of the Paris house of his family, and gave it to Mr. Chisholm to read. The sense of it was that a terrible financial crisis was impending, that the writer had . . . barely enough to meet his engagements, and that his Paris relatives should draw no more cheques or bills on him since he could not pay them. When Mr. Chisholm had read this letter, the financial magnate denounced once more the policy of *The Times* as catastrophic, insisted that the leading articles must cease at once, and that *The Times* should advocate neutrality.

Mr. Chisholm reported the interview at the daily editorial conference, and after Steed had given his opinion: 'It is a dirty German-Jewish international financial attempt to bully us into neutrality and the proper answer would be a still stiffer leading article tomorrow', Lord Northcliffe replied: 'I agree with you. Let us go ahead.' Next day the same financial magnate and his younger brother summoned Lord Northcliffe himself and

assured him that they had received such information of the overwhelming military and naval strength of Germany that, if England went to war, 'the British Empire would be swept off the face of the earth in a few weeks'. Therefore they implored him to use his influence to keep England neutral. They had made similar representations to the Chancellor of the Exchequer, Mr. Lloyd George, who appreciated the gravity of the situation. If Lord Northcliffe would set his face earnestly in favor of neutrality, all might yet be saved.

Steed goes on to say:

How Lord Northcliffe treated them he did not tell me; but I gathered from another quarter that their interview with him was very brief indeed.[1]

3. Alarm in London during the night of 31 July to 1 August; exchange of telegrams between Poincaré and King George V.
Grey was not entirely deaf to the alarmist cries of the financiers reported to the Cabinet by Lloyd George. What was the attitude of Asquith? His wife, Margot Asquith, writes that he returned from an interview with business men in the city saying:

They are the greatest ninnies I have ever had to tackle. I found them all in a state of funk.[2]

[1] Steed, II, pp. 8-12.
[2] *The Autobiography of Margot Asquith* (London, 1920-2), II, p. 161.

But he does not seem to have made any stand against Lloyd George's alarmist talk. In his diary for 30 July he notes:

The City, which is in a terrible state of depression and paralysis, is for the time being all against English intervention. The prospect is very black.[1]

It grew still blacker on the 31st. Russia had ordered general mobilization and Germany had proclaimed the *Kriegsgefahrzustand,* and demanded that Russia should agree to demobilize within twelve hours, failing which Germany herself would mobilize. This was much more serious news than appeared at first sight. If at the beginning London had not perceived the imminence of war because of Germany's concealment of the fact that for her mobilization meant war, a panic broke out when, at midnight on the 31st, the German Embassy made known Bethmann's telegram of 8.30 p. m. revealing the truth at last. After repeating the story of Wilhelm's intervention at Vienna at the Tsar's request and the frustration of his mediation by the Russian partial and then general mobilization, Bethmann concluded his message with the words:

We therefore told Russia that if she did not stop her warlike measures against Germany and Austria-Hungary within twelve hours we should mobilize, and that would mean war. We asked France whether in a Russo-German war she would remain neutral.[2]

This German message reached Asquith late in the night of 31 July. In his diary for 1 August he notes:

When most of them had left, Sir W. Tyrrell arrived with a long message from Berlin.

It looks as if there had been an unofficial meeting of Ministers at which Tyrrell expected to find Grey present. But he was not there, and Asquith continues:

We all set to work, Tyrrell, Bongie [Asquith's private secretary, M. Bonham Carter], Drummond and myself, to draft a direct personal appeal from the King to the Tsar. When we had settled it I called a taxi and, in company with Tyrrell, drove to Buckingham Palace at about 1.30 a. m. The King was hauled out of his bed, and one of my strangest experiences was sitting with him, clad in a dressing gown, while I read the message and the proposed answer.[3]

This was not an answer drafted by Asquith to be sent by King George to the Tsar. It was King George's own warm personal appeal to the Tsar 'to remove the misapprehension which I feel must have occurred and to leave still open grounds for negotiation and possible peace',

---

[1] Asquith, *Memories and Reflections,* II, p. 7.
[2] DD. III, 513; BD. XI, 372. Seep. 51.
[3] Asquith, *Memories and Reflections,* II, p. 7.

an appeal to which the Tsar replied after war was declared, as has been narrated above.[1] Lichnowsky records:

> At 2 a. m. I was called to the telephone and Mr. Asquith's private secretary informed me that the King had at once telegraphed to the Tsar appealing to him to stop the mobilization.[2]

Harold Nicolson relates:

> Shortly before midnight on that Friday, 31 July, Nicolson was awakened at his private house in Cadogan Gardens by an urgent message from the French Embassy.[8]

The message enclosed the already mentioned telegram of 12.30 p. m. on 31 July from Viviani reporting incorrectly that on the previous day, Friday, German patrols had twice penetrated the strip of French territory evacuated by French troops in their ten-kilometre withdrawal.[4]

This was alarming news, but probably about the same time Nicolson received the still more alarming German news because at 7 a. m. next morning, Saturday, 1 August, he sent across for General Sir Henry Wilson and together they went to Lord Haldane's house where Sir Edward Grey was staying. Wilson was at that time Director of Military Operations and in constant communication with General Foch and the French General Staff. Together with them he had worked out a scheme for the dispatch to France of a British Expeditionary Force if the need arose. He and French and the War Office in general were ardent advocates of the closest intimacy between the two armies. It was for this reason, that Nicolson sent for him to plead the cause of intervention with Grey. But Grey was still in bed, and Nicolson, unwilling to disturb his chief, returned home to breakfast, while Wilson dashed off on an excited errand to mobilize the leaders of the Unionist opposition, which Nicolson obviously could not do.[5]

The situation when Nicolson reached the Foreign Office seemed to be growing steadily more serious. The German overnight communiqué was casting the blame on Russia for the approaching war. The French overnight communiqué was accusing Germany of having already opened hostilities, and the President of the Republic was appealing to King George in the already mentioned letter, brought over on the evening of the 31st by William Martin, the *Chef du Protocol,* and appealing to England to make the public announcement of solidarity with France which alone could still save the peace. Forewarned of the

---

[1] BD. XI, 384 (CDD., p. 536), 490; *Int. Bez.* i. V, 451. See pp. 125-6.
[2] Lichnowsky, p. 13.
[3] Nicolson, p. 418.
[4] DF. 3. XI, 390 ; BD, XI, 338; See Vol. II, 647.
[5] Nicolson, pp. 396-7; 418-19.

arrival of this letter, Paul Cambon had arranged that William Martin should be received by the King before lunch.[1] But King George's answer had to be that desired by his Ministers. And Grey wanted it to be non-committal. So the King copied out in his own hand:

I most highly appreciate the sentiments which made you write me in such a cordial and friendly spirit. . . . I am happy to think that our two Governments have worked so harmoniously together in an endeavor to find a peaceful solution to the questions at issue. . . . I am not without hope that the terrible events which seem so imminent can be averted. I admire the coolness shown by you and your Government in refraining from extreme military measures on your frontiers and in taking up an attitude which cannot in any way be interpreted as a provocation. I am myself making every effort to find a solution which will in any case enable active military operations to be suspended and will give the Powers time to discuss among themselves with calmness. . . . As to the attitude of my country, events are changing so rapidly that it is difficult to foresee what will happen, but you may rest assured that my Government will continue to discuss frankly and freely with M. Cambon all points touching the interests of both peoples.[2]

4. *On the morning of 1 August Grey holds out to Lichnowsky a prospect of French and English neutrality.*

A more evasive reply than the above there could not be. Steed writes:

I have heard it whispered that the King afterwards called it 'my wretched letter'.[3]

But it exactly represented Grey's state of mind on the morning of 1 August. It was then that he took the disastrous step of which mention has been made in describing the scene at the Berlin Schloss shortly after 5 p. m. on 1 August immediately after the signing of the order for general mobilization whereby the German war machine was set in motion. Just as that very moment Lichnowsky's telegram, dispatched from London at n. 14 a. m. was received at the Schloss. It ran:

Sir E. Grey has just sent word by Sir W. Tyrrell that he hopes this afternoon to make a communication to me about the results of a Cabinet meeting now in progress, which may be of a nature to avert the great catastrophe. From Sir William's indications it seems to mean that if we were not to attack France, England would remain neutral and guarantee the passivity of France. I shall learn particulars this afternoon. Sir E. Grey has just called me to the telephone and asked whether I feel able to give an assurance that in the event of France's remaining neutral in a Russo-German war, we would not attack France. I assured him I could make myself

---

[1] Charles-Roux, *Trois Ambassades françaises* (Paris, 1928), p. 50.
[2] DF. 3. XI, 550; Poincaré, IV, pp. 503-4.
[3] Steed, II, p. 15.

responsible for that and he will use this statement at today's Cabinet meeting.[1]

For Berlin this was most joyful news. Here was an offer to the Central Powers that France and England would stand aside while they went ahead against Russia and Serbia. Kaiser, Chancellor and those around them at the Schloss were so elated that they never stopped to ask themselves whether they were dreaming or whether Grey had gone crazy. Moltke objected to changing his plan of campaign but was silenced and German acceptance was telegraphed on 1 August not only by Bethmann to Lichnowsky but also by Wilhelm to King George.[2] However, on that same 1 August there came a reply from King George:

> I think there must be some misunderstanding as to a suggestion that passed in friendly conversation between Prince Lichnowsky and Sir Edward Grey this afternoon when they were discussing how actual fighting between German and French armies might be avoided while there is still a chance of some agreement between Austria and Russia.[3]

It is clear that to undo the consequences of the message Grey had sent by Tyrrell and of the expressions used by Grey himself to Lichnowsky over the telephone, the King was being made to declare that there had been a 'misunderstanding' and to gloss over the actual facts. The proposals put forward by Grey, in a conversation, not of 'this afternoon' but of the morning, first through Tyrrell, and then by Grey himself over the telephone, were not at all of the nature indicated by King George. About a month later, after war had begun, Lord Robert Cecil asked in the Commons on 28 August whether the Foreign Secretary's attention had been called to the publication by the German Government of certain proposals which were alleged to have been made to secure French and English neutrality during the war. In reply Grey stated:

> It was reported to me one day that the German Ambassador had suggested that Germany might remain neutral in a war between Russia and Austria and also engage not to attack France, if we would remain neutral and secure the neutrality of France. I said at once that if the German Government thought such an arrangement possible I was sure we could secure it. It appeared, however, that what the Ambassador meant was that we should secure the neutrality of France if Germany went to war with Russia. This was quite a different proposal, and, as I supposed it in all probability to be incompatible with the terms of the Franco-Russian Alliance, it was not in my power to promise to secure it. Subsequently the Ambassador sent for my private secretary [Tyrrell], and told him that, as soon as the

---

[1] DD. III, 562. See pp. 171-2.
[2] DD. III, 575, 578. See p. 174.
[3] DD. III, 612. See p. 177.

misunderstanding was cleared up, he had sent a second telegram to Berlin to cancel the impression produced by the first telegram.[1]

In this statement, Grey (i) ascribes the initiative in the proposal to Lichnowsky; (ii) declares that he thought it to be an offer of German neutrality towards not only France but Russia. Which version is the more credible, this or Lichnowsky's telegrams? The very expressions used by Grey carry little conviction. If, against all probability, Lichnowsky had said that 'Germany might remain neutral in a war between Russia and Austria', he should have been sounded on that point and not on the proposal not to attack France, because an attack on France would have been a consequence of war with Russia, so that neutrality towards Russia would have carried with it neutrality towards France. Lichnowsky's own account of the episode is contained in his memorandum *My Mission to London,* written in 1916 and by an indiscretion published in Switzerland in January 1918.

Sir Edward still strove to find some way of avoiding the catastrophe. Sir W. Tyrrell called on me on the morning of 1 August to tell me that his chief still hoped to find a way out. Would we remain neutral if France did? I understood that we should then agree to spare France, but he had meant that we should remain altogether neutral—towards Russia also. That was the well-known 'misunderstanding'. Sir Edward had asked me to call in the afternoon. As he was at a meeting of the Cabinet, he called me up on the telephone, Sir W. Tyrrell having hurried to him at once. In the afternoon, however, he talked about Belgian neutrality and the possibility that we and France might face one another in arms without attacking.

This [proposal of the morning] was thus not a proposal at all, but a question without any binding force, as our interview, as I have already mentioned, was to take place soon afterwards. Berlin, however, without waiting for the interview, made this report the foundation for far-reaching measures.[2]

Out of regard and respect for Grey, Lichnowsky refrains from contradicting him, and reproaches Berlin with going ahead on the basis of something which did not amount to a proposal. But he does not admit that it was he who had misled Grey by holding out hopes of the possibility of German neutrality towards not only France but Russia. It is, moreover, obvious that he can hardly have misunderstood first Tyrrell and then Grey, who over the telephone had put the direct question. On all these grounds it may be regarded as certain that on the morning of 1 August Grey really believed in the possibility of promising Germany that France and England would remain neutral. The idea was in every sense absurd. It was inconceivable that France would betray her ally and leave her at the mercy of Austria and Germany, while it was easy to foresee

---

[1] Grey, II, 312; BD. XI, 419, note 2.   [2] Lichnowsky, pp. 75-6.

that, once victory in the east had been gained, Germany would turn her strength against France. Indeed, it has already been noted above that on that very evening of 1 August before receiving King George's telegram, hence while still under the illusion that England and France would perhaps remain neutral, Wilhelm told Szögyény 'that he had the impression that the mobilization of Germany had frightened France to an extreme degree' and that 'he was determined to settle accounts with France'.[1]

Once France had been beaten the same fate would sooner or later have overtaken Britain. It seems impossible that Grey can ever have entertained such an idea. And yet he did so. And even in his afternoon talk with Lichnowsky, in which the idea of French neutrality was dropped, he still put forward something uncommonly like it.

Lichnowsky went to this afternoon interview full of confidence. Before setting out he telegraphed at 2.10 p. m.:

Sir William Tyrrell has just now been here to say that Sir E. Grey will this afternoon make proposals to me regarding English neutrality, even for the eventuality of our being at war with both Russia and France.[2]

This telegram was again cheering news for the Kaiser. He underlined its closing phrase and minuted it: 'To be sent to Rome together with this afternoon's telegrams. As Italy will drag her feet (*zach mitgeben*) in the Triple Alliance so long as there is fear of enmity with England.' Tyrrell paid this second call on Lichnowsky somewhere about 1 p. m. and his words show that Grey still toyed with the idea of England's remaining neutral in a Four Power war. In Grey's afternoon talk with Lichnowsky the idea reappears somewhat toned down. Lichnowsky telegraphed his report of their conversation at 5.47 p. m. on 1 August:

He [Grey] said he had wondered whether it would not be possible in the event of a Russian war for us and France to remain armed without attacking each other. I asked whether he would be in a position to assure me that France would enter into a pact of that nature. As we did not mean either to destroy France or conquer parts of her territory, I could imagine that we would accept such an agreement, assuring us of the neutrality of Great Britain. The Minister said he would make inquiries but could not overlook the difficulty on both sides of keeping the army inactive.[3]

Accordingly, at 5.25 p. m. on 1 August, Grey telegraphed to Bertie:

German Ambassador here seemed to think it not impossible, when I suggested it, that after mobilization on western frontier French and German armies should remain, neither crossing the frontier as long as the other did not do so. I cannot say whether this would be consistent with French obligations under her alliance. If it were so consistent, I suppose French Government would not object to our engaging to

---

[1] D.A. III, 105. See pp. 176-7.   [2] DD. III, 570.   [3] DD. III, 596.

be neutral as long as German army remained on frontier on the defensive.[1]

As has already been remarked this is different from the proposal of the forenoon in not being based on the neutrality of France. However, it amounted to much the same in presupposing that the French army would remain inactive, while the German army would remain inactive towards France but not towards Russia. This shows that Grey was mistaken in telling the House of Commons on 28 August that the proposal had been 'that Germany might remain neutral in a war between Russia and Austria and also engage not to attack France if we would remain neutral and secure the neutrality of France'.

No! What he proposed to Germany on 1 August was that she was to attack only Russia while France and England remained neutral. A few hours later he amended his proposal as we have just seen, but it cannot be said that the latter proposal was less absurd than the former; indeed, it was more so. Only two alternatives existed. Either France was bound to aid Russia and therefore to attack Germany, or she was not so bound, and in that case why should she mobilize? Was she to do so simply to stand at ease while Germany hurled her full strength against Russia? And Germany, on her side, would be having to maintain the bulk of her forces in the west to guard against possible French attack, carrying on the war against Russia only with the remainder, which would be unequal to the task as long as the French army remained intact. The absurdity of this idea was at once perceived by the Kaiser, one of whose marginal notes to Lichnowsky's telegram runs: 'The fellow is mad or an idiot!' His footnote sums up:

My impression is that Mr. Grey is a deceitful cur who is scared of his own baseness and wrong policy and does not want to take sides openly against us but wants to be made to do so by us.[2]

This was of course absurd but, given the Kaiser's mentality, is understandable in view of the enormity of the whole idea. Even the English Ambassador at Paris could not believe his eyes when he read Grey's telegram. His own reply, dispatched at 1.15 a. m. on 2 August, inquires:

Do you desire me to state to French Government that after mobilization of French and German troops on Franco-German frontier we propose to remain neutral so long as German troops remain on the defensive and do not cross French frontier, and French abstain from crossing German frontier? I cannot imagine that in the event of Russia being at war with Austria and being attacked by Germany it would be consistent with French obligations towards Russia for French to remain quiescent. If French undertook to remain so, the Germans would first attack Russians and,

[1] BD. XI, 419.   [2] DD. III, 596.

if they defeated them, they would then turn round on the French. Am I to enquire precisely what are the obligations of the French under Franco-Russian alliance?[1]

This telegram reached London at 4.30 a. m. on 2 August. At 10.50 a. m. Grey instructed Bertie: 'No action required now on my telegram No. 297 of 1 August.'[2] But the episode proves not only the truthfulness of Lichnowsky's account but also the perturbation to which Grey was a prey on 1 August and which caused him to lose his head. Though his mind was not particularly acute, it cannot be believed that in normal circumstances he would have imagined this to be a possible solution of the difficulties confronting him. Indeed, he must have felt so embarrassed by Lord Robert Cecil's question in the Commons on 28 August that he gave a version of the incident which corresponded neither to the facts nor to his own ideas. However, years later, when his attention had been drawn to the inconsistency between his reply in the House on 2 August and his telegram to Bertie in Paris of 1 August, he wrote in an appendix to his memoirs:

In these last critical days and hours every suggestion that might have a chance of avoiding or localizing war was explored. Time was getting short and, in the effort to save it, confusion sometimes arose. My recollection of the misunderstanding that occurred on the telephone between Lichnowsky and myself is still clear, and is precisely as explained in the answer in Parliament. I do not recollect the circumstances of the telegram to Bertie, and cannot say with certainty exactly what was in my mind when I sent it. My impression is that it implied that the German and French armies should each, though mobilized, take no part in the war, so long as the other did not do so. But it may be that in the pressure of the time I made a suggestion without considering its full bearing, and that Bertie very justly pointed out that it was impracticable.[3]

There is no need to press the matter further. Grey's blunder of the forenoon is inexplicable. As regards the afternoon proposal one explanation is perhaps plausible, namely, that as the day went on Grey changed his mind about the earlier proposal and discreetly sought to beat a retreat by recasting his suggestion in the afternoon to Lichnowsky and Bertie in such a way as to render it impracticable, so that it would be dropped, as in fact it then was. This hypothesis finds support in the opening words of Grey's telegram to Bertie of 5.25 p. m.:

I have definitely refused all *ouvertures* to give Germany any promise of neutrality, and shall not entertain any such suggestion unless it were on conditions that seemed real advantages for France.[4]

[1] BD. XI, 453.	[3] BD. XI, 460.
[3] Grey, II, pp. 312–13.	[4] BD. XI, 419.

This was a misleading statement considering that it was he who had asked Lichnowsky

whether I feel able to give an assurance that in the event of France's remaining neutral in a Russo-German war, we would not attack France,[1]

in return for English neutrality. Thus not only had Grey not 'refused all *ouvertures* to give Germany any promise of neutrality', but had himself made an *ouverture,* which he could only regard as null and void if it were made *pro forma* to bury the more dangerous proposal of the forenoon. And in fact after their afternoon talk Lichnowsky regarded it as buried. At 8.26 p. m. he notified Berlin:

My today's telegram No. 205 cancelled by my later telegram No. 212 [of 5.47 p. m., after the talk]. As positive English proposal not forthcoming, your telegram needs no reply. I have therefore taken no further steps.[2]

And to exculpate Grey as far as he could the chivalrous Lichnowsky telegraphed at 6.28 a. m. on 2 August:

Sir E. Grey's suggestions, based on desire to procure neutrality of England for as long as possible, were made without previous consultation with France and in ignorance of mobilization and are now entirely dropped.[3]

5. *English warning to Germany against the violation of Belgium; Grey refuses to promise English neutrality in return for respect of Belgium.*

Let us now consider what reasons led Grey to drop his proposal of the forenoon. It is possible that he himself perceived its absurdity, but not very probable. One must not forget that on 1 August he sent Tyrrell a second time to Lichnowsky with the message

that Sir E. Grey will this afternoon make proposals to me regarding English neutrality, even for the eventuality of our being at war with both Russia and France.[4]

Was it that Grey was offended by the evasiveness of the German reply to his request for a pledge to respect the neutrality of Belgium? We have seen that the German Foreign Minister, in reply to Goschen's question late at night on 31 July, had answered that he must first consult the Kaiser and the Chancellor, and then when further pressed by Goschen he

gave me to understand he rather doubted whether they could answer at all, as any reply they might give could not fail, in the event of war, to have the undesirable effect of disclosing to a certain extent part of their plan of campaign. . . . He told me in confidence that Belgium had already committed certain acts which he could

---

[1] DD. III, 562. [2] DD. III, 603.
[3] DD. III, 631. [4] DD. III, 570. See p. 383.

only qualify as hostile. . . . He said that in any case it would be necessary for them to know what France replied to your enquiry.[1]

These words let it be understood that Germany intended to violate Belgian neutrality. Now, this telegram from Goschen had arrived at 3.30 a. m. on 1 August, so that Grey must have lead it, if not before he sent Tyrrell to see Lichnowsky in the forenoon, at least when he talked with Lichnowsky over the telephone. Moreover, he knew that Goschen had sounded Jagow about his proposal of the 31st for mediation by the 'four disinterested Powers' on a basis which, if accepted by Berlin, would assure Germany of English neutrality if war were to come.[2] He further knew of Jagow's reply that the German Government would only consider the proposal if Russia accepted the German ultimatum to countermand her mobilization within twelve hours.[3] Consequently other reasons must be sought to account for the change in Grey's attitude.

It was probably affected by the discussion that went on in the Cabinet on the morning of 1 August about which Asquith's diary notes:

The main controversy pivots upon Belgium and its neutrality. . . . Grey declares that if an out-and-out and uncompromising policy of non-intervention at all costs is adopted he will go. . . . Of course if Grey went I should go and the whole thing would break up.[4]

But it did not come to that. As Grey writes:

By 1 August a change in the point of view of the anti-war group was beginning to give shape to the attitude of the Cabinet as a whole. It is not possible to say with certainty how and why this change was being wrought. . . . My impression is that, as war became imminent, . . . they became more uneasy at the prospect of Britain sitting still and unmovable, while great events fraught with incalculable consequences were happening at her very doors.[5]

It has been noted above that at 5.30 p. m. on the 31st, on learning of the Russian general mobilization and the probability of German mobilization, Grey had telegraphed to the English Ambassadors at Paris and Berlin:

I still trust that situation is not irretrievable, but in view of prospect of mobilization in Germany it becomes essential to His Majesty's Government, in view of existing treaties, to ask whether French (German) Government is prepared to engage to respect neutrality of Belgium so long as no other Power violates it. A similar request is being addressed to German (French) Government.[6]

[1] BD. XI, 383. See pp. 54-5.   [2] BD. XI, 340. See Vol. II, p. 642.
[3] BD. XI, 385. See p. 54.   [4] Asquith, *Memories and Reflections,* II, pp. 7-8.
[5] Grey, II, p. 1.   [6] BD. XI, 348.

Grey must of course have reported to the Cabinet Jagow's unfavorable reply together with the French reply:

French Government are resolved to respect the neutrality of Belgium, and it would only be in the event of some other Power violating that neutrality that France might find herself under the necessity . . . to act otherwise.[1]

Certain it is that the Cabinet agreed upon an *aide-mémoire* which Grey read out to Lichnowsky at their afternoon talk:

The reply of the German Government with regard to the neutrality of Belgium is a matter of very great regret, because the neutrality of Belgium does affect feeling in this country. If Germany could see her way to give the same assurance as that which has been given by France it would materially contribute to relieve anxiety and tension here. On the other hand, if there were a violation of the neutrality of Belgium by one combatant while the other respected it, it would be extremely difficult to restrain public feeling in this country.[2]

This was a big step forward which Grey had prevailed upon his colleagues to take. To say that 'it would be extremely difficult to restrain public feeling in this country' if Germany violated Belgian neutrality and France did not, when it looked very likely that this was going to happen, was to intimate the probability of English intervention. But Morley was blind to this and in his notes on the debate of 1 August, which he wrongly dates 2 August, he writes:

Grey very properly asked leave to warn the German Ambassador that, unless Germany was prepared to give us a reply in the sense of the reply we had from France, it would be hard to restrain English feeling on any violation of Belgian neutrality by either combatant. This leave of course we gave him.

Morley goes on to say:

There was a general, but vague, assent to our liabilities under the Treaty of 1839, but there was no assent to the employment of a land force, and, I think, no mention of it.[3]

But if there were English feeling on any violation of Belgian neutrality which would be hard to restrain, how could it manifest itself except by a demand for English intervention in the war?

Once he had obtained the Cabinet's consent to the above statement being made to Lichnowsky, Grey in his afternoon talk with the Ambassador said nothing more of the proposals foreshadowed by Tyrrell in the forenoon and by Grey himself over the telephone. Lichnowsky's telegram narrates:

To the question whether, on condition we respected Belgian neutrality, he could give me a definite statement about the neutrality of Great Britain

---

[1] BD. XI, 382. See pp. 89-90.   [2] BD. XI, 448.   [3] Morley, p. 13.

the Minister replied that this was not possible, though this question would be of great importance with English public opinion. If we violated Belgian neutrality there would certainly be a swing round of opinion which would make it very difficult for the Government to adopt a benevolent neutrality. For the present there was not the least intention of making war on us. The desire would be to avoid this, if in any way possible. But it would be difficult to draw the line marking how far we could go without their intervening. He adverted again and again to Belgian neutrality, saying that it would play an important part.

It was at this point in the conversation that Grey, as has been shown above, touched on the possibility of France and Germany standing facing each other without attacking. Lichnowsky sums up the interview as follows:

My general impression is that they want to keep out of the war if at all possible, but the Foreign Minister's answer to Sir E. Goschen about Belgian neutrality has produced a bad impression.[1]

Even more emphatic is Grey's own account to Goschen of the words he used in answer to Lichnowsky's question 'whether, if Germany gave a promise not to violate Belgian neutrality, we would engage to remain neutral'.

I replied that I could not say that; our hands were still free, and we were considering what our attitude would be. All I could say was that our attitude would be determined largely by public opinion here, and that the neutrality of Belgium would appeal very strongly to public opinion here. I did not think that we could give a promise of neutrality on that condition alone. The Ambassador pressed me as to whether I could not formulate conditions on which we could remain neutral. He even suggested that the integrity of France and her colonies might be guaranteed. I said that I felt obliged to refuse definitely any promise to remain neutral on similar terms, and I could "only say that we must keep our hands free.[2]

This refusal of Grey's to promise English neutrality in return for a German pledge not to violate the neutrality of Belgium has been made into a capital charge against him by writers and historians hostile to him. The Kaiser calls him a 'deceitful cur'.[3] We will revert to the matter later on, but in the present writer's opinion Grey acted perfectly rightly. And in any case, while Germany on 1 August was blowing up bridges and setting her course for war, Grey up to the last moment worked for peace even when refusing to promise English neutrality in return for Germany's respecting Belgian neutrality.

To be sure, all through 1 August Grey continued to hope that things might come right, his hope being based on the

---

[1] DD. III, 596. See p. 384.   [2] BD. XI, 448.   [3] DD. III, 596.

but bogus resumption at the eleventh hour of direct conversations between Vienna and St. Petersburg.[1]

The resumption was notified on 1 August to the Foreign Office by the Russian Embassy from a telegram of Sazonov's telling that the Austrian Government had declared its readiness 'to enter upon a discussion of the substance of the ultimatum sent to Serbia'. Sazonov expressed his satisfaction and voiced a' wish that the negotiations should be carried on in London with the participation of the Great Powers.[2]

This cheering news led Grey to telegraph to Goschen at 3.10 p. m.:

Russian Government has communicated to me the readiness of Austrian Government to discuss with Russia, and readiness of Russia to accept, a basis of mediation, which is not open to objections raised to original formula suggested by Russia [an allusion to Sazonov's new formula communicated by Buchanan[3]]. I still believe that if only a little respite in time can be gained before any Great Power begins war it might be possible to secure peace. His Majesty's Government are carefully abstaining from any act that may precipitate matters, and I hope German Government may be able to make some use of the Russian communications referred to above to relieve tension. Things ought not to be hopeless while Russia and Austria are ready to converse.[4]

On 1 August Grey received another good piece of news which made him take action. Berchtold had lost no time in sending Mensdorff a copy of his telegram to Szögyény of 31 July expressing his readiness 'to examine more closely Sir E. Grey's proposal to mediate between ourselves and Serbia'.[5] This bogus offer was at once conveyed confidentially to Grey by Mensdorff.[6] Grey was so completely taken in that even after the war, in writing his memoirs, he still thought that 'when Austria found that the parallel of 1909 was not to be repeated and that things were serious, she began to try to get out of it'.[7] This, as has already been shown, was an entirely mistaken impression.[8] But it led Grey to telegraph to Buchanan at 6.30 p. m. on 1 August that

Austrian Government have informed German Government that, though the situation has been changed by the mobilization of Russia, they would ... be ready to consider favorably my proposal for mediation between Austria and Serbia. The understanding of this acceptance would naturally be that the Austrian military action against Serbia would continue for the present, and that the British Government would urge upon Russian Government to stop

---

[1] See Vol. II, pp. 681-3.
[2] *Int. Bez.* i. V, 348; BD. XI, 418. See Vol. II, p. 683.
[3] BD. XI, 393; *Int. Bez.* i. V, 343. See p. 57.
[4] BD. XI, 411.
[5] Oe-U. VIII, 11155. See Vol. II, p. 680.
[6] DA. III, 94.   [7] Grey, I, p. 332.
[8] See Vol. II, pp. 651-86, the chapter on the Austrian general mobilization.

the mobilization of troops directed against Austria, in which case Austria would naturally cancel those defensive military counter-measures in Galicia which have been forced upon Austria by Russian mobilization. . . . If in the consideration of the acceptance of mediation by Austria, Russia can agree to stop mobilization, it appears still to be possible to preserve peace.[1]

Telegrams to Bunsen and Goschen are further evidence of Grey's endeavors on 1 August to save the peace.[2] But all were doomed to failure for a variety of reasons: because Berchtold's offer to converse with St. Petersburg was not sincere; because it was practically impossible for Russia to revoke her mobilization, especially after the German ultimatum; because—and this is the most serious reason of all—Germany herself was mobilizing, and this for her meant going to war. Hence when in the last hours of 1 August Goschen communicated Grey's telegram to Jagow and spent a long time arguing with him that if Germany did not desire war on her own account she should hold her hand and continue to work for a peaceful settlement, Jagow replied:

The situation was now that . . . Russia had sent no answer. Germany had therefore ordered mobilization, and the German representative at St. Petersburg had been instructed . . . to inform the Russian Government that the Imperial Government must regard their refusal to answer as creating a state of war.[3]

Of this sudden deepening of the tragedy Grey was not yet aware. In his memoirs he writes :

I did most honestly feel that neither Russian nor French mobilization was an unreasonable or unnecessary precaution. In Germany . . . was the greatest army the world had ever seen, in a greater state of preparedness than any other, and what a spirit was behind? . . . How could anyone urge on France that the precaution of mobilization was unreasonable? For I believed the French and Russian mobilizations to be preparation, but not war. Indeed, the French, when they mobilized, did it with instructions that no troops were to go within ten kilometres of the German frontier. With Germany mobilization was something different. It was the last, and not the first word. . . . Mobilization was the word, and it was followed immediately by the blow.[4]

This was a fact, however, which Grey only realized after war had broken out. He can hardly be blamed for his ignorance seeing that even the German Navy Minister, Tirpitz, did not know the German plan of campaign. But this ignorance was a disaster, as has been shown above,[5] because the nature of German mobilization was one of the factors making straight for war, into which England was being drawn even though, almost

[1] BD. XI, 422. [2] BD. XI, 412, 417, 418.
[3] BD. XI, 458. [4] Grey, I, p. 331. [5] See Chapter V.

at the very moment when Germany was sending her ultimatum to Russia, Grey was still talking in a manner to discourage French hopes.

6. Paul Cambon's despair on the afternoon of 1 August; his request for at least the help of the British navy.

That on the morning of 1 August Grey held out the hope to Lichnowsky of France and England remaining neutral is proved by a remark made by Grey to Cambon in their afternoon conversation on that day.

After the Cabinet today I told M. Cambon that the present position differed entirely from that created by Morocco incidents. In the latter, Germany made upon France demands that France could not grant, and in connection with which we had undertaken special obligations towards France. In these, public opinion would have justified the British Government in supporting France to the utmost of their ability. Now the position was that Germany would agree not to attack France if France remained neutral in the event of war between Russia and Germany. If France could not take advantage of this position, it was because she was bound by an alliance to which we were not parties.[1]

The idea that Germany offered not to attack France if she remained neutral was suggested to Grey only by Lichnowsky's reply to his question over the telephone. It had no basis in the telegram asking for British neutrality sent by the Chancellor on the evening of 29 July.[2] Indeed, if it were not out of the question to ascribe to Grey artifices of which he was by nature incapable, the thought might suggest itself that Grey sent his message to Lichnowsky by Tyrrell and repeated it himself over the telephone in order to be in a position to talk to Cambon as he was now doing. He went on to add, as he telegraphed to Bertie:

This did not mean that under no circumstances would we assist France, but it did mean that France must take her own decision at this moment without reckoning on an assistance that we were not now in a position to promise.

M. Cambon said that he could not transmit this reply to his Government, and he asked me to authorize him to say that the British Cabinet had not yet taken any decision.

I said that we had come to a decision: that we could not propose to Parliament at this moment to send an expeditionary force to the Continent. Such a step had always been regarded here as very dangerous and doubtful. It was one that we could not propose, and Parliament would not authorize unless our interests and obligations were deeply and desperately involved.[3]

[1] BD. XI, 426.   [2] DD. II, 373. See Vol. II, p. 506.
[3] BD. XI, 426.

It can easily be imagined what impression these words must have produced on the distinguished French diplomatist, who had been one of the chief artificers of the Franco-British *Entente,* and now saw it crumbling at the critical moment when his country was embarking on a war in which without wholehearted British support she would probably be defeated.

Similar statements had been made by Grey in the preceding days, but then the danger of a breach of the peace was still problematical. After the evening of 31 July when Germany sent her ultimatum to France and Russia no further doubt was possible. Yet here was Grey evading the issue although the French Embassy on 1 August had sent the Foreign Office a copy of the Italian declaration that the present war was not a defensive but an aggressive war, and that for this reason the *casus foederis* [for Italy] under the term of the Triple Alliance did not arise.[1] France was, therefore, the victim of an aggression. Furthermore, under the agreement embodied in the exchange of notes in 1912 she had concentrated her navy in the Mediterranean, leaving the defense of her Channel and Atlantic coastline to the British navy. What was now to happen if England refrained from intervention? No wonder Cambon reminded Grey in no uncertain terms of the above facts, drawing attention to the danger of a German attack on the French coast. Grey replied that as long as Germany was not assured of English neutrality she would not venture to send her ships into the Channel for fear of English intervention. Cambon refused to take this for an answer.

You tell me today that you cannot yet . . . give me the slightest assurance that you will intervene. I shall not send on that reply, for it would fill my country with rage and indignation. In the absence of a formal alliance does there not exist for you a moral obligation to sustain us, to lend us at least the support of your navy, since it is on your advice that we have sent ours elsewhere?[2]

Grey admitted that a German attack on the French coast

might alter public feeling here, and so might a violation of the neutrality of Belgium. He [Cambon] could tell his Government that we were already considering the Belgian point, and that I would ask the Cabinet to consider the point about the French coasts. He could say that the Cabinet had not yet taken any decision on these points.[3]

With this slight assurance Cambon had to take his leave without having secured any definite guarantee. No wonder he looked back in after-years on those hours as 'the darkest hours of my career'[4]. But he let nothing of his despair be seen in his telegram of 6.24 p. m. on 1 August summarizing the talk. Like those of the previous days, it shows him

[1] BD. XI, 406.   [2] Recouly, pp. 52-3.
[3] BD. XT, 426.   [4] Recouly, p. 53.

concerned not to rob the French Government of all hope. He begins with an account of his appeal for English support especially in view of the fact that, in agreement with England, the French navy had been concentrated in the Mediterranean. To this Grey had replied that

Germany having requested a declaration of neutrality from England and not having obtained it, the British Government remained master of its action; if the Government did not appear favorable to a landing of English troops on the Continent, which, he thought, would not be well received by public opinion, there were other points on which intervention would doubtless appear justified.[1]

This was a very optimistic version of Grey's words, which at the most had held out a distant prospect of British naval protection. Grey's own report of them to Bertie runs:

As to the question of our obligation to help France, I pointed out that we had no obligation. France did not wish to join in the war that seemed about to break out, but she was obliged to join in it, because of her alliance. We had purposely kept clear of all alliances, in order that we might not be involved in difficulties in this way. It was most unreasonable to say that, because France had an obligation under an alliance of which we did not even know the terms, therefore we were bound equally with her, by the obligation in that alliance, to be involved in war. M. Cambon admitted that there was no obligation of this kind, but he urged very strongly the obligation of British interests. If we did not help France, the *Entente* would disappear; and, whether victory came to Germany or to France and Russia, our situation at the end of the war would be very uncomfortable. I admitted the force of this, but I said that it was for us to consider the point of what British interests required, and to deal with it in Parliament.[2]

This line of argument drove Cambon to unbosom his anxiety to Nicolson as he had done the previous evening.[3] Harold Nicolson describes the scene:

A few minutes later, white and speechless, he [Cambon] staggered into Nicolson's room. Nicolson went towards him and took his hands to guide him to a chair. 'Ils vont nous lâcher, ils vont nous lâcher', was all that the Ambassador could say. Nicolson went upstairs to interview Sir Edward Grey. He found him pacing his room, biting at his lower lip. Nicolson asked whether it was indeed true that we had refused to support France at the moment of her greatest danger. Grey made no answer beyond a gesture of despair. 'You will render us', Nicolson said angrily, 'a by-word among nations'. He then returned to M. Cambon. The Ambassador had by then recovered. He suggested that the moment had arrived to produce 'mon petit papier'. This document referred to the 1912 arrangement and made it

---

[1] DF. 3. XI, 532, Poincaré, IV, p. 487. The *Yellow Book* only publishes fragments of this telegram as No. 126 (CDD. p. 229).

[2] BD. XI, 447.   [3] See Vol. II, p. 649.

clear that France, relying on our word, had deprived her northern coasts of all means of defense. Nicolson advised him not to send in an official Note to this effect in view of the high tension then prevailing. He promised, however, to convey the reminder to Sir Edward.[1]

We do not know whether Nicolson actually ventured to raise the matter with Grey or whether Grey would have allowed it. The respectful language always used by Foreign Office officials in dealings with their chief would not make it seem likely. However that may be, the anecdote is not entirely true. Cambon had already produced his '*petit papier*' at his interview with Grey and received the assurance that the Cabinet would discuss the question of the French coasts. And in his note to Grey of 1 August Nicolson simply quotes Cambon as having

pointed out to me this afternoon that it was at our request that France had moved her fleets to the Mediterranean, on the understanding that we undertook the protection of her northern and western coasts. As I understand you told him that you would submit to the Cabinet the question of a possible German naval attack on French northern and western Ports, it would be well to remind the Cabinet of the above fact.

This note was minuted by Grey:

I have spoken to the Prime Minister, and attach great importance to the point being settled tomorrow.[2]

This meant that he meant to settle it in a sense favorable to France. At 11.15 p. m. on 1 August a telegram arrived from Buchanan saying:

German Ambassador handed to Minister for Foreign Affairs formal declaration of war this evening at 7 o'clock.[3]

Quickly decoded, the telegram was at once sent on to the Admiralty, where it was read by Churchill. He walked across to Downing Street, where he found Asquith already surrounded by Haldane, Crewe and perhaps other Ministers who had also learnt the news. The news, as Lichnowsky relates, filled London with dismay.

It was difficult to explain to Englishmen, with their somewhat vague ideas of military necessities, why Germany could not, as Russia had done, confine herself merely to a mobilization of her troops. The English interpreted the German declaration of war on Russia as conclusive evidence of the victory of the military party in Berlin.[4]

This was in fact the case, and Churchill relates:

I said that I intended instantly to mobilize the Fleet notwithstanding the Cabinet decision, and that I would take full personal responsibility to the

[1] Nicolson, pp. 418-9.   [2] BD. XI, 424.
[3] BD. XI, 445.   [4] Lichnowsky, p. 13.

Cabinet the next morning. The Prime Minister . . . said not a single word, but I was clear from his look that he was quite content.[1]

This mobilization meant no great change, because the First and Second Fleets had been in full preparedness for war and at their war stations for several days. All that was still needed were the Third Fleet ships to fulfill the roles assigned to them in the war plan. As Churchill walked down the steps of 10 Downing Street with Sir Edward Grey, the latter said: 'You should know I have just done a very important thing. I have told Cambon that we shall not allow the German fleet to come into the Channel.' Here Churchill has certainly made a slip. Grey may well have said that he was about to make that promise to Cambon, but not that he had already done so, because this was not true. Indeed, he could never have given an undertaking of such far-reaching importance without Cabinet consent. Churchill it is true went straight back to the Admiralty and gave the order to mobilize at 1.25 a. m. on 2 August, but that was another matter.[2]

7. The Conservatives advocate intervention; Bonar Law's letter to Asquith.

It was on Sunday, 2 August, that the Cabinet agreed to aid France by protecting the French coasts. Its consent was given under the pressure of events and with the encouragement of the Conservative Party. The promoters of the idea were a group of Unionist members in contact with Winston Churchill, who writes:

Each day as the telegrams arrived showing the darkening scene of Europe and the Cabinets ended in growing tension, I pulled the various levers which successively brought our naval organization into full preparedness. It was always necessary to remember that if Peace was preserved every one of these measures, alarmist in character and involving much expense, would have to be justified to a Liberal House of Commons. . . . I had also to contemplate a break-up of the governing instrument. Judged by reports and letters from members, the attitude of the House of Commons appeared most uncertain. On Thursday evening [30 July] I entered into communication with the Unionist leaders through Mr. F. E. Smith [later Lord Birkenhead] I informed him of the increasing gravity of the European situation. . . . I stated that no decision had been reached by the Cabinet. . . . I asked him to let me know where he and his friends stood on the supreme issue. He replied at once that he himself was unreservedly for standing by France and Belgium. After consulting with Mr. Bonar Law, Sir Edward Carson and others who were gathered at Sir Edward Goulding's house at Wargrave he sent me the . . . written assurance which I showed to Mr. Asquith the next morning (Saturday) [1 August].[3]

---

[1] Churchill, I, p. 217.   [2] Churchill, I, p. 217.
[3] Churchill, I, p. 215.

Lord Beaverbrook writes that Churchill was also in communication with F. E. Smith in an attempt to form a Coalition Government under Asquith which would neutralize the influence of the pacifists and above all of Lloyd George. But Bonar Law declined and the attempt failed.[1]

One of the most active interventionists, as has been said, was General Sir Henry Wilson, who early on the morning of 1 August had gone with Nicolson to call on Grey and then had 'dashed off on an excited errand to mobilize the leaders of the Unionist opposition'. Actually he had no need to dash off on an excited errand that morning since he had invited some friends to breakfast among whom were L. S. Amery, the Duke of Northumberland, and Leo Maxse, editor of the *National Review,* who in that periodical has narrated what went on at the breakfast:

We were naturally in despair. No one could see any daylight until one of our number suggested bringing in the Unionist Opposition to save the situation. The Party leaders had been conferring together at Buckingham Palace over the interminable Irish question. Could they not be persuaded to discuss the European crisis? It was not thought very hopeful, but it was the only hope. As there was no time to lose we there and then constituted ourselves into an informal 'Pogrom', as it was called under the inspiration of the General. . . . It was obviously 'unusual', not to say 'irregular', but then Great Wars only come once in a century, and we felt this to be a decisive moment in the history of the world. . . . It was very late, but it was not yet too late. As Ministers were wobbling the wrong way they might wobble the right way under sufficient pressure. The 'Pogrom' broke up for the day . . . but touch was kept by telephone.[2]

On leaving the breakfast Maxse and Amery went quickly to work. Maxse called on the young Conservative M.P., George Lloyd (later Lord Lloyd), who, as Steed narrates, towards midnight on Thursday, 30 July, came to his room at Printing House Square:

'It's all up', he said 'The Government are going to "rat".' . . .
'What are the Opposition leaders doing?' I asked.
'They are going into the country to play lawn tennis', he ejaculated bitterly.
'Balfour, Bonar Law, and the whole set of them. . . .'
'Can't you go and gather them?' I enquired.
'Maxse and I were thinking of that', returned my visitor. 'We might go in a motor-car and fetch them.'[3]

They went to fetch them, Lloyd and Lord Charles Beresford to Wargrave for Bonar Law, and Amery to Westgate for Sir

[1] Lord Beaverbrook, *Politicians and the War,* 1914–1916 (London, 1928), 1, pp. 22-3.
[2] L. J. Maxse, 'Retrospect and Reminiscence', *National Review,* August 1918, pp. 747-8.
[3] Steed, II, p. 7.

Austen Chamberlain, from whose *Memorandum* it is possible to reconstruct the events that followed.[x]

Chamberlain got back to London in the small hours of 1 August, was met at the station by George Lloyd and given the following news: George Lloyd had been in communication with M. Cambon and learnt from him that the Government were not supporting France. Cambon had exclaimed with great bitterness: 'Honor! Does England know what honor is?' Lloyd had come to the station straight from a meeting at Lansdowne House at which Lord Lansdowne, Leader of the Conservatives in the House of Lords, Bonar Law and Balfour were present. General Sir Henry Wilson had gone to the meeting with him. Wilson was in despair. Mobilization orders ought already to have been issued, but he could not get permission to take the most preliminary steps. Both Wilson and Lloyd had been distressed by their conversation with the leaders at Lansdowne House. Lloyd said: 'Balfour, of course, understands the position, but Bonar Law does not know what it means and Lansdowne does not seem to understand.' They had parted without taking any steps, and Lloyd put it to Chamberlain that he was the only person who could persuade them to move. Next morning, 2 August, at 9.15 Chamberlain was at Lansdowne House and found Lord Lansdowne as much alive as himself to the perils of the situation and convinced that for England to hang back now was for her to incur indelible disgrace and lasting danger and insecurity. Chamberlain proposed that the Unionists should send a letter, which he had already drafted, to Asquith offering 'the assurance of the united support of the Opposition in all the measures required by England's intervention in the war'. Lansdowne replied that at the meeting of the previous night the Unionist leaders had offered to see Asquith if he desired. They had no answer as yet and he was reluctant to take further steps. The two then went to Bonar Law's and found him also reluctant to take further steps unless Asquith invited them to see him. Chamberlain continued to urge that the leaders should either go to Downing Street and demand an audience of Asquith or should send him a letter. The matter was urgent. Cambon had told Lloyd that Grey was pleading the attitude of the Opposition as an excuse for inaction. It then came to light that there had been a misunderstanding. At dinner on Wednesday, 29 July, Nicolson had spoken as if it were a matter of course that England should join in at once with France and Russia. Thereupon Balfour characteristically had put the other side of the case, though, in fact, entirely agreeing with Nicolson. Nicolson had misunderstood Balfour and reported Balfour's objections to Grey as if they expressed his real mind.

---

[1] This 'Memorandum' first appeared in the *Sunday Times* of 1 December 1929 and -was later included in Sir Austen Chamberlain's memoirs, *Down the Years* (London, 1935), pp. 93-105.

Balfour had become aware of this and, failing to obtain an interview with Grey, had sent a message to Grey's private secretary to explain that he had been misunderstood. (Grey's own story is that Bonar Law came daily during the last week of July to ask what the news of the crisis was and said he doubted 'whether his party would be unanimous or overwhelmingly in favor of war, unless Belgian neutrality were invaded.[1]')

In the end Bonar Law said 'I am not sure that after all Austen's idea is not right. I think we ought to write to the Prime Minister', and they then agreed on a draft which ran:

> Lord Lansdowne and I feel it our duty to inform you that, in our opinion, as well as that of the colleagues whom we have been able to consult, any hesitation in now supporting France and Russia would be fatal to the honor and to the future security of the United Kingdom, and we offer H.M. Government the assurance of the united support of the Opposition in all measures required by England's intervention in the war.

8. *Lichnowsky's appeals; Cambon's angry words; the Cabinet on 2 August authorizes the protection of the French coasts.*

This important letter reached Asquith just before the Cabinet of 11 a. m. on Sunday 2 August. That morning at breakfast he had already had a visit from

> Lichnowsky, who was very émotionné and implored me not to side with France. He said that Germany, with her army cut in two between France and Russia, was far more likely to be crushed than France. He was very agitated, poor man, and wept.[2]

Lichnowsky on his side telegraphed Berlin at 1.23 p. m. on 2 August:

> I have just called on the Prime Minister and exhaustively discussed our standpoint with him. Tears several times stood in the old gentleman's eyes and he said to me. 'A war between our two countries is quite unthinkable.'[3]

Lichnowsky had gone to pay his call in a state of great anxiety. At 9.10 a. m. on that 2 August he had telegraphed an appeal to Berlin to refrain from violating Belgian neutrality because, if a war with Belgium resulted,

> the English Government would not be able to remain neutral very much longer in face of the storm of public opinion that is to be expected. Should we on the other

---

[1] Grey, I, p. 337. See pp. 366-7. In a footnote Grey writes: 'It has been said that I must have misunderstood Bonar Law. . . . He referred only to the opinion of the rank and file of the party. . . . I supposed that a large majority of the Conservative Party would support action to help France. As to Bonar Law's opinion he never expressed it to me at this stage. Nor do I remember that I expressed mine to him.'

[2] Asquith, *Memories and Reflections,* II, p. 8.

[3] DD. III, 676.

hand respect Belgian neutrality there is still a possibility of England's remaining neutral if we act with moderation in the event of a victory over France. As people here now think that the violation of Belgian neutrality is an eventuality to be reckoned with, I regard it as not impossible that England will in the immediate future take sides against us. Today, Sunday, a Cabinet meeting is to take place, an unheard of thing; and I assume that this question will be dealt with.[1]

But after Asquith's words Lichnowsky's dispatch of 1.23 p. m. expressed the conviction 'that for the present there is not the slightest intention of declaring war on us; that on the contrary, they prefer first to wait the course of events'. Asquith had added, however, that a neutral attitude on the part of the British Government would be greatly hindered by two things: the violation of the neutrality of Belgium; any attack by German warships on the unprotected northern coast of France. There would then occur 'a serious reversal of public feeling'.

Lichnowsky had also been to see Grey before the hour of the Cabinet meeting; Grey, however, had once more said that he could give no definite assurances.

But it was plain from his words that he would prefer to refrain from any intervention. We must not hide from ourselves the fact, however, that the good intentions of the Government, which undoubtedly exist, and the general friendly feeling towards Germany will, by the violation of Belgian neutrality, be put to a severe test, the outcome of which will be very doubtful for us, especially if we win brilliant victories over France or advance right to Paris.[2]

Asquith has also written his account, which partly confirms that of Lichnowsky:

I told him that we had no desire to intervene, and that it rested largely with Germany to make intervention impossible if she would (i) not invade Belgium and (ii) not send her fleet into the Channel to attack the unprotected north coast of France.

Was that the exact way he put it? He goes on to say:

Happily I am quite clear in my mind as to what is right and wrong: (1) We have no obligation of any kind either to France or Russia to give them military or naval help. (2) The dispatch of the Expeditionary Force to help France at this moment is out of the question and would serve no object. (3) We must not forget the ties created by our long-standing and intimate friendship with France. (4) It is against British interests that France should be wiped out as a Great Power. (5) We cannot allow Germany to use the Channel as a hostile base. (6) We have obligations to Belgium to prevent it being utilized and absorbed by Germany.[3]

[1] DD. III, 641.   [2] DD. III, 676.
[3] Asquith, *Memories and Reflection,* II, pp. 8-9.

Points 3 and 4 clearly took in all the rest and would bring England into the war even if Germany respected Points 5 and 6. But Asquith did not perceive this at the moment. Like Grey he dealt with problems one at a time and was being carried further than he meant to go. In any case, even while he was speaking to Lichnowsky the Germans had showed their hand by violating the neutrality of Luxemburg.

This news was telegraphed by Viviani to Cambon at 7.42 a. m. on 2 August.[1] On receiving it Cambon immediately asked for an appointment with Grey, who offered to see him at 3 p. m., but Cambon insisted on seeing him at once.[2] Cambon brought along a copy of the Treaty of London of 11 May 1867, by which the Powers, including Britain and Prussia, guaranteed the neutrality of Luxemburg. He no doubt thought it would carry weight with the Cabinet. But Grey seems only to have given him the answer he was to give in the afternoon after the Cabinet meeting, namely that, as Lord Clarendon had said in the House of Lords on 20 June, 1867, the Guarantee of Luxemburg was a collective guarantee, hence created quite different technical obligations from the guarantee of Belgium by the treaty of 1839, which was an individual guarantee. The English position had been stated afresh on 4 July 1867 by Lord Derby. In 1839

the Powers . . . bound themselves to uphold, not collectively but severally and individually, the integrity of the treaty. . . . By a collective guarantee it is well understood that, while in honor all the Powers who are parties to it severally engage to maintain, for their own part, a strict respect for the territory for which neutrality is guaranteed . . . yet a single Power is not bound to take up the cudgels for all the other Powers with whom she gave a collective guarantee.[3]

This train of argument filled Cambon with indignation and despair, which he voiced to the Foreign Editor of *The Times,* H. Wickham Steed, when the latter called at the French Embassy.

Steed relates:

Towards midday on Sunday, 2 August, I called upon M. Paul Cambon. Like his colleague, Count Benckendorff, he was utterly ignorant of the British Government's intentions. When I spoke to him of the violation of the neutrality of Luxemburg, which had been announced that morning, he pointed to a copy of the Luxemburg Treaty by which the signatory Powers guaranteed the neutrality of the Grand Duchy (jointly, but not severally) and exclaimed bitterly:

'There is the signature of England. I have asked Grey whether England means to respect it.' 'What did he say?' 'Nothing, nothing. I do not know whether this evening the word "honor" will not have to be struck out of the British vocabulary.'

---

[1] DF. 3. XI, 536.   [2] Charles-Roux, *Trois Ambassades Françaises,* pp. 57-8.
[3] Grey, II, pp. 3-6.

Six years later Steed reminded Cambon of this conversation:

'Did I say that?' asked M. Cambon quickly. 'It was a very stiff thing to
say.'
'Yes, M. l'Ambassadeur, you said it, and I, though an Englishman, took
no offence at it, for it was a very "stiff" situation and your responsibility was
terrific.' 'Ah', he continued. 'Those were the only three days of real
difficulty in all the years I have spent in London—the 1st, 2nd and 3rd of
August, 1914.'[1]

We have already seen that Cambon had used a similar phrase to
George Lloyd,[2] so that the thought must have been very much in his
mind during those days. But in telegraphing to his Government his
language was perfectly restrained. His telegram of 11.20 a. m. on
2 August simply states that he showed the text of the 1867 treaty to
Grey and gave him for the information of the Cabinet a copy of its
Article II guaranteeing the neutrality of Luxemburg. He remarked that
Jagow's language and the violation of Luxemburg foreshadowed an
intention of violating the neutrality of Belgium. Sir Edward Grey then
gave him two items of good news, firstly his own warning to Berlin
that English public opinion would not tolerate the violation of Belgium,
and secondly that British naval forces would prevent any operations
against the French coast.[3]

Grey explains how his new attitude came into being:

By 1 August a change in the point of view of the anti-war group was beginning
to give shape to the attitude of the Cabinet as a whole. . . . The first sign of this
trend of thought was the expression of an opinion that we could not stand the
German Fleet coming down the Channel, and, within sight and sound of our
shores, bombarding the French coast. It might be supposed that this suggestion
came as a tactical move from a pro-French quarter made and designed to shake or
sap the position of the anti-war section. It was no such thing. It came
spontaneously from the anti-war quarter and was based, first, simply on the ground
of feeling and sentiment.[4]

Here, however, Grey's memory has betrayed him. The new tendency
revealed itself in the Cabinet meeting of 1 August at which he received
the authorization to give Germany the serious warning against violating
Belgian neutrality which has been mentioned above.[6] In this warning
there was no word of the protection of the French coast, a point which
was raised for the first time by Cambon in the afternoon of 1 August
and met with Grey's approval but not that of the anti-war group.
Morley tells us:

[1] Steed, *Through Thirty Years,* II, pp. 13-14.   [2] See p. 398.
[3] DF. 3. XI, 579. See p. 388.   [4] Grey, II, pp. 1–2.
[5] See pp. 388—9.

We were all first alarmed on the Saturday evening [1 August]. Burns himself took the lead, to good purpose, and intimated in his most downright tones that the warning to Germany not to try it on against French coasts or ships in the Channel was more than he could stand, not only because it was practically a declaration of war on land, but mainly because it was the symbol of an alliance with France with whom no such understanding had hitherto existed. . . . This proceeding tonight was admirably frank and took full effect. Runciman, with an anxious face, speaking of the Cabinet that was appointed for Sunday morning, muttered to me as we left the room: 'I'm very much afraid this is going to break us up tomorrow.'[1]

Morley's statements would make it seem as if there was another Cabinet on the Saturday evening at which Grey brought up the question raised by Cambon in the afternoon. But there is no evidence of a second Cabinet meeting on 1 August. Asquith simply says:

We parted in fairly amicable mood and are to sit again at 11 tomorrow, Sunday.[2]

Moreover, Churchill's account makes it clear that the decision on the defense of the French coasts was made known to him by Grey in the small hours of Sunday, 2 August.[3] The fact is that memoirs written long after the event are not always reliable, and the more one reads Morley's *Memorandum* the more inaccurate one finds its dating and its accounts of Cabinet discussions. It is trustworthy as to the general trend but not as to chronological detail. In the present instance, he rightly says that there was opposition to the idea of guaranteeing the protection of the French coasts, but if the opposition was expressed on Saturday evening, it can only have been at a private gathering of the anti-war Ministers after they had learnt of the proposal.

9. The resignation of Burns and Morley; the Grey-Cambon conversation in the afternoon of 2 August.

Asquith's diary for 2 August gives the following account of the Cabinet meeting:

We had a long Cabinet from 11 till nearly 2 which very soon revealed that we are on the brink-of a split. We agreed at last with some difficulty that Grey should be authorized to tell Cambon that our fleet would not allow the German fleet to make the Channel a base of hostile operations. John Burns at once resigned, but was persuaded to hold on at any rate till the evening when we meet again. There is a strong party against any kind of intervention in any event. Grey of course, will never con-sent to this and I shall not separate myself from him. Crewe, McKenna and Samuel are a moderating intermediate body. Bonar Law writes that the

[1] Morley, pp. 7-8.   [2] Asquith, II, p. 8.
[3] Churchill, I, p. 217. See pp. 395–6.

Opposition will back us up in any measure we may take for the support of France and Russia. I suppose a good number of our own party in the House of Commons are for absolute non-interference. It will be a shocking thing if at such a moment we break up.[1]

This picture is very different from the one given by Grey, but leaves a truer impression of the way in which the fate of the war, and with it of the world, hung in the balance right up to the last.

The Cabinet—writes Churchill—sat almost continuously throughout the Sunday, and up till luncheon-time it looked as if the majority would resign. The grief and horror of so many able colleagues were painful to witness. But, what could anyone do? In the luncheon interval I saw Mr. Balfour, a veritable rock in times like these, and learned that the Unionist leaders had tendered formally in writing to the Prime Minister their unqualified assurances of support.[2]

Does this mean that Asquith had not read out Bonar Law's letter to the Cabinet? Grey writes:

It was at one of these last Cabinets that a message was read to us saying definitely that the Conservative front Opposition benches were ready to support a decision to stand by France. There was no mention of Belgium, and all credit must be given to the Conservative

---

[1] Asquith, *Memories and Reflections,* II, pp. 8-9. It may be noted that Cambon told Recouly Lord X. had been consulted during the Sunday morning Cabinet meeting on the economic consequences of a war. 'Lord X., said Paul Cambon smiling, later repeatedly assured me that he had advised intervention, but I have every reason to believe the contrary' (Recouly, p. 55). Lord X. is probably Alfred de Rothschild who at 3.45 p. m. on 1 August had telegraphed to the Kaiser: 'Sire, I am aware that Your Majesty is straining every nerve in favor of peace and it is because I am aware of this . . . that I venture to address Your Majesty at such a very critical moment. . . . Will Your Majesty send me a proposal which I could at once lay before my friends and which would be of such a nature as would find favor both at St. Petersburg and at Vienna?' (DD. III, 580). The Kaiser's footnote runs: 'An old, much respected acquaintance of mine! Between 75 and 80 years old!' But he did not answer. By the time the telegram reached him at 7.30 p. m., German mobilization was already under weigh. Did the Cabinet, next day, want to know the result of Rothschild's move, or simply his opinion on the situation? In speaking of his 'friends' he certainly meant Cabinet Ministers. But in the minutes of the Cabinet meeting of 2 August there is no trace of Rothschild's having attended it, as Cambon with absolute conviction affirms. It is of interest that this big London financier could telegraph thus to the Kaiser, by-passing the English Foreign Secretary. [At 6.43 p. m. on 27 July Rothschild had sent a first long telegram in English to Wilhelm, beginning: 'Sire, Your Imperial Majesty has on several occasions given me to understand that, if necessary, I might have the great honor of addressing myself personally to Your Majesty.' The essential section of this appeal runs: 'I am really anxious to tell Your Majesty that when the question of peace or war is perhaps evenly balanced in the scales it is towards your Majesty that the eyes of the world are directed, knowing the unequalled and unparalleled power Your Majesty wields and the unequalled and unparalleled desire which Your Majesty always expresses in favor of the maintenance of peace; it is therefore . . . having been for so many years a devoted and unswerving admirer of Your Majesty's policy that I ... beg to be allowed to lay most respectfully at your feet the heartfelt prayer that Your Majesty may continue to exercise that influence namely in the interest of universal peace . . .' Auswartiges Amt. A15273. Ed.]

[2] Churchill, I, p. 218.

leaders for their resolution and courage . . . when they had not before them, as we had before us, the compulsion of the imminent menace to Belgium. But the message was first read and laid aside; it could have no influence then on our discussion.[1]

But the question of Belgium was bound up with that of France, even if not, in Morley's words, on account 'of the plea that it would furnish for intervention on behalf of France'.[2]

Morley was less opposed than. Burns to giving protection to the French coast and this is perhaps the reason why Grey gives Morley's group the credit for the proposal.[3] Morley writes:

There were two lines of argument for this warning to Germany. (1) We owed it to France, in view of the *Entente,* and also of her value to us in the Mediterranean. (2) We could not acquiesce in Franco-German naval conflict in the narrow seas, on our door-step so to say. The authorization, however, was not unanimous. Burns, with remarkable energy, force, and grasp, insisted that this was neither more nor less than a challenge to Germany, tantamount to a declaration of war against her. He wound up with a refusal to be a party to it. . . . I said to Burns as we broke up at luncheon-time, 'I think you are mistaken in going on this particular proposal. The door-step argument makes a warning to Germany defensible, apart from French *Entente.* I expect that I am certain to go out with you, but on the general policy of armed intervention, as against diplomatic energy and armed neutrality, to which Grey has step by step been drawing the Cabinet on'. I made just as much impression on John Burns as I expected—that is, not the slightest.[4]

Simon and Lloyd George drove Morley to lunch at Lord Beauchamp's, where there were also Harcourt, Samuel, Pease, M'Kinnon Wood and perhaps Runciman.

The general voice was loud that 'Burns was right' and that we should not have passed Grey's proposed language to Cambon. They all pressed the point that the Cabinet was being rather artfully drawn on step by step to war for the benefit of France and Russia. If I, or anybody else, could only have brought home to them that the compound and mixed argument of French liability and Belgian liability must end in expeditionary force, and active part in vast and long-continued European war, the Cabinet would undoubtedly have perished that very evening, Lloyd George and Simon leading the schism.[5]

It is by no means certain that this is what would have happened. If Morley says so, there is no doubt that he believed it and that his pacifist

[1] Grey, II, pp. 10-11.   [2] Morley, p. 14.   [3] See p. 402.
[4] Morley, pp. 12-13. Spender writes that both Morley and Burns opposed the protection of the French coast (*op. cit.,* II, p, 89), but Morley's *Memorandum* shows that there was no trace of opposition on his part.
[5] Morley, pp. 14-15.

colleagues behaved in a way to make him think so. In actual fact, however, they had on the morning of 1 August authorized Grey to give Lichnowsky the warning against violating Belgian neutrality and on the morning of 2 August they had approved the promise to France, to protect her coasts. In any case, even if a few other Ministers had resigned, the pressure of European war would no doubt have led to the formation of a coalition Government of Liberal interventionists (Asquith, Grey, Churchill, Haldane, etc.) and Conservatives. Morley did not want to be the cause of such a far-reaching change. He said to his colleagues:

Personally my days are dwindling. I was a notorious peace-man and little-Englander, etc., my disappearance would be totally different from theirs; the future responsibilities to Asquith, to the party, to the constituencies, were quite different in their case, with their lives before them, and long issues committed to their charge. They made loud, prompt protest of course. Lloyd George and Simon were energetically decided at the end, as they had been at the beginning, to resist at all costs the bellicose inferences from the *Entente*.[1]

Morley knew them too well to take their protests over-seriously. Of Lloyd George in particular he comments: 'What exactly brought Lloyd George among us and what the passing computations for the hour inside his lively brain I could not make out.' But he had to wrestle with his own conscience all the afternoon before making up his mind to quit the Cabinet on public grounds, and finally, as the Cabinet of 6.30 p. m. rose, said quietly to Asquith that he feared that he, too, must go.[2]

Before this took place Grey had called on Cambon and handed him the following *aide-mémoire*:

I am authorized to give an assurance that if the German fleet comes into the Channel or through the North Sea to undertake hostile operations against French coasts or shipping the British fleet will give all the protection in its power.

This assurance is of course subject to the policy of His Majesty's Government receiving the support of Parliament and must not be taken as binding His Majesty's Government to take any action until the above contingency of action by the German fleet takes place.[3]

Cambon's account, as given to Recouly, runs:

It was only on the Sunday evening that Sir Edward Grey at last brought me the assurance for which I was waiting. He came and told me that the Government had decided to lend France the co-operation of the Navy. ... I heaved a sigh of relief, as you can well believe. I felt that the battle was won.

[1] Morley, p. 16.   [2] Morley, pp. 16-21.   [3] BD. XI, 487.

Everything was settled. In truth a great country does not wage war by halves. Once it decided to fight the war at sea it would necessarily be led into fighting it on land as well.[1]

But is it true that Cambon regarded the battle as already won? That he thought it about to be won is quite likely, but he had no grounds for regarding it as won, nor does any document show that he did so. No doubt in recalling events many years later he slightly confused their sequence. For example, it was not on the Sunday evening that Grey called with the *aide-mémoire* but in the early afternoon, perhaps immediately after the Cabinet meeting. Cambon can have been only half pleased with its decisions, because, after raising the question of Luxemburg and receiving the answer discussed above,[2] he asked what the Cabinet would say to the violation of Belgium. Grey summarizes his reply in his dispatch to Bertie of 4.45 p. m. on 2 August:

I said that was a much more important matter; we were considering what statement we should make in Parliament tomorrow, in effect whether we should declare violation of Belgian neutrality to be a *casus belli*. I told him what had been said to the German Ambassador on this point. I also explained how at the beginning of a great catastrophe such as this European war, of which no one could foresee the consequences, where we had such enormous responsibilities in our Empire as in India, or as regards countries in our occupation such as Egypt, when even the conditions of naval warfare and the possibility of protecting our coasts under these conditions were untried, it was impossible safely to send our military force out of the country.

M. Cambon asked whether this meant we should never do it.

I replied that it dealt only with the present moment. He dwelt upon the moral effect of our sending only two divisions. But I said that to send so small a force as two or even four divisions abroad at the beginning of a war would entail the maximum of risk to them and produce the minimum of effect.[3]

For Paul Cambon the big decisive question was whether England would send to France the Expeditionary Force which had been the subject of discussions between the two General Staffs. Its dispatch would have not only great moral but also great practical effect, as was to be demonstrated later by the important role it was soon to play in the victory on the Marne. For the moment, however, the Cabinet was against it. At 5.30 p. m. on 2 August Cambon reported to Viviani:

The Cabinet this morning discussed the contingency of sending an English force to the Continent. The majority of the Ministers took the view that, given the position in India and Egypt, England could not strip herself of her military forces. In reporting this decision to me, Sir Edward Grey said that it did not imply an

---

[1] Recouly, p. 55.   [2] See p. 401.   [3] BD. XI, 487.

absolute refusal to intervene on land, but that the Government left it open to review the question again according as the present conflict developed.

Cambon then reproduces Grey's *aide-mémoire* on naval intervention without any mark of pleasure. In reporting Grey's refusal to regard the violation of Luxemburg as a reason for going to war, Cambon remarks that the violation of Luxemburg is an argument worth advancing in anticipation of a violation of Belgium.

Belgian neutrality is regarded in England as so important that at this evening's Cabinet, called to draw up the terms of the statement to be made in the Commons tomorrow, Sir Edward Grey will ask for authorization to say that any violation of that neutrality would be regarded as a *casus belli.* . . . Sir Edward Grey says that the neutrality of the territory of that Power is not a Belgian but an English interest and that England must see that it is respected.

After speaking of the efforts made by big business men and the Governors of the Bank of England, more or less under the influence of German banking interests, to prevent England from siding against Germany, Cambon ends:

It is to be hoped that these mercantile considerations will not make the British Government forgetful either of its traditions of policy or of the general interests of England in the future.[1]

There was room for hope but no certainty because of the strong anti-war party in the Cabinet. Would the pacifist Ministers come round?

One encouraging factor was the sudden surge of public opinion in favor of war. Lloyd George writes in this connection:

The Army was not the only element that desired war. The populace caught the war fever. In every capital they clamored for war. The theory which is propagated today by pacifist orators of the more cantankerous and less convincing type that the Great War was engineered by elder and middle-aged statesmen who sent younger men to face its horrors, is an invention. The elder statesmen did their feckless best to prevent war, whilst the youth of the rival countries were howling impatiently at their doors for immediate war. I saw it myself during the first four days of August 1914. I shall never forget the warlike crowds that thronged Whitehall and poured into Downing Street, whilst the Cabinet was deliberating on the alternative of peace or war.[2]

Charles-Roux also relates that while the Cabinet was sitting and Cambon was waiting in Nicolson's room at the Foreign Office to hear the result of its discussions, a secretary from the French Embassy was sent to the Foreign Office to bring Cambon the latest news that German patrols had crossed the French frontier.

---

[1] DF. 3. XI, 612 See p. 376. Reproduced in part with considerable alterations as No. 137 of the *Yellow Book* (CDD., p. 235); Poincaré, IV, pp. 506-7.

[2] Lloyd George, I, pp. 64-5.

In the streets between Albert Gate and the Foreign Office knots of people were beginning to gather. There was a rush for newspapers. As the evening advanced, the excitement grew. Crowds gathered in front of Buckingham Palace singing *God Save the King* and in front of the French Embassy singing the *Marseillaise.* The King and Queen appeared on the balcony and were greeted with wild enthusiasm. At one o'clock in the morning there were still demonstrators outside the French Embassy. Their din prevented Paul Cambon from enjoying his well-earned rest. 'But', adds Charles-Roux 'how grateful he was to them all the same!'[1]

10. The Cabinet decides that the violation of Belgium would oblige England to intervene.

Cambon had yet another reason for feeling a sense of relief. On that evening the Cabinet decided that the violation of Belgian neutrality by Germany would oblige England to intervene. Morley relates of the 6.30 p. m. Cabinet:

Grey reported his conversation with Cambon. Burns said he must go. The Prime Minister still bespoke him for a talk at the close of the Cabinet. As we got up from our chairs I said quietly to Asquith that I feared I, too, must go. He looked at me with his clear, open eye. 'One favor at any rate', he said, 'I would ask you. Sleep on it.' 'Of course I will', I answered. I left him trying to deal with Burns—in vain.[2]

The other Ministers who at the luncheon hour had seemed inclined to bring about a Cabinet split rather than consent to war changed their attitude at the 6.30 p. m. Cabinet meeting, as Lord Crewe reported to the King on Asquith's behalf:

Sir Edward Grey gave an account of his. conversation with M. Cambon, to whom he gave the message of which Lord Crewe informed Your Majesty this afternoon,[3] adding a further statement of the reasons which at the present juncture make it impossible for Your Majesty's Government to send our military force out of the country, without pledging themselves either way for the future. The precise form of the statement to be made in Parliament tomorrow was not freely discussed, as Your Majesty's Ministers will meet again tomorrow morning. It was agreed, however, that no communication as regards restrictions on the employment of the German Fleet should be made to Germany beforehand, and that when the announcement is made it would be clear that the practical protection of the French coasts that would be involved is not only a recognition of our friendship with France, but is also imperatively required to preserve British interests. As regards Belgium, it was agreed, without any attempts to state a formula, that it should be

---

[1] Charles-Roux, *Trois Ambassades Françaises,* pp. 61-3.
[2] Morley, p. 21.
[3] This letter is not among those which have been made public.

made evident that a substantial violation of the neutrality of that country would place us in the situation contemplated as possible by Mr. Gladstone in 1870, when interference with Belgian independence was held to compel us to take action.[1]

At the meeting of 29 July the Cabinet was still undecided on this point. As Asquith wrote to the King:

It is a doubtful point how far a single guaranteeing State is bound under the Treaty of 1839 to maintain Belgian neutrality if the remainder abstain or refuse. The Cabinet consider that the matter, if it arises, will be rather one of policy than of legal obligation.[2]

At the morning meeting of the Cabinet on 2 August—writes Spender—Belgium proved to be the deciding factor:

Would Belgium resist or would she, like Luxemburg, submit after registering her protest with the Powers? In the latter event we could not . . . be more Belgian than the Belgians or compel them to submit to the horrors which forcible resistance would inflict on them for our convenience or that of France and Russia. To force her to yield her territory as the battleground of the European Armageddon would be a crime, and the more so as we were not in a position to offer her the immediate succor which she would need, if she decided to resist. The Peace group were strong on the point that a 'simple traverse' of a corner of Belgium by German troops would not be a cause of British intervention.[3]

By the time the Cabinet met again at 6.30 in the evening it was quite certain—as Spender writes—that the Germans were about to invade Belgium, and almost certain that the Belgians would resist.

The Belgian question was taken up once more and for the last time, and after 'heavy wrestling' it was agreed, as Lord Crewe reported to the King, 'that it should be made evident that a substantial violation of the neutrality of that country would place us in the situation contemplated as possible by Mr. Gladstone in 1870 when interference with Belgian independence was held to compel us to take action'. There were still loopholes. It might still be argued that the violation was not 'substantial', or that it did not interfere with Belgian independence, and several Ministers still clutched at these possibilities on the Sunday evening after the Cabinet had risen. But for the great majority the decision was taken that, if Belgium resisted, our entry into the war would be imperative.[4]

But by now the question whether Belgium would resist was settled. To Grey's inquiry of 31 July the Belgian Government had replied at 10.24 a. m. on 1 August that

---

[1] Spender, *Life of Lord Oxford and Asquith* II, p. 82.
[2] Spender, *ibid.*, II, p. 81.
[3] Spender, *ibid.*, II, pp. 89-90.
[4] Spender, *ibid.*, II, p. 91.

Belgium will to the utmost of her power maintain neutrality, and desires and expects other Powers to observe and uphold it. . . . that the relations between Belgium and the neighboring Powers were excellent and that there was no reason to suspect their intentions, but that Belgian Government believed that in case of violation they were in a position to defend the neutrality of their country.[1]

At 11.37 a. m. there followed the news that the decision had been taken to mobilize at once.[2] As Grey comments :

The announcement that, if her neutrality was assailed, she intended to defend herself was important. If she were to acquiesce voluntarily, or even under duress, in the passage of German troops, we should be entitled to send troops to vindicate the neutrality and resist the violation of it; but it was clear that an appeal from her for help, when she herself was fighting for what we were pledged to defend, would be peculiarly strong and moving.[3]

This meant that if the Germans entered Belgium—as seemed more than probable after Jagow's evasive answer to Goschen's question—Britain would intervene.

Things were at that point in London when the Brussels Government received the ultimatum from the German Minister and at once took its decision. We now proceed to speak of this ultimatum and to discuss in detail the Belgian question, which brought the British Empire into the European war with far-reaching consequences.

[1] BD. XI, 395.   [2] BD. XI, 415.   [3] Grey, II, p. 9-10.

CHAPTER IX

BELGIAN NEUTRALITY AND THE GERMAN ULTIMATUM

(1) *Belgium and the treaty of 1839. How England safeguarded Belgian neutrality in 1870 and 1887 (p. 412).* (2) *Belgian relations with France and Germany after 1870; the Schlieffen plan and the Barnardiston-Ducarne military agreements (p. 416).* (3) *Anglo-Belgian differences and Belgian sympathies for Germany (p. 420).* (4) *The views of Joffre and the French Government on the Belgian question (p. 425).* (5) *The Bridges episode; France gives up the plan of a maneuver through Belgium (p. 430).* (6) *An inquiry by Nicolson; and Grey's assurances to the Belgian Minister (p. 434).* (7) *Broqueville's military reforms; the satisfaction in Paris and London; Wilhelm and Moltke make bellicose speeches to King Albert (p. 437).* (8) *The Belgian Government's optimism before the presentation of the German ultimatum (p. 443).* (9) *The behavior of the German Minister at Brussels; the content of the German ultimatum (p. 448).* (10) *The Belgian Government decides on resistance and on the refusal of French armed assistance (p. 455).* (11) *The Belgian Government's reply to the German ultimatum (p. 463).* (12) *Lingering German hopes; the Belgian appeal to England and France (p. 469).*

1. Belgium and the treaty of 1839. How England safeguarded Belgian neutrality in 1870 and 1887.

For an understanding of the Belgian question and the position of England, France, and Germany in regard to Belgium it is necessary to go back into the past and give a rapid summary of the events following the creation of the Belgian State at the beginning of the nineteenth century.[1]

In redrawing the map of Europe after the fall of Napoleon, England and the Powers of the Holy Alliance had begun by depriving France of the Rhine frontier, to which she laid claim, and also of the Belgian provinces. These had been joined to Holland to form a 'bridgehead' for Europe, the defense of which against a French invader was entrusted

---

[1] On the Belgian question and the events leading up to the violation of Belgian neutrality, see: René Dollot, *Les origines de la neutralité de la Belgique et le système de la Barrière* (Paris, 1902); K. Strupp, *Die Neutralisation und die Neutralität Belgiens* (Gotha, 1917); Karl Hampe, *Das belgische Bollwerk, eine aktenmäszige Darlegung über Barrièrestellung, Neutralität und Festungspolitik Belgiens* (Stuttgart, Berlin, 1918); Bernhard Schwertfeger, *Die belgischen Dokumente zur Vorgeschichte des Weltkrieges,* 5 vols in 3 (Berlin, 1925), in *Amtliche Aktenstücke zur Geschichte der Europäischen Politik,* 1885-1914; Heinrich Pohl, *Der deutsche Einmarsch in Belgien* (Berlin, 1925); Johannes Victor Bredt, *Die belgische Neutralität und der Schlieffensche Feldzugplan* (Berlin, 1929); Karl Hosse, *Die engliscb-belgiscben Aufmarschpläne gegen Deutschland vor dem Weltkriege* (Vienna, 1930); Graf Max Montgelas, 'Die belgische Neutralität und der Schlieffensche Feldzugsplan', in *Berliner Monatshefte,* December 1931, pp. 1129-50; J. A. Wullus-Rudiger, *La Belgique et l'équilibre européen* (Paris, 1935).

in the first instance to Dutch and Belgian, later on to British and Prussian troops. But this settlement was not acceptable to the Belgian people, who, if they had never yet attained independence, had certainly played a leading part in European history since the thirteenth century. Liége, Brabant, and Flanders were proud of their ancient democratic traditions, while Bruges and Antwerp had been at the height of their glory in the Middle Ages. If her geographical position as the gateway to the west and the meeting-place of three great civilizations, those of England, Germany, and France, had brought upon Belgium the misfortune of being the cockpit of Western Europe, she had always shown a remarkable power of recovery from her hardships and now strove to render herself independent of Holland, who had always used her as a battlefield against France and had beggared Antwerp for the benefit of Rotterdam and Amsterdam.

In 1830 the Belgian people rose in revolt against Dutch domination and, to avoid a new war, the Powers agreed to make Belgium an independent buffer state. In order that Belgian independence should be brought into harmony 'with the interests and security of the other Powers and the preservation of the balance of power in Europe' it was laid down on 26 June 1831 that Belgium was to remain 'perpetually neutral'. The Powers (England, France, Prussia, Austria, and Russia) guaranteed 'this perpetual neutrality and therewith also the integrity and inviolability of her territory'. In 'just reciprocity' Belgium was under the obligation to observe the same neutrality towards the other States and not to disturb their tranquility, while always retaining the right to defend herself against aggression. The Powers had no great confidence in the viability of the new State and would have ended by yielding to Talleyrand's wish to dismember it had not this been stoutly opposed by Lord Palmerston, speaking on behalf of England, where for economic and political reasons the fate of Flanders had for centuries been regarded as a traditional English interest. It was at the wish of England that the choice of a ruler fell on Leopold of Saxe-Coburg-Gotha, a German prince who had made his home in England and was the widower of Princess Charlotte, daughter of the Prince of Wales.

The new King ascended the throne on 1 July 1831. On 2 August a Dutch army 50,000 strong invaded Belgium, whose newly formed and unprepared army could put up no effective resistance. Leopold I, who had become betrothed to Louis Philippe's elder daughter, called France to his aid and after a 'ten-day campaign' the Dutch forces withdrew. But the prompt French intervention was viewed with suspicion in England. On 15 August Lord Palmerston, rightly regarded by the Belgians as the 'Father of Belgium', threatened France with war unless the French troops were immediately withdrawn. France yielded to the threat, and on 14 October 1831 the London Conference, by the

Treaty of the Twenty-Four Articles, confined itself to placing the neutrality of Belgium under the guarantee of the five Powers without renewing the guarantee of her integrity and inviolability. With the support of the three Holy Alliance Powers, who withdrew from the conference, William I of Holland steadily refused until 14 May 1838 to ratify the treaty of 14 October 1831, Belgium in the meanwhile remaining in occupation of the Maestricht district and the Grand Duchy of Luxemburg, the right to which had been taken away from her by the conference. When William at last ratified the treaty, Belgium on her side had to give up these two districts. The treaty, which came into force on 19 April 1839, finally establishing the independence of Belgium, was to become the 'scrap of paper' torn up by Germany in 1914.

French aspirations to Belgium were not ended by the treaty. Louis Philippe sought to conclude a Franco-Belgian customs union as a prelude to annexation and only desisted at a threat of war from Lord Aberdeen. When Louis Napoleon came to power he, too, was widely believed to have designs of annexing Belgium, but he did not pursue them for fear of incurring the enmity of England. The Prussian victory at Sadowa in 1866 gravely weakened the position of France in Europe, and to restore her prestige Napoleon offered Prussia an offensive and defensive alliance allegedly inspired by the triumph of the nationality principle, so dear to his heart. This secret draft, known as the 'Benedetti treaty' of 1 September 1866, gave French consent to the union of the North German Federation with the South German states to form a German Federal Union in return for Prussian consent to the annexation to France of Luxemburg and Belgium. The idea had in reality originated with Bismarck, who as late as the beginning of 1867 was not averse to the cession of Belgium to France. He changed his mind when he perceived the possibility of winning the hegemony of Europe for Prussia.

In the period preceding 1870, when Britain was living in 'splendid isolation', neither the Government nor public opinion felt any inclination to take up arms in defense of Belgian independence. Army and navy were utterly unprepared. Britain, moreover, had never gone to war on the Continent except in alliance with another Power. For the rulers of Belgium, who had always relied on being unconditionally protected by England, it was an anxious situation. In August 1866 the Belgian Minister, van der Weyer, raised the question with Lord Stanley but received nothing more than promises of diplomatic support, and the young King Leopold II, who had succeeded his father in December 1865, in vain sought assurances from London. But when in 1870 the danger of war became imminent, the London Government reawakened to the importance of the Belgian question.

In order not to antagonize England at the moment when France was on the brink of war with Prussia, Napoleon III, on 15 July 1876, instructed the Duke of Gramont to give assurances to the English Ambassador and the Belgian Minister that in case of war France would respect Belgian neutrality in any event (*quand même*). At Berlin the same assurances were given by Thile, whereupon to discredit France in English public opinion Bismarck had the text of the Benedetti proposals published in *The Times* of 25 July. The publication aroused serious misgivings in London, and Paris at once sent word to Lord Granville that, though the draft was in Benedetti's handwriting, the proposal had originated with Bismarck and had given rise to conversations which had been dropped. Bismarck on his part let it be understood that if the draft treaty had not been made public, France after the completion of her own mobilization and that of Prussia would have proposed to Berlin that their two armies should flout unarmed Europe by putting the Benedetti proposals into execution. Under pressure from Belgium and from public opinion at home the Gladstone Government proposed to the German and French Governments that they should severally sign an agreement to last twelve months after the conclusion of the peace between France and Prussia. This agreement took note of the engagements given by France and Prussia to respect Belgian neutrality and laid down that in defense of Belgium against any State violating her neutrality the Queen of England engaged to send forces to fight at the side of the State which respected it. Amid cheers in the Commons, Gladstone, after a warm eulogy of Belgium, declared that the country would never

quietly stand by and witness the perpetration of the direst crime that ever stained the pages of history in the darkest ages, and thus become participators in the sin.

In September 1885 Bismarck took the precaution of asking Philip Currie, Permanent Under-Secretary at the Foreign Office, who was on a visit to Germany: 'Would England fight if Belgium was attacked?' Currie replied: 'No doubt, if she had an ally', adding that ever since he had been at the Foreign Office, Belgium and Constantinople had been looked upon as questions about which England would fight.[1] However, at the beginning of 1887, when war was within an ace of breaking out anew between France and Germany, Lord Salisbury seems to have forgotten the precedent of 1870. When Lord Vivian, the English Minister at Brussels, informed his Government that the Belgian Government had inquired whether it could count on English aid in case of war, repeating his request for instructions several times, the Foreign Secretary and Foreign Office maintained silence, a silence all the more disquieting for Belgium because articles appeared in the

[1] Lady Gwendolen Cecil, *Life of Robert, Marquis of Salisbury* (London, 1931), III, p. 259.

London press advising that England should keep out of the conflict, only ensuring that no territory was taken from Belgium. Fortunately war did not break out. Belgium received assurances from France and Germany that they would not violate her neutrality. Nay more, in *Die Post* of 24 February 1887, Bismarck published a semi-official article full of indignation against the English journalists who had imputed to Germany the plan of beginning a war by the violation of a European treaty merely because her General Staff had made plans along those lines.

They make a mistake—said the article—if they think that with us the conduct of policy is subordinated to the views of the General Staff rather than the contrary. Neither the neutrality of Belgium nor that of Switzerland will be violated by Germany. The leadership of the German State attaches far too much importance to its reputation as the strictest observer of the treaties which Europe has established for the preservation of peace.[1]

Bismarck might have added that Germany was encouraged to take that line by a knowledge of the friendly feelings shown towards her by the Belgians. The Second Empire's designs on Belgium, the defeat and decline of France, the creation and growing power of the German Empire, had, after 1870, created among the Belgians a mood of distrust and disparagement of France and trust and liking for Germany. Especially was this the case with the Catholic Conservative party which from 1884 governed the country, and it was also visible in its diplomatic relations. The hegemony of Germany seemed to be a guarantee of peace, ever the paramount interest of a small country whose sole safeguard was its neutrality. The tendency to draw closer to Germany was strengthened by a change of attitude towards England. This was caused in the first place in 1902 by the violent campaign carried on by Casement and Morel against Belgian rule in the Congo, at that time under the personal sovereignty of Leopold II. And soon afterwards, the formation in 1904 of the *Entente Cordiale* ended the possibility of England's holding the balance between France and Germany in defense of Belgian neutrality.

2. Belgian relations with France and Germany after 1870; the Schlieffen plan and the Barnardiston-Ducarne military agreements.

And yet the Belgian Government ought to have taken heed of a warning which reached it in 1904, before the conclusion of the Franco-British *Entente Cordiale*. As we have already seen, the elder Moltke's

---

[1] Bismarck's words need not be held up in reproach to Bethmann Hollweg. As early as 1859 Moltke had thought of attacking France through Belgium. Waldersee, who succeeded Moltke in 1888, was asked by Bismarck whether it would not be advisable for Germany in case of war to pass through Belgium. Waldersee thought not, regarding it as desirable that the initiative should be taken by France, and he convinced Bismarck that the best plan for a war on two fronts was that of Moltke designed for an attack on Russia.

plan of campaign had been to begin by taking the field against Russia, standing on the defensive in the west meanwhile. Waldersee had left this plan unchanged, but Schlieffen, who succeeded him in 1891, entirely reversed it. His opening attack was to be launched against France through Belgium. Leopold II got wind of this when on 26 January 1904 he paid a visit to Wilhelm at Berlin. Van der Elst, the Belgian Secretary General for Foreign Affairs from 1905 to 1917, records that Wilhelm said:

> For years and years I have sought in every way to bring about a *rapprochement* with France and each time I have held out the hand of friendship she has rejected my advances with disdain. . . . Now I have had enough of it. . . . The French want war. Well I they shall have it. As for your country, I advise you to prepare. Your army is inadequate, its strength bears no relation to the population figures. . . . In the tremendous struggle which is about to begin, Germany is certain of victory, but this time you will be forced to choose. If you are with us I will give you back the Flemish provinces which France took away in defiance of all law. I will recreate the Duchy of Burgundy for you. You will become sovereign of a powerful kingdom. Think over my offer and what may be in store for you.[1]

The shock and dismay which these words produced in Leopold have been described by Bülow. To him the Kaiser said that his words to King Leopold had been: 'Whoever, in the case of a European war, is not for me, is against me. . . . In the event of Belgium's not being on my side, I shall be actuated by strategical considerations only.' Bülow protested that 'until our enemies had violated Belgian neutrality, we ourselves could not disregard agreements we had solemnly sworn to uphold', but the Kaiser only answered: 'If that is how you think, I shall in case of war have to look round for another Chancellor.'[2]

Leopold lost no time in bringing the matter to the knowledge of the Brussels Government, but the latter seems not to have drawn the necessary conclusions. Certainly no warning was passed on to France. Paléologue, however, relates that the French General Staff soon afterwards came into possession of exact information on the plan of attack which in case of war the Germans were to carry out on France via Belgium. With romantic detail Paléologue relates that in 1904, when he was Deputy Assistant Director for Political Affairs at the French Foreign Ministry, a high-ranking German officer, whose name was never disclosed, but who 'seemed to be a general attached to the Great General Staff at Berlin', by a letter signed *Le Vengeur* made an offer, which was accepted, to hand over for a sum of 60,000 francs the new

---

[1] Baron van der Elst, 'La préméditation de l'Allemagne', in *Revue de Paris,* 1 April, 1923, pp. 530-1.

[2] Bülow, II, pp. 72 4.

plan of concentration adopted by the German General Staff against France, i.e., the Schlieffen plan. Paléologue says he learned particulars on 25 April 1904 from General Pendezec, the French Chief of Staff, who subsequently collected evidence of German preparations which corroborated the *Vengeur*'s revelations. In a note Paléologue adds that in December 1929, Pétain held an inquiry into the accuracy and authenticity of these revelations, but without result because on higher orders all secret documents of the military intelligence service had been burnt in August 1914. But Paléologue had passed on information of the contents of the documents quoted to Delcassé and Paul Cambon in 1904 and to Rouvier in 1905, to the great alarm of them all.[1]

The authenticity of the *Vengeur* document has been questioned by Armand Charpentier, who writes that it 'has every appearance of being a forgery by which some leading member of our General Staff and some diplomat or other at our Quai d'Orsay have been or have pretended to be taken in'. In 1904, when it is said to have fallen into the hands of the French General Staff, the Minister for War was General André, and his Chef de Cabinet General Percin. Charpentier had numerous conversations with General Percin between 1920 and the General's death, but never, in his many references to the invasion of Belgium, did the General mention the *Vengeur*'s revelations. Had he known of them he would have used them in his book entitled *Lille,* since they would have enabled him to arraign the incredible lack of foresight on the part of the French General Staff. Though possessed of information on the route to be taken by the German troops across Belgium to the French northern frontier, the General Staff not only failed to fortify that frontier but actually dismantled the principal forts, chief among which were those at Lille. Charpentier thinks that General Pendezec was taken in by a forger, possibly one of those who worked for Colonel Henry in that *Deuxiéme Bureau d'Information* which achieved such lamentable notoriety in the Dreyfus case. Probably the document, on subsequent examination by some more wide-awake officer, was found to be a forgery of similar type to those in the Henry collection, and was therefore destroyed. This would explain how it was not found in 1929 by General Pétain.[8]

But whether Pendezec was the dupe of a forger or not, the fact remains that the *Vengeur*'s revelations came very close to the truth, and that at the end of 1905 the French Commander-in-Chief, General Brugère, introduced into concentration plan XV a 'variant', the purpose of which—according to a letter written by his son, Raymond

---

[1] Maurice Paléologue, *Un prélude à l'invasion de la Belgique (Le Plan Schlieffen,* 1904), (Paris, 1932), pp. 23-7, 33, 99-100, 145.

[2] Armand Charpentier, 'Une histoire rocambolesque. Le document "Le Vengeur",' in *Évolution,* April 1933, pp. 193 ff.

Brugère, Counsellor at the French Embassy in Brussels, to Paléologue and by him published in the *Revue des Deux Mondes,* was to facilitate 'the rapid transport northwards of a considerable reserve force precisely in the case of a German offensive through Belgium'. Raymond Brugère claims for his father the credit for the exchanges of views and provisional (*éventuels*) agreements which followed between the French and English Staffs in anticipation of a possible invasion of Belgium by Germany. There is no reason to regard it as impossible that these measures were taken in consequence of the *Vengeur* revelations, even if, as Paléologue implies, no great weight were attached to these. He writes that Pendezec's successor, General Brun, in a conversation of 22 January 1906 about the Pendezec 'variant', drafted a few days earlier, remarked:

> Of course, if the *Vengeur* revelations are genuine, the center of gravity of our concentration would have to be moved much further north. . . .
>
> But is not the *Vengeur* laying a trap for us? Is he not perhaps feigning to have turned traitor? General Brugère still refuses to believe that the German General Staff has decided to cross Belgium to reach the Oise valley and fall on Paris. I confess that this encircling movement, which would necessarily involve both banks of the Meuse, also perplexes me by its extraordinary breadth (*envergure*).[2]

In the succeeding years, whether for that reason or another, Brugère's successors seem entirely to have forgotten the *Vengeur* document. A footnote in Vol. II of the 3rd Series of the *Documents Diplomatiques Français* runs:

> On 9 January 1912 the Supreme Council of National Defence had received a communication containing information to the effect that in case of war Germany would not hesitate to extend the area of operations of its armies to Belgium. To prepare against this threat it might from the military point of view be advisable to take the initiative in entering Belgium; but from the political point of view the move might carry with it the risk of modifying the attitude of England.[3]

No mention here of the 1904 revelations, of which Joffre was probably ignorant. Had he known of them or thought them important, he would certainly have made use of them in a conversation which he had on 11 October 1911 with the Foreign Minister, de Selves, and at his meeting on 21 February 1912 with Poincaré, certain other Ministers and Paléologue, when he made no allusion to the 1904 incident.[4]

However, it is true, as Paléologue states, that in 1906 the French and British General Staffs felt anxiety at the possibility of a German move

---

[1] *Revue des Deux Mondes,* 15 November, 1932, pp. 425-30.
[2] Paléologue, *Prélude d l'invasion,* pp. 156-7.
[3] DF. 3. II, p. 244. [4] See p. 428.

through Belgium. The Algeciras crisis at the beginning of that year led General Grierson, Director of Military Operations at the War Office, to have a talk with the French Military Attaché, Major Huguet, and then to write on 11 January 1906 to the Foreign Office:

> I think that, if there is even a chance of our having to give armed assistance on land to France or to take the field on her side in Belgium in consequence of a violation of Belgian territory by the Germans, we should have as soon as possible informal communication between the military authorities of France and/or Belgium and the General Staff.[1]

On 15 January Grey gave the authorization on the understanding that the talks should not be binding.[2] Next day Grierson instructed Lieutenant-General Barnardiston, the Military Attaché at Brussels, to open talks with the Belgian Chief of Staff, General Ducarne.

Ducarne, fully aware of the danger overhanging his country, obtained permission from his Government to enter upon exploratory and non-committal discussions. In his talks with Barnardiston he made, one clear reservation, namely, that Belgium would take up arms against any Power violating her neutrality and that the English should only enter Belgium after the violation of her neutrality by Germany. Plans were drawn up for the landing in Belgium of a British Expeditionary Force of 100,000 men, later raised to 150,000.

3. Anglo-Belgian differences and Belgian sympathies for Germany.

These agreements fell into the hands of the Germans in Brussels in the autumn of 1914, but, in publishing them, they omitted the essential feature just mentioned, namely, the reservation made by Ducarne. Major Hosse goes so far as to say:

> In 1906 the British and Belgian Staffs concluded a military agreement which, without receiving official confirmation, had binding force. . . . The two Governments were cognizant of the arrangements and approved them.[3]

The truth was that there was no alliance and no ratification. Barnardiston—as is stated in Ducarne's letter of 10 April 1906 to the Belgian War Minister, actually reproduced by Hosse—had given an undertaking that

---

[1] BD. III, 211. See Huguet, pp. 15-17.   [2] BD. III, 217.

[3] Karl Hosse, *Die englisch-belgischen Aufmarschplam gegen Deutschland vor dent Weltkriege* (Vienna, 1930), p. 47. The effrontery of German historians in their judgments on the Barnardiston-Ducarne agreement is incredible. Even Lutz writes: 'The Anglo-Belgian "discussions" of 1906 of which we are now well informed, were not consonant with the spirit of neutrality, especially in their one-sided tendency against Germany. Germany found herself admittedly in an *impasse* and from a purely strategic standpoint the invasion was justifiable' (Lutz, p. 524). In other words, if Germany meant to defeat France she had to pass through Belgium, but if the French, English, and Belgians took measures to prevent this, they were not playing the game.

the entry of the English into Belgium would only take place after the violation of our neutrality by Germany.[1]

Hence if no violation took place, the agreement would not become operative. It may be conceded that such an agreement was open to unfavorable interpretation and that to leave no room for misunderstanding and to cover all possible threats of violation Belgium should have made similar arrangements with France and Germany. But there is no justification for protest from that very nation whose actions were to prove how well advised England and Belgium were to discuss between themselves the problem of their military co-operation. The following German impression of English military opinion at that moment was reported to Bülow by Moltke on 23 February 1906:

> The change in the balance of power in Europe produced by a victorious Germany would be so great a national threat to England that she would be obliged to lay aside 'the desirable neutrality purposed by the Government'. It is taken for granted that in a Franco-German war Belgium will be drawn in on the side of France. The view is taken that a victorious Germany would have no interest in depressing France to a third-rate Power. . . . Instead Germany would indemnify herself with Belgium, possibly also annexing Holland. . . . The self-preservation of England demands her intervention in a Continental war in order to prevent any such German supremacy unless the German Government were to declare its readiness unconditionally to guarantee the independence of Holland and Belgium even if Belgium by force of circumstances ranged herself with France. That a victorious Germany could be expected to accede to this request is regarded, however, as impossible. If Germany at the outbreak of war refused the guarantee of Belgian and Dutch independence that would be asked of her, it would be any English Government's duty to take the side of France in order to protect Belgian independence.[2]

The views of the German General Staff are formulated in a memorandum sent by Moltke to Bethmann on 21 December 1912:

> Unless there is a change in the European political situation we shall be forced by Germany's central position to wage a war on several fronts, holding the defensive with smaller forces on the one side in order to take the offensive on the other. This other side can only be France. . . . And to take the offensive against France it will be necessary to violate Belgian neutrality. Only an advance through Belgian territory gives us the hope of attacking and beating the French army in the open field. In this way we shall find facing us the English Expeditionary Force and—unless we achieve a treaty with Belgium—the Belgian army. Nevertheless, this operation offers better prospects of success than a frontal attack against the fortified French eastern front.[3]

[1] Hosse, Annex No. 11.   [2] GP. XXI[2], 7226.
[3] Bredt, p. 55.

These documents show on which side of the scales the weight of German military opinion was thrown. The Belgians, on the other hand, whether from love of Germany or fear of her, soon came to regard the Barnardiston-Ducarne arrangements as compromising. They turned for advice to the diplomatist most trusted by the Belgian Government of the day, the germanophil Belgian Minister at Berlin, Baron Greindl, who on 20 June 1906 replied inveighing against the English 'intrigue' intended 'to protect us against a German attack which the German Government has never contemplated'.[1] Thus the agreement remained a dead letter and was dropped. Belgium thought she was sufficiently protecting herself by obtaining from the Hague Peace Conference of 1907 the recognition by a unanimous vote of the principle that the territory of neutral States was inviolable.

Nay more, owing to English opposition in 1908 to the annexation of the Congo by Belgium, Anglo-Belgian relations grew so bad that at the beginning of 1909 General Ducarne received instructions to work out a plan of concentration designed to meet an invasion of Belgium from the North Sea. The decision was taken to fortify Antwerp against attack from the British navy. An order was placed with Krupp for eight 280 mm. heavy guns, which were paid for in advance, but never delivered. The Germans made use of them in 1914.[2] This neglect of provision for her own defense was a grave dereliction on the part of Belgium and brought the direst consequences in its train. Her duty should have been to take measures for the protection of her territory and her neutrality. Such measures would have served as a deterrent, since any intending invader would understand that he could not hope to cross her territory and outflank the enemy lines almost without striking a blow. Her inaction created a situation which led both the Germans and the French to think that the best plan of campaign would be to cross Belgium in order to carry the offensive into enemy territory. Had the Belgian army been large and well organized, had Belgian fortifications been up to date and defended by heavy artillery, had Belgium made it widely known that she intended to defend her neutrality at all costs, in alliance at need with whichever Power refrained from violating that neutrality, she would have offered no temptation to anyone to invade her.

It must be added that Belgian negligence of essential measures of self-defense was a constant source of anxiety to the neighboring Powers who were guarantors of her neutrality. It even alarmed the German General Staff in 1887 when in a possible Franco-German war the French were thought to be contemplating a march through Belgium

---

[1] Wullus-Rudiger, p. 25.
[2] Wullus-Rudiger, pp. 24-5, 45, 67; Klobukowski, pp. 58-9.

and when she was in no state to prevent it. Bismarck was besought to take the matter up and asked for an exact account of the defensive possibilities of the country. He was only reassured when the Belgian Government obtained the necessary credits for the fortification of Liége and Namur.[1] But the greatest alarm was felt in London where at every international crisis thoughts turned to Belgium with the query what would be the position of England were Belgian neutrality to be violated and how much resistance would Belgium put up if invaded by Germany. Thus it came about that in 1908 Grey instructed the Foreign Office to draw up a memorandum on the following questions:

How far would England's liability under the treaty [of 1839] guaranteeing the neutrality of Belgium be affected, if (1) Belgium acquiesced in a violation of her neutrality; (2) if the other guaranteeing Powers or some of them acquiesced?

Eyre Crowe's lengthy memorandum brings out the following point:

The neutrality of Belgium was guaranteed not merely because it was a Belgian interest, but because it was an interest of the guaranteeing Powers. . . . It follows that the obligation of the guarantee was incurred not alone, nor exclusively, as towards Belgium, but also as towards the other guaranteeing Powers. . . . Great Britain is liable for the maintenance of Belgian neutrality whenever Belgium or any of the guaranteeing Powers are in need of, and demand, assistance in opposing its violation.

In concurring with this view Sir Charles Hardinge minuted:

The liability undoubtedly exists as stated above, but whether we could be called upon to carry out our obligation and to vindicate the neutrality of Belgium in opposing its violation must necessarily depend upon our policy at the time and the circumstances of the moment. Supposing that France violated the neutrality of Belgium in a war against Germany, it is, under present circumstances, doubtful whether England or Russia would move a finger to maintain Belgian neutrality, while if the neutrality of Belgium were violated by Germany it is probable that the converse would be the case.

This comment, if somewhat cynical, was pertinent, as Grey himself remarks:

I am much obliged for this useful minute; I think it sums up the situation very well, though Sir C. Hardinge's reflection is also to the point.[2]

It is noteworthy that Grey's questions envisaged the possibility that Belgium might actually not desire to remain neutral. The doubt

---

[1] Bredt, pp. 10-12. In this connection Bredt publishes a letter from Wilhelm I to Leopold II who, on 14 February 1887, had written giving an account of the measures taken by Belgium in defense of her neutrality. In his reply Wilhelm I remarks that the Belgian army was too weak and that its inadequate strength left the country open to attack (Bredt, pp. 12–13).

[2] BD. VIII, 311.

originated in the Belgian failure to take any measures for self-defense when it became apparent that Germany would be likely to march across Belgian territory, taken in conjunction with the extremely intimate and confidential relations which Belgium maintained with Germany. The *British Documents* bring evidence of many warnings given by the various British Military Attachés. During the Bosnian crisis the Military Attaché at Paris on 6 February 1909, reported his Spanish colleague as saying

that, in the event of war between France and Germany, Belgium had—to the best of his belief—decided to throw in their lot with Germany. . . . They were well aware that they were totally unable to defend their neutrality and thought that they would come better out of a conflict between their two powerful neighbors by joining that 'which they judged to be the more powerful.[1]

Grey forwarded this document to Brussels asking for the opinion of the British Military Attaché there. On 25 February 1909 the reply came back that in military circles

it seems to be generally hoped that France would be the first to cross the frontier, or, if it was a near thing, that the Belgian Government would try to make out that French troops were the first to violate Belgium's neutrality.[2]

On 21 February 1911 the British Military Attaché at Rome, Colonel Delmé-Radcliffe, in a long report on the military and political position of Switzerland, remarks:

The German Great General Staff . . . hopes to overwhelm its enemy by a strategical envelopment which will enable it to turn the formidable barrier of the French positions at Verdun, Toul, Épinal, and Belfort. Counting on the weakness of Belgium and the unarmed neutrality of Luxemburg, Germany has designed to turn these defenses by her right wing through Luxemburg and Southern Belgium.[3]

When the Agadir crisis arose the Foreign Office instructed the English Military Attaché, Lieutenant-Colonel Bridges, and the Chargé d'Affaires, Mr. Macleay, to raise the question of Belgian neutrality at Brussels. On 22 September 1911 Bridges quoted the Belgian Chief of Staff, Lieutenant-General Jungbluth, as saying: 'all possible steps had been taken that could be justified by the situation,' while Mr. Macleay, on 29 September, reported assurances from Davignon 'that the Belgian Government were absolutely determined to resist invasion from whatever direction it might proceed and in whatever portion of the Kingdom it might be attempted'.[4] But these assurances did not convince the British authorities.

[1] BD. VIII, 312.   [2] BD. VIII, 313.
[3] BD. VIII, 344.   [4] BD. VIII, 317, 318.

4. The views of Joffre and the French Government on the Belgian question.

A month later, on 19 October 1911, Bridges sent a pessimistic report on the line that would probably be taken by Belgium in the event of a German invasion.[1] He pointed out the inadequacy of Belgian military preparations, the need for which had been made amply clear when at the end of 1911 the question arose of an ostensibly Dutch, but really German, proposal for the fortification of Flushing. This, if carried out, would have prevented the English from making a landing there to oppose a German penetration of the country, and was thus incompatible with the spirit of the 1839 treaty. The Brussels Government felt misgivings and sent van der Elst, the Secretary General for Foreign Affairs, first on a semi-official visit to Schoen, the German Ambassador at Paris, whose wife was Belgian, and then to pay a call on Flotow, the German Minister at Brussels, to raise the question of statements appearing in certain newspapers in Belgium, France and England to the effect that in the event of a Franco-German war, Germany would violate the neutrality of Belgium. He suggested that a declaration in the Reichstag during a debate on foreign affairs would serve to calm public opinion. A few days later Bethmann sent answer by Flotow that 'Germany had no intention of violating Belgian neutrality, but that it would be difficult to make a public declaration to that effect because Germany would thereby weaken her military position in regard to France, who, secured on the northern side, would concentrate all her energies in the east.[2]

This was a specious excuse seeing that the 1839 treaty gave France the right to feel secure on the Belgian frontier, so that if Germany was unwilling to let her feel secure there, it was a sign that Germany herself was premeditating double dealing in that direction. But Brussels never thought of pursuing the implications of this brazen reply, the only excuse for which was the ingenuousness of the request and that it would never have done to let the truth be known or guessed. Fears were again felt in July 1911 when the dispatch of the *Panther* to Agadir seemed to presage a war provoked by Germany, and news came in supporting the view that the German General Staff planned to attack France through Belgium. Gaiffier, the Belgian Minister at Bucharest, was then instructed 10 ask the opinion of King Carol of Romania, whose reply of December 1911 runs:

---

[1] BD. VIII, 319.

[2] *First Belgian Grey Book*, 12; van der Elst, *art. cit.*, pp. 523-7. It seems, too, that Wilhelm, on a visit to Brussels in 1910 said to van der Elst: 'Belgium will never have anything to fear from us' and that he would never 'place her in an awkward position' (van der Elst, *art, cit.*, p. 529). At the unveiling of a statue at Aix-la-Chapelle in the summer of 1911 Wilhelm remarked to Delvaux de Teuffe, one of the delegation representing Belgium: 'You had lately, I believe, great alarms in your country—believe me they are needless.' And to another, General Heimburger: 'You did well to have confidence in us' (BD. VIII, 322).

In all frankness and with full conviction I answer that your territory will be violated and that no account will be taken of your neutrality.[1]

At the end of 1911 this possibility of violation was admitted even by the Belgian Minister at Berlin, Greindl, who five years earlier had stoutly denied it. But in a long dispatch of 23 December 1911, giving his opinion on a plan drawn up by General Ceulemans to meet a German invasion, Griendl remarked that a French invasion was no less probable and that 'the idea of an enveloping movement from the north has certainly entered into the arrangements of the *Entente Cordiale*'. In any case he thought the Belgian army ought not to

sacrifice itself for abstract principles, but husband its resources in order to remain capable, in the event of the invasion of Belgium, to preserve at least one point of Belgian territory where King and Government could find refuge, where the national flag would fly, where we should be sole masters, where we would admit no foreign garrison. . . . The construction of the fortresses of Namur and Liége offers us a chance of preserving until the peace not only the city of Antwerp, but all the center of the country, perhaps even the capital. . . . It is also necessary to consider the by no means improbable hypothesis that we ourselves might be compelled by events to become belligerents against our will. In that case we should have to let ourselves be guided only by consideration of our interests and by the degree of confidence we should feel in the Great Powers at war. What it is important to establish is that we should be absolutely free in our decision. Our neutrality would have been wrecked, or at least suspended, by the act of Great Powers bringing war into our country. The 1839 treaty is a contract binding on us only so long as it is honored by all parties. Contrary to an idea too widespread in Belgium, we should not be obliged to fight on the side of the foreign army whose entry into Belgium was anterior by a few hours to that of the adversary. We should have the absolute right to choose our allies, and if we do not have it, we must arrogate it to ourselves. The preservation of the country's existence, our primordial duty, cannot be at the mercy of a fortuitous case. . . . It is not necessary to suppose . . . that the invasion of Belgium must be accompanied by mental reservations hostile to our independence.[2]

In other words, for fear that the first to violate Belgian neutrality might be the Germans, Greindl was proposing that the Belgian army should offer them no resistance and should refrain from asking help from France and England on the ground that 'the Powers that would come to our help would be no less to be feared than the one which first invaded us'.[3] The Belgian army should retire on Antwerp and end up by making common cause with the German army, which would probably come out

[1] Wullus-Rudiger, pp. 39-40.

[2] Bernhard Schwertfeger, *Die belgischen Dokumente zur Vorgeschichte des Weltkrieges, 1885-1914. Zweiter Kommentarband. Der geistige Kampf um die Verletzung der belgischen Neutralität* (Berlin, 1925), pp. 143-55.

[3] Wullus-Rudiger, p. 41.

victorious, even though this course might conflict with the duties imposed on Belgium by the 1839 treaty. The man who could write like this had no reason to write slightingly of 'the no less perfidious than naive overtures of Colonel Barnardiston'.[1]

Fortunately the Belgian Government in 1914 did not follow Greindl's advice, though it was identical with that given later by General de Witte under the pseudonym of O. Dax in a publication which created a considerable stir.[2] When the time came the Belgian leaders decided that their army should sacrifice itself for an 'abstract principle', to its own great glory and the salvation of the country. Nevertheless, their eyes were not opened to German intentions until 2 August 1914 when the ultimatum from Berlin was put in their hands. And even then they were more mistrustful of France and England than of Germany.

The doubts about France were—it must be admitted—not entirely unjustified. Just as Germany could not easily overcome the line of French fortifications, so also for France it was not advisable to dash herself against the fortified German lines. It was also a suspicious circumstance that she had not erected similar fortifications along the frontier facing Belgium, knowing that there existed a probability of the German army's taking the offensive in that direction. In fact it cannot be said that the French Government took the necessary measures to meet this mortal danger. Until the appointment of Joffre as Chief of Staff on 28 July 1911 French plans of concentration were based on the theory of the defensive-offensive. Mention has been made above of the variant to Plan XV introduced by General Brugère in 1905 to meet an offensive coming from the direction of Belgium. At the time of Joffre's appointment the plan in force was No. XVI, which took no account of the danger from Belgium, and was based on the conviction that the German blow would be struck in the Metz-Toul-Verdun region. Joffre's predecessor, General Michel, had, it is true, proposed not only army reforms, which were rejected by the Government, but also a plan of concentration taking account of the possibility of a German violation of Belgium and moving the center of gravity of the French forces to the extreme left. Joffre, however, was less alive to the danger from Belgium and judged that

such a plan exposed us to a rupture either of our center or our right, and risked opening the heart of the country to the enemy.[3]

---

[1] Schwertfeger, *Die belgischen Dokumente zur Vorgeschichte dss Weltkrieges. 2ter Kommentarband* (Berlin, 1925), p. 147.

[2] *The Situation in Belgium in the Event of a Franco-German Conflict.* The book closed with the words: 'If the occasion arises we must not hesitate so to direct events as will cause our alliance with the stronger of the two belligerents to be justified by the facts' (Joffre, I, p. 54).

[3] Joffre, I, pp. 17, 18.

Taking into account the French temperament, which fights best when on the offensive and is apt to take alarm at early reverses, Joffre prepared a variation of Plan XVI, as a transitional step to a new plan.

A study of the German railway system and its detraining points had shown that platforms had been lengthened and other recent improvements made which would enable the main body of the German troops to detrain north of the Metz-Strasbourg line. This seemed to support the hypothesis of a German attack through Belgium. On the other hand, the statements repeatedly published by German writers as to the necessity of violating Belgium

might be merely a maneuver to draw us toward the north and leave us uncovered to the east, where the enemy might seek to obtain a rapid decision.[1]

Before he could work out a definite plan Joffre needed to be informed by the Government what would be the position of France with regard to the other European Powers and to what extent the other Powers would observe their agreements and their treaties of alliance or of neutrality. At a Council of National Defence on n October 1911 he raised the question with the Foreign Minister, de Selves. De Selves replied: 'In diplomacy we count on possibilities, never on certainties', whereupon

I replied by showing that, for example, from a strictly military point of view, our interests would suggest the carrying of the war into Belgium, but that this question was one which lay in the domain of diplomacy. M. de Selves answered that recently when war came so near to breaking out, the question of Belgium had been discussed between the Chief of the General Staff and himself, and it had been understood that we would hold ourselves ready to march into Belgium if the Germans themselves first violated her neutrality.[2]

On 16 October Joffre handed Paléologue, the Director of Political Affairs, a memorandum on the general situation containing the following passage:

By reason of the shortness of the frontier separating France and Germany and the numerous fortifications lining it on both sides . . . the Germans—and indeed the French—would have every advantage in developing their maneuver through Belgium. Moreover, the Belgian Army would be incapable of offering any opposition to a violation of its territory. The French General Staff has never thought that it could be the first to violate Belgian neutrality. Not only would this be a denial of our signature, but it would constitute a provocation capable of alienating Russia and England. However, from information in our possession we have reason to believe that the Germans do not intend to respect this neutrality as we do.

[1] Joffre, 1, p. 19.   [2] Joffre, I, pp. 38-9.

In view of the gravity of the question, it would be most useful for me to have the advice of the Council of National Defence regarding the authorization to be given to the Commander in Chief to extend his zone of operations into Belgium the moment he learns of the violation of that country by the Germans, and again, is there complete agreement regarding the interdiction against our troops being the first to violate Belgian neutrality?[1]

The Quai d'Orsay's reply of 20 October to this runs:

It is our duty to take no initiative which might be regarded as a violation of Belgium's neutrality. But it seems certain that Germany will march her troops across Belgian territory, and in that case we should take whatever measures are required by the necessity of defending ourselves.[2]

At a further meeting of the Council of National Defence on 9 January 1912 Joffre raised the question:

At the first news of the violation of Belgian territory by the Germans, may our armies penetrate Belgian territory?

And the Council unanimously gave him authorization to do so.[3]

In drawing up his new plan of concentration Joffre found himself placed in a dilemma by the heavily fortified region of Metz-Thionville.

It obliged us either to give up the initiative conferred by a strategic offensive . . . or else plunge at once into the hornet's nest that lay between Metz and Strasbourg. We could escape this dilemma in no other way than by orienting our operations towards Belgium; but this solution was permitted us only in the event of this country having been previously violated by the German armies. . . . It would be impossible for us to receive before the tenth or eleventh day, at the very earliest, information which would indicate the nature of the adversary's maneuver.[4]

By that time it would be too late. So Joffre brought the problem up at a secret meeting at the Quai d'Orsay on 21 February 1912 attended only by Poincaré, who a few days previously had become Prime Minister and Foreign Minister, Millerand, Minister for War, Delcassé, Minister of Marine, Paléologue, Director of Political Affairs, and the Army and Navy Chiefs of Staff, Joffre and Aubert.

Aubert explained the naval arrangements between the British Admiralty and the French Naval Staff. All operations in the North Sea, English Channel and Atlantic were reserved to the British fleet, while the French fleet would take charge of operations in the Mediterranean. Joffre's conversations with the British Staff had taken as a basis six infantry divisions, one cavalry division and two mounted brigades, a total of 125,000 men.

Taking the strictly military point of view . . . I then explained to the conference that if we could conduct our offensive across Belgium . . . the

[1] Joffre, I, pp. 39-41.   [2] Joffre, I, pp. 42-3.
[3] Joffre, I, pp. 47-8.   [4] Joffre, I, p. 49.

problem presented to us would be simplified. . . . Neither in Alsace nor in Lorraine do we find ground favorable for an offensive having immediate decisive results in view. The situation would be infinitely more advantageous if it were permissible for us to extend our left beyond our frontier into the Grand Duchy of Luxemburg. In this region we could develop all our means of action, and we would be passing far to the north of all the fortified systems constructed at great cost by our adversaries. In case of success our armies would throw the German masses back towards Southern Germany and directly menace their principal line of retreat as well as their communications with Berlin. Moreover, a movement through Belgium would make it possible for the British army to participate more efficaciously in our operations.[1]

Joffre adds that Millerand and Delcassé agreed 'with my conception of the results to be expected from a plan of operations aiming at offensive action across Belgian territory'.

But Poincaré pointed out that an invasion of Belgium by France would run the risk of setting against us not only Europe but the Belgians themselves, because of the difficulty of coming to an understanding with them beforehand, and under these conditions it seemed essential that our entrance upon Belgian territory be justified at least by a positive menace of German invasion. Indeed, it was this fear of an invasion of Belgium by the Germans which, in the first place, had led to the military arrangements with Great Britain. We, therefore, had to be sure that a plan based upon a march by us through Belgium would not have for its effect the withdrawal of British support from our side.[2]

Joffre asks himself the question: 'What was to be understood by a "positive menace"?' and concludes:

While the conference of 21 February 1912 resulted in stating the problem, it did nothing to solve it. . . . The Prime Minister without doubt had in mind all the warnings which the British had given us concerning Belgian neutrality.

At the time of the Anglo-French military conversations in 1906, when France promised to respect Belgian neutrality, Colonel Repington had uttered the warning words:

Do not let yourselves be tempted to enter Belgium upon a simple threat from Germany; it might be in the interests of that country to push you towards such a step.

And the warning had been repeated by Lord Esher in 1911.[3]

5. *The Bridges episode; France gives up the plan of a maneuver through Belgium.*

Nevertheless, soon afterwards Poincaré had the question thus raised by Joffre put to the Foreign Office. To Paléologue, Paul Cambon on 21 March 1912 reported having said to Nicolson that

[1] Joffre, I, pp. 49-51.   [2] Joffre, I, p. 51.   [3] Joffre, I, p. 51.

our two Governments might at some moment have to face the following question: 'If it were to be established beyond doubt that an army concentrated round Aix-la-Chapelle was preparing to enter Belgium . . . ought we to wait for the occupation of Belgium by the German army before advancing ourselves?' 'It is a serious question', said Sir Arthur. 'Yes, but it is one which will arise if we have the certainty of a march of German forces on Belgium.'[1]

On 28 March 1912 Poincaré himself wrote Paul Cambon asking him to raise the following matter with Downing Street:

> The essential point is that England should not engage to remain neutral between France and Germany even on the hypothesis of the attack seeming to come from us. To take only one example, could we rightly be held guilty of aggression if a concentration of German forces in the Aix-la-Chapelle region obliged us to cover our northern frontier by penetrating into Belgian territory?[2]

This telegram was received by the Chargé d'Affaires, Fleuriau, who put the French views to Nicolson. Fleuriau's dispatch of 4 April does not report Nicolson's reply to his inquiry.[3] In reality Nicolson did not know what answer to give. As we shall soon see, he himself tried in vain to find a solution.[4] Perhaps it is not beside the mark to see some connection between the problem raised by Joffre in Paris, the inquiry made in London by Poincaré and the so-called Bridges incident arising from a statement made by Bridges to General Jungbluth. On 23 April 1912, Bridges, the Military Attaché at Brussels, said to the Belgian Chief of Staff that if war had broken out at the time of Agadir England, as was her right and duty, would have landed troops in Belgium without waiting for the consent of the Brussels Government.[5]

Nobody, as it turned out later, had authorized Bridges to make such a statement, which was merely an expression of personal opinion entirely at variance with the English Government's intentions. However, from the point of view of treaty rights the project would have been well within the law. In the already quoted Greindl memorandum it is admitted that 'to enter our country the guarantor has no need of our permission. . . . The guarantee clause was inserted in the 1839 treaty more in the interests of the guarantors than in that of Belgium'. It was nevertheless obvious that only an actual violation of Belgian neutrality could justify one of the guaranteeing Powers in entering Belgium and that any preventive entry would wear the aspect of a violation. Hence Jungbluth replied—first on his own account and then on written instructions from the Foreign Minister—that England could not land troops without the consent of the Belgian Government, that

---

[1] DF. 3. II, 240.   [2] DF. 3. II, 269.   [3] DF. 3. II, 300.
[4] See pp. 435–6.   [5] *First Belgian Grey Book,* Appendix No. 4[2].

the Government was determined to defend its neutrality and was sole judge of the aid it would need.

Here Jungbluth was overstating, since if one of the guarantor Powers entered Belgium the others had the right to follow suit in their own interests if not in the interests of Belgium. But Jungbluth's reaction was exceeded by that of the War Minister, the germanophil Michel, who on 12 September 1912 said to the English Naval Attaché, Captain Kelly, that in his opinion not Germany but France and England would be the first to send their troops into Belgium.

He made it quite clear that in his opinion the danger of a breach of Belgian neutrality lay more from England than anywhere else.[1]

On 7 October 1912 General Michel told Bridges that from the time England entered on the *Entente Cordiale* her

position in Belgium had gone back and that in his opinion . . . in stepping down from her position of isolation [she had] lost prestige all over the world. . . . He had asked himself how Great Britain was going to employ her expeditionary force. . . . Belgium formed the only theatre where such a force could conceivably operate. Again, would Great Britain come to the assistance of Belgium if her neutrality were violated by the French? He thought not. Only in her own interest or in that of the French would she come. Great Britain for these reasons was a potential enemy. . . . In answer to my question as to the probable procedure in Belgium on a violation of territory, the Minister said that Belgian troops would march with all speed against the firstcomers, but that calling in of other Powers was a delicate matter, and he . . . was not in favor of it for the reason that it was often easier to get a policeman into your house than out of it.

Grey's minute to Bridges's report runs:

If Germany does not violate the neutrality of Belgium no one else will do so.[2]

He also took the matter up with France, as we learn from Joffre:

On 27 November 1912 General Wilson, with the approval of Sir Edward Grey, came to the French General Staff and informed us that the Foreign Office believed 'that Belgium was hesitating as to the attitude she would take in the case of war between France and Germany, and that she seemed to incline rather to the German side. Now—he added—if France should be the first to violate Belgian neutrality, the army of Belgium would certainly join the Germans, and the British Government would then be called upon to defend the neutrality of that country. This would place us in a very embarrassing position; therefore—he concluded—the French army has no interest whatever in being the first to violate Belgian neutrality.' This communication was of the very highest importance for it obliged me definitely to renounce all idea of a maneuver *a priori* through Belgium.[3]

[1] BD. VIII, 324.   [2] BD. VIII, 326.   [3] Joffre, I, p. 54.

There remains the query whether, after having to give up that idea, Joffre was well advised to pursue the project of an offensive against impregnable German fortifications and whether he should and could not have devised better means of countering the enemy's plan. The truth is that he had not grasped its implications and he frankly admits that the

error into which we were led bore heavily on the manner in which we organized our concentration,[1]

especially as for the first three weeks of the war he refused to modify his plan of action. This, however, lies outside our subject. The point that concerns us is that the French refrained from violating the neutrality of Belgium not so much from unwillingness to dishonor their signature as because they feared the effect of violation on their relations with England. If England had given consent, Joffre in all probability would have worked out a plan of concentration preparing for an offensive across Belgium, justifying it by the fact that the same maneuver was an essential part of the German war plan and that in order to paralyze the German plan he must not wait to let it develop. Would this justification have been nothing more than a mere pretext? Could it, in other words, perhaps have a sound basis? Bredt writes:

In 1914 the German General Staff definitely calculated that in the event of war the French would invade Belgium with their left wing. Colonel-General von Moltke had personally collected all the relevant information and indications and reached his conviction according to them.

But the meager and unconvincing evidence, quoted by Bredt,[2] is derived from Moltke himself, who laid down his views about the probable plan of campaign in a memorandum entitled *Strategic concentration and operative intentions of the French in a future Franco-German war:*

The idea of advancing on Belgium with their left wing appears in French military literature for the first time in the summer of 1911 and has latterly often been expressed. It is advocated especially by the Englishman Hilaire Belloc, and the former French Military Attaché in Brussels, Commander Duruy, and further by a French officer writing under the pseudonym of Landrecies who is in touch with Duruy. Their line of argument takes as its starting-point the assertion that the Germans in their advance through Belgium will be obliged in order to cover their right flank to take possession of the Liége-Namur line of the Meuse, in the first place attacking Liége. If in this struggle the Belgians were left to themselves they would scarcely offer serious resistance. Therefore the English and French will have to intervene and advance to the Meuse. . . . The German plan of operations is

---

[1] Joffre, I, p. 62.
[2] Bredt, p. 113. See also Montgelas, *Die belgische Neutralität und der Schlieffensche Feldzugplan,* KSF. December 1931, pp. 1136-7.

based on an unimpeded encircling movement by their right wing. This plan will be frustrated if this wing is pinned down on the Meuse by the above-indicated maneuvers of the English, Belgians and French. . . . How far the above information is correct cannot be proved. But it is probable that part of the French forces will advance to the Givet-Namur line of the Meuse.[1]

Probable, but not certain! Moltke's statement makes it clear that the plan of the offensive against Belgium did not assume an advance of the French main forces into Belgium for an attack against the Germans. Bredt says that it looks as if a discarded idea of Schlieffen's was still influencing Moltke.[2] More likely Moltke was seeking a justification for his ultimatum to Belgium. But even had the French advance been certain the memorandum admits that the maneuvers of the English, Belgians, and French would be intended only to foil the German encircling movement through Belgium. Moltke regards such maneuvers on their part as logical, hence probable, if not certain. This admission on the enemy's part seems to constitute a reproach leveled at the *Entente* leaders of preferring to risk losing the war rather than enter Belgium ahead of or simultaneously with the Germans. Was the reproach merited? From the strictly military standpoint it undoubtedly was, but not from the political point of view, since it would then have been difficult, if not impossible, to persuade public opinion in England and the rest of the world that the violation of Belgian neutrality by France was due to its violation by Germany.

6. An inquiry by Nicolson; and Grey's assurances to the Belgian Minister.

The Schlieffen plan had created a disturbing problem for the *Entente* military chiefs, though they had not realized its full gravity and did not know what measures to take to counteract its deadly effects,[3] especially as they were uncertain what attitude Belgium would adopt and knew her inability to defend herself. The dispatches reaching both London and Paris in 1912 sought to rouse them to a realization of the danger and deserved more attention than they received. Alarming also was the language of certain Belgian journals, among them *the XX Siècle,*

---

[1] Bredt, pp. 113-14.

[2] Bredt, p. 114.

[3] In this connection Bredt writes: The plans of the German general staff were well recognized and appreciated by the French and English. Germany's military position was fully understood, and from the purely military standpoint the plan of campaign met with nothing but approval. On one point, however, the enemy assumptions went astray. They reckoned with a march through southern Belgium, south of the Meuse and Sambre, not with the invasion of the whole of Belgium taking in Liége and the Meuse. Through this miscalculation it became possible for the Schlieffen plan to be fundamentally successful and for a victorious German advance to reach almost to the gates of Paris. But at that point the plan suffered shipwreck on the inadequacy of the leadership which on the Marne failed to make proper use of the auxiliary services *{der Amhilfen)* and suddenly lapsed into unjustified pessimism (Bredt, p. 210).

regarded as the organ of the Prime Minister, Broqueville, which asserted that the *Entente Cordiale* was 'as dangerous for Belgium in case of war as Germany could be'.[1] On 14 November 1912, speaking in the Chamber, Broqueville made the cryptic utterance:

One cannot lose sight of the fact that the grouping of the Powers has given rise to alliances and military understandings which in the event of a European war might deprive the granting of a guarantee of the value that can only be assured by the neutrality of the guarantor,

which seemed to mean that any guarantor Power on becoming belligerent would no longer have the right to defend Belgian neutrality by force of arms against violation by another guarantor Power, and that Belgium could play off one belligerent against the other. In reporting this on 16 November, the French Chargé d'Affaires, de Fontarce, added:

The question may well arise for us to know whether it is to our interest to accept such a thesis or whether, on the contrary, as the *Indépendence Belge* remarks, there is not reason to observe that the guarantee of neutrality was imposed on Belgium as much as granted to her, and that by this fact it confers on the guarantor Powers rights no less than duties.[2]

On 25 November 1912 the French Minister, Klobukowski, reported from Brussels that the *XX Siecle* had omitted a word in reproducing Broqueville's speech, the correct version of which should run'. . . the offer of a guarantee, the value of which could only *completely* be assured by the neutrality of the guarantor'.[3]

However that may be, the overall situation was such that Nicolson was asked by the English military chiefs to ascertain the probable attitude of Belgium in the event of French or British forces being obliged to defend Belgian neutrality. He put the question privately to Sir Francis Villiers, the English Minister in Brussels, in the following letter:

There is one point on which I have been for some time anxious to write you, but which pressure of business has continually prevented me from doing. I should much like to have your opinion as to whether, in the event of a European war, Belgium would be likely to be on our side or against us? What I mean is that, should we and France, for instance, be compelled to advance through Belgium for the purpose of repelling a German aggression in those quarters, whether we could count on Belgium receiving us as friends or enemies? It is a matter of some importance, though I quite understand that it will be difficult to give any decided answer to it. I was asked the question by our military people, and I said that I thought that, if anything, the balance inclined to Belgium regarding us as most unwelcome visitors, and

[1] DF.3.IV,385.   [2] DF.3.IV,476.   [3] DF.3.IV,565.

that she would be more likely to incline to Germany. You see that the point is that we and France might have to move troops across the Belgian frontier in order to meet the approach of German troops on the other side, and naturally it would be a matter of great importance to the military commanders if they felt that on their left flank they had friends and not dubious enemies. . . .[1]

This letter seems to show that, in spite of what General Sir Henry Wilson, with Grey's consent, had said to Joffre on 27 November 1912, the War Office was still studying possibilities of entering Belgium before the Germans to forestall their advance. The two phrases 'to advance through Belgium for the purpose of repelling[5] and 'in order to meet the approach' would seem to put the question how would Belgium behave if Anglo-French troops entered her territory before German troops for the purpose of opposing German aggression. It looks as if this were Grey's meaning, although his words are not explicit. Sir Francis Villiers made the Belgian view plain in his reply of 11 January 1913:

The views held, or at any rate expressed by the Government here is that so far as the guarantee of Belgian neutrality is concerned, the position has materially changed since the establishment of our *Entente* with the French. In the event of a European conflict England would be involved, Belgium would be included within the theatre of war, the neutrality of the country would not necessarily be taken into account, and might be violated by British forces as well as by those of the other belligerents. Belgium can, therefore, no longer depend upon the guarantee, but must provide for her own defense against three possible enemies instead of against two as before —that is to say against England as well as against France and Germany. . . . How far these feelings are really entertained it is difficult to judge. Their actual expression only began just at the time when the Belgian Government had made up their minds to propose a large increase of the army. . . . There is some distrust of us, due to the impatience, rapidly growing, at our delay in recognizing the annexation of the Congo. There is also on the part of the Government a leaning towards Germany. Our reception as friends or enemies, should we advance troops into Belgium to repel a German aggression, would depend upon circumstances. From my own observations and from conversations with Bridges I am of opinion that if we were to take action before the Germans actually entered Belgium, or in any case without agreement with the Belgian Government, or without an invitation from them, we should be considered to have violated the neutrality of the country and thus to be enemies. This would not be the feeling, I believe, among the people or in the army, but the Government would treat our troops as hostile, not probably to the extent of actively opposing us, but they would not afford any assistance or in any way facilitate our operations.[2]

[1] Nicolson, pp. 398-9.
[2] Nicolson, pp. 398-400. See also BD. VIII, 328, *n.*

Harold Nicolson says it was not the War Office but the Committee of Imperial Defence which prompted Sir Arthur Nicolson to write the letter, but this seems not to be so.[1] The policy of England is stated unambiguously in Sir Edward Grey's footnote to Bridges' report to Villiers of 8 October 1912:

If Germany does not violate the neutrality of Belgium no one else will do so.[2]

And he reaffirmed it to the Belgian Minister, Count de Lalaing, on 7 April 1913.

The Belgian Minister informed me that there had been talk in a British source which he could not name [Bridges?] of the landing of troops in Belgium by Great Britain, in order to anticipate a possible dispatch of German troops through Belgium to France. I said that I was sure that this Government would not be the first to violate the neutrality of Belgium, and I did not believe that any British Government would be the first to do so; nor would public opinion here ever approve of it. What we had to consider, and it 'was a somewhat embarrassing question, was what it would be desirable and necessary for us, as one of the guarantors of Belgian neutrality, to do if Belgian neutrality was violated by any Power. For us to be the first to violate it and to send troops into Belgium would be to give Germany, for instance, justification for sending troops into Belgium also. What we desired in the case of Belgium, as in that of other neutral countries, was that their neutrality should be respected; and as long as it was not violated by any other Power we should certainly not send troops ourselves into their territory.[3]

Sir Francis Villiers called on the Belgian Foreign Minister with this letter. Some days later it was returned to him by the Secretary General. Baron van der Elst, who reaffirmed the statement made by General Jungbluth to Colonel Bridges:

The Belgian Government take the view that intervention by England in case of a violation of our neutrality could only take place if we were in agreement on the principle of this intervention and its application.[4]

But from that time onward there was some improvement in the relations between the two countries.

7. Broqueville's military reforms; the satisfaction in Paris and London; Wilhelm and Moltke make bellicose speeches to King Albert.

The improvement—which was only slight because the Belgian Government still continued to incline more towards Germany— was due on the one hand to the recognition by England of the annexation to Belgium of the Congo Free State, and on the other

---

[1] BD. III, 221.
[2] BD. VIII, 326.
[3] BD. VIII, 330.
[4] Wullus-Rudiger, p. 90.

to the satisfaction felt in London and Paris that Belgium was beginning to take measures for her own defense. Her deficiencies in this respect had been pointed out by Poincaré to Guillaume, the Belgian Minister at Paris, when, on 23 October 1912, the latter had voiced the apprehensions felt in Belgium at the military preparations then in progress in Northern France. Poincaré said:

We have the certainty that the German army will seek to attack France by passing through the territory of Belgium; we must defend her [France].

As Guillaume assumed that only defensive measures were in question, Poincaré replied that France would be obliged to carry the war into Belgium if Belgium were not in a position to defend her neutrality against Germany.

I have every reason to believe—retorted Guillaume—that my Government is convinced of the need to strengthen its defense system,

whereupon he received the assurance from Poincaré

that France will never take the initiative of violating our neutrality.[1]

The question of military reform had been under discussion in the Belgian Parliament for years, but the combined opposition of the old Catholic Right and the Socialists had prevented anything being done. On 23 December 1909, however, King Albert succeeded to the throne. As General Galet, once his fellow student at the military academy and later his Officer-in-Waiting and military adviser during the war, relates, King Albert felt convinced that a European war would break out during his reign.[2] He therefore sought to remedy the gross deficiencies of Belgian military organization. Under his impetus much greater attention was paid to military problems than hitherto. In 1910 an Army General Staff was created under General Jungbluth. Next the reorganization of the army was taken in hand and the Prime Minister, Broqueville, became War Minister. In December 1912 he brought in a bill introducing general military service and providing for an army of 150,000 front-line troops, 130,000 to garrison the forts of Antwerp, Liége and Namur and 60,000 in the reserve. These measures would have taken at least ten years to come into full effect, and the law was passed only on 30 August 1913, so that when war broke out in 1914 army reorganization was in its very beginnings. From General Leman, the gallant defender of Liége, we know that material and moral conditions in the army were all but desperate.[3]

---

[1] Wullus-Rudiger, pp. 118-19.   [2] Galet, p. 1.

[3] On May 1, 1914, the French Military Attaché at Brussels, Commandant Génie, reported: the Belgian officers, themselves, whom one can talk with, admit that the Belgian army in 1914 could not be mobilized either in its new form which lacks cadre personnel, staffs, and material, or in its old form which has been broken up; it would be necessary to improvise an emergency organization (DF. 5. X, 192).

The King's efforts encountered opposition of every kind. Colonel (later General) Ryckel, of whom King Albert thought highly, had in 1911 worked out a plan of concentration on the left bank of the Meuse, but General Jungbluth's successor discarded it and obtained the transfer of Ryckel. At the end of 1913 the King obtained the latter's recall and nomination as Sub-Chief of General Staff. In April 1914 when the office of Chief of Staff fell vacant King Albert sought to have Ryckel appointed to it, but Broqueville objected and nominated Lieutenant-General de Selliers de Moranville. Selliers rejected Ryckel's plan of concentration and delayed the drawing up of one of his own, so that the beginning of the war found Belgium practically without a plan of campaign and with a command divided against itself.[1]

While the army was in this deplorable condition, the fortifications, as has already been said, lacked the 280 mm. heavy guns ordered from Krupps, and their defense works were so obsolete and so inadequate to resist the fire of German heavy artillery that they later became the tomb of their heroic defenders.

But all this only became subsequently apparent. At the time, both in France and in England, there was rejoicing that in some degree Belgium was taking measures to strengthen herself. In his annual report for the year 1913 even the skeptical and distrustful English Military Attaché, Bridges, wrote:

> The year 1913 has been a moving one for the army and marks a serious effort on the part of the Government to place the defenses of the country on a sound footing .... The general effect [of the sweeping reforms] has been to raise the morale of the army and the country and there is more prospect today of the Belgians fighting seriously to protect their neutrality than ever before in their history as a nation.[2]

Equal satisfaction was expressed in Paris, to which the French Military Attaché reported on 17 January that Broqueville had said in the Chamber:

> Belgium can tip the scales in this situation by allying with the one who has not violated against the one who has; our strength will then really be the guarantee of our independence.[3]

As the first to violate it would be Germany, and as her action would presumably bring in Belgium and England on the side of France, Joffre estimated that the forces at his command would be 'distinctly superior to those of the Germans' and reported in that sense to a conference held at the Quai d'Orsay on 12 October 1912.[4] But Joffre

---

[1] Galet, pp. 4-6, 17, 24, 36, 38–44. Galet further writes: 'Whoever may have been responsible for it, the fact remains that in 1914, "whatever the contingency, nothing was ready for the concentration of the army' (*op. cit.,* p. 40).
[2] BD. VIII, 331.   [3] DF. 3. V, 321; Joffre, I, p. 55.   [4] Joffre, I, p. 64.

continued to watch military developments in Germany with a feeling that war was bound to come.

My thoughts turned more and more anxiously towards Belgium. What attitude was she going to adopt? King Albert has given so many proofs of his loyalty to the Allied cause that today no one need hesitate to point out that his family relations and the tendency of his mental processes gave rise to some fear that he might turn towards our enemies. Moreover, the powerful Catholic Party of Belgium was germanophil, and the influences of this party might have a considerable bearing upon the decision of the Government.[1]

Joffre's misgivings were not without foundation. He might have added that the Germans, as Klobukowski records, had by 1912 made themselves masters of the Belgian international exchange market with its banks, commerce and shipping.[2]

A powerful influence in favor of Germany was exercised by the Belgian Catholic Party, which the Flemish vote had maintained in power for the last twenty-eight years. Notwithstanding the alarms of 1913, manifestations of German sympathies and of trust in Germany characterized the policy of the Belgian Government up to the last. On 29 April 1913 the German Socialist deputy Noske spoke in the Reichstag of the fear felt in Belgium that Germany might violate Belgian neutrality, saying that relations between the two countries would improve if the German Government gave the Belgian Government some reassurance in the matter. Jagow briefly replied:

The neutrality of Belgium is provided for by international agreements and Germany is determined to respect these agreements. I have nothing to add to the clear statement I have just made about our relations with Belgium.

The Socialist deputies Ledebour and Haase voiced doubts that this statement would dissipate Belgian misgivings. The War Minister, General von Heeringen, then stated:

Belgium plays no part in the causes which justify the proposed reorganization of the German military system. That proposal is based on the situation in the East. Germany will not lose sight of the fact that Belgian neutrality is guaranteed by international treaty.

On learning of Jagow's curt and chilling expressions the Belgian Government instructed Baron Beyens to ask for a further definition of their meaning in order 'to give them further amplitude, a more marked cordiality, a more noticeable sympathy for our country'. Beyens took the opportunity of a diplomatic reception to give this message to Jagow, who replied 'with a slightly irritated air that the Socialist deputies had

---

[1] Joffre, I, p. 121.
[2] Klobukowski, p. 22.

already several times pressed him to make his statement more specific but that he could add nothing to his words, which were sufficiently clear'.[1]

This episode, which might well have added to the Brussels Government's misgivings, passed unheeded. And the same must be said of the alarming statements made by the Kaiser and Moltke to King Albert during his visit to Berlin in November 1913. Beyens relates:

> The Kaiser discoursed at length on the political situation in Europe. He thinks it so bad, through the fault of France, that he regards war with her as inevitable and imminent. . . . The King tried to overcome this disastrous error of judgment. . . . All to no purpose. The Kaiser obstinately went on declaring that a conflict was inevitable and that he had no doubt of the crushing superiority of the German army. . . . Count Moltke also thinks war near and dwelt on the certainty of a German victory. War with France will rouse general enthusiasm in Germany.[2]

Galet records that on returning to Brussels the King gave him an account of these conversations, in which Moltke would seem to have gone even further than his Imperial Master:

> Small countries, such as Belgium, would be well advised to rally to the side of the strong if they wished to retain their independence.

'This'—comments Galet—'was more than intimidation; it was a shameless threat against the neutrality and independence of Belgium'.[3]

If this account is correct it would seem that either King Albert kept back from Beyens Moltke's most significant words referring to Belgium, or else that Beyens decided to keep them to himself, lest they might cause the Government to change its policy.

The attitude of Wilhelm and Moltke cannot be dissociated from the bellicose and intransigent spirit prevailing in Germany in July 1914. But what here concerns us is the purpose of the practically identical speeches made by the pair to King Albert, namely, to impress on him

---

[1] *First Belgian Grey Book.* Enclosure in no. 12; Baron Beyens. *Deux années à Berlin* 1912-14 (Paris, 1931), I, pp. 245-7. Acting on instructions Prince Hatzfeld, the German Plenipotentiary at Brussels, reiterated the statements made by Jagow and Heeringen to the Editor of the 'chief Belgian Catholic paper'. The latter in January 1913 had sent a petition to Wilhelm by registered post asking 'that the Kaiser should publicly bring the regulations of his army into harmony with the 1907 laws laying down the inviolability of neutral frontiers by belligerents'. In making his reply Hatzfeld added that the Germans 'had no interest in entirely dissuading the French from their outrageous suspicions against the Germans in the matter of the observance of these laws and treaties; that explains . . . why the petition has not received a more completely satisfying answer'. Needless to say the editor concludes: 'We none the less thanked the Kaiser and his representative for this, given the circumstances, sufficiently explanatory answer' (Wullus-Rudiger, *Appendix No.* 3, pp. 306-9).

[2] Beyens, II, 39- 40.

[3] Galet, p. 23.

that it was no use for the Belgians to resist the passage of German troops across their country[1] and the use the King made of these speeches. After pondering over the matter, King Albert confided the conversations to Beyens. Though Beyens, like his predecessor Greindl, admired Germany and regarded her hegemony as a guarantee of peace and prosperity in Europe, he volunteered to talk the matter over under the seal of secrecy with Jules Cambon, the French Ambassador to Berlin. This would give France a hint to be more careful of German susceptibilities or at least put her on her guard and thus avert the European conflagration to which a Franco-German war would lead. With King Albert's approval Beyens spoke with Cambon on 10 November and Cambon's report of their talk was sent off on 22 November. It is natural, Beyens had said,

that the King of the Belgians is disquieted by the possibility of a conflict which would involve the Crown and even the existence of his country, and that he is anxious to warn you. . . . It would therefore seem to him important to be watchful in order that, as far as possible, no incident may arise . . . . King Albert will be passing through Paris when he accompanies the Queen to the Riviera. He will then be able to talk all this over with M. Poincaré. . . . King Albert's personal integrity—comments Cambon—rules out *a priori* any idea of his making himself the spokesman of Germany. It is undoubtedly the emotion felt by him which Baron Beyens has conveyed to me.[2]

[1] It was perhaps not the first time that King Albert directly got wind of German intentions. Klobukowski tells of having learnt from a colleague in 1912 that on King Albert's visit to Berlin in 1910 the Crown Prince had asked: 'If one day Belgium were to be invaded, what would she do?' 'Her duty', said the King coldly. This answer elicited an unseemly burst of hilarity from the German prince. 'Her duty!'—he exclaimed—'What with? Can one at least hope that on that day you will be mindful of your German kinship?' 'I shall be mindful that I am Belgian', replied King Albert (Klobukowski, p. 34).

[2] Beyens, II, pp. 40-7; DF. 3. VIII, 517. This document with additions and suppressions figures as No. 6 in Ch. I of the French *Yellow Book,* entitled *Warnings.* When it was published in December 1914 and thus became known in Germany, Jagow asked Moltke for explanations. Moltke wrote in reply on 18 December 1914: 'I most emphatically deny having said that I regarded war as necessary and inevitable or that we must make an end of it (*cette fois il faut en finir*)', *Das deutsche Weissbuch über die Schuld am Kriege* (Berlin, 1927), p. 86; GP. XXXIX, note to 15658. Now while it is obvious that Jules Cambon had no reason then to ascribe words to Beyens which Beyens had never uttered, there is the further fact that Beyens, writing many years later but before the publication of the *Documents Diplomatiques Français,* corroborates Cambon's account. He further tells how he learnt from the French Military Attaché, Melotte, of the conversation, at the dinner in honor of King Albert, between Melotte and Moltke who was his right hand neighbor at table. To Melotte's remark: 'We are going to have a long period of peace', Moltke replied: 'Do not have any illusions. War with France is inevitable and much nearer than you think. We do not desire it. ... We shall wage it in order to have done with it. We are sure of being victorious. . . . We shall lose battles but shall win in the end . . . . As for England . . . When the last of our ships has been sunk, what, I ask you, will remain of the British Navy? We should lose our ships; England would lose the command of the seas which would pass for ever to America' (Beyens, II, pp. 47-53). This conversation was the subject of Beyens's report to Davignon of 25 November 1913.

Yet the question obtrudes itself. Was King Albert's emotion due to fear of invasion by Germany or by France? On 7 May 1914 the German Military Attaché, Major von Klüber, reporting to Berlin on his farewell audience of King Albert, narrates that he brought the conversation round to the possibility of an anti-German attitude on the part of the Belgians in a future Franco-German war. This elicited from King Albert the reply:

> You are very well informed. It is certainly true that at one time the French planned a *coup de main* against Namur at the first outbreak of war. But I know for certain that this plan has recently been changed, I presume in consequence of the Belgian army reforms. Now they are again carrying on espionage in the Semois valley, as we are perfectly aware. I well understand what General von Moltke told me at Potsdam and you tell me again now. I, too, regard the French danger as the worst and so do the nobility and the great majority of the Clerical Party.[1]

These words, if authentic, make it seem that King Albert feared France more than Germany. This would seem incredible if the documents did not prove that his Ministers displayed up to the last minute a friendliness and trustfulness towards Germany in striking contrast to the coldness and mistrust with which they treated France and England.

8. The Belgian Government's optimism before the presentation of the German ultimatum.

Notwithstanding all the information reaching Belgium about the German war plan and the things said to King Albert by Moltke, the Brussels Government, even when a European war looked imminent, firmly believed, or at least hoped, that Germany would honor the assurances given by her rulers that she would not break her solemn engagements and would spare the small nation which had shown her so much regard, attachment and esteem. Nevertheless,

> the passage of belligerents across Belgium had become the favorite theme of all the writings dealing with the future war. . . . The preparations for invasion, carried out in full daylight by the German Government, roused discussion. As early as 1911 there existed ten single- or double-track railways connecting the Eifel district with the Belgian frontier or the Grand Duchy of Luxemburg; four more were under construction, another four were contemplated. Most of these lines were useless for traffic and purely strategic. Fully equipped stations, platforms for troops entrainment, were built with customary German organization and method.[2]

It seems very strange that all these preparations awakened no misgivings. A possible explanation might have been found if it had been believed in Belgium that the German General Staff had two separate

---

[1] KSF. VIII, 1930, pp. 795-6.
[2] Baron Beyens, 'La neutralité belge' in *Revue des Deux Mondes*, 15 June 1915, pp. 734-6.

plans, one for a war with France involving the crossing of Belgium, another for a war with Russia in the event of aggression coming from Russia. But nothing shows that such a belief ever existed. On the other hand, it is quite clear that when the Austro-Serbian crisis arose Brussels had no premonitions of what it was likely to lead to, despite the warnings arriving from the Belgian Ministers at St. Petersburg, Vienna, and above all Berlin, that a most serious situation was developing.[1] And even when the threat of a European war was realized, the Brussels Government could or would not grasp that Belgium would be drawn into it.

The Apostolic Nuncio sent word to the King by a high official that the war *'passera en Belgique'*. But the Foreign Ministry attached no importance to the warning. As late as 25 July an International Certificate for Motor Vehicles was issued to King Albert for a foreign tour under his incognito as Count de Réthy. The same incredulity prevailed in Parliament. When as a precaution three classes of conscripts were called up on 28 July, two opposition leaders, happening to meet on the 29th, remarked that Broqueville was only issuing the call-up in virtue of his military law. There was not going to be a war and, if there were to be one, it would not affect Belgium. The Belgian Liberal press disapproved of the Austrian declaration of war on Serbia, while the Catholic press comment on it was favorable.

True, on 24 July the Foreign Minister, Davignon, circulated a note to the Belgian Ministers at Paris, Berlin, London, Vienna, and St. Petersburg to be presented to the signatory Powers of the 1839 treaty assuring them of Belgium's determination to fulfill the international obligations imposed upon her by treaty in the event of a war breaking out on her frontiers:

> The Belgian army has been mobilized and is taking up such strategic positions as have been chosen to secure the defense of the country and the

[1] *Second Belgian Grey Book,* 7, 8, 9, 12, 14. On the Belgian aspect of the crisis of July 1914, see:

Alfred de Ridder, *La Belgique et la guerre, Histoire Diplomatique* (Brussels, 1925); A Galet, *Albert, King of the Belgians in the Great War* (London, 1931); A. Klobukowski, *Souvenirs de Belgique,* 1911-1918 (Brussels, 1928); Léon Leclere, 'La Belgique à la veille de l'invasion' *(Revue d'Histoire de la Guerre Mondiale.* July 1926, pp. 193-216); Antonin de Selliers de Moranville, *Du Haut de la Tour de Babel* (Paris, 1925); Antonin de Selliers de Moranville, *Contribution à l'Histoire de la Guerre Mondiale* (Paris, 1933); C. de Woeste, *Mémoires pour servir a l'Histoire Contemporaine de la Belgique* 1894-1914, 2 volumes (Brussels, 1933); A. de Bassompierre, 'La nuit du 2 au 3 août, 1914 au Ministère des Affaires Ètrangères de Belgique' in *Revue des Deux Mondes,* 15 February 1916, pp. 884-906; also (Paris, 1916); Louis Comte Lichtervelde, 'La nuit du 2 août au Ministére de la Guerre' in *La Nation Belge* (Brussels) of 2 August 1921; Antonin de Selliers de Moranville, 'Le Conseil de la Couronne du 2 Août 1914' in *Le Flambeau* (Brussels) of 31 August 1921; J. Crokaert, 'L'ultimatum allemand du 2 août 1914', in *Le Flambeau* of 31 March 1922; L. van der Elst, 'La Reine Elisabeth. Souvenirs de Guerre', in *La Revue Belge* (Brussels) of 15 November 1929, pp. 570–97; *Mémoires du Lieutenant Général Baron de Ryckel* (Paris, Brussels, 1920).

respect of its neutrality. The forts of Antwerp and on the Meuse have been put in a state of defense. It is scarcely necessary to dwell upon the nature of these measures. They are intended solely to enable Belgium to fulfill her international obligations; and it is obvious that they neither have been nor can have been undertaken with any intention of taking part in an armed struggle between the Powers or from any feeling of distrust of any of these Powers.[1]

This was a purely precautionary measure on a level with the military call-up of three classes on 29 July. Davignon showed no anxiety and turned a deaf ear to any disturbing talk. Klobukowski gives a caustic sketch of him:

The Minister, M. Davignon, was very much an *honnête homme,* as they used to say in the eighteenth century, of extreme rectitude and imperturbable placidity. I enjoyed his society. In his room the sounds of the outside world seemed to arrive hushed and muted like distant echoes shorn of the urgency they had conveyed before entering. In his charming optimism M. Davignon must, I imagine, have held the view that things have only the importance one lets them have, and his philosophically equable temperament made him rate this pretty low. . . . In the anxious period we were passing through, which shook him somewhat out of his usual habits, his final remark invariably was: 'Let us hope it will turn out all right in the end.'[2]

Such being the temperament of the Minister in charge of the conduct of Belgian foreign policy, whose immediate colleague, moreover, was van der Elst, a reverential admirer of Germany, much about that policy that has already been told and still remains to be told becomes understandable.

As early as 27 July, Baron Fallon, the Belgian Minister at the Hague, had reported that the Jonkheer Loudon, Queen Wilhelmina's Foreign Minister, had sent for him and asked:

What steps has Belgium taken to meet the situation? The Minister for War desires to be informed of what has been decided in Brussels. You will understand that we are in the same position. We are equally threatened, for a German army might try to pass through Dutch Limburg in order to cross Belgium and yet avoid the Liége forts. Our defense should be a joint one. It would be advisable that the Minister of War should from now on be kept informed of the measures decreed in Brussels to meet the grave events which are threatening.[3]

---

[1] *First Belgian Grey Book,* 2; CDD., pp. 300-1.

[2] Klobukowski, pp. 63-4.

[3] Galet, p. 33; Selliers de Moranville, *Contribution à l'Histoire de la Guerre Mondiale 1914-1918* (Paris and Brussels, 1933), pp. 126-7, Selliers de Moranville writes that he only learnt of Fallon's telegram after the war. 'Yet the proper exercise of my functions would have required that I should be told of it. The same thing happened as regards most of the subsequent diplomatic and military communications sent direct to the King' *(ibid.,* p. 127). A further telegram from Fallon which reached the Government on 29 July was also not communicated to him *(ibid.,* p. 128).

The Dutch minister's concern was not without foundation. Schlieffen had originally planned to pass through Dutch Limburg, thinking he could do so with the consent of Holland. Moltke did not have this illusion and had given up the idea simply in order not to add Holland to his enemies and to retain the Dutch ports as channels of overseas communications.[1]

Galet's account continues:

On the following days Jonkheer Loudon more than once pressed for our reply, repeating that joint action was in our best interests and that Belgium could count on the closest co-operation of Holland. He emphasized that the defense of the Meuse was arranged for and the demolition of the bridges prepared, the railways guarded and that strong detachments were ready. As neutrals, we were unable to reply to these overtures until we were actually menaced.[2]

It was not at all true that Belgium's neutrality obliged her to wait for the *fait accompli* before taking steps to avert it. If there were no invasion, the counter-measures would not take effect; if invasion came they would be fully justified. The truth is that the Belgian Government was unwilling to look the danger in the face, however menacingly it loomed up ahead. By the time action was taken, it was too late. Galet relates:

On 3 August, when Baron Fallon again called on Jonkheer Loudon to ask that General Leman, the Governor of Liége, should have a consultation with the Governor of Maestricht, he was not received with the same cordiality as had been shown to him on the previous occasions, and his question was evaded. The Dutch Government had just received the pledge from the German Government that its territory would be respected.[3]

That being the way Davignon treated Holland, it may be imagined how distant he was with France and England. On 28 July 1914 he told Sir Francis Villiers

that the Belgian Government have carefully considered the various eventualities which may arise from the present European crisis and that they have determined to offer resistance to the utmost of their power should the integrity or neutrality of Belgium be assailed from any quarter,[4]

these words being intended less as an assurance to England than as a warning. And the Secretary-General at the Foreign Ministry, van der Elst, disquieted the French Minister, Klobukowski, on 27 July by declaring

that the Royal Government 'which has no mistrust towards anyone, which feels itself threatened by no one, but which is anxious to make its neutrality

---

[1] See pp. 239–40.
[2] Galet, p, 34.
[3] Galet, pp. 34-5.
[4] BD. XI, 243

respected', will employ all resources at the present hour available to it to defend its territory against any violation, from wheresoever it may come.

Klobukowski reminded van der Elst of the statement made in Parliament on 14 February 1913 by the Belgian Prime Minister, Broqueville, who was also Minister for War, that the Belgian army must be in a position to tip the scales in favor of that one of the Powers which should not first violate Belgian territory.[1] But it was an unwelcome reminder and van der Elst only replied: 'I have no recollection of this statement.'[2]

On 28 July Klobukowski gave the same reminder to the Belgian Foreign Minister; Davignon, who turned it off with the remark:

I do not very well remember what was said at that sitting. I will ask Baron de Broqueville to clarify his utterance; as far as I believe, he meant that Belgium wished to possess an army sufficiently strong for anyone to think twice before attacking it.[3]

Klobukowski came to the conclusion that

the Belgian Government has no intention of tying its hands by a decision on grounds of principle. . . . Inclined by temperament and interest to attach itself, the last resort, to the stronger side, it will . . . at the right moment 'fly to the aid of victory'. I add that its sympathies, its inclinations—I speak of the Government and not of the people, who in the Walloon districts are for us—lead it to favor the Germans rather than the French.

Klobukowski later reports that his impression was shared by his Romanian colleague, Djuvara, who expressed the opinion that

Belgium will no doubt make an honest effort to see that its territory is respected whatever the direction from which invasion comes, but purely to save its face; after a few engagements the order will be issued to retire on Antwerp and from there to watch the course of events.[4]

And this was also the impression of the French Military Attaché, Commandant Génie.[5]

Meanwhile the situation was growing increasingly critical. The first in Brussels to receive, by telephone on 31 July, news of the German proclamation of the *Kriegsgefahrzustand* was Klobukowski, who called at once on Davignon to say:

Without being instructed by my Government to make a statement, I felt I had authority to give him an assurance in case of need that the Government of the Republic would not be the first to violate Belgian territory. The Minister for Foreign Affairs replied that the Royal Government had always thought this would be so and thanked me.[6]

[1] See p. 439. [2] DF. 3. XI, 178. [3] DF. 3 XI, 292.
[4] DF. XI, 372. [5] DF. 3. XI, 373.
[6] DF. 3. XI, 418, 460; in LJF. No. 418 appears as No. 119, out is altered to state 'that the Government of the Republic would respect the neutrality of Belgium'.

The *First Belgian Grey Book,* records that Davignon further added:

We have also every reason to believe that the attitude of the German Government will be the same as that of the Government of the French Republic.[1]

Davignon's distrust of France was equaled by his distrust of England shown when on 31 July Grey telegraphed to Villiers:

In view of possibility of European war I have asked French and German Governments separately whether each is prepared to respect neutrality of Belgium provided no other Power violates it. In view of existing treaties you should inform Minister for Foreign Affairs and say I assume that Belgium will to the utmost of her power maintain neutrality and desire and expect other Powers to observe and uphold it.[2]

In giving the desired assurance Davignon begged Villiers to add

that the relations between Belgium and the neighboring Powers were excellent and that there was no reason to suspect their intentions, but that Belgian Government believed that in case of violation they were in a position to defend the neutrality of their country.[3]

This was as much as to say: Let England mind her own business. We have nothing to fear from Germany. Paul Cambon's comment runs:

This strange answer, which arrived as I was with Sir Edward Grey, gave us the idea that there was perhaps some secret arrangement between Germany and Belgium. In any case Sir Edward Grey points out that the neutrality of this Power's territory is not more a Belgian than an English interest, and that England is bound to see that it is respected.[4]

This was perfectly true, even if the Belgian Government preferred to forget the fact. It justified the final words of Grey's telegram which may have given Davignon offence.

9. *The behavior of the German Minister at Brussels; the content of the German ultimatum.*

One wonders what were the grounds for Davignon's sense of security! That somewhere in the Ministry for Foreign Affairs doubts were felt is evident from the conversation which took place on the morning of 31 July between van der Elst and the German Minister, Below-Saleske.

The Secretary General asked the German Minister if he knew of the conversation which he [van der Elst] had had with his [Below's] predecessor, Herr von Flotow.

---

[1] *First Belgian Grey Book,* 9; Klobukowski, p. 78.   [2] BD. XI, 351.
[3] BD. XI, 395; *First Belgian Grey Book,* 11.   [4] DF. 3. XI, 612.

As we have already seen, Bethmann Hollweg had on that occasion in 1911 instructed Flotow to declare 'that Germany had no intention of violating Belgian neutrality'. Van der Elst recalled that in 1913 Jagow had made reassuring declarations to the Budget Committee of the Reichstag respecting the maintenance of Belgian neutrality. Below replied 'that he knew of the conversation with Flotow and that he was certain that the sentiments expressed at that time had not changed'.[1] But he did not say on what grounds his certitude was based. Again, on 2 August, when the Brussels *Soir* asked Below whether it was true that he had in his Government's name declared to Davignon that Germany would respect Belgian territory, the German Minister replied:

I made no such statement, and personally I think that I had no need to do so since it was superfluous. With us the view has always prevailed that the neutrality of Belgium must not be violated. German troops will not cross Belgian territory. Grave events are about to take place. It may be that the flames will destroy your neighbor's roof, but your house will be spared.

In contrast to this ambiguity the attitude of France was the subject of a frank declaration made to Davignon by Klobukowski on 1 August:

I am authorized to declare that, in the event of an international conflict, the Government of the Republic, as it has always stated, will respect the neutrality of Belgium. In the event of this neutrality not being respected by another Power, the French Government, to secure its own defense, might find it necessary to modify its attitude.[2]

This statement was not authorized by Viviani, who had confined himself on 1 August to sending on to Klobukowski the reply he had given to Grey's inquiry as to the attitude that would be adopted by France in the event of a conflict with Germany. 'I declared that, as we had several times repeated to the Belgian Government, we intended to respect its neutrality.' The active Klobukowski thereupon telegraphed back: 'I have renewed to M. Davignon the declarations relative to the neutrality of Belgium.'[3] The French declaration was at once posted up in Brussels and 'produced a deep and excellent impression which cannot but strengthen the favorable attitude of the population towards us'. At 1 p. m. on 1 August Davignon's private secretary, Bassompierre, called on Klobukowski, who asked:

Has the Minister for Foreign Affairs received from the German Government similar assurances to ours about respect of the neutrality of Belgium? M. de Bassompierre answered after a moment's hesitation: 'Nothing so far, to my knowledge.'

---

[1] *First Belgian Grey Book,* 12. See pp. 425, 440.
[2] *First Belgian Grey book,* 15.
[3] DF. 3. XI, 465, 522.

A postscript to this dispatch runs:

As I sign this letter I learn from a good source of the following utterance of General Selliers de Moranville, Chief of Staff of the Belgian army: 'Belgium will defend herself against all aggressors, the lastcomers as well as the first-comers. We shall make no difference between them. ... If the Germans enter first we shall put up a strong resistance. If, after the Germans, come the French, we shall turn against them equally. Our interest is to make common cause with nobody.'[1]

This was too sweeping a statement on the General's part. Klobu-kowski's assurances must have sounded to Davignon like both a promise and a warning, while from Germany there came no counter-part, nothing but a disquieting silence. Added to this was a telegram of 1 August from Beyens in Berlin:

The English Ambassador has been instructed to inquire of the Minister for Foreign Affairs whether, in the event of war, Germany would respect Belgian neutrality, and I understand that the Minister replied that he was unable to answer the question.[2]

Thereupon Davignon instructed the Belgian Ministers at Paris, Berlin, London, Vienna and St. Petersburg to hand the respective Governments to which they were accredited the note circulated to them on 24 July assuring the Governments of Belgium's determination to fulfill the international obligations imposed upon her by treaty in the event of a war breaking out on her frontiers.[3] And in an effort to obtain a public assurance from Germany he sent Bassompierre on the afternoon of 1 August to call on Below-Saleske.

I was careful to warn the German Minister through M. de Bassompierre that an announcement in the Brussels press by M. Klobukowski would make public the formal declaration which the latter had made to me on 1 August. When I next met Herr von Below he thanked me for this attention, and added that up to the present he had not been instructed to make us an official communication, but that we knew his personal opinion as to the feelings of security, which we had the right to entertain towards our eastern neighbors.[4]

Davignon can hardly have felt that the personal opinion of Below was sufficient, and it may well be doubted whether the latter was being entirely straightforward. On 30 July a special messenger (Feldjäger) from Berlin had brought him a sealed envelope with orders not to open it until instructed by telegraph to do so.[5] Below must certainly have wondered what it contained and guessed that it related to Belgium in case of war. If he, therefore, proceeded to make reassuring statements

---

[1] DF. 3. XI, 501.   [2] First Belgian Grey Book, 14.
[3] First Belgian Grey Book, 2, 16.   [4] First Belgian Grey Book, 19; DD. III, 584.
[5] DD. II, 375, 376. See p. 453.

he must have done so thinking that either they would be borne out by facts or they would keep Belgium quiet and prevent her from taking measures detrimental to Germany.

King Albert perceived how needful it was to make Berlin break its silence. When about 2 p. m. on 31 July he learnt that Germany had proclaimed the *Kriegsgefahrzustand* he called a Cabinet meeting, at which he presided, to discuss the issuing of a mobilization order, which he regarded as urgently necessary. He encountered a certain amount of opposition, although, be it noted, Holland, which was less threatened, had already mobilized. But in the end his opinion prevailed and at 7 p. m. it was decreed that 1 August should be the first day of mobilization.[1] On learning on 1 August that France had engaged to respect Belgian neutrality but Germany had not done so, King Albert sent for van der Elst that same evening to discuss the drafting of a letter which he meant to send to Wilhelm. Translated into German by the Queen, the letter, dated the 1st, was sent off on 2 August. It said:

> For over eighty years since Belgium has been independent our country has conscientiously observed its international obligations, several times in most difficult circumstances, and the Imperial Chancellor in 1870 paid a glowing tribute to its correct and impartial attitude. Your Majesty and Your Government have on repeated occasions given us valuable proofs of Your friendship and sympathy, and authorized personages have given us assurances of respect for Belgian neutrality in the event of a fresh conflict. We then fully appreciated the political objection which prevented the publication of this declaration and we do not doubt that the feelings and intentions of the mighty Empire over whose destinies Your Majesty presides have remained unchanged towards us. The relations of kinship and friendship which closely bind our two families induce me to write You today asking You in this so grave hour graciously to renew the expression of these feelings towards my country.[2]

King Albert's misgivings were not shared by Davignon. When on 2 August Villiers warned him:

> We know that France has given you formal assurances, but Great Britain has received no reply from Berlin on this subject,

Davignon commented to the Ministers at Paris, London and St. Petersburg:

> The latter fact did not particularly affect me, since a declaration from the German Government might appear superfluous in view of existing treaties. Moreover, the Secretary of State [Jagow] had reaffirmed ... on 29 April 1913, 'that the neutrality of Belgium is established by treaty which Germany intends to respect'.[3]

---

[1] Galet, pp. 27-8.　　　　[2] DD. IV, 765.　　　　[3] *First Belgian Grey Book, 38.*

And to Villiers he gave the reply

that Belgian Government have no reason whatever to suspect Germany of an intention to violate neutrality. He says that Belgian Government have not considered idea of appeal to other guarantee Powers, nor of intervention should a violation occur; they would rely upon their own armed force as sufficient to resist aggression, from whatever quarter it might come.[1]

The heedlessness and levity revealed by these statements filled the *Entente* Ministers at Brussels with dismay. Convinced themselves that German aggression was a probability if not a certainty, they saw that the Belgian Government was not even considering the question of an appeal to the guarantee Powers in such an eventuality. Klobukowski telegraphed to Paris on 2 August:

This absence of a declaration from Germany and this tranquility on the part of Belgium give rise here to belief in the rumor of some sort of connivance between the two countries. Fresh information, which I regard as reliable, assures me that the King of the Belgians is believed to have received assurances personally from the German Kaiser, on condition that he proceeds, as in fact he has immediately done, to a general mobilization.[2]

And in a further message of the same day Klobukowski added:

I have been able to ascertain almost beyond doubt that the King of the Belgians, who had addressed himself to the German Kaiser . . . had received from him certain assurances of a tranquillizing nature. My informant added . . . that a condition had been attached to this good will on the part of Germany: general mobilization, as if in the Kaiser's mind . . . the first act of invasion was bound to come from France.[3]

But these suppositions were without foundation. The Belgian Government's behavior was entirely due to a failure co realize the danger overhanging their country. Crokaert, whose reconstruction of the events in Brussels during the night of 2/3 August is based on the most authoritative sources, opens his tale with the following words:

On Sunday, 2 August, 1914, Brussels spent its last day of peace delightfully. On the eve of a long and pitiless war Belgian public opinion evinced a singular quietude and an unshakeable optimism.

On that very evening when the German ultimatum had just been delivered to Davignon the King had sent Ingenbleek with a message of congratulations to Paul Hymans on his appointment as Minister. As Ingenbleek had left the Palace he had seen Davignon arriving accompanied by the Secretary-General, van der Elst. The two men joyfully took for granted that Davignon was bringing the King good news similar to that which Klobukowski had given him the day before,

[1] BD. XI, 476.   [2] DF. 3. XI, 586.   [3] DF. 3. XI, 630.

namely, the assurance from Germany that she would not be the first to violate Belgian neutrality.[1] The fact was that on the morning of that same day, the 2nd, a telegram from Eyschen, the Luxemburg Prime Minister, had announced the invasion of the Grand Duchy by German troops.[2] But even this event did not open the Belgian Government's eyes. Bassompierre relates that it was hoped that the English inquiry and the threat implicit in it would make Berlin think twice.

Judging from the latest telegrams might it not be supposed that the German forces concentrated along the frontier were edging their way towards the Moselle and that they would avoid setting foot on Belgian soil? Might the reasons put forward for the violation of the Grand Duchy, and which were not applicable to Belgium, give grounds for this supposition?[3]

While Brussels still indulged in such hopes, Below-Saleske received the instruction despatched from Berlin at 2.5 p. m. on 2 August to open the envelope sent to him on 30 July,'[1] and to present the ultimatum contained in it:

Reliable information has reached the Imperial Government of the intended deployment of French forces on the Givet-Namur stretch of the Meuse. It leaves no doubt as to the French intention to advance against Germany across Belgian territory. The Imperial Government cannot but fear that, in spite of the utmost good will, Belgium will be unable without assistance to repel a French invasion with sufficient prospect of success as to afford adequate guarantee against a threat to Germany. It is a dictate of self-preservation for Germany to forestall the hostile attack. Therefore the German Government would feel the deepest regret were Belgium to regard it as an act of hostility against herself if the steps taken by the adversary oblige Germany in self-defense likewise to enter Belgian territory.

To prevent all misunderstanding the Imperial Government makes the following declaration:

1. Germany purposes no acts of hostility against Belgium. If Belgium is willing to adopt benevolent neutrality towards Germany in the impending war, the German Government not only engages to guarantee in full measure the integrity and independence of the Kingdom at the conclusion of peace, but is even prepared to meet in the friendliest spirit any of the Kingdom's demands for compensation at the expense of France.

2. On the above conditions Germany engages to evacuate the territory of the Kingdom as soon as peace is concluded.

3. If Belgium maintains a friendly attitude, Germany is prepared, in co-operation with the Belgian authorities to purchase all the requirements of

---

[1] Crokaert, *Le Flambeau,* 1922, pp. 307-8.

[2] *First Belgian Grey Book,* 18.

[3] A. de Bassompierre, La nuit de 2 au 3 août, 1914, au Ministère des Affairs Étrangères de Belgique', in *Revue des Deux Mondes,* 15 February 1916, p. 893.

[4] DD. II, 375, 376; III, 648. See Vol. II, p. 503, Vol. III, p. 204.

her troops by payment in cash and to make good all damage which might be caused by German troops.

Were Belgium to put up opposition to the German troops, in particular causing obstruction by resistance at the Meuse fortifications, the destruction of railways, roads, tunnels, or other key-points, Germany will with regret be obliged to regard the Kingdom as an enemy. In this event Germany would not be able to undertake any obligations towards the Kingdom but would have to leave the later settlement of the relations between the two States to the arbitrament of the sword.

The Imperial Government entertains the definite hope that this eventuality will not arise and that the Royal Belgian Government will know how to take the appropriate measures to ensure that incidents such as those mentioned above do not take place. In this case the friendly ties binding the two neighbor States will become stronger and more enduring.

I beg Your Excellency to communicate the above immediately in strict confidence to the Belgian Government, requesting them to return an unambiguous answer within twenty-four hours. Will Your Excellency inform me at once by telegram of the reception accorded to your communication and the definitive reply of the Royal Belgian Government.[1]

As has been stated already, this document was drafted by Moltke on 26 July. It is so explicit that it has been regarded as proof positive of the German determination to go to war. Jagow, however, does not hesitate to claim that it was nothing more than a precaution, on a level with other measures taken by the enemy, and, in itself, meant nothing.[2]

On receiving Moltke's original draft, Stumm, the Director of the Political Section of the Foreign Ministry, at once introduced changes into it. Moltke's text made the French intention to cross Belgian territory come 'after union with an English expeditionary force', i.e., took for granted that English intervention which the Wilhelmstrasse was hoping to avoid. Therefore Stumm struck out the relevant words. In Moltke's draft of heading i, the second sentence begins: 'If Belgium is willing to take the side of Germany.' But Stumm thought this was asking too much and toned it down to a request for 'benevolent neutrality'. Moltke's draft merely offered to meet 'any of the Kingdom's demands for compensation'. Stumm added 'at the expense of France' this being a promise which, as we have already seen, Wilhelm had made to Leopold II in 1904.[3] But in asking for English neutrality on 29 July Bethmann had assured Goschen that 'in the event of a victorious war Germany aimed at no territorial gains at the expense of France' in Europe.[4] Grey rejected the request, but to avoid angering him it was

---

[1] DD. II, 376.
[2] Jagow, *Herr Poincaré,* KSF. VIII, July 1930, pp. 601-11.
[3] See p. 417.
[4] DD. II, 373; BD. XI, 293. See Vol. II, p 506.

judged advisable not to offer French territory to Belgium, and in the telegram sent on 2 August, but drafted on 31 July, instructing Below-Saleske to open the envelope, he was told only to say that if Belgium observed benevolent neutrality 'the German Government engages at the conclusion of peace to guarantee the possessions and independence of the Belgian Kingdom in full'. He was further told to carry out the instructions in the envelope that same evening at 8 p. m. German time (i.e., 7 p. m. Belgian time).

> Further, the reply is to be given within twelve, not twenty-four hours, i.e., by tomorrow [3 August] 8 a. m.
> Please assure Belgian Government urgently that, in spite of Paris's promises, all doubt as to the correctness of our news of French plan must be ruled out. . . . Belgian reply must be here by tomorrow afternoon 2 p. m., German time. Will Your Excellency immediately wire reply to us here and also, immediately on receiving it, send it to General von Emmich, Union Hotel, Aix-la-Chapelle, by one of the Embassy staff, preferably the Military Attaché, by car. Belgian Government must receive impression that all instructions in this matter only reached you today. I further advise your suggesting to Belgian Government that it might retire with troops to Antwerp and that, if desired, we might take over protection of Brussels against internal unrest.[1]

10. *The Belgian Government decides on resistance and on the refusal of French armed assistance.*

It is not needful to dwell at length on the hypocrisy and clumsy obtuseness displayed in this document by which the rulers of Germany thought to trick world opinion into believing that the German army had been unexpectedly compelled to enter Belgium because reliable news had been received that the French were invading that country. As if it were not self-evident that the German General Staff could embark on the venture of invading Belgium to take the French in the rear only as a result of having a plan of concentration, a railway network, and an organization planned long years in advance. The Chancellor, in his Reichstag speech on 4 August 1914, was to confess with brutal frankness:

> Necessity knows no law. Our troops have occupied Luxemburg and perhaps have already entered Belgian territory. That is a breach of international law. . . . France could wait, we could not.

And a long series of German documents and publications proves that the Schlieffen and Moltke plans never started from the assumption of a French invasion of Belgium, but always from the assumption that an invasion of Belgium was the only way in which France could be taken

---

[1] DD. III, 648.

by surprise and beaten by the German army before its attack was switched over to Russia.[1]

As an extra touch of knavery, the ultimatum was written in German so that the first thing the Belgian Government had to do was to have it translated. And this, be it noted, when the time allowed for the reply was only twelve hours—twelve night hours. The tragic scene deserves to be described in detail. At 6.30 p. m. Below-Saleske asked by telephone for an immediate interview in order to make an important communication. Just after 7 p. m. he entered Davignon's room pale and tottering.

Davignon asked with concern: 'What is the matter? Are you not well?' Below-Saleske replied with an effort: 'I came up the stair too quickly, it is nothing.' Then he added: 'I have a most confidential communication to make to you on behalf of my Government.' And drawing an envelope from his pocket, he handed it to Davignon. It was the ultimatum. Davignon with feverish anxiety opened, read and reread it. He paled and, trembling, overcome, at last understanding the treachery of Germany and the fate in store for Belgium, he faltered: 'No, surely? . . . No, it is not possible! . . .'The paper fell to the floor between the two men. Meanwhile Below-Saleske recovered his self-control and composedly summarized the purport of the note . . . insisting on Germany's will to peace and emphasizing the news of an impending French offensive through the Meuse valley. In the presence of such perfidy Davignon could not remain calm. In an agitated and vehement tone he poured out his indignation, the baselessness of the imputations against the loyalty of Belgium, the non-existence, the unlikelihood, of a French attack towards Namur. A few moments later Below-Saleske took his leave, carrying away the assurance that the German note would be discussed by the Cabinet without delay.[2]

Leclere records that Davignon said to him:

This is the last thing we could have expected; Germany, who used to call herself our devoted friend, offering us dishonor [3]

One cannot but say that if the rulers of Belgium had not been determined to shut their eyes this is exactly what they might have expected from Germany. It had been intimated to Leopold II by Wilhelm, and probably to King Albert by Moltke. It was only too apparent that as neither the French nor the Germans could

---

[1] It is not clear why Montgelas in a discussion of Bredt's book gives a list of pieces of evidence in possession of the German General Staff pointing to an intention on the part of France to violate Belgian neutrality as if they were the determining factor in the German invasion of Belgium. On the contrary it was anxiety aroused by the Schlieffen plan which made the English and French think they might have to enter Belgium at short notice, in order to forestall a German invasion (KSF. IX, December 1931, pp. 1136-7).

[2] Crokaert, in Le Flambeau, 1922, I, pp. 309-10.

[3] Léon Leclere, 'La Belgique à la veille de l'invasion', in *Revue d'Histoire de la Guerre Mondiale*, July 1926, p. 204.

penetrate the formidable defense lines protecting their respective frontiers, one or both of them would try to turn the defenses by crossing Belgium. To prevent this and compel them to respect the 1839 treaty the Belgian Government should have created a system of defenses strong enough to deter the Germans from contemplating any breach of treaty. They should, moreover, have maintained closer relations with England, because she, whether making common cause with France or not, had at least as much interest in the independence and neutrality of Belgium as had Belgium herself. But from 1870 onwards admiration for Germany and belief in her invincibility had become ingrained in the educated classes everywhere on the Continent. We Italians also, in the months preceding our entry into the war, were to find out how widespread and deeply rooted the feeling was. These considerations do not detract from the high credit due to Belgium. Given such a mentality it was all the more admirable that her leaders rid themselves of it at one stroke and resolved on stubborn resistance to an invasion which many observers had credited them with a willingness to tolerate, if not even to turn to profitable account.

After Below-Saleske's departure the Ministry officials sent for Broqueville and at once set about translating the German document, the phrasing of which presented considerable difficulty. At the end of an hour the translation was ready and was read out aloud by Bassompierre. A long, strained silence followed, broken at last by van der Elst's asking Broqueville: 'Well, M. le Ministre. Are we ready?' 'Yes', was the reply, 'we are ready. . . . But, there is a but; we have no heavy guns.' The truth was that much else was lacking as well as heavy guns! Broqueville went on to say: 'It is ten past eight, I am going to inform the King and ask him to summon the Ministers to the Palace.'

What did the King and his Minister say to each other? Nobody knows. Neither the Sovereign nor the Minister ever spoke of it to anyone. . . . But it is permissible to think that the King anticipated some sort of maneuver on the part of Germany. . . . As early as Saturday, 1 August, the King had had discussions on the position of Belgium with several Ministers of State, in particular with M. van den Heuvel, a professor of Louvain University and a specialist in international law.[1]

But though the German menace grew more visible, not even the King until the ultimatum made up his mind to offer immediate resistance concentrating his forces in the direction whence came the threat. As Galet writes:

He made clear his wish to maintain the divisions where they were up to the moment when the identity of the enemy should be revealed. Anxious not

---

[1] Crokaert, pp. 311-15.

to furnish Germany with any pretext arising from wounded susceptibilities, he enjoined the avoidance of any act which might be construed as hostile,[1]

This state of mind explains his telegram to Wilhelm on 1 August. But the receipt of the ultimatum 'ended all uncertainty on the part of the King—war was inevitable'.[2] A Cabinet meeting was summoned for 9 p. m. and a Crown Council for 10 p. m., the latter being composed of Ministers with portfolio, Ministers of State (i.e., ex-Ministers, members of Parliament, diplomatists and officials nominated as Ministers of State by the King), and military chiefs.

The Cabinet meeting, at which the King presided, was brief and, as Leclere writes, unanimous in deciding on the rejection of the German ultimatum.[3] The second meeting was much longer and more important. Galet writes of it:

In the mind of the King, who presided, this meeting was called together less with the object of deciding what reply should be given to the Germans —that was not in any doubt—than of impressing the responsible leaders of the nation with the gravity of the situation which would be brought about. He expressly warned the members that hostilities would assume a character of violence undreamed of by them, that the result of the reply they were about to frame would be a terrible ordeal for Belgium, and that it was essential not to do anything in a moment of passion, but to decide with a full realization of what they were committing the country to. On hearing the Imperial demands the meeting was swept by such a wave of patriotic indignation that in spite of the gloomy outlook for the future there was an immediate and impassioned expression of unanimity.[4]

The meeting asked for the text of the ultimatum to be read aloud a second time, and then Broqueville arose to speak. . . . In an eloquent summing up which would have put an end to all hesitation, if there had ever been .any, he epitomized his whole standpoint: 'If die we must, better death with honor. We have no other choice. Our submission would serve no end. The stake for which Germany has begun this war is the freedom of Europe. Let us make no mistake about it, if Germany is victorious, Belgium, whatever her attitude will be annexed to the Reich.'[5]

All those present were asked for an opinion, some speaking more at length than others. Especial weight attached to the words of M. de Woeste, the veteran leader of the Right, which had always been so friendly to Germany.

Perhaps he was seized with a certain hesitation in view of the immensity of the sacrifice we were about to make. But he recovered and gave final shape to his thought in the brief utterance: 'The answer must be: No.' All the other

---

[1] Galet, pp. 41-2.   [2] Galet, p. 32.
[3] Leclere, *art. cit.,* pp. 205-6.   [4] Galet, p. 46.
        [5] Crokaert, pp. 317-18.

members of the Council expressed themselves one after another in the same sense. Opinion was unanimous. The answer must be no.[1]

There then followed a discussion of the military situation during which the Chief of Staff, Lieutenant-General Selliers, informed the Council that the army was not ready and would be unable to give battle to the enemy and contain him; the cadres were incomplete; there was no heavy artillery; but it would be quite possible to carry out mobilization and concentration; Liége and Namur could hold out for a time and Antwerp could withstand a siege. As line of defense he proposed the Velpe. This view was opposed by the Sub-Chief of Staff, General Ryckel, whom the King called on to speak. In Ryckel's opinion the best line of defense along which the Belgian army should be concentrated was the one he had always advocated, namely, the Meuse line. It had always been rejected but perhaps there was still time to adopt it. From there the Belgian army could wage a war of defense or march on Aix-la-Chapelle, were the Germans to choose another line of attack.[2]

This brought to the surface the conflict not only between the Chief of Staff and his subordinate, but also between the Chief of Staff and the King, who thought highly of Ryckel, shared his opinions, and had not been able to get him appointed Commander-in-Chief. In the three preceding days the King had had a sharp difference of opinion with Selliers, whose idea was to concentrate the army in the center of the country, thus leaving two-thirds of its area without military protection and entrusting the defense of the forts of Liége and Namur entirely to their respective garrisons. King Albert and Ryckel both thought that the line of the Meuse, being much nearer the frontier, would cover the protection of almost the whole country, keeping communications with Antwerp open and making it possible to offer serious resistance. The contrary recommendations put forward by Selliers, asking even for the withdrawal of the III Division from Liége (though this was actually not carried out), plunged the King into despair, and made him feel that he had failed in his efforts to prepare Belgium to defend herself. Galet writes:

And now disaster was in sight. Nothing that he had intended was ready. The storm found Belgium without a plan, with a command divided against itself. The Ship of State was adrift, and the crew insubordinate.[3]

General Ryckel, after his account of his contribution to the discussion, writes:

When I had finished, the King addressed the assembly: 'I think, gentlemen,

[1] Crokaert, pp. 318-19.
[2] Galet, pp. 46-7; Selliers de Moranville, *Contribution,* pp. 163-4.
[3] Galet, pp. 41-4.

there can be no hesitation. We can do nothing but follow this plan which has been so wisely worked out.'[1]

But General Ryckel's statements are not borne out by the Belgian Chief of Staff, Selliers, who writes that on 31 July

His Majesty approved my plan of concentration in principle; however, anxious not to give Germany any pretext for declaring herself threatened by our army, the Sovereign thought that the plan was too visibly aimed at that Power and might awaken its susceptibilities. Accordingly, His Majesty expressed the desire to withdraw the position of our concentration by about the distance of one stage to the west, i.e., towards the interior of the country. . . . By these changes of detail in my concentration plan His Majesty hoped to produce the impression of threatening France as much as Germany.[2]

It is difficult to ascertain exactly what was said at the Crown Councils of 2 and 3 August. No report was drawn up, no notes taken. Not until 5 April 1915 did the King command van der Elst to collect the data necessary for writing up the Council minutes. Selliers tells us:

It would seem that Baron van der Elst was not successful in putting together a report of the Crown Council of 2 August. . . . As far as I know, only two accounts exist written by people present at the historic meeting; mine dating from the beginning of April 1915 in response to Baron van der

---

[1] Galet, pp. 46-7; *Mémoires du Lieutenant Général Baron de Kyckel* (Paris and Brussels, 1920, pp. 286-9). General Galet writes that if the Belgian army had been massed along the Meuse 'von Emmich's army would have been checked absolutely. We should have main tained our positions and not a German soldier would have reached the left bank; we should have avoided the isolated action of the 3rd Division, and we should have started the war with a resounding success, the effect of which on the German plan of campaign would have been incalculable' (Galet, p. 48). The Belgian army would have prevented the fall of Liége, which was essential for the evolution of the German plan, and would not have happened but for the isolation of the 3rd Division and for the fact that General Leman could not organize 'proper co-ordination between the defense of the intervals and that of the forts' (Galet, p. 57, 79-81). The Germans expected to find a small garrison at Liége and to take it by surprise in a night attack, gaining possession of bridges, tunnels and other constructions intact and thus opening the broad Hesbaye plain to the maneuver of the masses commanded by Generals Kluck and Bülow. But instead of this the mobilization and concentration of the Belgian 3rd Division was completed when General Emmich's army opened the attack, which failed on 5 and 6 August and had to be renewed with stronger forces before achieving success on 16 August.

[2] Selliers, *Contribution,* pp. 131-2. He further writes: 'Towards 2 p. m. on 1 August, Broqueville sent for me to talk over some changes in my arrangements. The Government —he said—wishes France and Germany to seem equally aimed at by our military measures' *(ibid.,* p. 148). The Selliers' concentration plan of July 1914, approved by the Government for the case of war with Germany, provided for the concentration of six army divisions and three cavalry divisions totaling about 117,000 men in the St. Trond-Eghezée-Hougaerde-Tirlemont quadrilateral; four front line divisions at St. Trond, Houtain-l'Eveque, Hannut, Eghezée respectively; two second line divisions at Tirlemont and Hougaerde, and a cavalry division in advance of the front line at Braives. At the King's wish on 31 July the concen tration was moved back one stage to the Louvain-Tirlemont-Perwetz-Wavre quadrilateral and the cavalry division was concentrated at Gembloux. On 3 August in deference to the King's desire another rearrangement was made: the 3rd division was ordered to Liége and the 4th to Namur *(ibid.,* pp. 103, 130-2, 177-8 ; Galet, pp. 40-8).

Elst's request, and the one in Baron de Ryckel's *Mémoires*. Both documents deal exclusively with the military matters discussed at the meeting.

Between the two accounts there are 'irreconcilable differences'. Selliers writes that he was asked the following questions:

> Can our army fight a defensive battle alone with a chance of halting the enemy? Is our army completely ready to meet the attack of the enemy? Reply—No, the war has caught us in the very act of reorganizing the army; our officer cadres, especially those in the reserve, are still inadequate; our field artillery is still below establishment; we have absolutely no heavy guns. Will the fortifications of Liége and Namur be able to hold out for a certain time? Yes. For a month. . . . Will the fortifications of Antwerp be able to stand a siege? Yes, but only with the support of the field army, because the construction of some of the encircling forts is not completed and the troops manning them are below strength.

In answer to a question from the King, Selliers outlined the conditions in which the Belgian army would co-operate with the Allied armies:

> (i) The Belgian army would undertake the guard and defense of the fortified places to the exclusion of Allied troops;
> (ii) Our army would operate in liaison and agreement with the Allies, but would not pass under the command of an Allied general.
> Asked in his turn . . . General de Ryckel, Sub-Chief of the Army General Staff, briefly expressed the opinion that our field army immediately on completing its concentration in the west and from the neighborhood of the fortified position of Liége, should immediately take the offensive, penetrate into the Rhine province, and march on Cologne. . . . Selliers pointed out the temerity of such an operation, which would expose our field army to untimely destruction, at the same time endangering the subsequent defense of the fortified position of Antwerp.[1]

If Ryckel's account meets with the approval of his former pupil General Galet,[2] Selliers describes it as *'un maquillage honteux et effronté de la vérité'*.[3]

> There was no word of the Velpe or Gèthe positions or of any plan of military operations. . . . General de Ryckel uttered his idea of an offensive towards Cologne as a *boutade,* not at all as a detailed and well thought out exposition, and the King expressed neither approval nor disapproval of it.[4]

In a view of the discrepancies between the Selliers and Ryckel versions of the Crown Council meeting, the survivors of those who attended it were asked by Selliers to express their opinion; five of them concurred with the Selliers account, some

---

[1] Selliers, *Contribution,* pp. 163-4.
[2] Selliers, *Contribution,* pp. 174-5.
[3] Selliers, *Contribution,* p. 174.
[4] Selliers, *Contribution,* pp. 173-4.

declined to give an opinion, others said they could not trust their memories. Broqueville wrote that Ryckel's version was *'en désaccord complet avec la réalité'.*[1] This controversy is a sample of the difficulties confronting historians when they investigate certain more obscure aspects of the July crisis and shows with what caution even first-hand accounts must be treated.

Coming back to the story of the Crown Council, the survey of the military situation was followed by a discussion of the attitude to be taken by Belgium towards the guarantor Powers. First of all the major question: would the Germans invade the whole of Belgium or confine themselves to occupying the district on the far side of the Meuse? In the former case would it not be imperative to ask for the intervention of the guaranteeing Powers? Crokaert, who records details of the discussion, throws no light on the line the Council proposed to take towards French and English offers of assistance in the event of the Germans occupying the whole country. He relates that Carton de Wiart outlined certain consequences that would emerge if the Germans did not violate the left bank of the Meuse, whereupon M. Liebaert pressed for the destruction of the Meuse bridges. This brought General de Ryckel to his feet with the protest: 'No, No! We must be able to drive the Germans back to where they belong.'[2] Crokaert adds:

> The King took the view that we could not formally join in on the side of our allies without making an agreement with them safeguarding our independence and the autonomy of our army,

which must never come under the command of a foreign general. Several voices were raised in protest against this, and Hymans condemned it in the telling phrase: 'When one is drowning one does not ask one's rescuer to show his credentials.' At that moment van den Heuvel arrived from Ghent and soon managed to get agreement for a middle course: Belgium would not appeal to her guarantors for military aid until Belgian neutrality had actually been violated. Until then she

---

[1] Selliers de Moranville, pp. 169–73.

[2] It is not quite certain that Ryckel did utter these words. In any case Galet gives a methodical account of bridges, tunnels, constructions demolished. He ends by saying: 'All this destruction . . . might have been conceived on a far greater scale . . . but such as it was it forced the Germans to concentrate on their own territory or in the Grand Duchy' (Galet, pp. 59-8). Crokaert relates that at Ryckel's words a voice asserted that 'the French would soon come to our aid with five army corps'. The King said that this was a rumor devoid of foundation (Crokaert, p. 322). It originated with the French Military Attaché and was reported to Grey by Villiers on 3 August (BD. XI, 521). On 15 April 1915 van der Elst inquired of Selliers whether the Crown Council discussed the question of help promised by France and Britain, in particular that of the five French army corps which were to come immediately to the aid of Belgium. Selliers wrote in reply that he had certainly heard them mentioned and thought possibly it was Klobukowski who had brought up the matter with either the King or Broqueville or Davignon. 'However'—he concludes—'my memory is not exact on this point' (Selliers, *Contribution,* p. 165).

would appeal to them only for diplomatic support.[1] We do not know on what authorities Crokaert bases this account of his and what is its value in view of the absence of official minutes and of first-hand evidence from men who had been present at the meeting. All we know from Selliers is that

there was, moreover, a long debate on the question of the reply to be given to the ultimatum, for it was still hoped that Germany could be induced to refrain from her aggressive intentions.[2]

11. *The Belgian Government's reply to the German ultimatum.*

By that time it was almost midnight and time was growing short for the work that had still to be done in drafting, revising and passing the text of the reply to be handed over seven hours later. The drafting was entrusted to three members of the Council: Carton de Wiart, Minister for Justice, van den Heuvel and Paul Hymans, Minister of State. They first set to work at a corner of the big table round which the members of the Crown Council were seated. But too many voices offered suggestions and advice, and in search of quiet they walked over to the Ministry for Foreign Affairs, where the Political Director, Baron Gaiffier, was putting the last touches to a preliminary draft which he had undertaken on his own initiative while the Crown Council was holding its discussion. This preliminary draft had already crystallized the essential points in logical order. The working out of the final text was a slow and laborious process at which Broqueville and Davignon, were silent spectators. To the restrained and impressive eloquence of its wording each of the three Ministers made his contribution.[3]

Hardly was the draft finished when in the small hours, about 1.30 a. m., Below-Saleske appeared once more and was received by van der Elst, to whom he said, on instructions from the German Government, that

this morning eighty French officers in Prussian officers' uniform in twelve motor-cars tried to cross the German frontier at Walbeck, west of Geldern,

and that

today in breach of international law France took belligerent action against us (bomb-throwing by airmen, border crossed by cavalry patrols).[4]

---

[1] Crokaert, pp. 321-3. Galet's account runs: 'Agreement was not so easily reached on another point—whether it was necessary to make an immediate appeal to France and England, guarantors of our neutrality, or whether it would be better to wait to approach these Powers until our territory should actually have been invaded. The King pronounced in favor of the second course, and after some lively discussion it was adopted by the majority of the assembly' (Galet, p. 50). This probably took place when the meeting was resumed.

[2] Selliers, *Contribution,* p. 164.   [3] Crokaert, pp. 324-7.

[4] DD. III, 677, 682, 709. See p. 208.

The allegations were without foundation, as was later proved, but the trick was no more barefaced and puerile than its predecessors. Baron van der Elst inquired where these incidents had taken place. 'In Germany', replied Below-Saleske. 'In that case I do not understand the object of your call', said van der Elst. Taken aback, Below hesitated, and then explained that acts of this nature might well foreshadow other breaches of international law and that French bad faith was a direct threat to Belgium. Crokaert narrates that van der Elst's indignant reply could be heard by the Ministers in Davignon's room.[1] At 9.48 p. m. on the 2nd Below had reported to Berlin that he had served the ultimatum, adding:

The Foreign Minister could not conceal his painful surprise at the unexpected communication,[2]

and at 3.5 a. m. on 3 August, announcing his delivery of the messages about the alleged French incidents, he remarked: 'However, I do not think that this will influence the Belgian reply, which in my opinion is likely to be in the negative.'[3]

By 2 a. m. the reply was ready for submission to the Crown Council, which met again at the Royal Palace. Carton de Wiart read out the text and it was at once unanimously approved by the Council without changes. The discussion was then resumed on the approach to be made to the guarantor Powers and van den Heuvel's temporizing proposal was adopted. At 2.30 a. m. the Council began to disperse. The approaching dawn was whitening the east. King Albert rose from his chair. 'Gentlemen'—he remarked—'this is the dawn of a dark day.' Then, after a pause, he added: 'But it promises to be a brilliant one.' Then, as if to himself: 'If we had been weak enough to yield, tomorrow in the streets of Brussels the people would have hanged us.'[4]

This was perhaps the thought which induced certain others of those present to make up their minds in favor of resistance. Among them was Greindl, who three and a half years earlier had advocated a very different attitude.[5] He left the Crown Council 'livid and ghastly, leaning on a friend's arm in order not to fall'.[6]

King Albert's thought, expressed in the words quoted above, finds confirmation in a passage in Klobukowski's dispatch of 5 August:

It is unquestionably under the irresistible impulse of public opinion that . . . the Ministry resigned itself in the last analysis to have recourse to the co-operation of the Powers guarantors of the neutrality of Belgium.

A footnote in the *Documents Diplomatiques Français* explains in regard to the signs of omission: 'Here the Commission thought

---

[1] Crokaert, p. 328. [2] DD. III, 695. [3] DD. III, 709.
[4] Crokaert, pp. 329-30. [5] See p. 426. [6] Crokaert, p. 330.

necessary to refrain from reproducing certain words relating to a personage.'[1] Can this be King Albert? Probably.

At 7 a. m. [Belgian time] de Gaiffier delivered the Belgian Government's reply at the German Legation, and the Military Attaché at once took it to General Emmich at Aix-la-Chapelle, where the General was awaiting it before launching the attack on Liége. At 10.55 a. m. on 3 August Below-Saleske telegraphed to Berlin that the Belgian Government rejected its demands and would forcibly oppose any violation of its neutrality. At 12.35 p. m. he telegraphed the full text of the reply to Berlin with the comment: 'Feeling towards Germany bad.'[3] This was an understatement. Indignation pierces through the very phrasing of the Belgian note, which, after briefly summarizing the German demands, continues:

This note has caused deep and painful astonishment to the King's Government. The intentions it ascribes to France are in contradiction with the formal declarations made to us on 1 August by the Government of the Republic.

Moreover, if, contrary to our expectation, Belgian neutrality should be violated by France, Belgium would fulfill all her international obligations and her army would offer vigorous resistance to the invader.

The treaties of 1839, confirmed by the treaties of 1870, vouch for the independence and neutrality of Belgium under the guarantee of the Powers, and notably of the Government of His Majesty, the King of Prussia.

Belgium has always been faithful to her international obligations; she has carried out her duties in a spirit of sincere impartiality; she has spared no effort to maintain and enforce respect for her neutrality.

The infringement of her independence with which the German Government threatens her would constitute a flagrant violation of international law. No strategic interest justifies such a breach of law.

Were it to accept the proposals laid before it, the Belgian Government would sacrifice the nation's honor while being false to its duties towards Europe.

Conscious of the part which has been played by Belgium in the civilization of the world for more than eighty years, the Government refuses to believe that Belgian independence can only be preserved at the price of the violation of her neutrality.

If this hope were disappointed, the Belgian Government is firmly resolved to repel every infringement of its rights by all the means in its power.[3]

Whatever the previous shortcomings of the Belgian Government, this reply which it returned to the German ultimatum is the noblest document produced by the whole crisis and redounds to the honor-both of those who were responsible for its substance and those who gave it its form, which in brevity and self-restraint—even if the self-restraint were due to a lingering hope that Germany might yet refrain from violating

---

[1] DF. XI, 773.   [2] DD. VI, 735, 779.
[3] DD. IV, 779; *First Belgian Grey Book,* 22.

Belgian neutrality—attains a solemnity worthy of the occasion. This was so clearly felt by the German Government that in the three editions of the German *White Book* it refrained from publishing the note, for which reason German public opinion felt amazed and indignant at the resistance put up by Liége.

However, the Belgian Government did not see fit to communicate the text of its reply to the Powers signatories of the treaty of 1839, Davignon merely telegraphing a brief summary of the German note and the reply to the Belgian Ministers abroad.[1] On the evening of 2 August the French Minister, Klobukowski, and the English Minister, Villiers, were not even informed of the ultimatum delivered by Below-Saleske. Klobukowski relates of 3 August:

> 8 a. m. Appearance at the Legation of Baron de Gaiffier, Director of Political Affairs, my former colleague at Cairo. He read me the ultimatum delivered to the Belgian Government at 7 p. m. on the previous day by the German Minister in the name of his Government . . . and also the Belgian Government's reply. . . . 'I am not leaving a copy of these documents with you', he said. 'I have not even my Minister's authority to communicate them to you.'[3]

Not until 8.20 a. m. on 3 August was Klobukowski able to telegraph to Paris:

> In reply to German Government's ultimatum about having to facilitate its military operations in Belgium, the Royal Government refuses and declares itself resolved vigorously to defend its neutrality guaranteed by treaty and in particular by the King of Prussia.[3]

At 10.40 a. m., after seeing Davignon at 10 a. m., he telegraphed more fully,[4] but only on 5 August was he able to send the text of the ultimatum and the Belgian reply.[5] At 9.31 a. m. on 3 August Villiers also briefly reported what had happened.[6] He later procured copies of the two notes and sent them to London by courier after telegraphing a summary at 5.46 p. m.[7] The Belgian Government's reserve was in accordance with the King's wish and the views of the Cabinet, which met again at 10 a. m. on 3 August and lasted until noon. Davignon laid before it a statement made to him that morning by Klobukowski after consultation with the English and Russian Ministers and which Davignon promised to submit to the Cabinet:

> Without being yet instructed by my Government to make a statement, but in view of its known intentions, I feel I am in a position to state that, if the Royal

[1] *First Belgian Grey Book,* 23.

[2] Klobukowski, p. 87. After seeing Gaiffier, Klobukowski gave a summary of events to the *Havas* correspondent and thus the world learnt the news (Klobukowski, p. 88).

[3] DF. 3. XI, 644.   [4] DF. 3. XI, 650; Klobukowski, p. 88.

[5] DF. 3. XI, 773 annexes.   [6] BD. XI, 521.   [7] BD. XI, 561.

Government made an appeal to the French Government as a Power guarantor of Belgian neutrality, we should at once respond to its appeal; if this appeal were not made, it is probable, unless of course the needs of self-defense gave rise to exceptional measures, that it would refrain from intervening until Belgium had carried out some effective measure of resistance.

At the end of the Cabinet meeting Davignon read Klobukowski a note in which the Belgian Government thanked the French Government for its offer and said that 'in the present circumstance we do not appeal to the guarantee of the Powers. Later the Royal Government will judge what is needful to do'.[1] On similar lines King Albert telegraphed on 3 August to George V: 'I make a supreme appeal to the diplomatic intervention of Your Majesty's Government to safeguard the integrity of Belgium.'[2]

Not content with declining 'for the time being' military aid from France, the Belgian Government also sought to guard against possible French advances into its territory even after the German ultimatum gave the guaranteeing Powers the right to intervene in defense of Belgian neutrality as being a direct interest of their own. Wullus-Rudiger relates:

As late as the afternoon of 3 August the order was issued to fire on all military aircraft. Up to the moment when the Germans crossed the frontier (4 August at 8 a. m.) the troops of the V armored division, detailed to oppose any violation of the southern frontier, had orders to fire on all French soldiers crossing it under arms.[3]

This explains the anxiety felt up to the last moment by the statesmen of the Triple *Entente*. As late as 3 August, Kudashev, the Russian Minister at Brussels, telegraphed to Sazonov that his French colleague was very pessimistic and feared that Belgian defense would be nothing more than a 'sham'.[4] Klobukowski also thought it suspicious that the Germans had not yet crossed the frontier and telegraphed at 5.23 p. m. on 3 August: 'It would be a good thing to let them take the initiative in the actual violation for which they are perhaps trying to make us responsible.' At 6.56 p. m. he again telegraphed:

The impression deepens that the ultimatum of Germany, who, after threatening, has not acted, is a maneuver to induce us to be the first to intervene in Belgium, thus causing an initial conflict between the Belgian army and our own.[5]

---

[1] *First Belgian Grey Book,* 24; DF. 3. XI, 664, 676. [2] *First Belgian Grey Book,* 25.
[3] Wullus-Rudiger, p. 120. [4] *Int. Bez.* I. V 498.
[5] DF. 5. XI, 680, 687. It is a question whether these anxious telegrams from Klobukowski were not the reason for the French Government's sending him 500,000 (gold) francs. At 32.35 p. m. on 4 August he telegraphed to Paris: 'I have just received from Lord Rothschild an order on the Banque Nationale for 500,000 francs on the Ministry of Finance's account. Kindly indicate use.' A footnote in the DF. runs: 'These funds were probably necessary to

Villiers, too, was not clear what was happening. At 7.2 p. m. on 3, August he telegraphed:

French Military Attaché has been assured on authority which he considers reliable that if Germany actually invades Belgium in force Belgian Government will appeal at once not only to France but also to England for military aid. They will not do this so long as Belgian soil is not violated by formidable bodies of German troops.[1]

Both the Belgian Government and King Albert still clung to the idea that the ultimatum was not Germany's last word. Lieutenant-General Galet writes:

The presentation of the ultimatum had not convinced us that Germany would actually enter our territory. If the Imperial General Staff had really intended to send its armies across Belgium, why did it disclose its plans so soon as the first day of mobilization, before concentration had begun? It was tantamount to a kindly warning to give the French time to take measures to meet the move. . . . Any offensive on the right, especially across Belgium, besides in all probability causing the extra complication of British intervention, would leave to the French army the whole of France in which to maneuver. . . . Was it not possible that the Great General Staff was only trying to provoke the French army to a deployment in the wrong direction by attracting its center of gravity to the north? And if this were correct, and the Germans did not invade our territory, where should we be, with the French and British armies on our soil? Could we avoid being dragged by them into the war? Before inviting foreign armies into Belgium it was necessary that invasion should have taken place.[2]

This train of argument is so specious that it carries no conviction. There is, moreover, in the surviving evidence, no trace of King Albert's having reasoned thus. Indeed, if he had, one would expect him to feel less indignation and alarm than he actually did. Leclere writes:

It was perhaps still legitimate to hope that at the last moment, when faced with the formal refusal of Belgium and the incalculable consequences that were bound to result from the violation of Belgian neutrality, Germany would renounce the project of allowing her troops to cross the frontier. All hope of this had not been given up at the Foreign Ministry in Brussels.[3]

Klobukowski also bears witness that

up to the last minute the Belgian Government thought that Germany would modify a plan which seemed both politically and strategically mistaken.[4]

facilitate the departure of the very many French people domiciled in Belgium. M. Klobukowski's question, however, seems to have received no reply' (DF. 3. XI, 722). If the funds were meant for another purpose Klobukowski clearly did not guess what it was.

[1] BD. XI, 562.   [2] Galet, p. 51.   [3] Leclere, art. cit., p. 212.
[4] Klobukowski, p. 89, note.

The Belgian statesmen seem to have been ignorant of the fact that a plan of war cannot be changed at the last minute. Neither politicians nor diplomats had any knowledge of military problems. Moreover, their eyes were blinded by awe and reverence for Berlin, which went so far that at midnight on 31 July General Leman was ordered not to construct field-works between one fort and another for fear of offending German susceptibilities. In the event this helped to bring about the early fall of Liége.[1] It was, moreover, feared that all hope of a German change of heart would vanish if the French or English were to enter Belgium first. Then again, by the 3rd the Kaiser must have received King Albert's letter, and the answer to it had to be awaited.

12. *Lingering German hopes; the Belgian appeal to England and France.*

At Wilhelm's request to Bethmann, the reply was drafted by Jagow and dispatched from the Schloss at 8.20 p. m. on 3 August. It ran:

If I had to put a serious question to Your Majesty's Government it was with the friendliest intentions towards Belgium but under the decisive compulsion of the hour in which Germany's fate is at stake. It still lies in Your Majesty's power to place our future mutual relations on the friendly footing foreshadowed in the terms offered. My feelings towards Your Majesty and your land remain unchanged.[2]

When the Kaiser sent this message, Berlin long since knew from Below-Saleske's first telegram, received at 1.10 p. m., that the Belgian Government was going to put up armed resistance to invasion by Germany. But while Brussels still trusted that Germany would not proceed with invasion, Berlin was no less confident that Belgium would not persevere in resistance.

This had been Moltke's assumption when, having taken on his shoulders the task of directing foreign policy, he got officials of the Foreign Ministry to put together an article for the press giving reasons for the invasion.[3] On learning the Belgian reply, he withdrew the article and instructed the Wilhelmstrasse on the afternoon of 3 August to notify the Belgian Government

that to our regret we shall be compelled by the negative attitude of the Royal Belgian Government towards our well-intentioned proposals to put into operation the security measures, which, as already explained, are unavoidably necessary against the French threat, by force of arms, if not possible otherwise. The notification is necessary as our troops will be entering Belgian territory tomorrow morning. I regard this declaration as sufficient, as Belgium has stated she will oppose armed resistance to any invasion. A declaration of war does not seem to me desirable, because I still reckon on coming

---

[1] Wullus-Rudiger pp. 205-6. [2] DD. IV, 783. [3] DD. IV, 781.

to an understanding with Belgium when the Belgian Government realizes the seriousness of the situation.[1]

At 10.35 p. m. on 3 August Jagow telegraphed Below-Saleske in the desired sense.[2] On 4 August Moltke sent another series of instructions to the Wilhelmstrasse to assure the Belgian Government:

Even after the invasion has taken place, you will continue to take the standpoint that Germany is at any time ready to stretch out the hand of brotherhood to Belgium and negotiate an acceptable *modus vivendi*. But basis of negotiation must be: opening of Liége to the march through of German troops, abstention from destruction of railways, bridges, key-points.

Jagow lost no time in sending these instructions to Below-Saleske.[3] The German General Staff, on its side, had ordered the first invading troops to behave in a friendly manner to the Belgian population, with the result that they entered Venders shouting *Vive la Belgique!* and at Spa they gave a concert opening with the 'Brabançonne'.[4] Their blandishments were wasted.

On receiving Jagow's telegram, sent at Moltke's behest on the evening of 3 August, Below-Saleske, who that same 3 August had sent a note to the Belgian press for the purpose of presenting as favorable an interpretation of the German ultimatum as possible to Belgian public opinion, wrote to Davignon at 6 a. m. on 4 August that the German Government

will find itself, to its deep regret, compelled to take—if necessary by force of arms—the measures of security indicated as indispensable in view of French threats.[5]

At 11 a. m. on 4 August Brussels learned that at 8 a. m. German advance troops had entered Belgium at Gemmenich. But the news had

---

[1] DD. IV, 788. On this point Lutz writes: 'Up to 3 August Moltke counted on coming to an understanding with Belgium as soon as the Belgian Government "realized the seriousness of the situation". In fact, despite assurances to the contrary, Brussels was probably not at the beginning determined to oppose the German march through Belgium with its entire armed strength' (Lutz, pp. 397–8). In support of this Lutz refers especially to a private letter written by Villiers to Nicolson on 12 August (BD. XI, 670, n.), but neither it nor Villiers's other reports justify the assumption that after the ultimatum Belgium had any hesitations about rejecting the German demand. She perhaps hoped that Germany would not invade, but from the beginning she was determined to resist invasion.

[2] DD. IV, 791.

[3] DD. IV, 804, 805.

[4] Wullus-Rudiger, p. 199. Beyens writes that the German Government did not expect resistance from Belgium. Liége was attacked by three corps of advance troops not provided with heavy artillery to demolish its forts. 'They thought they were going to enter through open gates with flags flying and drums beating, greeted as victors, almost as friends' ('La neutralité beige', in *Revue des Deux Mondes*, 15 June 1915, p. 743). Beyens does not perceive that this observation is a reflection on the Brussels Government, whose behavior was such as to give rise to this illusion on the part of the Germans.

[5] *First Belgian Grey Book*, 27,

not yet arrived when at the historic sitting of Parliament that morning the King, appealing to the Belgians to unite in resistance to aggression, once again, in spite of Below-Saleske's letter, voiced the hope 'that the events that were feared would not take place'. Broqueville read out the notes exchanged with the German Government together with a Government statement ending with the words: 'A country which defends its independence may be defeated, it will never be subjugated.' The voting was unanimous in favor of resistance and of the legislation thereby rendered necessary. When the news arrived of the violation of Belgian territory, the Cabinet decided to appeal to the guaranteeing Powers and the following note was sent to, the English, French and Russian Ministers at Brussels:

The Belgian Government regrets to have to announce to Your Excellency that this morning the armed forces of Germany entered Belgian territory in violation of treaty engagements. The Belgian Government is firmly resolved to resist by all means in its power. Belgium appeals to England, France and Russia to co-operate as guaranteeing Powers in the defense of her territory. There should be concerted and joint action to oppose the forcible measures employed by Germany against Belgium, and, at the same time, to guarantee the future maintenance of the independence and integrity of Belgium. Belgium is happy to declare that she will assume the defense of her fortified places.[1]

Davignon informed Below-Saleske that the Government had ceased to have official relations with him and enclosed passports for him and the Legation staff,[2] while King Albert at 4.15 p. m. on 4 August sent Wilhelm the following reply:

The feelings of friendship which I have expressed to Your Majesty and those which Your Majesty has many times lavished on me, the so cordial relations of our two Governments, the unfailingly correct attitude of Belgium, against which Germany has never been able to formulate the smallest grievance, prevent my

---

[1] *First Belgian Grey Book,* 40. This note reached Villiers almost at once, since he telegraphed it on to London at 4 p. m. on 4 August (BD. XI, 654). Klobukowski only received it at 10 p. m. (Klobukowski, p. 97). At 7.56 p. m. he telegraphed that he still knew nothing official of the Cabinet's decisions in regard to the guaranteeing Powers. Not until 11.15 p. m. did his telegram go off with news of the note handed him by Davignon (DF. 3. XI, 753, 758). One might be tempted to think that the delay was intentional, lest French troops should enter Belgium prematurely. In actual fact the appeal to the Powers was sent with much mistrust especially on the part of the King, who insisted on the inclusion of the final statement referring to the defense of the fortified places 'as a kind of safeguard of our sovereignty in the event of the troops of another country remaining in our country' (Galet, p. 63). But it is by no means certain that the hour of dispatch of Villiers's telegram is correct, for two reasons. Firstly if it had gone off at 4 p. m. on the 4th, it would have been received long before 12.50 a. m. on the 5th, since telegrams between Brussels and London generally took less than three hours. Secondly its Registry number is 29, i.e., it was later than No. 28 (BD. XI, 631), which went off at 6.38 p. m., arriving in London at 9.15 p. m.

[2] *First Belgian Grey Book,* 31.

supposing for an instant that Your Majesty would cruelly force us in front of the whole of Europe to choose between war and the loss of honor, between respect for treaties and neglect of our international engagements.[1]

In spite of this attitude on the part of Belgium and her King, the German Government after the fall of Liége made a further attempt to obtain their surrender. On 9 August, Fallon, the Belgian Minister at the Hague, telegraphed to Davignon that the Netherlands Foreign Minister had asked him:

to convey to you the following information, the United States Minister at Brussels having declined to do so! . . . Now that the Belgian army has upheld the honor of its arms by its heroic resistance to a very superior force, the German Government begs the King of the Belgians and the Belgian Government to spare Belgium the further horrors of war. The German Government is ready for any compact with Belgium which can be reconciled with their arrangements with France. Germany once more gives her solemn assurance that it is not her intention to appropriate Belgian territory to herself. . . . Germany is still ready to evacuate Belgium as soon as the state of war will allow her to do so.

The United States Ambassador has asked his colleague to undertake this attempt at mediation. The Minister for Foreign Affairs has accepted the mission without enthusiasm. I have undertaken it to oblige him.[2]

On 12 August Davignon telegraphed to Fallon:

Faithful to her international obligations, Belgium can only reiterate her reply to the ultimatum, the more so as since 3 August her neutrality has been violated, a distressing war has been waged on her territory, and the guarantors of her neutrality have responded loyally and without delay to her appeal.[3]

Not even this second rebuff was enough for the Berlin Government. Wullus-Rudiger relates:

At the time of the Battle on the Marne when the Belgian army had to retire on Antwerp, enticing proposals were again and again made through the medium of Woeste, the leader of the Catholic Party. Monsignor di Sarzana, the counsellor at the Brussels Nunciature, was also involved. Reverting to a proposal made by Wilhelm to Leopold II in 1904, Sarzana urged the conclusion of an understanding between Belgium and Germany which might lead to the recovery by Belgium of the Flemish regions of France.[4]

Did these moves betray a realization on the part of Germany that her violation of Belgian neutrality was a blunder? Certainly this was the feeling at the Wilhelmstrasse when on 4 August Beyens called on Jagow to ask for explanations in regard to die German ultimatum, Jagow's embarrassed reply ran:

[1] DD. IV, 837.
[3] *First Belgian Grey Book,* 71

[2] *First Belgian Grey Book,* 60.
[4] Wullus-Rudiger, p. 201. See p. 417.

Absolute necessity forced us to make this demand. . . . The passage through Belgium is a question of life and death for Germany. She has to be finished with France as quickly as possible, completely crush her before being able to turn next against Russia, or else she will herself be caught between the hammer and the anvil. We heard that the French army was preparing to pass by way of Belgium and attack our flank. We had to forestall her.

Beyens answered:

Contrary to what you believe, France has formally promised to respect our neutrality provided you do the same. What would you have said if, instead of spontaneously making this promise, she .had been ahead of you in making the same demand, if she had insisted on a passage through our country and we had yielded to her threats? Would you not have said that we were cowards, incapable of defending our neutrality, and unworthy of an independent existence ?

To this question Herr von Jagow did not reply.

But he could not do otherwise than admit:

Germany has no reproaches to address to Belgium, whose attitude has always been most correct.

And as Beyens said he was ready to ask for his passports, Jagow exclaimed:

But I do not want thus to break off my relations with you. We shall perhaps still have matters to discuss.

The German Under-Secretary of State, Zimmermann, put forward no pretexts in excuse of the violation of Belgium. He simply said

that the department for Foreign Affairs was powerless. Since the order for mobilization had been issued by the Kaiser, all power now belonged to the military authorities. It was they who had considered the invasion of Belgium to be an indispensable war operation.[1]

This was no doubt true, but it was also true that the civil authorities in Germany had throughout tamely surrendered to the military, who brought the country to defeat and certainly had no claim to such deference. When one reads the instructions issued by Moltke to the Wilhelmstrasse between 3 and 5 August one is amazed by their lack of the most elementary political and psychological insight.[2] One asks oneself how a great country like Germany could entrust her fate to such men. Schlieffen himself, distinguished general though he was, was completely incapable of assessing the effects that would be produced by an invasion of Belgium, or of realizing that a political constellation might arise calling for a plan of campaign which would leave Belgium untouched and not involve an offensive against France. As

---

[1] *Second Belgian Grey Book,* 51, 52 ; Beyens, II, pp. 269-73.
[2] DD. III, 662; IV, 804, 876.

Wilson said to the Belgian Chamber of Deputies on 19 June 1919: 'Belgium and her part in the war is in one sense the key of the whole struggle, because the violation of Belgium was the call to duty which aroused the nations.'[1] One might add that it was also the key of the peace treaty, for on the proposal of the American delegates Lansing and Scott it was laid down in the report presented to the Conference for Peace Preliminaries on 4 April, 1919, that the violation of Belgian neutrality 'must be condemned in explicit terms and its authors doomed to the execration of mankind'.[2]

Basing themselves on the Barnardiston-Ducarne discussions of 1906 and the conversation between Colonel Bridges and General Jungbluth of 1912, and misrepresenting the character of the former, the Germans have vainly sought to accuse and calumniate the little country that refused to submit to them. The truth is that the documents they found in Brussels only served to show how strong had been the preference for Germany in the attitude of the Belgian Government, whose faults in the eyes of the Belgian nation and of posterity were—let it be repeated—to have closed its eyes to the threat growing increasingly manifest on its eastern frontier; to have taken no adequate measures for the defense of the national territory; to have trusted Germany blindly to the very last while reserving suspicion and mistrust for those who least merited it. These faults were handsomely redeemed by the Government's display of integrity and courage. By their previous attitude and their abstention from all contacts with France and England, both Government and people deserved different treatment at the hands of the invader. In their own interests the Germans would have done better not to give way to resentment but seek by considerate treatment to efface the memory of the wrong they were doing to the country. Instead of this, Bethmann Hollweg, on 6 September 1914, told American correspondents of the United Press and Associated Press that after the first encounters Belgian girls had amused themselves putting out the eyes of German wounded.[3]

It is, however, not necessary to labor this point, since there were, and still are, Germans of unimpeachable credentials 'who have acknowledged the guilt of Germany. Moreover, at Versailles on 28 May 1919, it was unconditionally recognized as a 'wrong for which reparation must be made' in a note drawn up by Hans Delbruck, Max Weber, Montgelas, and Mendelssohn-Bartholdy.[4] Let it here suffice to quote

---

[1] The Public Papers of Woodrow Wilson, *War and Peace* (N.Y. and London, 1927), Vol. I, p. 511.

[2] *Das deutscbe Weissbuch über die Schuld am Kriege* (Berlin, 1927), p. 55.

[3] Beyens, 'La neutralité belge', in *Revue des Deux Mondes,* 15 June 1915, p. 727.

[4] *Das deutsche Weissbuch über die Schuld am Kriege* (Berlin), 1927, p. 71.

what has been written by Schoen, at that time the German Ambassador at Paris:

> The violence done to Belgium was not only a strategical and political error, it was also a breach of international law, as the competent authorities had to admit from the first. . . . It was both wrong and dishonorable, it exposed us to the contempt of the world, and furnished our enemies with weapons with which they fought us no less effectively than by force of arms. . . . To crush a weak country, protected by sacred treaties, is a crime against which the world's conscience revolts. Germany will have to bear this burden of atonement for generations to come.[1]

Over and above the moral damage, the invasion of Belgium brought on Germany the military damage of English intervention, which otherwise would not have taken place so immediately. This was acknowledged by the Kaiser himself on 1 August 1914 in a marginal note to a telegram from Below-Saleske alluding to Grey's request for an undertaking by Paris and Berlin to respect Belgian neutrality. He wrote: 'That is what English intervention against us will be determined by.'[2] In the following pages this will become more clearly apparent.

[1] Schoen, pp. 248-9.   [2] DD. III, 584.

CHAPTER X

BRITAIN AT WAR

(1) *Last German appeal to London for English neutrality* (p. 476). (2) *The Cabinet meeting of 3 August agrees on the statement to be made by Grey* (p. 481). (3) *Grey's speech in the House of Commons on the afternoon of 3 August* (p. 484). (4) *The sending of the English ultimatum to Berlin* (p. 489). (5) *The delivery of the ultimatum* (p. 495). (6) *London vainly awaits the German reply; proclamation of the 'state of war'* (p. 498). (7) *English reluctance to send troops to the Continent* (p. 502). (8) *The Council of War on 5 August decides to send the Expeditionary Force to France* (p. 508). (9) *Asquith's speech in the Commons on 6 August* (p. 512). (10) *Grey's ideas on the Belgian question and English intervention* (p. 517). (11) *Grey's share of responsibility for the war* (p. 523).

1. Last German appeal to London for English neutrality.

On 2 August at 12.30 p. m. Berlin was told that England had cut off cable communications with Germany. Tirpitz heard of the news first and at once inquired of Jagow whether they were to consider them selves as in a state of war with England. Jagow asked Goschen for explanations, and Grey at 5.25 p. m. telegraphed *en clair* to Goschen in reply

that delay has been due to extraordinary congestion. . . . I understand that lines are now working satisfactorily.[1]

Clearly Berlin was in a state of nerves that Sunday, the day on which at 2.5 p. m. the instruction went off to Below-Saleske to present the ultimatum to Belgium which might be expected to bring about the so much dreaded intervention of England. In a telegram reaching the Wilhelmstrasse at 11.47 a. m. Lichnowsky had said:

The question whether in a war with France we violate Belgian territory is probably of decisive importance for the neutrality of England. . . . As it is now believed here that the violation of Belgian neutrality will have to be reckoned with, I think it not impossible that England will in the immediate future take up position against us.[2]

This admonition on Lichnowsky's part led Jagow at 5.30 p. m. to telegraph in exculpation of Germany's action:

We have reliable information that French, in spite of their declarations, have concentrated large numbers of troops on Belgian frontier and are making preparations for invasion of Belgium. To forestall surprises we shall probably be compelled to take counter-measures.

[1] DD III, 654; BD. XI, 483.   [2] DD. III, 641. See p. 400.

In this case, if Belgium grants us benevolent neutrality, we shall give her an assurance that when the campaign ends we shall respect Belgian integrity to the full and make ample reparation for requisitionings and damage caused by us. It is to be hoped that England will regard German action as only self-defense against French menace. Even in the event of an armed conflict with Belgium, Germany will maintain the integrity of Belgium after conclusion of peace. Please communicate this to English Government, but not until tomorrow, Monday, morning,[1]

i.e., when London would have learnt of the ultimatum presented on Sunday evening at Brussels.

How could Berlin imagine that England would be hoodwinked by these explanations, knowing, as she did, that France had no intention of violating Belgian neutrality? But so it was, and the illusion was strengthened by Lichnowsky's next telegram of 1.23 p. m. on the 2nd, which arrived 6.48 p. m. and brought better news than its predecessor. Knowing that a decisive Cabinet meeting was to be held that Sunday he called on Asquith at breakfast-time that morning to make a supreme appeal. We have already seen the promising telegram, sent off after their talk, during which Asquith had uttered the words: 'A war between our two countries is quite unthinkable.'[2] Earlier than this telegram from Lichnowsky another from the Military Attaché had gone off at 12.19 p.m. to the German Army and Navy General Staffs reporting that Lichnowsky

had received the definite impression from a conversation with the Foreign Secretary that, if at all possible, England would like to stay neutral. In order not to create difficulties, it would be desirable if our Navy refrained from actions which might lead to incidents and be regarded as a challenge. This would in the first place include naval attacks on French north coast, left unprotected by France in reliance on England. Naval attacks on Russia are of no concern to England. For the time being the English will not approach German waters and expect reciprocity from us.[3]

Tirpitz approved the adoption of this suggestion and at 9.30 a. m. on 3 August Jagow telegraphed to Lichnowsky:

We can definitely state that a threat to the French north coast on our part will not take place as long as England remains neutral.[4]

Consequently Lichnowsky sent a communiqué to the English press saying that, if England remained neutral, Germany would refrain from naval action and would not use the Belgian coast as a base.[5]

[1] DD. III, 667.
[2] DD. III, 676. See p. 399.
[3] DD. III, 669.
[4] DD. III, 714, 715.
[5] DF. 3. XI, 670. Cambon ended his dispatch: 'I am having the reply made that respect of coast is not respect of territorial neutrality and that the German ultimatum is already a violation of that neutrality.'

Bethmann Hollweg also made his contribution towards propitiating England by a longish telegram, sent off at 12.55 a. m. on 3 August, casting all the blame on Russia.[1] This line of argument was thought to be Germany's strong suit. At 6.15 p. m. on 1 August, Dr. Hammann, Counsellor at the Foreign Ministry, had telegraphed a request to Ballin, the Chairman of the Hamburg-America line to give publicity to the theme: 'Russia alone foists a war on Europe which nobody wants but herself.'[2] Ballin approached *The Times* on 2 August, but Steed spoke strongly against the publication of the message, which he suspected of emanating from the Kaiser.[3]

However, Kuhlmann, Counsellor at the German Embassy in London and a future Foreign Minister, was successful in persuading the *Westminster Gazette* of 3 August to publish an adroitly phrased statement to the effect that England could be more useful to France by remaining neutral than by coming in, since she did not want to send her handful of divisions to the Continent, where they would be no use, and therefore could only be helpful to France at sea. If England remained neutral Germany was prepared to abstain from attacking France in the north by sea. What good would it be, therefore, for England to intervene when, by staying out, she could give France powerful diplomatic support to bring the war to an end? A tissue of sophistries! Without that handful of divisions France would never have won the Battle of the Marne. Without the command of the sea exercised by England to the detriment of her enemies and the benefit of her allies, her allies would have lost the war. The arguments might possibly have carried some weight if France alone had been at issue. But the French question had been thrust into the background by that of Belgium, and whatever Grey may have said on that morning of 3 August to raise Lichnowsky's hopes, the message sent by Jagow can have done nothing to make him change his views.

There is no trace of the Grey-Lichnowsky talk of 3 August in the *British Documents,* but Grey refers to it in his memoirs, wrongly placing it at 2 p. m., after the Cabinet meeting and before his appearance at 3 p. m. in the Commons, whereas we know that it took place in the forenoon before the Cabinet from a Cambon dispatch[4] and also from the fact that Lichnowsky's lengthy report on it was sent off in cipher at 1.2 p. m.[5] Grey writes half apologetically for not having told Lichnowsky what had been the Cabinet's decision and thus dissipating his illusions:

His first words told me that he brought nothing from Berlin. He asked what had the Cabinet decided? What was I going to say in the House of Commons?

---

[1] DD. III, 696.   [2] DD. III, 572.   [3] Steed, II, p. 17.
          [4] DF. 3 XI, 670   [5] DD. IV, 764.

Was it a declaration of war? I answered that it was . . . a statement of conditions. . . . I would have told him personally anything, for no man had worked harder to avert war than Lichnowsky . . . but he was bound to telegraph whatever was said to Berlin. . . . He asked, was the neutrality of Belgium one of the conditions? . . . He then implored that we should not make Belgian neutrality one of the conditions, he knew nothing, he said, of the plans of the German General Staff . . . but it might be that it was part of the plan for German troops to go through one small corner perhaps of Belgium. I was sure what he said of his own want of knowledge of German military plans was true . . . but I could say nothing. . . . It was the last time that I saw him at the Foreign Office, and the vision of it is clear now—he standing in front of the door that he had entered, and I standing with him, hard pressed for time, and ready to go out.[1]

From Grey's silence to his question whether Belgian neutrality would be a *sine qua non* of English non-intervention, Lichnowsky gained the impression

that he would like, if at all possible, to go on remaining neutral. I gave him the following assurance: (i) that even in the event of a conflict with Belgium we should maintain the integrity of Belgian territory, (ii) that in the event of English neutrality we should not approach France in the Channel and on her northern coast with our navy. . . . I still hope that on this basis it will be possible to reach an agreement, as it is realized here that a conflict with us will yield no advantage to either France or Belgium. Whether it can be avoided depends mainly on feeling in the Cabinet and on public opinion, which might perhaps be unduly upset by our action in Belgium. I repeat, even today there is a desire to remain neutral and in this there is expectation of our support.[2]

At this juncture it no longer mattered that Grey was not frank with Lichnowsky. But his reserve is another instance of the way he always failed to speak plainly to him, thus misleading the German Government one may truly say, right up to the very last moment. Thus it came about that the telegram reporting the conversation of 3 August sent Bethmann into raptures. It had

---

[1] Grey, II, pp. 12–14. Grey saw Lichnowsky once more on 5 August. During the night Lichnowsky had received his passports and at Grey's wish called at his home to say goodbye (Lichnowsky, p. 15). It was a poignant parting and Lichnowsky wrote that Grey described the decision as the hardest he had ever had to take in his life, but that England would not suffer more by intervening than by remaining neutral. She could always make her will felt by a threat to withdraw from the war. And she could make no pacts with a country which had broken its pledges. He would always be prepared to mediate when Germany wished to end the war. 'We do not want to crush Germany', he had added, 'but to restore peace as soon as possible.' The Kaiser's marginal note ran: 'canting liar, slippery as an eel' *(Die auswärtige Politik des deutschen Reiches,* Berlin, 1928, IV, 850-2). In his memoirs Lichnowsky deplores that this confidential interview was made public. By so doing 'Bethmann Hollweg unfortunately destroyed the last chance of gaining peace through the mediation of England'. And he goes on to tell: 'The arrangements for our departure were perfectly dignified and calm ... A special train took us to Harwich where a guard of honor was drawn up for me. I was treated like a departing sovereign' (Lichnowsky, p. 76).

[2] DD. IV, 764.

reached Berlin at 4.33 p. m. but was only given at 9 p. m. to the Chancellor, who wrote in the margin of the reply telegram: 'I regret that No. 234 was only submitted to me at 9 o'clock.' He was, indeed, eager to reply to Lichnowsky, whose message conveyed that, even after the ultimatum to Belgium of the previous evening, the bridges between London and Berlin were still standing. That meant the game was not lost; there was still hope that Grey might identify himself with the German standpoint in the event of a war on two fronts. In that case a frank statement was called for. Accordingly, out of the abundance of his heart, the Chancellor wrote:

Please say to Sir Edward Grey that if we have taken the step of infringing Belgian neutrality we have been forced thereto by the duty of self-preservation. We were in a military impasse. We, who had hitherto confined ourselves to the most essential military defensive measures, have by the unfortunate Russian mobilization found ourselves suddenly in danger of being engulfed by inundations from east and west, since France, too, has already made strong military preparations. The procedure of French mobilization has shown that mobilization fatally leads to war. Wedged between east and west we have had now to resort to every means of defending our existence. It is not an intentional breach of international law, but only the act of a human being fighting for his life. Say that I have devoted all my endeavors as Imperial Chancellor to bringing about gradually and in co-operation with England a state of affairs which would render it impossible for the civilized nations of Europe madly to tear one another to pieces, and that, by her criminal playing with fire, Russia has thwarted these endeavors. I am firmly hoping that England by her attitude in this world crisis will lay a foundation upon which after it is ended we can jointly achieve what now has been destroyed by Russian policy.[1]

Not a word about the German invasion of Belgium being due to the necessity of forestalling a French invasion, as had been the story all along and as the Chancellor himself was to say in the Reichstag the following day! Here is the avowal that, in order not to succumb in a war on two fronts, Germany must pass through Belgium. It was not she who on that account was responsible for the war, but Russia, who had caused the failure of all efforts for peace. As if Grey was not aware that Berlin had rejected every proposal for conciliation and insisted that Russia must agree to the localization of the Austro-Serbian conflict! It is not known what happened to this last appeal from the Chancellor, sent off at 10.25 p. m. on 3 August. Lichnowsky may well have thought it too compromising, its avowal that Germany was violating Belgian neutrality for her own convenience running counter to previous appeals and to yet another message from Jagow on the morning of 4 August reiterating that Germany had to

[1] DD. IV, 790.

enter Belgium to forestall a French attack via Belgium.[1] To this message we will return later.[2] We now turn our attention to the events leading up to Grey's speech in the Commons.

2. The Cabinet meeting of 3 August agrees on the statement to be made by Grey.

Before the Cabinet met at 11 a. m. on 3 August Asquith had received a call from the two Conservative leaders, Bonar Law and Lord Lansdowne, who had asked the previous evening for an interview. The reason for this given by Austen Chamberlain is that on the 2nd Bonar Law had received a communication from Asquith stating that the Government was under no obligations to France. It looks as if the message contained the same six headings that, as we have already seen, figure in Asquith's diary for 2 August.[3]

In certain respects these six points were mutually incompatible and the Conservative leaders received the impression that the Government was looking for pretexts not to intervene in the war. Hence their call on Asquith, whom they found tired and obviously anxious to be rid of them as soon as possible. They pressed the question and went away with the impression that the memorandum did not reflect Asquith's real views, and that he was with Grey and Churchill, but was mainly anxious to keep the Cabinet together. Asquith mentioned the German ultimatum to Belgium, whereupon Law and Lansdowne asked: 'Is that not a reason for acting at once?' Asquith replied that the Government did not yet know whether the statement was true, but in any case they were agreed that neither on military nor on political grounds ought the Expeditionary Force to be sent at once. When this was repeated to the group of Conservatives waiting at Lansdowne House, Balfour very pertinently asked *when* they had arrived at that decision. 'It is wholly inconsistent with what we know of their plans at the time of Agadir.'

A note from Winston Churchill, handed to Balfour while we were together, explained that Grey had made his announcement about the fleet to the French Ambassador only, and that it had not been communicated to the German Ambassador, who would learn it only from the declaration made this afternoon in the House of Commons. I held up my hands in horror at this slipshod way of conducting affairs.[4]

As we have already seen from Lord Crewe's letter to King George V, the Cabinet on 2 August had decided 'that no communication as regards restrictions on the employment of the German Fleet should be made to Germany beforehand'.[5] And Grey wrote to Cambon:

I hear Churchill told your Naval Attaché that my communication to you this afternoon was also made to the German Ambassador. This is quite

---

[1] DD. IV, 810. [2] See p. 492. [3] See p. 400.
[4] A. Chamberlain, *Down the Years,* pp. 100–3 [5] See pp. 409–

wrong; nothing has been said to any foreign representative, except yourself or will be said until a public statement is made.[1]

Suppose—exclaimed Austen Chamberlain on hearing this—the German fleet comes out not knowing of our intentions—is the British Admiral to fire a shot across its bows and order it to go back?

I said—he continues— . . . that affairs at the War Office were in some confusion owing to the fact that the Prime Minister had no time for his departmental duties as Secretary of State [for War] and suggested that Kitchener, who left London at 11.30 this morning [for Egypt], might well be kept and used at the War Office. . . . Balfour sent an immediate note to Winston.[2]

And in fact Kitchener was stopped at Dover and put in charge of the War Office. Asquith was mainly occupied that morning in trying to hold the Cabinet together, for he had just received the resignations of Morley and Simon, following on that of Burns, Morley proposing, however, to come to the Cabinet of that day, 3 August. He saw Lloyd George before it and told him he had sent in his resignation. Lloyd George seemed astonished: 'But if you go, it will put us who don't go, in a great hole.' Morley goes on to state:

My impression is that he must have begun the day with one of his customary morning talks with the splendid *condottiere* [Churchill] at the Admiralty, had revised his calculations . . . and found in the German ultimatum a sufficiently plausible excuse.[3]

However, Lloyd George's change of front was much more probably connected with the swing round in public opinion which he so vividly describes as taking place during the first four days of August, 1914.

The war had leapt into popularity between Saturday and Monday. On Saturday the Governor of the Bank of England called on me, as Chancellor of the Exchequer, to inform me on behalf of the City that the financial and trading interests in the City of London were totally opposed to our intervening in the war. By Monday there was a complete change. The threatened invasion of Belgium had set the nation on fire from sea to sea.[4]

Accordingly a complete change took place also in Lloyd George, who had known for several days that the Belgian question had arisen but writes as if this were not the case:

Had the question of defending the neutrality and integrity of Belgium been raised there would not have been a dissentient voice on that issue. Lord Morley and John Burns might conceivably have stood out. Of that I am not convinced, had a decision on that point alone been reached in time as a means of circumscribing the area of war and possibly of persuading Germany of the futility of waging it at all under conditions which would

---

[1] DF. 3. XI, 626.   [2] A. Chamberlain, *Down the Years,* p. 104.
[3] Morley, pp. 23-4.   [4] Lloyd George, I, pp. 65-6.

have been unfavorable to her preconcerted military schemes. But such a proposal was never submitted to our judgment. . . . The policy I urged upon my colleagues was not one merely of passive non-intervention. . . . I proposed that we should take immediate steps to increase and strengthen our army . . . so that . . . none of the belligerents could afford to disregard our appeal. Had Germany respected the integrity of Belgium this would have been the wisest course to pursue. . . . France . . . . could have concentrated all her strength on defending a frontier of 250 miles protected by formidable fortresses. . . . Had Britain been able to throw into the scale a well-equipped army of a million men to support her fleet, Germany would have hesitated before she rejected terms of peace.[1]

But all this is wisdom after the event. The documents show that the question of Belgium came into the foreground as early as 29 July[2] and Lloyd George told Morley on 3 August that 'the news of Germany bullying Belgium' had changed Runciman's line and his own. Though this change had no direct bearing on the course of events, it marks how the momentum of the crisis swept aside not only Lloyd George's opportunist pacifism, itself of little worth in the light of his bellicose speech at the time of Agadir, but also the more sincerely held convictions of the other Ministers who remained in the Cabinet. Only Burns and Morley left it.

Morley describes what went on at this Cabinet meeting where Asquith announced not only the resignations of Burns and Morley but the further prospect that Simon and Beauchamp would leave the Cabinet. It also seemed probable that a majority in the Cabinet and of the Liberals in the House leant in that direction, too. Asquith was only prevented from taking the same line by the fact that 'nothing would induce him to separate from Grey' and that he did not think the Conservatives would be capable of dealing with the crisis. The idea of a coalition had occurred to him, 'but Coalitions have hardly ever turned out well in our history'. Morley then declined to withdraw his resignation. 'Simon followed, but with much emotion, quivering lip and tears in his eyes. He was even firmer than I [Morley] was.'[3] Asquith's diary for 3 August records:

We had a rather moving scene in which everyone all round said something, Lloyd George making a strong appeal to them not to go, or at least to delay it. Anyhow, they all agreed to say nothing today and to sit in their accustomed places in the House.[4]

Simon and Beauchamp did more. They withdrew their resignations, yielding to the counsels of Asquith, who the same day wrote to the King:

[1] Lloyd George, I, pp. 71-3.
[2] See p. 410.
[3] Morley, pp. 24-7.
[4] Asquith, *Memories and Reflections,* II, p. 20.

The Cabinet met today. Its time was exclusively occupied with a consideration of the diplomatic situation and of the statement to be made in the
afternoon in the House of Commons by Sir E. Grey. That statement presents,
exactly and exhaustively, the case put forward by the Government as the
result of the full and anxious Cabinet consultations of the last three days.[1]

3. *Grey's speech in the House of Commons on the afternoon of 3 August.*

The Cabinet meeting ended at 2 p. m., and at 3 p. m. Grey rose
in the House to make his speech on the line the Government
proposed to take. Its main points are as follows:

We have consistently worked with a single mind, with all the earnestness
in our power, to preserve peace. . . . In the present crisis . . . there has
been a disposition—at any rate in some quarters on which I will not dwell—
to force things rapidly to an issue, to the great risk of peace. . . . I do not
want to dwell on that . . . and to say where the blame seems to us to lie,
which Powers were most in favor of peace, which were most disposed to
risk or endanger peace, because I would like the House to approach this
crisis in which we are now from the point of view of British interests, British
honor, and British obligations, free from all passion as to why peace has
not been preserved. We shall publish Papers as soon as we can regarding
what took place last week when we were working for peace. . . . I come
first, now, to the question of British obligations. . . . The Triple *Entente*
was not an alliance—it was a diplomatic group. The House will remember
that in 1908 there was a crisis, also a Balkan crisis, originating in the annexation of Bosnia and Herzegovina. The Russian Minister, M. Izvolsky, came
to London. . . . I told him . . . I did not consider that public opinion
in this country would justify us in promising to give anything more than
diplomatic support. . . . In this present crisis, up till yesterday, we have
also given no promise of anything more than diplomatic support. . . . I
must go back to the first Moroccan crisis of 1906. That was the time of the
Algeciras Conference. . . . I was asked the question whether, if that crisis
developed into war between France and Germany, we would give armed
support. . . . I said, in my opinion, if war was forced upon France then on
the subject of Morocco—a question which had just been the subject of
agreement between this country and France . . . —in my view public
opinion in this country would have rallied to the material support of France.
. . . I expressed that view . . . almost in the same words to the French
Ambassador and the German Ambassador. . . . That position was accepted
by the French Government, but they said to me. . . . 'You will not be able
to give that support, even if you wish to give it when the time comes, unless
some conversations have already taken place between naval and military
experts.' There was force in that. . . . I authorized these conversations to
take place. . . . As I have told the House, upon that occasion a General
Election was in prospect. I had to take the responsibility of doing that
without the Cabinet. . . . I consulted Sir Henry Campbell-Bannerman, the

[1] Spender, II, p. 82.

Prime Minister, Lord Haldane, Secretary of State for War, and the present Prime Minister, who was then Chancellor of the Exchequer . . . and they authorized that on the distinct understanding that it left the hands of the Government free whenever the crisis arose. . . . The Agadir crisis came [in 1911] and throughout that I took precisely the same line that had been taken in 1906. But subsequently, in 1912, . . . it was decided that we ought to have a definite understanding in writing . . . that these conversations which took place were not binding upon the freedom of either Government; and on 22 November 1912 I wrote to the French Ambassador. . . . 'We have agreed that consultation between experts is not and ought not to be regarded as an engagement that commits either Government to action in a contingency that has not yet arisen and may never arise.' . . . The present crisis . . . has not originated as regards anything with which we had a special agreement with France. . . . It has originated in a dispute between Austria and Serbia. . . . No Government and no country has less desire to be involved in war over a dispute with Austria and Serbia than the Government and the country of France. They are involved in it because of their obligation of honor under the definite alliance with Russia. . . . We are not parties to the Franco-Russian Alliance. We do not even know the terms of that Alliance. . . . I now come to what I think the situation requires of us. For many years we have had a long-standing friendship with France. . . . But how far that friendship entails obligation . . . let every man look into his own heart, and his own feelings, and construe the extent of the obligation for himself. I construe it myself as I feel it, but I do not wish to urge upon anyone else more than their feelings dictate as to what they should feel about the obligation. The House, individually and collectively, may judge for itself. I speak my personal view, and I have given the House my own feeling in the matter. The French Fleet is now in the Mediterranean, and the northern and western coasts of France are absolutely undefended. The French Fleet being concentrated in the Mediterranean, the situation is very different from what it used to be, because the friendship which has grown up between the two countries has given them a sense of security that there was nothing to be feared from us. . . . My own feeling is that if a foreign fleet, engaged in a war which France had not sought, and in which she had not been the aggressor, came down the English Channel and bombarded and battered the undefended coasts of France, we could not stand aside and see this going on practically within sight of our eyes, with our arms folded, looking on dispassionately, doing nothing! . . . But I also want to look at the matter without sentiment, and from the point of view of British interests. . . . Let us suppose the French Fleet is withdrawn from the Mediterranean; . . . let us assume that out of that come consequences unforeseen which make it necessary at a sudden moment that in defense of vital British interests we should go to war; let us assume that Italy, who is now neutral, because, as I understand, she considers that this war is an aggressive war . . . departs from her attitude of neutrality at a time when we are forced . . . to fight; what then will be the position in the Mediterranean? . . . We have not kept a fleet in the Mediterranean which is equal to dealing alone with a combination of other fleets in the Mediterranean. . . . In these compelling circumstances yesterday afternoon I gave to the French Ambassador the following statement: 'I am authorized to give an assurance that if the German Fleet comes into the Channel or through the North Sea to undertake hostile operations against the French coasts or shipping, the British Fleet will give all the protection in its power. This assurance is, of course, subject to the policy of His Majesty's Government receiving the support of Parliament, and must not be taken as binding His Majesty's Government to take any action until the above contingency of action by the German Fleet takes place.' I read that to the House . . . as binding us to take aggressive action should that contingency arise. . . . I understand that the German Government would be prepared, if we would pledge ourselves to neutrality, to agree that its fleet would not attack the northern coast of France. . . . But it is far too narrow an engagement for us. There is the more serious consideration— becoming more serious every hour—there is the question of the neutrality of Belgium. . . . The governing factor is the treaty of 1839. . . . In 1870, when there was war between France and Germany, the question of the neutrality of Belgium arose. . . . Prince Bismarck gave an assurance . . . that the German Confederation and its allies would respect the neutrality of Belgium, it being always understood that that neutrality would be respected by the other belligerent Powers. . . . The people who laid down the attitude of the British Government were Lord Granville in the House of Lords, and Mr. Gladstone in the House of Commons. Lord Granville on 8 August 1870 used these words: 'We might have explained to the country and to foreign nations that we did not think this country was bound either morally or internationally or that its interests were concerned in the maintenance of the neutrality of Belgium. . . . It is a course which Her Majesty's Government thought it impossible to adopt . . . with any due regard to the country's honor and to the country's interests'. . . . The honor and interests are, at least, as strong today as in 1870.

Grey then informed the House of his inquiry whether the French and German Governments respectively were prepared to respect the neutrality of Belgium, of the immediate French assurances, the German evasive reply and the news of a German ultimatum to Belgium. He read out King Albert's appeal to King George for 'diplomatic intervention to safeguard the integrity of Belgium', and went on to quote Gladstone's memorable words:

'We have an interest in the independence of Belgium which is wider than that which we may have in the literal operation of the guarantee. It is found in the answer to the question whether . . . this country . . . would quietly stand by and witness the perpetration of the direst crime that ever stained the pages of history, and thus become participators in the sin?'

If—continued Grey—it be the case that there has been anything in the nature of an ultimatum to Belgium, asking her to compromise or violate her neutrality, whatever may have been offered to her in return, her independence is gone if that holds. If her independence goes, the independence of Holland will follow. I ask the House, from the point of view of British interests, to consider what may be at stake. If France is beaten in a struggle of life and death, beaten to her knees, loses her position as a great Power, becomes subordinate to the will and power of one greater than herself—consequences which I do not anticipate, because I am sure that France has the power to defend herself with all the energy and ability and patriotism which she has shown so often—still if that were to happen, and if Belgium fell under the same dominating influence, and then Holland, and then Denmark, then would not Mr. Gladstone's words come true, that just opposite to us there would be a common interest against unmeasured aggrandizement of any Power?

It may be said, I suppose, that we might stand aside, husband our strength, and then, whatever happened in the course of this war, at the end of it intervene with effect to put things right, and to adjust them to our own point of view. . . . I do not believe, for a moment, that at the end of this war, even if we stood aside and remained aside, we should be in a position, a material position, to use our force decisively to undo what had happened in the course of the war, to prevent the whole of the West of Europe opposite to us—if that had been the result of the war—falling under the domination of a single Power, and I am sure that our moral position would be such as to have lost us all respect. . . . I think it is due to the House to say that we have taken no engagement yet with regard to sending an expeditionary armed force out of the country. Mobilization of the Fleet has taken place; mobilization of the Army is taking place; but we have as yet taken no engagement, because I do feel that, in the case of a European conflagration, such as this is, unprecedented, with our enormous responsibilities in India and other parts of the Empire, or in countries in British occupation, with all the unknown factors, we must take very carefully into consideration the use which we make of sending an Expeditionary Force out of the country until we know how we stand. . . . I have put to the House and dwelt at length upon how vital is the condition of the neutrality of Belgium. What other policy is there before the House? There is but one way in which the Government could make certain at the present moment of keeping outside this war, and that would be that it should immediately issue a proclamation of unconditional neutrality. We cannot do that. We have made the commitment to France that I have read to the House. . . . The Belgian Treaty obligations, the possible position in the Mediterranean, with damage to British interests, and what may happen to France from our failure to support France—if we were to say that all these things mattered nothing . . . we should, I believe, sacrifice our respect and good name and reputation before the world, and should not escape the most serious and grave economic consequences. . . . We believe we shall have the support of the House at large in proceeding to whatever the consequences may be. . . . I have put the vital facts before the House, and if, as seems not improbable, we are forced, and rapidly forced, to take our stand upon these issues, then I believe, when the country realizes what is at stake, what the real issues are, the magnitude of the impending dangers in the West of Europe, which I have endeavored to describe to the House, we shall be supported throughout, not only by the House of Commons, but by the determination, the resolution, the courage, and the endurance of the whole country.

'No distinction of phrase or thought', comments Lloyd George. In his *Twenty-five Years* Grey produces a series of very much more forceful arguments to prove the necessity of British intervention[1] than appear in his speech of 3 August, where he refrained from using even the documents already at his disposal. His speech only lightly touched on the German request for neutrality. Had he quoted the actual German text and his own reply, as did Asquith on 6 August,[2] the effect would have been very different. In fact he tells us:

> At first it was in my mind to read to the House Bethmann Hollweg's bid for our neutrality, and the reply made to it; but this was deliberately discarded. To read that would tend to stir indignation, and the House ought to come to its decisions on grounds of weight, not of passion.[3]

The argument is specious. The German request for neutrality had a bearing which it was vital for the House to know. The present writer, in reading the speech, has the impression that in spite of everything Grey still showed, as he had shown all through the crisis, a certain hesitation in shouldering the full burden of his own responsibilities and refrained from giving the House a strong lead in the hope of getting a vote in favor of war without the exercise of pressure. Hence his insistence on the fact that the Government had not tied the hands of Parliament, his declaration that he did not contemplate the dispatch to the Continent of an Expeditionary Force, his silence on the behavior of Germany and Austria, who had rejected all suggestions for conciliation, his omission of much else that would have been relevant. It was surely a strange appeal to say that he did not wish 'to urge upon anyone else more than their feelings dictate as to what they should feel about the obligations' to help France! In a matter of such capital importance it was the Government's duty to make its own attitude plain and ask the House to support it. Nevertheless, Grey's sincerity and simplicity, the restraint of his language, the force of his arguments, the goodness of his cause, of which most of his hearers were convinced before they came to hear him, all combined to earn him the enthusiastic applause of the great majority of both Liberals and Conservatives and silenced the handful of pacifists.

Before the House rose Grey received a note from the Belgian Legation summarizing the German ultimatum and the Belgian categoric rejection, which he read out after his speech was over. In his book he remarks: 'If this communication had been received before I went to the House it would . . . certainly have strengthened the statement very much.'[4] It is not clear why he did not get it in time, seeing that it figures in the *British Documents* as arriving earlier than a telegram from

---

[1] Grey, II, Chap. XVIII.   [2] See pp. 512-14.
[3] Grey, II, p. 14.   [4] Grey, II, p. 17.

Villiers which reached the Foreign Office at 10.55 a. m. on 3 August, four hours before Grey's speech began, and gave definite news of the German ultimatum, adding the fact not mentioned in Grey's actual speech that 'Belgium had refused categorically'.[1] But even if not fully informed of the events in Brussels, the House realized that it was not a question of going to war over the Austro-Serbian quarrel, or even purely for the sake of Belgium, but rather that the outbreak of a European conflagration raised questions of life and death for all the Great Powers and called for unlimited sacrifice from each one of them. Strange to say, Lichnowsky did not realize the full bearing of Grey's speech. He, who from the first had been so clear-sighted, shrank at the critical moment from facing the facts and still clung to vain hopes, partly perhaps because of lack of plain speaking from Grey. Beginning with his telegram of 1 August foreshadowing English neutrality,[2] Lichnowsky's dispatches of the last days show him tragically pursuing a chimera. While Grey was still delivering his speech on 3 August Lichnowsky sent off details of its statements on the defense of the French coast,[3] and at 10 p. m. he gave his impression of the speech as a whole as indicating

that the English Government for the time being does not contemplate intervening in the conflict and abandoning its neutrality. . . . In my opinion we can receive the speech with satisfaction and regard it as a big success that England is not immediately joining her *Entente* associates. . . . This attitude would be greatly facilitated if Belgian territory could be evacuated again in a short time and without fighting.[4]

When next morning Lichnowsky read the speech as a whole he realized he had been too optimistic, but even then only went so far as to telegraph:

I must modify my opinion of yesterday in the sense that I do not think we can much longer reckon on the neutrality of England. . . . What form British intervention will take and whether it will be immediate, I cannot judge. But I do not see how . . . the British Government can retreat unless we are in a position to evacuate Belgian territory with the utmost dispatch. . . . The news received yesterday of the invasion of Belgium by German troops has caused a complete reversal of public opinion to our disadvantage. The appeal of the King of the Belgians with its moving words has greatly deepened this impression.[5]

4. *The sending of the English ultimatum to Berlin.*

It cannot be ruled out that Grey's inaction after his speech led Lichnowsky into misjudging the situation and failing to realize that

---

[1] BD. XI, 521. [2] DD. III, 562. [3] DD. IV, 784.
[4] DD IV, 801. [5] DD. IV, 820.

war was a matter of hours. One would have expected that as soon as the speech was over it would have been followed on the 3rd by a stern intimation to Berlin not to allow its troops to enter Belgium and a warning that England would regard the violation of Belgian neutrality as a *casus belli*. Churchill narrates that when Grey had ended his speech

neither he nor I could remain long in the House. Outside I asked him, 'What happens now?' 'Now,' he said, 'we shall send them an ultimatum to stop the invasion of Belgium within twenty-four hours.'[1]

But the ultimatum did not go off until 2 p. m. on 4 August, and in the event the German Government was given only five hours in which to reply. The moment to give the stern warning would have been that very evening of the 3rd, before the German invasion had begun and when there was still time to call it off if Germany were anxious to avoid English intervention at all cost. When he came round to the belief that the invasion of Belgium was imminent, Grey had the support of Churchill, Lloyd George and Asquith.[2] But even without this, why did he delay so long in notifying the enemy of what he would do? The Schlieffen plan fixed the beginning of the invasion for the morning of the third day of mobilization, in this case 4 August, so that on the evening of 3 August or even as late as the small hours of 4 August there would still have been time to stop it. After that it was too late.

It may be objected that before sending Germany an ultimatum the consent of the Cabinet would have had to be obtained, but on the following day this formality seems to have been omitted.[3] After Grey's speech another Cabinet was held on the evening of the 3rd. The subject discussed at it we learn from Cambon's dispatch of 12.17 a. m. on 4 August:

Sir Edward Grey told me confidentially that at this evening's Cabinet it was decided that instruction will be sent tomorrow to the English Embassy at Berlin to ask the German Government to withdraw its ultimatum to Belgium; 'if they refuse,' added the Foreign Secretary, 'it will be war'.[4]

This finds confirmation in Asquith's *Memories and Inflections:*

On Monday 3 August, it was decided to dispatch a telegram to Germany requesting her to give us an assurance that the neutrality of Belgium would be respected.[5]

This means that on the evening of 3 August what was under discussion was not something in the nature of an ultimatum but only a request to Berlin not to invade Belgium. And what is more, the decision

---

[1] Churchill, I, p. 220.
[2] Churchill, I, p. 220; Lloyd George, I, pp. 73-4; Asquith, *Genesis,* p. 215.
[3] See p. 494.   [4] DF. 3. XI, 712.
[5] Asquith, *op. cit.,* II, p. 10.

was taken to dispatch this request not that same evening, as would have been natural and necessary, but the following morning. One might suspect that the intention was to wait until Germany declared war on France, lest England find herself at war before France. But this cannot be the reason because on the evening of the 3rd London already knew that Germany had that very evening sent an ultimatum to France.[1] And even had it been the reason for delaying the ultimatum all hesitation should have vanished next morning. But what went off at 9.30 a. m. on the 4th instead of an ultimatum was a telegram to Goschen telling him of the German ultimatum to Belgium and the Belgian refusal to yield, and ending mildly:

His Majesty's Government are bound to protest against this violation of a treaty to which Germany is a party in common with themselves, and must request an assurance that the demand made upon Belgium will not be proceeded with, and that her neutrality will be respected by Germany. You should ask for an immediate reply.[2]

No hint of a threat of war!

Had Lichnowsky known of this document when about the same time he was telegraphing his own impressions to Berlin he would have expressed himself still more optimistically than he did. Even assuming that this was the right tone for a first approach to Germany, it ought to have been sent off at least fourteen hours earlier, i.e., about 7.30 p. m. on the 3rd. It is, of course, true that no words would have restrained the German Government from violating Belgian neutrality after war had been declared against France when the only plan for a war with France was the Schlieffen plan. But of this London was then in ignorance and there was a general hope that Germany would not violate Belgium. All the more reason for prompt action lest fresh events frustrate that hope. One seeks in vain in Grey's memoirs for an explanation of his feeble and belated request to Berlin, although one will be discussed later on which may seem to fit the facts.[3]

We must now turn our attention to Grey's activities on the morning of 4 August. After the telegram to Goschen he at 10.45 a. m. circularized instructions to the Ministers at Brussels, the Hague, and Christiania:

You should inform Government to which you are accredited that if pressure is applied to them by Germany to induce them to depart from neutrality, His Majesty's Government expect that they will resist by any means in their power, and that His Majesty's Government will support them in offering such resistance, and that His Majesty's Government in this event are prepared to join Russia and France, if desired, in offering to the Government to which you are accredited at once an

---

[1] BD. XI, 563.　　　　[2] BD. XI, 573.　　　　[3] See pp. 520-1.

alliance for the purpose of resisting use of force by Germany against them, and a guarantee to maintain their independence and integrity in future years.[1]

The words 'an alliance' were toned down to 'common action' by a telegram of 12.30 p. m. Moreover, Paris and St. Petersburg were asked to take similar steps at the three northern capitals[2] and 'to join His Majesty's Government in their guarantee to respect the integrity and independence of Sweden now and hereafter if the latter remains neutral during the war'.[3] But at 2 p. m. Grey changed his mind and cancelled all these instructions,[4] though Villiers had already carried out his and reported at 6.38 p. m. the 'lively satisfaction' with which they had been received.[5]

Grey's change of mind was no doubt due to a fresh development, the news received at 11 a. m. from the Belgian Legation of Germany's having notified Brussels that she 'would carry out, if necessary by armed force, the measures announced'.[6] At 11.20 a. m. came confirmation in a telegram from Villiers stating that

as the Belgian Government have declined the well-intentioned proposals submitted to them by the Imperial Government, the latter will, deeply to their regret, be compelled to carry out, if necessary by force of arms, the measures considered indispensable in view of the French menaces.[7]

There was thus no more doubt of Germany's intentions, and they were confirmed by a telegram from Jagow of 10.20 a. m. on 4 August, a copy of which was handed to the Foreign Office by Lichnowsky at 12 noon.

Please dispel any mistrust that may subsist on the part of the British Government with regard to our intentions by repeating most positively formal assurance that, even in the case of armed conflict with Belgium, Germany will, under no pretence whatever, annex Belgian territory. Sincerity of this declaration is borne out by fact that we solemnly pledged our word to Holland strictly to respect her neutrality. It is obvious that we could not profitably annex Belgian territory without making at the same time territorial acquisitions at the expense of Holland. Please impress on Sir E. Grey that German army could not be exposed to French attack across Belgium, which was planned according to absolutely unimpeachable information. Germany had consequently to disregard Belgian neutrality, it being for her a question of life or death to prevent French advance.[8]

This appeal, drafted in English by Stumm and telegraphed *en clair* so that it might reach Grey without delay, was in fact delivered a little more than an hour and a half after dispatch. It betrays the anxiety of the German leaders about the threat of English intervention and is minuted by Stumm: 'Dispatched at the urgent wish of General von

[1] BD. XI, 580.   [2] BD. XI, 578.   [3] BD. XI, 576.
[4] BD. XI, 595.   [5] BD. XI, 631.   [6] BD. XI, 581.
[7] BD. XI, 584.   [8] DD. IV, 810; BD. XI, 587.

Moltke.' Now Moltke had foreseen not only Belgian resistance but also English intervention. It looks as if at the moment of launching his plan of war he perceived how dangerous it was and therefore how mistaken. Indeed, in his Memorandum to the Foreign Ministry of 2 August he had already written:

> It is not our object to smash *zertrümmern)* France, but only to defeat her. The neutrality of England is of such importance to us that this concession can be made to her.[1]

Another point worthy of note is that, to strengthen the appeal, Stumm resorts to an argument which reflects little credit on its authors. England need not fear, it suggests, that we shall break this new engagement as we have broken the one given in 1839 and recently renewed. Even if we wanted, we could not do so because of the pledge we have given to Holland (as if that could not be broken too!). The end of the message, motivating the German invasion of Belgium by the need to forestall a French attack, may have been meant as a corrective to Bethmann's telegram of the previous evening to Lichnowsky which, as we have seen, the latter never communicated to Grey, while he sent on the new appeal at once.[2]

Such an appeal was not likely to persuade Grey not to send the ultimatum. And it is a fact not to be forgotten that England sent her ultimatum to Germany (i.e., decided to go to war in support of Belgium) before knowing whether the Brussels Government was willing to be succored by the guarantor Powers. Her consent, communicated in a telegram from Villiers, only reached the Foreign Office at 12.50 a. m. on 5 August, whereas the ultimatum to Germany left London at 2. p. m. on the 4th.[3]

---

[1] DD. III, 662.   [2] DD. IV, 790. See p. 480.

[3] Barnes maintains that the ultimatum was sent only after Grey received the circular letter of Davignon to the Ministers of England, France and Russia appealing for the aid of the guarantor Powers: 'On 3 August he [Grey] was thrown into a panic when he learned that the Belgian Government appealed to England merely for diplomatic intervention against Germany . . . Belgium had also given definite information that it preferred to attempt to resist Germany unaided. . . . [On the 4th] he practically went to the extreme of demanding that Belgium ask for military aid of the *Entente.* . . . The Belgian Government took the hint and replied, "... There should be concerted and joint action to oppose the forcible measures taken by Germany against Belgium". As soon as this reply was received from Belgium, Grey breathed easily for the first time since 2 August' (Barnes, pp. 555–6). Barnes has to write his history this way to fit his thesis, but the documents belie him. To prove that the English ultimatum was dispatched after the arrival of Davignon's letter, he quotes No. 40 of the *First Belgian Grey Book* which bears no indication of the hour of dispatch and omits Villiers's telegram forwarding Davignon's letter, which bears the indication that it was dispatched from Brussels at 4 p. m. (see note on p. 471) arriving in London at 12.50 a. m. on 5 August, when not only the ultimatum had been sent, but war had begun. Moreover it is a fact that Davignon's letter was not in the least written in answer to Grey's offer. The Belgian Government's decision to ask the aid of the guarantor Powers was taken immediately on learning of the German invasion of Belgian territory.

Asquith's diary for 4 August relates:

We had an interesting Cabinet, as we got the news that the Germans had entered Belgium[1] and had announced that if necessary they would push their way through by force of arms. This simplifies matters. So we sent the Germans an ultimatum to expire at midnight requesting them to give a like assurance with the French that they would respect Belgian neutrality. They have invented a story that the French were meditating an invasion of Belgium and that they were only acting in self-defense, a manifest and transparent lie.[2]

It would be a mistake to take these words as meaning that the ultimatum was under discussion at the Cabinet of 4 August. Asquith nowhere expressly says so, and Churchill actually denies it:

Before the Cabinet separated on Monday morning, Sir Edward Grey had procured a predominant assent to the principal points and general tone of his statement to Parliament that afternoon. Formal sanction had been given to the already completed mobilization of the Fleet and to the immediate mobilization of the Army. No decision had been taken to send an ultimatum to Germany or to declare war on Germany, still less to send an army to France. These supreme decisions were never taken at any Cabinet. They were compelled by the force of events, and rest on the authority of the Prime Minister.[3]

Probably at the evening Cabinet of 3 August, not mentioned by Churchill, Grey and Asquith were given a free hand to take the decisions 'compelled by the force of events'. Spender notes:

There is curiously no letter to the King recording the Cabinet of 4 August, but the recollection of the survivors is that the drafting of the ultimatum was left to Asquith and Grey, and that the consequential steps were taken for granted.[4]

This shows that, had Grey so wished, he could very well have done on the evening of the 3rd what he waited to do until 2 p. m. on 4 August, i.e., have sent on the 3rd the telegram to Goschen which he sent only on the 4th:

We hear that Germany has addressed note to Belgian Minister for Foreign Affairs stating that German Government will be compelled to carry out, if necessary by force of arms, the measures considered indispensable. We are also informed that Belgian territory has been violated at Gemmenich. In

[1] Villiers telegraphed the news at 1 p. m. and confirmed it at 3.25 p. m. by telegrams reaching London at 4.20 p. m. and 7.10 p. m. respectively (BD. XI, 611, 624). But the Foreign Office had learnt of it much earlier, so that Grey was able to make use of it in the ultimatum sent off at 2 p. m. He probably heard it from the Belgian Legation to which Davignon had telegraphed it (*First Belgian Grey Book,* 39).

[2] Asquith, *Memories and Reflections,* II, p. 21.

[3] Churchill, I, p. 220.

[4] Spender, II, p. 93.

these circumstances, and in view of the fact that Germany declined to give the same assurance respecting Belgium as France gave last week in reply to our request made simultaneously at Berlin and Paris, we must repeat that request, and ask that a satisfactory reply to it and to my telegram[1] of this morning be received here by 12 o'clock tonight. If not, you are instructed to ask for your passports and to say that His Majesty's Government feel bound to take all steps in their power to uphold the neutrality of Belgium and the observance of a treaty to which Germany is as much a party as ourselves.[2]

5. *The delivery of the ultimatum.*

While this telegram was on its way the Chancellor was making his speech in the Reichstag justifying the German invasion of Belgium by the need to forestall a French invasion and saying that 'as long as England remains neutral our fleet will not attack the northern coast of France and that we will not violate the territorial integrity and independence of Belgium'.[3] This passage of the speech was telegraphed at 4 p. m. to Lichnowsky *en clair,* evidently in the hope of its being intercepted. And in fact it was the censor, and not Lichnowsky, who communicated it to the Foreign Office.[4] Meanwhile Goschen had received Grey's telegram of 9.30 a. m.[5], and called on Jagow that afternoon of the 4th to inquire in the name of his Government whether the Imperial Government would refrain from violating Belgian neutrality. His lengthy report of 6 August describes the events of that memorable afternoon.

Herr von Jagow at once replied that he was sorry to say that his answer must be 'No', as, in consequence of the German troops having crossed the frontier that morning, Belgian neutrality had already been violated. Herr von Jagow again went into the reasons why the Imperial Government had been obliged to take this step—namely, that they had to advance into France by the quickest and easiest way, so as to be able to get well ahead with their operations and endeavor to strike some decisive blow as early as possible. It was a matter of life and death for them, as if they had gone by the more southern route they could not have hoped, in view of the paucity of roads, and the strength of the fortresses, to have got through without formidable opposition, entailing great loss of time. This loss of time would have meant time gained by the Russians for bringing up their troops to the German frontier. . . .

During the afternoon I received your telegram and . . . informed the Secretary of State for Foreign Affairs that unless the Imperial Government could give the assurance by 12 o'clock that night that they would proceed no further with their violation of the Belgian frontier . . . I had been instructed to demand my passports. . . . Herr von Jagow replied that to his great regret he could give no other answer. . . . I gave His Excellency a

---

[1] BD. XI, 573. See p. 491.   [2] BD. XI, 594.   [3] See p. 224.
[4] BD. XI, 612.   [5] BD. XI, 573.

paraphrase of your telegram . . . and asked him whether . . . it were not possible even at the last moment that their answer should be reconsidered. He replied that if the time given were even twenty-four hours his answer must be the same. I said that in that case I should have to demand my passports. This interview would have taken place at about 7 o'clock. In a short conversation which ensued Herr von Jagow expressed his poignant regret at the crumbling of his entire policy and that of the Chancellor, which had been to make friends with Great Britain and then, through Great Britain to get closer to France. . . .

I then said that I should like to go and see the Chancellor. . . . He begged me to do so. I found the Chancellor very agitated. His Excellency at once began a harangue which lasted for about twenty minutes. He said that the step taken by His Majesty's Government was terrible to a degree, just for the word 'neutrality', a word which in war-time had so often been disregarded —just for a scrap of paper, Great Britain was going to make war on a kindred nation who desired nothing better than to be friends with her. All his efforts in that direction had been rendered useless by this last terrible step, and the policy to which, as I knew, he had devoted himself since his accession to office, had tumbled down like a house of cards. What we had done was unthinkable, it was like striking a man from behind while he was fighting for his life against two assailants. He held Great Britain responsible for all the terrible events that might happen! I protested strongly against that statement and said that in the same way as he and Herr von Jagow wished me to understand that for strategical reasons it was a matter of life and death for Germany to advance through Belgium and violate her neutrality, so I would wish him to understand that it was, so to speak, a matter of 'life and death' for the honor of Great Britain that she should keep her solemn engagement to do her utmost to defend Belgium's neutrality if attacked. . . . The Chancellor said: 'But at what price will that compact have been kept. Has the British Government thought of that?' I hinted to His Excellency, as plainly as I could that fear of consequences could hardly be regarded as an excuse for breaking solemn engagements, but His Excellency was so excited, so evidently overcome by the news of our action and so little disposed to hear reason, that I refrained from adding fuel to the flame by further argument.[1]

Goschen on his side must have been deeply distressed, as we can gather from Bethmann Hollweg's subsequent account of their interview, which ends:

Sir Edward Goschen, who was so much struck by my excitement, ought at least to have finished the story and told that, as he said goodbye, he burst into tears and asked to be allowed to remain awhile in my anteroom because he could not let himself be seen in such a state by the Chancery staff.[2]

If it was strange that an Englishman should thus burst into tears, tears were also shed in Sazonov's room at St. Petersburg, by Lichnowsky and Asquith in London, and by others elsewhere, as we shall

---

[1] BD. XI, 671.   [2] Bethmann, I, p. 180.

see. If Below-Saleske did not actually burst into tears, he looked as if he were about to faint when handing the German ultimatum to Davignon. Goschen's emotion entirely redounds to his honor, while Bethmann's chagrin at the failure of his schemes, vented in the words 'a scrap of paper', has ever since been regarded by world opinion as the loss of a battle for Germany.

After Goschen had left, the Wilhelmstrasse must have been in some doubt whether his request for his passports was equivalent to a declaration of war. In Grey's ultimatum the word 'war' did not occur, but only the euphemistic phrase 'take all steps in their power to uphold the neutrality of Belgium'. To clear the matter up

at about 9.30 p. m. Herr von Zimmermann, the Under-Secretary of State for Foreign Affairs, came to see me. . . . He asked me casually whether a demand for passports was equivalent to a declaration of war. I said . . . that there were many cases where diplomatic relations had been broken off and nevertheless war had not ensued, but that in this case he would have seen from my instructions . . . that His Majesty's Government expected an answer to a definite question by 12 o'clock that night, and that in default of a satisfactory answer they would be forced to take such steps as their engagements required. Herr Zimmermann said that that was in fact a declaration of war. . . . In the meantime, after Herr Zimmermann left me, a flying sheet, issued by the *Berliner Tageblatt,* was circulated stating that Great Britain had declared war against Germany. The immediate result of this news was the assemblage of an exceedingly excited and unruly mob before His Majesty's Embassy. . . . When the crash of glass and the landing of cobble-stones into the drawing-room, where we were all sitting, warned us that the situation was getting unpleasant, I telephoned to the Foreign Ministry . . , and an adequate force of mounted police, sent with great promptness, very soon cleared the street. . . . Herr von Jagow came to see me and expressed his most heartfelt regrets at what had occurred. . . . On the following morning, 5 August, the Emperor sent one of his aides-de-camp to me with the following message: 'The Emperor has charged me to express to Your Excellency his regret for the occurrences of last night but to tell you at the same time that you will gather from these occurrences an idea of the feelings of his people respecting the action of Great Britain in joining with other nations against her old allies of Waterloo. His Majesty also begs that you will tell the King that he has been proud of the titles of British Field-Marshal and British Admiral, but that in consequence of what has occurred he must now, at once, divest himself of those titles'.[1]

On the morning of 6 August Goschen left the German capital. While these events were taking place on the evening of 4 August at Berlin, Asquith in London was giving news to the House of the sending of the ultimatum.

[1] BD. XI, 671.

The House—he writes—took the fresh news today very calmly and with a good deal of dignity, and we got through all the business by half-past four.[1]

When Asquith returned to his room at the House of Commons he was joined by his wife, Margot, who writes:

'So it is all up ?' I said. He answered without looking at me: 'Yes, it's all up.' I sat down beside him. . . . Henry sat at his writing-table, leaning back, with a pen in his hand. . . . I got up and leant my head against his; we could not speak for tears.[2]

These episodes are full of significance. Whether scenes of tears or of temper, they characterize the men and their attitudes. They throw light on the inmost feelings of those whose actions brought so much tragedy upon the world. Grey was as much in despair as Asquith when at 3 p. m. on 4 August he received the call of the United States Ambassador, W. H. Page.

Overwrought the Foreign Secretary may have been . . . but there was nothing flurried or excited in his manner; his whole bearing was calm and dignified, his speech quiet and restrained; he uttered not one bitter word against Germany, but his measured accents had a sureness, a conviction of the justice of his course, that went home in almost deadly fashion . . . if there was one note in his bearing that predominated all others, it was a solemn and quiet sincerity. . . . There was a touch of finality in his voice. . . . 'Germany has violated the neutrality of Belgium. That means bad faith. . . . It will not end with Belgium. Next will come Holland, and, after Holland, Denmark. This very morning the Swedish Minister informed me that Germany had made overtures to Sweden to come in on Germany's side. . . . England would be forever contemptible if it should sit by and see this treaty violated. . . . We have told Germany that, if this assault on Belgium's neutrality is not reversed, England will declare war.' There was a moment's pause, and then the Foreign Secretary spoke again: 'Yet we must remember that there are two Germanys. There is the Germany of men like ourselves—of men like Lichnowsky and Jagow [!!]. Then there is the Germany of men of the war party. The war party has got the upper hand. At this point Sir Edward's eyes filled with tears. 'Thus the efforts of a lifetime go for nothing. I feel like a man who has wasted his life.' . . . 'I came away', the Ambassador afterward said, 'with a sort of stunned sense of the impending ruin of half the world.'[3]

6. London vainly awaits the German reply; proclamation of the 'state of war'.

Though there were these scenes of despair, we have other accounts from Asquith (even if he did say to his wife that it was all up), from

[1] Asquith, *Memories and Reflections,* II, p. 21.
[2] Margot Asquith, *The Autobiography of,* II, p. 195.
[3] B. J. Hendrick, *Life and Letters of W. H. Page* (London, 1923), I, pp. 313-14.

Churchill, and from Lloyd George which show that not all the members of the Cabinet were convinced that Berlin would return a refusal.

Would Germany—writes Lloyd George—realize what war with Britain meant, arrest the progress of her armies, change her strategy, and perhaps consent to a parley? I low much depended on the answer to these questions! . . . Hour after hour passed and no sign came from Germany. . . . Shortly after 9 o'clock I was summoned to the Cabinet Room for an important consultation. There I found Mr. Asquith, Sir Edward Grey, and Mr. Haldane all looking very grave [Spender says that Margot Asquith, Tyrrell and Churchill were also present][1] Mr. M'Kenna arrived soon afterwards. A message from the German Foreign Office to the German Embassy in London had just been intercepted. It was not in cipher. It informed the German Ambassador that the British Ambassador in Berlin had asked for his passports at 7 p. m. and declared war.[2] . . . Should this intercept be treated as the commencement of hostilities, or should we wait until we either heard officially from Germany that our conditions had been rejected, or until the hour of the ultimatum had expired? We sat at the green table in the famous room where so many historic decisions had been taken in the past. . . . Should we declare war now, or at midnight? The ultimatum expired at midnight in Berlin. . . . It meant eleven o'clock according to Greenwich time. We resolved to wait until eleven. Would any message arrive from Berlin before eleven informing us of the intention of Germany to respect Belgian neutrality? . . . As the hour approached, a deep and tense solemnity fell on the room. No one spoke. It was like awaiting the signal for the pulling of a lever which would hurl millions to their doom—with just a chance that a reprieve might arrive in time. Our eyes wandered anxiously from the clock to the door, and from the door to the clock, and little was said. Boom! The deep notes of Big Ben rang out into the night the first strokes of Britain's most fateful hour since she rose from the deep. . . . There was no doubt or hesitation in any breast. But let it be admitted without shame that a thrill of horror quickened every pulse.[3]

Outside the crowd struck up 'God save the King', and Churchill sent the war telegram 'Commence hostilities against Germany' to the ships and establishments under the White Ensign all over the world, hoping especially that the *Goeben* in the Mediterranean might be caught and sunk right at the beginning.[4]

Grey was also one of those who waited in the room at 10 Downing Street. He writes:

I was there in touch with the Foreign Office to certify that no satisfactory reply had come from Berlin, though this was, after all that had happened, a foregone conclusion, and a matter of form. . . . Midnight came. We were at war.[5]

---

[1] Spender, II, p. 93.   [2] DD. IV, 848.   [3] Lloyd George, I, pp. 73-7.
                   [4] Churchill, I, pp. 223, 229.   [5] Grey, II, p. 18.

Neither Grey nor his colleagues would have felt such suspense if the refusal or silence of Berlin had been taken for granted. But is it certain that they waited until midnight before regarding themselves as at war with Germany?

Harold Nicolson, who was a junior clerk at the Foreign Office at the time, writes:

It was expected that the German Government would return no reply to this ultimatum and that a state of war would arise at 11 p. m. . . . A communication was thus prepared for delivery to Prince Lichnowsky when the ultimatum expired. The text of this communication was as follows: 'The result of the communication made at Berlin having been that His Majesty's Ambassador has had to ask for his passports, I have the honor to inform Your Excellency that in accordance with the terms of the notification made to the German Government today His Majesty's Government consider that a state of war exists between the two countries as from today 11 o'clock p. m. I have the honor to enclose passports for Your Excellency, Your Excellency's family and staff.'[1]

This message was obviously written after the intercepted telegram had revealed that Goschen had asked for his passports, and was certainly ready when

one of the Private Secretaries dashed in to say that Germany had declared war on England. It was then 9.40 p. m., and the Note prepared for Prince Lichnowsky was hurriedly re-drafted and typed. The amended version began with the words: 'The German Empire having declared war upon Great Britain, I have the honor, etc' The passports were enclosed in this amended letter, and Mr. Lancelot Oliphant. . . was despatched to Prince Lichnowsky. He returned at 10.15 A few minutes later an urgent telegram arrived *en clair* from Sir Edward Goschen at Berlin. It reported that the Chancellor had informed him by telephone that Germany would not reply to the ultimatum, and that, therefore, to his infinite regret a state of war would arise by midnight.[2]

This last statement, however, is a slip on Nicolson's part. No such message was ever telephoned by Bethmann. On the other hand, on 4 August Goschen sent two reports summarizing conversations with Jagow and the Chancellor, neither of which reached Downing Street from Berlin.[3] Hence on that evening of 4 August the Foreign Office was without news from the Ambassador and must have learnt from some other source of its mistake in writing: 'The German Empire having declared war, etc'.

The Foreign Office were appalled at this information. Immediate inquiries were made as to how the previous information had been received. . . . It was ascertained that this information was based on an intercepted wireless

---

[1] Nicolson, p. 423.   [2] Nicolson, p. 424.   [3] BD. XI, 666, 667 and note.

message by which German shipping were warned that war with England was imminent. . . . The Foreign Office then realized with acute horror that they had handed to Prince Lichnowsky an incorrect declaration of war. It was decided that at any cost this document must be retrieved and the right one substituted. It was decided that the youngest member of the staff should be selected for this invidious mission, and the choice therefore fell on Nicolson's youngest son [Harold Nicolson]. . . . It was by then some five minutes after eleven. . . . The Foreign Office clerk stated that there had been a slight error in the document previously delivered and that he had come to substitute for it another, and more correct, version. Prince Lichnowsky indicated the writing table in the window. 'You will find it there', he said. The envelope had been but half opened, and the passports protruded. It did not appear that the Ambassador had read the communication or opened the letter in which the passports had been enclosed. He must have guessed its significance from the feel of the passports and have cast it on his table in despair. A receipt had to be demanded and signed. . . . 'Give my best regards', he said, 'to your father. I shall not in all probability see him before my departure.'[1]

Singular as this story may sound, it finds some confirmation in a letter of Walter H. Page.

I went to see the German Ambassador at 3 o'clock in the afternoon [of 5 August]. He came down in his pyjamas, a crazy man. I feared he might literally go mad. . . . This interview was one of the most pathetic experiences of my life. The poor man had not slept for several nights.[2]

It seems curious that Lichnowsky should have abstained from reading the letter accompanying the passports and explaining the grounds on which these were sent, i.e., why war was being declared. Perhaps his friendship for Grey rendered it too poignant, and certainly he never spoke of it to Berlin. On the other hand, the behavior of the English Government in the whole matter was no less singular. It waited over twenty-four hours after Grey's speech before sending the ultimatum; it allowed a bare minimum of time for a reply (from 7 p. m., when Goschen handed it to Jagow, to midnight); it asserted merely on the authority of an intercepted and unchecked telegraphic message that Germany had declared war on England. What would it have done' if the intercepted telegram had been untrue and Germany agreed to withdraw her troops from Belgium? In the light of later knowledge it is obvious that Germany could not have done so, but at that time nobody knew this and many thought that this is what she might do.

---

[1] Nicolson, pp. 423-6. There existed another rumor to the effect that on being handed his passports on the ground that Germany had declared war on England, Lichnowsky declined to take delivery of them 'on the ground that he had no information that his country had declared war on us' (J. D. Gregory, *On the Edge of Diplomacy,* London, 1928, p. 69). But obviously Nicolson's story is the right one.

[2] Hendrick, *op. cit.,* I, p. 306.

The same sort of mistake had been made three days earlier by the German Chancellor. In instructing Pourtalès to declare war on Russia unless she agreed to demobilize, he overlooked the possibility that, as in fact happened, he might find himself without a reply and therefore not able to be sure whether the two countries were at war or not.[1] The only excuse for such mistakes is that the statesmen of that day lacked the experience to know that if an Ambassador was ordered to deliver an ultimatum, and to declare war should the terms of the ultimatum be rejected, he would probably be unable to communicate with his own Government once war was declared. The only way to avoid this contingency would have been to keep the ultimatum separate from the declaration of war, so that the latter was not issued until the Government learnt from its Ambassador that the terms of the ultimatum had not been accepted. Then there would be no need to wait for a reply before knowing whether or not it was war. But neither Berlin in regard to St. Petersburg nor London in regard to Berlin waited for the rejection of the ultimatum before declaring war. The result, was that they found themselves in a dilemma which might have had disastrous consequences.

7. *English reluctance to send troops to the Continent.*

The truth is that in the last tragic hours confusion reigned everywhere. Thus when London declared war it was not known what kind of war would have to be fought, at sea only, or also on land. Grey had always said to Paul Cambon that there could be no idea of sending an expeditionary force to France. As late as 2 August Asquith had written in his *Contemporary Notes:* 'The dispatch of the Expeditionary. Force to help France at this moment is out of the question and would serve no object.'[2] Spender explains:

The qualification 'at this moment' is important. On 2 August it was far from clear what the enemy's plan of campaign was to be. . . . The development of the German attack through Belgium required all plans to be reconsidered, and made it an imperative necessity to reinforce the French as quickly as possible. Asquith faced up to the new situation at once, but the decision which had to be taken was by no means so easy as it seemed afterwards. It had been one of the principles of orthodox strategy till then that the enemy's fleet must either be disposed of in battle or safely sealed up in its own ports before the army could be transported oversea.[3]

By 2 August the invasion of Belgium was expected, but the truth is that neither Asquith nor Grey was in favor of sending troops and did not motivate their refusal with the reasons given by Spender, as we

---

[1] See p. 193.   [2] See p. 400.
[3] Spender, II, p. 104.

shall shortly see.[1] Evidence of this is to be found in a dispatch of Paul Cambon's, sent in two parts at 6.19 and 7.28 p. m. on 4 August. As late as the afternoon of 4 August, when German troops were already in Belgium and the ultimatum had been sent to Germany,

Grey asked me to come and see him immediately in order to tell me that the Prime Minister would today make a statement in the House of Commons that Germany had been invited to withdraw her ultimatum to Belgium and to give her answer to England before midnight. *Secret.* I asked Sir Ed. Grey what his Government would do if Germany replied in the negative. 'War', he replied. 'How will you make war? Will you immediately embark your expeditionary force?' 'No, we shall blockade all the German harbors. We have not contemplated the dispatch of a military force to the Continent. I explained to you that we needed our forces to assure our defense at certain points and that public opinion was not in favor of an expedition.' 'Your explanations', I answered, 'did not seem satisfactory to me and it does not seem to me that you ought to stop at such flimsy considerations. Public opinion, too, is not what it was three days ago. It asks for war with all resources. The moment is decisive, a statesman would seize upon it. You will be forced by public opinion to intervene on the Continent, but, to be effective, your intervention must be immediate.' I showed him on the map the dispositions for our defense and the necessity for our left to be protected in the event of the violation of Belgian neutrality: I added that, by the agreements between our General Staffs, the shipment of material and supplies was to begin on the second day of mobilization, which lasts for five days, and that every moment lost would cause complications in the execution of our plan. I asked the Foreign Secretary to apprise the Prime Minister and Cabinet of these considerations. This he promised to do.[3]

It is probably in consequence of this telegram, the parts of which arrived in Paris at 9.15 and 10.40 p. m. on the 4th, that Poincaré, with Joffre's approval, wrote thanking King George for his answer to Poincaré's earlier letter, expressing appreciation of Grey's speech in the Commons and asking for information as to English intentions of military co-operation. 'If it were possible to land immediately military units in France bound for Belgium. . . . this measure . . . would have a most salutary effect in Belgium and France.'[3] It does not appear that this letter, which Poincaré dates the 4th but which is perhaps of the 5th,[4] had any effect on the English Government. Probably Grey

---

[1] See pp. 504-5.

[2] DF. 3. XI, 754; Poincaré, IV, pp. 535-6. The LJF. reproduces only the first few lines of this dispatch as No. 153.

[3] Poincaré, IV, pp. 534-5.

[4] Even if not prompted by Cambon's telegram, which Poincaré cannot have read earlier than midnight, it is impossible to see how this letter can have been written on the 4th, seeing that it says 'H.M. King Albert has appealed for our aid and yours'. Now the appeal, made not by King Albert but by the Belgian Government, was made known to Klobukowski at 10 p. m. and was by him communicated to Paris at 11.15 p. m. by a telegram reaching

was very much more influenced by his talk with Cambon. However, evidence is lacking to clear up how it came about that on 5 August Asquith and Grey changed their attitude and agreed to the dispatch of the Expeditionary Force to France, a measure which may probably be regarded as being of decisive influence on the course of the war in that it enabled the lightning German advance to be stopped on the Marne. No doubt Paul Cambon's telegrams from London would do much to clear up the point if they were made public. It is surprising to find that Volume 3 XI of the *Documents Diplomatiques Français* reproduces no telegrams from London between 4 August and 11 August. There is one, dispatched at 12.12 a. m. on 5 August, reporting only the absence of a German reply to the ultimatum and the Admiralty notification to the Fleet that war began at 11 p. m. on 4 August.[1] We know, for example, from Poincaré that Paris received two telegrams from Cambon during the night of 5-6 July.[2] It would be well if the editors of the French collection would at least explain the reason for this lacuna. Even if Cambon had gone to Paris, which does not seem to have been the case, there would have been somebody taking his place. The English Government's real reasons for not wanting to send the Expeditionary Force to France are given by Grey both in his memoirs and in his talk with Cambon. First and foremost it was thought that public opinion was against it, and the idea was so ingrained that the political leaders were taken by surprise when they learnt the real state of feeling in the country. Writing in his diary for 4 August Asquith notes:

> It is curious how going to and from the House we are now always escorted and surrounded by cheering crowds and loafers and holiday-makers.[3]

But it is undoubtedly true that there was considerable division of opinion as to the advisability of sending the little British army to fight in France. Churchill writes:

> The differences which had prevailed about entering the war were aggravated by a strong cross-current of opinion, by no means operative only in the Cabinet, that if we participated it should be by naval action alone. Men of great power and influence, who throughout the struggle labored tirelessly and rendered undoubted services, were found at this time resolutely opposed to the landing of a single soldier on the Continent.[4]

the Quai d'Orsay at 12.45 a. m. on the 5th which Poincaré cannot therefore have received before the early hours of the 5th. Of the six telegrams from Klobukowski which Poincaré reproduces consecutively on pp. 536-8, this and the one preceding it are the only ones of which he does not give the times of dispatch and receipt. An oversight perhaps? Incidentally Poincaré does not tell us how, when, or by whom this letter of his was conveyed to the King.

[1] DP. 3. XI, 770.   [2] Poincaré, V, p. 18.
[3] Asquith, *Memories and Reflections,* II, p. 20.   [4] Churchill, I, p. 231.

The reason is given by Grey:

> The landing of even a small German force [in England], after the Expeditionary Force had gone, and before the Territorial Army was ready, might do irreparable harm.[1]

There was no substance in this apprehension. Either Britain retained the mastery of the seas and then the Germans could never carry out a landing, or she lost it and then she would have to accept the fact of defeat. Another suggestion is mentioned by Grey, namely,

> that the British Expeditionary Force should be kept in reserve till the first shock of the German onset was over. Then there would be a critical moment at which the dispatch of the British Force would be not only effective but decisive.[2]

This suggestion is worth no more than the other. The crucial issue was to withstand the first shock, and to this end the Expeditionary Force, numerically small but in every respect of first-rate quality, was soon to show that it could play an outstanding part. The German General Staff undervalued it. Grey quotes Tirpitz as his authority for saying that

> on the outbreak of the war the German military authorities told the Navy not to make an effort to prevent the British Army from landing in France because, if it did land, the German Army could deal with it.[3]

But it was valued for the fine thing it was by the French military chiefs, who realized as well as the British Command that its presence in France 'would make the whole difference and would ensure success'.[4]

Indeed, without it the Germans would have been victorious on the Marne.

Perhaps it is that experience of war has now opened the eyes of the veriest layman to military questions in their many aspects, but in reading what Grey has written one has the impression that the English

---

[1] Grey, II, p. 64.

[2] Grey, II, p. 65.

[3] Grey, II, p. 27; Tirpitz, II, p. 290.

[4] Grey, II, p. 66. General Huguet, who went to London in December 1904 as French Military Attaché, writes: 'From my first contact with it I came to the conviction that the South African war had served it as an excellent training school. I do not believe there then existed in all Europe a single army in which the instruction of the non-commissioned officers had reached such a high level, in which the rank and file—in the cavalry as well as in the infantry—were so well trained in handling their arms and taking advantage of the terrain. Their clothing and equipment were speedily copied by most of the continental armies. Experience of warfare had taught . . . the formidable effect of the machine gun and the usefulness of high caliber, long range artillery. When we were thinking the 75 mm. gun good enough for most fighting work every British division was equipped not only with its field gun firing a heavier, more powerful shell than our own but also with 18 heavy 125 mm. howitzers firing a 27 kilogram shell, and 4 direct fire guns with a range of 9,500 meters firing a shell of the same weight' (Huguet, pp. 15-14).

political leaders lacked the very rudiments of military knowledge and reasoned with an incoherence which beggars description. Of the extraordinary Council of War at Downing Street on 5 August Churchill writes:

> I do not remember any gathering like it. . . . Decision was required on the question: How should we wage the war that had just begun? Those who spoke for the War Office knew their own minds and were united. The whole British Army should be sent at once to France, according to what may justly be called the Haldane Plan. Everything in that Minister's eight years' tenure of the War Office [Haldane was still in the Cabinet, though no longer at the War Office] had led up to this and had been sacrificed for this. To place an army of four or six divisions of infantry thoroughly equipped with their necessary cavalry on the left of the French line within twelve or fourteen days of the order to mobilize, and to guard the home island meanwhile by the fourteen Territorial divisions he had organized, was the scheme upon which . . . he had concentrated all his efforts and his stinted resources. . . . It represented approximately the maximum war effort that the voluntary system would yield . . .; and mobilization schemes, railway graphics, time-tables, the organization of bases, depots, supply arrangements, etc., filling many volumes, regulated and ensured a thorough and concerted execution. . . . All that remained to be done was to take the decision and give the signal.[1]

But at the critical moment the courage to give the signal was lacking. Instead of the order to mobilize 'and embark' of the original plans, only the order to 'mobilize' was given.

The expert in English military questions, General Huguet, the French Military Attaché in London during the critical period stretching from the end of 1904 to the beginning of 1911, gives a very enlightening description of the attitude of the English towards their army. Up till 1914 the army never played a part of national importance comparable with what was to be its role in 1914-18. The military chiefs lamented that the country had never known invasion, which would have brought home the necessity of being strongly armed. After the South African War Lord Roberts campaigned in vain for conscription. The only result achieved was that the best use was made of the scanty forces obtained by voluntary recruitment. And precisely because these forces were small and costly there was reluctance to let them go abroad. In the event of a European conflagration most people thought that the English share of the fighting must be done on the high seas and not on the Continent. There was no realization that naval warfare was not enough and that the command of the seas did not give the assurance of victory, although that was the lesson of the struggle with Bonaparte. After Trafalgar England

---

[1] Churchill, I, pp. 231-2.

was mistress of the seas, but it was another ten years before Napoleon was defeated. Without Waterloo Trafalgar would have been useless.

While this was understood by the best military authorities and by a few other leading figures, most public men and public opinion generally had no inkling of it. Even on the General Staff, General Grierson, who had initiated the conversations with the French and Belgian General Staffs, had in 1906 been replaced by a general who let them drop. Not until 1910, when General Sir Henry Wilson, to whose qualities Huguet pays the highest tribute,[1] was appointed Director of Military Operations, were the studies for Anglo-French military co-operation resumed and brought to a satisfactory conclusion. Wilson's frequent visits to Paris led to the clearing up of all doubtful points. In the preceding years the British General Staff had intended that the Expeditionary Force should land at Antwerp, the defense of Belgium being the ground for its dispatch to the Continent. But the French regarded Belgium as a secondary theatre of operations and were supported in this by the British naval authorities, who wanted to close the Straits of Dover and opposed a landing at Antwerp. Hence it was only with Wilson that the final agreements were concluded, and it was planned that the Expeditionary Force should land at Boulogne, Le Havre and Dunkirk and be concentrated in the triangle Maubeuge-Busigny-Hirson to act in concert with the Belgian forces against the enemy flank.

The German plans for the violation of Belgium were believed to be much less extensive than they actually proved to be, and the forces much inferior to those actually employed. The French General Staff was badly misinformed as to the enemy position and movements. It expected to find itself up against at most under twenty front-line army corps instead of the actual thirty-six. It estimated at a maximum of twelve to fifteen army corps the *masse de maneuver* detailed to carry out the enveloping movement through Luxemburg and Belgium, the truth being that there were 27J army corps as well as cavalry and *Landwehr.* The result was that the British Army found itself in danger of being enveloped and had to retreat instead of attacking. It managed, however, to link up with the extreme French left, and this, as Huguet writes, was of

capital importance in saving the French V Army from a threat of envelopment of such strength and magnitude that escape from it could only have been effected with the greatest difficulty, that it is doubtful whether the situation could have been restored on the Marne, and that the history of the first months of the war would have taken a very different course from what it did.[2]

[1] Huguet, pp. 33-5.   [2] Huguet, pp. 19-36, 51-2.

But the merit for this belongs to the military, not to the political leaders, who at the moment ordered only the mobilization of the land forces and not their embarkation.

8. *The Council of War on 5 August decides to send the Expeditionary Force to France.*

From Wickham Steed we have Haldane's own account of the issuing of the order for the mobilization of the Expeditionary Force. First published in the *Review of Reviews* for March 1924, it was recalled by Steed in a letter to *The Times* of 4 April 1936, and runs:

At that time Sir Edward Grey was staying with me at this house. After dinner on Sunday, 2 August, a dispatch came saying that Belgium was likely to be invaded. We talked it over and then walked across to No. 10 Downing Street to see the Prime Minister, Mr. Asquith. Grey agreed with me, as did Asquith, that minutes might count not as hours but as years if the Germans were really to invade Belgium. . . . It was clear that, in a great crisis, the Prime Minister could not attend to the War Office in addition to his ordinary work. Therefore he asked me to take over, and gave me written authority to issue orders to the generals. We decided that night to mobilize the Expeditionary Force next morning; and the generals were convened for 11 a. m. in my old room at the War Office. Asquith wrote a note on the Sunday night, 2 August, to the French Ambassador, M. Paul Cambon, telling him of our decision, which, of course, was only contingent—a precaution against the eventuality of a German invasion of Belgium. . . . Next morning I gave the generals four orders. . . . While Grey was making his great speech in the House of Commons (3 August) mobilization was actually proceeding. So well did the machine work, that after the German invasion of Belgium and the declaration of war on 4 August, the first units of the Expeditionary Force actually landed in France on 5 August. Thus our men were there before the Germans.

In *The Times* of 6 April 1936 Brigadier-General Sir James Edmonds queried the date, 3 August:

I have before me the photograph of the order. . . . It is in Mr. Asquith's handwriting on half a sheet of notepaper, and runs: 'The Cabinet approves of mobilization. Please put the necessary machinery, messages, etc., in order: the proclamation will be made tomorrow [4 August]'. H.H.A. 3 August 1914.

To this in *The Times* of 7 April Steed replied that the note quoted by Edmonds 'reads like a reply to some inquiry which the Chief of Imperial Staff may have made of Mr. Asquith'. And in *The Times* of 8 April Major-General Sir Frederick Maurice, who had Lord Haldane's papers in his possession for the purpose of writing his biography, corroborated Steed's account, adding that the note reproduced by

Edmonds was taken by Haldane to the War Office on the morning of 3 August when he assembled the Army Council, showed them Mr. Asquith's authority, and issued the order for mobilization.

Which date is correct? The matter is of no great importance, but since every detail of the crisis leading to the First World War has been and will continue to be a subject of discussion, it is perhaps worth while to express an opinion on it. There can be no question that Haldane who revised the account both in MS. and in proof, told the story as Steed gives it and left notes among his papers to the same effect. What has to be seen is whether his memory did not deceive him, as it did when he said that the first units of the Expeditionary Force landed in France on 5 August. As we shall see, the decision to dispatch the force was only taken on 6 August and the landing began on 10 August. The reasons for doubting the first statement of his are as follows. He states that he convened the generals at 11 a. m. on the 3rd. How could he, if there was a Cabinet at that hour? Above all, how can it be believed that on the evening of the 2nd, when Morley had first spoken of resigning and had been asked by Asquith to think better of it, Asquith could have taken upon himself to order mobilization without the consent of the Cabinet? Indeed, Churchill tells us that at the Cabinet of Monday morning, 3 August, formal sanction was 'given to the already completed mobilization of the Fleet and to the immediate mobilization of the Army'.[1] There still remains the question to be cleared up of Asquith's note of 2 August to Cambon. If England were mobilizing her Expeditionary Force and the news came straight from the Prime Minister, Cambon would not have lost a minute in telegraphing so important and encouraging a decision to his Government. He did not do so. Only somewhere about midnight on the 3rd, by a telegram dispatched at 12.17 a. m. on the 4th, did he telegraph to Viviani:

> You can announce that the mobilization of the English Fleet is completed and that orders are already issued for the mobilization of the land army.[2]

This was an allusion to a decision taken by the Cabinet on the morning of the 3rd and notified to the War Office on the half-sheet of notepaper of which Edmonds speaks in his letter to *The Times,* and which Haldane probably brought with him to the meeting with the generals. The note stated that mobilization would be proclaimed on the 4th. And in fact at 11.35 a. m. on the 4th Cambon telegraphed afresh:

> The mobilization of all the metropolitan forces of the English army has just

---

[1] Churchill, I, p. 220.
[2] DF. 3 XI, 712.

been ordered. The first mobilization day will begin in the night of 4/5 August.[1]

There was still another fact which throws doubt on the accuracy of Haldane's version, namely, the action of General Wilson. Chamberlain notes down on 4 August:

Milner telephoned me at 10 o'clock this morning to ask me if I could join him. I found that he had learned from General Henry Wilson that whilst the Government had at last given the order to mobilize, they had given it in an incomplete form. The full order would be 'mobilize and embark'. The order actually given was 'mobilize'. The result of this, according to Wilson, would be that railway arrangements would be disorganized and that the eventual dispatch of an Expeditionary Force would be delayed a further four days. Milner was very anxious that the Opposition should put fresh pressure on the Government.[2]

Now if mobilization had been ordered on the 3rd the zealous Wilson would never have waited till the 4th to set Lord Milner in motion, knowing that he, Chamberlain and other Opposition leaders would act at once. And in fact Chamberlain tells us:

Balfour agreed to write to Haldane and press the case for the immediate dispatch of 100,000 men. . . . It took some time to bring Bonar Law to the same conclusion, and it was then too late to convey the letter to Asquith in time to be of any use, as we had been given to understand that the decisive Cabinet would be held at 2 o'clock.[3]

In actual fact the decision was taken", not on the 4th and not by the Cabinet, but at an Extraordinary Council of War convened at Downing Street in the afternoon of the 5th. 'I do not remember any gathering like it', comments Churchill.[4] And Asquith notes in his diary for the 5th:

After the House I had a War Council, a rather motley gathering: Lord Roberts, Kitchener, Ian Hamilton, French, Douglas Haig, etc., with Haldane, Grey, Winston and myself. We discussed the strategic situation and what to do with the Expeditionary Force, and adjourned till tomorrow, when we shall have over a representative of the French General Staff.

---

[1] DF. 3. XI, 731. Cambon was not correctly informed in saying that the first day of mobilization would begin in the night of 4–5 August. General Huguet, who was sent by Messimy to London on 6 August as leader of the French military mission with the Expe ditionary Force and had a first-hand knowledge of the facts, writes: 'The decision for military intervention was taken by the Government on 5 August; according to arrangement the English mobilization was to be four days behind ours, in fact it was seven, the first day having been fixed for Sunday 9 August, which corresponded to our eighth day of mobili zation. But from that moment on operations went forward as laid down with perfect regularity and precision. Advance units arrived on the second day, the first fighting troops landed on the fifth and were in the concentration areas on the seventh (Saturday, 15 August)' (Huguet, p. 37).

[2] Chamberlain, *op. cit.,* p. 104.   [3] Chamberlain, *op. cit.,* p. 105.

[4] Churchill, I, p. 231.

August 6. We had our usual Cabinet this morning and decided with much less demur than I expected to sanction the dispatch of the Expeditionary Force of four divisions.[1]

The real decision, in fact, was taken at the Council of War on 5 August and notified to Paris in the night of 5/6 August by two telegrams which are unaccountably omitted from Vol. 3 XI of the *Documents Diplomatiques Français,* and of which we only know from Poincaré, who writes:

At the gathering of the British War Council, held this afternoon . . . it was decided that another meeting will be held tomorrow at 5 p. m. and that our General Staff would be requested at once to send an officer to give explanations about the disposition of our army to facilitate the study of the best way of employing an English Expeditionary Force. Now at last the London Cabinet is resolutely taking the decision to intervene on land and to concert with us on military questions.[2]

These telegrams were not known to Messimy when on the morning of the 6th he sent for Huguet and asked him to go to London to exercise pressure on his 'English friends'. Huguet arrived on the evening of the 6th and learned at once from Paul Cambon that the decision to dispatch the Expeditionary Force had been 'taken the previous day. He writes:

All the members of the Government were present, as well as the chief military and naval authorities. From one who had been present I later learnt some particulars of what took place. Mr. Asquith opened with a survey of the situation: the German violation of Belgian neutrality, the British declaration of war, the promise of naval co-operation. He recalled the discussions which had taken place between the French and British General Staffs and stated the purpose of the meeting: Is it a case for dispatching our Expeditionary Force to France too? . . . The meeting remained undecided until the moment when the Prime Minister, turning to Mr. Winston Churchill, put the direct question: 'If we send our army to France can you safeguard our territory from invasion with the navy alone?' This was the point on which everything hung. Mr. Winston Churchill reflected for a moment and then answered firmly: 'Yes I can . . . but I think some regular troops should provisionally be kept in England until the Territorial Army is able to take over the defense.' This settled the question.[3]

---

[1] Asquith, *Memories and Reflections,* II, p. 25.
[2] Poincaré, V, p. 18.
[3] Huguet, pp. 44-5. At the War Council on 5 August Lord Roberts again raised the question whether the landing force should not be based on Antwerp to strike at the flank and rear of the German invader, but the Admiralty raised objections and the War Office said they had no such plan worked out (Churchill, I, p. 232), for the reasons explained above. Nevertheless when Antwerp was about to fall one infantry and one cavalry division were landed there in hot haste, too late to prevent the surrender. They managed, however, to withdraw to Flanders and take part in the battle of Ypres.

It was decided to send four infantry and cavalry divisions immediately and to keep the other two infantry divisions at home for dispatch later. In fact the agreement between the two General Staffs did not extend to the sending of these two divisions, although the French had pressed for this. The one who would have been willing to dispatch the entire army was Haldane, who was expected to be put again in charge of the War Office in the emergency. Contrary to the wishes of Asquith and Grey he was not given the appointment because of the unjust suspicion that he was pro-German. In his stead public opinion clamored for Lord Kitchener, who at the first meeting of the War Council made his colleagues' blood run cold by prophesying a long struggle which would be won not at sea but on land and for which Britain would have to raise an army of millions of men and maintain them in the field for several years. Churchill writes:

> These words were received by the Cabinet in silent assent; and it is my belief that had Lord Kitchener proceeded to demand universal national service to be applied as it might be required, his request would have been acceded to. He, however, proposed to content himself with calling for volunteers, and in the first instance to form six new regular divisions.[1]

9. *Asquith's speech in the Commons on 6 August.*

Thus it was that in his speech in the Commons on 6 August Asquith, on Kitchener's behalf, asked for 'power to increase the number of all men of all ranks, in addition to the number already voted, to no fewer than 500,000'.[2] In this speech he had no need to give reasons justifying the dispatch of the Expeditionary Force to the Continent. Nor was there any necessity to keep the matter from the enemy's knowledge, the announcement being implicit in Asquith's request for the large increase in military forces. The speech met with no opposition. The Government had all along overestimated the difficulty of persuading public opinion as regards the need for intervention.

No doubt public opinion was by degrees molded by Grey's speech on the 3rd, by the immediate publication of the English *White Paper,* and finally by Asquith's speech of the 6th, more eloquent in its appeal

---

[1] Churchill, I, p. 234. See also Grey, II, pp. 68-70. On 7 August 1914 Kitchener told Huguet that he expected the war would last three years. In August 1915 he said: 'With the new fighting method's introduced by the Germans, it is no longer three years that the war is going to last but four or five years, perhaps even more. The British effort will in consequence have to be intensified and prolonged. . . . England has not yet put forth her full effort but will do so by degrees and in the end will turn the scales in our favor' (Huguet, pp. 50-1). Owing to the falling out of Russia it was in the end the American battalions which turned the scales, but this does not alter the fact that it was Kitchener who from the first foresaw how hard the struggle would be and how great an effort it would demand, although he was regarded by those who knew him best as a general of mediocre ability and limited experience and knowledge (Huguet, pp. 47-8).

[2] Spender, II, p 116.

than that of Grey. In it Asquith paid a glowing tribute to Grey's efforts on behalf of peace, evidence of which was furnished by the diplomatic documents published in the *White Paper.* From the *White Paper* Asquith quoted the terms offered by Germany in return for English neutrality as given in Goschen's dispatch of 29 July,[1] a dispatch which Grey, from an excess of scruple typical of him, had refrained from using in his own speech. What did that proposal amount to? Asquith asked the House. It amounted to the betrayal not only of France, but also of Belgium, to whose appeal

we should have been obliged to say that, without her knowledge, we had bartered away to the Power threatening her our obligation to keep our plighted word. . . . What are we to get in return? A promise—nothing more; a promise be it observed . . . given by a Power which was at that very moment announcing its intention to violate its own treaty and inviting us to do the same.

Asquith then gave the House a summary of Grey's reply to the German offer, and commented:

I regard the proposals made to us as proposals we might have thrown aside without consideration and almost without answer. Can anyone doubt that in spite of great provocation my right hon. friend, who had already earned the title—no-one ever more deserved it—of the peace-maker of Europe, persisted to the very last moment of the last hour in that great and beneficent but unhappily frustrated purpose? I am entitled to say, and I do say on behalf of this country—I speak not for party, but for the country as a whole—we made every effort that a Government could possibly make for peace. This war has been forced upon us. And what is it that we are fighting for? . . . I can reply in two sentences. In the first place, to fulfill a solemn international obligation—an obligation which, if it had been entered into between private persons in the ordinary concerns of life, would have been regarded as an obligation not only of law, but of honor, which no self-respecting man could possibly have repudiated.

I say, secondly, we are fighting to vindicate the principle, in these days when material force sometimes seems to be the dominant influence and factor in the development of mankind, that small nationalities are not to be crushed, in defiance of international good faith, by the arbitrary will of a strong and overmastering Power. I do not believe any nation ever entered into a great controversy—and this is one of the greatest history will ever know—with a clearer conscience and stronger conviction that it is fighting, not for aggression, not for the maintenance even of its own selfish interest, but in defense of principles the maintenance of which is vital to the civilization of the world, and with the full conviction, not only of the wisdom and justice, but of the obligations which lay upon us to challenge this great issue.[2]

[1] BD. XI, 293. See Vol. II, p. 519.
[2] Spender, II, pp. 111-15.

In these inspiring words and with the vow that the United Kingdom would throw all its vast resources into the coming struggle Asquith nobly laid down the principles for which his country and its allies were about to do battle, principles in virtue of which their cause finally triumphed. It is Asquith's supreme merit to have felt and expressed these principles from the outset. Herein he shows himself a finer figure than Grey, for whom the Austro-Serbian conflict was a matter of no interest and who would not have lifted a finger to save Serbia from being crushed by Austria if this could have been done without bringing Russia upon the scene.[1]

Spender rightly says that when this last and greatest crisis came, it was not, in Asquith's view,

an entanglement, but an open clash of forces and ideas, in which Great Britain, however technically free, was bound to make her choice. The question, as he saw it, was not whether she was bound to France, but whether, bound or free, she could possibly remain a spectator while the Central Powers worked their will upon Europe.[2]

Asquith's influence was a very powerful factor in carrying the policy of intervention. Grey testifies:

Had it not been for Asquith the outbreak of war might have found us with a Cabinet in disorder or dissolution, impotent to take any decision.[8]

But—it will be objected—was it not for the sake of Belgium that England came in? Here there is some truth in the accusations of certain historians who charge Grey with having led the country to believe itself pledged by the 1839 treaty to go to the help of Belgium, which was not the case. The point deserves attention as one which occupied a prominent position in the discussions to which the outbreak of the European war gave rise.

The writers who maintain that the 1839 treaty gave England the right to go to war in defense of Belgium but did not make it an obligation for her to do so are asserting what nobody denies, since on 29 July 1914 the Cabinet ruled that 'the matter, if it arises, will be rather one of policy than of legal obligation', as Asquith wrote to the King on 30 July.[4] But would the political aspect not be such as to render it necessary to go to war? Those historians who plead the cause of German innocence, of whom Barnes stands in the forefront, maintain that, even if the respect of Belgian neutrality was a supreme British interest, it could have been safeguarded by a promise of neutrality on the understanding that Germany did not violate the treaty of 1839, but that Grey refused to give this promise because he wanted a pretext for

[1] BD. XI, 98. See Vol. IT, pp. 329-30.   [2] Spender, II, p. 100.
[3] Grey, II, 242.   [4] Spender, II, p. 81. See p. 410.

going to the aid of France. To gain this pretext, though well knowing that Germany would go through Belgium, he hypocritically demanded on 31 July that Germany and France should engage to respect Belgian neutrality, whereupon Germany returned a refusal, which Barnes regards as quite natural.

She would have been most foolish to surrender this one great potential lever on British neutrality without trying to secure some reciprocal British assurance. The astute procedure was to be non-committal in regard to Grey's question about Belgian neutrality on the 31st, and then attempt, through direct negotiation, to get England to promise neutrality if Germany would respect Belgian territory. This was exactly what Germany proceeded to do. On 1 August Prince Lichnowsky . . . proposed to Grey that England remain neutral on condition that Germany keep out of Belgium. Upon Grey's refusal, he then asked Grey to formulate the conditions under which England would remain neutral. Grey refused this also.[1]

Let us overlook the fact that in disregard of all moral considerations Barnes attaches no importance to the circumstance that Germany had solemnly pledged herself to respect Belgian neutrality and that the observance of this pledge could not be made use of as a bargaining-counter. But what must be said is that, in support of his thesis, Barnes makes the assertion:

In 1927 von Jagow stated to the writer that Lichnowsky's proposal about Belgium was authorized from Berlin and that the greatest blunder of Lichnowsky was his failure to publish the offer in the British papers.[2]

It is quite obvious that Barnes has completely misunderstood what Jagow was saying to him. Although telling the truth was not Jagow's strong point, he can never have told Barnes that if England had remained neutral Germany would have given up the plan of attacking France through Belgium. The following reasons prove Barnes to be mistaken:

(i) Germany had no other plan of campaign than that of Schlieffen-Moltke; and the military chiefs were firmly convinced that only this plan would render it possible to win a war on two fronts.

(ii) If Lichnowsky had received instructions to offer German neutrality towards Belgium in exchange for English neutrality, some trace of this would have turned up among the German diplomatic documents.

(iii) Had the German Government really meditated making such an offer, Bethmann on 29 July, in making his notorious request to Goschen for English neutrality, would never have been 'non-committal' in regard to Grey's question about Belgium; and when on 31 July Goschen, on instructions asked Jagow for a promise of respect for

---

[1] Barnes, pp. 546-52. [2] Barnes, p. 554.

Belgian neutrality, the 'astute procedure' would in that case have been to welcome the proposal with open arms.

(iv) Had Jagow possessed evidence proving that Germany had promised England that if she remained neutral, Germany would respect Belgian neutrality, he would have shouted it from the housetops in 1914 and not waited for Barnes to elicit it from him thirteen years later.

Hence when on 27 August 1914 Grey was asked whether he had notified the Cabinet of Lichnowsky's inquiry, he was quite correct in answering that it was a personal and not an official one. And in fact, if he had answered it in the affirmative, Berlin would have had to disavow its own Ambassador. We need only recall Moltke's despair when faced with the possibility of having to fight a war on a single front against Russia alone, while France remained neutral.[1] Though on this point he might conceivably have yielded, however much against the grain, one thing that he could never have done was to agree to improvising in a matter of hours a new plan of concentration and attack against France, leaving Belgium untouched. There is no doubt, therefore, that Lichnowsky was acting without instructions, not intentionally so but from excess of zeal, and that when he did act thus it was too late for war to be prevented. His telegram conveying Grey's refusal reached the Wilhelmstrasse at 10.2 p. m. on 1 August, after mobilization had been ordered, i.e., war had begun.

The fact that Lichnowsky's inquiry was made in a private capacity did not dispense Grey from making it known to the Cabinet, and in fact, contrary to Lutz's assertion,[2] he did report it together with his own refusal. This is made clear in Morley's *Memorandum* where, writing of 2 August, he notes:

I do not recall whether it was at the morning or the afternoon Cabinet that Grey told us of his talks with Lichnowsky; I remember noting that it seemed a great pity, while 'keeping our hands free' [Grey's phrase], not to take advantage of the occasion for more talk and negotiation. It was worth trying at any rate, instead of this wooden *non possumus* even though

---

[1] See p. 176.

[2] Lute, p. 397. Lutz admits that Lichnowsky was speaking purely in a private capacity and adds: 'Berlin, it is true, would certainly not have guaranteed Belgian neutrality in a war on two fronts.' Lutz adds that on 4 August Lerchenfeld, the Bavarian Envoy, wrote from Berlin in this connection: 'The Chief of General Staff slates that at the price of respecting Belgium even English neutrality would be too dearly bought, as the war of offence against France is only feasible along the line of Belgium' (Lutz, p. 397; DD. IV, *Anhang IV*, No. 33). A further letter of Lerchenfeld's on 5 August is still more explicit about Moltke's view: 'The accession of England to the enemy undoubtedly worsens our position, because the provisioning of the civil population might become difficult if the war were to last on. This point caused him a certain anxiety. In spite of this he had strongly advised against buying English neutrality at the price of respecting Belgian territory' (DD. IV, *Anhang IV*, No. 35).

Lichnowsky's ideas of suggestions were merely personal and unauthorized by instructions.[1]

To this it may be replied that Grey never denied or hid from his colleagues that he favored intervention in support of France, while his pacifist colleagues never openly dared to maintain that the violation of Belgian neutrality ought to be accepted. Moreover—and this is by far the most important point which Barnes and the others of his persuasion never consider—even if Grey and the Government had been against intervention, it would have been a colossal blunder for them to have pledged their country to neutrality in return for nothing more than respect of Belgian neutrality by Germany. By so doing they would have given Germany a free hand not only to take the French colonies but to remake the map of Europe at will and ultimately to hurl her strength against England, very possibly with the co-operation of the Powers who regarded themselves as betrayed by her. No matter what their ideas, even if they regarded neutrality as the right course, the English Government would have had to abandon it when the interests of the country made that necessary. Time after time in the preceding years Germany had tried to obtain a promise of neutrality in a possible European war. Never had Grey, been prepared to make it, well knowing that to do so would be an act of suicide on Great Britain's part. Was it likely that he would change his mind when the conflict was breaking out?

10. Grey's ideas on the Belgian question and English intervention.

While recognizing that it was a paramount English interest to rally to the support of Belgium and that the English leaders neither could nor should fetter their freedom of action by giving any advance promise of neutrality even though they might be opposed to intervention, one cannot but ask oneself the question whether Grey did not perhaps instinctively feel that the defense of Belgian neutrality was the one ground on which he could overcome the repugnance existing in England to entering a Continental war at the side of France, as he deemed it indispensable for her to do in order to safeguard the position of the British Empire in the world, and whether, in order to bring his country into the war, he did not exploit the violation of Belgian neutrality by Germany which was to be anticipated. This accusation has been leveled against Grey by all sorts of politicians and historians who regard English intervention as a crime or a blunder, beginning with Morley, who declares:

The Belgian question took its place in today's [2 August] discussion, but even new only a secondary place. . . . The precipitate and peremptory blaze about

[1] Morley, pp. 13-14.

Belgium was due less to indignation at the violation of a treaty than to natural perception of the plea that it would furnish for intervention on behalf of France, for expeditionary force, and all the rest of it. Belgium was to take the place that had been taken before, as pleas for war, by Morocco and Agadir.[1]

First of all one remark. Assuming that Grey acted as his opponents say he did, he cannot be blamed for this by those who think that it was a paramount interest of England to intervene at once with her whole strength in the general war which her Government had failed to prevent. But it has still to be seen whether it is in fact true that he did play the Belgian card with such consummate political and diplomatic skill that for more than a week he contrived to mislead not only his colleagues, but also the Foreign Office officials and the French and Russian Ambassadors into believing that he was averse to plunging England into a war provoked by Balkan squabbles in which she had no interest and in which France took part purely in virtue of an alliance to which Great Britain was not a party, while all the time he was really in favor of intervention and was getting his way by making play astutely with the Belgian card.

Morley asserts that Belgium played 'only a secondary part' through-out the deliberations of the Cabinet. But—as Spender remarks—'this is at variance with the records and with the memories of surviving members of the Cabinet',[2] and it does not at all mean that the Belgian question was of secondary importance. Sir Herbert Samuel, who was then in the Cabinet, writes:

> It is true that the Belgian aspect did not bulk so largely; but that was because the circumstances were quite clear; no serious difference of opinion was expressed; there was little occasion for argument. With regard to intervention on behalf of France the case was different.[3]

Lloyd George also confirms :

Had the question of defending the neutrality and integrity of Belgium been raised there would not have been a dissentient voice on that issue. Lord Morley and John Burns might conceivably have stood out. Of that I am not convinced had a decision on that point alone been reached. . . .[4]

What remains to be seen is whether Grey did not perhaps take advantage of the unanimity among his colleagues to lead them on into intervention on behalf of France, which he so much desired.

Appearances would seem to support this assumption. He abstained from asking the Cabinet to make any pronouncement either for or

[1] Morley, pp. 13-14.
[2] Spender, *Life of Lord Oxford and Asquith,* II, p. 99.
[3] *Manchester Guardian Weekly,* 26 October 1928, p. 325.
[4] Lloyd George, I, p. 71

against such intervention, realizing that it would give rise to differences of opinion. He further omitted to warn Germany and France immediately against violating Belgian neutrality as, according to certain of his critics, he should have done without waiting so long as the 31 July. Lloyd George writes:

It is a misfortune that Sir Edward Grey did not play sooner and more boldly this card of our treaty pledges to Belgium. It might have averted the war altogether.[1]

This view is shared by Hermann Lutz, who writes:

The line taken by the British Government at the outbreak of the 1870 war might have commended itself as one to be imitated by a Foreign Secretary making every endeavor . . . to keep the peace between the Great Powers. A Government statement that in the event of any infringement of Belgian neutrality—as was decided in 1870—Belgium would receive armed protection could not give offence anywhere and would have been an effective method of making the Central Powers beat a retreat if made in time.[2]

But it was not made in time, and the reason was not because Grey did not believe the Germans would go through Belgium. He himself records:

I remember saying more than once, to colleagues inside or outside the Cabinet, that it did not matter whether the decision was to go to war or to demand conditions from Germany. Conditions meant war just as surely as a declaration of war. Respect for the neutrality of Belgium must be one of the conditions, and this Germany would not respect.[3]

This shows that Grey knew beforehand what would be the outcome of his three moves. The first was that of 31 July when though the situation was beyond repair he asked Paris and Berlin 'to engage to respect neutrality of Belgium so long as no other Power violates it'.[4] The second was on 1 August when with Cabinet consent he warned Germany that 'if there were a violation of the neutrality of Belgium by one combatant while the other respected it, it would be extremely difficult to restrain public feeling in this country'.[5] The third was on 2 August when he secured Cabinet consent for a statement in the House that the violation of Belgian neutrality would constitute a *casus belli*.[6] By this piecemeal procedure and, between its second and third stages, a promise to France to give her the full protection of the British navy against any German naval attack,[7] Grey overcame the opposition of the majority of the Cabinet and brought them all, except the two who resigned, round to the view that war was unavoidable.

---

[1] Lloyd George, I, p. 67,   [2] Lutz, p. 526.   [3] Grey, II, p. 10.
[4] BD. XI, 348. See p. 387.   [5] BD. XI, 448; DD. III, 596. See p. 389.
[6] See p. 409.   [7] See p. 409.

Nor is this all. Even after his victory in Parliament and in the country, he still—as has been shown—took no immediate steps to give Germany a stern warning that if she did not respect Belgian neutrality, Great Britain would declare war on her. He waited until the invasion had begun before telegraphing his ultimatum as late as at 2 p. m. on 4 August. Why this? One might be tempted to think that, feeling war between Germany and France to be inevitable, he did not want Germany to refrain from entering Belgium and thus deprive him of that pretext for going to the aid of France. But this view is at variance with Grey's whole temperament and outlook. There was no duplicity in him. He was of limited intelligence, and the respect he commanded was due to his integrity and honesty, which won him confidence because it was the very negation of diplomatic finesse. He groped so much in the dark from 24 July on, he tumbled so slowly to the facts of the situation created by the Austrian ultimatum to Serbia, that there can be no question of consummate ability carrying out the bidding of an iron will. He was anything but that. In him, as Paul Cambon said to Recouly,[1] there were two men at odds the one with the other, the foreign minister and the pacific idealist. The foreign minister sided with France against Germany. The idealist, who often overbore the politician, strained every nerve to find some way of escape other than war. Hence his repugnance to giving pledges to France or threatening Germany; hence his strange proposals to Lichnowsky on 1 August, intended to keep France and Germany from going to war, so that England might thus remain neutral. It is difficult to determine at what point and to what degree he realized that the Belgian question might turn the scales in favor of France in the event of a general conflagration. In all probability, even if he used the Belgian question as a 'pretext' for intervention, he did so simply and naturally and without guile.

The truth is that neither for Grey nor for his colleagues of either persuasion was Belgium a mere 'pretext'. All that has been already said about the antecedents of the Belgian question, all that still finds acceptance today, only serves to show that for Britain the question of Belgium was a major issue. She could not do otherwise than face the problem of going to war in defense of two paramount interests. In the first place she could not break up the Triple *Entente* by refusing her support to France, if not also to Russia. In the second place she could not look on while Germany established herself on the Belgian coast. As British public opinion awoke to the second of these interests sooner than to the first, partly because of the moral issue involved, it was natural for Grey to lay greater stress on this aspect, if only as a means

[1] Recouly, pp. 45-6.

of getting his views on the other aspect accepted. But unless the present writer is mistaken, Grey spoke more artlessly, more simple-heartedly than is often believed. 'There was little for me to do—he writes— circumstances and events were compelling decision.'[1]

And this is very likely how it was. There are, however, two matters to which this interpretation will not apply. One—in the opinion of the present writer—is Grey's delay, whether of his own volition or at the suggestion of Nicolson or Crowe, in telegraphing the English ulti- matum to Berlin, presumably for fear that Germany might be tempted to buy British neutrality by abstaining from passing through Belgium, thus making it much more difficult for Grey to carry the country into a war on the side' of France. In fact it is open to doubt whether England would have come in so quickly, had not the German violation of Belgian neutrality played into the hands of France and her English sympathizers. Lloyd George is one of many who think that she would have stayed out.[2] And this was probably true, at any rate for the time being. Indeed, had Germany declared that she would not only respect Belgium but would also not attack France and would only defend her- self against French attack—as she would certainly have done if she had had any other plan available than the Schlieffen-Moltke plan—and had France taken the first step in going to war in fulfillment of her engagements as Russia's ally, the English Liberal Government would most probably have failed to bring the country in in support of a France who had not been attacked and who went to war of her own accord.

The other omission which was perhaps intentional on Grey's part was that he did not, right from the beginning, follow Gladstone's precedent in 1870 and raise the question of Belgium with both France and Germany. Indirectly he puts forward an excuse for this when he writes:

I remember saying more than once, to colleagues inside or outside the Cabinet, that it did not matter whether the decision was to go to war or to demand conditions from Germany. . . . Respect for the neutrality of Belgium must be one of the conditions, and this Germany would not respect.[3]

If that was what he thought, it was his duty for obvious tactical reasons to have sent Germany a warning, even though not expecting it to be heeded. In actual fact it very probably would have been heeded. Germany was well aware that she herself could not on the spur of the moment wage any other war than the one laid down in the Schlieffen- Moltke plan. Had she received warning before the Austrian declaration of war on Serbia that an invasion of Belgium would bring England in

---

[1] Grey, II, p. 10. [2] Lloyd George, I, p. 66, [3] Grey, II, p. 10.

against her, rather than have this happen she would in all likelihood have put a stop to the Austrian declaration, the original cause of the mobilizations and thus of the general conflagration. However, it is by no means certain that Grey was convinced right from the outset that the Germans were going to march through Belgium. It would be strange if he was certain of this when no one else was. The Belgians were not so, as we have seen. But neither was the French General Staff. If it had been, it would have made quite different preparations to meet the German onslaught. We know from Joffre that as late as the evening of 1 August 'there reigned the most complete uncertainty as to what it would be possible to do'.[1] Probably Grey only began to believe the invasion of Belgium certain in the very last days after it was foreshadowed in the Chancellor's bid for English neutrality of which he learnt on 30 July. This would explain why he never thought till then of taking the momentous step of inquiring of Paris and Berlin, as he did on 31 July, whether each was prepared to respect the neutrality of Belgium provided no other Power violated it. Then Jagow's evasive reply could not but confirm his worst suspicions. It would have been better if the idea had occurred to him sooner, but his was a slow-moving mind.

There were other occasions when for the same reason he failed to come to clear conclusions enabling him to take appropriate action quickly. For instance, on 24 July his first reactions were that the Austro-Serbian conflict was of no concern to him and that no obligation or interest would cause England to intervene in any European conflict to which it might give rise. He saw no objection to Russia's mobilizing and thought that the other Powers might intervene to save the peace after the completion of mobilization. Not until the morning of the 31st did he talk to Lichnowsky in terms which, if used earlier, might well have averted the tragedy:

> I said to German Ambassador this morning that if Germany could get any reasonable proposal put forward which made it clear that Germany and Austria were striving to preserve European peace, and that Russia and France would be unreasonable if they rejected it, I would support it at St. Petersburg and Paris and go to the length of saying that if Russia and France would not accept it His Majesty's Government would have nothing more to do with the consequences; but, otherwise, I told the German Ambassador that if France became involved we should be drawn in.[2]

Grey's slowness of intuition is not admitted by some of the best English authorities, who incline to the explanation of the Government's inaction put forward by Spender:

---

[1] Joffre, I, p. 130.
[2] BD. XI, 340. See Vol. II, p. 642.

The dominant idea of all sections of the Cabinet was that Great Britain alone was in a position to mediate with relative impartiality between the European groups. She had performed this function to complete satisfaction in the previous year, and they hoped that she would be permitted to perform it again in the new crisis. But this role required her to remain uncommitted, so long as the slightest hope of peace remained, and necessarily excluded the strong declaration on the side of France and Russia which those Powers naturally desired. . . . To urge mediation, to keep on urging it, and to exhaust every possibility, however remote or unpromising, of building bridges between the two European groups was what the public expected of a Liberal Government, and the only line on which either Cabinet or national unity could have been secured.[1]

The speciousness of this argument, which would absolve the English Government of all responsibility, is patent. In any major crisis England could act as supreme arbiter only by offering or denying her armed assistance to the Powers who were her friends. As Grey told the House on 3 August, she saved the peace in 1906 and 1911 by threatening Germany with war, and in 1908-9 by telling Russia that over the annexation of Bosnia-Herzegovina she would give diplomatic but not military support.[2] If in 1914 she failed to save the peace, the reason is that she did not speak clearly until it was too late.

11. Grey's share of responsibility for the war.

Grey shows himself not inaccessible to this reproach, nay even to a sense of remorse. Several times in his book he brings forward excuses which fail to convince.

The pledge [to France and Russia] simply could not have been given sooner than it was. To give it on my own initiative, without consulting the Cabinet, was, of course, out of the question. To do so would have been criminal, for such a pledge would have been worthless. The Cabinet, in the earlier days, was not prepared to give such a pledge, and, with the existing state of feeling in Parliament and the country, it was not in a position to give it. . . . If any of us had pressed for a pledge to be given in the earlier days of that week, we should have divided the Cabinet. . . . The violation of Belgium, when it came, would have found us with a divided Cabinet; . . . with a House of Commons and a country paralyzed by division of opinion. . . . Looking back on it all, it seems to me that the course actually followed in those critical days was the only one that could have led to the entry of Britain into the war, immediately, wholeheartedly and with practical unanimity.[3]

The obvious reply to this is that the best course to have followed was one leading to peace, not to war, and that to preserve peace there was not the slightest need to give pledges to

---

[1] Spender, II, p. 97.   [2] Grey, II, pp. 294-309   [3] Grey, II, pp. 40-1.

France and Russia, but on the contrary to warn them both, and Germany too, that they must not be unyielding in their demands, otherwise France and Russia would find themselves threatened with English neutrality and Germany with English intervention. And that Grey could have taken this line no matter if the Cabinet was divided is proved by the fact, which can never be often enough repeated, that this is precisely the line he did take with Germany, giving a hint on 29 July and speaking more plainly on 31 July, when it was too late, while Russia and France received no warning from him at all. He never seems to have understood the effect that the threat of English intervention would have in Germany. He writes:

> Germany would naturally have preferred that we should not come in. . . . Everything we know goes to prove that the German military authorities calculated on a war, not of years, but of months, during which they would not be seriously hurt by anything the British Army could do, that they thought they could deal easily with the British Expeditionary Force if it came: in other words, that their plans covered the risk of Britain coming in. . . . If this were so, an early intimation that we should join France and Russia would not have prevented war.[1]

But it is obvious that Great Britain was redoubtable on account not so much of her army as of her navy. An abundance of evidence is available to prove beyond all shadow of doubt that what the Kaiser and the German political leaders feared above everything was British intervention and that they clung to the hope of British neutrality.

Victor Naumann relates that on the afternoon of 4 August he was in Stumm's room at the Wilhelmstrasse discussing the situation with him.

> The English decision was being awaited with the greatest anxiety. As we were in conversation about it Herr von Jagow entered Stumm's room and called him out. I shall never forget Jagow's face at that moment; his features showed, I will not say horror, but an expression of anguish which had awakened in him. When Herr von Stumm returned after a considerable time, he too was pale and said to me: 'England has declared war on us.'[2]

This happened on the evening of 4 August after Germany had declared war on Russia and France and presented the ultimatum to Belgium, and still Berlin was not fully convinced of English intervention. This fact in itself is sufficient to show what a responsibility rested on the shoulders of the London Government, particularly on the Minister in charge of Great Britain's foreign policy.[3]

[1] Grey, II, pp. 42-5.

[2] Victor Naumann, *Dokumente und Argumente* (Berlin, 1928), p. 25.

[3] Those who regard English intervention as a blunder and a crime can quote the authority of Lloyd George who, forgetting that in his *War Memoirs* he had written: 'I never doubted that, if the Germans interfered with the integrity and independence of Belgium, we were in honor bound to discharge our treaty obligations to that country' (*ibid.,* Vol. I,

p 51), published on 29 March 1936, an article, referred to in a letter to *The Times* of 30 March 1936, in which he stated that 'a military plan worked out by contacts between the General Staffs of Great Britain and France . . . landed the Empire ultimately in 3,300,000 casualties and a debt of £8,000 m. It shattered our export trade for 22 years. It has not yet recovered . . . Beware of military entanglements'. Mr. Duff Cooper, whose letter draws attention to this article, comments: 'The plain meaning of this statement is that if it had not been for these military arrangements Mr. Asquith's Government, in which Mr. Lloyd George was Chancellor of the Exchequer, would not have taken part in the war of 1914. And, further, the obvious deduction is that we should have been very wise to have kept out of it.' In *The Times* of 31 March, Lloyd George replied: 'Mr. Duff Cooper has missed the point of the article by me which he criticizes in your issue today. My contention was that the military arrangements entered into between the Powers had the effect in 1914 of cutting short the negotiations by which they sought to avert the crisis, and thus precipitated the Great War. Had it not been for the professional zeal and haste with which the military staffs set in motion the plans which had already been agreed between them the negotiations between the Governments, which at that time had hardly begun, might well have been continued, and war could, and probably would, have been averted,' To this Duff Cooper retorted in *The Times* of 1 April: 'Mr. Lloyd George's second statement is worse than his first and reflects still graver discredit on the responsible British Ministers in 1914 We are now solemnly assured on the high authority of one who was then Chancellor of the Exchequer and subsequently Prime Minister that these gentlemen allowed the professional zeal of their military advisers to cause the break down of negotiations 'which had hardly begun' and through which 'war could, and probably would, have been averted'. . . . 'While awaiting an answer it is well to remember that war was declared on 4 August, after the German troops had crossed the Belgian frontier, and that the first recorded meeting between the Cabinet and their naval and military advisers took place on 5 August.' On 2 April Lloyd George replied with a long letter described by Duff Cooper on 3 April as 'the smoke screen with which he has thought fit to mask his retreat from an impossible position' and in which Lloyd George claimed that the military convention 'was a part of the tangle of military arrangements which thwarted all the efforts for peace'

This is untrue The truth is that it was the Russian mobilization which set the others in motion and that once the machinery of mobilization had begun to work, the military gained the upperhand of the political authorities. The Russian partial mobilization was suggested by Sazonov before the military came on to the scene and was the consequence of the Austrian declaration of war on Serbia. The military agreements, in particular the Anglo-French convention, cannot in the least be said to have exercised any influence on the outbreak of the European war. Huguet writes in this connection: 'It is certain that the studies undertaken at that time did not bind the English Government . . . It is not less certain that a considerable number of officers were called upon to participate in them. The result was that the feeling grew up among these that in the event of war they would be intervening on our side and their joint studies appeared to them as constituting a moral if not formal engagement, from which England could not default. This consideration . . . was later to have a certain influence on the Government's decision' (Huguet, pp. 38-9). This last statement is to be doubted. There is no evidence that Grey and Asquith ever regarded the Anglo-French military agreements as forming one of the reasons in favor of intervention. Huguet himself writes: 'It is incontestable that neither the existence of the *Entente Cordiale* nor the military agreements entered upon would in 1914 have had the power to bring about the adherence of England, had they not been joined by the violation of Belgian neutrality' (Huguet, p. 30). Furthermore it is obvious that what weighed more than the military agreements themselves was what caused them, namely the existence of the Triple *Entente* which, failing English intervention, would have broken up, leaving England isolated.

CHAPTER XI

AUSTRIA AT WAR WITH THE TRIPLE ENTENTE

(1) *Vienna is notified of the proclamation of the* Kriegsgefahrzustand *in Germany (p. 526).* (2) *Germany requests Austria-Hungary to attack Russia immediately; Berchtold's statements; Conrad's opposition (p. 529).* (3) *The Austrian declaration of war on Russia (p. 532).* (4) *Grey's attitude to Austria-Hungary; Berchtold's desire to postpone the rupture with England (p. 534).* (5) *France decides to break off diplomatic relations with Vienna on the ground of a baseless report that an Austrian army corps had been dispatched to Alsace-Lorraine (p. 539).* (6) *France and England declare war on Austria-Hungary (p. 542),*

1. *Vienna is notified of the proclamation of the* Kriegsgefahrzustand *in Germany.*
It has been related in detail above how at the moment when Berlin decided to proclaim the *Kriegsgefahrzustand* and send St. Petersburg the ultimatum which would lead to war, a serious misunderstanding arose between Conrad and Moltke in which Moltke asked whether Austria was going to leave Germany in the lurch in a war against Russia.[1] The misunderstanding was soon cleared up, but the Monarchy waited until 6 p. m. on 6 August before sending Russia a declaration of war as Germany had done at 7 p. m. on 1 August, i.e., five days earlier. Was this delay due to hesitation on the part of Austria at the last minute when the resumption of direct conversations with St. Petersburg caused a *détente* between the two capitals which as we have seen, raised many hopes?[2] This has found a certain amount of credence. But it would be foolish to imagine that after all that had happened Austria could hesitate to follow her ally in taking the extreme decision, though she did so unwillingly and though Berchtold was taken aback by German precipitation.

He realized that the situation had grown rapidly worse when he learnt on 31 July from Tschirschky that the *Kriegsgefahrzustand* had been proclaimed and that an ultimatum was about to be sent to Russia demanding the suspension of mobilization.[3] In telegraphing news of the proclamation to Tschirschky at 1.45 p. m. on the 31st the Chancellor had added that mobilization would follow 'probably' (*voraussichtlich*) in forty-eight hours, that it inevitably meant war, and that Germany expected the Monarchy's immediate active participation in hostilities against Russia.[4] But the 'probably', which recurred also in a telegram

---

[1] See pp. 46–8. [2] See Vol. II, pp. 681-6.
[3] DA. III, 80. [4] DD. II, 479.

from Szögyény,[1] left an opening for the thought that all hope was not lost. The word ultimatum was not used in the telegrams and it was not made clear that Germany was going to take the initiative in declaring war on Russia. Nor did Wilhelm's telegram of 4.5 p. m. on the 31st to Francis Joseph give the impression that this was to be the next step. It said:

I reckon with 2 August as first day of mobilization and am prepared in fulfillment of my obligations under the alliance to begin war immediately against Russia and France.[2]

The impression given by these words is of a Germany prepared to go to war if Austria were to be attacked by Russia, as logically she would expect to be. Only in the small hours of 1 August, when the Conrad-Moltke incident took place, did Vienna begin to know the truth. At 2.20 a. m. on 1 August Moltke informed Conrad by telephone that Germany had sent a twelve-hour ultimatum to Russia and France, expiring at 4 p. m. on 1 August, that if Russia did not agree to demobilize, war would be declared on her immediately, and that her compliance was not expected.[3] At 8 a. m. on 1 August the Ballplatz received Szögyény's telegram saying that Pourtalès had handed a note to the Russian Government setting a time-limit of eighteen hours for the return of a declaration revoking mobilization.[4]

It is difficult to say how far these messages created the impression that immediate war was certain. But they must deeply have disturbed Berchtold, who was by temperament unfitted to shoulder the responsibility of bringing on a European war. On 1 August he received calls from Shebeko and Dumaine, the Russian and French Ambassadors. Shebeko in vain tried to gain his acceptance of the formula, given by Sazonov to Pourtalès in the night of 29/30 July, to the effect that if Austria declared her readiness to drop from the ultimatum the points infringing Serbian sovereign rights, Russia would engage to stop all military preparations.[5] But Shebeko went away with the impression that Berchtold would not be averse to accepting a conciliatory proposal compatible with his own *amour propre* and Austrian prestige.[6] The impression was erroneous. Berchtold was merely playing for time and waiting for Berlin to make the next move. To Dumaine, who blamed Germany for the failure of the Austro-Russian negotiations for a peaceful solution, Berchtold retorted that the dispute had been aggravated by the Russian general mobilization.

Instead of pursuing the discussion of conditions for an arrangement, he talked of nothing else but the situation of Germany in regard to France and Russia. My

---

[1] Oe-U. VIII, 11130.　　　　　　　[2] DD. III, 503. See p.45
[3] See pp. 45-7.　　　　　　　　　　[4] DA. III, 82.
[5] See Vol. II, pp. 561-2.　　　　　　[6] *Int. Bez.* i. V, 418.

pressing insistence on his obtaining from Berlin a momentary abstention until it becomes evident that no ground for an understanding exists between Vienna and St. Petersburg encountered discouragement from him. 'The situation is too obscure', he said in ending.[1]

Of these two talks Berchtold drew up a report, which caused some offence in Berlin,[2] showing that both Ambassadors had complained of Germany's aggressive attitude without arousing any protest from him. In sending this report to Berlin on 3 August Tschirschky added:

Today the Russian Ambassador [*sic*] Kudashev . . . asked a junior member of the Ballplatz staff whether Austria was not under obligation to support Germany against Russia. . . . There is no doubt . . . that this ingenuous-sounding question and the ostentatious non-provocation of the Monarchy also on the military field (the Russians have withdrawn their troops two kilometres behind the frontier) aim at driving a wedge between ourselves and Austria.[3]

This was an overstatement, but there is no doubt that Sazonov still had lingering hopes of Austria, for on the evening of 1 August after receiving the German declaration of war (this fact emerges from the serial numbers of the relevant Russian documents, which unfortunately do not bear the indication of their hours of dispatch and receipt) he telegraphed to Shebeko:

If a rupture of relations takes place also between ourselves and Austria, you will have to come here with the whole Embassy staff, asking your Spanish colleague to undertake (the custody of our interests in Austria-Hungary. Till now, however, we have received no pronouncement to this effect from the Austro-Hungarian Ambassador, remain therefore in relations with Austria.[4]

It seems singular that Sazonov should still have been doubtful of the possibility of a rupture 'also' with Austria, at a time when Russia was already at war with Germany. But this doubt of his and the sequence of the documents reveal how, when it came to the point, St. Petersburg hesitated to be the first to open hostilities. Russia had mobilized to prevent Austria from crushing Serbia; it should therefore have fallen to her to take action against the Monarchy. But she still hung back. And if Austria had been able she would have done the same. As it was she did not at once declare war, for reasons we must now consider, and she betrayed acute embarrassment as to how to declare war without appearing to be in the wrong.

[1] DF 3. XI, 555.
[2] DA. III, 99.
[3] DD, III, 704.
[4] *Int. Bez.* i. V, 394.

2. Germany requests Austria-Hungary to attack Russia immediately; Berchtold's statements; Conrad's opposition.

On the morning of 2 August Vienna received a telegram from Szögyény reporting a conversation with Wilhelm, before whom he had laid Francis Joseph's reply to Wilhelm's appeal of 31 July.[1] Wilhelm had written that he had not yet received an answer to his request to Russia that she should demobilize and that the Tsar had telegraphed to him that 'the mobilization of the Russian army by no means meant war'.[2] The word 'war' had not appeared in the Kaiser's message. Nevertheless, hostilities had already begun. At 6.35 a. m. on 2 August Bethmann telegraphed to Tschirschky:

> We are in a state of war with Russia, Russian troops having yesterday crossed our frontier at several points and perpetrated hostilities. We had also instructed the Imperial Ambassador at St. Petersburg, in the case of an unsatisfactory response to our demand, to declare war yesterday afternoon, but have received from the Ambassador news neither of Russia's reply to our demand nor of delivery of declaration of war. We expect of Austria fulfillment of her allied obligations and immediate vigorous intervention against Russia.[3]

Tschirschky executed his instructions that same morning, as we know from the fact that at 2 p. m. Bunsen telegraphed to Grey:

> German Ambassador, on leaving the room of the Minister for Foreign Affairs as I was about to go in this morning, read me a telegram just received by him from Berlin stating that, Russian troops having crossed German frontier at several points, German Government considered that state of war with Russia existed. I then saw Minister for Foreign Affairs, who admitted that Austria must consider herself in same position towards Russia.[4]

But how did she take up that position? Was she able to do so immediately? In an interview which Luciano Magrini had with Berchtold in the presence of Hoyos on 29 October 1933, Berchtold declared that up to the last minute, even after the German proclamation of general mobilization, he still believed that a slight hope existed of avoiding a European war. He went on to say:

> I was completely ignorant of the fact that for Germany mobilization meant immediate entry into war. We did not know that the German plan of war implied from the first mobilization day offensive military operations and violation of the neutrality of Belgium, and we hoped that if the worst came to the worst England would remain neutral. If I had been aware that Germany would violate the neutrality of Belgium I should have been in no doubt that we must from the outset count on English intervention. Not until late in the evening of 3 August did I learn from a telegram of Szögyény's that the German General Staff had conceived the plan, 'which could not now be modified', of attacking France through Belgium.

---

[1] See pp. 45-6, 176-7.   [2] DA. III, 101.   [3] DD. III, 627.   [4] BD. XI, 493.

Szögyény added that upon his observing to the Wilhelmstrasse that the violation of Belgian neutrality would drive England to range herself with our adversaries, he was answered that 'now the word was with the military and it was no longer possible to raise objections with them'. The telegrams from Szápáry and Szögyény of the morning of 2 August gave no grounds for thinking that war had broken out between Germany and Russia. According to Szápáry there were still possibilities of diplomatic negotiation, and Sazonov had told him that the Tsar had given Wilhelm his word that the army would not move as long as a conversation with Austria continued.

A second telegram from Szápáry reported that Sazonov had told Pourtalès the Tsar had given Kaiser Wilhelm assurances of so formal a nature that there was no reason for anxiety on the subject of Russian general mobilization. Szögyény, in his turn, reported having been informed by Kaiser Wilhelm that the Tsar had telegraphed that 'the mobilization of the Russian army did not mean war'. I was therefore not a little surprised when about noon Tschirschky informed me that the Russians had opened hostilities and that Germany, being thus attacked, expected of Austria-Hungary an immediate, vigorous attack on Russia. I at once informed Conrad, who showed surprise and annoyance at the premature outbreak of the war and insistently qualified the vigorous and immediate offensive action which Tschirschky with unremitting pressure seemed to demand of us as inopportune, dangerous and impossible. Conrad deplored that Germany should so late have decided to clarify her attitude towards Russia. He could not understand her haste. It was as much to Germany's interest as to our own that Austria-Hungary should not fall into the mistake of a premature big offensive which could not be undertaken with the peace-time troops then available in Galicia. Conrad remarked that only on the previous day had the order for general mobilization been signed by the Emperor. The mobilization and concentration of the troops in Galicia would take time. Over-hasty action would lead to a reverse and imperil the success of mobilization. And since partial mobilization had presupposed only the case of war with Serbia, now it would be necessary for six divisions mobilized on the Serbian front to be transferred to the Russian front; but first of all one must wait for them to assemble in the zone laid down for partial mobilization. It was necessary to gain time, and if Russia did not declare war on us, that was all to the good; but Conrad thought it would be a great mistake for us to declare it, seeing that we were not ready and that we should run the risk of seriously disorganizing the mobilization of our army. He asked me to tell Berlin that we raised no objection to the necessity of war with Russia, and that in all eventualities Germany would find us staunchly at her side; only we thought it necessary for our declaration of war to be postponed as long as possible in order to enable the Monarchy to get through the first days of general mobilization without difficulty. As for a vigorous offensive, it could not take place until the troops had been assembled in Galicia. About 4 p. m. a telegram from Szögyény informed me that Russian troops—according to what he had been told by Jagow—had crossed the frontier at Schwidden, attacking Germany, who consequently regarded herself as at war with Russia. Jagow had added that no declaration of war would be made by Germany. I am in the dark about the reasons for which Jagow concealed from Szögyény that the declaration of war had been delivered to Sazonov by Pourtalès at 7 p. m. on the previous day. Perhaps if he had admitted that the initiative in declaring war lay with Germany, he could not have made Germany appear as the one who had been attacked.

In the evening of 2 August and the morning of the 3rd Tschirschky persisted in asking me for an immediate declaration of war on Russia and the opening of a military offensive, while Conrad firmly maintained his point of view. Fresh appeals from the Chancellor came to me through Szögyény. Above all, Berlin pressed that we should at once attack Russia in force, which Conrad declared he could not do. On the evening of 3 August I submitted to the Emperor the text of a declaration of war to be presented to Sazonov by Szápáry 'the day after tomorrow or as circumstances demand one of the succeeding days according to the political and military situation'.

Berlin must have been notified by telephone—as was done occasionally between the two capitals—of the reasons for the Austrian delay, for at 5.30 p. m. on 3 August Tschirschky telegraphed to Jagow:

As Your Excellency knows, Austrian declaration of war on Russia has only been postponed in order to be undisturbed as long as possible in the concentration in Galicia.

The embarrassment in which the German move had placed the Monarchy is shown in the next sentence:

Vienna would like to avoid incurring the odium of aggression through a spontaneous declaration of war on Russia, and wonders whether Austria could not allege the Russian attack on Germany as a ground for war also for the Monarchy in consequence of the alliance. As the declaration of war can hardly be delayed for more than a few days, a statement of Berlin's views on the question of the declaration of war would be received with thanks.[1]

On 4 August the Kaiser wrote in the margin 'Yes' to the Austrian query about the ground to be alleged for the declaration of war. But before knowing his opinion Bethmann Hollweg at 11.40 a. m. on 4 August had angrily telegraphed to Tschirschky:

We are compelled by Austria's action to go to war and may expect that Austria will not try to gloss over this fact, but will publicly proclaim that threat of intervention (mobilization against Austria) in Serbian conflict forces Austria to war.[2]

The reason for the Chancellor's wrath is obvious. By his inquiry Berchtold had put his finger on a very sore spot with Bethmann, namely, the serious blunder made by Germany in breaking off the negotiations for a settlement which were in

[1] DD. IV, 772.   [2] DD. IV, 814.

progress and declaring war on Russia and France.[1] By proposing to place the responsibility for resorting to war on Russia 'to avoid incurring the odium of aggression', Berchtold was indirectly censuring the opposite course willed by the Chancellor, a course which had encountered considerable opposition even at Berlin. Bethmann's rebuttal of the reproof took the form of reminding Vienna that it was Austrian action which had caused Germany to go to war and requesting that the Russian mobilization against Austria be alleged as the Austrian reason for declaring war.

3. *The Austrian declaration of war on Russia*

In the afternoon of 4 August the Wilhelmstrasse was notified by the Austrian Embassy that the Austrian declaration of war on Russia was to be dispatched the following morning.[2] At 12.45 p. m. on the 5th Forgach called on Conrad to say that at noon on 6 August the declaration of war would be delivered at St. Petersburg.[3] In reality it was not delivered until 6 p. m. on that day.[4] It remained in the form submitted to Francis Joseph on 3 August, not amended on the lines desired by Bethmann, and ran:

> On the instructions of his Government, the undersigned, the Austro-Hungarian Ambassador, has the honor to inform his Excellency the Russian Minister for Foreign Affairs as follows:
>
> In view of the threatening attitude adopted by Russia in the conflict between the Austro-Hungarian Monarchy and Serbia; and of the fact that, according to a communication from the Berlin Cabinet, Russia has seen fit, as a result of that conflict, to open hostilities against Germany; and whereas Germany is consequently at war with Russia; Austria-Hungary considers herself also at war with Russia from the present moment.[5]

The phrasing was skilful in casting the blame for the general war on Russia for having mobilized and then, according to Berlin, opened hostilities against Germany. But as this accusation was not founded on fact, and in any case Germany had on the previous day handed Russia a declaration of war based on other grounds, the Austrian reasons fell to the ground, whereas the fact remained that the initiative in going to war was taken by Germany while Austria joined in on grounds not so much of a conflict with Russia as of the alliance which bound her to Germany. In other words, had Germany not declared war, Austria would not have done so either. The Russian mobilization was not a sufficient reason for her to go to war, any more than was Austrian mobilization for Russia, and German mobilization for France.

It was the Schlieffen plan which had obliged Germany to reply to the enemy mobilization not only by mobilizing herself but also by

---

[1] See pp. 186-92.   [2] DD. IV, 860.   [3] Conrad, IV, p. 177.
[4] Russian *Orange Book*, 79.   [5] DA. III, 124; *Int*. Bez. 2. VI, 12.

opening hostilities and had thus compelled the Chancellor to declare war on Russia and France. Fischer states that neither Berchtold nor even Conrad knew of

the obligation resting on the German General Staff to make war immediately in the event of Russian mobilization.[1]

'Obligation', of course, in virtue of the ambitious Schlieffen plan, which, even had it offered the perfect military solution, was none the less an acute menace to world peace and to Germany herself. Nobody, not even Conrad, then suspected that mobilization meant the opening of hostilities, and Berchtold, who by temperament was anything but inclined to want a major war, must certainly have regretted in his heart of hearts that war had come about by Germany's action in burning her boats. This would explain his words to Shebeko and Dumaine when he talked with them on 1 August and the tone of the Austrian declaration of war. It would also explain Shebeko's telegram of 3 August replying to Sazonov's of 1 August:

So far I have received no explanation from the Austrian Government about the rupture of relations with us, so I am remaining in contact with the directors of Austrian policy; there is confirmation of the conjecture voiced by me before our breach with Germany that Austria would not be unwilling to negotiate with us for a possible way out of the dangerous situation created by her ultimatum to Serbia. In Forgach's words, the position became critical from the moment when the *ukaze* about our general mobilization appeared. All this points to the fact that war with us was not wanted here; it is greatly dreaded, and they are annoyed at the boorish challenge thrown at us by Germany, making a general war inevitable. The mood is without doubt one of deep depression.[2]

But there could be no going back, Writing about those days in later years, Shebeko relates:

Knowing that in politics as in private life the most unexpected reversals are possible . . . I set myself the task of persuading the Austrian statesmen of the folly of their conduct even from the point of view of Austrian interests. . . . It seemed to me at moments that my interlocutors began to perceive the madness of their policy; but . . . the feeling that the solution of the problem had slipped out of their fingers and now depended only on Berlin; the certainty that—even if they tried to stop themselves on the slippery slope—their ally, who had thrown down the gauntlet to Russia and France, would never allow it; all these factors obliged them to confine themselves to generalities which had no other purpose than to gain them time to finish arming and concentrating their troops. . . . On 5 August Count Berchtold finally informed me that the allied relationship binding Austria to Germany unfortunately obliged him to break off his relations with me and

---

[1] Fischer, pp. 269-70.   [2] *Int. Bez.* i. V, 495.

at the same time to recall Count Szápáry from St. Petersburg. . . . The text of the Austrian declaration of war on Russia and Count Berchtold's words on 5 August at Vienna . . . suffice in themselves to reveal the dominant role assumed by Germany in the last days of the crisis.[1]

No doubt it was Germany who in the last days cut communications with the opposite shore. But the first to take up an unyielding attitude had been Austria, who had rejected all mediation and insisted on going to war with Serbia, expecting from Russia a compliance and acceptance of the *fait accompli* which was out of the question. Hence Shebeko is mistaken in writing that Austria would have been not unwilling to negotiate for a settlement. She would have done so had Germany insisted on it, but Bethmann was either unwilling or unable to insist. And when he surrendered to Moltke's pressure, the wrongdoing of Austria faded into the background, thrown into the shade by the aggressive action of Germany. Thus a false impression arose of an Austria who would have been willing to yield, and this impression later influenced the way in which the Monarchy was treated, at least by England.

4. *Grey's attitude to Austria-Hungary; Berchtold's desire to postpone the rupture with England.*

Notice must be taken, in this connection, of the strange illusion cherished for some time by certain *Entente* diplomatists, that it was possible to be at war with Germany without being at war with Austria. On 3 August Bunsen telegraphed to Grey that Dumaine

does not know whether Franco-German war necessarily entails a state of war between France and Austria. He fears, however, that circumstances may compel him to leave Vienna at any moment. . . . I feel in doubt as to whether possible contingency of war between England and Germany would cause me to be immediately withdrawn from Vienna.[2]

Shebeko wrote to Sazonov on 1 August that while the Italian Ambassador, Avarna, made no secret of his distaste for the way Austria was behaving,

I cannot unfortunately say the same of the English Embassy in Vienna. Its members openly express their sympathies for Austria.[3]

And in a retrospective survey of 1 October 1914 Dumaine commented that the Bunsens, who were enjoying life in Vienna, where they had been living for only eight months, 'dreaded for personal reasons the eventuality of a rupture with Austria-Hungary'.[4] But on 4 August Dumaine himself reported having talked to Macchio on the 3rd, adding:

[1] Shebeko, *Souvenirs* (Paris, 1936), pp. 271-2, 278; *Int. Bez.* ii. VI, 7.
[2] BD. XT, 5S2,   [3] *Int. Bez.* i, v, 419.   [4] DF. 3. XI, 704.

I tried everything to get him to see that his Government is the dupe of Berlin; without the ruthless German intrusion, satisfactory arrangements might yet have been concluded with Russia, thus sparing Austria a fearful war. I even hinted that, as the situation did not oblige one to leave Vienna immediately, I might stay on unless relations were to be entirely broken off.[1]

And even after Berchtold told Shebeko that the Austrian Ambassador was being recalled from St. Petersburg, Bunsen reported: 'French Ambassador is still in doubt.'[2]

Grey also shared the illusion. He writes: 'When Austria found that . . . things were serious, she began to try to get out of it.'[3] This impression was due in some measure to the great popularity of Mensdorff, the Austrian Ambassador in London, but still more to the friendly feelings entertained both in England and in France towards the Dual Monarchy. Indeed, in the second phase of the war these feelings manifested themselves in ways that were very disquieting to Italy. This is the explanation of Grey's words to Mensdorff in notifying him of the English ultimatum to Germany on 4 August. Mensdorff thus summarizes them:

Grey, deeply moved, said he saw no necessity for the moment to make a communication to the I. and R. Government and no cause for quarrelling with us so long as we do not go to war with France. In any case he hoped that we would not attack without observing the formality of a declaration of war. He was not recalling Sir M. de Bunsen.

If we went to war with France, it would be difficult for England, as France's ally, to co-operate with her in the Atlantic and not in the Mediterranean. His whole communication was in the most friendly tone and actuated, I fully believe, by the desire to avoid a conflict with us. Tyrrell afterwards, in reply to a remark of mine, said that for the time being the French Mediterranean fleet was not heading in the direction of the Adriatic.[4]

On 4 August Grey telegraphed to Rodd in Rome: 'I do not suppose we shall declare war upon Austria unless some direct provocation is given, or she declares war on us',[5] and to Bunsen in Vienna:

We shall presumably be at war with Germany tomorrow. . . . But I understand Austria not at present to be at war with Russia or with France, and I do not therefore contemplate instructing you to ask for your passports or to address any communication to the Austrian Government."

On the 7th Grey telegraphed to Bunsen: 'Austrian Ambassador is still here without instructions, and I have no further instructions to send you at present.'[7]

[1] DF. 3. XI, 747.   [2] BD. XI, 661.   [3] Grey, I, p. 332. See p. 390.
[4] DA. III, 131, 156.   [5] BD. XI, 591.   [6] BD. XI, 618.
[7] BD. XI, 663.

In reply to an anxious inquiry from St. Petersburg on 6 August as to how much naval support could be expected from France and England, Grey told Benckendorff on the 8th that he really wished to declare war on Austria as soon as possible.

He is simply waiting for the French declaration of war. France, he said, has not yet taken this step because her fleet is busy covering the very considerable transport of troops from Algeria to France. Until the French fleet is free, the English squadron occupied with the pursuit of important German cruisers [*Goeben* and *Breslau*] is too weak to engage the Austrian fleet.[1]

Berchtold on his side was also undecided, whether because the Supreme Command opposed a rupture until the navy was ready, or because he was weighing the possibilities of a bright idea which made it expedient that the state of war with Britain should be delayed as long as possible. In the afternoon of 4 August Rear-Admiral Raisp, the Naval Representative with the Army Supreme Command, called on Conrad to say that as a result of Italy's defection the Austrian navy was in danger of being destroyed in the Adriatic by the Anglo-French fleet, twelve times its strength, and could give only fictitious protection to the coast of the Monarchy. But it could render real service in the Black Sea. Conrad writes that he thought

any scheme that might speed up the adherence of Bulgaria and Turkey so important, that I telegraphed Admiral Haus, who was in supreme command of the Navy, to ask his opinion. . . . With Rear-Admiral Raisp I went to see Count Berchtold to get his view. The Minister approved and sent a note to Constantinople with instructions to obtain free passage through the Dardanelles from the Grand Vizier, and to point out that the Austrian fleet would be a protection also to Constantinople. A request would be addressed to Berlin for the inclusion of the German vessels *Goeben* and *Breslau* in the enterprise. In the evening Count Hoyos personally inquired when in view of the above conversation the declaration of war should go off. I replied that this would depend on when the fleet reached the Black Sea—in three days.[2]

On 5 August came Admiral Haus's reply. It was unfavorable on grounds that a coaling station would have to be secured, that the fleet might be attacked en route by superior forces, and that the navy was not prepared for special missions. Berchtold's letter to Conrad on receiving the news is worth quotation as showing how things were managed in the Monarchy.

I am unpleasantly surprised by the news that Haus put so many difficulties in the way of your brilliant plan! Its execution would be of decisive influence on the final attitude of Romania and Bulgaria, who are apprehensive of the Russian vessels on their coast. If Odessa were bombarded, Bessarabia would be freed. The two

[1] *Int. Bez.* ii. VI[1] , 13, 35.　　　　[2] Conrad, IV, p. 174.

Governments in Bucharest and Sofia are rather hesitant and need a military demonstration to keep them securely with us. Haus seems to be treating the matter very clumsily, forgetting that he is open to attack by foreign forces even in the Adriatic.[1]

If Berchtold saw this, why did he not bring pressure to bear on Haus, who had not put the fleet into readiness though he had known for a month that there was the possibility of war? But Berchtold was incapable of such vigorous action. In fact, on 5 August Tschirschky received instructions from Jagow to make 'urgent representations' that Austria should send declarations of war to France, Russia, and England,[2] this being in reply to a message from Tschirschky of 4 August

that *Goeben* and *Breslau*, endangered by English superiority, Urgently need support of Austrian fleet, which it is formally difficult for Austria to give without a declaration of war.[3]

Berchtold reacted at 1.40 a. m. on 5 August by sending Szögyény the full text of Mensdorff's dispatch, quoted above, for communication to the German Government, adding that Austria had no interest in exposing her fleet needlessly to destruction and needed it to prevent English or French landings on the Dalmatian coast, but was nevertheless prepared

to give priority to the bonds of alliance with the German Empire and, at its wish, enter into war with England as soon as our navy has completed its preparations.[4]

His telegram crossed with one from Szögyény, sent off at 3.50 a. m. on 5 August,

Imperial Chancellor and Secretary of State ask me to request Your Excellency urgently to send the declaration of war not only to Russia and France but *immediately* to England.[5]

Unable any more to evade the issue Berchtold asked Francis Joseph for authorization to declare war on France and England, His report to the Emperor ended:

The German Imperial Chancellor today urgently requested me by Count Szögyény to declare war on France and England as soon as possible. For the sake of the maintenance of friendly feeling on the part of our ally, the German Empire, I regard it as very necessary to keep in step with the German Government in every way and not let the suspicion arise in German public opinion that we inclined to be backward in the fulfillment of our duties under the alliance.[6]

---

[1] Conrad, IV, pp. 178-9.   [2] DD. IV, 874.
[3] DD. IV, 870.   [4] DA. III, 135; DD. IV, 877, 878,
[5] DA. III, 138.   [6] DA. III, 147.

The Emperor's assent was given on 6 August. In notifying Szögyény thereof, Berchtold sent the following message for Bethmann:

It goes without saying that we shall in every way fulfill our obligations under the alliance and declare war on France and England. At present our fleet is in process of being made ready. The Third and Fourth Division, manned by reservists, will not be at full strength until tomorrow and will need at least four or five days more to be ready for war. Our Supreme Command fears that a declaration of war on France would automatically result in the appearance of the French and English fleet in the Adriatic and their establishing themselves at Cattaro; Montenegro would then certainly take sides against us. And yet our fleet would be sacrificed if it had to enter the war before the completion of its preparations. Thus very serious military considerations speak against an immediate declaration of war; and though I do not overlook the fact that the impression produced by our delay is unfortunate, I share the opinion of the military authorities that a premature declaration of war would entail far worse positive disadvantages. ... In spite of all the above arguments, I would, in defiance of all our military authorities, declare war on France and England tomorrow, if the Imperial Chancellor still insists, but would beg Bethmann to consider that even a slight success of our fleet may be expected a few days hence rather than today, and that for ourselves and Germany it is infinitely more important to achieve such success than to go forward at once with the declaration of war.[1]

To this on 6 August Szögyény's reply ran:

Imperial Chancellor requests me to inform you that after consulting the Chiefs of the Army and Navy General Staffs he agrees to postponement of our declaration of war on England and France, but definitely reckons on these declarations of war taking place after the completion in five days from now of the war preparations of the navy, i.e., on the 12th August at the latest.[2]

On 11 August Szögyény telegraphed to Berchtold that the German Government and the two German General Staffs now left it to Berchtold's discretion if and when he should declare war on France and England, provided there was no change in the situation, and this was further expounded by Tschirschky as follows:

By 'change in the situation' the Berlin Cabinet means: (i) intervention of the French Mediterranean fleet in the North Sea, because then the Austrian navy could attack strongly in the Mediterranean and against Algiers; (ii) the event of the German cruiser *Goeben* taking refuge in Pola.[3]

Berchtold gratefully welcomed Tschirschky's elucidation and observed to him that it was important for Germany, too, that the Austrian navy

[1] DA. III, 151.
[2] DA. III, 153.
[3] DA. III, 171, 172.

should remain intact as long as possible, especially in view of Italy. . . . Were Italy to contemplate action against us, it would be very necessary for the Austrian navy to be able to intervene with undiminished strength.[1]

5. *France decides to break off diplomatic relations with Vienna on the ground of a baseless report that an Austrian army corps had been dispatched to Alsace-Lorraine.*

In France the general feeling of friendliness towards Austria was no less strong than in England, but matters took a different turn from the first both for military reasons and because of the need to show solidarity with the Russian ally. On 3 August the French Ambassador at Berne had heard from a Swiss officer that a train-load of Austrian soldiers had been seen crossing Germany and that they were troops from Innsbruck traveling to Alsace.[2] On 4 August Doumergue, the new French Foreign Minister, inquired at Vienna whether the report was true and received from the French Military Attaché the answer that similar rumors were circulating also in Vienna.[3] On the 4th Berchtold said in conversation to Dumaine that happily there was no possibility of French and Austrian troops meeting in combat. But a rumor was circulating in Vienna that the XIV army corps of Innsbruck was being sent to Alsace-Lorraine, while Bavarians were to go to Galicia.[4] On the 5th Dumaine reported the recall of the Austrian Ambassador, Szápáry, from St. Petersburg and the impending departure from Vienna of the Russian Ambassador, Shebeko, adding:

The dispatch, which is hardly any longer in doubt, of an Austrian army corps to Alsace-Lorraine would seem to make the continuance of my mission impossible.[5]

On 6 August Macchio sent for Dumaine and read him two telegrams from Paris reporting that Austrian shops were being looted by the Paris mob without police interference, that Austrian nationals were being turned out of hotels and restaurants, and that the Embassy was filled with refugees.

Baron Macchio said to me in conclusion that the recall of Count Szécsen has not been decided, the Ambassador's presence seeming to be useful for the maintenance or the restoration of calm. As to the participation of Austro-Hungarian contingents in operations in Alsace-Lorraine, he incidentally said he knew nothing, while agreeing that the question was one for the military authorities.[6]

Thereupon on 8 August Doumergue sent to Szécsen and asked him to get his Government to clear up the matter of the Austrian troops in Alsace, of whose presence there the French Government was now

---

[1] DA. III, 171, 172.   [2] DF. 3. XI, 701.
[3] DF. 3. XI, 756.   [4] DF. 3. XI, 771.
[5] DF. 3. XI, 772.   [6] DF. 3. XI, 776.

certain. Dumaine, on his side, was also to raise the question again with the Ballplatz.[1] On 9 August Berchtold telegraphed to Szécsen:

The news of participation of our troops in the Franco-German war is invented from beginning to end,[2]

and the same day Dumaine also reported:

Count Berchtold has just declared in the most precise terms that the information reaching the French Government is without any foundation and that there has never been a question of transporting Austro-Hungarian troops to the French frontier.[8]

To this Doumergue replied on 10 August at 1.10 a. m.:

If the Austrian troops have not been transported to the actual French frontier, they are nevertheless in a neighboring region where we must regard them as being in support of German troops which are acting against us. Please point this out to Count Berchtold and beg him to give you the assurance that no Austro-Hungarian force has been transported to the west out of Austrian territory.[4]

Doumergue still remained unconvinced and at 12.45 p. m. on 10 August telegraphed to Dumaine *en clair:*

Count Szécsen has brought me his Government's reply, which differs somewhat from the one made to you. While you were told that there were no Austrian troops on the French frontier, Count Szécsen said to me that there was no participation of Austro-Hungarian troops in the Franco-German war. This reply and the one made to you do not give us the assurance that there has been no dispatch of Austro-Hungarian troops to the west of Germany outside Austrian territory. These troops, whose presence in Germany is absolutely confirmed, by enabling her to dispose of the effectives they replace on German territory, must indisputably be regarded *de jure* and *de facto* as acting against us. In these conditions it is impossible for the representative of France to remain in Austria. I beg you therefore to ask for your passports and to leave without delay with your Embassy staff.[5]

Doumergue had spoken in similar terms to Szécsen that morning, so that the Ambassador had to ask for his passports and leave. Though allowing it to be true that Austrian troops were not actually at the French frontier, Doumergue said he had information that an Austro-Hungarian army corps had been moved to Germany and their presence there enabled the Germans to use their own troops elsewhere.[6]

It was a specious argument, and in talking to Izvolsky the same day Doumergue said that

---

[1] DF. 3. XI, 780; DA. III, 163.   [2] DA. III, 165.
[3] DF. 3. XI, 782.   [4] DF. 3. XI, 783.
[8] DF. 3. XI, 784.   [6] DA. III, 169.

the main reason which had induced him to hasten the diplomatic break with Austria was our reference to the necessity of resisting a possible move on the part of the Austrian navy.[1]

At 2.35 p. m. on the 10th, Dumaine, having inquired of Berchtold by letter and received an immediate reply, telegraphed to Doumergue:

Count Berchtold states in formal terms that no Austro-Hungarian force has been transported to the west outside Austrian territory,[2]

and when on n August Berchtold received Dumaine's farewell call he did not fail to

certify once again that the information on which the French Government based its rupture of relations was an invention from beginning to end.[3]

This was true. Even though on 6 August Austria had acceded to Moltke's request for a battery of 305 mm. heavy, guns, Conrad had declared that he needed every man against Russia, Serbia, and Montenegro.[4] Moreover, as 4 August was the first day of general mobilization in the Monarchy, Austrian troops could not have been sent to Germany at that moment by the overburdened German railways.

There would have been plenty of time to wait for the categoric reply which Dumaine was asked to, and did in fact, obtain.

If at the beginning the French Government really believed that Austria was sending troops to Germany, it used the pretext later as a proof of its solidarity with Russia, on whom Austria had declared war. As Poincaré writes:

Be that as it may, Austria is now at war with a nation allied to France; the Austrian fleet is cruising in the Adriatic, is blockading the Montenegrin coasts, and Russia is beginning to regard our attitude towards her enemies as ambiguous. M. Sazonov insistently asks M. Paléologue whether our Mediterranean fleet is to remain indefinitely idle in front of the Austrian squadron.[5]

France, therefore, could not do otherwise than give Russia the support so urgently asked for, while at the same time motivating her own declaration of war by a hostile act on the part of Austria. The reason of this is contained in a dispatch from Izvolsky of 5 August:

Count Szécsen shows no intention of asking for his passports. Doumergue thinks this a trick to provoke France into taking first step towards a rupture and to draw Italy's attention to this as constituting the *casus foederis*. It is felt here that both France and Russia must act particularly prudently towards Austria and give her no grounds for accusing them of being the aggressors.[6]

---

[1] *Int. Bez.* ii. VI^r, 57.   [2] DA. III, 170; DF. 3. XI, 785.   [3] DA. III, 173.
[4] Conrad, IV, 192.   [5] Poincaré, V, p. 56.   [6] *Int.. Bez.* ii. VI^1, 6.

Dumaine, writing from Vienna on 12 August, had the same impression of Berchtold's moves.[1] But, as an interpretation of events, this does not bear investigation. Italy had given certain definite assurances to France, but her refusal to recognize the *casus foederis* was based on reasons which had nothing to do with the actions of France. Berchtold was marking time for military reasons and therefore gave Paris those assurances regardless of whether they were consonant with his engagements towards his ally, Germany. On 4 August Conrad had written him: 'A premature declaration of war against France might bring French ships upon us in the Adriatic.'[2] before the Austrian navy was ready. Mensdorff's dispatches from London, moreover, were making it plain to Berchtold that war with France would entail the war with England, which he so much wished to stave off. But so anxious was Paris to ensure Italian neutrality that it made pretence of being attacked by Austria as a precaution whereby the blame for its own declaration of war on the Monarchy could be laid on the shoulders of the Monarchy itself.

6. *France and England declare war on Austria-Hungary*

Thus the French declaration of war made great play with the alleged dispatch of Austrian troops to the German frontier, which was quite untrue, had been categorically denied, and was not based on any authoritative source. To Mensdorff it was communicated by Grey in conjunction with the English declaration of war. This did not come as a surprise. As early as 7 August Mensdorff had telegraphed to Berchtold:

I saw Grey this afternoon. I thought he was going to notify me of the rupture of our diplomatic relations. But he told me he had sent no instructions to Bunsen and that therefore the latter would stay in Vienna till further orders 'unless you want to precipitate matters'. I protested against this supposition. . . . I again did all I could to reopen the question whether it was really indispensable for ourselves and England to go to war. 'Would it not be better to limit the area of hostilities? Would it not be useful if two Powers, one of each group, remained in touch?' To all this he would not say much: 'I cannot speak of the future, only of the present.' I had the clear impression that if we are to be at war with France we shall also be so with England.[3]

The rupture in Franco-Austrian relations took place on 10 August. Shortly before that Crowe had said to the Counsellor of Embassy, Trauttmansdorff, that it was illogical and inconceivable that the fiction of peace between the Monarchy and England could be maintained. 'Yet I am still here and Bunsen still in Vienna', comments Mensdorff in

---

[1] DF. 3. IX, 791.   [2] Conrad, IV, p. 175.   [3] DA. III, 159.

a dispatch of 12 August.[1] The ink on it can hardly have been dry when there arrived the declaration of war from Sir Edward Grey. It ran:

At the request of the French Government, who are not in a position to communicate direct with your Government, I have to make to you the following communication:

The Austro-Hungarian Government, after declaring war on Serbia, and thus taking the first initiative to the hostilities in Europe, has, without any provocation on the part of the Government of the French Republic, extended the war to France:

(1) After Germany had in succession declared war on Russia and France, the Austro-Hungarian Government has joined in the conflict by declaring war against Russia, which was already fighting on the side of France.

(2) According to information from numerous trustworthy sources Austria has sent troops to the German frontier in circumstances which amounted to a direct menace to France.

In view of these facts the French Government is 'obliged to inform the Austro-Hungarian Government that it will take all measures which make it possible for it to answer these actions and these threats.

Sir Edward Grey's message added:

As a breach with France has been brought about in this way the British Government feels itself obliged to announce that Great Britain and Austria-Hungary will be in a state of war as from 12 o'clock tonight.[2]

Thus the war of words between France and Austria ended in the same way as that between Austria and Russia. Austria, forced to declare war on Russia, France, forced to declare war on Austria, were both mainly concerned, Austria to put the blame on Russia, France to put the blame on Austria. Each was above all anxious not to appear as the aggressor, a consideration which Germany under the exigencies of the Schlieffen plan had been obliged to discard. The reasons alleged for these two declarations of war may be regarded as the overture to all the debates and polemics on war guilt which have never died down since. The French Government, in breaking with Austria, neatly cast the blame on the Central Powers without mentioning the word 'war' but only 'all measures which make it possible for them to answer these actions and these threats'. One can only say that the legend of the Austrian troops sent to Alsace-Lorraine forms a worthy counterpart to that of the bombs on Nuremberg, with the difference that the bombs on Nuremberg had a terrible sequel while for the time being nothing happened between the Monarchy and the two Powers which on 12 August declared war on it. Indeed, in 1917–18 conversations actually took place with a view to saving the Monarchy from doom.

[1] DA. III, 174.
[2] DA. III, 175; CDD., p. 532.

The partings between Grey and Mensdorff, Bunsen and Berchtold foreshadowed possibilities of contacts being renewed at a later date. Grey's letter to Mensdorff of 12 August runs:

I cannot express the sorrow which I feel in having to make to you personally the announcement contained in my official letter. . . . I should like to see you to say good-bye, and to shake hands, and to assure you how much my personal friendship remains unaltered.[1]

Mensdorff's telegram had not yet been received by Berchtold when at noon on 12 August Bunsen, on instructions from Grey, announced to him that

in view of the fact that we had some time ago declared war on Russia and were now at war with France, the English Government on its part was obliged to declare war on us and to announce that from 12 o'clock midnight it regards itself as at war with the Monarchy.

Berchtold objected that

our diplomatic relations with France were broken off, but we were till now not at war with the Republic. . . . In tones of emotion the Ambassador replied that he was carrying out his mission with a heavy heart, . . . and that there were no differences between England and the Monarchy which could in the least justify the conflict. . . . I assured him . . . that the two States . . . were closely associated politically and morally by traditional sympathies and common interests.[2]

How little ground there was for this last assertion, how worlds apart were the moral interests of Austria and England, came to light on 26 August when Austria declared war on Belgium on the ground that

Belgium, having refused to accept the proposals made to her on several occasions by Germany, is lending her military co-operation to France and Great Britain.[3]

With good reason did Davignon reply on 29 August:

The Government waited, not only until the ultimatum had expired, but also until Belgian territory had been violated by German troops, before appealing to France and England, guarantors of her neutrality under the same terms as Germany and Austria-Hungary, to co-operate in the name and in virtue of the treaties in the defense of Belgian territory. . . . Germany herself has recognized that her aggression constitutes a violation of international law.[4]

[1] BD. XI, 673.
[2] DA. III, 176.
[3] DA. III, 181, 182.
[4] *First Belgian Grey Bonk,* 78.

Though the cordial farewells exchanged between the English and Austrian diplomatists had for purely momentary reasons no counterpart in the exchanges between the French and Austrian diplomatists, they had implications going beyond the words actually used. They were premonitory symptoms of a tendency on the part of England and France to regard the war as a war mainly against Germany and the conflict with Austria as a side issue. Thus they expended their joint efforts on beating the stronger enemy, when an all-out offensive against the Austrian front would have yielded better results and markedly shortened the war.

CHAPTER XII

ROMANIAN NEUTRALITY

(1) *More disappointments for the Central Powers (p. 546). (2) Berchtold and Conrad fear that Romania will leave the Triple Alliance; first impressions at Bucharest after the Sarajevo murder (p. 550). (3) The equivocal Romanian first reaction to the Austrian ultimatum to Serbia (p. 555). (4) Bratianu's advice to Belgrade; Romanian concern at the prospect of Bulgarian territorial aggrandizement (p. 559). (5) Vienna's vague assurances; the shifts and evasions of King Carol and Bratianu (p. 560). (6) Bratianu's final maneuver; the German promise of Bessarabia (p. 564), (7) Russian and French activity at Bucharest; the Russian promise of Transylvania (p. 568). The Romanian Crown Council of 3 August decides on neutrality (p. 572). Romania renounces respect of the Treaty of Bucharest and abandons Serbia to Bulgarian aggression (p. 575).*

1. *More disappointments for the Central Powers.*

The neutrality of Italy and the intervention of England were the two greatest disappointments for Germany as she hovered on the brink of a grim war on two fronts. But other disappointments were in store for her and her ally, who had built on the support of minor Powers which was either denied them or only given in part later on. The Kaiser voiced German hopes on the eve of the war to the Austrian Military Attaché, Bienerth, whom he received in audience at 5 p. m. on 31 July:

Kaiser Wilhelm explained his efforts to gain active allies. To King Carol of Romania he had telegraphed that, as head of the House of Hohenzollern, he counted on active support in fulfillment of the written treaty. Count Hutten-Czapski, who had just returned from Romania, expressed to Kaiser Wilhelm the fullest conviction that Romania would actively intervene on the side of the Triple Alliance. . . . He had further telegraphed to the King of Bulgaria in decided terms the demand that he should range himself with Austria in the general conflict. . . . He was in the act of concluding a secret treaty with Turkey, pledging Turkey to go into action against Russia with five army corps under the supreme command of Liman von Sanders and the leaders of the military mission now totaling sixty officers. . . . As regards Greece, he—Kaiser Wilhelm—had sent the King a telegram that he 'would break off all relations' with him if Greece sided with Russia. He further reminded the King of Greece that his country would be defenseless against the superiority of the Austro-Hungarian and Italian fleets. . . . His aide-de-camp, Lieutenant-Colonel von Kleist, was on his way to the King of Italy with a letter in which Kaiser Wilhelm urgently asked King Victor Emmanuel to fulfill the treaty by mobilizing his total land and sea forces and sending the promised army group across the Alps.

From the intervention of Italian troops on German soil against France he expected mainly a great moral effect. . . . Germany would have to throw her main forces first against France, and only after the latter's defeat could she take the offensive against Russia, hence Austria-Hungary must bear the first Russian onslaught. . . . He was convinced that Germany would have to reckon with England's active intervention against the Triple Alliance; God alone knew how the German fleet would stand up to the Anglo-French fleet that was four times its strength.[1]

Moltke too, in his gamble, was counting on many cards when on 2 August he asked the Wilhelmstrasse to publish the treaty with Turkey who must declare war on Russia as soon as possible. If England became an adversary, endeavors must be made to kindle revolt in India, Egypt and South Africa. Sweden must be induced to mobilize all her forces and attack as soon as possible on the Finnish frontier. To this end all her wishes, so far as they were compatible with German interests, must be granted, including the retrocession of Finland. If Sweden agreed to co-operate with Germany, Copenhagen must be told of it and invited to do likewise. Similarly Norway. Austria must be asked whether she would put the existing agreements with Bulgaria into operation. The attitude of Greece and Romania must also be ascertained. Japan was to be invited to use the favorable opportunity to realize all her aspirations in the Far East. To this end she must, if need be, receive a promise of German help. Persia was to be invited to throw off the Russian yoke and if possible make common cause with Turkey.[2]

Germany felt quite sure of Sweden. Conrad relates that on 26 July Tschirschky said to him and Berchtold:

Sweden had told M. Poincaré that if there were to be a war with Russia she would unquestionably take the side of the Triple Alliance.[3]

Of all these varied hopes not one was fulfilled at once. Turkey joined the Central Powers in November 1914, Bulgaria not until October 1915. Romania declared herself neutral, and then in 1916 attacked Austria. Greece, too, finally rallied to the *Entente,* while the Scandinavian countries remained neutral. Instead of the projected revolts in India and Egypt hosts of Indian volunteers fought against Germany. Gandhi himself enrolled in the British Army. But the most serious and painful of all these disappointments for the Central Powers was the defection of Romania. Coming on top of the defection of Italy and the intervention of England, it made the cause of the Central Powers look morally bad and militarily anything but secure.

[1] Oe-U. VIII, 11133, 11134.
[2] DD. III, 662. See p. 198.
[3] Conrad, IV, p. 131.

Let us see how things developed in Romania. The story is of special interest to Italians, who at the outbreak of the war were in a similar position to that of the Romanians. But it is also of general interest as throwing light on one of the most important aspects of the situation out of which the war arose. As Fay well observes: 'The Serbian question has received a great deal more attention from writers, because it ultimately became the occasion of the World War; but, next to it, nothing bothered the heads of the men at the Ballplatz more seriously than this Romanian question in the months before the war.'[1] War broke out in consequence of Serbian irredentism, which had found its reason and sustenance in the annexation of Bosnia-Herzegovina and the oppression of the Slav element within the Monarchy. As has been said, the only solution of the Austrian problem would have been a generous measure of federalism or at least of trialism. But both trialism and federalism encountered the opposition of the Magyar ruling class, which was unwilling to lose the dominance it enjoyed under dualism. So that in the end the Southern Slavs achieved their unity, not within the Monarchy, but in conflict with it. This same Magyar ruling class, moreover, drove Romania first to neutrality and then intervention against the Monarchy, thus making the greatest contribution to its dissolution.

After centuries under Turkish suzerainty the two Principalities of Moldavia and Wallachia had been occupied by Russia in 1808, but by the Peace of Bucharest in 1812 were restored to the Sultan with the loss of Bessarabia, it being detached from Moldavia, to which it had always belonged, and ceded to Russia. A southern strip of Bessarabia was recovered by Moldavia through the Treaty of Paris in 1856. In 1859 the Principalities achieved personal union under Prince Alexander Cuza and in 1862 a single government was formed for the two countries. In 1866, on the abdication of Prince Alexander, Prince Charles of Hohenzollern-Sigmaringen was elected *hospodar* of a united Romania. Though Romania had fought on the Russian side in the Russo-Turkish war of 1877, Southern Bessarabia was taken away from her again by Russia in the Peace of San Stefano, while Romania received the Dobruja from the Sultan, a territorial settlement which was ratified by the Treaty of Berlin in 1878. In 1881 Prince Charles was crowned as King Carol of an independent Romania. Under the influence of its Hohenzollern ruler, educated in Germany and deeply attached to her, the new kingdom gravitated into the orbit of the Central Powers. On 30 October 1883 it concluded with Austria a secret alliance which was joined on the same day by Germany and on 15 May 1888 by Italy. It was several times renewed, the last time being on 5 February 1913

[1] Fay, 1, p. 480.

under the conservative Maiorescu Government. At the time of its conclusion the treaty had fulfilled the needs of the moment, but though it still accorded with the King's sympathies and those of the Conservative leaders, it only continued in existence because it remained a dead secret. Public opinion would never have tolerated it because of the treatment meted out by Hungary to the three million Rumanes in Transylvania and also because in the Balkan wars Austria had supported Bulgaria against Romania.

In Transylvania the Rumanes formed the overwhelming majority of the population. Economically and socially oppressed by the Magyar magnates, under-represented in the Hungarian parliament, they nursed grievances which had increasing repercussions in Romania and gave rise to an irredentism less violent in its manifestations than that of the Southern Slavs but strong enough to cause a permanent rift between the two countries. Permanent, because, as has been well observed by Diamandy, who was Romanian Minister in St. Petersburg at the outbreak of the war, Hungary was incapable of creating conditions for the Transylvanian Rumanes which would have satisfied them.

> The Hungarian element was a minority in the state. To maintain its dominating position it had to hold down the other nationalities. . . . The introduction of sweeping democratic reforms, putting these nationalities on the same footing as the Magyar element, would have deprived the Hungarian element of its supremacy.[1]

This explains but does not justify a state of affairs which was further aggravated by the difficulties in Austro-Romanian relations arising from the Balkan wars of 1912-13.

The victories won by Bulgaria at the end of 1912, while seeming to assure her predominance in the Balkans, had thoroughly alarmed Bucharest and given rise to a demand for compensation to redress the balance. This demand took the shape of a claim to a strip of the Dobruja which would improve the frontier assigned to Romania by the Congress of Berlin in 1878 in compensation for the loss of Bessarabia. Bulgaria, on bad terms with Romania, regarded this claim as blackmail to which she was not prepared to yield. The Romanian Government appealed to the Central Powers for support, which Germany gave effectively but which Austria, bound as she was hand and foot to Bulgaria, could only make a feint of giving. The dispute was submitted to the arbitration of the St. Petersburg Conference, which on 19 May 1913 ruled that Silistria should go to Romania.

This ruling, which three months earlier would have satisfied the Romanians, now came too late. The St. Petersburg decision was

---

[1] C. J. Diamandy, 'La grande guerre vue du versant oriental', *Revue des Deux Mondes,* 15 December 1927, p. 802.

violently attacked, and Austrian admonitions not to unite with Serbia and Greece against Bulgaria fell on deaf ears. In vain did Berchtold 'urgently warn' Bucharest that

in view of the open and deep-seated conflict between the Monarchy and Serbia, the military co-operation of Romania with Serbia and Greece was incompatible with the alliance,

and that in the event of a Serbo-Bulgarian conflict the Monarchy might be obliged to take up arms against Serbia.[1] King Carol replied that if Austria wanted to create a Big Bulgaria at the expense of Serbia, Romania relied on Serbia to prevent this and that the alliance would be shaken if Vienna tried to prevent Romania from vindicating her rights.[2] Far from promising neutrality in a Serbo-Bulgarian conflict, he intimated that he would occupy the Turtukai-Balchik line. And in fact, when in the night of 29/30 June 1913 the Bulgarian army treacherously attacked the Serbian and Greek forces, Romania mobilized and went to war, entering the southern Dobruja and threatening Sofia. Defeated, abandoned by Austria, advised by Berchtold himself to sue Bucharest for peace, Bulgaria had to surrender. The armistice of 10 July was followed by the Treaty of Bucharest of 10 August 1913, which gave Romania the Turtukai-Balchik line with a good slice of territory formerly belonging to Bulgaria.[3]

These gains Romania owed, not to her Austrian ally, who even endeavored to obtain the revision of the treaty of 10 August, but to Germany and Russia. The latter, deeply offended by the advent to power in Bulgaria of the Austrophil Radoslavov, had skilfully exploited the situation to attract Romania into her orbit, making her forget the old scar of Bessarabia over the fresh-flowing wound of Transylvania, with such success that Izvolsky wrote to Sazonov on 14 August, 1914:

I have thought and still think that your diplomatic masterpiece has been the detachment of Romania from Austria, always a dream of mine, but one which I had never managed to make come true.[4]

2. Berchtold and Conrad fear that Romania will leave the Triple Alliance; first impressions at Bucharest after the Sarajevo murder.

Vienna had no illusions about the fact that Romania was lost to the Triple Alliance. On the eve of the Sarajevo murder Romania headed the list of Austrian worries, and it figures in the memorandum taken to Berlin by Hoyos on 5 July 1914.[5] On 1 July, the day Berchtold was having the memorandum drafted, he wrote to Conrad:

[1] Oe-U. VI, 6630, 7103.   [2] Oe-U. VI, 7153, 7189.
[3] R. W. Seton-Watson, *A History of the Romanians* (Cambridge, 1934), Ch. XIV has a helpful account of 'Romania and the Balkan Problem' (1908-14).
[4] LN. II, p. 133.   [5] Oe-U. VIII, 9984. See Vol. I, pp. 535-7.

I have had a memorandum drafted for His Imperial Majesty and H.M. Kaiser Wilhelm dealing with the whole set of Balkan questions, especially the relation of Romania to the Monarchy and the Triplice from the political point of view. . . . The paper needs supplementing by a short note showing the consequences arising from the neutrality and possible eventual hostility of Romania in a European war from the military point of view. . . . I beg Your Excellency to prepare a note for me dealing with these issues for use in Berlin.[1]

Conrad promptly replied on 2 July that

the more favorable case of simple neutrality on the part of Romania would be equivalent to the loss of 20 divisions, i.e., about 400,000 men, while the entry of Romania into the ranks of the enemies of the Triplice would mean a loss on our part of 40 divisions, i.e., about 800,000 men. . . . Till now in a Triplice war the Austro-Hungarian army has had to bear the chief burden of the fight against Russia, in order to make it possible for the allied German army to win swiftly a decisive victory over France. This difficult task for our main forces had prospect of success only so long as the co-operation of the Romanian army could be counted upon. . . . As the Monarchy must in future be more than ever determined to concentrate all forces on the decisive main blow against Russia, it is urgently necessary to block all road and rail communications leading from Romania into the Monarchy by permanent fortifications to prevent an unhindered invasion of Transylvania. . . . The Monarchy . . . would have to begin its measures against Romania without delay and complete them, for only an open treaty of alliance binding Romania to the Triplice Alliance could count as a guarantee against possible eventual hostility. The slightest doubt on this point would make it imperative to take military precautions without delay.[2]

A warning such as this might well have made Berchtold pause before embarking upon a course of action which might bring about a European war. Conrad's note was accompanied by a table showing the estimated military strength of the two camps. The combined forces of Russia, France, Serbia, Montenegro, and Romania were given as 133 frontline and 84½ second-line divisions, making a total of 217½. The combined forces of Germany, Austria-Hungary, and Italy were given as 122 front-line and 38 second-line divisions, making a total of 160. But if Italy fell out the total would be reduced by 34 divisions. This was just what was the case a month later (except that the 20 Romanian divisions did not at the beginning form part of the *Entente* forces), as might easily have been foreseen. A keener perception of the line likely to be taken by Italy and Romania in a crisis arising out of an ultimatum to Serbia sent to give a pretext for attacking her would have shown the advisability of a course which was the opposite of the one chosen. The horror aroused by the Sarajevo crime would have been used to enlist all possible

---

[1] Oe-U. VIII, 9976.   [2] Oe-U. VIII, 9995.

sympathies, those of Russia above all, in favor of a knockout blow to Pan-Serb propaganda. Had that been done, Romania would have supported the Monarchy. Czernin writes:

The first impression [of the assassination of Francis Ferdinand] in Romania was one of profound and sincere sympathy and genuine consternation. Romania never expected by means of war to succeed in realizing her national ambitions; she only indulged in the hope that a friendly agreement with the Monarchy would lead to the union of all Romanians, and in that connection Bucharest centered all its hopes in the Archduke and heir to the throne. His death seemed to end the dream of a Greater Romania, and the genuine grief displayed in all circles in Romania was the outcome of that feeling. The much maligned Take Jonescu, on learning the news while in my wife's drawing-room, wept bitterly; and the condolences that I received were not of the usual nature of such messages, but were expressions of the most genuine sorrow. . . .

The ultimatum and the danger of war threatening on the horizon completely altered the Romanian attitude, and it was suddenly recognized that Romania could achieve her object by other means, not by peace, but by war—not with, but against the Monarchy. I could never have believed it possible that such a rapid and total change could occur practically within a few hours. Genuine and simulated indignation at the tone of the ultimatum was the order of the day, and the conclusion universally arrived at was: 'Austria has gone mad'.[1]

Very similar in substance is the report sent to Sazonov on 4 July by the Russian Minister at Bucharest, Poklevski. It is indirectly a tribute to the figure of Francis Ferdinand:

The Romanian people on both sides of the Carpathians looked on the Archduke as their sincere friend, and this opinion was fully shared by statesmen of all parties here, who a few years ago had an opportunity in Sinaia of gaining a personal acquaintance with the Archduke's views and his desire to reconcile the mutually hostile Hungarian and Romanian nations. To him was ascribed, not without reason, the initiative in the negotiations which were carried on first by the Prime Minister Lukács and later by Count Tisza with the Rumane National Committee in Transylvania for the purpose of clarifying and satisfying the demands of the Rumane population of Hungary in the religious, administrative and educational field. It is true these negotiations produced no results and are now broken off, but Romanian public opinion on both sides of the Carpathians in no way ascribes the failure to Archduke Francis Ferdinand, but solely to the irreconcilable chauvinism of the Magyars. It is, moreover, beyond doubt that some of the statesmen and politicians here, bred in the old traditions, hoped that after his accession the Archduke would succeed in realizing his plans for the Rumane population in Hungary and thereby render it possible for Romania to revert to her previous policy of close friendship with Austria

[1] Czernin, pp. 86-7.

. . . . Reading the articles in the press one might think at first that under the emotion of the sad event at Sarajevo warm feelings for Austria had been reawakened in Romania. But in my opinion such a conclusion would be mistaken. Even in the press utterances the thought is apparent that with the Archduke's death hope for an improvement in the state of Rumanes in Hungary has vanished. . . . . The most impulsive of the Romanian statesmen, Filipescu, declared to me on the day of the Sarajevo tragedy that the death of Archduke Francis Ferdinand was from the Romanian standpoint a powerful impetus to the further strengthening of friendship with Russia.[1]

This was all the more so after the Austrian ultimatum to Serbia, which produced the impression in Bucharest that Austria had, to use Czernin's expression, 'gone mad'. Nor was it less mad on her part and that of Germany to imagine that Romania and Italy, having been kept in the dark about their decisions, would follow at their heels in a venture so contrary to their own interests. As early as 3 July Czernin warned Vienna:

M. Bratianu *re* conflict with Serbia. Prime Minister tells me Sazonov said to him that in a war between the Monarchy and Serbia Russia could not stay quiet but would have to declare war on us. I report this as is my duty, but add that I have the very distinct impression that Bratianu fears the infamous murder at Sarajevo might lead to war with Serbia and is trying to intimidate us in order to prevent this.[2]

On 10 July, receiving Czernin in audience, King Carol said he was convinced that official circles in Serbia condemned the outrage as much as he did, and that the Serbian Government would carry out searching investigations, but he thought it understandable if Serbia would not allow investigations by Austrian officials in Belgrade. He himself was anxious for a peaceful settlement of the dispute. From conversations with Bratianu and other Ministers he found that they shared his own feeling that 'since the murder of the Heir Apparent the future of Austria-Hungary looked very dark and gave cause for the greatest pessimism'. This news alarmed Vienna and was communicated in full to Berlin on 13 July. But Jagow did not take it seriously and wrote to Tschirschky:

That so cautious a politician as King Carol has been capable of mentioning to the Austrian Minister the possibility of the collapse of his country is hard to believe. . . . Moreover, the way in which this utterance is reported betrays extreme diplomatic dilettantism on the part of the writer.[3]

Czernin's report was, in fact, quite accurate and showed a much better understanding of the situation in Romania than did the men at Vienna and Berlin, who had not even made up their minds what

---

[1] *Int. Bez.* i. IV, 81.   [2] Oe-U. VIII, 10007.
[3] Oe-U. VIII, 10172, 10175, 10176, 10195; DD. I, 39.

they wanted. The Austrian memorandum and Francis Joseph's letter had been written to persuade Wilhelm that Bulgaria must be made to enter the Triplice, a thing Germany had always refused to contemplate. Under the impact of the Sarajevo outrage Wilhelm had allowed himself to be persuaded and as early as 6 July Bethmann had telegraphed instructions to Waldburg, the German Chargé d'Affaires at Bucharest, to ask for an audience of King Carol, communicate the substance of Francis Joseph's letter to him, and say that Germany agreed to the accession of Bulgaria to the Triple Alliance on condition that accession was compatible with the terms of the alliance binding the Central Powers to Romania. Waldburg was to ask King Carol to consider whether he could not loosen his ties with Serbia and make a stand against the agitation carried on in Romania against the territorial integrity of the Monarchy. Any agreement between Bulgaria and the Triplice would include an explicit guarantee of Romanian territorial integrity.[1]

This was what Vienna had claimed to desire. But on second thoughts Berchtold had changed his mind. On 8 July he telegraphed Szögyény that it was better to say nothing at Bucharest of an intention to bring Bulgaria into the Triplice,

because in the event of developments involving an action against Serbia, the above-mentioned communication to Bucharest might lead to an unfriendly attitude towards us on the part of Romania.[2]

But it was too late to turn back, and Jagow, thinking that Waldburg would probably have already carried out his instructions of the 6th, telegraphed him on the 9th to say at his audience with King Carol that

Count Berchtold does not for the moment intend to make a *démarche* at Sofia for the conclusion of an alliance with Bulgaria and will only advise quietness there. Count Berchtold has been actuated in this matter by considerations of friendliness towards the ally Romania and the expectation that, in the event of a conflict, Romania will discharge her alliance obligations to the full.[3]

Waldburg carried out his instructions on 10 July and reported to Berlin:

When there was mention of Russian efforts to found a new Balkan League aimed directly against Austria-Hungary, His Majesty interrupted me with the remark that nothing was known to him of such an intention on the part of Russia.[4]

The King went on to say that the moment was unfavorable for an approach to Bulgaria such as Francis Joseph suggested. Before any loosening of Romanian ties with Serbia would be possible, public opinion in Romania would have to be conciliated by Hungarian

---

[1] DD. I, 16. [2] Oe-U. VIII, 10126.
[3] DD. I, 21. [4] DD. I, 28, 41.

concessions to the Rumanes in Transylvania. Count Tisza had given promises in this sense, but the expectations thus raised had not been fulfilled. Vienna seemed to have lost its head, and the situation was serious, though not beyond hope. 'About the political capacity of Count Berchtold His Majesty spoke in no flattering terms.' He sharply denied that he would ever lend himself to the acquisition of Transylvania by conquest, and when after the luncheon the subject cropped up again, he said, turning to the Crown Prince Ferdinand, who was present: 'You and 1 will not live to see that, your son may, perhaps.'[1]

3. The equivocal Romanian first reaction to the Austrian ultimatum to Serbia.

If Berchtold was worth little, Bethmann and Jagow were no better, and they were equally responsible for keeping Romania and Italy in the dark about the decision to settle with Serbia once for all. By telegrams of 20 and 22 July the Austrian Legation at Bucharest received instructions to tell King Carol and Bratianu on the afternoon of Thursday, 23 July, and not earlier, that on that very afternoon the Serbian Government would be presented with a note containing demands to be accepted within twenty-four hours. The telegrams added that the note would be communicated to the Powers on the 24th. Only on that day was Czernin to acquaint the Romanian Government of the actual text of the note because 'We must make sure that the Romanian Government is not able on the Thursday to make contact with individual Cabinets'.[2] The same instructions were issued by Berchtold to Merey, who, being unwell, sent Ambrozy to Fiuggi at 4 p. m. on. the 23rd to make the first general announcement to San Giuliano, and about noon on the 24th sent the text of the note to De Martino by the hand of Ambrozy.[3] In actual fact, Romania was more considerately treated than Italy since Czernin read the text to King Carol on the 23rd, while the Consulta received it only on the 24th. This was done 'on verbal instructions' from Berchtold, as we learn from Czernin's dispatch of 24 July.[4] Czernin had left Bucharest on 12 July, returning just before the presenting of the ultimatum. In the meantime he had been in Vienna and Ischl for consultations with Berchtold and Francis Joseph and had probably pointed out to Berchtold that it was not becoming to keep the note secret from the King of Romania until the 24th.

[1] DD. I, 41, 66. He said very much the same thing to Marghiloman a fortnight later in answer to the question 'whether he considered the question of Transylvania to be ripe enough to risk everything for it.' 'No', he said, 'but in twenty years Austria would break up owing to Hungary's attitude' (Seton-Watson, *Romanians,* p. 473).

[2] Oe-U. VIII, 10402, 10482.

[3] See Vol. II, pp. 311-13.

[4] Oe-U. VIII, 10588.

But this trifling attention could not undo the impression produced by the ultimatum, and things were made worse by the fact that in the days preceding its delivery Czernin on his return from Vienna had intimated that a note was to be dispatched but at a later date and quite different in form. Bratianu's indignation was voiced in an article in *Epoca*.[1] King Carol, it is true, had already understood the seriousness of the situation and in his diary for 21 July had noted that he had spoken with Beldiman, the Romanian Minister at Berlin.

I have authorized him to say at Berlin that Austrian policy places us in great embarrassment. War on the horizon on account of Serbia, whose nerve is being worn down by Vienna and above all by Budapest. Situation serious.[2]

The situation was still more serious than King Carol realized, and he was made aware of this on the morning of the 23rd by Fasciotti, the Italian Minister at Bucharest, who warned him that Vienna was going to present unacceptable demands in order then to declare war on Serbia and begged him to urge at Vienna that the demands presented should be such as Serbia could accept.[3] Not many hours later, at 6 p. m., the perusal of the note showed King Carol how truly Fasciotti had spoken. Czernin writes:

I had been instructed to read the ultimatum to him the moment it was sent to Belgrade, and I shall never forget the impression it made on the old King when he heard it. He, wise old politician that he was, recognized at once the immeasurable possibilities of such a step, and before I had finished reading the document, he interrupted me, exclaiming: 'It will be a world war.' It was long before he could collect himself and begin to devise ways and means by which a peaceful solution might still be found. . . . The terrible distress of mind felt by the King when, like a sudden flash of lightning from the clouds, he saw before him a picture of the world war may be accounted for because he felt certain that the conflict between his personal convictions and his people's attitude would suddenly be known by all.[4]

The conversation lasted several hours. The account of it sent by Czernin to Vienna relates that King Carol was thrown into consternation by the ultimatum to Serbia, exclaiming: 'In a week's time we may have a European war.' It put an end to his plans for intervention at Belgrade, St. Petersburg and perhaps Vienna to bring about mutual concessions which would save the peace. He criticized the most

---

[1] Oe-U. VIII, 10725.

[2] C. J. Diamandy, 'Ma Mission en Russie', in *Revue des Deux Mondes,* 15 February 1929, p. 816.

[3] DD. I, 135. Three days earlier in conversation with the German Chargé d'Affaires, Waldburg, Fasciotti had advised against Austria's presenting unacceptable terms at Belgrade, thus obliging Russia to intervene and had added that 'Italy was not for the moment financially in a position to wage war' (DD. I, 177. See p. 262).

[4] Czernin, pp. 87-8, 90.

extreme demands of the note relating to the control of the press and the presence of Austrian officials in Serbia. Remembering that Sazonov had said to him at Constantza: 'Russia absolutely needs peace but we cannot allow anyone to touch Serbia because public opinion would be so roused that my position would become very difficult', King Carol clearly saw that war could not remain localized between Austria and Serbia. 'His sympathies are on our side'—continues his report—'but he knows that his country will not make it easy for him to carry out the treaty of alliance.' Czernin would have liked to clarify this point but could not because to his great regret Berchtold on 22 July had expressly instructed him to refrain from doing so. The general impression left by this part of the conversation was: 'The King believes there will be a European war and he hopes that it will be possible to maintain the treaty.' He foresaw that one result of a general war would be the creation of a Big Bulgaria at the expense of Serbia, but Czernin reassured him: 'If Bulgaria is made bigger, Romania can perhaps get something too', and felt that this had made a good impression on King Carol.[1]

Czernin had a conversation with Bratianu too on the 24th. Bratianu also deplored the note to Serbia as showing that Austria wanted a war, and went so far as to ask whether Austria could be sure of her army, whether the Slavs of the Monarchy might not make common cause with Serbia. Czernin proudly denied such a possibility, adding that the Triple Alliance with its associate Romania was strong enough to hold Russia and France in check. But Bratianu let the matter drop and inquired what were Austria's intentions as regards Serbia, Czernin answered that Serbia would be forced to accept the Austrian demands but that Austria had no intention to annex Serbian territory. Czernin's summing up of Bratianu's attitude runs:

I have the conviction that in a war between Serbia and the Monarchy Romania will remain neutral. If the big conflagration comes, M. Bratianu will be in favor of not intervening and awaiting the outcome. . . . The King will oppose a breach of the treaty. Which trend will prevail is hard to foresee. In any case I do not think that, as far as can be foreseen, Romania will turn against the Monarchy unless drawn directly by Bulgaria and Turkey into a war which would place the country on the side of our enemies.[2]

Czernin's dispatches show that the Romanian leaders were no less at fault than those of Italy in withholding the warning which it would have been necessary to give if they had meant to deter Austria from going to extreme lengths against Serbia and thus bringing about a European war.

[1] Oe-U. VIII, 10588, 10589, 10592.
[2] Oe-U. VIII, 10590, 10593.

They failed to make it plain that in such a war they would refuse to recognize the *casus foederis* and would not march with the Central Powers. Like San Giuliano, Bratianu was playing a game of cunning, going to even greater extremes, as we shall see, to the extent of deceiving Czernin by tricks of dubious political morality, with the result that he encouraged Bulgarian aggression on Serbia to the detriment of the most obvious Romanian interests. No doubt Romania's position was more difficult than that of Italy since she was threatened from three directions. If she marched with Austria she would go against public opinion and help towards the aggrandizement of the feared and hated Bulgaria and the destruction of her ally Serbia while at the same time exposing herself to Russian invasion. From intervention on the side of Russia and France she was held back, not only by a certain reluctance to flout the King's feelings and a lack of confidence in the success of the Dual Alliance, but also by fear of joint attack by Bulgaria and Austria. Even neutrality was not immune from serious risks, involving, as it must, the desertion of Serbia and a free hand for Bulgaria, even if it did not also call down the vengeance of the victors. But just because a European conflagration raised such terrifying problems the Romanian Government should have made the utmost effort to avert it. Here, as in so many other cases, an honest, straightforward policy was the wisest.

But it demanded courage, and courage was not among the endowments of Bratianu, who at once ruled out the possibility of siding with Russia and Serbia against an Austrian move so manifestly in conflict with Romanian interests. To Pašić's request for advice he unhesitatingly replied advising full acceptance of the ultimatum terms. He told this on 25 July to the Russian Minister, Poklevski, who on instructions from Sazonov had called to ask—too late—for Romanian support of the proposal to prolong the time-limit of the ultimatum. Bratianu added that he could not advise differently in view of the fact that Romania was not in a position to give Serbia armed assistance where Romanian interests were not involved.[1] On 25 July the respected and influential French Minister, Blondel, pressed the Romanian Foreign Minister, Porumbaro, for a clarification of the Romanian attitude. For this purpose the Council of Ministers was summoned and on 27 July a formula was handed to Blondel which can be summarized as follows: solidarity with Serbia and Greece in support of respect for the Treaty of Bucharest if Bulgaria violated it; non-intervention between Austria and Serbia as long as Austria did not modify the *status quo* set up by that treaty.[2] But that formula, covering solely the immediate interests of Romania, especially in regard to Bulgaria, refrained from replying to the main question of how Romania would act in the event of a

---

[1] *Int. Bez.* i. V, 23, 72.   [2] DF. 3. XI, 154, 172, 232.

general European war. Poklevski put the question on 25 July to Bratianu, who parried it by saying that in such an event a decision would be reached after consultation not only with the Cabinet but also with the Opposition leaders, and that it was first necessary to ascertain what line Russia would take and what would be her aims.[1]

4. Bratianu's advice to Belgrade; Romanian concern at the prospect of Bulgarian

In immediately advising Serbia to accept all the terms of the ultimatum Bratianu forestalled the belated proposal made to Rodd by San Giuliano on 28 July.[2] Nay more, as early as 25 July Bratianu put forward the solution of the *Halt in Belgrade* which Wilhelm was to send to Vienna on 28 July, and which would have prevailed, had it not been wrecked by the mobilizations. On the 25th Czernin telegraphed to Vienna, and confirmed on the 26th, that he had been asked by Bratianu whether,

as the time-limit had expired, it would not be possible to make a halt after the eventual invasion by our troops and, with the assurance that we purpose no permanent annexation, resume negotiations with Serbia while maintaining provisional occupation.[3]

One wonders whether the Kaiser got wind of the idea before suggesting it to Jagow.

Be that as it may, Bratianu put it forward because he did not want Serbia to be territorially diminished for the benefit of Bulgaria, which, after being shorn of so much territory, was a source of keen anxiety to him. His anxiety was shared by the King, who again received Czernin on the evening of the 26th after learning the Serbian reply to the ultimatum, which seemed to him tantamount to full acceptance.

The King asked outright whether I knew for certain that no territorial changes of Serbian land were intended and emphasized that such would be unacceptable to Romania. . . . Raising his voice in an energetic way quite unusual with him, the King yesterday categorically declared that a 'Big Bulgaria' would be quite unacceptable to him, for the Balkan equilibrium established by the Peace of Bucharest must in all circumstances be upheld.[1]

The King raised his voice because he sensed that Vienna indeed intended, for the benefit of Bulgaria, to overturn the equilibrium established by the Treaty of Bucharest, and that Bulgaria would use the occasion to retake all the territory she had lost in the second Balkan war. This explains his and Bratianu's repeated requests for positive assurances from Austria as to the future attitude of Sofia. These

---

[1] *Int. Bez.* i. V, 72.   [2] See Vol. II, pp. 417-8.
[3] Oe-U. VIII, 10662, 10725.   [4] Oe-U. VIII, 10795, 10796, 10798.

assurances were repeatedly given by Vienna, reaffirmed on Austria's behalf by Berlin, and elicited from Sofia by Vienna and Berlin without, however, calming the two statesmen's fears.[1]

Something very much more convincing would have been needed to reassure them and counteract the influence of Poklevski, whose attitude —as Czernin remarked on 27 July—'is reminiscent of the Hartwig school'. It is no use—urged Czernin—to utter generalities such as 'We abhor a policy of conquest'; 'We do not purpose the annexation of Serbia'; 'We shall always bear the interests of Romania in mind', etc.

Nobody in Romania believes that when we actually have Serbia prostrate we shall content ourselves with acceptance of the 'Note', leaving the now existent Big Serbia intact. . . . Nobody seems in doubt that we have assigned, perhaps even promised, a large slice of Serbia to the Bulgarians. So if it is Your Excellency's intention to preserve Romania at least as a neutral Power in the event of the expected further complications, I regard it as absolutely necessary to indicate now as soon as possible the territory that is to be assigned to her.[2]

But Berchtold thought he could hold Romania to observance of the treaty by fine words alone. After the rupture of Austro-Serbian diplomatic relations on the evening of 25 July, preluding the declaration of war on Serbia, he had telegraphed on the 26th telling Czernin to assure Bucharest that

Austria-Hungary's vigorous action will be of benefit to the entire Triple Alliance and thus to its associate Romania. . . . Mindful of our obligations as allies, we should in the further course of events take no decisions affecting the interests of Romania without making previous contact with her. If Russia acted aggressively against us we should count on the loyal co-opera-tion of Romania as being our ally. But we cherish the confident hope that Russia will not raise the great question of a world war. Then the fate of the whole of Central Europe, Austria-Hungary, and Germany would be at issue, and their destruction would result in the complete abandonment of Romania to Russia and Slav domination.[3]

5. *Vienna's vague assurances; the shifts and evasions of King Carol and Bratianu.*

On 28 July, after war had been declared on Serbia, Berchtold reiterated:

With all means at our disposal we shall seek to hold Bulgaria to strict neutrality, At present we have not the slightest reason to doubt the explicit assurances on this point given by the Bulgarian Government.

Then, in allusion to the treacherous attack made on 29 June

---

[1] Oe-U. 10661, 10663, 10720, 10785, 10795, 10796, 11006, 11189, 11190.
[2] Oe-U, VIII, 10798.   [3] Oe-U. VIII, 10721.

1913 by the Bulgarian army against the allied Greek and Serbian armies, Berchtold added that

> a Bulgarian aggression against Romania would not seem more than a venture *à la Danev*. In such an event we should leave Bulgaria to her wretched fate.

This dispatch was circulated also to Tarnowski in Sofia, but with the suppression of its most vital sentence—the threat to leave Bulgaria to her fate,[1]

Francis Joseph, on his part, telegraphing on 28 July to King Carol to say he had ordered his army to open hostilities against Serbia, added:

> Your long friendship and the intimate relationship between us offer me security that in this grave hour you will show sincere understanding of the decisions I have taken.[2]

How could King Carol show and induce Bratianu to show understanding when Hungary was showing so little under-standing for Romanian feelings? On 28 July Tisza telegraphed to the Ballplatz:

> All that we have gained in prestige from our firm attitude with Serbia will be lost if we let ourselves be intimidated by Romania. We hold Romania in check through Bulgaria, have nothing to fear from her, and will place our future relations with her on a satisfactory and solid basis only by a firm, impressive bearing. We can give her a guarantee against attack from Bulgaria and emphasize that we will give consideration to the balance of power in the Balkans, but that an entirely new juridical situation has been created by the war provoked by Serbia. . . . Were Romania not to honor her pledges as an ally we should be released from all obligations and could shape our Balkan policy independently of Romanian interests.[3]

Neither Vienna nor Berlin shared this opinion, but their appeals were powerless against Hungarian inflexibility.

Before receiving Francis Joseph's telegram King Carol had on 27 July again received Czernin in audience. Acting on instructions contained in the above-mentioned telegram of 26 July[4] to give assurances that Austria would 'take no decisions affecting the interests of Romania without making previous contact with her', Czernin noted the King's satisfaction with this assurance, but added in his report:

> In the event of Russia's intervening against us the King said we could unfortunately scarcely reckon on military support from Romania. Russia . . . would see to it that the Romanian army would be fully occupied on the Bulgarian frontier. . . . Moreover, the question of the Rumanes in Transylvania has so greatly stirred Romanian public feeling against Hungary that co-operation between the two armies is practically impossible.

---

[1] Oe-U. VIII, 10874, 10875.   [2] Oe-U. VIII, 10873.
[3] Graf Stefan Tisza, *Briefe* (Berlin, 1928), I, pp. 43-4.   [4] Oe-U. VIII, 10721.

King Carol would raise the matter with the Government and the Opposition leaders.

> In so saying, the King, who was agitated as I had never yet seen him, assured me that, if he could but follow his own inclination, his army would unquestionably fight on the Triplice side, but he could not do so because in the last year so much has changed that he is not in a position to carry out the treaty. He requested me, nevertheless, to announce to Your Excellency that even in the Russian conflict he would observe strict neutrality, and no power in the world would ever make him take up arms against the Monarchy. . . . Finally His Majesty added the remark that his impression was that Vienna and Berlin wanted the war with Serbia, and the question whether or not a world war was to arise lay entirely in the Monarchy's hands. At best the following two steps might at the eleventh hour avert a general conflagration. After our invasion of Serbian territory we might again demand the total acceptance of our Note, which it might be hoped Serbia would then accept. In the second place the official declaration that we do not plan aggression would make a great impression at St. Petersburg. The Tsar and M. Sazonov were still pacific, but the military party clamoring for war was daily gaining ground.[1]

In this document it is interesting to note the King's renewal of the suggestion, already put forward by Bratianu, of the *Halt in Belgrade* which it would have been so much to Vienna's interest to consider and adopt, and his tacit assumption that the issue of peace and war lay in the hands of the Monarchy, hence that if the European conflagration broke out, the prime responsibility for it would rest with the Monarchy. (The King did not know that the Monarchy was being urged on by Berlin to make war on Serbia.) We will, however, not linger on this point but will continue the narrative of events. A later telegram of 28 July from Czernin reported:

> The German Chargé d'Affaires tells me that H.M. the King said to him today that he could not fully carry out the terms of the treaty of alliance against Russia, as he was able to mobilize at most two army corps. Remainder of army was needed against Bulgaria.[2]

Thus, even though with only a small portion of the Romanian army, King Carol was promising to range himself with the Central Powers. The Romanian Minister Beldiman, on returning to his post on 26 July, had assured Jagow that 'King Carol will not change his policy towards the Triple Alliance', and Jagow had cautiously commented: 'It is true the Minister saw the King prior to the outbreak of the Austrian *démarche* at Belgrade'[3] the date of the audience being, as we have seen,[4] 21 July. Obviously the King's various utterances and

---

[1] Oe-U. VIII, 10876, 10877.   [2] Oe-U. VIII, 10879.
[3] DD. I, 193.   [4] See p. 556.

those of his Ministers were explained, as Czernin perceived, by the desire to abstain from hoisting his colors for as long as possible. While assuring Berlin of some measure of armed support, he told Czernin bluntly on 28 July that Romania did not intend to honor the treaty. Czernin writes:

I cannot quite understand this divergence of statements. Whether the King hoped to intimidate me so that my reports should reflect the opinion that a possible world war would end badly for us, or whether the King does not realize the intimate exchange of ideas taking place between Vienna and Berlin, one thing is certain, namely . . . that at the best we can count on only a small part of the Romanian army. . . . However, at my last conversation with Your Excellency you were good enough to say that the complete neutrality of Romania would in itself be a great gain, and I am firmly convinced that Romania will not take up arms against us as long as the present King reigns.[1]

There can be no doubt that both King Carol and Bratianu— the latter especially—were practicing evasion. After giving Jagow the firm assurances quoted above, Beldiman on 26 July sent the Wilhelmstrasse a very equivocal note:

The Royal Romanian Government, which by the speed of events may find itself in the position of discharging its duty under the alliance, attaches the greatest importance to receiving, in the closest agreement with the German Empire, such timely information as will enable it to take necessary political and military measures, particularly to prepare public opinion in the country for possible far-reaching decisions affecting Romania.[2]

The note concluded with the statement that it had been written on instructions from the King and Bratianu. Something similar was said by Bratianu on the 28th to Czernin when he reproached Austria with not having given him advance news of the note to Serbia 'because as War Minister he must make certain preparations before mobilizing against Russia'. Czernin's comment runs:

I attach no importance to Bratianu's words now after the King's important statements and only report the conversation to illustrate the ambiguity in ruling circles here. Incidentally, I mention that, owing to misleading reports from its Minister, Berlin is mistaken in expecting active collaboration from Romania.[3]

But Berchtold preferred the optimism of Berlin and its representative at Bucharest to the pessimism of Czernin, to whom he telegraphed on 29 July:

Let us not assume that King Carol's utterances reported by you on the subject of Romania's probable attitude in a war between the Monarchy and

---

[1] Oe-U. VIII, 10956.   [2] DD. I, 208.   [3] Oe-U. VIII, 10878.

Russia represent His Majesty's last word. We still confidently hope that Germany's influence in Bucharest will succeed in making King Carol change his mind and inclining him to loyal fulfillment of his accepted obligations as an ally.[1]

Germany was not slow in making her influence felt, as is shown by a series of telegrams from Jagow to Waldburg, expressing confidence in Romania's loyalty, giving assurances on behalf of Bulgaria, and denying the existence of Bulgarian war preparations,[2] and by telegrams from Waldburg reporting his conversations with the King on 28, 29 and 30 July, the latter being particularly important. On 29 July Jagow had telegraphed:

> Matters are coming to a head in that Russia has today ordered mobilization of Kazan, Kiev, Moscow, Odessa. Austria can hardly do otherwise than mobilize against Russia. Perhaps the conflict might still be averted by a Romanian *démarche* at St. Petersburg or possibly by a direct telegram from King Carol to Tsar in which Romanian engagements are revealed.[3]

The suggestion of this *démarche* had been made to Jagow by Berchtold, who on 28 July had telegraphed to Szögyény that it might be useful 'to put pressure on Russia from Romania', taking the form of

> a solemn *démarche* at St. Petersburg (possibly even a secret telegram from King Carol to Tsar Nicholas) or the publication of the alliance, stating that in the event of a European conflagration Romania would fight on the side of the Triple Alliance against Russia.[4]

Berchtold can scarcely have imagined that such a declaration would cause Russia to give way, but it would have served to compromise King Carol.

6. Bratianu's final maneuver; the German promise of Bessarabia.

There was, however, not the slightest chance that King Carol would thus compromise himself. He had always steadily refused to publish his engagements with the Triplice. Could it be imagined that he would do so at this juncture! Therefore he adroitly avoided the question. To Francis Joseph's telegram of 28 July announcing the declaration of war on Serbia and making no request for Romanian fulfillment of the treaty,[5] Carol replied on the 29th with wishes for 'the speedy and favorable issue of the war' and for the preservation of the peace of Europe.

> At the same time I cherish the desire that the balance of power in the Balkan peninsula achieved by my country with so much sacrifice may remain intact.[6]

[1] Oe-U. VIII, 10952.   [2] DD. I, 214; II, 316, 321.
[3] DD. II, 389.   [4] Oe-U. VIII, 10863.
[5] Oe-U. VIII, 10873.   [6] Oe-U. VIII, 11014.

To a request of 30 July from Waldburg, on instructions from Jagow, that he should telegraph to the Tsar, King Carol replied that the Russian partial mobilization was only a gesture to calm public opinion, that it would be awkward for him to send a telegram to the Tsar, that disquieting news was coming in from Bulgaria, that a dispatch from England intimated that an Austrian attack on Russia would not leave her indifferent, and finally that

he was endeavoring to prepare public opinion for a possible war with Russia, but he once more pointed out the great difficulty of fulfilling his obligations under the alliance.[1]

Czernin on the same day reported that Waldburg had asked for publication of the treaty. 'As was to be expected, His Majesty sought excuses and declared he would consult with Bratianu'.[2] With Czernin that day the King was more explicit.

His Majesty avoids a direct answer but declares fulfillment 'virtually impossible' for him. He could mobilize against Russia at most one or two army corps, which being 400 km. away from our army would certainly be defeated. The Russian fleet would destroy Constantza. . . . Romania would succumb, and then revolution would at once break out. My objection that these were all possible eventualities when the treaty was made produced no impression. I declared I could not accept rejection of the treaty as a last word. . . . King Carol declared that the decision did not lie with him alone, all the Ministers and both Opposition leaders must give their vote. Cabinet meeting on this subject in the coming days, but feeling of the majority of the Ministers against co-operation with the Monarchy. . . . His Majesty hopes that after the occupation of Belgrade, which might be retained as a gage, we would accept fresh negotiations.[3]

It is strange to see that in spite of the King's plain language and a low opinion of Bratianu, Czernin on 30 July still placed some reliance on the latter's words. On that day Czernin reported to Vienna that Bratianu had suppressed the publication of a telegram to a Romanian newspaper from its correspondent in Hungary saying that the Hungarian authorities had made numerous arrests among Rumane notables in the Banat. Czernin added the advice: 'In view of Germany's forthcoming attempt to obtain the publication of the treaty, fresh irritation against the Monarchy is to be deprecated'.[4] Still on the same day Czernin telegraphed to Tisza:

The university professor Stere of Jassy is going with Bratianu's approval to Vienna to meet leaders of our Rumanes there. The object of his journey, he says, is to promote a demonstration by our Rumanes in favor of the Austro-Hungarian Monarchy. On a basis of the demonstration of loyalty by

[1] DD. II, 463   [2] Oe-U. VIII, 11040, 11044.
[3] Oe-U. VIII, 11045, 11046.   [4] Oe-U. VIII, 11039

our Transylvanian Rumanes he wants to get up a big anti-Serbian and anti-Russian demonstration in Bucharest and show that even the Rumanes in the Monarchy share this standpoint and in a grave hour stand firm by their fatherland. As M. Bratianu in connection with recent events undoubtedly desires to influence public opinion here in our favor, I should be grateful if you would follow the matter with benevolent interest.[1]

This is an episode which justifies doubts as to the *bona fides* of Bratianu's tactics. There are certain national feelings with which no one has a right to play tricks. Never would an Italian Minister have dared, either on Italian soil or in the unredeemed territories, to get up a demonstration of Trentini or Triestini in favor of Austria. Why did Bratianu go to such lengths to calm Austrian anxiety? It looks as if this maneuver, which would not actually be put into execution, was intended to delay publication of the treaty until it had been decided what course would be taken by the country in the event of a European war. But the fact remains that Czernin's suspicions of Bratianu were somewhat allayed. Another apparently reassuring sign was that Tarnowski at Sofia, also on 30 July, induced the Bulgarian Premier, Radoslavov, to instruct the Bulgarian Minister, Radev, to declare at Bucharest that that as long as Romania did not side against Austria, she would have nothing to fear from Bulgaria.[2] And in fact Radoslavov telegraphed telling Radev to inform Bratianu that 'Bulgaria is resolved to observe neutrality until the end of the war between Austro-Hungary and Serbia and cherishes the sincere wish to remain in friendly contact with the Bucharest Cabinet. If, however, in the event of a general conflagration Romania were to swing away from the Triplice, Bulgaria would find herself compelled to change her attitude towards Romania.'[3] Radev carried out these instructions during the night of 30/31 July, but they had no effect on the situation, which on the 31st was plunging headlong towards war.

On the 30th Bethmann had sent the Kaiser a telegram for King Carol which went off on the morning of the 31st. After summarizing the reasons which forced Germany to range herself with Austria, the telegram ended:

In this grave hour my thoughts fly to you who have created a civilized state on Europe's eastern march and thereby erected a dam against the Slav tide. I am confident that as King and Hohenzoller you will remain loyal to your friends and fulfill your engagements under the alliance to the utmost.[4]

On the proclamation of the *Kriegsgefahrzustand* on the 31st Berlin deemed it advisable in view of the imminence of war to back up the Kaiser's appeal with some tempting promise. At 6 p. m. on that day

---

[1] Oe.-U VIII, 11042.   [2] Oe-U. VIII, 11102.
[3] Oe-U. VIII, 11140.   [4] DD. II, 472.

Jagow instructed Waldburg, the Chargé d'Affaires at Bucharest, to tell King Carol and Bratianu without delay that

if war with Russia were unavoidable, the Imperial Government, in the event of a favorable outcome, would use its influence in order that, as reward for the fulfillment of its engagements and for active participation in the war on our side, Romania should receive Bessarabia.[1]

Waldburg carried out his instructions on 1 August. The King told him that the Italian Minister had just officially announced that in the impending general war Italy did not regard herself as bound by her alliance since she regarded the provocation as coming from Austria. King Carol added that the same clause existed also in his treaty, and that he was summoning a Crown Council to decide what line was to be taken. Less honest than the King, Bratianu assured Waldburg that he would do everything possible to fulfill the treaty engagements, while enlarging on the Austrophobia of Romanian public opinion. He asked that Hungary should give assurances to its Rumanes in Transylvania that more rights would be granted them after the war.

As regards Bessarabia, Bratianu declared that it would only be of value to Romania if Russia were made to cede other territory to Austria and Germany and be so weakened that this province would actually remain permanently with Romania.[2]

Next day the German Minister, Waldthausen, returned to his post at Bucharest and Bratianu complained to him that he had never received previous warning and had had no time to counteract the anti-Austrian feeling in the country.

He voiced the idea that Romania might in the first place declare that she would not attack Bulgaria if Bulgaria attacked Serbia. By this as many Austrian army corps would be set free for use against Russia as equaled the Romanian army. . . . He would like best if Russia attacked Romania, since this would bring about a change in public opinion.[3]

Clearly fear deterred the Romanian Premier from refusing to recognize the *casus foederis,* as was his right and duty, and led him to permit the enemy Bulgaria to attack the friend Serbia, so that in the event of victory the Treaty of Bucharest would have been modified at the expense of Serbia to the serious disadvantage of Romania. The deal offered by him was neither profitable nor honest, but that did not prevent him from proposing it. Bethmann, however, would have liked still more. On 2 August, when war had broken out, he asked for 'the immediate mobilization of the Romanian army and its entry into war against Russia'.[4] On 3 August he announced:

[1] DD. III, 506. [2] DD. III, 582.
[3] DD. III, 699. [4] DD. III, 646.

Auspicious negotiations with Bulgaria for conclusion of an alliance. Please tell King and ask if formal undertaking by Bulgaria to give up Dobruja so long as Romania remains with Triplice would satisfy him and Romania would then move with us against Russia.[1]

Another telegram from Jagow of the same day announced the signing of an alliance with Turkey.[2] Francis Joseph also put pressure on King Carol by a telegram which is recorded in the King's diary for 2 August:

The Emperor Francis Joseph telegraphs me somewhat too energetically that both as officer and King I ought to keep my word and march side by side with his army against Russia.[3]

All in vain. The King and Bratianu told Waldthausen on the 3rd that the Crown Council was to meet that very day to take a decision and that the King would very strongly advocate mobilization.[4]

7. *Russian and French activity at Bucharest; the Russian promise of Transylvania.*

Such was the situation between Romania and the Central Powers before the meeting of the Crown Council. We must now turn our attention to what was going on between Romania and the Triple *Entente*. Something of it has already been told. As regards England the account is of the briefest. On 1 August the English Minister at Bucharest, Sir George Barclay, reported:

I have refrained from advising neutrality as I feel uncertain as to the attitude of Romania. . . . Romania's avowed objection to remaining neutral is that in the general settlement she may suffer. The fact that Great Britain has advised neutrality might diminish this fear.[5]

That same evening Grey replied: 'We cannot give advice.'[6] In this reply there is the whole man with his lack of decision, his failure to realize what the situation demanded, whether to save the peace or win the war.

Let us now turn our attention to the action of Russia. On 26 July Sazonov instructed Poklevski to tell Bratianu that Russia was doing everything possible to compose the Austro-Serbian conflict, but that if she failed she could not remain neutral and leave Serbia to her fate.

We think that all sympathies and future hopes must necessarily intimate to Romania that her interests lie with Serbia. If Austria flings herself today on Serbia with the accusation of irredentism, the same fate will overtake Romania tomorrow, or else she will have to renounce for ever the realization of her national ideal.[7]

---

[1] DD. III, 729.   [2] DD. III, 743.
[3] Diamandy, *Ma Mission en Russie,* p. 817.
[4] DD. III, 786.   [5] BD. XI, 416.
[6] BD. XI, 432.   [7] *Int. Bez.* i. V, 85.

Poklevski carried out his instructions on the 27th but, apart from pro-Serbian protestations, elicited nothing from Bratianu, who eluded the question as he had done two days earlier.[1] This made Sazonov feel anxious, all the more as he had at once learnt of the note handed by Beldiman to Berlin on the 26th.[2] On 28 July he informed Poklevski of it, adding: 'We are unwilling to believe this information since, if it were true, it would convict Romania of unparalleled deceitfulness.'[3] But on the 28th Poklevski was able to send more reassuring news. Bratianu had called on him to say that he was not authorized to make any official statement about Romanian policy in the event of a European war but

speaking personally he thought he could state that Russia at all events need not expect any hostile move on the part of Romania. . . . Through Bratianu's words could be perceived . . . the fear that if Romania remained neutral she would after the war was over be exposed to chicanery both from Russia and from Austria.[4]

On 29 July Sazonov telegraphed back assurances to calm such fears:

In the event of an actual armed conflict between Austria and Serbia our intervention is to be expected in order not to permit the annihilation of Serbia. This will be the aim of our war with Austria, if such a war proves to be unavoidable. . . . Will you put the categoric question to Bratianu as to what attitude Romania will adopt, giving him to understand that we do not rule out the possibility of advantages for Romania if she joins us in a war with Austria. We should like to know what are the Romanian Government's views on this point.[5]

Indeed, after Nicholas II on the 29th telegraphed thanking King Carol personally for his efforts to save peace,[6] Sazonov himself on 30 July sent a message to Bratianu expressing readiness to support the annexation of Transylvania to Romania, and on the 31st, he again reverted to the subject:

We have positive data pointing to the possibility of armed action on the part of Romania jointly with Austria against us. Be prepared . . . for all eventualities and secure the inviolability of the secret archives by sending them in time to Odessa. Certain signs indicate that the possibility exists for us to secure the non-intervention, or even the open transition of Romania to our side by offering commensurate compensation. As such compensation we would declare our willingness to promise our support for the acquisition by Romania of Transylvania.[7]

The Russian Minister, Poklevski, on his part sent a long pessimistic dispatch on the same day to St. Petersburg reporting that Bucharest society and part of the Romanian press anticipate 'that Romania will

[1] *Int. Bez.* i. V, 148.   [2] DD. I, 208.   [3] *Int. Bez.* i. V, 165.
[4] *Int.* Bez. i. V, 199.   [5] *Int. Bez.* i. V, 216.
[6] *Int. Bez.* i. V, 215, 280.   [7] *Int. Bez. i.* V, 341.

remain neutral and that the King has decided to proceed in league with Germany'. Both he and Blondel had received information that the King was threatening to abdicate unless Romania sided with the Triplice. The King's attitude was motivated by 'the existence of a defensive treaty with Austria in the form which I have communicated' and by a 'belief in the superiority of the Triplice forces and the conviction that the Triplice can give Romania adequate guarantees against Bulgaria'. However, 'one can say with certainty that public opinion here is hostile to Austria', the army too being pro-Russian. Blondel and Poklevski had made a joint call on Bratianu, who reiterated that 'Romania was not bound in any way' and that her attitude would be decided by the forthcoming Grand Council. After Blondel had left, Bratianu had discussed the offer of Transylvania with Poklevski, asking whether France and Britain would consent to its being given to Romania. 'I answered that our Allies would have regard to promises made by us.' Three days later Sazonov was to telegraph that Poincaré had said to Izvolsky 'that in order to exercise pressure on Romania in the desired sense, Transylvania must be offered to her'.[1] But already Bratianu showed he was taking the offer very much to heart:

> He begged me not to attach any credence to the rumors going around the town and sought to persuade me that the possibility of co-operation with us was not to be ruled out. . . . I do not, like Your Excellency, believe in the possibility of 'unparalleled deceitfulness' on the part of Romania.[2]

But Poklevski did not feel entirely reassured any more than Blondel, who at 1.10 a. m. on 31 July telegraphed that after the Cabinet of the 30th the Government issued a communiqué: 'that Romania will remain neutral as long as the present situation does not change.' Blondel pointed out to several members of the Cabinet that 'in the event of a conflict between Austria-Hungary and Russia, Romania might depart from her neutrality. My interlocutors under different forms confessed to me that the question had indeed been raised whether Romania could remain neutral and whether the victor would not make her pay for her abstention. . . . I have become convinced that certain members of the Cabinet hesitated to come out clearly in favor of neutrality'. The King was exercising persuasion both at Vienna and Belgrade in favor of the *Halt in Belgrade*.[3]

The discerning French Minister had perceived the unwisdom of Sazonov's and Poklevski's request for immediate Romanian intervention on the Russian side and he asked only for her neutrality. He persuaded Poklevski that it was best to proceed carefully and 'as it were, by stages'. For more than an hour on 31 July in the presence of

---

[1] *Int. Bez.* i. V 481.   [2] *Int. Bez.* i. V, 365.   [3] DF. 3. XI, 379.

Poklevski he advocated neutrality 'as the only solution which would not jeopardize Romania's future'. Bratianu 'expressed the fear that the interested Powers would bear a grudge against Romania for her inaction'. Poklevski 'was able to give an assurance that Russia, for her part, would be grateful for abstention, which in present circumstances would be regarded as a token of friendship'.[1] But Bratianu declined to commit himself, and Sir George Barclay telegraphed on 31 July to Grey:

My French and Russian colleagues, who had until now been hopeful as to attitude of Romania in event of general conflict, are now very anxious.[2]

Their anxiety lasted over the following days, despite the fact that Bratianu, on learning on 2 August of the German declaration of war on Russia and giving the news to Poklevski, asked whether Russia would regard the observance of neutrality by Romania as a friendly gesture and was gratified by Poklevski's affirmative answer.[3] The question showed which way the wind was blowing, but Poklevski, who still pressed for Romanian intervention on the side of the *Entente*, remained mistrustful and telegraphed again that same day:

The-attitude of the Romanian Government is really ambiguous and causes us serious anxiety. It still oscillates strongly and a definite decision has clearly not been reached.[4]

Before the Crown Council meeting of 3 August Poklevski talked with almost all the leading political figures and reported to St. Petersburg that German and Austrian threats and promises were causing dismay among them.

Take Jonescu would make no concrete statement about neutrality and only uttered the opinion to me that Romania in any case was done for, for whatever she decided she would either be wiped off the face of the earth or become something like a Russian or Hungarian province. His agitated and depressed mien and many other indications make me apprehensive of a Crown Council decision today highly unfavorable to ourselves.[5]

[1] DF. 3. XI, 446, 633.
[2] BD. XI, 350.
[3] *Int. Bez.* i. V, 469.
[4] *Int. Bez.* i, V, 470.
[5] *Int. Bez.* i, V, 502. It is hard to realize that neither Poklevski, nor Blondel, nor even Sazonov knew that Romania had been allied to the Triplice for thirty years and that the alliance had been renewed only the previous year. After the Constantza meeting Blondel telegraphed to Paris that Sazonov had declared himself convinced that there was no alliance between Austria and Romania, that at most only verbal agreements had passed between the two Sovereigns and that Romania's hands were free. Blondel added that four Roumanian Cabinet Ministers had corroborated Sazonov's opinion, challenging any one who affirmed the contrary, to produce the treaty if there were one (DF. 3. X, 416). No secret was ever better kept, but to achieve this even the Foreign Minister, Porumbaro, had to be kept in the dark.

This narrative gives some idea of the uncertainty which prevailed up to the last regarding the attitude of Romania. If one considers that among the diplomatists of the two opposing groups still greater uncertainty reigned as to the intentions of England and Italy, one can gain some idea of the far-reaching effects resulting from the behavior of the three countries on whose aid or neutrality the opposing camps gambled right up to the last minute. Had they only made their intentions clear in good time, the crisis of 1914 would never have ended in war. They could have done so easily enough, had the political leaders from the outset mustered courage to pursue the policy dictated by the obvious interests of their respective countries. So self-evident is this that one is amazed to find the diplomacy of both sides incapable of grasping so elementary a principle. But, as has been remarked above, the spirit of a nation is the most elusive thing for a foreigner to understand, and never more so than when that foreigner is one of the 'well-informed', who in the nature of things move in select circles where the last thing they are able to get at is the unvarnished truth.

8. The Romanian Crown Council of 3 August decides on neutrality.

These reflections receive confirmation from the unanimity prevailing at the Crown Council of 3 August, which was attended by the Crown Prince and all the Romanian political leaders. Many versions have been given of what took place at it, but a careful reconstruction of it has been made by George Fotino.

The object of the Crown Council was not to decide on which side Romania would range herself. It was not a question of ascertaining how to espouse the cause of the Allies but of how not to make common cause with the Central Powers, to which she was bound by a treaty. . . . This memorable meeting opened with an appeal from the aged Sovereign to his counselors, which ran: 'The world war has broken out; the struggle is engaged. On its issue will depend the future map of Europe and the fate of nations. In this struggle there will be victors and vanquished. And irrevocably the neutrals will be among the vanquished. . . . Romania must fulfill the treaty binding her to the Triple Alliance. This treaty has for decades secured unquestionable advantages for Romania. . . . The political parties, each in turn, have followed the same policy. To change it today would be to repudiate both our signature and our past.'[1]

King Carol, himself, anticipated the victory of the Central Powers. He did not believe that England would come into the war, thus causing his niece, the future Queen Marie, to exclaim in exasperation: 'In this house they just do not understand a thing!'[2]

[1] G. Fotino, 'Une séance historique au Conseil de la Couronne' (3 août 1914), in *Revue des Deux Mondes,* 1 August 1930, pp. 529-41.
[2] Take Jonescu, *Souvenirs* (Paris, 1919), p. 46.

But the Crown Council did understand, and a deep silence followed the King's speech. The King turned towards Bratianu, but he asked to speak last and the Opposition was called on to express its views. The aged Theodor Rossetti, the doyen of former Prime Ministers, said: 'Certainly, treaties have to be respected, but so far as I can see these do not oblige Romania to act', and he advocated neutrality. He was followed by another former Prime Minister, Carp, who spoke against neutrality: 'Sooner or later we shall be invaded by one side or the other. Moreover, why hesitate? The victory of the Triple Alliance is assured. . . . The triumph of Slavism would be fatal to our country.' Carp's speech made a deep impression and to counteract it the leader of the Conservative party, Marghiloman, asked the King to read out the text of the treaty. This stated clearly that the *casus foederis* would arise for Romania 'si l'Autriche-Hongrie etait attaquee . . . sans provocation aucune de sa part'. Marghiloman then commented: 'Our allies have not been attacked, they themselves have attacked; there is, therefore, no *casus foederis*. . . . Public opinion must also be taken into account, it will not hear of a war on the side of the Triple Alliance. . . . What Austria imposes on Serbia today may be imposed on us tomorrow by Hungary. . . . I am for neutrality. In any case, let us await the decision of Italy. If she interprets the text in the sense of non-application of the *casus foederis,* who would comprehend a different interpretation on our part? Certainly not the country.'

John Lahovary, another Conservative member, spoke strongly in favor of neutrality, ending by expressing doubts of the victory of the Triplice, which the neutrality of Italy would contribute to render still less a foregone conclusion. Carp, who had listened with great impatience to this speech, broke in: 'I assure you that Italy will enter the war immediately.' The King could have cleared the matter up there and then, since, as has already been said,[1] he had told Waldburg, the German Chargé d'Affaires, that Fasciotti had received instructions from the Italian Government to announce that in the impending general war Italy did not regard herself as bound by her alliance since she regarded the provocation as coming from Austria.[2]

But Fotino's account, corroborated by a fact of which we shall soon take cognizance, shows that the King kept this vital piece of information to himself, calling on the former Conservative Minister Gradisteanu to speak next. 'This war[1]', said Gradisteanu, 'appears to us to be a Hungarian war. . . . Let us therefore remain neutral.' He was followed by the leader of the Conservative Democratic party, Take Jonescu. It has been asserted that he proposed co-operation with France and Russia, but this is not so. What he said was: 'After thirty

[1] See p. 567.   [2] DD. III, 582.

years of alliance with her [Austria] and Germany, we cannot fight on the side of Russia. After long and painful reflection I see only one possibility for Romania: armed neutrality.' Bratianu summed up on behalf of the Government: 'We ask for the neutrality of Romania. The treaty . . . does not bind us to take arms. Even if it did so, Romania could not allow her fate to be decided without her having been previously consulted. . . . Romania could not take up arms in a war aiming at the annihilation of a small nation. The question of the Rumanes of Transylvania dominates the whole situation. . . . If in questions of secondary importance it is possible to disregard public opinion, in the decisive hours of the national life one cannot flout it. At the present moment one can only go to war if the conscience of the nation approves. It does not. Let us, therefore, remain neutral. Italy will probably take up the same position. The war will be a long one; let us await the course of events. We shall have the chance to say our word.'

The King seemed more and more depressed, and Carp asked leave to speak again. His tone was aggressive. 'You are afraid.'—he shouted at Bratianu—'You have not the courage to take responsibility. You find it convenient to shelter behind public opinion.' Carp's thesis was that the statesman is the sole master of his nation's destiny; the nation cannot impose its will on those who govern it. At the height of the discussion the door opened and an usher brought Bratianu a telegram confirming the neutrality of Italy. The King, who already knew this, made a gesture of resignation and did not speak. Carp, still unabashed, accused his opponents of deserting their King in the hour of need. The King tried a last appeal: 'Gentlemen, I feel myself personally bound to the Central Powers. If you think that the good of Romania requires another foreign policy, I am ready to withdraw.' He cast a glance around. Nobody moved. After a painful silence Lahovary spoke: 'Does Your Majesty not see that Austria-Hungary in not informing you has treated Your Majesty as a vassal?' This was too much for the King's pride, and after further discussion he asked his counselors to pronounce for or against neutrality. One after another they pronounced for neutrality, with the single exception of Carp. 'I find', said the King, 'that the representatives of the country with all but unanimity demand the neutrality of Romania. As a constitutional monarch I submit to your vote, gentlemen. But I fear that the prestige of Romania will emerge diminished from today's meeting and that you will repent of the decision that has been taken.'

These particulars of the discussion which went on at the Crown Council meeting are not without interest as showing at whose door the immediate responsibility for the outbreak of war was at that moment felt to lie. Men of all parties both in Bucharest and in Rome had at once the clear impression that the provocation came from Austria, it not being likely that Russia would countenance an attack on Serbia. What an incalculable benefit it would have been had Berlin and Vienna been told in time that they would be left to run the risks of the venture alone! But not even the Council's decision gave Bratianu the courage to talk plainly to his allies. At the end of the meeting the King withdrew to his room and sent for Marghiloman and Take Jonescu to undertake with him the drafting of the communiqué for the *Official Gazette* and the communication to be handed to the representatives of the Central Powers. The communiqué stated that 'the Crown Council discussed the steps to be taken by Romania in the present circumstances. It was almost unanimously decided that Romania would take all measures necessary for the defense of her frontiers'. The communication handed to Waldburg and Czernin ran as follows :

After a warm appeal from the King to put the treaty into operation the Crown Council with one dissentient declared that no party could take responsibility for such a step. The Crown Council resolved that in view of the fact that Romania had been neither warned nor consulted in connection with the Austro-Hungarian *démarche* at Belgrade, the *casus foederis* did not arise. The Crown Council further resolved that military measures should be taken for the security of the frontiers, whereby the Austro-Hungarian Monarchy would be benefited since its frontiers would be covered for several hundred leagues.

After the Crown Council the Cabinet continued discussions alone and, in order to secure a more speedy effect by its *White Book,* decided to renounce the standpoint of the Treaty of Bucharest and allow Bulgarian intervention in Serbia, a measure which would enable Austria-Hungary to withdraw at once from the Serbian theatre of war several army corps equivalent in number to those Romania could dispatch to the Pruth [i.e., against Russia]. This, incidentally, would be the only way [for the Romanians] to ensure safety with regard to Bulgaria where Russian influence allows of no certainty. Of course all this will hold good only if this attitude on the part of Romania is regarded by the two Empires as consonant with friendly relations. To demand more of the King's chivalrous feeling would be to outstep the bounds of the possible.[1]

9. *Romania renounces respect of the Treaty of Bucharest and abandons Serbia to Bulgarian aggression.*

If the moral law has any validity in international relations it must be agreed that Bratianu and those responsible with him for the decisions embodied in the above document were not actuated by over-many scruples. In the first place, though the Crown Council decided on neutrality, they had not, as had Italy, the courage to tell the Central Powers that neutrality was the course chosen by Romania. The

[1] DD. IV, 811.

existence of the *casus foederis* was denied, not on grounds that the European conflagration had been caused by the action of Austria, but on grounds that Bucharest had not been consulted over such action. And 'the King's chivalrous feelings' were put forward as an excuse. Blondel reported to Paris on 3 August:

> The Council, out of deference to the King, it is said, was unwilling to use the expression neutrality, which would have been more exact. I regret this, for it would have been easier with this expression to return a refusal to the solicitations of Austria.[1]

And in speaking of the Crown Council to Czernin on 6 August, King Carol told him:

> Contrary to all expectation those present had pronounced almost unanimously against the application of the treaty on the ground that the *casus foederis* did not arise for Romania, and had declared themselves in favor of neutrality. The attitude of Italy had unfortunately strongly influenced this decision. His Majesty had raised strong objections to this interpretation. . . . In the end the King had at least managed to prevent an unqualified declaration of neutrality and had demanded that the wording should run that Romania would defend her frontiers. In which direction was obviously clear. All joining in with Russia was with the same unanimity rejected as unthinkable.[2]

The chief motive of Bratianu's prudence is to be sought in his fear of the Central Powers, whose victory was widely regarded as certain. It was certainly fear of their anger which made him depart from what were regarded as the guiding principles of Romanian policy, the observance of the Treaty of Bucharest and the prevention of Bulgarian aggrandizement, and led him to propose the formulation embodied in the second part of the document.

This formulation was tantamount to telling Austria: 'We shall not object to Bulgaria's attacking Serbia and altering the Treaty of Bucharest to suit herself. Any such co-operation of Bulgaria with Austria would enable Austria to withdraw from the Serbian and dispatch towards the Russian front a number of Austrian army corps equivalent to those which, if Romania had respected the treaty, she would have been able to send against Russia. Thus the neutrality of Romania will not harm the Monarchy, which consequently should regard such generosity on the part of Romania as a token of sincere friendship.' How this line of conduct was to be reconciled with the declarations made at the Crown Council it is difficult to see. It would

---

[1] DF. 3, XI, 633; the date, 2 August, is probably a slip for 3 August. See DD. IV, 811.
[2] *Österreichisch-ungarisches Rotbuch. Diplomatische Aktenstüke betreffend die Beziehungen Österreich-Ungarns zu Rumänien in der Zeit vom 22. Juli 1914 bis 27. August 1916* (Vienna, 1916), 7.

have helped towards an Austrian victory and was supremely ungenerous towards Serbia, with whom there existed a *de facto* alliance and for whose safety Romania ought to have felt the deepest concern. But fear is a bad counsellor, and Bratianu had a big dose of it. If he had reasoned things out he would have become convinced of a truth, soon perceived in Italy, namely, that both Romania and Italy would pay dearly for their neutrality and that it was therefore to their supreme interest that victory should not go to the Central Powers.

Naturally the *Entente* Powers were never told by Bratianu of the free hand given to Bulgaria to fling herself upon Serbia; had they been told, the reactions of St. Petersburg and Paris would have been very pronounced. Even Blondel remained in the dark about this change in the attitude of Romania, expressing satisfaction at the decision in favor of neutrality and describing it to Paris as 'the best solution for the moment' on the ground that if Turkey and Bulgaria were to commit an aggression, Romania would necessarily take sides against them in defense of the terms of the Treaty of Bucharest,[1] the very opposite of the actual fact. In regard to the impression produced on the Central Powers and their diplomatic representatives one point must be borne in mind. The great collection of Austrian diplomatic documents published in 1930 only goes down to 31 July 1914, and therefore does not reproduce the correspondence of Czernin and Berchtold after 31 July. But when Romania came in on the side of the *Entente,* Austria published a *Red Book* which contains the few documents mentioned here. They are insufficient to throw full light on the attitude of Vienna, but when taken together with the German documents they give some idea of the reception accorded to the Romanian decision in the respective Chancelleries.

In ending his report of 4 August on what Bratianu had told him of the Crown Council proceedings, the German Minister Waldthausen wrote:

> In order not to worsen the situation for us, I advise on no account to publish the treaty. Perhaps it may be possible at a later stage of the war to bring about the intervention of Romania against Russia.

Wilhelm's marginal note to the dispatch runs:

> Even before the war our allies are dropping off us like rotten apples! An utter collapse of German and Austrian foreign diplomacy. This should and could have been avoided.[2]

True, but only by refraining from sending Serbia the ultimatum which Wilhelm himself had desired.

---

[1] DF. 3. XI, 633.   [2] DD. IV, 811.

As matters now stood with Romanian as with Italy, there was nothing to be done but to put a good face on the bad business, especially as the renunciation of respect for the Treaty of Bucharest was in itself a notable concession on the part of Bratianu. Accordingly on 4 August Berchtold telegraphed to Czernin:

In full agreement with the Berlin Cabinet I request Your Excellency to intimate at once to M. Bratianu that the two Central Powers appreciate the decisions of the Romanian Crown Council, regard them as in keeping with friendly relations, and Romania as still our ally. We shall therefore in further developments give full consideration to Romanian interests and confidently anticipate that Romania will defend her Moldau frontiers and repel any possible invasion by Russia.[1]

From Jagow on 4 August Waldthausen received two messages. The first ran:

On our information it may definitely be expected that if the case were to arise Turkey and Bulgaria would assist Romania in the conquest of Bessarabia.[2]

The second said:

In thanking M. Bratianu for communication please tell him that we regard Romanian attitude as in keeping with our friendly relations and hope subsequently for active co-operation on the part of Romania.[3]

The German and Austrian Ministers executed their instructions on 5 August, and Bratianu's feeling of relief from a nightmare is perceptible in Czernin's dispatch of that day:

The declaration made by Herr von Waldthausen and myself produced an *excellent* impression on M. Bratianu. Prime Minister thanked in the King's name and his own and emphasized his satisfaction that the interests of Romania were being given consideration by both the Empires in so difficult a situation. He said that our declaration had done more to bind the three Powers together than all the other events of the past forty years.[4]

As for King Carol, he was so affected after the Crown Council that he took to his bed, as he told Waldthausen on 4 August before knowing of Jagow's reassuring message. Not everything that he said to Waldthausen in excuse of himself and his country can be regarded as true. For instance, he asserted that

a great sensation had been caused by the Italian declaration of neutrality made before the meeting of the Crown Council; but for that he would have won acceptance for co-operation with the Triple Alliance.[5]

---

[1] *Oe-U. Rotbuch, Rumänien*, 5.   [2] DD. IV, 830.
[3] DD. IV, 847.   [4] *Oe-U. Rotbuch, Rumänien*, 6.
[5] DD. IV, 868.

We know for certain that, however much the King thought fit to put the responsibility for his country's decision on Italy, the contrary was true. The Italian declaration of neutrality was made known to the Crown Council, not before it began, but at its end, after all speakers except Carp had spoken in favor of Romanian neutrality on grounds unconnected with the Italian attitude. Despite this fact the King repeated the same statement on 6 August to Czernin, as we have seen, adding that 'he still firmly hoped that . . . the possibility would arise for Romania to join in'.

The general impression gained by Czernin was:

Here they are trying to gain time until the outcome of the European war begins to grow clear. If we are the victors (and this is the King's expectation) Romania will join in with us. Only if, contrary to expectation, the fortunes of war were to go against us, and the slogan, here so popular, of the 'carving up of the Monarchy' were to revive all the instincts against us prevailing here, then Romania would also stake her claim, though I believe that in this case the King would rather abdicate than have a hand in it.[1]

Indeed, on 4 August Carol had assured Waldthausen that 'any action against Austria on the part of Romania was definitely ruled out as long as he was King'.[2] But his days were numbered. The strain caused by the conflict between his personal convictions and his people's attitude undoubtedly shortened his life. Czernin writes:

The last weeks of his life were a torture to him; each message that I had to deliver he felt as the lash of a whip. . . . I recollect one particularly painful scene where the King, weeping bitterly, flung himself across his writing-table and with trembling hands tried to wrench from his neck his order *Pour le mérite*.

Czernin expresses the view that if King Carol had been as strong a character as he was an able diplomatist he would have called Carp to power and Carp would have brought Romania into the war on the side of the Central Powers. 'The blood shed in victorious battles for the common cause would have created the unity which should have been the foundation of the alliance but never came into being.'[3] Czernin's over-simplified view of the situation was utterly wide of the mark. Never could the Romanians have been induced to fight shoulder to shoulder with the Hungarians. It was in Hungary that the opposition to the cession of Transylvania to Romania originated. This opposition was not especially Tisza's. Any other Hungarian politician in his position would have taken the same line. But up to the last moment Tisza believed that Romania would never dare to attack the Monarchy. He regarded Czernin's reports as too pessimistic, and wrote in one of

---

[1] *Oe-U. Rotbüch, Rumänien*, 7.   [2] DD. IV, 868.
[3] Czernin, pp. 90, 94.

his answers: 'Whoever tries to seize even one square meter of Hungarian soil will be shot.' Czernin comments sadly:

It is a terrible but just punishment that poor Hungary, who contributed so much to our definite defeat, should be the one to suffer the most from the consequences thereof, and that the Romanians, so despised and persecuted by Hungary, should gain the greatest triumphs on her plains.[1]

Nor was it even certain that Austria could feel sure of Romania as long as King Carol lived. As early as 5 August 1914, Sazonov offered the Romanian Government a formal military alliance under which in exchange for Romania's entry into the war

Russia engaged not to cease from war against Austria-Hungary until the districts of the Austro-Hungarian Monarchy inhabited by a Rumane population should be reunited to the Romanian Crown.[2]

This, it is true, was rejected by the Romanian Government, but among the last lines penned by King Carol in his diary before his death on 10 October we read:

28 September. All the men in political life want us to go into Tran sylvania. . . .
29 September. Bratianu . . . has won over Costinescu by telling him that in the event of Russian victory Sazonov guarantees the Rumane provinces of Hungary and is willing to give this pledge in writing. The Crown Council is to be summoned; *on doit être seulement sûr que la neutralité sera votée?*

On 2 October, by an exchange of letters between Sazonov and Diamandy, an agreement was signed by which Romania promised Russia benevolent neutrality, Russia, in return, guaranteeing the territorial integrity of Romania and recognizing her rights to annex the Rumane regions of the Austro-Hungarian Monarchy excepting the Bukovina.[4]

A week later, on 10 October, King Carol breathed his last, and under his successor Romania ended by ranging herself with the *Entente.* She was invaded and forced to surrender. But the 'dismemberment of the Monarchy', carried out on a full scale, came in the end to her rescue, so that, in spite of the Romanian leaders' many fears and the reprehensible maneuvers prompted thereby, their policy was crowned with success. But this does not mean they would not have been well advised to take a more straightforward line which would better have served the paramount aim of preserving peace. What they could or would not see was that, being in the same position as Italy in regard to

---

[1] Czernin, pp. 97, 107, 108.
[2] Diamandy, *Ma Mission en Russie,* pp. 806-9.
[3] Diamandy, *Ma Mission en Russie,* pp. 812-20.
[4] Diamandy, *Ma Mission en Russie,* pp. 812-20.

the Central Powers and having the same interest in not letting Serbia be crushed, they ought to have approached the Italian Government with a proposal for joint action to warn Vienna and Berlin against unleashing a war in which neither Italy nor Romania would join.[1] If they had presented a joint set of demands to the Central Powers they would have gained in moral prestige and material strength. Their cause would have become merged with that of safeguarding the peace of Europe. They would have become champions of the loyal fulfillment of treaties, and this would have guaranteed them against the reprisals so much feared by them both.

It might be thought that the initiative in such a course should have come from Italy. But this is not the case. Which ever of the two capitals first realized the need ought at once to have made the suggestion to the other and been assured of the fullest acceptance. The need was from the first understood by both of them, but neither had the courage and honesty to put up a fight against the decisions of Vienna and Berlin lest they draw down vengeance upon their own heads. They elected to go their separate ways, taking a course which would in good earnest have drawn down the vengeance of the Central Powers had theirs been the victory.

[1] In this connection Radev, the Bulgarian Minister at Bucharest, telegraphed his Government on 27 July: 'The Italian Minister after his conversation with Bratianu today intimated to me that in the event of a general war Romania was disposed to fall in with the line taken by Italy. The two states were in the same position, since they on the one hand had engagements with Austria and on the other had no interest in going to war' (*Bulgarian Documents,* 217, KSF., 1928, p. 244). But Bratianu's words were not binding nor did they suggest joint action or previous consultation as to how to save the peace. From Rome on 2 August the Bulgarian Minister, Rizov, reported: 'I have learnt in strict confidence that Romania has proposed to Italy that they should jointly go to the assistance of Germany and Austria but that Romania has been convinced that the destruction of Serbia ought not to be allowed' (*Bulgarian Documents,* 259, KSF., 1928, p. 254). There does not seem to be any foundation for these reports, Romania never had the slightest intention of ranging herself with the Central Powers, and a subsequent telegram of Rizov's of 4 August reports the uncertainty felt in Rome about what Romania was going to do. 'The King of Romania is said to be insisting on their joining with Austria. The Romanian Government is said to be in favor of neutrality' (*Bulgarian Documents,* 278, KSF., 1928, p, 259).

CHAPTER XIII

BULGARIA BETWEEN TRIPLE ALLIANCE AND TRIPLE *ENTENTE*

1. *The Sarajevo outrage and projects of an Austro-Bulgarian alliance.*

When after some five centuries of oppression the Bulgarians were
freed from Turkish domination by Russia, the Treaty of San Stefano
of 3 March 1878 granted full satisfaction to their territorial aspirations.
But the Congress of Berlin, fearing that the new principality would
become a Russian fief, considerably reduced its territory. Among other
things it put Macedonia once more under the Turkish yoke, thereby
perpetuating a situation to end which Bulgaria, Greece, and Serbia
composed their differences, entered into alliance and went to war in
1912. Public opinion all over the world viewed their endeavor with
sympathy, and their victory would have been a benefit to Europe as a
whole but for the fact that squabbles arose over the sharing out of the
spoils and culminated in a treacherous attack by the Bulgarian army
against the Serbs and Greeks in the night of 29/30 June 1913. It ended
with the utter defeat of the aggressor at the hands of the Serbs, Greeks,
and Romanians, who were later joined also by the Turks. This attack,
put Bulgaria in the wrong, relegating to the background the misdeeds
of Serbia, who had also refused to submit the dispute to the arbitration
of the Tsar. The man directly responsible for the attack was King
Ferdinand of Bulgaria, who planned it with General Savov without
the knowledge of the Prime Minister, Danev.

Ferdinand of Saxe-Coburg-Gotha had come to the throne in 1887
against the wish of Russia. He had never been in a position to pursue
a pro-Austrian and pro-German policy, which would perhaps have
better suited his inclinations but not those of the Bulgarian people,
who owed their liberation to Russia and still looked to her for the
fulfillment of their national aspirations. Ferdinand, therefore, sought to
effect a reconciliation with the Tsar, and once Alexander III was no
longer in the way, achieved it in 1896 with Nicholas II. In 1902 he
concluded a military agreement with Russia and in the crisis of 1908–9

received full Russian support when he threw off the nominal sovereignty of the Turks. He renewed the agreement at the end of 1909 and later joined in the Balkan alliance which had been formed under Russian auspices. But Ferdinand was deemed clever, crafty and unprincipled and was trusted by nobody either in Bulgaria or elsewhere. He was strongly disliked by Wilhelm, Francis Ferdinand, and King Carol. It has been narrated above that after his betrayal of the Slav cause by his disregard of the Tsar's advice that Serbia and Bulgaria, as was laid down in their treaty of alliance, should submit their differences to the Tsar's arbitration, Ferdinand lost Russian support and had to submit to the humiliating Treaty of Bucharest. He attributed his failure to the absence of Austrian intervention, on which he claimed to have relied.[1]

The murder of the Austrian Heir Apparent, by removing one of Ferdinand's enemies, opened up fresh horizons. He undoubtedly anticipated that the Monarchy would react to it in a way from which Bulgaria could draw profit. And if a general war were to result Bulgarian co-operation would become valuable and would be sought after by both camps. In the meantime he must move warily and not commit himself. By good luck Bulgaria had not yet bound herself to Austria, nor would this be advisable as matters stood.

If such were the thoughts of the Bulgarian Sovereign—and his behavior justifies this assumption—he probably did not guess to what extent from the first the possibility of an alliance between the Central Powers and Bulgaria bulked large in the exchanges of ideas that went on between Berlin and Vienna and to what decisions such an alliance would lead. The memorandum brought to Berlin by Hoyos on 5 July had, as we have seen, sought to prove the necessity of such an alliance, a necessity steadfastly denied by Germany until on 5 July it was unexpectedly admitted by the Kaiser.[2] On 6 July Zimmerman telegraphed to Michahelles, the German Minister at Sofia, informing him of this change in German policy and empowering him to support, if so requested, his Austrian colleague's efforts to bring Bulgaria into the Triple Alliance.[3] But in the meanwhile Berchtold changed his mind and on 8 July informed Tschirschky that 'on mature reflection he had come to the conclusion that it would be wiser for the time being not to conclude the projected alliance with Bulgaria chiefly because it might perturb Romania'.[4] Hence on 9 July Jagow telegraphed to Michahelles that for the moment Austria was advising Sofia to keep quiet.[5]

The question will later on[6] be discussed whether Berchtold's change of mind was due only to fear of perturbing Romania. What here

---

[1] See Vol. I, pp. 448–53, 491-4.   [2] See Vol. 11, p. 159.
[3] DD. 1, 17.   [4] DD. 1, 19.   [5] DD. I, 22.
[6] See pp. 593–5.

concerns us is that he was anxious not to hasten a decision and that in the memorandum for Berlin he stated that the terms of a treaty with Bulgaria 'would have to be drawn up carefully'.[1] This chopping and changing did not meet with the approval of Tarnowski, the Austrian Minister at Sofia, whom Berchtold recalled for consultations on 7 July[2] and who left Sofia at the very moment when he was to have taken steps to conclude the alliance. Certainly by the time he returned to Sofia there would be no chance of his finding the Bulgarian Government as eager as it had been to bind itself to the Triplice. On 12 July Flotow reported to Berlin having heard from San Giuliano that

in Bulgaria, according to a message from the Italian representative at Sofia, there was apprehension of a Russian *coup de main* against King Ferdinand.[3]

At that moment, when a German loan was under negotiation, the atmosphere in the Bulgarian capital was extremely tense, and the scheming Russian Minister, Savinsky, a diplomat of the Hartwig type, had a hand in creating the tension. That Ferdinand was aware of and alarmed by the state of affairs is revealed by a telegram sent by him on 14 July to the Bulgarian Minister at St. Petersburg, Dimitriev, intercepted and decoded by the Russian Foreign Ministry. It said that the German loan was not to Ferdinand's liking, that Savinsky was plotting against his life and was in touch with Bulgarian and Serbian anarchists for a repetition of the Sarajevo outrage and continued:

Russia is much mistaken, for with my death its last hope of influencing Bulgaria would be gone.[4]

The Bulgarian Prime Minister, Radoslavov, also felt that his life was threatened, and on 16 July the French Minister at Sofia, Panafieu, telegraphed to Paris:

The Prime Minister this morning had the opposition leaders summoned by the Chief of Police who . . . told them they would be made answerable for his safety with their own lives.

Panafieu added the comment:

Bulgaria is reliving the worst days of the Stambulovist regime; it is M. Genadiev who is certainly the one who inspires the Government.[5]

Savinsky on 22 July wrote confidentially to Sazonov that Genadiev was doing everything he could to discredit Russia, to the point of trumping up bogus plots against the King's life by terrorist agents purporting to be in the employ of the Russian legation. Forged documents, manufactured to support the allegations, included letters from would-be assassins offering their services.[6]

---

[1] See Vol. I, p. 537.   [2] Oe-U. VIII, 10107.   [3] DD. I, 38.
[4] *Int. Bez.* i. IV, 219.   [5] DF. 3. X, 521.   [6] *Int. Bez.* i. IV, 333.

At that juncture Tarnowski returned to his post from Vienna with the draft of an Austro-Bulgarian treaty of alliance. In order to bring it into line with the Austro-Romanian treaty, the draft contained an article by which Bulgaria would recognize as binding her frontier with Romania laid down by the Treaty of Bucharest.[1] But the draft was not to be presented immediately, perhaps because, as has been said, Berchtold had not made up his mind to go forward with it, or else because it was hoped that Bulgaria would take the first step in asking for an alliance. This was in fact what happened in a conversation which Tarnowski had with Radoslavov on 16 July. The Prime Minister began by asking what Tarnowski had brought back from Vienna

and whether I thought that the Bulgarian Government could with success now renew its proposal for a formal association with us. The position of the Government was weakened by the fact that in foreign policy it was hanging in the air, and the Opposition reproached the Cabinet with running after the Triplice for years. Now the business of the loan was formally settled the moment had come to put Bulgaria's relations with the Monarchy definitely in order. . . . A military agreement would perhaps be the best arrangement. I answered inviting him to submit suggestions. . . . He said he would consult with Tonchev and Genadiev and submit a draft. To judge by my interlocutor's expressions it looks as if he would be in no great hurry to do so.[2]

Still less in a hurry was the man who really determined Bulgarian foreign policy, King Ferdinand himself, and who, as Radoslavov told Tarnowski on 16 July, was about to go abroad. Tarnowski realized that no decisions would be taken by the Government in the King's absence.[3] Berchtold in perturbation telegraphed back on 17 July that the King should be induced not to leave the country at this inappropriate moment. Tarnowski was to explain to the King's Private Secretary, Dobrovich, that the King would do well to await the outcome of the impending Austrian *démarche* at Belgrade. Tarnowski carried out these instructions on 18 July.[4]

2. *King Ferdinand's tergiversations.*

One wonders whether the King really meant to leave Sofia to escape proposals from Vienna or whether his impending departure was not perhaps announced to make the Austrian Minister show his cards, as in fact happened. The latter is the more credible hypothesis. Writing on 29 July the English Minister at Sofia, Bax-Ironside, reported:

I gather that General Markov, Bulgarian Minister in Berlin, wrote to King Ferdinand on 7th July that the Ballplatz were preparing a note of

[1] Oe-U. VIII, 10389, *n*.   [2] Oe-U. VIII, 10310.
[3] Oe-U. VIII, 10311.   [4] Oe-U. VIII, 10366.

such a stiff nature for the Serbian Government that no independent State could accept it . . . War between Austria, Serbia and Montenegro was considered as a foregone conclusion.[1]

The existence of this revelation is not confirmed by the documents, but in any case Tisza made such a threatening speech on 15 July as could not fail to open King Ferdinand's eyes, if they had not been opened already. On 18 July Dobrovich told Tarnowski that the King had meant to put off his journey until after the Austrian *démarche* at Belgrade, but that 'in the last few days there was an impression here that Austria-Hungary had now given up the *démarche,* so the King now thought he could leave'.[2] Thus the *démarche* was expected and the Austrian Minister was only being asked to confirm it. On his doing so there was no more word of the King's journey. But this did not mean any less reluctance on Ferdinand's part to tie himself to Austria and give up his unfettered freedom to await the further course of events. Tarnowski saw this, or at least feared it. When Radoslavov on 19 July told him:

It is not enough for the Government to want an alliance with us, the King must also be in agreement.

Tarnowski ended his report with the words:

God grant . . . that I do 'not have to lament what I have always deplored, namely, that by the fault of Germany we did not sooner regulate our relations with Bulgaria by treaty, especially the unfortunate handling of the loan negotiations.[3]

Yet more anxious was Tarnowski on 20 July when Radoslavov had still not given him news of the King's attitude to an alliance. His report runs:

Bulgaria, whose attitude will be of decisive importance to us, is today absolutely free and it would not be impossible for the King to upset the calculation on which our plan is based. I therefore sought to persuade the Prime Minister to ascertain King Ferdinand's attitude quickly so that we may gather whether to fear double-dealing on the King's part.

Radoslavov thereupon sounded Tarnowski about what Vienna was planning against Serbia, and Tarnowski parried by saying that before knowing whether the King shared the views of his Prime Minister it would be premature to say more. 'When I am told that the King is at one with the Government, I would perhaps confide many things to the Prime Minister which will make him rejoice.' Once more Tarnowski voiced his regret 'that we did not settle our relations with Bulgaria by treaty before we decided on a punitive policy towards Serbia'.[4]

[1] BD. XI, 653.   [2] Oe-U. VIII, 10366.
[3] Oe-U. VIII, 10389.   [4] Oe-U. VIII, 10421-3.

Berchtold replied on 21 July that it would be technically impossible to conclude an alliance with Bulgaria before settling with Serbia, but that if there were to be war between the Monarchy and Serbia, it would be of great importance that Bulgaria should remain neutral in order not to jeopardize the localization of the war.[1] On 23 July Berchtold reiterated this injunction, adding instructions to meet the eventuality of war with Russia:

> We still reckon on the possibility of Romania's acceding to the Triplice or at least remaining neutral as long as Bulgaria does not intervene in the conflict. In the event of war with Russia it would be important to persuade the Bulgarian Government to give Bucharest assurances of neutrality both directly and through us. I am aware that it may prove difficult to dissuade Bulgaria from premature military action aiming at the occupation of Macedonia. You might mention in conversation . . . that at the appropriate moment the Monarchy would bear in mind Bulgaria's historic claim to Macedonia. . . . If Romania should adopt a hostile attitude towards us we would then have to count on the fullest measure of support from Bulgaria. You would then change your tone and in the name of the Austrian Government give the fullest assurances that the Monarchy and its allies would employ all their resources to obtain the fulfillment of Bulgarian territorial claims. In any case it would be desirable that Macedonian Comitaji in Bulgaria should begin intensive activities, officially disavowed by the Government.[2]

Tarnowski can hardly have felt much satisfaction over these instructions. There was no reason whatever why the alliance with Bulgaria should not be concluded without waiting for the settlement of accounts with Serbia. And was it so desirable and necessary that Bulgaria should keep out of the conflict except in the case of Romania's joining in on the enemy's side? Was Bulgarian intervention on the side of the Triplice incompatible with that of Romania, or at least with Romanian neutrality? These are questions which will be discussed further on.[3] Another factor which added to Tarnowski's anxieties on 23 July was the King's refusal to grant him an audience on grounds of Tarnowski's unfriendly attitude at the time when Francis Ferdinand had refused to see Ferdinand.[4]

It was a trumped up pretext, the King in reality fearing that Tarnowski would broach awkward questions and seek to extract promises. That this was so is shown by Tarnowski's dispatch of 25 July:

> From utterances of Prime Minister [Radoslavov] and Finance Minister [Tonchev] I today had the impression that His Majesty may have expressed himself not quite so unreservedly in favor of accession to the Triplice.[5]

---

[1] Oe-U. VIII, 10462.
[2] Oe-U. VIII, 10550.
[3] See p. 596.
[4] See Vol. I, p. 493; Oe-U. VIII, 10556.
[5] Oe-U. VIII, 10691.

On the same day the German Minister, Michahelles, telegraphed to Berlin in the opposite sense:

Prime Minister told me that, now the loan is arranged, the Government is stronger and able to begin to pursue an independent political line in seeking accession to the Triplice. . . . The King is greatly pleased and has ordered him to draw up a proposal.

Wilhelm annotated the last sentence: 'I'm sure he is', and urged speed.[1] But Michahelles had none of Tarnowski's grasp of the situation at Sofia.

The audience for which Tarnowski had in vain asked was for the purpose of acquainting the King of the ultimatum presented at Belgrade on 23 July, and the communication was therefore made on the 24th to Radoslavov, who described it as 'perhaps a great and unexpected piece of good fortune for Bulgaria', adding that 'Bulgaria must officially observe neutrality', that 'advantage to Bulgaria could only result from our success', and that 'the Bulgarian Government . . . would do nothing against my advice or without my knowledge'.[2] Radoslavov and his colleagues had visions of regaining the Macedonian territory ceded to Serbia. To make sure the Prime Minister, Finance Minister, and War Minister asked Tarnowski for an interview in which they sounded him as to what territorial gains Bulgaria might expect to make. Tarnowski, not being in a position to make any promises, 'managed with considerable difficulty to keep the Ministers in their previous good mood'.[3]

In reality Bulgaria had no reason to join in the Austro-Serbian conflict, from which she could derive great advantage without the risk of bringing Romania and Greece down on her. Moreover, not only Berlin and Vienna but also St. Petersburg advised her to remain neutral,[4] while Bucharest and Athens in a joint *démarche* reminded her of the inviolability of the Treaty of Bucharest and warned her that, if she were to attack Serbia, Greece and Romania would move against Bulgaria.[5] Even Pašić, in a talk with the Bulgarian Minister at Nish on 27 July, made vague promises that there would be 'good consequences' for Bulgaria if she created no unpleasant complications.[6] The Bulgarian Government without hesitation pledged itself to observe strict neutrality and circulated this information to the Bulgarian representatives abroad on 28 July.[7] That same day Tarnowski reported appeals to Radoslavov from the Russian Minister, Savinsky, invoking the Slav sentiment of the Bulgarians, and saying:

[1] DD. I, 162.   [2] Oe-U. VIII, 10623.
[3] Oe-U. VIII, 10846.   [4] Bulg. 210.
[5] BD. XI, 224, 267, 371-   [6] Bulg. 218; Oe-U. VIII, 10844.
[7] Bulg. 226.

Bulgarians must stand by Serbs, who after all are brothers. . . . If Bulgaria were on the side of Serbia the Balkan League would be reconstituted, since Romania and Greece would join in. . . . Prime Minister says he answered . . . Bulgarians feel themselves Slavs, but first of all Bulgarians . . . and Bulgaria would remain absolutely neutral.[1]

In reality Radoslavov went still further with Savinsky, saying 'that he would of course take Macedonia with both hands', and giving Savinsky the impression that

if and when Austria were to attack Serbia, Bulgaria will certainly send her Comitaji to Macedonia. . . . With their practical common sense the Bulgarians mean to look round and then decide according to the course of events what side it would be more profitable for them to join.[2]

That being the situation Berchtold's imperious telegrams requesting that Bulgaria should engage with Romania to observe the strictest neutrality if Romania should join the Central Powers were unnecessary. On 29 July Tarnowski easily persuaded Radoslavov to give Bucharest through Radev the fullest assurances provided that Romania remained with the Triplice.[3] And on 28 July Tarnowski gave the Bulgarian Prime Minister, Radoslavov, and his colleagues at the War Ministry and Foreign Ministry the awaited all-clear signal to begin Comitaji action in Macedonia.[1]

3. Failure of the first feelers for an Austro-Bulgarian alliance.
Less smooth progress was made with the preliminaries of the alliance for which on 16 July Radoslavov had promised to present a draft. He had, indeed, composed one and submitted it to the King, but on 30 July had still not received it back. Ferdinand had gone off on a motor tour. 'Characteristic nonchalance!' was Tarnowski's comment.[5] However, on 31 July Ferdinand returned to the capital and on 2 August Radoslavov laid the draft before the Austrian and German representatives. Its text was brief and to the point.

1. The Triplice will guarantee Bulgaria's present territory against attack from whatever side it may come. 2. The Triplice will give Bulgaria support in her aspirations for future territorial acquisitions in regions in which she possesses historic and ethnographical rights and which are under the dominion of a State not belonging to the Triplice. Thus if Romania goes with the Triplice, she will have nothing to fear from Bulgaria, and, in the case of later territorial changes, Bulgaria will seek acquisitions only in the west. If Romania goes over to Russia, Bulgaria would have a free hand to reassert her claims to the Dobruja.[6]

[1] Oe-U. VIII, 10921.   [2] *Int. Bez.* i. V, 251, 254.
[3] Oe-U. VIII, 10874, 11006, 11102, 11140. See p. 566.
[4] Oe-U. VIII, 10922.   [5] Oe-U. VIII, 11105.
[6] DD. III, 673.

But it was one thing to put forward a project of alliance and another to sign it. Let us now see how events developed.

It is not directly known how this document was received at Vienna because, as has been said above, the Austrian documents of the *Red Book* of 1919, save for a few in Vol. III, only go down to 31 July. But a little light is shed by the German documents. Berlin after the declaration of war on Russia was impatient to get allies. Jagow on 1 August drafted a telegram to Tschirschky saying: 'Austrian delays might force Bulgaria over into the camp of our enemies', though the telegram was never actually sent and a footnote explains that the matter was 'dealt with elsewhere'.[1] The same day Jagow telegraphed to Michahelles at Sofia:

> We press at Vienna for immediate understanding with Bulgaria over her attitude to threatening European conflict. Please support strongly relevant measures of your Austrian colleague.[2]

When on 2 August Bethmann received Radoslavov's draft he hastened that very evening to accept it. But as the Bulgarian Premier had not informed the Italian Minister about it, leaving Berlin and Vienna to explain matters to Rome, Bethmann hit on the device that the treaty should not be made with the Triplice as such but that separate treaties should be signed with Germany and Austria respectively, and that it should be made clear that Bulgarian aspirations were not directed against Turkey. These fresh instructions, were, however, to await further confirmation.[3] A copy of them was at the same time telegraphed to Tschirschky with the request to press at Vienna for corresponding instructions to be sent immediately to the Austrian Minister at Sofia.[4] At 11.55 a. m. on 3 August Bethmann instructed Michahelles to negotiate, but before actually concluding, 'to wire what active obligations, particularly on the military field, Bulgaria proposes to undertake'.[5] On 4 August Michahelles wired back the proposed text:

> Bulgaria engages in present European conflict, on request from Germany, to take military measures with all her forces against any neighboring State which is on the side of the enemies of the German Empire.[8]

Jagow telegraphed back on 5 August:

> Formula agreed. Likewise agreed that Bulgaria goes to war with Serbia.[7]

Berlin now felt so sure of having won Bulgaria for the Central Powers that on 5 August Jagow sent a special messenger to Sofia with a document signed by the Kaiser giving Michahelles full powers to

---

[1] DD. III, 555.   [2] DD. III, 549.   [3] DD. III, 697.
[4] DD. III, 698.   [5] DD. III, 728.   [6] DD. IV, 857.
[7] DD. IV, 873.

conclude the alliance and accompanying it with a deed of ratification also bearing the royal signature.[1] In fact, however, the alliance was not concluded until 6 September 1915, thirteen months later, and Bulgaria only took the field against Serbia on 7 October 1915.

This delay had a considerable influence on the course of the war in the Balkans. On 23 August 1914 the Serbs were able to repulse the Austrian forces under General Potiorek, which had crossed the Drina, and to penetrate into Bosnia. Potiorek regained the offensive on 6 November and occupied Belgrade. But on 3 December the Serbs opened a counter-offensive which routed the Austrians, who lost 130 heavy guns and 40,000 taken prisoner. A concentration of sixteen divisions, four of which were Bulgarian, six Austrian and six German, was necessary to initiate in October 1915 the campaign which enabled the Central Powers to crush the Serbian Army, invade the country and link up with Turkey across Serbia and Bulgaria. Had the Bulgarians entered the war at the beginning this result might have been achieved a year earlier without any set back to Austria. It may be affirmed that if the Austro-Bulgarian alliance had been concluded in 1913 and Conrad had been able in good time to work out a plan of co-operation with the Bulgarian army, the forces that were at the beginning concentrated on the Save and arrived too late in Galicia, would probably, at least in part, have been ready on the spot in Galicia.

This is proved by a perusal of the Conrad-Moltke correspondence of that period. On 5 August Moltke wrote to Conrad:

> Concentrate your entire strength against Russia. Surely even Italy cannot be so foul as to fall on us from behind. Let the Bulgarians loose against Serbia and let the pack kill one another off. Now there can be but one objective: Russia![2]

It was all very well for Moltke to give orders like this, but Conrad could not carry them out to the extent of diverting his attention entirely from Serbia. Hence on 10 August he replied:

> Here too the main objective is the decision in the north by the full deployment of all available forces. At the same time the situation calls for a successful stroke in the Balkans as soon as possible. Success there would be assured if Bulgaria would immediately take the field against Serbia. We are using all levers to induce Bulgaria to do so, but she hesitates and apparently would like to wait for us to pull the chestnuts out of the fire for her. She quite overlooks the consideration that by immediate joint action with us she could rid herself of the Serbs for all time. There is no strong man in Bulgaria to impose such a decision.[3]

---

[1] DD. IV, 865, 866.
[2] Conrad, IV, p. 195.
[3] Conrad, IV, p. 195.

On 9 August Conrad telegraphed to the Austrian Military Attaché, Laxa, at Sofia:

Use every means to get Bulgarians as soon as possible to make a powerful drive against Kragujevac from Pirot-Zaječar line, but not to go in for negotiations with Turks and Romanians about vague co-operation.[1]

This was because a telegram of 6 August from Moltke had advised the Bulgarians not to move against Serbia but to co-operate with Turkey against Russia.[2]

But, even if every means was used, it was too late to secure Bulgaria for an all-out offensive against Serbia and thus enable Austria to deploy larger forces against Russia. The matter should have been attended to in good time. If before the Sarajevo outrage Germany was responsible for its not having been done, it was Austria who caused the delay after the crime. It will be remembered that Berchtold's memorandum 24 June 1914 had touched on the possibility of a treaty with Bulgaria which would have to be drawn up carefully,[3] and then, when Germany agreed to an alliance,[4] had asked Berlin not to press forward with the matter for the time being.

This had taken place the day after the meeting of the Council of Joint Ministers of 7 July at which Tisza, at that time opposed to any action that might lead to war, had pointed out that Germany's assent to the accession of Bulgaria to the Triplice had opened the way to a Balkan policy full of promise. Indeed—he continued—an alliance between Bulgaria and Turkey and their accession to the Triplice would create a counterpoise to Romania and Serbia, forcing the former perhaps to return to the Triplice. Berchtold had replied that in his opinion Romania could not be won back so long as the pan-Serb agitation went on, since it brought pan-Romanian agitation in its train, and Romania could only take measures against this if she felt isolated in the Balkans by the extinction of Serbia and realized that she could find support only in the Triplice. Furthermore, not a step had been taken towards the accession to the Triplice of Bulgaria. The Radoslavov Government would be willing, but was not strong, and might be overthrown by a movement of public opinion. Then there was the difficulty that Germany agreed to negotiations with Bulgaria only on condition that they should not adversely affect the interests of Romania. These requirements would not be easy to fulfill.[5]

These arguments in themselves reveal Berchtold's lack of enthusiasm for an alliance with Bulgaria.

[1] Conrad, IV, p. 190.   [2] Conrad, IV, p. 190.
[3] See Vol. I, p. 537.
[4] See Vol. II, p. 139.
[5] Oe-U. VIII, 10118; See Vol. II, pp. 164-70.

4. Berchtold proposes limits to Bulgarian co-operation in order not to antagonize Romania.

After war broke out Berchtold's lack of enthusiasm was even more marked. At 5.30 p. m. on 4 August Michahelles telegraphed to Berlin:

My Austrian colleague is still without instructions about the concluding of a treaty of alliance with Bulgaria: I therefore wait in order that the treaties may be worded in similar terms.[1]

This seems to conflict with Tschirschky's dispatch of 12.30 p. m. from Vienna:

Count Tarnowski has today been empowered, if his German colleague receives similar instructions, to inform Bulgarian Government that R. and I. Government is prepared to accept in principle the two propositions laid down by Bulgaria. As regards the text of the final treaty the Austro-Hungarian representative will receive exact instructions and be directed to remain in constant touch with his German colleague.[2]

Once again it is a mere acceptance in principle, since Berchtold kept the wording of the final treaty in his own hands. His delaying tactics so exasperated Berlin that on 5 August Jagow telegraphed to Tschirschky:

Michahelles reports that Austro-Hungarian Minister is still without instructions about treaty of alliance. Please urge Vienna to empower its representative immediately to conclude without delay in concert with Michahelles, who has detailed instructions.[3]

From this it is clear that after 5 July, when Wilhelm, in deference to the wish of Vienna, agreed to letting Bulgaria join the Triplice, the roles were reversed and Vienna now hung back. Nay more, to ward off Conrad's pressure for the immediate conclusion of an alliance with Sofia, Berchtold put forward the excuse of opposition from Berlin which no longer existed. Conrad's diary for 3 August notes:

Count Berchtold called at my room and we discussed the situation. . . *Myself:* 'If Romania leaves us in the lurch we have no other choice than to hold on to Bulgaria.' *Count Berchtold:* 'What are we to do with the Bulgarians?' *Myself:* 'Let them loose on the Serbs.'[4]

This although no plan had been prepared for Austro-Bulgarian military co-operation. The following morning Berchtold told Conrad of the Romanian Government's decision to remain neutral, and went on to say that

Germany hoped Romania in the later course of events would join the Central Powers and therefore advised not engaging Bulgaria since then Romania would certainly not join. . . .

---

[1] DD. IV, 857. [2] DD. IV, 798.
[3] DD. IV, 872. [4] Conrad, IV, p. 171.

Myself: In order not to fall between two stools and gain neither the cooperation of Bulgaria against Serbia nor the accession of Romania, let us grasp Bulgaria firmly and give amicable explanations to Romania.[1]

This was precisely what Berlin was urging, while Berchtold was pretending the contrary. Did he perhaps on the morning of 4 August not yet know of the Chancellor's appeal to him, sent by telegram to Tschirschky at 1.15 a. m. on 3 August, a telegram which must certainly have been in Tschirschky's hands on the morning of the 3rd?

We have already seen that as early as 1 August Jagow had drafted a telegram for Tschirschky ending with the words: 'Will Your Excellency urgently press Count Berchtold for an immediate understanding with Bulgaria',[2] and that the telegram was never sent, probably because some other solution was adopted. One thing, however, is certain, namely, that on 3 August Tschirschky took no steps to carry out the instructions received from Berlin, or at least made no report of having done so to Berlin. Nay more, on the morning of the 4th, in speaking with Conrad, he altered the truth in the same way as Berchtold. This is how Conrad reported the matter to Berchtold the same day:

As I was leaving you this morning I ran into the German Ambassador and we discussed the Romanian decision, which he read out to me. I gained the impression that Germany is rather averse to the idea of setting Bulgaria on Serbia. As against this I can but repeat what I expressed to you orally, namely, that it is of pre-eminent importance for us to have Romania on our side. . . . Romania herself has expressed the idea that she would be fulfilling her Triplice obligations in raising no objections to a Bulgarian attack on Serbia to ease things for us.

Conrad's clear-sightedness reveals itself further in his prescient remark:

Just imagine what would happen if in the coming few days we were to suffer a military reverse over there! The entire political situation would thereat tilt over in our disfavor.[3]

Meanwhile, after having given Conrad an impression which was the reverse of what Berlin intended, Tschirschky paid his call on Berchtold and, on returning to the Embassy at 12.30 p. m., dispatched the already quoted telegram reporting Berchtold's temporizing instructions to Tarnowski.[4]

One cannot but think that Berchtold and Tschirschky were of one mind in regarding an immediate alliance with Bulgaria as a false move, and one wonders whether consideration for Romania was the sole reason for their attitude. German opposition to the accession of

---

[1] Conrad, IV, pp. 173-4. [2] DD. III, 555. See p. 590.
[3] Conrad, IV, p. T75. [4] DD. IV, 798. See p, 593.

Bulgaria to the Triplice had undoubtedly been based on the fear of alienating Romania, and Berchtold in putting forward the idea to Germany had always been careful to lay down, as he did in the memorandum sent by the hand of Hoyos, that any treaty with Sofia must be so worded as not to be incompatible with the Monarchy's engagements under its alliance with Romania. Berlin and Vienna were agreed that Bucharest should be informed of the negotiations with Sofia. But Vienna, having no illusions as to the Romanian attitude, had all along acted with scant conviction, and one does not see why at the decisive moment Austria displayed so much more regard for Romanian susceptibilities than Germany, even going to the length of not wanting the alliance with Bulgaria which now seemed indispensable.

Moreover, in agreeing to the alliance, Germany had never intended the Bulgarian role to be as limited as Berchtold laid down when, as we have seen, he wrote on 23 July to Tarnowski:

> We still reckon on the possibility of Romania's acceding to the Triplice or at least remaining neutral as long as Bulgaria does not intervene in the conflict. In the event of war with Russia it would be important to persuade the Bulgarian Government to give Bucharest assurances of neutrality both directly and through us. . . . If Romania should adopt a hostile attitude towards us we would then have to count on the fullest measure of support from Bulgaria.[1]

Nothing could be more suspect than these instructions. When had Berlin and Vienna ever laid down such limits to Bulgarian co-operation? Bethmann's ideas about it were on very different lines from this.

It is hard to see what basis Berchtold had for his opinion. Was it conceivable that Romania would side with Russia if Bulgaria took the field as an ally of Austria? It is highly doubtful. What was more probable was that Romania would be, unlikely to make common cause with Russia, if she were afraid of being attacked by Bulgaria. In other words, Bulgarian intervention would more likely make Romania join in with her allies, the Central Powers, or at least maintain strict neutrality. Berlin deemed the former mote probable, as is clear from Jagow's dispatch to Michahelles of 5 August, which ended:

> Bulgaria's accession to Triplice will presumably lead to active intervention of Romania against Russia.[2]

He was not mistaken, since Bucharest really feared Bulgaria, a fact which should have made Berchtold play his Bulgarian card with greater daring.

Even admitting that until 3 August consideration for Romania may have been a reason for hesitation about concluding the Bulgarian

---

[1] Oe-U. VIII, 10550. See p. 587.   [2] DD. IV, 865.

alliance, all such reasons had vanished by 4 August when the Romanian Government not only proclaimed neutrality but, afraid of its own decision, agreed to a Bulgarian attack on Serbia, calling attention to the benefit thereby accruing to Austria, who could now withdraw from the Serbian front a number of army corps equal to those Romania would have dispatched to the Russian front if she had come into the war.[1]

Well then? Here we are confronted with one of the many mysteries which a close examination of the documents brings to light but does not enable us to solve. Historians have not stopped to inquire why, after imploring Germany for over a year to allow Austria to safeguard herself in the Balkans by allying with Bulgaria, Berchtold no longer wanted the alliance when Berlin was willing and anxious for it. But the point was worth raising because considerations connected with Romania fell to the ground once Romania gave consent to a Bulgarian attack on Serbia. We are therefore forced to conclude that Vienna had other reasons for not wanting to bind itself for the moment to Bulgaria. Here the field is open to induction. It might be thought that in the event of victory Berchtold wanted to hold open the possibility of swallowing Serbia whole and was therefore unwilling to promise Bulgaria the territory she claimed. But it seems considerably more likely that he was disinclined to promise Bulgaria big concessions for fear of thereby putting difficulties in the way of a peace by compromise. Had he not on 22 July sent word by Hoyos to the Austrian Minister at Stockholm that 'the accession of Sweden to the Triplice would involve us in too far-reaching obligations'?[2] One must never lose sight of the fact that Berchtold was a man of irresolute, wavering character, feeling himself overwhelmed by the momentous decisions he was called upon to take, incapable of strong action, averse from bold decision, moving through the crisis more like a sleepwalker.

In noting that Berchtold threw obstacles in the way of an immediate alliance with Bulgaria one must agree that, even had he behaved otherwise, it would have been difficult, if not impossible, to attach Bulgaria to the Triplice once Ferdinand had sensed the use Austria was likely to make of the Sarajevo outrage. Moreover, as Panafieu wrote to Paris on 29 July:

> The painful memories of 1913 have certainly taught him a lesson. . . . The King would infuriate the whole of public opinion and risk his throne and his life if he were to put himself at enmity with Russia.[3]

He could not make his decision until sure which side was going to win. In 1915, as in 1913, he miscalculated the chances. But in July 1914

---

[1] DD. IV, 811. See p. 575.   [2] Oe-U. VIII, 10504.   [3] DF. 3. XI, 300.

there were so many elements of uncertainty as to the outcome of the struggle that neutrality seemed to him the safest course. Italy and Romania had detached themselves from the Central Powers, while England was coming in against them; Turkey, whose solidarity with them had been proclaimed, was remaining neutral; Austria had declared war on Serbia on 28 July but had not attacked. And there was the further problem that if Bulgaria were called upon to take sides against Russia she might find herself left to fight Serbia single-handed, an ordeal which she would not have cared to face. The utmost caution was imposed not only by the Central Powers' scant chances of victory but also by the bad financial and military state of the country consequent on the two Balkan wars and by the existence of a strong current of feeling friendly to Russia. The conclusion to be drawn is that Bulgarian neutrality was not brought about by Berchtold's indecision, unjustifiable as it was. What did tip the scales were the repeated refusals of Berlin to accept the Bulgarian proposals put forward as early as May 1913.

5. Russian threats and pressure at Sofia.

The reasons which moved the Sofia Government to decline the proposals of the Central Powers operated with still greater force against Russian pressure, a pressure in which Slavophil circles at St. Petersburg also took a hand. On 31 July the Bulgarian Minister at the Russian capital, General Radko Dimitriev—a Russophil who at once enlisted in the Russian army and later held an important command in Galicia— wrote to his Government:

I have just been handed a resolution from the Russian [Slavophil] Charitable Society inviting us to send a delegate to Nish to negotiate with the Serbs about our future frontiers in the event of Austria's disintegrating, as is the firm anticipation here.[1]

This appeal was an acknowledgment that Bulgarian aspirations in Macedonia were well founded. The same thought was in Sazonov's mind when on 31 July, even before receiving the German ultimatum, he telegraphed to the Russian Chargé d'Affaires in Serbia, Strandtmann:

Inquire discreetly of the Serbian Government whether it does not think the moment suitable, perhaps by our mediation, to put out feelers for an understanding with Bulgaria in order to ensure not only its effective neutrality but even its military support by consenting to territorial compensation in the event of Serbia's receiving an equivalent elsewhere.[2]

[1] Bulg. 246.
[2] *Int. Bez.* i. V, 339.

This move was sympathetically received on 2 August by Pašić, but

he foresees serious difficulties with Serbian public opinion in this matter and, above all, exaggerated demands from the Bulgarians. . . . He will place his hopes on our help and at need on our moderating influence at Sofia.[1]

Next day, when war had broken out, Pašić said to Strandtmann that

the Bulgarians would regard Serbian proposals as a sign of weakness and ask too much. . . . He would be very grateful for a Russian initiative at Sofia. It might be based on Slav solidarity and Bulgaria's duty to go hand in hand with Russia in her own interest. The Bulgarians would answer any such initiative on our part ... by raising the question of compensation. . . . They should then be asked what their claims would be in return for active aid. Pašić hopes that the demands thus formulated by the Bulgarians . . . might form a basis for direct negotiations between Serbia and Bulgaria under the immediate supervision and guarantee of Russia.[2]

On receiving the earlier of Strandtmann's two telegrams Sazonov had anticipated Pašić's suggestions by telegraphing that same 3 August to Savinsky at Sofia:

At the moment of grave decisions through which we are now passing Bulgaria's behavior will determine Russian relations with her perhaps for all time. The leaders of Bulgarian policy have it in their power to dissipate all misunderstandings, give fresh strength to the links between Bulgaria and Russia, and emerge from the coming ordeal with national aspirations pretty well fulfilled. For this it will be necessary for Bulgarian policy to be sincerely and honestly brought into harmony with the intentions of Russia. Bulgaria will derive practical advantages therefrom in the event of territorial acquisitions being made by Serbia. But if, on the contrary, Bulgaria were to set about raising trouble in Macedonia and harboring evil designs against Serbia, such behavior would, in the view of Russia's entry into war, be regarded as an open act of hostility against Russia, and a gulf will open up between the two countries for ever. Bulgarian leading statesmen fear personal responsibility for the country's further policy, and we should like to think that, mindful of the best traditions of her history, Bulgaria will not be unfaithful to them, and will definitely declare that she means to enter into immediate negotiations with us to bring our respective views into harmony.[3]

Sazonov's expressions do not make it clear whether in speaking of 'the coming ordeal' he was asking Bulgaria to come into the war on the side of Russia. However, he read out to Dimitriev the instructions that were going off to Savinsky, and Dimitriev on 4 August telegraphed to Sofia:

At this important historic moment Bulgaria is being asked to give up neutrality and join the Slav common cause. Neutrality is regarded as an attitude hostile to this cause. He [Sazonov] tells me that the Serbs have already become extremely compliant and that we might

---

[1] *Int. Bez.* i. V, 472.   [2] *Int. Bez.* i. V, 505.   [3] *Int. Bez.* i. V, 484.

count on considerable territorial compensation at the winding-up of the war. I explained to him that after all that had happened it would be difficult to induce the Bulgarian nation to go to the help of Serbia. He replied that this would not be expected of them, our contingent could be given another task.[1]

Savinsky, however, did not interpret his Minister's instructions in that sense. On receiving Sazonov's telegram of 3 August he immediately asked for an audience of King Ferdinand, which was granted probably on 5 August and lasted an hour and a half. The published Russian diplomatic documents do not reproduce Savinsky's dispatch, but there exists a long letter of 15 August from him giving Sazonov a detailed account of the conversation. This account shows that Savinsky refrained from any request for Bulgarian co-operation, merely asking for benevolent neutrality. He first read out the text of Sazonov's instructions of the 3rd and followed it up by a sharp crack of the Russian whip over Ferdinand's head, reproaching him with keeping the pro-Austrian Prime Minister, Radoslavov, in power, refusing a loan from France, and accepting one from Germany, a course which betrayed that there was some understanding between Bulgaria and Austria, and going on to say:

As long as Russia was not at war this policy, though criminal, was a crime only against Bulgaria, but now it becomes inadmissible towards ourselves.

Bulgaria could not expect to gain anything from Austria, who had been deserted by her own allies, Italy and Romania, and had scant chances of winning the war.

If victory is granted us, one of Russia's cares would be to establish a real solid equilibrium in the Balkan peninsula; . . . then if Bulgaria behaves irreproachably towards Russia, it is certain that this will not be forgotten. . . . Serbia herself felt that it would be only just that your benevolence towards her during the war should be rewarded.

Even if—continued Savinsky—contrary to expectation, the victory were to go to Austria

she would reduce Bulgaria, who would be no longer needful to her, to an impotent vassal state which could no longer hinder the realization of the age-old Austrian desire for Salonika and the Aegean. . . . All the good that Bulgaria can hope for in the future can come to her only from Russia, as has always been the case in the past; in return we ask nothing more from her than to remain honestly neutral till the end of the war, not to make trouble in Macedonia, and not to plot against Serbia. On my remarking that I knew in great detail that the formation of armed bands in Bulgaria was being encouraged and that certain of them had crossed the Serbian frontier, the King said: 'This is absolutely a surprise for me. I thought, I was sure, that

[1] Bulg. 282.

the movement no longer existed.' In saying this the King was wittingly telling a lie, for I know with certainty that the Palace supplies the chieftains of these bands with funds.

The same day I had conversations with Radoslavov and Genadiev. . . . I laid stress on the monstrousness of the fact that Bulgaria did not rise as one man on learning of the Russian declaration of war. Russia does not need her aid, on the contrary, she asks her to stay quiet, but the bare idea that at such a moment the Bulgarian Government can be other than at one with Russia is infamous from the moral and criminal from the political point of view, for . . . it is her own existence that Bulgaria is calling in question. At the end my two interlocutors had to acknowledge that my reasoning was correct.[1]

6. Serbian and Russian promises rejected by the Bulgarian Government as inadequate.

While this was going on at Sofia Sazonov took another step forward by telegraphing on 5 August to Strandtmann:

We think that Bulgarian co-operation regardless of the outcome of the war can only be secured by ceding at once Ištip and Kočana with the territory reaching to the Vardar. If she fights the war to victory Bulgaria will receive the so-called debatable territory . . . specified in Article 2 of the secret annex to the Serbo-Bulgarian treaty of 13 March 1912. If Bulgaria shows reluctance to take military action, she might after our winning the war be rewarded for conscientious observation of neutrality by Kočana and Ištip and territory as far as the Vardar. Serbia will have to engage now with Russia to do this and Russia will communicate this pledge to Bulgaria. When you say this to Pašić make our general standpoint clear: having embarked on a war which calls for the exertion of all her strength, a war necessitated by the defense of Serbia and leading with God's help to the fulfillment of Serbian national aspirations, Russia does not doubt that the Serbian Government will without hesitation respond to her ardent desire to restore the fraternal relationship between all Slav peoples, above all between Serbia and Bulgaria. The sacrifices which Serbia will have to make are nothing in comparison with what she will be able to gain.[2]

This was very true, but the time to speak thus to the Serbian Government was earlier, while it still feared that it was going to be left to its fate and would have been willing to give pledges in return for military aid. It has already been shown that Pašić readily welcomed Sazonov's move of 31 July. But he had to reckon with the *Black Hand,* the army, the nationalists, and his own colleagues. To Strandtmann, who called on 6 August to carry out the instructions of 5 August, Pašić said that

to his great regret he could have not the slightest illusions as to the attitude of his Cabinet colleagues to the proposal. In their present form they would not accept it, of that he was convinced, for when with his closest friends on

---

[1] *Documents Diplomatiques Secrets Russes,* 1914-1917 (Paris, 1928), pp. 111-15.
[2] *Int. Bez.* ii. VI[1], 2.

whom he could depend he touched on the question of bringing Bulgaria over to our side by the granting of territorial compensations, he met with decided opposition on the following grounds: Bulgaria's situation was such that she could not take action against Russia without endangering her own existence. Greece and Romania had undertaken to cover Serbia against Bulgarian attack and made this known to Bulgaria. Though relations between Bulgaria and Turkey had considerably improved lately, inextinguishable mistrust prevailed between them. . . . One could not but feel anxiety over joint action between armies which a year ago had been fiercely fighting each other. Finally, one could not foresee the impression which the news of territorial concessions in return for military aid would produce on the Serbian troops, who would dislike the whole idea. . . . In these circumstances he [Pašić] would think it necessary to secure the 'benevolent' neutrality of Bulgaria. If Your Excellency thought possible, Russia might say to Bulgaria that she would receive territorial compensation, the extent of which it would be better not now to specify, if she genuinely observed neutrality and Serbia won the war. Solely for Your Excellency's information Pašić confidentially told me the general line of the new frontier which he plans.[1]

This would have given the Bulgarians Ištip and Radovic but not the Vardar line. As is easy to imagine, the reasons alleged by the Serbian Premier for declining Bulgarian co-operation were without substance. At the moment when he brought them forward the Romanian Government had already agreed to Bulgaria's attacking Serbia in the rear, though the attack was not made until many months later. But had it never taken place and had Bulgaria made common cause with the Triple *Entente,* even at need taking the field against Turkey, the European war would have gone differently. What remains to be seen is whether even the greatest concessions made by Serbia would ever have induced King Ferdinand to make common cause with Russia, hating her as he did, and convinced as he was that victory would go to the Central Powers.[2]

Savinsky carried out his instructions of 3 August and received the reply to his request for Bulgarian neutrality on 8 August. In the absence of concrete Russian proposals, which would have had to be on a scale sufficient to outweigh the offers made by

---

[1] *Int. Bez.* ii. VI[1], 19.

[2] *Fatal Years* contains the following angry but not unjustified comment on Ferdinand. 'The European war provided Ferdinand with the opportunity, as he thought, of re-establishing his position shaken by the disastrous results of his policy in 1913 and of avenging himself on Serbia for his defeat. Even more than Serbia he hated Russia, which he regarded as chiefly responsible for the Bucharest peace, unfavorable to Bulgaria, and the failure of his Byzantine dream. By furthering the cause of Germany in the Balkans he hoped to resuscitate in his person the Constantinople Basileus or at any rate to find an occasion for displaying the Byzantian stage costume he had procured beforehand. Those who knew King Ferdinand will probably not dispute this suggestion. Everyone remembers the universal indignation that prevailed in Russia at the news of Ferdinand's fresh treachery—the second since 1913' (Sazonov, *op. cit.,* pp. 229-30).

Austria and Germany, the Bulgarian reply was, as might be expected, evasive.

The Bulgarian Government meditates neither the attainment of national aspirations nor territorial aggrandizement. It is concerned with the country's safety and only considers what means are to be employed to avert the evil fate of war from our unhappy country. . . . The Bulgarian Government will sincerely and with the utmost willingness meet the desire of the Imperial Government not to provoke unrest in Macedonia and do all in its power not to allow the formation of armed-bands or their entry into Serbian territory. It goes without saying that the Bulgarian Government can take no responsibility for tumults that might break out in Macedonia instigated by Serbian subjects under Serbian jurisdiction.[1]

Sazonov justifiably remarked to the Bulgarian Minister, Dimitriev, on 9 August that he could not regard a reply as sincere which contemplated the possibility of disturbances in Macedonia such as could be provoked only by Bulgarian Comitaji. After another conversation with Radoslavov on 9 August and one with the War Minister, Savinsky telegraphed to St. Petersburg:

It seems to me essential that to win over Bulgaria to our side we must without losing a moment, make written proposals, not necessarily entering into detail, but indicating the main lines of Bulgaria's future territorial gains.[2]

Writing to Savinsky on 9 August describing his conversation with Dimitriev Sazonov showed a greater sense of urgency than hitherto:

I said that at the present moment any ambiguity would be extremely dangerous and that I would request him [Dimitriev] to warn his Government of the consequences of any kind of action against Serbia. . . . These consequences would be disastrous for Bulgaria.[3]

And in this talk Sazonov said clearly what Russia asked of Bulgaria, namely, benevolent neutrality and resistance to any offensive on the part of Turkey.[4] In return for these two services Sazonov would guarantee to Bulgaria the acquisition of Ištip and Radovic. And—he continued—

in the event of a victorious war, giving Serbia considerable territorial gains, we should of course consider the possibility of further satisfaction for Bulgaria.[5]

On the same day (9 August) Sazonov followed this up with another telegram to Savinsky:

---

[1] *Int. Bez..* ii. VI[1], note to 41; Vasil Radoslavov, *Bulgarien und die Weltkrise* (Berlin, 1923), pp. 137-8.
[2] *Int. Bez.* ii. VI[1], 46.   [3] *Int. Bez.* ii. VI[1], 41.
[4] Bulg. 282. See p. 599.   [5] *Int. Bez.* ii. VI[1], 41.

You will tell the Bulgarian Government we expect a prompt and straight answer to our proposal of neutrality, together with an undertaking to prevent action on the part of Turkey. Unless we receive a perfectly straight answer or if the reply is delayed, we warn the Bulgarian Government that Russia reserves full freedom of action in virtue of her alliance with Serbia, laying responsibility for the consequences on those directing the present Bulgarian policy.[1]

The idea of using Bulgaria to paralyze Turkey was a good one, and Pašić's reception of Strandtmann's proposals on 6 August made it possible for Sazonov to offer Bulgaria Ištip and Radovic in reward for such service. While even by adequate concessions it would have been difficult to get the Bulgarian army forthwith to make common cause with the Serbian, it seemed as if it would be relatively less difficult to induce Bulgaria to fall on Turkey in order to retake Adrianople, assuming that to be needful, since Turkey would be hardly likely to join in with the Central Powers unless she felt sure of Bulgaria. But even on the best supposition Sofia would have had to be given much more liberal promises of restitution of the territories torn from her in the second Balkan war. A telegram of 7 August from Strandtmann shows that Pašić clearly realized this:

In Pašić's opinion, if Bulgaria consented to act against Turkey, Greece would receive a guarantee 'against any possible aggressive intentions' on Turkey's part. This might induce her later on 'in return for commensurate compensation' to cede perhaps Kavala in South Albania to Bulgaria.[2]

This message from Strandtmann formed the subject of circular instructions from Sazonov on 10 August to the Russian Ministers at Athens, Bucharest and Nish approving of Pašić's idea:

We regard it as extremely desirable that Serbia and Romania, jointly with ourselves, should bring influence to bear on the Greek Government to obtain equivalent compensation for Bulgaria if the Epirus is assigned to Greece.[3]

But Greece declined to entertain the proposal by which Pašić sought to divert Sazonov's attention from the inadequacy of the concessions offered by Serbia. In any case the Bulgarian Government had no desire for an agreement with Russia and on 12 August declined the proposals made by Savinsky on the 11th acting on his instructions of the 9th:

In view of the fact that nothing has taken place to alter its earlier decisions and fully conscious of its responsibility to the nation, the Council of Ministers resolved to inform the Russian Minister that Bulgaria will continue to observe the strictest neutrality and will watch over the defense of its territory.[4]

---

[1] *Das Zaristiscbe Russland im Weltkrieg* (Berlin, 1927), pp. 68-9.
[2] *Int. Bez.* ii. VI[1], note to 51.
[3] *Int. Bez.* ii. VI[1], 51.   [4] *Int. Bez.* ii. VI[1], 81.

No other answer was indeed possible in view of the fact that, as we shall soon see, under pressure from the Central Powers an agreement with Turkey had been brought about on 6 August. Tarnowski was at once informed of this answer together with Sazonov's telegram to which it was the reply. Both were at once telegraphed to Berchtold.[1] Bulgaria's behavior towards Russia, of course, fed the hopes of Berlin and Vienna. Conrad records that on 11 August Tarnowski telegraphed from Sofia:

Here the expectation is to be witness of a swift and brilliantly executed punitive expedition; we, as you know, were until recently declaring that we would of course deal with Serbia single-handed, and Bulgaria was simply to keep quiet. Had we from the beginning prepared opinion here for our wanting Bulgarian co-operation in the event of the war not remaining localized, the impression of disappointment over our action against Serbia, would have been avoided. . . . From the moment I was apprised I was apprehensive of the situation which might result from our beginning war before making an alliance with Bulgaria and achieving an understanding with Turkey.[2]

Tarnowski was a luckless Cassandra with his gloomy forebodings. The very report he sent on 14 August on the firmness of the Bulgarian Government towards Russian pressure seemed to belie them. That same day Conrad announced to the Bulgarian Military Attaché, Major Tantilov, that the Austrian offensive against Serbia had begun, adding:

Unless Bulgaria intervenes quickly she will be too late. This is her one chance to rid herself of Serbia by settling accounts with her now. We have our interests in the Adriatic. You have yours in the Aegean. I do not see why there should be another State between us and you. If you do not start soon, you will be too late. We have already made a big advance.[3]

The Bulgarians waited, and did not regret having done so, because, as has been mentioned above, the Serbs repulsed the Austrian offensive. It lies outside the scope of the present work to trace the efforts of the two belligerent groups to win Bulgaria over. In the end the Central Powers were successful. But they could, with greater advantage, have done so from the very beginning and much more easily than their enemies, had their diplomacy at Sofia, no less than at Bucharest, Constantinople, and Rome, proved more equal to its task.

[1] Conrad, IV, p. 210.
[2] Conrad, IV, p. 201.
[3] Conrad, IV, p. 211.

CHAPTER XIV

THE TURKISH ALLIANCE WITH GERMANY AND OTTOMAN HESITATIONS

1. Russian and German relations with Turkey.

The Ottoman Empire, which had been in a state of increasing decay since the beginning of the nineteenth century, was in a disastrous condition after the Balkan war of 1912. The Anglophil Grand Vizier Kiamil Pasha had hoped that the Powers would come to his country's rescue, but the Powers advised him to cede to his enemies everything conquered by them, even Adrianople. It was at this juncture that the Young Turks, who had been waiting their chance to seize power, marched on the Porte under the leadership of Talaat and Enver, murdered the War Minister, Nazim Pasha, forced Kiamil to resign, and installed as his successor Mahmud Shevket Pasha, who formed a cabinet of the most influential members of the notorious Committee of Union and Progress. At the head of this committee of some forty members were Enver, Talaat, and Djemal. These men in 1908 had been the authors of a revolution claiming to work for the regeneration of the country, but in reality rendering its condition worse than before, since they were still more corrupt, more unscrupulous, and more brutal than their predecessors.

The Second Balkan War enabled Enver to take advantage of the defeat of Bulgaria and march on Adrianople, recapture the city and retain it for Turkey in spite of Russian protests. But the Maritza line was not enough to provide a basis of security for the Ottoman Empire, now almost driven out of the European continent and thrown back on its possession of Asiatic provinces, backward, poverty-stricken, and bled white. The Young Turks sought to infuse new strength into the Empire by calling in foreign experts to reorganize its finances, tariffs, police, navy and army. The French General Baumann was entrusted with the reorganization of the police, and the English Admiral Limpus with that of the navy.

As for the army, the Grand Vizier on 22 May 1913 approached the Kaiser through Wangenheim with a request that a German general should be placed in charge of its reorganization.[1] The choice fell on General Liman von Sanders, and it was arranged that he with a staff of forty-two German officers should run the military academy. He was to be a member of the War Council, have control of appointments, be authorized to impose punishments, hold inspections, and in addition command the First Army Corps stationed at Constantinople. This meant in practice that the Turkish army and capital were placed in the hands of Germany. These arrangements roused intense indignation at St. Petersburg. The ultimate supreme aim of Russian policy and the object of all her wars with Turkey for the two preceding centuries was the possession of Constantinople and the Straits, coveted for sentimental, military, and economic reasons, especially as giving free passage from the Black Sea to the Mediterranean. And if this goal did not seem attainable for the moment and it had been necessary not to attempt more than make repeated efforts to obtain the opening of the Straits, Russia could never allow another Power to establish itself at Constantinople and put an end to her own aspirations. Hence the Russian warning to Bulgaria at the end of 1912 when it looked as if the Bulgarian advance would carry its forces as far as the Bosporus. Hence also the protest in November 1913 against the Liman von Sanders mission, which Russia might perhaps have gone to the length of regarding as a *casus belli,* had she been better prepared militarily, had she received stronger support from England and France, and had the Prime Minister, Kokovtsov not been opposed to a war. The matter was patched up by a compromise under which Liman von Sanders was not put in command of the Constantinople Army Corps and was made, instead, Inspector-General of the Turkish army.

That the Russian apprehensions were justified is beyond doubt. Through the Baghdad railway and the control of the army, Germany had acquired a predominant position in Turkey which would enable her to prevent the realization of Russian traditional aspirations. Taube says very truly that the Liman von Sanders affair

contributed greatly to [Sazonov's] all too nervy handling of the Serbo-Austrian crisis which in those tragic days of July 1914 precipitated the final catastrophe. . . .
As a result of this affair the openly hostile attitude of the Russian Navy Ministry towards Turkey in the Straits question spread to the Foreign Ministry, which till then had shown great circumspection in its handling of this historic problem.[2]

Even without the Liman von Sanders mission the Turks would

---

[1] GP. XXXVIII, 15440.
[2] Taube, *Der grossen Katastrophe entgegen* (Leipzig, 1937), p. 285.

have been attracted towards Germany. Their hereditary enemy was Russia. Ever since the time of Peter the Great they had feared her who had so much contributed to the liberation and development of the Balkan states, had laid claim to Constantinople and also nourished designs on Armenia. In the past they had always found a protector in England, but she had now become virtually an ally of Russia, and since her occupation of Egypt had no more confidence in the future of the Ottoman Empire. Only Germany, who had no desire to take territory from the Turks could save them. Not but that among the Young Turks there were some who would have preferred to ally with the Triple *Entente* rather than with the Triple Alliance, but they were a minority and carried less weight than those who inclined towards Germany. Furthermore, when the crisis of July 1914 broke out some of the *Entente* supporters went over to the opposite camp. One of these converts, the Navy Minister, Djemal Pasha, writes:

> Germany, whatever else might be said, was the only Power which desired to see Turkey strong. Germany's interests could be secured by the strengthening of Turkey, and that alone. Germany could not lay hands on Turkey as if she were a colony, for neither the geographical position nor her resources made that possible. The result was that Germany regarded Turkey as a link in the commercial and trading chain, and thus became her stoutest champion against the *Entente* Governments, which wanted to dismember her, particularly as the elimination of Turkey would mean final 'encirclement' of Germany. . . . Thus we had two groups of Powers before us, the ideal of one of which was to get us in its power, while the aim of the other was to make friendly approaches to us in view of certain prospective advantages, and to conclude an alliance with us based on equal rights and obligations. Could this offer be rejected?[1]

2. *Turkey betwixt alliance with Greece and alliance with Bulgaria.*

However, the Turks who inclined towards Germany were non-plussed by the favor shown to Greece by Wilhelm and his Government, both of them desirous of a rapprochement between Turkey, Greece, and Romania which would isolate Serbia. It had been Venizelos who, anxious for German support in settling the question of the islands, over which Turkey had not accepted the Powers' decision, took the step on 17 April 1914 of proposing to the Chancellor a settlement based on recognition of the Sultan's nominal suzerainty over the islands of Chios and Mitylene and the conclusion of an alliance between Greece and Turkey.[2] The idea found favor with Berlin and on 2 May Jagow recommended it to the German Ambassador

---

[1] Djemal Pasha, *Memories of a Turkish Statesman, 1913-1919* (London, 1922), p. 113.
[2] GP. XXXVI², 14564.

in Turkey, Wangenheim.[1] But Wangenheim, who had a profound knowledge of Turkish conditions and exercised great influence at Constantinople, wrote back on 7 May that Turkey for many reasons tended rather towards alliance with Bulgaria and Romania than towards Greece.

Romania, Turkey, and Bulgaria formed militarily a single territorial unit; their armies totaled two million men and might enable them to be independent of the Great Powers. Against Romania and Bulgaria the Turks felt no antipathy, knowing that these countries had no designs on Constantinople, while it was to their interest that the Straits should not be in the possession of a Great Power. On the other hand, they hated Greece, who, as they knew, had aspirations for Constantinople. An alliance with Greece could not protect Turkey against the dangers she feared from Russia, and might well hasten an accord between Russia and Bulgaria, whereas if Turkey were linked with Romania and Bulgaria and covered in her rear by the Triple Alliance, the Russian threat would lose substance.[2]

In so clear a situation it seems incredible that Berlin should have persisted in pressing for co-operation with Romania and Greece rather than with Bulgaria and Turkey, which would have been easy to obtain. In spite of Turkish intervention in the Second Balkan War, Sofia and Constantinople were already seriously beginning to talk of an alliance in the first days of September 1913 when the Bulgarian delegates arrived to conclude the peace whereby Bulgaria was to resign herself to the loss of Adrianople. On 5 September the Grand Vizier told Wangenheim that from his first meeting with the delegates he gained the impression that Bulgaria was more anxious to achieve an alliance with Turkey than to secure possession of Adrianople and the Maritza line.[3] Bulgaria was thinking primarily of a war of *revanche* against Greece, while Turkey was determined on no account, even were it to cost her a war, to allow the four large islands close to the coast of Asia Minor to go to Greece.[4] What was in the wind, therefore, was a secret offensive alliance, whose basis, as the Austrian Ambassador to Constantinople, Pallavicini, telegraphed to Berchtold on 30 October 1913, would have been as follows: if Bulgaria did not feel sure of Romanian neutrality, Turkey would act alone against Greece; if Bulgaria felt secure as regards Romanian neutrality, Bulgaria and Turkey would attack Serbia and Greece.[5] The agreement was to be signed on 22 or 23 December 1913,[6] but at the last moment Bulgaria drew back in fear of both Romania and Russia. She put forward the demand that there was to be no war for four years unless with the

[1] GP. XXXVI[2], 14582.   [2] GP. XXXVI[2], 14587.
[3] GP. XXXVI[1], 1321   [4] Oe-U. VII, 8550, 8592, 8607.
[5] Oe-U. VII, 8777, 8778.   [6] Oe-U. VII, 9116.

certainty of Romanian neutrality The Turks on the other hand were in a hurry and planned to go into action in the spring of 1914[1] As a further safeguard against any threat from Romania, Sofia threw out the suggestion that both Turkey and Bulgaria should join the Triple Alliance.[2] At that time, however, Germany was opposed to the accession of Bulgaria to the Triple Alliance In March 1914 the Turkish Government put out fresh feelers at Bucharest for an agreement with Bulgaria and Romania, but realized that for the moment condition^ were not propitious [3]

So these negotiations were dropped and in their stead, at the behest of Berlin, others were begun for a Turko-Greek alliance, though with how little conviction may well be imagined To bring about their failure the Grand Vizier and Foreign Minister, Said Halim Pasha, on 29 April put forward the demand that, as a result of the alliance, Greece should recognize the Sultan's sovereignty, not only over Chios and Mitylene, as Venizelos had proposed, but over all the islands assigned to Greece by the Powers with the exception of Crete.[4] The tension between the two countries became such as to give rise to fears of war In the first days of July 1914 Enver inquired of the Bulgarian Minister, Toshev, whether in a conflict with Greece, which seemed imminent, Turkey could count on Bulgaria, receiving a reply in the negative.[5] However, it had been arranged that the Grand Vizier should have a meeting with Venizelos at Brussels, when the Sarajevo crime and Francis Joseph's letter to Wilhelm accompanying the Austrian memorandum caused the policy of Berlin to swing round to approval of Bulgarian accession to the Triple Alliance as advocated in that memorandum which at the same time advocated the promotion of an alliance between Bulgaria and Turkey regarded as desirable by both these countries.

At the discussion which took place on 6 July at the Wilhelmstrasse between Bethmann and Jagow on the one hand and Hoyos on the other, the Chancellor—as Szögyény reports—expressed the opinion

that it would be better for the moment to negotiate and settle only with Bulgaria, leaving it for future decisions whether Turkey and possibly Greece were to be brought into alliance with Bulgana Imperial Chancellor remarked that in view of the extensive German interests in Turkey her accession would be particularly desirable [6]

Berchtold telegraphed these opinions on 10 July to Pallavicini,[7] who on 12 July telegraphed back from Constantinople that 'at the moment predominant part of authoritative circles here may be described as friendly to the Triplice', but urging speedy

[1] Oe-U. VII, 9010.   [2] Oe-U. VII, 9131.   [3] Oe-U. VII, 9464.
[4] GP XXXVI[2], 14578.   [5] Oe-U. VIII, 10081.   [6] Oe-U. VIII, 10076.
[7] Oe-U. VIII, 10179.

action.[1] Berchtold on 13 July sent this news on to Szögyény, telling him to suggest to Jagow that Turkish statesmen should be sounded by both Germany and Austria on the possibility of a Turkish rapprochement with the Central Powers, 'since I have the impression that Sofia is again feeling concern about the Turkish attitude'.[2] There was no cause for this impression and Berchtold probably only alleged it as a means of bringing pressure to bear on Berlin. In fact that same day he received a report from Pallavicini of a conversation in which the Grand Vizier opined 'that the present moment, when Austria had all sympathies on her side, was favorable for a final settlement of accounts with Serbia, . . . the other Balkan States would hardly stand aside, and Bulgaria in particular would certainly use the occasion for an attack on Serbia. In his opinion, Turkey, whose interests were practically identical with those of Bulgaria, would not stand in her way'.[3]

3. *Germany at first refuses to ally with Turkey.*

The opinions expressed to the Austrian Ambassador by the Grand Vizier show how well disposed Turkey was towards the cause of the Central Powers. But at that moment her accession to the Triplice was opposed by the Wilhelmstrasse in spite of what the Chancellor had said to Hoyos and Szögyény on 6 July. On 14 July Jagow's reply to Szögyény was that

for the next few years Turkey could only be a liability on account of her poor military state. She would be in no position to take the field against Russia. . . . She would be sure to make demands on us. We could certainly not give her definite protection against, for instance, a Russian attack on Armenia. . . . If Romania were to remain true to the Triplice, and Bulgaria perhaps seek accession to our group, that would influence the attitude of Turkey.[4]

Once more, as in the preceding years, the Germans showed little understanding of the Balkan situation. The influence determining the German attitude at that moment was that of Wangenheim, then in Berlin. After his return to Constantinople on 15 July he again sent a report on 18 July advising against the accession of Turkey to the Triplice.[5] And he brought Pallavicini round to this opinion, though Pallavicini's dispatch of 16 July advised that 'everything should be done to prevent Turkey's joining the power group of our opponents. My German colleague seems to me to underestimate this latter danger.'[8] On 18 July Pallavicini himself wrote warning against the possibility of an alliance between Turkey, Greece and Romania which would

[1] Oe-U. VIII, 10217.   [2] Oe-U. VIII, 10237.   [3] Oe-U. VIII, 10243.
[4] DD. I, 45; Oe.-U. VIII, 10297.   [5] DD. I, 71.   [6] Oe-U. VIII, 10303.

necessarily be directed against Bulgaria and also against Austria. He advised that everything should be done to bring about a rapprochement between Turkey and Bulgaria, giving up as impracticable Wangenheim's idea of one between Turkey and Romania.[1] This impression received further confirmation from conversations which Pallavicini had with the Grand Vizier, Talaat, and Enver severally on 20 July. They each expressed the view that this was the last chance for Austria to restore her prestige as a Great Power with the Balkan peoples and Turkey. Not only Bulgaria but also Romania and Turkey would range themselves unreservedly with the Triplice if Austria were to give Serbia a good lesson. At the wish of Germany and Romania and against her better judgment, Turkey had been on the point of making an alliance with Greece. This alliance would not come to pass if Austria by forceful action bound Bulgaria to her. From what the three Turkish Ministers said Pallavicini gained the impression that the Triple *Entente,* Russia especially, was now working for an alliance between Turkey, Greece, and Romania. If on the contrary successful efforts were now made to bring about an alliance between Bulgaria and Turkey, the latter country, even without formal accession to the Triplice, would be prevented from passing over to the opposite camp.[2]

This danger was very much less than Pallavicini thought. A perusal of the documents leaves the impression that the three Turkish statesmen spoke as they did in order to scare him and further their own designs for a rapprochement not with Greece but with Bulgaria and through her with the Triple Alliance, since what they wanted was to feel themselves secure on the Bulgarian frontier. On 20 July the Grand Vizier sent for the Bulgarian Minister, Toshev, and told him of his forthcoming meeting with Venizelos in Holland or Belgium, saying that there was no question of an alliance with Greece and asking what would be the Bulgarian attitude in the event of a conflict between Austria and Serbia.[3] And on 22 July Enver Pasha raised the question of Turkey's accession to the Triplice directly with Wangenheim, saying that

Turkey needed the backing of one of the Great Power groups. A small minority in the Committee [of Union and Progress] wanted an alliance with Russia and France. . . . The majority of the Committee, headed by the Grand Vizier with Talaat Bey, Halil, and himself, did not want to become vassals of Russia and was convinced that the Triplice was stronger than the *Entente* and would be the victors in a world war. He could therefore affirm that the present Turkish Government urgently desired to join the Triplice and only if rebuffed by it would with a heavy heart decide in favor of a pact with the Triple *Entente.* . . . At the moment two possibilities

---

[1] Oe-U. VIII. 10355. [2] DD. I. 99; Oe-U. VIII, 10409, 10412.
[3] DD. I, 102, Oe-U. VIII, 10453.

of secondary alliances lay open to Turkey: an alliance with Greece, which would be a half-way house to the Triple *Entente,* and an alliance with Bulgaria, leading over to the Triple Alliance. The Cabinet inclined therefore towards agreement with Bulgaria on condition that the alliance was under the patronage of the Triplice or at least of one Triplice Power. . . . Now as a consequence of the Austro-Serbian tension the situation had grown critical. The Grand Vizier was about to negotiate with Venizelos for an alliance. But it would be easier for him to decline the Greek offer if there were a prospect that Turkey and Bulgaria as a *bloc* might stand in a similar relationship to the Triplice as Romania in the past. The Porte could not wait for the outbreak of a war in the Balkans.

Wangenheim objected that

the economic recovery of Turkey would be prejudiced by such an alliance. . . . As a member of the Triplice Turkey would have to reckon with the open hostility of Russia. The Turkish eastern frontier would be the weakest spot in the strategic dispositions of the Triplice and the natural point of attack for Russia. The Triplice Governments would doubtless hesitate to shoulder burdens for which Turkey today could make no adequate return. Even Turkey and Bulgaria as a *bloc* would scarcely be of any value to the Triplice as an ally. . . . Enver Pasha listened attentively but stressed again and again that if the Triplice prevented the alliance between Bulgaria and Turkey, the friends of the Triple *Entente* in the Committee would gain the upper hand.[1]

The German Ambassador's objections did not show great acumen. He was blind to the fact that it was to his country's interest to bind all available forces to itself and prevent them from going over to the enemy; nay more, that a Turkish alliance would prevent Russia from receiving supplies and communicating with her allies via the Mediterranean besides putting great pressure on Bulgaria. Wilhelm at once perceived Wangenheim's mistake and disapprovingly annotated his dispatch: 'Theoretically correct but at the present moment mistaken! Now it is a question of getting hold of every musket in the Balkans that is prepared to go off *for* Austria against the Slavs, thus a Turko-Bulgarian alliance leaning on Austria is most certainly to be agreed to!' And on 23 July the Kaiser's wrath was aroused by a dispatch from Wangenheim saying:

Margrave Pallavicini had been instructed by his Government to warn the Grand Vizier against concluding an alliance with Greece. . . . The Grand Vizier assured my Austrian colleague most emphatically that he would make no alliance with M. Venizelos and that in the event of war Austria could count on Turkey as on Bulgaria. . . . Finally the Grand Vizier repeated the desire expressed to me by Enver Pasha yesterday that formal entry into the Triplice might be made possible for Turkey. Margrave Pallavicini, who had

[1] DD. I, 117.

in the meantime discussed the question with me, replied that an alliance with Turkey would at the moment impose too great a burden on the Triplice. The Triplice could not defend Turkey against everybody.

'Rubbish', commented the Kaiser, adding 'Wangenheim must definitely reply welcoming Turkish accession to the Triplice', because otherwise Turkey would go over to the Franco-Russian group and be closed to the influence of the Central Powers.[1] And on reading Wangenheim's dispatch of 22 July on board the *Hohenzollern* the Kaiser commanded Wedel on the 24th to telegraph to the Wilhelmstrasse that while regarding Wangenheim's reasoning as

theoretically correct, he is of the opinion that at the present moment on grounds of expediency advantage must be taken of Turkey's inclination towards the Triplice. So if Stamboul actually means to conclude alliance 'under the patronage of the Triplice or of one Triplice Power' let it really try to bring Romania and Bulgaria together and place itself at Austria's disposal.

This instruction was sent by Jagow to Wangenheim on the same day.[2]

4. *The signing of the pact of alliance between Germany and Turkey on 2 August 1914.*

Wangenheim was not long in bringing the affair off. The Austrian ultimatum to Serbia had aroused great enthusiasm at Constantinople, and when Pallavicini had read it to the Grand Vizier on 24 July, the latter's comment had been that 'the decidedness of the Austrian Government's attitude even exceeded his expectations', and that, if a general conflagration were to result, Turkey could not do otherwise 'than join the Triplice in company with Bulgaria'. He had long been trying for an alliance with Bulgaria, but she had drawn back at the last moment. Now in the changed circumstances he hoped to be successful. He would be able to place troops at Bulgaria's disposal in the event of her being attacked by Romania.[3]

Wangenheim, accordingly, dropped his objections to the alliance, telegraphing on 27 July that the proposal had been made.[4] And in the night of 27/28 July the Grand Vizier sent for Wangenheim and asked him to transmit to the Kaiser his Sovereign's request that Germany would conclude a secret, short-term, defensive and offensive alliance with Turkey against Russia. 'The *casus foederis* would arise if Russia should attack Turkey, Germany or Austria-Hungary, or if Germany or the Triplice should go to war with Russia. Against countries other than Russia, Turkey needs no protection. . . . Turkey would engage

---

[1] DD. I, 149, Oe-U. VIII, 10452, 10489.   [2] DD. I, 141, 144.
[3] Oe-U. VIII, 10598, 10673.   [4] DD. I, 276.

to find a form whereby at the outbreak of war the supreme direction of the Turkish army and actual command of a quarter of the army would be transferred to the Military Mission.'[1]

At 9.30 p. m. on the 28th Bethmann replied that the Kaiser accepted the Grand Vizier's proposal on the following terms:

(i)   Both Powers pledge strict neutrality in present conflict between Austria-Hungary and Serbia.

(ii) If Russia were to intervene actively in the war, so that the *casus foederis* would arise for Germany in regard to Austria, the *casus foederis* would also arise for Turkey.

(iii) Germany will in the event of war leave the Military Mission in Turkey. Turkey ensures the actual exercise of the supreme command by the Military Mission, (iv) Germany guarantees integrity of Turkey's present territory against Russia.

(iv) The treaty is valid for the present Austro-Serbian conflict and the possible international complications arising therefrom.[2]

He says he had thought of a seven-year duration but was prepared in the extreme case to allow the treaty to run concurrently with General Liman's contract, i.e., till the end of 1918.[3]

Then came 31 July when already Russia had proclaimed general mobilization, arousing the apprehensions of Constantinople and causing Wangenheim to telegraph at 3 p. m. to Berlin:

If we mean to conclude with Turkey, it is high time. We might otherwise have 300,000 Turks against instead of with us.

The dispatch went on to say that General Liman was beginning to doubt whether the Turks would declare in favor of Germany and that Pallavicini regarded Austrian hesitations about Bulgaria as an 'over-refinement'.[4] It is clear that all three men were in a state of nerves over this critical matter. The Chancellor, too, was in much the same state, and after proclaiming the *Kriegsgefahrzustand* at 3 p. m. on 31 July he telegraphed at 6.15 p. m. to Wangenheim:

Please inform Grand Vizier without delay that we agree to the duration of the treaty till 1918, as desired by the Porte, and are ready for immediate conclusion. . . . It must, however, first be ascertained whether in the present war Turkey can and will undertake some action worthy of mention against Russia. In negative case alliance would obviously be useless and not to be signed.[5]

The signing took place at 4 p. m. on 2 August.[6] The treaty, which was later joined by Austria, was on the lines laid down by the Chancellor. It carried the provision that, unless denounced

---

[1] DD. II, 285.   [2] DD. II, 320.   [3] DD. III, 411.
[4] DD. III, 517.   [5] DD. III, 508.   [6] DD. III, 726.

by one of the contracting parties six months before the date of expiry, the treaty would be renewed for a further five years.[1]

The conclusion of this treaty caused much satisfaction to Moltke. At the beginning of his long memorandum of 2 August for the guidance of the Wilhelmstrasse he wrote:

> The treaty with Turkey is to be made public immediately. Turkey is to declare war on Russia as soon as possible.[2]

But this was not Constantinople's idea. All that Turkey did was to mobilize on 3 August and proclaim armed neutrality. On that same day Wangenheim telegraphed:

> Enver and Liman would like to declare war on Russia immediately. . . . Grand Vizier . . , against this because (1) Turkish mobilization . . . is not completed; (2) Bulgaria's attitude is not yet clear, and without Bulgaria direct intervention against Russia is not possible; (3) we fear that after declaration of war England might commandeer the *Sultan Osman I* [building with Armstrong Whitworth in England].

Wangenheim added that the Bulgarian Minister, who, with Wangenheim's and Pallavicini's support, was to have resumed negotiations with the Porte, was still without instructions. 'Everything hangs on the speed of the Bulgarian decisions and actions.'[3]

But Berlin was in a hurry and none too sure of Turkey's word. Hence Jagow telegraphed on 4 August:

> England will possibly declare war on us today or tomorrow. To prevent the Porte from deserting us at the last moment under the impression of the English move, Turkish declaration of war against Russia today if possible appears of the greatest importance.[4]

But this telegram crossed with one from Wangenheim:

> Grand Vizier tells me Bulgarian Minister has still made no overtures for a possible *entente*. He has the impression that Bulgaria will make her attitude depend on that of Romania. The essential thing now is to bring Romania and Bulgaria together as soon as possible.[5]

The truth was that for reasons which have been discussed in the preceding chapter Bulgaria did not want to commit herself. On 21 July the Grand Vizier asked Toshev 'what would be Bulgaria's attitude on the outbreak of an Austro-Serbian war',[6] to which on 24 July the Bulgarian Government replied that 'Bulgaria would not intervene

---

[1] DD. III, 733. [2] DD. III, 662. [3] DD. III, 795.
[4] DD. III, 836. [5] DD. III, 854 [6] DD. I, 102.

without previously coming to an understanding with Turkey'.[1] This meant little, and Austria was endeavoring to get considerably more. On 21 July Pallavicini advised Toshev:

Ally yourselves with the Turks for joint action with Austria-Hungary in the event of others intervening on behalf of Serbia.[2]

But Sofia did not budge. Late on 30 July Berchtold instructed Tarnowski to suggest informally that Radoslavov should 'pick up again the dropped thread of a rapprochement with Turkey'.[3] Radoslavov's reply on 31 July was .that the Grand Vizier had gone to meet Venizelos in Munich, that Turkey was beginning to mobilize, and her policy was 'nebulous'. Tarnowski said reassuringly that his news of the Turkish attitude towards Bulgaria was good, whereupon Radoslavov said he would talk with Turkey, 'but first wanted formally to perfect the union of Bulgaria with Germany'.[4] Late that same evening Radoslavov soothingly told Tarnowski that he had in the meantime received good news from Constantinople: the Grand Vizier had given up the journey to Munich and a commercial treaty had been signed. He, Radoslavov, had already given Toshev instructions on the lines suggested by Tarnowski to open discussions with Turkey for concerted behavior on the part of the two States.[6] By way of encouragement Jagow telegraphed to Sofia and Bucharest on 3 August that the Turko-German alliance had been signed.[6] On 3 August Toshev was still without instructions, and on the morning of 4 August nothing definite had happened. On 6 August, however, a treaty was signed at Sofia by Radoslavov on behalf of Bulgaria and by Mehmed Talaat on behalf of Turkey. Its existence remained a deep secret until it was divulged to Wangenheim on 17 December 1914 by Halil Bey. The treaty contained seven articles and its text ran as follows:

Art. i. The Ottoman Empire and the Kingdom of Bulgaria promise reciprocally peace and friendship. The two States engage mutually to respect their territories.

Art. ii. In the event of one of the High Contracting Parties being attacked by one or several Balkan States, the other Contracting Party, on request from its ally, shall declare war on the assailant or assailants and attack the assailant or assailants immediately with all its available armed forces.

Art. iii. The High Contracting Parties engage not to undertake armed action against one or several Balkan States without previous agreement. In the event of one of the parties being under the necessity of declaring war on a Balkan State without having previously consulted its ally or without having obtained its ally's consent, the latter shall maintain benevolent neutrality if it does not desire to co-operate militarily.

---

[1] DD. I, 147.   [2] Bulg., 195.   [3] Oe-U. VIII, 11096.
[4] Oe-U. VIII. 11186.   [5] Oe-U. VIII, 11193.   [6] DD. IV, 743.

Art. iv. All military co-operation between the two High Contracting Parties shall be regulated by a special military convention which shall also cover the conditions in which the troops of the one party may cross the territory of the other.

Art. v. Bulgaria declares that the terms of the present treaty concerning her entry into military offensive action in agreement with Turkey can only come into force after Bulgaria has obtained an adequate guarantee from Romania, either by a triple agreement between Turkey, Romania, and Bulgaria, or by a special understanding between Romania and Bulgaria on a basis of neutrality.

Art. vi. The mobilization of the Bulgarian army will take place at the moment judged opportune by the Bulgarian Government. The latter shall inform the Imperial Ottoman Government thereof and will let the latter know the day on which it will be able to order military operations.

Art. vii. The duration of the present convention is fixed until the final liquidation of the present European war and the demobilization of the armies. However, it may continue in force for a duration of five years if not denounced by one of the parties within three months after the demobilization of the Turkish and Bulgarian armies.

The existence and tenor of the present treaty shall be guarded in the deepest secrecy.[1]

5. *Turkey does not go to war; she declares neutrality and makes a feint of negotiating with Russia.*

In spite of this treaty Turkey did not join the war on the side of the Central Powers until 3 November 1914, after the German Admiral, Souchon, as a way of overcoming the Grand Vizier's last hesitations and creating a state of war, had on 29 October bombarded Odessa, Sebastopol and Novorossisk. It is well known that not all members of the Turkish Government were in favor of making war on Russia and that those suspected of sympathies with the *Entente* were only told of the alliance after it was signed. But even those who favored the alliance seemed half to regret having bound themselves to Germany. The reasons for their fears and hesitations are easily imagined if one considers how alarming the situation appeared immediately afterwards. The swift intervention of England and the Italian and Romanian declarations of neutrality made the victory of the Central Powers look less certain than had been believed. Moreover, Bulgaria, who had been expected to attack Serbia at once, made no sign of moving. Clearly it was advisable to wait and see, meanwhile keeping Russia dangling, concealing the alliance from her and fobbing her off with promises. From a reliable source Sazonov had received secret information of negotiations between Turkey, Bulgaria and Austria and on 25 July had

---

[1] From the copy of the treaty preserved in the German Foreign Ministry Archives, *Abteilhung 4, Beziehungen zur Türkei von 1914.—Bulgarien* No. 17. A.S. 2976. [Ed.]

telegraphed to Constantinople drawing the Russian Ambassador Giers'
attention to them.[1] The following day Giers replied:

> So far neither I nor the French Ambassador observe indication of a wish on the
> part of the Porte to take immediate action,

and that for the moment it was pursuing a policy of wait and see.[2] On
1 August Giers reported having been told by the Grand Vizier that the
Austrian Ambassador was endeavoring to persuade Turkey to make
common cause with Austria but that in his opinion Turkey ought to
keep out of the conflict. Giers, however, was convinced that Turkey
would not let the first favorable chance slip to further her own interests, provided the chance were to offer itself.[3] On 2 August Giers
sought out the Grand Vizier to ask an explanation of the rumors about
Turkish mobilization and received the answer that it was being
proclaimed for fear of action on the part of Bulgaria.[4] On 4 August the
Grand Vizier told Giers that the Cabinet on the previous day had
decided on strict neutrality, that the Bosporus and Dardanelles were
to be mined, and that only merchant ships would be allowed through.[5]
On 5 August Enver Pasha went to the length of offering the Russian
Military Attaché, Leontiev, an actual military alliance, suggesting that
Russia might use the Turkish army 'to neutralize this or that Balkan
State which in any way intended to move against Russia, and also for
the support of the armies of the Balkan States against Austria'. Leontiev
inquired what concessions would be asked in return, and Enver replied
that for Turkey they would consist of the Aegean islands and Western
Thrace.[6]

This was an obvious maneuver on the part of Enver Pasha to
conceal the alliance with Germany, and in support of the maneuver
the Bulgarian Minister Toshev called on Giers on 5 August to give it
as his opinion

> that the moment had come for Bulgaria to return to the Russian orbit of influence
> and join with the other Balkan States. . . . He doubted the possibility of the
> Bulgarian army fighting side by side with the Serbs. But he was certain that Bulgaria
> would not side against Serbia and that she would honestly maintain the strictest
> neutrality during the present crisis. But she would wish to have guarantees that she
> would not be attacked by Turkey, and as such would regard a mutual pact on the
> part of Greece, Turkey, Bulgaria and Romania not to enter the war. A pact of this
> kind would be the nucleus of a Balkan *bloc* against Austria. In exchange for their
> neutrality the Balkan countries should receive territorial compensation. On this
> compensation Toshev's views are identical with those expressed today to

---

[1] *Int. Bez.* i. V, 50.   [2] *Int. Bez.* i. V, 109.
[3] *Int. Bez.* i. V, 439.   [4] *Int. Bez.* i. V, 478, 479.
[5] *Int. Bez.* i. V, 557.   [6] *Int. Bez.* ii. VI[1], 8.

our military agent [Leontiev], which proves with certainty that Turkey and Bulgaria, supported by Germany and Austria, have been holding discussions on common action in the present crisis. . . . I suppose it is fear of German non-success and the passionate desire to gain some tangible profit from this war that prompts Turkey and perhaps Bulgaria to make advances to us at this moment. Though putting no trust in their sincerity, I think they must not be repulsed, for we should throw them into the arms of our enemies.[1]

In a further dispatch of 5 August Giers reports:

Toshev made a pretty transparent allusion to an understanding . . . said to have been concluded between Turkey and Germany in connection with their joint machinations against us. . . . I do not deny the possibility of such an understanding, but it cannot have any import for the moment on account of the state of the Turkish army.[2]

On 9 August, after another interview between Enver and Leontiev at which Enver pressed for a Russo-Turkish alliance, Giers reiterated his plea that Russia should accept Enver's proposals: 'Even if Enver is not entirely sincere, our acceptance will clarify the situation.'[3] But this opinion was not shared by Sazonov, who on 10 August telegraphed to Giers:

Pending a reply from Sofia keep in mind that in conversations with Enver we must gain time. Remember that possible action on the part of Turkey against us directly gives us no anxiety. At the same time, while maintaining the entirely friendly tone of the discussions with the Turks, endeavor to intimate to them that actions on their part which do not receive our sanction will jeopardize the whole of Asia Minor, whose existence we, in alliance-with France and England, hold in our hands, while they are not in a position to harm us.[4]

In after-years Sazonov expressed a juster appreciation of the situation when he wrote in *Fateful Years* that:

In 1914 Turkey's attitude to the war was a matter of first-rate importance to all the belligerent countries. The possibility of Turkey siding with the Central Powers was particularly dangerous to Russia, for in that case the Black Sea would be open to the enemy's fleet, and a considerable part of our army needed on the Western front would have to be retained on the Turkish frontier, and, the Black Sea being closed, we should be cut off from direct communication with our allies and be paralyzed economically, having nothing but the distant and in every way inconvenient port of Archangel for an outlet.[6]

[1] *Int. Bez.* ii. VI¹, 9; *Documents diplomatiques secrets russes,* pp. 69-70.
[2] *Documents diplomatiques secrets russes,* pp. 69-70.
[3] *Int. Bez.* ii. VI¹, 48, 49.
[4] *Int. Bez.* ii. VI¹, 50; *Documents diplomatiques secrets russes,* p. 76.
[5] Sazonov, p. 227.

Then why did Sazonov telegraph to Giers: 'Possible action on the part of Turkey against us directly gives us no anxiety'? He may have not wanted to enter into engagements with the Porte, hoping that the outcome of the European war would settle the problem of Constantinople and the Straits in Russia's favor. There was, moreover, a belief that Turkey would not venture to take sides against the Triple *Entente,* which was so much stronger in the Mediterranean than the Triple Alliance. These were very rash assumptions, but there are some, such as Morgenthau, the United States Ambassador in Turkey from 1913 to 1917, who are convinced that Turkey would never have entered the war if the *Goeben* and the *Breslau* had not entered the Straits and joined the Turkish fleet.

6. *The entry of the* Goeben *and* Breslau *into the Bosporus and the consequences thereof.*

At the moment of the outbreak of the European war the *Goeben,* a powerful German battle-cruiser of the latest type, and the *Breslau,* a swift light cruiser, were in Mediterranean waters. After making their presence felt on 4 August by firing a few rounds against the Algerian coast they touched at Messina on the 5th and thence made for the Aegean, having received orders to proceed to Constantinople. At Naxos they ran out of fuel, but the German Minister at Athens persuaded Venizelos to allow them to coal up, so that, leaving Naxos at 3.45 a. m. on 10 August, the two warships reached the entrance to the Straits about 5 p. m. The Turkish Government, asked by the German Government to give free passage to German and Austrian vessels, ought not to have allowed them to pass, and at first the Grand Vizier had qualms because, as Enver told Wangenheim on 4 August, Turkish relations with Bulgaria were still not clarified.[1] But his qualms were due only to the desire to exploit the situation in order to extract further concessions. Since the granting of asylum to the two cruisers would be regarded as a dangerous infringement of neutrality to the disadvantage of the *Entente,* the Grand Vizier asked for commensurate compensation, the terms of which are recorded by Wangenheim in a dispatch of 6 August. They include a German promise of support for the abolition of the capitulations, the territorial integrity of Turkey, the restoration of the islands, a rectification of her eastern frontier, and appropriate reparations.[2] As the two cruisers were being chased by a British squadron and there was not time to await a reply from Berlin, Wangenheim on 6 August took the responsibility of accepting the Turkish terms on condition 'that Turkey should come into war together with the Triplice Powers' and that when the terms came into force Germany

---

[1] DD. IV, 852.

[2] Carl Mühlmann, *Deutschland und die Turkei* (Berlin, 1929), pp. 96-7.

was in a position 'to dictate her will to the belligerents'.[1] On the conclusion of the agreement the *Goeben* and the *Breslau* were to have free passage, and in fact reached Constantinople at 8.30 p. m. on 10 August piloted through the minefields by a tug.

Four hours later the English squadron appeared at the mouth of the Straits. It could have acted much more speedily and sunk the enemy units; it could, moreover, have forced the Straits in order to attack and sink them in the Sea of Marmora. It is not necessary here to inquire into the reasons why this was not done and the two vessels were allowed to escape, but the omission had the most fateful consequences. The Turkish Government feared that the *Entente* would declare war unless the two warships were disarmed, while at the same time it was unwilling and unable to deprive itself of them and fail in the execution of the agreements made with its German ally. The Council of Ministers met at midnight on 10 August and decided to declare that the *Goeben* and the *Breslau* had been purchased by Turkey. The two cruisers were given Turkish names and added to the Ottoman navy, which by their acquisition became stronger in the Black Sea than the Russian navy. The latter, therefore, was unable to attack Constantinople or to threaten Turkish supremacy in the Black Sea.

Morgenthau comments:

I am convinced that when the judicious historian reviews this war and its consequences, he will say that the passage of the Strait by these German ships made it inevitable that Turkey should join Germany at the moment that Germany desired her assistance and that it likewise sealed the doom of the Turkish Empire.[2]

A.-F. Frangulis, a political opponent of Venizelos, whom he accuses of having enabled the two warships to escape the pursuit of the British squadron by allowing them to recoal, goes still further than Morgenthau:

It is known that their arrival at the Golden Horn played a decisive part in Turkey's entry into the war on the side of the Central Powers. It is also known what this entry of Turkey into the war meant: it meant Russia cut off from her allies, the Russian collapse, revolution, Bolshevism all rendered possible; it meant the 200,000 dead at the Dardanelles, the war carried into Asia, upheaval throughout the Near East. Finally Greece herself became the latest victim of that far-off act, all the consequences of which even today [1926] cannot be said to be at an end.[3]

Frangulis is impelled by political passion to exaggerate the guilt of Venizelos. It was the English Government, as Frangulis himself

---

[1] Mühlmann, *op. cit.*, pp. 44-6.
[2] *Ambassador Morgenthau's Story* (London, 1918), p. 80.
[3] Frangulis, I, p. 129.

records, which suggested to the Greek Prime Minister not to depart from observance of the usages of international law and therefore to let the warships have the coal necessary for their return to their nearest national harbor. Moreover, notwithstanding the refueling, the British fleet could well have taken more speedy and effective action, as has been said above. But Frangulis is not alone in attributing so decisive an importance to the entry of the *Goeben* and the *Breslau into* the Bosporus. The able French Minister of Marine, Georges Leygues, speaking in the Chamber on 23 June 1920, went so far as to say:

> The presence in the Mediterranean of the *Goeben* and the *Breslau* for a few-days, the fact of these cruisers taking refuge in Constantinople, sufficed to modify all the factors of the Near East problem, lengthening the duration of the war by several years and setting the catastrophe of Russia in motion.[1]

It may be a matter for argument whether Turkey would not in the end have made common cause with the Central Powers even if the *Goeben* and the *Breslau* had not entered her waters. But this event certainly influenced her conduct greatly.

As Giers telegraphed to St. Petersburg on 12 August:

> The arrival of the *Goeben* and *Breslau* alters the situation here not to our benefit. . . . It has considerably strengthened the self-esteem of the Turks and may inspire them with temerity for the most extreme steps.
>
> Following your instructions I will endeavor to gain time, but must give it as my opinion that a decision should be taken without delay if we contemplate the possibility of joint action with Turkey, as even tomorrow it may perhaps be too late. I am convinced that an agreement with Turkey will only make it easier to come to terms with Bulgaria, whereas if we wait for an answer from the Bulgarians, of whose sincerity we can but be doubtful, we shall lose hold of both Turkey and Bulgaria and have them both as our enemies.[2]

This was very true. And not only Russia, but also France and England, entirely misapprehending what had been decided by Turkey, allowed themselves to be hoodwinked into believing the assurances of the Turkish Government, attaching insufficient importance to disquieting signs and to the resentment that would necessarily be aroused by the English Government's commandeering of the two dreadnoughts ordered by Turkey in English shipyards and on the point of being delivered to her.[3]

Leaving aside the meager and almost certainly incomplete documentation published in the *Documents Diplomatiques Français* 3, XI, let us note that on 4 August Grey telegraphed to Beaumont, the English Chargé d'Affaires at Constantinople:

---

[1] Frangulis, I., p. 129.   [2] *Int. Bez.* ii. VI[1], 84.   [3] Churchill, I, p. 209.

You should earnestly impress upon Grand Vizier that Turkish interest would best be served by maintaining a strict neutrality. If Turkey were to be drawn into the war as an ally of Germany and Austria the gravest consequences would follow. You must, however, be careful to give to your communication the character of good advice from Turkey's oldest friend, and avoid anything to give rise to an impression that we are threatening.[1]

Nor did his tone change after the *Goeben* and *Breslau* incident. On 12 August Churchill wrote to Grey:

In all the circumstances, the Admiralty agree that the sale or transfer of these two vessels to the Turkish flag should be allowed, provided that the transfer is *bona fide* and permanent. The essential condition to insist on is that all the German officers and men of the crews of both ships must without exception be at once repatriated to Germany under parole not to serve again during the war.[2]

And on 16 August Grey wrote to the English Chargé d'Affaires, Beaumont:

As soon as French and Russian Ambassadors are similarly instructed, you are authorized to declare to Turkish Government that if Turkey will observe scrupulous neutrality during the war England, France, and Russia will uphold her independence and integrity against any enemies that may wish to utilize the general European complication in order to attack her.[3]

On 17 August Churchill again wrote to Grey:

The situation about *Goeben* and *Breslau* is extremely unsatisfactory. . . . We have to keep two British [battle] cruisers, which are urgently needed elsewhere, waiting with other vessels outside the Dardanelles.[4]

But up to the last the Triple *Entente* Powers failed to realize that Turkey had thrown in her lot with Germany. Their eyes were not opened until 3 November 1914, when the Ottoman Empire entered the war. Not that it would have been easy to prevent this from happening, but certainly to be successful any such attempt would have had to combine bolder action by the British fleet with far stronger diplomatic pressure from the three *Entente* Powers. From the point of view of the conduct of operations it would have been an immense advantage to find out where Turkey stood before she had time to make her preparations.

---

[1] BD. XI, 589.
[2] Churchill, I, pp. 482-3; Frangulis, 1, pp. 126-7.
[3] *White Paper, Miscellaneous*, No. 13 (1914), Cd. 7628.
[4] Churchill, I, p. 483.

CHAPTER XV

THE NEUTRALITY OF GREECE

(1) *The Serbo-Greek treaty of alliance; the Serbian attitude towards a war between Greece and Turkey (p. 624).* (2) *Venizelos refuses recognition of the* casus foederis *in an Austro-Serbian war (p. 627).* (3) *The feeling in Athens; the decision in favor of neutrality (p. 630).* (4) *Pressure from the Kaiser to obtain Greek support meets with resistance from King Constantine (p. 634).* (5) *Venizelos favors alliance with the Triple* Entente; *Russia asks Greece to make territorial concessions to Bulgaria; Greece refuses (p. 640).* (6) *An incomprehensible* démarche *by Streit; Greece joins with the Triple* Entente (*p. 643*).

1. *The Serbo-Greek treaty of alliance; the Serbian attitude towards a war between Greece and Turkey.*

Until the accession of King Constantine Greece had always gravitated in the orbit of the Triple *Entente.* Greece owed her resurgence to France, Russia and England, who since the battle of Navarino had never ceased to be her protectors. The friendly attitude towards these three Powers had become still more marked during the Venizelos Ministry and in the course of the First Balkan War when Greece relied above all on the Triple *Entente* for the fulfillment of her national aspirations in the Epirus and the Aegean islands. But after the assassination of King George at Salonika in 1913 he was succeeded by King Constantine, who had finished his education in Germany by serving in a regiment of the Guards and had then carried on his military training at the Academy of War and on the German General Staff. He had married a sister of the Kaiser and sent his own sons to be educated in Berlin, making no secret of his German sympathies and his reverential admiration for everything German.

To announce his accession to the European Courts Constantine selected the former Prime Minister Theotokis, known as a friend and admirer of the Kaiser, an opponent of Venizelos, and father of the Greek Chargé d'Affaires at Berlin. Theotokis went to Berlin on a secret mission from the King behind the back of Venizelos and on 18 June 1913 assured Jagow on behalf of Constantine that Greece was ready at any time to join the Triple Alliance provided she were sure of protection against the superior might of Bulgaria. He went on to say that the Slavs were the natural enemies of Greece, who ought to have Salonika as far as Kavala and Seres.[1] Jagow replied that he must first consult Germany's allies. In reply to his inquiry he received on

---

[1] GP. XXXV, 13450.

20 June unfavorable replies from both Berchtold and San Giuliano.[1] Nor could this be otherwise. It was the eve of the Second Balkan War, and Berchtold, as we know, was staking everything on Bulgaria. San Giuliano, in any case, was unreservedly hostile to Greece. Both therefore, had good reasons for replying that they were doubtful of the value of the Greek offer in view of Venizelos's frankly favorable attitude to the *Entente.*

Their doubts seem to have been shared by Jagow, who in his report to the Kaiser of 21 June wrote that he had telegraphed to Quadt, the German Minister at Athens, asking for his impressions. Quadt had replied that Theotokis's statements that Greece was intending to join the Triplice were in flat contradiction to everything Venizelos had ever said to him. 'Venizelos by an alliance only seeks to join with Romania and Turkey, keeping Greece out of any possible complications between Great Powers.'[2] As soon as Venizelos heard of Theotokis's proposals to Berlin he ordered Zaimis, the Greek Minister at Vienna, to say to Berchtold that 'Greece was quite prepared to cultivate good relations with the Triplice Powers, but must avoid becoming involved with the concerns of the Great Powers. "What we desire"—were Zaimis's actual words—"is not to be pushed around by either group".' On 24 June Berchtold replied that Austria could not contemplate a rapprochement with Greece, who had made an alliance with Serbia, 'the most anti-Austrian element in the Balkans'.[3] During July the members of the Triple Alliance still continued to discuss this alliance with Greece, and on 31 July Flotow reported that San Giuliano still opposed it and that his skepticism had been reinforced by Giolitti's asking 'whether he really attached serious importance to a Greek scrap of paper'.[4] On 2 August 1913 Jagow replied to Flotow's telegram:

> Greece on her part has directly offered to join the Triplice. We have asked for postponement of the decision until end of Balkan disorders. Greece has complied for the time being, but not changed intention as to the orientation of her policy.[5]

It is not clear how the idea of union with the Triplice was compatible with the treaty of alliance between Serbia and Greece. This had been concluded on 1 June 1913 and had a wider scope than Berchtold realized. In Article I the two States promised mutual support with their total military resources not only in the case of a surprise attack on the Greek or Serbian army by strong forces of the Bulgarian army, but also in the case of a war between one of them and a third Power. This Power could be none other than Austria, since in the case of a war with

---

[1] GP. XXXV, 13451, 13453.   [2] GP. XXXV, 13452.
[3] GP. XXXV, 13457.   [4] GP. XXXV, 13473.
[5] GP. XXXV, 13473. n.

Italy Greece could not receive aid from Serbia because Serbia was without a fleet. As we know, in the night of 29/30 June 1913 Bulgaria unexpectedly attacked the Greek and Serb lines. The alliance at once became operative and Bulgaria was completely defeated. In the peace negotiations at Bucharest Greece demanded Seres and Kavala. The assignment of Kavala to Greece was opposed not only by Austria, who wanted to indemnify Bulgaria for military aid withheld in the war, but also by Russia. Sazonov, who regarded Bulgaria as a dangerous rival to Russia in the question of the Straits and Constantinople, felt that these big demands on the part of Greece were a still more danger-ous threat. But Russian opposition remained without effect because Germany and France wanted Kavala to go to Greece.[1]

Having won victory and made the Peace of Bucharest on 8 August 1913, King Constantine went on a journey to Berlin, Paris, and London. On 7 September at the ceremony at which Kaiser Wilhelm conferred the baton of a German Field-Marshal upon him, Constantine made a speech in which he said:

Our victories are due to the vigor of our troops and also to the principles I and my officers have learnt of the art of war at Berlin.[2]

The French Government and press took strong exception to such a demonstration of pro-German sympathies, and this led Venizelos on 11 September to assure the French Chargé d'Affaires that, far from associating itself with the words to which objection had been taken, the Government wanted them to be forgotten, and would request the King to make a speech in France which would give full satisfaction there.[3] On 19 September Venizelos told the Chargé d'Affaires that

he has received an assurance from the Sovereign that during his stay in Paris he would do everything possible to efface the unfortunate impression created by his Berlin speech.[4]

And actually the toasts exchanged on 21 September between Poincaré and Constantine were marked by the greatest cordiality.

In reporting the Berlin speech the French Chargé d'Affaires at Berlin commented:

We must henceforth reckon on finding a Court influence in Greece hostile to France. There may, however, be no need to fear it so long as M. Venizelos remains Prime Minister.[5]

But in the spring of 1914, when the question of the Aegean islands was under discussion because Turkey had refused to abide by the decision arrived at by the arbitrating Powers on 31 January 1914,

---

[1] See Vol. I, pp. 462-6.   [2] DF. 3. VIII, 131.
[3] DF. 3. VIII, 139.   [4] DF. 3. VIII, 169.
[5] DF. 3. VIII, 131.

Venizelos appealed to the protection of Germany. On 17 April 1914, still further disquieted by the fact that Turkey had purchased from Brazil an ironclad under construction in a British shipyard and had ordered another from the same source, Venizelos asked the Chancellor to back a solution of the Turko-Greek conflict based on Greek recognition of the nominal sovereignty of Turkey over the islands of Chios and Mitylene and on the conclusion of an alliance between Turkey and Greece.[1] The proposal was warmly welcomed by Germany, and under pressure from Berlin the Turkish Government consented to negotiate. But it made counter-proposals which Greece could not accept and intensified its persecution of the Greeks living in Asia Minor. This was the point which had been reached when on 24 May the Greek Government sent instructions to the Greek Minister at Constantinople to break off diplomatic relations with Turkey unless mass deportations were stopped and a guarantee given that the lives and property of the Greeks in Asia Minor would be respected.[2] At the same time the Greek Government informed the Serbian Government that, if Turkey did not give satisfaction, an ultimatum would be sent her threatening war and that if Bulgaria intervened in any such war Greece would invoke the *casus foederis*. On 16 June Pašić replied that the alliance was defensive in character and expressed the hope that the Græco-Turkish question would be peacefully settled by the mediation of the Great Powers. The Serbian army, the Serbian people and Serbian finances could not stand a war, whereas Bulgaria had been set on her feet again by Austria and was well equipped.[3] This reply cannot be regarded as a breach of treaty. The alliance did not oblige one partner to follow the other blindly into any adventure. Serbia had the right to be consulted by Greece before Greece made war and to explain what difficulties stood in the way of her giving support. Nor did Athens at the time take exception to the Serbian answer. Frangulis explains this by the fact that, owing to the intervention of the Powers, the conflict with Turkey took a peaceful turn.[4] But if Athens had objected to the Serbian interpretation of the treaty obligations, these objections should have been lodged in Belgrade at that time.

2. *Venizelos refuses recognition of the* casus foederis *in an Austro-Serbian war.*

Greece did not protest because she could not object to the interpretation given to the treaty by Serbia; moreover, she herself was soon afterwards to default on her own engagements in circumstances very different from those in which Serbia had found herself. Serbia had raised well-founded objections to a Græco-Turkish war provoked by a Greek ultimatum. The Serbian note ended:

[1] See p. 609.
[3] Frangulis, I, pp. 132-3.
[2] Frangulis, I, p. 112.
[4] Frangulis, I, p. 134

The Serbian Government considers that its duty towards its country and its vital interests is to draw its allies' attention to all the serious dangers which will arise as soon as Greece breaks with Turkey and goes to war at sea.[1]

Greece, on the contrary, refused recognition of the *casus foederis* when Serbia was attacked by Austria, How she did this can be seen by referring not only to the documents in the two *White Books* published by the Venizelos Government with omissions and some mutilations but also to those reproduced by Frangulis. In March 1921 Frangulis was entrusted by the then Foreign Minister, G. Baltazzi, with the task of examining the original documents in the Foreign Ministry Archives to ascertain the truth about the attitude taken by Greece in the European war. Baltazzi believed that Venizelos and his friends had invented a series of legends damaging to the King and to those who supported and vindicated his action. Frangulis, a jurist and historian who had held Cabinet office and had been the representative of Greece at the League of Nations, ably carried out his task in his two volumes, *La Grèce, Son Statut International, Son Histoire Diplomatique.* Though his political bias prevented his work from being impartial, there can be no question of the authenticity of the documents published by him.

When, on 23 July, Austria sent her ultimatum to Belgrade, Venizelos was absent on a journey to meet the Grand Vizier at Brussels and conclude an agreement with him about the Aegean islands and an alliance with Turkey.[2] These conversations for the settlement of the dispute over the islands had been suggested by the *Daily Telegraph* correspondent Dillon.[3] On 24 July at Trieste Venizelos learnt of the Austrian ultimatum and at once understood its gravity. He grasped the imminence of an Austro-Serbian, perhaps of a European war and knew that the *casus foederis* would undoubtedly arise for Greece. But he did not see how Greece could possibly recognize it without exposing herself to most serious danger. In a speech to the Greek Lower House on 26 August 1917 he relates how in July 1914 he spent many sleepless nights revolving in his mind the difficulties that must arise from the fact that his country's ally, Serbia, plunged into the European war, would be in no position to come to the help of Greece in the eventuality of an attack from Turkey and Bulgaria. Far from being able to aid Serbia against Austria, Greece would herself be in danger from the fact that Serbia would be unable to concentrate the 150,000 men in the region laid down in the military agreement covering a war against Bulgaria. Article I of the text of the alliance laid this down clearly; but how could the terms be kept?[4]

---

[1] Frangulis, I, p. 134.   [2] See p. 616.   [3] DF. 3 X, 519.
[4] M. Catacciolo, *L'intervento della Grecia nella guerra mondiale e l'opera della diplomazia alleata* (Rome, 1925), pp. 27-30.

Venizelos, therefore, telegraphed from Trieste on 24 July to the Greek Foreign Minister, Streit:

My absence from Athens provides plausible reasons for postponing any immediate reply in the event of Serbia's asking for the application of our alliance. Pending this reply you might, if necessary, suggest that if, as it seems, the responsibility of Serbia in the Sarajevo tragedy is established, it will be necessary for the Serbian Government to display extreme conciliatoriness, if it wishes to avoid the reproach of provocation. This necessity appears the more imperious in that, according to her own statements at the moment of the acute phase in our dispute with Turkey, Serbia was not ready for war.[1]

The following morning from Munich Venizelos reverted to this point in another telegram to Streit:

While reserving our opinion as to the application of the treaty of alliance which in present circumstances seems to be ruled out by the provocative conduct of Serbia, it would be necessary for you to leave no doubt in the mind of your interlocutors as to our determination not to look on with folded arms at a Bulgarian attack on Serbia. It would be impossible for us to tolerate such an attack, which might lead to the aggrandizement of Bulgaria and the calling in question of the Treaty of Bucharest.[2]

To this Frangulis makes the comment:

It seems to be the opinion of M. Venizelos that the conduct of Serbia, who in accepting the Austro-Hungarian ultimatum had sacrificed everything, even her own sovereignty, was provocative conduct.[3]

Actually Serbia never accepted all the terms of the ultimatum. In any case, when Venizelos telegraphed on the morning of 25 July, he could not possibly know the text of the Serbian reply which was in process of being drafted at Belgrade. What is certain is, however, that at that moment only Austria was asserting the responsibility of Serbia in the Sarajevo crime and that Venizelos was taking advantage of this assertion, which he ought to have accepted with reserve, to deny Serbia recognition of the *casus foederis* in respect of war with Austria. When this telegram came to be published in the Greek *White Book* the words 'which in present circumstances seems to be ruled out by the provocative conduct of Serbia' were omitted either in order not to accuse Serbia or not to acknowledge that, if there were no provocation, the *casus foederis* must arise for Greece. Whatever the reason, the fact remains that Venizelos at that moment was taking no exception to Serbia's refusal a month earlier to support Greece in the war she was planning to start against Turkey, nor did he do so in another telegram, still from Munich, sent on 26 July to Alexandropulos, the Greek Minister at Belgrade.

---

[1] Frangulis, 1, p. 136.   [2] Frangulis, I, p. 136–7; Gr. 14.
[3] Frangulis, I, p. 137.

Alexandropulos had telegraphed on 25 July to say that Pašić had just asked him

whether the Serbian Government can count on the armed support of Greece, (i) in the case of Serbia's being attacked by Austria, (ii) in the case of Serbia's being attacked by Bulgaria.[1]

On 26 July Venizelos replied:

I must consult the King and the Government before giving a definite reply. But I authorize you to say to H. E. [Pašić] that I give you my personal views. . . . As to the possibility of a war between Austria and Serbia, I firmly hope that . . . it will be avoided thanks to H. E.'s conciliatory spirit; . . . but if war were to break out we should make a decision as soon as we were in possession of all the data, taking into account our own capacity to render assistance; in regard to the eventuality of an attack on Serbia by Bulgaria I am determined to advise the King and the Government to send all our forces against Bulgaria.[2]

3. *The feeling in Athens; the decision in favor of neutrality.*

After the Austrian declaration of war on Serbia on 28 July, Venizelos from Munich telegraphed on the 29th telling Streit to instruct Alexandropulos:

If in a localized Austro-Serbian war we can stay neutral, we must not forget that our alliance binds us to mobilize 40,000 men immediately. It is, however, to the joint interest of Serbia and Greece not to take this step immediately as liable to provoke a Bulgarian general mobilization, which might have serious consequences. . . . Our attitude corresponds exactly with that decided on in our joint interest by the Serbian Government at the moment of our crisis with Turkey. . . . Consideration must also be given to the possibility of a general war with a view to deciding our policy in advance. My considered opinion is that in such an event the Government must on no account let itself be induced to range itself in the opposite camp to Serbia and co-operate with her enemies. It would be contrary both to Greek vital interests, her good faith as an ally and the dignity of the State. On no pretext would I depart from this policy.[3]

Thus the Greek position was outlined in regard to Serbia and indirectly in regard to the two warring camps. Greece was to remain neutral, only intervening against Bulgaria if the latter attacked Serbia, this being the least Greece could do under the terms of her treaty with Serbia, and it being, further, a vital Greek interest to prevent infringement of the Treaty of Bucharest. The telegram contains an allusion to the precedent of the Serbian refusal of aid, but the analogy is patently specious. Serbia had

---

[1] Gr. 12.
[2] Frangulis, I, p. 137; Gr. 15,
[3] Frangulis, I, p. 139; Gr. 17.

in 'the joint interest' raised timely objections to any war against Turkey provoked by Greece. Greece, on the contrary, was defaulting on her pledges at the very moment when the case arose which the treaty had been designed to meet, i.e., when Serbia was attacked by a third Power. And here was Venizelos graciously declaring that in his opinion 'the Government must on no account be induced to range itself in the opposite camp to Serbia and co-operate with her enemies'. Steering clear of recognition of the *casus foederis* in an Austro-Serbian war and regarding the Græco-Serbian alliance as *de facto* if not *de jure* a purely Balkan affair, Venizelos was undoubtedly voicing the public opinion of the country, which had no intention of sacrificing itself for Serbia. As on 27 July the Austro-Hungarian Minister, Szilassy, telegraphed from Athens:

> Not a single voice is raised to demand actual defense of the one and only ally. M. Venizelos's sympathies for Serbia are purely platonic and anything but profound. . . . What is most clear is that the idea of Greek intervention is regarded with positive horror and they are waiting to see what Bulgaria will do.[1]

Streit, sharing the King's views rather than those of Venizelos, assured Szilassy that the country was just as friendly to Austria as it was to Serbia. And on 28 July, when Szilassy read out to him the telegram from Berchtold giving Greece the reasons for which Austria was taking action against Serbia,[2] Streit replied

> that he quite understood our action and that the King, to whom I had our note to the Great Powers communicated together with the enclosures, was beside himself with indignation against the Serbs. M. Streit . . . again assured me that Greece would attempt nothing that would jeopardize the localization of a possible war . . . the treaty with Serbia was a 'Balkan treaty', the *casus foederis* would arise if one of the contracting parties were attacked by Bulgaria.[3]

On 28 July Bulgaria announced her neutrality,[4] on 31 July, however, in telling the German Chargé d'Affaires, Bassewitz, 'that Bulgaria will observe neutrality', Streit added that this would hold good only if the war remained localized between Austria and Serbia, not if a general war developed.[5] Now in a general war there was a danger that the Central Powers would seek and obtain the support of Bulgaria and Turkey, indeed Streit had got wind of negotiations opened by Austria to that end. He raised the matter with Bassewitz on 29 July, saying he could not believe this news was correct, since it would denote a policy at variance with that of Germany.[6]

---

[1] Oe-U. VIII, 10779. [2] Oe-U. VIII, 10777.
[3] Oe-U. VIII, 10861. [4] DD. II, 336, 381.
[5] DD. III, 538. [6] DD. II, 360.

On the same day Streit told Szilassy that since his accession King Constantine had twice sent a message to King Peter advising him to place his relations with the Monarchy on as friendly a footing as possible. Streit further declared that Greece would observe strict neutrality. He mentioned reports that Bulgaria was preparing to attack Serbia and Greece with bands 12,000 strong but said that these reports would not cause Greece to mobilize 'since the Greek Government was anxious not to give the impression that it was bound to take some sort of position towards the Serbian conflict. . . . At the worst, the purpose would be, not intervention in the present war, but only an action against Bulgaria to "impose neutrality upon her in maintenance of the Treaty of Bucharest".' Szilassy expressed it as a personal opinion that 'Greece might receive part of Serbia and I found my interlocutor very accessible'.[1] That same day Streit looked 'visibly relieved'[2] when Szilassy gave him Berchtold's message of the 29th that Austria had received a pledge of absolute neutrality from Bulgaria.[3] Berchtold on the 31st told Szilassy, still speaking personally, to continue talks with Streit 'on the possible assignment to Greece of a bit of Serbia, and to try to win him over to this idea'.[4]

Things had reached that point when Venizelos, informed by a telegram from the Kaiser to Constantine and the latter's reply, which we shall examine in a moment, decided to go and watch the situation on the spot and returned to Athens, although both Streit and the King, who were hand in glove and no doubt wanted to keep him out of things, had telegraphed urging him not to return, as Bulgaria showed no signs of moving.[5] Meanwhile the crisis was growing more acute and a European war was approaching. Venizelos must have discovered that, in spite of the instructions telegraphed by him from Munich on the morning of 29 July as to the reply to be given to Pašić's request for Greek support of 25 July, Streit had done nothing. Frangulis offers no explanation of this inaction, but in view of Streit's sympathies and the fact that he resigned from the Cabinet a month later because of differences with the Prime Minister, it is legitimate to assume that he wanted an anti-Serbian line to be taken. Bosdari, the Italian Minister at Athens, narrates that Streit gave it as his opinion that the treaty of alliance did not contemplate the case of an Austro-Serbian conflict, which was the reverse of the truth.[6] On Venizelos's return a Cabinet

---

[1] Oe-U. VIII, 11017.   [2] Oe-U. VIII, 11019.
[3] Oe-U. VIII, 10935   [4] Oe-U. VIII, 11115.
[5] BD. XI, 222. That the King did not desire the return of Venizelos is shown by Streit's words to Szilassy on 28 July. 'In the strictest confidence as proof of Greek sincerity he would say that H.M. the King had telegraphed Venizelos not to return but to have the meeting with the Grand Vizier when the latter starts out on his journey' (Oe-U. VIII, 10861).

[6] A. de Bosdari, *Delle guerre balcaniche, della grande guerra* (Milan, 1928), p. 103.

was held which supported the line taken by him, and on 2 August Streit telegraphed instructions to Alexandropulos to inform Pašić that

without entering into an examination of the obligations resulting from its alliance with Serbia . . . the Greek Government is convinced that it is fulfilling its whole duty as friend and ally by the decision it has taken to maintain benevolent neutrality towards Serbia and to hold itself ready to repel any aggression on the part of Bulgaria towards Serbia. Far from being useful to Serbia, the participation of Greece in the present war would greatly harm her. In becoming a belligerent Greece would only contribute to her ally forces weak in comparison with the enemy's might, while inevitably condemning her to see Salonika, the only port of supply open to her, subject to decisive attack from Austria. Furthermore, the entry of Greece into the war would fatally weaken the strength of her army, which in the joint interest it is important to preserve intact to keep Bulgaria in order.[1]

This document does not attempt to claim, as Streit did, that Greece was not under an obligation to side with Serbia against Austria. Its line of argument was that her intervention would do Serbia more harm than good, alleging objections that actually existed when the treaty was made but had lost force in August 1914 when if the Austrian navy were to attack Salonika it would have had to run the gauntlet of the Franco-British fleet. The truth is that in making the treaty Greece had undertaken more than she could perform. To carry out her pledges she would have had to detach forces which were needed, indeed proved insufficient, for her own self-defense against Bulgaria. This was understood by Serbia, who did not press for Greek help against Austria. It is difficult to understand how Venizelos came to consent to such a treaty, the impracticability of which was accentuated by the annexed military convention, engaging Serbia, as has been said above, to concentrate 150,000 men on the Bulgarian front in the event of war with Bulgaria. How could Serbia concentrate this force if she had to defend herself against Austria? On 30 July Streit actually dared to ask Serbia to withdraw part of her strength from the Austrian frontier and send them towards Bulgaria to intimidate her and prevent her mobilizing. The Serbian Government replied that, as Austria had taken the offensive, it did not know what forces it had at its disposal but that there were 20,000 to 30,000 men in Macedonia able to deal with the situation. The Greek request was renewed on 17 August when the Serbian Government was told that if Turkey alone attacked, Greece could manage alone, but if Bulgaria joined in Serbia must come to the rescue with at least 100,000 men. Pašić replied that Serbia could not detach troops from her Austrian frontier unless the danger became imminent, and that if it did become imminent she intended first to concert with the *Entente* Powers on the steps to be taken.[2] From this reply Frangulis

---

[1] Frangulis, I, pp. 140-1; Gr. 18.   [2] Frangulis, I, pp. 155-7.

draws the conclusion that Greece was not false to her word and that it was Serbia who under the pressure of events failed to honor her engagements.[1] And in fact on 21 September 1915 Venizelos sent for the *Entente* diplomatic representatives and told them that the King and Chief of Staff regarded Greece as free from all obligations towards Serbia since she was not able to send the 150,000 men to the Greek front as laid down in the military convention in the case of war with Bulgaria.[2] In reality, just as Greece was not able to aid Serbia when she was attacked by Austria, so Serbia when engaged with Austria could not spare 100,000–150,000 men for the defense of Greece against Bulgaria. But the first to default on her engagements was Greece.

4. Pressure from the Kaiser to obtain Greek support meets with resistance from King Constantine.

While this was going on between Serbia and Greece, Germany, misled by her confidence in King Constantine and perhaps also by the behavior of Venizelos, who had tried to make an alliance with Turkey under the aegis of Germany, was not satisfied with Greece's offer to remain neutral only so long as Bulgaria refrained from attacking Serbia, and put forth more far-reaching demands. On 23 July Jagow telegraphed to Bassewitz, the German Chargé d'Affaires at Athens:

Tension between Austria and Serbia makes military conflict not impossible. In that case Bulgaria would hardly let slip the opportunity for an attack on Serbia. Flow far Turkey would then remain quiet is doubtful. . . . Timely detachment of Greece from Serbia advisable, lest Greece be drawn into conflict.[3]

In other words, as Jagow said to Theotokis on 25 July, Greece should remain neutral even if Bulgaria entered the Austro-Serbian conflict.[4] Venizelos, who that morning had arrived in Munich, telegraphed on the contrary to the Greek Minister at Berlin instructing him to inform the German Foreign Ministry of the Greek Government's intention to oppose any Bulgarian armed intervention against Serbia.[5] That same day at Athens the Greek Foreign Minister, Streit, told Bassewitz that Greece would not intervene in an Austro-Serbian conflict but

about the Greek attitude to possible intervention by Bulgaria or Turkey M. Streit did not think he could today express an opinion as so much depended on the circumstances in which the intervention occurred. The maintenance of the Treaty of Bucharest was a cardinal question for Greece. In this connection she could make no statements respecting Greece which might cost her the loss of Serbian friendship.[6]

[1] Frangulis, I, pp. 157–8.   [2] Crawfurd Price, *Venizelos and the War* (London, 1917), p.98.
[3] DD. I, 122; Gr. 11.   [4] Gr. 13.
[5] *Int. Bez.* i. V, 62.   [6] DD. I, 189.

Wilhelm in the meantime was making much more far-reaching demands on King Constantine. From Constantinople on 23 July Wangenheim had telegraphed a rumor gathered by Liman von Sanders that Greece 'was making feverish preparations for a landing in Turkey'. To this Wilhelm had appended a marginal note directing that the German Minister at Athens, Quadt, should on his behalf personally convey this news to Constantine, adding

that I appeal to his honor as a ruler and a colleague of mine. . . . His Majesty ought not on petty personal grounds to attack a Triplice friend whom I value when that friend is about to support Austria against the Slavs. On the contrary, H.M. ought to range himself on the side of Austria, or else my friendship is at an end.[1]

This marginal note and Jagow's telegrams give the impression that Berlin was under the illusion that Greek support could be counted upon. The documents, as far as they are known to us, do not justify this illusion. But we do not know what letters passed between Wilhelm and King Constantine, nor what they had said to each other when they met in Berlin in September 1913 and in Corfu in March 1914. An outburst of the Kaiser's to the Greek Minister at Berlin which we shall presently consider[2] makes it seem not impossible that Constantine, jealous of the popularity of Venizelos, whom he disliked, encouraged the hopes of his august brother-in-law, who deemed that a sovereign could do what he pleased regardless of the will of the Government. Typical of this attitude is Wilhelm's answer on 8 September 1913 to an inquiry from Conrad whether Germany were seeking closer political relations with Greece.

Kaiser Wilhelm: We shall have Greece on our side.

Myself: That would be very nice, but popular feeling there is in favor of France, not Germany.

Kaiser Wilhelm: Now after victory the King can do as he likes in his own country. He will carry out the policy he wants.[3]

Vienna did not feel the same confidence and on 4 June 1914 Francis Joseph said to Conrad:

The German Kaiser is flirting with Greece, and the end will be that the whole affair will turn to our disadvantage.[4]

This was a pessimistic view, but the fact remains that in August 1914 not one of the Balkan States embraced the cause of the Central Powers and that at the height of the crisis Constantine refused Wilhelm his support as soon as he learnt of Wilhelm's marginal note,[6] telegraphed

---

[1] GP. XXXV[2], 14647. [2] See p. 637.
[3] Conrad, III, 432. [4] Conrad, III, 702.
[5] GP. XXXVI[2], 14647.

to Berlin by Wedel and sent on by Berlin to Bassewitz in Athens. In the lengthy reply, which Constantine handed to Bassewitz on 27 July the King firmly denied that Greece was intending to attack Turkey and continued:

I do not see how Turkey can help Austria without allying with Bulgaria. But if Bulgaria intervenes that would result in increased power for another Slav State in the Balkans and one which is a special menace to the non-Slav States. This would upset the Bucharest Treaty and the balance of power in the Balkans. It would be a threat to our interests and, I imagine, run counter to German interests in the Near East. In such an event I would not side with Austria against the Slavs as Your Majesty's telegram says.[1]

In fact Greece joined with Romania to warn Bulgaria that her intervention would not be tolerated,[2] and on 28 July Streit expressed himself in the same sense in a telegram to Theotokis.[3] Constantine's reply was not at all to the liking of Berlin, and Bethmann laid before the Kaiser the draft of a telegram which Wilhelm approved and which was sent off on 31 July. It ran:

So long as the conflict is confined to Austria and Serbia neither Turkey nor Bulgaria will, of course, be allowed to intervene. If a general European conflagration develops, not only they but all the Balkan States will have to make their choice. I assume that the very memory of your murdered Father will hold you and Greece back from taking sides with the Serb assassins against my person and the Triplice. Even purely from the point of view of Greek self-interest it seems to me that the place for your country and dynasty is beside the Triplice. . . . No one has followed the remarkable rise of Greece under your leadership with more grudging eyes than Russia. Never will Greece have a better chance than now under the powerful protection of the Triplice to throw off the tutelage which Russia seeks to assert over the Balkans.

If against my confident expectation you take the enemy side, Greece will be exposed to immediate attack from Italy, Bulgaria, and Turkey, and our own personal relationship will probably suffer permanent injury.[4]

On 2 August the King replied:

It never entered our heads to help the Serbs. But it also does not seem to me possible to join with their enemies and attack them, since they are after all our allies. It seems to me that the interests of Greece demand absolute neutrality and maintenance of the *status quo* in the Balkans as created by the Treaty of Bucharest. If we abandoned this standpoint Bulgaria would enlarge herself by the annexation of the parts of Macedonia recently acquired by Serbia, embrace our entire northern frontier and become a big menace to us. These considerations compel us . . . together with Romania to make every effort to hold Bulgaria back from intervention.[5]

[1] DD. I, 243.   [2] See p. 588.
[3] Frangulis, I, p. 138; Gr. 16.   [4] DD. II, 466; III, 504.
                 [5] DD. III, 702.

On reading this document on 3 August the Kaiser was moved to indignation, venting his annoyance in marginalia of the following tenor:

Tell Athens I made the alliance with Bulgaria and Turkey for the struggle with Russia and will treat Greece as an enemy unless she joins us at once. . . . If Greece does not come in with us at once she will lose her position as a Balkan Power, not get our support for her wishes, and be treated as an enemy.

Wilhelm announced to Theotokis, the Greek Minister at Berlin, on 4 August

that an alliance has today been concluded between Germany and Turkey; Bulgaria and Romania are also ranging themselves on the side of Germany; the German vessels now in the Mediterranean are to join the Turkish fleet for joint action. From the above His Majesty will see that all the Balkan States are ranged on the German side in the struggle against Slavism.

Reminding King Constantine that Greece had been able to retain Kavala thanks to support from himself, Wilhelm appealed to the King to order the mobilization of his army so that they could 'march hand in hand against the common enemy, Slavism'. Otherwise reported Theotokis,

if Greece does not range herself on Germany's side there will be a breach between Greece and the Central Powers. Finally His Majesty told me that what he asks of us today is to put into effect all that Your Majesty and he had so often discussed *touching the necessity of combating Slavism in the Near East. The Bulgaria/is, according to His Majesty, are not Slavs but Tartars.*[1]

Frangulis states that the words in italics were suppressed in the *White Book* in order to insinuate that the King had gone so far as to promise Greek adherence to the Triplice. Nevertheless, the full text itself makes it seem probable that Constantine's assurances did not fall short of the Kaiser's expectations.

Certainly the King's devotion to Germany, kept constantly aflame by his Queen, the Kaiser's sister, knew no bounds and led him to believe implicitly in the certainty of a German victory. That, however, does not mean that in July 1914 he wanted Greece to range herself with the Central Powers. Not that he had any freedom of movement when the head of the Government was a man like Venizelos, whose prestige and popularity were immense. It is true that on 13 August Venizelos told the Russian Minister, Demidov, that

it was not without difficulty that he had persuaded the King to maintain Greek neutrality in view of the engagements with Serbia under their alliance.[2]

---

[1] Frangulis, I, pp. 146-7; Gr. 19.   [2] *Int. Bez.* ii, VI[1], 92. See p. 640.

But there was no truth in this statement, and Venizelos may have made it merely to put pressure on the *Entente*. The telegram to Wilhelm, sent when Venizelos was absent from Greece, shows that the King was from the outset determined to object to Bulgarian intervention. This decision in itself would have made it impossible for him to join with the Central Powers, as did also his alliance with Serbia. Even though he never contemplated discharging his obligations under that alliance, he went so far as to tell the Kaiser that he could not go over to the opposite camp. Neutrality was thus the role that suited him best and was most popular with the Greeks.

Writing to clear King Constantine's memory of the imputation of having taken a treasonable attitude towards the *Entente* Powers, his brother, Prince Nicholas of Greece, gives the following account.

At the time the war broke out, Prince Nicholas, with his wife and children, was in Russia paying a yearly visit to his mother-in-law, the Grand Duchess Vladimir. On his return to Greece by a roundabout route Prince Nicholas hastened to see the King towards the beginning of September and found him filled with indignation at Germany's attitude.

He told me that the Kaiser had strongly urged him to join forces with Germany and had appealed to him as a brother-in-law and a Field-Marshal of the German army. . . . 'It is extraordinary!' he said. 'Does he take me for a German? And because he has given me a Field-Marshal's baton, does he imagine that I am under any obligation towards him? If that is so, I am ready to return it at once. Besides, he seems to forget his geography and that Greece would cease to exist within twenty-four hours after she had declared herself Germany's Ally. What folly! Whoever heard of such a thing! No. We are Greeks, and the interests of Greece come first. For the present, at any rate, it is imperative that we should remain neutral. But as to joining Germany, such an eventuality is and always will be an impossibility.' . . . At this early period, King Constantine and M. Venizelos, in spite of small differences of opinion, were in agreement as to the policy to be pursued. But, alas, it cannot be denied that a latent difference of opinion did, nevertheless, exist, owing chiefly to the fact that whereas the King and members of the General Staff estimated that the European war would be a long and arduous business, M. Venizelos prophesied that it would be over in a couple of weeks to the entire advantage of the *Entente*. . . . King Constantine, being aware of the real inclinations of Turkey and Bulgaria, had no doubts whatsoever that the endeavors of the *Entente* to secure Turkey's neutrality and Bulgaria's adhesion were destined to failure.[1]

Nevertheless, after Italy's entry into the war in May 1915, when at the end of August it became apparent that Bulgaria was about

---

[1] H.R.H. Prince Nicholas of Greece, *Political Memoirs* 1914-1917. *Pages from My Diary* (London, 1928), pp. 18, 22-9.

to intervene on the side of the Triple Alliance, King Constantine said to the Italian Ambassador, Alessandro Bosdari, that the war would be a disaster for Greece,

that the Germans were everywhere victorious and would be more so as time went on. He could not understand how Italy could have embarked on such a risky undertaking. The recent offer of the Quadruple Alliance to Greece was a fraud and he meant to remain neutral to prevent Greece being crushed by the Bulgarians and Turks.[1]

It is not within the purview of the present work to enter into the controversy between the Venizelists and King Constantine's adherents, whose mutual recriminations would involve us in a study of events that came later. Here it will suffice to reproduce the telegram sent by Constantine to Theotokis on 7 August in answer to the one sent him in the name of Wilhelm:

The Kaiser knows that my personal sympathies and political opinions draw me to his side. I shall never forget that it is to him that we owe Kavala. Nevertheless, after mature reflection it is impossible for me to see how I could be useful to him if I immediately mobilized my army. The Mediterranean is at the mercy of the united English and French fleets. They would destroy our battle fleet and our merchant navy, they would take our islands from us, above all they would prevent the concentration of my army, which can only be effected by sea since no railway yet exists. Without being useful to him in any way we would be wiped off the map. I am forced to think that neutrality is imposed upon us, which might be useful to him, together with the pledge not to touch his friends among my neighbors so long as they do not touch our local Balkan interests.[2]

This document, which Frangulis with his German sympathies abstains from quoting, reveals both the attachment of King Constantine to the German cause and his opinion that so long as the English and French fleets had the command of the sea it was impossible for Greece to range herself with the Central Powers. Let us confine ourselves to this observation without pursuing the matter further, and let us proceed to note that, taking his cue from his Royal master, Streit on 8 August guardedly telegraphed to Theotokis: 'as long as Bulgaria does not attack Serbia, bringing the Treaty of Bucharest into operation', Greece had to decide not to depart from her neutrality, but that in the case that 'Bulgaria were to prepare to attack Serbia, the action of Greece would be limited to holding her in check to keep her neutral'.[3] But Berlin was not content with this formula, which had already been used by Streit on 29 July when talking with Szilassy.[4] Quadt, the German Minister to Athens, acting on instructions, threatened Streit on 12 August that

---

[1] Bosdari, *op. cit.*, p. 130.
[2] Gr. 21.
[3] Frangulis, I, p. 154.
[4] See p. 632.

he would ask for his passports unless the Greek Government promised unconditional neutrality if Serbia were attacked by Bulgaria. Venizelos told the Russian Minister, Demidov, that Streit had returned a categoric refusal to the German demand.[1] But Streit's own telegram to Theotokis of 12 August, like his earlier one, was couched in a minor key.[2]

5. Venizelos favors alliance with the Triple Entente; *Russia asks Greece to make territorial concessions to Bulgaria; Greece refuses.*

At that time two policies were being pursued in Greece, that of the King and Streit, and that of Venizelos. In contrast to the King, Venizelos believed in the victory of the *Entente* and wanted to seek its protection, fearing, moreover, that Greece could not resist of her own strength, especially when Serbia was being palled upon to settle accounts with Austria. With this idea he sought on 2 August to elicit proposals from the *Entente* by making the following declaration to the French Chargé d'Affaires:

If the European situation led to a general conflagration, Greece would in no case be found in a camp opposed to that of the Triple *Entente*. As regards her eventual active participation, before deciding she will wait to receive the advice of those three Powers.[3]

But no such advice was forthcoming, while, on the other hand, the situation had been rendered still more disquieting by the news that Turkey had mobilized.[4]

Therefore on 7 August, immediately on the return of the Russian Minister, Demidov, to Athens (the English and French Ministers were also away on leave at the moment of the crisis), Venizelos called on him to say

that he regarded the moment as more than favorable for the reconstitution by Russia of a Balkan *bloc* against Austria. He thought the Russian Government might at once offer all members of it appropriate compensation: Transylvania to Romania, Bosnia-Herzegovina and Northern Albania to Serbia, Macedonia up to and including Monastir to Bulgaria. . . . Greece would only claim southern Albania. . . . The coast with Valona could go to Italy. Such a combination, thought Venizelos,

---

[1] *Int. Bez.* ii. VI[1], 92.   [2] Gr. 25.   [3] DF. 3. XI, 577.

[4] Bosdari writes: 'This news again threw the Greek political world into the greatest uncertainty, and, partly to do something to calm the alarm of public opinion, it was decided to call three classes to the colors. . . . On 13 August the former Prime Ministers were summoned to a discussion on the attitude of Greece particularly in consequence of the Turkish mobilization. It resulted in a reaffirmation of Greek neutrality. Suddenly Turkey, possibly to distract attention from her true intentions of formally allying with Germany [of which Bosdari had already forewarned Rome, as he had also given forewarning of the Austro-Bulgarian alliance], invited Greece to a meeting at Bucharest to discuss the questions left in abeyance because the meeting between Venizelos and the Grand Vizier had not taken place. Zaimis went as the Greek delegate. But the meeting produced no result' (Bosdari, *op. cit.,* pp. 105-6).

would satisfy them all and weld them together against the common enemy. This proposal demanded rapid action and would have to emanate from us, he said, asking that his name be not brought in as he does not know how Serbia would take it. Venizelos is completely convinced of the righteousness of our cause and has no doubts of the triumph of the Triple *Entente*'s arms.[1]

On 11 August Venizelos reverted to this proposal, which would result in the renunciation by Serbia of Macedonian territory, but he intimated that since Serbia would be gaining territory from Austria she could not do less than indemnify Bulgaria for remaining neutral, and she would lose the territory in Macedonia anyway if Austria were to be the victor. The offer of immediate restitution of Ištip and Kočana 'would probably cause a revulsion of feeling in Bulgaria which the Radoslavov Government would perhaps not be able to resist'.[2]

However, just at the moment when Venizelos was trying to revive the Balkan league at the expense of Serbia, Pašić was thinking that the small concessions to Bulgaria he had promised to Sazonov were quite enough, and that Greece on her part should offer something to Bulgaria. On 7 August, Strandtmann had telegraphed to Sazonov Pašić's suggestion that Greece should offer Kavala to Bulgaria in return for compensation in Southern Albania. Sazonov replied on the 10th that the idea was excellent,[3] and reported to Demidov on the 12th that he had said to the Greek Minister at St. Petersburg that

Serbia has already embarked on the consideration of possible compensations. It is now the turn of Greece, all the more so as in the event of a successful war she can reckon on the Epirus.[4]

Demidov did not think it wise at that moment to ask Greece to make territorial concessions. On 13 August he telegraphed:

Venizelos is addressing to Russia, England, and France an appeal that if as a result of her agreement with Serbia Greece becomes involved in war through an attack by Bulgaria or Turkey, the Powers should regard her as an ally having the same rights as Serbia and give her help and support. Venizelos would like to receive an offer to this effect from the Triple *Entente* Powers, but as he has not been empowered to take this step by the King and is acting without the latter's knowledge and perhaps against his secret wishes, he asks for the initiative to come from us so as to give him a further strong argument with the King in support of his stubborn efforts. Having, not without difficulty, obtained from the King the preservation of Greek neutrality notwithstanding the engagements with Serbia, he would further like to make it possible that, in the event of Bulgaria's coming over to our side, Greece could also join the *bloc* in common action. . . . I regard it as

---

[1] *Int. Bez.* ii. VI[1], 29.   [2] *Int. Bez.* ii. VI[1], 68.
[3] *Int. Bez.* ii. VI[1]. 51 and *n*.   [4] *Int. Bez.* ii. VI[1], 71.

extremely desirable to accede to this request of Venizelos. In fine I would think it dangerous at this moment before the decisive and overt passing over of Greece to the *Entente* side to touch on the delicate question of concrete concessions by Greece.[1]

Two days later, on 15 August, Demidov urged afresh that to ask Greece to cede territory would be playing into the enemy's hands, since the possession of Kavala 'had become a national question in the fullest sense of the word'.

On Venizelos—who, with all the strength of his prestige and his convictions struggles against the vacillating King, the influence of the Queen, the intrigues of the German Minister, the pro-German Court camarilla, the General Staff, and also some members of the Cabinet, not excepting the Foreign Minister—on Venizelos my statement had a depressing effect from the very first word. He greatly hopes that we will not ask of him something he cannot fulfill, though fearing that your conversation with the Greek Minister, which has certainly been already reported to the Foreign Minister, will be made use of with the King. In reality the Bulgarian and Romanian choice of policy will mainly depend on our early successes in the field. Do you not think it possible to hold back with concrete proposals about concessions and leave Venizelos time to steer Greece definitely into Triple *Entente* waters?[2]

Demidov was quite right. It is true that Bulgaria ardently desired to recover the Macedonian territory, taken from her by Serbia, and Kavala, taken by Greece. But if Serbia, threatened in the rear, could not but make considerable concessions, Greece was in another position since Bulgaria and Turkey would be restrained by the Central Powers. Thus to ask Kavala from her after her hard fight for it the previous year would be, indeed, as Demidov said, to play into the enemy's hands, just as it would alienate Italy to promise Southern Albania to Greece. Hence Pašić's suggestion, adopted by Sazonov, would offend both Greece and Italy and weaken Venizelos's influence with the King. The astute Pašić had carefully refrained from making the proposal to Athens himself, and had put it forward at St. Petersburg in order to draw off Sazonov's attention from the concessions which Russia had a right to demand of Serbia in whose defense she had gone to war. And in fact Sazonov did not make further demands on Pašić, mistakenly thinking that the inadequate Serbian offer of Ištip and Radovic could be supplemented by a Greek offer of Kavala, that very Kavala which a year previously he had in vain tried to get assigned to Bulgaria. He probably had the further thought that the cession of Kavala would weaken the Greeks in the Aegean and distract their attention from the mirage of Constantinople.

[1] *Int. Bez.* ii. VI[1], 92.   [2] *Int. Bez.* ii. VI[1], 105.

The London and Paris Governments took no interest in the matter, and let things take their course. Grey approved of Venizelos's proposals for the Balkan *bloc* and even of Sazonov's idea of asking Greece to give up Kavala.[1] In Poincaré's *Au Service de la France* there are traces of disapproval of Russian policy felt in Paris.[2] But neither Paris nor London understood that, while for the moment it was impossible to bridge the wide gulf between Greece and Bulgaria, it was to the interest of the Triple *Entente* to win over Greece in order to be able to launch her immediately against Turkey if Turkey joined the side of the Central Powers. It is probably true that the Ottoman Government would have hesitated to intervene if it had known that it would be attacked by Greece. 'Greece'—wrote Demidov on 19 August—'may well be able to render us valuable service, for instance if Turkey were to attack'. This the Tsar annotated on 23 August: 'Undoubtedly'.[3] The British Government, on the other hand, under the illusion that Turkey was able and willing to remain neutral, was in no hurry to grasp Venizelos's outstretched hand. On 17 August the English Chargé d'Affaires, Erskine, was instructed to return the following answer which committed England but did not commit Greece:

I think Greece may reserve herself as long as Turkey remains neutral. If Turkey departs from an attitude of neutrality we shall be ready to support Greece as an ally.[4]

The French Government's reply, received on 18 August, ran:

For the moment we think that all the efforts of Greece should be directed towards making Turkey keep promised neutrality and avoiding everything that might lead the Turkish Government to abandon it.

All that the Russian Government did was to express its 'lively satisfaction and sincere thanks'.[5]

6. *An incomprehensible* démarche *by Streit; Greece joins with the Triple* Entente.

This is as far as Frangulis's account takes the story. But the Russian diplomatic documents contain the following extraordinary telegram from Demidov of 18 August:

Following on my yesterday's conversation with the Foreign Minister about the attitude that would be taken by Greece in the European conflict, he called on me today to declare officially that in full agreement with the King the Government had decided at the first invitation from us to come in openly on the side of the Triple *Entente* with all sea and land forces. Greece, said the Minister, is completely at our disposal and the moment of her entry

---

[1] *Int. Bez.* ii. VI[1], 75.   [2] Poincaré, V, pp. 40, 71, 101.
[3] *Int. Bez.* ii. VI[1], 127 *n.*   [4] Frangulis, I, pp. 152-3.
[5] Frangulis, I, pp. 152-3.

depends entirely on us. Until that moment Venizelos asks us to keep this decision secret.[1]

In the light of Streit's previous conduct and the King's views this move seems utterly incomprehensible. Nor do later documents throw light on it, because the publication of the Russian documents, especially of those that should have come out in Vol. VI, is not exhaustive, and neither the footnote to the dispatch nor the telegrams following it explain the enigma. In fact the telegrams following merely make it more mysterious, though it is outside our task to pursue this matter since it concerns events after the outbreak of the war which only interest us in so far as throwing an indirect light on the period under survey. Here all we need note is that on 28 August the English and French representatives at Athens asked Demidov to join them in making the following declaration to the Greek Government:

> If Turkey joins Germany and Austria the three Powers will accept and support Greece as an ally; if Bulgaria joins Austria in attacking Serbia, and Greece is drawn in by her alliance, the three Powers will give her all assistance in their means. At the same time the three Powers would suggest to the Greek Government that it would do well to raise with Bulgaria the question of compensations such as might induce her to join in on the side of Greece, and that Greece could give if she received advantages elsewhere.[2]

But on 5 September Demidov reported that Venizelos sent for the English Chargé d'Affaires and told him in confidence that

> within forty-eight hours he would very probably ask the Foreign Minister to resign because the latter was not in agreement with his policy of friendship with the Triple *Entente*. Elliot told Venizelos that the *Entente* representatives were about to make a communication to the Foreign Minister. . . . Elliot asked Venizelos whether in the circumstances he would prefer our making it direct to him or postponing it. He vehemently replied that if the communication had anything to do with concessions we could make it to the Foreign Minister for in that case it would be he, Venizelos, who would go.[3]

This is not the place to continue the story. It is enough to say that nothing was done by the time that Turkey went to war on 3 November 1914. Nor could anything be achieved when the diplomacy of the three *Entente* Powers, far from pursuing a united and well thought out policy, drifted along in the wake of the incoherent, ineffective moves of the impulsive Sazonov, who uttered alternately threats and promises, dreaming of agreements and impossible territorial exchanges between the exasperated Balkan States which had been unable to reach an accord a year previously. He had no idea what was or was not possible

---

[1] *Int. Bez.* ii. VI[1], 127.
[2] *Int. Bez.* ii. VI[1], 179.
[3] *Int. Bez.* ii VI[1], 225.

to obtain and put Greece on the same level as Serbia, while obviously he had a right to demand far more of Serbia than of Greece. Thus the *Entente* Powers failed to gain the immediate support of Greece, whose place, in view of the feelings and interests of the Greek people, was at their side. True that even with a wiser policy they might not have won her over because the King would never have allowed it. But this does not hide the fact that their policy played into the King's hands rather than into those of Venizelos.

CHAPTER XVI

MONTENEGRO MAKES COMMON CAUSE WITH SERBIA

(1) *Russian distrust of Cetinje; King Nicholas's feelers for an agreement with Austria-Hungary (p. 646). (2) The question of Serbo-Montenegrin union (p. 648). (3) King Nicholas's pro-Austrian attitude after the Sarajevo outrage (p. 650). (4) Berchtold's anxious telegrams to influence Montenegro's decision (p. 653). (5) King Nicholas's telegram to Prince Alexander; Montenegro mobilizes (p. 655). (6) Berchtold's final appeal; the Montenegrin Skupština decides on intervention on the side of Serbia; the King dragged into the war (p. 658).*

1. Russian distrust of Cetinje; King Nicholas's feelers for an agreement with Austria-Hungary.

It may seem excessive to devote space to the attitude of little Montenegro and its Sovereign towards the danger of a European war. But in fact the record of its behavior and that of the Balkan States in general throws much light on the situation leading to the war. It must be remembered that on the eve of the war Austrian statesmen were greatly perturbed over the projected union between Serbia and Montenegro, a problem which the crushing of Serbia would have settled once for all.

To understand the situation that had developed in July 1914 it must be borne in mind that since the autumn of 1912 Russia had regarded Montenegro as a vassal State. For the ten preceding years she had maintained a military agent, General Potapov, at Cetinje with the title of 'Controller of the Subsidy' of 1,800,000 crowns granted annually by Russia to the little State. The Russian Military Mission, consisting of General Potapov, a colonel, and two captains, had armed, equipped, and drilled the Montenegrin army, trying to give it semblance of cohesion. Between Russia and Montenegro there also existed a military convention binding Montenegro not to take action without previous accord with Russia. But in October 1912, King Nicholas, without listening to the advice of St. Petersburg, was the first of the Balkan States to cut short all hesitation and declare war on Turkey. As a sign of displeasure the Russian Government withdrew the annual subsidy, with the result that at the beginning of September 1913 the Cetinje Cadet School could not reopen for lack of funds and at the beginning of 1914 only unusable fragments remained of all the equipment that had been provided in the past by Russia. Supplies and munitions were non-existent, the barracks were empty, the officers lived idle at their homes. About the end of January 1914 General Potapov went off on long leave after learning that the King, without the knowledge of the Montenegrin Government, had personally entered into secret negotiations with the Austrian Government, 'definitely directed against the policy of Russia and France in the Balkans'.[1]

Intrigues between the King of Montenegro and Austria were not a new thing. Baron Giesl, who was Austrian Minister at Cetinje during the Balkan Wars, told the present writer that in October 1911 after the Italian declaration of war on Turkey the King, probably aspiring to the throne of Albania, offered him to ally with the Monarchy with the words: 'We are the falcons of Montenegro and we want to open the road to the Austrian eagles.' But Aehrenthal declined the proposal. What road was Nicholas proposing to open to the Austrian eagles?

To understand what was in his mind it must be remembered that Cetinje and Belgrade were rivals for the title and mission of the 'Piedmont of the Balkans'. After the accession of Peter Karageorgević, and still more after Serbia's great victories in the two Balkan Wars, the hopes of the free Serbs and of the Southern Slavs in Austria-Hungary converged on Belgrade and, as a first step, they aspired to the union of Serbia and Montenegro under the Karageorgević dynasty.[2]

This danger had been foreseen by King Nicholas even before the Balkan Wars and he had sought to parry it by soliciting the friendship and support of Austria-Hungary. Giesl told the present writer that as early as 8 June 1912 King Nicholas, in return for an indemnity of twenty million kronen, had agreed to cede the Lovčen to Austria-Hungary, but then the Montenegrin Government had refused to sanction the deal.

On 1 December 1912 Giesl reported to Vienna that the King summoned him by telegram to Rijeka and proposed an agreement with Austria-Hungary:

King Nicholas frankly admits that there is growing discontent in the country, that the party calling itself *Narodna Stranka* is carrying on a vigorous agitation in favor of Serbia, and that Montenegro is in a very unfavorable position. The threat to his dynasty from the rivalry with the Karageorgevićs is acute, but he says he is determined to accept the challenge and fight it out. . . . The King strongly emphasized that he meant to remain the first figure in the Serb world or else abdicate and withdraw to America. He would, however, in this case first proclaim his son Peter 'King of all Serbs' at Prizrend; they had better not drive him to desperation! But since the 'Serb peril' was also a threat to Austria, as was proved by the demonstrations in Dalmatia, Croatia and Bosnia, our interests were identical, and we ought to ally for joint defense against the threat. He therefore offered the Monarchy

---

[1] DF. 3. IX, 99.　　　　[2] See Vol. I, p. 509.

an agreement for the purpose of carrying on a joint struggle against Serbia and as compensation for us a promise from him to maintain peace on the Dalmatian and Herzegovinian frontier! When I asked him what he understood by the aid that was to be given by us he . . . specified the wherewithal . . . to build roads and railways, carry out harbor improvements. . . . As soon as peace was concluded we must openly take his part and support his claim to the Sanjak against Serbia. . . . All occupied territory, particularly Scutari and San Giovanni di Medua, must be left in his possession.[1]

On 23 December 1912 the Austrian Military Attaché at Cetinje, Major Hubka, wrote in a letter to Conrad that King Nicholas might be open to persuasion to make a permanent change of policy and cede the Lovčen to Austria in return for commercial and economic concessions and the assignment of Scutari and the coastal strip as far as the Drin to Montenegro. Thereupon Conrad on 24 December wrote a letter to Berchtold in which after mentioning the aversion felt by the Montenegrin Royal Family for the Serbian Royal Family and the danger of Montenegro's being absorbed into Serbia, he suggested that the moment was ripe for offering Montenegro 'close alliance with the Monarchy'.

If it were possible to bring about an open breach between Serbia and Montenegro it would seem to me advantageous because then a cleavage would be made in the Slav world and Russia would lose her role as Pan-Slav protecting Power. I am viewing this also from the military standpoint. . . . Giesl should be in a position to give a decisive opinion on the matter.

On 26 December Berchtold replied:

Serbo-Montenegrin relations are the subject of our close attention and the playing off of King Nicholas against his son-in-law would fit calculations quite well if Nicholas were not just acting the comedian and meant it in earnest. But when one takes this unreliable Balkan Macchiavelli at his word, as Giesl has tried to do, he comes out with quite unacceptable proposals. . . . We have no intention of letting Montenegro have Scutari . . . the focus of Albanian Catholicism.[2]

2. The question of Serbo-Montenegrin union.

After the Second Balkan War the question of Serbo-Montenegrin union moved into the foreground.[3] Had there been no opposition from the King of Montenegro, the union of the countries would have been quickly and easily achieved. Austria-Hungary was opposed to it because by increasing the territory and prestige of Serbia it would constitute another important step towards the attainment of Southern

---

[1] Oe-U. V, 4733. [2] Conrad, II, pp. 402-6.
[3] See Vol. I, pp. 508-18.

Slav unity outside the Monarchy, in other words towards the dissolution of the Monarchy. In Russia, on the other hand, the union was ardently desired. But although King Nicholas had been advised by Russia to conclude a treaty of union with Serbia based on the preservation of his dynasty and had written Peter Karageorgević a grandiloquent letter to this effect,[1] Sazonov thought it wise not to precipitate events. Patience was needful because Austria-Hungary might go to the length of war to prevent it. Union must be prepared by slow transitions. Intimacy must first be established between the Belgrade and Cetinje Governments, beginning in the field of administration. The two States would wait to proclaim their political union until outside circumstances were favorable.[2]

Sazonov remained faithful to this prudent policy even after the Sarajevo murder. On 7 July he telegraphed to the Russian Minister at Belgrade enjoining extreme circumspection in questions liable to increase tension and create a dangerous situation:

> We therefore think it desirable to pause in the negotiations for Serbo-Montenegrin rapprochement, which has already attracted the attention of the Austro-Hungarian and even of the German Government.[3]

In February 1914 the Russian General Staff had proposed the grant to Montenegro of an annual subsidy of 4,500,000 rubles to provide for a Montenegrin army of up to 60,000 men with Russian instructors.[4] King Nicholas had greeted this proposal[5] with joy. He was in no position to look a gift horse in the mouth, because army pay was in arrears and the officers might soon be giving trouble. But the idea was not received with equal enthusiasm by the Russian Foreign Ministry, whose spokesman, Neratov, at a conference with the General Staff on 13 April, expressed concern

---

[1] See Vol. I, pp. 514-15.   [2] DF. 3. X, 141. See Vol. I, p. 514.
[3] *Int. Bez.* i. IV, 112.   [4] Bogičević, *Aits. Pol. Serb.* II, 904.
[5] *Int. Bez.* i. I, 185. Bogičević (*ibid.,* 977, p. 564) reproduces a letter of 23 May 1917 in which Plamenac asserts that the renewal of the subsidy to Montenegro which had been suspended in 1911 was frustrated by the intrigues of Pašić who had supplanted Montenegro at St. Petersburg. In April 1914— the letter continues—King Nicholas told Plamenac that the Russian Military Attaché at Cetinje had officially notified him of the renewal of the subsidy with the payment of arrears. The Military Attaché had explained that in Russia there was an expectation of war. 'We were in consternation' adds Plamenac and goes on to tell that after the Sarajevo crime, Gavrilović, the Serbian Minister at Cetinje, had assured him: 'Do not fear anything. Russia will not leave us in the lurch.' Plamenac comments: 'M. Pašić is not extremely intelligent but he is cunning and unscrupulous, . . . if he had not been sure of Russia he would have done a deal with the honor of Serbia.' The purpose of this letter was to accuse Russia of having premeditated the war. Light is thrown on the figure of Plamenac by a speech of his recorded in a dispatch of Delaroche-Vernet, the French Minister at Cetinje, of 26 May 1914: 'We have already given the map of the Balkans several jabs of the pen knife; perhaps in a not too distant future we will give it some more. I hope France is preparing, or rather, as she is ready now, will remain so, and that Russia will continue her reorganization and military preparations' (DF. 3. X, 286).

lest an army be created which might take action against the future fusion of Montenegro with Serbia or prove to be an effective weapon in King Nicholas's hands for actions not desired by us.[1]

But the General Staff had its way (though nothing came of it, because when the July crisis arose the question had still not been settled) and Sazonov on 22 April gleefully told Paléologue that he had got King Nicholas to agree 'almost with joy' to the process of dying by inches.[2]

It is hard to understand how Sazonov could cherish such an illusion. On 29 May Delaroche-Vernet, the French Minister at Cetinje, reported the King's having said in reply to a question from the Greek Minister: 'So long as I am alive Montenegro shall not lose its individuality.'[3] Even apart from King Nicholas's resentment towards Russia for suspending the subvention, his jealousy and hatred of the Serb Royal House, and his own perfidious and tortuous character, it was pretty obvious that any promise made by him was determined by his fear of opposing the current favorable to union and a wish to hide his real intentions. At the bottom of his heart he could not be otherwise than averse from letting his realm be swallowed up by Serbia, and he thus felt drawn politically towards Austria, whose interest it was to prevent Serbo-Montenegrin union. Moreover, he expected that in the event of a European war, victory would go to the Central Powers. And the question remains whether from the Austrian point of view Berchtold was wise to rebuff his approaches and refuse him Scutari instead of trying to strengthen his throne, buying, his friendship with liberal subsidies instead of demanding the Lovčen which Nicholas had no power to give. On 4 August Conrad wrote to Berchtold:

> If Montenegrin neutrality were really to be had for money it would be of the greatest value to us; in return for neutrality, so precious to us, one might easily let them have Scutari.[4]

That being so, would it not have been more far sighted in 1912-13 to make this and other concessions part of a policy which would have won Montenegro away from Serbia and made independence practicable and desirable for her?

3. *King Nicholas's pro-Austrian attitude after the Sarajevo outrage.*

Berchtold was to perceive his mistake in July 1914 when he made greater efforts to gain the neutrality of Montenegro than that of Italy. As one reads the Austro-Hungarian diplomatic documents one is astonished to find that the diplomatic correspondence between Vienna

---

[1] *Int. Bez.* i- II, 209.
[2] DF. 3. X, 141. See Vol. I, p. 514.
[3] DF. 3. X, 304.
[4] Conrad, IV, 176.

and Cetinje is equal In volume to that between Vienna and Rome. Twice in the correspondence with Rome one finds Berchtold instructing Merey to ask San Giuliano to use his influence to keep Montenegro neutral.[1] Asked by Luciano Magrini to explain why Berchtold attached so much importance to the neutrality of so small a State, Hoyos replied that its importance was not military but political. In the previous year during the Scutari crisis Berchtold had had experience of Russian sensitiveness on the subject of Montenegro and had come to the conclusion that if Montenegro were to remain neutral Russia would feel less impelled to intervene. But this explanation does not carry conviction, since, even if Montenegro stood aside, Russia would not think it any the less necessary to go to the help of Serbia, on which she founded her hopes of Southern Slav union. One cannot but conclude that Berchtold hoped to use Montenegrin abstention to wreck all prospects of union between Serbia and Montenegro. In truth, had Montenegro refused to help Serbia, a feeling of enmity would have arisen between the two States which Austria would have rendered permanent by aggrandizing Montenegro at the expense of Serbia.

Easy as it might be to win over the King to the side of Austria, it was an impossible undertaking to sever the Montenegrins from the Serbs. After the Sarajevo murder the French Minister telegraphed that Government circles in Cetinje had welcomed the crime 'with secret satisfaction' and that the King 'does not approve of the gesture in itself but is delighted with its result'.[2] It Is probable that the disappearance of the Archduke was no grief to Nicholas. However, on 5 July the Austrian Secretary of Legation, Lothar Egger, Ritter von Möllwald, wrote in a private letter:

> The King's bearing in the recent week of mourning has been so strikingly friendly to Austria that one wonders what is the reason. First he came to the Legation and left his card. Two days later he sent for me and spoke of His Imperial Majesty and the Sarajevo disaster in warm tones which cannot be reproduced in a letter. He even spoke of the Queen's tears. In the last twenty-four hours he has prevented the planned demonstration in front of the Legation by forbidding all Montenegrins

---

[1] It was to Italy's interest that Montenegro should side with Serbia. But San Giuliano, obsessed by the fear that Montenegrin intervention would cause Austria to occupy the Lovčen, sought to prevent intervention lest it should serve as a pretext for the occupation. This is the explanation of his instructions to Carlotti to beg Sazonov to keep Montenegro neutral *(Int. Bez.* i. V, 183, 237), as if it were not obvious that Russia, at war with Austria, would do the very opposite. In reality San Giuliano underestimated the pressure he could put on Vienna to prevent any Austrian occupation of the Lovčen. On 4 August Berchtold actually telegraphed to Merey that Austria did not intend to attack Montenegro, and that if attacked by Montenegro, Austria in deference to Italian apprehensions would refrain from seizing the Lovčen. Merey was to ask San Giuliano 'whether he would not be disposed to renew his counsels of neutrality at Cetinje'. And San Giuliano declared his readiness to fulfill the Austrian request (DA. III, 129, 140).

[2] DF. 3. X, 464, 474.

to take part in it and in his patriarchal way has himself provided for the 'policing of the streets'. He has thereby put himself directly at variance with the majority of his subjects, who are extremely excited over the demonstrations (in Bosnia-Herzegovina).[1]

The anti-Austrian demonstration took place the next day, when the King in his car himself drove back the demonstrators, so that they did not reach the Legation.[2]

He did not, perhaps could not, hand over Mehmedbašić, one of the Sarajevo conspirators arrested in Montenegro, in response to Berchtold's request because there were persons who contrived his escape. But his Foreign Minister, in his own and the King's name, was so profuse in apologies that the incident had no sequel, and Berchtold spoke appreciatively of Montenegro's innocence of the crime.

On 16 July Berchtold telegraphed to the Austro-Hungarian Minister, Otto, to mention unobtrusively in conversation with the King that while the Sarajevo investigation had brought to light clues leading to Belgrade, none had been found leading to Montenegro. It was due to the King that the Montenegrin Government, unlike that of Serbia, had not closed its eyes to the machinations of Pan-Serb propaganda in its midst. Otto might add that

the Austrian Government as a special mark of favor was about to procure for the Montenegrin Government an advance installment of the international loan on terms which would not be too great a burden on the Montenegrin Treasury.[3]

Otto did not find an immediate pretext for requesting an audience of the King, but on 21 July he had an excellent occasion in connection with the Lovčen. On the morning of the 19th the *Temps* had published the statement that Austria intended to take possession of the Lovčen by a surprise attack against which Montenegro had concentrated 10,000 men. Szécsen at 12.38 p. m. had telegraphed the news to Vienna,[4] and on the 20th at 2.45 p. m. Berchtold instructed Otto to make the news, 'which you can of course categorically deny', the ground on which to request an audience.[5] On 21 July Berchtold telegraphed to Otto:

Today's evening issue of the *Wiener Fremdenblatt* gives a semi-official *démenti* which you should bring to the notice of the Foreign Minister.[6]

Thereupon Otto that same day called on Plamenac with the good news, asking for an audience at which the King evinced extreme satisfaction both at the *dementi* and the contents of Berchtold's telegram of

---

[1] Oe-U. VIII, 10062. [2] Oe-U. VIII, 10079.
[3] Oe-U. VIII, 10300. [4] Oe-U. VIII, 10386.
[5] Oe U. VIII, 10403. [6] Oe-U. VIII, 10449.

the 16th. 'He seemed to see in them an indication that the era of misunderstandings was over and that he, his Government, and the country with our help would soon see better days.'[1] On the 22nd Otto wrote a long report to Vienna summarizing his various talks with the King and Plamenac in the course of which the King had observed that

apart from transient misunderstandings the best relations had always existed between Montenegro and the Monarchy. . . . He had joined the Balkan League, which, as far as Montenegro was concerned, was never directed against Austria-Hungary but solely against Turkey. When the [Balkan] war came and with it the invasion of the Sanjak by Serbian troops, Montenegro had also been obliged 'to invade it in order not to let it fall entirely into Serbian hands. But mindful of his duties towards the Monarchy the King had not failed to send his formal apologies several times to Vienna through the Austrian Legation at Cetinje and explain the reasons which quite against his will had obliged him to extend his military operations to this territory. . . . In these circumstances the 'hands off' Scutari had fallen on him and his country like a bolt from the blue. . . . Were Montenegro to receive the Bojana, nay more, the Drin as its frontier, the danger of union with Serbia would be ended, and at the same time the Monarchy would gain among its neighbors on its southern frontier a friend on whom it could unconditionally rely if only because this friendship was also in Montenegro's own interests. In the opposite case sooner or later the absorption of the lesser by the greater would inevitably come to pass, the very thing that we [Austria] had always declared we could not tolerate, namely, Serbia on the Adriatic, augmented possibly by Northern Albania.[2]

From this document, as from another to come,[3] one concludes that Plamenac shared the King's friendly feelings for Austria and hostility towards Serbo-Montenegrin union. It is not far-fetched to suppose that Nicholas had guessed or been informed of Austrian intentions towards Serbia and was hoping to turn them to his 'own advantage.

4. Berchtold's anxious telegrams to influence Montenegro's decision.

The next day was 23 July, the day on which Belgrade was presented with the Austrian ultimatum sent by Berchtold to Otto on the 20th with instructions to communicate its text to the King and the Montenegrin Government together with the message that Vienna 'made a very clear distinction between Montenegro and Serbia' and was sure 'that by her attitude towards the *démarche* that has just taken place at Belgrade Montenegro will dissociate herself from the tendencies which led to the events of 28 June'.[4] On the 24th Otto communicated, first to the King and then to Plamenac, the ultimatum

[1] Oe-U. VIII, 10450; DP. 3. X, 544; XI, 31.   [2] Oe-U. VIII, 10486.
[3] See pp. 656-7.   4 Oe-U. VIII, 10402.

together with the Austrian note to the Powers, and reported to Vienna that on both they had

made a deep impression and aroused mixed feelings. On the one hand keen satisfaction at the tribute paid to Montenegro, on the other the unuttered but clearly visible apprehension that, in the event of an armed conflict between the Monarchy and Serbia, the Kingdom quite against its will might be drawn into it by public opinion or affected by it in one way or another. His Majesty expressed the hope that the Serbian Government would be sensible enough to yield all along the line, although certain points would be hard to accept.[1]

Cracks were beginning to show in the card castle of hopes reared by the Monarchy and the Montenegrin King. The situation was exactly as described by Otto. The King was opposed to making common cause With Serbia to the point of telling the Russian Minister Giers that

he thoroughly understood and approved of the Austrian action except for the demand for the admission by the Serbian Government of Austrian officials to the supplementary investigation on Serbian territory.[2]

But he feared that public opinion would demand intervention against Austria. The Foreign Minister, Plamenac, on the other hand, on 24 July told the Italian Minister, who had expressed a hope that Montenegro would stand aside from the Austro- Serbian conflict, 'that his country could not thus betray Serbia'.[3] On the same day Plamenac told Delaroche-Vernet:

'I think that the Austro-Hungarian army will soon enter Serbian territory.' 'What will you do then?' I asked. 'We shall prepare M. Otto's passports', he replied. 'If there were no other link between Serbia and ourselves, the ties of blood are stronger than anything. I have been saying so recently to the Italian and Austrian Ministers. No power could prevent Serbs and Montenegrins from fighting side by side.'[4]

And on 25 July Plamenac said the same thing to the German Chargé d'Affaires, Zech.[5] Did he speak thus to extract promises and concessions from Austria? On 24 July the Austrian Military Attaché, Hubka, wrote:

King and Cabinet willing to remain neutral if Austria-Hungary promises concessions to Montenegro. Positive decisions in the matter not yet taken [in the absence of the Prime Minister and War Minister, Vukotić].

Conrad minuted: 'Do not be sparing with the money'[6] and next day sent a note to the Ballplatz recommending that concessions of all sorts be offered the King, including prospects of pecuniary assistance.[7]

---

[1] Oe-U. VIII, 10594.   [2] *Int. Bez.* i. V, 77.   [3] DF. 3. XI, 17.
[4] DF. 3. XI, 24.   [5] DD. I, 195.   [6] Oe-U. VIII, 10595.
[7] Oe-U. VIII, 10702.

Berchtold at once instructed Otto to offer the Montenegrin Government an advance of 6 million kronen on behalf jointly of Austria-Hungary and Italy.[1] Otto, who on the 25th warned Vienna: 'The Ministers are agitating for solidarity with Serbia in the event of war',[2] executed his mission on the morning of the 26th, and, though the French Minister, Delaroche-Vernet, reported on the same day: 'This offer has not been accepted',[3] Nicholas assured the German Military Attaché on 27 July 'that he would do everything to avoid war with Austria'.[4]

It was the eve of the critical 28 July when Austria was to declare war on Serbia, and on the 27th Berchtold instructed Otto to inform the King personally of the rupture of diplomatic relations with Belgrade, telling him:

> To our regret and much against our will we have been placed under the necessity of forcing Serbia into a radical change of her hitherto hostile attitude by the most drastic means. . . . We fully understand the delicate position of the King . . . but since we do not pursue a policy of conquest . . . we trust that the King in his wisdom will not take any hasty step which might be detrimental to the friendly feelings prevailing here towards himself and his country. . . . According to the development of events we would at the appropriate moment certainly show consideration for the interests of Montenegro, whose existence and prosperity as an independent State we have at heart,[5]

In a telegram following immediately after, Berchtold asked Otto to press his case with the King and report immediately on the Montenegrin attitude and desires.[8] Via Sofia on 28 July Berchtold got wind of a declaration of the Montenegrin Minister at Belgrade that his country would co-operate with Serbia and telegraphed to ask for German support at Cetinje,[7] which Jagow gave on the same day,[8] recommending neutrality and the localization of the conflict.

5. King Nicholas's telegram to Prince Alexander; Montenegro mobilizes.

The tension created by the ultimatum was increased by the expulsion ordered at an hour's notice by the Austrian military authorities on 26 July of all Montenegrins, women and children included, living in the Cattaro district. The incident led to protests from Plamenac and explanations from Berchtold. Telegraphic communications were also cut between Cetinje and Cattaro.[9] On 28 July Delaroche-Vernet

---

[1] The relevant dispatches are not published in the collection of Austro-Hungarian diplomatic documents. But see DF, 3. XI, 105, *note.*
[2] Oe-U. VIII, 10667.   [3] DF. 3. XI, 105.   [4] DD. II, 284.
[5] Oe-U. VIII, 10799.   [6] Oe-U. VIII, 10800.   [7] DD. II, 306.
[8] DD. II, 322.
[9] Oe-U. VIII, 10801, 10886, 10958, 11048, 11052, 11145.

reported to Paris that the Montenegrin Government was arming and expelling all Austrian subjects resident in Montenegro and that the Cabinet of the previous evening had decided that the country would join her fate with that of Serbia.[1] The German Chargé d'Affaires, Zech, on 28 July reported similar news from Cattaro.[2] Promises had been made to Serbia in an exchange of telegrams between Prince Alexander and King Nicholas published on 28 July 1914 by the Cetinje newspaper *Glas Crnogorca*. The Prince's ran:

> Great joy fills me to learn—though I never doubted it—that Montenegro declares her solidarity with Serbia in the defense of the Serbian people. ... I send my greeting to my beloved and cherished Grandfather and the valorous Montenegrin army.

The King's reply ran:

> Sweet are the sacrifices one makes for the truth and for the nation's independence. . . . My Montenegrins are already at the frontier, prepared to fall in the defense of our independence. Long live my dear grandson to be the joy of his dear father and myself. Long live the valiant Serbian army. Long live our cherished Serbdom.[3]

There was no sincerity in these words, which did not prevent King Nicholas from negotiating with Austria, as we shall now see.

Mobilization was announced on the evening of the 28th in a special edition of the *Official Gazette* on grounds of Austrian troop concentrations on the Montenegrin frontier. In informing Vienna of it on the 29th Otto reported that the Skupština was summoned for 1 August, that the Prime Minister was back, and that he himself was still endeavoring to keep Montenegro neutral.[4] On 28 and 29 July Otto had long conversations with Plamenac, who explained to him that the King had been absent and thus not able to receive him and hoped that Otto would not renew the request, which would make his position difficult now that news had come in of Serbian blood being shed in the fighting that had begun. Otto did not insist and Plamenac then said that

His Majesty and the Government were still determined to observe strict neutrality 'unless we are swept away by public opinion'. The position of King and Government would be strengthened if we were to make a declaration here as has been done at Berlin and Rome that the war with Serbia was not a war of conquest. During his reign of over fifty years the King of Montenegro had almost quadrupled the size of his country, nevertheless even at its present size he was not able to stand on his own feet and depended on foreign help, an untenable position in view of the great territorial changes

---

[1] DF. 3. XI, 182.   [2] DD. II, 358.
[3] *Montenegrische Dokumente zum Ansbruch des Weltkrieges,* in KSF., November 1931, pp. 1107-8.
[4] Oe-U. VIII, 10959.

in the Balkans in the last two years in which Montenegro came off so badly. We had done Montenegro grave wrong in arresting her attempt to expand southward after giving her repeatedly to understand that we approved of this expansion. Montenegro, it is true, had been guilty of several lapses in regard to the Monarchy, but on the whole her behavior had always shown that we could in our own interest easily win her as a good, devoted, and grateful friend. H.M. the King and the Government still counted on us and placed reliance on Your Excellency. . , . His Majesty and the Government would ask Your Excellency whether the Austro-Hungarian Government was willing and able to offer Montenegro a guarantee of her further independent existence. She would regard as such a guarantee the assurance of an aggrandizement of Montenegro such as would enable her to continue her existence in complete autonomy and independence without the foreign help of the past alongside the other Balkan States, especially Serbia. The Foreign Minister's statements, summarized above, are the result of long consultations with the King and the Prime Minister. He asked for very confidential handling and speedy, even if only provisional, reply, in allusion to the Skupština, which meets the day after tomorrow.[1]

The tone of this conversation, the tenor of the statements and requests made by Plamenac and his eagerness for a speedy reply betray that the King and his Foreign Minister, if not the Prime Minister also, were on the 29th still hesitating to support Serbia and negotiating with Austria. From their own point of view they were not wrong to do so. It must be remembered that on the 29th they could still not be sure that Russia would go to war and could think that the conflict would remain localized. Had that been so, Serbia and Montenegro would have headed for destruction if they had stood out against Austria, and their rulers would have lost their thrones. It must also be remembered that on 25 July the Russian Minister, Giers, said to the King that the latter's 'long years of experience as a statesman would suggest a course of action to him which would spare Montenegro the unspeakable misfortune that a war would entail'. Sazonov set matters right on the 27th with a telegram:

If Austria proves intractable and falls on Serbia Russia will not be indifferent to Serbia's fate. We are of the opinion that Montenegro must more than ever bring her policy into harmony with that of Serbia in their common cause. On that will depend Russia's future attitude towards Montenegro.[2]

These are fine words but if the war had remained localized, help from Montenegro would not have availed to save Serbia, whereas neutrality might have brought great gain to Montenegro, whom Austria had an interest to aggrandize at the expense of Serbia, thus putting a stop to Serbo-Montenegrin union to the great satisfaction of King Nicholas.

[1] Oe-U. VIII, 10961.
[2] *Int. Bez.* i. V, 77, 118.

It is true that to the German Chargé d'Affaires, Zech, Plamenac spoke in somewhat different terms on 30 July, while giving assurances that Montenegro did not intend to attack Austria:

He attached no weight to Austrian promises, she has been making them for thirty-five years and never kept any. No wonder Austria was lavish at the present moment with unavoidable promises. In the circumstances it would be particularly unpleasant for the Monarchy to be involved in war with Montenegro as well, for Russia would never look on passively at a conflict between Austria and two Slav countries. . . . The Minister further declared that Montenegro could not quietly watch the dismemberment of Serbia. Surrounded by Austria on all sides, Montenegro would be doomed to disappear.[1]

If this was a device to induce Berlin to exercise influence on Vienna it succeeded, for Jagow at once sent Zech's message on to Vienna,[2] Plamenac was still maneuvering when on 30 July, deploring the declaration of war on Serbia, he asked Austria for assurances of territorial *désinteressement,* and when on 31 July he told Otto that Montenegro would be able to remain neutral only so long as Russia remained so, and that if Russia intervened she would definitely have to follow suit, but in actual practice would withdraw from this obligation by declaring that her situation made it impossible for her to carry on a war.[3] King Nicholas was equally lacking in candor when he told Giers on 30 July that there was no doubt about Montenegro's decision to take her stand with Serbia.[4]

6. Berchtold's final appeal; the Montenegrin Skupština decides on intervention on the side of Serbia; the King dragged into the war.

Meanwhile, alarmed by Montenegrin mobilization, Berchtold telegraphed on the 30th to Otto to say that he must know exactly how matters stood and asking Otto's opinion whether to make further promises or, as the Military Attaché proposed, to send an ultimatum.[5] But when the Military Attaché reported that the Montenegrin Government thought it could get the Skupština to vote for neutrality if Austria engaged not to annex Serbian territory, to assure the independence of Montenegro, give her adequate financial assistance and some increase of territory, Berchtold, who had received Otto's telegram on the 29th, replied on the 31st:

As Montenegrin neutrality would be of great importance to us, will you on the basis of the above report, endeavor to influence the Government so that the Skupština decides on neutrality. You might point out afresh that we are waging

[1] DD. 11, 476.   [2] DD. II, 476 n.
[3] Oe-U. VIII, 11051, 11053, 11147.   [4] *Int. Bez.* i, V, 370.
[5] Oe-U. VIII, 11049.

no war of conquest against Serbia; in the Balkan wars we had given proof that aspirations for territorial expansion were far from our thoughts, and today, too, we meditated no permanent seizure of Serbian territory. We had a genuine interest in the independence of Montenegro, therefore, by maintaining a correct, neutral attitude she could reckon with certainty on our championship of her independence in the future also. You might observe in this connection that in the defense of Montenegrin independence we can count on the support of Italy. After the end of the present conflict Montenegro, in return for her neutral attitude, can count not only on ample financial aid from the Monarchy but also on our putting no obstacles in the way of her acquiring territory in the direction of the Sanjak of Novibazar and that any Montenegrin wishes in connection with Albania would—within the framework of an agreement with Italy—find favorable consideration from us.[1]

This telegram reached Cetinje on 1 August. But about noon on the previous day news had spread like wildfire of the Russian general mobilization, and also a rumor that a Russian army corps had invaded Galicia.[2] As Eduard Czegka, the Keeper of the Vienna *Kriegsarchiv,* writes, the news of the Russian general mobilization entirely changed the situation and made it impossible to rein in the war faction.[3] The Skupština met on 1 August and left no doubt as to the will of the great majority in the country to go to war with Austria at once in support of Serbia. Applause greeted all the speakers, who unanimously declared in favor of war. Dr. Nicholas Škerović said that Austria must be annihilated and that the moment had come to drive her from the Balkans. Mitar Vučetić expressed amazement that an Austro-Hungarian Minister could still be in Cetinje and asked for a declaration of war on Austria. An opposition motion was carried in favor of war on the Monarchy at the side of their brother Serbs.

This vote did not bind the Cabinet, for at the same time the Skupština passed a vote of confidence in the Government and left it a free hand. How would this be used? The Austrian Military Attaché, Hubka, tells us that at midnight the King received delegates from the Skupština in the courtyard of the palace. 'He thanked them in arid words for their patriotic behavior but at the same time exhorted them to calmness and prudence. Disappointed and downcast, the people's representatives left the courtyard and dispersed into Kafana [cafés] where they went on talking politics.'[4]

Did King Nicholas still imagine he could retain control of the situation with the help of Austrian promises? Berchtold's telegram containing them was received by Otto after the Skupština had voted.

[1] Oe-U. VIII, 11143.
[2] G. von Hubka, *Kritische Tage in Montenegro,* KSF., January 1931, p. 40.
[3] E. Czegka, *Die Mobilmachung im Sommer, 1914*, KSF., January 1936, p. 18.
[4] Hubka, *art. cit.,* p. 41.

Plamenac confined himself to saying that he would report them to the King and return an answer next day.[1] But that same day, 1 August, Plamenac intimated to the French Minister, Delaroche-Vernet, that he was only awaiting the completion of mobilization to hand Otto his passports.[2]

This, to be sure, did not yet mean war. On 30 July Nicholas had said to the Russian Minister, Giers, that if the Austrians did not attack, the Montenegrins would not do so either,[3] a course entirely in accordance with the wish expressed to Plamenac by the Ministers of France, Italy, and Serbia.[4] On 1 August Plamenac told Giers that he had said something similar to Otto and had added that if there were war between Russia and Austria the whole country would stand by Russia. Giers drew the conclusion from this conversation that Montenegro greatly feared war with Austria and that Austria was anxious not to precipitate a war with Montenegro.[5] Plamenac told Giers of Berchtold's offer and on 2 August Giers telegraphed that there would be a discussion that day about the reply to be sent to Austria and the question of handing Otto his passports.[6]

Plamenac's reply to Otto does not figure in either the Austrian or the German collections of diplomatic documents. In the Austrian collection there is only a telegram of 6 August from Gravosa, by which Otto announced that at 5.30 p. m. on 5 August the Montenegrin Government had handed him a note saying that it found itself obliged to resort to arms for the defense of the Serb cause and that his mission at Cetinje had ended.' But the actual text of the Montenegrin note was published in 1929. It runs:

On 24 [sic] July last the Austro-Hungarian Government handed the Serbian Government a note in which it demanded nothing less than the alienation of Serbia's sovereignty to the benefit of the Monarchy. To save the peace of Europe and spare it the horrors of war, the Government of Serbia in reply to the note made all the concessions compatible with the dignity of an independent State. The Austro-Hungarian Government was not willing to declare itself satisfied with this unprecedented condescension and on 28 July declared war on Serbia and for the last week has been trying to invade her territory, threatening her independence and that of the whole Serb nation. On 1 August Germany, the ally of the Austro-Hungarian Monarchy, also declared war on Russia, Montenegro's protectress. Bound to Serbia by solid ties of consanguinity, attached to Russia by indissoluble bonds of age-old gratitude, menaced in her own turn, as is proved by all the aggressive measures taken by Austria-Hungary for the last fortnight along her Dalmatian and Herzegovinian frontier, the expulsion of Montenegrins from the Monarchy, the

[1] Oe-U. VIII, 11148.   [2] DF. 3. XI, 531.
[3] Int. Bez. i. V, 370.   [4] DF. 3. XI, 540.
[5] Int. Bez. i. V, 436.   [6] Int. Bez. i. V, 474.
[7] DA. III, 158.

seizure of sailing vessels, the armed attack on the Sanjak frontier—Montenegro finds herself forced to declare that she cannot remain neutral in this struggle and that she must herself resort to arms in order to contribute to the defense of the freedom of the Serb people.[1]

This declaration was anything but to the liking of the King, who had assented to it rather than lose his throne. Conrad reproduces a report from Otto saying that King Nicholas 'is watched like a prisoner; he would like to stay neutral but dare not move a muscle', and that 'there was a rumor that the King was keeping a vessel ready for flight'.[2] Further, Major Hubka writes that the King asked him to call before his departure and told him he had never believed it possible that he would have to take arms against the so venerated Francis Joseph.

God is my witness that I never willed the war, for I know what is at stake. Destiny fulfills itself; it is stronger than the human will.[3]

Fate led Montenegro to merge with Serbia in the new Yugoslav State. Austria went to her doom, and the King of Montenegro would not have saved his dynasty by taking her side. But Montenegro's intervention was yet another disappointment for the Monarchy, whose leaders had shown more readiness to satisfy Montenegrin aspirations than to tranquillize Italy by an unhesitating acceptance of her interpretation of Article VII of the treaty. From blunder to blunder they led their country to destruction.

[1] A. Rappaport, *Montenegros Eintritt in den Weltkrieg,* KSF. October 1929, pp. 962-3.

[2] Conrad, IV, pp. 206, 317-18.

[3] Hubka, *art. cit.,* p. 43. After the war when the Montenegrin National Assembly, meeting at Podgorica, unanimously voted for the union of Montenegro with Serbia, ex-King Nicholas wrote a letter to President Wilson against the Serbs in which he said: 'Perfidious as they are, I was the first to hold out a hand to them, being the first to declare war on Austria, though convinced that the provocation came from their side by the Sarajevo murder and their *Black Hand.* The crime perpetrated against the Archduke and his wife was the cause of the world's mourning twenty million victims today. A terrible thought that that country is not willing to realize the crime that has been committed and for which it, just as much as Wilhelm, is responsible before the world' (Luciano Magrini, *Il Montenegro. La fine di un regno,* Milan, 1922, p. 43).

CHAPTER XVII

THE ATTITUDE OF THE OTHER STATES

1. *Swedish hostility to Russia and tendencies towards alliance with Germany.*
Besides having hopes of support from the Balkan States Germany firmly relied on the co-operation of Sweden. In a report of 12 June 1912 Beaucaire, the French Minister at Copenhagen, noted:

Of the three Scandinavian nations, Sweden alone seems capable and appears to be preparing herself to play an active role in the event of a major international conflict. Not only is her population twice that of Denmark or Norway, not only are her financial resources more considerable, but she also has stronger military and naval forces at her disposal. . . . Rightly or wrongly the fear of a Russian offensive from the north has gained greater credence in Sweden in the course of recent years. This belief is encouraged by the Germans, who neglect nothing to sow mistrust between Sweden and Russia. . . . It is also necessary to point to a recent movement in favor of a union under German auspices of the three Scandinavian countries which would then join the Triple Alliance. The German Empire would thus attract into its orbit nearly 12 million men of superior race. At the same time it would gain undisputed control of the entrance to the Baltic, of the Norwegian fjords, and of Sweden, which could be made to play in regard to Russia the same function of creating a diversion as at the time of Richelieu and Mazarin she played for France against the Empire. This plan has recently been the theme of various publications extensively commented on in the press. It seems, however, still a long way from being realized. . . . The populations of the three countries are in the mass resolutely pacific and feel fortunate in being able to remain outside major European conflicts. In Denmark and Norway these feelings are deep-rooted, and it would, I think, be impossible to gain acceptance by public opinion there for war operations of an offensive character. In Sweden the mentality of the governing classes and of the influential nobility may still bring back to life hankerings after military glory. The memory of Gustavus Adolphus and Charles XII is cherished as a national cult.[1]

While the Conservatives were in power the Government was under pressure from the military party and the Action party, but when the Liberals succeeded them the Government drew back from the idea of seeking support from Germany and seemed mainly preoccupied by the fear of being dragged into a European war. However, in February 1914 the Government of the pacifist Staaf came into conflict with the Crown and made way for the Hammarskiöld-Wallenberg ministry, which, while claiming to be above party, introduced an armament program eagerly demanded by public opinion. The pro-German current, whose major representative was Sven Hedin, regained the upper hand and military circles revived the project of an alliance with Berlin.[2]

The purpose of armament could only be defense or offence against Russia, who gave provocation by the Russification of the Finnish and Swedish population of Finland, by military measures on the Swedish frontier, by organizing in Sweden an espionage service which was betrayed by the imprudence of the Russian Military Attaché, and by threatening to fortify the Aland islands. Russia on her part was led into these precautions by fear of a possible Swedish attack in the event of a European war. The opinion was widely held that if Russia became involved in a major war the Swedish army would invade Finland and threaten St. Petersburg from the north with the consent of Finland, which for three centuries had shared a common life with Sweden on a footing of equality and whose middle classes still spoke Swedish and chafed under Russian rule. Nothing would be more natural than that Sweden should create a diversion across Finland, a region which a victorious Germany would have willingly restored to Sweden. No less natural was it that Russia should take measures to frustrate this. On 10 January 1914, Thiébaut, the French Minister at Stockholm, noted:

> The Swedes seek to reorganize their forces only in order to be in a position to defend their neutrality against all violence from whatever quarter. 'Only one thing', said Count Ehrensvärd once to me, 'could throw us into the arms of Germany, the fortification of the Aland Islands, which would put us under Russian guns'. There is clearly a misunderstanding between Sweden and Russia which is going from bad to worse, and it is no less evident that German diplomacy encourages this

[1] DF. 3. III, 93; Herre, in KSF. May 1933, p. 474.
[2] As late as 7 April 1914, Chevalley, the French Minister at Christiania, reported a lecture given there by Sven Hedin proposing an alliance of Sweden and Norway with Germany. One of the warmest advocates of this alliance was the notorious German General Bernhardi (DF. 3. X, 82).

misunderstanding for its own advantage. . . . It is to Germany's interest that Russia should tie up part of her forces in Finland.[1]

On 12 May Thiébaut returned to the theme:

Perhaps it is no more than a misunderstanding. The Pan-German press has adroitly inflamed it by seeking to prove to the Swedes that Russia is pursuing her age-old dream of an outlet to blue water, that she has found the road barred in the Far East, on the Persian Gulf, in the Bosporus, that she will finally be led into seeking an ice-free harbor in Norway and assuring access to it by the occupation of Swedish Lapland, only an alliance with Germany being able to guarantee Sweden against this perhaps not far distant aggression. There are only too many people in Sweden (the Court, the Army, the Navy) ready to accept this thesis.

Thiébaut's suggestion was that Poincaré should take advantage of his St. Petersburg visit to obtain pacific assurances from the Russian Government which he would take with him to Stockholm before proceeding to Copenhagen.[2]

The suggestion was adopted. On 1 July Izvolski wrote to St. Petersburg:

In a conversation with me M. Poincaré said he thought these visits would be of some use to Triple *Entente* policy and he meant to make every effort particularly in Sweden to clarify the true aims of this policy.[3]

On 23 July Sazonov telegraphed to Nekludov, the Russian Minister in Sweden:

Poincaré has made the offer to use his visit to Stockholm to reassure the Swedish Government as to the hostile intentions ascribed to us. I answered that we had already given the most positive assurances that such intentions did not exist but that it would not be otherwise than useful if the Swedes were to hear once more the confirmation of our pacific attitude towards them from a friend and ally of Russia.[4]

Poincaré's intervention on behalf of Russia during his visit to Stockholm also took in the vexed question of the espionage carried on in Sweden by Russian officers in official positions.[5] The Swedish Foreign Minister, Wallenberg, told Viviani in conversation:

If Russia persists in her conduct towards us, she will throw us into the arms of Germany in spite of ourselves.[6]

Later on the same day, 25 July, Wallenberg had a talk with the German Minister, Reichenau, during which he expressed 'lively approval' of the Austrian ultimatum to Serbia, adding that

---

[1] DF. 3. IX, 52. [2] DF. 3. X, 221. [3] *Int. Bez.* i. IV, 44.
[4] *Int. Bez.* i. V, 3. [5] DF. 3. XI, 231. [6] Poincaré, IV, pp. 313-14.

the timing of the ultimatum had been very skilfully done, as the President of the French Republic was on the high seas. Today, during M. Poincaré's visit, they had of course to keep up a pretence here, but if Russia were to intervene on behalf of Serbia and thereby bring about a Russo-German war, then the present Government with H.M. the King at its head would not for one moment remain in doubt on whose side they would have to stand.[1]

And on the same day (the 25th) a similar message was sent by the Austrian representative to Vienna:

At today's reception the Royal Princes and the statesmen present expressed their satisfaction to me over our Belgrade *démarches,* remarking particularly on their timeliness. The King gave the German representative [Reichenau] to understand that, in the event of a conflict, Sweden's position would undoubtedly be with the Triple Alliance.[2]

That very day, the 25th, Wallenberg was assuring the Russian Minister, Nekludov, that

whatever might be the further development of events, Sweden would have regard above all to the defense of her neutrality and of her friendly relations with all her neighbors.[3]

And in fact in the crisis of July 1914 the behavior of Sweden was as suspicious and disquieting to the *Entente* as it was encouraging to Germany. The account sent to Conrad by Col. Straub, the Austrian Military Attaché at Stockholm, on 3 July, shows the Swedes as very well informed. The Swedish press clearly realized the serious consequences of the disappearance of the Archduke, who had been the only man capable of stemming the centrifugal tendencies among the subject peoples of the Monarchy. It understood how big a blunder Austria had committed by the renunciation of the Sanjak of Novibazar. One paper had gone to the length of heading an article *Finis Austriae.* Others had expressed a hope that Berchtold would be replaced by a man who would tenaciously and fearlessly use the power that he actually had at his command to the advantage of the dynasty and the State.[1] But Berchtold was incapable of being either tenacious or fearless. His private letter of 22 July to Hadik, the Austrian Minister at Stockholm, is another proof of this fact. Though avowing that 'at the outbreak of European war a natural identity of interests would arise between Sweden and the Triplice Powers', he would 'not regard direct arrangements with Sweden in view of a possible *casus belli* as in the Austrian

---

[1] *Auswärtiges Amt. Abteilung A. Die Stellung Schwedens im Falle eines Krieges. Neutralitäts-frage. Schweden.* No. 26. AS. 1385. [Ed].
[2] *Int. Bez.* i. V, 141. This telegram does not figure in the official collection of Austrian diplomatic documents. It was relayed by Berchtold to Szápáry on the 27th and intercepted and deciphered by the Russians.
[3] *Int. Bez.* i. V, 104. [4] Conrad, IV, pp. 26-7.

interest, and thought that the accession of Sweden to the Triplice would impose far too extensive obligations on us'.[1]

This identity of interests was strongly felt by certain currents of Swedish public opinion. As Herre writes:

The approach of the world war fanned hatred of Russia to a blaze. The Teutonic race was regarded as being in danger, and they felt a call to rally to the cause of their sister nation in resistance to the hereditary Slav enemy. They were convinced that after a victory over Germany the Tsarist Empire would establish itself on the North Sea littoral even if Sweden remained outside the conflict. . . . There was actually a revival of certain ambitions and desires that Finland might be regained if Sweden entered the war in good time. These arguments did not remain without effect on the people, and even the Government did not remain insensible to them. They were received expectantly in Germany. In the Army Command they awakened hopes that if war broke out Sweden would go into action as an ally.[2]

2. German pressure at Stockholm; Wallenberg's declarations to the Russian and English Ministers.

The German documents do not throw full light on the line taken by the German Government at this juncture. In Jagow's preliminary telegram giving notice of the Austrian ultimatum to Reichenau, the German Minister at Stockholm, on 23 July, he had said that if localization of the conflict proved impossible 'we hope that Sweden will understand how serious for her own fate is the hour that has struck'.[3]

This telegram anticipated an idea which the Kaiser from on board the *Hohenzollern* expressed to Berlin on 25 July:

If the situation grows more acute and tension increases between ourselves and Russia, H.M. the Kaiser and King wishes the question of confidence to be addressed immediately to Denmark and Sweden.[4]

Was this conceived as an ultimatum? Reichenau's reply to Jagow is not among the published documents. The next German document is another telegram from Jagow of 28 July after the Austrian declaration of war on Serbia. It runs:

A Swedish declaration of neutrality would probably render any subsequent change of attitude on the part of Sweden more difficult.[5]

On 30 July Bethmann Hollweg telegraphed to Reichenau:

We have reason to believe that England will very soon take part in the war on the side of the Dual Alliance. In the event of English intervention it is urgently

---

[1] Oe-U. VIII, 10504.   [2] Herre, KSF. May 1933, p. 479.
[3] DD. 1, 123.   [4] DD. I, 173.
                    [5] DD. II, 319.

necessary that the Swedish declaration of neutrality should reserve freedom of action.[1]

These two last telegrams, if closely examined, make it apparent that there is a lacuna in the documents which might be explained by the hypothesis that negotiations were carried on through the Swedish Minister at Berlin. It is already singular that there should have been no reply to the first of these three telegrams, that of Jagow to Reichenau of 23 July. Those of 28 and 30 July, asking for Sweden to reserve freedom of action in declaring her neutrality, point to the existence of exchanges of ideas in view of possible later intervention by Sweden especially in the event of English intervention. Reichenau seems not to have played a part in such exchanges of ideas for on 31 July he telegraphed:

In order to direct our efforts towards the right objective it would be important for myself and the Military Attaché to be informed whether and in what direction the Supreme Command thinks of Swedish co-operation, assuming it to be obtainable.[2]

Now the ideas of the Supreme Command are laid down in that memorandum sent by Moltke to Jagow on 2 August and noted above.[3]

Sweden must be induced to mobilize all her forces and send her 6th Division as soon as possible to the Finnish frontier. By her movements Sweden must seek to awaken and prolong Russian fears of an advance through Finland and a possible landing of Swedish forces on the Russian coast. We must unhesitatingly grant all her wishes for the recovery of Finland or anything else as far as is compatible with German interests.[4]

Was this a new proposal or the confirmation of proposals already under discussion between Berlin and Stockholm?
The German historian, Paul Herre, writes:

The details of these negotiations after the last days of July are not properly known. Far-reaching assurances were certainly given of satisfaction for the most ambitious national aspirations including even the recovery of Finland, as the reward of co-operation. While in all parties and classes feeling against Russia grew steadily stronger, the Government maintained an attitude of coolness and reserve against increasing pressure from outside and inside. The most important question was what England would do.[5]

Wallenberg made a disquieting statement to the English Minister, Esme Howard, as the latter telegraphed to Grey on 2 August:

I asked Minister for Foreign Affairs today whether he could now give me categorical assurances regarding neutrality. His Excellency replied that Sweden was determined to maintain neutrality as long as possible. I asked

---

[1] DD. II, 406.   [2] DD. III, 520.   [3] See p. 198.
[4] DD. III, 662.   [5] Herre, KSF. May 1933, p. 482.

if there were conditions in which Sweden might abandon neutrality. He replied that he greatly feared that, if Great Britain joined Russia, Sweden would be forced to take the other side. If Sweden were placed in such a position as to be obliged to choose sides their Government would be forced by public opinion to go against Russia.

It is not clear why Sweden felt bound to opt for one side or the other and intervene against Russia precisely in the event of England's entering the war, but this was undoubtedly the view taken by Wallenberg. For when Howard assured him

that in any case Great Britain would not violate Swedish neutrality and asked whether, if Germany did so, Sweden would resist, he merely repeated that if England took part in war Sweden would have to do so, he feared.[1]

A week earlier, on 26 July, Wallenberg had assured the Russian Minister, Nekludov, that 'whatever might be the further development of events, Sweden would have regard above all to the defense of her neutrality and of her friendly relations with all her neighbors'. And he repeated the same assurances to Nekludov on the 29th.[2] But Sazonov attached no importance to them because on 27 July the Russians had deciphered a telegram of Berchtold's to Szápáry relaying a dispatch from Stockholm to Vienna, which ran:

At today's reception the Royal Princes and the statesmen present expressed their satisfaction to me over our Belgrade *démarches,* remarking particularly on their timeliness. The King gave the German representative [Reichenau] to understand that, in the event of a conflict, Sweden's position would undoubtedly be with the Triple Alliance.[3]

This telegram does not figure in the official collection of Austrian diplomatic documents. Among the Russian documents, moreover, there is a wireless message of 30 July from the Russian Admiralty Chief of Staff to Essen, the Commander of the Russian Baltic forces:

According to reasonably reliable news reaching us an agreement was signed between Germany and Sweden on 25 July, therefore we must regard Sweden as a probable enemy.[4]

On 1 August Sazonov telegraphed this news to Nekludov,[5] who on the 2nd replied that Wallenberg had again affirmed the intention of Sweden to remain neutral. Only such an event as the participation of England in the war would lead to a departure from neutrality, for then Sweden would be 'between the hammer and the anvil'. However, England apparently was not going to enter the war, so that the occasion

[1] BD. XI, 511.   [2] *Int. Bez.* i. V, 104, 250.
[3] *Int. Bez.* i. V, 141.   [4] *Int. Bez.* i. V, 330.
                    [5] *Int. Bez.* i. V, 387.

would not arise.[1] These statements seemed so disquieting to Esme Howard that he took the matter up again with Wallenberg on 3 August:

Fearing some misapprehension as to the Minister for Foreign Affairs' communication of yesterday, I submitted in writing the substance of it as reported in my telegram,[2] and asked if it was correct. He has requested me to transmit it in following rather milder form:—

1. If England did not go to war, he was positive that Sweden's neutrality could be maintained.

2. If England did go to war, he feared that extreme circumstances might arise which would force Sweden to choose one side or the other, and it was his private opinion, considering public opinion here, that it was impossible for Sweden to fight on the same side as Russia.[3]

This formula might seem a little less blunt than the other, but its anti-British tendency was no less plain even though masked by an anti-Russian declaration. Unless England moved, Sweden did not propose to move either. Russia seemed not to enter into Swedish calculations unless the view taken at Stockholm was that without the intervention of England Russia would be beaten, while with it she would be victorious. But in the latter case Swedish support of Germany would not suffice to change the fortunes of war.

3. *The Swedish declaration of neutrality.*

One thing certain is that Wallenberg's statement to Howard has to be viewed in conjunction with the Chancellor's telegram of 30 July:

We have reason to believe that England will very soon take part in the war on the side of the Dual Alliance. In the event of English intervention it is urgently necessary that the Swedish declaration of neutrality should reserve freedom of action.[4]

Between the two documents there is such accordance as to reveal at least the embryo of an agreement between Berlin and Stockholm which never actually materialized but which Wangenheim at Constantinople regarded so much as a certainty that on 3 August the English Minister at Sofia telegraphed to Grey:

German Ambassador at Constantinople informed Grand Vizier that Sweden would also be found on their side.[5]

Berchtold, too, told Conrad on 3 August that 'Sweden has promised active intervention against Russia, she says she will invade Finland'.[8]

---

[1] *Int. Bez.* i. V, 464, 465.   [2] BD. XI, 511.
[3] BD. XI, 570.   [4] DD. II, 406. See pp. 666-7.
[5] BD. XI, 564.   [6] Conrad, IV, p. 171.

Was there perhaps the intention of masking the agreement, if it were concluded, with a German ultimatum to Sweden as a way of carrying out the Kaiser's wish for 'the question of confidence to be immediately addressed to . . . Sweden'.[1]

Both Stockholm and Christiania in those days regarded an ultimatum as imminent. On 3 August Howard telegraphed to Grey:

Norwegian Minister has just told me no ultimatum has been presented here yet respecting Swedish neutrality. I understand, however, that both Swedish and Norwegian Governments have discussed possibility, and that Swedish Government is very doubtful whether it can oppose Germany successfully. He said that he was of the opinion that whatever line Sweden took Norway must also take.[2]

In reality this was not so. On 2 August Reichenau was reporting to Berlin:

M. Wallenberg stated that his Norwegian colleague had agreed that Norway should keep in step with Sweden as long as possible, and that if their ways should part neither country should in any circumstances turn its weapons against the other.[3]

This agreement with Norway shows that on 2 August the Swedish Government was still toying with the idea of joining eventually with Germany. On 4 August on the contrary it proclaimed unconditional neutrality, and that same day the King twice said to Nekludov:

Sweden is not bound to any State by any sort of agreements or treaties; . . . only violence could force Sweden to abandon the attitude she had adopted. I reaffirmed to the King that Russia had no intention whatsoever of infringing Swedish neutrality in any way and on the contrary had the most sincere and friendly feelings towards Sweden.[4]

What remained to be seen was whether English intervention, which had not yet taken place on the morning of 4 August, would change Stockholm's decision. On that 4 August when Sweden announced her neutrality the Swedish Minister in London called to inform Grey

that it was Sweden's settled desire to maintain her neutrality; but he was to add that, were she forced into the impending European war, it would be impossible for her to take the side of Russia owing to all the distrust that had been created in Sweden by Russian spying. I expressed satisfaction at hearing that Sweden intended to maintain her neutrality; and I said that, if

---

[1] DD. I, 173. See p. 666. On 30 July Reichenau reported Wallenberg as having said that if England were not to maintain neutrality he 'would regard it as quite natural if we were to send an ultimatum to the Swedish Government' (*Auswärtiges Amt. Schwedens Neutralität. Ko-operation. 23.7.14–2.5.15.* No. 9. AS. 1517). [Ed.]

[2] BD. XI, 567.

[3] DD. III, 692.

[4] *Int. Bez.* i. V, 549.

she did so, it would be my object to get Russia and France to join with me in a guarantee to respect the independence and integrity of Sweden.[1]

And the same day Grey telegraphed to Paris and St. Petersburg:

> It is most urgent that French and Russian Governments should express to Sweden their willingness to join His Majesty's Government in their guarantee to respect the integrity and independence of Sweden now and hereafter if the latter remains neutral during the war. It should be added that if Sweden takes active sides with Germany we shall be freed from all obligation towards her.

In repeating this to Stockholm he added: 'You should make such declarations on behalf of His Majesty's Government.'[2]

A necessary precaution in view of the possibility, implied in the Swedish Ambassador's words to Grey, that Sweden might intervene against the Triple *Entente*! That Berlin went on cherishing this hope as late as 8 p. m. on 4 August is shown by Jagow's telegram to Reichenau:

> English Ambassador has just asked for his passports. Inform Government immediately,[3]

that being the contingency which it was expected would bring Sweden into the war. But Sweden made no move, observing strict neutrality even to the point of refusing to accede on 5 August to the German request to close its waters in the Sound by mines as Denmark consented to do.[4] Indeed, Swedish neutrality ended by being almost favorable to the Triple *Entente*.[5]

Any temptation felt by the Swedish Government to co-operate with Germany must no doubt have been subdued by the assurances and veiled threats emanating, on Grey's initiative, from London, Paris, and St. Petersburg. But the decision for neutrality ante-dated these measures and was taken either because the Swedes perceived at what a disadvantage the Central Powers were embarking on war or, still more probably, because they could not well act otherwise than did Denmark and Norway, even though they did contemplate such a possibility. In the event the three States declared their neutrality after previous consultation and agreement.[6] Herre writes:

> In the hour of crisis the Scandinavian peoples felt they were a band of brothers in spite of their different points of view and this in itself was a factor favoring an attitude of neutrality in which they gave one another mutual support.[7]

---

[1] BD. XI, 642.   [2] BD. XI, 576.   [3] DD. IV, 843.
[4] See p. 675.   [5] Herre, KSF., May 1933, p. 483.
[6] BD. XI, 475; DD. IV, 789.   [7] Herre, KSF., May 1933, p. 479.

Indeed, only on this condition could the three States maintain their solidarity, since Norway and Denmark not only were determined to remain neutral, but were at heart much more in sympathy with the *Entente* cause than with that of the Central Powers.

4. Norway's sympathies for the Entente; *the Anglophil character of Norwegian neutrality.*

Norway gravitated particularly towards England. Her neutrality was never in doubt and had an influence on Stockholm's decision, just as Stockholm had an influence in checking any fancies Christiania may have had for making common cause with England. On 31 July Chevalley, the French Minister at Christiania, telegraphed to Paris information reaching him from a high source that Norway was preparing to defend herself against any possible British attack on Christiansund and German attack on Bergen.[1] And on 1 August Findlay, the British Minister at Christiania, reported: 'The Government has taken the necessary steps to safeguard Norwegian neutrality.'[2] From England there was nothing to be feared, but there seemed some likelihood of an ultimatum from Germany, and, as has been already mentioned,[3] Howard on 3 August reported that 'the Swedish Government is very doubtful whether it can oppose Germany successfully' and 'that whatever line Sweden took Norway must also take'. In view of the extreme importance for England of not having the Germans established on the opposite shore of the North Sea, Grey on 4 August at 10.45 a. m. sent a circular telegram to Brussels, The Hague, and Christiania urging that

if pressure is applied to them by Germany to induce them to depart from their neutrality, His Majesty's Government expect that they will resist by any means in their power, and that His Majesty's Government will support them in offering such resistance, and that His Majesty's Government in this event is prepared to join Russia and France, if desired, in offering to the Government to which you are accredited at once an alliance [corrected to 'common action' by a telegram of 12.30 p. m.] for the purpose of resisting use of force by Germany against them, and a guarantee to maintain their independence and integrity in future years.[4]

A telegram of 4 p. m. revoked these instructions,[5] but in any case Norway had resolved to discharge her duty. At 8 p. m. on 5 August, Chevalley, the French Minister at Christiania, wrote to Paris:

It is possible that a German ultimatum has been today presented to Sweden and announced to Norway,

---

[1] DF. 3. XI, 393.   [2] BD. XI, 434.   [3] See p. 670.
[4] BD. XI, 580. See pp. 491-2.   [5] BD. XI, 593.

but that Ihlen, the Foreign Minister, had declared that
even under German menace, Norway would defend her neutrality.[1]

The Belgian example had found imitators, and her invasion was not calculated to improve the position of Germany in the public opinion of the Scandinavian countries.

Norwegian neutrality was friendly towards England though without outstepping the bounds of neutrality. Would England have liked something more? At 1.45 p. m. on 5 August Grey sent the following telegram to the English Ministers at the Hague and Christiania:

> The Belgian Government have appealed to Great Britain, France, and Russia to co-operate as guarantors in defense of her territory, and His Majesty's Government regard themselves as engaged in common action to uphold the treaty with Belgium and her independence, integrity, and neutrality. His Majesty's Government believe that the issue involves in effect the separate existence in full independence, not only of Belgium, but of other neighboring States. In this issue His Majesty's Government would be glad to join in common action with Netherlands (Norwegian) Government, with the object of securing the full independence, liberty, and integrity of every State that will join in common action to defend itself. His Majesty's Government believe that on the result of this war depends the question whether Great Britain, France, and all the countries bordering on the North Sea shall maintain their existence as before this war.[2]

Grey does not specify in what this 'common action' was to consist. But such a suggestion, thrown out at the moment when Great Britain was entering the war, seems, however restrained its wording, like an appeal for general support, the extent of that support to be determined by the two Chancelleries to which the appeal was addressed. In the case of Norway it took the form of benevolent neutrality, which was rewarded after the war by the gain of the long-coveted Spitzbergen group of islands.

5. *Danish fear of Germany and declaration of neutrality.*

Denmark was even more determined than Norway to remain neutral. Not that the Danish people had the same feelings towards the two camps, but they felt powerless to assert their rights against the German colossus, gladly as they would have done so, since the Schleswig question was still an open wound, aggravated by the harsh Prussian policy of denationalization. Section 5 of the Treaty of Prague of 1866 had laid down: 'The populations of the North Schleswig districts shall again be reunited with Denmark if they manifest the wish by a freely expressed vote.' Twelve years later, in 1878, Prussia struck out this

[1] DF. 3. XI, 768. [2] BD. XI, 656.

paragraph with the consent of Austria, who thus repaid the support received from Bismarck at the Congress of Berlin in the question of Bosnia-Herzegovina.

However, at the outbreak of the war Denmark had no thought of being able to liberate the Schleswig Danes by making common cause with the Triple *Entente*. It would have meant letting herself be invaded, with the hope of salvation at the hands of the victors if Germany were defeated. Intervention on the side of the *Entente* was a course that nobody would have ventured to choose, that nobody asked the Government to take. By remaining neutral the Danes could achieve their desires if, as actually happened, Germany lost the war. Yet their position was no easy one, placed, as they were, between Germany and England and directly threatened by the former in so violent a manner that their radical and pacifist Government, headed by Zahle, treated Germany with the utmost deference for fear of evil consequences. Bapst, the French Minister at Copenhagen, wrote with truth to Paris on 29 July that

in the event of the war having a repercussion in the direction of the Baltic the present Danish Minister would give this neutrality a character clearly favorable to the views of Germany.[1]

And this is what in fact happened.

On 29 July Sir Henry Lowther, the English Minister at Copenhagen, wrote to Grey that Scavenius, the Minister for Foreign Affairs,

informed me that whatever turn events might take, the attitude of Denmark would be one of strict neutrality. His Excellency said that the attitude of Great Britain was of paramount importance to this country, and, provided that the strict neutrality of Great Britain were assured, he did not anticipate trouble for Denmark in the event of a European war. Were the contrary the case the geographical position of Denmark would bring her within the danger zone, which caused some feeling of apprehension.[2]

This apprehension increased when on 29 July Jagow telegraphed to Brockdorff-Rantzau, the German Minister at Copenhagen:

In a European conflagration we have no intention to endanger the integrity of the Danish State. But the fortunes of war might, without our wish or participation, result in an extension of operations to Danish waters. Denmark must realize the seriousness of the situation and come to a decision on the attitude she will adopt in this event.[3]

Thereupon on 31 July the Danish Minister in Berlin, Count G. Moltke, gave a verbal undertaking of benevolent neutrality, and Jagow assured him

[1] DF. 3. XI, 296   [2] BD. XI, 646.   [3] DD. II, 371.

that, so long as Denmark remained neutral and was in a position to do so, we did not intend to include Danish territory and waters in our war operations (provided our opponents did not do so) and that we further did not intend to infringe the integrity of the Danish Kingdom. We advised Denmark to secure her harbors, etc., against occupation by the English or Russian navies.[1]

The anxiety of Copenhagen not to offend Berlin reached such a pitch that on 31 July Scavenius sent Kruse, a Foreign Ministry official, to tell Rantzau that Germany need not be alarmed if Denmark called up about 1,400 men for the navy and 1,300 men for the naval fortifications.[2] Next day the Danish Minister in Berlin handed a note to the Wilhelmstrasse to announce that his Government was about to call up 10,000-15,000 men to put the Danish army on a footing equal to the peace strength of other Powers, but would, as Brockdorff-Rantzau had suggested, wait to do so until mobilization had been proclaimed in Germany, although the military authorities desired it to be done immediately.[3] And when the Minister of War, the well-known anti-militarist Munch, yielded to the military authorities' demand for the call-up of another 18,000 men, Scavenius instructed the Minister to convey his excuses to Berlin,[4] where, despite the Danish assurances, a certain amount of trepidation was felt. To the dispatch of 1 August the Kaiser wrote the marginal comment: 'The next proof (*Beweis*) will be the crossing of our frontier',[5] fearing no doubt that England would egg on Denmark to seize the occasion to recover Schleswig. However, on 4 August Rantzau wrote from Copenhagen:

Contrary to current rumors that English assurances have been given to Denmark in the event of war with Germany, M. de Scavenius declares with absolute definiteness that neither by England nor by Russia has any such *démarche* yet been made.[6]

And when Denmark proclaimed her neutrality on 4 August Rantzau reported:

General mobilization, which was expected here, is still withheld by the Government in spite of strong current demanding it for the protection of the country and the maintenance of neutrality.[7]

Finally, when England intervened in the war, Denmark acceded to the German request to close the Great Belt and the Sound by mines, although by international agreements the seaways were always to be left open to traffic. In 1907 the British Government had declared that any closure would be a breach of neutrality, but now it registered no protest, partly

[1] DD. III, 494, 662.   [2] DD. III, 532.   [3] DD. III, 560.
[4] DD. III, 616, 724.   [5] DD. III, 616.   [6] DD. IV, 846.
[7] DD. IV, 855.

perhaps because it knew that the Germans intended to mine some of the Danish waters. The closing of the straits, especially of the Great Belt, was, as Guy-Charles Cros writes,

of fundamental importance to Germany, who feared a British naval attack on her naval base at Kiel, and it is highly probable, if not certain, that in the event of a refusal the Germans would have taken matters into their own hands, since, as Bethmann Hollweg had declared in connection with the violation of Belgian neutrality, 'necessity knows no law'.[1]

This danger was averted by the prudence of the Government, which firmly rejected the pressure of public opinion, in the main hostile to Germany. Neutrality was skilfully maintained throughout the war, during which, in view of the *Entente's* need to keep the seaways open, Denmark might well have suffered the fate of Greece. But once Germany was defeated national fervor broke all bounds. At the Peace Conference Denmark asked and obtained that the fate of Schleswig should be decided by a plebiscite, which in 1920 resulted in the return of North Schleswig to Denmark.

6. The Dutch Government's firm stand towards Germany.

The Dutch attitude towards Germany showed greater firmness. Paul Herre in his article on *Die mitteleuropäischen Staaten* and their attitude in the July crisis writes that the attitude of Holland was dictated by hostility towards Belgium as a rival and by the calculation that in the event of war not Holland but Belgium would be threatened, hence it would be best to leave her to face the danger alone.[2] This was, however, not the case.

Leaving apart the bloodshed which had marked the separation between Holland and Belgium in 1830-1 and the estrangement of Holland from England and France resulting from this event, serious ill-feeling had arisen in 1909 over the fortification of Flushing. The Dutch Government was then accused of wanting to close the Scheldt in time of war in order to prevent the British from going to Antwerp in support of Belgium in the event of her invasion by Germany. It seemed as if Holland were obeying injunctions from Germany, since the Kaiser was known to be dissatisfied with the state of Dutch coastal defenses. Grey, however, was not disquieted He wrote on n October 1909 that 'the Dutch fear Germany much more than us' and that 'Holland must prove to Germany that she can prevent her country being seized by us and used as a base against Germany'.[3] Moreover, Belgium had other

---

[1] 'La question du Slesvig de 1914 à 1919', in *Revue d'histoire de la guerre mondiale* (Paris), January 1928, p. 35.
[2] Paul Herre, KSF., July 1933, p. 677.
[3] BD. VIII, Grey's minute to 539.

harbors in which the English could land. Thus, though Holland rigidly upheld her sovereignty over the Scheldt and refused to consider projects which would have been of benefit to Antwerp, the two Governments, if not the two peoples, had long since buried the resentments left by separation of 1830-1, and in 1914 were on terms of intimacy and mutual trust.[1]

When the threat of war became manifest the Dutch Foreign Minister, Loudon, though expressing optimism in conversations with the English and French Ministers,[2] vainly sought, as has already been said, to approach the Belgian Government with a view to concerted action. On 27 July, Fallon, the Belgian Minister at The Hague, reported to Brussels that Loudon had asked him what steps were being taken by Belgium to meet the threat of a European war, saying:

> You will understand that we are in the same position. We are equally threatened, for a German army might try to pass through Dutch Limburg in order to cross Belgium and yet avoid the Liége forts. Our defense should be a joint one. It would be advisable that the Minister of War should from now on be kept informed of the measures decreed in Brussels to meet the grave events which are threatening.[3]

These words reveal that Holland anticipated a German invasion of Belgium and felt by no means sure that she herself would be spared.[4] But in July 1914, though not less in the dark than Belgium as to Germany's real intentions, the Dutch Government displayed greater awareness and determination to resist any violation of its neutrality than did the Government of Belgium. In the days following the 27th Loudon several times pressed the Belgian Government for an answer to his inquiry, pointing out that it was to the Belgian interest to concert with Holland, who was heartily willing to co-operate, and naming the steps which Holland was prepared to take in her own defense. It is not clear whether Loudon would have gone so far as to offer Belgium Dutch support, even if he had known that Germany did not mean to attack Holland, but it is hardly likely. As far back as 19 October 1910 the then Dutch Foreign Minister, van Swinderen, had assured Buchanan:

> As regards the question of a close understanding with Belgium ... the Netherlands would never consent to anything in the shape of a political or military *entente*.[5]

Holland clearly ran much less risk of invasion than Belgium and did not wish to lose the advantages of her less exposed position. This does not mean that Davignon should not at once have grasped the helping

---

[1] Wullus-Rudiger, p. 180.   [2] BD. XI. 195; DF. 3. XI, 140.
[3] See p. 445.   [4] See pp. 238-40.   [6] BD. XI, 571.

hand held out to him, but instead of doing so he did not even mention the offer to the Belgian Chief of Staff or see Loudon again until 3 August when Brussels was in the throes of disaster while The Hague was sure of not being attacked.[1]

However, before having this assurance the Dutch Government rightly took alarm and prepared with the utmost energy to defend the country and resist invasion. Between 28 July and 3 August a series of measures of all kinds was reported to London by Chilton and to Paris by Pellet. On 31 July all classes of army and navy reservists were called up and all regiments were at full strength.[2] On 2 August Chilton reported

that Dutch troops on the German frontier are being heavily reinforced and that they will fire on the Germans the moment they cross.[3]

On the 3rd he wired that all available troops were being moved to the province of Limburg.[4]

But the need for action never arose. On 30 July Jagow sent Müller, the German Minister at The Hague, a sealed envelope containing a copy of the ultimatum to Belgium; on 2 August he laid down the lines on which Müller was to justify the invasion of Luxemburg. A quarter of an hour later he again telegraphed instructing Müller to open the sealed envelope and notify the Dutch Government of the German ultimatum to Belgium, pretending that all instructions relating to this matter had only just reached him. Müller was further to say that the German Government definitely reckoned on the Netherlands observing benevolent neutrality towards Germany. 'On this condition the neutrality of the Netherlands will be fully respected by Germany.'[5] Half an hour later Jagow, hoping to produce an impression at The Hague as well as at Brussels, dished up the story of the eighty French officers in Prussian uniforms crossing the German frontier at Walbeck in twelve motor cars. 'This constitutes a most serious breach of neutrality on the part of France.'[6]

7. German assurances at The Hague; Dutch neutrality.

At 9 a. m. on 3 August Müller executed his instructions. Loudon thanked him for the communication 'without pronouncing himself for the time being' and promised to look into the affair of the eighty officers.[7] Berlin, which received this telegram at 1.37 p. m., must have felt uneasy about the Dutch attitude, for a memorandum sent by the General Staff to the Wilhelmstrasse on 1 August contains the statement:

---

[1] Selliers de Moranville, pp. 126-9.   [2] DF. 3. XI, 422; BD. XI, 375.
[3] BD. XI, 478.   [4] BD. XI, 527.
[5] DD. II, 426; III, 671, 674.   [6] DD. III, 677. See p. 463.
[7] DD. IV, 738.

Holland is forced by England to take the side of the Triple *Entente.* Mobilization of army, home guard and navy has been ordered.[1]

Not until 1.17 a. m. on 4 August did Müller's next telegram reach Berlin with the news:

The Minister for Foreign Affairs this afternoon [3 August] made the statement that the Netherlands would on principle strictly maintain neutrality towards all quarters. The Netherlands Government relies unconditionally on Germany's not infringing Dutch neutrality in any way. (Kaiser: We don't mean to.)

Müller added that the Dutch Government had no knowledge of the affair of the eighty French officers.[2]

The wording of the telegram implies that Loudon's statement was not made personally to Müller but sent as a message. In any case his attitude was dignified and betrayed nothing of the relief that he must have felt on learning that Holland was not to share the fate of Belgium. The sense of relief resulted in the strictest observance of neutrality, so that when on 3 August, after the delivery of the ultimatum at Brussels, the Belgian Minister asked Loudon to allow General Leman, commanding the fortress of Liége, to consult with the Governor of Maestricht, Loudon evaded the request.[3] Once the war had begun, the German Government on its side gave its word of honor scrupulously to respect Dutch neutrality.[4]

It is of interest to note that neither on 3 nor on 4 August did Loudon vouchsafe information to the *Entente* representatives at The Hague of Müller's statement and the reply made to it, and this despite the fact that the press of 3 August was alleging that Holland, too, had received an ultimatum. The silence of 3 August was followed on the 4th by a statement to Chilton:

'Chef de Cabinet' at Ministry for Foreign Affairs told me this morning that German Government had not presented an ultimatum respecting neutrality to Netherlands Government, as reported in yesterday's papers. If they do, Netherlands Government will give same reply as Belgian Government have given.[5]

Why was there no word of the fact that twenty-four hours earlier Berlin had engaged to respect Dutch neutrality? And why the same silence with the French Minister?[6] The result of this strange behavior was that London on 4 August was still in ignorance of the fact that Dutch neutrality was not to be violated. It may be objected that

[1] DD. III, 609.
[2] See p. 446
[5] BD. XI, 604.
[2] DD. IV, 797.
[3] Herre, KSF., July 1933, p. 678.
[6] DF. 3 XI, 739.

Bethmann Hollweg's notorious statement to Goschen late on 29 July contained the promise:

We shall respect the neutrality and integrity of Holland as long as it is respected by our opponents.[1]

This undertaking postulated British neutrality, failing which it would not be binding. Feeling anxious on this point Grey on the morning of 4 August sent the British Minister at The Hague the same telegram as had been dispatched to Brussels and Christiania urging them to resist any German pressure to depart from neutrality by any means in their power and offering an alliance with the Triple *Entente?*

Chilton executed his instructions in the afternoon of 4 August before receiving the telegram canceling them.[3] Only then did Loudon break his silence

to tell you that he has received a formal assurance from the German Government that they will not violate neutrality of Netherlands if Netherlands maintain their present neutral attitude.

On returning to revoke his instructions, Chilton saw the Chef de Cabinet, 'who said he regretted communication must be cancelled, as it was an agreeable one'.[4] That same day the Netherlands Minister in London informed Grey

that Germany had given a most satisfactory assurance as regards Dutch neutrality. . . . I said that I had thought of making a proposal to them, in case Germany should put pressure on them to depart from an attitude of neutrality. As this contingency had not arisen, I need say nothing more at present.[5]

It is not clear whether Grey perhaps withdrew his proposal after learning that Holland would be respected. At any rate, perhaps on second thoughts, he sent to the Governments at Christiania and The Hague on 5 August the appeal 'to join in common action . . . with the object of securing the full independence, liberty, and integrity of every State that will join in common action to defend itself'.[6]

Further reactions in Holland were similar to those of Norway. Herre remarks:

Only a small group of discerning men showed understanding for the position in which the unpopular neighboring nation found itself in the great struggle. The great majority [of the Dutch people] sympathized more or less openly with the *Entente.* The old mistrust of Germany received fresh sustenance from the violation of Belgian neutrality.[7]

[1] DD. II, 373; BD. XI, 293. See Vol. I, pp. 506-7.
[2] BD. XI, 580. See pp. 491-2.   [3] BD. XI, 593. See p. 492.
[4] BD. XI, 632.   [5] BD. XI, 639.
[6] BD. XI, 656. See p. 673.   [7] Herre, KSF., July 1933, p. 678.

8. *The German invasion of Luxemburg.*

The Grand Duchy of Luxemburg had been created by the Congress of Vienna and, although part of the Germanic Confederation, was placed under the sovereignty of King William I of Holland. In 1831 after Belgium had broken away from Holland the Grand Duchy was divided into two parts. The larger, western part was joined to Belgium. The other part, which spoke a German dialect, remained a Grand Duchy with William I as its ruler and in 1842 became a member of the German *Zollverein*. When William III of Holland was on the point of ceding his rights to Napoleon III and war between France and Germany was threatening, the Powers intervened and by the Treaty of London of 11 May 1867 collectively guaranteed the neutrality of the Grand Duchy, which, while remaining a member of the German *Zollverein*, became independent. At the death of William III in 1890 the personal union between the Kingdom of Holland and the Grand Duchy came to an end, and the new Grand Duke belonged to the House of Nassau.

Schlieffen did not hesitate a moment to include the Grand Duchy in his plan of campaign, brushing aside the obstacle of its neutrality. In his opinion the violation of the Grand Duchy would not give rise to more than platonic protests. Joffre foresaw this danger and regarded Luxemburg as a vassal state of Germany. Hence on 9 January 1912 he had the following questions raised at a meeting of the French Council of National Defence:

At the first news of the violation of Belgian territory by the Germans, may our armies penetrate Belgian territory? Have they the right to disregard the neutrality of Luxemburg?

The Council replied unanimously in the affirmative.[1] But the little country seemed unconscious of the danger overhanging it on both sides. It was quite powerless to resist its two strong neighbors, least of all its German friends.

At the outbreak of the crisis Eyschen, the Prime Minister of the Luxemburg Government, was at Évian-les-Bains and decided to return to his post only in the night of 29/30 July. In the forenoon of 31 July he called at the French and German Legations to ask for an assurance that their respective Governments would issue an official declaration pledging themselves to respect Luxemburg neutrality.[2] That same day he sent a protest to the Wilhelmstrasse against the cutting off of food supplies and other necessities from Germany despite the Grand Duchy's membership of the *Zollverein*.[3] On 1 August he telegraphed to Jagow

---

[1] Joffre 1, pp. 47–8. [2] DF. 3. XI, 407: DD. III, 486. See p. 202.
[3] DD. III, 511.

that Prussian officers and other ranks had that day occupied the Luxemburg station of Ulflingen and torn up the railway track. He assumed
that there had been some mistake and expected an apology but pressed
all the more for a statement that Luxemburg neutrality would be
respected so long as it was not infringed by another Power. On
2 August he told Buch that the German officers and other ranks had
been fetched away from Ulflingen in cars by Germans who said the
whole thing was a mistake.[1]

We know that this was not so. The German mobilization order
signed in Berlin at 5 p. m. on 1 August signaled the immediate beginning of operations among which figured the occupation of Luxemburg
by the German 16th Division. Thus the officers and men who about
7 p. m. on the 1st had occupied Ulflingen station were acting under
orders and preparing for the invasion. But when it seemed that England
was going to remain neutral if Germany did not attack France, Wilhelm
without Moltke's consent had telegraphed to the 16th Division not to
enter Luxemburg.[2] It was certainly the receipt of this order, when the
16th Division was already on the move, that led to the evacuation of
Ulflingen station. As soon as the misunderstanding as to the English
attitude was cleared up Wilhelm sent for Moltke in the middle of the
night and promised to follow the lines laid down by the General Staff.
It was Moltke who then telegraphed to the 16th Division to advance
according to plan.[3]

On the morning of 2 August Eyschen realized that the invasion had
begun on a large scale. He protested to Buch, telegraphed two protests
directly to Berlin, and had a further protest telegraphed to the Kaiser
by the Grand Duchess Marie Adelheid.[4] These telegrams crossed with
one from Bethmann Hollweg to Buch saying that it was a question
'purely of measures for the security of the Luxemburg railways under
our management against French attack'.[5] This was not the pretext
Moltke wanted to have put forward, as is clear from a draft for a note
to Luxemburg dictated by him on 2 August, and used by Jagow as
the basis of his reply to Eyschen at 2.10 p. m. on 2 August:[6]

> The military measures have to our great regret been rendered necessary by the
> fact that according to reliable information French forces are advancing on Luxemburg.
> We had to take the measures for the protection of our army and the security of the
> railways. . . . Unfortunately, in view of the imminent danger there was no time for
> previous consultation with the Luxemburg Government.[7]

Moltke's draft had contained the offer of a guarantee

---

[1] DD. III, 602, 606, 619.   [2] See p. 176.   [3] See pp. 177-8.
[4] DD. III, 637, 638, 644, 647.   [5] DD. III, 640.   [6] DD. III, 639.
[7] DD. III, 649. See p. 203.

that if Luxemburg on its part did not carry out hostile acts against Germany or her troops, the Luxemburg State will be unconditionally confirmed in its present integrity on the conclusion of peace.

But Jagow pared this down to an assurance of 'full compensation for the damage caused by us'.

The commander of the German 8th Army Corps, General Tulff von Tscheepe und Weidenbach, on 3 August posted up notices printed in Koblentz in French and German saying:

France, having violated the neutrality of Luxemburg, has opened hostilities from Luxemburg soil against German troops, as has been ascertained beyond doubt.[1]

Here once more recurs the device of attributing responsibility for the war to the other side. But none knew better than Eyschen that the statement was false, and on the morning of 3 August he telegraphed to Bethmann Hollweg and Jagow:

This is based on an error. On Luxemburg soil absolutely no French forces are present, nor is there any sign whatever of a threat to neutrality on the part of France. On the contrary, on Saturday evening, 1 August, the railway track on French soil was torn up near Mont Saint Martin Longwy.[2]

The Germans did not confine themselves to occupying railways. They carried out a full-scale invasion, requisitioning motor- and horse-drawn vehicles and supplies, and placing the whole country under martial law.[3] General Fuchs, commanding the 16th Division, had orders to arrest certain high officials, but before doing so asked confirmation of his orders from Berlin[4] and also instructions what to do about the French Minister, Mollard, who had not yet left.[5] Receiving no reply, he had Mollard sent to the frontier on 4 August.[6] It was Eyschen himself who at 8.30 a. m. notified Mollard of the German demand for his expulsion. Mollard left at 2.15 p. m. and reached Paris in his own car on 5 August. Similar treatment was meted out to the Belgian Minister.

On the morning of 2 August Mollard had notified Viviani of the violation of Luxemburg neutrality,[7] and Viviani had at once passed on the news to London.[8] We have seen how Paul Cambon hastily procured a copy of the 1867 treaty and called on Grey with it, expecting the news of the violation to make a great impression on him. We have further seen how Grey had replied that what Luxemburg had was a collective guarantee; that no one of the signatory Powers had an obligation to defend Luxemburg unless all the signatory Powers did so; that no Power had an obligation to act separately and without the

[1] DF. 3. XI, 709, annex 1.   [2] DD. III, 730.   [3] DF. 3. XI, 709
[4] DD. III, 684.   [5] DD. IV, 787.   [6] DD. IV, 842.
[7] DF. 3. XI, 560.   [8] DF. 3. XI, 563.

others; that the Luxemburg obligation was as slight as the Belgian was formidable; that England could if she wished make the German invasion a reason for going to war, but it was not an obligation. We have seen, too, the storm of indignation these arguments aroused in Paul Cambon.[1]

What still has to be seen is how far the indignation of the French Government was sincere and legitimate. It is a fact that when at 5.15 p. m. on 31 July Paris learnt of Eyschen's request to Mollard for an assurance that France would not violate Luxemburg neutrality, the French Government did not immediately reply. It almost seems as if Joffre hesitated to give the undertaking, for Viviani waited until German troops had invaded Luxemburg before telegraphing to Mollard at 4.20 p. m. on 2 August:

> Kindly declare to the President of the Council that in conformity with the Treaty of London of 1867 the French Government intended to respect the neutrality of the Grand Duchy of Luxemburg as it has shown by its attitude. However, the violation of this neutrality by Germany is of a nature to oblige France henceforward to let herself be guided in regard to this by the consideration of her defense and her own interests.[2]

This telegram reached Mollard only at 7.55 p. m. on 3 August.[3] The French declaration did not fully satisfy Luxemburg. On 4 August Eyschen replied:

> Permit me to remark that the French Government's decision is based solely on the deed of a third Power for which the Grand Duchy was assuredly not responsible. Consequently the rights of Luxemburg must remain intact. The German Empire has formally declared that only a temporary occupation of Luxemburg was in its intention.[4]

This makes it clear that the Luxemburg Government had fully acquiesced in the *fait accompli* and was solely concerned with preventing a clash between the combatants on its own territory. Eyschen sent no further protest to Berlin, nor did he recall the Luxemburg Minister, and his passivity was approved by the Chamber of Deputies on 3 August. Herre maintains that:

> Sympathies and antipathies played no part in this attitude; it would scarcely have been different if France had been the first to infringe neutrality.

But he, himself, provides the reason for doubting this assertion by adding:

---

[1] See pp. 401, 407. Eyschen notified Grey and Viviani of his protest to Berlin and Jagow's reply. Grey answered: 'The serious matters to which they allude will engage the earnest attention of His Majesty's Government' (BD. XI, 466, 467, 554; DF. 3. XI, 565, 588, 709).

[2] DF. 3. XI, 591.   [3] DF. 3. XI, 710.   [4] DF. 3. XI, 769, annex 1.

The decisive factor was the economic and financial connections with Germany. This explains the willingness to accept not only the invasion but also the four years of German occupation on a footing of friendly relations with the German authorities and troops. It is unjustified to attribute the responsibility to the Grand Duchess's German origins or the pro-German sympathies of the Minister of State. Their attitude was shared by the Luxemburg population, which allowed the German troops to invade without hostility, even to some extent welcoming them with joy.[1]

9. *Tie neutrality of Switzerland.*

Neutrality had always been the fundamental principle of Switzerland in international relations. After the short-lived Napoleonic domination, her neutrality was guaranteed by the Powers who by the Declaration of Paris of 20 November 1815 affirmed that 'the neutrality and inviolability of Switzerland and her independence of all foreign influence respond to the true interests of Europe'. To defend herself against any possible violation the Swiss Confederation had created a highly efficient army capable of acting as a deterrent even to any great Power which might seek to attack it or traverse its territory. But after 1870 German influence and a German spirit had gained ground in the little country, seventy-five percent of whose population was of Teutonic language, to the extent of raising doubts as to whether in the event of war it would maintain its neutrality.

On this subject Colonel Delmé-Radcliffe, British Military Attaché at Rome and Berne, a witness whose good faith is above suspicion, sent the War Office a lengthy memorandum on 17 November 1909. In this monograph the question is raised:

Is Switzerland now disposed to defend, to the very utmost and against everybody, her neutrality? . . . I now think the real truth to be that Switzerland has become so permeated with German sentiment that she is ceasing to be a separate nation, except in the political sense. . . . The feeling of the bulk of the population for Italy is distinctly unfriendly. . . . To the outsider the grounds for this extreme contempt and hostility of the Swiss towards the Italians appear insufficient. . . . To an impartial foreign observer it would appear that if any country is animated with entirely peaceful intentions towards another it is Italy in regard to Switzerland. . . . Were Italy regarded by Germany and Austria as an integral portion of the Triple Alliance, and as a nation entitled to full consideration as an ally, it is inconceivable that Switzerland should have been induced to regard her with so much suspicion. . . . A deep-rooted bitterness against France is still extant . . . The existing Swiss fortifications are directed exclusively against France and Italy. . . . How thoroughly the Swiss are preparing themselves for the eventuality of having to fight France or Italy innumerable facts tend to show.[2]

[1] Herre, KSF., February 1934, p. 154.
[2] BD. VIII, 335.

In a further memorandum of 17 September 1901 Colonel Delmé-Radcliffe writes of Austro-Swiss Staff talks in which a part was played by a map containing 'a line representing the "rectification" of the Swiss frontier' with Italy.[1] And on 21 February 1911 he reported a conversation with General Pollio, the Italian Chief of Staff:

> The day before yesterday, after lunch at my house. . . . His Excellency, who was formerly Military Attaché at Vienna, said that he had habitually looked upon it as a fundamental axiom that Switzerland had no desire but to maintain her neutrality. . . . . But all the evidence . . . especially since he himself had been appointed Chief of the General Staff, had forced him most reluctantly . . . to the conclusion that an entirely different situation must now be faced. . . . He said that it was infamous that Switzerland should show such hostility towards Italy. . . . 'Italy is the most pacific country on the face of the globe, and I give you my word of honor that no responsible statesman in Italy wishes to annex even a hand's breadth of Swiss or Austrian territory.'[2]

The minutes appended to these reports by Crowe and Grey show that they were regarded as being of unusual interest and were communicated by Grey to the French Government. In April 1911 echoes of French and English perturbation reached the ears of Ruchet, the President of the Swiss Confederation, who gave the most formal assurance that no military understanding existed between Switzerland and any of her neighbors.[3] In actual fact all that Conrad had obtained from the Swiss, as he relates in his memoirs, was the assurance that they would not allow the Italians to enter Swiss territory to turn the Stelvio position by taking the road through the Tauferer valley.[4] This fact was alluded to by Delmé-Radcliffe, who added that the Italian Government had thoughts of asking Berne for an equivalent assurance in respect of Austria, but did not do so. 'The reason for not asking for it is not known. It may have been timidity.'[5]

To form an opinion as to the value of Colonel Delmé-Radcliffe's observations let us first look at the line taken by Switzerland in the crisis of July 1914.

The danger of a general conflagration could not but cause her the greatest anxiety. The country depended on imports for its grain, coal and other products of basic necessity. How could it hold out in a war of any length, and what would be the repercussions of such a war on its three linguistic communities, whose sympathies would be drawn in divergent directions towards those of their own tongue among the belligerents? On 27 July the Swiss Minister, Carlin, called on Nicolson

---

[1] BD. VIII, 341.   [2] BD. VIII, 344.
[3] Wullus-Rudiger, p. T84.   [4] Conrad, I, p. 206.
                    [5] BD. VIII, 335.

to say that his Government had telegraphed in regard to the situation, being extremely anxious as to the position of Switzerland in the event of the European conflict. . . . M. Carlin observed that the Serbian Government seemed to have conceded practically all the Austrian demands.[1]

This was the view taken by the whole Swiss press, which pointed out that the key to the situation was in the hands of Germany. On the evening of 31 July, when the situation was seen to be desperate, Lardy, the Swiss Minister in Paris, asked the Federal Government's permission, which was at once granted, to report to the French Government what he had been told by the Romanian Minister, Lahovary. Dining with Lahovary at their club, the Austrian Minister Szécsen had intimated to him

that if a friend of Serbia, France for example, were in the name of Serbia to ask for the Austrian terms, there would be chances that Vienna would reply.[2]

But by that time the situation was beyond repair.

However, as Grant Duff wrote to Grey on 29 July:

There is, I think, no question that this country will strictly maintain her neutrality, but any infringement of her frontier will be met with armed force.[3]

In fact, as soon as the news arrived on the afternoon of 31 July that Germany had declared the *Kriegsgefahrzustand,* the Swiss Federal Council decided to mobilize. The relevant decree was signed on 1 August and messages were sent to Paris and Berlin stating:

The sole object of this measure is the maintenance of Swiss integrity and neutrality. . . . A formal declaration of neutrality will be sent later.[4]

On 3 August the Federal Assembly approved the measures taken by the Federal Council, granting it full powers and unlimited credit. The command of the army was entrusted to Colonel Wille as the senior corps commander. Neutrality was proclaimed on 4 August.[5]

It was in no danger of violation because Germany, the only Power which would have thought of violating it, was conducting her operations via Belgium. On 2 August the Swiss Government complained to Romberg, the German Minister at Berne, that Uhlan patrols had made use of a Swiss road, on the pretext that it was an international highway. But Zimmerman hastened to proffer apologies and assurances that the mistake would not recur.[6] In Jagow's circular telegram of 3 August giving the German pretexts for invading Belgium, the copy sent to Berne carried the special instruction: 'and renew the assurance of the strictest respect for Swiss neutrality'. The original bears the marginal

---

[1] BD. XI, 172.
[2] DF. 3. XI, 503. See pp. 92-7.
[3] BD. XI, 324.
[4] DF. 3. XI, 429, 501; DD. III, 589.
[5] DF. 3. XI, 735.
[6] DD. III, 681, 70T.

note in Rosenberg's hand: 'The Chief of the General Staff agrees.'[1] On the morning of 3 August Romberg carried oat these instructions, whereat Beau, the French Minister at Berne, wrote to Paris: 'I know that a similar declaration is expected of the French Government', an assurance which Viviani hastened that same day to give.[2]

There were two points on which there existed the possibility of complications between the two countries. The Congress of Vienna had, within the terms of Swiss neutrality, also neutralized that part of Savoy south of the Lake of Geneva belonging to the Kingdom of Sardinia and had laid down that in case of war the area was to be occupied by Switzerland. This territory had passed to France, and when the declaration of Swiss neutrality was communicated to her, she made reservations on the right of Switzerland to occupy them. But since the Berne Government made no use of this right, all went smoothly. The other possible complication might have arisen if the Germans had wanted in case of war to use the Baden Station in Bâle. However, France received assurances that Switzerland would oppose its use with all her forces, and the Germans in any case felt no need to use it, since they were intending to pass through Belgium.[3]

Swiss neutrality was maintained throughout the war and was not endangered by the intervention of Italy in 1915, although this added to Swiss difficulties. What has been said here would seem to show that the fears of the English Military Attaché, though shared by General Pollio and—it must be added—by the Italian Government and well-informed Italian public opinion, were devoid of foundation. In reality they were well founded in respect of the Swiss army chiefs but not of the political leaders, and it was public opinion which had the last word. As regards the army chiefs there is no doubt that by their origins, their views, their training and general attitude they might well warrant serious doubts. Delmé-Radcliffe had remarked that:

> Colonel Corps-Commandant Wille, Commander of the 3rd Army Corps, the man who, in the event of war, would certainly be appointed general and commander-in-chief of the Swiss army, comes of a Hamburg family, and is a naturalized, not a born Swiss. His wife was a Countess Bismarck, a niece of the Chancellor's. . . . The pro-German influence of such a man can be easily understood. Another example is the Chief of the General Staff, Divisional-Colonel von Sprecher-Bemegg. This man comes from the Graubünden, where he has a property. He has many relations in the Austrian army, including a brother who is a general.

How these Swiss military circles understood neutrality is shown in an article published in the French-Swiss *Revue Militaire Suisse* which states:

---

[1] DD. III, 703.   [2] DF. 3. XI, 654, 684.
[3] Herre, KSF. March 1934, pp. 296-7.

If anxiety on behalf of our independence obliges us to declare ourselves on one side or another in an international quarrel, and counsels us to act defensively against one or other of our neighbors, we are absolutely within our rights by international law to take such action.[1]

This theory would have made it very easy to cast neutrality aside, and it is by no means sure that the General Staff would not have done so, had it been possible. The 'Two Colonels' scandal, which broke out at the end of 1915 and beginning of 1916, gives grounds for thinking this. At that time it was brought to light that Colonel Egli, the second in command of the General Staff, and Colonel Wattenwyl, head of one of the principal services of the General Staff, were regularly sending official and other information from Swiss sources to the German Military Attaché, Busso von Bismarck. Further, they got their cipher clerk, Langie, at first without his suspecting it, to work for Germany.[2] This scandal confirmed the fears of the Italian General Staff. Cadorna writes that 'we could fully rely on the straightforwardness of the Federal Government' about which 'no doubt could possibly arise', since it was clearly to the interest of the Swiss Confederation to make its neutrality respected. But 'we could not feel the same confidence in the army chiefs'. As the great majority of them were German Swiss 'was it not to be feared that an instinctive sympathy for the cause of the Central Powers might perhaps even lead them to force the hand of the Federal Government?' All the more so since General Wille's relations with Germany and those of Colonel Sprecher with Austria were common knowledge, and since the 'Two Colonels' scandal . . . 'was not of a nature to dispel suspicions and inspire tranquility'. Cadorna goes on:

In the light of facts all these anxieties were later to prove devoid of foundation and the attitude of Switzerland throughout the war was irreproachable. Nevertheless, at the time these anxieties loomed large and weighed continually like an incubus during the development of operations. They made it necessary all the time to have in mind the possibility of Swiss neutrality being violated and to consider measures to meet the eventuality, especially as, though remote, it would, had it materialized, have placed the whole army suddenly in extreme danger.[3]

It is not our concern here to enter into details of the precautions taken by the Italian High Command to meet the danger, nor into the story of Federal Councilor Hoffmann, who in 1917 tried to bring Germany and Russia to make peace. The neutrality maintained by the Swiss Government and people throughout the war redounds to their

[1] BD. VIII, 335.
[2] Wullus-Rudiger, p. 185.
[3] Luigi Cadorna, *Altre pagine sulla grande guerra* (Milan, 1925), pp. 29-32.

honor and shows how great an advantage the existence of the Swiss Confederation is to the States surrounding it and to the peace of Europe.

10. *The ancient ties of alliance between England and Portugal; Lisbon's solidarity with London.*

The Anglo-Portuguese alliance dates back to the fourteenth century, with special confirmation on 14 October 1899 of certain articles of treaties of 1642 and 1661.[1] Such a tie left no doubt as to what would be the attitude of the Lisbon Government. On 1 August the Portuguese Prime Minister told German pressmen that 'there was no doubt that Portugal would discharge her obligations towards England under the alliance'.[2] But the Government was itself not quite sure of the extent of its obligations, and so on 1 August Freire de Andrade, the Foreign Minister, telegraphed to Teixeira Gomes, the Portuguese Minister in London, instructing him to inquire at the Foreign Office 'about our attitude in view of our direct obligations resulting from treaties with Great Britain' and whether 'for the enemy we can be regarded as allies of Great Britain'.[3] Next day Andrade pressed for a reply to the question. It was necessary 'to declare our attitude, which I know we should desire to be one of neutrality, but I cannot declare it without knowing whether England, to whom we are bound by treaties, does not desire some different manifestation from us'.[4]

Similarly on 3 August the Foreign Minister told the Austrian Minister that Portugal hoped to remain neutral, but that she had an alliance with Great Britain which she would not ignore.[5] On 3 August Gomes received a note from Sir Eyre Crowe:

I am authorized by Sir Edward Grey to say that H.M. Government would earnestly beg the Portuguese Government to defer for the present issuing any declaration of neutrality.[6]

And on 4 August Grey telegraphed in the same sense to Sir Lancelot Carnegie.[7]

But Lisbon was impatient to reach a decision and on 4 August the Prime Minister, speaking in the name of the President of the Republic, requested Carnegie 'to assure His Majesty's Government of Portugal's intention and desire to act in complete co-operation with Great Britain in whatever course the latter may adopt'.[8] On the same day Grey telegraphed to Carnegie that

---

[1] BD. I, 118.   [2] DD. III, 617.
[3] *Livro Branco, Portugal no conflito europeu* (Lisbon, 1920), 1.
[4] *Livro Branco*, 2.   [5] BD. XI, 565.
[6] *Livro Branco*, 5.   [7] BD. XI, 590.
[8] BD. XI, 601.

in case of attack by Germany on any Portuguese possession, His Majesty's Government will consider themselves bound by the stipulations of the Anglo-Portuguese Alliance. For the present His Majesty's Government would be satisfied if the Portuguese Government refrained from proclaiming neutrality.[1]

The Portuguese Government accordingly confined itself to not declaring neutrality, while the press and public opinion were in favor of war. On 7 August the Senate and Chamber approved the line taken by the Government, voting it full powers and proclaiming their solidarity with England.[2] Before the year was out Portuguese troops were operating against the Germans in Africa. But it was not until 9 March 1916 that Germany declared war on Portugal on the ground that at the request of England she had sequestered thirty-six German vessels anchored in the Tagus.

11. The neutrality of Spain.

In the collections of diplomatic documents on the origins of the war the attitude of Spain remains in obscurity. The *Documents Diplomatiques Français* contain only three documents relating to Spain. The *Deutsche Dokumente* have but one. It seems as if the indifference of Spain towards what went on in Europe was matched by the indifference of the belligerent States towards the attitude of Madrid, and that the Triple Alliance, like the Triple *Entente,* knowing the military weakness and pacific tendencies of the Spanish, felt only a faint interest in a country which from the outset seemed securely neutral. In a report sent to Paris on 27 July Mathieu de Vienne, the French Chargé d'Affaires at Madrid, remarked that 'foreign policy counts very little in the day-to-day preoccupations of most people; . . . there is perhaps not another country in Europe which concerns itself less with its neighbors'. The Prime Minister, Dato, advised a group of Spanish journalists 'that in your articles you should make a point of calming opinion and explaining to the public how far removed we are from the international cataclysms that are being so glibly announced'. Only a few journals commented on the crisis. The *Diario Universal,* the organ of the former Prime Minister, Romanones, made a simple allusion to 'consequences so remote for the moment that there is no need to speak of them'. The opposition paper *Tribuna* made the crisis an occasion for attacking the Government: 'Really anything may be feared, and the only thing not to be done is exactly what the Cabinet is doing; ignore the whole affair and take no precautions.' The *Liberal* went to the length of putting the blame on Austria, reproaching her with 'her

---

[1] BD. XI, 610.

[2] *Papers Relating to the Foreign Relations of the United States, 1914 Supplement, The World War* (Washington, 1928), pp. 76-7.

selfishness, her hypocrisy, her haughtiness without reason, making her hated by European public opinion'. It poured ridicule on those timid spirits 'who speak of a secret pact with France engaging to throw a hundred thousand men into the fray'.[1]

There was in reality no secret pact between France and Spain, and if Paris had not known Alphonse XIII's sympathies for France and the predominantly pro-French feelings of the Spanish people, there might well have been some anxiety on the part of France about her Pyrenean frontier. But on 1 August the French Ambassador at Madrid reported that the Minister of State had that day renewed the assurances already repeatedly given by the King 'that we might in all security withdraw our forces from our Pyrenean frontier'.[2]

That same day Ratibor, the German Ambassador at Madrid, telegraphed to Berlin: 'the Spanish Minister of State in reply to a question told the Austrian Ambassador that the Spanish Government will maintain absolute neutrality'. To this the Kaiser wrote in the margin: 'Then it must not allow through transport for troops from Morocco.'[3] The Kaiser's marginal note was prompted by a telegram from the German Chargé d'Affaires at Tangiers reporting statements in Casablanca newspapers that 20,000 men were to be held in readiness for embarkation for France.[4] The news was correct, for on 31 July, General Lyautey, the French Resident General in Morocco, had telegraphed to Paris that he could at once dispatch twenty battalions and six mounted batteries, some of them raised in Eastern and Western Morocco. These units could embark between the third and thirteenth day from receipt of sailing orders if the transport vessels arrived in good time. There would then still be forty battalions left in Eastern and Western Morocco.[5] One does not understand what opposition the Kaiser expected from Spain, seeing that the French Government had made no request to the Madrid Government for transport facilities for these troops, who would not have to cross Spanish Morocco or Spain but would embark at Casablanca and Oran direct for France. All that Geoffray had asked of Madrid was that purchases made by private firms on behalf of the French Government should not meet with obstacles.[6]

While the Spanish Government reaffirmed its strict neutrality, King Alfonso XIII made no secret of his sympathies for France. On 4 August, in receiving Geoffray in audience he said he was sorry to be the head of a country too weak to enter the fray.

Having French blood in his veins he followed with admiration the efforts made by the Government of the Republic in its endeavor to assure the maintenance of

---

[1] DF. 3. XI, 174.   [2] DF. 3. XI, 519.   [3] DD. III, 615.
[4] DD. III, 618.   [5] DF. 3. XI, 424.   [6] DF. 3. XI, 519.

peace and the fine patriotic movement which manifested itself on the occasion of the mobilization. King Alfonso XIII added that his Government was about to proclaim the neutrality of Spain but that he would do all in his power to render service to us as far as was possible. He asked me in confidence whether I personally thought that an initiative on his part in favor of peace would have any chance of success. I replied that any overture from the King of Spain would be received with due consideration by the French Government and would be in harmony with the desire, manifested by us many times in these last days, to avoid the shedding of blood; but that I had not many illusions about the reception it would meet with from Germany at the present moment. His Majesty . . . told me in strict confidence that he would try to obtain a suspension of constitutional guarantees from the Government; this would give him a much freer hand. . . . In taking leave of me . . . His Majesty said that France was defending the independence of the Latin nations and hence of Spain.[1]

It is not known whether the King made the request to the Government to suspend the constitutional guarantees. Since no such measure was taken, it must be presumed that, if the King asked for it, the Cabinet refused it. Throughout the war Spain maintained a wary neutrality.

12. *Japan intervenes on the side of the* Entente.

Article I of the Anglo-Japanese alliance, in the revised text of 13 July 1911, laid down:

Whenever, in the opinion of either Great Britain or Japan, any of the rights and interests [in the regions of Eastern Asia and of India] referred to in the preamble of this Agreement are in jeopardy, the two Governments will communicate with one another fully and frankly, and will consider in common the measures which should be taken to safeguard those menaced rights or interests.

Article II ran:

If by reason of unprovoked attack or aggressive action, wherever arising, on the part of any Power or Powers, either High Contracting Party should be involved in war in defense of its territorial rights or special interests [in the regions of Eastern Asia and of India] mentioned in the preamble of this Agreement, the other High Contracting Party will at once come to the assistance of its ally, and will conduct the war in common, and make peace in mutual agreement with it.[2]

On 1 August 1914 Grey wrote in a dispatch to Tokyo:

I told the Japanese Ambassador today that the situation in Europe was very grave. We have not yet decided what our action should be, but under certain conditions we might find it necessary to intervene. If, however, we

---

[1] DF. 3. XI, 746.   [2] BD. VIII, 436.

did intervene, it would be on the side of France and Russia, and I therefore did not see that we were likely to have to apply to Japan under our alliance, or that the interests dealt with by the alliance would be involved.[1]

On the same day Jagow telegraphed to Tokyo from Berlin:

War with Russia will scarcely be avoidable. We are convinced that the Japanese Government with a just appreciation of the great moment will draw the necessary consequences for Japan.[2]

In Moltke's already mentioned memorandum for the Foreign Ministry of 2 August, in which with utter incomprehension of the true situation he disposed of States as if they were pawns in a game of chess, he wrote of Japan:

Japan is to be invited to use the favorable opportunity now to satisfy all her aspirations in the Far East, preferably by military action against Russia, who is tied down in the European war. Wishes which Japan may possibly think attainable with German assistance must be accorded to her. We can promise Japan everything she desires of us in this respect.[3]

Such illusions on the part of Germany were soon dispelled by the Japanese Foreign Minister, who told the German Ambassador, Count Rex, on 2 August that

he regards relations with Russia as very friendly and does not reckon on any deterioration. . . . Japan desires to remain neutral as long as possible; she is well disposed towards us; of course the final decision of Japan depends on England. If England claims Japanese help in East Asia or India then Japan must intervene. . . . This might happen if there were a German attack on British territory, for example Hong Kong.[4]

On 4 August Kato spoke in the same sense to the Russian Ambassador, Malevski:

The Foreign Minister has just confirmed what he said to the English Ambassador yesterday. Japan will not declare her neutrality but will wait to see what attitude Great Britain will adopt in the present crisis.[5]

And on 5 September Kato read out in Parliament a declaration of 4 August which ended with the statement that the Japanese Government, while hoping to maintain neutrality, 'is giving the greatest attention to the different aspects of the situation'.[6] Japan had old scores to pay off on Germany on account of the latter's hostility at the time of the Treaty of Shimonoseke (17 April 1895) and also of Kaiser Wilhelm's

---

[1] BD. XI, 436.   [2] DD. III, 545.   [3] DD. III, 662.

[4] DD. III, 785. On the subject of Russo-Japanese relations it must be added that the collection of Russian documents contains the draft of an agreement, not to say alliance, between the two countries which came to nothing. Tokyo certainly promised to help Russia: 'Japan says she is ready to help us all' (*Int. Bez.* i. VI[1], 10, 116).

[5] *Int. Bez.* i. V, 569.

[6] *Japan und der Kriegsausbruch 1914, Parlamentsreden,* KSF., November 1931, p. 1077.

campaign against the 'yellow peril'. She would be glad to profit by the occasion to take territory away from Germany. On 2 August, Greene, the English Minister at Tokyo, wrote:

Japanese vernacular papers are now discussing the possibility of Japan being invited to support her ally in defense of her interests in the Far East. The view generally taken seems to be that Japan will gladly accept responsibility.[1]

Kato's speech to Parliament on 5 September contained the statement:

At that moment German warships and auxiliary cruisers were cruising in East Asiatic waters and greatly threatening our own and our ally's trade, while at the same time in Kiao-Chow, the German leased territory in China, warlike preparations were being made the aim of which was obviously to make that place the basis of German operations in East Asia. Grave apprehensions, therefore, could not but arise with regard to the maintenance of peace in the Far East.[2]

Now it is clear, as we shall soon see, that a word to Germany would have sufficed to hold her back from carrying the war into Far Eastern waters. But after Port Arthur, Kiao-Chow was the second largest gateway giving access to northern China and was situated in the province of Shantung, which was an abundant producer of raw materials, such as iron and coal, which Japan lacked.

However, England showed no sign pf making the desired request for Japanese collaboration. Grey's dispatch of 1 August had, in fact, ruled out the probability of its becoming necessary. On 3 August Kato with fervor replied:

His Majesty's Government may count upon Japan at once coming to assistance of her ally with all her strength, if called on to do so, leaving it entirely to His Majesty's Government to formulate the reason for, and nature of, the assistance required.[3]

That very day, under the pressure of events, the Foreign Office changed its mind. Acting on an opinion given by Tyrrell, Grey telegraphed to Greene:

At present moment, when war with Germany is a possibility, it might be well for you to warn Japanese Government that, if hostilities spread to Far East, and an attack on Hong Kong or Wei-hai-wei were to take place, we should rely on their support.[4]

This telegram was laid before the Tokyo Cabinet, whose reply on 4 August was one of full consent. Indeed, so eager was Japan to intervene that Kato added:

[1] BD. XI, 499.   [2] KSF. November 1931, p. 1078.
[3] BD. XI, 571.   [4] BD. XI, 534, 549.

In the hypothetical cases, such as a capture of a British merchant ship or a case involving, perhaps, a question of Chinese or Russian territorial waters, the Imperial Government would wish to have the opportunity of considering it and consulting with His Majesty's Government before taking definite action.[1]

Grey in thanking told the Japanese Ambassador:

How much I had been impressed by the way in which Japan, during the Russo-Japanese war, demanded nothing of us under our alliance with her except what was strictly in accord with the Treaty of Alliance; . . . and now we in turn should avoid, if we could, drawing Japan into any trouble.[2]

The words seem to contain a hint of anxiety over the ally's excessive zeal. How impatient Japan was to intervene is apparent in Page's dispatch of 11 August to the American Secretary of State:

Sir Edward Grey informs me that Japan finds herself unable to refrain from war with Germany. . . . Japan assures Britain that she is anxious to respect both the neutrality and the integrity of China. The Anglo-Japanese treaty binds both parties to it to respect her integrity.[3]

On that same day MacMurray, the American Chargé d'Affaires in China, telegraphed:

Japanese Chargé d'Affaires reliably quoted as saying that his Government would welcome an opportunity to participate in taking Kiao-Chow and that an expedition for that purpose is available immediately.[4]

On the other hand Guthrie, the American Ambassador in Japan, telegraphed on the same date:

Counsellor of German Embassy informs me that his Ambassador anticipates proposition from Japan for neutralization of Orient. Ambassador has no direct communication with Berlin and he requests you to inform his Government and says he advises this arrangement and desires instructions.[8]

That same 11 August the American Secretary of State, Bryan, replied to Guthrie:

The Department doubts whether it may properly and lawfully become a medium of communication between a belligerent Government and its own diplomats.

But simultaneously he telegraphed to Gerard, the Ambassador in Berlin:

Discreetly ascertain the views of the German Government as to the possibility of circumscribing the area of hostilities and maintaining the *status quo* in the Far East.[6]

---

[1] BD. XI, 637. [2] BD. XI, 641.
[3] *Papers relating to the Foreign Relations of the United States, 1914 Supplement, The World War* (Washington, 1928), pp. 167-8.
[4] *Ibid.*, p. 166. [5] *Ibid.*, p. 166. [6] *Ibid.*, p. 167.

Gerard's reply of 13 August stated that Germany did not seek war with Japan, and put forward a set of terms relative to circumscribing War in the East.[1] This dispatch left Berlin at 8 p. m., arriving in Washington at 9.40 p. m. on 14 August. We do not know if it was communicated to the Japanese Government. Certainly the latter must have scented something and feared it would find its hands tied, for on 15 August it cut short all hesitation and sent the German Government the following ultimatum:

Considering it highly important and necessary in the present situation to take measures to remove all causes of disturbance to the peace in the Far East and to safeguard the general interests contemplated by the agreement of alliance between Japan and Great Britain, in order to secure a firm and enduring peace in Eastern Asia, establishment of which is the aim of the said agreement, the Imperial Japanese Government sincerely believe it their duty to give advice to the Imperial German Government to carry out the following two propositions:

(1) To withdraw immediately from the Japanese and Chinese waters German men-of-war and armed vessels of all kinds and to disarm at once those which cannot be withdrawn;

(2) To deliver on a date not later than 15 September 1914 to the Imperial Japanese authorities without condition or compensation the entire leased territory of Kiao-Chow, with a view to eventual restoration of the same to China.

The Imperial Japanese Government announce at the same time that in the event of their not receiving by noon, 23 August 1914, the answer of the Imperial German Government signifying an unconditional acceptance of the above advice by the Imperial Japanese Government, they will be compelled to take such action as they may deem necessary to meet the situation.[2]

Needless to dwell on the irony of the word 'advice'! On 19 August MacMurray, the American Chargé d'Affaires in China, telegraphed from Peking:

I learn that the German Chargé d'Affaires has been discussing . . . the possibility of immediately retroceding Kiao-Chow directly to the Chinese Government. I also learn that the Chinese Government has now been warned to discontinue such *pourparlers*.[3]

On 20 August MacMurray telegraphed:

British Minister informed the Chinese that his Government could not now recognize such a transfer.[4]

---

[1] *Papers relating to the Foreign Relations of the United States, 1914 Supplement, The World War*, pp. 169-70.
[2] DA. III, 179; *Int. Bez.* 2. VI, 108; *Papers relating to the Foreign "Relations of the United States, 1914 Supplement, The World War*, p. 170.
[3] *Ibid.*, p. 172.   [4] *Ibid.*, p. 173.

In fact Germany made no reply to Japan within the given time-limit, having decided not to do so, and Japan declared war on her on 23 August.

It is difficult to say to what degree England advised, permitted or merely suffered the action of Japan. On n August, Page, the Ambassador in Great Britain, telegraphed to Bryan:

Sir Edward Grey has conferred with me about suggestions that he says you have made through the British Embassy at Washington concerning the possible neutralization of the Pacific Ocean. He fears that so sweeping an arrangement could hardly be made. But suggestions from the United States to England and Germany to agree that *status quo* in China be maintained by each of them would be a great advantage if agreed to.[1]

This suggestion did not on the face of it rule out the possibility that London desired the Japanese action against Kaio-Chow. But it does not give grounds for asserting, as Japanese writers have done, that on 7 August the English Ambassador at Tokyo asked for immediate Japanese intervention.[2] In his speech of 5 September Kato declared:

In response to an appeal for aid from her ally at a time when the East Asia trade, regarded by Japan and England as one of their special interests, was subject to constant menace, Japan, who regards that alliance as the fundamental principle of her foreign policy, cannot do otherwise than accede to the request and play her part. In the Government's opinion, moreover, it is a serious impediment to the maintenance of lasting peace in East Asia that Germany, whose interests are opposed to those of the Anglo-Japanese alliance, possesses a base for her powerful activities in a corner of the Far East; furthermore, this conflicts with the more immediate interests of our own Empire. The Government therefore, decided to accede to the English request and, if the necessity arises, to go to war with Germany. When the Emperor had given his sanction to this decision, it was at once communicated to the English Government. There followed a full and free exchange of views between the two Governments and thus it was decided to take measures necessary for the protection of the general interests laid down in the treaty of alliance.[3]

[1] *Papers relating to the Foreign Relations of the United States, 1914 Supplement, The First World War*, pp. 165-6.
[2] It seems as if Japan would have liked not to break with Austria. In the harbor of Tsingtao (Kiao-Chow bay) the Austrian warship *Kaiserin Elisabeth* was lying. A series of dispatches of 24–26 August to the State Department tell of Austrian instructions that the cruiser should disarm and the crew go into internment at Shanghai. 'Japan seems agreeable to the proposal.' But then came an order from Francis Joseph to the Commander of the vessel 'to take up flight together with German Navy'. (*Papers relating to the Foreign Relations of the United States, 1914 Supplement, The World War*, p. 170.) On 24 August Berchtold telegraphed telling the Austrian Ambassador, Müller, to ask for his passports (DA. III, 180).
[3] KSF., November 1931, pp. 178-9.

Kato's language is not very explicit, but it would seem that London was informed by Tokyo of the decisions taken and gave them its approval. What is not clear is whether the approval was motivated by fear of opposing Japan's wishes or whether England also wanted Germany to be expelled from that 'corner of the Far East'. The part played by a British detachment in the siege of the fort of Tsingtao makes it seem as if England wanted to get the Germans out while not letting the Japanese install themselves in their place. In the end the Japanese had to restore Tsingtao to China in 1922.

13. The United States and Wilson's last effort to save peace.

It now remains to speak of the United States and of its President's effort to save the peace of Europe when, alas, war had already broken out.

In the afternoon of 28 July, the day on which Austria declared war on Serbia, Herrick, the United States Ambassador in Paris, telegraphed to Bryan:

Situation in Europe is regarded here as the gravest in history. . . . I believe that a strong plea for delay and moderation from the President of the United States would meet with the respect and approval of Europe.[1]

Bryan telegraphed asking Page in London:

Is there in your opinion any likelihood that the good offices of the United States if offered under Article 3 of the Hague Convention would be acceptable or serve any high purpose in the present crisis?[2]

Page replied:

I informally requested Sir Edward Grey yesterday that if the good offices of the United States could at any time or in any possible way be used, please inform me. He expressed his thanks and said he would do so. I am renewing the suggestion today.[3]

But Page did not renew the suggestion that day and, indeed, did not see Grey again until the afternoon of the 31st. After their talk he reported that Grey

again expressed his great gratitude for the suggestion of offering the good offices of the United States in case they could be used. After the failure of his proposal of an ambassadorial conference to prevent Austria from going to war with Serbia, he made proposals looking to the localization of hostilities and he has yet received no responses. Grey asked me if the United States has offered its good offices at Vienna or St. Petersburg or Berlin.[4]

[1] U.S.A., pp. 18-19.   [2] U.S.A., p. 19.
[3] BD. XI, 259; U.S.A., pp. 19-20.   [4] BD. XI, 370; U.S.A., pp. 24-5.

On the evening of 1 August Bryan replied:

Suggestion made to the British Government through you has not been communicated to any other Government but the President asked you to let us know if there is the slightest intimation that such a suggestion might be effective elsewhere.[1]

On the evening of 3 August Page reported:

My very definite opinion is that there is not the slightest chance of any result if our good offices be offered at any Continental capital. This is confirmed by the judgment of the British Foreign Office. We may have a chance after the war has reached a breathing-space.[2]

But Wilson did not give up the attempt. On the evening of 4 August he telegraphed to Francis Joseph:

Great and Good Friend! As official head of one of the Powers signatory to the Hague Convention, I feel it to be my privilege and my duty under Article III of that convention to say to Your Majesty, in a spirit of most earnest friendship, that I should welcome an opportunity to act in the interests of European peace, either now or at any other time that might be thought more suitable as an occasion, to serve Your Majesty and all concerned in a way that would afford me lasting cause for gratitude and a period of happiness.[3]

Between the evening of the 4th and the morning of the 5th Wilson sent out the same appeal to the Tsar, the Kaiser, King George V, and Poincaré. On 6 August Wilson, the American Chargé d'Affaires at St. Petersburg, telegraphed Sazonov's reply that 'offer comes too late for Russia, should have been made earlier'. Sazonov had added: 'Audience with the Emperor uncertain on account of numerous engagements and approaching departure for Moscow where he will remain some time.'[5] Not until 26 August did the Chargé d'Affaires receive the Tsar's reply:

Appreciating the humanitarian sentiments which dictated this step His Majesty has deigned to command me to transmit to the President his sincere thanks. Russia did not desire war and did everything to avoid it, but from the moment this war was imposed upon her she cannot fail to defend her rights by force of arms. Under these circumstances it seems for the moment premature to contemplate the possibility of peace.[6]

Poincaré, who describes the President's proposal as 'well intentioned, to be sure, but timid and embarrassed',[7] returned a still more evasive reply on 6 August:

[1] U.S.A., p. 29.
[3] U.S.A., p. 42; DA. III, 146.
[5] U.S.A., p. 45.
[2] U.S.A., p. 37.
[4] U.S.A., p. 42, *n*. 1.
[6] U.S.A., pp. 78-9.
[7] Poincaré, V, p. 27.

For its preservation the Government has made every sacrifice compatible with its dignity and its honor. . . . It was attacked at the same time that the territory of neutral Powers was being violated. I highly appreciate the thought, which in this instance as in others, has inspired the head of the great American Republic. You may be certain that the French Government and people see in this act a new evidence of the interest you bear in the destiny of France.[1]

Page was received by King George on 7 August:

His Majesty expressed most earnestly his thanks and requested me to convey them to the President. He talked long and appreciatively and he expressed the hope that an occasion would come when the President's offer of mediation might be accepted.[2]

On the same day Francis Joseph received the American Ambassador, Penfield, and placed a message in his hands thanking the President and saying:

Austria-Hungary will certainly accept with gratitude and in concert with its allies the mediation of your Government at such time as the honor of the flag will permit and when the objects of the war shall be attained.[3]

Most lengthy of all was the Kaiser's reply of 14 August, giving in six paragraphs his version of the events leading up to the war and ending with the words: 'I am most grateful to the President for his message.'[4]

One may feel tempted to wonder whether things would have turned out differently and whether the American move would have had a. chance of saving the peace, had it been made on the 29th immediately after it was suggested by Herrick, and had Page supported it more vigorously in London than he did. It seems hardly likely. The American Ambassador, James W. Gerard, narrates that on 30 July he had a talk with the Belgian Minister, Beyens, and the French Ambassador, Jules Cambon, in the garden of the French Embassy. They both agreed that nothing could prevent war except the intervention of America.

Acting on my own responsibility I sent the following letter to the Chancellor : 'Your Excellency,—Is there nothing that my country can do? Nothing that I can do towards stopping this dreadful war? I am sure that the President would approve any act of mine looking towards peace.' To this letter I never had any reply.[5]

It is right to remember that relations between the United States and Europe were not then what they became after the war, and the American President did not yet enjoy the prestige he was later to acquire. Wilson's appeal did not carry

---

[1] U.S.A., p. 48. [2] U.S.A., p. 50.
[3] U.S.A., pp. 49-50; DA. III, 146. [4] U.S.A., pp. 60-1.
[5] James W. Gerard, *My Four Years in Germany* (London, New York, 1917), pp. 88-9.

enough authority to influence the course of events and was made when the European States, flung into the maelstrom of war, and wholly dominated by the will to fight and to win, had no realization of the length of the struggle, the destruction of life and property it was to cause, and the train of evil consequences it was to bring in its wake. European diplomacy, which in the course of the July crisis had so often demonstrated its ineptitude, was henceforth silent. It was now the turn of the big guns to speak.

BIBLIOGRAPHY

1. DIPLOMATIC DOCUMENTS

GENERAL COLLECTIONS

Carnegie Endowment for International Peace. Division of International Law: *Diplomatic documents relating to the outbreak of the European War.* With an introduction by James Scott Brown, Parts I and II. (New York, 1916.) *Official diplomatic documents relating to the outbreak of the European war.* (New York, 1916.) *Collected diplomatic documents relating to the outbreak of the European war.* (London, 1915.)

AUSTRIA-HUNGARY

Diplomatische Aktenstücke zur Vorgeschichte des Krieges 1914. (Vienna, 1915.) *Österreichisch-ungarisches Rotbuch.*

Diplomatische Aktenstücke betreffend die Beziehungen Österreich-Ungarns zu Italien in der Zeit vom 20. Juli 1914 bis 23. Mai 1915. (Vienna, 1915.) *Österreichisch-ungarisches Rotbuch.*

Diplomatische Aktenstücke betreffend die Beziehungen Österreich-Ungarns zu Rumänien in der Zeit vom 22. Juli 1914 bis 27. August 1916. (Vienna, 1916.) *Österreichisch-ungarisches Rotbuch.*

Republik Österreich. Staatsamt für Äusseres: *Diplomatische Aktenstucke zur Vorgeschichte des Krieges 1914. Ergänzungen und Nachträge zum österreichisch-ungarischen Rotbuch* (28. Juni bis 27. August 1914). 3 volumes. (Berlin and Vienna, 1919.)

PRIBRAM, A. F. *The Secret Treaties of Austria-Hungary, 1879-1914.* 2 volumes. (Cambridge (Mass.) and London, 1920-1.)

Österreich-Ungarns Aussenpolitik von der bosnischen Krise 1908 bis zum Kriegsausbrucb 1914. Diplomatische Aktenstücke des österreichisch-ungarischen Ministeriums des Äussern. Ausgewählt von Ludwig Bittner, Alfred Francis Pribram, Heinrich Srbik und Hans Uebersberger, bearbeitet von Ludwig Bittner und Hans Uebersberger. 8 volumes. (Vienna, 1930.)

PHAROS (pseud, of Pater Puntigam). *Der Prozess gegen die Attentäter von Sarajevo, nach dem amtlichen Stenogramm der Gerichtsverhandlungen.* (Berlin, 1918.)

MOUSSET, ALBERT. *Un drame historique: l'attentat de Sarajevo. Documents inédits et texte intégral des sténogrammes du procès.* (Paris, 1930.)

Il delitto di Sarajevo (Bologna, 1930) [text of the verdict].

BELGIUM

Royaume de Belgique: Ministère des Affaires Étrangères: *Correspondance diplomatique relative à la guerre de 1914 (24 juillet-29 août).* (Paris, 1914.) *First Belgian Grey Book.*

Royaume de Belgique. *Correspondance diplomatique relative à la guerre de 1914.* II. (Paris, 1915.) *Second Belgian Grey Book.*

Belgische Aktenstücke 1905-1914. Berichte der belgischen Vertreter in Berlin, London und Paris an den Minister des Äussern in Brüssel. (Berlin, 1915.)

Die belgischen Gesandtschaftsberichte aus den Jahren 1905 bis 1914. (Munich, 1916.)

Amtliche Aktenstücke zur Geschichte der Europäischen Politik 1885-1914: *Die belgischen Dokumente zur Vorgeschichte des Weltkrieges.* Ed. By Bernhard Schwertfeger. 5 volumes, 2 supplements, 2 volumes of commentary. (Berlin, 1925.)

BULGARIA

Ministère des Affaires Étrangères: *La question bulgare et les états balkaniques. Exposé et documents.* (Sofia, 1919.) In English: Ministry of Foreign Affairs, *The Bulgarian Question and the Balkan States.* (Sofia, 1914.)

Diplomaticheski dokumenti po namesata na Bulgariya v evropeyskata vqyna. (Sofia, 1920-21.) A selection translated into German in *Kriegsschuldfrage* (Berlin), March, 1928, pp. 227-59, under the title: *Die Bulgarischen Dokumente zum Kriegsausbruch 1914.*

FRANCE

Ministère des Affaires Étrangères: *La guerre européenne. Documents diplomatiques 1914. Pièces relatives aux négotiations qui ont précédé les déclarations de guerre de l'Allemagne à la Russie (1 août 1914) et à la France (3 août 1914). Déclaration du 4 septembre 1914.* (Paris, 1914.) *French Yellow Book.*

Ministère des Affaires Étrangères: *L'alliance franco-russe. Origines de l'alliance 1890-1893. Convention militaire, 1892-1899, et convention navale, 1912.* (Paris, 1918.)

Ministère des Affaires Étrangères: *Les accords franco-italiens de 1900-1902.* (Paris, 1920.)

Ministère des Affaires Étrangères, Commission de publication des documents relatifs aux origines de la guerre de 1914: *Documents diplomatiques Français (1871-1914).* 1re série, 1871-1900, Volumes I-X; 2me série, 1901-1911, Volumes I-XI; 3me série, 1911-1914, Volumes I-XI. (Paris, 1929.) In progress.

GERMANY

Aktenstücke zum Kriegsausbruch. Dem deutschen Reichstag vorgelegt am 4. 8. '14. Mit nachträglichen Ergänzungen. (Berlin, 1914.) *German White Book.*

Vorläufige Denkschrift und Aktenstück zum Kriegsausbruch. (Reichstag,13. Legislaturperiode, II Session 1914.) (Berlin, 1914.)

Das deutsche Weissbuch über die Schuld am Kriege (mit der Denkschrift der deutschen Viererkommission zum Schuldbericht der Allierten und Assoziierten Mächte). (Berlin, 1927.)

Urkunden des deutschen Generalstabes über die militärpolitische Lage in den letzten Jahren vor dem Kriege. Hat der deutsche Generalstab zum Kriege getrieben? (Berlin, 1919.)

Die deutschen Dokumente zum Kriegsausbruch. Vollständige Sammlung der von Karl Kautsky zusammengestellten amtlichen Aktenstücke mit einigen Ergänzungen. Edited by Graf Max Montgelas and Walter Schücking. 4 volumes. (Berlin, 1927.)

Verfassungsgebende deutsche Nationalversammlung 15. und deutscher Reichstag 12. Ausschuss: *Beilagen zu den stenographischen Berichten über die öjfentlichen Verhandlungen des Untersuchungsausschusses.* Unterausschuss No. I: *Zur Vorgeschichte des Weltkrieges. Schriftliche Auskünfte deutscher Staatsmänner.* No. II: *Militärische Rüstungen und Mobilmachungen.* (Berlin, 1921.)

The German White Book concerning the Responsibility of the Authors of the War. Edited by J. B. Scott. (New York, 1924.) Translation of *Deutschland schuldig? Deutsches Weissbuch über die Verantwortlichkeit der Urheber des Krieges.* (Berlin, 1919.)

Bayerische Dokumente zum Kriegsausbruch und zum Versailler Scbuldspruch. Edited by Pius Dirr. (Munich and Berlin, 1928.)

Die grosse Politik der europdischen Kabinette 1871-1914. Sammlung der diplomatischen Akten des Auswärtigen Amtes. Edited by Joh. Lepsius, A. Mendelssohn-Bartholdy, Friedrich Thimme. 40 volumes. (Berlin, 1922-7.)

Die auswärtige Politik des deutschen Reiches 1871-1914. Gekürzte Ausgabe der amtlichen grossen Aktenpublikation der Deutschen Reichsregierung. Unter der Leitung von Albrecht Mendelssohn-Bartholdy und Friedrich Thimme. 4 volumes. (Berlin, 1928.)

SCHWERTFEGER, BERNHARD. *Die diplomatischen Akten des Auswärtigen Amtes 1871-1914. Ein Wegweiser durch das grosse Aktenwerk der deutschen Regierung.* 8 volumes. (Berlin, 1925-27.)

Deutsche Gesandtschaftsberichte zum Kriegsausbruch 1914.—Berichte und Telegramme der badischen, sächsischen und württembergischen Gesandtschaften in Berlin aus dem Juli und August 1914. Im Auftrag des Auswärtigen Amtes herausgegeben von August Bach. (Berlin, 1937.)

GREAT BRITAIN

Foreign Office.—Correspondence respecting the European Crisis. [Cd. 7467] (Miscellaneous No. 6, 1914) (House of Commons Sessional Papers, 1914, vol. CI, 1). (London, 1914.)

— Despatch from His Majesty's Ambassador at Berlin respecting the Rupture of Diplomatic Relations with the German Government. [Cd. 7445] (Miscellaneous No. 8, 1914) (House of Commons Sessional Papers, 1914, vol. CI, 95). (London, 1914.)

— Despatch from His Majesty's Ambassador at Vienna respecting the Rupture of Diplomatic Relations with the Austro-Hungarian Government. [Cd. 7596] (Miscellaneous No. 10, 1914) (House of Commons Sessional Papers, 1914, vol. CI, 101). (London, 1914.)

Foreign Office.—Correspondence respecting Events leading to the Rupture of Relations with Turkey. [Cd. 7628] (Miscellaneous No. 13, 1914) (House of Commons Sessional Papers, 1914-16, vol. LXXXIV, 179). (London, 1914.)

— Despatch from His Majesty's Ambassador at Constantinople summarizing Events leading up to the Rupture of Relations with Turkey, and Reply thereto. [Cd. 7716] (Miscellaneous No. 14, 1914) (House of Commons Sessional Papers, 1914-16, vol. LXXXIV, 273). (London, 1914.)

— Letter of July 31, 1914, from the President of the French Republic to the King respecting the European Crisis, and His Majesty's Reply of August 1, 1914. [Cd. 7812] (Miscellaneous No. 3, 1915) (House of Commons Sessional Papers, 1914-16, vol. LXXXIII, 1003). (London, 1915.)

— Collected Diplomatic Documents relating to the Outbreak of the European War. [Cd. 7860] (Miscellaneous No. 10,1915) (House of Commons Sessional Papers, 1914-16, vol. LXXXIII, 33). (London, 1915.)

Great Britain and the European Crisis. Correspondence and Statements in Parliament together with an Introductory Narrative of Events. (London 1914.) *British Blue Book.*

Diplomatische Kriegsrüstungen. Dokumente zu den englisch-russischen Verhandlungen über ein Marineabkommen aus dem Jahre 1914. (Berlin, 1919.)

British Documents on the Origins of the War 1898-1914. Edited by G. P. Gooch and Harold Temperley. 11 volumes. (London, 1926-38.)

GREECE

Ministère des Affaires Étrangères de Grèce: *Documents diplomatiques 1913-1917. Traite d'alliance gréco-serbe; invasion germano-bulgare en Macédoine.* (Athens, 1917.)

Ministère des Affaires Étrangères: *Documents diplomatiques 1913-1917. Traite d'alliance gréco-serbe; invasion germano-bulgare en Macédoine. Supplément.* (Athens, 1917.)

Un livre noir. Correspondence telegraphique entre les souverains déchus de Grèce et de Berlin. Édition de l'Association des Hellènes Libéraux de Lausanne. (Lausanne, 1918.)

PORTUGAL

Portugal no conflito europeu I^a Parte. Negoções até a declaração de guerra. Documentos apresentados ao Congresso da República em 1920 pelo Ministro dos Negócios Estrangeiros. (Lisbon, 1920.) Portuguese *White Book.*

ROMANIA

Ministère des Affaires Étrangères: *Les évènements de la péninsule balkanique. L'action de la Roumanie. Septembre 1912–août 1913.* (Bucharest, 1913.)

Ministère des Affaires Étrangères: *Le traité de paix de Bucarest du 28 juillet/10 août 1913, précédé des protocoles de la Conférence.* (Bucharest, 1913.)

RUSSIA

Ministère des Affaires Étrangères *Recueil de documents diplomatiques. Negotiations ayant précédé la guerre, 10/23 juillet-24 juillet/6 août 1914.* (Petrograd, 1914.)

Russisches Orangebuch. Teil I. *Verhandlungen vom 10./23. Juli bis zum 24. Juli/ 6. August 1914;* Teil II. *Verhandlungen mit der Türkei vom 19 Juli/1. August bis 19. Oktober/ 1 November* 1914. (Berlin, 1916.)

LALOY, ÉMILE. *Les documents secrets des Archives du Ministère des Affaires Étrangères de Russie.* (Paris, 1920.)

SIEBERT, BENNO VON. *Diplomatische Aktenstüke zur Geschichte der Entente-politik der Vorkriegsjahre.* 2 volumes. (Berlin, 1921.)

The Falsifications of the Russian Orange Book, published with an introduction by Baron G. von Romberg. (London, 1923.)

Un livre noir. Diplomatie d'avant guerre d'après les documents des Archives Russes 1910-1917. 3 volumes in 6 parts. (Paris, 1922-1934.)

How the War began in 1914. Being the Diary of the Russian Foreign Office from the 3rd to the 10th of July, 1914. With a foreword by S. D. Sazonov and an introduction by Baron Schilling. (London, 1925.) *Schilling's Diary.*

IZVOLSKI. *Der diplomatische Schriftwecbsel Iswolskis 1911-1914. Aus den Geheimakten der russischen Staatsarchive.* Edited by Friedrich Stieve. 4 volumes. (Berlin, 1926.)

Iswolski im Weltkriege. Der diplomatische Schriftwechsel Iswolskis aus den Jahren 1914-1917. Neue Dokumente aus den Geheimakten der russischen Staatsarchive. Nebst einem Kommentar von Friedrich Stieve. (Berlin, 1926.)

Les Allies contre la Russie, avant, pendant et après la guerre mondiale. By Zaiontchkovsky and fifteen others. Preface by Victor Margueritte. (Paris, 1926.) See also *Revue d'histoire de la guerre mondiale* (Paris, 1926), pp. 266-8.

Rossiya v mirovoy vojne. Volume I, with an introduction by M. N. Pokrovsky: Russia and Turkey; Russia and Bulgaria; Russia and Romania; Russia and Italy. (Leningrad, 1925.) Translated into German as: *Das zaristische Russland im Weltkriege. Neue Dokumente aus den russischen Staatsarchiven über den Eintritt der Türkei, Bulgariens, Rumaniens und Italiens in den Weltkrieg. Mit einem Vorwort von A. von Wegerer.* (Berlin, 1927.)

Documents diplomatiques secrets russes 1914-1917. D'après les archives du Ministère des Affaires Étrangères à Petrograd. (Paris, 1928.)

BENCKENDORFF, ALEXANDER, GRAF VON. *Diplomatischer Schriftwechsel.* Edited by Benno von Siebert. 3 volumes. (Berlin and Leipzig, 1928.)

RAFFALOVIC, ARTHUR. *'L' abominable vénalité de la presse.'* D'après les documents des archives russes 1897-1917. (Paris, 1931.)

Mezhdunarodnye Otnosheniya v epochu imperialisma. Selected by M. N. Pokrovski and published by the Central Executive Committee of the Soviet Union. Series i, Volumes I-V: From the beginning of 1914 to the outbreak of war. Series ii, Volumes VI-IX: From the outbreak of war to 1917. (Moscow, 1931-8.)

Translated into German as: *Die internationalen Beziehungen im Zeitalter des Imperialisms. Dokumente aus den Archiven der Zarischen und der Provisorischen Regierung.* Edited by Otto Hoetsch. (Berlin, 1931-40.)

SERBIA

Correspondance diplomatique du Gouvernement serbe, 16/29 juin–3/16 août 1914. (Paris, 1914.)

BOGHITSCHEWITSCH [BOGIČEVIĆ], MILOS. *Die auswärtige Politik Serbiens, 1903-1914.* 3 volumes. (Berlin, 1928-31.)

TURKEY.—See GREAT BRITAIN

UNITED STATES OF AMERICA

Department of State. *Diplomatic Correspondence with Belligerent Governments relating to Neutral Rights and Commerce.* (Washington, 1915.)

Department of State. *Diplomatic Correspondence with belligerent Governments relating to Neutral Rights and Duties, nos. 2, 3.* (Washington, 1915-16.)

Diplomatic Correspondence between the United States and Germany, August 1, 1914-April 6, 1917. Edited, with introduction and analytical index, by James Brown Scott. (New York, 1918.)

Department cf State. *Papers relating to the Foreign Relations of the United States. Supplements: The World War, 1914–18.* 9 volumes. (Washington, 1928-33.)

Department of State. *Papers relating to the Foreign Relations of the United States, 1918: Russia.* 3 volumes. (Washington, 1931-2.)

Department of State. *Papers relating to the Foreign Relations of the United States, 1914–20: Lansing papers.* 2 volumes. (1939-40.)

2. MEMOIRS, CRITICAL STUDIES, ETC.

ADAMOW, E. A. *Die europäischen Mächte und Griechenland während des Weltkrieges.* (Dresden, 1932.)

ADAMOW, E. A. *Die europäischen Mächte und die Türkei während des Weltkrieges. Die Aufteilung der asiatischen Türkei.* (Dresden, 1932.)

ADDISON, CHRISTOPHER. *Four and a half Years. A Personal Diary from June 1914 to January 1919.* (London, 1934.)

ALBERTI, ADRIANO. *Il Generale Falkenhayn. Le relazioni tra i capi di S.M. della Triplice.* (Rome, 1924.)

ALDROVANDI MARESCOTTI, LUIGI. *Guerra diplomatica. Ricordi e frammenti di diario, 1914-1919.* (Milan, 1937.)

ALDROVANDI MARESCOTTI, LUIGI. *Nuovi ricordi e frammenti di diario per far seguito a 'Guerra diplomatica, 1914-1919'*. (Milan, 1938.)

ANRICH, ERNST. *Die englische Politik im Juli 1914. Eine Gesamtdarstellung der Julikrise.* (Stuttgart-Berlin, 1934.)

ANRICH, ERNST. *Europas Diplomatic am Vorabend des Weltkrieges.* (Berlin, 1937-)

Armées Françaises (Les) dans la grande guerre. 9 volumes and annexes. (Paris, 1922-31.)

ARMSTRONG, HAMILTON FISH. 'Three Days in Belgrade. July 1914', in *Foreign Affairs,* January 1927. (New York.)

ARTHUR, SIR GEORGE COMPTON ARCHIBALD. *The Life of Lord Kitchener.* 3 volumes. (London, New York, 1920.)

ASQUITH, HERBERT HENRY. *The Genesis of the War.* (London, 1923.)

ASQUITH, HERBERT HENRY, Earl of Oxford and Asquith. *Memories and Reflections, 1852-1927.* 2 volumes. (London, 1928.)

ASQUITH, HERBERT HENRY. *Fifty Years of British Parliament,* 2 volumes. (London, 1926.)

ASTON, SIR GEORGE. 'The Entente Cordiale and the military conversations', in the *Quarterly Review* (London), April 1932, pp. 363-83.

AULARD, A. 'Ma controverse avec le professeur Delbrück', in *Revue de Paris,* 1 May 1922, pp. 28-43.

AVARNA DI GUALTIERI, CARLO. *L'ultimo rinnovamento della Triplice.* (Milan, 1924.)

BACH, AUGUST. 'Die letzten Versuche zur Erhaltung des Friedens in Paris am 31. Juli und 1. August 1914', in *Kriegsschtildfrage* (Berlin), February 1928, pp. 204-15.

BACH, August. 'Jaurès Ermordung', in *Berliner Monatshefte,* September 1929, pp. 880-98.

BACH, AUGUST. 'Die französische Regierung und die russische Mobilmachung 1914', in *Kriegsschuldfrage* (Berlin), August 1923, pp. 30-3.

BACH, AUGUST. 'König Georgs Telegram an den Zaren', in *Berliner Monatshefte,* December 1932, pp. 1221-9.

BAERNREITHER, JOSEPH MARIA. *Fragments of a Political Diary.* (London, 1930.)

BAGGER, EUGENE S. *Francis Joseph. Emperor of Austria.* (London, New York, 1927.)

BALFOUR, ARTHUR JAMES, Earl of. *Chapters of Autobiography.* (London, 1930.)

BAMBERG, FELIX. *Geschichte der orientalischen Angelegenheit im Zeitraum des Pariser und des Berliner Friedens* (Berlin, 1892). *Storia della questione orientale dalla pace di Parigi alia pace di Berlino.* (Milan, 1906.)

BARETLLES, BERTRAND. *Le rapport secret sur le Congrès de Berlin adressé à la S. Porte par Karathéodory Pacha.* (Paris, 1919.)

BARNES, HARRY ELMER. *The Genesis of the World War. An introduction to the problem of war guilt.* (New York, 1929.)

BARRÈRE, CAMILLE. 'L'Italie et l'agonie de la paix en 1914', in *Revue des Deux Mondes* (Paris), 1 October 1926, pp. 545-62.

BARRÈRE, CAMILLE. 'Le prélude de l'offensive allemande de 1905', in *Revue des Deux Mondes* (Paris), 1 February 1932, pp. 634-41.

BARRÈRE, CAMILLE. 'Les responsabilités du Prince de Bülow', in *Revue des Deux Mondes* (Paris), 1 May 1931, pp. 89-101.

BARRÈRE, CAMILLE. 'Souvenirs diplomatiques. La Chute de Delcassé', in *Revue des Deux Mondes* (Paris), 1 August 1932, pp. 602-18, and 1 January 1933, pp. 123-33.

BARRÈRE, CAMILLE. 'Lettres à Delcassé', in *Revue de Paris,* 15 April 1937, pp. 721-63.

BASSOMPIERRE, ALBERT DE. 'La nuit du 2 au 3 août 1914 au Ministère des Affaires Étrangères de Belgique', in *Revue des Deux Mondes* (Paris), 15 February 1916, pp. 884-906.

BAUER, HANS. *Sarajevo. Die Frage der Verantwortlichkeit der serbischen Regierung an dem Attentat von 1914.* (Stuttgart, 1930.)

BEAVERBROOK, WILLIAM MAXWELL AIKEN, LORD. *Politicians and the War 1914-1918.* 2 volumes. (London, 1928, 1932.)

BEAZLEY, SIR C. R. *The Road to Ruin in Europe, 1890-1914.* (London, 1932.)

BENSON, E. F. *The Outbreak of War, 1914.* (Manchester, 1933; New York, 1934.)

BERCHTOLD, LEOPOLD, GRAF. 'Russia and the World War', in *Contemporary Review* (London), April 1928, pp. 422-32.

BERTIE OF THAME, FRANCIS LEVESON, LORD. *The Diary 1914-18.* 2 volumes. (London, 1924.)

BETHMANN HOLLWEG, THEOBALD VON. *Betrachtungen zum Weltkriege.* 2 volumes. (Berlin, 1919-22.)

BEYENS, NAPOLÉON EUGÈNE LOUIS, BARON. *L'Allemagne avant la guerre. Les causes et les responsabilités.* (Brussels and Paris, 1915.)

BEYENS, NAPOLÉON EUGÈNE LOUIS, BARON. *'La semaine tragique.* (Paris, 1915.) Reprint of articles from *Revue des Deux Mondes,* 1 June 1915, pp. 481-506, and 15 June 1915, pp. 721-746.

BEYENS, NAPOLÉON EUGÈNE LOUIS, BARON. 'Albert I chez Guillaume II', in *Revue des Deux Mondes* (Paris), 15 June 1930, pp. 819-38.

BEYENS, NAPOLÉON EUGÈNE LOUIS, BARON. 'La neutralité belge', in *Revue des Deux Mondes* (Paris), 15 June 1915, pp. 721-46.

BIBL, VICTOR. *Die Tragödie Österreichs.* (Leipzig, 1937.)

BIENVENU-MARTIN, JEAN BAPTISTE. 'Mon interim de Chef du Gouvernement (15-29 juillet 1914)', in *Revue de France,* 15 août 1933, pp. 639-52.

BILINSKI, L. R., VON. *Wspomnienia i dokumenty, 1846-1922.* 2 volumes. (Warsaw, 1924-5.)

BISMARCK, OTTO, PRINCE. *Gedanken und Erinnerungen.* Volksausgabe. 2 volumes. (Stuttgart and Berlin, 1905.) *Bismarck the man and the statesman: being the reflections and reminiscences of Otto, Prince von Bismarck.* 2 volumes. (London, 1898.)

BISSOLATI, LEONIDA. *La politica estera dell' Italia dal 1897 al 1920. Scritti e discorsi.* (Milan, 1923.)

BITTNER, LUDWIG. 'Die schwarze Hand', in *Berliner Monatshefte,* January 1932, pp. 63-4.

BLOCH, CAMILLE. *Les causes de la guerre mondiale. Précis historique.* (Paris, 1933.)

BOGHITSCHEWITSCH (BOGIČEVIĆ), MILOS. *Causes of the War.* (London, 1920.)

BOGHITSCHEWITSCH, MILOS. *Le colonel Dragutin Dimitriević Apis.* (Paris, 1928.)

BOGHITSCHEWITSCH, MILOS. *Le procès de Salonique.* (Paris, 1927.)

BOGHITSCHEWITSCH, MILOS. 'Mord und Justizmord. Aus der Geschichte des Mordes von Sarajevo und des Konigreiches Jugoslavien', in *Süddeutsche Monatshefte* (Munich), February 1929, pp. 331-70.

BOMPARD, Louis MAURICE. 'Le conseil de Potsdam du 5 juillet 1914 et les confidences de l'ambassadeur Wangenheim', in *Revue d'histoire de la guerre mondiale* (Paris), January 1930, pp. 44-50.

BONIN LONGARE, LELIO, CONTE. 'Ricordi di Vienna nei primi anni della Triplice Alleanza', in *Nuova Antologia* (Rome), 16 November 1932, pp. 145-68.

BOSDARI, ALESSANDRO. *Delle guerre balcaniche, della grande guerra e di alcuni fatti precedenti ad esse.* (Milan, 1928.)

BOURGEOIS, E. and PAGÈS, G. *Les origines et les responsabilités de la grande guerre. Preuves et aveux.* (Paris, 1921.)

BOURGEOIS, EMILE. *Manuel historique de politique étrangère.* Volume 4, *La politique mondiale (1878-1919). Empires et nations.* (Paris, 1926.)

BRANDENBURG, ERICH. *Von Bismark zum Weltkrieg.* (Leipzig, 1939.) *From Bismarck to the World War.* (London, 1933.)

BREAL, AUGUSTE. *Philippe Berthelot.* (Paris, 1937.)

BREDT, JOHANN VICTOR. *Die belgische Neutralität und der Schlieffensche Feldzugsplan.* (Berlin, 1929.)

BRENTANO, LUJO. *Die Urheber des Weltkrieges.* (Munich, 1922.)

BUCHANAN, SIR GEORGE. *My Mission to Russia and other Diplomatic Memories.* 2 volumes. (London, 1923.)

BUCHANAN, MERIEL. *The Dissolution of an Empire.* (London, 1932.)

BÜLOW, BERNARD, PRINCE. *Memoirs 1905-9.* 4 volumes. (London and New York, 1931-2.)

BÜLOW, B. W. VON. *Die ersten Stundenschläge des Weltkrieges. Eine Zeittafel der wichtigen Vorgange bei Kriegsausbruch mit Hinweisen auf die einschlägigen Urkunden.* (Berlin, 1922.)

BURIAN, COUNT STEPHAN. *Austria in Dissolution.* (London, 1925.)

CABURI, FRANCO. *Francesco Giuseppe. La sua vita e i suoi tempi.* 2 volumes. (Bologna, 1920.)

CADORNA, LUIGI. *La guerra al fronte italiano.* 2 volumes. (Milan, 1921.)

CADORNA, LUIGI. *Altre pagine sulla grande guerra.* (Milan, 1925.)

CAILLAUX, JOSEPH. *Agadir. Ma politique extérieure.* (Paris, 1919.)

CAILLAUX, JOSEPH. *Devant l'hisloire. Mes prisons.* (Paris, 1920.)

CAILLAUX, JOSEPH. *D'Agadir à la grande pénitence.* (Paris, 1933.)

CALLWELL, SIR C. E. *Field-Marshal Sir Henry Wilson, Bart. His Life and Diaries.* 2 volumes. (London, 1927.)

CAMBON, JULES. 'Fin d'ambassade à Berlin 1912-1914', in *Revue des deux Mondes* (Paris), 15 June 1927, pp. 760-93.

CAMBON, JULES. 'Le Prince de Bülow et ses Mémoires', in *Revue des deux Mondes* (Paris), 15 April 1931, pp. 751-65.

Cambon, Paul, ambassadeur de France (1843-1924) par un diplomate. (Paris, 1937)

CARACCIOLO, M. *L'intervento della Grecia nella guerra mondiale e l'opera della diplomazia alleata.* (Rome, 1925.)

CECIL, ALGERNON. *British Foreign Secretaries 1807-1916. Studies in Personality and Policy.* (London, 1927.)

CECIL, GWENDOLEN. *Life of Robert, Marquis of Salisbury.* 4 volumes. (London, 1931-2.)

ČEROVIĆ, Bozo. *Bosanski omladinči i Sarajevski atentat.* (Sarajevo, 1931.)

CHAMBERLAIN, AUSTEN. 'When War came. Action of the Opposition Leaders. A Contemporary First-hand Record,' in *Sunday Times* (London), 1 December 1929.

CHAMBERLAIN AUSTEN. *Down the Years.* (London, 1935.)

CHARLES-ROUX, FRANÇOIS. *Trois ambassades Françaises à la veille de la guerre.* (Paris, 1928.)

CHARPENTIER, ARMAND. 'Les responsabilités de M. Poincaré', in *Évolution* (Paris), April 1926.

CHARPENTIER, ARMAND. 'Une histoire rocambolesque. Le document "Le Venseur"', in *Évolution* (Paris), April 1933, pp. 193-204.

CHELARD, RAOUL. *Responsabilité de la Hongrie dans la guerre mondiale 1914-1918. Souvenirs personnels et documents inédits.* (Paris, 1930.)

CHIALA, LUIGI. *Pagine di storia contemporanea.* 3 volumes. (Turin, 1892-8.)

CHLUMECKY, LEOPOLD, FREIHERR VON. *Erzherzog Franz Ferdinands Wirken und Wollen.* (Berlin, 1929.)

CHLUMECKY, LEOPOLD, FREIHERR VON. *Österreich-Ungarn und Italien. Das Westbalkanische Problem und Italiens Kampf um die Vorherrschaft in der Adria.* (Leipzig, 1907.)

CHOPIN, JULES (pseud. J. E. Pichon). *L' Autriche-Hongrie 'Brilliant Second'.* (Paris, 1917.)

CHURCHILL, WINSTON LEONARD SPENCER. *The World Crisis.* 6 volumes. (London, 1923-31.)

CHURCHILL, WINSTON LEONARD SPENCER. *My Early Life. A Roving Commission.* (London, 1930.)

CLEMENCEAU, GEORGES. *France facing Germany.* (New York, 1922.)

CONRAD VON HOTZENDORF, FRANZ, GRAF. *Au meiner Dienstzeit 1906-1918.* 5 volumes. (Vienna, 1921-1925.)

CONRAD, GINA. *Mein Leben mit Conrad von Hotzendorf.* (Leipzig, 1935-)

CORTI, EGONE CESARE. 'Il conte Corti al Congresso di Berlino', in *Nuova Antologia* (Rome), 16 April 1925, pp. 351-61.

CREWE, ROBERT MARQUESS OF. *Lord Rosebery.* 2 volumes. (London, 1931.)

CRISPI, FRANCESCO. *Memoirs of Francesco Crispi.* 3 volumes. (London, 1912-14.)

CRISPI, FRANCESCO. *Questioni internazionali.* (Milan, 1913.)

CROKAERT, J. 'L'ultimatum allemand du 2 août', in *Le Flambeau* (Brussels) 31 March 1922.

CROZIER, PHILIPPE. 'L'Autriche d'avant-guerre', in *Revue de France* (Paris, 1921), pp. 268-308, 560-89, 576-617.

CURATOLO, G. E. *Francia e Italia. Pagine di storia 1849-1914.* (Turin, 1915.)

CZEGKA, E. 'Die Mobilmachung Montenegros im Sommer 1914', in *Berliner Monatshefte,* January 1936, pp. 3-23.

CZERNIN, OTTOKAR, COUNT. *In the World War.* (London, 1919.)

DANILOF, YOURI. *La Russie dans la guerre mondiale (1914-1917).* Préface du Maréchal Foch. (Paris, 1927.)

DANILOF, YOURI. 'Juillet 1914 en Russie. Souvenirs personnels', in *Monde Slave* (Paris), April 1931, pp. 62-84.

DANILOV, YOURI. 'La mobilization russe in 1914', in *Revue d'histoire de la Guerre Mondiale* (Paris), October 1923, pp. 259-66.

DELBRÜCK, CLEMENS VON. *Die wirtschaftliche Mobilmachung in Deutschland 1914.* (Munich, 1924.)

DELBRÜCK, HANS. *Der Stand der Kriegsschuldfrage.* (Berlin, 1924.) DEMARTIAL, GEORGES. *L'Évangile du Quai d'Orsay.* (Paris, 1926.)

DEMARTIAL, GEORGES. 'L'état de la question des responsabilités de la guerre en France', in *Évolution* (Paris), 15 March 1926.

DEMARTIAL, GEORGES. 'Les responsabilités de la guerre. Histoire d'un mensonge', in *Évolution* (Paris), May 1931.

DEMARTIAL, GEORGES. 'Réponse a un point d'interrogation', in *Berliner Monatshefte,* January 1933, pp. 63-5.

DENIS, ERNEST. *La Grande Serbie.* (Paris, 1919.)

DERUSSI, G. C. 'Politica bulgara si Jon J, C. Bratianu in preajma marelui razboi', in *Democracia* (Bucharest 1931), February, pp. 34-5; March, pp. 3-14.

D'EUDEVILLE, JEAN. *1912: Préface de la guerre.* (Paris, 1938.)

DIAMANDY, C. J. 'La grande guerre vue du versant oriental. Un nouvel "homme malade" en Europe', in *Revue des Deux Mondes* (Paris); I, 1912-1914, 15 December 1927, pp. 781-804; II, *A Constanza,* 1 January 1928, pp. 129-43; III[I] and II *Ma mission en Russie,* 15 February 1929, pp. 794-820; 15 November 1930, pp. 421-32.

DICKINSON, GOLDSWORTHY LOWES. *The International Anarchy 1904-1914.* (London, 1926.)

DJEMAL, AHMET, PACHA. *Memories of a Turkish Statesman, 1913-1919.* (London, 1922.)

DOBROROLSKI, SERGEJ KONSTANTINOVIC. 'La mobilization de l'armée russe en 1914', in *Revue d'histoire de la guerre mondiale* (Paris, April-July, 1923); *Die Mobilmachung der russischen Armee 1914.* (Berlin, 1922.)

DOBROROLSKI, SERGEJ KONSTANTINOVIC. 'Die Kriegsbereitschaft der russischen Armee im Jahre 1914', in *Kriegsschuldfrage* (Berlin), January, 1925, pp. 27-38.

DOBROROLSKI, SERGEJ KONSTANTINOVIC. 'Noch einiges von der russischen Mobilmachung im Jahre 1914', in *Kriegsschuldfrage* (Berlin), April 1924, pp. 78-89.

DOLLOT, RENE. *Les origines de la neutralité de la Belgique et le système de la Barrière.* (Paris, 1902.)

DRIAULT, EDOUARD. *Le Roi Constantin.* (Versailles, 1930.)

DROSOS, DEM. I. D. *La fondation de l'alliance balkanique.* (Athens, 1929.)

DUMAINE, ALFRED. *La dernière ambassade de France en Autriche. Notes et souvenirs.* (Paris, 1921.)

DUMBA, KONSTANTIN. *Dreibund und Entente-Politik in der Alten und Neuen Welt.* (Vienna, 1931.)

DUPIN, GUSTAVE. *Le regne de la bête.* (Paris, 1925.)

DUPIN, GUSTAVE. *M. Poincaré et la guerre de 1914. Études sur les responsabilite's.* (Paris, 1931.)

DURHAM, MARY EDITH. *The Sarajevo Crime.* (London, 1925.)

ECKARDSTEIN, HERMANN, FREIHERR VON. *Diplomatische Enthüllungen zum Ursprung des Weltkrieges. Bruchstücke aus meinen politischen Denkwürdig-keiten.* (Berlin, 1919.)

ECKARDSTEIN, HERMANN, FREIHERR VON. *Lebenserinnerungen und politische Denkwürdigkeiten.* Three volumes. (Leipzig, 1919-21.)

ECKARDSTEIN, HERMANN, FREIHERR VON. *Personliche Erinnerungen an König Eduard. Aus der Einkreisungszeit.* (Dresden, 1927.)

EGGELING, BERNHARD VON. *Die russiscbe Mobilmachung und der Kriegsausbruch. Beiträge zur Schuldfrage am Weltkriege.* (Berlin, 1919.)

EISENMENGER, VICTOR. *Archduke Francis Ferdinand.* (London, 1931.)

ELST (VAN DER), BARON. 'La préméditation de l'Allemagne', in *Revue de Paris*, 1 April 1923, pp. 521-31.

ERENYI, GUSTAV. *Graf Stefan Tisza. Ein Staatsmann und Martyrer.* (Vienna, 1935.)

EULENBURG-HERTEFELD, PHILIPP, FURST ZU. *Aus 50 Jahren. Erinnerungen, Tagebücher und Briefe.* (Berlin, 1923.)

EWART, JOHN S. *The Roots and Causes of the Wars (1914 to 1918).* 2 volumes. (New York, 1925.)

FABRE-LUCE, ALFRED. *La victoire* (Paris, 1924.)

FABRE-LUCE, ALFRED. *Caillaux.* (Paris, 1933.)

FARAMOND DE LAFAJOLLE. *Souvenirs d'un attaché naval en Allemagne et en Autriche.* (Paris, 1932.)

FAY, SIDNEY BRADSHAW. *The Origins of the World War.* 2 volumes. (New York, 1948.)

FISCHER, EUGEN. *Die kritischen 39 Tage von Sarajevo bis zum Weltbrand.* (Berlin, 1928.)

FISHER OF KILVERSTONE, JOHN ARBUTHNOT, LORD. *Memories.* (London, 1919.)

FISHER OF KILVERSTONE, JOHN ARBUTHNOT, LORD. *Records.* (London, 1919.)

FITZROY, SIR ALMERIC. *Memories.* 2 volumes. (London, 1925.)

FOCH, FERDINAND, MARÉCHAL. *The Memoirs of Marshal Foch.* (London, 1931.)

FOERSTER, WOLFGANG. 'Die deutsch-italienische Militarkonvention', in *Kriegsschuldfrage* (Berlin), May 1927, pp. 395-416.

FOERSTER, WOLFGANG. *Graf Schlieffen und der Weltkrieg.* (Berlin, 1925.)

FOERSTER, WOLFGANG. *Aus der Gedankenwerkstatt des deutschen Generalstabes.* (Berlin, 1931.)

FOTINO, GEORGES. 'Une séance historique au Conseil de la Couronne (3 août 1914)', in *Revue des Deux Mondes* (Paris), 1 August 1930, pp. 529-41.

FRAKNOI, WILHELM. *Die ungarische Regierung und die Entstehung des Weltkrieges.* Auf Grund aktenmässiger Forschung dargestellt. (Vienna, 1919.)

FRANGULIS, A. F. *La Grèce: son statut international, son histoire diplomatique.* 2 volumes. (Paris, 1934.)

FRANKE, LYDIA. *Die Randbemerkungen Wilhelm II in den Akten der auswärtigen Politik als historische und psychologische Quelle.* (Strasbourg, 1934, Dissertation.)

FRANTZ, GDNTHER. *Russlands Eintritt in den Weltkrieg.* (Berlin, 1924.)

FREYTAG-LORINGHOVEN, HUGO, FREIHERR VON. *Menschen und Dinge wie ich sie in meinem Leben sah.* (Berlin, 1923.)

FRIEDJUNG, HEINRICH. *Das Zeitalter des Imperialismus 1884 bis 1914.* 3 volumes. (Berlin, 1919-22.)

GACINOVIG, VLADIMIR. *Spomenica Vladimira Gacinovica.* (Sarajevo, 1921.)

GALET, EMILE JOSEPH. *Albert, King of the Belgians in the Great War.* (London, 1931.)

GARVIN, JAMES LOUIS. *The Life of Joseph Chamberlain.* 3 volumes. (London, 1932-4.)

GATTI, ANGELO. *La parte dell' Italia. Rivendicazioni.* (Milan, 1926.)

GERARD, JAMES WATSON. *My Four Years in Germany.* (New York, 1917.)

GERARD, JAMES WATSON. *Face to Face with Kaiserism.* (New York, 1918.)

GERIN, RENE and POINCARÉ, RAYMOND, *Les responsabilités de la guerre. Quatorze questions par René Gerin; quartorze réponses par Raymond Poincaré.* (Paris, 1930.)

GERIN RENE. *Les responsabilités de la guerre de 1914; Mémoires pour l'histoire de la guerre mondiale.* (Paris, 1930.)

GHIKA WLADIMIR, PRINCE. 'Les origines de la guerre: autour du drame de Sarajevo', in *Revue Universelle* (Paris), 15 April 1921, pp. 129-41.

GIACCARDI, A. 'La prima offensiva francese in Tunisia', in *Storia e Politica internazionale* (Rome), 31 December 1939, pp. 757-80.

GIESL, WLADIMIR, FREIHERR VON. *Zwei Jahrzehnte im Nahen Orient.* (Berlin, 1927.)

GIOLITTI, GIOVANNI. *Memoirs of my Life.* (London, 1923.)

GOOCH, GEORGE PEABODY. *History of Modern Europe 1878-1919.* (London, 1923.)

GOOCH, G. P. *Before the War. Studies in Diplomacy.* 2 volumes. (London, 1936-1938.)

GOOCH, G. P. *Recent Revelations of European Diplomacy.* (London, 1940.)

Gooss, RODERICH. *Das Wiener Kabinett und die Entstehung des Weltkrieges.* (Vienna, 1919.)

Gooss, RODERICH. *Das österreichisch-serbische Problem bis zur Kriegserklärung Österreich-Ungarns an Serbien, 28. Juli 1914.* (Berlin, 1930.)

GOPČEVIČ, SPIRIDION. *Österreichs Untergang die Folge von Franz Josefs Missregierung.* (Berlin, 1920.)

GOUTTENOIRE, DE TOURY. 'Le Congrès de la Ligue des Droits de l'Homme', in *Évolution* (Paris), November 1932.

GRAHAM, STEPHEN. *St. Vitus Day.* (London, 1930.)

GRELLING, RICHARD. *La campagne 'innocentiste' en Allemagne et le traité de Versailles.* (Paris, 1925.)

GREY, SIR EDWARD, LORD GREY OF FALLODON. *Twenty-five Years 1892-1916.* 2 volumes. (London, 1925.)

GREY, SIR EDWARD, LORD GREY OF FALLODON. *Speeches on Foreign Affairs 1904-14.* (London, 1931.)

GRIESTNGER, JULIUS ADOLF, FREIHERR VON. 'Die kritischen Tage in Serbien. Erinnerungen', in *Berliner Monatshefte,* September 1930, pp. 838-55.

GUÉCHOFF [GESHOV], IVAN EVSTRATIEV. *La genèse de la guerre mondiak. La débâcle de l'alliance balkanique.* (Berne, 1919.)

GUILLAUME II. *Tableaux d'histoire comparée de 1878 a l'explosion de la guerre de 1914* (Paris, 1923). *Comparative History, 1878-1914* (Tables of dates and events) (London 1922). See also Wilhelm II.

GUYOT, RAYMOND. *La première Entente Cordiale.* (Paris, 1926.)

HALDANE, RICHARD BURDON, VISCOUNT. *Before the War.* (London, 1920.')

HALDANE, R. B., VISCOUNT. *An Autobiography.* (London, 1929.)

HALLER, JOHANNES. *Aus dem Leben des Fürsten Philipp zu Eulenburg-Hertefeld.* (Berlin, 1924.)

HAMMANN, OTTO. *Der neue Kurs. Erinnerungen.* (Berlin, 1918.)

HAMMANN, OTTO. *Zur Vorgeschichte des Weltkrieges. Erinnerungen aus den Jahren 1897-1906.* (Berlin, 1919.)

HAMMANN, OTTO. *Um den Kaiser.* (Berlin, 1919.)

HAMMANN, OTTO. *Bilder aus der letzten Kaiserzeit.* (Berlin, 1922.)

HAMPE, KARL. *Das belgische Bollwerk, eine aktenmässige Darlegung über die Barrierestellung, Neutralität und Festungspolitik Belgiens.* (Stuttgart-Berlin, 1918.)

HASSELL, ULRICH VON. *Tirpitz. Sein Leben und Wirken mit Berücksichtigung seiner Beziehungen zu Albrecht von Stosch.* (Stuttgart, 1920.)

HELMREICH, E. C. 'Die tieferen Ursachen der Politik Berchtolds im Oktober 1912', in *Berliner Monatshefte,* March 1932, pp. 218-44.

HENDRICK, H. J. *Life and Letters of W. H. Page.* 3 volumes. (New York, 1922-5.)

HENRY, MAURICE. *Les causes de la neutralité de la Suisse et son attitude pendant La guerre de 1914-1918.* (Geneva, 1934.)

HERRE, PAUL. *Die kleinen Staaten Europas und die Entstehung des Weltkrieges.* (Munich, 1937.)

Histoire diplomatique de l'Europe (1871-1914) [Manuel de politique européenne] publié sous la direction de Henri Hauser par J. Ancel, L. Cahen, R. Guyot, A. Lajusan, P. Renouvin et H. Salomon. 2 volumes. (Paris, 1929.)

Histoire politique de la grande guerre, 1914-1918, by A. Aulard, E. Bouvier, A. Ganeur. (Paris, 1924.)

History, *The Cambridge History of British Foreign Policy 1783-1919.* Ed. By Sir A. W. Ward and G. P. Gooch. Volume III, 1866-1919. (Cambridge, 1923.)

HOHENLOHE-SCHILLINGSFURST, ALEXANDER, PRINZ VON. *Aus meinem Leben.* (Frankfurt A. M., 1925.)

HOHENLOHE-SCHILLINGSFURST, CHLODWIG, FÜRST ZU. *Denkwüdigkeiten der Reichskanzlerzeit* [1894-1905]. 3 volumes. (Stuttgart, 1931.)

HOIJER, OLOF. *Le Comte d'Aehrenthal et la politique de violence.* (Paris, 1922.)

HOLSTEIN, FREDRICK VON. *Lebensbekenntnis in Briefen an eine Frau.* (Berlin, 1932.)

HOLSTEIN, FRITZ VON. *Gespräcbe und Briefe 1907-1909.* Eingeleitet und herausgegeben (aus den Papieren Hermanns von Rath) von Heinrich Otto Meisner, in *Preussische Jahrbücher* (Berlin). Vol. 228: Heft I, pp. 1-13; Heft II, pp. 111-21; Vol. 229: Heft I, pp. 165-72; Heft, III pp. 229-96.

HOSSE, KARL. *Die englisch-belgischen Aufmarschpläne gegen Deutschland vor dem Weltkriege.* (Vienna, 1930.)

HOYOS, ALEXANDER, GRAF. *Der deutsch-englische Gegensatz und sein Einfluss auf die Balkanpolitik Österreicb-Ungarns.* (Berlin-Leipzig, 1922.)

HOYOS, ALEXANDER, GRAF. 'Russia's Pre-war Policy', in *Contemporary Review* (London), May 1929, pp. 587–93.

HUBKA, G., VON. 'Kritische Tage in Montenegro', in *Berliner Monatshefte,* January 1931, pp. 27-45.

HUGUET, CHARLES JULIEN. *L'intervention militaire britannique en 1914.* (Paris, 1928.)

HULDERMANN, B. *Albert Ballin.* (Berlin, 1922.)

IORGA, NIKOLAE. 'Comment la Roumanie s'est détachée de la Triplice. D'après les documents austro-hongrois et des souvenirs personnels', in *Revue historique du Sud Est europeen* (Bucharest), July-September 1933, pp. 232-307.

IOTZOFF, DIMITRI. *Zar Ferdinand von Bulgarien.* (Berlin-Schonberg, 1927.)

ISAAC, JULES. *Un débat historique, 1914. Le problème des origines de la guerre.* (Paris, 1933.)

ISAAC, JULES. *Paradoxe sur la science homicide et autres hérésies.* (Paris, 1936.)

ISWOLSKY, ALEXANDRE. *Mémoires.* (Paris, 1923.)

JÄCKH, ERNST. *Kiderlen-Wächter, der Staatsmann und Mensch. Briefivechsel und Nacblass.* 2 volumes. (Stuttgart, 1924.)

JAGOW, GOTTLIEB VON. *Ursachen und Ausbruch des Weltkrieges.* (Berlin, 1919.)

JAGOW, GOTTLIEB VON. *England und der Kriegsausbruch. Eine Auseinandersetzung mit Lord Grey.* (Berlin, 1925.)

JAGOW, GOTTLIEB VON. 'Die deutsche politische Leitung und England bei Kriegsausbruch', in *Preussiche Jahrbücher* (Berlin), July 1928, pp. 6-10.

JAGOW, GOTTLIEB VON. 'Die deutsche Politik 1913 und 1914 vor dem Weltkriege', in *Süddeutsche Monatshefte* (Munich), July 1924, pp. 241-8.

JAGOW, GOTTLIEB VON. 'Herr Poincaré', in *Berliner Monatshefte,* November 1931, pp. 1074-81.

JAGOW, KURT. *Das Drama der 13 Tage.* (Berlin, 1924.)

'Japan und der Kriegsausbruch 1914. Parlamentsreden', in *Berliner Monatshefte,* November 1931, pp. 1074-81.

JEHAY, COMTE FR. DE. *L'invasion du Grand-Duché de Luxembourg en août 1914.* (Paris, 1916.)

JEVTIĆ, BORIVOJE. *Sarajevski Atentat.* (Sarajevo, 1924.)

JOFFRE, JOSEPH JACQUES CESAIRE. *The Memoirs of Marshal Joffre.* 2 volumes. (London, 1932.)

JONESCU, TAKE. *Some Personal Impressions.* (London, 1919.)

JOVANOVIC, LJUBA. 'Posle Vidov-dana 1914 Godine', in *Krv Sloventsva* (Belgrade, 1924). 'The Murder of Sarajevo', reprinted from the *Journal* of the British [now Royal] Institute of International Affairs (London), March 1925.

JUDET, ERNEST. *Georges Louis.* (Paris, 1925.)

KANNER, HEINRICH. *Kaiserliche Katastrophenpolitik.* (Vienna, 1922.)

KANNER, HEINRICH. *Der Schlüssel zur Kriegsschuldfrage.* (Munich, 1926.)

KAUTSKY, KARL. *Wie der Weltkrieg entstand.* (Berlin, 1919.) *The Guilt of Wilhelm Hohenzollern.* (London, 1920.)

KERR, MARK, ADMIRAL. *Land, Sea and Air.* (London, 1927.)

KIBALTCHICHE, VICTOR (Pseud. Serge). 'La vérité sur l'attentat de Sarajevo', in *Clarte.* (Paris, May 1925.)

KJELLÉN, RUDOLF. *Dreibund und Dreiverband.* (Munich, 1921.)

KOKOVTZOF, WLADIMIR NIKOLAJEWITSCH, COUNT. *Out of My Past. The Memoirs of Comte Kokovtzof.* (London, 1935.)

Krv Sloventsva, 1914-1924. Spomenica desetogodišnjice Svetskog Rata. (Belgrade, 1924.)

KUHL, H. VON. 'Ost-oder Westaufmarsch 1914', in *Kriegsschuldfrage* (Berlin), October 1923, pp. 73-7.

KUHLMANN, RICHARD VON. *Thoughts on Germany.* (London, 1932.)

KUTSCHBACH, ALBIN. *Der Brandherd Europas; 50 Jahre Balkan-Erinnerungen.* (Leipzig, 1929.)

LAMOUCHE, LÉON. *Quinze ans d'histoire balkanique (1904-1918).* (Paris, 1928.)

LANCKEN, WAKENITZ OSCAR, FREIHERR VON. *Meine dreissig Dienstjahre 1888-1918. Potsdam, Paris, Brüssel.* (Berlin, 1931.)

LANGER, WILLIAM L. *The Diplomacy of Imperialism, 1890-1902.* 2 volumes. (New York, 1951.)

LANGER, WILLIAM L. *European Alliances and Alignments 1871-1890.* (New York, 1950.)

LANGER, WILLIAM L. 'The European Powers and the French Occupation of Tunis', in *The American Historical Review,* October 1925, pp. 55-78; January 1926, pp. 251-65.

LAZAREWITSCH, DOBROVOI. *Die Schwarze Hand* (Lausanne, 1917), *La main noire* (Lausanne, 1917).

LECLERE, LÉON. 'La Belgique à la veille de l'invasion', in *Revue d'histoire de la guerre mondiale* (Paris), July 1926, pp. 193-216.

LEE, SIR SIDNEY. *King Edward VII. A Biography,* 2 volumes. (London, 1925-7.)

LEGER, LOUIS. *Histoire de l'Autriche-Hongrie.* (Paris, 1920.)

LICHNOWSKY, KARL MAX, FÜRST VON. *My Mission to 'London 1912 to 1914.* (London, 1918.)

LICHNOWSKY, KARL MAX, FÜRST VON. *Heading for the Abyss. Reminiscences.* (London, 19Z8.)

LICHTERVELDE, LOUIS, COMTE DE. *Le 4 août 1914 au parlement belge* (Brussels-Paris, 1918). *August the fourth, 1914, in the Belgian Parliament.* (London, 1918.)

LIMAN VON SANDERS, OTTO. *Five Years in Turkey* (Annapolis, 1927). *Fünf Jahre Türkei* (Berlin, 1920.)

LINDOW, ERICH. *Freiherr Marschall von Bieberstein als Botschafter in Konstantinopel 1897-1912.* (Danzig, 1934.)

LLOYD GEORGE, DAVID. *War Memoirs.* 6 volumes. (London, 1933-36.)

LONĆAREVIĆ, DUŠAN A. *Jugoslaviens Entstehung.* (Vienna, Zurich, 1929.)

LOUIS, GEORGES. *Les Carnets de Georges Louis.* 2 volumes. (Paris, 1926.)

LUDENDORFF, ERICH. *Wie der Weltkrieg 1914 'gemacht' wurde.* (Munich, 1934.)

LUMBROSO, ALBERTO. *Le origini della guerra mondiale.* (Milan, 1928.)

LUTZ, HERMANN. *Die europäische Politik in der Julikrise 1914. Gutachten.* (Berlin, 1930.)

LUTZ, HERMANN. 'Das Entscheidende über den "Halt in Belgrad"', in *Berliner Monatshefte,* July 1927, pp. 679-88.

LUTZ, HERMANN. 'Moltke und Präventivkrieg', in *Kriegsschuldfrage* (Berlin), November 1927, pp. 1107-20.

MACCHIO, KARL, FREIHERR VON. *Wahrheit! Fürst Bülow und ich in Rom 1914-1915.* (Vienna, 1931.)

MACH, RICHARD VON. *Aus bewegter Balkanzeit 1879-1918. Erinnerungen.* (Berlin, 1928.)

MADOL, HANS ROGER. *Ferdinand von Bulgarien. Der Traum von Byzanz.* (Berlin, 1931.)

MAGRINI, LUCIANO. *Il tramonto della Triplice Albania. Alla vigilia della guerra.* (Milan, 1908.)

MAGRINI, LUCIANO. *La Serbia invasa.* (Milan, 1922.)

MAGRINI, LUCIANO. *Il Montenegro. La fine di un regno.* (Milan, 1922.)

MAGRINI, LUCIANO. *La caduta e l'assassinio dello Zar Nicola II.* (Milan, 1928.)

MAGRINI, LUCIANO. *Il dramma di Sarajevo. Origini e responsabilità della guerra europea.* (Milan, 1929.)

MANDL, LEOPOLD. *Die Habsburger und die serbische Frage.* (Vienna, 1918.)

MARGHILOMAN, ALEXANDRU. *Note politice 1897-1924.* 5 volumes. (Bucharest, 1927.)

MARGHIEOMAN, ALEXANDRU. 'L'intervention roumaine. Extraits des notes', (I. *Le Conseil de Couronne du 2/3 août 1914*. II. *Le Conseil de Couronne du 27 août 1916*), in *Revue d'histoire de la guerre mondiale* (Paris), 1928, pp. 157-66.

MARGUERTTE, VICTOR. *Les criminels*. (Paris, 1925.)

MARGUTTI, ALBERT VON. *La tragédie des Habsbourg*. (Vienna, 1919.)

MARTIN, WILLIAM. *Les hommes d'état pendant la guerre*. (Paris, 1929,)

MASARYK, THOMAS. *Vasić-Forgach-Aehrenthal*. (Vienna, 1911.)

MAXSE, L. J. 'Retrospect and Reminiscence', in *The National Revue*. (August, 1918.)

MAXSE, L. J. *Politicians-on the Warpath*. (London, 1920.)

MELAS, GEORGE M. *Ex-King Constantine and the War*. (London, 1920.)

MESSIMY, ADOLPHE-MARIE. *Mes souvenirs; jeunesse et entrée au parlement—ministre des colonies et de la guerre en 1911 et 1912: Agadir—minisire de la guerre du 16 juin au 26 août 1914: la guerre*. (Paris, 1937.)

MICHON, GEORGES. *The Franco-Russian Alliance 1891-1917*. (London, New York, 1929). *L'alliance franco-russe (1891-1917)*. (Paris, 1931.)

MICHON, GEORGES. *La préparation à la guerre. La loi des trois ans, 1910–1914*. (Paris, 1935.)

MOLDEN, BERCHTOLD. *Alois Graf Aehrenthal. Sechs Jahre äussere Politik Österreich-Ungarns*. (Stuttgart and Berlin, 1917.)

MOLTKE, HELMUTH VON. *Erinnerungen. Briefe. Dokumente 1877-1916*. Edited by Eliza von Moltke. (Stuttgart, 1922.)

MONTGELAS, MAX GRAF. *The Case for the Central Powers*. (London, 1925.)

MONTGELAS, MAX, COMTE. 'Le 30 juillet 1914 à Berlin et à Petersbourg', in *Évolution* (Paris), November 1926.

MONTGELAS, MAX. 'Der angebliche Bombenwurf bei Nürnberg', in *Kriegs-schuldfrage* (Berlin), July 1927, pp. 672-5.

MONTGELAS, MAX. 'Das Plaidoyer Poincarés, in *Kriegsschuldfrage* (Berlin), February 1928, pp. 133-70.

MONTGELAS, MAX. 'Die belgische Neutralität und der Schlieffensche Feld-zugsplan', in *Berliner Monatshefte,* December 1931, pp.1129-50.

MONTS, ANTON, GRAF. *Erinnerungen und Gedanken des Botschafters Anton, Graf Monts*. Edited by Karl Fr. Nowak und Friedrich Thimme, (Berlin. 1932.)

(MONTS, ANTON, GRAF) THIMME, FRIEDRICH. 'Fürst Bülow und Graf Monts. Ein vervollständigter Briefwechsel, in *Preussische Jahrbücher* (Berlin). I. January-March 1933, pp. 193-219; II. April-June 1933, pp. 17-34, 97-123, 199-235.

(MONTS, ANTON, GRAF) THIMME, FRIEDRICH. 'Graf Monts und Luzzatti (Briefmaterial Monts)', in *Europäische Gespräche* (Berlin), October 1931, pp. 449-78.

MORGENTHAU, HENRY. *Ambassador Morgentbau's Story.* (New York, 1918.)

MORHARDT, MATHIAS. *Les preuves.* (Paris, 1924.)

MORLEY OF BLACKBURN, JOHN, VISCOUNT. *Memorandum on Resignation, August 1914.* (London, 1928.)

MOUKHTAR, PASHA, *La Turquie, l'Allemagne et l'Europe depuis le traité de Berlin jusqu'à la guerre mondiale.* (Paris, 1924.)

MÜHLMANN, CARL. *Deutschland und die Türkei 1913-1914.* (Berlin, 1929.)

MÜNZ, SIGMUND. *Fürst Bülow: der Staatsmann und Mensch. Aufzeichnungen, Erinnerungen und Erwägungen.* (Berlin, 1930.)

MUSCHLER, REINHOLD CONRAD. *Philipp zu Eulenburg, Sein Leben und seine Zeit.* (Leipzig, 1930.)

MUSULIN, ALEXANDER, FREIHERR VON. *Das Haus am Ballplatz. Erinnerungen eines Österreichisch-ungarischen Diplomaten.* (Munich, 1924.)

NAUMANN, VICTOR. *Profile. 30 Porträtskizzen aus den Jahren des Weltkrieges nach persönlichen Begegnungen.* (Munich, 1925.)

NAUMANN, VICTOR. *Dokumente und Argumente.* (Berlin, 1928.)

NEKLUDOFF, ANATOLIJ VASILIEVIC. *Diplomatic reminiscences* (London, 1920). *Souvenirs diplomatiques. En Suède pendant la guerre mondiale* (Paris, 1926).

NEVINS, ALLAN. *Henry White. Thirty Years of American diplomacy.* (New York, 1930.)

NICHOLAS (H.R.H. PRINCE NICHOLAS OF GREECE). *Political memoirs 1914-1917. Pages from my Diary.* (London, 1928.)

NICHOLAS II, TSAR OF RUSSIA. *Archives secrètes de l'empereur Nicolas II.* (Paris, 1928.)

NICHOLAS II, TSAR OF RUSSIA. *Journal intime de Nicolas II (juillet 1914-juillet 1918).* (Paris, 1934.)

NICOLAI, WALTER. *Gebeime Mächte* (Leipzig, 1923). *The German Secret Service* (London, 1924).

NICOLSON, HAROLD GEORGE. *Sir Arthur Nicolson, Bart., First Lord Carnock. A Study in the Old Diplomacy.* (London, 1930.)

NIKITSCH-BOULLES, PAUL. *Vor dem Sturm. Erinnerungen an Erzherzog-Tronfolger Franz Ferdinand. Von seinem Privatsekretär.* (Berlin, 1925.)

NINČIĆ, MOMČILO. *La crise bosniaque (1908-1909) et les puissances européennes.* 2 volumes. (Paris, 1937.)

NOLDE, BORIS. *Ualliance franco-russe. Les origines du système diplomatique d'avant-guerre.* (Paris, 1936.)

NOULENS, JOSEPH. 'Le Gouvernement français à la veille de la guerre 1913-1914', *in Revue des deux Mondes (Paris),* 1 February 1931, pp. 608-21.

Österreich-Ungarns letzer Krieg 1914-18. Herausgegeben vom Österreichischen Bundesministerium für Heereswesen und vom Kriegsarchiv. Unter der Leitung von Edmund Glaise-Horstenau. 7 volumes. (Vienna, 1931-38.)

OLDOFREDI, HIERONYMUS. *Zwischen Kriegimd Frieden. Erinnerungen.* (Vienna, 1925.)

OMAN, CHARLES W. C. *The Outbreak of the War of 1914-18.* (London, 1919.)

ONCKEN, HERMANN. *Das deutsche Reich und die Vorgeschichte des Weltkrieges.* 2 volumes. (Berlin, 1933.)

PALEOLOGUE, MAURICE. *An Ambassador's Memoirs.* 3 volumes. (London, 1923-5.)

PALEOLOGUE, MAURICE. *Un prélude à l'invasion de la Belgique. Le plan Schlieffen,* 1904. (Paris, 1932.)

PALEOLOGUE, MAURICE. *Un grand tournant de la politique mondiale (1904-1906).* (Paris, 1934.)

PALEOLOGUE, MAURICE. 'Sur le chemin de la guerre mondiale (fevrier-mars 1913)', in *Revue des deux Mondes* (Paris), 1 October 1933, pp. 481-506.

PALEOLOGUE, MAURICE. *Guillaume II et Nicholas II.* (Paris, 1935.)

PEVET, ALFRED. *Les responsables de la guerre.* (Paris, 1922).

PFEFFER, LEO. *Istraga u Sarajevskom atentatu.* (Zagreb, 1938.)

PICHON, JEAN. *Les origines orientales de la guerre mondiale.* Préface du Général E. Brémond. (Paris, 1937.)

PITREICH, MAX FREIHERR VON. 1914; *Die militärischen Probleme unseres Kriegsbeginnes. Ideen, Gründe und Zusammenhänge.* (Vienna, 1934.)

POHL, H. *Der deutsche Einmarsch in Belgien.* (Berlin, 1925.)

POINCARÉ, RAYMOND. *Au service de la France, Neuf années de souvenirs.* 10 volumes. (Paris, 1926-1933.)

POINCARÉ, RAYMOND. *The Origins of the War.* (London, 1922.)

POINCARÉ, RAYMOND. 'The Responsibility for the War', in *Foreign Affairs* (New York), October 1925, pp. 1-19.

POLETIKA, N. P. *Saraevskoe Ubijstvo.* (Leningrad, 1930.)

POMIANKOWSKI, JOSEF. *Der Zusammenbruch des Ottomanischen Reiches. Erinnerungen an die Türkei aus der Zeit des Weltkrieges.* (Zurich-Leipzig-Vienna, 1928.)

POPOVIĆ, ČEDAR A. 'Organizacija "Ujedinjenje ili Smrt"', in *Nova Evropa* (Zagreb), 11 June 1927, pp. 396-405.

POPOVIĆ, ČEDAR A. 'Rad Organizacije "Ujedinjenje ili Smrt"', in *Nova Evropa* (Zagreb), September 1927, pp. 139-52.

POPOVIĆ, ČEDAR A. 'Sarajevski Atentat, i organizacija "Ujedinjenje ili Smrt"', in *Nova Evropa* (Zagreb), 26 July 1932, pp. 394- 414.

POPOVICI, AUREL C. *Die vereinigten Staaten von Gross-Österreich.* (Leipzig, 1906.)

POURTALÈS, FRIEDRICH, GRAF. *Meine letzten Verhandlungen in Sankt Petersburg.* (Berlin, 1927.)

POZZI, HENRI. *Black Hand over Europe.* (London, 1935.)

POZZI, HENRI. *Les coupables.* (Paris, 1935.)

PRIBRAM, A. Zwei Gespräche des Fürsten Bismarck mit dem Kronprinzen Rudolf von Österreich', in *Österreichische Rundschau* (Vienna), January, 1921.

PRINCIP, GAVRILO. *Ein geschichtlicher Beitrag zur Vorgeschichte des Attentats von Sarajevo. Gavrilo Princips Bekenntnisse.* (Zwei Manuscripte Princips, Aufzeichnungen seines Gefängnispsychiaters Martin Pappenheim aus Gesprächen von Feber bis Juli 1916 über das Attentat, Princips Leben und seine politischen und sozialen Anschauungen). (Vienna, 1926.)

Princip 0 Sebi. (Zagreb, 1926.)

Propyläen-Weltgeschichte. Edited by Walter Goetz. Volume IX: *Die Entstehung des Weltstaatensystems.* Volume X: *Das Zeitalter des Imperialisms 1890-1933.* (Berlin, 1933, 1937.)

PUAUX, RENE, *Le mensonge du 3 août 1914.* (Paris, 1917.)

RADOSLAVOF, VASIL. *Bulgarien und die Weltkrise.* (Berlin, 1923.)

RAPPAPORT, A. 'Montenegros Eintritt in den Weltkrieg', in *Berliner Monatshefte,* October 1929, pp. 941-66.

RECOULY, RAYMOND, *Les heures tragiques d'avant-guerre.* (Paris, 1922.)

REDLICH, JOSEPH. *Emperor Francis Joseph of Austria.* (New York, 1929.)

RENAULT, ERNEST. *1914-1919. Histoire populaire de la guerre d'après les documents officiels et officieux et les témoignages des plus hautes personnalités militaires ayant commandé et combattu au front.* 3 volumes. (Paris, 1921, 1923-4.)

RENOUVIN, PIERRE and APPUHN. *Introduction aux tableaux d'histoire de Guillaume II.* (Paris, 1922.)

RENOUVIN, PIERRE. *The Immediate Origins of the War (28 June–4 August, 1914).* (New Haven, 1928.)

RENOUVIN, PIERRE. *La crise européenne et la grande guerre (1914-1918).* (Paris, 1934)

RENOUVIN, PIERRE. 'Les engagements de l'alliance franco-russe', in *Revue d'histoire de la guerre mondiale* (Paris), October 1934, pp. 297-310.

REVENTLOW, ERNST, GRAF. *Politische Vorgeschichte des Grossen Krieges.* (Berlin, 1919.)

RIDDER, ALFRED DE. *La Belgique et la guerre. Histoire diplomatique.* (Brussels, 1928.)

RODZIANKO, MICHAIL VLADMIROVIC. *The Reign of Rasputin.* (London, 1927.)

ROLOFF, GUSTAV. 'Englands Anteil an der Kriegsschuld', in *Kriegsschuldfrage* (Berlin), October 1928, pp. 917-50.

ROLOFF, GUSTAV. 'König Georg von England und der Ausbruch des Weltkrieges', in *Berliner Monatshefte,* October 1931, pp. 927-38.

ROSEN, FRIEDRICH. *Aus einem diplomatischen Wanderleben.* 2 volumes. (Berlin, 1931-2.)

BIBLIOGRAPHY 725

Rosen, Roman Romanovich, Baron von. *Forty Years of Diplomacy.* 2 volumes. (London, 1922.)

Ryckel, Baron de. *Mémoires.* (Brussels, 1920.)

Salandra, Antonio. *I discorsi della guerra.* (Milan, 1922.)

Salandra, Antonio. *La neutralità italiana* (1914). (Milan, 1922.)

Salvatorelli, Luigi. *La Triplice Alleanza.* (Milan, 1939.)

Salvemini, Gaetano. *Dal patto di Londra alla pace di Roma.* (Turin, 1925.)

Salvemini, Gaetano. *La politica estera di Francesco Crispi.* (Rome, 1919.)

Salvemini, Gaetano. 'La politica estera della Destra', in *Rivista d'Italia* (Rome), 15 November 1924, pp. 345-70; 15 January, pp. 182–210, 15 February, 1925.

Sandonà, Augusto. *L' irredentismo nelle lotte politiche e nelle contese diplotnatiche italo-austriache.* 3 volumes. (Bologna 1932-8.)

Savinsky, Aleksandr Aleksandrovic. *Recollections of a Russian diplomat.* (London, 1927.)

Savinsky, Aleksandr Aleksandrovic. 'Guillaume II et la Russie. Les lettres et dépêches à Nicolas II. 1903-1905', in *Revue des deux Mondes* (Paris), 15 December 1922, pp. 765-802.

Savinsky, Aleksandr Aleksandrovic. 'L'entrevue de Buchlau', in *Monde Slave* (Paris), February 1931, pp. 218-27.

Sazonov, Serge Dimitrievic. *Fateful Years, 1909-1916.* (London, 1928.)

[Sazonov.] *Rings um Sasonow. Neue dokumentarische Darlegungen zum Ausbruch des grossen Krieges durch Kronzeugen.* Herausgegeben und eingeleitet von Eduard Ritter von Steinitz. (Berlin, 1928.)

Schaper, Theobald von. 'Generaloberst von Moltke in den Tagen vor der Mobilmachung und seine Einwirkung auf Österreich', in *Kriegsschuldfrage* (Berlin), August 1926, pp. 514-49.

Schäfer, Theobald von. 'Wollte Generaloberst von Moltke den Präventivkrieg?', in *Berliner Monatshefte,* June 1927, pp. 543-60.

Shebeko, Nikolaj Nikolaevic. *Souvenirs. Essai historique sur les origines de la guerre de 1914.* (Paris, 1936.)

Schmitt, Bernadotte E. *The Coming of the War.* 2 volumes. (New York, 1930.)

Schmitt, Bernadotte E. *The Annexation of Bosnia, 1908-1909.* (Cambridge and New York, 1937.)

Schoen, Wilhelm Ed., Freiherr von. *The Memoirs of an Ambassador* (London, 1922.)

Schoen, Wilhelm, Ed. Freiherr von. 'Die deutsche Kriegserklarung an Frankreich am 3. August 1914', in *Die deutsche Nation* (Berlin), July 1922, pp. 547-5 3-

Schücking, Walter. *Die völkerrechtliche Lehre des Weltkrieges.* (Leipzig, 1918.)

SCHULTHESS. *Europäischer Geschichtskalender.* (Munich.) Annual publication.

SCHWEINITZ, HANS LOTHAR VON. *Denkwürdigkeiten.* 2 volumes. (Berlin, 1927.)

SCHWEINITZ, HANS LOTHAR VON. *Briefwechsel des Botschafters General von Schweinitz,* (Berlin, 1928.)

SCHWERTFEGER, BERNHARD. *Der Weltkrieg der Dokumente. Zehn Jahre Kriegsschuldforschung und ihr Ergebnis.* (Berlin, 1929.)

SEGRE, ROBERTO. *Vienna e Belgrado 1876-1914.* (Milan, 1935.)

SEIGNOBOS, CHARLES. *Histoire politique del l'Europe contemporaine.* (Paris, 1926.)

SELLIERS DE MORANVILLE, ANTONIN. 'Le Conseil de la Couronne du 2 août 1914', in *Le Flambeau* (Brussels, 21 August, 1921), pp. 449-69.

SELLIERS DE MORANVILLE, ANTONIN. *Du haut de la Tour de Babel.* (Paris, 1925.)

SELLIERS DE MORANVILLE, ANTONIN. *Contribution à l'histoire de la guerre mondiale 1914-1918.* (Paris, 1933.)

SETON-WATSON, R. W. *The Rise of Nationality in the Balkans.* (London, 1917.)

SETON-WATSON, R. W. *Sarajevo.* (London, 1926.)

SETON-WATSON, R. W. *A History of the Romanians.* (Cambridge, 1934.)

SEYMOUR, CHARLES. *Intimate Papers of Colonel House.* 4 volumes. (London, New York, 1926-8.)

SIEGHARDT, RUDOLF. *Die letzten Jahre einer Grossmacht. Menschen, Volker, Probleme des Habsburger Reichs.* (Berlin, 1932.)

SIXTE DE BOURBON, PRINCE. *L'offre de paix séparée de l'Autriche.* (Paris, 1920.)

SOSNOSKY, THEODOR. *Franz Ferdinand der Erzherzog-Thronfolger. Ein Lebensbild.* (Munich, 1929.)

SPALAIKOVIC, MIROSLAV. 'Une journée du ministre de Serbie à Petrograd. Le 24 juillet 1914', in *Revue d'histoire diplomatique* (Paris), April-June 1934, pp. 131-46.

SPEARS, EDWARD LOUIS. *Liaison 1914; a Narrative of the Great Retreat.* (London, 1930.)

SPENDER, JOHN ALFRED. *Life, Journalism and Politics.* 2 volumes. (London, 1927.)

SPENDER, JOHN ALFRED. *Fifty Years of Europe. A Study in Pre-war Documents.* (London, 1933.)

SPENDER, J. A. and ASQUITH, CYRIL. *Life of Herbert Henry Asquith, Lord Oxford and Asquith.* 2 volumes. (London, 1932.)

SPICKERNAGEL, WILHELM. *Fürst Bülow.* (Hamburg, 1921.)

STAAL, GEORGES FREDERIC CHARLES, BARON. *Correspondance diplomatique de. M. de Staal* (1884-1900). 2 volumes. (Paris, 1929.)

STANOJEVIC, STANOJE. *Die Ermordung des Erzherzoges Franz Ferdinand.* (Frankfort, 1923.)

STEED, HENRY WICKHAM. *The Hapshurg Monarchy.* (London, 1913.)

STEED, HENRY WICKHAM. *Through Thirty Years, 1892-1922.* (London, 1924.)

STIEVE, FRIEDRICH. *Deutschland und Europa 1890-1914.* (Berlin, 1928.)

STIEVE, FRIEDRICH. *Isvolsky and the World War.* (London, 1926.)

STIEVE, FRIEDRICH. *Im Dunkel der europäischen Geheimdiplomatie.* (Berlin, 1926.)

STIEVE, FRIEDRICH and MONTGELAS, MAX. *Russland und der Weltkonflikt.* (Berlin, 1927.)

STRUPP, KARL. *Die Neutralisation und die Neutralität Belgiens.* (Gotha, 1917.)

STÜRGKH, JOSEPH, GRAF. *Erinnerungen.* (Leipzig, 1927.)

SUCHOMLINOF, W. A. *Erinnerungen.* (Berlin, 1924.)

[Sukhomlinov trial]. *Die russische Mobilmachung im Lichte amtlicher Urkunden und der Enthüllungen des Prozesses.* (Berne, 1917.)

SZÁNTÓ, ALEXANDER. *Apis, der Führer der 'Schwarzen Hand'. Ein Beitrag zum Kriegsschuldproblem.* (Berlin, 1928.)

SZÁPÁRY, FRIEDRICH, GRAF. Chapter in *Erinnerungen an Franz Joseph I, Kaiser von Österreich.* Ed. by E. R. von Steinitz. (Berlin, 1931.)

SZÉCSEN, NIKOLAUS, GRAF. 'Ein vergeblicher Versuch für die Erhaltung des Fricdens im Sommer 1914', in *Kriegsschuldfrage* (Berlin), February 1926, pp. 66-70.

SZILASSY, JULIUS, BARON. *Der Untergang der Donaumonarchie. Diplomatische Erinnerungen.* (Berlin, 1921.)

TABOUIS, GENEVIÈVE. *The Life of Jules Cambon.* (London, 1938.)

TARTALIA, OSKAR M. *Veleizdajnik.* (Zagreb, 1928.)

TARTALIA, OSKAR M. 'Dragutin Dimitriević "Apis"', in *Nova Evropa* (Zagreb), 26 July 1927, pp. 67-74.

TAUBE, MICHAEL. *Der grossen Katastrophe entgegen.* (Leipzig, 1937.)

THIMME, FRIEDRICH. *Front wider Bülow. Staatsmänner, Diplomaten und Forscher zu seinen Denkwürdigkeiten.* (Munich, 1931.)

TIRPITZ, ALFRED VON. *Erinnerungen* (Berlin-Leipzig, 1927). *My Memoirs,* 2 volumes (London, 1919).

TIRPITZ, ALFRED VON. *Politische Dokumente.* 2 volumes. Vol. I: *Der Aufbau der deutschen Wehrmacht.* Vol. II: *Deutsche Ohnmachtspolitik im Weltkriege.* (Berlin, 1924, 1926.)

TIRPITZ, ALFRED VON. 'Warum kam eine Flottenverständigung mit England nicht zustande?', in *Süddeutsche Monatshefte* (Munich), November 1925, pp. 95-126.

TISZA, STEFAN VON. *Briefe 1914-1918.* Herausgegeben und mit einer Einleitung versehen von Oskar von Wertheimer. (Berlin, 1928.)

TITTONI, TOMMASO. *Italy's Foreign and Colonial Policy.* (London, 1914.)

TITTONI, TOMMASO. *Il giudizio della storia sulle responsibilità della gnerra.* (Milan, 1916.)

TITTONI, TOMMASO. *Nuovi scritti di politica interna ed estera.* (Milan, 1930.)

TOMMASINI, FRANCESCO. *L'Italia alla vigilia della guerra. La politica estera di Tommaso Tittoni.* 5 volumes. (Bologna, 1934-41.)

TOSCANO, MARIO. *Il Patto di Londra.* (Bologna, 1931.)

TROTHA, ADOLF VON. *Grossadmiral von Tirpitz; Flottenbau und Reichsgedanke.* (Breslau, 1932.)

TROTHA, FRIEDRICH VON. *Fritz von Holstein als Mensch und Politiker.* Eingeleitet von Friedrich Thimme. (Berlin, 1931.)

TRYWDAR-BURZYNSKI, LOUIS DE. *La crépuscule d'une autocratie. Quelques crises en Allemagne.* (*Extraits de souvenirs*). (Florence, 1926.)

TCHARYKOV [CHARIKOV], NIKOLAI VALERIANOVIC. *Glimpses of High Politics through War and Peace (1855-1929).* (London, 1931.)

TSCHUPPIK, KARL. *The Reign of the Emperor Francis Joseph, 1848-1916.* (London, 1930.)

ULLRICH, RICHARD. "'Herrn Paléologues Meldung der russischen allgemeinen Mobilmachung', in *Berliner Monatshefte,* August 1933, pp. 781-3.

VALENTIN, VEIT. *Deutschlands Aussenpolitik von Bismarcks Abgang bis zum Ende des Weltkrieges 1890-1918.* (Berlin, 1921.)

VALENTINI, RUDOLF VON. *Kaiser und Kabinettschef Nach eigenen Aufzeichnungen und dem Briefwechsel dargestellt von Bernhard Schwertfeger.* (Oldenburg, 1931.)

VIRUBOVA, ANNA. *Souvenirs de ma vie* (Paris, 1927). *Journal secret 1909-1917* (Paris, 1928).

VIVIANI, RENE. *Réponse au Kaiser.* (Paris, 1923.)

WAHL, ADALBERT. *Deutsche Geschichte von der Reichsgründung bis zum Ausbruch des Weltkriegs (1871-1914).* 4 volumes. (Stuttgart, 1926-36.)

WALDERSEE, ALFRED, GRAF VON. *Denkwurdigheiten.* Bearbeitet und herausgegeben von Heinrich Otto Meisner. 3 volumes. (Stuttgart-Berlin, 1922-3.)

WALDERSEE, ALFRED, GRAF VON. *Aus dem Briefwechsel des Generalfeldmarschalls.* Edited by Heinrich Otto Meisner. 2 volumes. (Stuttgart-Berlin-Leipzig, 1928.)

WALDERSEE, ALFRED, GRAF VON. 'Von Deutschlands militärpolitischen Beziehungen zu Italien', in *Berliner Monatshefte,* July 1929, pp. 636-64.

WEGERER, ALFRED VON. *A Refutation of the Versailles War Guilt Thesis.* (New York, London, 1930.)

WEGERER, ALFRED VON. *Der entscheidende Schritt in den Weltkrieg.* (Berlin, 1931.)

WEGERER, ALFRED VON. *Der Ausbruch des Weltkrieges.* 2 volumes. (Berlin, 1939-)

WEGERER, ALFRED VON. 'Zu den Memoiren des Generals von Falkenhayn', in *Kriegsschuldfrage* (Berlin), August 1927, pp. 784-5.

WEGERER, ALFRED VON. 'Die russische allgemeine Mobilmachung und das deutsche Ultimatum an Russland', in *Kriegsschuldfrage* (Berlin), November 1928, pp. 1061-4.

WERTHEIMER, EDUARD. *Graf Julius Andrassy.* 3 volumes. (Stuttgart, 1910-13.)

WIESNER, FRIEDRICH VON. 'König Alexander von Jugoslavien und die Attentäter von Sarajevo', in *Kriegsschuldfrage* (Berlin), September 1926, pp. 639-61.

WIESNER, FRIEDRICH VON. 'Die Schuld der serbischen Regierung am Mord von Sarajevo', in *Kriegsschuldfrage* (Berlin), April 1928, pp. 307-95.

WILHELM II, KAISER. *The Kaiser's Letters to the Tsar.* Edited by N. F. Grant. (London, 1920.)

WILHELM II, KAISER. *Ereignisse und Gestalten aus den Jahren 1878-1918* (Leipzig-Berlin, 1922). *My Memoirs, 1878-1918* (London, 1922).

WILHELM (KRONPRINZ). *Erinnerungen.* (Berlin, 1922.)

WINDISCHGRAETZ, LUDWIG, PRINZ. *Vom Roten zum Schwarzen Prinzen.* (Berlin, 1920.)

WITTE, SERGEJ JULIEVICH, COUNT. *Memoirs of Count Witte.* (New York, London, 1921.)

WOESTE, COMTE CHARLES DK. *Mémoires pour servir à l'histoire contemporaine de la Belgique, 1894-1914.* 2 volumes. (Brussels, 1933.)

WOLFF, THEODOR. *Das Vorspiel.* (Munich, 1924.)

WOLFF, THEODOR. *The Eve of 1914.* (London, 1935.)

WULLUS-RUDIGER, I. *La Belgique et l'équilibre européen.* (Paris, 1935.)

ZEDLITZ-TRUTSCHLER, ROBERT, COUNT. *Zwölf Jahre am deutschen Kaiserhof.* (Stuttgart, 1924.)

ZIBERT, J. A. *Der Mord von Sarajevo und Tiszas Schuld am Weltkriege.* (Laibach, 1919.)

ZWEHL, HANS VON. *Erich von Falkenhayn, General der Infanterie. Eine biographische Studie.* (Berlin, 1926.)

INDEX